WINSTON S. CHURCHILL
1874–1965

Churchill at Lille, 28 October 1918

WINSTON S. CHURCHILL

by

MARTIN GILBERT

VOLUME IV

1916–1922

HEINEMANN : LONDON

William Heinemann Ltd
15 Queen St, Mayfair, London W1X 8BE

LONDON   MELBOURNE   TORONTO
JOHANNESBURG   AUCKLAND

434 13010 9
First published 1975

Printed and bound in Great Britain by
Richard Clay (The Chaucer Press) Ltd
Bungay, Suffolk

Contents

PART THREE: AT THE COLONIAL OFFICE,
1921–1922

Illustrations

1. Frontispiece: Churchill at Lille, 28 October 1918
   [*Imperial War Museum*]

Section 1 (between pages 144 and 145)

2. Churchill and his wife in 1919
   [*Churchill Press Cutting Albums*]
3. Churchill visits a munitions works, Glasgow, October 1918
   [*Radio Times Hulton Picture Library*]
4. Churchill speaking to munitions workers
   [*Radio Times Hulton Picture Library*]
5. Churchill with women munitions workers
   [*Radio Times Hulton Picture Library*]
6. Churchill in a munitions works
   [*Radio Times Hulton Picture Library*]
7. The avenue of trees at the Chateau Verchocq
   [*Martin Gilbert archive*]
8. The Chateau Verchocq
   [*Martin Gilbert archive*]
9. Churchill, his brother and Eddie Marsh, Lille, 28 October 1918
   [*Imperial War Museum*]
10. Lloyd George at Lympne, a photograph taken in 1920
    [*Sybil, Lady Cholmondeley and Mr Wakefield*]
11. Haig and Rawlinson, a photograph taken on 19 March 1920
    [*The Press Association Ltd*]
12. Clemenceau
    [*Bibliothèque Nationale, Paris*]
13. Foch
    [*Ministry of Defence, Paris*]
14. Loucheur, Churchill, Lloyd George and Bernard Baruch, Paris, 1919
    [*Churchill Photograph Albums*]

Maps

Preface

THIS volume spans six years of Winston Churchill's life, from December 1916 to November 1922. For all but six months of this period he was a member of Lloyd George's Cabinet, first at the Ministry of Munitions, then at the War Office and finally at the Colonial Office. Among the challenges with which he had to deal were the demobilization of the armies in January 1919, the British intervention against Bolshevism in Russia, the civil war in Ireland and the problems created by Britain's new Middle East territories. He was also called upon by Lloyd George during several crises, including the German breakthrough in March 1918 and the Chanak crisis of September 1922. During these six years, Churchill's power of organization, of hard work and of oratory, reached a high point, recognized by his colleagues and respected by his critics. He was a leading advocate of economy in defence expenditure, and of appeasement in European affairs. His parliamentary speeches sustained the Government in several moments of crisis. In his public speeches he emerged as a leading opponent of the Labour Party, and as the determined enemy of any future Labour administration.

For six years Churchill was actively involved in many diverse and complex problems. He tackled each one with boldness, and sought definite solutions. Some of his policies were extremely well-received, others were criticized and condemned. But he himself believed that all his actions were in harmony, and that they were based upon a true understanding of the nature of events. His view of the world was increasingly pessimistic; but he was convinced that with foresight, and active policies, it could still be guided towards a calmer future. Of his own abilities to be that guide, he had no doubts.

In this volume my aim has been to describe Churchill's precise role in each episode, however controversial. I have also tried to show the full range of his opinions, which were sometimes extreme, and often provoked fierce protests. It would have been impossible to give a fair and rounded picture of Churchill's life during these six years without using evidence and documents which are scattered in a wide range of public archives and private papers. Less than half the documents used in this volume come from the Churchill collection: the majority, including many of his own more important private letters, have had to be found in other sources, these include: the Royal Archives at Windsor; the Admiralty, Air Ministry, Cabinet Office, Colonial Office, Foreign Office and War Office papers at the Public Record Office, London; the archive of *The Times*, London; the Central Zionist Archives, Jerusalem; and, in individual archives, the Amery papers (in private possession), the Margot Asquith papers (in private possession); the Baldwin papers (Cambridge University Library); the Beaverbrook papers (Beaverbrook Library, London); the Bonar Law papers (Beaverbrook Library, London); the Austen Chamberlain papers (Birmingham University Library); the Cowdray papers (in private possession); the Curzon papers (India Office Library, London); the Derby papers (in private possession); the Esher papers (Churchill College, Cambridge); the H. A. L. Fisher papers (Bodleian Library, Oxford); the Haig papers (the National Library of Scotland, Edinburgh); the Lady (Ian) Hamilton papers (in private possession); the Hankey papers (Churchill College, Cambridge); the Hodges papers (in private possession); the Colonel House papers (Yale University Library); the Lady Islington papers; the T. E. Lawrence papers (Bodleian Library, Oxford); the Shane Leslie papers (in private possession); the Lloyd George papers (Beaverbrook Library, London); the Countess Lloyd-George papers (Beaverbrook Library, London); the Loucheur papers (Hoover Institution, Stanford, California); the Lothian papers (Scottish Record Office, Edinburgh); the Edward Marsh papers (in private possession); the Milner papers (Bodleian Library, Oxford); the Edwina Mountbatten papers (in private possession); the Northcliffe papers (*The Times* archive, Printing House Square, London); the Rawlinson papers (Churchill College, Cambridge); the Rumbold papers (Bodleian Library, Oxford); the Ruppin papers (in private possession); the Sacher papers (in private possession); the Samuel papers (Prime Minister's Office, Jerusalem); the Philip Sassoon papers (in private possession); the Savory papers (in private possession); the C. P. Scott papers (British Museum); the Spears papers (in private possession); the Sykes papers (in private possession); the Trenchard papers (in private possession); the Thurso papers (Churchill College, Cambridge); the Weizmann papers (The Weizmann Institute, Rehovot, Israel); and the Henry Wilson papers (in private possession and at the Imperial War Museum, London). Also, the Crewe papers (Cambridge University Library). The source of each document quoted is given in the List of Sources, starting on page 917.

Many people have helped me in the search for documents and materials. In particular I should like once again to express my thanks to Baroness Spencer-Churchill, who generously gave me the benefit of her recollections, and who answered my many queries. I should also like to thank the following for their kind help, and for valuable reminiscences of the period: Sir Reader Bullard; Sybil, Marchioness of Cholmondeley; Peregrine S. Churchill; Sir Gerard Clauson; the late Sir Herbert Creedy; the late Jessie Crosland; the late Gilbert Hall; Sir John Hathorn Hall; H. Norman Harding; the late G. E. R. Gedye; Colonel A. P. Hodges; Major-General F. E. Hotblack; the late Countess Lloyd-George of Dwyfor; Brigadier Charles Roberts; Mrs Hannah Ruppin; Lieutenant-General Sir Reginald Savory; Sir Geoffrey Shakespeare; the late Major-General Sir Edward Louis Spears; Sir Garnet Wilson and Major-General George Wood. In the seven years before his death Randolph S. Churchill used often to set down his own recollections of his father; I have drawn on this material for a childhood memory. I should like also to thank Winston S. Churchill MP who gave me access to his grandfather's press cutting and photograph albums, and the Hon. Lady Soames who provided me with copies of Churchill's correspondence with his wife.

I am most grateful to all those who gave me access both to archives and to information, whether for use in the text itself, or for the biographical notes. For help in providing material used in this volume I should like to thank Niels-Peter Albertsen, Assistant Press and Cultural Attaché, Royal Danish Embassy, London; P. A. Alsberg, State Archivist, Prime Minister's Office, Jerusalem; the Rt Hon Julian Amery; His Excellency the United States Ambassador, Mr Walter Annenberg; Paul Apostolidis, First Secretary, Greek Embassy, London; Major-General J. M. W. Badcock; Lieutenant-Colonel A. J. Barker; the 6th Marquess of Bath; B. S. Benedikz, Sub-Librarian, University Library, University of Birmingham; Mrs Mary Bennett, Principal of St Hilda's College, Oxford; the Dowager Countess of Bessborough; Robin Bidwell, Middle East Centre, University of Cambridge; Dr Richard Bingle, India Office Library, London; Pierre-Louis Blanc, Cultural Counsellor, French Embassy, London; D. C. Brech, Archivist, Royal Air Force Museum, Hendon; Baroness Budberg; Dr H. Cahn; Mr Bernard Cheeseman, Library and Records Department, Foreign and Commonwealth Office, London; Anthony Crosland; A. G. Davey, Army Records Centre, Hayes, Middlesex; Miss J. Davidson, Ministry of Defence (Air), London; John Davidson, Director of Information and Research, Conservative and Unionist Central Office, Edinburgh; His Excellency the

French Ambassador, M. Jaques de Beaumarchais; Pierre de la Gorce; G. Dethan, Archives and Documentation, Ministry of Foreign Affairs, Paris; Dr Christopher Dowling, Imperial War Museum, London; Dr Michael Dunnill; J. R. Ede, Keeper of the Public Records, Public Record Office, London; Admiral Fliche, Chef du Service Historique de la Marine, Paris; George Georghallides, Cyprus Research Centre, Nicosia; Dr Michael Glenny; Mrs Ruby Hall; Dr Michael Heymann, the Central Zionist Archives, Jerusalem; Peter Holdsworth, Chief Librarian, *Telegraphy and Argus*, Bradford; Dr Derek Hopwood, Middle East Centre, Oxford; Dr Michael Hoskin, Keeper of the Archives, Churchill College, Cambridge; S. J. P. Howarth, S. Pearson & Son Limited, London; Stephen Inwood, Department of Documents, Imperial War Museum, London; J. Laloy, Director of Archives and Documentation, Ministry of Foreign Affairs, Paris; Miss Jane Langton, Royal Archives, Windsor; Franz G. Lassner, Director of Archives, Hoover Institution on War, Revolution and Peace, Stanford, California; Professor A. W. Lawrence; Iris, Lady Leslie; Colonel Marsauche, Service Historique, Ministry of Defence, Paris; Julian L. Meltzer, Weizmann National Memorial, Rehovot, Israel; His Excellency the Turkish Ambassador, Turgut Menemencioglu; I. J. Miller, Executive Secretary, The Zionist Federation of the United Kingdom, London; Francisco Moita, Counsellor, the Portuguese Embassy, London; Elizabeth Monroe; Mario Montuori, Director, The Italian Institute, London; Mlle C. Morel, Assistant Librarian, Institut Français du Royaume-Uni, London; Admiral of the Fleet Earl Mountbatten of Burma; Andrew W. Mudie; His Excellency the Irish Ambassador, Donal O'Sullivan; Hugh Ozanne; Charles G. Palm, Assistant Archivist, Hoover Institution on War, Revolution and Peace, Stanford, California; Alan Palmer; Ian V. Paterson, County Clerk, County of Lanark; H. G. Pearson, Departmental Record Officer, Home Office, London; Mrs Agnes F. Peterson, Hoover Institution on War, Revolution and Peace, Stanford, California; Mr N. Petsalis-Diomidis; J. Gordon Phillips, Archivist, *The Times*; Roger Pierrot, Le Conservateur en chef, Bibliothèque Nationale, Paris; Sir Anthony Rumbold; J. F. Russell, Department of Manuscripts, National Library of Scotland, Edinburgh; Mrs Miriam Sacher; Susan Sjoblom, Personnel section, Royal Ministry for Foreign Affairs, Sweden; Admiral Giovanni Sleiter, Ministry of Defence, Rome; Professor Stefan Stefanescu, Institutul de Istorie, 'N Iorga' Bucharest; S. J. Stephenson, N. M. Rothschild & Sons Ltd; Bonar Sykes; A. J. P. Taylor; D. M. Torbet, City Librarian, Dundee; T. P. Tracey, Ministry of Defence (Air), London; the 2nd Viscount

Trenchard; the late Dr Wayne Wilcox, Cultural Attaché, Embassy of the United States of America, London; Mrs I. Wagner, Librarian, The Labour Party Library, Transport House, London; Major Cyril Wilson; and Mrs D. Wynn, Commonwealth War Graves Commission, Maidenhead, Berkshire. I should also like to thank all those who have given me permission to quote material in which they own the copyright.

I am grateful to Jerry Moeran of Studio Edmark, and his assistant, Miss Jean Hunt, for preparing the photographs for publication; to T. A. Bicknell, cartographer, for his work on the maps; and to Miss Mary Tyerman, who worked for two months in the British Museum Newspaper Library at Colindale, and also helped scrutinize the proofs. I am grateful to Mrs Judy Holdsworth, Mrs Charmian Allam, Miss Elizabeth Norman and Miss Molly Minett, who did the typing at different stages of the work.

I should like to thank the Winston Churchill Travel Foundation, whose travel grant made it possible for me to visit several important archives in Jerusalem, and to gather much new material for the Palestine chapters.

At the proof stage I was much helped by the criticisms and suggestions of Professor Chimen Abramsky, Dr Sidney Aster, Dr Christopher Dowling, Joe Haines, Miss Elizabeth Monroe, Lord Samuel, Ivor Samuels and Dr Bernard Wasserstein.

I should like finally to thank Miss Susie Sacher, who helped with research and gave good advice for over three years, working in the Public Record Office for material on Churchill's ministerial career, examining national and local newspapers for the whole of the period, working in several major private archives and making many important suggestions about the style and content of the volume. Her work and encouragement have been of the utmost help in the writing of this volume.

Merton College   MARTIN GILBERT
Oxford
19 February 1974

PART ONE

MINISTER OF MUNITIONS, 1917–1918

1

The Shadow of the Dardanelles

B Y the beginning of December 1916 Churchill had been out of office for more than a year. Following his removal from the Admiralty in May 1915 he had sometimes despaired of ever holding an important Cabinet position again. He alone had been held responsible for the failure of the British naval attack of the Dardanelles, and many people had blamed his lack of judgement for the suffering and slaughter of the Gallipoli campaign. He had found no solace, during the summer of 1915, in being Chancellor of the Duchy of Lancaster, a Cabinet post devoid of all administrative work, and incapable of satisfying his ambition. 'I do not want office,' he had written to his friend Archibald Sinclair[1] on 5 July 1915, 'but only war direction: that perhaps never again. Everything else—not that. At least so I feel in my evil moments.' Later in his letter he told Sinclair:

I am profoundly unsettled: & cannot use my gift. Of that last I have no doubts. I do not feel that my judgements have been falsified, or that the determined pursuance of my policy through all the necessary risks was wrong. I wd do it all again if the circumstances were repeated. But I am faced with the problem of living through days of 24 hours each: & averting my mind from the intricate business I had in hand—wh was my life.

In November 1915 Churchill had resigned from the Government, rejoined the army and gone to the western front. In January 1916 he had been given command of an infantry battalion. With Sinclair as his

[1] Archibald Henry Macdonald Sinclair, 1890–1970. Entered Army, 1910. 4th Baronet, 1912. Captain, 1915. 2nd in Command of the 6th Royal Scots Fusiliers, while Churchill was in command, January–May 1916. Squadron-Commander, 2nd Life Guards, 1916–17. Major, Guards Machine Gun Regiment, 1918. Served under Churchill, Ministry of Munitions, 1918–19; Churchill's personal Military Secretary, War Office, 1919–21; Churchill's Private Secretary, Colonial Office, 1921–2. Liberal MP, 1922–45. Secretary of State for Scotland, 1931–3. Leader of the Parliamentary Liberal Party, 1935–45. Secretary of State for Air in Churchill's wartime Coalition, 1940–5. Created Viscount Thurso, 1952.

second-in-command, he had tried to absorb himself in front-line duties. But politics still dominated his thoughts, and by the end of March 1916 he had decided to return to the House of Commons, even if it meant a long period in opposition. 'Is it not damnable,' he had written to his brother Jack[1] on 15 July 1916, 'that I should be denied all real scope to serve this country, in this tremendous hour?'

Throughout the summer and autumn of 1916 Churchill's main activity had been the preparation of his case for the Dardanelles Commission of Enquiry, to which, on September 28, he had given evidence. Throughout October he had watched while others gave evidence, had challenged every statement with which he disagreed and had urged those who had supported the campaign to come forward in his defence. 'Everything I hear about the D'lles Commission encourages me,' he had written to Sinclair on November 29. 'The interim report cannot now be long delayed and I have good hopes that it will be a fair judgement. I sh'd like to have it out as soon as possible. But the days slip away.'

On December 7 Lloyd George[2] had become Prime Minister, at the head of a new all-Party Coalition, committed to the vigorous prosecution of the war. But he had offered Churchill no place in his administration. Although he had a high regard for Churchill's talents, and wanted to make use of them, the Conservatives, on whom he depended for support, insisted on Churchill's exclusion from office. This veto reflected more than a decade of Conservative hostility.

Churchill had counted on Lloyd George's accession to office for his own return to the Cabinet, and was bitter not to be included in the new Government. On December 10 he wrote to Sinclair:

The papers will have apprised you of the course of events, & you will have learned from them of the downfall of all my hopes and desires. These have not been unworthy, for I had an impulse & a gift to give to the war energies of the country. But my treasure is rejected. If I cd reconcile the turn of

[1] John Strange Spencer Churchill, 1880–1947. Churchill's younger brother, known as Jack. A stockbroker. Major, Queen's Own Oxfordshire Hussars, 1914–18. Served at Dunkirk, 1914; on Sir John French's staff, 1914–15; on Sir Ian Hamilton's staff, 1915; on General Birdwood's staff, 1916–18.
[2] David Lloyd George, 1863–1945. Liberal MP, 1890–1931. Chancellor of the Exchequer, 1908–15. Minister of Munitions, May 1915–July 1916. Secretary of State for War, July–December 1916. Prime Minister, December 1916–October 1922. Independent Liberal MP, 1931–45. Created Earl Lloyd-George of Dwyfor, 1945.

events and of newspaper opinion with the true facts & the true values I shd be hopelessly downcast. But I am sure that these judgements are unjust and I have a good conscience & am confident of my record. Still you who know me so well will understand how unpleasant it is to me to be denied all scope in action at this time of all other times.

Of course I have every right to complain of L.G. who weakly & faithlessly bowed to Northcliffe's[1] malevolent press. But this is not the hour when personal resentments however justified must influence conduct or colour opinion. I shall remain absolutely silent!

It was unlucky that the D'lles report shd have been delayed until after the crisis; for I am still hopeful that it will give a turn to public opinion. But everything has turned out ill for me since the war began. Perhaps we are now at the nadir.

It will be odd now on the direct opposition Bench with all the furious ex Ministers arriving. I expect they will soon be vy anxious to be civil to me. But I intend to sit in the corner seat in a kind of isolation.

Later in his letter Churchill gave Sinclair his impression of Lloyd George's Cabinet:

The new Government is a weak one—so far as ability is concerned and largely inexperienced. Political considerations alone have ruled the formation of the War Council, & except L.G. not one of its members possesses any aptitude for war or knowledge of it. The exclusion of the Admiralty & War Office from the War Council shows an utter lack of comprehension of the interplay of forces. The difficulties before them are enormous, & only disasters lie ahead for many months.

On December 10, as a gesture of friendship and encouragement, Lloyd George asked Sir George Riddell[2] to take Churchill a message. Riddell told Churchill that Lloyd George had no intention of keeping him out of office, and would try to make him Chairman of the Air Board. Lloyd George added, however, that the Dardanelles Commission Report would have to be published first. As the Report was unlikely to be ready until the summer of 1917, the offer held out no immediate hope of office. Riddell gave Churchill Lloyd George's message on December 11, and in his diary recorded Churchill's reaction. 'I don't

[1] Alfred Charles William Harmsworth, 1865–1922. Newspaper proprietor. Bought the *Evening News* (1894), *Daily Mail* (1896), *Daily Mirror* (1903), *The Times* (1908). Created Baronet, 1903. Created Baron Northcliffe, 1905. Chairman, British War Mission to the United States, 1917. Director of Propaganda in Enemy Countries, 1918. Created Viscount, 1918.

[2] George Allardice Riddell, 1865–1934. Began work in London as a boy clerk in a solicitor's office. Solicitor, 1888. Chairman of the *News of the World*, 1903. Knighted, 1909. Member of the Admiralty War Office and Press Committee, 1914. Liaison officer between the Government and the Press, 1914–18. Created Baronet, 1918. Created Baron, 1920.

reproach him,' Churchill had replied. 'His conscience will tell him what he should do. Give him that message and tell him that I cannot allow what you have said to fetter my freedom of action. I will take any position which will enable me to serve my country. My only purpose is to help defeat the Hun, and I will subordinate my own feelings so that I may be able to render some assistance.'

Churchill would have liked to become Chairman of the Air Board. For over a year he had been advocating a united air policy, under a single Minister. Although the post was not in the War Cabinet, Conservative opposition could not be overcome. On December 20 the new First Lord of the Admiralty, Sir Edward Carson,[1] wrote to the Conservative leader, Andrew Bonar Law:[2] 'I shd greatly fear friction if the appt is made. I much dislike having to seem opposed to the suggestion as my personal inclination is towards utilising Churchill's undoubted ability—especially so as he's so down in his luck at present—but I hope some other, more suitable opportunity may be found.' That same day Churchill wrote to Sinclair, describing Lloyd George's offer, and adding:

Since then I hear this arrangement bruited in various secret & well informed quarters. I have not seen him however, tho he threw a note across the floor last night asking me to come. I do not want to have a chatterbox talk. Unless I am *really* wanted I do not want to join them. However painful it is not to have work to do against the enemy, one must just wait. There is nothing to be gained by eagerness. The matter now hangs I suppose in the balance. . . . But for the war nothing wd induce me to take office.

I look back a gt deal to our Plugstreet days, & wish I cd have cut myself more adrift from London & its whirlpools and been more content with the simple animal life (& death) wh the trenches offered. When I am *absolutely* sure there is no prospect of regaining control or part of it here, I shall turn again to that resort & refuge: & after all I have learned in disillusionment I think I cd do better. It is a mellow picture in retrospect. But I was always tormented by the idea that gt opportunities were slipping by at home.

And this is a fact. If I had stayed Chancellor of the Duchy and shut my

<hr>

[1] Edward Henry Carson, 1854–1935. Conservative MP, 1892–1921. Knighted, 1900. Solicitor-General, 1900–6. Leader of the Ulster Unionists in the House of Commons, 1910–21. Attorney-General, May–October 1915. First Lord of the Admiralty, December 1916–July 1917. Minister without Portfolio in the War Cabinet, July 1917–January 1918. Created Baron, 1921.

[2] Andrew Bonar Law, 1858–1923. Born in Canada. Brought to Scotland at the age of twelve. Conservative MP, 1900–10 and 1911–23. Parliamentary Secretary, Board of Trade, 1902–5. Leader of the Conservatives in the House of Commons, 1911. Secretary of State for the Colonies, May 1915–December 1916. Chancellor of the Exchequer, 1916–19. Lord Privy Seal, 1919–21. Prime Minister, 1922–3. Two of his three sons were killed in action.

mouth & drawn my salary, I shd today be one of the principal personages in direction of affairs. That was a costly excursion. Still I cannot regret it. Under a fair pretence of fine words, there is a gt *déconsidération* of all who wear uniform. They are discounted as persons 'under the law'. Not one of these gallant MPs who has fought through the Somme at the heads of their battalions, stands a chance agst less clever men who have stopped & chattered at home. This is to me the most curious phenomenon of all. It is quite inexplicable to me.

Churchill still hoped that when the Dardanelles Commission Report was published, his political fortunes would improve. Meanwhile, he held aloof from all opposition groupings. 'I have been enveloped in courtesies by the ex Liberal Ministers,' he told Sinclair in his letter of December 20, 'but I remain quite unattached.' 'Everyone seems to think,' Churchill's former Private Secretary Edward Marsh[1] wrote to Sinclair on the following day, 'the report will be much in his favour. If only he'd stayed out with you, I expect he wd now be at the top of the tree, & I shd be back with him. Let us all beware of Impatience!'

On December 23 Churchill left London for Blenheim, where he spent Christmas and New Year with his family. It was the second consecutive New Year during which he had held no political office. Lord Fisher,[2] whose resignation in May 1915 had precipitated the crisis leading to Churchill's fall, was likewise without any official employment. On January 25 Fisher celebrated his seventy-sixth birthday. That same day Churchill wrote to congratulate him on his 'continued enjoyment of perennial youth and vigour'. His letter went on:

Like you I have seen no one political. One is quite powerless as far as the war is concerned. It is a pity, because a descent on the German coast, the bringing in of Denmark and the entry & domination of the Baltic wd secure a decisive victory for the Allies, who otherwise will be forced to far less satisfactory alternatives after far greater sacrifices. Our common enemies are all powerful today & friendship counts for less than nothing.

I am simply existing.

[1] Edward Howard Marsh, 1872–1953. Known as 'Eddie'. Entered Colonial Office as a 2nd Class Clerk, 1896. Private Secretary to Churchill, December 1905–November 1915. Assistant Private Secretary to Asquith, November 1915–December 1916. Private Secretary to Churchill, 1917–22 and 1924–9. Private Secretary to successive Secretaries of State for the Colonies, 1929–36. Knighted, 1937.

[2] John Arbuthnot Fisher, 1841–1920. Known as 'Jackie' and, because of his somewhat oriental appearance, 'the old Malay'. Entered Navy, 1854. First Sea Lord, 1904–10. Admiral of the Fleet, 1905. Created Baron, 1909. Retired, 1911. Head of the Royal Commission on Fuel and Engines, 1912–14. Re-appointed First Sea Lord, October 1914; resigned, May 1915. Chairman of the Admiralty Inventions Board, 1915–16.

Throughout the early months of 1917, Churchill's thoughts were entirely dominated by the Dardanelles. 'I had a short talk with Winston about the Dardanelles Report,' Sir Maurice Hankey[1] wrote in his diary on February 16. 'He said he was satisfied, but the tone of his voice indicated disappointment.' During February Churchill wrote two long memoranda for the Dardanelles Commission of Enquiry, setting out his reasons for supporting the Gallipoli campaign even after he had left the Admiralty in May 1915. In the first memorandum Churchill criticized what he described as the 'series of delays' in reinforcing the troops on the Gallipoli Peninsula during the summer of 1915, and wrote bitterly of the Coalition Government which Asquith[2] had formed in May 1915, as a Government 'based purely upon a balancing of personal and party claims, united neither by any common conception of action, nor of comradeship, nor by mutual confidence, nor even by partisanship'. And he continued: 'It robbed the country at once of a responsible Opposition and an alternative Administration. It suppressed utterly for the time being all effective criticism within the House of Commons and transferred this function with the immense power which has followed from it to the press.' Churchill went on to point out that the poor quality of the Divisions at Gallipoli, though known to the War Office, had not been revealed to the Cabinet until it was too late. 'If ever there was an operation in the history of war,' he concluded, 'which once having been taken should have been carried through with the utmost vigour and at the utmost speed it was the military attack on the Gallipoli Peninsula.'

In his second memorandum of February 1917, Churchill criticized the Government's policy after the failure of the August offensive. In September and October 1915, he insisted, the Government should have renewed the military offensive on the Gallipoli Peninsula and sent sufficient reinforcements and munitions to make victory certain. The failure was not a military, but a political one. 'It is no good coming along afterwards,' he wrote, 'and applying to these events the light of after-knowledge and the assumptions of plenary power. The future was then unknown. No one possessed plenary power.' And he continued:

[1] Maurice Pascal Alers Hankey, 1877–1963. Entered Royal Marine Artillery, 1895. Captain, 1899. Retired, 1912. Secretary to the Committee of Imperial Defence, 1912–38. Lieutenant-Colonel, Royal Marines, October 1914. Secretary to the War Council, November 1914–May 1915; to the Dardanelles Committee, May–November 1915; to the Cabinet War Committee, December 1915–December 1916. Knighted, 1916. Secretary to the War Cabinet, 1916–18; to the Cabinet, 1919–38. Created Baron, 1939. Minister without Portfolio, 1939–40. Chancellor of the Duchy of Lancaster, 1940–1. Paymaster-General, 1941–2.

[2] Herbert Henry Asquith, 1852–1928. Liberal MP, 1886–1918 and 1920–4. Home Secretary, 1892–1905. Chancellor of the Exchequer, 1905–8. Prime Minister, 1908–16. Created Earl of Oxford and Asquith, 1925. His eldest son was killed in action, 1917.

The wishes of foreign Governments, themselves convulsed internally by difficulties the counterpart of our own, were constantly thrusting themselves athwart our policy. No one had the power to give clear brutal orders which would command unquestioning respect. Power was widely disseminated among the many important personages who in this period formed the governing instrument. Knowledge was very unequally shared. Innumerable arguments of a partial character could be quoted on every side of all these complicated questions. The situation itself was in constant and violent movement. We never at any time possessed the initiative; we were always compelled to adapt ourselves to events.

All the time, however, clear and simple solutions existed which would speedily have produced the precious element of victory. They were not, however, solutions within the reach of anyone not possessed of commanding power.

On February 21, while the Dardanelles Commission was reading Churchill's final submissions, the Navy Estimates debate in the House of Commons gave him a chance to voice his opinions on the current conduct of the war. His mind was still on the Dardanelles. Criticism had its place, he told the House of Commons, but the only criticism that was justified in wartime was 'criticism before the event'. And he went on: 'Nothing is more easy, nothing is cheaper, nothing is more futile than to criticise the hazardous and incalculable events and tendencies of war after the event has occurred.'

On March 5, during the Army Estimates debate, Churchill advocated a Secret Session of the House of Commons, to enable Ministers to explain their policies in greater detail, and to enable MPs to be more critical. 'The House of Commons,' he asserted, 'would be to blame and failing in its duty if upon all these great questions connected with manpower, the supply of men, and our military policy, they do not insist upon some serious discussion in which the Ministers could take part, and in which hon. Members could really address themselves to questions in which the life and fortunes of the country depend.' But Lloyd George declined Churchill's advice.

In his speech on the Army Estimates Churchill argued that insufficient use had been made of Indian and African manpower. From Africa, he believed, as many as 300,000 men could have been recruited for labour services in the war zone, thus freeing an equivalent number of British soldiers for the front line. The failure to find new sources of manpower would, he declared, gravely hamper the military campaigns of 1918: 'I say quite frankly, I have a feeling of despair, because it does seem to me that the House of Commons, by not grappling with these questions, by not following them up with intense attention and even ferocity, is allowing power to slip from its hands and is allowing itself to be made a useless addition to the Constitution.'

Churchill then outlined his own plans for the campaigns of the future, aimed at saving life, but at the same time ensuring victory. He was insistent that new techniques of mechanical warfare must be developed. 'Machines save life,' he asserted, 'machine-power is a substitute for man-power, brains will save blood, manoeuvre is a great diluting agent to slaughter.' Unless new 'manoeuvre devices' were developed, he went on, 'I do not see how we are to avoid being thrown back on those dismal processes of waste and slaughter which are called attrition'. Churchill then warned the Government not to repeat the tactics of the Somme offensive of 1916. 'I hope,' he said, 'that they will not launch out on vast offensives of the kind we had last year unless they are certain that the fair weather months at their disposal and the reserves they command relatively to the enemy are such as to give an indisputable result.' The Allies had no right 'to count upon events turning decisively and immediately in our favour'. Preparation should now be made for the campaign of 1918. No source of manpower should be neglected. Mechanical aids should be developed 'which require intense exertion of thought'. The skilled production of weapons should proceed 'at its very height'. By such methods, Churchill concluded, 'we can make victory a certainty in 1918. There is still time for that. Do not let us always be behind the march of events. We are doing in 1917 what we ought to have done in 1916 or even in 1915. Do not let it be said when 1918 arrives that we find ourselves in agreement at last with all those measures which it would have been proper to take in 1917.'

Churchill's immediate political prospects still seemed to depend on the verdict of the Dardanelles Commission of Enquiry. On February 15, in a friendly gesture, Lloyd George had lent him a draft copy of the first section of the Report, which Churchill in his turn showed to Sir George Riddell. 'After I had skimmed it,' Riddell recorded in his diary that same day, 'he asked my candid opinion. I told him I thought he had come well out of the inquiry, but that the document would be damaging to Asquith and Kitchener.'[1] But Churchill pointed out to

[1] Horatio Herbert Kitchener, 1850–1916. Entered Army, 1868. Commander-in-Chief of the Egyptian Army, 1892–8. Knighted, 1894. Defeated the Dervishes at Omdurman, 1898. Created Baron Kitchener of Khartoum, 1898. Commander-in-Chief, South Africa, 1900–2. Created Viscount, 1902. Commander-in-Chief, India, 1902–9. Field-Marshal, 1909. British

Riddell that the evidence on which the report was based was not to be published, although it contained, Churchill said, 'proof that when we stopped the naval operations the Turks had only three rounds of ammunition'.

The Report made it clear that Asquith had been as anxious as any of his Cabinet to attack and defeat Turkey, and that Lord Kitchener had not informed his colleagues in sufficient detail of the military plans for April and August 1915. Although Churchill himself was not singled out for blame in the Report, he was angered because many of the charges that had been levelled against him were not fully answered. On March 10 he wrote to Lloyd George, protesting against the excisions and distortions of the Report. Riddell delivered the letter personally. 'I assert,' wrote Churchill, 'that quotations from the evidence included in the body of the Report do not in numerous cases represent the evidence given before the Commission.'

For the Commission itself, Churchill prepared a series of notes on the Report, in which he listed the omissions which, in his view, needed to be remedied. In a covering letter to the Commissioners he set out his main grievance, that the Report had failed to set the Dardanelles campaign into the general context of the war:

It seems to me very necessary for the Commission to bear in mind the circumstances in which their inquiry is pursued. The enterprise has ended in defeat and failure. The Army has been withdrawn. The positions which they had won by so much effort and sacrifice have been yielded to the enemy. The hopes, the legitimate expectations, the chances of battle have vanished away; only the slaughter, the suffering and the waste remains. . . .

A great volume of prejudice and not unnatural vexation has gathered round the story of the expedition. All tongues are freed. The natural tendency of the Commission is to look for faults and errors and it is not surprising that they should find them.

It is important therefore that some standard bearing a true relation to the episodes of the Great War should be kept in mind and that in surveying the military operations on the Gallipoli Peninsula and the many horrible and melancholy circumstances connected with them it should not be assumed that elsewhere throughout the theatres of war everything has gone smoothly and well; that other plans have not miscarried; that other battles have been fought without painful incidents, confusion or mischance; that loss of life on the Gallipoli Peninsula was more deplorable and more preventable than loss of life elsewhere; that its suffering and carnage are unparalleled.

Agent and Consul-General in Egypt, 1911–14. Created Earl, 1914. Secretary of State for War, 5 August 1914 until drowned at sea 5 June 1916.

Churchill then turned to the events on the western front, telling the Commission:

In the attack of the 1st of July on the German positions North of the Somme nearly 70,000 British troops were killed and wounded and of these nearly half were killed or missing and of the missing—nearly 20,000—all except a few hundreds perished miserably and by inches where they fell. Except at the Southern end of the line the whole plan of attack failed, and after five months continuous fighting sustained by unprecedented supplies of men and ammunition scarcely any of the original objectives assigned to the first day's operations had been attained. The sanguine expectations which led on three or four occasions to many thousands of Cavalry being brought up to gallop through some gap in the enemy's line were shown to be utterly out of contact with reality at any point. For the sake of a few miles of ground devoid of strategic significance nearly 600,000 British casualties have been sustained and the efficiency of our Army in the West sensibly and permanently diminished. These operations were based upon a complete and admitted miscalculation of the German reserves, the error amounting to nearly two millions of men. In consequence the Spring campaign of 1917 opens with a greater equality of forces in the West than was the case when the battle of the Somme began.

Nevertheless with a good Press sedulously manipulated & employed and the effective support of the governing forces, these operations have been represented as a long series of famous and memorable victories and the initial disaster of the 1st of July has been established in the public mind as a brilliant triumph. A fifth of the resources, the effort, the loyalty, the resolution, the perseverance vainly employed in the battle of the Somme to gain a few shattered villages and a few square miles of devastated ground, would in the Gallipoli Peninsula, used in time, have united the Balkans on our side, joined hands with Russia, and cut Turkey out of the war. The choice was open to us; we have built our own misfortune and no one can tell what its limits will be.

Churchill did not expect to be vindicated for some time. His letter ended:

Public opinion is unable to measure the true proportion of events. Orthodox military opinion remains united on the local view that victory in 1915 could only be found by pouring out men and munitions in frantic efforts to break the German entrenchments in the West. The passage of a few years will throw a very different light on these events. They will then be seen in a truer proportion and perspective. It will then be understood that the capture of Constantinople and the rallying of the Balkans was the one great and decisive manoeuvre open to the allied armies in 1915. It will then be seen that the ill-supported armies struggling on the Gallipoli Peninsula, whose efforts are now viewed with so much prejudice and repugnance were in fact within an ace of succeeding in an enterprise which would have abridged the miseries of the World and proved the salvation of our cause. It will then seem incredible that a dozen old ships, half a dozen divisions, or a few hundred thousand shells were allowed to stand between them and success. Contemporaries have condemned the men who tried to force the Dardanelles—History will condemn those who did not aid them.

The Dardanelles Report was to be debated in the House of Commons on March 20. Churchill spent six days preparing his speech. When he lunched with the editor of the *Manchester Guardian*, C. P. Scott,[1] on March 16, he could talk, Scott recorded, 'of nothing but Dardanelles Report' which was, he told Scott, 'curiously careless and inaccurate'. During their talk, Scott asked Churchill whether he was willing to join Lloyd George's Government. 'Not in any subordinate capacity—,' Churchill replied, 'only in one of the chief posts.' Scott asked if he would accept the War Office. 'Yes,' said Churchill, 'that would do very well.'

The Debate on the Dardanelles Commission Report opened in the House of Commons on the afternoon of March 20. The House was crowded. For the first time since the outbreak of the war, a military operation was being made the subject of thorough scrutiny and open debate. In his speech Churchill welcomed the Report as 'at any rate, an instalment of fair play' and went on to say, of the Commissioners:

They have swept away directly, or by implication, many serious and reckless charges which have passed current broadcast throughout the land during the long months of the last two years. They have reduced these charges within the limits of modest and sober criticism, and, further, by laying before the nation, the general outlines of the story—a long, tangled, complicated story—they have limited the responsibilities which have been thrown on me and under which I have greatly suffered.

. . . the current of public opinion and the weight of popular displeasure, were mainly directed upon me, who was at that time responsible for the Admiralty. The burden that I have hitherto borne alone is now shared with the most eminent men which this country has produced within the lifetime of a whole generation in Parliament, in the Army, or the Fleet.

But Churchill went on to criticize severely specific quotations in the Report, elaborating in even greater detail on the criticisms that he had

[1] Charles Prestwich Scott, 1846–1932. Editor of the *Manchester Guardian*, 1872–1929. Liberal MP, 1895–1906. A friend of Lloyd George, who often sought his advice.

sent to Lloyd George on March 10, and to the Commissioners in early
March. His discussion of the specific documents and orders took more
than half an hour. 'I elaborate these details to the House,' he explained,
'first of all to defend myself against the false impression spread abroad
by building up a story out of these little clippings and snippets from
documents and evidence, which do not represent the documents and
which do not represent the evidence,' but also to defend 'other interests
besides my own'. He went on:

I am defending the Government of which I was a member. I am defending
the chief under whom I served, and who had acted on the advice which I had
tendered. I am defending the authority and dignity of the Admiralty, because,
believe me, you could do it no greater injury than to weaken the confidence
of the officers and men of the Fleet in the orders they get from the Admiralty
by favouring the impression that those orders had been made in a reckless,
careless, amateur, and a haphazard way.

Churchill reiterated the arguments he had used in his letter to the
Commissioners, and begged his critics to look at the naval attack on the
Dardanelles with a greater sense of proportion. 'I may be accused of
being reckless or sanguine,' he went on, 'but I shall plead that if I am it
is because the sense of proportion with which I have judged this War
from the very beginning, is different in important aspects from the
accepted standard.'

Towards the end of his speech, Churchill raised the question of the
Turkish shortage of heavy gun munitions at the moment when the
British naval attack was broken off. 'It was not possible for me to lay all
the information I possessed on this subject before the Commission,' he
told the House of Commons; the result was that in the Report itself
there was nothing but 'a dark, vague and cryptic sentence to the effect
that there was information that the forts were running short of ammunition'. This, he believed, as he had earlier written to Lloyd George, did
not show how near the naval attack might have been to success, and
ignored altogether the influence that this information had had upon
even Lord Fisher's determination to persevere with the attack. 'One day
the truth will be known . . .' Churchill continued, 'and surely it is
prudent, it would be prudent, to wait before passing final judgment on
the action of those who were responsible for these operations, until these
all-important facts can be ascertained with historical certainty.'

Churchill continued his speech with a detailed denunciation of those
who had disrupted the planning of the Dardanelles by their criticism,
and ended:

My recollection, looking back on this story, is that it was one long struggle from the beginning to the end—one long, agonising, wearying struggle to get every ship, every soldier, every gun, and every round of ammunition for the Dardanelles. When this matter is passed in final review before the tribunal of history, I have no fear where the sympathies of those who come after us will lie. Your Commission may condemn the men who tried to force the Dardanelles, but your children will keep their condemnation for all who did not rally to their aid.

On March 22, two days after his Dardanelles speech, Churchill sent Sir Archibald Sinclair a detailed account of his feelings:

The war weighs heavy on us all & amid such universal misfortune & with death so ubiquitous & life so harsh, I find a difficulty in setting pen to paper. I have liked to think you have been bored & not in danger, & I hope this condition will continue. I share it—so we are fellow sufferers. I remain inactive & useless on the edge of the whirlpool. I see a good deal of L.G. and hear how things are going. But otherwise I keep clear of the whole governing machine except F.E.[1] The Asquithians are all vy kind & friendly: but here again I keep a separate dwelling.

You will be glad to hear that the House of Commons is coming to hand again. The three speeches I have made this year have all been vy well received. The Dardanelles debate especially was vy successful to me personally. The grouping of forces in the House are becoming increasingly favourable. The Dlles report has forced all who care about K's memory (and they are many) to join with all who adhere to orthodox Liberalism in defence of that operation: and I thus have strong bodies of public opinion between me & the malevolence of Tory Press. This is likely to govern my affairs.

Churchill went on to tell Sinclair that Lloyd George was planning 'to force an election'. But, he said, there was 'no justification' for such a course, and 'I am doing all I can to prevent such a disastrous course both by supporting the Government in the prosecution of the war, & by protesting against such a course'.

On April 3 Churchill again criticized the Government's military policy. Speaking in the House of Commons, he spoke of the misuse of wounded men. 'It is perfectly clear,' he said, 'that men invalided out of the Army for ill-health while on active service, and considered permanently disabled from that ill-health, should not be called up and sent

[1] Frederick Edwin Smith, 1872–1930. Known as 'F.E.'. One of Churchill's closest friends. Conservative MP, 1906–19. Head of the Press Bureau, August 1914; resigned, October 1914. Lieutenant-Colonel, attached to the Indian Corps in France, 1914–15. Solicitor-General, May 1915. Knighted, 1915. Attorney General, 1915–19. Created Baron Birkenhead, 1919. Lord Chancellor, 1919–22. Created Viscount, 1921. Created Earl, 1922. Secretary of State for India, 1924–8.

to the front while there are, as we all know, quite young and active men in many industries throughout the country within the age limit who have not yet been out to the front at all.' And he added angrily: 'Everybody knows it. Everybody feels it.'

Churchill's concern for a rapid development of mechanical warfare was accentuated in the first week of April, when he learnt of the impending British offensive east of Arras. Writing in the *Sunday Pictorial* on April 8, he warned that victory could not be obtained 'simply by throwing in masses of men on the western front', and argued that mechanical inventions could become, if properly used, 'a substitute for men'.

On April 9—Easter Monday—the British Army launched its spring offensive. By April 11 the Germans had been driven back nearly four miles, along a fourteen-mile front. That day Churchill wrote to Sinclair —who had been taken ill and was thus unable to take part in the battle:

My dear,

I am so sorry to hear of yr illness & I know how vexed you will be to be out of the fight. Never mind. Cavalry have no rôle on the western front. There will be no galloping through, & even catastrophe will be prevented by the unfailing interposition of preliminary hard facts.

This battle seems to have been well organised and the Artillery (fed by the abused L.G. & other 'politicians') has proved once again overwhelming on the limited area exposed to its attack. But the secondary stages are vy costly, and the forward movement must be gradual—i.e. step by step.

Meanwhile there is much to cause anxiety. Russia! The Submarines!! The German Reserve Army!!! (if it really exists). All these are factors of *fundamental* uncertainty.

It is vy joyous reading of this brilliant *episode*. 11,000 Huns glad to accept life at the hands of our small army. One likes to dwell on it, altho I fear the *tendencies* are no longer so favourable as they used to be. Still America— dear to your heart & mine, is please God a final makeweight.

Do not fret or chafe. Just do what is yr appointed task & may Heaven protect you till better days dawn—& even after that—is the prayer of yr sincere friend W.

On April 17 the House of Commons debated the Government's suppression of a series of articles in the *Nation*, in which it had been asserted that the British troops on the western front had been outmanoeuvred by the German 'tactical' withdrawal in Champagne, and that the German retreat had been a prudent act. The first of the articles, written on March 3, had been widely reprinted in Germany. The Government decided not to allow the others to appear.

Lloyd George defended the suppression in a passionate speech. Churchill then rose to defend the *Nation*. But before he could speak, Lloyd George left the Chamber, a fact on which Churchill commented with much sarcasm. As for the articles themselves, he declared, they were 'absolutely immaterial and innocent'; everything in them made 'mild reading compared with the Dardanelles Report from the point of view of public confidence'. If such reports could not be published, it would soon lead 'to a universal harmonious chorus of adulation from morning to night about whatever was done, until some frightful disaster took place'. The Government's action betrayed 'an undue love of power and an undue love of the assertion of arbitrary power'.

During his speech, Churchill appealed to Bonar Law to take note, on Lloyd George's behalf, of the deep concern of the House of Commons. When Bonar Law interrupted to say: 'We will judge that by the Division,' Churchill was stung to anger. 'Do not look for quarrels,' he replied, 'do not make them; make it easy for every party, every force in this country, to give you its aid and support, and remove barriers and obstructions and misunderstandings that tend to cause superficial and apparent divergence among men whose aim is all directed to our common object of victory, on which all our futures depend.' Above all, Churchill insisted, the Government must deal 'fairly and justly' with criticism, and not reply to it with 'the kind of rhetoric or argument which might do very well on public platforms, but is entirely unsuitable to the cool discussion in the House of Commons'.

Lloyd George knew that Churchill's aim was to return to a position of authority, but that if no place were found for him, he would continue to attack the Government's war policy. Towards the end of April he had discussed the possibility of Churchill's employment with the Minister of Munitions, Dr Christopher Addison.[1] Lloyd George suggested that Churchill might join the Ministry of Munitions as the Chairman of a Committee, or Board, to examine the development of mechanical aids to warfare.

[1] Christopher Addison, 1869–1951. Hunterian Professor of Anatomy, 1901. Liberal MP, 1910–22. Parliamentary Secretary to the Board of Education, 1914–15. Parliamentary Secretary, Ministry of Munitions, 1915–16. Minister of Munitions, 1916–17. Minister in Charge of Reconstruction, 1917. President of the Local Government Board, 1919. Minister of Health, 1919–21. Minister without Portfolio, 1921. Labour MP, 1929–31; 1934–5. Minister of Agriculture and Fisheries, 1930–1. Created Baron, 1937; Viscount, 1945. Secretary of State for Commonwealth Relations, 1945–7. Paymaster-General, 1948–9. Lord Privy Seal, 1947–51. In 1924 he published his diaries in two volumes, entitled *Politics from Within*.

At Lloyd George's suggestion, Addison met Churchill twice, and discussed the question with him. 'It appears to me,' Addison wrote to Lloyd George on April 27, 'that the most effective way of giving effect to your suggestions and making the fullest use of Mr Churchill's services, on the lines on which he feels free to assist, (viz:—without undue advertisement and without attaching to him special executive responsibilities) would be to form a small *ad hoc* Committee under his Chairmanship which should consider and discuss (1) the general question of the Tank programme, both as to numbers and types, and any other suggestions with regard to mechanical devices which may be worth considering.' Addison added that the Ministry of Munitions would give Churchill 'any facilities that might be required'. But nothing came of this suggestion. Two days later, when Lloyd George spoke at the Guildhall, his Secretary, Frances Stevenson,[1] noted that Churchill, who was present, looked 'very sulky'. Everyone she spoke to 'remarked how surly he was looking, and he left quite alone'.

In the first week of May, Churchill sought out his cousin, Frederick Guest,[2] the Coalition Liberal Chief Whip. They discussed the growing Parliamentary opposition to Lloyd George's Government, and the fact that Liberal, Labour and Irish Nationalist MPs were grumbling about the conduct and prospects of the war. If these three Parties were to unite against Lloyd George, and if Asquith were to mount a direct Liberal challenge, Conservative support alone would not be enough to sustain the administration. Churchill suggested to his cousin that Lloyd George should take the initiative, and summon a secret Session of the House of Commons.

Guest informed Lloyd George of Churchill's advice. A secret Session was announced for May 10. Asquith, who was unprepared for such an opportunity, did not seek to exploit it. No member of Asquith's opposition group asked to open the Debate. The task therefore fell to Churchill, whose main appeal was a repetition of what he had been saying openly for more than six months: that there should be no premature offensive in France. The United States had entered the war on April 2;

---

[1] Frances Louise Stevenson, 1888–1972. Schoolteacher. Private Secretary to Lloyd George, 1913–43. She married Lloyd George in 1943. Countess Lloyd-George of Dwyfor, 1945. She published her memoirs, *The Years That Are Past*, in 1967. Her only brother was killed in action on the western front, May 1915.

[2] Frederick Edward Guest, 1875–1937. The third son of 1st Baron Wimborne; Churchill's cousin. Served in the South African War as a Captain, Life Guards, 1899–1902. Private Secretary to Churchill, 1906. Liberal MP, 1910–29. Treasurer, HM Household, 1912–15. ADC to Sir John French, 1914–16. On active service in East Africa, 1916–17. Patronage Secretary, Treasury, May 1917–April 1921. Secretary of State for Air, April 1921–October 1922. Joined the Conservative Party, 1930. Conservative MP, 1931–7. Known as 'Freddie'.

but American troops could not be ready for action in Europe until 1918. 'Is it not obvious . . .' he asked, 'that we ought not to squander the remaining armies of France and Britain in precipitate offensives before the American power begins to be felt on the battlefields?' He proceeded to give his reasons: 'We have not the numerical superiority necessary for such a successful offensive. We have no marked artillery preponderance over the enemy. We have not got the numbers of tanks which we need. We have not established superiority in the air. We have discovered neither the mechanical nor the tactical methods of piercing an indefinite succession of fortified lines defended by German troops.' Then he returned once more to his plea: 'Shall we then in such circumstances cast away our remaining man power in desperate efforts on the Western Front before large American forces are marshalled in France? Let the House implore the Prime Minister to use the authority which he wields, and all his personal weight, to prevent the French and British High Commands from dragging each other into fresh bloody and disastrous adventures. Master the U-boat attack. Bring over the American millions. And meanwhile maintain an active defensive on the Western Front, so as to economize French and British lives, and so as to train, increase and perfect our armies and our methods for a decisive effort in a later year.'

In his reply, Lloyd George refused to commit himself against a renewed offensive. Nor did he tell the House of Commons the extent to which he was already committed. Shortly after he had finished speaking, he and Churchill met by chance behind the Speaker's chair. 'In his satisfaction at the course the Debate had taken,' Churchill later recalled in *The World Crisis*, 'he assured me of his determination to have me at his side. From that day, although holding no office, I became to a large extent his colleague. He repeatedly discussed with me every aspect of the war and many of his secret hopes and fears.'

A few days later Churchill decided to visit the French front to see for himself the military situation. Lloyd George agreed to support his visit, and when the two men lunched together at Walton Heath on Sunday May 19, Lloyd George wrote to the French Minister of War, Paul Painlevé,[1] asking him to give Churchill 'every facility' for visiting the

---

[1] Paul Painlevé, 1863–1933. Mathematician; Professor in the Faculty of Sciences at Lille, 1886; at the Sorbonne, 1891. Elected to the Chamber of Deputies, 1906, as an independent Socialist. Minister of Public Instruction and Inventions, October 1915–December 1916. Minister of War, March 1917–September 1917. Prime Minister, and Minister of War, 12 September–13 November 1917 (when he was succeeded as Prime Minister by Clemenceau). President of the Chamber, 1924. Prime Minister for the second time, April, June–November 1925. Minister of War, 1925–6. Minister of Air, 1930–1 and 1932–3.

front. That evening, Frances Stevenson recorded in her diary Lloyd George's reasons for drawing closer to Churchill once more:

He says he wants someone in who will cheer him up and help & encourage him, & who will not be continually coming to him with a long face and telling him that everything is going wrong. At present, he says, he has to carry the whole of his colleagues on his back. They all come to him with their troubles and trials, instead of trying to relieve him of anxiety. D [Lloyd George] feels that he must have someone a little more cheerful to help him to cope with all these mournful faces—Bonar Law not the least of them. I think D. is thinking of getting Winston in in some capacity. He has an intense admiration for his cleverness, & at any rate he is energetic and forceful. D. has seen him once or twice lately & I think they have talked things over. Churchill is very loath to associate with the Asquithites. He hates McKenna[1] & was telling D. that McKenna simply gloated when the submarine losses were high. . . .

I don't know whether D. is seriously thinking of taking Churchill on, as he knows his limitations and realises that he is eaten up with conceit. 'He has spoilt himself by reading about Napoleon', said D. to me.

During the spring of 1917 Churchill had bought a small home in the country, Lullenden, in Sussex. It cost him £6,000, which he raised by selling £5,000 of Pennsylvania Railroad stock, and a £1,000 Exchequer War Bond. He liked to spend each weekend at Lullenden, relaxing with his family and painting. His nephew Peregrine,[2] who was four years old at the time, later recalled:

We had a game called the bear game. Uncle Winston used to prop up his paintings against the wall, to make a tunnel, and then he would chase us through the tunnel.

We had three German prisoners at Lullenden working on the farm. One day we were taken ill with food poisoning. The prisoners were arrested and taken away. We had pet rabbits. One night they were served up for dinner.

Churchill's son Randolph[3] also remembered Lullenden. He was six years old at the time of its purchase. Forty-four years later he recalled

[1] Reginald McKenna, 1863–1943. Liberal MP, 1895–1918. President, Board of Education, 1907–8. First Lord of the Admiralty, 1908–11. Home Secretary, 1911–15. Chancellor of the Exchequer, May 1915–December 1916. Chairman, Midland Bank, 1919–43.

[2] Henry Winston Spencer Churchill, 1913– . Known as Peregrine. Jack Churchill's younger son. Inventor and Company Director.

[3] Randolph Frederick Edward Spencer Churchill, 1911–68. Churchill's only son. His godfathers were F. E. Smith and Sir Edward Grey. Conservative MP, 1940–5. Major, British mission to the Yugoslav Army of National Liberation, 1943–4. Journalist and historian; author of the first two volumes of this biography.

how his father would set off through the woods, 'and we all had to chase him. Once he disturbed a nest of bees or perhaps wasps and passed through unscathed. All of us children however, in hot pursuit were badly stung. . . .' Randolph also remembered an outdoor version of the bear game:

Father was the Bear. We had to turn our backs and close our eyes and he would climb a tree. All us children—six or seven perhaps—had then to go and look for Bear. We were very much afraid but would advance courageously on a tree and say: 'Bear! Bear! Bear!' And then run away. Suddenly he would drop from a tree and we would scatter in various directions. He would pursue us and the one he caught would be the loser.

On Saturday May 26 Churchill left England for his visit to France. The French high command entertained him as they had done over two years before, when he was a Cabinet Minister; they listened to his opinions and responded to his enthusiasm. Under the auspices of the French Ministry of War, he was taken to the battlefields of 1916—to Verdun, the Argonne and the Vimy Ridge. 'There was no danger,' Churchill wrote to his wife on May 29, '& hardly the sound of a gun.' He dined with General Fayolle,[1] whose Army corps he had visited in December 1915, and who had since been given the much wider command of an Army Group. 'Instead of 3 Divisions,' Churchill explained to his wife, 'he commands 41! So he has gone up in the world. It was pleasant to find complete agreement on all military questions. Indeed I think the French soldiers see vy clearly the truths of this front.' The tour was exhausting: 'We have been travelling very long distances in motor cars,' he told his wife, 'and in continuous movement from daylight till night: & I expect this will continue.'

While in Paris, Churchill saw Marshal Foch,[2] who had been removed

[1] Marie Emile Fayolle, 1852–1928. Entered the French Army, 1875. Professor, Ecole de Guerre, 1897–1907. General of Brigade, 1910. Commanded the 33rd Corps, 1915–16; the 6th Army, 1916–17; the Centre Group of Armies, 1917; the Group of Armies of Reserve, 1917–18; the French Occupation Forces on the Rhine, 1918–20. Marshal of France, 1921.

[2] Ferdinand Foch, 1851–1929. Lieutenant, French Army, 1873. Professor, Ecole Superieure de Guerre, 1894–1900; General Commanding the Ecole, 1907–11. Commanded the XXth Corps, based on Nancy, 1913–14. Commanded the 9th Army, at the battle of the Marne, September 1914. Deputy to the Commander-in-Chief, during the 'race to the sea', October 1914. Honorary knighthood, 1914. Commanded the Group of Armies of the North, 1915–16. Deprived of his command after the battle of the Somme. Recalled, Generalissimo of the Allied Forces, France, April–November 1918. Marshal of France, August 1918. Appointed British Field-Marshal, 1919. His only son was killed in action, 22 August 1914.

from his fighting command after the unsuccessful and costly French offensive in Artois in the spring of 1915. Churchill saw Foch in his office near Les Invalides—'Certainly no one ever appeared less downcast or conscious of being at a discount,' he later recorded, in an article published in the *Pall Mall* magazine in July 1929; and his article continued:

He discussed with the utmost frankness and vigour the whole scene of the war, and particularly those Eastern spheres in which I had been so much interested. His postures, his captivating manner, his vigorous and often pantomimic gestures—comical, if they had not been fully expressive—the energy of his ideas when his interest was aroused, made a vivid impression upon me. He was fighting all the time, whether he had armies to launch or only thoughts.

After two days in the French battle zone, Churchill made plans for his journey northwards, to the British front. 'Evidently,' he wrote to his wife in his letter of May 29, 'all the claws of the military pussy cat are withdrawn into their sheaths and a soft purring sound is plainly audible.'

Before leaving for the British front, Churchill spent two days in Paris, staying at the Ritz. On May 29 he lunched with Lord Esher[1] at the Café des Ambassadeurs. Also at the lunch was Sir Henry Wilson,[2] who wrote a full account of the conversation in his diary:

Winston in great form & evidently in high favour with L.G. so I expect he will soon be employed again. He is very keen (& rightly so) that the navy should fight instead of doing nothing & he has great plans for bringing on fights by laying mine fields close up against enemy ports. Then his great plan for the moment is to delay any attempt at a decision on this front till the Americans come over—say 12–15 months. He developed this at length using both good & silly arguments all mixed up. . . .

Winston was very keen to get ½ Salonica Garr^n on flat-bottomed boats to be used for sudden descents here & there. There is the germ of a good idea there, but I besought him not to go out of Salonica without bargaining about it.

So we have a great lunch & long talk, and it always amuses me to talk to Winston. . . .

[1] Reginald Baliol Brett, 1852–1930. Liberal MP, 1880–85. Secretary to the Office of Works, 1895–1902. 2nd Viscount Esher, 1899. A permanent member of the Committee of Imperial Defence, 1905–18. In 1915 he was sent to Paris as Liaison Officer between the British and French War Offices.

[2] Henry Hughes Wilson, 1864–1922. Entered Army, 1884. Director of Military Operations, War Office, 1910–14. Lieutenant-General, 1914. Chief liaison officer with the French Army, January 1915. Knighted, 1915. Commanded the 4th Corps, 1916. Chief of the Imperial General Staff, 1918–22. Field-Marshal, July 1919. Created Baronet, August 1919. Ulster Unionist MP, 1922. Shot dead by two Sinn Feiners on the steps of his London house.

On May 30 Churchill lunched with Painlevé. Several senior French officials had been invited to meet him.[1] One of the Englishmen who was present at the lunch, Sir Henry Norman,[2] sent Lloyd George an account of his own conversation with Churchill on May 31. 'I asked Churchill if his visit to the French front had modified his pessimistic outlook, as expressed in the secret session. He said it had only confirmed him in his views!' Churchill was still convinced that the correct time for an offensive was 1918, not 1917. In his letter to his wife of May 29 he had written: 'It has all been vy pleasant, but never for a moment does the thought of this carnage & ruin escape my mind or my thoughts stray from the supreme problem. I am much stimulated by the change and movement, & new discussions with new people, & I am vy full of ideas.'

On the morning of May 31 Churchill left Paris for the British front, where he spent the whole of June 1. On June 2 he lunched with Sir Douglas Haig[3] at St Omer. In his diary Haig recorded that Churchill had argued in favour of postponing the offensive until the summer of 1918, but that during their discussion he had seemed 'most humble'. Haig had received, however, a most critical letter about Churchill, written by Lord Esher on May 30:

My dear Douglas,
    A true appreciation of Winson Churchill,—of his potential uses,—is a difficult matter.
    The degree in which his clever but unbalanced mind will in future fulfil its responsibilities is very speculative.
    He handles great subjects in rhythmical language, and becomes quickly enslaved by his own phrases.
    He deceives himself into the belief that he takes broad views, when his mind is fixed upon one comparatively small aspect of the question.
    At this moment he is captured by the picture of what *1918* may bring forth in the shape of accumulated reserves of men and material, poured out

---

[1] Among those at the lunch were the Under Secretary of State for Munitions, Louis Loucheur, and the Chief of the French Naval Staff, Vice-Admiral de Bon.

[2] Henry Norman, 1858–1939. Journalist. Assistant editor, *Daily Chronicle*, 1895; resigned from journalism, 1899. Liberal MP, 1900–10 and 1910–23. Knighted, 1906. Assistant Post-master-General, 1910. Chairman, War Office Committee on Wireless telegraphy. Created Baronet, 1915. Liaison officer of the Ministry of Munitions with the Ministry of Inventions, Paris, 1916. Chairman of the Imperial Wireless Telegraphy Committee, 1920. Member of the Broadcasting Committee, 1923. Director of several colliery companies.

[3] Douglas Haig, 1861–1928. Entered the Army, 1885. Knighted, 1909. Chief of Staff, India, 1909–11. Lieutenant-General, 1910. Commander of the 1st Army Corps, 1914–15. His successful defence of Ypres, 19 October–22 November 1914, made him a national figure. Commanded the 1st Army at Loos, November 1915. Succeeded Sir John French as Commander-in-Chief, British Expeditionary Force, 19 December 1915. Field-Marshal, January 1917. Created Earl, 1919.

from England in one great and final effort; while, at the same time a million Americans sweep over Holland on to the German flank.

He fails to grasp the meaning to France, to England, to Europe, of a postponement of effort—through the long summer that was crammed full of artificial expectations—and a still longer winter. . . .

It seems not unlikely that L. George will put Winston into the Government, or give him some showy position. There have been pourparlers between L.G. and the Tories on the subject: but Winston told me no details. He appeals to L. George, because he can strike ideas into colour and imagery. But his ideas are 'Transpontine' that is to say too melodramatic; and nothing but steadiness and the very coolest appreciation of the factors in the problems of the war and its settlement can give us the position we ought to occupy at the War's end. . . .

The power of Winston for good and evil is, I should say, very considerable.

His temperament is of wax and quicksilver, and this strange toy amuses and fascinates L. George, who likes and fears him.

You will find much that he has to say about the navy both interesting and valuable. All that he has to say about the army valueless. It may be worth your while to instruct him. Of this you will be the best judge.

To me he appears not as a statesman, but as a politician of keen intelligence lacking in those puissant qualities that are essential in a man who is to conduct the business of our country through the coming year. I hope therefore that he may remain outside the Government.

2

'A Dangerously Ambitious Man'

WHILE Churchill was still in France, several newspapers announced categorically that on his return he would be brought into the Cabinet as Chairman of the Air Board. Downing Street refused to confirm or deny the report. There was an immediate spate of protest. On June 3 the *Sunday Times* declared that Churchill's appointment to any Cabinet post would be 'a grave danger to the Administration and to the Empire as whole'. The leading article continued: 'Whatever his friends and admirers may say or think of him, his public record has proved beyond all argument or doubt that he does not possess those qualities of balanced judgement and shrewd far-sightedness which are essential to the sound administrator. . . .'

Two of Lloyd George's Conservative Ministers, Lord Curzon[1] and Lord Derby,[2] were quick to complain about the rumoured appointment. 'As you know,' Curzon wrote to Bonar Law on June 4, 'some of us myself included only joined Ll.G on the distinct understanding that W.Ch was not to be a member of the Govt. It is on record, and to the pledge I and I think all my colleagues adhere.'

Lord Derby went to see Lloyd George on June 8 to make his protest. Immediately after the meeting he wrote to reinforce his arguments. Churchill's inclusion in the Government, he wrote, could only be 'a source of weakness'. Derby was only prepared to accept Churchill in the

[1] George Nathaniel Curzon, 1859–1925. Conservative MP, 1886–98. Under-Secretary of State for India, 1891–2; for Foreign Affairs, 1892–8. Viceroy of India, 1898–1905. Created Earl, 1911. Lord Privy Seal, May 1915–December 1916. President of the Air Board, 1916. Lord President of the Council and Member of the War Cabinet, 1916–19. Secretary of State for Foreign Affairs, 1919–22. Created Marquess, 1921. Lord President of the Council, 1924–5.
[2] Edward George Villiers Stanley, 1865–1948. Conservative MP, 1892–1906. Postmaster General, 1903–5. 17th Earl of Derby, 1908. Director-General of Recruiting, October 1915. Under-Secretary of State at the War Office, July–December 1916. Secretary of State for War, December 1916–18. Ambassador to France, 1918–20. Secretary of State for War, 1922–4.

Cabinet on three conditions, which Lloyd George had apparently agreed to, and which Derby set out in his letter:

(1) that he was not a member of the War Cabinet and did not attend any meetings unless specially summoned for business connected with the Board; (2) that his duties as Chairman of the Board were the same as those of Lord Cowdray[1] and that he had nothing to do with either personnel, tactics or the nomination of the War Office representatives on the Board; and (3) that he received no War Office telegrams other than those which were in any way connected with his particular department.

Derby added that he doubted whether Churchill would ever agree to accept 'a comparatively minor position', or agree 'to do his own work without interfering with other peoples''.

A third Conservative Minister, Lord Milner,[2] was likewise angered at the thought of Churchill's appointment. On June 30 Sir Henry Wilson recorded a conversation with Milner in his diary: 'He told me he was getting on well with LG on the whole, although he had very difficult times now and then; that only a few days ago he nearly resigned over some subject which he was afraid would come up again. I thought it was Winston. . . .'

Not all Lloyd George's colleagues were as hostile as Curzon, Derby and Milner. Dr Addison shared Lloyd George's desire to see Churchill's talents used in the interest of the State. On June 4 he had written to Lloyd George about the Air Board: 'I feel that we should get Winston in & the more it is talked about the more opportunity there is for opposition to gather. I should advise acting quickly in this so as to get the ice broken.' Addison was also willing to hand over the Ministry of Munitions to Churchill. 'Give me three weeks,' he added, 'and I could get the estimates over & shape things here through my new Board of Directors so as to pave the way for Winston if you wished him to follow me.' Lord Rothermere[3] also wrote to Lloyd George at this time:

[1] Weetman Dickinson Pearson, 1856–1927. Head of the firm of S. Pearson & Son Ltd., engineering contractors. Completed the Blackwall Tunnel under the Thames, 1894; and created Baronet at the opening ceremony. Liberal MP for Colchester, 1895–1910. Created Baron Cowdray, 1910. He had a controlling interest in the Mexican oilfields. Supervised the construction of the Gretna Green munitions factory, 1915–16. Created Viscount, 1917. President of the Air Board January–November 1917. His youngest son was killed in action on 6 September 1914.
[2] Alfred Milner, 1854–1925. Under-Secretary for Finance, Egypt, 1889–92. Chairman of the Board of Inland Revenue, 1892–5. Knighted, 1895. High Commissioner for South Africa, 1897–1905. Created Baron, 1901. Created Viscount, 1902. Member of the War Cabinet, December 1916–18. Secretary of State for War, 1918–19; for the Colonies, 1919–21.
[3] Harold Sidney Harmsworth, 1868–1940. Younger brother of Lord Northcliffe, with

. . . you know I hold the view very strongly that if you saw your way to appoint Winston to the Air Board it would by reason of his driving power be popular particularly under yourself as you alone of all his friends can control him. Misfortune has chastened him. He really is very attached to you and it seems a calamity that his knowledge and energy should be lost to the nation at this crisis.

If you make this appointment you can rely upon me using all the influence I have to support it. . . .

On June 8 Christopher Addison recorded in his diary: 'I advised LG that if he wanted to get Winston in to put him into the Air Board at once, otherwise he only gave opportunity for opposition which is very strong in the Unionist Party.' But Lloyd George made no announcement. During the day Lord Curzon wrote angrily to Lloyd George:

My dear Prime Minister,

May I again and for the last time urge you to think well before you make the appointment (W Ch) which we have more than once discussed? It will be an appointment intensely unpopular with many of your chief colleagues—in the opinions of some of whom it will lead to the disruption of the Govt at an early date—even if it does not lead as it may well do to resignations now.

Derby, who opened the subject to me of his own accord this evening & who has spoken to you, tells me that it will be intensely unpopular in the Army.

I have reason to believe the same of the Navy.

Is it worthwhile to incur all these risks and to override some of those who are your most faithful colleagues & allies merely in order to silence a possible tribune of the people whom in my judgment the people will absolutely decline to follow?

He is a potential danger in opposition. In the opinion of all of us he will as a member of the Govt be an active danger in our midst.

On June 8, Sir George Younger,[1] who knew the temper of the Tory Party, warned Lloyd George that Churchill's inclusion in the Government 'would strain to breaking point the Unionist Party's loyalty to you'. Younger's letter listed new and old complaints:

His unfortunate record, the utter futility of his criticisms of your War Policy at the last Secret Session, and his grave responsibility for two of the greatest

---

whom he had helped to establish the *Daily Mail* and *Evening News*. Created Baronet, 1912. Proprietor of the *Daily Mirror*, 1914. Created Baron Rothermere, 1914. Launched the *Sunday Pictorial*, 1915. Director-General of the Royal Army Clothing Factory, 1916. President of the Air Council, 1917–18. Viscount, 1919. Two of his three sons were killed in action.

[1] George Younger, 1851–1929. President of the National Union of Conservative Associations in Scotland, 1904. Conservative MP, 1906–22. Created Baronet, 1911. Chairman of the Conservative Party Organization, 1916–23. Treasurer of the Conservative Party, 1923–9. Created Viscount, 1923. Chairman, George Younger & Sons, Brewers, Ltd.

disasters in the War have accentuated the distrust of him which has prevailed both in the House and outside of it for a long time past, and I feel certain that his inclusion in the Government would prove disastrous to its fortunes. I believe the Unionist Party in the House would unanimously back this opinion and I am certain that our great organisations in the country of which, as you know, I am Chairman would strongly assert it.

The protests in the Cabinet continued. The man whom Churchill would have replaced at the Air Board, Lord Cowdray, warned Lloyd George, in a letter on June 9, that Churchill would take over a thriving department and would then make sure 'that he, and he alone, gets all the credit from the very brilliant achievements of the Air Service'. Churchill was 'a dangerously ambitious man' who would be led by the success of the Air Board 'to think that he was the most important man (in the eyes of the country) in the Government & therefore the proper man to make a bid for the Premiership'. If he went to the Air Board, Cowdray concluded, he would be a 'grave danger, both to the country & to yourself'.

The rumour of Churchill's appointment to the Air Board had reached the United States. From New York, Lord Northcliffe telegraphed to Churchill, on June 13: 'Many congratulations on your appointment.' But Northcliffe's telegram was premature. Lloyd George had in fact made Churchill no offer of a Cabinet place. 'The latest attempts to hustle Mr Churchill into the Ministry,' noted the *Morning Post*, 'have failed.'

On June 18 Lloyd George invited Christopher Addison to lunch with him at 10 Downing Street, and spoke of the strong Conservative opposition to giving Churchill the Air Board. Lloyd George had another scheme. 'He is going to try,' Addison wrote, 'to get him into the Duchy of Lancaster. . . .' Later that same day Lloyd George sent Frederick Guest to see Churchill, and to offer him a place in the Cabinet as Chancellor of the Duchy of Lancaster, with elaborated functions. Churchill declined.

That night Guest sent Lloyd George an account of the interview. Churchill, he wrote, was prepared 'to try to help to beat the "Hun" in either of the following capacities. 1. To assist you in council in the War Cabinet, if necessary without salary. 2. To accept charge & responsibility for any War Department, as long as he has powers to actively assist in the defeat of the enemy.' He was not prepared, however, to accept a sinecure.

Guest encouraged Lloyd George not to be deflected by Conservative hostility. 'Your will & influence with your Tory colleagues,' he wrote in

his letter on June 18, 'is greater than you have credited yourself with
. . . sooner or later you will have to test it—why not now?'

Lloyd George waited for the Air Board controversy to fade away.
Churchill continued to publish his criticisms of the Government's war
policy. On June 10, in an article in the *Sunday Pictorial*, he reiterated his
belief that there should be no British offensive until the arrival of large
numbers of American troops. Two weeks later, on June 24, in a further
article, he demanded a new aggressive naval policy. The Royal Navy
had failed to utilize its full power, he asserted. But, he went on, 'once
true war-thought has taken possession of the mind of power, the means
to translate it into action are rarely found lacking'. Without a British
naval initiative, he insisted, the Germans would be free to intensify their
submarine attacks, and Britain's war making abilities would be put in
jeopardy.

On June 30 Churchill went to his constituency, Dundee, with Lloyd
George, who was to receive the Freedom of the city. In his speech at the
ceremony, Churchill told the assembled citizens of Lloyd George's
achievements. 'I have known my right honourable friend the Prime
Minister,' he said, 'for what is to me a very large portion of my human
life—nearly 14 years—and I rejoice to be present in this ancient, famous
city of Dundee, war scarred, war bitter, but not war weary, which has
decided, through its principal magistrates to offer him the greatest
honour at its disposal.' Later in his speech, Churchill praised Lloyd
George's power of 'not allowing himself to be diverted by the innumerable multitude of superficial incidents and phenomena which in every
direction, on every hand, confuse and baffle the eye'. The Prime
Minister, he declared, knew how to search 'patiently and penetratingly
for those deeply underlying causes which are affecting the war'.

On July 9 Churchill spoke in the House of Commons from the
Opposition benches. Once more he was critical of the Government's
war policy. Speaking on the question of air raid warnings, he declared:

There ought to be a clear instruction from the Government as to what
people are to do when an air raid takes place. I have no doubt a great many
Members have been guilty of the foolish conduct of going out on balconies, or
into the streets or open places, to see what is going on, and I dare say some
will be foolish to do so again; but there ought to be perfectly clear guidance
by the Government and the authorities that when an air raid takes place it is
the duty of every person to go into his house, or any available building, and
to seek such accommodation in the lower parts of those buildings as is
convenient. . . .

I do not think the Government need be ashamed of changing their mind or of modifying their policy. We are all in this business together, and the important point is to find out what is the best thing to do.

A week after Churchill's speech, Lloyd George invited him to join the Government, asking him, at 10 Downing Street on July 16, what post he would like. 'I said at once,' Churchill recalled in *The World Crisis*, 'that I preferred Munitions.' Lloyd George accepted Churchill's choice. Addison agreed to move to the specially created post of Minister of Reconstruction, a Ministry which was not to be in the Cabinet. Lloyd George also took the opportunity of appointing Edwin Montagu[1] Secretary of State for India. Both these appointments were announced in the Press on July 18.

The news of Churchill's entry into the Government provoked an immediate controversy. The first Ministerial protest came from Lord Derby, who went to see Lloyd George that same morning. Derby's Private Secretary, Herbert Creedy,[2] described the interview in a note written later that day:

Lord Derby said he wished to speak quite frankly; he had seen the appointments in the paper for the first time that morning & thought that, in view of the misgivings he felt, he ought to tender his resignation.

The Prime Minister expressed his complete satisfaction with Lord Derby's conduct of the administration of the War Office & begged him not to consider such a step. He thought he had left it to Mr Bonar Law to inform his Unionist colleagues of the new appointments. Mr Churchill would not be permitted to interfere with the War Office, as it would be his duty to supply that for which the War Office asked him, and the assurances given when it was in contemplation to make him President of the Air Board would hold good now that he was at the Ministry of Munitions.

Mr Lloyd George added that in matters of this kind he must exercise the prerogative of the Prime Minister to appoint those whom he thought likely to help him. He was in great need of men to go round the country in the next three months to expound the policy of the Government, and, if denied their assistance, he would much sooner resign himself now. Lord Derby repeated

---

[1] Edwin Montagu, 1879–1924. Liberal MP, 1906–22. Financial Secretary to the Treasury, February 1914–February 1915; May 1915–July 1916. Chancellor of the Duchy of Lancaster, February–May 1915; January–June 1916. Minister of Munitions, July–December 1916. Secretary of State for India, June 1917–March 1922.

[2] Herbert James Creedy, 1878–1973. Joined the War Office as a Clerk, 1901. Private Secretary to successive Secretaries of State for War, 1913–20. Knighted, 1919. Secretary of the War Office, 1920–4. Under-Secretary of State for War, 1924–39.

that he thought a great mistake had been made which would do the Prime Minister much harm, but, so long as Mr Churchill refrained from all interference with regard to the conduct of the war & confined himself to the business of his Department, he (Lord Derby) would not press his resignation.

The *Morning Post* voiced the complaints of many Conservatives in a fierce editorial. Churchill's appointment, it declared, 'proves that although we have not yet invented an unsinkable ship, we have discovered the unsinkable politician'. While First Lord of the Admiralty, the paper continued, Churchill had 'committed at least two capital blunders which cost the nation many thousands of lives and an appalling loss of prestige': these blunders were the attempt to save Antwerp, and the attack on the Dardanelles. 'Both expeditions,' declared the *Morning Post*, 'were managed more or less personally by Mr Churchill, whose overwhelming conceit led him to imagine he was a Nelson at sea and a Napoleon on land.'

The Colonial Secretary, Walter Long,[1] wrote personally to Lloyd George on July 18 to voice his discontent:

My dear Prime Minister,
   I hope you will pardon me if I say that I was greatly surprised to read some of the new appointments in today's Papers. Of course the selection of his Colleagues is a matter solely for the P.M. & one in which he is not expected to consult his subordinates & in ordinary conditions this rule works admirably & there are obvious remedies open to those who may find it difficult to cooperate with new colleagues. But these times are not ordinary. When you did me the honour to press me to join your Government you told me you did so because you considered that I represented the largest number of the Party to which I belong & you said they would be greatly guided by my actions.
   Again when you contemplated making somewhat similar changes a short time ago you were good enough to send for me & ask my views. I made it clear that my objections were based on general & public grounds & you were also good enough to say you would see me again before making any appointment. I have however heard nothing more of the matter. I therefore find myself in a somewhat awkward position. I had, & have, no sort of objection to Churchill or Montagu on personal grounds, I admire the great abilities of both, but I felt, & feel, that the inclusion of the former as M/M would weaken your Gov. & would certainly make it extremely difficult for many of my friends to continue their support. . . .

----

[1] Walter Hume Long, 1854–1924. Conservative MP, 1880–1921. President of the Local Government Board, 1900–5. Chief Secretary, Ireland, 1905. Created the Union Defence League, the leading anti-Home Rule organization, 1907–14. President of the Local Government Board, May 1915–December 1916. Secretary of State for the Colonies, 1916–19. First Lord of the Admiralty, 1919–21. Created Viscount, 1921.

Conservative hostility did not abate. On July 18 Leopold Amery[1] wrote in his diary: '. . . the bringing in of Churchill and Montagu into the Government has shaken its prestige and reputation seriously'.

Churchill's friends who were serving at the front were particularly glad to learn of his appointment. On July 20 Major-General Seely[2] wrote from Flanders: 'I am so glad, not only for your sake who at last have an outlet for energies and talents, but even more for all of us who want so badly just what you can give.'

Several of those who wrote to Churchill were disappointed that he had not been given wider scope for his abilities. 'I am full of hope,' wrote Lord Esher on July 24, 'that you, with your fiery energy and keen outlook, will presently take all aeroplane construction into your Dept. If you do not obtain control of this branch of munitions we shall have the worst possible time next year.' Churchill's aunt Cornelia,[3] however, sent him a word of warning. 'My advice,' she wrote on July 18, 'is to stick to munitions and don't try & run the Govt!'

The dispute over Churchill's appointment continued for several weeks. No political appointment, the *Morning Post* announced on July 19, had ever created 'such widespread bitterness'. Some Conservatives looked to Bonar Law to lead their protest, but he would not do so. Yet Lloyd George had not himself told Bonar Law of Churchill's appointment, or discussed it with him in advance. Although Bonar Law was angry, he made every effort to dampen the hostility of his followers, for he feared a revived Asquithian opposition in which Churchill would take a leading part. Lloyd George played on these fears. 'I think you ought to know,' he wrote to Bonar Law on 10 Downing Street notepaper, 'that Asquith told Winston that if he came in he would put him in at the Admiralty.'

[1] Leopold Charles Maurice Stennett Amery, 1873–1955. A contemporary of Churchill at Harrow. Fellow of All Souls College, Oxford, 1897. Served on the editorial staff of *The Times*, 1899–1909. Conservative MP, 1911–45. Intelligence Officer in the Balkans and eastern Mediterranean, 1915–16. Assistant Secretary, War Cabinet Secretariat, 1917–18. Parliamentary Under-Secretary, Colonial Office, 1919–21. First Lord of the Admiralty, 1922–4. Colonial Secretary, 1924–9. Secretary of State for India and Burma, 1940–5.

[2] John Edward Bernard Seely, 1868–1947. Liberal MP, 1900–22; 1923–4. Under-Secretary of State for the Colonies, 1908–11. Secretary of State for War, 1912–14. Resigned in March 1914, following the Curragh incident. Commanded the Canadian Cavalry Brigade, 1915–18. Gassed, 1918, and retired from Army with rank of Major-General. Under-Secretary of State to Churchill, Ministry of Munitions and Deputy Minister of Munitions, 1918. Under-Secretary of State for Air, 1919. Created Baron Mottistone, 1933. His eldest son was killed at Arras in 1917.

[3] Lady Cornelia Henrietta Maria Spencer-Churchill, 1847–1927. Churchill's aunt; eldest daughter of the 7th Duke of Marlborough. She married in 1868, Ivor Bertie Guest (1835–1914), who was created 1st Baron Wimborne in 1880.

On July 22 Lord Derby wrote to Sir Philip Sassoon:[1] 'There is no doubt that the appointment of Winston and Montagu is a very clever move on Lloyd George's part. He has removed from Asquith his two most powerful lieutenants and he has provided for himself two first-class platform speakers and it will be platform speakers we shall require to steady the country which is at present very much rattled by that distinguished body the House of Commons. . . .'

On being appointed Minister of Munitions Churchill had been obliged, in accordance with constitutional practice, to seek parliamentary re-election. Speaking to his constituents at Dundee on July 21, he could not hide his bitterness at his long exclusion from office. 'In a period of Titanic events', he said, men should be judged 'by the earnestness and loyalty of their efforts, not simply by their power to achieve impossibilities'. During his speech Churchill referred to the 'incomparable opportunities' created by the entry of the United States into the war; but he went on to assert: 'We are the heart, the centre, of the League of Nations. If we fail, all fail. If we break, all break.'

---

[1] Philip Albert Gustave Sassoon, 1888–1939. Succeeded his father as 3rd Baronet, 1912. Conservative MP, 1912–39. Private Secretary to Sir Douglas Haig, 1914–18. Parliamentary Private Secretary to Lloyd George, 1920–2. Trustee of the National Gallery, 1921–39. Under-Secretary of State for Air, 1924–9; 1931–7. First Commissioner of Works, 1937–9.

3

Minister of Munitions

ON July 18 the outgoing Minister of Munitions, Dr Addison, informed the senior staff of the Ministry of Churchill's appointment. 'I did my best to make things welcome for Winston,' he wrote in his diary. '. . . from what I could learn they were not very friendly to the idea of Winston's coming.' Addison believed, however, that this hostility would soon wear off, 'for there is no more capable Chief of a department than he is, as they will soon find out'. On July 24 Addison spent much of the morning 'installing Churchill' at the Ministry of Munitions, and going over the Munitions Programme with him. That afternoon he introduced Churchill to the permanent staff.

One member of the staff, Harold Bellman,[1] later recalled the meeting in his memoirs:

Those who attended from the secretariat fully expected a stormy scene. When the company was assembled Winston arrived, was received rather coldly, and opened by stating that he had perceived that 'he started at scratch in the popularity stakes'. He went on boldly to indicate his policy and to outline his proposals for an even swifter production of munitions. As he elaborated his plans the atmosphere changed perceptibly. This was not an apology. It was a challenge. Those who came to curse remained to cheer. The courage and the eloquence of the new minister dispelled disaffection and the minister took up his task with a willing staff. It was a personal triumph at a critical juncture.

As many Conservatives feared, Churchill was eager to involve himself in as wide a range of discussions as possible. On the afternoon of July 22

[1] Harold Bellman, 1886–1963. Served with the Railway Clearing House, 1900–15. Principal Assistant, Establishment Department, Ministry of Munitions, 1915–19. Assistant Secretary, Abbey Road Building Society, 1920; Secretary, 1921; subsequently Chairman of the Abbey National Building Society. Knighted, 1932. President of the International Union of Building Societies, 1934–8. Member of the Ministry of Health Central Housing Advisory Committee, 1935–47. He published his memoirs, *Cornish Cockney*, in 1947.

he telephoned to the War Cabinet's Secretary, Sir Maurice Hankey, who lived nearby, and asked him to come to tea with him at Lullenden. That night Hankey recorded in his diary:

. . . I had an interesting walk & talk with him, rambling round his wild & beautiful property. Lloyd George had given him my War Policy report & he was already well up in the whole situation and knew exactly what our military plans were, which I thought quite wrong. He had breakfasted with Lloyd George that morning. On the whole he was in a chastened mood. He admitted to me that he had been 'a bit above himself' at the Admiralty, and surprised me by saying that he had no idea of the depth of public opinion against his return to public life, until his appointment was made. He was hot for an expedition to Alexandretta but I put all the objections and difficulties to him.

That evening, when Hankey was gone, Churchill wrote to Lloyd George about the future strategy on the western front. In his letter he deplored 'a renewed offensive in the west', and urged Lloyd George to try to 'limit the consequences' of any attack that might already have been decided on. Lloyd George was about to cross to France to discuss war policy with the French. Churchill ended his letter on a personal note: 'Don't get torpedoed; for if I am left alone your colleagues will eat me.'

On July 25, the Director-General of Munitions Supply, Sir Frederick Black,[1] wrote to Churchill urging a complete reorganization of the different Munitions departments. After studying Black's letter, Churchill realized that more than fifty departments had long been competing with one another for both labour and materials, and had often acted without reference to Black himself, who was theoretically in command of the hierarchy. Sir Laming Worthington-Evans[2] had also submitted a memorandum to Churchill, on July 22, in which he advocated the right of direct access to the Minister by the head of each department.

Churchill was at once impressed by the need for radical changes in

[1] Frederick William Black, 1863–1930. Entered the Colonial Office, 1880; transferred to the Admiralty, 1883. Served in Malta and Ceylon. Director of Naval Stores, Admiralty, 1903–6. Knighted, 1913. Director-General of Munitions Supply, 1915–17. Acting Chairman, British War Mission to the USA, November 1917–February 1918. Director of Navy Contracts, 1918–19. Resigned from the civil service, 1919. A Managing Director of the Anglo-Persian Oil Company, 1919–23. President of the Institute of Petroleum Technologists, 1919.

[2] Laming Evans, 1868–1931. Conservative MP, 1910–31. Inspector of Administrative Services, War Office, 1914–15. Controller, Foreign Trade Department, Foreign Office, 1916. Assumed the prefix surname of Worthington, 1916. Known as 'Worthy'. Created Baronet, 1916. Parliamentary Secretary Ministry of Munitions, 1916–18. Minister of Blockade, 1918. Minister of Pensions, 1919–20. Minister without Portfolio, 1920–1. Secretary of State for War, 1921–2 and 1924–9.

his Ministry, and began to work out a comprehensive scheme aimed at greater efficiency, and a speedier process of decision-making. On July 26 he had to leave London for Dundee, to conduct a brief election campaign: all new Ministers had to seek re-election on their appointment. Two days later he returned to London, and on the afternoon of July 29 he unfolded his plans to Lloyd George and Sir George Riddell, who had motored together to Lullenden to see him. Riddell recorded in his diary:

He had just returned from Dundee and gave us a minute account of his doings. He said he proposed to reorganise the Ministry on the lines discussed when I called to see him on the day of his appointment. He has evidently been working hard to master the work of his new Department and displayed considerable knowledge of the situation. He pointed to the necessity for proper co-ordination between the Departments using steel and other materials, so that a programme might be agreed upon, having due regard to the supplies available. The P.M. agreed upon the necessity for this reform.

Churchill, Lloyd George and Riddell then discussed the problem of United States munitions production:

Winston read cablegrams from Northcliffe, with whom he was now upon terms of intimate association. From them and other documents to which he referred, it appeared that the Americans are doing badly. Their constructional policy is said to be defective and ill-planned. . . .
Winston said he was of opinion that the present state of affairs urgently demanded one of two things—a British campaign by L.G. to endeavour to induce this country to increase its efforts during the next twelve months, or an American campaign to endeavour to induce the Americans to expedite their preparations. For the latter it would be necessary for L.G. to go to America.

Churchill reiterated his belief that the Allies should 'mark time until next year, when the Americans will be ready'. Riddell noted that 'Winston painted while he talked, and seemed to have progressed in the former art'. He also showed Riddell his potato field, 'and explained that he had helped to plant and cultivate it'.

On July 29 the Dundee election result was declared. Churchill was re-elected with a majority of 5,266. On the following day he returned to London from Lullenden. The reorganization of his Ministry was his immediate concern. He was determined to carry out a complete overhaul of the departmental organization, and to set up an efficient secretariat at the centre. A word of warning came from General Smuts,[1] who

---

[1] Jan Christian Smuts, 1870–1950. Born in Cape Colony. General, commanding Boer Commando Forces, Cape Colony, 1901. Colonial Secretary, Transvaal, 1907. Minister of Defence, Union of South Africa, 1910–20. Second-in-Command of the South African forces that defeated the Germans in South-West Africa, July 1915. Honorary Lieutenant-General

wrote on July 31: 'Now that you are well in the saddle (and with such a majority) you must not ride too far ahead of your more slow going friends.'

On August 1 Churchill took his seat in the House of Commons. He was received, *The Times* reported, 'with some cheers'. Later that same day he took the initiative in trying to resolve a serious labour dispute which had begun in Scotland a year and a half before, in March 1916. A number of trade union leaders who worked at Beardmore's Munition Works, and at other munition factories in the Clyde district, had organized a series of strikes, and brought all work to a halt. As a result they had been arrested, and forbidden to remain at the Works, or to reside in Glasgow. From the moment they had been deported from the city, they demanded to be allowed to return, and to continue to work in the munition factories. But three successive Ministers of Munitions, Lloyd George, Edwin Montagu and Dr Addison, had refused. When Dr Addison had tried to effect a compromise, Sir William Beardmore[1] had demanded guarantees that they would abstain from any shop floor demonstrations. On August 1 Churchill intervened, telegraphing to his Chief Labour Adviser, Sir Thomas Munro:[2]

Please go and see Sir William Beardmore and explain to him that I think it would be better to take these men back as a matter of course without raising any question of sentiment or principle on so small a point. If they do not really want reinstatement but only a political grievance this will soon become apparent in their daily work. If Sir William does not share my view I hope he will at once come to see me as trouble may easily be fomented on this point.

Sir Thomas Munro was unable to influence Sir William Beardmore towards moderation. But Churchill persevered in his attempt to find a solution. On the afternoon of August 7 he saw the leader of the deportees, David Kirkwood.[3] In his memoirs, *My Life of Revolt*, Kirkwood recalled

commanding the imperial forces in East Africa, 1916–17. South African Representative at the Imperial War Cabinet, 1917 and 1918. Prime Minister of South Africa, 1919–24. Minister of Justice, 1933–9. Prime Minister, 1939–48.

[1] William Beardmore, 1856–1936. Shipbuilder. Founder and Chairman of William Beardmore and Co. Ltd., Engineers. A patron of Antarctic exploration, Sir Ernest Shackleton, gave his name to the Beardmore Glacier. Created Baronet, 1914. President of the Iron and Steel Institute, 1917. Between 1906 and 1919 his firm built 4 battleships, 7 cruisers, 12 destroyers, 13 submarines and 24 hospital ships. Created Baron Invernairn, 1921.

[2] Thomas Munro, 1866–1923. County Clerk of Lanarkshire, 1904. Knighted, 1914, the first County Clerk either in England or Scotland to receive this distinction. Chief Labour Adviser, Ministry of Munitions, 1916–18. Adviser to the Demobilization Branch, Ministry of Labour, 1919. Treasurer of the Lanark Education Authority from 1919 to his death.

[3] David Kirkwood, 1872–1955. Trained as an engineer on the Clyde. Active in the Trade Union movement, Clydeside. Deported from the Clyde, 1916, for organizing a protest against

the meeting, which took place that afternoon in Churchill's room at the Hotel Metropole, the headquarters of the Ministry in Northumberland Avenue:

I had formed an opinion of Winston Churchill as a daring, reckless, swash-buckler individual who was afraid of no one. . . . I expected arrogance, military precision, abruptness. When he appeared, I knew I was wrong. He came in, his fresh face all smiles, and greeted me simply, without a trace of side or trappings. I felt I had found a friend.

'How do you do, Mr Kirkwood? I have heard a good deal about you,' he said.

'I dare say you have,' I replied.

'Yes, and I want you to know that, whatever happens, nothing is to be allowed to stand in the way of the production of the munitions of war.'

'Quite right,' I said.

Then he rang a bell, saying: 'Let's have a cup of tea and a bit of cake together.'

What a difference so small a thing can make! . . . Here was the man, supposed never to think of trifles, suggesting tea and cake—a sort of bread and salt of friendship. It was magnificent. We debated over the teacups.

'Well, what about it?' he asked.

'I will tell you,' I replied. 'The Government deported me without cause. I have had redress for those wrongs. I realize that what was done to me was done because we were at war. "I waive the quantum o' the sin"'—at which he screwed up his face—'but I am unemployed. I am a highly skilled engineer, idle since May. I want you to put me back in Beardmore's whether Beardmore wants me or not.'

I have seldom seen a man look so astonished. His brows came down. He looked at me and said:

'Look here, Kirkwood, you have a great reputation, but you are not living up to it. I expected you to be a reasonable man. You are the most unreasonable man I ever met in all my life. Here am I, three weeks in my job, and you ask me to put you back in Beardmore's whether he wants you or not, into the Works he has built up over a lifetime.'

'Yes, that is so,' I said. 'It may seem a strange request. I've told you I have forgiven all that was done to me, but this is doing it all over again. I am treated as if I was a traitor to my country. There is no worse injury could be done to a Scotsman. You have got to do this thing or I'll go out from here and from the Isle of Wight to John o'Groats I'll advocate a down-tool policy . . .'

He whipped round with flashing eyes: 'You must not mention that here,

---

an increase in house rents. A Member of the Glasgow Town Council, 1918–22. Labour MP for Clydebank Dumbarton Burghs, 1922–50; for Dumbartonshire, 1950–1. Privy Councillor, 1948. Created Baron, 1951. In 1935 he published *My Life of Revolt* (with a foreword by Churchill).

Kirkwood. I will not tolerate it. Remember you are in the Ministry of Munitions.'

'I would say it, Mr Churchill, were it in the Court of Heaven, and not only say it, sir, but I'm going to do it.'

He sat back in his chair, looked straight into my eyes and roared with laughter. Then he said:

'By Jove, and I believe you would! But there's no good in getting heated about it. You feel wronged and only one thing can change that feeling. Well, why not? Let us see what we can do in the next two or three days, and it won't be my fault if you are not back in Beardmore's.'

Three days after his interview with Churchill, Kirkwood was offered the job of manager in the Beardmore Mile-End Shell Factory. Within six weeks, as a result of a bonus scheme devised by Kirkwood, shell production at Mile-End was the highest in Britain.

The facts of Churchill's settlement were kept secret; but within a week details had been leaked to the Press. In a leading article on August 18 the *Morning Post* denounced the method by which the settlement had been reached:

The incurable itch to do something striking, something away from the beaten track, has already been too much for Mr Churchill. . . . He has already celebrated his tenure of his new office by extending the hand of fellowship to the Clyde deportees. A gang of as dangerous and desperate agitators as ever fomented trouble in the labour world. . . .

Throughout Churchill's first months at the Ministry of Munitions, the *Morning Post* persevered with its campaign to undermine Churchill's authority. On August 3 it declared:

That dangerous and uncertain quantity, Mr Winston Churchill—a floating kidney in the body politic—is back again at Whitehall. We do not know in the least what he may be up to, but from past experience we venture to suggest that it will be everything but his own business. . . . Neither the War Office nor the Board of Admiralty is likely to be safe from his attentions.

Throughout the first two weeks of August Churchill was seeking to master the problems of his Ministry, and examining the various proposals put forward for its reorganization. On August 2 he wrote to A. J. Balfour,[1] urging him to arrange for a more efficient system of communication with Lord Northcliffe's American Mission, and pointing out: 'A strict routine may, here and there, cause some inconveniences, but

[1] Arthur James Balfour, 1848–1930. Conservative MP, 1874–85; 1885–1906; 1906–22. Prime Minister, 1902–5. First Lord of the Admiralty, 1915–16. Foreign Secretary, 1916–19. Lord President to the Council, 1919–22; 1925–9. Created Earl, 1922.

these are not comparable to those which arise when a considerable number of persons push cheerily ahead on their own affairs without knowledge of what others are doing, or in concert with them.' On August 3 he wrote to his statistical adviser, Walter Layton,[1] seeking detailed information about the Tank programme 'on a single sheet of paper':

How many tanks, and of what patterns, are to be ready month by month for the next 12 months? By whom, and to what extent, have these programmes been approved? How much steel do they require? How much do they cost? How much labour skilled and unskilled do they require in these 12 months? What are the principal limiting factors in material and class of labour? Apart from the number of Tanks, what quantity of spares, and what maintenance plant are required? Give the money value or weights of materials or proportion of labour required or whichever of the three is the most convenient and representative. Let me know the number of people in the Tank Department, the principal salaries paid, and the aggregate of salaries paid per annum. Show particularly any part of Tank production which overlaps aeroplane production, i.e. any transferable margin, whether of skilled mechanics or of ball bearings, etc. in which these two branches of production are clashing competitors. Show also the proportion of steel, of money, and of skilled and unskilled labour proposed to be absorbed in Tank production in these 12 months compared with the general Budget of the Ministry.

'I shall be quite content,' Churchill added, 'if many of these figures are approximate only.'

Churchill continued his work during the weekend. On Sunday August 5 he wrote to his senior medical adviser, Sir George Newman,[2] from Lullenden about the need for a short handbook summarizing the various welfare projects organized by the Ministry. 'I should like to see a proof of the Handbook when it is ready,' he wrote, 'and I hope every endeavour will be made to keep it short, simple and practical, and that the various points will be brought out by the use of special types of

    [1] Walter Thomas Layton, 1884–1966. Lecturer in economics, University College, London, 1909–12. Represented the Ministry of Munitions on the Milner Mission to Russia, 1917. Statistical Adviser, Ministry of Munitions, 1917–18. Unsuccessful Liberal candidate at the Elections of 1922 and 1923. Editor of *The Economist*, 1922–38. Knighted, 1930. Chairman, *News Chronicle* Ltd., 1930–50; Vice-Chairman, *Daily News* Ltd., 1930–63. Head of the Joint War Production Staff, 1942–3. Director, Reuters Ltd., 1945–53. Created Baron, 1947. Vice-President, Consultative Assembly of the Council of Europe, 1949–57. Deputy Leader of the Liberal Party in the House of Lords, 1952–5. Director, Tyne-Tees Television Ltd., 1958–61.
    [2] George Newman, 1870–1948. Bacteriologist. Demonstrator at King's College, London, 1896–1900. Chief Medical Officer, Board of Education, 1907–35. Knighted, 1911. Chairman, Health of Munitions Workers Committee, 1915–18. Medical Member, Central Control Board (Liquor Traffic), 1915–19. Chief Medical Officer, Ministry of Health, 1919–35. Author of several medical works, including *Hygiene and Public Health* (1917).

printing and plenty of spacing.' Having worked all Sunday, Churchill returned to London, where he addressed a Minute to his Director-General of Labour Supply, Sir Stephenson Kent,[1] about the Sunday working being done in munitions factories. 'I am in principle strongly opposed to Sunday work,' he wrote, 'except in emergencies. It usually results in workmen receiving double wages for working on Sunday, and taking Monday off.'

Churchill respected and encouraged the autonomy of his officials, while at the same time questioning them closely and frequently. On Sunday August 12 he explained his method of work in a letter to Sir Laming Worthington-Evans. 'Pray do not hesitate to come to me if you feel in difficulties,' he wrote, 'but be masters of the question & formulate yr own policy.'

On August 14 Churchill asked the House of Commons for permission to introduce his first Munitions of War Bill on the following day. He apologized for bringing such important business forward so late in the Session, but explained that he had been engaged 'in constant negotiation and enquiry' for the past three weeks. The aim of the Bill, he explained, was 'output on the one hand and industrial peace on the other'. He feared that any further delay in settling the demands of munitions workers 'might be made a cause of ill-will and difficulty and discontent which would far exceed the advantages of a longer period of negotiation'.

Churchill introduced his Bill on the evening of August 15. In his speech to the House of Commons he urged support for the clauses which enabled special wage awards to be made to skilled men, which prevented the restriction of piece rates, and which forbad the penalization of workmen for belonging to trade unions or taking part in a trade dispute. At the end of his speech Churchill defended this policy in a short peroration:

. . . We cannot win this War unless we are supported by the great masses of the labouring classes of this country. We cannot possibly win unless they sustain us and go with us, and unless they do so with a loyal and spontaneous determination we must expect disastrous results. We believe that a great and overwhelming majority in all parts of the country are determined to stand by the cause and carry the War to a victorious conclusion. Basing myself on that,

[1] Stephenson Hamilton Kent, 1873–1954. A contemporary of Churchill at Harrow. In the Coal Trade before 1914. Director-General, Munitions Labour Supply, 1917. Knighted, 1917. Head of a Munitions Mission to the United States, 1917. Member of Council (Labour Group), Ministry of Munitions, 1918. Controller-General of Civil Demobilisation and Resettlement, Ministry of Labour, 1918–19. High Sheriff of Sussex, 1924.

I feel that this particular measure, if it removes any suspicion of want of good faith or want of sympathy will, even though it may be alleged that in some respects it is prejudicial to output, give us back in other directions a much richer harvest than we should have reaped from adopting a more narrow interpretation of this question.

No sooner had Churchill settled down to the routine work of his Ministry, than his Cabinet colleagues began to question the scope of his activities. On the morning of August 15, he had been invited to Lord Derby's room at the War Office to attend a meeting of the War Cabinet at which munitions were to be discussed. As he was not a member of the War Cabinet, he was meant to give his opinion only when it was asked for. But on the question under discussion, the possible allocation of British field guns to Russia, he gave his views unasked. Lord Derby was outraged at what he regarded as an encroachment on his own rights as Secretary of State for War, and persuaded the Chief of the Imperial General Staff, Sir William Robertson,[1] to join him in a written protest to Lloyd George. Robertson, in signing the letter, wrote separately to Lord Derby: 'All I want is to be allowed to do my own work without interference by Winston & others.' On August 16 Derby's letter was delivered at 10 Downing Street. In it, Derby attacked Churchill directly:

I submit that, as he is not a member of the War Cabinet, and as his functions are really those of supply of munitions to the War Office and other Government Departments, subject to the approval of the War Cabinet, such a procedure on his part is not only inconvenient, but also quite irregular. . . .

The possible despatch of field guns to Russia was not the only War Cabinet decision in which Churchill had become involved on August 15. During a second War Cabinet that afternoon, at which Derby was not present, the discussion had turned to the possible release of naval guns from the Admiralty to the War Office. As neither Derby, nor any Admiralty representative was at the meeting, Churchill was able to express his opinion unchallenged by either service Minister. But, later

[1] William Robert Robertson, 1860–1933. Entered Army as a Private, 1877. 2nd Lieutenant, 1888. Major-General, 1910. Director of Military Training, War Office, 1913–14. Knighted, 1913. Quarter-Master-General, British Expeditionary Force, 1914–15. Chief of Staff, British Expeditionary Force, 1915. Chief of the Imperial General Staff, 1915–18. Commander-in-Chief, Home Forces, 1918–19. Commander-in-Chief, British Army of Occupation on the Rhine, 1919–20. Created Baronet, 1919. Field-Marshal, 1920.

that day, when the First Lord of the Admiralty, Sir Eric Geddes,[1] learnt of what had happened, he, like Derby before him, was outraged, writing direct to Lloyd George in protest:

My fears as regards the Minister of Munitions are somewhat fortified by what has passed in conversation with him upon several occasions, and at recent meetings of the War Cabinet and Cabinet Committees. He has shewn that he contemplates an extension of his functions beyond what I have ever understood them to be, and an infringement of mine which I should view with great concern. When serving on the Committee appointed by the Cabinet to deal with the subject of Steel and men for Shipbuilding, of which Lord Curzon was chairman, I was obliged to make representations to him on the subject of Churchill's concern in purely Admiralty matters. . . .

Were it not that such dealings as I have had with Churchill have been most cordial, I would almost feel that there was a personal aspect to his interference in Admiralty matters since I have been appointed First Lord, but I am quite sure that such a feeling would be wrong, and that it is only due to his keenness and previous knowledge of the Admiralty that the difficulties which I foresee may arise. . . .

On receiving Geddes' letter, Lloyd George summoned him to 10 Downing Street. But Geddes was not mollified. Indeed, after he had seen Lord Derby later that day, both men decided to threaten resignation if Churchill's authority was not severely curtailed.

Angered by this hostility, Churchill wrote Lloyd George a seven-page letter of protest on August 19. Although he finally decided not to send the letter, it strongly expressed his feelings:

My dear Prime Minister,
    It will I think be necessary for the War Cabinet to give a decision on the relations of the Ministry of Munitions & the Admiralty & War Office.
    My view is that the M of M has nothing to do with strategy & tactics & that he shd express no official opinion on such subjects unless he is invited to be present as a Minister of the Crown at a meeting of the War Cabinet where such matters are raised, or is authorised by the Prime Minister to draw up a paper dealing with them.
    On the other hand in the sphere of *materiel* the Minister of Munitions is entitled to review & examine the whole of our resources and to express his convictions as to the best use that can be made of them. For instance if the new shipbuilding programme requires a large cut to be made in the quanti-

[1] Eric Campbell Geddes, 1875–1937. An engineer on India railways before 1914. Deputy Director-General of Munitions supply, 1915–16. Knighted, 1916. Inspector-General of Transportation, in all theatres of war, 1916–17. Honorary Major-General, and honorary Vice-Admiral, 1917. Conservative MP, 1917–22. First Lord of the Admiralty, 1917–18. Minister of Transport, 1919–21. President of the Federation of British Industries, 1923, 1924.

ties of shell steel provided for the Army, it is right for the M of M to know what the Admiralty position in shell steel & ammunition is, & to state the facts statistically & comparatively to the War Cabinet. Or again if long range guns are urgently needed by the army, it is open to the M of M to draw attention to the very large reserves of such guns now being discarded by the Admiralty, & to indicate the use that could be made of them on land. Or again if the Admiralty claim entire control of the oxygen supplies & use oxygen for purposes far less refined & important than some of those under the charge of the M of M with consequent peril to our whole aeronautical supply, it shd be open to the Minister to draw attention to the relative merits of the competing services & to use all such arguments as may be necessary in that connexion. It is of course for the War Cabinet to judge: & there is certainly no harm in their hearing the facts on both sides.

At present the Admiralty claim a super priority upon all supplies; not only as respects the most urgent and vital parts of that immense business, but even in regard to comparatively commonplace needs. They assert the doctrine that the least important Admiralty needs shd rank before the most urgent claims of the Army or of Aeronautics. In my view there shd be a frank & free discussion on the merits in each case & a loyal & friendly effort by departments—even after a little plain-speaking—to do the best they can by the public cause. . . .

This episode confirmed the Conservatives' belief that Churchill would never restrict his activities to his own Department. 'There are some ugly rumours,' Walter Long wrote to Bonar Law on August 23, 'about WC & interference in *War* policy—I believe that if this materialises it will end this Gov. The feeling here & *in France* is very strong. . . .'

Churchill's plans for the reorganization of the Ministry of Munitions were complete by mid-August. On August 18, exactly four weeks after he had been appointed, he issued a memorandum to the Press, giving details of the changes. After three years of war, Churchill explained, the need was no longer for emergency expedients and 'the suspension of all ordinary rules'. The time had come, 'by more economical processes, by closer organization, and by thrifty and harmonious methods, to glean and gather a further reinforcement of war power'.

Instead of the fifty existing semi-autonomous departments, each headed by its own Director-General, Churchill set up a Munitions Council of eleven Members. Each Member of Council was directly responsible to Churchill himself; each was in overall charge of several related aspects of Munitions production, previously the concern of five or six Director-Generals.

To replace the virtual autonomy of the old departments in purchasing materials and organizing production methods, Churchill also set up a Council Secretariat to provide the Ministry with a centralized, co-ordinating administration. This Secretariat, Churchill explained in his memorandum of August 18, would contain 'a strong element of trained Civil Servants, thoroughly acquainted with official methods and inter-departmental relations'. Its responsibilities would be 'to concert the action of the various departments and authorities concerned in each class of business'. It would also be used for 'the recording of action and the circulation of information of all kinds'. On September 15 Churchill appointed his former Admiralty Secretary, James Masterton Smith,[1] to take charge of the Council Secretariat. He also set up his own private office to help him in the day to day conduct of business, and Edward Marsh returned once more as his Principal Private Secretary.

From September to December 1917 the Munitions Council met once a week. But from its first meetings, the Council found that some of the problems discussed at each meeting involved only two or three Members of Council. Churchill therefore decided to set up Council Committees, made up of the relevant Council Members and two or three other officers of the departments concerned. Seventy-five such Council Committees were set up, between August 1917 and November 1918. These Committees reported their findings and decisions direct to Churchill. On December 11, at a meeting of the Munitions Council, Churchill declared:

. . . Speaking for myself, I practically always approve a Council Committee report exactly as it comes. I think I have hardly ever altered a word, and I read each report through with great attention, and see the decision on the question which I know is ever so much better than I could have produced myself if I had studied the question for two whole days; and it would be quite impossible for me to do that.

By September 4 the reorganization of the Ministry was complete. That day Churchill held a conference of his principal advisers. 'What is your war plan?' he asked them, and he went on: 'If you know what your war plan is it is quite easy to parcel out your material.' Churchill

---

[1] James Edward Masterton Smith, 1878–1938. Entered Admiralty, 1901. Private Secretary to five First Lords: McKenna, 1910–11; Churchill, 1911–15; Balfour, 1915–16; Carson, 1916–17; Sir E. Geddes, 1917. Assistant Secretary to Churchill at the Ministry of Munitions, 1917–19 and at the War Office, 1919–20. Knighted, 1919. Appointed by Churchill Permanent Under-Secretary of State, Colonial Office, 1921. Retired, 1924.

went on to emphasize the overriding need to create an expanding, rational programme of aircraft building. The air, he said, had too long been 'the drudge of the other services', and he continued: 'there are only two ways left now of winning the war, and they both begin with A. One is aeroplanes and the other is America. That is all that is left. Everything else is swept away.'

Churchill was pleased by the rapid success of his reorganization, and relished the work involved. 'This is a very heavy Department,' he wrote to Lloyd George on September 9, 'almost as interesting as the Admiralty, with the enormous advantage that one has neither got to fight Admirals or Huns! I am delighted with all these clever business men who are helping me to their utmost. It is very pleasant to work with competent people.'

4

'Give Me the Power'

O N 10 September 1917 Churchill's new Munitions Council met to discuss steel production. Several Members of the Council were worried by the lackadaisical attitude of both management and workers in the steel industry. Churchill decided to intervene directly, and to put his full Ministerial authority behind an appeal to all Steel companies to change their attitude. That day he himself drafted a letter which was sent to the heads of every steel company in Britain. In it he declared:

The foundation upon which all our chances of Victory stand is Steel. The greatest possible quantities are required not only to hurl at the enemy in the form of shells, but to build the cargo ships vitally needed to replace those sunk by submarines and so safeguard us against famine and ruin. . . .

Steel is not only our principal means of war, but it is our best chance of saving the lives of our soldiers. This is a war of Machinery; and generalship consists in using machinery instead of flesh and blood to achieve the purposes of strategy and tactics. Every man or manager who is engaged in Steel Production is directly engaged in smiting down the enemy and bringing the war to a speedy close. And although he may not share the perils and sufferings of the fighting troops, he can win for himself the right to share their honour when victory is attained.

On Wednesday September 12, two days after writing this appeal, Churchill left London for France. It was his first visit abroad since he had become Minister of Munitions, and he planned to discuss the problems of munitions supply with both the British Commander-in-Chief, Sir Douglas Haig, and with the French munitions experts. During his visit, Churchill was accompanied by Edward Marsh, who recorded their progress in his diary.[1]

[1] Each time he was in France, Marsh kept a special diary, which he then sent to a young friend of his in the Royal Naval Air Service, Sub-Lieutenant David Davies (who, as Ivor Novello, made his first stage appearance in London in 1921).

Churchill and Marsh reached Calais at noon. After lunch, they drove to Cassel, and from there continued eastwards, to the battle area. As Marsh wrote:

We had been told that Messines was 'unhealthy' so we didn't go there, and preferred Wytschaete which was reported 'quiet'. But no sooner did we begin to walk along the Ridge than 6″ shells began to burst around us. One of our batteries must have been firing at the Huns yesterday or this morning, and they were trying for their revenge. Columns of smoke rose from the ground, 60–100 yards from us, and bits of shell fell quite close—5 or 6 yards off— while all the time our own shells were whistling and shrieking over our heads. . . .

Winston lent me his excellent field-glasses, through which I could see the emplacement of the Boche lines, about 3000 yards off in plain—and several towns, including the utter ruin of Ypres.

Winston soon began to think it was silly to stay there, and we began picking our way back through the stumps and round the shell-holes of Wytschaete wood. The shells were still falling, all in a radius of about 150 yards—we saw one burst about 30 yards in front of a huge lorry packed with troops which went on as if nothing had happened.

From Wytschaete, Churchill and Marsh returned towards the coast, reaching St Omer that evening, and dining with Sir Douglas Haig. In his diary Marsh recorded:

Winston didn't get going, and dinner was dull, especially at first. Later on there was a rather interesting discussion, about tanks, and the possibilities of a huge aerial offensive next year. Haig thinks highly of tanks, in their proper place. He told us of a little enterprise of Gen. Maxse's[1] which would normally have cost 600–1000 casualties—but owing to the tanks there were only 15.

After dinner Churchill talked strategy with Haig and Sir Launcelot Kiggel,[2] both of whom were anxious to learn if Churchill was still an advocate of military action in the east. They were relieved to find, as Haig wrote in his diary that night, that Churchill 'is all in favour of concentrating our efforts against the western front'. While the three

[1] Ivor Maxse, 1862–1958. Entered Army, 1882. Served as a Major in the Sudan, 1897–99, and in South Africa, 1899–1900. Brigadier-General, 1914. Went to France in Command of the 1st Guards Brigade, 12 August 1914. Major-General, commanding the 18th Division, October 1914–January 1917. Commanded the 18th Army Corps, January 1917–June 1918. Knighted, 1917. Inspector-General of Training to the British Army in France, 1918–19. General, Commanding Northern Command, 1919–23.

[2] Launcelot Edward Kiggell, 1862–1954. Entered Army, 1882. Served in the South African War, 1899–1902. Brigadier-General, 1909. Director of Staff Duties, War Office, 1909–13. Commandant, Camberley Staff College, 1913–14. Director of Home Defence, War Office, 1914–15. Chief of the General Staff, British Armies in France, December 1915–January 1918. Knighted, 1916. Lieutenant-General, 1917. Lieutenant-Governor of Guernsey, 1918–20.

men were talking, news was telephoned from Paris that a new Government had been formed, headed by the former Minister of War, Paul Painlevé.

On Thursday September 13, Churchill remained at St Omer. After lunch he continued his discussions on strategy with Haig and Kiggel. Both Generals wanted to know whether Lloyd George really believed that the war could be won on the western front, and how far their own efforts in the offensive were being supported by the Cabinet. In his diary Haig wrote: 'Winston admitted that Lloyd George and he were doubtful about being able to beat the Germans on the western front.' But Haig had confidence in his policy of persistent attack, and had ordered a renewed assault on the German trenches for September 20.

After his discussion with Haig and Kiggel, Churchill was driven to Poperinghe, for tea with his brother Jack, who was serving on the Anzac Staff. On the way back to St Omer he passed large numbers of troops moving forward to the assembly areas. 'Many of them recognized Winston and cheered and waved their hands,' Marsh wrote in his diary. 'He was as pleased as Punch.'

Churchill remained at St Omer throughout Friday September 14, in discussion with Haig. 'He and Winston seemed to warm to each other as the visit went on,' Marsh wrote, 'and at our last luncheon Haig was quite genial and cracked several jokes.' But, Marsh added, 'the tone of GHQ is tremendously optimistic, so much that I found other people were quite irritated'. During the afternoon, Churchill had a long talk with senior members of Haig's Staff, about the shortage of guns. 'I have no doubt,' Haig wrote in his diary that night, 'that Winston means to do his utmost (as Minister of Munitions) to provide the army with all it requires, but at the same time he can hardly stop meddling in the larger questions of strategy and tactics; for the solution of the latter he has no real training, and his agile mind only makes him a danger because he can persuade Lloyd George to adopt and carry out the most idiotic policy.' Haig had no doubts that the drive towards Passchendaele would be the prelude to a further and significant advance across German-occupied Belgium. Churchill was still convinced that Britain's offensive powers would not be sufficiently overwhelming until 1918, and that to continue the attack in 1917 was to court disaster.

On the evening of September 15 Churchill and Marsh left St Omer for Amiens. On the following morning they spent several hours amid the ruins and devastation of the Somme battlefield.

During the early afternoon, at Arras, Churchill discussed in conference the question of the supply of poison gas. When the conference was over he and Marsh drove back again towards the front. They had only gone a little way when, as Marsh wrote:

Winston was attracted by the sight of shells bursting in the distance—irresistible! Out we got, put on our steel helmets, hung our gas-masks round our necks, and walked for half-an-hour towards the firing, there was a great noise, shells whistling over our heads, and some fine bursts in the distance—but we seemed to get no nearer, and the firing died down, so we went back after another hour's delay. Winston's disregard of time, when there's anything he wants to do, is sublime—he firmly believes that it waits for him.

Shortly after six o'clock Churchill and Marsh reached Péronne. At midnight they arrived in Paris, where rooms were awaiting them at the Ritz.

On the morning of Monday September 17 Churchill met the new French Minister of Munitions, Louis Loucheur,[1] who urged the setting up of an Inter-Allied Munitions Council. 'I will do everything in my power to facilitate the settlement of this matter. . . .' Churchill wrote to Loucheur on his return to the Ritz. 'The question is most urgent & shd be pressed from day to day, with the sole object of presenting to the US the joint agreed proposals of the Allies, in whose decision the accord of England & France shd play a dominating part. . . .'

That evening Churchill dined in Paris with several Americans. 'Winston very eloquent,' Marsh wrote in his diary, 'on the necessity of bringing every possible American soldier over to France as soon as possible, and training them here or in England instead of in America—so as not to waste transport during the time of training.'

On Tuesday September 18 Churchill drove out of Paris to discuss with French artillery experts the problem of transporting heavy artillery on the already congested railway lines. That evening he and Marsh dined at Amiens. After dinner they drove to the coast, and were brought back to Dover in a destroyer.

Shortly after Churchill's return to London, the problems of munitions shortages made themselves felt in several ways. On the night

---

[1] Louis Loucheur, 1872–1931. Engineer, contractor and munitions manufacturer. One of the first French businessmen to receive political office during the war. Under-Secretary of State at the Ministry of Munitions, December 1916–April 1917. Minister of Munitions, 1917–20. Elected to the Chamber of Deputies, 1919. Helped in the drafting of the economic section of the Treaty of Versailles, 1919. Minister for the Liberated Areas, 1921; Minister of Trade, 1924; Minister of Finance (for seventeen days), 1925; Minister of Trade, 1926; Minister of Labour, 1928. Author of the 'Loucheur Law' of 1928 to help deal with housing crises by building low-priced houses with the help of public funds.

of October 1, several German aeroplanes successfully penetrated London's defences for the third time in three nights. At a meeting of the War Council on the following morning Churchill warned that anti-aircraft barrages 'could not be continued indefinitely, owing to the great wear and tear of the guns and the heavy expenditure of ammunition'. Two days later, on October 3, Sir Douglas Haig telegraphed to Lord Derby that he was seriously worried about the supply of 6-inch howitzer ammunition. 'This howitzer,' he explained, 'is more generally used than any other weapon, and has for all descriptions of artillery work proved itself invaluable. Recent successes have been due to a large extent to the ample supply of ammunition which has hitherto been available. . . .' Any reduction in supply of ammunition for the howitzer would, he warned, 'hamper present offensive operations'.

Derby sent Haig's appeal to Churchill. But Churchill had no means of increasing howitzer shell production. Adequate supplies had hitherto been bought in the United States. But the Americans had decided to decrease production. On October 5 Churchill sent a copy of Haig's telegram to Lord Northcliffe, adding to it an urgent message, which, he said, 'carries the highest authority', to the effect that the United States' decision was causing 'grave anxiety'. The War Cabinet, he added, 'urge that you will make every endeavour to induce United States Government to authorise the placing of the contracts asked for by the Ministry of Munitions'. The supply of this ammunition, he concluded, 'is of vital importance for the Allied cause'. That same day, the British case was put with much force by a member of the British Mission in Washington, Robert Brand,[1] to the Commissioner in charge of raw materials on the War Industries Board, Bernard Baruch,[2] who agreed to produce a million 6-inch shells. Brand telegraphed the news to Churchill from New York, adding that he would 'go ahead at once with negotiations', and would press the War Industries Board to provide a further million shells as soon as the United States' own needs were met. These orders,

---

[1] Robert Henry Brand, 1878–1963. 4th son of the 2nd Viscount Hampden. Served in South Africa under Lord Milner, 1902. Member of the Imperial Munitions Board of Canada, 1915–18. Deputy-Chairman of the British Mission in Washington, 1917–18. Financial adviser (to Lord Robert Cecil) at the Paris Peace Conference, 1919. Financial Representative of South Africa at the Genoa Conference, 1922. Head of the British Food Mission, Washington, 1941–4. British Treasury Representative, Washington, 1944–6. Created Baron, 1946. His only son was killed in action in 1945.

[2] Bernard Mannes Baruch, 1870–1965. Of Jewish parentage; born in New York. Financier. Chairman, Allied Purchasing Commission, 1917. Commissioner in Charge of Raw Materials, War Industries Board, 1917–18. Chairman of the War Industries Board, 1918–19. Economic Adviser to the American Peace Commission, 1919. Member of the President's Agricultural Conference, 1922. American Representative on the Atomic Energy Commission, 1946.

essential if Haig's army were to be adequately armed, were among the most expensive of the war. Between August 1914 and November 1918 the British Government spent £914 million on gun ammunition, of which more than a fifth was for 6-inch howitzer shells.

Churchill's responsibility for the production and purchase of guns and gun ammunition led, on October 9, to his appointment to a War Cabinet Committee 'to consider the allocation of guns in relation to the demands put forward by our own armies and by those of the Allied Governments'. Lord Curzon was appointed chairman of the committee; Balfour, Churchill and Derby were its other members, and Leopold Amery its secretary.

That evening Churchill addressed over four thousand munitions workers at the Ponders End munitions factory. During his speech he spoke of the importance of the American contribution to the war effort. The United States armies, he declared, were 'perhaps the most powerful of all, certainly the most welcome to us here, our cousins, our brothers, the great Republic of the United States'. In such company, he added, Britain could continue the fight 'assured that the purposes which we serve will not be frustrated, and hopeful that the conflict will not be prolonged'. And he concluded:

. . . It was not a war only of armies, or even mainly of armies. It was a war of whole nations. . . . It was also a supreme conflict of moral and political ideals. The German War Lords said that their system of militarism and Caesarism had enabled them for more than three years to make head against almost the whole world. But was it not also true to say that this same system and the policy which emerged from it, had brought the whole world against them? And would it not also be proved true that the weight of the whole world would overwhelm them, and the condemnation of the whole world would wither them and their system, and all that it stands for, and all that stands to it?

Churchill's speech provoked an immediate reaction in Germany itself. The German Foreign Minister, Richard von Kühlmann,[1] speaking in the Reichstag, warned that British statesmen should learn by experience not to talk about annihilating German militarism. 'Mr Churchill especially,' he added, 'in looking back upon his earlier expedition, which aimed at Constantinople and resulted in failure . . .

[1] Richard von Kühlmann, 1873–1949. Entered the Berlin Foreign Office, 1893. Counsellor of the German Embassy in London, 1908–14. Secretary of State for Foreign Affairs, 1917–18. An advocate of a negotiated peace, he tried to arrange for negotiations with Sir William Tyrrell, in Holland in the summer of 1918 and was dismissed by the Kaiser.

should have been taught that even the thin wall can turn the dream of victory into defeat if this wall consists of men. . . .'

The Allocation of Guns Committee met at the War Office on October 10. It was decided, Leopold Amery noted in his diary, that insufficient raw materials existed to fulfil 'the enormous Russian demands for machine guns', and that supplies both to Russia and Rumania would have to be cut down. Amery's diary entry continued:

I talked with Churchill coming away. Under the influence of a successful speech to a large meeting of munitions workers the night before he was very sanguine about the labour situation, and inclined to think that the great thing was to keep the machinery oiled by satisfying them, as regards pay, etc., even if it involved progressive depreciation of all their money values.

Amery was much impressed by Churchill's achievements during his first three months as Minister of Munitions, and in particular by his insistence upon the development of special mechanical methods of fighting. On October 31 he was shown a memorandum by Churchill urging a rapid increase in both the research and production of trench mortars and tanks. 'Whatever his defects may be,' Amery noted in his diary, 'there is all the difference in the world between the tackling of a big problem like this by a man of real brain and imagination, and its handling by good second rate men like Robertson and Haig, who still live in the intellectual trench in which they have been fighting.'

On becoming Minister of Munitions, Churchill was confronted by serious industrial unrest. Since the spring of 1916, when Asquith's Government had imposed strict embargoes on wage increases, pieceworkers in munitions factories had been able to earn considerably more than skilled workers, whose wages were fixed. Under Government regulations it was impossible for skilled workers to transfer to piece-work in order to earn more. In March 1916 this discrepancy had been brought to Dr Addison's attention by the skilled workers at Sheffield, who were earning three pounds a week, while the piece-workers, former 'gardeners and coachmen', were earning at least six pounds. That March, the Amalgamated Society of Engineers had asked for an extra ten-shillings a week for skilled men; in July 1916 Addison had awarded a three-shillings increase. The grievance of the skilled workers was only briefly assuaged. During 1917 discontent spread throughout the munitions factories, not only to engineering workers, but to all trades.

On 21 August 1917, Churchill had appointed a Representative Committee to examine the discrepancy of wages between skilled and piece-workers, and chose Major Hills[1] as its chairman. On September 6, the Hills Committee had submitted its interim report, arguing in favour of substantial wage increases for skilled men. That same day, after reading their interim report, Churchill wrote to the Chairman of the Labour Committee of the Munitions Council, Sir Charles Ellis:[2] 'we are morally bound to improve the rates of the skilled time-worker'. But he added that he did not see any moral obligation to raise skilled workers' wages to the same level as that of piece-workers. 'The amount of improvement,' he wrote, 'must be decided with reference to the interests of the State, as it is clear that the Treasury and the Cabinet must have the final word. . . .' On September 21 the Hills Committee reported again, recommending that the wage increase should be between 10 and 15 per cent and that it should be limited to engineering workers, who, it judged, were the worst affected by the differential between skilled wages and piece-work rates.

On September 22, Churchill accepted Major Hills' conclusion. He hoped that the other Ministries concerned, the Ministry of Labour and the Admiralty, would do likewise. Both these Ministries had agreed to send representatives to sit on the Hills Committee. But neither Ministry approved the report, for they were afraid that the wage increases which the Hills Committee recommended for engineering workers would be demanded, sooner or later, by all skilled workers. The Hills Committee had itself recognized this problem, which Churchill referred to a special Committee of his own, within the Ministry of Munitions, headed by Sir Charles Ellis. The conclusion which Sir Charles Ellis' Committee reached was that the increase should be limited to certain engineering workers only. Such an increase would itself cost the State £3,765,000. If all engineering workers were included, the cost would be £5,700,000. If the scheme were extended beyond the engineering trades, and shipyard workers were included, the

[1] John Waller Hills, 1867–1938. Solicitor. Conservative MP, 1906–18, 1918–22 and 1925–38. A Director of the Midland Railway Company, 1910–22. Captain, 4th Battalion, Durham Light Infantry, 1914; Major, 1915. Acting Lieutenant-Colonel, commanding the 20th Battalion, Durham Light Infantry, July 1916. Wounded, 30 September 1916, and returned to his Parliamentary duties. Chairman of the West Midland Commission on Industrial Unrest, 1917. Financial Secretary to the Treasury, 1922–3. Privy Councillor, 1929.

[2] Charles Edward Ellis, 1832–1937. Barrister, Inner Temple, 1878. Director, John Brown & Co. Ltd., shipbuilders, 1890. Director-General of Ordnance Supply, Ministry of Munitions, 1915–17; Knighted, 1917. Chairman, Labour Committtee of the Munitions Council, 1917. Member of the Royal Commission on Awards to Inventors, 1919–27. Vice-President, Institute of Naval Architects.

cost would rise to £6,565,000. If iron and steel workers were added, the total cost would be £8,500,000.

Churchill discussed these figures with Major Hills and Sir Charles Ellis before the War Cabinet met on October 12. During the meeting he recommended the least expensive scheme; a 15 per cent increase limited to 165,000 engineering workers in three classes: those in the tool-room, maintenance and supervising groups. But the War Cabinet feared that if this limited scheme were adopted, there would be an immediate snow-balling of wage demands. It was decided instead to set up a special committee, consisting of two members of the War Cabinet, Lord Milner and George Barnes,[1] to consult the departments concerned that same afternoon, and to put forward an independent proposal. The Milner–Barnes Committee reported back to the War Cabinet that evening. It overruled Churchill's proposal, and advised that the wider engineering scheme should be adopted; a $12\frac{1}{2}$ per cent increase for moulders as well as tool-room, supervising and maintenance classes, a total of 250,000 men. The cost would be £5,700,000. This the War Cabinet accepted, and the increases were announced on October 13.

The battle for Passchendaele opened on October 12. The British front line was a mile and a quarter from the village. But each time the British tried to advance, they were met with intense machine gun fire, and by October 24 they were still a mile from their objective. That day, the Italian Army was crushed at Caporetto by German and Austrian troops, and within twelve hours over a million Italian soldiers were in retreat.

It was not until Sunday October 28 that the first accurate news of the Italian disaster reached England. Churchill was spending the day at Lullenden. Lloyd George, who was at Walton Heath, telephoned with the news, and asked him to motor over at once to see him. 'He showed me the telegrams,' Churchill recalled in *The World Crisis*, 'which even in their guarded form revealed a defeat of the first magnitude.'

Lloyd George set off almost immediately for Italy. At the same time five French and five British divisions were hurried to the Italian front. The first of these troops reached the Italian front on November 10.

[1] George Nicholl Barnes, 1859–1940. Apprenticed as a machine tool worker at the age of eleven. Worked in the London Docks as a construction worker. General Secretary, Amalgamated Society of Engineers, 1896–1908. Chairman, National Committee of Organized Labour for Old Age Pensioners, 1902. Labour MP, 1906–22. Minister of Pensions, December 1916–August 1917. Member of the War Cabinet, May 1917–January 1919. Minister without Portfolio, August 1917–January 1920. He published *From Workshop to War Cabinet* in 1923.

Their effect was immediate. The German and Austrian forces were checked on the line of the Piave river, and the danger that Italy would be forced out of the war was averted. But on the western front, November 10 saw the final day of the battle at Passchendaele. The village itself was captured, but the offensive came to a halt. Although British troops now controlled all the high ground of the Ypres salient, nearly a quarter of a million men had been killed or wounded. On November 10 alone, the last day of the attack, 3,000 men had been killed and 7,000 wounded.

The exhaustion of the British armies in the Ypres salient and the sudden unforeseen demands of the Italian front threw great strains upon the Ministry of Munitions during the winter of 1917. Churchill hustled forward the activities of his Council. New plant for the manufacture of poison gas shells, he wrote on November 2, must be laid down 'without delay', and Treasury approval obtained 'as an urgent war necessity'. Why, he asked on November 5, was aeroplane engine production 20 per cent below forecasts: 'Pray let me know what is holding you up.' That same day he learnt that deliveries of new and repaired guns had been less in October than in September: 'What is the cause of this?' he wrote. 'Is it due to lack of guns to repair? Please let me have a report.' On November 7 he proposed to his Munitions Council the setting up of specific reserves of munitions to meet particular emergencies. 'We should be careful,' he warned, 'not to dissipate our strength or melt it down to the average level of exhausted nations. It will be better used with design by us than weakly dispersed.'

Churchill was increasingly frustrated by the attitude of others. On November 15 he informed his friend General Barnes:[1] 'Hitherto both the Naval and the Military Authorities have altogether underrated bombing possibilities, and steadily discouraged the construction of bombing machines.' To the Shipping Controller, Sir Joseph Maclay,[2] who had proposed major reductions in the construction of special concrete barges needed to bring iron-ore from Spain, he wrote with acerbity that same day:

---

[1] Reginald Walter Ralph Barnes, 1871–1946. Entered Army, 1890. Lieutenant, 4th Hussars, 1894. Went with Churchill to Cuba, 1895. Captain, 1901. Brigadier-General, commanding the 116th Infantry Brigade, and the 14th Infantry Brigade, 1915–16. Commanded the 32nd Division, 1916–17 and the 57th Division, 1917–19. Major-General, 1918. Knighted, 1919.

[2] Joseph Paton Maclay, 1857–1951. Shipowner. Member of the Glasgow Town Council. Commissioner for Taxes, City of Glasgow. Created Baronet, 1914. Shipping Controller (later Minister of Shipping), 1916–21. Member of the Committee on National Expenditure, 1921. Created Baron, 1922.

... I must impress upon you that the supplies of iron-ore from the North of Spain are a matter literally of life and death to the British army in the field and to the whole munition output by which that army is sustained. The reduction which you are forced to suggest in the paper on Shipping, which you have so kindly sent me, would be fatal to our war effort alike in 1918 and 1919. . . .

I certainly could never acquiesce in seeing the whole Munitions programme ruined and the striking power of our army vitally affected. I earnestly hope that no question of departmental procedure will be allowed to stand in the way of a vehement effort being made, not only by this but by every other channel, to avert the catastrophe which you foresee.

On Sunday November 18 Churchill left London for Paris, to discuss the serious situation with the French and Italian Ministers of Munitions, Louis Loucheur and General Dallolio.[1] On the Monday, Dallolio pressed for an increase in munitions supply from both Britain and France. Later that day Churchill telegraphed to Lloyd George:

... Italian demands are of extreme urgency for re-equipment of second army and replacement of losses in others. I consider them on the whole moderate and I believe they can be met generally without serious detriment to our own programmes. Loucheur has been authorised by French Government to contribute an equal quantity and is prepared to do so immediately, subject to our taking similar action. . . . Question is one of policy, not of detail. If you decide in principle to give aid demanded jointly with the French I am sure details can be arranged satisfactorily.

As a continuation of his telegram, Churchill sent Lloyd George a list of the Italian demands. Dallolio had asked for 150,000 rifles, 75 million rounds of small arm ammunition, 2,000 machine guns with 20 million rounds of ammunition, 1,300 eighteen-pounder guns, 300 medium guns or howitzers, 40 heavy howitzers and 40 tanks. All these demands were additional to the needs of the British troops in Italy.

At the War Cabinet on November 19 Churchill's telegram was the subject of some controversy. Lord Derby telegraphed directly to Churchill that evening, angry that no War Office representative was present at the Paris negotiations. 'I am therefore,' he informed Churchill, 'sending the Master General of Ordnance[2] to Paris tomorrow to be

[1] Alfredo Dallolio, 1853–1952. Entered the Italian Army as an artillery officer, 1872; Major-General, 1910. Director-General of Artillery, Ministry of War, 1910–17. Senator, 1917. Minister of State for Arms and Ammunition, 1917–18. General Commander of Army Artillery, 1918–20. Lieutenant-General, 1923. President of the Committee for National Mobilization (later the Committee for Civil Mobilization), 1923–39.

[2] William Thomas Furse, 1865–1953. Son of an archdeacon of Westminster. Entered Royal Artillery 1884. Assistant Adjutant General for Transport, South Africa, 1899–1900. Major-

present at the conference on behalf of the Army Council. Please engage
a room for him at your hotel.'

On November 20, while awaiting General Furse's arrival in Paris,
Churchill went to the Chamber of Deputies. A week earlier Painlevé's
Government had been defeated, and Georges Clemenceau[1] had suc-
ceeded him both as Prime Minister and as Minister of War. From the
diplomatic box, Churchill witnessed the return of Clemenceau to the
Chamber after an absence of eight years.

In his speech to the Chamber, Clemenceau declared that his aim was
to carry on 'the war, and nothing but the war'; pacifist propaganda
would be dealt with by courts martial; there were to be 'no more
pacifist campaigns—no more German intrigues—neither treason nor
half treason—war, nothing but war'; his Government had only one
aim, 'to conquer'. In an article in the *Strand* magazine in December
1930, Churchill recalled the impression which Clemenceau's speech had
made upon him:

. . . he ranged from one side of the tribune to the other, without a note or
book of reference or scrap of paper, barking out sharp, staccato sentences as
the thought broke upon his mind. He looked like a wild animal pacing to and
fro behind bars, growling and glaring; and all around him was an assembly
which would have done anything to avoid having him there, but having put
him there, felt they must obey. Indeed it was not a matter of words or reasoning. Elemental passions congealed by suffering, dire perils close and drawing
nearer, awful lassitude, and deep forebodings, disciplined the audience. The
last desperate stake had to be played. France had resolved to unbar the cage
and let her tiger loose upon all foes, beyond the trenches or in her midst.
Language, eloquence, arguments were not needed to express the situation.
With snarls and growls, the ferocious, aged, dauntless beast of prey went into
action. . . .

On Wednesday November 21 Churchill and General Furse discussed
Italian munition needs with Loucheur, and later in the day with
Loucheur and Dallolio together. Churchill sent a telegram that day to
both Lloyd George and Derby, describing the outcome of the talks. The
bulk of Italy's needs would be provided by France, but Britain would

General Commanding the 9th (Scottish) Division, 1915–16. Master-General of Ordnance,
War Office, 1916–19. Hon. Member of the Munitions Council, 1917–19. Knighted, 1917.
Lieutenant-General, 1919. Member of the Army Council, 1920.

[1] Georges Clemenceau, 1841–1929. Mayor of Montmartre, 1870. Member of the Chamber
of Deputies, 1876–93 and 1902–29. Radical journalist; editor of *Justice*. Minister of the
Interior, 1906. Prime Minister, 1906–8. Prime Minister and Minister of War, November
1917–January 1920. In *Great Contemporaries* (1937) Churchill wrote: 'Happy the nation which
when its fate quivers in the balance can find such a tyrant and such a champion.'

supply 150,000 rifles, 200 machine guns and 175 medium guns. As for tanks, Churchill explained: 'We have stated that we consider 40 tanks if sent at all should be complete with British personnel and as part of British force and that this is a matter for General Staff.'

As soon as Churchill returned from France, he was involved in problems which had arisen as a result of the War Cabinet's decision of October 13 to give a 12½ per cent increase in wages to engineering workers. The fears expressed in October that workers in other industries would demand similar increases were proved to be well-founded. Despite a Press notice issued on October 27, which tried to explain that the increase was not in any sense a general award, demands for an extension of the bonus soon arose from all sections of industry. On November 4 a meeting of engineers at Oldham, Churchill's former constituency, passed a resolution demanding the extension of the bonus to all men 'from draughtsmen to labourers'. During the first two weeks of November there were strikes at munitions factories in Salford, Manchester, Derby and Burnley. The 12½ per cent award was judged to be the cause. But the award was not universally condemned. In the House of Commons on November 6, a Labour member, William Anderson,[1] declared:

We have at this moment a much better atmosphere, in which there is far less industrial tension than there was sometime back. . . . I hold no brief for the present Minister of Munitions. I believe he has his personal and political detractors—I am not concerned with them one way or the other—but in my opinion he has brought courage and a certain quality of imagination to the task of dealing with labour questions. . . . Because of that the situation has perceptibly improved, and I hope he will go in the same direction. . . .

The demands for a wider bonus continued. On November 9 a conference representing half a million unskilled munitions workers demanded that the bonus be extended to them. Churchill was receptive to this appeal, writing to Lord Milner on November 10 that although the case of the semi-skilled and unskilled 'was in no wise involved in my original pledge and is no part of the "Skilled Workers Grievance" it has a very solid case of its own behind it, and we must expect that there will

[1] William Crawford Anderson, 1877–1919. Trade Unionist and pacifist. Labour MP for Sheffield, 1914–18. Member of the National Administrative Council of the Independent Labour Party.

be serious agitation to secure its recognition in some form or other. . . .'
Churchill went on to defend the record of his Ministry:

I think it is not untrue to say that the relations of the Ministry of Munitions
with labour have greatly improved in the last few months, and the maintenance of this atmosphere is of great importance to our output . . . the
efficiency of our output shows a steady increase every week. Although disputes
and stoppages, when collected together in a weekly report, make a gloomy
picture, it must be remembered that they are only the comparatively small
exceptions to the vast mass of production which is flooding steadily forward. . . .

The War Cabinet was to discuss again the scope of the 12½ per cent
award. In his letter to Milner, Churchill made it clear where his sympathies lay:

Demands of the workers for increases of wages are not, in my opinion, disproportionate to what is natural and reasonable in all the circumstances of
the present situation, and certainly they are not in excess of the increases
either in the cost of living or in the degree of effort which has been forthcoming. . . .

Lord Milner and George Barnes reconvened their War Cabinet
Committee, and, on November 15, proposed that the 12½ per cent
advance should be extended to both semi-skilled and unskilled workers,
not only in the engineering industry, but also in the foundry, boiler-
making and shipbuilding trades. This proposal was put to the War
Cabinet on November 21. Churchill, who was present, argued strongly
in its support. The War Cabinet approved. It also decided to appoint
George Barnes as chairman of a special Government Labour Committee, with powers to interpret the original 12½ per cent order of October
13 as far as other industries were concerned. Barnes' Committee found
the industrial agitation so widespread that it favoured an announcement that the bonus had been a mistake, and suggested that the whole
award might best be withdrawn, and rearranged. But from the discussions at the War Cabinet on November 27, it was clear that such a
step would be politically disastrous.

Churchill continued to assert that it was not only a question of
equity, but also of justice, that the bonus should be extended even
more widely. The Cabinet decided to grant the extensions, and Barnes'
Committee was instructed to work out the details. On the following day
Churchill answered questions in the House of Commons about the
bonus, and explained the War Cabinet's new decision. The original

plan, he said, had covered 300,000 men and would have cost £6,500,000; the revised plan now covered 900,000 men and would cost about £14,000,000. 'It remains to be seen,' he added, 'whether these very substantial advances, involving serious cost to the State, will be accepted in the spirit in which they have been made by the Government, namely, that of loyal and earnest cooperation for the vital objects of the War.'

At the end of November Churchill was again in France. During his visit, he confirmed the arrangements, which he had proposed on his previous visit, for the establishment of a British gun carriage factory at Creil, north of Paris, so that heavy guns could be repaired and modified without having to be sent back to Britain. He also undertook, at the request of Bernard Baruch, the Commissioner in charge of raw materials on the United States War Industries Board, both to find and to buy, for the United States, all the war materials they would need when their troops reached Europe. Churchill bought these materials wherever he could find them, in France, in Spain, and even in Canada.[1]

One reason for Churchill's visit to France was the decision of an inter-allied body, the Commission on Food Supplies, to release two million tons of shipping to help the French and Italians import food from across the Atlantic. This decision had been insisted upon at the end of October by the French Minister of Commerce, Clémentel.[2] Churchill had not been consulted about it in advance, nor had he been informed when it was made, although 1,550,000 of the tonnage allocated to France and Italy was to be cut off the Ministry of Munitions' share. On learning of what had been decided, he had written angrily to the Shipping Controller, Sir Joseph Maclay, on November 21 that these decisions:

have shattered our means of furnishing the armies in the field with the ammunition they require for 1918. They will also force me to notify to the French and Italians an entire suspension of the allocation to them of steel

[1] While Churchill was Minister of Munitions, Great Britain provided the United States with 164 heavy guns, 1,800 trench mortars, 300,000 grenades, 15,000 rifles, 11,000,000 rounds of ammunition, 4,553 lorries and ambulances, 2,219 motor cycles and bicycles, 811 motor cars, 452 aeroplanes and 18 tanks.

[2] Etienne Clémentel, 1862–1936. Deputy, Puy-de-Dôme, 1898. Minister of Colonies, 1898. Minister of Commerce, 1916–20. Helped to establish the Inter-Allied Wheat Executive, 1916, and the Inter-Allied Maritime Transport Council, 1917. Senator, 1918. President and founder of the International Chamber of Commerce, 1919. Minister of Finance, 1924.

products of all kinds, although used exclusively for military purposes. This
will unquestionably create a serious diplomatic position. I was informed in
Paris that the French were astonished at the liberality of our concessions to
them in the matter of food.

Churchill wrote to Loucheur and Dallolio on similar lines. His warnings were effective. Both Loucheur and Dallolio prevailed upon their
respective Governments to reduce their food import quotas.

Confronted by the possibility of an enormous reduction in the amount
of shell steel reaching Britain from the United States, Churchill had
taken immediate action within his own sphere of authority. In a departmental Minute he set out his emergency proposals:

There must be great masses of iron in one form and another scattered about
the country. Take for instance all the park and area railings. I should suppose
there were 20,000 tons of iron in the Hyde Park railings alone, while the
weight of metal in the area railings of the London streets must be enormous.
The same is true of many great towns throughout the country. Then there is
the building material of unfinished buildings, girders, etc. which would be
worked up into other urgently needed Works of Construction for military
purposes. A few strands of barbed wire could be used to protect areas and
enclosed parks. Drastic action will help to rouse people to a sense of the
emergency and of the magnitude of the effort required. Thirdly, there are the
battlefields. There must be 700,000 or 800,000 tons of shell-steel lying about
on the Somme battlefields alone. The collection of this is vital. The proper
machines must be constructed. A smelting plant should be set up on the
battlefields.

Let me have definite recommendations for immediate action on all these
points with the least possible delay, and advise me as to the composition of a
suitable committee, not consisting of members of Council, which can carry
out any policy decided on.

Churchill remained in France from November 20 until December 4.
While in Paris, he arranged with Loucheur and Dallolio for the estab-
lishment of an Allied Munitions Council, for which the Foreign
Office had given its approval. He also persuaded Loucheur to agree to
the establishment of a combined Anglo-American Tank factory at
Bordeaux, whose task, Sir Henry Wilson recorded in his diary on De-
cember 3, would be 'to assemble parts sent over from us & from
America, to turn out 1500 big tanks by about July–Aug'.

During October, stimulated by Sir Henry Wilson, Churchill had
reiterated his belief in the need to expand the scope and scale of
mechanical warfare. On October 30 he had lunched in London with his

friend the Duke of Westminster,[1] a pioneer in the use of armoured cars. Sir Henry Wilson, who was present, recorded in his diary: 'Winston's paper is admirable & full of ideas.' On December 8, Churchill circulated his paper to the War Cabinet. In it he advised that tanks should be used, 'not only as a substitute for bombardment', but also as 'an indispensable adjunct to infantry', and he compared the victory at Cambrai, in which tanks had played the major part, with the Passchendaele offensive. In Flanders, he wrote, from August to November of that year, 54 square miles had been gained and 300,000 men killed or wounded, at a cost in ammunition of £84 million. At Cambrai, from November 20 to December 6, over 42 square miles had been gained, fewer than 10,000 men killed or wounded and only £6,600,000 spent on ammunition. In Flanders 465,000 tons of shell had been expanded, a severe drain on British resources; the battle of Cambrai had used up only 36,000 tons of shell. Churchill went on to point out further advantages of a great reliance upon the tank, and to comment upon the army's persistent faith in the need for cavalry:

Powerful as the tanks have proved themselves in surprise offensives on suitable ground, they are still more valuable in counter-attack. In this case they would be moving over ground with which they were familiar, and against an enemy necessarily unprepared with any special arrangements to receive them. They are immune from panic, and in their advance must carry forward with them the infantry counter-attack. It would be lamentable if, for want of men at this stage of the war, and with its lessons so cruelly written, we should not be allowed to develop these weapons to our highest manufacturing capacity. Are we really to keep in being, at a time when every man is precious, when every ton of stores counts, 30,000 or 40,000 cavalry with their horses, when these admirable cavalrymen would supply the personnel for the greatest development of mechanical warfare both for offence and defence in tanks, in armoured cars, and on motor-cycles that has ever yet been conceived? . . .

It was not on tanks alone that Churchill believed the army should rely. In a public speech at Bedford on December 11 he declared: 'Masses of guns, mountains of shells, clouds of aeroplanes—all must be there. . . .' Churchill was convinced that lives would be saved, and victory brought nearer, if the idea of attrition, the pitting of men against

[1] Hugh Richard Arthur Grosvenor, 1879–1953. Known as 'Bendor'. 2nd Duke of Westminster, 1899. ADC to Lord Roberts, South Africa, 1900–2. Commanded an armoured car detachment, Royal Naval Division, 1914–15. Personal Assistant to the Controller, Mechanical Department, Ministry of Munitions, 1917. His half-brother, Lord Hugh Grosvenor, a Captain in the Household Calvary, was killed in action in November 1914.

men, were abandoned, and a war of metal and machines put in its place. Ten years later he wrote in *The World Crisis*:

Accusing as I do without exception all the great ally offensives of 1915, 1916 and 1917, as needless and wrongly conceived operations of infinite cost, I am bound to reply to the question, What else could be done? And I answer it, pointing to the Battle of Cambrai, '*This* could have been done'. This in many variants, this in larger and better forms ought to have been done, and would have been done if only the Generals had not been content to fight machine-gun bullets with breasts of gallant men, and think that that was waging war.

Throughout December Churchill pressed his colleagues to give every possible priority to tank production, and to transfer a large proportion of cavalry officers to tank duties. To Archibald Sinclair, himself a cavalryman, Churchill wrote on December 29:

. . . The cavalry myth is exploded at last & there is every prospect of these splendid regiments being given a fair opportunity on the modern field. I am strongly pressing that the cavalry shd be put by regiments into the Tanks both heavy & chasers, & this view is meeting with a great deal of acceptance. I advise you to apply for Tanks, & I will assist in any way I can to further yr wishes.[1] It wd be a thousand pities if the cavalry were simply dispersed as drafts among the infantry. The future life of this arm after the war depends upon their discarding the obsolete horse, & becoming associated with some form of military machinery having a scientific & real war value. It is not fair to blame the cavalry. I blame those who assign impossible tasks & absurd conditions to brave men.

It looks as if the failure of the Submarine attack as a decisive factor must leave the Germans no resources but a great offensive in the West. In spite of their reinforcements from the Russian front they will be inferior in a. numbers b. morale c. ammunition & d. reserves. I wish them the joy of it. An elastic defence with strong 'one-day battle' counter blows at their points, & tank led counter attacks on the flanks of hostile salients; a good army of maneouvre behind our front; & steady influx of Americans ought to make in combination a singularly cheerless outlook for the Hun general staff. Thank God our offensives are at an end. Let them make the pockets. Let them traipse across the crater fields. Let them rejoice in the occasional capture of placeless names & sterile ridges: & let us dart here & there armed with science & surprise & backed at all points by a superior artillery. That is the way to break their hearts & leave them bankrupt in resources at the end of the 1918 campaign. I look forward with good hopes to the coming clash; & to the opportunity of a good peace at the end of it.

We must not be done out of our world victory by wordy generalties.

[1] Sinclair was unable to find a place with the Tanks. He transferred instead to the Guards Machine Gun Corps.

France has got to win & know that she has won, & Germany has got to be beat & know that she is beaten. I do not think there will be any weakness here or in America. For me Alsace Lorraine is the symbol & test of victory.

Arm yourself therefore my dear with the panoply modern science of war. Make catsmeat of these foolish animals who have broken your hearts so far. Embark in the chariots of war & slay the malignants with arms of precision.

I will try vy hard to come to see you when next I come to France: or give you rendezvous in Paris. At present I am submerged by Labour difficulties— & have to fight for breath.

Throughout the winter the Ministry of Munitions was troubled by continued industrial unrest on the part of the part-time workers, who still resented the $12\frac{1}{2}$ per cent increase in the wages of skilled workers. There were further strikes in demand of an extension of the bonus. At a meeting of the War Cabinet on December 24, Churchill spoke with feeling on behalf of the strikers. According to the Minutes of the meeting:

Mr Churchill said that the perpetual agitation for further increases in wages was due very largely to the fact that wage earners were convinced that enormous profits were being made both by the employers and by profiteers engaged in trade and exchange. He was convinced that one of the only means of stopping these demands would be for the Government to take the whole of the excess profits instead of only 80 percent. . . .

Such a radical policy did not commend itself to a predominantly Conservative Cabinet. On December 31 Churchill circulated a memorandum on the labour situation to the War Cabinet. But the War Cabinet decided against publication. The memorandum was an appeal for moderation:

This is no time either for wage-scrambling or for profiteering. The idea that any class has a right to make an excess profit out of the war must be combated wherever it appears and by every means open to the State. Under the existing law four-fifths of the excess profits are taken by taxation. It is impossible to rest satisfied with this provision, and every practicable means will be employed by the Government to secure to the service of the country all excess profits made during this time of suffering.

Advances of wages have recently been given by the Government to definite sections of workmen in the engineering and shipbuilding trades. These advances arose out of an intention to remedy the contrast between the wages of skilled time workers in certain munitions industries which had grown up during the war. But in practice it was found impossible to keep the grant within the original limits, and as soon as one class was satisfied another felt entitled to make demands. The Government cannot, in the interests of the country, go further on this road. To do so would be to throw an undue burden on British finance, and if applied all round would lead to a rise of prices deeply injurious to the poorer classes of workers, and only wipe out the benefit of those who had received the advance. . . .

While the war lasts Advances of Wages can only be given on proof of increased cost of living, or in the form of payment by results, or for some very exceptional cause. This applies equally to private employers, who must not consider themselves at liberty to make unauthorised advances to their work-people, the cost of which in many cases is thrown on the State. The best way in which the mass of the British people can be helped through the present grave period in our national fortunes is, not by raising wages all round, but by keeping down the cost of living by every means in human power. . . .

The New Year opened with increased industrial unrest. At a War Cabinet on January 1 Sir Eric Geddes drew attention to the growing ill-feeling throughout the country. A strike of semi-skilled workers at Sheffield was only settled on January 3 by an offer of a pound advance in the pre-war rate, plus the $12\frac{1}{2}$ per cent. On January 4 the electrical workers threatened strike action unless the $12\frac{1}{2}$ per cent were extended to all workers in establishments doing government work. That same day, George Barnes told the War Cabinet that 'telegrams from all quarters continue to pour in' about unfair wage differentials, and that these telegrams were 'more and more threatening'. Churchill took independent action, inviting representatives of the iron and steel trades to the Ministry of Munitions. An agreement was reached, which was explained in an official statement from the Ministry on January 5. According to the statement: 'The agreement lays down a general scale of bonuses under which all the workers will be treated alike.'

Churchill's intervention was resented by George Barnes, who believed that the Ministry of Labour ought to be conducting all negotiations concerned with wages. Lloyd George supported Barnes, and the negotiations were transferred to the Ministry of Labour, while remaining under Barnes' overall supervision as a Member of the War Cabinet. Churchill protested immediately to Lloyd George, writing on January 7: 'I am sure I cd have succeeded in winding up the business satisfactorily had the necessary powers been given to me.' Eight days later, on January 15, Barnes told a Glasgow audience that the industrial unrest had arisen because of Churchill's 'butting in' with the $12\frac{1}{2}$ per cent wages award. As a result of Churchill's actions, Barnes added, the

Government had been living 'on the top of a veritable volcano'. Churchill was incensed by Barnes' remarks; it was a travesty of the facts to claim that he was responsible for the 12½ per cent award.

During the third week in January Lloyd George authorized Barnes to work out a final wages settlement in collaboration with the Ministry of Labour. Churchill was excluded from the discussions. At a meeting of the War Cabinet on January 21, Barnes suggested an immediate 7½ per cent bonus for all piece-workers, and to this Lloyd George gave his approval. But Churchill continued to protest. In a note that same day he declared: 'There is no excuse for shirking the laborious and practical business of insisting on the revision of low piece-rates and dealing with exceptional cases on their merits.' He feared also, he added, a demand for similar wages increases on the part of women workers. On January 22 Churchill protested direct to Lloyd George:

My dear Prime Minister,

Really you ought to put the winding up of this 12½% business in my hands. I am sure I can do it with better chances of success than any other department. It is an odious job; but it ought not to be shirked.

At the employers deputation you spoke to me of the importance to *me* of reaching a good settlement & then immediately afterwards you handed all over to the unsympathetic hands of the Ministry of Labour who have neither the staff nor the capacity to handle it.

We are steadily getting through our difficulties in the enormous munitions area, & with a fair chance I am confident we can deal with the shipyard cases.

After all this is a fair offer & a bold one. If you do not let me help you in a difficulty of this kind I shall soon cease to be of much use—if indeed I am not a burden already.

Now do I beg you take a short & simple course. Say 'The Minister of Munitions began this & he must settle it up'.

Give me the power & I will settle it up. But if it is simply to be muddled away by Barnes & an understaffed Labour Department, then I shall have to publish the true facts of the original order.

How many people know for instance that Milner & Barnes took the *crucial* decision to widen the schedule before any public announcement *in my absence*.

Yours always
W

At Churchill's special request, the War Cabinet was summoned again on the morning of January 23. A few minutes before the meeting opened, he handed Ministers copies of his note of January 21. But neither this, nor his private protest to Lloyd George, were of any avail. The War Cabinet accepted Barnes' assertion that any delay in making the $7\frac{1}{2}$ per cent award would only lead to an increase in unrest, and the award was announced to the Press that afternoon.

Churchill feared a German offensive during the spring of 1918, against which the Allied forces might crumble. Reading the intelligence reports from eastern Europe, he realized that the Germans, no longer confronted by the Russian army, would be able to transfer two or even three million men to the western front.[1] His fears were increased that the Government were not taking adequate steps, either to raise manpower, or to develop mechanical aids. On January 19 he sent Lloyd George a set of figures to illustrate the lack of initiative in finding men for the army, together with a critical covering letter:

My dear Prime Minister,

I hope you are not closing your mind to these facts. The war is fought by divisions, & I think that is a true way of counting forces. Next to that 'rifles' i.e. fighting infantrymen are the test & with them guns, light, medium & heavy. I do not like the tendencies displayed in these paras. which show very serious accumulation of forces & still more possibilities in the future.

I don't think we are doing enough for our army. Really I must make that point to you. We are not raising its strength as we ought. We ought to fill it up at once to full strength.

It is very wrong to give men to the Navy in priority to the Army. To me it is incomprehensible. The imminent danger is on the Western front: & the crisis will come before June. A defeat here will be *fatal*.

Please don't let vexation against past military blunders (which I share with you to the full) lead you to underrate the gravity of the impending campaign, or to keep the army short of what is needed. You know how highly I rate the modern defensive compared with offensive. But I do *not* like the situation now developing and do not think all that is possible is being done to meet it.

Fancy if there was a bad break!

Look what happened to Italy. One night may efface an army—men at once—at all costs, from Navy, from Munitions, from Home Army, from Civil Life. Stint food and commercial imports to increase shells, aeroplanes & tanks.

Wire and *concrete* on the largest possible scale.

A good plan for counter blows all worked out beforehand to relieve pressure at the points of attack when they manifest themselves.

---

[1] The first act of the Bolsheviks, on seizing power in Russia in November 1917, had been to remove Russia from the war, and to open peace negotiations with the Germans at Brest-Litovsk. The negotiations were concluded, and a peace-treaty signed, in March 1918.

If this went wrong—everything would go wrong. I do not feel sure about it. The Germans are a terrible foe, & their generals are better than ours.

Ponder & then *act*.

Yours always

W

Churchill continued to warn of the dangers of the coming months. On January 26 he wrote to the Minister of Air, Lord Rothermere, urging him not to allow his orders to drop below 4,000 aeroplane engines a month. 'It may well be considered worthwhile,' he added, 'to raise production to 5,000, or even 6,000 engines per month.' It seemed essential, he added, 'to go on building up the size and scale of our Air Forces'.

On the evening of Saturday February 16 Churchill crossed over to France, to discuss the supply of ammunition, tanks and poison gas with the army commanders. During his visit he was worried that his wife might be caught in a German air raid. 'This vy clear weather & the state of the moon,' he wrote to her on February 17, 'will certainly expose you to danger. I do wish you would not delay to send the children out of town. . . . It made me feel vy anxious last night to see how bright & quiet the night was.' He was glad to be in France, 'without a care', as he wrote, 'except that I do not like to think of you & the kittens in London. Better be safe than sorry.'

Churchill had to cut short his visit and return to London on February 18, to answer questions at the Ways and Means Committee, during the Supplementary Estimates debate in the House of Commons. In answer to a strong complaint from the Liberal MP for North-East Lanark, James Duncan Millar,[1] about 'absolutely deplorable' housing conditions in parts of Lanarkshire, he declared:

My hon. Friend will realise that we have reached a phase in the struggle in which material, even more than labour, becomes the limiting factor, and, in regard to housing, the particular kind of labour is also very severely drawn upon. We have the greatest difficulty in meeting the urgent claims which are made upon us for the improvement of the housing conditions, having regard to the even more imperious demands for works and construction connected with the development of the Air Service, steel works, and every service directly associated with the War. . . .

Churchill had been angered for some months by pessimistic reports in the Press, and by questions in the House of Commons, which implied

---

[1] James Duncan Millar, 1871–1932. Advocate of the Scots Bar, 1896; Senior Advocate Depute, 1913–16. Liberal MP, 1910 and 1911–18. Liberal National MP, 1922–4 and 1929–32. Knighted, 1932.

that all munitions workers were discontented, and munitions production endangered. He took the opportunity of the debate to answer these criticisms:

. . . Before I sit down I should like to impress one point upon the Committee and upon those outdoors. We read in the newspapers repeatedly about strikes, and officials and Members of Parliament and others who are concerned with our production are always getting news of strikes and disturbances and fermentation in the great world of munition labour. But we forget the vast area which continues to work day after day, week after week, and month after month with absolutely unbroken regularity, and with ever increasing efficiency and skill.

It is a great pity that the nation and other countries should not realise the widespread and unswerving loyalty and resolution with which the production of munitions is being maintained by the 2,500,000 or 3,000,000 men and women continually engaged upon it, or that there should be any fear in the mind of the public, or of those who are their guides in public criticism, that the whole mass of labour is swaying uneasily in that field of industry, and that there is a general air of discontent and laxity of purpose throughout this great area. Nothing could be more erroneous. . . .

On Thursday February 21 Churchill returned to France. He spent the day north of Arras—'a long jolly day roundabout the Vimy district', as he described it to his wife in a letter that evening. He had been 'walking in mud for 5 hours & no lunch! Now I am going to snooze before dinner. . . .' Because of the clear weather, he was again worried about German air raids on London. That night he slept 'in a chateau hitherto untouched by shellfire'.

Churchill spent the next day with his friend General Barnes, and was joined by his brother Jack. The three of them lunched with General Birdwood,[1] after which Churchill visited the trenches at Ploegsteert where he had served as a battalion commander for five months in 1916. He described the scene in a letter to his wife two days later:

. . . Everything has been torn to pieces & the shelling is still at times severe. The British line has moved forward about a mile, but all my old farms are mere heaps of brick & mouldering sandbags. The little graveyard has been filled & then smashed up by the shells. I missed Plugstreet's church. We ran past the place where it had stood without recognising it! My strong dugout

[1] William Riddell Birdwood, 1865–1951. Lieutenant, Royal Scots Fusiliers, 1883. General Officer commanding the Australian and New Zealand Army Corps (ANZAC), 1914–18. Lieutenant-General commanding the ANZAC landing, Gallipoli, April 1915. Commander-in-Chief, Allied Forces at the Dardanelles, October 1915–January 1916. Knighted, 1915. Field-Marshal, 1925. Commander-in-Chief, India, 1922–30. Master of Peterhouse, Cambridge, 1931–8. Created Baron, 1938.

however wh I built at Lawrence farm has stood out the whole two years of battering, & is still in use. So also are the cellars of the convent wh I drained & called the 'conning tower'. Otherwise utter ruin. . . .

Throughout the morning of Saturday February 23, Churchill worked on munitions files with a shorthand writer. Then, at noon, he set off to the north to see something of the Ypres salient. He described the expedition in his letter to his wife of February 25:

. . . I had not been in Ypres for 3 years. It has largely ceased to exist. As for the country round & towards the enemy—there is absolutely nothing except for a few tree stumps in acres of brown soil pockmarked with shell holes touching one another. This continues in every direction for 7 or 8 miles. Across this scene of desolation wind duckboard tracks many of them in full view of the enemy; & all about it as we walked now here now there occasional shells were pitching or bursting in the air, & our guns hidden in mud holes flashing bright yellow flames in reply.

We stopped our motor for lunch on the Ypres-Menin road & I was eating sandwiches & drinking beer when General Hunter-Weston[1] drove up coming back from a tour round the line. He is an old acquaintance of mine: a tremendous chatter-box & vy much chaffed in the Army for his ornate manner. He is the general who made the speech in the H of Commons the other day beginning, 'I am a plain blunt soldier'. Also you remember when the man was drunk in the trenches & they hid him from the general by putting him on a stretcher covered with a blanket, he said 'Hunter-Weston salutes the honoured dead', & passed on—hoodwinked. Well—anyhow he commands an Army corps in this neighbourhood, and took much trouble to explain the terrain to me. He got into my car & we lunched together. Meanwhile however the Huns began to fire. The spot is a favourite one—& is called 'Hellfire corner'. Big shells whined overhead & burst with vy loud bangs behind us. Nobody paid the slightest attention. The soldiers went on mending the roads & cooking their dinners & the traffic rolled to and fro. As we left the car to begin our walk a shell came just over our heads and burst about 20 yards away. Only one man was hurt a little further up the road.

Then we walked for miles (I have walked five hours at least each day) over these duckboards till finally we got to Glencorse wood & Polygon wood. These consist of a few score of torn & splintered stumps only. But the view of the battlefield is remarkable. Desolation reigns on every side. Litter, mud,

[1] Aylmer Hunter-Weston, 1864–1940. Entered Royal Engineers, 1884. Served on Kitchener's staff in the Sudan, 1898. Chief Staff Officer to Sir John French's Cavalry Division in South Africa, 1900. Brigadier-General commanding 11th Infantry Brigade, August 1914; promoted Major-General for distinguished service in the field. Commanded the 29th Division at the landing on Cape Helles, April 1915; promoted Lieutenant-General for the successful landing. Commanded the VIIIth Corps at the Dardanelles and in France, 1915–18. Knighted, 1915. Conservative MP, 1916–35. Known as 'Hunter-Bunter'.

rusty wire & the pock marked ground. Very few soldiers to be seen mostly in 'pill boxes' captured from the industrious Hun. Overhead aeroplanes constantly fired at. The Passchendaele ridge was too far for us to reach but the whole immense arena of slaughter was visible. Nearly 800,000 of our British men have shed their blood or lost their lives here during $3\frac{1}{2}$ years of unceasing conflict! Many of our friends & my contemporaries all perished here. Death seems as commonplace & as little alarming as the undertaker. Quite a natural ordinary event, wh may happen to anyone at any moment, as it happened to all these scores of thousands who lie together in this vast cemetery, ennobled & rendered forever glorious by their brave memory.

One vy odd thing is the way in wh you can now walk about in full view of the enemy & in close rifle shot. Both at Avion (near Lens) & yesterday at Polygon wood we were within a few hundred yards of the German line & partially or wholly exposed. Yesterday in fact the duckboard track led us to within 500 yards of a vy strongly held Hun position at Polderhoek Chateau. It was like walking along a street—not a scrap of cover or even camouflage. Still people kept coming and going & not a shot was fired. In my days at Plugstreet it wd have been certain death. But I suppose they are all so bored with the war, that they cannot be bothered to kill a few passers by. We on the other hand shoot every man we can see.

On the way back we passed the lunatic asylum blown to pieces by the sane folk outside!

A vy nice young officer acted as my guide—he had the V.C. & M.C. and was a vehement pro-Dardanellian where he had fought.[1]

I saw one other vy remarkable sight wh I must tell you of tho this letter is becoming far too long. I saw what looked like an enormous cloud of dark smoke in the air, wreathing & twisting & curling & uncurling, & darkening & thinning out again. It was millions of starlings. They feed on the battlefields and collect every evening into this swarm, and dance their ballets till dark. I have never seen anything like it. . . .

Churchill spent the night of February 23 at the headquarters of the Cavalry Corps, and remained there throughout Sunday February 24 with Archibald Sinclair. He spent the following Monday in the battle zone, and on Tuesday was in Paris on munitions business. That evening he dined at the Ritz. Among those present was the British Ambassador to France, Sir Francis Bertie,[2] who reported Churchill's remarks in his diary:

[1] Robert Gee, 1876–1960. Enlisted as a private, Royal Fusiliers, 1893. Served in the ranks for over twenty-one years. Commissioned as a 2nd Lieutenant, May 1915. Served at Gallipoli, 1915. Captain, September 1915. Served on the Staff of the 29th Division, 1915–18 (thrice wounded). Awarded the Military Cross, 1916; the Victoria Cross, 1917. Conservative MP, 1921–2 and 1924–7. Much to the embarrassment of the Conservative Whips, he 'disappeared' in 1926, only turning up several years later, in Western Australia.

[2] Francis Leveson Bertie, 1844–1919. Second son of 6th Earl of Abingdon; uncle of Lady

. . . Winston's views are peculiar. At one moment he said that the war ought
not to be continued a day beyond what might be necessary to free Belgium
and to obtain for France, not necessarily the whole of Alsace Lorraine, but
such part of it as would not enable her to feel and say that she had been
deserted by England and justify her in seeking another friend. As to the
German Colonies, South Africa might come to an arrangement to keep
German S.W. Africa, in return for some other German Colony taken by us.
German East Africa ought to be restored to Germany. The argument that it
might be used to threaten our road to India as a base for submarines was not
sustainable, for submarines could work without such bases. Germany must
have coaling stations and Colonies, and it cannot be expected that she could
be restricted to Europe. . . .

So struck had Bertie been by Churchill's views that he returned to
them in his diary on the following day:

Winston was very self-contradictory yesterday. He said that the war is a
European war and the results must be European. I suggested that what he
meant was that the decision of the war would be in Europe. To this he said
Yes, but added that nothing outside Europe *mattered*. He then went on to say
that if Germany breaks up Russia, we must break up Turkey. The inverse of
this is that, if Germany let go her hold of portions of Russia seized, we will
give up Palestine and Mesopotamia, and desert the Arabs of Arabia and
leave them to settle accounts with Turkey. . . .
    Winston in regard to the war prospects said that we are fast gaining the air
superiority over the Germans, that we shall, he expects, be able to get over
the submarine difficulty and then be in a position to treat with Germany if
she be reasonable. I think that he is in hopes of being top dog, by standing in
with the Labour Party. . . .

On the evening of February 27 Churchill returned to England.

At the beginning of March Churchill redoubled his efforts to impress,
both upon the public and the Government, the dangers of the coming
months, and the methods essential to combat them. On March 4 he
told a meeting of the Anglo-French Society at the Mansion House:

. . . We are now in the hush before the great battles in the west recommence.
In a few weeks, perhaps in a few days, certainly in a few months, the German
hordes, released from Russia, must either hurl themselves in attack upon the

---

Gwendeline Churchill. Entered the Foreign Office, 1863. Knighted, 1902. British Ambassador
Rome, 1903–5; Paris, 1905–18. Created Baron Bertie of Thame, 1915. Viscount, 1918.

British and French armies, or must expose the fact that they were incompetent to deliver a great offensive.

On the following day Churchill completed a memorandum for the War Cabinet in which he asked: 'How are we going to win the war in 1919?' and went on to set out a detailed argument in favour of a mechanically superior army. This army, he believed, would make if possible, in 1919, an offensive 'essentially different in its composition and method of warfare from any that have yet been employed on either side'. If such an offensive could be devised, dominated by tanks and aircraft, it would lead, he wrote, to a type of war 'proceeding by design through crisis to decision—not mere waste and slaughter sagging slowly downwards into general collapse'. To this end, Churchill set up a Tank Board within the Ministry of Munitions, and later persuaded his friend Jack Seely to take charge of it. Churchill instructed the Board to plan on a massive and expanding scale. By April 1919 it was to produce 4,459 Tanks; by September 1919, a total of 8,883. Only by this means, Churchill believed, could a decisive victory be secured by the end of 1919.

There were other mechanical factors on which Churchill laid stress in his memorandum of March 5. The results would be decisive, he wrote, if either side 'possessed the power to drop not five tons but five hundred tons of bombs each night on the cities and manufacturing establishments of its opponents'. He wanted to reduce reliance on infantry and artillery, to increase the use of air power by half, to quadruple the use of tanks, and to multiply the use of poison gas five times. Tanks and gas, he insisted, were only being used at present 'on a miniature and experimental scale'. The need was for a new impetus towards mechanical and chemical warfare. 'The resources are available,' he wrote, 'the knowledge is available, the time is available, the result is certain: nothing is lacking except the will.'

Trench warfare, Churchill insisted, could never lead to victory. Every British attack in 1915, 1916 and 1917 had been in vain; nothing had been achieved but 'a series of costly experiments, each of which has shown us the chance we have lost and exposed our thoughts to the enemy'. Merely to throw more men against each other face-to-face was no answer. 'Surely,' Churchill asked, 'we ought to have a plan for which we can strive, and not simply go carrying on from day to day and from hand to mouth in the hopes of something turning up before we reach the final abyss of general anarchy and world famine.'

Churchill sent his memorandum to all Cabinet Ministers. On March

8 Sir Maurice Hankey recorded in his diary a visit to Churchill at the
Ministry of Munitions to discuss 'a wonderful scheme he has worked
out for a tremendous development of mechanical warfare to smash the
Germans on the western front next year!' That same day Sir Eric
Geddes wrote to Churchill from the Admiralty:

I have been most interested in reading your inspiring paper on *Munitions
Programme, 1919*.
I hope it will bring great thoughts to the minds of those who dictate our
tactics. You have a great gift of expression and to one who has not studied the
problem your arguments are very convincing.
I wish you every success in trying to get a decision for 1919. . . .

Churchill had feared that Geddes would resent his memorandum. In
his reply on March 10 he defended its circulation:

. . . Whatever office I held or even if I were out of the Government, I should
do that. If I thought the Cabinet were going seriously wrong I should remon-
strate with them, and if that proved useless or unwelcome, I should resign and
say what I had to say in the House of Commons. I could never divest myself
of that general responsibility. After all, the object is to find out what is the
best thing to do, and counsel and criticism are necessary processes to that end.

On March 8 Lloyd George summoned Churchill to 10 Downing
Street, and asked him to set out his Tank proposals. Sir Henry Wilson,
who had just succeeded Sir William Robertson as Chief of the Imperial
General Staff, described the meeting in his diary:

After lunch L.G. had an enormous Tank Comm^ee at which Winston said he
would build 4000 tanks by Ap:1919. This will require at least 100,000 men.
Geddes doubted if Winston could get the steel. I doubted if I could get the
men, but we decided to go on with the tanks which I think on the whole was
wise. There seems to be 3 answers to Tanks (a) Low flying aeroplanes (b) guns
(c) mines. . . .

Churchill's appeal for a massive increase in the production and use of
tanks and gas, and his warning that no offensive should be launched
until 1919, did not impress the military authorities in France. Sir
Douglas Haig continued to believe in the power of infantry and artillery
to succeed in the offensive. At the meeting at 10 Downing Street on
March 8, Sir Henry Wilson had declared that the Germans could
always confront the Tank with an insuperable obstacle, the land mine.
At a meeting of the War Cabinet three days later, to which Churchill
had not been summoned, Wilson told those present—Lloyd George,
Lord Milner, Barnes, Bonar Law, General Smuts, A. J. Balfour and

Lord Derby—that the War Office had examined Churchill's proposals about poison gas, but could not support them. Serious limitations, he pointed out, were placed on the offensive use of poison gas 'by the fact that the force employing it was prevented from penetrating into the gassed area for a time sufficient to enable the enemy to organise his defence'.

As soon as Churchill learnt of Sir Henry Wilson's remarks that land mines would prove an insuperable obstacle to a massive tank attack, he set about trying to find a solution. On March 16, in a thousand-word Departmental memorandum, he urged that a 'serious effort must be made to face the question of the frustration of tanks by means of land mines and buried shells'. It was essential, he added, that 'foresight and vigilance' must be exercised to make sure that the efforts to increase the Tank programme were not wasted. It was necessary to make a special effort to 'overcome the misgivings lately excited in military minds, and also cope with the real danger should it manifest itself'.

In his memorandum Churchill made various suggestions, including a 'large steel hammer' extending twenty feet in front of a tank, which, on reaching the mined area, 'could strike the ground heavy blows sufficient to spring off the shell'. He also asked if it might not be possible for the gun on the tank itself to be sufficiently depressed to fire on 'the suspicious ground in front'. Another method he outlined was to have a special Tank in each group with an armoured undercarriage strong enough to resist the explosions, 'and thus clear away a minefield'. Or again, he wrote:

... an ordinary tank might push a heavy roller, or series of rollers, in front of it, or might carry them in a kind of tray from which they would be allowed to drop on the ground in front of the tank when the known limits of the minefield are reached. . . . Or again, a vehicle might be designed which a tank could tow along with it, which, actuated by wires from the tank, could move ahead and by this way explode minefields.

Churchill ended his memorandum by pointing out that these 'crude ideas are only intended to excite the scientific mind and lead to the production of definite solutions'. Two committees, he instructed, should at once be formed, one from the Trench Warfare Department, the other from the Mechanical Warfare Department, to study the question. These two committees, he added, 'should acquaint each other with the fruits of their reflections and meet together to arrive at joint solutions'.

To Churchill's chagrin, there was much renewed talk of peace-making during March. When the Allied Ministers came to London to discuss war strategy on March 14, rumour at once made peace the object of their visit. On March 15 the Paymaster General, Sir Joseph Compton-Rickett,[1] spoke in public in such a way as to imply that the Government were seriously considering a negotiated peace. Churchill's cousin, Lord Wimborne,[2] was excited by the thought that peace might be possible, writing on March 16 from Viceregal Lodge, Dublin:

My dear Winston,

I keep wondering whether the conditions you surmised are in any way maturing. The Compton-Rickett Speech has set the world a-speculating. It is even reported that *all* the allied prime ministers are in London!

You know my strong conviction, to which I think your own views now incline to share.

I tremble lest another chance be lost through obstinacy, over confidence, or personal vanity. I cannot feel that Russia has any claim upon us, or see why we all should ruin ourselves on behalf of Bolshevism. As to any accumulation of German power in the end it is more than set off by the English speaking solidarity.

I really *earnestly* pray you use your influence in the direction of sane accommodation. How disproportionate, to calm reflection, do all human quarrels appear in contrast to their shattering results. A ruined world will curse this frenzied age in years to come!! . . .

Churchill replied to Lord Wimborne on March 18:

Alas My dear Ivor for yr hopes.

C Rickett's speech had no such significance; nor has the gathering of the Prime Ministers any other object but the prosecution of the War, wh it seems to me will certainly continue on a gt scale; for we are reinforced by America & Germany by the capture of Russia.

The Germans are in no mood for reason and I shd greatly fear any settlement with them unless & until they have been definitely worsted. At present they think they have won. . . .

[1] Joseph Rickett, 1847–1919. The Chairman of several coal trade companies, 1890–1902. Liberal MP, 1895–1906 and from 1906 until his death. Knighted, 1907. Took the additional surname of Compton, 1908. Privy Councillor, 1911. President of the National Council of Evangelical Free Churches, 1915. Paymaster-General, 1916–19.

[2] Ivor Churchill Guest, 1873–1939. Conservative MP, 1900–6. Liberal MP, 1906–10. Created Baron Ashby St Ledgers, 1910. Paymaster-General, 1910–12. Lord in Waiting, 1913–15. 2nd Baron Wimborne, 1914. Lord Lieutenant of Ireland, 1915–18. Created Viscount Wimborne, 1918.

5

'Within an Ace of Destruction'

CHURCHILL crossed over to France on Monday March 18. It was his fifth visit since he had become Minister of Munitions eight months before. On reaching St Omer he went straight to Haig's headquarters, where he discussed the serious military situation with several senior members of Haig's staff. A German attempt to break through the trench lines was expected at any time, but north of the Oise, the British troops were outnumbered by nearly two to one.

After spending the night at St Omer, Churchill drove early the next morning to Tank headquarters at Montreuil, where he outlined his plans for a major increase in Tank production during 1919. From Montreuil he drove back to St Omer where he lunched with Haig, and explained his policy. Haig was critical of Churchill's plan to send 4,000 Tanks to the western front in 1919: 'This is done,' he wrote in his diary that night, 'without any consideration of the manpower situation and the crews likely to be available to be put into them.'

After lunch, Haig took Churchill into his study, and explained on a map the military situation as he saw it. 'Though nothing was certain,' Churchill later recorded in *The World Crisis*, 'the Commander-in-Chief was daily expecting an attack of the first magnitude.' Haig viewed the coming battle, Churchill recalled, 'with an anxious but resolute eye'. But he also complained strongly to Churchill, first about the War Cabinet's decision for the British to take over, at Clemenceau's insistence, a fifty-mile section of the French front, and then about the pressure that had been put on him to assign a large portion of his troops to a General Reserve, which could be called upon in an emergency either by the French or British forces. Churchill suggested that as Haig believed the main German attack would come against the British front, he would surely get all the advantage of the General Reserve, but Haig's discontent could not be assuaged. Before Churchill left Haig's room, he was told the precise balance of forces. North of the River Oise, 110 German divisions faced 57 British divisions. To the south, 85 German divisions faced 95 French, and in the east, 4 German divisions faced 9 American.

Churchill's conversation with Haig ended at about 3 o'clock. He had no further official work at St Omer for two days, when he was to attend a chemical warfare conference, and decided to visit his old Division, the Ninth, whose Commander, General Tudor,[1] had been a friend of his since they had both been subalterns together in India twenty years before.

General Tudor's headquarters were in the ruined village of Nurlu, and were part of the front against which the German attack was expected. Churchill and the Duke of Westminster drove there from St Omer, reaching Nurlu at seven o'clock. 'When do you think it will come?' Churchill asked Tudor. 'Perhaps tomorrow morning,' Tudor replied, 'perhaps the day after. Perhaps the week after.' That night Churchill slept at Tudor's headquarters, less than seven miles from the trenches.

On Wednesday March 20 Tudor took Churchill to see every part of his defences. They inspected the medium artillery positions behind Havrincourt, and in the afternoon went to part of the line held by South African forces at Gauche Wood. To reach Gauche Wood, they had gone, not by the communications trenches, but over the fields. In his diary Tudor wrote: 'I said that up to now we could not have walked in the open like this without being chased . . . the Hun must have had orders to keep things quiet on our front; it was typical of him to overdo it, practically telling us his attack is imminent.'

That night Churchill slept again at Nurlu. Before he went to bed, Tudor said to him: 'It is certainly coming now. Trench raids this evening have identified no less than eight enemy battalions on a single half-mile of front.'

Churchill woke up early on the morning of Thursday March 21. It was a few minutes after four o'clock, and he lay in bed for about half an hour, musing. All was silent; and then, at about twenty to five, he heard six or seven loud explosions several miles away. His first thought was that they must be British 12-inch guns firing at the Germans; but they were German mines, exploding under the British trenches. 'And then,' Churchill later recalled, 'exactly as a pianist runs his hands across the

[1] Henry Hugh Tudor, 1871–1965. Entered Army, 1890. Brigadier-General commanding the Artillery of the 9th (Scottish) Division, 1916–18. Major-General commanding the 9th Division, 1918. Commanded 'Black and Tans', Ireland, 1921; Palestine, 1922. Knighted, 1923.

North Sea

Dover

Dover Strait

Dunkirk

Ostend

Passchendaele

Calais

Poperinghe

Ypres

Boulogne

Cassel

Kemmel

M

St Omer

Méteren

W

Menin

Hazebrouck

B

P

Lys

A

GERMAN-
OCCUPIED
BELGIUM

Verchocq

Béthune

Lille

Montreuil

La Bassée

Loos

St Pol

Lens

Hesdin

Vimy

Drocourt

Frévent

Arras

Doual

Doullens

Bapaume

Cambrai

Abbeville

Somme

Havrincourt

Le Cateau

Bazuel

Flixecourt

Albert

Ancre

Nurlu

G

Busigny

Lamotte

Péronne

Bohain

Brancourt

Amiens

Somme

St Quentin

Drury

Moreuil

GERMAN-
OCCUPIED
FRANCE

Montdidier

Beauvais

Lassigny

Noyon

Oise

Matz

CHEMIN DES DAMES

Compiègne

Aisne

Creil

Oise

Soissons

Villers
Cotterets

Fère-en-
Tardenois

Rheims

Château
Thierry

Seine

Le Bourget

Paris

Marne

M Messines
W Wytschaete
P Ploegsteert
A Armentieres
B Bailleul
G Gauche Wood

────── The front line on 20 March 1918

▓▓▓▓▓ German conquests between 21 March and 17 July 1918

0 5 10 15 20 25 30

Scale in miles

© Martin Gilbert

THE WESTERN FRONT DURING 1917 AND 1918

keyboard from treble to bass, there rose in less than one minute the most tremendous cannonade I shall ever hear.'

The German offensive had begun. The artillery barrage was strong and effective. Nearly all the telegraph cables linking the divisional headquarters with the forward zone were cut. Wireless stations were destroyed. Artillery positions and machine gun posts were bombarded with gas shells. 'Through the chinks in the carefully prepared window,' Churchill recalled, 'the flame of the bombardment lit like flickering firelight my tiny cabin.' He dressed quickly, and hurried to the head-quarters Mess. On the duckboards, outside the Mess, Tudor approached him. 'This is *it*,' he said. 'I have ordered all our batteries to open. You will hear them in a minute.' But, as Churchill recalled, 'the crash of the German shells bursting on our trench lines eight thousand yards away was so over-powering that the accession to the tumult of nearly two hundred guns firing from much nearer could not be even distinguished'.

It was still over an hour before daylight, and from Tudor's Head-quarters, Churchill watched the relentless artillery bombardment. Shortly after six o'clock the German infantry began its attack. A thick fog over much of the front bewildered the defenders. With 750,000 men the German armies intended to crush entirely the British force of only 300,000. The South Africans were driven from Gauche Wood, and both to the north and to the south of the Ninth Division, the German attack was immediately successful in breaking through the British front line. Churchill wanted to remain at Ninth Division headquarters, and Tudor had no objection. But the Duke of Westminster urged him to leave at once. 'With mingled emotions,' Churchill later recalled, 'I bade my friends farewell and motored without misadventure along the road to Péronne.' By early afternoon Churchill had reached St Omer. 'It was as well they did go,' Tudor wrote in his diary; for by nightfall the road to Péronne was impassable.

Churchill remained at St Omer for the rest of March 21, and on Friday March 22 was in conference all day at the Chemical Warfare School. The German advance continued without respite. Everywhere the British were forced to leave their front line trenches. The Fifth Army was driven back almost ten miles. Haig turned for help to the General Reserve, of which he had been so critical. On March 22 the first French troops were rushed northwards. But the impetus of the German attack was too strong; by the afternoon of Saturday March 23, the Fifth Army had retreated to the Somme. To the north, the Third Army was under increasing attack. Havrincourt and Nurlu had fallen to the Germans that day. 'Weather absolutely perfect for the Germans,' Churchill's friend, Brigadier-General Spiers,[1] wrote in his diary. 'They are bombarding Paris with a long-range gun. . . .'

The success of the German attack caught the War Cabinet unawares. From Haig's headquarters, Sir Philip Sassoon wrote bitterly to Lord Esher:

This is the biggest attack in the history of warfare I wd imagine. . . . The situation is a very simple one. The enemy has got the men and we haven't. For two years Sir DH has been warning our friends at home of the critical condition of our manpower; but they have preferred to talk about Aleppo & indulge in mythical dreams about the Americans.

The Director of Military Operations at the War Office, Major-General Maurice,[2] wrote in his diary that day:

. . . 5th Army have lost many prisoners and guns. All our drafts in France are already exhausted and by stripping England of men we can just about replace our casualties. War Cabinet in a panic and talking of arrangement for falling back on Channel ports and evacuating our troops to England.

On reaching London, Churchill went straight to the War Office to learn the latest news, arriving shortly after midday on March 23. Sir Henry Wilson, 'with the gravest face' as Churchill later recalled, showed him the telegrams from France and explained the position on a map. Then both men walked to 10 Downing Street, where they found Lloyd George sitting in the garden, together with Lord French.[3] Lloyd George took Churchill aside, and asked him how it would be possible to hold any positions on the battlefront now that the carefully fortified lines had been broken, and with troops who were in retreat. 'I answered,' Churchill later wrote, 'that every offensive lost its force as it proceeded.

[1] Edward Louis Spiers, 1886–1974. Joined Kildare Militia, 1905. Captain, 11th Hussars, 1914. Four times wounded, 1914–15. Liaison officer with French 10th Army, 1915–16. Head of the British Military Mission to Paris, 1917–20. In 1918 he changed the spelling of his name to Spears. National Liberal MP, 1922–24; Conservative MP, 1931–45. Churchill's Personal Representative with French Prime Minister and Minister of Defence, May–June 1940. Head of British Mission to General de Gaulle, 1940. Head of Spears Mission to Syria and the Lebanon, 1941. First Minister to Syria and the Lebanon, 1942–4.

[2] Frederick Barton Maurice, 1871–1951. Entered Army, 1892. Colonel, 1915. Director of Military Operations, 1915–18. Major-General, 1916. Knighted, 1918. Principal, Working Men's College, St Pancras, 1922–33. Professor of Military Studies, London University, 1927. Principal, Queen Mary College, London University, 1933–44. Author of many historical works. In 1899 he married Edward Marsh's sister Helen Margaret.

[3] John Denton Pinkstone French, 1852–1925. Entered Navy, 1866. Transferred to Army, 1874. Lieutenant-General, commanding the Cavalry in South Africa, 1899–1902. Knighted, 1900. Chief of the Imperial General Staff, 1912–14. Field-Marshal, 1913. Commander-in-Chief of the British Expeditionary Force in France, August 1914–December 1915. Commander-in-Chief, Home Forces, 1915–18. Created Viscount, 1916. Lord Lieutenant of Ireland, 1918–21. Created Earl of Ypres, 1922.

It was like throwing a bucket of water over the floor. It first rushed forward, then soaked forward, and finally stopped altogether until another bucket could be brought. After thirty or forty miles there would certainly come a considerable breathing space, when the front could be reconstituted if every effort were made.'

When the War Cabinet met at 10 Downing Street at four o'clock, Lloyd George asked Churchill to remain, although he was not a member. The urgent question was, where could men be found to check the onrush of German troops? Sir Henry Wilson recorded in his diary: 'For hours I insisted on the importance of taking a long, broad view of the future of conscription on *everyone* up to 50 & of course on Ireland. I think I did good & Winston helped like a man. Smuts was good but more cautious, Milner disappointing. BL ditto. AJB rather uninterested. Curzon not there.'

The War Cabinet meeting ended at about six o'clock. As it broke up, news came in of further retreats. 'Our casualties in the battle are going to be huge,' Hankey recorded in his diary.

Throughout Sunday March 24 the German attack continued. The Fifth Army was driven across the Somme, and Péronne was occupied by the Germans. To the north, the Third Army was driven from Bapaume, and fell back towards the River Ancre.

Churchill spent the afternoon of March 24 at 33 Eccleston Square. The grave events of the past forty-eight hours had served only to strengthen his resolve to combat panic and demoralization. Hoping to encourage Lloyd George, he wrote to him during the afternoon:

My dear Prime Minister,
    The following steps seem appropriate to the situation:—
    1. 50,000 trained men from the Fleet including the bulk of the Marines.
    2. The age raised to 55.
    3. Ireland like all the rest of us.
    4. The American army to form on existing British & French *Cadres* in so far
       as it is unable to enter the line by divisions.
    5. The King shd be allowed to go to the Front.
These steps are additional to the obvious administrative measures wh are indicated by the Ministry of National Service. You must not accept any statement that 10,000 men a day is the limit of cross-channel conveyance. It is quite untrue. There are a score of expedients that can be adopted.
    The above also applies to the transport of munitions. Whatever is available & needed can & must be carried to France.
    Parliament shd be called together with the utmost despatch & on yr initiation; & shd then be told *that practical measures are being taken* & must be insisted on.

There are of course two problems, (a) the immediate reforming of a front & (b) the enduring through the summer. I do not think the first insoluble if the *lift* is given, and proper steps are taken.

The second will be still harder to surmount; but after all the forces are not hopelessly unequal:

Violent counsels & measures must rule.

Seek the truth in this hour of need with disdain of other things. Courage & a clear plan will enable you to keep the command of the Nation. But if you fall below the level of the crisis, your role is exhausted. I am confident you will not fail. Lift yourself by an effort of will to the height of circumstances & conquer or succumb fighting.

I am sure this situation can be retrieved.

Even if the land war collapsed the sea, the air, & the United States will give us the means of victory.

But now is the time to risk everything; & to run risks for their very sake. You can count on the support of yr fellow countrymen in all forms of vehement action.

Your sincere friend
W

Churchill did not send this letter. Instead, he invited Lloyd George to dine with him at 33 Eccleston Square. Lloyd George brought Sir Henry Wilson with him, and after dinner they were joined by Sir Maurice Hankey. In *The World Crisis* Churchill recalled: 'I never remember in the whole course of the war a more anxious evening.' Lloyd George's resolution, he added, was 'unshaken under his truly awful responsibilities'. That night Sir Henry Wilson recorded in his diary:

. . . Winston backed me up *well* when I pressed L.G. *hard* to really conscript this country & Ireland. I finished by saying to L.G. 'You will come out of this bang top or bang bottom' and Winston cordially agreed. I want L.G. to summon Parliament, conscript up to 50 years of age & *include* Ireland. I am not sure that he sees the full gravity of the situation yet.

A moving day. We are very near a crash. L.G. has, on the whole, been buoyant. BL most depressing, Smuts talked much academic nonsense, Winston a *real* gem in a crisis, & reminded me of Aug: 1914.

On Monday March 25 the news from France was worse. By reaching the Somme, and pressing towards Amiens, the Germans were trying, as General Maurice wrote in his diary, 'to separate us from the French'. The War Cabinet met at eleven in the morning, 'an anxious meeting', according to Hankey. Churchill was again present, and informed them that he was going to appeal to all munitions workers to give up their Easter holidays, and that he would release men from the factories for the front.

That afternoon Churchill received a group of English, Colonial and American journalists who had just completed a tour of munitions factories in Birmingham. He spoke with enthusiasm of the efforts of munitions workers. 'A good deal of writing appears in the newspapers,' he said, 'and a good many comments are made on the assumption that we have a sulky population reluctantly and grudgingly doing their work. I say that we have a loyal, strong, valiant and resolute people who love their country and mean to bring it successfully out of this peril. That is the only foundation on which we stand and by which we shall undoubtedly be sustained.' It was, Churchill added, a 'very grave and serious time'.

When Hankey went to Downing Street early that evening, the news, he recorded in his diary, 'seemed better, and we both felt more cheerful'. And he went on to record that 'Balfour & Churchill whom I found in company with the PM, were ridiculously optimistic'.

On Tuesday March 26 the Third and Fifth Armies fell back towards the Ancre. That morning Churchill telegraphed to all munitions factories:

A special effort must be made to replace promptly the serious losses in munitions which are resulting from the great battle now in progress. It should be our part in the struggle to maintain the armament and equipment of the fighting troops at the highest level. Our resources are fortunately sufficient to accomplish this up to the present in every class of munitions. But it is necessary to speed up the completion and despatch of important parts of the work in hand. I rely upon every one concerned in the manufacture of tanks to put forward their best efforts. There should therefore be no cessation of this work during the Easter holidays. . . .

Later that morning, Churchill assured the War Cabinet that two thousand guns of every type would be ready to be sent to France by April 6. When the meeting ended, Lloyd George asked Churchill, Lord French and Sir Maurice Hankey to remain behind. Hankey recorded in his diary: 'French was most bitter about Haig, who, he said, was no judge of men, had surrounded himself with stupid people & bad Corps Commanders. . . . He considered Haig had badly let down the army in shattering it in the hopeless Flanders offensive.'

Sir Henry Wilson had spent the whole of March 26 in France. At midday, he was at Doullens. There, at a conference held between Clemenceau, Loucheur, Foch, Pétain,[1] Milner and Haig, it was agreed

---

[1] Henri Philippe Benoni Omer Joseph Pétain, 1856–1951. Commanded an Infantry Regiment, August 1914; an Army Corps, October 1914; the 2nd Army, June 1915. In

that Foch should co-ordinate the Allied efforts to halt the German advance.

At seven in the evening, while Churchill was still at 10 Downing Street, Milner and Wilson crossed from Boulogne to Folkestone by destroyer, reaching London at a quarter to eleven. Churchill and General Maurice were at Victoria Station to meet them. They then drove to Downing Street, where Wilson told Lloyd George 'the chances are now slightly in favour of us'.

During the night the German advance continued. Churchill spent the night in the Ministry of Munitions building in Northumberland Avenue, and at breakfast time on March 27 went to see Lloyd George at Downing Street. Sir Henry Wilson, who joined them for breakfast, recorded in his diary that he warned Lloyd George 'that if we blocked the Boches in their attack they would turn on Italy in May or June, & then come back to us in the autumn. Winston agreed.' At a meeting of the War Cabinet that morning, Wilson described his visit to France '& wound up by saying the chances were in our favour now'. But on that same day German troops reached the outskirts of Montdidier. There was a desperate need to find more men to halt this relentless advance.

The War Cabinet met again during the afternoon of March 27. Milner, Curzon and Churchill pressed Lloyd George to extend conscription to Ireland. But opinion was divided, and no decision was reached. It was also decided to send a further Division to France, and to order General Allenby[1] to adopt the offensive in Palestine, in the hope of creating a major, if distant diversion.

In response to Churchill's appeal, a flood of telegrams reached the Ministry of Munitions during March 27. 'The munitions workers of Liverpool,' read one, 'assure you that there will be no loss of output and are ready to show the fighting army what the industrial army can achieve.' From Birtley, the Belgian refugees who were engaged in

---

charge at the siege of Verdun, 1916. Chief of the General Staff, April 1917. Commander-in-Chief, May 1917–November 1918. Vice-President, Supreme War Council, 1920–30. War Minister, 1934. Ambassador in Madrid, 1939–40. Prime Minister, 16 June 1940; he negotiated the armistice with Germany, 22 June 1940. Chief of State, 1940–4. Condemned to death after the liberation of France, 1945; the sentence was commuted to life imprisonment.

[1] Edmund Henry Hynman Allenby, 1861–1936. Entered Army, 1882. Major-General, 1909. Commanded 1st Cavalry Division, British Expeditionary Force, 1914. Commanded the Cavalry Corps, 1914–15. Commanded 5th Army Corps, 1915. Knighted, 1915. Commanded 3rd Army, 1915–17. Lieutenant-General, 1916. General, 1917. Commander-in-Chief, Egyptian Expeditionary Force, 1917–19. Received the surrender of Jerusalem, 9 December 1917. Drove the Turks from Palestine at the Battle of Megiddo, 19 September 1918. Created Viscount Allenby of Megiddo, 1919. Field-Marshal, 1919. High Commissioner for Egypt and the Sudan, 1919–25. His only son was killed in action in France in 1917.

munitions production telegraphed their determination 'to still further increase the production of those shells which are urgently required'.

Churchill again slept at the Ministry. When he awoke on the morning of Thursday March 28, the news from France was worse. With their heavy guns the Germans would soon be able to threaten the Amiens–Paris railway from the outskirts of Montdidier; they had recaptured the whole Somme battlefield of 1916, and had occupied the town of Albert. Churchill hurried to Downing Street, where he found Lloyd George in bed, 'a grey figure' as he later recalled, 'amid a litter of telegrams and reports'. The Allied armies were in disarray. There was every danger that the Germans would drive a wedge between the French and British forces. The British might then be driven back, northwards, towards the Channel ports. The French, isolated and in retreat, might not be able to hold their front, and Paris would then be at risk. In such circumstances Clemenceau might have no other course but to surrender.

Lloyd George wanted first-hand evidence that the French and British armies still had the stamina to fight back. He had to be certain that the hopes which Milner and Wilson had reported were not mere chimeras. Early that morning he decided to send Churchill to France to examine the situation on his behalf. He knew that Churchill shared his views about the need to defeat Germany, and that he was in frequent contact with the senior French and British officials in France, both military and civilian. He therefore asked Churchill if he could 'get away for a few days to France'. Churchill said that he could. Lloyd George then explained that he wanted Churchill to ask Foch direct whether the French army would be willing to make 'a vigorous attack' on the southern flank, in order to relieve the pressure on the British forces. Churchill himself believed this could be done by what he called the 'upward punch' of the French armies then south of the Oise.

During the morning Lloyd George telegraphed to Clemenceau:

Now that General Foch is practically in charge of the combined operations on behalf of the Allied Gov^{nts}, the Prime Minister & the War Cabinet are anxious to be in the closest touch with him during these critical days. They have therefore deputed Mr Churchill to proceed to Head Q^{rs} to-day where he will remain for the present, so that, should there be any form of assistance which in the judgement of Gen. Foch could be rendered by the British Gov^{nt}, he can immediately communicate direct with the British Government.

Churchill made immediate arrangements to cross to France. The Southern Railway Company prepared a special train at Charing Cross. The Admiralty alerted a destroyer to take him across the Channel.

Churchill asked the Duke of Westminster to travel with him. He then telephoned Sir Henry Wilson for a talk about the military situation. As there was no time for Wilson to go to the Ministry of Munitions, he went instead to Charing Cross station, where Churchill was already in his train. On learning that Churchill was being sent on a mission to Foch, Wilson was extremely angry. 'I told him I *could* not agree & must have this changed,' Wilson wrote in his diary. Churchill must go, he insisted, 'to Clemenceau, *not* to any soldier'.

Sir Henry Wilson returned to the War Office and set about the task of keeping Churchill away from Foch. He spoke to Bonar Law, who agreed that it would be wrong for Churchill to go to Foch's head-quarters, and who put this joint protest to Lloyd George. But Lloyd George had no intention of cancelling Churchill's mission. In order to mollify Bonar Law, he decided instead to send Churchill direct to Clemenceau in Paris. If Clemenceau would agree to a French offensive, Foch would carry it out. While Churchill was still travelling southwards towards the coast, Lloyd George sent an urgent message to his private secretary, J. T. Davies:[1]

Find out which station Winston Churchill has gone to (Dover or Folke-stone) & send a phone message to be delivered to him telling him that on reflection I have come to the conclusion he had better stay in Paris & not at French Head Quarters. He had better therefore go straight to Clemenceau ascertain position & report here. If Clemenceau agrees he could then visit French GHQ but not stay there. . . .

By midday, Churchill and the Duke of Westminster had reached Folkestone, where a destroyer was waiting to take them to Boulogne. From Boulogne they drove to Haig's new headquarters at Montreuil. Churchill later described the scene in a magazine article which he published in 1926:

. . . The rain streamed down in torrents in the silent, empty streets of this peaceful little old-world town. From this point sixty British divisions—more than half in bloody action—were being directed. From La Bassée southward the battle was at its intensest pitch. The remains of the Fifth Army were streaming back across the old crater fields of the Somme towards Amiens. Byng[2] with the Third Army was in full grapple. From every part of the

[1] John Thomas Davies, 1881–1938. Private Secretary to Lloyd George from 1912 to 1922. Knighted, 1922. A Director of the Suez Canal Company from 1922 until his death. Also a Director of the Ford Motor Company.
[2] Julian Hedworth George Byng, 1862–1935. Entered Army, 1883. On active service in the Sudan, 1884; in South Africa, 1899–1902. Major-General, 1909. Commanded the Troops in Egypt, 1912–14. Commanded the 3rd Cavalry Division, 1914–15; the Cavalry Corps, 1915;

British front, from every depot and school in the rear, every division of which could be spared, every reserve that could be discovered, every man who could shoulder a rifle, were being scraped together and rushed forward by rail and motor to stop the terrible tide of German advance.

All this I knew. Yet how oddly the calm, almost somnolence, of this supreme nerve centre of the Army contrasted with the gigantic struggle shattering and thundering on a fifty thousand yard front fifty or sixty miles away. The ordinary routine of the bureaus was proceeding. There was an utter absence of excitement or bustle. The Commander-in-Chief was taking his afternoon ride. No one not acquainted with the conditions of the Great War would have believed it possible that one of the largest and most bloody and critical battles in the history of the world was in fact being skilfully and effectively conducted from this spot.

While at Montreuil, Churchill saw Haig's Chief of Staff, Sir Herbert Lawrence,[1] in his office at the Military School. As they talked, news of troop movements were continually being telephoned in to the office. 'The main battle was devouring his reserves,' Churchill later recalled, 'the enemy were still pouring through the gap; their front advanced continuously; every division taken from the quieter sectors invited a new blow in the weakened areas.' Lawrence told Churchill that in the past week the British had lost more than 100,000 men killed or captured, and over 1,000 guns. The worst news was of heavy German troop movements towards the hitherto unattacked northern part of the British line. Much now depended upon what the French would do. If they attacked from the south, into the flank of the advancing German armies, they might still force the Germans to lessen the depth of their thrust. But if the French moved elsewhere, or did not move at all, the Allied armies would be forced apart.

On a map, Lawrence showed Churchill the location of the French

---

the 9th Army Corps, 1915–16; the 17th Army Corps, 1916; the Canadian Corps, 1916–17, the 3rd Army, 1917–19. Knighted, 1915. General, 1917. Created Baron, 1919, and granted £30,000 by Parliament for his war service. Governor-General of Canada, 1921–6. Created Viscount, 1926. Commissioner, Metropolitan Police, 1928–31. Field Marshal, 1932.

[1] Herbert Alexander Lawrence, 1861–1943. 4th son of the 1st Baron Lawrence. Entered the Army, 1882. Served as an Intelligence Officer at the War Office and in South Africa, 1897–1902. Retired from the Army, 1903, and entered the City. A Member of the Committee of the Ottoman Bank, 1906 and a Director of the Midland Railway, 1913. Rejoined the Army, 1914. Major-General, 1915, on active service at Gallipoli, in command of the 127th (Manchester) Brigade. In the summer of 1916 he commanded the troops that drove the Turks from Sinai. Commanded the 66th Division at Passchendaele, 1917. Knighted, 1917, Chief of Staff, GHQ France, January–November 1918. Lieutenant-General, 1918. General, 1919. Member of the Royal Commission on the Coal Industry, 1925. Chairman of Vickers, 1926. Chairman and Managing Director of Glyn Mills & Co, merchant bankers, 1934–43. Both his sons were killed in action, one in May 1915, the other in September 1916.

divisions. Several had moved up to Beauvais in the British zone of armies. 'But,' Churchill wrote, 'what their main intention was, or what their power to execute it was, he did not profess to know.' All Lawrence could say was: 'No doubt they are doing their best.' It was Churchill's task to find out what 'their best' might be, and to urge them to attack northwards.

Churchill and the Duke of Westminster set off from Montreuil towards Paris. They drove through Amiens, which was already under bombardment from the German heavy guns. From Amiens they drove towards Beauvais. 'The mist and the rain blanketed the flashes of the guns,' Churchill recalled, 'and the throbbing of the motor drowned the distant cannonade.' The streets of Beauvais were crowded with French troops; an Army Corps headquarters had just been set up in the town. Troop trains were arriving continuously at the railway station. The two men reached Paris at midnight, and slept, as Churchill later recalled, 'in the luxuries of an almost empty Ritz'.

Before going to bed, Churchill had received a visit from Leopold Amery, who handed him Lloyd George's telephone message, instructing him, as Amery recorded in his diary, 'to stick to Paris and not go directing strategy at GHQ'. Amery remained with Churchill for a while, noting:

We had a good talk while he wallowed in a hot bath and then went to bed. (Winston is an extraordinary shape and wears a long nightgown!). He had found our GHQ very worried about Montdidier and the French and down, in the mouth generally—also evidently without information of what the French were doing. His own preoccupation was whether the French were only counter-attacking piecemeal or were getting everything together for a really big stroke. He reports well of the War Cabinet, though they are still very worried about Ireland, mainly because LG doubts if Irish conscripts will fight. Bonar too was facing the storm all right, though, as WC said, he is a vessel with very low free board and the deep waters roll over his soul very easily.

On the morning of Friday March 29 Churchill saw the head of the British Military Mission, Major-General Sackville-West,[1] and the senior British liaison officer with the French, his friend General Spiers. Telling them of his mission, he then asked them their personal opinion

---

[1] Charles John Sackville-West, 1870–1962. Entered Army, 1889. Served as a Captain in South Africa, 1899–1900. Twice wounded on the western front, 1914–16. Major-General, 1917. British Military Representative of the Allied Military Committee, Versailles, 1918–19. Knighted, 1919. Military Attaché, Paris, 1920–24. Lieutenant-Governor of Guernsey, 1925–29. Succeeded his brother as 4th Baron Sackville, 1928.

of the French situation. 'There is no doubt,' Churchill telegraphed to
Lloyd George after his conversation, 'the French realise the gravity of
the next ten days and we need not assume that they are not exerting
themselves.' But he went on to explain that as many of the French infantrymen were being moved forward by motor lorry, they often did not
have their 'artillery and impedimenta' with them. As a result there was
'no immediate prospect of any strong French punch developing on a
great scale as we had hoped from behind their present covering troops'.

Churchill had to convince Clemenceau of the need for a rapid and
substantial French advance. Shortly before sending his telegram to
Lloyd George, he had sent General Spiers to see Clemenceau, and to
explain to him the purpose of his visit. Clemenceau sent back the reply:
'Not only shall Mr Winston Churchill see everything, but I will myself
take him tomorrow to the battle and we will visit all the Commanders
of Corps and Armies engaged.'

That afternoon Churchill saw Loucheur, and at six in the evening he
called to see Clemenceau. Immediately on leaving Clemenceau, he
telephoned Lloyd George to give an outline of his discussions. At ten in
the evening he telegraphed more fully:

... I had a most satisfactory talk with Clemenceau and every personal
facility will be accorded to me. Spiers has been very helpful. I also saw Loucheur
who has been continually with the Armies. These men know the real intentions of the French Government and I am completely reassured as to their
policy. It is quite right. What I cannot judge is whether they will be able to
carry it out. But at any rate there is a clear, bold policy being pushed to the
utmost limit with all available resources and with the agreement of all concerned. Put briefly it is the upward punch of which I spoke to you. Spiers'
telegram of this afternoon will give you the number of divisions to be
employed. How far fact will correspond with intention I cannot yet tell. The
plan which I have been shown is worthy of the French Army. I don't know
what the Hun is going to do. ...

During his day in Paris, Churchill had learnt that Haig intended to
pull the broken Fifth Army out of the line, and reconstitute it entirely.
In his telegram to Lloyd George he passed on this news, and also his own
advice:

... I think there is a big task for you that the rebuilding of the Army is
backed by all the power of the State. Munitions will be abundant but you
will have to find gunners, technical troops, Officers, Sergeants, besides the
enormous drafts. It is a problem deserving your personal study, because in a
month or six weeks this Army, such as it is, might well be the Army of Reserve
and a great factor now counting for very very little. ...

Churchill had no doubts as to the state of French morale. 'They are in good confidence here,' he told Lloyd George. 'Clemenceau of course a tower of strength and courage.'

During his talk with Loucheur, Churchill had learnt that the Germans were expected to be able to put a million new men in the field by the end of 1918, to replace the casualties of the summer and autumn. This information added a further urgency to the Allied need for American troops to join the battle. The Commander of the United States troops in Europe, General Pershing,[1] was refusing to send his troops piecemeal into action, or to let them join British or French units as they arrived in Europe. He wanted to hold them back until he could form a single United States Army. 'Pershing's one idea,' wrote General Maurice in his diary on March 28, 'is to have a great army of his own which will be ready when the war is over.'

Lloyd George was determined that American troops should join the battle at once, and that as new troops arrived from the United States they should be put into the line without delay. He decided to by-pass Pershing, and appeal direct to President Wilson.[2] Lloyd George wanted Wilson to send 120,000 United States infantrymen to Europe each month for four months, and to allow each American Brigade, as it arrived, to be attached to a British or French Division. 'In no other way,' Lloyd George insisted, 'can the hundreds of thousands of trained and half trained men, now in America, be made available in this struggle, for they cannot be organised into separate units in time.' Unless such action was taken, Lloyd George warned, 'we shall simply give Germany a chance to deliver a knock-out blow, with which they hope to win the war'.

Churchill supported Lloyd George's appeal to President Wilson. In his telegram to Lloyd George on the evening of March 29 he promised to get Clemenceau 'to back your admirable telegram . . . by a message tomorrow, and by his seeing Baker.[3] This is a vital matter.' That night, from the Ritz Hotel, Churchill sent Clemenceau a copy of Lloyd George's telegram, together with a covering note:

[1] John Joseph Pershing, 1860–1948. Entered the United States Cavalry, 1886. Served in the Apache and Sioux Indian campaigns, 1886, 1890–1 and in the Spanish-American War, 1898. In command of US troops sent into Mexico, 1916–17. Commander-in-Chief, American Expeditionary Forces in Europe, 1917–19. Chief of Staff, US Army, 1921–4.

[2] Woodrow Wilson, 1856–1924. President of the United States, 1912–21. In December 1916 he sought to persuade the belligerents to negotiate peace, but in April 1917, following repeated German sinkings of US ships, he obtained a declaration from Congress that a state of war existed with Germany.

[3] Newton Diehl Baker, 1871–1931. Lawyer; City Solicitor, Cleveland, Ohio, 1902–12; Mayor of Cleveland, 1912–16. United States Secretary for War, 1916–21. Member of the Permanent Court of International Justice at the Hague, 1928.

My dear President,

Here is the text of the telegram to America.

The Prime Minister wished me to appeal to you to back it all you can by a message of your own. He also asks that, if your approve, you shd see Mr Baker American Minister of War and persuade him to telegraph in support of these proposals.

Yours sincerely,
Winston S. Churchill

At ten in the evening General Spiers telegraphed from Paris to Sir Henry Wilson. His draft read:

1) Clemenceau has told G^n Pétain that for political reasons he insists that the American Div available sd be engaged at the earliest possible moment.
2) G^n Pershing has informed G^n Pétain that all the American Army in France is at his disposal to do what he likes with
3) M. Clemenceau is most optimistic, his morale is superb, he is convinced that the Germans are now held but states he wd fight if necessary every foot of the way back thro' Amiens & then thro' Paris. He has adopted Foch's point of view that no more ground must now be given
4) Mr Churchill has made a good personal impression on Clemenceau.

That night Clementine Churchill, who had been without news of her husband since he had left thirty-six hours before, wrote from London: 'I long for news. Montdidier looks bad. Please do not even go within range of shellfire. I am sure it will not help your mission.' And she added: 'I hear rumours that you will not be home for some time?'

Shortly after Clementine Churchill sent off this letter, Lloyd George telephoned her with news. Her husband, he said, was confident of the outcome of the battle. 'I am so relieved that you are confident,' she wrote on the following day from Lullenden, 'as the newspapers, tho' repeating again & again that we are "holding them", are rather depressing.' She had read in the Press that the Germans were daily shelling Paris with a long distance gun. One shell, hitting a church in Paris on Good Friday, had killed eighty of the congregation. 'I do hope,' she wrote, 'that when the long range guns start firing you take cover.'

At ten on the morning of Saturday March 30 Lloyd George went to see Sir Henry Wilson at the War Office, and told him, as Churchill had asked him to, of Churchill's two telegrams from France. 'The news is not so good,' Wilson wrote in his diary, 'as the Bosches have pushed the French out of Montdidier & have got nearly into Moreuil. Winston, from Paris, reports well on the Tiger, & on the pace at which the French are coming up.' At the War Cabinet that morning, Lloyd George read out portions of both Churchill's telegrams. Not all Ministers approved. 'Tonight in our walk,' Wilson wrote in his diary, 'Milner referred to this & said he was going to tell LG that either he (M) must have LG's full confidence or else he would leave the Govt.' Wilson commented: 'I agreed with Milner. This sending Winston over —first, with the idea of his going to Foch which I killed, & then to Clemenceau is a direct snub to Milner. . . .'

At eight that morning Churchill had presented himself at the Rue St Dominic, Clemenceau's headquarters. 'Five military motor cars,' he later recalled, 'all decorated with the small satin tricolours of the highest authority, filled the courtyard. . . .' Clemenceau emerged from the building, accompanied by several senior Generals, and greeted Churchill in fluent English:

I am delighted, my dear Mr Winston Churchill, that you have come. We shall show you everything. We shall go together everywhere and see every-thing for ourselves. We shall see Foch. We shall see Debeney.[1] We shall see the Corps Commanders, and we will also go and see the illustrious Haig, and Rawlinson[2] as well. Whatever is known you shall know.

Clemenceau set off in the first car, Churchill and Loucheur in the second. The staff officers filled the others. 'As soon as we cleared the barriers of Paris,' Churchill recalled, 'we proceeded at a rate of about seventy kilometres an hour, or over. The cars leaped and bounded on the muddy roads. The country, scarred by successive lines of entrench-ments, flashed past as we rocketed northwards.' Churchill had much to discuss with Loucheur. Many of the Allied munitions factories, in-cluding the principal aeroplane workshops, would be within range of German guns if the advance were to continue much farther. It would then be essential to move the factories well to the south of Paris. But the labour needed to prepare the new factories could not be spared from the existing factories. The moment the emergency made it essential for the

[1] Marie-Eugène Debeney, 1864–1943. Entered the French Army, 1886. Chief of Staff of the 1st Army, 1914–15. Général de Brigade, 1915; Général de Division commanding the 7th Army, 1916–17. Major-General of the Group of Armies of the North and North-East, 1917. Commanded the 1st Army, 1917–19. Chief of the General Staff, 1924–6.

[2] Henry Seymour Rawlinson, 1864–1925. Entered Army, 1884. On Kitchener's staff in the Sudan, 1898. Brigadier-General, 1903. Major-General commanding the 4th Division, September 1914; the 7th Division & 3rd Cavalry Division, October 1914; the IV Corps, December 1914–December 1915. Knighted, 1914. Lieutenant-General commanding the Fourth Army, 1916–18. General, 1917. Created Baron, 1919. Commanded the forces in North Russia, 1919. Commander-in-Chief, India, 1920–5.

labour to be transferred, aeroplane production would be disrupted, at the very moment when it was most needed. 'The hostile front was coming now so near to the capital,' Churchill recalled, 'that all these complications stared us in the face.'

Shortly before ten o'clock the convoy of cars reached Beauvais, and drew up in front of the Town Hall. Churchill later recalled how:

Clemenceau got out. We all got out. We marched quickly up the steps of a stone staircase to a big room on the first floor. The double doors were opened and before us was Foch, newly created Generalissimo of all the Allied Armies on the western front. After brief greetings we entered the room. With Foch was Weygand,[1] together with two or three other officers. Our party numbered about a dozen. The doors were shut. . . .

On the wall of the conference room was a map about two yards square, showing that part of the front threatened by the German breakthrough, from the north of Arras to the outskirts of Rheims. Churchill's account continued:

General Foch seized a large pencil as if it were a weapon, and without the slightest preliminary advanced upon the map and proceeded to describe the situation. I had heard of his extraordinary methods of exposition; his animation, his gestures, his habit of using his whole body to emphasise and illustrate as far as possible the action which he was describing or the argument which he was evolving, his vivid descriptiveness, his violence and vehemence of utterance. For this style he had been long wondered at, laughed at, and admired in all the schools of war in which he had been Professor or Chief. He spoke so quickly and jumped from point to point by such large and irregular leaps that I could not make any exact translation of his words. But the whole impression was conveyed to the mind with perfect clearness by his unceasing pantomime and by his key phrases. I cannot attempt to reproduce his harangue, but this was his theme.

'Following the fighting of the 21st, the Germans broke through on the 22nd. See where they went. First stage of the invasion. Oh! oh! oh! How big!' He pointed to a line on the map.

'On the 23rd they advanced again. *Deuxième journée d'invasion. Ah! ah!*' Another enormous stride. 'On the 24th. *Troisième journée. Aié! Aié!*'

But the fourth day there was a change. The lines on the map showed that the amount of territory gained by the enemy on the fourth day was less than

[1] Maxime Weygand, 1867–1965. Entered the French Army as a Cavalry Officer, 1887. Chief of Staff to General Foch, 1914–23. He received an honorary knighthood in 1918. Head of the French Military Mission to Poland, 1920. French High Commissioner in Syria, 1923–4. Commander in Chief of the French Army, 1931–5 and May–June 1940. Minister of National Defence, June–September 1940. Governor-General of Algeria and Delegate-General of the Vichy Government in French Africa, 1940–1. Imprisoned by the Germans, 1942–5; subsequently imprisoned in France, 1945–8.

that which they had gained on the third day. The famous Commander turned towards us and swayed from side to side, using his hands as if they were the scales of a balance.

'*Oho!*' he said. '*Quatrième journée. Oho! Oho!*'

We all knew that something had happened to the advancing flood. When he came to the fifth day, the zone was distinctly smaller. The sixth and the seventh zones were progressively smaller still. Foch's voice had dropped almost to a whisper. It was sufficient for him to point to the diminishing zones and with a wave of the hand or a shrug of the shoulder to convey the moral and meaning which he intended.

Until finally, '*Hier, dernière journée d'invasion,*' and his whole attitude and manner flowed out in pity for this poor, weak, miserable little zone of invasion which was all that had been achieved by the enemy on the last day. One felt what a wretched, petty compass it was compared to the mighty strides of the opening days. The hostile effort was exhausted. The mighty onset was coming to a standstill. The impulse which had sustained it was dying away. The worst was over. Such was the irresistible impression made upon every mind by his astonishing demonstration, during which every muscle and fibre of the General's being had seemed to vibrate with excitement and passion of a great actor on the stage.

And then suddenly in a loud voice 'Stabilisation. Sure, certain, soon. And afterwards. Ah, afterwards. That is my affair.'

He stopped. Everyone was silent.

Then Clemenceau, advancing, '*Alors, Général, il faut que je vous embrasse.*'

No more was said. The visitors left the Town Hall, returned to their cars and drove off to the north. Their objective was Sir Henry Rawlinson's headquarters, at Drury, some twelve miles south of Amiens, on the Amiens–Beauvais road. When they arrived, large, fresh shell holes in the nearby fields showed that the Germans were near. Rawlinson's task was to regroup the broken Fifth Army within his own Fourth Army, and to hold the line intact, even while it was being forced relentlessly back.

Rawlinson invited the visitors to luncheon. 'An improvised, but substantial collation,' Churchill recalled, '(meat, bread, pickles, whisky and soda) was set out on the table. But Clemenceau would not have this until his contribution of chicken and sandwiches of the most superior type had been produced from the last of his cars.' Hardly had they finished than Sir Douglas Haig arrived, accompanied by Sir Herbert Lawrence. Haig and Lawrence then went with Clemenceau to an adjoining room, while Rawlinson, Loucheur and Churchill waited. Rawlinson told Churchill that his army had at last won a small success: 'Jack Seely with the Canadian Cavalry Brigade has just stormed the Bois de Moreuil.' Churchill asked if Rawlinson would be able to make and hold a new front line. 'No one can tell,' Rawlinson replied. 'We have hardly anything between us and the enemy except utterly exhausted, disorganised troops. . . . All the Fifth Army infantry are dead from want of sleep and rest. Nearly all the formations are mixed or dissolved. The men are just crawling slowly backwards; they are completely worn out.' Some of the British troops had been fighting, and retreating, continuously for ten days.

While Rawlinson explained the extent of the demoralization to Churchill, Haig was urging Clemenceau for immediate reinforcements. 'Clemenceau is in full accord with me,' Haig recorded in his diary, 'and gave orders for the French to support us energetically, and cross the Ancre. . . . I sincerely hope that Clemenceau will get his order carried out!'

Haig and Clemenceau then rejoined Rawlinson, Churchill and Loucheur. 'Evidently all had gone well,' Churchill recalled. 'The "Tiger" was in the greatest good humour. Sir Douglas, with all his reserve, seemed contented. The staff telephones were working vigorously in an adjoining room.' Clemenceau then spoke in English to the assembled company: 'Very well, then it is all right. I have done what you wish. Never mind what has been arranged before. If your men are tired, and we have fresh men, our men shall come up at once and help you.'

Clemenceau's decision offered immediate relief to the hard pressed British troops, who were, as Churchill telegraphed to Lloyd George that night, 'worn out and deadened by what they have gone through' Instead of a separate French offensive further south, to divert the German pressure, there would now be direct French assistance where the British line was most weak. His offer made, and accepted, Clemenceau then told Rawlinson: 'I claim my reward.' When Rawlinson asked what he meant, Clemenceau replied: 'I wish to pass the river and see the battle.' Rawlinson protested that beyond the river the situation was uncertain. 'Very well,' said Clemenceau, 'we will re-establish it. After coming all this way and sending you two divisions, I shall not go back without crossing the river.' Clemenceau was insistent; Rawlinson did not refuse. Summoning Churchill and Loucheur to follow him, Clemenceau entered his car. 'A few shells will do the General good,' he said, pointing to his military Chef du Cabinet, General Mordacq.[1] Churchill recorded the sequel in his article of 1926:

[1] Jean Jules Henri Mordacq, 1868–1943. Born at Clermont-Ferrand. Entered the French Army, 1889. Colonel Commanding the 88th Infantry Brigade, October 1914; the 90th Infantry Brigade, March 1915. Général de Brigade commanding the 24th Infantry Division,

So we all got into our cars again and set off towards the river and the cannonade. We soon began to pass long trickles and streams of British infantry in the last stages of fatigue; officers and men sometimes in formation but more often mingled. Many of these walked as if they were in a dream, and took no notice of our file of brightly flagged cars. Others again, recognising me, gave me a wave or a grin as they would no doubt have done to George Robey[1] or Harry Lauder,[2] or any other well known figure which carried their minds back to vanished England and the dear days of peace and party politics.

At length we reached the river. The artillery fire was now fairly close. Near the bridge was a large inn. A French brigadier, pushing on in front of his troops, had already established himself in some of its rooms. The rest of the place was filled with British officers from twenty different units; for the most part prostrate with exhaustion and stunned with sleep. A Provost Marshal, I think, was serving whisky to enable them to get up and crawl onwards, as soon as possible. Clemenceau had a few words with the French brigadier. As we got back into the motors he called to me, and I came to the side of his car.

'Now,' he said, 'Mr Winston Churchill, we are in the British lines. Will you take charge of us? We will do what you say.'

I said, 'How far do you want to go?'

He replied, 'As far as possible. But you shall judge.'

So I made my car, which was now third in the procession, come up to the front, and seating myself next to the driver, map in hand, pushed on across the bridge. The straggling houses on the other side soon gave way to open country. At the first cross roads I turned to the right, i.e. to the south, and followed an avenued road which ran roughly parallel to the river Luce on the enemy's side of which we now were. This road led to the Bois de Moreuil, and I thought we might possibly get in touch with some of Seely's Canadians. The guns were firing now on every side. The flashes of the British and French batteries concealed in wooded heights behind the river were every moment more numerous. The projectiles whined to and fro overhead. On our left towards the enemy was a low ridge crowned with trees about three hundred

January 1916–November 1916. Chef de Cabinet to the Minister of War, with the rank of Général de Division, November 1917–November 1918. Commanded the 30th Army Corps, Army of the Rhine, 1920. He published *Le ministère Clemenceau, journal d'un temoin* in 1933.

[1] George Robey, 1869–1954. Apprenticed as an Engineer, 1886–90. Music hall artist, actor and producer. Known as 'the Prime Minister of Mirth'. First appeared on the music hall stage in 1891. Served in the Motor Transport Service, 1914–18; organized entertainments for war charities, and raised £500,000. Member of the General Advisory Council of the BBC, 1937. Entertained troops throughout England, 1939–40.

[2] Harry MacLennan Lauder, 1870–1950. As a boy, worked in a flax mill and then, for ten years, in a coal mine. Made his career as comedian and songwriter. First appeared on the Scottish stage in 1882; in London in 1900. Organized concerts for charitable purposes, 1914–18; he also gave concerts on the western front. Knighted, 1919. His songs included 'I love a lassie' and 'Stop yer tickling, Jock'. His only son, Captain John Lauder, was killed in action on the western front in December 1916.

yards away. Among these trees a few dark figures moved about. The study I had made of the map before leaving Rawlinson's headquarters led to the presumption that these were the mixed forces scraped from the schools which Colonel Carey[1] commanded. If so, it was at once our front line and our last line. What lay beyond that, I could not tell. Rifle fire was now audible in the woods, and shells began to burst in front of us on the road and in the sopping meadows on either side. The rain continued, as always, to pour down and the mists of evening began to gather.

I thought on the whole that we had gone quite far enough. If anything happened to this thin line on the top of the hill—we had no means of knowing how near the enemy was to it or what would happen—it might be quite impossible to go back by the road parallel with the front, by which we had come. It would be very awkward if a sudden retirement of the line made it necessary for the Prime Minister of France to retreat directly across the fields and ford the river (if indeed it was fordable—about which I knew nothing). And so I stopped the procession of cars and suggested to Monsieur Clemenceau that we could get as good a view of what was going on from the side of the road as from anywhere else. The Bois de Moreuil or its neighbouring woodlands lay before us at no great distance. The intervening ground was dotted with stragglers, and here and there groups of led horses—presumably of Seely's brigade—were standing motionless. Shrapnel continued to burst over the plain by twos and threes and high explosive made black bulges here and there. The 'Tiger' descended from his automobile and climbed a small eminence by the roadside. From here we could see as much as you can ever see of a modern engagement without being actually in the firing line, that is to say, very little indeed.

We remained for about a quarter of an hour questioning the stragglers and admiring the scene. No shell burst nearer to us than a hundred yards. Loucheur and Clemenceau were in the highest spirits and as irresponsible as schoolboys on a holiday. But the French staff officers were increasingly concerned for the safety of their Prime Minister. They urged me to persuade him to withdraw. There was nothing more to see, and we had far to go before our tour of inspection was finished. The old 'Tiger' was at that moment shaking hands with some weary British officers who had recognised and saluted him. We gave these officers the contents of our cigar cases. I then said that I thought we ought to be off. He consented with much good humour. As we reached the road a shell burst among a group of led horses at no great distance. The group was scattered. A wounded and riderless horse came in a staggering trot along the road towards us. The poor animal was streaming with

[1] George Gias Sandeman Carey, 1867–1948. Entered the Royal Artillery, 1886. Brigadier-General, Royal Artillery, 27th Division BEF, 1915; 11th Corps, 1915–17. Brigade Commander, 139th Infantry Brigade, 1917–18. His special 'Force' of 2,500 British Engineers and 500 Americans who had never been in action before, was sent to the front on 26 March 1918 and disbanded, its work done, four days later. Divisional Commander, 20th Division, 1918–19. Officer Commanding the Troops in Jamaica, 1920–2.

blood. The 'Tiger', aged seventy-six, advanced towards it and with great quickness seized its bridle, bringing it to a standstill. The blood accumulated in a pool upon the road. The French General expostulated with him, and he turned reluctantly towards his car. As he did so, he gave me a sidelong glance and observed in an undertone, '*Quel moment délicieux!*'

Clemenceau, Churchill and Loucheur returned to Drury. From there, they drove north to Amiens, and beyond Amiens to the headquarters of General Debeney, who was commanding the French army then building up the front on the right of Rawlinson's weary troops. 'A long animated discussion took place,' Churchill recalled, 'between the Commander and the two French Ministers.' Debeney was confident that he could hold his own sector of the front for twenty-four hours, when reinforcements would arrive. The group then drove back to Beauvais, where they joined General Pétain in the French headquarters train, in the siding of Beauvais station. Pétain's mood was confident, his advice reassuring, as Churchill recorded:

Here all was calm and orderly. Pétain and his staff received the Prime Minister with the utmost ceremony. We were conducted into the sumptuous saloons of this travelling military palace, and a simple but excellent dinner was served in faultless style. We had already been exactly twelve hours either touring along the roads at frantic speeds or in constant exciting conversation with persons of high consequence. Personally I was quite tired. But the iron frame of the 'Tiger' appeared immune from fatigue of any kind or in any form. He chaffed Loucheur and the Generals with the utmost vivacity, breaking at a bound from jokes and sallies into the gravest topics without an instant's interval, and always seeking the realities amid the cool sparkling ripple of his conversation.

Said Pétain at one moment, 'A battle like this runs through regular phases. The first phase through which we are now passing is forming a front of any kind. It is the phase of men. The second phase is that of guns. We are entering upon that. In forty-eight hours we shall have strong artillery organisations. The next is ammunition supplies. That will be fully provided in four days. The next phase is roads. All the roads will be breaking up under the traffic in a week's time. But we are opening our quarries this evening. We ought just to be in time with the roads, if the front holds where it is. If it recedes, we shall have to begin over again.'

After dinner with Pétain at Beauvais, Clemenceau, Churchill and Loucheur drove back to Paris, reaching the city at one o'clock on the morning of Sunday March 31. 'Clemenceau,' Churchill recalled, 'alert and fresh as when we started, dismissed me.' In a letter to his wife during March 31, Churchill wrote of Clemenceau: 'The old man is vy gracious to me & talks in the most confidential way. He is younger even than I am! . . . .' And he continued:

He is an extraordinary character. Every word he says—particularly general observations on life & morals—is worth listening to. His spirit & energy indomitable. 15 hours yesterday over rough roads at high speed in motor cars. I was tired out—& he is 76!

He makes rather the same impression on me as Fisher: but much more efficient, & just as ready to turn round & bite! I shall be vy wary.
        'This battle fares like to the morning's war,
            When gathering clouds[1] contend with growing light'
(You shd read the passage in Henry VIth part III).

On reaching Paris Churchill had telegraphed the story of the day's events to Lloyd George. The British divisions, he warned, were 'in many cases only skeletons; many stragglers'. Fortunately the Cavalry Corps had 'reserved its strength' and was near at hand. The French, he went on, were sending reinforcements to the weakest points on the British front 'as fast as they can come up. . . . Nothing more can be done than what they are doing.' The German forces, although tired, were still strong; the most that the combined British and French forces could expect to do was 'to slow down the advance'. Churchill's telegram continued:

Thirdly: Enemy from his present position can shell Amiens and long stretches of Amiens-Paris railway by bringing up medium long range guns. This he will certainly do in a few days. Amiens already much damaged by bombing and much deserted. I don't expect we shall get much more out of it, anyhow, as a base or railway centre.

Fourthly: Our Armies require to be strengthened by every conceivable means. I wonder if there are any spare Brigades of Home Defence troops. There are a great many Officers and men in the Machine Gun schools. You ought to scrub your whole Military organisation and also the Navy in order to diminish superiority of the enemy.

Fifthly: Clemenceau will prepare his telegram to Wilson tomorrow 31st. He is favourable and so is Loucheur: Baker is no longer in Paris. I will press this point again tomorrow morning. Clemenceau is extremely cordial and confidential to me and splendid in his resolution and buoyancy. He insisted on smelling blood and powder today and only my prudence prevented him from doing more. . . .

Churchill returned to the Ritz, and to bed. His telegram was finally sent off from Paris at four in the morning, reaching the Director of Military

---

[1] Shakespeare in fact wrote 'dying clouds'.

Intelligence, Major-General Macdonogh,[1] in London at half past eight. It was at once decyphered, and sent to Lloyd George at 10 Downing Street.

Throughout the morning of Sunday March 31 Churchill discussed, with Sackville-West and Spiers, the question of manpower. They were all agreed that it was essential for the United States troops to be sent over, and used, with the greatest possible speed. Churchill then wrote to Clemenceau, in an attempt to persuade him to telegraph to President Wilson in support of Lloyd George's request:

My dear President,
   I should like to be able to tell Lloyd George what you will do about the American telegram. This is the moment to press Mr Wilson. It will be all the better if your telegram strikes a different note & comes from a different point of view, so long as it has the same object namely 120,000 Americans a month. Let us strike while the iron is hot. I don't see how else we can get the life energy which the armies will need this summer. I propose starting out again this morning at about 10.30, but of course I can put this off if you want to see me. It was a memorable day yesterday in your company & I was touched by the kindness & confidence with which you have received me.

Yours sincerely,
Winston S. Churchill

Clemenceau asked to see Churchill at noon. Together they drafted a telegram to Jean Jusserand[2] in Washington, for immediate transmission to President Wilson.

Yesterday, on the Moreuil Front, accompanied by Mr Winston Churchill, who has been sent here by Mr Lloyd George to ascertain the precise military situation, I was able to ascertain for myself the magnificent attitude of the Allied troops and to reassure myself that we shall soon check the tremendous effort of the German troops, amongst whom Austrian and Bulgarian troops have been reported. I am now able to inform you that, whatever happens, we shall contest the ground step by step, and that from today onward we are

---

[1] George Mark Watson Macdonogh, 1865–1942. Lieutenant, Royal Engineers, 1884; Major-General, 1916. Director of Military Intelligence, 1916–18. Knighted, 1917. Adjutant-General, 1918–22. Lieutenant-General, 1919. Member of the Royal Commission on Local Government, 1923–9. President of the Federation of British Industries, 1933–4. Member of the Central Committee for the Regulation of Prices, 1939–41. Member of the Finnish Aid Bureau, 1940. A Director of several companies; Chairman of Scammell Lorries Ltd.

[2] Jean Adrien Antoine Jules Jusserand, 1855–1932. Diplomat and literary historian. Entered the French Foreign Ministry, 1878. Counsellor of Embassy, London, 1887–90. Minister to Denmark, 1898–1902. Ambassador to the United States, 1902–25.

certain of stopping the enemy, without being able to say exactly where and when.

Notwithstanding this, the situation is of the utmost gravity and it is my duty therefore to associate myself with Mr Lloyd George in asking you to see President Wilson and to beg him in the name of the French Government, as Lord Reading[1] has already done in the name of the British Government, to be so good as to give immediate instructions so that 120,000 American Infantry may be embarked monthly for Europe, from now onwards till the end of July. The present state of affairs compels me, moreover, to give the very fullest support to Mr Lloyd George's request. . . .

Churchill telegraphed a copy of Clemenceau's appeal to Lloyd George. Then, with Clemenceau's approval, he set off alone for his second journey to the battle zone. Before going he lunched at the Ritz with the Duke of Westminster and Leopold Amery. Amery recorded in his diary the Duke's private remark about Churchill's visits to the front, that he 'couldn't realize that he wasn't popular on these occasions, just because people received him politely'. During the lunch, Amery recorded:

I talked over Irish conscription with Churchill who is sound on it—complained that if only my party had not insisted on hounding him out of the front rank he might have saved the country from so many disastrous hesitations. . . .

During his visit to the front on March 31, Churchill saw the Commander-in-Chief of the French 3rd Army, General Humbert,[2] and the Commander of the Group of Armies of Reserve, General Fayolle. That night he dined again with Pétain at Beauvais. The events of the past twenty-four hours seemed to bear out Pétain's confidence of the previous evening. At midnight, on his return to Paris, Churchill telegraphed to Lloyd George:

. . . No serious attack took place to-day, which can only be due to heavy Hun losses yesterday, and on Southern side of angle, namely Montdidier-Lassigny.

[1] Rufus Daniel Isaacs, 1860–1935. Liberal MP, 1904–13. Knighted, 1910. Solicitor-General, 1910. Attorney-General, 1910–13. Entered Cabinet, 1912. Lord Chief Justice, 1913–21. Created Baron Reading, 1914; Viscount, 1916; Earl, 1917. Special Ambassador to the USA, 1918. Viceroy of India, 1921–6. Created Marquess, 1926. Secretary of State for Foreign Affairs, 1931.

[2] Georges Louis Humbert, 1862–1921. Entered the French Army, 1883. Served in Indo-China, 1885; Madagascar, 1895 and Morocco, 1913–14. Général de Division, 1914. Commanded the 32nd Army Corps, 1914–15; the Army of Lorraine, 1915; the 3rd Army, July 1915–June 1919. Inspecteur Général (Paris), 1919. Governor of Strasbourg and Commandant of Alsace, 1919–21.

French are now well established and solidly backed with guns. Southwards thrust does not now cause anxiety.

Time has been very valuable on Montdidier-Somme sector and whole position should be greatly strengthened by to-morrow morning. Fifth Army has lost a little ground and French are grumbling. There is always some friction at junction of Armies and when this junction is critical point of hostile attack difficulties become pronounced.

Rawlinson wishes to withdraw his men to re-organise, and the French declare that he should hold on to the very small portion of the front in his charge. I think these difficulties will settle themselves. General Fayolle expects battle to continue in critical condition for good many days, but every day gained adds to our advantages. The enemy, however, is already shelling various Railway stations on the main Amiens-Paris line. Every phase of a battle like this brings its own problem—first, men: then, field guns; then, heavy guns; then, munitions. Now roads are coming into view. These difficulties are however present on the other side too.

At nine in the morning of Monday April 1, Churchill telegraphed to Lloyd George again:

It is considered certain here that the Germans will pursue this struggle to a final decision all through the summer and their resources are at present larger than ours. It would be fatal to be lulled by the talk of depression in Germany leading to peace. Every effort must be made if we are to escape destruction. . . .

The joint Anglo-French appeal to President Wilson was successful. During the morning of April 1 Lord Reading telegraphed from Washington with the news that Wilson would send 480,000 American soldiers to France, at the rate of 120,000 a month. Churchill saw Clemenceau again that evening, and reported the conversation to Lloyd George by telegram at midnight:

Clemenceau wants you, if you can, to come here at once. Considerable difficulties about the high command which you will readily understand have arisen. There has been a serious misunderstanding between the three commanders Foch, Haig, Rawlinson about the responsibility for the front at the junction of the armies. . . . To-day Clemenceau has personally adjusted some of the difficulties, but he now asks me to remind you of your promise to come and appeals to you to do so. I think it very desirable. You and he together can make a good settlement and no-one else can. It will be also a good thing for you to take a view of the British situation from a different stand-point.

Please telephone me what you will do, early to-morrow. I shall remain here meanwhile. Many congratulations on your American achievement.

Lloyd George was given Churchill's telegram when he awoke on the morning of Tuesday April 2, and at once made plans to leave for France. At seven in the evening he and Sir Henry Wilson left London for Folkestone, where they spent the night. At 7.15 on the morning of April 3 they crossed over to France. Churchill met them at Boulogne and travelled with them as far as Montreuil. But Wilson had insisted that Churchill should play no part in the military discussions, and Churchill spent the rest of the day on munitions business. Meanwhile, Lloyd George and Wilson were joined by Haig, and drove from Montreuil to Beauvais, where Clemenceau and Foch were waiting for them. Discussions began at three o'clock, in the Town Hall. General Spiers acted as interpreter. Two American Generals, Pershing and Bliss,[1] were also present. In his diary, Sir Henry Wilson recorded the subsequent discussions:

LG said the British Public wanted Foch to have real power. . . . Bliss said Foch must be given—if he had not already got them—powers for the future as well as for the present. I drafted a part of the Tiger's new declaration . . . a para of rights of appeal of each C in C to his Gov! if he received *from Foch* any 'Instructions' which he thought would endanger his army. The American Gov! with Pershing and Bliss' approval was added to the final line & everyone agreed. . . . DH then urged an early French offensive. LG & I pressed this on Foch, & Clemenceau & Foch agreed.

That evening, Lloyd George and Wilson drove from Beauvais to Boulogne, dining at the roadside near Montreuil. At Boulogne they were joined by Churchill and the Duke of Westminster. They crossed the channel at once, reaching London at two-thirty in the morning. Churchill's mission was over. Two days later, on April 6, he wrote to Asquith—whose son Arthur[2] was about to join the Ministry of Munitions:

. . . I have just got back from the French battle-front which I have been watching for the last week on behalf of the Govt. I saw all the generals & was

[1] Tasker Howard Bliss, 1853–1930. Entered the United States Army, 1875. Professor of Military Science at the Naval War College, 1885–8. On active service in Puerto Rico during the Spanish-American war, 1898. Brigadier-General, 1901. Assistant Chief of Staff, US Army, 1909; Chief of Staff, 1917. General, 1917. American Military Representative on the Supreme War Council, Versailles, 1917–19. American Commissioner, Paris Peace Conference, 1919. He received an honorary knighthood from King George V in 1918.

[2] Arthur Melland Asquith, 1883–1939. Known as 'Oc'. Sudan Civil Service, 1906–11. In business, 1911–14. Enlisted in the Royal Naval Volunteer Reserve, 1914. Served in the Royal Naval Division at Antwerp, Dardanelles and western front, 1914–16. Four times wounded. Served in the Ministry of Munitions, 1918; in the Ministry of Labour, 1919. Company director.

given the fullest information. The position is for the moment quite stabilized. The line of battle is now regularly formed & satisfactory arrangements have been made at the junction of the armies. The main strength of the French army stands between Paris & the further advance of the enemy. Amiens of course will be under long range fire, & its extremely important communicns are compromised tho not at present interrupted. Both sides are now supremely interested in resolving the battle in their southern area & will make it a trial of strength like Verdun only more so. We must also expect to be attacked from La Bassée to Arras. If the enemy succeeded there it wd be vy unpleasant. If he does not succeed, at least he wd keep our reserves tied down. These are the most likely developments.

The American troops—as soldiers & not as divisions—will be needed in large numbers if we are to survive the summer, & so will every man we can claw out of these islands.

I have been able to replace everything in the munitions sphere without difficulty. Guns, Tanks, aeroplanes will all be ahead of personnel. We have succeeded in pulling the gun position round so completely since last summer that we can deliver 2000 guns as fast as they can be shipped.

It has been touch & go on the front. We stood for some days within an ace of destruction.

6

'No peace till victory'

ON his return from France, Churchill was angered to learn that the International Red Cross had tried, during the first week of April, to assert its influence against the use of poison gas. The French Government at once intimated to the Red Cross that they would be willing to give up using poison gas if the Germans were also willing to abandon it. On April 6 Churchill wrote in protest to Loucheur:

I am much concerned at the attitude taken by the French representatives at the Conference held last week on the Red Cross suggestion of the willingness of the German Government to abandon the use of poison gas. Apparently France is strongly in favour of our offering to give up this form of warfare, or at any rate of accepting a German offer. I do not believe this is to our advantage. I hope that next year we shall have a substantial advantage over them in this field. Anyhow I would not trust the German word. They would be very glad to see us relax our present preparations, allow our organisation to fall into desuetude; and then after an interval, in which they had elaborated new methods, they would allege that we had broken the arrangement and, perhaps even without this pretext, resume gas-warfare on the largest scale.

I am on the contrary in favour of the greatest possible development of gas-warfare, and of the fullest utilisation of the winds, which favour us so much more than the enemy. . . .

Churchill's argument prevailed. The use of poison gas continued. Between April and August 1918 the production of gas shell increased by over a hundred per cent, from 350 tons a week to 795 tons a week. By May 1918 over a third of the shells fired by the British Army were gas shells.

During the first week of April, the German troops made their final plans for a new attack further to the north, along the River Lys. Their aim was to cut off Ypres from the south, seize the high ground of Kemmel and capture Hazebrouck, an important Allied railway junction. The attack began after midnight on April 7, with an intense gas bombardment. Over 30,000 shells, including mustard gas, were directed on Armentières. The German troops advanced shortly before dawn on April 9. The main attack came against the Portuguese 2nd Division, which was unable to withstand so fierce an assault. By noon almost all the Portuguese had disappeared from the battlefield. Two thousand had been killed, six thousand had been taken prisoner and fourteen thousand had fled. The British First Army could not hold the broken line. 'Situation very critical,' General Spiers wrote in his diary for April 10. 'Germans attacking more & more to the North. . . . British foresee possibility of having to retire on Channel ports which would mean severance with French & German objective gained.'

Throughout April 11 the German advance continued. By nightfall Armentières was in German hands, and Ploegsteert, where Churchill had served, and which had been under Allied control since November 1914, fell to the advancing armies.

By April 17 the Germans had reached the limits of their advance. Mount Kemmel had been attacked, but had not fallen. The Ypres salient had been much reduced but Ypres itself was still in British hands. That day Churchill telegraphed to the head of the Tank factory at Birmingham, Dudley Docker:[1]

Express again to all hands my satisfaction at the admirable deliveries. Tell them confidentially not for publication that the losses of tanks have been larger than previously reported but that they have exacted a heavy toll from the Huns in many cases and helped our infantry notably. Explain to them that during the uncertainty of the battle and its intense fierceness, it is not possible for the Tank Corps to make deliveries regularly.

The roads are congested, depots are moving, everyone is involved in the fight. When the lull comes there will be a general refitting and that is the moment for which we must have ready the largest possible numbers. I am watching for this moment very carefully. They must not be put off their efforts if tanks accumulate temporarily. The Army is fighting for its life and we are standing by to put new weapons in their hands the very instant they turn to us. Let there be no misunderstanding therefore but only confidence and full steam ahead.

As well as urging public effort, Churchill sought to guide Lloyd George during the critical weeks. On April 18 he sent Lloyd George a memorandum, marked 'Very Secret', in which he analysed the strategic

---

[1] Frank Dudley Docker, 1862–1944. Chairman of the Metropolitan Carriage, Wagon & Finance Company, Birmingham. Director of the Birmingham Small Arms Company Limited, and of the Midland Bank Ltd.

decisions which would have to be taken if the German offensive continued. 'It is imperative . . .' he wrote, 'to face the situation in advance and have a clear and profoundly considered view.' The 'vital question' was, he wrote, *whether we should let go our left hand or our right*'; abandon the Channel ports, or abandon all contact with the French front line. Churchill pointed out that if one looked at a map of the whole of France it became clear 'that however important the Channel, the Channel ports and Flanders may be, they and all the ground we hold are only a fragment of the country and nation we are defending'. Churchill's memorandum continued:

If the Germans could succeed in sweeping us from the Channel ports and capturing Dunkirk, Calais, and Boulogne, they gain all those very great advantages which have so often been explained. They can command the Straits of Dover, close the Port of London to all except northabout traffic, render Dover Harbour uncomfortable, bombard a large part of Kent and Sussex, and deprive our armies of their nearest and most convenient bases. But they would remain confronted by the mass of the still unbeaten British and French armies along a line from the neighbourhood of Abbeville so much shortened that, even with greatly reduced forces, it could be solidly held. And behind these armies would be the whole of France open for dilatory retirement or manoeuvre. Until those armies were forced to lay down their arms the land war would not be ended. If France wished to make peace, the facilities of retreat open to the British in several directions to the sea or to neutral territory would afford bargaining power to make a military convention providing for the repatriation of that army; and France would be bound to insist on that, even at territorial loss to herself. Therefore, great as are the advantages which Germany would gain by the conquest of the Channel ports, there would be no reason why the war could not be indefinitely prolonged after their loss, provided the French and British armies remained united.

If, on the other hand, the Germans divide the British and French armies from each other at Abbeville, forcing us to let go our right hand and shut ourselves up in a Torres Vedras, they will have the following choice open to them, viz: whether to wire in and so mask the British and throw their whole force against the French and Paris, or alternatively to hold the French in check while they drive the British into the sea. What would their choice be? What was it at the beginning of the war? Did they not absolutely disdain the Channel ports while there was a chance of taking Paris and smashing the main army? Had we any difficulty in deciding, when it came to the pinch in those days, whether our—then little—army should cover the Channel ports, or hold on firmly to the French and fight the main battle out in their company?

Although the British army thrown back on the Channel ports might be seriously weakened, yet to drive it into the sea, or to destroy it in its entrenchments, would require an enormous effort. For the Germans to lay siege to such an army, with the almost intact French army striking at their backs, would seem to be an unwise proceeding. '*Frappez la masse*' is a maxim to which the Germans have always given an understanding allegiance. And that would be their shortest road to end the war. It therefore seems probable that they would have the weakened and exhausted British army cooped up in its lines around the Channel ports, and try the main conclusion with the French army. On the morrow of such a victory the British army would be at their disposal. They could deal with it at their convenience.

All this appears to follow the elementary lines: Divide the enemy's forces into two parts: hold off the weaker part while you beat the stronger: the weaker then is at your mercy.

Churchill continued his analysis with a series of questions:

Do not all these considerations go to show that the vital and supreme need is for us to keep connection with the French? Does not experience generally show that armies which can get separated from the main army are disposed of at leisure? Is not the sound rule to stand together, retire together, turn together, and strike together, as we did at the Marne? What would have been the position of a British army which, after Mons, had retreated on the Channel ports, if in its absence the battle of the Marne had been lost by the French? How long would the Belgian army have held out if they had been cut off in Antwerp? What happened to the Roumanian army once it was isolated?

'Happily,' Churchill concluded, 'these black alternatives are not yet before us, and there are good hopes they will never be.' But it was necessary to make plans 'promptly' in order to be prepared for the worst.

Churchill was still convinced that the war could be won within twenty-four months. On April 22 he wrote to the Duke of Westminster, who was going to Madrid to see King Alfonso:[1]

. . . I hope you will tell the King that I am absolutely confident of the final result. I do not think there will be any compromise. It will be a clear-cut result. Everything shows that the English-speaking world is settling down to war & becoming more fiercely devoted to it month by month. Presently the British will be more bitter than the French. Later on the Americans will be more bitter even than the English. In the end we shall beat the heart out of Prussian militarism. . . .

[1] Leon Fernando Maria Jaime Isidoro Pascual Antonio, 1886–1941. Posthumous son of King Alfonso XII of Spain, he was proclaimed King at birth (as Alfonso XIII). He married Victoria Eugenie, a granddaughter of Queen Victoria, in 1906. Narrowly escaped death in a bomb incident in Paris, 1905; and again on his wedding day in Madrid, 1906. Fired at three times, but escaped unhurt, in Madrid, 1913. He fled the country following the Republican majority in the 1931 municipal elections. He died in exile in Rome.

Three days later, on April 25, Churchill spoke in the House of Commons about the military crisis and munitions production. He could offer the House, he said, 'a fairly good report'. Although 1,000 heavy guns and 5,000 machine guns had been lost or destroyed since March 21, there were, a month later, 'more serviceable guns as a whole, and more of practically every calibre, than there were when the battle began'. He had indeed been able to send Sir Douglas Haig 'more than twice as many guns as have been lost and destroyed in the battle'; the same, he said, was true of aircraft. As for Tanks, he had been able 'to replace every tank that has been lost by newer and better patterns of Tanks as fast as the Army can take delivery'. The Ministry of Munitions, he told the House, had expected the German offensive to begin in the third week of February, not in the third week of March, and had made its calculations accordingly.

The present problem, Churchill explained, was manpower. Since May 1917 the Ministry of Munitions had released 100,000 men for the Army, and since the German offensive of March 21 this rate had risen to 1,000 a day. Churchill appealed for men to enrol as War Munition Volunteers, and praised what had already been done. Over 1,500 firms had given up their Easter holidays at his request. The working men and women did not deserve the 'carping and croaking which goes on about the attitude of labour towards the War'. A 'gigantic transformation' had taken place in industry. Under the pressure of war, British industry was achieving every day 'a higher organization and a more modern outfit'.

Churchill had special words of praise for the women who made munitions. Nearly three-quarters of a million women were employed under the Ministry of Munitions by April 1918. 'It is a striking fact,' he said, 'that more than nine-tenths, and in many branches far more than nine-tenths, of the whole manufacture of the shells which constitute the foundations of the power and terror of the British Artillery, are due to the labours of women—of women who before the War never saw a lathe.' Churchill ended his speech, which had taken an hour and a half to deliver and had covered many aspects of munitions production, with a confident appeal:

I wonder what impression the House has derived from the numerous facts—pregnant, selected facts—which I have laid before it! I hope that it is the same impression which is continually borne in upon me as the War advances and difficulties and dangers gather, as the fury of the storm mounts higher and higher in seemingly inexhaustible violence—it is a profound conviction which grows in my heart from the study of the phenomena presented by the

War, from everything I learn the strength, the massive solidity, and the inexhaustible resources of this great nation, this wonderful Island, battling for its life and for the life of the world.

Ask what you please, look where you will, you cannot get to the bottom of the resources of Britain. No demand is too novel or too sudden to be met. No need is too unexpected to be supplied. No strain is too prolonged for the patience of our people. No suffering or peril daunt their hearts. Instead of quarrelling, giving way as we do from time to time to moods of pessimism and of irritation, we ought to be thankful that if such trials and dangers were destined for our country we are here to share them, and to see them slowly and surely overcome.

On April 27 Churchill crossed over to France on munitions business, staying for three days at Haig's headquarters and learning at first hand of the continuing need for heavy gun ammunition. On April 30 he returned to England. That evening Haig wrote in his diary: 'For the time being he is most friendly and is doing all he can to help the Army. He has certainly improved the output of the munitions factories very greatly, and is full of energy in trying to release men for the Army, and replace them by substitutes.'

On his return to London, Churchill found two telegrams from the United States, in which the War Industries Board appealed for British artillery. The American troops on whom so much seemed to depend could not be provided with adequate artillery from American sources. Churchill wrote to Loucheur with a request for French help in providing the Americans with the large number of heavy guns for which they had asked. 'In my view,' Churchill wrote, 'we must do everything in our power to encourage the United States to pour troops into France as rapidly as possible, by making them feel that there will be no lack of artillery from one source or another to sustain American infantry when they enter the line of battle.' British stocks, he explained, had been seriously depleted by the need to supply Italy after the Caporetto 'disaster'. The artillery losses between March 21 and April 4 had likewise exposed the Ministry of Munitions 'to unexpected strains'. Nevertheless, Churchill still hoped to be able to provide the Americans with the 208 heavy guns which he had, in November 1917, promised to manufacture. Now it was a question of finding more. Britain could supply a further fifty guns; he wanted France to make a similar extra effort.

Churchill was becoming increasingly dissatisfied with the political situation in England. On April 15, before going to France, he had drafted a letter to Lloyd George, urging him to 'fortify' himself by setting up 'a proper Cabinet of responsible Ministers'. A War Cabinet was adequate, he added, for 'the day to day settlement of military & administrative business relating to the war, & to relieve other Ministers of their responsibilities in these respects. But the high policy of the State ought not to be settled by so narrow & unrepresentative a body as yr War Cabinet. . . .' Churchill insisted that the time had come for Lloyd George 'to form a political instrument for definite purposes', such as negotiations with Austria-Hungary, or the passing of a Home Rule Bill for Ireland. Failure to set up such a Cabinet would lead, Churchill concluded, 'to grave risk of collapse'. Churchill held back this letter. But on May 3 he raised these matters with Lloyd George himself, and after their conversation he drafted a letter which he sent to Lloyd George on May 4:

My dear Prime Minister,
    I always do my very best to help you & to give you my true opinion & advice when you ask for it. But I cannot undertake any responsibility for policy. Under the present system the War Cabinet alone have the power of decision & the right of regular & continuous consultation. Their burden cannot be shared by departmental ministers occasionally invited to express an opinion on particular subjects or phases.
    Certainly I will never accept political responsibility without recognised regular power.
    I do not seek this power. As you know I do not think the new system which Carson invented of governing without a regular Cabinet is sound or likely to be successful.[1] But I am quite content in this war crisis to continue to serve you & the Government to the best of my ability in an administrative capacity, without troubling myself about political or party combinations, & to offer you personally in your intense labours for the national safety every aid & encouragement that a sincere friend can give.
    It was a very warm-hearted & courageous act of yours to include me in yr Government in the face of so much Conservative hostility, & I have ever had yr interests at heart. But I shd fail in the frankness which our long & intimate friendship requires were I not—in view of our serious conversation yesterday —to make my position clear.

Yrs always
W

[1] In November 1916 Sir Edward Carson had urged Asquith to set up a small War Cabinet, the Ministers of which would be entirely free from Departmental duties. Asquith had declined to take Carson's advice, but when Lloyd George became Prime Minister in December 1916 he had at once established just such a system, and Carson himself had been a Member of the new War Cabinet (as Minister without Portfolio) from July 1917 until January 1918.

Churchill saw Lloyd George again on May 14, and they discussed
Churchill's suggestion. Churchill elaborated on his scheme for the setting up of a Cabinet which would be able to discuss and initiate policy,
independently of the War Cabinet. But Lloyd George felt that the existing system was adequate for time of war. On May 15 Churchill sent him
a further letter, reiterating his proposals, and pointing out that in the
present Cabinet 'all the traditional great offices except the India Office
are filled by Tories', while all the Liberal Ministers, with the exception
of Montagu, were excluded from real responsibility. Churchill warned
Lloyd George that he would lose his political control, and forfeit all
chance of pursuing a Liberal social policy, if he allowed the Conservative
Ministers to continue to dominate the administration. In advising a
drastic reconstruction, Churchill stressed that his principal object was
not self-advancement, but Lloyd George's own future as an effective
political force:

It would greatly facilitate your task, both from the point of view of offices
& persons, if I remained outside. This I should be quite ready to do. You
would then be able to say to the minor Tory offices, 'How can you claim to
come in when the Ministry of Munitions is out?' Other Liberal Colleagues cd
not be offended if they were left outside with me. I should not take such an
arrangement in any way as a slight. I am quite content to serve during the
war as an official in a purely administrative post without involving myself in
political cares or party bitterness.

My only desire is to take part in the war, & I shall always be very grateful
to you for giving me such interesting work. It wd be a great relief to me to be
freed from the necessity of coming to decisions in political & party matters
which would be at once premature & final. That is why I have so often
disappointed you when our conversation has turned on party organisation &
election preparations. I shd therefore be very glad to facilitate the creation of
a political Cabinet, by remaining exactly as I am.

That such a step is necessary both to the national interests & to your own, I
am absolutely sure. How can you expect to form a party capable of real
political action, without fusion of groups & an effective sense of corporate
responsibility? At present you have two collections of non-responsible office
holders, who never mingle as colleagues, who rarely meet as officials, & who
have to be breakfasted in separate cages for fear their mutual prejudices shd
overcome them; while you pass anxiously & with soothing & deprecative
words from one to the other. As long as the war issue is the sole one on wh
Parlt has to vote, you may keep the thing going by your personal efforts & by
debating triumphs; even so you have to fight for yr life from month to month.
But such an arrangement wd never stand the test of a political issue, nor
would it be possible to build up any new effective party machinery behind it.

Despite Churchill's appeal, Lloyd George continued to determine war policy through his War Cabinet, and Churchill remained a departmental Minister. As with so many of his suggestions to Lloyd George, he did not even receive a reply.

During the spring and early summer of 1918, Churchill's visits to France became more frequent and more prolonged. On the western front he could gauge the needs of the armies; at Haig's headquarters he could talk to those who had to provide those armies with the reinforcements they needed; in Paris he could co-ordinate munitions policy with the French and Italian Governments, and supervise the work of his factories in France. During the second week in May he decided to set up a permanent headquarters for himself in France, and on May 10 wrote from London to Haig with a formal request:

It wd be a convenience to me if I cd have a permanent lodging assigned to me in France somewhere in the zone of the armies. I do not like trespassing on yr unfailing good nature & hospitality each time I come over, tho' I shd hope you wd always let me come to see you when I am there & you are not too busy.

My liaison officer might be allotted a few rooms or a small house somewhere in the neighbourhood of GHQ & I cd stay there in ordinary circumstances when I had occasion. If you have no objection the arrangements cd vy easily be made. Perhaps you will let me know.

Of course I do not want to visit the Army on any other footing but that of your guest with all that that implies; but I shd like to be a guest who is never likely to be a burden. . . .

Haig was sympathetic to Churchill's request, and soon found Churchill a suitable headquarters, the Chateau Verchocq.

On May 18 Churchill was in Paris, attending the Inter-Allied Munitions Conference. On the following morning his work was finished, and he wanted to return to London as quickly as possible. No regular air service existed between Britain and France. But Churchill went to Le Bourget aerodrome to see if there was anyone returning to England. A test pilot, Captain Patteson,[1] was about to return to his base, No. 7 Aircraft Acceptance Park, at Kenley, from where new aeroplanes were tested, and then flown to France. Patteson took Churchill back with

---

[1] Cyril Patteson, 1888– . 2nd Lieutenant, Royal Engineers, October 1914. Awarded the Military Cross for bravery at Suvla Bay, Gallipoli, 1915. Lieutenant, 1st Battalion, South Wales Borderers, May 1916. Seconded to the Royal Flying Corps, February 1917. Served in France in No. 60 Squadron, March 1917; then in No. 29 Squadron. Temporary Captain (Flight Commander), October 1917. Served with No. 7 Aircraft Acceptance Park, Kenley, 1918. Acting Major, Royal Air Force, October 1918. Commanded No. 1 Communications Squadron, October 1918 to July 1919.

him. While waiting for Churchill's official car to arrive, and drive him back to Lullenden, Patteson entertained Churchill in his cottage close to the aerodrome. Another pilot, Lieutenant Hall,[1] later recalled the sequel:

With considerable initiative Patteson took the opportunity to suggest to Mr Churchill that a passenger-carrying squadron should be formed for the specific use of people, like himself, in a hurry. Mr Churchill agreed. Patteson was placed in command of it and raised to the rank of major. He was given a free hand as to type of machine and he chose the D.H.4 with a Rolls-Royce engine, and on the move from Kenley to Hendon he took some of his test pilots with him. . . .

Shortly, the Minister visited Hendon to see how the new squadron was progressing. He was accompanied by Major General Seely who appeared to be on very friendly terms with him. The engine of a nearby machine was started up and Mr Churchill proceeded to climb into the passenger's seat, forgetting to remove the cigar he was smoking. Seely questioned the wisdom of this at which Mr Churchill scrambled back out again, and placed his cigar on the aerodrome turf at our feet. The atmosphere was good humoured and Seely thereupon began to recite—'The Minister, placing his cigar upon a brick and regardless of all personal risk, climbs fearlessly into his aeroplane . . .'

The new air service squadron was named No. 1 Communication Squadron. Its aircraft were put at the disposal of any senior politicians or service personnel whose official duties took them to France. Patteson himself offered to fly Churchill to France whenever necessary.

Shortly before the outbreak of war, Churchill's mother had met a member of the Northern Nigerian Civil Service, Montagu Porch,[2] with whom she had gone sight-seeing in Rome. In 1914 Porch had enlisted in the Nigerian Regiment, and joined the Cameroons Expeditionary Force.

---

[1] Gilbert Hall, 1890–1972. Entered the Army as a 2nd Lieutenant, August 1914; fought on the western front, 1915–16. Transferred to the Flying Corps, January 1917; flew at the battle of Arras as an Observer, April 1917. Became a pilot, June 1917. Served with No. 1 Communication Squadron, 1918. Retired from the Royal Air Force as a Lieutenant, 1919.

[2] Montagu Phippen Porch, 1877–1964. Served with the Middlesex Yeomanry in the South African War, 1900. Graduated from Magdalen College, Oxford, 1902. Served with the Egyptian Exploration Fund, 1904–5, crossing the Sinai desert by camel to collect ancient stone implements. Assistant Resident, Northern Nigeria, 1906; 3rd Class Resident, 1912. Lieutenant, Nigerian Regiment, Cameroons Expeditionary Force, 1914–15. Acting Resident, Zaria (Nigeria), 1915–18. After his marriage to Lady Randolph, he resigned from the Nigerian Civil Service to live in London. Went to the Gold Coast on business, 1921. He married again in 1926, and lived in Italy. On his wife's death in 1938 he returned to England.

In 1916 he returned to England on leave. In April 1918 Lady Randolph and Porch became engaged. Porch was twenty-three years younger than Lady Randolph—and three years younger than Churchill. On May 31 Colonel Repington [1] recorded in his diary: 'Lady R charming about her future. Mr Porch quite good-looking and intelligent. They get married tomorrow and go to Windsor for the weekend. Winston says he hopes marriage won't become the vogue among ladies of his mother's age.' Lady Randolph was sixty-four. The wedding was held at the Harrow Road Register Office on June 1. Before the wedding Montagu Porch wrote to Churchill, from the Connaught Hotel, Mayfair:

Dear Winston,

I am very glad you are able to come to our Wedding—It seems almost incredible that today, when the World is in anguish, I should be allowed so much happiness.

I would now assure you that this, the most important step in my life is not taken in the dark. I have carefully considered the position from every point of view—your Mother's financial affairs are understood.

I love your Mother, I can make her happy. Her difficulties and obligations from henceforth will be shared by me—so willingly.

I thank you for your kindness and consideration. We shall be good friends.

Yours very truly
Montagu Porch

Churchill and his wife were among those who signed the Register. After the wedding, Montagu Porch returned to Nigeria. His wife, who announced that she would continue to be known as Lady Randolph Churchill, had to stay in London. 'She took steps to get a passport to Nigeria,' the newspaper *West Africa* reported after her death in 1921, 'but Downing Street refused because of the submarine peril. . . . She pleaded over and over again, but permission was withheld.'

On May 27 the German forces had begun the third of their offensives, against the British and French forces along the Chemin des Dames. The French troops retreated in disorder. By nightfall the Germans had advanced nearly twelve miles into the Allied lines. For six successive days they continued to advance, capturing Soissons on May

[1] Charles à Court Repington, 1858–1925. Entered Army, 1878. Lieutenant-Colonel on Kitchener's staff at Omdurman, 1898. Forced to resign his commission because of a personal indiscretion involving another officer's wife. Military Correspondent of *The Times*, 1904–18. Military Correspondent of the *Daily Telegraph*, 1918–25.

29 and Fère-en-Tardenois on June 2. The important town of Chateau Thierry, on the Marne, was threatened.

On June 3 Churchill made his first flight to France with his new air service. Captain Patteson was his pilot. On the following day Churchill sent his wife an account of his activities:

My darling,

I had a touching vision of you & yr two kittens growing rapidly smaller and the aerodrome & its sheds dwindling into distant perspective as I whirled away.

It was a vy beautiful & wonderful journey. We crossed the Channel at 1400 & in one hour from leaving you we reached Hesdin 6 miles away from GHQ.

Sunny[1] arrived all right in the evening & we were hospitably entertained by the C in C.

I spent the afternoon with Jack, & had tea with the Oxfordshire Hussars. Now I am off to my Conference & then on to Paris.

The Flying business is vy different now to those earlier days. Kenley near Godstone (not Penshurst) is the nearest aerodrome for Lullenden. I will send you a message when I return & you can motor in there to meet me if you will.

Tender love & many kisses from

Yr ever loving
W

PS   I shall learn the situation when I reach Paris. It is evidently a vy anxious one.

On June 2 Chateau Thierry fell to the Germans. Throughout June 3 and 4 the situation remained grave. 'I do not like the outlook,' Sir Maurice Hankey wrote in his diary on June 4. 'The Germans are fighting better than the allies, and I cannot exclude the possibility of disaster. I see very difficult times ahead.' On June 6 Churchill wrote to his wife from Paris:

Beloved darling,

An air raid is in progress & I am due & overdue for bed. So these lines will be few but to the point. Much work has come upon me here & I have found the days all too short. I have seen very many interesting & influential people & transacted a good deal of business satisfactorily.

You can judge the general situation for yrself. On the whole I am hopeful.

---

[1] Charles Richard John Spencer-Churchill, 1871–1934. Churchill's first cousin. 9th Duke of Marlborough, 1892. Paymaster-General of the Forces, 1899–1902. Staff Captain and ADC to General Hamilton during the South African War, 1900. Under-Secretary of State for the Colonies, 1903–5. Lieutenant-Colonel, Queen's Own Oxfordshire Hussars, 1910. Employed at the War Office as a Special Messenger, 1914–15. Joint Parliamentary Secretary, Board of Agriculture and Fisheries, 1917–18.

But the fate of the capital hangs in the balance—only 45 miles away. Next time I come here (if there is a 'next time') you must really try to accompany me. You must prepare a good cause under the shelter of the YMCA (*Y*'a *Moyens Coucher Avec*) (as Loucheur calls it) & spend a few jolly days in this menaced but always delightful city.

I shall not leave here finally till Monday morning & Monday, Tuesday & perhaps Wednesday I shall be with the Army. D. V. Weather permitting & the rest of it I propose to fly to Kenley Aerodrome Wed or Thursday. I will send you notice. Try to be at Lullenden so that we can be together. Kenley is near Godstone.

Tender love to you & all dear & dearest ones

Yr devoted
W

On June 6 the German attack was halted, and both French and British units were able to make small counter attacks. But the battle was a serious defeat for the Allies. Nearly 30,000 British troops had been killed or wounded, while the French had over 95,000 casualties. Equally demoralizing, more than 60,000 British and French troops were taken prisoner. On June 8 Churchill visited the centre of the French line north of Compiègne. 'The presage of battle was in the air,' he recalled in *The World Crisis*. 'All the warnings had been given, and every-one was at his post. The day had been quiet, and the sweetness of the summer evening was undisturbed even by a cannon shot. Very calm and gallant, and even gay, were the French soldiers who awaited the new stroke of fate. By the next evening all the ground over which they had led me was in German hands, and most of those with whom I had talked were dead or prisoners.'

On June 9, the Germans attacked for the fourth time since March 21, seeking to cross the river Matz and to capture Compiègne. Here the defence was borne entirely by the French troops whose positions Churchill had visited on the previous day. In contrast to the rout of May 27 on the Chemin de Dames, the French retreated in good order. On June 10 Churchill wrote to his wife from Paris:

My darling one,

The vy critical and deadly battle on the Montdidier-Noyon front has raged all day, & the latest accounts (5.30 p.m.) are apparently satisfactory. There is no surprise here, but a blunt trial of strength—the line strongly held with troops & good reserves at hand. If the French cannot hold them back on this sector, it is not easy to see what the next step on our part shd be. I am hope-ful. Both the generals Fayolle & Humbert who I saw yesterday, & who are certainly vy capable men, were soberly confident & hoped they wd be attacked.

I go to GHQ tomorrow & hope to return to you Wednesday. But it may be Thursday. If you are at Lullenden, I will come on there & spend the night of Wed. Thursday is my Air dinner.

I have brought you a little present in Paris, wh I shall shew you when I arrive.

The young flying officer has won my heart. His wife was there the other day when we started. He is vy gallant, & vy *battered*.

Tender love my dearest soul to you & all yr chicks.

Two Bertha shells arrived within 150 yards today. They are pop gun affairs & not in the least alarming.

Your always loving
W

On June 11 the French were able to launch the first of a series of counter-attacks, which were repeated on June 12 and again on June 13. On June 13 Churchill flew back to England. A month later, on July 7, he explained to Archibald Sinclair that, as a result of his return flight, he 'vy nearly finished an eventful though disappointing life in the salt waters of the channel'. Luckily, he added, 'we just fluttered back to shore'. Lullenden, he pointed out, was only an hour's flight from Haig's headquarters—'But one must have careful engine supervision.'

Sir Douglas Haig encouraged Churchill's visits to France. 'We shall always be glad to see you out here,' he wrote on June 20, 'whenever you can find the time to come.' Churchill reciprocated by dealing directly with GHQ whenever they had particularly urgent munitions needs; on June 17 he had given instructions for the manufacture of 1,000 tons of high explosive shell per week.

Churchill was still convinced that the War Cabinet was not acting with enough energy in its search for victory. Twice during June, he wrote to Lloyd George with advice on policy. The first of his letters, on June 15, was intended to strengthen Lloyd George's own resolve:

My dear Prime Minister,

I trust you will continue to press with all yr strength for the marrying of American divisions to our shattered cadres. This is the true line; & also for afterwards the value will be immeasurable. If you insist I am sure you can carry it through.

Yours always
W

Two days later, on June 17, Churchill wrote again, worried because the War Cabinet's decision to deport German civilians from China had been reversed, following French pressure. 'I am sure it is against your inclination,' he wrote, 'to back down before German threats of reprisals about clearing German women & children out of China . . . . we have an absolute right to clear the Huns out of China. This makes an enormous difference in the future. Preparations for it are far advanced. To give way just because the Germans threaten to ill-use Belgians is weakness.' Churchill was also angered by the War Cabinet's public announcement that no British air raids would take place over Germany on Corpus Christi day. 'Do put your foot down on this,' he wrote. 'It is *abject.*'

On behalf of his department, Churchill fought against any further transfer of factory workers from Tank production to the front. On July 6, in a memorandum which he sent to Lloyd George before circulating it to the War Cabinet, he warned of 'the very serious consequences that will arise from the continual drafting of skilled men into the Army. . . .' The United States, he urged, must now provide the majority of new troops, as there were ten million American males between the ages of 20 and 30. 'If we are to obtain any effective superiority in numbers,' he wrote, 'it can only be by American aid.' The American troops, he pointed out, depended upon British munitions production for their fighting efficiency:

. . . The first million who have come have been almost entirely equipped by Britain and France. But for the fact that we were able to supply them with artillery, machine guns, rifles, trench mortars, &c., and to feed them with munitions of all kinds, no use in the present crisis could have been made of this first million. My latest report from America states that the American Army in France will be almost entirely dependent during the whole of 1918 on British & French artillery production. If we are to continue to put, as we must do, the most extreme pressure upon the American Government to pour its men over, we must be in a position to guarantee them thorough and immediate equipment when they arrive, and ample supply thereafter. . . .

The withdrawal of men from factories to the front had affected all branches of munitions production, not only tanks, but poison gas and aeroplanes. During the first week of July, Churchill had planned to produce over 1,000 aeroplane engines. But the shortage of skilled labour had resulted in under 700 being produced. One firm was about to produce an anti-aircraft height finder. But thirty skilled mechanics had been withdrawn, postponing production of an instrument which, Churchill wrote, 'if the men had been left at their work, would in a very few months have made possible the release of 30 men many times over from anti-aircraft batteries in the Field'. The worst blow, however, to munitions production had been in Tank production; to this Churchill returned with some bitterness at the end of his memorandum:

... A programme was approved, at a special meeting of the War Cabinet presided over in February by the Prime Minister, for the urgent construction of tanks. That programme represented what I then considered to be the maximum effort we could make in this field. It is rapidly falling into arrears. Meanwhile, however, the War Office, on the urgent demand of the Army in the field, have demanded 400 additional tanks, and if the plans which are favoured by the Chief of the Imperial General Staff are to attain fruition, still larger increases will be required.

In spite of all the opposition to tanks and the mishandling of this policy at every stage, they have now taken a firm root, and every week affords further evidence of their immense utility. I have now received a most urgent demand through M. Loucheur, from General Foch for 300 large tanks to be delivered to the French in July, August and September. The only thing that has been done to assist me in this matter has been to take hundreds of men from the manufacture of tanks, thus dislocating the whole of the Metropolitan Works, with the result that for the sake of getting enough men to make a couple of Companies of infantry the equipment of perhaps four or five battalions of tanks will be lost. Considering that one tank is worth hundreds of men, and, properly used, may conceivably be worth a whole battalion, I must avow myself unable to comprehend the processes of thought which are at work.

In sending this protest to Lloyd George on July 9, Churchill added a covering note in which he warned: 'We cannot go on indefinitely without producing effects which will be bad and stupid. ... I am being pressed now to make releases which will be most injurious, and wasteful of our war effort. In some directions we have already gone too far.'

Churchill held back his memorandum until July 12, when he circulated it to the War Cabinet. But the War Office insisted that the need for soldiers was still so urgent that even Tank production must take second place. On July 15 Churchill telegraphed to Loucheur that he could not provide France with any Tanks at all. Two days later, he appealed direct to the Deputy Chief of the Imperial General Staff, Major-General Harington:[1]

---

[1] Charles Harington, 1872–1940. Known as 'Tim'. Entered Army, 1892. Served in the South African and First World Wars; Major-General, 1918. Deputy Chief of the Imperial General Staff, 1918–20. Knighted, 1919. Lieutenant- General Commanding the Army of the Black Sea, 1920. General Officer Commanding the Allied Forces of Occupation in Turkey, 1920–3. General, 1927. Governor and Commander-in-Chief, Gibraltar, 1933–8. He published *Tim Harington Looks Back* in 1940.

. . . The conditions of this war are perpetually changing every 3 or 4 months, and a new view has to be taken and readjustments made. As the gale blows now from this quarter and now from that, a different setting of the sails is necessary, though the object of the voyage and the principles of navigation are unaltered. Therefore I consider now and for some time to come you ought not to withdraw men so as to weaken my production of munitions. The Irish should be conscripted; munition workers who go on strike should be conscripted; above all, the Americans should be brought in not only in their own formations but as battalions attached *en passant* to every British brigade for training.[1] All these things can be achieved if enough people with knowledge go on pressing continually above all not taking 'No' for an answer. . . .

Harington was sympathetic to Churchill's plea. But the decision on manpower rested with the War Cabinet. On July 19 Churchill appealed to the War Cabinet in strong terms. It was 'really impossible', he said, to release men from munitions factories at the pace required by the War Office. 'The output of tanks had fallen by one half,' he said. 'The men were resisting dilution and delaying output, and there was considerable discontent. . . .'

Churchill's appeal was unsuccessful. The members of the War Cabinet preferred to support Lord Milner's contention that the need was for men immediately, not machines in the future.[2] Lloyd George did not want to risk extending conscription to Ireland. The munitions factories would have to continue working below strength. On July 22 Churchill expressed his anger at the decision in a letter to Lloyd George, which went unanswered:

Questions wh the Prime Minister's conscience shd be asking him:—
1. Am I not one of the original founders of Tanks?
2. What am I doing to push them forward now?
3. Am I doing enough?
4. Can I not do more with my great power?
5. Are they going to be frittered away in more incidental fighting next year 1919—as in every other year?
6. Have I not still got time to get a move on?

[1] Churchill had long been an advocate of such a course. According to the Cabinet Minutes for 4 January 1918: 'Mr Churchill said that the United States Government had declared their willingness to intervene in the war. It should be pointed out to them that by their plan of forming complete Divisions under General Pershing in France, they would be intervening, but that they would intervene on a still larger scale if they could agree to the embodiment of American Battalions in British Brigades.'

[2] In July 1917 there were seven members of the War Cabinet: Lloyd George, Bonar Law, Curzon, Arthur Henderson, Lord Milner, General Smuts and George Barnes.

Churchill's work had become so exacting that he now lived at the Ministry of Munitions building in Northumberland Avenue. Living at the Ministry, he explained in a letter of June 18, 'has many conveniences from the point of view of getting work done. It enables me to work up to the last moment before dinner, to get papers when I come back after dinner, and to begin with shorthand assistance as early as I choose in the morning.' Each weekend when he was not in France he took his work to Lullenden.

In the third week of June Churchill prepared a major review of war policy, which was circulated to the War Cabinet on June 22. His memorandum opened with a description of the first three and a half years of war, and strong criticism of the policy of offensives on the western front during 1915 and 1916: 'This campaign', as he described it, 'of agony and disaster'. His main proposal was for a major offensive on the western front in 1919, 'choosing the period of climax', as he explained, 'and subordinating, as far as pressure of circumstances will allow, every intervening event to that supreme purpose'. The plans for 1919 must not be delayed until the winter. 'Unless while we are fighting for our lives this summer,' he wrote, 'we can look ahead and plan for 1919, we shall be in the same melancholy position next year as we are this.' Churchill ended his memorandum by asking:

Do the means of beating the German armies in the West in 1919 exist? Can the men be procured? If so, the mechanisms can be prepared. We still have the time. Have we the will-power and the command to look ahead and regulate action accordingly?

On July 4, the 142nd anniversary of the declaration of American independence, Churchill was the principal speaker at a meeting of the Anglo-Saxon Fellowship at the Central Hall, Westminster. 'When I have seen during the past few weeks,' Churchill said, 'the splendour of American manhood striding forward on all the roads of France and Flanders, I have experienced emotions which words cannot describe.' Britain's reward for answering the appeals of Belgium and France in 1914 was not territorial or commercial advantage, he said, but the 'supreme reconciliation' of Britain and the United States. 'We seek no higher reward,' he declared, 'than this supreme reconciliation. That is the reward of Britain. That is the lion's share.'[1]

[1] Throughout the years of Lloyd George's premiership Churchill was emphatic about the need for good relations between Britain and the United States. On 14 February 1921, at a

Churchill also spoke lyrically of the coming of war in 1914. 'I am persuaded,' he said, 'that the finest and worthiest moment in the history of Britain was reached on that August night, now nearly four years ago, when we declared war on Germany.' The purposes of the war, Churchill continued, did not admit of compromise. The war had become 'an open conflict between Christian civilisation and scientific barbarism'. It was a struggle 'between right and wrong'. Because of this, 'Germany must be beaten; Germany must know she is beaten; Germany must feel she is beaten. Her defeat must be expressed in terms and facts which will, for all time, deter others from emulating her crime, and will safeguard us against their repetition.' But, Churchill went on, the Germans must be treated, once the war was over, 'with wisdom and justice'. The same principles for which the Allies were fighting must be used 'to protect the German people'. When German militarism was destroyed, he declared, 'the German people will find themselves protected by those simple elemental principals of right and freedom against which they will have warred so long in vain'. Churchill then made his final appeal: 'No compromise on the main purpose, no peace till victory, no pact with unrepentant wrong.'

Churchill's oratory was effective. 'I am overjoyed at your wonderful success,' his friend Lord Beaverbrook[1] wrote when the speech was ended. 'You have done immense service.' Two days later Beaverbrook wrote again: 'You yourself must have been conscious of the extent to which you moved and stirred your great audience. . . .' Churchill's speech, Beaverbrook added, would be printed in pamphlet form and distributed throughout the United States. The speech was widely reported. Later in the month Sir Archibald Sinclair, who, like Churchill, had an American mother, wrote from the western front:

---

time of Anglo-American friction over Ireland, he wrote to his wife: 'It was uphill work to make an enthusiastic speech about the United States when so many hard things are said about us over there and when they are wringing the last penny out of their unfortunate Allies.' 'All the same,' he added, 'there is only one road for us to tread, and that is to keep as friendly with them as possible, to be overwhelmingly patient and to wait for the growth of better feelings which will certainly come. . . .' Two months later Churchill urged his Cabinet colleagues not to be carried too far by their dislike of American naval policy. 'It would be a ghastly state of affairs,' he told the Cabinet on 30 May 1921, 'if we were to drift into direct naval rivalry with the United States.'

[1] William Maxwell Aitken, 1879–1964. A Canadian financier. Conservative MP, 1910–16. Knighted, 1911. Canadian Eye-Witness in France, 1915; Canadian Representative at the Front, 1915–16. Newspaper proprietor: bought the *Daily Express*, his largest circulation newspaper, in December 1916. Created Baron Beaverbrook, 1917. Chancellor of the Duchy of Lancaster and Minister of Information, 1918. Minister for Aircraft Production, 1940–1. Minister of State, 1941. Minister of Supply, 1941–2. Lord Privy Seal, 1943–5.

... I remember sounding you upon the possibility of drawing closer to the States on that first walk we took together at Maxine's[1] years before the war. How delighted I was when you treated the idea seriously & not as an impracticable dream. It was certainly absolutely true of all Englishmen & Scotsmen with recent American connections & probably of the vast majority of thinking men in our country that they will be willing to regard the complete understanding & co-operation with America as our highest reward— 'the lion's share'.

Next to that sentiment I liked best the insistence on the necessity of victory & the impossibility of compromise: and especially I was delighted (and not a little surprised, I confess!) at the declaration that the principles, for which we are fighting, will be Germany's (and Russia's, Winston!) protection when the final peace comes to be made. Of course, I remember you used to say that 'Germany for the Germans' was our battle cry, but lately I have thought that you had gone over to the camp of the 'practical statesmen'. This splendid declaration of democratic ideals thrilled me. It is the best counterpart of the President's utterances which has proceeded from Europe. . . .

'If all goes well,' Churchill wrote to Sinclair on July 11, 'England and U.S. may act permanently together. We are living 50 years in one at this rate.'

During the summer the production of munitions was threatened by serious labour unrest. On June 26 a strike had broken out among woodworkers at the Alliance Aeroplane Works which halted aircraft production. On the previous day, the factory's owner, Samuel Waring,[2] had announced that a shop steward who had summoned a meeting of workmen during working hours was to be dismissed, and the workers' shop committee banned from the factory floor. On July 3 the Unions involved in aircraft production agreed to an appeal by the Ministry of Munitions to resume work on the following day, and to accept Churchill's direct arbitration. But at the Works themselves, unofficial representatives of the men persuaded them not to return to work, and from

---

[1] Jessie Dermot, 1868–1940. Born in Maine, USA. She adopted the name 'Maxine Elliot' for her stage career. In 1914 she organized a Belgian Relief Barge, from which in fifteen months, she fed and clothed some 350,000 refugees.

[2] Samuel James Waring, 1860–1940. Established the business of Waring & Sons in London, 1893. Sought to promote a New English Renaissance of decorative art. Amalgamated his business with that of Gillow. Organized several munitions factories, 1914–18, for the production of aeroplanes, aeroplane engines and general war equipment. Founded the British Aerial Transport Company, 1917; its first regular service, between London and Birmingham, was inaugurated on 30 September 1919. Created Baronet, 1919; created Baron, 1922.

July 4 the trouble spread throughout the London area. On July 9 Churchill issued a three-point statement to the Press:

1) That the strike is not only illegal but is unauthorised by the Trade Unions;
2) That arbitration was accepted by the Trade Union leaders, and has been brought to nought by certain persons not representative of any recognised labour organisation; and
3) That the interruption of work is a serious interference with the output of munitions.

That evening Churchill met the Union leaders of the London District Aircraft Committee at the Ministry of Munitions. They too deplored the strike; but they pointed out that the dismissal of the shop steward was only a small symptom of a deeper discontent. The Alliance Aeroplane Works management had for several months refused to recognize the rights of any of the shop floor representatives.

Throughout the afternoon and early evening of July 10 Churchill presided over a series of conferences at the Ministry of Munitions, to discuss the dispute with all concerned. After six hours of negotiation, he announced his decision: the Alliance Aeroplane Works would be taken over by the Government. Its owners, Waring and Gillow, were censured by the Ministry of Munitions in a statement issued that evening. 'It is believed by the workmen,' the statement read, 'that the firm in question has opposed the legitimate development of the shop steward and shop committee movement. The Minister, without pronouncing a final opinion, has formed the view that this belief is not wholly unfounded.'

On July 11 *The Times* commented that there was 'no precedent for such a measure' as Churchill's decision to assume control of the Alliance Aeroplane Works. Not only did it enable Churchill to remove a recalcitrant management, it also gave him the power to end the strike by direct Ministerial action. In the Ministry's statement the strikers were reminded 'that as soon as the firm against whom they have struck has been taken over by the Government, they are no longer strikers but merely unemployed or idle workmen. It is accordingly the duty of these men and all others on strike in sympathy to resume work immediately. Failing such resumption, the Minister will use his powers against them under the Defence of the Realm Act and the Munitions of War Acts.' The strikers returned to work, their principal grievances met by Churchill, who reinstated the shop steward, and allowed the shop committee to continue its activities.

At the beginning of the third week of July, a further labour dispute

threatened to disrupt Tank production. On July 16 Churchill gave the
War Cabinet an account of the dispute, which arose when men were
transferred, against their will, from one factory to another, often with a
reduction in wages. This had become necessary, since March, because
over 100,000 munitions workers had been conscripted. Churchill told
the War Cabinet that 'he wished to be free to proceed against persons
conspiring against the State, and to withdraw from them the protection,
which they now enjoyed, from recruitment for the army'. He agreed
that it would be an 'illegitimate use of the Military Service Acts to
compel workmen to put up with industrial conditions against which
they were striking in the ordinary way', but this dispute, he stressed,
was not one over working conditions or trade union rights. The War
Cabinet supported Churchill's request for stern measures. According to
the Minutes of the discussion, 'stress was laid on the importance of
victory being assured in any struggle with the disaffected men'.

On July 19 the Executive Council of the Amalgamated Society of
Engineers met Churchill at the Ministry of Munitions. He told them
that their members must return to work. Later that day he issued a
statement to the Press:

Without the power to regulate to a certain extent the appointment of our
available labour between the various firms engaged on various classes of war
material, it will be quite impossible for the output of munitions in the present
difficult and critical circumstances to be maintained.

Persons, therefore, who incite others to cease work in these circumstances
are exposing themselves to very grave responsibilities with regard to their
countrymen and with regard to the law. . . . It is hoped that the high
standard and fine record throughout munition industries during the war,
and especially during these months of extreme national danger, will not
be marred by a dispute which, if prolonged, must necessarily lead to grave
consequences.

This statement appeared in the Press on Saturday July 20. On the
following Monday, July 22, the War Cabinet again discussed the
threatened strike, and again supported Churchill's appeal for firm
action. It was clear, he declared, 'that the Government had reached a
point where to shrink from using these powers would be disastrous to the
whole future of their relations during the war'. If the present situation
were firmly handled, those relations would be, he believed, 'immensely
improved. . . .'

During July 22 reports reached Churchill from Scotland Yard that
strikes were imminent in Coventry and Manchester. On July 23, in
defiance of their Union's instructions, 12,000 skilled men stopped work

at Coventry. On the following day the strike spread to all munitions factories in Birmingham. Tank production was at once affected. At noon on July 24 the War Cabinet met to decide on the Government's action. Serious though the strikes were, Churchill told the War Cabinet, the main impression he had gained 'was one of hesitation, as if the men were not quite certain of their powers'. On the other hand, 'the promoters of discord were strenuously endeavouring to rouse the workmen'. The 'only weapon' the Government could use, he went on, was to threaten to conscript the strikers, and to be prepared to carry out its threat.

During the War Cabinet discussion, the Minister of Labour, George Roberts,[1] urged that the men should be 'fully seized of the implications of their conduct if they struck work'. He was not sure, the Minutes recorded, 'that the patriotic elements amongst the workmen had not grasped the character of the strike in which they were asked to join'. He wanted Churchill to consult the Trade Union Advisory Committee before taking any 'drastic step'. Sir Stephenson Kent then admitted that 'it was conceivable that many might be moved to strike if provoked by the threat of the Military Service Acts'.

Lloyd George intervened in the discussion with a strong statement in support of Churchill's proposed action. According to the Minutes of the meeting, 'the Prime Minister emphasised the importance of the State winning in the struggle with the strikers. If to put men into the Army would help the State to win, then they should not hesitate to use the Military Service Acts. . . .' But Lloyd George went on to suggest that Churchill's solution should be delayed to see if the workmen themselves 'would fall into hostile groups'.

The War Cabinet decided that Churchill should meet the Trade Union Advisory Committee, warn them of the action the Government were prepared to take, and urge them to settle the dispute themselves. 'I talked to Winston about the strike . . .' Sir Henry Wilson wrote in his diary on July 24, '& he wants to put the strikers into the ranks at once.'

The strike continued. At breakfast at Bonar Law's house on July 25, Churchill was, as Christopher Addison recorded in his diary, 'out hotfoot against the strikers, his prescription being a simple one, viz., that their exemptions should be withdrawn and that they should be called

---

[1] George Henry Roberts, 1869–1928. Son of an agricultural labourer. Joined the Independent Labour Party, 1886. Labour MP, 1906–18. Parliamentary secretary to the Board of Trade, 1916–18. Minister of Labour, 1917–18. Food Controller, 1919–20. Unsuccessfully contested Norwich as a Conservative candidate, 1923.

up for military service. There was considerable demur, with which I agreed, to using the Military Service Act as an agent in an industrial dispute. Opinion was almost solid that it would be better to proceed as the law provided against the promoters of the strike. Kellaway[1] told me at the House afterwards, that he too had serious misgivings as to Winston's prescription.'

During July 26 the crisis worsened. At Birmingham, the workers of the Birmingham Electric Supply Department passed a unanimous resolution to stop work at midnight on July 30. That same day 300,000 munitions workers in Leeds threatened to stop work in four days time. The news of this threat was telegraphed to Churchill that night. Lloyd George himself decided to intervene, issuing a stern warning 'on behalf of his Majesty's Government'. Any men who were not back at work on July 29, he declared, 'will be deemed to have voluntarily placed themselves outside the area of munitions industries. Their protection certificates will cease to have effect from that date, and they will become liable to the provisions of the Military Service Acts.'

Lloyd George's warning was effective. By the morning of July 30 the strikers returned to work. In the Press, Churchill and Lloyd George were praised for their firm handling of a potentially disastrous situation. 'At the Cabinet,' Sir Henry Wilson wrote in his diary on July 30, 'Winston reported that the Coventry strike was at an end, a satisfactory result of Govt remaining stiff.'

Churchill continued to warn against war-weariness and defeatism. On August 3 he drafted a message to his constituents, explaining his feelings. Lord Lansdowne,[2] he wrote, had advised that 'we shd now endeavour to make peace with Germany upon honourable terms . . . & that we shd now try to make a territorial bargain with Germany & her allies wh wd spare mankind the suffering & slaughter & economic waste through wh they must otherwise plough their way'. Such a proposition,

---

[1] Frederick George Kellaway, 1870–1933. Liberal MP, 1910–22. Joint Parliamentary Secretary, Ministry of Munitions, 1916–21; Secretary, Department of Overseas Trade, 1920–1. Postmaster-General, 1921–2.

[2] Henry Charles Keith Petty-Fitzmaurice, 1845–1927. 5th Marquess of Lansdowne, 1856. Governor-General of Canada, 1883–8; Viceroy of India, 1888–93; Secretary of State for War, 1895–1901; Foreign Secretary, 1900–5. Minister without Portfolio, May 1915–December 1916. In 1917 he publicly advocated a negotiated peace with Germany. His second son, Lord Charles Mercer Nairne, was killed in action in France, 30 October 1914.

Churchill declared, was 'undoubtedly a serious one, but it is not one wh those who take the contrary view need be afraid of facing'. His letter went on:

For what is the contrary view? It is in a sentence that *this war has got to be won & that it is not won yet.* These twin hard facts will be found to dominate every form of argument not arising from despondency or treason. Let us not pretend that we have won yet. Let us not delude ourselves by thinking that there is any substitute for victory. To enter upon a struggle like this, to proclaim that vital & sacred issues are at stake, to cast the flower of the nation's manhood into the furnace, to wage war by land and sea for four devastating years, & then to discover that the foe is so stiff that after all a reasonable accommodation is expedient, & shd be brought about as quickly as possible is not, however it may be disguised, anything wh resembles 'an honourable peace'. To set out to redress an intolerable wrong, to grapple with a cruel butcher, & then after a bit to find him so warlike that upon the whole it is better to treat him as a good hearted fellow & sit down & see if we can't be friends after all, may conceivably be a form of prudence but that is the very best that can be said for it.

But is it even prudent? To judge this we must look out upon the vast field of the war & try however inadequately to compute its awful balances. Stated vy broadly the following is the salient fact of the war situation:—The *Appearance* of power is with the enemy & the *Reality* of power is with us. . . .

Churchill went on to explain that whereas Germany had won 'scores of battles', had occupied Belgium, Serbia, Rumania and Poland, had 'overthrown Russia', and had 'gripped tight in her hands' the three other enemy states—Bulgaria, Turkey and Austria-Hungary—the reality was that the German people themselves had suffered enormously in achieving these conquests. 'The strain upon the life energies of the German people,' he declared, 'cannot be less than three times what we in the British islands have yet been called upon to endure. . . . If we are steadfast, they must collapse.'

For several weeks, over 10,000 American soldiers had been reaching Europe each day. The German assault of March 18 had not produced any decisive result, despite nearly five months of effort and loss. Since the March attack began, the Allies had won aerial control of the western front. 'All the world is marching against Germany & her confederates,' Churchill wrote. 'All the continents, all the oceans, all the men in all the lands are leagued against the guilty nation. We have but to persevere to conquer. That is the reality.' And he continued:

A Peace made now would for all time register & rivet upon the world the appearance of German power taken at its culminating point. It wd forever deny the other nations all their heritage in Reality. A peace upon the accomplished facts of German triumph, at the hour when German triumph is tottering would shut out for many years from mankind their native basic right. They have the right & they have the strength. Are they to forego the right, & disperse the strength before the hollow pomp of German military assertion? Are we to doom our children to accept for all time the Germans at their own valuation, at their highest valuation, at their most extravagant valuation; to stamp these false values forever upon the world & to blot out from the account our immense, and if we give them play, overwhelming resources? To do so will be to defraud & defile the destiny of man. . . .

7

'The sort of life I like'

AT the War Cabinet on the morning of Thursday August 8, Sir Henry Wilson announced that a British offensive had begun in France, and that it was hoped that Tanks would play a major part in its success. Churchill was eager to witness this important moment in Allied fortunes, and flew to France during the afternoon of August 8. 'We had a very pleasant fly over,' he wrote to his wife two days later, 'and passed fairly close to Lullenden. I could follow the road through Croydon and Caterham quite easily. We came down at Lympne Aerodrome and watched all the machines starting for France. About fifty were being sent off that night.' From Hesdin aerodrome, Churchill was driven to the Chateau Verchocq, arriving in time for dinner. It was the first time he had stayed in the Chateau, and he described it in his letter to his wife of August 10:

. . . The Chateau is very comfortable—simple but clean. I have a charming room, filled with a sort of ancient wood-carved furniture that you admire and which seems to me to be very fine and old. The grounds contain avenues of the most beautiful trees, beech and pine, grown to an enormous height and making broad walks like the aisles of cathedrals. One of these must be nearly half a mile long. The gardens are very pretty, though of course there are not many flowers. . . .

By nightfall the Fourth Army, commanded by Sir Henry Rawlinson, had broken through the German front line, capturing 400 guns, and taking nearly 22,000 prisoners. That night Churchill telegraphed to Sir Douglas Haig: 'I am so glad that it has all come right. I was always sure it would this year. Please accept my sincere congratulations on today's brilliant event.' Haig telegraphed his reply on the following morning. 'I shall always remember with gratitude,' he said, 'the energy and foresight which you displayed as Minister of Munitions, and so rendered our success possible.' Churchill sent Haig's telegram to his wife on the following day. 'It is certainly very satisfactory,' he wrote, 'to have succeeded in gaining the confidence and good-will of the extremely difficult and to some extent prejudiced authorities out here. There is no doubt that they have felt themselves abundantly supplied.'

On the morning of August 9 Churchill set off by car to the headquarters of the Fourth Army, at Flixecourt, near Amiens. He was much delayed by columns of German prisoners who crowded the roads. Writing to his wife on the following day he described the scene:

. . . On our way to the battle-field we passed nearly 5,000 German prisoners, penned up in cages or resting under escort in long columns along the roadside. Among them were more than 200 officers. I went into the cages and looked at them carefully. They looked a fairly sturdy lot, though some of them were very young. I could not help feeling sorry for them in their miserable plight and dejection, having marched all those miles from the battle-field without food or rest, and having been through all the horrors of the fight before that. Still, I was very glad to see them where they were. . . .

Churchill arrived at Flixecourt in time to lunch with Rawlinson. After lunch he asked Rawlinson if he could go any nearer to the battle. East of Amiens, a road ran due east, through Villers Bretonneux, to the front line. 'It is being shelled,' Rawlinson told him, 'but there is no congestion, you can go along it as far as you care.' Churchill asked his ·brother John to accompany him, as both escort and guide. They drove without incident as far as the village of Lamotte, which, on the previous morning, had been five thousand yards behind the German front line. 'As they were shelling the village, and trying to shell the road,' Churchill wrote to his wife on the following day, 'we moved the car down a side road about half a mile, where we found a safe place for it, and then we walked about on the battlefield, picking our way with discretion.' In his letter, Churchill described the scene of the previous day's battle:

. . . The ground everywhere was ploughed up by shells, but nothing to the same extent as the Somme and Ypres battle-fields. The tracks of the Tanks were everywhere apparent. There were very few dead to be seen, most of them having been already buried; but generally speaking I do not think there can have been much slaughter, as the enemy seems to have yielded very readily. . . .

Throughout August 10, Churchill worked at Montreuil, discussing with Haig's staff the apparent superiority of German over British shells. 'The German shells have false noses,' he wrote that evening to his wife, 'which make them go much further than ours, and the question is, Why

have we not developed these earlier? There is no doubt that we have
fallen behind. . . .' Churchill assured the senior officers at Haig's headquarters that he would do all he could to improve the quality of the
British shells during 1919.

As soon as he reached the Chateau Verchocq on the evening of
August 10, Churchill wrote to General Seely about the superior
German shells. 'It is not at all creditable to us,' he declared, 'that the
Germans should be firing these shells of every nature as a matter of
regular practice while we are still fumbling with experiments.'

Churchill realized at once that the victory of August 8 was far more
than a temporary one. In his letter of August 10 he wrote to his wife:

. . . The events which have taken place in the last 3 days are among the most
important that have happened in the war, and, taken in conjunction with the
German defeats on the Marne and at Rheims, entitle us to believe that the
tide has turned. Up to the present there must be at least 30,000 prisoners in
our hands, with several hundred guns. In addition, Montdidier is surrounded
and the troops holding it are cut off. This may largely increase our captures.
On the front of three armies, the fourth British and the first and third
French, several hundred thousand men have been marching forward for
several days through liberated territory. Our cavalry are still out in front, and
in some parts of the line there are at the moment no Germans left. The
Australian armoured cars rushed through the moment the front was broken
and attacked the headquarters of the transport and everything they could find
in rear. They have reached the headquarters of an Army Corps and shot four
of the staff officers. At another place they found the German troops in a
village at their dinners and ran down the whole street firing in through the
windows upon them, doing tremendous execution.

I am so glad about this great and fine victory of the British Army. It is our
victory, won chiefly by our troops under a British Commander, and largely
through the invincible Tank which British brains have invented and
developed. Haig has done very well, and it does not follow that we are at the
end of our good fortune yet. There are great possibilities in the situation if
they can be turned to account. One American regiment has taken part on
our front in this battle. Would you believe it—only three American Divisions
were in the line at any one moment between Rheims and Soissons. They
certainly had a good press. That is one reason why I rejoice that we should
have won a great success which no one can take from us. . . .

Churchill also wrote to Lloyd George from the Chateau Verchocq on
the evening of August 10. 'Of course, there is always the danger that
local impressions may be misleading,' he explained, 'but everything I
could see and hear inspired me with the very greatest confidence and
pleasure. It seems to me this is the greatest British victory that has been

won in the whole war, and the worst defeat that the German army has
yet sustained. How thankful you must be after all the anxieties through
which we have passed.'

The purpose of Churchill's letter to Lloyd George was to warn about
several serious shortcomings in the British armoury. There could be no
doubt, he wrote, that the British shells were inferior to the German, that
there was insufficient poison gas, that the aeroplane engines had not
fulfilled expectations, and that the most recent Tank models had not
been entirely satisfactory. 'It is only by looking these facts in the face,'
Churchill told Lloyd George, 'especially the unpleasant ones, that one
finds the means to overcome the difficulties and avoid mishap.' In his
letter, Churchill told Lloyd George of his plans and requirements:

. . . I am very hopeful that with Seely's authority and drive, and Maclean's[1]
very high qualifications and experience, we shall realise the full programme
which I promised you at the beginning of the year by the required date.
Meanwhile there are plenty of tanks for the comparatively small numbers of
officers and men which have hitherto been provided. To handle the tanks
which we shall certainly make by next June, at least 100,000 men will be
required for the Tank Corps. The tanks also will fail in their full effect if the
cross-country vehicles are not simultaneously ready. I hope you will continue
to study this aspect, which is all-important. I see no reason why, if we take the
steps which are open to us now, we should not win a decisive military
victory in the West next year. . . .

On Sunday August 11, Churchill again visited the battlefields east of
Amiens. Three days later he sent his wife an account of what he saw:

. . . The Germans were hardly firing at all, while our batteries thundered
away. There were more German dead lying about than in the other sector wh
I visited, & all our dead cavalry horses dotted the country side & disfigured
the scene. We saw one of our message balloons (like those at Richmond)
brought down in flames, the observers just skipping out in their parachutes
in time. . . .

Clementine Churchill was expecting her fourth child in October.
'The War news continues good,' she wrote to her husband on August 13,

[1] James Borrowman Maclean, 1881–1940. Educated as an engineer. Worked for several
years on the Clyde. Entered the Ministry of Munitions as Director of Shell Production, 1915.
Subsequently Controller of Gun Manufacture and Technical Adviser to the Ordnance Group.
Appointed by Churchill to be Controller of the Mechanical Warfare Department, 1917.
Controller of Tank Production, and Chairman of the Tank Production Committee, 1918.

'but it seems to me that "the Victory" is now complete & that for the
present nothing more is to be expected? I do hope we shall be careful
not to waste our men in pushing now that the spurt is finished.' Four
days later, when Churchill received his wife's letter, he replied: 'Your
remark about not throwing away our men shows you to be a vy wise &
sagacious military pussy cat.' On August 15 Clementine Churchill
wrote again, from Mells in Somerset:

Thank-you for a most interesting account of what is going on in France—
How much better you describe things than the most brilliant Newspaper
Correspondent. But I forget! You were one once—but that was before I
knew you. . . . This is a delicious place wherein to rest and dream & I feel my
new little baby likes it—Full of comfort beautiful things, sweet smelling
flowers, peaches ripening on old walls gentle flittings & hummings & pretty
grandchildren. But under all this the sadness & melancholy of it all. Both the
sons dead, one lying in the little Churchyard next to the House carried away
at sixteen by Scarlet Fever, and other sleeping in France as does the Husband
of the best loved daughter of the House Katherine Asquith.[1] Both their
swords are hanging in the beautiful little Gothic Church beside long inscrip-
tions commemorating long dead Horners who died in their beds. . . .

For five days from August 13 Churchill was in Paris, living at the
Ritz, and attending a series of meetings on munitions problems. 'Conferences all day,' he wrote to his wife on August 14, 'and many people to
see.' On August 15 he presided at a meeting of the Inter-Allied Munitions Council, writing to his wife that evening:

It is quite an impressive gathering—the 4 great nations assembled along
the tables with their ministers & generals etc. We arranged that each gt
power shd represent one of the little powers (so as to restrict numbers).
France took Greece. Italy was given Serbia, the US Belgium, & we look after
the Portuguese so we are like four kangaroos each with an infant in the pouch.
Ours is rather a dirty brat I am afraid.

During a break in the conference during the day Churchill went to
see Clemenceau. Two days later he wrote to his wife of how the French
Prime Minister 'was full of complaints about the British manpower
plans'. Churchill added: 'I am also disquieted by what I know, & think
we are not making sufficient provision.'

In his letter to his wife on August 15, Churchill described the
'tropical brilliancy' of the weather in Paris. It was 'provoking', he told
her, 'to be cooped up in a conference hour after hour'. But on August 16

[1] Katherine Frances Horner. Daughter of Sir John Horner of Mells, Somerset. In 1907 she
married Asquith's eldest son Raymond, who was killed in action on the Somme in 1916. Her
brother Edward was killed in action in 1917.

he and Loucheur attended a further conference, at which they persuaded the senior United States' war supplies purchaser, Edward Stettinius,[1] to agree to Britain and France providing the steel, tank engines and guns for the American Third Army. The principal problem was to find the materials and manpower to complete the Anglo-American Tank factory at Chateauroux. That same day Churchill telegraphed to Sir Douglas Haig to enlist his help. 'Can you assign me a thousand German prisoners of war,' he asked, 'for the completion of the Anglo-American tank factory at Chateauroux?' On the following day Churchill wrote bitterly to his wife:

The Anglo-American Tank factory at Chateauroux for wh I was let in by that foolish Colonel Stern[2] is in a fair way to become an international scandal. I cannot secure either the labour or the organisation necessary for its completion. Meanwhile the material for the Tanks is nearly ready, & the Tanks are badly wanted. It is causing me much embarrassment & may be the cause of bringing me back to Paris towards the end of the week.

Churchill continued to fight against the transfer of men from munitions factories to the front, and for a higher priority for Tank production. But his view was not supported by those whom he most admired, and whom he believed were his supporters. On August 29, Sir Henry Rawlinson wrote emphatically to Sir Henry Wilson: 'All you have got to do is to keep our infantry up to strength and not waste manpower in tanks and aviation. They won't win the war for you as the infantry will. We cannot beat the Boche without infantry. Tanks, aeroplanes etc are great helps, but they cannot and will not win the war for us by themselves, so do not let Lloyd George think they will. . . .' Churchill himself had already tried to enlist Lloyd George's support. On August 17 he telegraphed from Paris:

I shall be in France all next week, and if you are passing through would very much like to see you. I wish particularly to talk to you about man power

---

[1] Edward Riley Stettinius, 1865–1925. United States industrialist; President of Sterling & Co, Machine Manufacturers (1905), and of the Diamond Match Co (1909). In charge of the J. P. Morgan & Co. Agency for the Purchase of War Supplies, 1915–17. United States Surveyor-General of Purchases, 1917–18. Second Assistant Secretary of War, 1918. Senior United States War Supplies Purchaser in Europe, 1918. (His son Edward R. Stettinius Jnr. was Special Assistant to President Roosevelt, 1941–2 and Secretary of State, 1944–5.)

[2] Albert Stern, 1878–1966. Lieutenant, Royal Naval Volunteer Reserve (Armoured Car Division), 1914. Secretary to the Landship Committee, Admiralty, 1916. Major, Machine Gun Corps, Heavy Branch, 1916. Head of the Tank Supply Committee, Ministry of Munitions, 1916; Director-General, Mechanical Warfare Department (rank of Lieutenant-Colonel), 1917; Commissioner, Mechanical Warfare, Overseas and Allies, 1918. Knighted, 1918. Member of the London Committee of the Ottoman Bank, 1921–64. Chairman, Special Vehicle Development Committee, Ministry of Supply, 1939–43.

proposals which I have been thinking about a great deal. Try and give me a rendezvous. Winston.

But the message that came back from Lloyd George's secretary, William Sutherland,[1] was not encouraging. 'Prime Minister went to Criccieth on Saturday,' he wrote, 'and is unlikely to be back from North Wales before the end of the week.'

While in Paris, Churchill saw much of Stettinius with whom, he wrote to his wife on August 17, he had established 'excellent relations'. On August 15 he had given a dinner to the Italian munitions representatives, and made them a speech 'in the kind of French they understand & speak themselves'. On August 16 Loucheur took Churchill and Stettinius to Chateau Thierry, scene of the Germans' furthest advance in March. They lunched with General Mangin,[2] who had led the successful French counter-attack on June 11. 'Of course,' Churchill wrote to his wife, 'the General was confident the Germans were about to collapse. In fact he used exactly the same sort of language I heard almost on this vy spot (Villers-Cotterêts) from Sir John French almost 4 years ago! I hope it is less premature now.'

On August 18, while he was still in Paris, Churchill sent Loucheur a long written appeal for closer Anglo-French co-operation in the design and manufacture of long-distance bombing planes. It was essential, he wrote, to draw up plans in such a way as to ensure that, during the autumn, Britain and France would be able 'to discharge the maximum quantity of bombs upon the enemy'. Churchill regarded bombing as essential for victory, telling Loucheur:

. . . It will be disastrous if after having made for all these months immense preparations to bomb Germany—not only the Rhine but Westphalia—and having our organisation and plant perfected in all respects except one, the effort should be rendered abortive through the lack of that one, viz, a comparatively small number of Liberty engines.

This is the moment to attack the enemy, to carry the war into his own country, to make him feel in his own towns and in his own person something of the havoc he has wrought in France and Belgium. This is the moment, just

[1] William Sutherland, 1880–1949. Secretary to the Cabinet Committee on Supply of Munitions, 1915. Private Secretary to Lloyd George, 1915–18; Parliamentary Secretary, 1918–20. Liberal MP for Argyllshire, 1918–24. Knighted, 1919. A Junior Lord of the Treasury, 1920–2. Chancellor of the Duchy of Lancaster, April–October 1922.

[2] Charles Marie Emmanuel Mangin, 1866–1925. Entered the French Army, 1888. Served in western Africa, 1906–12 and in Morocco, 1912–13. Général de Brigade, commanding the 5th Infantry Division, 1914–16. Général de Division, commanding the 2nd Army Corps, 1916; the 6th Army, 1916–17. Commanded the 9th Army Corps, December 1917–June 1918; the 10th Army, June–November 1918. President of the Consultative Committee for Colonial Defence, 1921–2. Inspector General of Colonial Troops, 1922.

before the winter begins, to affect his morale, and to harry his hungry and dis-spirited cities without pause or stay. While the new heavy French machines, of which you were speaking to me will strike by night at all the nearer objectives, the British, who alone at the moment have the experience, apparatus and plans already made to bomb not only by night but in broad daylight far into Germany, must be assured of the means to carry out their role.

On the evening of August 18, Churchill returned to the Chateau Verchocq. His wife had returned from Mells to Lullenden. 'I am glad you are having such full and fruitful days,' she wrote to him that evening. 'It must be exhilarating to be in the actual atmosphere of victory.' Churchill stayed at his Chateau for six days. Edward Marsh arrived from England to join him, and a new pilot, Lieutenant Hall, was ordered to put himself and his aeroplane—a DH4—at Churchill's disposal. Fifty years later, Hall recalled:

I was informed of the exact position of the Chateau and was to land at the nearest suitable aerodrome to it, and to telephone the Chateau on my arrival when a car would be sent to pick me up. The car turned out to be a Rolls Royce with an English-speaking chauffeur and on reaching the Chateau I was allotted a bedroom by Mr Marsh, the Minister's private secretary, who seemed to be in charge of everything. Ablutions were performed by means of an old-fashioned jug and basin, with no hot water in evidence, when presently two gentlemen looked into the room and asked if they could have a wash too. Both were strangers to me and later I knew them to be Lord Weir [1] and Sir Maurice Bonham Carter. [2] Going downstairs I met Mr Churchill and his brother John in the uniform of a Major.

In the evening we all assembled in the dining room for a meal. Being the youngest there I felt a little nervous. . . .

At that first meal Mr Churchill sat at the head of the table and acted as host. Food was not too plentiful in that fourth year of the war and the first course was a plain and wholesome Shepherd's Pie. Mr Churchill referred to it as 'minced meat under a glorious cloud of mashed potatoes', and it tasted all the better for that. . .

Mr Churchill did most of the talking, with the others joining in when they had something to contribute. The subject was, of course, the war and the way the war was being conducted. I remember being astonished to hear that the

[1] William Douglas Weir, 1877–1959. Shipping contractor and pioneer motor car manufacturer. Scottish Director of Munitions, 1915–17. Controller of Aeronautical Supplies, and Member of the Air Board, 1917. Knighted, 1917. Director-General of Aircraft Production, Ministry of Munitions, 1917–19. Created Baron, 1918. Secretary of State for Air, April–December 1918. Adviser, Air Ministry, 1935–9. Created Viscount, 1938. Director-General of Explosives, Ministry of Supply, 1939. Chairman of the Tank Board, 1942.

[2] Maurice Bonham Carter, 1880–1960. Called to the Bar, 1909. Private Secretary to H. H. Asquith, 1910–16. Married Asquith's daughter Violet, November 1915. Knighted, 1916. Assistant Secretary, Ministry of Reconstruction, 1917; Air Ministry, 1918.

Ministers of State at home were far from satisfied. Mention was made of the appalling losses of lives at Ypres, the Somme and at Arras, with very little gain in the matter of territory, which after all must have been the object for launching these assaults on the Germans. Thousands of men had died and their loss had been generally accepted as inevitable in modern warfare. But were they inevitable? The discussion continued along these lines for some time and what interested me most was the feeling of remorse and sincere concern expressed for the relatives at home. They did care!

The conversation changed to a brighter topic when Mr Churchill started to tell us about the preparation of his speeches. Apparently he went through a routine, even to making gestures with arms and hands, and I believe before a mirror, in the seclusion of his study at home. He informed us that some years ago he had suffered injury to his shoulder in an accident, and he was always cautious on the platform in case he should put his shoulder out of joint just at the peroration of his speech, which would have ruined the show!

Then he turned to the subject of tanks, the new surprise weapon that was to confound the enemy. . . . Mr Churchill called for suggestions for getting tanks across rivers. 'Rivers,' he explained 'which, by the dispensation of Almighty God run east and West in France, instead of north and south, and thereby add to our difficulties.' We were all trying to think this one out when he broke in again:—'Now I in my simple way can think of no fewer than six different methods of getting tanks across rivers. Firstly, there shall be certain self-sacrificing tanks that shall plunge into the river and lie on the river-bed, and so form a bridge over which their more fortunate comrades shall cross in safety.' On seeing the smile on his face we realised this was a joke and I cannot note now remember what useful suggestions, if any, were made to surmount the problem.

One could never predict what Mr Churchill would come out with next. During a lull he suddenly, without any warning, uttered the word 'stunt'. 'Stunt' he repeated, 'that is a remarkable word, and it has come to stay.' He then asked each of us to define the word 'stunt'. Lord Weir was the first to make the attempt followed by the rest all round the table. By this time we had reached the coffee stage of the meal and one could not help noticing Mr Churchill's habit of rolling his cigar across the top of his coffee cup. The cigar was held between the first finger and thumb of each hand and he practised this untiringly and I think unconsciously for long periods, meanwhile commenting on our efforts to define this wonderful new word 'stunt' that had come over to us from America.[1]

During one dinner at the Chateau Verchocq, Churchill began to

[1] According to the Oxford English Dictionary, the word 'stunt' was first found in American college slang in about 1878, but was of unknown origin. Among its meanings were: 'a feat undertaken as a defiance in response to a challenge', and 'an enterprise set on foot with the object of gaining reputation or signal advantage'. The word also had a military usage: 'An attack or advance'.

recite, from memory, several of the war poems of Siegfried Sassoon.[1]
This was something he did quite often. On August 10 Lord Esher had
written to Philip Sassoon: 'By the way, *who* is Siegfried Sassoon. . . .
Winston knows his last volume of poems by heart, and rolls them out on
every possible occasion.' Lieutenant Hall recalled a recitation at the
Chateau:

We all listened attentively. I had never heard of Sassoon or his poems and we
were soon told something of this man's history. It was obvious that the
Minister held the greatest admiration for Sassoon as a man, as a soldier and
as a poet. We quickly realised that the main theme of the poems was anti-war,
the futility of war and the misery war brought. We heard that the Generals
were seriously worried at the damage to morale these poems might inflict on
the troops, and that it would be preferable for Sassoon to remain in England,
out of harm's way. Mr Churchill then stated that on our return to England
he intended to get in touch with Sassoon and to make some amends to him,
possibly I believe by offering him a job in the Ministry of Munitions. I feel
sure it was Winston's brother John who thereupon exclaimed 'I should leave
that man alone if I were you. He might start writing a poem about *you*,' to
which Mr Churchill immediately replied 'I am not a bit afraid of Seigfried
Sassoon. That man can think. I am afraid only of people who cannot
think.'

On August 21 Churchill went to Frevent to see Sir Douglas Haig. A
new British offensive had been launched towards Bapaume. Lieutenant
Hall recorded Churchill's departure from the Chateau Verchocq:

About mid-morning I was sent for to receive my orders for the day. On
reaching his bedroom I met Mr Marsh, his secretary, pacing up and down
the landing within easy reach, if needed. I later learned it was nothing
unusual for him to be hauled out of bed in the middle of the night if the
Minister happened to require his services.

On entering the bedroom I found Mr Churchill stretched on his bed in his
dressing gown, face downwards and with his feet on the pillow. In that
uncomfortable position he was writing, with a newspaper as a makeshift
table. A used breakfast-tray lay nearby and a framed portrait of his wife. . . .

---

[1] Siegfried Sassoon, 1886–1967. Of Jewish descent. Novelist and poet. A friend of Edward
Marsh. Enlisted in the Sussex Yeomanry, 3 August 1914. Went to the western front in
November 1915, with the Royal Welch Fusiliers. Awarded the Military Cross for his heroism
in bringing back the wounded after a raid opposite Mametz, 1916. Fought in the battle of the
Somme, 1916. Wounded in the neck during the battle of Arras, April 1917. While convalescing
in Britain, June–July 1917, he made a formal protest against the war, and threw his Military
Cross into the Mersey. Served in Palestine, March–May 1918, and on the western front,
July 1918. Wounded in the head, July 1918. He published his first volume of war poetry,
The Old Huntsman, in May 1916, and *Counter Attack* in July 1918. His younger brother was
killed at Gallipoli in August 1915. His volume *Siegfried's Journey* was published in 1945.

Churchill reached Haig's advanced headquarters at noon and stayed for lunch. In his diary Haig wrote of Churchill:

. . . He is most anxious to help us in every way, and is hurrying up the supply of '10 calibre-head' shells, gas, Tanks, etc. His schemes are all timed for 'completion in *next June*!' I told him we ought to do our utmost to get a decision this autumn. We are engaged in a 'wearing out battle', and are outlasting and beating the enemy. If we allow the enemy a period of quiet, he will recover, and the 'wearing out' process must be recommenced. In reply I was told that the General Staff in London calculate that the decisive period of the war cannot arrive until next July. . . .

Churchill stayed at Frevent throughout the afternoon, returning by air to the Chateau Verchocq with Lieutenant Hall, who later recorded:

It was dusk when we landed and his first remark was about the sunset we had just seen. At the aerodrome we found a group of young airmen, some little more than boys, waiting to take off on a night bombing raid. The engines of their machines were warming up and Mr Churchill strolled over for a chat. Later, as we moved away, he asked if I thought they looked depressed, as all were subdued and silent, and he then said—'You know, the people at home have no idea what these lads are going through.' And he then asked if I had noticed what a fine face one of the youths had. . . .

By August 26 the British troops on the Somme had recaptured most of the ground lost to the Germans during March and April. By August 31 the Fourth Army had captured 32,000 prisoners, 456 heavy guns and 3,100 machine guns and trench mortars.

Churchill had returned to England on August 24. On the evening before his return he wrote to his wife:

My darling,
A line only to tell you that unless the weather is bad I shall fly over tomorrow (Saturday) afternoon to Penshurst Aerodrome & hope to be with you for dinner. Do not be the least worried if I do not turn up as a landing in a field somewhere out of the way is always a possibility. If the weather is bad I shall not cross.
The battle is now general along the whole front from the Scarpe to Soissons & 3 British & 4 French armies are attacking. . . .
I am quite alone here. It is vy jolly moving about so freely with the armies, & yet being able to do my work regularly.
I look forward to the joys of Lullenden however with much delight.

Churchill spent only two weeks in England before returning again to France. While he was in London, he attended several meetings of the

War Cabinet. On September 7 he learnt that the Chilean Government, the major source of Allied supplies of nitrates, had accepted his request that the whole of Chile's nitrate production should be sold to the Allies. Nitrates were an essential ingredient in the manufacture of explosives, and the Chilean Government had been reluctant to commit itself so completely to the Allied cause. For nearly a year Churchill had been in charge of these negotiations, not only for Britain, but also for France and the United States.

The September agreement with Chile enabled Churchill to give the French and United States Governments the quantities they required, and still retain sufficient for British needs. That evening he telegraphed enthusiastically to Bernard Baruch in Washington: 'I am going to begin discussing the 1919 production quite shortly and I should be glad if you would let me know as soon as possible what your monthly requirements will be. . . .' As the United States purchases of nitrates were over five times as large as that of Britain, Churchill's conduct of the negotiations was of even greater value to the United States than to Britain. 'When we met in Paris during the Peace Conference,' Churchill recorded in *The World Crisis*, 'I found that Mr Baruch apparently considered me an authority upon the deeper technical aspects of the nitrate trade. He one day asked me my advice upon an urgent and complicated question concerning it. But reputations are easier lost than gained. I thought I would let well alone, and disengaged myself with suitable modesty.'

After lunch on September 7, Churchill went to St Margaret's Bay, near Dover, to spend the afternoon with his wife and three children. Then, while she drove back to Lullenden, he was flown by Captain Patteson from Lympne to France. 'We sailed across the Channel through a fierce storm,' he wrote to his wife on the following day, 'and were over the other side in about 11 minutes.' And he urged her not to worry over his revived interest in flying. 'It gives me a feeling of tremendous conquest over space, & I know you wd love it yourself.'

Churchill reached the Chateau Verchocq in time for dinner with his brother. On the morning of Sunday September 8 he worked, in bed, at his munitions papers. September 12 would be the tenth anniversary of his marriage; in his letter to his wife of September 8, which he hoped would reach her in time, he wrote: 'I am vy happy to be married to you my darling one, & as the years pass I feel more & more dependent on you & all you give me.'

From the Chateau Verchocq, Churchill flew to Haig's headquarters at Montreuil where he lunched with Haig and his senior advisers. 'They are all convinced,' Churchill wrote to his wife on the following day, 'of the bad *morale* of the German army. The demeanour of the prisoners toward their captive officers, the demeanour of the officers themselves, the talk of the wounded etc, are all quite different from anything yet experienced here. One must always discount the sanguine opinions of the Army. Still there is an end to every task, & some day the optimists will be right.'

That evening Churchill returned to the Chateau Verchocq. On the following day he was shown over the Drocourt-Queant lines, which had been captured by the British only two weeks before. He described his visit in a letter to his wife on the following day:

. . . Everywhere the soldiers received me with the broadest of grins & many a friendly shout or hand wave. I think I value the spontaneous & unmerited goodwill of these heroic men more than the Garron Tower estates.¹ But do not be alarmed, I am not going to renounce them. Why shd we not enjoy both?

The ruin of the countryside was complete. A broad belt of desert land stretches across the front in some places 30 miles wide without a tree that is not a blasted stump or a house that is not a heap of bricks. Everywhere pain & litter & squalor & the abomination of desolation. Everywhere too the enemy flung shells at random—now here now there, to wh the working, sleeping, eating, bathing, loitering, marching soldiers paid not the slightest attention. Most of our dead are already buried, but a number of German blue grey bundles still lie about. . . .

Churchill had asked his pilot, Captain Patteson, to join him during the visit to the battle area. Before becoming a pilot, Patteson had fought on the Somme as an infantry officer. 'The reappearance of scenes wh he had left for so long,' Churchill wrote to his wife, '& his old terrible memories of the Somme, upset him altogether. He did not get frightened. He got positively ill and almost incapable of thought or action. Is it not odd when he is so skilful & resourceful & fearless in the air!'

That evening Churchill returned again to the Chateau Verchocq. On the following morning he wrote to his wife:

My darling one—I remember that this letter shd reach you on the 12th September. Ten years ago my beautiful white pussy cat you came to me. They

¹ Churchill stood to inherit this Northern Irish property through the will of his great-grandmother Frances Anne, second wife of the 4th Marquess of Londonderry. In the years before 1914 the estates brought in an income of some £4,000 a year, and were valued at over £55,000. In September 1918 only Lord Herbert Vane-Tempest stood between him and the inheritance. Lord Herbert was killed in a railway accident in 1921.

have certainly been the happiest years of my life, & never at any moment did
I feel more profoundly & eternally attached to you. I do hope & pray that
looking back you will not feel regrets. If you do it [is] my fault & the fault of
those that made me. I am grateful beyond words to you for all you have given
me. My sweet darling I love you vy dearly.

Your own unsatisfactory
W

Throughout September 10, Churchill worked at the Chateau Verchocq. During the day he wrote a long letter to Lloyd George, pointing
out that the expenditure of ammunition had become so high since Haig
had taken the offensive, that there was grave danger of a serious
shortage in 1919. If the advance continued at its existing speed, he
added, there would also be a heavy demand early in 1919 for steel rails,
for as the armies advanced the railways were being resorted to as the
best means of hurrying troops to the front. Churchill went on to discuss
the problem of manpower, warning Lloyd George that the search for
new sources of manpower for the ground fighting was going to affect the
air programme adversely:

. . . There is a considerable set-back here against the Air. There is no doubt
that the demands of the Air Force on men and material are thought to be
much in excess of the fighting results produced. There is no doubt that if
Haig had to choose between 50,000 men for the Infantry and 50,000 men for
the Air Force, he would choose 50,000 men for the Infantry. The reason is
not that a man in the air is not worth more than a foot soldier, but that a man
in the Air Force is not a man in the air, and that anything from 50 to 100 men
are required in the Air Force for every one man fighting in the air.

The magnificent performances and efficiency of the squadrons cannot be
accepted as the final test. Everything ought to pay a proportionate dividend
on the capital invested, and it is from this point of view that the Air Force
should be tested. How much flying, for instance, is done by the RNAS for the
45,000 first-rate fighting men and skilled men they employ? How many
bombs are dropped? How many submarines are sunk? How many flights are
made? How many Huns are killed for the enormous expenditure of national
energy and material involved? Again, take the balloons and the airships. Let
a similar test be applied to them. . . .

Churchill told Lloyd George that plans for expanding the Air Force
might have to be cut back considerably. 'You really cannot afford,' he
wrote, 'to let any part of your organisation fail in this culmination
period to produce continuously war results equal to its demand on the
public resources.' But he did not want Lloyd George to cut back Tank
production, and argued strongly for an increase in the number of men
allocated to the Tank Corps:

2. Churchill and his wife in 1919

3–6. Churchill visiting munitions works in Glasgow, October 1918: a sequence of four photographs. Churchill told the workers: 'Defeatism must be stamped out with all the vigour of public opinion.'

7. The Chateau Verchocq. On August 1918, Churchill wrote to his wife of 'avenues of the most beautiful trees, beech and pine, grown to an enormous height and making broad walks like the aisles of cathedrals'. This photograph was taken in 1969

8. The Chateau Verchocq: from a photograph taken in 1969

9. Churchill, his brother and Eddie Marsh at Lille, 28 October 1918

10. Lloyd George at Lympne, a photograph taken in 1920

12. Clemenceau

11. Haig and Rawlinson, a photograph taken on 19 March 1920

13. Foch

14. Loucheur, Churchill, Lloyd George and Bernard Baruch in Paris, 1919

. . . Up to the present there have only been about 18,000 men in the Tank Corps, and they have only had 600 or 700 Tanks to use in action. It is universally admitted out here that they have been a definite factor in changing the fortune of the field and in giving us that *tactical* superiority, without which the best laid schemes of strategists come to naught. It is no exaggeration to say that the lives they have saved and the prisoners they have taken have made these 18,000 men the most profit-bearing we have in the army. As for the demand which Tanks have made up to the present on material and skilled labour, it is indeed a very modest one. I am having graphics prepared which will illustrate these facts.

It has now been settled to raise the Tanks to 55,000 men. This is only about half what will be needed for the Tanks I shall actually have ready by the summer of next year. Although my outputs are only about half what I had expected, General Elles [1] of the Tank Corps tells me 'that the Tanks they have will see out the Tank men this year'. The Tank men are killed and wounded in considerable numbers, and the permanent wastage of the personnel is high, whereas the Tank in any victorious battle recovers very quickly from his wounds and hardly ever dies beyond the hope of resurrection. A few months sojourn in the grave is nearly always followed by a re-incarnation, so long, that is to say, as he is not snaffled by the powers of evil. Apart from the above, the fatigue on the Tank crews in action is very great, and the idea of the same crew working double relays of Tanks will certainly not carry us very far. . . .

Churchill set out what he described as 'four new circumstances' which would make the Tank 'an invaluable weapon' during the fighting of 1919. These were:

(1) Greatly increased numbers. They will be able to afford to have a considerable proportion knocked out in each battle and yet have enough left at every point to secure success.
(2) They have never yet developed smoke appliances with which they are being fitted. Smoke as an aid to the attack, and particularly to Tank attack, is only in its infancy. It is going to receive an enormous expansion next year.
(3) They have never yet been used in darkness; but that was the original idea which I had when they were conceived. Hitherto they have not been capable of negotiating the accidents of ground by night, but with better Tanks, and a proportion, though only a proportion, of larger Tanks, night operations will

[1] Hugh Jamieson Elles, 1880–1945. Entered Royal Engineers, 1899. Served in the South African War, 1901–2. Deputy Assistant Quarter-master-general, 4th Division, 1914. Brigade Major, 10th Division, 1915. Wounded in action, 1915. Lieutenant-Colonel commanding the Tank Corps in France, 1916–19. Promoted Brigadier-General, 1917; Major-General, 1918. Knighted, 1919. Commandant of the Tank Corps Training Centre, 1919–23. Director of Military Training, War Office, 1930–3. Lieutenant-General, 1934. Master-General of Ordnance, War Office, 1934–37. General, 1938. Chairman of the International Sugar Council, 1938–45. Regional Commissioner for South-West England, 1939–45.

become possible at points where trench warfare has given place to open fighting.

(4) The tactical manoeuvring power of the Tank and its combined training with infantry are developing fast and will yield immensely improved results. Tanks are not opposed to infantry: they are an intimate and integral part of the infantryman's strength. . . .

To emphasize his argument, about the future importance of the Tank, Churchill described to Lloyd George his visit to the battle area on the previous day:

. . . I walked over the Drocourt-Queant line and went on up to the extreme high watermark of our attack. I noticed several remarkable things. The Drocourt-Queant trench was strongly held with Germans, and it was a very fine, strong, deep trench. In front of it was a belt of wire, nearly 100 yards broad. This wire was practically uncut and had only little passages through it, all presumably swept by machine guns. Yet the troops walked over these terrific obstacles, without the wire being cut, with very little loss, killed many Germans, took thousands of prisoners and hundreds of machine guns.

Three or four hundred yards behind these lines was a second line, almost as strong and more deceptive. Over this also they walked with apparently no difficulty and little loss. Behind that again, perhaps a mile further on, were just a few little pits and holes into which German machine guns and riflemen threw themselves to stop the rout. Here our heaviest losses occurred. The troops had got beyond the support of the Tanks, and the bare open ground gave no shelter. In one small space of about 380 yards wide nearly 400 Canadian dead had just been buried and only a few score of Germans.

In his letter to Lloyd George, Churchill set out clearly what he believed the Government's future military policy should be:

The moral appears to be training and Tanks, short advances on enormous fronts properly organised and repeated at very short intervals, not losing too many men, not pushing hard where there is any serious opposition except after full preparations have been made. It is the power of being able to advance a reasonable distance day after day remorselessly rather than making a very big advance in a single day that we should seek to develop. This power can only be imparted by Tanks and cross country vehicles on the largest scale.

You would have been shocked to see the tragic spectacle of the ground where our attack for the time being withered away. It was just like a line of seaweed and jetsam which is left by a great wave as it recoils.

On September 10 Churchill again visited the battle zone, accompanied by Walter Layton. On the following day, from the Chateau Verchocq, he sent his wife an account of his activities:

My darling,

The days are wonderful & the news scarcely less bright. We took Layton out yesterday to see the new attack wh was launched between Arras & Albert. We were taken to a coign of vantage by the general[1] commanding the N. Zealand division. At the time I left they had taken in this small part of the battle front several hundred prisoners without losing more than 50 men! Haig with whom I lunched was vy hopeful about the situation & vy appreciative in his references to Tanks & my share in them. It was & *is* substantial. Layton returns today by the aeroplane wh brings this letter & my pouches.

I am off to see A. Sinclair who is rather near the line. Jack dines tonight as last night. In the full moonlight the Hun airmen buzz continually & the heavy crash of falling bombs rattles our windows. We are however not likely to be molested in the chateau.

Tomorrow I have to see a battery of our new guns—the first yet made—in the line on its trial.

I look forward so much to seeing you all at Lullenden Saturday afternoon. Probably I shall arrive at Penshurst.

Your ever loving husband
W

In the four weeks since August 10, the British had captured over 77,000 German prisoners and 800 heavy guns. 'There had never been such a victory in the annals of history,' Sir Douglas Haig wrote in his diary on September 10, 'and its effects are not yet apparent. . . . The discipline of the German army is quickly going, and the German Officer is no longer what he was. *It seems to me to be the beginning of the end.*' When Churchill sent Seely to see Haig on the evening of September 10, to ask for Tank production and training to be given priority, Haig was unsympathetic. 'I told him,' Haig recorded in his diary that night, 'we ought to aim at finishing the war *now* and not to delay the provision of Tanks until experiments showed we had a perfect design.'

On September 11 Churchill drove from the Chateau Verchocq to Paris, as the weather was too bad for flying. 'I was alone,' Churchill wrote to his wife on the following day, '& took the road by Montdidier in order to see the ruin the war had brought on this unlucky town. For an hour we ran through devastated, shell pitted facias—scraggy shreds of woods—along the road where Clemenceau & I had stood on that melancholy April day when the whole front was quivering & buckling

[1] Andrew Hamilton Russell, 1868–1960. Educated at Harrow and Sandhurst. Colonel, New Zealand Expeditionary Force, 1914. Served, and wounded, at the Dardanelles, 1915. Knighted, 1915. General, commanding the New Zealand Division, 1918. President of the New Zealand Returned Soldiers' Association, 1921–4 and 1926–35. Inspector-General, New Zealand Forces, 1940–1, and member of the New Zealand War Council. One of his two sons was killed at the Battle of El Alamein in 1942.

back. Montdidier is a heap of ruins. But bad as it is, it does not reach the utter destruction of Bailleul & Meteren in the North. There the British artillery has been at work—regardless of expense—& nothing but red smears of brickbats mark the site of what was in the spring thriving townships. . . .'

On the morning of September 12, while Churchill was on his way to Paris, the Americans launched their first offensive of the war. Attacking behind smokescreens, by nightfall they had advanced several miles into the St Mihiel salient. That night Churchill dined with General Spiers. 'Painlevé is coming,' Churchill wrote to his wife before the dinner. '*On est très méchant pour lui.* I shall try to console him.' Churchill also told his wife something of his immediate munitions plans. 'I am trying also,' he wrote, 'to arrange to give the Germans a good first dose of the Mustard gas, before the end of the month. Haig is vy keen on it & we shall I think have enough to produce a decided effect. Their whining in defeat is vy gratifying to hear.'

But Churchill's main thoughts on his wedding anniversary were with his wife:

Ten years ago my dearest one we were sliding down to Blenheim in our special train. Do you remember? It is a long stage on life's road. Do you think we have been less happy or more happy than the average married couple?

I reproach myself vy much for not having been more to you. But at any rate in these ten years the sun has never yet gone down to our wrath. Never once have we closed our eyes in slumber with an unappeased difference. My dearest sweet I hope & pray that future years may bring you serene & smiling days, & full & fruitful occupation. I think that you will find real scope in the new world opening out to women, & find interests wh will enrich yr life. And always at yr side in true & tender friendship as long as he breathes will be your ever devoted, if only partially satisfactory W

Between reaching the Chateau Verchocq on September 7, and re-turning to Verchocq from Paris a week later, Churchill had received no letter from his wife. Captain Patteson, on the other hand, had received a letter every day. On September 15 Churchill wrote to his wife:

My darling,

Eddie received my instructions to convey to you my reproaches yesterday. Up to this moment I have not had a single letter. Really it is unkind. Mails have reached me with gt regularity & swiftness by aeroplane or messengers. They have comprised all manner of communications but never one line from the Cat. The Canary on the other hand receives each day through my bag a bulky screed from his mate. You have certainly given me no chance to *answer* yr letters. You have deprived yourself of any opportunity for accusing me of not having read them. When I reflect on the many and various forms which yr naughtiness takes, I am astonished at its completeness & its versatility. So there!

Having put down my barrage on yr trenches, let me explain further why I have not returned home. . . . The US have now accepted my large artillery offer—more than 2,000 guns—out of wh they will be able to arm perhaps 15 additional divisions or nearly half a million men, in time for the crisis of next year. We must finish it then. On the other hand I am negotiating to get 2 or 3,000 Liberty motors for our air force, particularly for the bombing of Germany by the Independent force.

My days here have been fruitful in business & I have got a lot of things moving wh were otherwise stuck. The hamper of mustard gas is on its way. This hellish poison will I trust be discharged on the Huns to the extent of nearly 100 tons by the end of this month—I find each day lots to do, & lots to see. Indeed I have not done half the things I wanted to do yet. In the mornings or afternoons I sit here quietly looking at my papers—or I can sally out in my car to some friend up in the line. Or I can get someone I want to talk shop to, to come & dine here. Meanwhile the work arrives in steady consignments, & the telephone & aeroplane keep me in the closest touch. It is just the sort of life I like—Coming out here makes me thoroughly contented with my office. I do not chafe at adverse political combinations, or at not being able to direct general policy. I am content to be associated with the splendid machines of the British Army, & to feel how many ways there are open to me to serve them. . . .

Churchill signed his letter: 'You ever devoted though vilely neglected Pig.' He returned to London two days later, on September 17, after ten days in France.

On September 18 Edward Marsh asked Churchill for a personal favour. A literary friend of his, John Squire,[1] had asked if he could meet Churchill, and Churchill agreed to see him in the lounge of the Savoy Hotel. After the encounter, Squire wrote to Marsh:

Ten thousand thanks, he was fascinating—and I didn't entirely expect it, although I had heard him a hundred times. One couldn't get far with him at first meeting. He has enormous qualities, especially the primary quality of courage; one defect—the defect of romanticism—or rather, since romanticism may be good, of *sentimentalism*. You don't sum up Russia by calling Lenin[2]

[1] John Collings Squire, 1884–1958. Poet and literary critic. Literary Editor of the *New Statesman*, 1913–17; acting Editor, 1917–18. Editor of the *London Mercury*, 1919–34. A Governor of the Old Vic, 1922–6. Knighted, 1933. The author of over thirty books.

[2] Vladimir Ilich Ulyanov, 1870–1924. Known as 'Lenin'. Son of an inspector of schools. In 1887 his elder brother was executed for the attempted assassination of Alexander III. Joined a Marxist circle in Kazan, 1887; banished to Siberia, 1897–1900; founded the

a traitor, or by calling munition workers well-fed malcontents. That is melodrama. I have met many politicians; this is the first one who was *alive*.

A few days later, Churchill asked Marsh to reciprocate the favour, and to introduce him to Siegfried Sassoon. Marsh arranged for Sassoon to leave his convalescent home for a few days, and stay with him in London at his rooms in Gray's Inn. On Sassoon's third day in London, he went to see Churchill in his office at the Hotel Metropole. Sassoon recorded his encounter with Churchill in his book *Siegfried's Journey*:

His manner was leisurely, informal, and friendly. Almost at once I began to feel a liking for him and to forget that I was with one whom I had hitherto thought of as an unapproachable public figure. He had heard from Eddie that I was keen on hunting, and was pleased that we had that in common. The only other fox-hunting poet he knew was his old friend Wilfrid Blunt,[1] with whose political opinions, he added with an expressive smile, he profoundly disagreed. He then made some gratifying allusions to the memorable quality of my war poems, which I acknowledged with bashful decorum.

Having got through these preliminaries, he broached—in a good-humoured and natural way—the subject of my attitude to the War, about which—to my surprise—he seemed interested to hear my point of view. Still more surprising was the fact that he evidently wanted me to 'have it out with him'. Overawed though I was, I spotted that the great man aimed at getting a rise out of me, and there was something almost boyish in the way he set about it. My shy responses were, however, quite out of character with the provocative tone of the war poems, which may have led him to expect an exhibition of youthful disputatiousness. It would, of course, have been absurd for me to match myself against such a pre-eminent controversialist and war historian. I am not by temperament an arguer, and have always found difficulty in producing logical ideas rapidly. Such quickness does not belong to a reflective mind.

Nevertheless he was making me feel that I should like to have him as my company commander in the front line, and under the influence of his candid geniality I was discarding shyness and well on the way towards behaving as my ordinary self. There came a point, however, when our proceedings

---

Russian Social Democratic Labour Party, 1898. Emigrated to western Europe, 1900. Leader of the Bolshevik (majority) section of his Party from 1903. In 1912 he severed relations with all other Parties and factions. With only a brief return to Russia in October 1905, he lived in exile in Europe from 1900 to 1917. Returned to Russia, April 1917. Chairman of the Council of People's Commissars (Prime Minister) from the revolution of October 1917 until his death.

[1] Wilfrid Scawen Blunt, 1840–1922. Served in the Diplomatic Service, 1858–70. Travelled throughout the Middle East, 1877–81. Took part in the Egyptian National Movement, 1881–2. A leading supporter of Indian and Egyptian self-government, and of Irish Home Rule. Imprisoned for two months in Ireland, for calling a meeting in a banned district, 1882. On his Sussex estate (of some 2,000 acres) he bred Arab horses.

developed into a monologue. Pacing the room, with a big cigar in the corner of his mouth, he gave me an emphatic vindication of militarism as an instrument of policy and stimulator of glorious individual achievements, not only in the mechanism of warfare but in spheres of social progress. The present war, he asserted, had brought about inventive discoveries which would ameliorate the condition of mankind. For example, there had been immense improvements in sanitation.

Transfixed and submissive in my chair, I realized that what had begun as a persuasive confutation of my anti-war convictions was now addressed, in pauseful and perorating prose, to no one in particular. From time to time he advanced on me, head thrust well forward and hands clasped behind his back, to deliver the culminating phrases of some resounding period. It was the spontaneous generation of a speech which would probably be fully reported in the press before I was many weeks older. Before this he had definitely offered to find me a post in his Ministry if I wanted one, and had told me to think it over.

He now spoke with weighty eloquence of what the Ministry was performing in its vast organisation and output, and of what it might yet further achieve in expediting the destruction of the enemy. In love with his theme, he was elaborating a full-bodied paragraph when the secretarial countenance of Eddie appeared in the doorway to the ante-room, announcing that Lord Fisher had arrived. But the information went unheeded. The Winstonian exposition continued until Eddie reappeared with an apologetic intimation that Lord Fisher was growing restive. As I went out I was introduced to the famous Admiral—a small man with a queer Mongolian face, who had obviously come there with lots to say. . . .

Had he been entirely serious, I wondered, when he said that 'war is the normal occupation of man'? He had indeed qualified the statement by adding 'war—and gardening'. But it had been unmistakable that for him war was the finest activity on earth.

8

The Coming of Victory

ON September 28 the Bulgarian Government surrendered unconditionally to the Allied forces. Churchill learned the news in
Paris, where he was attending a meeting of the Inter-Allied Munitions
Council. While he was in Paris there were further British successes on
the western front, culminating in the capture of over 10,000 German
prisoners and 200 heavy guns, and on October 1 he wrote to Haig to
congratulate him on the success of his Armies. Two days later Haig
replied:

My dear Mr Churchill,
Very many thanks for your kind letter of 1st Oct, and for your friendly
remarks on the doings of our splendid army. I am more than grateful for the
kindly sympathy which you extended to me during the anxious time we
passed through in the spring and for the immense vigour with which you set
about providing us with munitions of war. . . .
I hope everything will be done to *maintain* the army at full strength in
order to beat the enemy as soon as possible. In my opinion it is of the highest
importance to keep on pressing the enemy at every possible point; because, if
we allow him any breathing time at all, he will be able to reorganise his
forces, to construct new defences, to make new plans, and much of the work
of 'wearing him out' will have to be started afresh.
Yours very truly
D. Haig

Throughout the second week of October, Churchill was in Scotland
and the North of England, touring munitions factories. On October 7 he
spoke to munitions workers in Glasgow about their efforts. 'Let every
munition worker,' he said, 'everyone who is concerned in the production of shells, figure to himself in imagination this spectacle of the
artillery holding the front by the fire of the shells they send them.'

At the end of his speech, Churchill warned against too great an expectation of an early victory:

I cannot say that I am over-sanguine at the present time of the speedy termination of the conflict. I cannot feel any degree of assurance that our righteous and indispensable war aims will at the present time receive that recognition which they require, nor can I feel that, having regard to the time which must elapse before the winter weather comes in France and Flanders, we have any right to count upon an immediate decision of a final character there. It may be that events will be better than we have any right to hope for now, but we must not count or build upon too favourable a development of events. We have started out to put this business through, and we must continue to develop to the utmost every resource that can make certain that whatever may be the course of the war in 1918, the year 1919 will see our foe unable to resist our legitimate and rightful claims. . . .

That night, when Churchill spoke to an audience of 5,000 people at St Andrews Hall, Glasgow, he deprecated a negotiated peace. 'We must be on our guard,' he warned, 'lest the results of our exertions should be brought to nought by Hun cajolery. . . .' On the following day he told a meeting organized by the Glasgow Corporation that defeatism 'should be stamped out . . . with all the vigour of public opinion'.

Speaking in Sheffield on October 11, Churchill praised Lloyd George for the courage and energy with which, in March 1918, he had 'laid his hand on every resource which was within reach'. But he went on to say that he did not think 'our dangers are at an end', and to ask:

. . . What is the use of supposing the Germans have repented? What is the use of supposing that they are sorry for what they have done? All they are sorry for is that it has not succeeded. If we wanted any proof that the German heart, the heart of the German militarists who are directing and controlling the policy of Germany, is as black as it ever was, we have only to read of the sinking of the latest passenger ship with its helpless burden of civilian passengers consigned to a watery grave.[1] No, we should not at this stage, mix sentiment with a solution of the serious state problems which lie before us. . . . It is our duty to make sure that our men's lives have not been sacrificed in vain, and that we shall not be confronted with a renewal of the struggle. It is only in that sense and with that object that we must insist on effectual guarantees.

On October 15 Churchill was in Manchester. That morning it was announced in the newspapers that President Wilson had refused a

---

[1] On October 10 a German submarine had torpedoed a British passenger steamer off the Irish coast, with the loss of nearly 300 lives. A few hours later the Irish Mail Boat *Leinster* was torpedoed and sunk, with the loss of 450 passengers, mostly women and children. Neither ship had been armed.

German request for an armistice. 'That stern and formidable answer,' Churchill declared, 'will be wholeheartedly endorsed throughout all the countries and nations of the Allies.' During the following week the Allied advance continued. On October 17 Douai was occupied by troops of the British Eighth Corps, commanded by Sir Aylmer Hunter-Weston. That same day Sir William Birdwood entered Lille, which had been under German occupation for over four years.

On October 20, desperate to win some favour with the Allies before beginning negotiations, the Germans announced the end of their submarine campaign against merchant ships. But the Allies did not relax their military efforts. Throughout October, British, French and Belgian aeroplanes bombed military targets in Germany with an intensity hitherto unknown. Railway junctions, steel works, chemical factories and aerodromes were the principal targets. Metz, Frankfurt, Coblenz, Bonn, Mainz and Karlsruhe were among the principal objectives.

On October 25 Churchill left England for France, and for five days he toured the liberated areas. Edward Marsh, who accompanied him, again kept a diary of events.

Churchill and Marsh had intended to fly to France, but as the weather was too misty, they travelled by train and boat. At Boulogne they were met by a Rolls-Royce provided by the Duke of Westminster, and driven to the Chateau Verchocq. The journey took longer than planned, as Marsh recounted in his diary:

First a tyre burst with one of those loud reports which make one think one has been assassinated—and then, in the village itself, Winston gave the chauffeur a wrong direction, left instead of right, at a cross-road. The chauffeur (an admirable man called Patterson who had been driving at the front since August 1914) preferred not to back, but to go on till he could turn the car—and on we went in the dark, on and on literally for kilometres between the close hedges of the roadside, it must be the original 'long lane that has no turning'. It's impossible to imagine anything alternately more comical and provoking. The climax of Winston's cursing was, 'Well, it's the most absolutely f—ing thing in the whole of my bloody life.' At *last* we came to a possible spot, turned, and got to the chateau about ½ an hour later than we otherwise should. Archie Sinclair, who is to be appointed liaison officer between Munitions Inventions and the front, turned up to dinner, luckily late himself—I went to bed early, leaving him and Winston to gossip.

On Saturday October 26 Churchill, accompanied by Sinclair and Marsh, drove through St Pol and Arras to the battlefield of Le Cateau, where they inspected the scene of the fighting. Then, as Marsh wrote:

We motored down into le Cateau, and on by the Bazuel road, which would soon have taken us close up to the Front, but we were stopped by a railway bridge which had been blown up by the Germans and fallen clean across the road—a large repairing party were at work on it, but it was quite impassable. This settled a quarrel which had been raging all day between Winston and Archie. Archie had promised his Colonel to be back before luncheon, and was determined not to be very late. Winston on the other hand wanted to go on with the joy-ride indefinitely.

The broken bridge put Archie in a strong position, and he positively refused to be taken any further afield. Winston yielded very sulkily, and we turned for a south-easterly round, parallel to our latest advance, through Busigny and Bohain, dropping Archie at Brancourt. He and Winston parted quite coldly, and when I tried to defend him by saying it was because he was so terribly honourable, Winston snapped, 'It isn't honourable, it's asinine. I shall take no more interest in him.'

Churchill and Marsh then drove back to Arras, and from there, after yet another puncture, reached Verchocq. During the day Churchill had driven over 150 miles. On reaching the Chateau, he presided over a conference of senior gas officers. 'There was good talk between the Arch-Poisoners,' Marsh noted.

On the morning of Sunday October 27, Churchill set off again to another of the battlefields, further north. His brother John joined him, and they drove, first to Béthune, then eastwards to Lille. During the journey they passed the battlefield of La Bassée, reaching Lille at noon. Lille had been liberated only ten days before. Churchill lunched there with Sir Reginald Barnes, and dined at the Hôtel de l'Europe, where he spent the night.

The citizens of Lille had asked to honour the British army, and a march past of British troops was planned for October 28. Sir William Birdwood took the salute in the Grande Place, and Churchill was asked to be present on the saluting stand.[1]

Churchill had to leave the march past before its end, as he had been invited to lunch with General Tudor at his headquarters in Harlebeke. 'In the dining room,' Marsh wrote, 'the last German officer left in the town had been killed a week before. The floor was stained with his blood, and his last two revolver shots had made a hole in the cornice and cracked a looking-glass in the hall.' After lunch Tudor drove Churchill towards the front line. When they were only five miles from the front,

---

[1] Among the British Officers present, standing just in front of Churchill on the saluting base, was the Chief of Staff of the 47th London Division, Colonel Montgomery (later Field Marshal Viscount Montgomery of Alamein).

Churchill was excited to see the church tower of Ingoyghem, from which, he insisted, he would have a good view of the front. Marsh wrote in his diary:

The General didn't at all want to take us up it, but Winston coaxed him, and we climbed up the broken staircase to the belfry, where we got a wonderful view into the German lines, running through a village ½ a mile away. While we were looking, the sound of guns began, and we saw shells bursting in the German village. Evidently the Huns would retaliate, so we began a dignified retreat. It was only the beginning of a tremendous strafe (quite unexpected by the General, who would certainly not have let us go there if he had known) and as we walked back to the motor shells whizzed over our heads every second—and sure enough German shell began dropping in the village we had just left. Suddenly the General smelt mustard gas, and made us stuff our handkerchiefs into our mouths till we got back to the motor.

Churchill and Marsh returned to Tudor's headquarters to spend the night. 'While we were at dinner that evening,' Tudor recorded in his diary, 'a Hun plane dropped a fairly large bomb in the street fairly near the house, but that was the only one dropped.' Churchill's visits, Tudor added, 'are always a great treat and a tonic to me and my staff'.

On the morning of October 29, Churchill and Marsh left Tudor's headquarters for Bruges. Their drive nearly ended in disaster. Instead of retracing their steps to Courtrai, and then taking the road direct to Bruges, they tried to use the Ghent road, believing that the front line ran parallel to it some six miles to the east. In a letter to General Tudor on November 4, Churchill described what then took place:

. . . I ought to have enquired about the actual direction of the line, instead of proceeding on a general impression. I did not know that it 'jinked' in so very markedly towards Vive St Eloi, and consequently sailed along the Ghent Road until I got to Beveren, under the impression that I was running almost parallel to the Front, whereas apparently we were directly approaching it. We then luckily turned off, looking for a pontoon bridge across the Lys, and eventually found ourselves in the village of Desselghem. Here I was puzzled to see a peasant suddenly throw himself down behind the wall of a house, and something seemed to be very odd about his gesture. Still, so strong was my impression that we were nearly 10,000 yards from the line that I did not draw any true conclusions from the incident.

The next moment, however, a shell burst about 50 yards ahead of the car, and women and children and soldiers began running about in all directions holding their hands to their faces. I then thought it must be an aeroplane

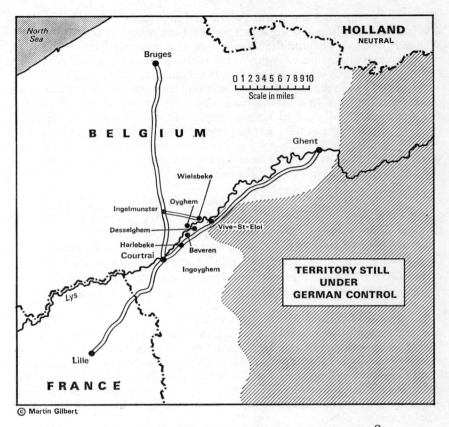

© Martin Gilbert

THE LILLE–GHENT SECTOR IN OCTOBER 1918

dropping bombs, and as the explosion made such a very large cloud of whitish smoke, I thought they must be gas bombs.

Two or three seconds later a whole series of explosions occurred all round us. I had a momentary impulse, through being still under the impression that we were attacked by a low flying aeroplane, that it would be better to stop in the village as we might be followed in our large and flaunting car and hunted down in the open country. Very luckily, however, I let the car run on, for the very spot where I had thought of pulling up to make enquiries was struck by another shell almost immediately.

In a few minutes we were in the open country and out of it. We then waited and watched the village being shelled from the banks of the Lys, and it was then clear that it was artillery fire and not bombs, as the shells could be heard distinctly coming from the north. I continued to speculate stupidly upon the odd habits of the Huns in firing such a very long-range battery upon an obscure village 10,000 yards behind the lines and we then proceeded, still with this in mind, to cross the Lys near Oyghem and work our way up towards Wielsbeke station, from which we turned west to Ingelmunster.

As far as I can make out, Wielsbeke station was very little more than 2,000 yards from the front line. At any rate, all down the first three miles of the Ingelmunster Road we had another rapid series of shells to enliven our journey, and it was not till I got to Bruges that I found out where the line actually ran. Really I would not have believed that after all these years one would be so stupid as to motor near the Front without knowing exactly how the line ran. However, all's well that ends well. . . .

Later in his letter to Tudor, Churchill reflected that, as his car was going at forty miles an hour, he might soon have run straight into the German lines, adding: 'What mugs we should have been!'

Churchill and Marsh reached Bruges in time for lunch. From there they drove due south to Passchendaele, through an area which had been under German rule for four years. From Passchendaele they drove to Ypres. In his diary Marsh described the last part of the journey:

We took a turn down the Ypres–Menin road as far as Hellfire Corner, and then drove into Ypres. When I saw it in March 1915 it was still a town— now there is nothing left but here and there a shapeless mass of bricks—except that the tower of the Cloth Hall is still recognizable, and still beautiful in its pale greys and yellows; and the lovely west door of the Cathedral has even some of its carvings left. Winston wants to turn that group of buildings into a cemetery, with lawns and flowers among the ruins, and the names of innumerable dead.

From Ypres, Churchill and Marsh drove on again to the Chateau Verchocq. Their day's journey had taken them over a hundred miles. They spent the night at the Chateau, and on the following day, October 30, flew back in separate aeroplanes to England.

Churchill's return to England coincided with the surrender of Turkey. 'It was yesterday that Turkey gave in,' Edward Marsh wrote to a friend on October 31, 'and it will be Austria tomorrow—"a drizzle of empires", Winston calls it, "falling through the air".'

Austria-Hungary surrendered on November 3. Four days later, on November 7, a German delegation approached the French lines and asked to be allowed to negotiate an armistice with Marshal Foch.

While the German armistice was being negotiated in France, Lloyd George was busy with domestic politics. He wanted to ensure that, once the war was over, he could maintain his position as Prime Minister. When the Coalition had been set up by Asquith in May 1915, it had been dominated by Liberal Ministers, but since December 1916 the Conservatives had been in a majority in the Cabinet. Asquith wanted a return to the two Party system, with himself leader of the Liberal Party. Lloyd George needed as many Liberals as possible in his Cabinet, if he were to be able to maintain the Coalition with himself at its head. On November 6 he asked two of his senior Liberal Ministers, Churchill and Montagu, to lunch with him at 10 Downing Street. 'It became obvious,' Montagu wrote that evening, 'that the Prime Minister was anxious to find out whether he could rely on our support, and it became obvious that the Prime Minister, both from personal affection and, rightly, from the importance attached to him, determined to devote his fishing expedition to landing Winston Churchill.' Montagu's account continued:

. . . Winston began sulky, morose and unforthcoming. The Prime Minister put out all his weapons. He addressed him with affection as 'Old Man'. He reminded him of their campaigns. He said that so well did he know him that he knew before he said anything that there was something about which he was unhappy. (This showed great perspicacity on the part of the Prime Minister, partly because Winston's face had all along been as sullen as you can possibly see it, and partly because for the last six months to my knowledge Winston has been speaking, if not open treason, open disgruntlement, which must have reached the Prime Minister's ears.)

Winston began with a dispassionate judicial analysis of the reasons for and against a General Election, ending with the advice that a General Election should be held. I was then asked my opinion, and I said that apart from all merits of the question, having regard to public attention and opinion on the subject, it was too late in my opinion to avoid it.

Finally, in a torrent of turgid eloquence, Winston exposed his hand. Never, he said, would he allow any personal consideration to weigh with him. He was prepared to serve the State in whatever capacity he thought most advantageous to the State. Opposition was great fun, although opposition to the present Prime Minister would be very distasteful to him. But he would accept it cheerfully if it were forced upon him. And he then began his usual arguments against the great men in the present Cabinet, the impossibility of the present machinery, the degradation of being a Minister without responsibility for policy, and so on. I have heard it so often before.

The Prime Minister waved it all aside, told him that this was a war measure for war purposes, that with the end of the war the War Cabinet came to an end, that he had made up his mind to have a Gladstone-like Cabinet of something between 10 and 12 and that this present machinery would cease

and that all the important Ministers would be in the Cabinet either because of
their Offices or because of their position.

The sullen look disappeared, smiles wreathed the hungry face, the fish was
landed. . . .

Lloyd George left the room, leaving Churchill and Montagu together. 'Winston was in the seventh heaven of delight,' Montagu noted.
But then Montagu reminded Churchill that in July 1917 he had said he
was only joining Lloyd George's Government for the period of the war,
and that as 'Conservatives were always Conservatives', he would return
after the war to his Liberal friends. Churchill replied 'that once he
joined Lloyd George, he joined him forever, that he had always been
Lloyd George's man and that he owed nothing to anybody else'.

Churchill was delighted that Lloyd George had agreed to set up a
Cabinet of twelve, and assumed that he would be invited to join it. That
evening he was asked by Lloyd George to dine at 10 Downing Street, to
discuss future policy with several other leading Liberal politicians.[1]
Lloyd George told his guests that he had decided on his post-war policies. The Coalition would continue. The Conservatives would be asked
to accept 'a very advanced social programme' in continuation of the
Liberal achievements before 1914, but there would be a number of
Tariff measures to placate them, and a Home Rule Bill which Montagu suspected Lloyd George had already negotiated with the Conservatives.

Lloyd George was determined to preserve the Coalition. Montagu
recorded how: 'He said at one moment rather sharply to Winston, but
intending it for us all, that in the course of a few days he was entitled to
know who were going on with him and who were not.'

Churchill was upset by Lloyd George's remark. He wanted a specific
assurance that he would be included in the post-war Cabinet, and this
Lloyd George was not prepared to give him. On November 7 he wrote
to Lloyd George stating his position, and offering if necessary to leave
the Government:

My dear Prime Minister,

I am vy grateful to you for letting me do such interesting war-work at the
M of M during the last sixteen months. I have tried my hardest to contribute
something toward the great result now being so fully achieved under yr
energetic & sagacious leadership. If the end of the war comes now, I am of

---

[1] Those present were Gordon Hewart (Solicitor General), H. A. L. Fisher (President of the
Board of Education), Christopher Addison (Minister of Reconstruction), Robert Munro
(Secretary of State for Scotland), Frederick Guest, Lord Reading, Montagu and Churchill.

course quite ready to do anything wh may be necessary in the proper winding-up of the Ministry & in the immediate resettlement of industry—provided that such shd be your wish.

It is not possible for me however to take the very serious & far-reaching political decision you have suggested to me without knowing definitely the character & main composition of the new Govt you propose to form for the period of reconstruction. I was vy glad to find that you take the view wh I hold so strongly that as soon as the war is over we shd return to the system of a regular Cabinet composed of the holders of the principal offices of State acting together with collective responsibility. Such a Cabinet shd I think especially at this time be primarily based upon the House of Commons & shd not contain unrepresentative or reactionary elements. Without wishing in any way to intrude upon yr decisions I feel that I cannot choose my own course without knowing who yr chief colleagues wd be.

There is also a personal aspect wh I cannot exclude. I am vy anxious not to be an embarrassment to you in any way. I do not wish to be pressed by yr good nature on reluctant Conservatives. Nothing but misfortune wd attend a Govt in the days & difficulties like these wh did not at the outset start in a spirit of loyal political comradeship. Please believe therefore that I shd make no complaint whatever on quitting the Govt now or at the end of the war, & that I shd leave with no other feeling but that of friendship towards you & of admiration for yr work in this supreme struggle & glorious outcome.

Yours always

W

Lloyd George was offended by Churchill's letter, replying on November 8:

My Dear Winston,

After the conversation we had on Wednesday night, when we arrived at an understanding on questions of policy, your letter came upon me as an unpleasant surprise. Frankly it perplexes me. It suggests that you contemplate the possibility of leaving the Government, and you give no reason for it except an apparent dissatisfaction with your personal prospects. I am sure I must in this misunderstand your real meaning, for no Minister could possibly adopt such an attitude in this critical moment in the history of our country. I am confronted with a problem as great as that of the war—fuller of difficulties and as vital to the people of the country. If you decide to desert me just as I am entering upon this great national task—although you have been good enough repeatedly to assure me that no one else could in your judgment do it as well—the responsibility must be yours.

What is your grievance? It cannot be policy. You know that I have not invited you to commit yourself to anything on Economic issues or Home Rule to which Mr Asquith and his colleagues had not already committed the Liberal Party, without any protest from you either at the time or subsequently.

Is it your associates in the Government? If so, which of them? It is a Coalition Government; you knew that when you joined it. You joined the Asquith Government which was also a Coalition; and the only difference between that Coalition and the present is that for Lansdowne and Selborne[1] have been substituted Milner and Cave.[2]

It cannot be that you will not serve in a Coalition Government of which I am the head, and in which Mr Asquith is not represented, because you took that decision over a year ago. It cannot be that you consider that Coalition may be essential in war but that in peace you ought to revert to Party Government. For years you have urged the Coalition of Parties for reconstruction, and you have recognised that in the great task of reconstruction which confronts us a Coalition of Parties is essential to success.

You say that before you come to 'the very serious and far-reaching political decision' which I invited you to take you must know how the Government is to be constituted. Surely that is an unprecedented demand! The choice of the Members of the Government must be left to the Prime Minister, and anyone who does not trust his leadership has but one course, and that is to seek leaders whom he can trust.

If you are dissatisfied with your personal position, may I point out that it is better than your position in the Asquith Government. You know when there was a vacancy in the Ministry of Munitions Asquith was urged to appoint you to the post, but the position given to you was that of the Duchy of Lancaster.

I have fully recognised your capacity, and you know that at the cost of a great deal of temporary dissatisfaction amongst many of my supporters I placed you in the Ministry of Munitions which during the war was one of the most important posts in the Government.

I should deeply and sincerely regret if anything came to sever a political and personal friendship which has now extended over fourteen years, but this is no time for half-hearted support.

The task I have in front of me when the war is over will require the whole-hearted loyalty, support and energy of all my colleagues. If you are assailed with personal doubts this you cannot give, and therefore it is right that you should make up your mind now.

Ever sincerely
D. Lloyd George

---

[1] William Waldegrave Palmer, 1859–1942. Liberal MP, 1885–6. Liberal Unionist MP, 1886–92. Succeeded his father as 2nd Earl of Selborne, 1895. First Lord of the Admiralty, 1900–5. High Commissioner for South Africa, 1905–10. President of the Board of Agriculture, 1915–16. His brother Robert was killed in action in Mesopotamia in January 1916.

[2] George Cave, 1856–1928. Conservative MP, 1906–18. Knighted, 1915. Solicitor General, 1915–16. Home Secretary, 1916–19. Created Viscount, 1918. Lord Chancellor, 1922–4 and 1924–8. Chancellor of Oxford University, 1925–8. An Earldom was to have been conferred upon him in 1928, but he died before the patent was passed; his widow was accorded the title of Countess.

Churchill's one desire was to be given a responsible place in the new administration. On November 9 he replied to Lloyd George:

My dear Prime Minister,

You have certainly misconceived the spirit in wh my letter was written. If you read the speech I made on the same day to the representatives of the Boards of Management you will see how far I am from contemplating any 'desertion' of you or yr Government during this critical period in wh my Department is so prominently concerned.

My difficulty arises from the fact that an election is about to be fought the result of wh will profoundly affect political relationships & political issues for several years to come, & that you have pointedly invited me to make a speedy & a definite choice in regard to it. It is just because I do not wish to be a 'half-hearted supporter' that I have ventured to ask for some further re-assurance from you. I do not feel that it is unbecoming in me to ask for this on public & on personal grounds. You have several times told me of yr intention when Peace comes to create a regular Cabinet on something like the Glad-stonian model. You have not yet told me whether you wd wish me to become a member of it. Yet I must say quite frankly that once the war and the first crisis of reconstruction are over, I shd not feel able to take a part in political responsibilities no matter how interesting or important the office I held with-out a seat at the council table at wh we have sat together for so many years.

I do not think it wd be right for me to exercise any influence I may possess in Parliament or the country on political issues without a recognised or legiti-mate share in political power. Rather than hold office without real responsi-bility I wd prefer to be a private member when you can dispense with my services, & in the meanwhile remain *politically* uncommitted in any special sense.

You are quite right in saying there is no present disagreement in policy between us. I consider the Government is entitled to claim full freedom of action within the scope of the Paris Resolutions during this extraordinary period whenever a case is made out on the merits. I have always shared yr view that Home Rule shd be given to that part of Ireland who so earnestly desires it & cannot be forced upon that part which at present distrusts it. I agree also that an election is necessary at the earliest moment. I shall cer-tainly say this at the election in any circumstances.

But do you not think I am justified in asking for some general description of the complexion of the Government you propose to form as to the balance of parties in it. After all the future depends at least as much on the character of the instrument as on the precise formulas used in regard to particular questions. Some measure of confidence & consideration might I think be extended by you to one who if he comes at all will come with heart & hand. I was distressed by the tone of yr reply on this point. You have never found me wanting in respect for the position of a Prime Minister.

Lastly—for I am afraid this letter is unconscionably long—am I unreasonable in wishing to feel that yr principal Conservative colleagues are genuinely willing to have me act with them? Do please remember what has taken place in the past, when yr Government was formed. . . .

I do not desire to be brought simply by yr goodwill into a hostile circle. It wd only lead to much unhappiness. I understand fully the many difficulties you surmount with unfailing courage. May I not count on yr sympathetic comprehension of mine?

Yours always

W

Lloyd George had not yet begun to reconstruct his Cabinet, and therefore could not offer Churchill a new post. But on the evening of Sunday November 10 he invited Churchill to a special Cabinet to discuss the imminent surrender of Germany. Present at the Cabinet were four members of the War Cabinet—Lloyd George, Bonar Law, George Barnes and Smuts—plus Milner, Balfour, Sir Eric Geddes, Churchill and Sir Henry Wilson. Lloyd George read out two telegrams from Clemenceau, describing the interviews between Foch and the German Armistice Commission. During the Cabinet meeting, several telegrams were brought in, saying that the Kaiser[1] had escaped to Holland, and that several German towns were in the hands of revolutionaries.

At five o'clock on the morning of November 11 the German Armistice Commission at Compiègne finally accepted the Allied terms. The Germans agreed to halt all military activity on land, sea and air, by eleven o'clock that same day; to evacuate Belgium, France, Luxembourg and Alsace Lorraine within fourteen days; to remove their troops from the Rhineland; to allow the Allied and United States armies to occupy all of Germany west of the Rhine as well as the principal crossings of the Rhine; and to surrender immediately to the Allies a vast quantity of military stores.

During the morning, Churchill presided over a meeting of the heads of departments at the Ministry of Munitions. They discussed the sale of surplus munitions stocks, and agreed that the Labour department of the Ministry should be transferred to the Ministry of Labour. There was some discussion about the conversion of munitions factories to peace time production. Shortly before eleven o'clock, Churchill returned to his room. In *The World Crisis*, he described the ensuing scene:

It was a few minutes before the eleventh hour of the eleventh day of the eleventh month. I stood at the window of my room looking up Northumberland Avenue towards Trafalgar Square, waiting for Big Ben to tell that the

[1] Wilhelm II, 1859–1941. First cousin of George V. Succeeded his father as German Emperor, 1888. Abdicated, 9 November 1918. In exile in Holland from 1918 until his death.

War was over. My mind strayed back across the scarring years to the scene and emotions of the night at the Admiralty when I listened for these same chimes in order to give the signal of war against Germany to our Fleets and squadrons across the world. And now all was over! The unarmed and untrained island nation, who with no defence but its Navy had faced unquestioningly the strongest manifestation of military power in human record, had completed its task. Our country had emerged from the ordeal alive and safe, its vast possessions intact, its war effort still waxing, its institutions unshaken, its people and Empire united as never before. Victory had come after all the hazards and heartbreaks in an absolute and unlimited form. All the Kings and Emperors with whom we had warred were in flight or exile. All their Armies and Fleets were destroyed or subdued. In this Britain had borne a notable part, and done her best from first to last.

The minutes passed. I was conscious of reaction rather than elation. The material purposes on which one's work had been centred, every process of thought on which one had lived, crumbled into nothing. The whole vast business of supply, the growing outputs, the careful hoards, the secret future plans—but yesterday the whole duty of life—all at a stroke vanished like a nightmare dream, leaving a void behind. My mind mechanically persisted in exploring the problems of demobilization. What was to happen to our three million Munition workers? What would they make now? How would the roaring factories be converted? How in fact are swords beaten into ploughshares? How long would it take to bring the Armies home? What would they do when they got home? . . .

And then suddenly the first stroke of the chime. I looked again at the broad street beneath me. It was deserted. From the portals of one of the large hotels absorbed by Government Departments darted the slight figure of a girl clerk, distractedly gesticulating while another stroke of Big Ben resounded. Then from all sides men and women came scurrying into the street. Streams of people poured out of all the buildings. The bells of London began to clash. Northumberland Avenue was now crowded with people in hundreds, nay, thousands, rushing hither and thither in a frantic manner, shouting and screaming with joy. I could see that Trafalgar Square was already swarming. Around me in our very headquarters, in the Hotel Metropole, disorder had broken out. Doors banged. Feet clattered down corridors. Everyone rose from the desk and cast aside pen and paper. All bounds were broken. The tumult grew. It grew like a gale, but from all sides simultaneously. The street was now a seething mass of humanity. Flags appeared as if by magic. Streams of men and women flowed from the Embankment. They mingled with torrents pouring down the Strand on their way to acclaim the King. Almost before the last stroke of the clock had died away, the strict, war-straitened, regulated streets of London had become a triumphant pandemonium. At any rate it was clear that no more work would be done that day. Yes, the chains which had held the world were broken. Links of imperative need, links of discipline, links of brute force, links of self-sacrifice, links of terror, links of honour which had held our nation, nay, the greater part of mankind, to grinding toil, to a compulsive cause—every one had snapped upon a few strokes of the clock. Safety, freedom, peace, home, the dear one back at the fireside—all after fifty-two months of gaunt distortion. After fifty-two months of making burdens grievous to be borne and binding them on men's backs, at last, all at once, suddenly and everywhere the burdens were cast down.

Clementine Churchill, who was expecting her fourth child that week, arrived at the Ministry of Munitions, to be with her husband at that historic moment. They decided to go together to 10 Downing Street, to offer their congratulations to Lloyd George. On entering their car, some twenty people jumped excitedly upon it, and a wildly cheering crowd surrounded them as they drove slowly forward. That night Churchill dined at 10 Downing Street with Lloyd George. The only other guests were F. E. Smith and Sir Henry Wilson. Churchill later recalled, in *The Aftermath*, how the conversation 'ran on the great qualities of the German people, on the tremendous fight they had made against three-quarters of the world, on the impossibility of rebuilding Europe without their help'. His own mood, he wrote, 'was divided between anxiety for the future and desire to help the fallen foe'. The news that evening was of near-starvation in Germany, and the continuing spread of Bolshevism in Russia. Churchill suggested that Britain immediately rush 'a dozen great ships crammed with provisions' into Hamburg. Lloyd George, he wrote, 'balanced the project with favouring eye'. That night Sir Henry Wilson noted in his diary: 'We discussed many things but principally the coming General Election!' And he added: 'LG wants to shoot the Kaiser. Winston does not. . . .'

Eleven years later, in *The Aftermath*, Churchill recalled the emotions of that first day of peace, and the excitement of the victory celebrations:

Who shall grudge or mock these overpowering entrancements? Every Allied nation shared them. Every victorious capital or city in the five continents reproduced in its own fashion the scenes and sounds of London. These hours were brief, their memory fleeting; they passed as suddenly as they had begun. Too much blood had been spilt. Too much life-essence had been consumed. The gaps in every home were too wide and empty. The shock of an awakening and the sense of disillusion followed swiftly upon the poor rejoicings with which hundreds of millions saluted the achievement of their hearts' desire. There still remained the satisfactions of safety assured, of peace restored, of honour preserved, of the comforts of fruitful industry, of the home-coming of the soldiers; but these were in the background; and with them all there mingled the ache for those who would never come home.

9

Electioneering and Cabinet Making

W HEN the war ended on 11 November 1918, Lloyd George had been Prime Minister for almost two years. Of the nine Ministers who had served at different times in his War Cabinet, he alone had been a member of the Liberal Party. Of the other eight ministers in the War Cabinet, five had been Conservatives, two Labour and one, Smuts, did not belong to a British political party. In the Cabinet itself, at the end of the war, the Liberals held only eight places, as against fourteen Conservative and two Labour. Many members of the Liberal Party bitterly resented the way in which Lloyd George had had become dependent upon Conservative support, and wished, with Asquith's leadership, to regain the power which they had lost when Asquith had resigned in December 1916.

Confident that he could keep his Coalition together in peace as in war, and that he could gather enough Liberal and Labour support to maintain with ease his control over all three parties in Parliament, Lloyd George decided to call an election before the Peace Conference opened in Paris. But many Liberals resented Lloyd George's plan to continue at the head of a predominantly Conservative administration, and the Asquithian Liberals prepared to challenge him at the polls.

On November 18 Churchill appealed to his constituents to support the Coalition Government, whatever their political views:

The victory wh has been won amid these hazards does not belong to any party or to any class. It belongs to all. Every household in the land has borne its share; most bear its scars; many have gained especial honour. We have always moved forward together in a company of many millions of British men & women. The result of these labours is national property. It must on no account be squandered. It must be guarded as a sacred trust. Britons must stand together & hold for all what has been won by all.

During the course of his speech Churchill referred to the question of German reparations. He advised moderation, not wishing to drive Germany into an extreme position:

Whom are we to deal with in Germany? Will those we should deal with this month be in power next month? Will the next Government be bound by any obligations contracted by this one? What will the next Government be? Will it be a Bolshevist anarchy completing the ruin of the German nation, or will it be a military government crouching for a spring at the Rhine? Evidently we must proceed with great care and vigilance, seeking so to influence matters that a government might be created in Germany strong enough to shoulder the burden of reparation and yet not capable of renewing the war. Such a problem will tax to the utmost limits all the resources of wisdom, of virtue and of statecraft which the victorious Powers command. It will never be solved unless they stand together armed and active, resolved not to be defrauded of their just rights on the one hand nor to be drawn into extravagances by the fullness of their victory on the other.

Churchill's moderate sentiments provoked an immediate protest. A leading Dundee Liberal, James Foggie,[1] writing to him on November 21, explained the strong anti-German feeling in the constituency:

Now that we have beaten the Germans we must deal with them as they did to the French in 1870–1871. You must be able in your address on Tuesday to explain 'Unconditional Surrender'.

I think the great card to play & one which will give you a huge victory, is that you declare, 'that Germany must pay this country & the other allied Nations, all expenses caused by the War'.

Germany started the War, & has been defeated, therefore it stands to reason she must pay. Had Germany beaten our Empire she certainly without any doubt, would have made us pay all expenses.

Dundee will stand nothing else. Dundee has given over 30,000 soldiers. Almost 10% over 3,000 have been killed.

Churchill replied on the following day, defending his position, and that of the Government, in favour of a negotiated, rather than an imposed or harsh, settlement:

I am in cordial sympathy with your feeling that we must not allow ourselves to be deprived of the full fruits of victory. But do you think that you are quite right in saying that we ought to impose upon Germany the same sort of

---

[1] James K. Foggie, 1866–1947. A Dundee art dealer, active in local politics; for several years he was a Liberal representative on the Dundee City Council.

terms as they imposed upon France in 1871? Surely the forcible annexation by Germany of Alsace-Lorraine against the will of the people who lived there and who wanted to stay with France was one of the great causes at work in Europe all these years to bring about the present catastrophe. If we were now to take provinces of Germany inhabited by Germans who wished to stay with Germany, and hold them down under a foreign government, should we not run the risk of committing the same crime as the Germans committed in 1871 and bringing about the same train of evil consequences? . . . The Allies have demanded from the Germans Reparation, i.e. payment by them for the damage which they have done. This may easily amount to more than £2,000,000,000. They have not asked them to pay for the expenses of the war which I see have been calculated at £40,000,000,000. The reason why they have not done so is because they believed that it was physically impossible for them to pay, and that a Treaty drawn up on that basis would be found afterwards to be valueless. . . .

Churchill's support for Lloyd George was also not approved by a constituency which had been strongly pro-Asquithian throughout the war. On November 23 the *Dundee Courier* warned of 'the rush and hush by which the election has been engineered and is to be pushed through', and described Churchill as 'one of the barnacle Ministers who are determined to cling to the rock of political power at all costs'. Lord Beaverbrook, a Conservative, and until three weeks before a Cabinet colleague, wrote to Churchill on November 26:

Speaking to you as a friend, I think you are making a mistake. You have accepted the Coalition compromise as a necessary expedient for carrying on the King's Government but not from the heart. Its policy is not really to your mind. Believe me, any man makes a great mistake who compromises on great issues of principle however pressing the necessity may appear to be, and I believe you would have been wiser to take the alternative course.

Although Churchill accepted a predominantly Conservative and Unionist Coalition, he had already tried to liberalize the content of Lloyd George's election programme. On November 20 he had made several alterations in the Government's election manifesto, designed to make it more Liberal in content; and on November 21 he had suggested the inclusion in the manifesto of a promise to enquire into war profits, writing to Lloyd George:

The old Tories have nothing to fear from it, & everybody else except the profiteerers will be enchanted. Why *should* anybody make a great fortune out of the war? While everybody has been serving the Country, profiteerers & contractors & shipping speculators have gained fortunes of a gigantic charac-ter. Why shd we be bound to bear the unpopularity of defending old Runciman's[1] ill-gotten gains? I wd reclaim everything above say £10,000 (to let the small fry off) in reduction of the War Debt.

Churchill's fourth child, a daughter, had been born four days after the armistice. She was christened Marigold Frances, but known to her parents as 'the Duckadilly'. Marigold's birth had been a difficult one, and Churchill was anxious to remain in London with his wife and children. But on November 25 he hurried to Dundee to rally support for himself, and for the Coalition.

At a speech in the Kinnaird Hall on November 26, Churchill set out his election pledges to the Dundee Liberal Association. On the platform he was supported both by the leader of the Dundee Liberals, Sir George Ritchie,[2] and by the Chairman of the Dundee Unionists, Sir George Baxter.[3] In his speech Churchill insisted on the importance of maintaining the Liberal principles of justice, freedom, tolerance and humanity 'which, not less than our Fleets and Armies, have carried our fame into every land'. It was, he argued, British political ideals, British institutions, the 'British way of doing things', which had to be preserved. 'Let us be very careful,' he warned, 'not to catch the infection of German ideas at the moment when we have defeated the German armies. . . . Let us preserve our great and old renown as the first of the free and liberal nations of the world, as the birthplace of Parliaments, as the pioneer of popular government, and as an unfailing fountain of enlightened thought and humanitarian sentiment.'

Churchill then turned to the question of reparations. He still refused to accept the popular demand that the Germans should pay all the expenses incurred by the Allies during the war, but he was firm in his attitude to Germany's responsibility for the war:

Practically the whole German nation was guilty of the crime of aggressive war conducted by brutal and bestial means. It is no use their pretending that their late Government is solely to blame. They were all in it, and they must all suffer for it. In particular, individuals against whom definite breaches of the

---

[1] Walter Runciman, 1847–1937. Shipowner. Created Baronet, 1906. President of the United Kingdom Chamber of Shipping, 1910–11. Liberal MP, 1914–18. Created Baron, 1933. Father of Walter Runciman (Churchill's Cabinet colleague from 1908–16). In his will he left £2,388,453, on which £1,176,130 were paid in death duties.

[2] George Ritchie, 1849–1921. Grocer's apprentice, 1865. Opened his own wholesale grocery and provision business in the 1880s. Elected to the Dundee Town Council, 1889. Finance Convenor, 1892–3. City Treasurer, 1895–1906. President of the Dundee Liberal Association, 1907–21. Knighted, 1910.

[3] George Washington Baxter, 1853–1926. Chairman of the Dundee and District Liberal-Unionist Association, 1886–1910. Unsuccessful Unionist candidate, 1895, 1908 and 1910. Knighted, 1904. Chairman of the Dundee Unionist Association, 1910–19. Created Baronet, 1918. President of the Scottish Unionist Association, 1919.

laws of war on land and sea can be proved or who can be proved to have treated prisoners with cruelty should be brought to trial and punished as criminals, however highly placed. Alsace-Lorraine must be completely restored to France. Poland must be reconstituted a nation with access to the sea, and Germany must give up her Polish provinces. None of the German colonies will ever be restored to Germany, and none of the conquered parts of Turkey will ever be restored to Turkey. Whoever has them, they will not. Reparation must be made by Germany to the utmost limit possible for the damage she has done. I cordially sympathise with those who say 'Make them pay the expenses of the war'. If the Allies have not claimed this it is for one reason only. It is not physically possible for them to do so. . . .

Churchill went on to point out how much of the world was 'in various stages of anarchy and starvation', how in Germany, there was 'a population already famishing and a government in revolution'. It was these facts, he told his audience, that were the real suffering which Germany had brought upon itself. 'People call for the punishment of Germany,' he said, 'and are afraid that she will get off lightly. They need not alarm themselves. That punishment will be terrible beyond all previous record.'

Churchill called for a national effort in peacetime no less determined than that of wartime:

Why should war be the only purpose capable of uniting us in comradeship. Why should war be the only cause large enough to call forth really great and fine sacrifices? Look at the wonderful superb things people will do to carry on a war and to win a victory. Look what they will give up. Look what toils they achieve—what risks, what sufferings, what marvellous ingenuity, and what heroic and splendid qualities they display. All for war. Nothing is too good for war. Why cannot we have some of it for peace? Why is war to have all the splendours, all the nobleness, all the courage and loyalty? Why should peace have nothing but the squabbles and the selfishness and the pettiness of daily life? Why if men and women, all classes, all parties, are able to work together for five years like a mighty machine to produce *destruction*, can they not work together for another five years to produce *abundance*?

All the arts and science that we used in war are standing by us now ready to help us in peace. All the organised power which moved the fleets and armies, which hunted the submarines in the depths of the sea, which made us the victors in the air, which produced unlimited munitions of every intricate kind—all the clever brains, true brave hearts, strong unwearied hands—all are available. Only one thing do we require—a common principle of action, a plain objective, that everyone can understand and work for, as he worked to beat the German. Without this we cannot succeed. But surely we have a common purpose? Surely this period of reconstruction may be looked upon as if it were a part of the war? Surely if the sense of self-preservation enabled us to combine to conquer the same sense of self-preservation should enable us to restore and revive our prosperity? . . .

In his peroration Churchill declared:

Five years of concerted effort by all classes, like what we have given in the war, but without its tragedies, would create an abundance and prosperity in this land, aye, throughout the world, such as has never yet been known or dreamt of. Five years of faction, of bickering, of class jealousies and Party froth, will not merely not give us prosperity, it will land us in utter and universal privation.

The Choice is in our own hands. Like the Israelites of old, blessing and cursing is set before us. To-day we can have the greatest failures or the greatest triumph—as we choose. There is enough for all. The earth is a generous mother. Never, never did science offer such fairy gifts to man. Never did their knowledge and organisation stand so high. Repair the waste. Rebuild the ruins. Heal the wounds. Crown the victors. Comfort the broken and broken-hearted. There is the battle we have now to fight. There is the victory we have now to win. Let us go forward together.

Throughout Churchill's speech there had been much heckling. 'The meeting last night,' he wrote to his wife on November 27, 'was the roughest I have ever seen in Dundee,' and he went on to explain why:

Usually at elections when each side has its champions, the opposition go to their own meeting and let off steam in cheering sentiments which they admire; but now, when there is practically no effective opposition or counter-case being unfolded, all the extremists crowded to my meeting, filling it an hour and a half before the advertised time, in order to make a demonstration on their own. Both outside and inside the hall there was a good deal of disorderly hostility, consisting almost entirely of Bolshevik elements. Another current was the discharged soldiers who pressed their own interests. I think I was very successful in dealing with one of the most turbulent meetings I have ever addressed, but I had to scrap entirely my speech and trust in the main to interruptions and rejoinders, a good many of which came off. We had a great struggle to get into the hall in a very hostile mob. I was afraid for a few moments that Sir George Ritchie would be knocked down. However with great agility he seized his assailant by the throat and succeeded in forcing him under the wheels of a motor-car, whence he was rescued by Archie with some difficulty. The only uncertain element is the great one, this enormous electorate composed of so many of the poorest people in the country. I am pretty confident, however, that we shall secure very large majorities indeed. . . . There is no doubt that my handling of the meeting last night was a gt success & that the whole position is becoming orderly & solid.

Churchill left Dundee in the night sleeper on November 28, reaching London on the following day, and leaving Jack Seely behind to continue the campaign on his behalf. On December 3 he returned to Dundee, and on the following day he wrote to a former Liberal MP, Sir Robert Perks,[1] reiterating his moderate approach to reparations. 'I do not consider that we should be justified,' he wrote, 'in enforcing any demand which had the effect of reducing for an indefinite period the mass of the working class population of Germany to a condition of sweated labour and servitude, as such a state of things would re-act on our own labour standards in this country in one form or another.'

Speaking at Lochee, in his constituency, on December 4, Churchill tried to switch the emphasis from foreign to domestic issues. He chose a radical theme. 'His announcement that the Government has definitely decided to nationalize the railways,' declared the *Dundee Advertiser* on December 5, 'is the most important concerning domestic policy that has been made for many years . . . on the whole we think the news will be received with satisfaction.'

Churchill returned to London on December 7. Three days later he returned to Dundee, where he repeated his demand for the rapid nationalization of the railways. So long as the railways were in private hands, he said, 'they had to be managed from the point of view of immediate and direct profit'. But, he went on, 'it might even pay the State to run the railways at a loss if by developing industries, creating new ones, reviving agriculture, and placing the trader in closer contact with his markets, they stimulated a great development at home'. Britain, he asserted, 'could not face the great questions of land settlement, new industries and extended production unless they had control of the means of transportation'. Churchill then set out his general view of capitalism:

They were all aware of the state of mind of some people who vilified the capitalist system, but it was the only system that had been invented as a substitute for slavery.

There was a great distinction between capital and monopoly. Socialism attacked capital. But if the capitalist system were to survive, as he believed it would, as the mainspring of every form of civilisation, it was essential there should be just laws to regulate the acquisition of wealth.

Monopolies should be controlled in the general interest. Taxation should be levied so far as possible in proportion to ability to pay. There should be

---

[1] Robert William Perks, 1849–1934. Railway lawyer. Liberal MP, 1892–1910. Treasurer of the Liberal League, 1902. Chairman of the Metropolitan District Railway, during conversion from steam to electricity, 1902–6. Created Baronet, 1908. First Vice-President, union of Methodist Churches, 1932–3. A leading advocate of the Channel Tunnel.

discrimination between earned and unearned incomes, and, last and most important of all, the great mass of the toilers should be assured of decent minimum standards of life and labour, which would enable them to secure the means of rearing a family in health and honour.

On December 11 Churchill spoke to some 800 of his constituents at Broughty Ferry. The first two-thirds of his speech was devoted to peace-making, and to the problems of the 'oppressed nationalities, held down under alien domination, trying to get free or get back to the larger groupings of their own race to which they belonged'. The frontiers of Europe, he said, must be redrawn 'in broad conformity with the group-ings of the populations'. He spoke also of the importance of 'a permanent League of Nations to render future wars impossible', and urged that such a League must concentrate above all on preventing secret arma-ments.

On December 12, at a final rally of his supporters, Churchill stressed the need for a united front at the Peace Conference. 'The last lingering hope of the Hun,' he declared, 'was that the British people would be found disunited.' On December 13 he sent his wife an account of the closing phases of the campaign.

We had a big wind up last night in the Kinnaird Hall, and I made a most successful speech to an almost entirely friendly audience. The opposition were present, but their interruptions only gave me opportunities of which I took the fullest advantage. Mr Scrymgeour[1] is counting on some support from among the women, but our information is that this will not be formidable. Everything we can hear from the soldiers, and the demeanour of all Service men met with, indicates that their voting will be enormously Coalition. Brown,[2] the second Labour candidate, is in full retreat from the Bolshevism of a fortnight ago. His placard today is 'Vote for Brown and bury Bolshevism'. I am contemplating a counter-placard 'Vote against Bolshevism and bury Brown'.

Altogether I think the chances of a great majority are very good, and it is not impossible that it may be the greatest majority ever yet recorded at a British election. Still, a majority of one is sufficient. Sir George Ritchie is quite satisfied with the course of the contest, and places the figure very high, so high indeed that I will not commit myself to it on paper before the event.

Asquith is having a very rough time in East Fife, and is being subjected to

[1] Edwin Scrymgeour, 1866-1947. The son of a pioneer of the Scottish Temperance Movement. Inaugurated the Prohibition Party in Dundee, November 1901, and fought six elections at Dundee as a Prohibitionist candidate. He was finally elected (by defeating Churchill) in 1922, and remained an MP until 1931.

[2] James S. Brown. Member of the Dundee Trades Council, 1917. Unsuccessful Labour Candidate for Dundee, 1918. President of the Dundee Trades and Labour Party, 1920.

abominable baiting by a gang of discharged soldiers. I do hope it will be all right for the poor old boy. I have been sorely tempted to take up the cudgels for him, but it would have caused many complications here and elsewhere. . . .[1]

Both the local papers have been working splendidly, and have shown the greatest cleverness in their advocacy. There is no doubt that my time has been in every respect well-spent. I shall drive twice round the constituency tomorrow morning and visit all the polling booths, and then catch the 2.47 to Edinburgh, where I shall dine. There is no use my remaining here after darkness sets in.

Churchill had taken the opportunity, on December 12, of visiting the Leuchars Air Station, where he had spoken to several of the young pilots. On December 13 he invited two of them to lunch with him in Dundee, a welcome break in the tumult of the election campaign. That day he wrote to his wife:

One of them is only 21, and has risen to Colonel by his ability rather than by any great prowess in the field. The other has killed 39 Huns, and has a very great reputation as an 'Ace'. It is rather strange for these youths having what undoubtedly must be the greatest and finest part of their lives, with all its tremendous experiences in the region of action lying behind them while yet at an age when most young men are still at their books.

Polling took place on December 14. But the results were not announced until December 28, to allow the soldiers' votes to be counted. Before the results were known, Lloyd George asked Churchill whether he wanted to go to the War Office or the Admiralty. In *The World Crisis* Churchill recalled how, after a night at Blenheim, he had decided on the Admiralty. But Lloyd George would make no final decision, and in a further discussion that week he suggested that Churchill might become Secretary of State for War, combining the War Office with the Air Ministry. Churchill was attracted by this suggestion, but on December 27 Leopold Amery wrote direct to Lloyd George from the Offices of the War Cabinet:

Don't put Churchill in the War Office. I hear from all sorts of quarters that the Army are terrified at the idea. What he needs is a field for adventure and advertisement, and the field that would give him most scope in both directions is the Air Ministry with its interesting potentialities, both commercial and strategical, or, failing that, the Colonial Office, minus the Dominions, where there is a great field for constructive administrative and economic policy. . . .

[1] Asquith was in fact defeated at East Fife by the Conservative candidate, thus losing his seat after thirty-two years. He returned to the House of Commons in February 1920, after a by-election at Paisley, just outside Glasgow.

In the week before Christmas, Churchill discussed with Lloyd George the other ministerial appointments. Lloyd George asked Churchill to put his views in writing, which he did on December 26. He wanted as many Liberals as possible in the Cabinet, and set out his ideas on its composition:

My dear Prime Minister,

Here is the letter about the new Government wh you have asked me to write you.

I assume that Asquith & his friends will stop outside. I hope however that bitterness will be assuaged by his going to the Peace Conference. I consider that if you are the leader of the majority of the Liberals you shd become leader of the Liberal party & that this issue shd be raised as soon as possible. The two matters may perhaps be made mutually to help each other.[1]

Unless someone of real political consequence like Asquith becomes Lord Chancellor it does not seem to me necessary to include that office in the limited Cabinet you have in mind. The Lord Chancellor cd if you found it convenient be treated as a high judge & as Speaker of the House of Lords rather than as a politician.

I assume secondly a Cabinet composed of the leading political figures who follow the Prime Minister holding between them all the principal offices of State. Having regard to the offices which must be represented I do not see how this can be less than 14 or 15. Of this I suppose the Unionists wd constitute at least half.

You wd no doubt wish to have near you 3 or 4 men of experience & party weights unburdened by departments &c & Bonar Law as Leader of the House (Query as 1st Lord of the Treasury) Curzon Lord President, Milner (or Rufus) Lord Privy Seal & Barnes Duchy of Lancaster. Thus yr War Cabinet system wd be merged in the larger body required for peace purposes without being definitely abandoned. The old sinecure offices are intended to supply this non-departmental element in the Cabinet & by using them the foreign term 'Minister without portfolio' can be avoided.

The Secretaries of State are it seems to me fairly obvious now; but there is a point about Jews wh occurs to me—you must not have too many of them. Montagu represents the Indian policy of the Government & therefore counts for more than a mere administrator. After Peace is settled Balfour will probably retire & surely then Rufus shd be his successor at the Foreign Office. Indeed I shd like to see him join the Government now as Lord Privy Seal—a close & old friend at yr side. The advent of the Infant Samuel[2] to the Home

[1] Asquith did not go to the Paris Peace Conference, although he himself asked Lloyd George if he could go. Nor would he give up the Leadership of the Liberal Party, even when it became clear that Lloyd George commanded the support of a majority of Liberal MPs. No Asquithian Liberal was invited to join the Coalition.

[2] Herbert Louis Samuel, 1870–1963. Liberal MP, 1902–18; 1929–35. Chancellor of the Duchy of Lancaster, 1909–10. Postmaster-General, 1910–14. President of the Local Govern-

Office shd be considered in the light of the two above-mentioned facts. Three Jews among only 7 Liberal cabinet ministers might I fear give rise to comment.

Churchill went on to advise Lloyd George about several other Ministerial posts:

. . . Milner wd be vy good at the Colonies. He ought to be given 50 millions a year to develop our tropical possessions, & at least 20 millions worth of orders for ironmongery ought to be placed promptly in the Munition works. Walter Long on this plan wd go to the Admiralty wh I expect he wd enjoy vy much.[1] For the Home Office I suggest Fisher.[2] You need a new man in the Cabinet & his political attainments are superior to those of any other officers of high rank. I think he is the best of all yr discoveries. . . .

Next, Churchill turned to his own future; he still wanted above all to go to the Admiralty, but accepted that this could not be:

You tell me that you have destined for me the task of dispersing & liquidating our Armies & Air Force & of building from the residue the armies & the aviaries of the future. I had as you know other ideas but I will do my best to serve you as you wish. It is a vy important & difficult task & you do me honour in choosing me for it. . . .

The rest of Churchill's letter, a further four pages, dealt with all the remaining Cabinet appointments. Of their friend F. E. Smith he wrote: 'I hope you will find it possible to include the Attorney General in the Cabinet. He can help you vy much with the Tory democrats. His exclusion wd I think chill a loyal friendship. He can earn £20–25,000 a year from an entirely independent position. . . .'[3]

For another of his friends, Churchill also sought a Ministerial appointment:

Pensions wd be filled by Jack Seely. The main policy is *Cash* wh comes from the Treasury on the decision of the Cabinet. Its execution requires a sympathetic figure—'one who knows what they went through', who

---

ment Board, 1914–15. Home Secretary, January–December 1916. Knighted, 1920. High Commissioner for Palestine, 1 July 1920–2 July 1925. Home Secretary, 1931–2. Created Viscount, 1937.

[1] Lord Milner did become Colonial Secretary, and Walter Long First Lord of the Admiralty.

[2] Herbert Albert Laurens Fisher, 1865–1940. Historian. Member of the Royal Commission on the Public Services of India, 1912–15 and of the Government Committee on alleged German outrages, 1915. Liberal MP, 1916–26. President of the Board of Education, 1916–22. A British delegate to the League of Nations Assembly, 1920–2. Warden of New College, Oxford, 1925–40. He published his *History of Europe* in 3 volumes in 1935. Governor of the BBC, 1935–9. Order of Merit, 1937. He died after being run down by a lorry, while on his way to preside at an Appeal Tribunal for conscientious objectors.

[3] Lloyd George in fact decided to make F. E. Smith Lord Chancellor, and he was raised to the peerage as Baron Birkenhead.

understands how to talk to them, & someone who can stand Parliamentary badgering. It involves dealing with a mass of detail in a humane & warm hearted spirit—not entirely without knowledge of politics. . . . If you are not attracted by this plan perhaps you will consider Seely for Postmaster-General. I do not think he will take an under-Secretaryship, now that Peace has come. . . .[1]

Churchill also suggested that his cousin Lord Londonderry[2] might be made Under-Secretary of State for War, to be Churchill's own spokesman in the House of Lords. 'It is important when dealing with the Army,' Churchill explained, 'to have the social side not entirely unrepresented. You yourself found Derby an assistance in this respect. If these young men of great worldly position are sincerely desirous of aiding a democratic & progressive policy, I think it is right to associate them directly with the Administration. . . .' Churchill's letter ended:

I hope you will endeavour to gather together all forces of strength & influence in the country & lead them along the paths of science & organisation to the rescue of the weak & poor. That is the main conception I have of the Victory Government & from it we may draw the prosperity & stability of the Empire.

I appreciate vy much indeed your having wished me to write fully to you on all these interesting points.

Yours always
W

On December 28 the election results were published. The Coalition Conservatives had won 335 seats, the Coalition Liberals 133, the Coalition Labour, 10; a total of 478 seats for Lloyd George. Opposed to him were 73 Sinn Fein, 63 Labour, 28 Liberal, 23 Conservative, 25 Irish Unionist and 7 Irish Nationalist MPs. The Liberal Party share of the vote had fallen from fifty per cent in December 1910 to twenty-five per cent in December 1918, making the Conservatives once more the dominant party in the state, for the first time in thirteen years. Churchill himself had been returned by what the *Dundee Advertiser* called 'an immense majority' of 15,365.

On the morning of December 29 Churchill went to 10 Downing

---

[1] Seely did agree to become an Under-Secretary, at the Air Ministry, and was given effective day-to-day responsibility for air policy, under Churchill's overall control.

[2] Charles Stewart Henry Vane-Tempest-Stewart, Viscount Castlereagh, 1878–1949. Conservative MP, 1906–15. Succeeded his father as Marquess of Londonderry, 1915. Served on the western front as 2nd in Command, Royal Horse Guards, 1916–17. Succeeded Seely as Under-Secretary of State for Air, 1920–1. Minister of Education and Leader of the Senate, Government of Northern Ireland, 1921–6. Returned to Westminster as First Commissioner of Works, 1928–9 and 1931; and as Secretary of State for Air and Lord Privy Seal, 1931–5.

Street, where Lloyd George asked him finally to decide between War and Air, or the Navy. That same day he replied from the Ministry of Munitions:

My dear Prime Minister,

I realise that you ought to have a speedy answer to the question you put to me this morning abt going to the WO or the Admy.

My heart is in the Admy. There I have long experience, & any claim I may be granted in public good will will always rest on the fact that 'The Fleet was ready'.

In all the circumstances of the present situation I think I shd add more weight to yr administration there than at the War Office.

There will be a good reason for connecting the Air with the Admy, for though aeroplanes will never be a substitute for armies, they will be a substitute for many classes of warships. The technical development of the air falls naturally into the same sphere as the mechanical development of the Navy; & this becomes increasingly true the larger the aeroplane grows.

There, I have no doubt what my choice shd be.

Yrs
W

Cabinet-making began at once. 'I am still in slight suspense as to where Winston & I shall be this time next week,' Edward Marsh wrote to Lord Esher on 1 January 1919—'Anyhow it will be somewhere that gives him a good chance.' On January 3 Bonar Law wrote to Lloyd George to say that he had put Churchill in the list of new Ministers 'as I believe you think this is best & I am not sure that it is not right, though it will not be popular. . . .' The new Cabinet was not finally decided upon until January 9. 'Tonight we hear that Winston comes to the WO,' Sir Henry Wilson wrote in his diary.

When the news that Churchill was to become Secretary of State for War and Air was known publicly, there was adverse comment in the Press. If, declared Lord Northcliffe's *Daily Mail* on January 11, the news meant that 'we are to return to the chaos from which we were delivered in 1917 with the formation of an Air Ministry . . . this union under such a man as Mr Churchill is asking for trouble, and is a sure cause of future mischief. . . .' The ultra-Conservative *Morning Post* was critical that Churchill had even the War Office to control, declaring, in a leading article on the same day:

Mr Churchill began in the Army; but he found early occasion to leave it, and his departure, we have heard, was not regretted. Since then he has wandered far, but we have watched his brilliant and erratic course in the confident expectation that sooner or later he would make a mess of anything he undertook. Character is destiny; there is some tragic flaw in Mr Churchill which determines him on every occasion in the wrong course. . . .

It is not only that he has vaster opportunities for mischief, but calamitous theories to put into practice. The Army is now in a state in which knowledge, tact, and cordial relations with officers and men are essential. Mr Churchill has that little knowledge which is dangerous; he has no tact, and his relations with the General Staff and with the Army as a whole are not in the least likely to be cordial. It is an appointment which makes us tremble for the future.

AT THE WAR OFFICE, 1919–1921

10

Demobilization

A T the time of the armistice in November 1918 there were nearly three and a half million British soldiers under arms. For two months, in France and Flanders, in Italy and Greece, in Palestine and Mesopotamia, officers and men demanded to be brought home. In camps throughout England they clamoured to return to civilian life. On January 4, a week before Churchill became Secretary of State for War, there were demonstrations by soldiers at Dover and Folkestone demanding immediate demobilization. These demonstrations continued for three consecutive days. On January 7 the War Office announced its demobilization rules. Only men with immediate offers of work would be allowed to leave the Army. A soldier who had served for four months, but had been offered an industrial job, could come home. A soldier who had served for four years, but had been offered no job, must remain in uniform. For three million men this scheme offered no prospect of an early return home, and the unrest continued. On January 9 Sir Douglas Haig telegraphed from France to the War Office, warning that Army morale was in danger of disintegration if the scheme of January 7 were allowed to stand.

On the morning of January 10, Churchill's first day as Secretary of State for War, Sir Henry Wilson went to see him at his room in the Ministry of Munitions to discuss the demobilization crisis. Churchill feared that the unrest would spread to camps throughout Britain. He also feared that widespread disobedience would encourage Bolshevism in Britain. Wilson recorded in his diary how Churchill wanted to bring back from France 'all reliable troops, i.e. Household & Cavalry, Yeomanry, Home County Rgts: etc'.

On January 11 Churchill telegraphed to Sir Douglas Haig, asking him to come as soon as possible to London for consultations. 'In conjunction with Eric Geddes,' Churchill telegraphed 'we can then survey the whole position and take definite decisions which are clearly needed.'

On the afternoon of January 12 Churchill saw Sir Henry Wilson, and suggested holding up the demobilization of all men who had served less than two years in France. On this basis, he pointed out, those who had served longest would be released first. 'There is much to be said for his argument. . . .' Wilson noted in his diary that afternoon. 'We must do something drastic to stop the present stampede. . . .'

The problem of demobilization was complicated by the urgent need to organize several Armies of Occupation. In Germany itself the British Government had taken over one of the three Zones of Occupation into which the western provinces of Germany had been divided. Troops had also to be maintained in Palestine, Mesopotamia and India, as well as in England. Sir Douglas Haig estimated that over a million men would be needed for the Armies of Occupation.

On the morning of January 15, Churchill asked Sir Henry Wilson, Sir Douglas Haig, Sir William Robertson, Sir Eric Geddes and Sir Robert Horne[1] to meet him at the War Office. In his diary, Haig re-recorded the course of the discussion. Churchill expressed the view that an Army of Occupation ought to be formed at once 'on some simple principle' and that the remaining forces, both in France and elsewhere, should be demobilized 'as rapidly as possible'. He then asked Haig, who was sitting next to him, for his opinion, and Haig stated that the existing demobilization orders and counter-orders 'had produced a very bad effect on the troops'. The existing army, Haig warned, 'was rapidly disappearing' and if something was not done at once to create an Army of Occupation, 'the Germans would be in a position to negotiate another kind of peace'. There followed an acrimonious exchange between Churchill and Horne, which Haig recorded in his diary:

Sir R. Horne and others pointed out the very serious effect on the public, on the Chambers of Commerce, on the Trades Unions, and other influential trades bodies, if the Demobilisation Scheme were to be now scrapped and another substituted for it. Already great trouble had arisen. Churchill said that he was prepared to face all this in order to get a lasting Peace. Sir R. Horne seemed chiefly to blame for these demobilisation blunders.

[1] Robert Stevenson Horne, 1871–1940. Lecturer in Philosophy; barrister. Assistant In-spector-General of Transportation, with rank of Lieutenant-Colonel, 1917. Director of Department of Materials and Priority, Admiralty, 1917. Director, Admiralty Labour Department, 1918. Third Civil Lord of Admiralty, 1918–19. Knighted, 1918. Conservative MP, 1918–37. Minister of Labour, 1919. President of the Board of Trade, 1920–1. Chancellor of the Exchequer, 1921–2. Delcined office under Bonar Law and turned to the City for employment, where he became Chairman of the Great Western Railway Company, the Burma Corporation, the Zinc Corporation and the Imperial Smelting Corporation, and a Director of many other companies. Created Viscount Horne of Slamannan, 1937.

At Churchill's suggestion, two committees were set up, one under Haig and the other under Sir George Macdonogh, to report within 48 hours on how the Army of Occupation ought to be formed. He urged them to pay special attention to the cost of the extra pay involved for those who were not regular soldiers, but conscripts who would have to be induced to give up their claim to an early demobilization. 'Winston very clear & good,' Wilson noted in his diary.

Haig had also been impressed by Churchill's advocacy of the Armies' case, recording in his diary:

I thought Churchill showed up well at this Conference and by taking this great responsibility so soon after taking over his new Office he made it clear, I think, that he not only has courage, but foresight and a knowledge of Statesmanship. All of these qualities most of his colleagues seem to have lacked so lamentably throughout this war.

With Lloyd George already in Paris for the opening of the Peace Conference, Churchill feared delay in obtaining Cabinet approval for his scheme. On Thursday January 16, while his two committees were still at work, he wrote to the new Chancellor of the Exchequer, Austen Chamberlain,[1] urging an early Cabinet decision, if possible on Monday January 20. Speed, he wrote, 'is very important and under the present pressure the Army is liquefying fast and if we are not careful we will find ourselves without the strong instrument on which our policy in Europe depends in the next few months'.

Austen Chamberlain deprecated haste, replying on January 16:

You are fortunate, if I may judge from your letter, in being able to concentrate on one problem for the moment. Here there are so many questions of equal urgency and so many people from outside the public offices whom it is my business to see that I cannot get on as fast.

Until I see the paper which you propose to circulate on Saturday, and which by the way will not reach me till Sunday morning, I cannot tell what issues are involved in it. But I would beg in any case for a little more time for their consideration before we come to a Cabinet discussion.

At eleven on the morning of January 17 Churchill and his advisers met again at the War Office. The two committees had reached their conclusions. Both Haig and Macdonogh were agreed that all men who had enlisted in 1914 and 1915 would be demobilized as soon as trans-

---

[1] Joseph Austen Chamberlain, 1863–1937. Conservative MP, 1892–1937. Chancellor of the Exchequer, 1903–5. Unsuccessful candidate for the leadership of the Conservative Party, 1911. Secretary of State for India, 1915–1917. Minister without Portfolio, 1918–19. Chancellor of the Exchequer, 1919–21. Lord Privy Seal, 1921–2. Foreign Secretary, 1924–9. Knight of the Garter, 1925. First Lord of the Admiralty, 1931.

port could be arranged to bring them home; a total of 2,200,000 men. All men who had joined the army after 1 January 1916 would be retained as part of the Armies of Occupation. All those who were to be retained would be given extra leave, and substantial increases in pay. Sir Douglas Haig, Sir Eric Geddes and Sir Robert Horne each agreed to this scheme, and Churchill promised it his full ministerial backing.

The War Cabinet met at noon, and again in the afternoon, with Bonar Law in the chair. Churchill explained his scheme in detail, and pointed out that in order to retain all men conscripted in 1916, and 1917 and 1918, it would be necessary to retain compulsory military service, a potentially unpopular move. That evening Bonar Law sent Lloyd George full details of the scheme, which he described as 'as good a proposal as is possible'.

That evening Wilson discussed with Churchill the need to hurry the scheme forward as a matter of urgency. 'I told him,' he recorded, 'that when we had got our scheme through the War Cabinet on Tuesday both he & I ought at once to go over to Paris & get LG to agree to it & get it out without a moment's delay. We are sitting on the top of a mine which may go up at any minute.' That evening Edward Marsh wrote to Lord Esher: 'We are settling down by degrees. It is rather a racket but W is bearing up well & I think he has made a good start.'

On the morning of January 18 the army scheme was circulated to all Cabinet Ministers and War Office departments. At the same time, Churchill also drafted a lengthy letter to Lloyd George, explaining the scheme, and the reasons for it. He intended to send this letter by air to Paris, so that it would reach Lloyd George during January 19. 'I do not think you will get the military authorities to function properly,' Churchill wrote, 'until they are reassured that they are not going to be left without an army.' Under the existing scheme, he added, 'the discipline of the whole Army is being rotted—every platoon simultaneously—by the pulling out of people in ones and twos without any relation to what the ordinary man regards as fair play'. Once the plan for the Armies of Occupation was agreed to, Churchill pointed out, and 'strong forces of moderate dimension' set up for the military needs of Britain, it would then be possible 'to push the others out of doors as fast as they want to go, or even faster'. His letter continued:

I am very anxious about the state of the Army, both in France and at home: it is better now than it was ten days ago, and I hear from various quarters that the statement we prepared and which you issued before I came into office had a very steadying effect. The papers also have seen the red light and have been trying to help as much as possible instead of exciting discontent. But I hear bad reports from J. H. Thomas[1] about the railwaymen; from Haig about the general discontent of the Army in France; and from Robertson so far as home is concerned. French is very worried about the Irish situation, and I have had to slow down the rate of demobilising the few efficient troops we have in that country.

It is really of vital importance to me to get this large scheme of mine settled. A broad and bold handling of the whole problem is required, and I think I have succeeded in grasping it and in evolving a comprehensive and far-reaching plan.

You cannot do better than read the explanatory statement which I have prepared with my own hands and which, subject to certain minor alterations which discussion will suggest, represents the policy I recommend. This statement I want to publish in time to catch the Sunday papers at the end of this week, and I am arranging to prepare the Editors and Proprietors beforehand by conferences and personal interviews, which will occupy the greater portion of my time. I am asking Henry Wilson to go over on Tuesday with the scheme and to obtain your assent to it. If you see objections to it, I will come over myself and discuss it with you. . . .

Together with this letter, Churchill prepared to send Lloyd George his detailed explanatory memorandum, in which he stressed that the Armies of Occupation 'must be strong enough to extract from the Germans, Turks and others, the just terms which the Allies demand'. Such Armies, he added, would have to be 'strong, compact, contented, well-disciplined', if Britain was to make sure that 'we are not tricked of what we have rightfully won'. It was Marshal Foch, Churchill pointed out, who had suggested the figure of 1,150,000 men as the number needed to guard British interests during the period between armistice and peace. The release of the men not needed, Churchill insisted, must appeal 'to a sense of justice and fair play'; for this reason the main considerations chosen to entitle a man to release were length of service, age and wounds. 'If anyone has to stay,' he wrote, 'it must be those who are not the oldest, not those who came the earliest, not those who have suffered the most.'

In his memorandum, Churchill went on to explain that under the plan, young soldiers of 18 who were still in training in England would be sent at once 'to help guard the Rhine Bridgeheads', thereby enabling

[1] James Henry Thomas, 1874–1949. Began work as an errand boy at the age of nine; subsequently an engine-cleaner, fireman, and engine-driver. Labour MP for Derby, 1910–31; National Labour MP, 1931–6. General Secretary, National Union of Railwaymen, 1918–24, and 1924–31. President of the International Federation of Trade Unions, 1920–4. Vice-Chairman of the Parliamentary Labour Party, 1921. Secretary of State for the Colonies in the first Labour Government, 1924. Minister of Employment and Lord Privy Seal, 1929–30. Secretary of State for the Dominions, 1930–5; for the Colonies, 1935–6.

an equal number of men 'old enough to be their fathers', to return home. This scheme would also enable the young soldiers 'to see the German provinces which are now in our keeping and the battlefields where the British army won immortal fame'.

Churchill was unable to send his letter and its enclosures by aeroplane to Paris. The weather was so bad that all channel crossings, both by air and sea, had come to a halt. The documents were too long to send by telegram. He therefore telegraphed to Lloyd George on the evening of January 19 to explain both the difficulties of communication, and, in brief, the scheme itself. 'Without your approval,' he urged, 'all action is paralysed.' Were there to be any further delay, he warned, there would be 'nothing left' of the Army but a 'demoralized and angry mob'.

Before Churchill's telegram reached Paris, he himself was surprised to receive a strongly worded protest from Lloyd George, who had learnt of the scheme in outline from Bonar Law's letter of January 17, and felt he had not been properly consulted. 'The PM was much annoyed,' Sir Maurice Hankey wrote to his deputy, Thomas Jones,[1] on January 18. Lloyd George's letter to Churchill was a forceful rebuke:

I have just heard that you propose bringing before the Cabinet on Tuesday the question of continuing military service for an army of 1,700,000. I am surprised that you should think it right to submit such a scheme to my colleagues before talking it over or at least before submitting it in the first instance to me. It is hardly treating the head of the Government fairly. This is a question not of detail but of first class policy which may involve grave political consequences (it might even produce trouble in the Army) & I ought to have been consulted in the first instance. A memo ought have been sent to me by aeroplane which would have reached me in a few hours.

Please let me know something of your plan at once.

Churchill received Lloyd George's protest on January 20. He at once telegraphed to Lloyd George in defence of his procedure:

Your letter of the 18th instant wh I am very sorry to receive I naturally supposed that you would wish the matter thrashed out here first as obviously the whole scheme had to be brought over to Paris for your consideration and I presume also for approval by Cabinet Colleagues there. Any discussion here could only be purely provisional and designed to clear the way for the case

[1] Thomas Jones, 1870–1955. Lecturer in Political economy at Glasgow University. Joined the Independent Labour Party, 1895. Professor of Economics, Belfast, 1909. Secretary of the National Health Insurance Commission (Wales), 1912. First Assistant Secretary (later Deputy Secretary) to the Cabinet, 1916–30. Member of the Unemployment Assistance Board, 1934–40. President of the University College of Wales, Aberystwyth, 1945–54. Author and administrator.

being put before you in the most convenient form and with preliminary
difficulties swept away. Arrangements had been made to send the whole
scheme to you tomorrow by aeroplane together with my full explanatory
memorandum and either Henry Wilson or I or both of us proposed to come
over Wednesday. Considering the number of departments involved and the
all important share of the Treasury it would have seemed to me quite futile to
come to Paris without obtaining preliminary agreement here. . . .

Briefly the scheme consists in releasing two men out of three and paying the
third man double to finish the job. I am extremely anxious about the present
state of the army and am serving you to the very best of my ability in preparing a comprehensive scheme for your approval.

Lloyd George was not mollified. He still felt that he should have been
consulted about the scheme before it was taken to the Cabinet. During
the afternoon of January 21, Sir Henry Wilson saw Bonar Law, and
then recorded in his diary: 'He told me that LG was angry with
Winston but I explained he had no reason to be.' Churchill himself saw
Bonar Law at six that evening, and explained again both the scheme,
and its urgency. While Churchill was talking to Bonar Law, Wilson
was discussing the scheme with Haig. Wilson recorded in his diary: 'he
is in absolute agreement with me about the necessity of carrying it out'.
Shortly after six o'clock that evening, Lloyd George's Private Secretary,
J. T. Davies, who was at 10 Downing Street, telephoned to the War
Office with a message for Churchill from Paris:

With reference to your telegram, the Prime Minister thinks the figures are
extravagant and far beyond the necessities of the case. If it were published to
the Army that such numbers are to be compulsorily retained, there will be
trouble.

If the German Army is to be demobilized, it is absurd to retain so big an
Army, and German demobilization must be the first step.

The Prime Minister will be glad to see you on Thursday. Meanwhile the
less haste, the greater speed.

As soon as Churchill received this further rebuke he informed Henry
Wilson of what had happened. 'I saw Winston at 7 o'c.,' Wilson wrote
in his diary. 'He had just received a message from LG strongly objecting
to our scheme. He must be *made* to agree. . . . LG won't let Winston
place our scheme before the Cabinet tomorrow but has no objections to
all the members meeting in "conversations". This will give him the
chance of denying, later on, that we put our scheme before the Cabinet.'

Churchill decided to proceed at once with the 'conversations' which
Lloyd George was prepared to allow. On the morning of January 22 he
wrote to Bonar Law to arrange a meeting for three that afternoon in

Bonar Law's room in the House of Commons. Before the meeting, Sir Henry Wilson, General Macdonogh and General Harington looked closely at the scheme in an attempt to prune the numbers needed for the Armies of Occupation. 'We went over our figures & total of 1,200,000,' Wilson wrote in his diary, 'which we might reduce a little but not much. LG writes, wires & telephones from Paris that our figures are fantastic.'

At three that afternoon Churchill went to Bonar Law's room, bringing with him Haig, Wilson, Macdonogh and General Hitchcock.[1] The other Ministers present were Sir Eric Geddes, Walter Long, Austen Chamberlain and Sir Robert Horne. Bonar Law began the discussion by announcing that, on Lloyd George's personal instructions, no decision was to be taken about the demobilization scheme without his participation and suggestions. Churchill then stated the case for the scheme as it stood. Wilson emphasized the urgency of making a public announcement of what they intended to do. The situation was so bad, he explained, 'that even now we dare not give an unpopular order to the troops'. Discipline, Wilson added, 'was a thing of the past'. Haig then declared emphatically, as he recorded in his diary, that if the existing orders were continued, 'by the *middle* of February there will be no organised Army of Occupation. How then can our Government hope to dictate peace terms to the Germans?' Wilson's account of the meeting continued:

Much talk round the plan but Winston & I stuck to it & in the end got an unwilling assent to our proposals. Austen very frightened of the expense. B.L. very determined not to express an opinion. Curzon not present so F.O. not represented. No secretary so no record of the proceedings as B.L. was so frightened of any decision.

As soon as Churchill returned to the War Office he made plans to go to Paris on the following day, in order to put his scheme personally to Lloyd George. He also wrote to Bonar Law in an attempt to enlist his support:

Mr dear Bonar Law,
    I do think you might write a line to the PM to tell him
        (a) that there was a general feeling that something very like this would
            have to be done at once and that Eric Geddes & Horne from their
            end were in agreement with the scheme,

[1] Basil Ferguson Burnett Hitchcock, 1877–1938. Entered Army, 1897. On active service in South Africa, 1899–1900. Director-General of Mobilization, War Office, 1918–19 (with the rank of Brigadier-General). Major-General, in charge of Administration, Aldershot Command, 1921–5. Commanded the 55th (West Lancs) Division, 1926–8; the 4th Indian Division, 1928–30. Lieutenant-General, 1930. Knighted, 1932.

(b) that it is admitted that numbers must be scrutinized further, and
(c) that the pay must be largely increased above present rates but the
   exact amount is under discussion between the various Departments
   affected and the Treasury.

Please do your best to impart to him the impression which I understood you
to have formed, viz., that action is imperative and that no one could suggest a
less objectionable plan.

Please give me a nice and helpful letter to take. I guarantee you a triumphant success in the House of Commons, if nothing goes wrong elsewhere.

Yours ever,
W

On the morning of January 23 Churchill crossed over to France,
accompanied by Sir Douglas Haig, Sir Henry Wilson and General
Macdonogh. All three were 'absolutely agreed', Wilson recorded in his
diary, 'that compulsion is necessary and that our total figure of about
1,200,000 is approximately correct & that no time is to be lost'. Lloyd
George discussed the scheme with them at lunch on January 24. 'We
now discussed it freely,' Haig recorded in his diary, 'and he was quite in
agreement with our views, except that he thought the numbers proposed might be reduced. Churchill put his case with tact, and clearly.'
Within an hour Lloyd George had agreed to Churchill's scheme,
'except', as Wilson recorded, 'that he wants us to keep only 10 Divs in
France instead of 15. . . . So this is splendid.'

Lloyd George's approval was decisive. Churchill and his advisers
went at once to Sir Henry Wilson's room in the Villa Majestic where,
for three hours, they settled the procedure for putting the scheme into
action. Churchill then returned to see Lloyd George, who gave the procedure his approval. Later that evening, Churchill sent Macdonogh
back to London to explain the full details of the scheme to Bonar Law
and Austen Chamberlain.

Churchill and Wilson planned to return to London on January 27, to
obtain final Cabinet sanction to the scheme on the following day at
three o'clock, and to announce the scheme to the Press at five o'clock.
From that moment, Wilson wrote in his diary on January 24, 'the great
adventure of "compulsing" a million men in the time of peace to serve
abroad will have begun'. There was not a moment to lose, he added,
'as all our power over the Army is slipping away'. That night Churchill
wrote to his wife: 'have made good progress with my business & the
generals are quite content'.

While Churchill was working out the final details of the scheme in
Paris on the morning of January 25, General Macdonogh was explain-

ing it to Bonar Law in London. Bonar Law was not content, and at once wrote in protest to Lloyd George. He had spoken, he informed Lloyd George, to three politicians, H. A. L. Fisher, Sir Laming Worthington-Evans and Major Baird.[1] Each had taken the view, he wrote, that to continue compulsory military service 'would be regarded by the public as inconsistent with the speeches made by the candidates at the election'. No one, Bonar Law told Lloyd George, was a better judge of the 'political dangers than you are'. But, he added, 'I doubt whether you fully realise the political dangers of the course proposed'. Bonar Law was particularly worried by the proposal to explain the scheme to the Press, which, he wrote, 'I believe to be Churchill's idea'.

Bonar Law's letter reached Lloyd George in Paris on the morning of January 27. He at once sent it to Churchill with the covering note: 'Please consider very carefully.' That afternoon Churchill sent Lloyd George a 1,300 word answer to Bonar Law's complaints. 'Compared to the French and American forces,' he pointed out, 'our contingent will be extremely small. We are thus reducing our burden by regularising our organisation.' In his letter, Bonar Law had asked Lloyd George to hold up Churchill's scheme until the Armies of Occupation could be built up on a voluntary basis, avoiding altogether the need to continue conscription. 'It is quite absurd,' Churchill wrote in his reply, 'to expect that these vitally necessary forces can be provided during the present year on a voluntary basis. This can only be provided on a compulsory basis pending the creation and organisation of voluntary forces, about which no time will be lost.'

Churchill strongly challenged Bonar Law's request not to announce the scheme publicly. It was quite wrong, he insisted, to 'live from hand to mouth and from month to month as if we were nursing a guilty secret in the hopes of something turning up to remove the difficulties'. It would be a mistake, he added, to 'shrink from stating the true facts to the public'.

Churchill ended his letter by protesting that Bonar Law had included Major Baird in the list of the three 'politicians' whom he had consulted: 'I really think it a pretty strong order that the opinion of the late Under Secretary to the Air Board should be cited in this connection. I should

[1] John Lawrence Baird, 1874–1941. Entered Diplomatic Service, 1896. Acting Agent and Consul-General, Abyssinia, 1902. Conservative MP, 1910–25. Served as an Intelligence Officer (Major) on the western front, 1914–15. Parliamentary Secretary to the Air Board, December 1916–January 1919. Succeeded his father as 2nd Baronet, 1920. Parliamentary Under-Secretary of State, Home Office, 1919–22. Minister of Transport, 1922–4. Created Baron Stonehaven, 1925. Governor-General of Australia, 1925–30. Chairman of the Conservative Party Organization, 1931–6. Created Viscount, 1938.

have thought that Baird was sufficiently occupied in deciding whether he would or would not serve as Under Secretary for Munitions.'

Lloyd George accepted Churchill's arguments. That same day, Churchill sent Lord Northcliffe, under a pledge of secrecy, the full details of the scheme, together with a long covering letter in which he set out the reasons for it, and appealing to Northcliffe to do all in his power to support it. 'I do not myself fear at all the course of such a policy,' Churchill added, 'provided that a strong lead is given and that the reasons which make each step necessary are fully and frankly explained.' As soon as Northcliffe received Churchill's letter he telegraphed, from Menton in the South of France: 'All my newspapers will do exactly what you wish on the subject,' and his principal editors were instructed by telegram to publicize and to support the scheme.

With his scheme accepted by Lloyd George, Churchill left Paris with Sir Henry Wilson by the 10.30 train on the evening of January 27, reaching Boulogne at eight the following morning. Churchill wanted to fly back to England from Boulogne, but the weather was too stormy, and the two men continued by boat and train, reaching London at two on the afternoon of January 28. The Cabinet met an hour later. Churchill was tired after his long journey, but explained his scheme once again, 'not very clearly', Sir Henry Wilson noted in his diary. The Cabinet accepted the scheme, for it had, at last, Lloyd George's imprimatur. On the following day Churchill wrote to Lloyd George:

The general feeling of the Cabinet was clearly that the important decision of principle was the continuance of compulsion for the interim period, that this decision was inevitable, and that, once taken, the question of numbers to a hundred thousand or two one way or the other would not make any difference to our Parliamentary or other difficulties. . . .

At five o'clock, as soon as the Cabinet had ended, Churchill returned to the War Office where he explained the scheme to the Press. In his letter of January 29 he told Lloyd George:

The newspaper men took it all like lambs. A. P. Nicholson[1] said he was surprised at the moderation of the figure and that we could get through with so few. I did not tell how the troops would be disposed between the different theatres, and they are naturally keeping Germany well to the front in their very helpful articles.

Everything is to be launched to-morrow and we must await the result. . . .

[1] Arthur Pole Nicholson, 1869–1940. Parliamentary Correspondent of *The Times*, 1908–13. Lobby Correspondent of the *Daily News*, 1914–19. Political Correspondent of the *Daily Chronicle*, 1920–3. Chairman of the Journalists Parliamentary Lobby Committee, 1921–2. Political Correspondent of the *Westminster Gazette*, 1924–9.

On January 30 the details of Churchill's scheme were published in the Press. As he had advised, there was no prevarication or vagueness. Conscription would be retained for the million men needed to form the Armies of Occupation. All men who enlisted before 1916 would be demobilized at once. No one over forty need be retained. In subsequent demobilizations, those who had been wounded would have priority. 'You will be interested to hear,' Frederick Guest wrote to Lloyd George on January 30, 'that Winston's statement re an Emergency Army has been extremely well received; even the Daily News finds it hard to criticise.' Sir Henry Wilson, who returned to Paris on January 31, noted in his diary: 'All my reports seem to think that the men like our Armies of Occupation scheme.' Among Cabinet Ministers, only Austen Chamberlain protested, writing to Churchill on January 30 that 'the burden which you impose upon the Exchequer is measured not only by the number which you ultimately retain, but also by the number which, at the outset, you include within the net'. He felt that the Cabinet's approval for 900,000 men in the Armies of Occupation was in excess of what was needed, and that 800,000 men would be sufficient.

Before Churchill could answer Austen Chamberlain's complaint, a serious crisis arose in France. It had been created by the original demobilization scheme, now abandoned. In Calais, on January 30, five thousand British troops, who had just arrived from England, demanded to be sent back at once. 'Their attitude,' Haig wrote to Churchill on January 31, 'was threatening, insubordinate & mutinous.' On learning of the mutiny, Haig had at once surrounded the camp with two loyal Divisions, complete with machine guns, and had given orders for the mutiny to be brought to an end. 'All preparations were finished yesterday,' Haig informed Churchill in his letter of January 31. 'The camp was then surrounded by machine guns, and General Sandilands[1] at the head of his Brigade (104th) marched into the camp with fixed bayonets, drove the mutineers towards one end, and arrested the 3 ringleaders. . . .'

The mutinous troops were sent off by train to their Divisions throughout France and the occupied zone of Germany. Haig informed Churchill that if immediate action had not been taken, 'the consequences wd have been most far reaching'. In his opinion, he added, it was essential for the three ringleaders to suffer 'the supreme penalty'. If they were not sentenced to death, he wrote, 'the discipline of the whole Army will suffer,

---

[1] Henry George Sandilands, 1864–1930. Entered the army, 1884; Colonel, 1913. Served through the war on the western front (mentioned in despatches five times). Brigadier-General, Commanding the 104th Infantry Brigade, 1918. Retired, 1919.

both immediately & for many years to come'. Churchill did not agree. That afternoon he telegraphed to Haig: 'Unless there was serious violence attended by bloodshed or actual loss of life, I do not consider that the infliction of the death penalty would be justifiable.' In his telegram he went on to explain why he did not support Haig's view that the men must be shot. 'The death penalty,' he wrote, 'should be used only under what may be called life and death conditions, and public opinion will only support it when other men's lives are endangered by criminal or cowardly conduct.'

Haig resented Churchill's intervention. 'I have power by Warrant,' he wrote in his diary on February 1, 'to try by Court Martial and shoot in accordance with Army Act; and no *telegram* from S of S can affect my right to do what I think is necessary for the Army.' But, as Churchill advised, no death sentences were passed on the Calais mutineers.

The pace of demobilization proceeded as quickly as the railway facilities would allow. By January 17 some 530,000 officers and men had already been demobilized; between then and January 31 a further 450,000 had been sent home.

On March 3 Churchill introduced his first Army Estimates to the House of Commons. At the start of his speech he appealed to the House to understand the difficulties with which the War Office was confronted. 'We are,' he said, 'half way between peace and war.' And he continued:

The greater part of Europe and the greater part of Asia are plunged in varying degrees of disorder and anarchy. Vast areas in both these Continents, inhabited by immense and once thriving populations, are convulsed by hunger, bankruptcy, and revolution. The victorious Allies, on whom there rests the responsibility for enabling the world to get to work again, are themselves exhausted in a very serious degree; and all these elements of difficulty and uncertainty vitiate or threaten to vitiate our calculations.

At every point must be added the enormous tangle of winding up the War effort, and adjusting with as little waste as possible the complications of wartime finance. . . .

Churchill went on to stress the overriding financial considerations, which he realized would dominate all future military policy:

The Estimates of this year are made by events; the Estimates of next year will, I hope, be made by policy. . . .

With the passing of war and the disorder which war carries in every sphere
of Government and of private life, finance will once more become the limiting
factor. Every scheme for our future Army and for our future Air Force must
be decided by what it will cost, and by the relation of its total cost to the
resulting war power. Over and over again nations have won wars and then
declined through the disorder of their finances.

Good finance is the golden key to national prosperity and I can assure the
House that I shall do my utmost to secure substantial reductions in military
forces, for without those reductions good finance is impossible.

Churchill went on to summarize his proposals in four parts. Continued demobilization of the 'Armies that won the war'. The establishment, on the basis of war-time compulsory service, of Armies of
Occupation in Germany of approximately 900,000 men, the setting up
of a Volunteer Regular Army and the recruiting of 'the permanent
after-war Army, built up out of new, young recruits, who have to be
trained, who have to be nourished and developed by good feeding, and
who have to reach the age of twenty before they can be sent to the
East. . . .'

At the end of his speech, Churchill declared:

There are two maxims which should always be acted upon in the hour of
victory. All history, all experience, all the fruits of reasoning alike enjoin
them upon us. They are almost truisms. They are so obvious that I hardly
dare to mention them to the House. But here they are. The first is:

'Do not be carried away by success into demanding or taking more than is
right or prudent.'

The second is:

'Do not disband your army until you have got your terms.'

The finest combination in the world is power and mercy. The worst
combination in the world is weakness and strife.

There are some men who write and speak as if all we had to do at this
critical and perilous juncture was to set our demands at the maximum that
appetite can suggest, and to reduce our armed power to the minimum that
parsimony or impatience can dictate. The Government take exactly the
contrary view on both points.

We plead earnestly for the maintenance in these times of trouble of a strong
armed Power, to be used with sober and far-sighted moderation in the
common good.

Believe me, it is far the cheapest, far the safest, and far the surest way to
preserve for long and splendid years the position which our country has
attained.

During the summer Lloyd George became impatient at what he saw
as a slackening of the pace of demobilization, and on August 20 he

wrote to Churchill to complain. In his reply at the beginning of September, Churchill admitted that there had indeed been delays. But he went on to give thirteen specific reasons why demobilization had not always been as speedy as he had hoped:

First. The delay in reaching the settlement with Germany which required us to hold till the middle of July 10 divisions in good order on the Rhine, and made it necessary as a precaution to have the elements of 3 more divisions available in France and Flanders.

Secondly. The failure to reach any settlement with Turkey and the continuous deterioration of the position throughout the Turkish Empire caused by the activities of the Greeks and the Italians.

Thirdly, by the unrest in Egypt due largely to internal causes.

Fourthly. The unrest in Palestine and Syria due to French designs upon the latter province.

Fifthly. The disorders in India and the threatening situation on the Afghan frontier.

Sixthly, by the situation in Ireland requiring the retention of between 50 and 60,000 men.

Seventhly, by the need of preparing for certain action in the event of a strike by the Triple Alliance in accordance with directions received from the Cabinet.

Eighthly. The delay in securing the repatriation of the German prisoners of war and in effecting the repatriation of the Turkish prisoners of war numbering approximately half a million.

Ninethly. The shipping stringency.

Tenthly. The delay in disposing of the immense quantities of stores scattered over all the theatres of war.

Eleventhly. The fact that demobilisation must proceed according to some plan which does not strike the soldiers as grossly unfair. It is here necessary to observe that the army was in a state of general incipient mutiny in January and February of this year. It has been restored to a condition of good discipline and contentment by following in the main the principle of releasing the men with the longest service before the newcomers. Any departure from this principle must be made with the very greatest caution. . . .

Twelfthly. The time necessarily required to create a new volunteer army, battalion by battalion, and send them out to India and the East to relieve the conscription troops now in occupation.

Thirteenthly. All the above problems have been complicated by the difficulty of arriving at fixed conclusions as to the size and cost of the post-war army, and by the uncertainty of the political as well as the military policy in Palestine, Mesopotamia and generally towards the Turkish Empire.

Churchill went on to point out that some of the delays had also arisen because several senior War Office personnel had been on holiday. 'After the strain of the last five years,' he wrote, 'it has been impossible to deny some spell of leave to the War Office Staff . . . many of whom have not had a holiday since the beginning of the war.' And he added: 'I have also found it necessary to take a fortnight's change in Scotland myself, but this of course implies no cessation in my work, which has proceeded continually and will so proceed without the intermission of a day.'

Churchill continued to defend his efforts. 'The demobilization of the armies has been a work of immense magnitude and difficulty,' he wrote to Lloyd George a few days later. 'How foolish to suppose that the armies which it took more than four years to spread about all over the world could be brought home again by a wave of the wand.'

Six weeks later the demobilization scheme was completed. On October 17, at a meeting of the Finance Committee of the Cabinet, Churchill reported that in the eleven months that had passed since the Armistice, an average of 10,000 men had been discharged every day. The daily military expenditure had fallen from just over £4,000,000 a day in January 1919 to only £1,250,000 in September. It was true to say, he added, 'that the Army had melted away. . . .'

11

Secretary of State for Air

CHURCHILL'S double appointment as Secretary of State for Air as well as for War caused surprise, and even anger in several quarters. 'The precise significance and scope of joining up the War Office and the Air Board are not yet clear,' *The Times* declared on January 11. 'If it is meant we are to return to the chaos from which we were delivered in 1917 with the formation of an Air ministry, separate and distinct from the other two services, this union under such a minister as Mr Churchill is asking for trouble and a sure cause of future mischief. . . .' But Churchill had no intention of weakening the autonomy of the Air Force, and in a departmental note on January 12 he explained the fundamental tenets of his policy. 'The Air Force,' he wrote, 'is the arm wh stands alone & midway between the land & sea services. Where they clash, it rules. Given superior thinking power & knowledge it must obtain the primary place in the general conception of war policy.'

On January 14 Lord Northcliffe's *Daily Mail* warned its readers of the likelihood of friction between the Admiralty and the War Office about aircraft production: 'We shall have air proposals bandied to and fro between Mr Walter Long, the new First Lord of Admiralty, Mr Churchill at the War Office, and General Seely who has to fetch and carry for Mr Churchill. This is a grotesque arrangement, unless the object is to evade all responsibility.' *The Times*, another of Lord Northcliffe's newspapers, after praising Churchill's qualities, asked:

> But can any single man cover the huge span of both these Departments of the Army and the Air? We gravely doubt it . . . the Air Ministry will demand the constant exercise of a keen and fresh imagination. The future greatness of the country depends in no small measure on this imaginative divination of the future of air power; there are a mass of legal questions to settle and detailed regulations to draw up; and, besides all this, there is the

enormously important commercial side of aviation. One horse, one man; we doubt even Mr Churchill's ability to ride two at once, especially two such high-spirited and mettlesome creatures.

On January 16 Churchill learnt from the First Sea Lord, Admiral Beatty,[1] that there was indeed hostility within the Admiralty towards his Air powers, and fears for the future of the naval air arm. Two days later Churchill wrote direct to Walter Long in self-defence:

I feel that having undertaken at the wish & suggestion of the PM the dual responsibility for the WO & the Air Ministry I am entitled to a little breathing space & time to look round. I should feel it rather hard on me if, without any change in the status character & organisation of the Air Force having occurred, & without my being given the time to formulate any policy, the Admy were to take alarm & commit themselves to a retrogressive policy.

I am fairly confident that I shd be able to propose to you arrangements wh both in form & fact will be satisfactory to the Admiralty; & as a colleague I ask that there shd be frank & friendly discussion between us before a difference between Departments is published to the wide circle of Govt Depts. With yr long experience of affairs I am sure you will recognise the reasonable nature of my request.

Long was not mollified by Churchill's explanation, and in a letter to Lloyd George on February 1, he explained his misgivings:

Don't misunderstand me: there is not hostility to Winston, on the contrary, the courage, the ability and the clearness of vision which have marked his treatment of army questions have already won him immense support, and, as I told you in my last letter, I am confident he will have no difficulty in carrying his proposals through parliament; but everyone asked how can he be the head of two great departments? . . .

Later in his letter to Lloyd George, Long asked whether it would 'not be well to restore the Air Ministry' to its former independence. And he continued:

You have an excellent man in Seely—keen and knowledgeable—and if this were done hostility would disappear and, as time goes on, you could see what is the proper policy for the future. On the other hand if things are allowed to remain as they are there will be very serious difficulty quite early in the coming session. We shall no doubt be able to overcome it by temporising, but it will not diminish, and, in the meantime, the efficiency of our fighting services must suffer.

[1] David Beatty, 1871–1936. Entered Navy, 1884. Rear-Admiral, 1910. Churchill's Naval Secretary, 1912. Commander of the 1st Battle Cruiser Squadron, 1913–16. Knighted, 1914. Vice-Admiral, 1915. Commander-in-Chief of the Grand Fleet, 1916–18. First Sea Lord, 1919–27. Created Earl, 1919. Admiral of the Fleet, 1919.

When Walter Long wrote this letter, Churchill had only been Secretary of State for Air for twenty-one days, precisely the same period that Long himself had been First Lord. Lloyd George was not impressed, and allowed Churchill to continue to devise a policy, and to obtain the personnel he needed.

At the beginning of February Churchill decided to ask Sir Hugh Trenchard[1] to become Chief of the Air Staff. Trenchard was telephoned early in the morning of February 4, and asked to go to see Churchill at once. In an autobiographical note written some years later he recalled:

I went over and saw him at about 10 o'clock at the War Office. He said he wanted me to go back as Chief of the Air Staff and organise the Royal Air Force for the future and carry out the demobilisation etc.

I demurred very much at doing this because I felt he and I would not agree on the policy to be carried out. He said he did not see why we should not agree and he wanted me to do it. . . .

Anyhow, Winston said you go away and write down what you think your policy ought to be, and I will do the same. We will exchange our notes and then meet again the next day. I wrote down my notes very shortly and sent them over, saying that I did not think he would agree, but I got nothing from him. The next morning he rang up and said would I go and see him. I went over and he said 'Well I have got your note on what you think the policy should be', and I said 'Yes, but I have not got yours'. 'Well,' he said, 'I had no time to write, but I see nothing in yours that I disagree with.' This was such a typical Winston move that I admit I was puzzled. We talked a lot about things and it really came down to the only thing we looked as if we were going to disagree on was the titles. He said I must accept, and he pressed me to, so I agreed. . . .

In his memorandum, Trenchard had proposed three 'Air Lords' responsible to the Secretary of State; the First to be in charge of military aviation, the Second of civil aviation and the Third of air production. The three Air Lords, together with the Secretary of State, and two Under-Secretaries, would form an Air Council. As for the air service itself, Trenchard set out his views briefly and clearly:

[1] Hugh Montague Trenchard, 1873–1956. Entered Army, 1893. Active service, South Africa, 1899–1902 (dangerously wounded). Major, 1902. Assistant Commandant, Central Flying School, 1913–14. Lieutenant-Colonel, 1915. General Officer Commanding the Royal Flying Corps in the Field, 1915–17. Major-General, 1916. Knighted, 1918. Chief of the Air Staff, 1919–29. Air-Marshal, 1919. Created Baronet, 1919. Air Chief Marshal, 1922. Marshal of the Royal Air Force, 1927. Created Baron, 1930. Commissioner, Metropolitan Police, 1931–5. Created Viscount, 1936. His elder son, and both his stepsons, were killed in action in the second world war.

The Royal Air Force would be composed of officers with permanent commissions and officers from the Navy and Army seconded for four years. The men would be permanently in the Air Service.

All new officers would have to learn to fly and no officer joining after this date would be considered for an appointment in the Air Force who had not learnt to fly.

Training would have to be specialised and I would recommend that one should, as far as one can see at present, train pilots as fighting pilots (land and sea), reconnaissance pilots (land and sea), bombing pilots (these would probably be common to both), and torpedo pilots. Each type of pilot would have a different badge like a corps, the service consisting of various arms, such as Bombing, Fighting, Reconnaissance, etc.

It is important to keep the training units distinct from the service units. Some of the squadrons would be at full strength and some only cadres and these should be periodically changed, i.e. full strength squadrons reduced to cadres, and cadre squadrons increased to full strength and sent to certain camps for war training.

There should be an Inspector General of the Air Force, but he should not have a seat on the Air Council.

By their emphasis on military aviation, Trenchard's ideas fitted in with Churchill's. But they were at variance with the hopes of the existing Chief of the Air Staff, Major-General Sir Frederick Sykes,[1] who wanted civil aviation to be given the higher priority. Under Trenchard's scheme, the Department of Supply and Research would be under service control, a view Churchill shared. Churchill also envisaged an important role for air power in the future defence of the Empire, and in particular of the Turkish territory in the Middle East which had come under British control since the Turkish surrender three and a half months earlier.

On February 8 Churchill explained his ideas to Walter Long:

In the first place, the fact that I hold the seals of two offices in no way implies the absorption of the Air Force in the Army. This arrangement is in principle temporary. It is of great convenience during the process of demobilisation that the Air Force and the Army can be guided step by step from one point of view. The practical course of business is greatly simplified and expedited thereby.

[1] Frederick Hugh Sykes, 1877–1954. Entered Army, 1901. Severely wounded in the South African War. Learned to fly, 1911. Commander, Royal Flying Corps, Military Wing, 1912–14. Major, 1912. Chief Staff Officer, Royal Flying Corps, France, 1914–15. Colonel Commanding the Royal Naval Air Service, Eastern Mediterranean, 1915–16. Brigadier-General, 1917. Deputy-Director of Organization, War Office, 1917. Major-General, 1918. Chief of the Air Staff, 1918–19. Knighted, 1919. First Controller-General of Civil Aviation, 1919–22. In 1920 he married Bonar Law's daughter Isabel. Conservative MP, 1922–8 and 1940–5. Governor of Bombay, 1928–33.

Secondly, the whole future garrisons of the British Empire have to be reviewed in the light of the war and the increased responsibilities cast upon us by our victory. It is desirable that in this review the disposition of the Air Forces and those of our garrisons should be regulated in harmony from a single standpoint, in order that the fullest use may be made of the new army especially—in the East and in the Middle East—and that economy of expense and personnel may be effected to the utmost.

(3) Meanwhile the future independence of the Air Force and Air Ministry will be in no way prejudiced. Nor will it be in any way 'militarised'. On the contrary, I propose deliberately to 'de-militarise' it and to enhance its distinctive character by every reasonable means.

For instance, I contemplate eliminating altogether all military ranks and titles and establishing new titles appropriate to a new service and a new element standing midway between the two parent services and catering for the needs of both. . . .

On February 9 Churchill offered Sir Frederick Sykes the post of Air Member in charge of Civil Aviation. The two men met on the following afternoon. In answer to Sykes' criticisms, Churchill declared, as Sykes later recalled, that there was 'no difference in policy, but certain variations in method'. Sykes did not agree with Churchill's analysis, and in his letter of acceptance on February 10, reiterated his belief in the need to give priority to civil aviation. 'I hope,' he wrote, 'the time will shortly arrive when civil aviation can be placed on its own basis.'

On February 12, in the House of Commons, a Liberal MP, Captain Wedgwood Benn,[1] brought a motion of no confidence in Churchill's air policy. The great danger of combining the two offices, he asserted, was that the Air Force would become entirely submerged by the Army, and would be used merely as an adjunct to War Office policy. In answer to Benn, a pioneer aviator, Colonel Moore-Brabazon,[2] asked the House of Commons to approve Churchill's appointment, declaring: 'He does enjoy the confidence of most people interested in the air. He has imagination, and I believe he has the movement at heart.' Churchill defended his policy in a brief speech, arguing that it would save Govern-

[1] William Wedgwood Benn, 1877–1960. Liberal MP, 1906–18 and 1918–27. A Junior Lord of the Treasury, 1910–15. Served with the yeomanry at Gallipoli, 1915, and with the Royal Naval Air Service in the eastern Mediterranean, 1916–17. DSO (1917), DFC (1918). Joined the Labour Party, 1927. Labour MP, 1928–31 and 1937–42. Secretary of State for India in the second Labour Government. Served in the Royal Air Force, 1940–5. Created Viscount Stansgate, 1942. Secretary of State for Air, 1945–6.

[2] John Theodore Cuthbert Moore-Brabazon, 1884–1964. Pioneer motorist and aviator; holder of pilot's Certificate No. 1. Won the *Daily Mail* £1,000 for flying a circular mile, 1909. Lieutenant-Colonel in charge of the Royal Flying Corps Photographic Section, 1914–18. Conservative MP, 1918–29 and 1931–42. Chairman, Air Mails Committee, 1923. Minister of Transport, 1940–1; of Aircraft Production, 1941–2. Created Baron, 1942.

ment money to have a single Secretary of State for the two Ministries, and to limit the Air Ministry's own highest political appointment to the salary of an Under-Secretaryship.

In a direct answer to Wedgwood Benn's criticisms, Churchill declared emphatically that 'the integrity, the unity, the independence of the Royal Air Force will be sedulously and carefully maintained'. There was, he added, 'not the slightest intention of merging them in the Army, of merging the administration of the Royal Air Force in the War Office, of subordinating it to the War Office, or of derogating from its separate, independent state as a Royal Air Force'. As for civilian aviation, he explained, it had not been split up between 'all the different Departments—the Board of Trade, the Foreign Office, or whatever it may be— as some people had suggested', but would be 'definitely placed in the sphere of the Air Ministry', under the control of Sir Frederick Sykes, who had 'patriotically consented to retire from the military profession, and to take civilian garb, in order to emphasise the civilian character of this Department'.

During the course of his speech, Churchill warned that 'much harm may easily be done' by overestimating the 'capacity and capability' of aviation. It would not help the development of commercial aviation, he said, 'if we begin by teaching the public to expect from it all sorts of performances which, although they are now within view, are certainly not yet within reach'.

Later in the debate, Wedgwood Benn withdrew his motion. Three days later, on February 15, Churchill—who was then in Paris—learnt that Walter Long had been urging his Cabinet colleagues to restore the control of the Royal Naval Air Service to the Royal Navy. Churchill acted swiftly to forestall any such Admiralty action, telegraphing that afternoon to General Seely:

Resist strongly any proposal to remove any form of flying from control of Air Ministry. You should point out that the whole future of Air Ministry depends upon its having the necessary body and substance which can only be supplied if, so far as the Government is concerned, functions of all kinds connected with the air are vested with it. On no account allow an adverse decision of this kind to be taken in my absence here. Make a direct appeal to Prime Minister to give me an opportunity of making my case known.

Seely acted on Churchill's behalf, not only in this instance, but in the months that followed, drafting legislation, preparing estimates and supervising the activities of the Air Council. Churchill himself concentrated on the evolution of policy, and in particular on maintaining the

independence of the Royal Air Force. At the end of February he wrote
to his friend F. E. Smith—who had just been created a Peer[1]—to
explain how his work was progressing:

There is no question of subordinating the Royal Air Force to the Army or
to the Navy or of splitting it into two and dividing it between the Army and
the Navy. In order to emphasise the distinct and independent character of
this branch of the fighting services, uniform and ranks and titles have been
deliberately differentiated from those prevailing in the Army and the
Navy.

The whole organisation of the Air Force as a separate force, and of the Air
Ministry as a separate ministry, has proceeded without intermission. A
complete scheme for the post-war organisation has been elaborated during
the year and is now very far advanced. When the Estimates for 1920 are
introduced it will be possible to lay before the House this scheme in full
detail, and it will then be seen that all the varied functions of the Royal Air
Force and its complex organisation have been fully provided for, including its
work with the Navy, its work with the Army and its work as an independent
strategic factor. We have aimed throughout the year at creating a separate
permanent Air Service affording as good a career and as good opportunities
of advancement to officers and men as either the Army or the Navy. . . .

In his letter to Lord Birkenhead, Churchill pointed out that as the
Air Force was at that moment less than a seventh the size or cost of
either the Army or the Navy, a separate Minister would be an extravagance. But, he added, it might well be 'that in the years that are to
come the importance of the Air Force will grow at the expense of the
other two Services, until possibly, as some people think, it will take the
prime place in our defensive organisation'. It was at such a time,
Churchill believed, that a separate Secretary of State for Air would be
needed.

On March 3 there was a setback to Churchill's hopes for the rapid
evolution of a detailed air policy. On that day, Trenchard wrote to say
that he had contracted Spanish influenza, and was not well enough to
continue as Chief of the Air Staff. He therefore tendered his resignation,
explaining in his letter why he could not go on:

I do not think I have the guts to pull it through now. I am played out and
I am sorry I took the job as it must be most inconvenient to you. It is worrying
me very much indeed and I feel that there are many things not going right
until you have put in my successor.

[1] F. E. Smith had been appointed Lord Chancellor on 10 January 1919, and created 1st
Baron Birkenhead on 3 February 1919.

Perhaps in six or nine months time if I have recovered I can be of use in a small way again, but at present I feel I am not fit to do work. The doctor does not think I shall be fit for 3 weeks or a month or maybe longer.

Churchill had too much faith in Trenchard's abilities to let him go after less than three weeks. Trenchard had already influenced him in the decision to make Egypt the centre of Air Force activity in the Middle East with bases at Baghdad and Karachi, and shared Churchill's vision of air power playing a decisive part in imperial defence. On the same day that Trenchard wrote offering to resign, Churchill replied, refusing his resignation:

My dear Trenchard,
I appreciate warmly the motive wh prompts you to write as you have done.
I think after all yr hard work you ought to take a month or six weeks leave & then let me know how you feel. There is not the slightest difficulty in carrying on for that time. In any case I cd not think of losing yr greatly valued services until I was satisfied you were physically unfit.
I do not believe for a moment that you will not be in good health & spirits long before the six weeks I prescribe are over.
I am looking forward so much to working with you; but you must really get quite fit before you come back.

Yours very sincerely
WSC

During the first week in March, the Air Council prepared the Air Estimates for the following year. Churchill decided that Seely should introduce them to the House of Commons, writing to him on March 5:

I think the expense will cause a shock, following as it does upon the enormous demands of the Army and also the Navy Estimates, which touch nearly 150 millions. Everything must therefore be done to try for a reasonable figure. I have provisionally approved the estimates on a basis of 100 squadrons and 27 millions expenditure, apart from 37 millions liquidation charges.
I am very anxious that a start should be made with the Baghdad permanent air station, as well as with the Cairo and Karachi stations, and I think we ought to take money in the Estimates for these purposes, cutting off the set sum from other heads so that the aggregate is not exceeded. . . .

Clementine Churchill did not approve of her husband holding two Ministerial offices. On March 9, when he was again in France, she wrote to him at length, setting out her feelings. She had dined two days before at Philip Sassoon's house, and had sat next to the Commander of

the Royal Air Force in France, Major-General Salmond.[1] In her letter
she described their conversation:

He said that the *best* men were going off as they of course are offered jobs
by civilian firms so that he feared that unless something is done quickly the
country (I mean the Government) will have nothing but the stumers. The
good men *want* to stay with the Air Force but are naturally tempted by good
offers. They go to Salmond & ask his advice.

Darling really don't you think it would be better to give up the Air &
continue *concentrating* as you are doing on the War Office. It would be a sign
of real strength to do so, & people would admire it very much. It is weak to
hang on to 2 offices—you really are only doing the one. Or again if you
swallow the 2 you will have violent indigestion!

It would be a tour de force to do the 2, like keeping a lot of balls in the air
at the same time. After all, you want to be a Statesman, not a juggler—If I
were you I would go to Ll G & say you only want to do the WO & suggest
Northcliffe as S & S for the Air—That will dispose of the Seely difficulty &
make N a friend for life. You are being so splendid at the WO & I don't want
there to be one weak spot in the armour. . . .

Churchill had no intention of giving up his double office, nor of
recommending Lord Northcliffe as his successor. The Air Council did
the routine work to his satisfaction, and without impinging on his War
Office responsibilities. Seely represented him in Paris on the Aviation
Committee of the Peace Conference. His only serious problem was
Trenchard's continuing illness. On March 16 Trenchard wrote to say
that he was still 'very weak', and would not be of any use until the end
of April. Once again he offered to resign. Two days later Churchill
replied: 'There is no question whatever of anyone taking your place,
and I have no intention of acting upon your various offers to resign,
which arise from your high sense of duty. I am sure you have most
valuable work to do for the Flying Service, and we will hold the fort
until you are restored.'

On March 13 Seely introduced the Air Estimates in the House of
Commons. The total asked for by the Air Ministry was £66,500,000, of
which £63,000,000 was for Military Aviation. Had the war still been in

[1] John Maitland Salmond, 1881–1968. Entered the Army, 1901. On active service in
South Africa, 1901–2. Instructor, Central Flying School, 1912. Lieutenant-Colonel, 1915.
Major-General, 1917. Director-General of Military Aeronautics, 1917–18. Major-General
Commanding the Royal Air Force in France, 1918–19. Knighted, 1919. Air Officer Com-
manding Inland Area, 1920–2. Air Officer Commanding the British Forces in Iraq, 1922–5.
Air Marshal, 1923. Air Officer Commanding-in-Chief, Air Defence of Great Britain, 1925–9.
Air Chief Marshal, 1929. Chief of the Air Staff, 1930–3. Marshal of the Royal Air Force,
1933. Director of Armament Production, Ministry of Aircraft Production, 1940.

progress, Seely declared, the total figure would have been £200,000,000. The Royal Air Force, he said, was being put on a peacetime basis, with approximately 5,300 officers and 54,000 men, and 102 squadrons. Of the total sum asked for, £3,000,000 would be set aside for experiment and research into civil aviation. This was only 6 per cent of the total sum. Yet with this, Sir Frederick Sykes would have to plan air routes in Britain and abroad, examine and advise on all schemes for commercial aviation, and superintend the registration and licensing of aircraft and pilots. During the debate which followed Seely's speech, Wedgwood Benn spoke bitterly of the low priority given to civil aviation, and pointed out that for months the United States Government had been operating an aerial postal service.

Trenchard returned to the Air Ministry in the first week of May. Throughout the summer he worked to evolve an effective organization for the new service. 'I am working night and day,' he wrote to General Salmond in June, 'and Mr Churchill is doing all he can to help. . . .' Trenchard and Churchill were absorbed in the problems of Military Aviation. Civil Aviation suffered. On May 1, the day on which civilian passenger flights were formally inaugurated, *The Times* had published a caustic leader on the neglect shown towards civil aviation. The blame, it felt, lay not with Churchill, but with Austen Chamberlain, the Chancellor of the Exchequer:

We have always doubted whether General Sykes, the Controller-General, was being given the powers which are essential for his task. . . . The Treasury are still boggling over General Sykes's staff requirements. Only the main appointments to the Department of Civil Aviation have been sanctioned as yet, and these only provisionally. . . .

The Government are not dealing fairly with General Sykes and his Department, and they must be warned that the country will not tolerate these dilatory methods any longer.

Churchill's own priority remained strongly for Military Aviation. On June 10 he completed a series of notes on the Royal Air Force in which he set out as his main aim the creation of 'a thoroughly efficient RAF which will last year after year in a good condition and be a credit to the country'. It was essential, he wrote, to follow up a suggestion which Trenchard had made about introducing 'something like the regimental system of the Army into the RAF, thus preserving the identities of the more famous squadrons'. Churchill proposed 'definite units of a permanent character possessing their own *esprit de corps* with good strictly managed messes, the officers of which know each other, and where there is a strong public opinion on questions of behaviour. A ceaseless fluctuation of individuals cannot be allowed. . . .' A good training college was needed, which, Churchill wrote, should be 'filled by competitive examination, preferably from the public schools'. He then listed the four principal features which he believed should predominate in the training of RAF officers:

(i) The discipline and bearing of an officer and a gentleman.

(ii) War studies: not only air war but war as a whole.

(iii) Technical instruction in mechanics of the kind given at Dartmouth with special reference to aviation needs.

(iv) A certain amount of flying instruction to be regarded as a privilege in the first year, and only obligatory in the second year. During the first year cadets would begin to specialise either on the technical or the flying side. All must be technical and all must fly, but the emphasis will be different according to aptitudes. . . . We must aim at having some of the very best practical engineers and technicians trained in our own hands and offer them good permanent careers. As there will only be one Air College it must really in a way play the part both of Woolwich and Sandhurst.

Churchill emphasized the need for good schools of mechanics, who, he said, 'must be caught early'. Although the trade unions had played 'a very valuable part in national life', he added, 'it would never do for the RAF to become *wholly* dependent upon their craftsmen. . . . We should aim at a minimum of training at least one-third and preferably one-half directly ourselves. . . .'

On June 19 there was a brief discussion in Cabinet about air casualties. Seely, who always spoke on routine air matters, told the Cabinet that in the past three weeks there had been one casualty for every thousand miles flown. Churchill could not believe that the figures could be so high, and interjected to tell his colleagues that Seely must have meant hours, not miles. Yet even this was too alarmist a figure, as Churchill wrote to Seely on June 20:

I have since had an opportunity of getting a report on the figures, a copy of which I enclose. You will see that you have mixed up ordinary deaths from influenza and other causes in the Royal Air Force with the flying casualties, and that the figure of 1,200 which I had so incautiously accepted from you includes all these. The actual fatal casualties up to the end of last month did not exceed 263 including casualties abroad, some of which at any rate must have been sustained under war conditions.

I do not think it possible to leave the Cabinet under the false impression which we have created in their minds, and I am therefore circulating the report with a suitable apologia.

The Air Ministry was small and new; it had few friends. On July 2 the House of Commons Select Committee on National Expenditure examined Trenchard about the use of aeroplanes by members of the Ministry. The tone of the questioning was hostile. In a letter to Churchill that day, Trenchard gave an account of the questioning of the Committee's chairman, Sir Frederick Banbury,[1] and of his own riposte:

He asked me who, in the Air Ministry, had aeroplanes for flying about, and I said that various officers had, and that I encouraged this. He also asked what Civil Members had aeroplanes, and whether I thought this necessary. I said that I deprecated being asked this question, but my view was that it was most necessary for the Secretary of State, and the Under Secretary of State, to have machines and travel by air, as it gave confidence to the Air Service, and it helped morale considerably. I also pointed out that if Sir Frederick Banbury became Air Minister that I should also strongly recommend that he travelled about by aeroplane!!

During the summer of 1919 Churchill began once more to take flying practice, and resumed the attempt to gain a pilot's licence, which he had begun when First Lord of the Admiralty, before the war. Early in 1914, at his wife's urgent request, he had given up learning to fly. The death of one of his young instructors, immediately after a flying practice, had led her to insist that he fly no more. But with the improved aircraft of 1919, and the increased opportunity provided by his continual official visits to France, he was tempted to try again. His flights in 1914 had been extensive, and he had nearly completed the flying time needed to obtain him his licence. Churchill was exhilarated by his renewed flying activities. One of the pilots whom he had known before the war, Colonel Scott,[2] frequently flew with him to France. They would leave Kenley or Croydon aerodrome in a DH4, and, flying at between twelve and four-

[1] Frederick George Banbury, 1850–1936. Chairman of the Great Northern Railway. Created Baronet, 1902. Conservative MP for Peckham, 1892–1906, and for the City of London, 1906–24. Created Baron Banbury of Southam, 1924. His only son, a Captain in the Coldstream Guards, was killed in action in September 1914. He was succeeded as 2nd Baron by his grandson, who was born posthumously in May 1915.
[2] Alan John Lance Scott, 1883–1922. Barrister. Lieutenant, Royal Flying Corps, 1915; seriously injured in a flying accident, as a result of which he had to be lifted into his cockpit each time he flew. Major commanding 60 Squadron, March/April 1917. Wounded, April 1917. Lieutenant-Colonel commanding 11th Wing, 2nd Brigade, Royal Flying Corps, 1917–18. Appointed Commandant, Central Flying School, 1918, by which time he had shot down thirteen German aircraft. Wing Commander, 1919. Air Secretary and Private Secretary to Churchill, and later to Frederick Guest, Air Ministry, 1919–22. Died of pneumonia.

teen thousand feet, reach the Paris aerodromes at Buc or Le Bourget within two hours. 'No tedious railway journey,' Churchill later recalled, 'no delays of transhipment, no apprehensions of seasickness! In these very fast war machines one travelled as on a magic carpet.' Nor did a crash landing at Buc aerodrome in June deter him from continuing his flights. There seemed no reason why he should not obtain his license before the end of 1919.

On Friday July 18, after a full day's work at the War Office, Churchill and Colonel Scott drove to Croydon aerodrome for a routine practice. The aeroplane had dual controls, and as usual Churchill took the machine off the ground himself. It rose to seventy or eighty feet without difficulty, and Churchill then turned it to the right, the first of two half circles needed to gain a safe height to pass over the high elm trees bordering the aerodrome. The right turn was perfect. The aeroplane's speed had reached sixty miles an hour. Churchill moved into the second, left turn, and began gently to centre the guiding-stick in order to resume an even keel. Five years later[1] he recalled the sequel:

To my surprise the stick came home at least a foot without producing the slightest effect. The aeroplane remained inclined at about 45 degrees and began gradually to increase its list. 'She is out of control' I said through the microphone to my pilot. Instantly I felt the override of his hand and feet on stick and rudders, as by a violent effort he sought to plunge the machine head-downwards in the hope of regaining our lost flying speed. But it was too late. We were scarcely 90 feet above the ground, just the normal height for the usual side-slip fatal accident, the commonest of all. The machine rushed earthwards helplessly. Above two hundred feet there would have been no danger; in fact at a thousand or fifteen hundred feet we had over and over again deliberately stalled the machine, made it fall out of control, waited till the side-slip turned (as all side-slips do) into the ultimate nose dive, and then as the speed increased to eighty or a hundred miles an hour and the controls began again to answer, had pulled her gently out into a normal flight.

But there was no time now. I saw the sunlit aerodrome close beneath me, and the impression flashed through my mind that it was bathed in a baleful yellowish glare. Then in another flash a definite thought formed in my brain, 'This is very likely Death'. And swift upon that I felt again in imagination the exact sensations of my smash on the Buc Aerodrome a month before. Something like that was going to happen NOW! . . .

The aeroplane was just turning from its side-slip into the nose dive when it struck the ground at perhaps fifty miles an hour with terrific force. Its left wing crumpled, and its propeller and nose plunged into the earth. Again I felt

[1] In an article, 'Why I Gave Up Flying', printed in *Nash's Pall Mall* magazine in July 1924, and subsequently published in book form in *Thoughts and Adventures* (1932).

myself driven forward as if in some new dimension by a frightful and overwhelming force, through a space I could not measure. There was a sense of
unendurable oppression across my chest as the belt took the strain. Streams of
petrol vapour rushed past in the opposite direction. I felt, as a distinct phase,
the whole absorption of the shock. Suddenly the pressure ceased, the belt
parted and I fell forward quite gently on to the dial board in front of me.
Safe! was the instantaneous realization. I leapt out of the shattered fuselage
and ran to my companion. He was senseless and bleeding. I stood by ready to
try to pull him out should the machine catch fire. Otherwise it was better to
leave him till skilled help arrived.

Churchill owed his life to Colonel Scott's presence of mind. In the few
seconds before their aeroplane had hit the ground, Scott had switched
off the engine, thus preventing an explosion. Two hours after the crash,
Churchill presided at a dinner in the House of Commons in honour of
General Pershing, and made a speech of welcome. 'This was plucky,'
Lord Riddell recorded in his diary four days later. And he added:
'Winston's forehead was scratched and his legs were black and blue.'

Churchill's friends begged him not to fly again. Lord Haldane,[1] who
had been present at the dinner in the House of Commons, wrote to him
on July 19:

My dear Winston,
    I want to add a line to what I said to you last night.
    Your life is too valuable to be risked by flying. You have boundless
courage, physical and moral (e.g. your courage in this latter regard in standing up for me as you did last night & on previous occasions). But the question
is one of what is right in the public interest.
    Sooner or later you will have another smash, how bad we cannot tell and if
it comes it will be a bad business not only for your family but for the public.
    Therefore, as a moralist who meditates, I say you ought to give up flying,
much as I know it attracts you.
    There are not days in which the country can spare you, and to avoid risk
becomes in these circumstances a public duty.

Churchill's relative, Lady Londonderry,[2] also wrote. Her husband had
nearly been killed a few weeks earlier while flying:

---

[1] Richard Burdon Haldane, 1856–1928. Liberal MP, 1885–1911. Secretary of State for
War, 1905–12. Created Viscount, 1911. Lord Chancellor, first under Asquith, 1912–15; then
under Ramsay MacDonald, 1924.

[2] Edith Helen Chaplin, 1879–1959. A daughter of the 1st Viscount Chaplin, and a grand-
daughter of the third Duke of Sutherland. She married Lord Londonderry (then Viscount
Castlereagh) in 1899. Founder and Director of the Women's Legion, 1915–19. Colonel-in-
Chief, Women's Volunteer Reserve, 1914–15. Created Dame Commander of the British
Empire, 1917 (the first women to be so appointed). A close personal friend of the first
Labour Prime Minister, Ramsay MacDonald.

My dear Winston,

I do hope you are really all right. I had such a fright over Charles the other day that I feel dreadfully for Clemmy—Must you do this. *Please* dont—good people are so scarce—I really think it rather evil of you—but I do hope you have not been hurt. Charley and I both send you our love—he is vy seedy, I am afraid there is something the matter with his kidneys—He has been in great pain and it is not much better now—Au revoir—and do be careful.

Churchill decided to abandon his search for a pilot's licence. He reproached himself also for being the cause of Colonel Scott's suffering. But to his relief, Scott not only recovered, but was able to walk better after his second accident than he had before. With Trenchard's approval, Scott was made a Commander of the Bath, and a few months later Churchill appointed him to the post of Air Secretary and Private Secretary, Air Ministry.

Since February 1919 Churchill had been considering the merits of merging the three fighting services, Army, Navy and Air Force, into a single Ministry of Defence, under a single Minister. On February 12, in the House of Commons, he had stressed the importance of a Ministry of Defence. But in his speech he had emphasized the long-term nature of such a development:

There can be no Ministry of Defence, however good that may be in theory, and as an ultimate ideal, actually there can be no Ministry of Defence until you have created a staff of extra-officers who have grown up year after year having studied the question of war and the defence of the Empire from the general point of view, and unless that staff have gradually gained the confidence of their respective branches and are familiar with all the branches.

You have to build up a great body of combined war thought, capable of producing professional, expert leaders to advise the Government, not from an Army point of view or a Navy point of view, but generally over the whole field of war.

Until you possess that body of officers, believe me, it is idle to speculate on the possibilities of a Ministry of Defence. That is a task which certainly cannot be accomplished and achieved until not merely the officers have been trained, but have grown up and are in such a position in their respective Services as will entitle them to the confidence of their comrades and their profession. It is a matter for a good many years' work.

However, nothing in what has been done in the association of the Air Force and the Army under the conditions I have specified, with entirely separate offices, is inconsistent in any way with that ideal, if it be thought to be possible. It may be said that two-thirds of the road has already been covered. . . .

Churchill told the House of Commons that it was Lloyd George who had 'instructed' him to raise the issue of a Ministry of Defence. His own instinct was for caution. On March 1, in a letter to Lord Birkenhead, he had written of how Seely was one of those who believed that 'a combination of the three services' was the 'true solution'. But four months later, Churchill had become an ardent advocate of such a scheme. On July 11 he discussed it with Lloyd George during a visit to Criccieth. Sir Henry Wilson, who was present, described the conversation in his diary:

We then had a long discussion on a Secretary of State for Defence to include Navy, Army, Air & Supplies. Winston & I warmly advocated it, LG put up all the objections he could think of but they were not very strong and in reality in the end, as he admitted to us later in the day, rested on the difficulty of getting Walter Long out of the Admiralty. Our conversation was interesting & Winston & I were satisfied with it.

One of the new S of S great difficulties will be to find 3 good Under Secretaries. Winston who already sees himself as Minister of Defence! suggested Hugh Cecil[1] for WO, Freddie Guest for Air & no one yet for Admiralty. . . .

There was a further discussion at Criccieth about the need for a Ministry of Defence on July 12. Wilson recorded Lloyd George's comments:

More talk with LG this morning. He quite agrees about the Defence Minister but has grave doubts as to whether he can move Walter Long, especially now that Walter is bitten with the charms of the 'Enchantress'! Winston says the Enchantress costs £80,000 a year![2]

On July 31 Sir Henry Wilson wrote to Lloyd George, urging that such a Ministry should be set up at once. But, he wrote in his diary that night, 'he doesn't seem to have gripped the situation'. On August 4 Churchill himself wrote to Lloyd George, urging an immediate decision in favour of a Ministry of Defence, as an essential part of the Government's financial, as well as military, policy:

[1] Lord Hugh Richard Heathcote Gascoyne Cecil, 1869–1956. Known as 'Linky'. Fifth son of the 3rd Marquess of Salisbury. Conservative MP, 1895–1906; 1910–37. Provost of Eton, 1936–44. Created Baron Quickswood, 1941. A leading member of the Church Assembly.

[2] The *Enchantress* was the official Admiralty yacht, used by successive First Lords both for work and relaxation. Churchill himself had spent many months on board the *Enchantress* between 1911 and 1914, inspecting naval bases and dockyards and visiting British naval installations in the Mediterranean.

We have got (a) to define the duties of the Army Navy & Air Force in the next five or ten years, i.e. what are their responsibilities to be (b) to discuss with the experts the measures & forces necessary to discharge those responsibilities & (c) to fix and distribute the money required. . . . But nothing can be done in this field unless either you can yourself preside at a vy lengthy & intricate inquiry between the services: or unless you devolve yr task on a Minister of Defence with whom alone you & the Treasury will deal. It is quite impossible for me to cut the Army & Air Force down as I am trying to do if the Navy—the sister profession—is to have a free run. . . .

The army has definite additions to its responsibilities & the Air Force is a new arm. But the Navy must be reduced in accordance with the altered state of the world & of other maritime powers. . . .

It seems to me that even if you decide against a Ministry of Defence, you wd be wise to make a change at the Admiralty. Beatty cannot be kept in the cold indefinitely, & new men shd come in pledged beforehand to a new basis of action & new financial limits.

Do not in settling these matters consider my personal wishes in any way. So long as a proper Cabinet is formed I am quite happy where I am & have plenty of vy interesting work. But all these questions are interwoven & you cannot deal with Finance until you have dealt with the services; & Finance will not brook delay.

Moreover every scheme for the reorganization of our defensive forces is hung up at the present time. We cannot make any good general plans—apart altogether from the scale—until the relations between the 3 services are settled. Therefore yr 4th gt question wh also awaits decision urgently is *Our Defensive System.*

I am full of sympathy for you in the immense burden wh you bear, and that after so many intense exertions. But if you are to have the rest wh is needed for you to recover yr full buoyancy and creative power, it is essential that you shd beforehand give the decisions wh will allow yr lieutenants to act effectively.

Lloyd George was attracted by Churchill's arguments in favour of a Ministry of Defence. On November 9 he explained to Sir George Riddell the advantages of Churchill's proposal. 'If this plan were adopted,' Riddell reported Lloyd George as saying, 'the efforts of the three services would be coordinated and they would not be competing against each other'. Lloyd George added that there would not be another European war 'at any rate, for ten years'; meanwhile the Ministry of Defence would 'consolidate' Britain's military position.

No action was taken to combine the three services. But Seely, who had himself been a supporter of such a scheme eight months earlier, now feared that it was a pointer to the eventual whittling away of an independent Air Ministry. On November 10, he resigned. 'Although we part company officially,' he wrote to Churchill that day, 'you will know that you always have in me a firm friend. May all good fortune attend you now and always.'

Seely had wanted an independent Air Ministry, not only freed from fear of absorption in a Ministry of Defence, but also separated from the War Office. Under such an arrangement, he could hope for a return to the Cabinet, as Minister for Air. The post of Under-Secretary had long ceased to appeal to him. On November 11 Churchill replied personally to his letter of resignation:

My dear Jack,

I am grieved to receive yr letter; but after our numerous talks I feel there is no more to be said.

I did whatever was in my power wh sincere & old friendship suggested to assist yr return from the military to the political arena. Had greater offices been in my sphere of influence, I wd have found one for you. As it was I was able only to secure for you the best in my power. That after trial and consn you do not find it possible to retain this will always be a source of deep regret to me.

I cannot accuse myself in any way; but that does not at all lessen the disappt wh I feel at the course you have taken or my conviction that yr own interests wd have pointed differently.

Yours always
W

In his resignation speech in the House of Commons on November 12, Seely spoke bitterly of how the Air Ministry was virtually an 'annexe' of the War Office, and how, as a result, the Royal Air Force suffered. Seely was succeeded as Under-Secretary of State by Churchill's cousin, Lord Londonderry, who was both a friend and an admirer of Trenchard, and who was able to give the Air Ministry an air of high social respectability.

Throughout 1919 Sir Frederick Sykes had striven, despite his small budget, to speed the development of civil aviation. On March 4, in a letter to Churchill, he pressed for a lump sum to be allocated to his department. 'I wish to urge the fact that the formation of a department such as this in time of peace is without precedent,' he wrote. Periodic adjustments of funds, under Treasury pressure, would, he argued, lead to 'every kind of difficulty', and would seriously hamper pioneer work, if not make it impossible.

Sykes' argument did not prevail. Military aviation, not civilian flying, was Churchill's priority. Sykes persevered against a background of financial neglect. On April 30 he published the 'Air Navigation Regulations for Civil Flying in the United Kingdom'. These governed every aspect of civil aviation, including standards for passenger aircraft. On June 15 the first aeroplane to fly the Atlantic landed in County Galway; it was only ten years since the first aeroplane had crossed the Channel. The Atlantic crossing, the prelude to commercial exploitation, had been stimulated by a *Daily Mail* offer of £10,000 for the first successful flight. It was Churchill who, as Secretary of State for Air, handed the two pilots their cheque. In July, Sykes set out for Churchill his three proposals for future civilian flights:

(1) England to Australia via Egypt, India, and the East Indian Archipelago.
(2) England to the Cape via Cairo.
(3) Shorter flights to European countries and places in the British Isles, viz: Glasgow, Dublin, Amsterdam, Lisbon via Madrid, and Cologne.

Much more slowly than Sykes wanted, these routes were surveyed, aerodromes established, stores and spares laid down, and international agreements obtained. On July 19, a weekend service was opened from London to Brussels. On August 25, the world's first daily commercial service was begun. A single pilot and a single passenger set off from Hounslow for Le Bourget, with a cargo of newspapers, grouse and Devonshire cream. The journey took two and a half hours. By the end of September over 52,000 passengers had been carried in scheduled civil fiights, operated by private companies, without Government subsidy. 250 aeroplanes had been certified as airworthy, and capable of passenger transport; 374 pilots had been given certificates; 300,000 miles had been flown. A regular cross-channel mail service was started on November 10. On December 11 the first England–Australia flight was completed in less than thirty days, showing the feasibility of Sykes' first flight proposal.

On December 27, survey work began on the establishment of the Cape to Cairo air route. But, despite these successes, Sykes was discontented at the almost total subordination of the needs of civilian flying to that of military aviation. Over twenty years later, writing in his memoirs, he expressed his pent up bitterness:

As a matter of fact, practically nothing was done to help the civil side. The problems, for example, connected with the development of the flying-boat which I repeatedly urged and which I regarded as equally important to the military side as to the civil, were almost completely neglected in spite of the obvious importance of flying-boats for the Empire air routes and no progress was made in aids to flying in fog and at night, which were essential for commercial aviation, and necessitated constant research and experiment. Since nothing was done, we were soon far behind other countries in blind flying and in landing at night, which in war must present almost as great a hazard to night bombing as anti-aircraft fire. The money allotted to me was quite inadequate to enable me to make any grant for research, as it was insufficient to allow me properly to maintain my Department, including the Meteorological Services, which had to be financed by my Department, although it served the country as a whole.

It was not Sykes alone who was dissatisfied by the lack of funds available for the air service. In the spring of 1919 Trenchard had thrown his support behind an ambitious scheme for air routes throughout the Middle East, and across Africa. The scheme had been drawn up by the commander of the Royal Air Force, Middle East, Major-General Salmond. On April 10 Salmond informed Trenchard that when he had explained his scheme at the Air Ministry, 'Winston expressed general approval.' Six weeks later, on May 21, Trenchard and Salmond finalized details of the first of the routes. Salmond returned to Cairo. From there, he pressed Trenchard to agree also to a Cairo to Cape Town route, and to the acceleration of plans for a regular air mail service from Cairo to Karachi. Trenchard approved Salmond's enthusiasm. But Churchill could not authorize the expenditure involved, and on September 5 Trenchard telegraphed to Cairo: 'I am afraid from your many telegrams that you have not got the atmosphere that is reigning here. That atmosphere is, economy at all cost. . . .'

Trenchard went on to warn Salmond that there could be no expenditure on air routes 'unless it is vitally necessary', that the Cairo to Cape route could not be advanced 'in any way', and that even on the Cairo to Karachi route 'the original idea of running the mail backwards and forwards must be held up for the present'. Trenchard ended his telegram: 'The whole business at present must be viewed in the light of economy, and even so it will be very doubtful if I shall have enough money to run the squadrons in India or Egypt.'

During 1920 Churchill and Trenchard found one sphere in which they were able to work closely together. In order to economize on the cost of imperial defence, Churchill had suggested transferring the control of Mesopotamia from the War Office to the Air Ministry, and governing the country by means of aeroplanes and armoured cars. On 29 February 1920 he wrote to Trenchard:

I shall be glad if you will, without delay, submit a scheme and state whether you consider the internal security of the country could be maintained by it. It is not intended that the force holding Mesopotamia should be sufficient to guard it against external invasion. It would be proportioned solely to the duty of maintaining internal security. . . .

It appears to me that this might well be obtained by having a series of defended areas in which air bases could be securely established. In these air bases, strong aerial forces could be maintained in safety and efficiency. An ample system of landing grounds judiciously selected would enable these air forces to operate in every part of the protectorate and to enforce control, now here, now there, without the need of maintaining long lines of communications eating up troops and money.

In his letter to Trenchard, Churchill examined in some detail the way in which Air Force control would operate:

The air bases should be well-defended areas of a permanent character— probably a ring of blockhouses with a certain number of tanks or moveable structures to supplement them and a system of carefully sited machine guns sweeping the approaches. They should in nearly every case be accessible by river. The landing grounds would appear to be sufficiently defended by one or more of the Moir pill boxes which could be erected to protect the aero-dromes and the storehouses and afford a temporary refuge for the small party of officers and mechanics who would be stationed there, for whom no doubt comfortable barracks would be built.

Not only must the air force be able to operate from the air by bomb and machine gun fire on any hostile garrison, but it must possess the power to convey swiftly two or three companies of men to any threatened point where ground work is required, and to maintain them. The construction of special aeroplanes for this purpose, and indeed for all other purposes incidental to any scheme must be the subject of special study. You will naturally make the tools you require for the job and exactly those tools *ad hoc*. The question of chemical bombs which are not destructive of human life but which inflict various degrees of minor annoyance should also be the subject of careful consideration.

Churchill urged Trenchard to put forward 'a practical scheme' which would commend itself to the Cabinet. This Trenchard proceeded to do. Every aspect of the problem excited Trenchard's imagination and stimulated his inventiveness. On 12 March 1920 Trenchard submitted his detailed scheme. There were two particular problems which the scheme highlighted. 'We have to develop the design of the supply aeroplane for carrying stores to isolated posts,' Trenchard explained, 'and the infantry-carrying aeroplane for the transportation of considerable numbers of men.'

Trenchard was prepared to push forward such developments, and welcomed the challenge which they presented. Churchill therefore took the question of Air Force control of Mesopotamia to the Cabinet, became its principal advocate and won approval for its implementation.

Throughout 1920 Churchill accepted without dissent the detailed policies which Trenchard put forward. But Trenchard's plans for expansion were continually frustrated by the Treasury's call for economy, and on Churchill, as Secretary of State for War, the Treasury's pressure was continual and almost irresistible. Trenchard never abandoned his appeals for special consideration; the Air Force, he believed, would only reach its full potential if it were given greater priority. In March 1921 he prepared a lengthy memorandum on the future role of air power, in which he insisted that the true value of the air force was not as an adjunct to the army or the navy, but as 'a primary and independent arm', with a definite part to play both in national and in imperial defence. To this end, it would need far greater funds than at present it was receiving.

In his memorandum, Trenchard set out in detail what he saw as the potential of air power both for defence and for offence. It was not 'a flight of the imagination' he declared, to say that shore-based aircraft could operate 'over a large portion of the trade routes of the Empire'. He also envisaged the use of aircraft, on a hitherto unconceived scale, to bomb ships and to drop torpedoes. As for the invasion threat, this, Trenchard believed, would be much reduced if air power were properly developed. 'No nation,' he wrote, 'would attempt such a task as an oversea invasion in the face of superior air forces capable of interfering with its vital communications.'

Churchill was excited by Trenchard's vision, which accorded with his own. 'Trenchard's whole submission,' he wrote to his Cabinet colleagues on a covering note, 'is so self-evident as to require no argument.' But a visionary air policy was not so easily pushed forward, and when Churchill gave up the Air Ministry on 1 April 1921, Trenchard had still to fight on against much opposition in search of the understanding and drive needed to make the Royal Air Force a major factor in the defence policy of successive Governments.

12

Russia in Turmoil

F ROM January 1919 Churchill's work at the War Office was dominated by the civil war in Russia, and by the presence of British troops alongside the anti-Bolshevik forces. For more than a year he had been an implacable critic of Bolshevism. In October 1917, when the Bolsheviks had seized power, and announced that Russia would leave the war, he had been incensed by what he considered an act of treachery by an ally. In a public speech at Bedford on 11 December 1917, he had declared: 'Russia has been thoroughly beaten by the Germans. Her great heart has been broken, not only by German might, but by German intrigue; not only by German steel, but by German gold.' And he continued: 'It is this melancholy event which has prolonged the war, that has robbed the French, the British and the Italian armies of the prize that was perhaps almost within their reach this summer; it is this event, and this event alone, that has exposed us to perils and sorrows and sufferings which we have not deserved, which we cannot avoid, but under which we shall not bend.'

On 26 December 1917, while still Minister of Munitions, Churchill had been invited to the War Cabinet to discuss the munitions problems created by Russia's withdrawal from the war. He stated that the Ministry of Munitions were doing all they could to 'damp down' the production of war materials allocated to Russia, but that they did not intend at present to regard Russia as 'an entirely gone' concern. A nucleus of the Russian programme would be kept in operation, he said, in order that full production could be restored 'in the event of a change in the situation'. Later in the discussion the question arose of the formation of an anti-Bolshevik force of Russians. According to the Minutes of the meeting:

Mr Churchill said he understood that a number of Russian officers were most anxious to be kept together, either in France or England, as a Russian unit to form a rallying point to those Russians who remained loyal to the *Entente*. In his opinion such a nucleus would be a valuable political asset.

British policy towards the Bolsheviks was evolved without Churchill's participation. On 14 December 1917 the War Cabinet had decided to pay any anti-Bolshevik Russians such money as they required 'for the purpose of maintaining alive in South-East Russia the resistance to the Central Powers'. The money would be paid 'so long as the recipients continued the struggle'. On December 26, after pressure from Clemenceau, the War Cabinet agreed that the French should direct all Allied activity against the Bolsheviks in the Ukraine, while the British were allotted the Armenian, Cossack and Caucasian regions 'as the British sphere' of anti-Bolshevik activity. This 'Convention of December 1917', as it was known, set the pattern for subsequent British involvement inside the boundaries of the former Russian Empire.

In the early months of 1918 Churchill was anxious to find some means of stimulating munitions production in England. The decision of the Bolsheviks to make peace with Germany made it inevitable that the Germans would concentrate all their troops for a massive attack in the west. On 23 February 1918 he wrote to his friend Lord Beaverbrook, who was then Minister of Information:

I am increasingly convinced that there can be no more valuable propaganda in England at the present time than graphic accounts of the Bolshevik outrages and ferocity, of the treacheries they have committed, and what ruin they have brought upon their country and the harm they have done to us and to our fighting men. It seems to me that the papers should be encouraged to give much publicity to all the news which reaches us of the chaos and anarchy in Russia. There is a strong feeling among British workmen that these wretches have 'let us down', and without overdoing it I think this absolutely true conception should be sustained by a constant stream of facts.

The War Cabinet met several times during February to decide what to do about the vast stock of British military supplies which had been sent to Russia in 1916 and 1917. Most of these supplies were stored, unprotected, at the northern ports of Archangel and Murmansk. In order to prevent them falling into German hands, Lloyd George decided, in March, to send British troops to protect them.

On 26 March 1918 the Bolshevik Government in Moscow agreed with the Allies to allow some 60,000 Czech prisoners of war—most of them captured by the Russians on the Austrian front in 1915—to leave

Russia along the Trans-Siberian railway to Vladivostok. The Allies wanted these Czech troops to fight against the Germans on the western front. By May 25 more than 10,000 of the Czechs had reached Vladivostok; the remaining 50,000 were scattered along several thousand miles of the Trans-Siberian railway, travelling eastwards. But on the following day Bolshevik troops attacked a unit of Czech artillery at Irkutsk. The Czechs retaliated in self-defence. Fighting between Czechs and Bolsheviks broke out in several towns, and by June 6 the Czechs were in possession of all the railway stations between Omsk and Krasnoyarsk, a distance of over eight hundred miles. Far from leaving Russia, they now controlled a vital part of her communications.

On learning that plans were still being made to evacuate the Czechs from Siberia by sea from Vladivostok, Churchill wrote to Lloyd George on 17 June 1918: 'It is certainly against your instinct & conviction to shift the Czecho-Slovak Corps from Russia to France.' Five days later, on June 22, he elaborated his views in a Cabinet memorandum, in the course of which he warned his colleagues:

If we cannot reconstitute the fighting front against Germany in the East, no end can be discerned to the war. Vain will be all the sacrifices of the peoples and the armies. They will only tend to prolong the conflict into depths which cannot be plumbed. We must not take 'No' for an answer either from America or from Japan. We must compel events instead of acquiescing in their drift. Surely now when Czech divisions are in possession of large sections of the Siberian Railway and in danger of being done to death by the treacherous Bolsheviks, some effort to rescue them can be made? Every man should ask himself each day whether he is not too readily accepting negative solutions.

Lloyd George already supported the policy which Churchill advocated. Clemenceau was likewise eager to see Bolshevism contained, and a new eastern front established in Russia. On 2 July 1918 Lloyd George and Clemenceau appealed jointly to President Wilson to give military support to the Czech forces in Siberia. Three days later the United States agreed to send troops to Russia. Henceforth, every allied Government helped to strengthen anti-Bolshevik forces. On July 16 the former British liaison officer with the Russian army, General Knox,[1] was instructed by the War Cabinet to go to Vladivostok, and to take charge of British military interests there. 'What we wanted,' Lord

---

[1] Alfred William Fortescue Knox, 1870–1964. 2nd Lieutenant, 1891. ADC to the Viceroy of India (Lord Curzon), 1899–1900 and 1902–3. Lieutenant-Colonel, 1911. Military Attaché, Petrograd, 1911–18. Major-General, 1918. Chief of the British Military Mission to Siberia, 1918–20. Knighted, 1919. Conservative MP for Wycombe, 1924–45.

© Martin Gilbert

THE INTERVENTION I

EASTERN SIBERIA

TRANS-SIBERIAN RAILWAY

JAPANESE

Lake
Baikal

Krasnoyarsk   CZECHS

Irkutsk

Vladivostok
AMERICANS
BRITISH
CANADIANS

Yellow
Sea

MONGOLIA

KOREA

Gobi
Desert

SINKIANG

CHINA

The Russian Imperial frontier in 1914
Area under Bolshevik control in January 1919
Anti-Bolshevik military activity in January 1919

0   250   500   750

Scale in miles

SIBERIA, 1918–1919

Robert Cecil[1] explained to the War Cabinet, 'was that friendly elements among the Russian troops should be collected and formed into an army.' A Labour MP, Colonel Ward,[2] was given command of two British battalions which landed at Vladivostok, where American, Japanese, French and Italian troops were already assembling. During July a further 7,000 Allied troops, mostly British, and under British command, landed at Murmansk and Archangel.

Even after the murder of the Tsar on 17 July 1918, Lloyd George was reluctant to institute a policy of greater military involvement against the Bolsheviks. 'Liberty,' he told the War Cabinet on July 22, 'meant that the Russian nation should have the right of setting up any Government they chose. If they chose a Republican Government, or a Bolshevist Government, or a Monarchical Government, it was no concern of ours. . . .' Yet British troops were already helping local anti-Bolshevik administrations at Batum on the Black Sea and at Baku on the Caspian Sea, while the British troops in northern Russia were giving food and finance to the local Russian authorities there, who had set up an anti-Bolshevik administration. In Siberia, the Allied troops sent to help the Czechs had come into direct armed conflict with Bolshevik troops, and in southern Russia the French were giving material as well as moral support to the anti-Bolshevik armies which had been brought together under several former Tsarist generals.

During August 1918 the Czech troops extended their control along the Trans-Siberian Railway helped by the Allied forces sent to protect them, including Colonel Ward and his two British battalions. At Omsk, the anti-Bolshevik Russians struggled to set up their own administration.

On 31 August 1918 Bolshevik troops forced their way into the British Embassy building in Petrograd. Their entry was resisted by the British Naval Attaché, Captain Cromie,[3] who, after killing three Bolshevik

[1] Lord Edgar Algernon Robert Cecil, 1864–1958. Third son of the 3rd Marquess of Salisbury. Independent Conservative MP, 1911–23. Under-Secretary of State for Foreign Affairs, 1915–16. Minister of Blockade, 1916–18. Created Viscount Cecil of Chelwood, 1923. Lord Privy Seal, 1923–4. President of the League of Nations, 1923–45. Chancellor of the Duchy of Lancaster, 1924–7. Nobel Peace Prize, 1937.

[2] John Ward, 1866–1934. Began work at the age of twelve as a railway navvy. Fought in the Sudan Campaign of 1885. Joined the Social Democratic Federation, 1886. Founded the Navvies' Union, 1886. Member of the Management Committee of the General Federation of Trade Unions, 1901–29; treasurer, 1913–29. Labour MP, 1906–22. Served on the western front as a Lieutenant-Colonel, Middlesex Regiment, 1915–16, having recruited five labour battalions. In 1918, while he was at Vladivostok with two battalions of the Middlesex Regiment, he supported Kolchak's revolt. Liberal MP, 1922–9.

[3] Francis Newton Allen Cromie, 1882–1918. Entered the Royal Navy as a midshipman, 1898; served in the China Expedition, 1900. Commanded the submarine E19, which forced

soldiers, was himself shot dead. 'The archives were sacked and everything was destroyed,' the Danish Minister in Petrograd[1] telegraphed to Copenhagen on September 2. 'Captain Cromie's corpse was treated in a horrible manner. Cross of St George was taken from the body and subsequently worn by one of the murderers. English clergyman was refused permission to repeat prayers over the body.' The Danish Minister's telegram was transmitted to London on September 3. Churchill was distressed by this news, which confirmed his belief in the barbarity of the Bolsheviks. As soon as he read the telegram he drafted a paper for the War Cabinet. Cromie, he wrote, was 'a very gifted man, of exceptionally high professional attainments', whom he had known personally before 1914. And he continued:

I earnestly hope that the Government, in spite of its many pre-occupations, will pursue the perpetrators of this crime with tireless perseverance. Reprisals upon various Bolshevik nonentities who happen to be in our hands are of no real use, though they should be by no means excluded. The only policy which is likely to be effective, either for the past or the future, is to mark down the personalities of the Bolshevik Government as the objects upon whom justice will be executed, however long it takes, and to make them feel that their punishment will become an important object of British policy to be held steadily in view through all the phases of the war and of the settlement. The exertions which a nation is prepared to make to protect its individual representatives or citizens from outrage is one of the truest measures of its greatness as an organised State. The fact that men are dying in thousands in fair war must not deaden us to the entirely different character of an act of this kind.

At its meeting on September 4 the War Cabinet decided to send a telegram to the Soviet Government, 'threatening reprisals' against Trotsky,[2] Lenin 'and the leaders of that Government' if the lives of British subjects were not safeguarded. Churchill was present at this War

a passage into the Baltic, September 1915. Brought German shipping in the Baltic to a halt for a whole week in October 1915. In Command of the English Flotilla in the Baltic, 1916–18.

[1] Harald Roger Scavenius, 1873–1939. Joined the Danish Foreign Office, 1900. Envoy to St Petersburg, 1912–20. Danish Foreign Minster, 1920–2. Envoy to Rome, 1923–8; to the Hague, 1928–39.

[2] Lev Davidovich Bronstein, 1879–1940. Son of a Jewish farmer. Studied mathematics at Odessa University, 1896. Gave up his studies to devote himself to revolutionary activity. Exiled to Siberia, 1898; escaped to England, 1902, with a forged passport in the name of 'Trotsky'. Joined the Mensheviks against Lenin, 1903. Returned to Russia, 1905. Again deported to Siberia, he again escaped, to London, in 1907. In exile in Vienna and Paris. Expelled from Paris, 1916, he went to New York. Returned to Russia, 1917, where he was reconciled to Lenin and became head of the Petrograd Soviet. Directed the armed uprising of 7 November 1917. Commissar for Foreign Affairs, 1917–18; for Military Affairs, 1918–25. Expelled from the Communist Party by Stalin, 1927. In exile in Turkey (1929), Norway (1936), and Mexico, where he was assassinated, probably on Stalin's orders.

Cabinet, but there was no record of his having spoken. At a further meeting of the War Cabinet on September 6 he declared 'that we should under no circumstances allow the Allied control of the Trans-Siberian Railway to be forfeited'.

With Germany's defeat imminent, doubts grew that the intervention in Russia should go on. When the War Cabinet met on October 18, Balfour pointed out that the main justification of the intervention had been 'to prevent German aggression and absorption of that country'. Several members of the War Cabinet challenged Balfour's attitude. General Smuts declared that Bolshevism was 'a danger to the whole world', and added that Britain was 'already committed at Murmansk, Archangel, and in Siberia'. Lord Robert Cecil added that he 'hated the idea of abandoning to Bolshevik fury all those who had helped us'; but he could not see how Bolshevism could be destroyed by 'military interference'.

When the War Cabinet met on November 10, the day before the Armistice with Germany, Churchill was asked to attend. He declared emphatically: 'We might have to build up the German Army, as it was important to get Germany on her legs again for fear of the spread of Bolshevism.' At an emergency conference at the Foreign Office on November 13, presided over by Balfour, and attended by two other members of the War Cabinet, Milner and Cecil, ten decisions were reached, each one in favour of continued British intervention in Russia. These included the continued occupation of Murmansk and Archangel; recognition for the Russians at Omsk who had set up an anti-Bolshevik administration; the maintenance of British troops in Siberia; military assistance for General Denikin[1] and his anti-Bolshevik forces in South Russia; the occupation of the Baku–Batum railway in the Caucasus and the despatch of munitions to the three Baltic states of Latvia, Lithuania and Estonia—each of which had been part of Tsarist Russia until 1917.

At the War Cabinet on November 14, Balfour pressed his colleagues to accept these proposals. He made a particularly strong plea on behalf of the former Baltic, Polish and Ukrainian provinces of Russia, insisting that Britain 'could not allow them to be overwhelmed by Central Russia, as these states contained populations of different race, language, and religion, and were, on the whole, more civilised and cultivated than

---

[1] Anton Ivanovich Denikin, 1872–1947. Entered the Tsarist Army in 1887; served in the Russo-Japanese War, 1904–5. Deputy Chief of Staff, February 1917. Commander of the Western Front, March 1917; of the South Western Front, May 1917. Commander-in-Chief of the Armed Forces of the South (anti-Bolshevist), 1918–19. Escaped first to Constantinople, then to France, 1920. Emigrated to the United States, 1945.

the Great Russians'. Lloyd George supported Balfour. According to the Minutes of the meeting: 'The Prime Minister stated that he was in entire agreement with the Foreign Secretary as to the general line of policy to be pursued.'

Lord Milner asked the War Cabinet if they would accept as a principle of British policy that where there was already in existence an anti-Bolshevik Government, Britain should support it, provided it was in the interests of the British Empire to do so—'that is to say, east of the Don and the Volga'. The War Cabinet accepted this principle. Lloyd George then gave his own opinion of the Bolshevik danger:

The Prime Minister said that it was important that the public in England should realise more fully what Bolshevism meant in practice. France was more secure against Bolshevism, owing to the existence of a large population of peasant proprietors. Here we had a great, inflammable, industrial population, and it was very desirable that our industrial population should know how industrial workers had suffered equally with the rest of the population of Russia at the hands of the Bolsheviks.

Churchill shared Lloyd George's view of the dangers of Bolshevism. On November 26, in a speech to his constituents at Dundee, he declared:

Russia is being rapidly reduced by the Bolsheviks to an animal form of Barbarism. The cost of living has multiplied 37 times. The paper money will not buy food or necessaries. Civil war is proceeding in all directions. The Bolsheviks maintain themselves by bloody and wholesale butcheries and murders carried out to a large extent by Chinese executioners and armoured cars. Work of all kinds is at a standstill. The peasants are hoarding their grain. The towns and cities only keep themselves alive by pillaging the surrounding country. We must expect that enormous numbers (probably more than we have lost in the whole war) will die of starvation during the winter. Civilisation is being completely extinguished over gigantic areas, while Bolsheviks hop and caper like troops of ferocious baboons amid the ruins of cities and the corpses of their victims.

By the end of December 1918 there were more than 180,000 non-Russian troops within the frontiers of the former Russian Empire, among them British, American, Japanese, French, Czech, Serb, Greek and Italian. Looking to these troops for military and moral support, and depending on them for money and guns, were several anti-Bolshevik armies of 'White' Russians, amounting to over 300,000 men. On every front the Bolsheviks were being pressed back towards Moscow. In

Siberia, Admiral Kolchak[1] had seized the leadership of all anti-Bolshevik activity east of the Urals. On all fronts the British, whose initial concern had been to keep Russia as an active ally in the war against Germany, had been drawn into a civil war between the Bolshevik and anti-Bolshevik Russians. The arms which they had sent to be used against Germany had been handed over to the anti-Bolshevik Russians, for use against the poorly armed Bolshevik forces. British troops, sent only to guard those arms, were being involved in the civil war, not only as advisers, but also as participants. Churchill had not been responsible for any of these decisions. But he had approved them. In a memorandum written at the end of 1918 he declared:

Most people wish to get free from Russia & to leave her to work out her own salvation or stew in her own juice assisted by any good advice we may have to spare. Nobody wants to intervene in Russian affairs. Russia is a vy large country, a vy old country, a vy disagreeable country inhabited by immense numbers of ignorant people largely possessed of lethal weapons & in a state of extreme disorder. Also Russia is a long way off. We on the other hand have just finished an important & expensive war against the Germans. We have won this war. We do not want to have a new war. On the contrary the war we have just won was as we have repeatedly declared a war to end war. We have not paid the bill for that one yet. It is far too soon to start out on another. We wish now to bring home our soldiers, reduce our taxes & enjoy our victory. On these points there is general agreement here.

Unhappily events are driving in a different direction, and nowadays events are vy powerful things. There never was a time when events were so much stronger than human beings. We may abandon Russia: but Russia will not abandon us. We shall retire & she will follow. The bear is padding on bloody paws across the snows to the Peace conference. By the time the delegates arrive she will be waiting outside the door. 'Am I to have no share in yr rejoicing & yr prosperity. I bled for you. I consumed my strength in yr cause. But for my sufferings you wd have perished. Are you really going to leave me to "stew in my own juice"?'

On 31 December 1918 Lloyd George invited Churchill to attend a meeting of the Imperial War Cabinet at 10 Downing Street. The aim of

---

[1] Alexander Vasilievich Kolchak, 1870–1920. A Crimean Tartar by birth. Served in the Russian Imperial Navy. Played a leading part in the siege of Port Arthur, 1905. Vice-Admiral, 1916. Commander-in-Chief of the Black Sea Fleet, 1916–17. Minister of War in the Siberian 'All Russian Government' (anti-Bolshevik), 1918. Declared himself 'Supreme Ruler', November 1918. Resigned the leadership of the anti-Bolshevik forces in favour of General Denikin, December 1919. Shot by the Bolsheviks at Irkutsk, 7 February 1920.

the meeting was to formulate British policy towards the Bolsheviks. During the meeting Lloyd George warned that the Allied position was 'highly unsatisfactory'. The Allies, he said, 'were neither interfering effectively in Russia nor evacuating it'. He felt that the first essential task at the Paris Peace Conference would be to work out 'a definite Allied policy' towards Russia. He proposed no British or Imperial initiative either way.

Churchill argued in favour of joint action by all the Allied powers, and he was confident that such action would succeed. The minutes recorded his remarks:

He was all for negotiation, with the object of securing a satisfactory settlement without fighting. But he considered that there was no chance of securing
such a settlement unless it was known that we had the power and the will to
enforce our views. What we should say to the Russians was that if they were
ready to come together we would help them: and that if they refused, we
would use force to restore the situation and set up a democratic Government.
In his view, Bolshevism in Russia represented a mere fraction of the population, and would be exposed and swept away by a General Election held under
Allied auspices. A decision on this question was urgent. It was the only part
of the war which was still going on, and if we ignored it we should come
away from the Peace Conference rejoicing in a victory which was no victory,
and a peace which was no peace: and in a few months we should find ourselves compelled to gather our armies again. . . .

Lloyd George was opposed to using Allied troops either to destroy Bolshevism, or to force the Russians to negotiate with each other. The farthest he was prepared to go was to help those border States in the Baltic and the Caucasus which were struggling to be independent from Russia, and which contained non-Russian majorities. He appealed to the Imperial War Cabinet to give him the authority, while in Paris, to bring all Allied military intervention to an end. 'Russia was a jungle,' he warned, 'in which no one could say what was within a few yards of him. In any case nothing could be worse than having no policy, and it was better to proceed resolutely on a wrong hypothesis than to go on hesitat-ing as the Allies had been doing.' Lloyd George then outlined the policy he wished to advocate in Paris. The minutes of the meeting recorded:

He was definitely opposed to military intervention in any shape. In the first
place, it appeared to him a tremendously serious undertaking. The Germans,
who had occupied only a relatively small part of Russia, within striking
distance of Petrograd and with practically nothing in front of them, had
found themselves unable, either to go to Petrograd or to save the situation in
the west, while all the time they and the Austrians had something like a

million men stuck in that morass, the greater part of whom they had not even yet succeeded in disentangling.

In our case the Allies were on the mere fringe of Russia, with less than 100,000 troops. The Bolsheviks had raised their forces to 300,000, which might exceed 1,000,000 by March, and had greatly improved their organisation. Where were we to find the troops with which to march into the heart of Russia and occupy the country? . . .

Our citizen army were prepared to go anywhere for liberty, but they could not be convinced that the suppression of Bolshevism was a war for liberty.

Lloyd George then explained his wider fears:

For Russia to emancipate herself from Bolshevism would be a redemption, but the attempt to emancipate her by foreign armies might prove a disaster to Europe as well as to Russia. The one thing to spread Bolshevism was to attempt to suppress it. To send our soldiers to shoot down the Bolsheviks would be to create Bolsheviks here. The best thing was to let Bolshevism fail of itself and act as a deterrent to the world. . . .

Lloyd George asked the Cabinet 'to support him in refusing to countenance any military intervention. . . .' Then he took up a suggestion made earlier by Sir Robert Borden[1] that 'representatives of all sections of Russia', Bolshevik, non-Bolshevik and anti-Bolshevik, should be invited to appear before the Peace Conference 'with a view to composing their differences'. The Imperial War Cabinet endorsed Lloyd George's remarks and accepted his proposal. But they also agreed with Lord Robert Cecil that if the Bolsheviks were to attack adjoining countries such as Poland and Rumania, the British and Imperial Governments 'would have to take measures to assist these countries in defending themselves'. Such assistance, it was felt, need not involve military intervention. Thus, on the eve of Churchill's becoming Secretary of State for War, it was agreed that no attempt should be made to overthrow Bolshevism by force.

Despite the decision not to intervene inside Russia, the future of British troops already on Russian soil had not been dealt with. On 21 January 1919, in a memorandum for the War Cabinet, Sir Henry Wilson pointed out that if these troops were to stay in North Russia, they would need to be reinforced. If reinforcements could not be sent, it might, he warned, be necessary to reduce the area under Allied control, and such action would then expose Finland to Bolshevik attack from the

[1] Robert Laird Borden, 1854–1937. Canadian Prime Minister, 1911–20. Knighted, 1914. First overseas Minister to receive summons to meeting of British Cabinet, 14 July 1915. Representative of Canada at Imperial War Cabinet, 1917–18. Chief Plenipotentiary Delegate of Canada at the Paris Peace Conference, 1919. Represented Canada on Council of League of Nations. Chairman of Sixth Committee of the League Assembly, 1930.

east. Even at present, Wilson emphasized, extra personnel were needed to enable the railway running south from Murmansk to be maintained; extra engineers were needed to prepare proper winter housing facilities; and at least a thousand extra men had been requested by the senior British officer at Murmansk, General Maynard,[1] for such tasks. Wilson supported Maynard's request. During the remaining winter months the temperature would remain well below zero. There were frequent snow blizzards, and little daylight, making the despatch of extra personnel a matter of urgency. At Archangel, the senior British officer, General Ironside,[2] had begun to train Russian soldiers in order to augment his force. But he had experienced, Wilson wrote, 'a little difficulty' with these troops, and needed reinforcements from Britain of both technical personnel and infantry, to secure his position. Wilson warned that any withdrawal from the existing position at either Murmansk or Archangel 'will expose considerable numbers of the Russian population, who have supported the Allied force, to massacre by the Soviet troops'. In his conclusion he stressed the 'urgent necessity' of reaching a decision, 'on the policy to be adopted'. 'Every day's delay,' he added, 'adds to the risk which is already serious.'

On January 3 the *Daily Express* warned its readers that there were 'ominous signs' that the Government were about to commit Britain to a 'gigantic campaign' against Russia. In its leading article the newspaper declared:

We are sorry for the Russians, but they must fight it out among themselves. Great Britain is already the policeman of half the world. It will not and cannot be the policeman of all Europe. We want to return to industry and to restore the ravages of war. We want to see our sons home again. In fact, we want peace. The frozen plains of Eastern Europe are not worth the bones of a single British grenadier.

[1] Charles Clarkson Martin Maynard, 1870–1945. 2nd Lieutenant, 1890. On active service in Burma, 1889–92, the Tirah, 1897, South Africa, 1900–1; and the Great War. Brigade-Commander, 1915–17. Commander-in-Chief of the Allied Forces at Murmansk, 1918–19. Knighted, 1919. Major-General, 1923. He published *The Murmansk Venture* in 1928.

[2] William Edmund Ironside, 1880–1959. 2nd Lieutenant, Royal Artillery, 1899. On active service in South Africa, 1899–1902. Major, 1914. Staff Officer, 4th Canadian Division, 1916–17. Commandant of the Machine Gun Corps School, France, 1918. Brigadier-General Commanding the 99th Infantry Brigade, 1918. Major-General commanding the Allied Troops, Archangel, 1918–19. Knighted, 1919. Head of the British Military Mission to Hungary, 1920. Commanded the Ismid Force, Turkey, 1920; the North Persian Force, 1920–1. Lieutenant-General, 1931. Quartermaster-General, India, 1933–6. General, 1935. Governor and Commander-in-Chief, Gibraltar, 1938–9. Head of the British Military Mission to Poland, August 1939. Chief of the Imperial General Staff, 1939–40. Commander-in-Chief, Home Forces, to prepare against invasion, May 1940. Field-Marshal, 1940. Created Baron, 1941. In 1953 he published *Archangel 1918–19*.

Murmansk

FINLAND

Archangel

Dvina

Kotlas

Petrograd

Baltic Sea

Viatka

Smolensk   Moscow   Kazan

CZECHS
KOLCHAK

Warsaw
POLAND

Tula

Chernigov   Orel
Kursk

Voronezh

Orenburg

Kiev
Kharkov
Poltava
Odessa
UKRAINE

Don

Donetz

Volga

RUMANIA

Dniester

Nikolaev
Kherson

Tsaritsyn

COSSACKS

BULGARIA

Varna

Don
COSSACKS

Astrakhan

THRACE

Black
Sea

Novorossisk

Caspian Sea

Constantinople

COSSACKS
Caucasus

GEORGIA

TRANSCASPIA

Prinkipo

Batum

TURKEY

Kars

DAGHESTAN

ARMENIA

AZERBAIJAN

Baku

Enzeli

Hamadan   PERSIA

—·—·— Russia's 1914 frontiers

▲▲▲ The line of the anti-Bolshevik armies in January 1919

0   100 200 300 400 500

Scale in miles

© Martin Gilbert

THE ANTI—BOLSHEVIK FORCES IN EUROPEAN RUSSIA, 1919

The War Cabinet met to discuss Russia on January 10, the day on which Churchill accepted Lloyd George's offer of the War Office. The main discussion was about how to halt the spread of Bolshevism westward. Sir Henry Wilson pointed out that during the past week 'there had been signs of unrest in the Army at home, and it was notorious that the prospect of being sent to Russia was immensely unpopular'. The War Cabinet also had before it a message from Marshal Foch, who stated that it was essential for Britain and France to give aid to Poland against the Bolsheviks. Foch argued 'that it was to the interest of the Associated Governments to stop the advance of Bolshevism before it penetrated Austria and Germany'. Churchill supported Foch's appeal, urging his colleagues not to 'stand aside and let Poland go to pieces'. He then suggested that the defeated German army should be used to check the westward advance of Bolshevism. 'It might be advisable,' he said, 'to let Germany know that if she were prepared to organise her Eastern front against the ingress of Bolshevism, the Allied Governments would raise no objection.' 'It was a matter of serious consideration,' he added, 'whether we should not now decide to bolster up the Central Powers, if necessary, in order to stem the tide of Bolshevism.'

The discussion then turned to the question of Siberia. Bonar Law said that Sir Henry Wilson had recommended the withdrawal of the two British battalions near Omsk. But Wilson seemed to have changed his mind, for he intervened to say that any such withdrawal 'meant breaking faith with the French and the Czecho-Slovaks'. Churchill spoke next, deprecating the withdrawal of the two battalions. 'If they were taken away,' he said, 'the fabric we had been trying to construct would fall to pieces. The Czechs would go, Kolchak's army would disappear, and the French would withdraw.' But no decision was reached; the War Cabinet decided that the Siberian question, as well as the containment of Bolshevism, 'must await the decision of the Associated Governments as to their general policy in Russia'.

Sir Henry Wilson was furious at the War Council's prevarication. 'Absolutely no policy,' he wrote in his diary. From that day, he was Churchill's senior adviser on military affairs. But he did not entirely share Churchill's point of view. 'The more I think about Russia,' he wrote in his diary on Sunday January 12, 'the more convinced I am that we (British) should keep out of the scrum. If the Americans & French like to go in, let them.' On some policies, however, he and Churchill were in full agreement. 'At the same time,' Wilson added, 'we should order the Boches to hold up Bolshevism. . . .'

Lloyd George, who had arrived in Paris for the Peace Conference, asked Wilson to lunch with him on January 12. 'We discussed Russia,' Wilson recorded. 'LG is opposed to knocking out Bolshevism. He does not like my proposal to arm Russian prisoners now in Germany even if they express a wish to go and fight ag^t the Bolshevists.'

On January 13, the Imperial War Cabinet met in Paris, with Lloyd George in the chair, to discuss future action in Russia. Sir Henry Wilson, who was present, wrote in his diary: 'It was quite clear that the meeting favoured *no* troops being sent to fight Bolshevists but on the other hand to help those States which we considered were Independent States by giving them arms, etc.'

Although Lloyd George and the War Cabinet were moving towards a policy of total withdrawal of all British troops from Russia, no final decision had been made; Churchill had now to deal with the day-to-day problems which the presence of troops involved. On January 14, his first official day as Secretary of State for War, there were already seven British Generals holding military commands on Russian soil. Each of these Generals, and the 14,000 British troops which they commanded, had been sent to Russia during 1918, with the Cabinet's approval, while Milner had been Secretary of State for War.[1]

On reaching the War Office on January 14, Churchill telegraphed to General Maynard and General Ironside in North Russia, to explain why it was necessary for their troops to remain in Russia:

It is not a question of their fighting value but of the moral effect. It would be better to risk a few thousand men (though there would be no risk if the railway could be put right) than to allow the whole fabric of Russo-Siberian resistance to Bolshevism to crumble. What sort of a Peace (!) shd we have, if all Europe & Asia from Warsaw to Vladivostock were under the sway of Lenin?

On the afternoon of January 15, at a meeting with fifty journalists in the War Office, Churchill spoke of the need for keeping up the existing British forces in Russia. On January 18 he agreed to Sir Henry Wilson's proposal to send out Press Correspondents to both Murmansk and Batum, in the hope that publicity for the soldiers' work in Russia would help win support in Britain for what they were doing. On January 20 he had several interviews with Wilson, and then dined with him at the

---

[1] Major-General Maynard had taken command of the British troops at Murmansk on 23 June 1918; Major-General Sir Alfred Knox at Vladivostok on 16 July 1918; Major-General Malleson in Transcaspia in mid-July 1918; Major-General Thomson at Baku on 17 November 1918; Major-General Ironside at Archangel on 19 November 1918, and Major-General Poole in the Caucasus on 3 December 1918.

Turf Club. That night Wilson noted in his diary: 'Winston all against Bolshevism, & therefore, in this, against LG.'

Lloyd George still favoured conciliation rather than intervention. While he was in Paris he decided, with the support of Woodrow Wilson, to invite the Bolsheviks to peace talks on the Turkish island of Prinkipo, near Constantinople. Churchill learned of this decision when he reached Paris on January 23, hoping to obtain Lloyd George's support for his demobilization scheme, and on the morning of January 24 expressed his anger to General Spiers. That evening Mary Borden [1] recorded in her diary that Spiers 'had long talk with Winston who said he had a row with LG, while the latter was shaving, about Russia. It seems it was LG's idea to invite Bolsheviks to Prinkipo & Wilson rushed in and took it all on himself.' Mary Borden added: 'Winston told LG one might as well legalize sodomy as recognize the Bolsheviks.'

On January 27, Churchill sent Lloyd George a strongly worded letter about the urgent need for a clear policy both in north and south Russia. He now accepted Lloyd George's reluctance to become embroiled with the Bolsheviks, and asked to be instructed to evacuate North Russia. But he pressed Lloyd George to continue to send material help to South Russia, Transcaspia and Siberia. In his letter Churchill wrote:

I am distressed by the military telegrams from Russia. We have very small forces (about 14,000) there. They are exerting a great influence, particularly in Siberia, because they are thought to be the vanguard of Britain. They are nothing of the sort. Individual officers and soldiers are keeping large towns and districts up to their duty against the Bolsheviks by giving the impression that 'Britain is behind them'; whereas long ago Britain has quitted the field.

We are at the present moment heavily and indefinitely committed in all sorts of directions, and we have, as far as I can see, not the least intention of making good any of them.

From the mere War Office standpoint, I object very much indeed to keeping soldiers in the field who are denied the transport, the technical services, the doctors, the hospital staffs and even the mules that they require according to their numbers. But that is what we are doing. These poor men are writing cheques on our account and in our name which we have neither the intention nor the means to honour. They have written a good many already.

It seems to me most urgent for us to frame and declare our *policy*. 'Evacuate at once at all costs' is a policy; it is not a very pleasant one from the point of view of history. 'Reinforce and put the job through' is a policy; but un-

[1] Mary Borden,   –1968. Daughter of William Borden of Chicago. She married General Spiers (her second husband) on 30 March 1918. She published over twenty books under her maiden name, including her first novel in 1924. Head of the Hadleigh–Spears Mobile Field Hospital Unit, France, 1939–40.

happily we have not the power—our orders would not be obeyed, I regret to
say.

Therefore, we must confine ourselves to modest limits. I offer the following
advice:—

(1) With regard to Murmansk and Archangel. Withdraw these forces as
soon as the ice allows, using the interval to wind up commitments there and
offering persons compromised there through working with and for us a refuge
in our ships. Meanwhile, however, equip and sustain those forces with the
small technical details and medical staff they require for their welfare, using
discreetly for this purpose all our present powers under the Military Service
Acts. All told the details needed do not exceed 1,000.

(2) South Russia, Transcaspia and Siberia.
These comprise enormous regions into which it will be disastrous for us for
Bolshevism to penetrate. Here we have called into being during the war, in
reliance upon our promises and encouraged by our aid, Russian armies which
are fighting themselves in an indifferent manner with varying fortunes—but
still fighting. We are very heavily compromised with Denikin and the Omsk
Government. We have only got two battalions in Siberia, and they are everywhere being paraded as symbols of the British power.

I consider, in view of what you have told me, that the anti-Bolshevik
Russians should be told that they have got to shift for themselves, that we
wish them well, but that all we can do is to give them moral support by the
presence of such volunteers—officers and men—who are ready to serve in
these theatres, and material in money, arms and supplies.

I hold most strongly that, after all that has happened, we cannot cut these
anti-Bolshevik Russian armies suddenly off the tap of our supplies. As long as
they are able to go on fighting effectively, we should continue to aid them
with arms, supplies and volunteers. We should fix now the quota of arms and
supplies, but should give no guarantee as to the number of volunteers.

If they are suppressed or throw up the sponge, we should, of course, withdraw and disinterest ourselves in all that may follow.

All the telegrams show that this matter requires your personal attention.
At present we are extending our commitments, curtailing our contributions,
and not even maintaining our own men, who have been sent there by
compulsion, as British soldiers should be maintained by the Government
responsible for their proper usage.

Churchill awaited Lloyd George's decision. But Lloyd George had
decided to wait until after the conference at Prinkipo between the
different Russian groups, although it was not certain whether the conference would ever take place. Churchill enlisted Sir Henry Wilson's
support, and Wilson wrote a commentary to Churchill's letter, which
was sent, with the letter, to Lloyd George. 'With all you say I entirely
agree,' wrote Wilson. 'For *months* I have been writing papers about

Russia with no result.' Wilson recognized that the problem of coming to a clear decision was 'enormously complicated by our Allies', and would be further delayed 'until the Prinkipo affair is exploded'. Wilson gave his own opinion of what should be done; it was not at all far removed from Churchill's. 'I am in favour,' he wrote, 'of being ready i) to quit Murmansk & Archangel next summer; ii) of quitting Omsk *now* if the French agree; iii) but of strengthening our hold on Batoum–Baku–Krasnovodsk–Merv line.' Churchill shared Wilson's doubts about the intervention at Omsk. 'Our policy in Siberia is too nebulous,' he wrote in a War Office minute on January 29, '& our prospects too gloomy. . . '

The commanders at Murmansk, Archangel and Batum clamoured for reinforcements in order to maintain their positions intact. On January 30 Sir Henry Wilson ordered three battalions from Salonica and one from Egypt to reinforce the British garrison at Batum, 'Winston agreeing', he noted in his diary. Wilson also wanted Churchill to persuade Lloyd George, as a matter of urgency, to send a further 2,500 men to North Russia. On January 31 he sent Churchill a four-page memorandum stressing the need for a swift decision. Every day's delay in not sending reinforcements, he wrote, 'added to the risk, which was already serious'. Wilson went on to state emphatically that the decision to invite the Bolsheviks to Prinkipo 'has had the inevitable result of discouraging the Russian troops now in the process of organisation in North Russia, to say nothing of the Allied forces there, some of whom at least leave much to be desired in the way of discipline, training and fighting spirit'.

On February 3 Churchill telegraphed to Lloyd George to ask that the Cabinet decision of January 10 'against sending more men to Russia' should be modified to enable the electricians, railwaymen and medical personnel needed in North Russia to be sent out at once. Until the Allies decided to withdraw their troops from Russia, Churchill declared, the responsibility 'for their proper maintenance, nourishment and support' rested with the War Office, and that as Secretary of State for War, he was determined 'to take whatever measures are possible to give effect to the military advice I receive and make sure that our troops are not ill-treated or cast away'. Churchill's telegram ended:

The alarming rumours which are circulating in London about the safety of our troops in North Russia are not justified by the facts, but the situation may rapidly deteriorate and people will not tolerate their beloved ones being left to their fate on this desolate coast without resolute efforts being made to succour them. These measures will be equally necessary whether the decision of the Allied Governments is to withdraw in the summer or go on with the operation. . . .

The War Office General Staff had prepared a detailed memorandum on the situation in North Russia, a copy of which was sent to Lloyd George by Churchill on February 4. In it, the General Staff pointed out that the Allied position in North Russia had, since January 19, been under attack by superior Bolshevik forces, and that they had been forced to retreat at several points.[1] If no further troops were sent out, the General Staff warned, there was the risk of 'a grave disaster to our own and Allied troops, for whose safety the British Government is primarily responsible'. A Bolshevik success in North Russia would, they concluded, 'give to the Bolshevik cause an impetus which would be felt not only in Siberia and South Russia but throughout the civilized world'.

Lloyd George accepted the War Office arguments, and on February 5 sent Churchill a telephone message to say that any reinforcements needed 'to secure the health, comfort and nourishment of troops should be sent without delay'. He also gave his interpretation of the War Cabinet's decision of January 10. 'The Cabinet decision that no re-inforcements should be sent to Russia,' he said, 'was due to the fact that they were advised by their military advisers that there was considerable unrest in the Army on the subject of Russia and that the despatch of further troops might have serious results. . . .' By agreeing to the despatch of further troops, Lloyd George himself now reversed the Cabinet's policy of withdrawal. Churchill, however, was cautious in implementing this decision, telegraphing to Lloyd George on February 5:

Opinion here is that *morale* of Army is much improved now from what it was three weeks ago. Full reports are not yet available, but there is a growing feeling of confidence. I hope it will not be long before anxieties in this respect at least may be greatly diminished. Meanwhile I ought to tell you that, since my telegram of the 3rd, two messages have been received from Murmansk & Archangel of a more encouraging nature as regards the daylight, and, secondly, showing that medical conditions have been greatly improved by exertions made locally. I am therefore having the question of the strength of any drafts that may be required carefully re-examined.

Churchill continued to urge caution when he wrote to his senior advisers, General Harington and General Thwaites,[2] on February 6, in

[1] The number of Allied troops in North Russia was less than that of the Bolsheviks: 6,220 British, 5,300 Russians, 5,100 Americans, 1,680 French and 25 Italians; a total force of 18,325, of whom, 11,195 were fighting troops. The Bolsheviks had 22,700 men at their disposal, of whom over 18,000 were fighting troops.
[2] William Thwaites, 1868–1947. 2nd Lieutenant, Royal Artillery, 1887; Lieutenant-Colonel, 1914. Served on the western front, 1915–18. Commanded the 141st Infantry Brigade, 1915–16; the 46th Division, 1916–18. Major-General, 1918. Director of Military

answer to their proposals for sending arms and equipment to the anti-
Bolshevik armies:

It is highly important to know what the Russians can & will do for themselves.

If they put up a real fight, we ought in my view to back them in every
possible way. But without them it is no good our trying.

Be vy careful not to let our wishes colour our statements.

When the War Cabinet met on February 12, Churchill asked for an
immediate decision; either a properly organized intervention, or withdrawal. The Minutes of the meeting recorded his appeal:

The Secretary of State for War said that we were committed in various
directions in Russia. We had forces both in the north and in the south of
Russia, and in Siberia. The men there were entitled to know what they were
fighting for, and were entitled to proper support from home. Our enterprises in
all these directions were crumbling. The situation in the north was not yet serious, although it might very easily become so. The Bolsheviks were getting
stronger every day. In the South, General Denikin's army had greatly deteriorated. Krasnoff[1] was discouraged, and believed the Allies had thrown them over
completely. The situation in Siberia was exactly the same. There was complete disheartenment everywhere. The Great Powers were still delaying the
decision on this matter. If we were going to withdraw our troops, it should be
done at once. If we were going to intervene, we should send larger forces
there. . . .

Churchill added that his personal belief was 'that we ought to intervene'. Lloyd George replied that he had always understood the War
Office's view to be that 'if we were going to do any good, we should need
a million men at least, and these should be despatched in the spring'.
Churchill said that he did not suggest a British military intervention 'on
that scale', but that it was necessary 'to try and keep alive the Russian
forces which were attempting to make headway against the Bolsheviks'.
Lloyd George returned to the question of numbers. A successful British
intervention, he said, would need 'half a million men advancing from

---

Intelligence, September 1918–April 1922; Director of Military Operations and Intelligence,
April–October 1922. Knighted, 1919. General Officer commanding the 47th Division (TA),
1923–6; British Army on the Rhine, 1927–9. Director-General, Territorial Army, 1931–3.

[1] Peter Nikolaevich Krasnoff, 1869–1947. A General in the Tsarist Army, he went to the
Don after the October Revolution, and organized an anti-Bolshevik Don Army, receiving
military aid first from the Germans, and then from the Allies. He twice attacked Tsaritsyn,
but failed to capture it, and eventually put his Don Army under Denikin's command. In
1919 he emigrated to Germany. In 1945 he was captured by the Red Army, sentenced to
death for collaboration with the Germans, and hanged.

Odessa or through Poland'. He believed that if Britain tried to limit her involvement to sending the anti-Bolshevik Russians guns and equipment, it would still be necessary to send at least 150,000 British troops to help them. Churchill agreed with Lloyd George 'that intervention on a large scale was not possible'.

The Chancellor of the Exchequer, Austen Chamberlain, told the War Cabinet that he doubted the chances of 'any good results', as the anti-Bolshevik forces were 'untrustworthy', the English troops in Siberia were 'very tired' and even the Czechs were now 'less willing to fight'. Churchill reiterated his view that 'if we had no effective means of helping these people, the sooner they were told the better it would be'. But, he warned, if the Allies would not help Russia now, Japan and Germany would 'certainly do so', and after a few years 'we should see the German Republic, united with the Bolsheviks in Russia and the Japanese in the Far East, forming one of the most powerful combinations the world had ever seen'.

Lord Curzon suggested sending volunteers of other nationalities as well as British. 'The Swedish Minister,'[1] he said, 'had mentioned to him the possibility of getting Swedish volunteers.' But Austen Chamberlain was critical of further intervention. As President Wilson had said that he was opposed to intervention, Britain and France would, he warned, 'have to sustain the whole cost'. Nor could the anti-Bolshevik forces, in his opinion, survive 'for a moment' by themselves. For the third time at the meeting, Churchill asked his colleagues to authorize him either to intervene directly with British troops, or to help the anti-Bolshevik forces with guns and equipment, 'or to withdraw'. But Lloyd George proposed the same solution as he had a month earlier on January 10: it was essential, he said, for the decision to be made in Paris, and with the personal involvement of President Wilson. 'It was a question which could not be decided here in London,' he insisted, 'but they should send an expression of their opinion to Paris.'

President Wilson was due to leave Paris, for America, on Saturday February 15. It was therefore necessary to have the discussion with him on February 14. Meanwhile, Lloyd George asked Sir Henry Wilson to prepare a statement showing the military effect of each of the three possible policies: full intervention; aid to the anti-Bolsheviks; and withdrawal. Churchill himself sent a long note to Wilson, in which he asked him to assume, in his calculations:

[1] Count Anton Magnus Herman Wrangel, 1857–1934. Swedish Minister to Brussels and the Hague, 1900–4; to Petrograd, 1904–6; to London, 1906–20. Swedish Delegate to the Paris Peace Conference, 1919; Minister for Foreign Affairs, 1920–1.

(a) that the Prinkipo Conference will not take place and that the Allied Governments will instead make a united appeal to all loyal Russians to exert themselves to the utmost against the Bolsheviks;

(b) that no troops can be sent from this country by compulsion to carry on the war in Russia.

The War Cabinet met again at noon on February 13. 'I refused to give any opinion,' Sir Henry Wilson wrote in his diary, 'of how much chance we should have of beating the Bolsheviks if we back the Esthonians, Poles, Denikin etc. There are too many unknown quantities for me to offer an opinion.'

At six o'clock that evening the Cabinet met for a second time that day, in Lloyd George's room in the House of Commons. According to the minutes of the meeting, Churchill reiterated his opinion that 'the only chance of making headway against the Bolsheviks was by the use of Russian armies'. There were, he said, nearly half a million anti-Bolshevik Russians under arms, and the Russians themselves planned to double this figure. 'If we were unable to support the Russians effectively,' he added, 'it would be far better to take a decision now to quit and face the consequences, and tell these people to make the best terms they could with the Bolsheviks.' Later in the discussion he declared: 'We were not dealing with facts that were at all certain. We were endeavouring to animate the wavering hands of the Russian forces, which were all that we could rely on. The Russian morale depended upon the Allies having a decided policy and carrying it out energetically.' Churchill went on to speak of the possibility of the Allies deciding to declare war on the Bolsheviks 'by a united declaration in Paris'. If this were done then British forces would have a part to play at Archangel, and Murmansk, in the Ukraine, Esthonia and the Caucasus. There would be 'no difficulty', he said, 'in finding the necessary volunteers'.

It was clear, Wilson wrote in his diary, 'that neither LG nor the Cabinet would throw their hearts into beating the Bolsheviks by means of Esthonians, Denikin etc & so I insisted there was only one course left and that was to clear out. . . . I am all in favour of declaring war on the Bolsheviks, but the others, except Winston, won't.'

At half past five on the morning of February 14, Churchill, accompanied by Sir Henry Wilson, left London by train for Paris. Their mission was to ask Clemenceau and President Wilson what policy Britain should pursue.

At the end of a War Office Minute of February 12, Henry Wilson had written: 'We think that if an atmosphere of help to our comrades were created, coupled with the knowledge of officers volunteering in

great numbers, much of the difficulty would be overcome.' Churchill
read Wilson's note during the journey to Paris, commenting on it, in
red pencil:

> Policy first.
>   Atmosphere second.
>   Then & not till then
>   Action.
> There is no policy at present.

13

Mission to Paris

CHURCHILL and Sir Henry Wilson reached Newhaven early on the morning of February 14, crossing at once to Dieppe in the destroyer *Plucky*, which had been alerted to receive them, and motoring without a break from Dieppe to Paris. During the journey, Wilson's car was involved in an accident which smashed the windscreen and broke half the steering wheel. Cold and wet, the two men reached Paris at three in the afternoon. At half past six that evening, Clemenceau informed President Wilson that he was summoning an emergency meeting of the Council of Ten, at the request of A. J. Balfour. As well as Clemenceau and Balfour, those present included Churchill, Sir Henry Wilson, Lord Milner, Sir Maurice Hankey and Philip Kerr[1] for Britain; Marshal Foch and Pichon[2] for France, Baron Sonnino[3] for Italy; and General Bliss and President Wilson for the United States. The meeting opened at 7 p.m., in Pichon's room at the Quai d'Orsay. Balfour told the Council that a decision had to be reached about the forthcoming meeting between the Bolsheviks, the anti-Bolsheviks and the Allies at Prinkipo. On February 4 the Bolsheviks had agreed to come to Prinkipo; it was up to the Allies to decide how to respond. Balfour asked

[1] Philip Henry Kerr, 1882–1940. Worked as a Civil Servant in South Africa, 1905–8. Editor, *The Round Table*, 1910–16. Secretary to Lloyd George, 1916–21. Secretary of the Rhodes Trust, 1925–39. Succeeded his cousin as 11th Marquess of Lothian, 1930. Chancellor of the Duchy of Lancaster, 1931. Chairman of the Indian Franchise Committee, 1932. Ambassador in Washington from 1939 until his death.

[2] Stephen Pichon, 1857–1933. Radical Deputy, 1885–93. Ambassador to Haiti, 1894; to Brazil, 1896; to China, 1898–1901. Resident General, Tunis, 1901–6. Senator, 1906–24. Three times Foreign Minister: October 1906–February 1911; March–December 1913 and November 1917–January 1920. One of the signatories of the Versailles Treaty.

[3] Sidney Sonnino, 1847–1922. Born in Alexandria, Egypt, of a Florentine father and an English mother. Italian Minister of Finance, 1893–6. Twice Prime Minister of Italy for a hundred days, in 1906, and 1909–10; Foreign Minister, November 1914–June 1919. Second Italian Delegate (Orlando was the First) at the Paris Peace Conference, January–June 1919. Senator, 1920. A distinguished Dante scholar and bibliophile.

Churchill to explain to the Council 'the present views of the British Cabinet'. In his book *The Supreme Control*, Hankey later recalled that Churchill opened the proceedings 'with great moderation'.

Churchill began by pointing out the 'great anxiety' about the Russian situation expressed at the Cabinet meeting on the previous day, and he went on to explain that:

In view of the imminent departure of President Wilson, the Cabinet had asked him to go over and obtain some decision as to the policy on this matter. Mr Lloyd George had expressed a wish to know whether the Allied policy which had led to the suggestion of the meeting at Prinkipo was to be pursued or, if not, what policy was to be substituted for it. If it were possible to go on with the original policy, so much the better, but if only the Bolsheviks were to attend the Conference, it was thought that little good would come of the meeting. . . .

Churchill also asked the Council to give a decision on the military aspects of the intervention:

Great Britain had soldiers in Russia who were being killed in action. Their families wished to know what purpose these men were serving. Were they just marking time until the Allies had decided on a policy, or were they fighting in a campaign representing some common aim? The longer the delay continued, the worse would be the situation of the troops on all the Russian fronts. The Russian elements in these forces were deteriorating rapidly because of the uncertainty of the support they might expect from the victorious Allies. The Allied troops were intermingled with these Russian troops, which were weakening and quavering, and they were themselves becoming affected. . . .

If the Prinkipo meeting did not lead to a 'cessation of arms' in Russia, Churchill concluded, 'this unsatisfactory condition might last an indefinite time'.

Clemenceau spoke next. A matter of such importance, he argued, 'could not be settled at a short and unexpected meeting'. He said no more, but was followed by President Wilson, who offered the meeting his 'personal thoughts' on the subject. He was opposed to any further Allied intervention in Russia, and said so bluntly:

. . . the troops of the Allied and Associated Powers were doing no sort of good in Russia. They did not know for whom or for what they were fighting. They were not assisting any promising common effort to establish order throughout Russia. They were assisting local movements, like, for instance, that of the Cossacks, who could not be induced to move outside their own sphere. His conclusion, therefore, was that the Allied and Associated Powers ought to withdraw their troops from all parts of Russian territory.

President Wilson then spoke of the Prinkipo meeting. Its aim, he said, was to find out 'what the people in Russia were thinking and purposing to do'. He was quite prepared to send an American representative to meet the Bolsheviks. But he pointed out that when the Bolsheviks agreed to come to Prinkipo, they had raised a number of issues which were, Wilson said, 'insulting'. These were 'repayment of debts, concessions and territorial compensations'.

Churchill spoke once more. It was essential, he declared, to institute a clear-cut policy. The complete withdrawal of all Allied troops was, at least, 'a logical and clear policy', but he feared that its consequences 'would be the destruction of all non-Bolshevik armies in Russia', a total of half a million men, whose numbers were increasing. 'Such a policy,' he continued, 'would be equivalent to pulling out the linch-pin from the whole machine. There would be no further armed resistance to the Bolsheviks in Russia, and an interminable vista of violence and misery was all that remained for the whole of Russia.' President Wilson was not impressed by Churchill's argument. 'The existing Allied forces,' he said, 'could not stop the Bolsheviks,' nor were any of the Allies 'prepared to reinforce its troops'. When Baron Sonnino asked whether the Allies might not at least continue to supply arms to the 'non-Bolshevik elements', Wilson observed that up until then the non-Bolshevik Russians 'had made very little use of them when they had them'.

Churchill made a further attempt to rouse support for a more active Allied policy. He accepted that 'none of the Allies could send conscript troops to Russia'. But he thought that the Allies might agree to send 'volunteers, technical experts, arms, munitions, tanks, aeroplanes, etc'. President Wilson was sceptical of Churchill's suggestion, and said so bluntly, as the minutes of the meeting recorded:

PRESIDENT WILSON understood the problem was to know what use would be made of these forces and supplies. In some areas they would certainly be assisting reactionaries. Consequently, if the Allies were asked what they were supporting in Russia they would be compelled to reply that they did not know. Conscripts could not be sent and volunteers probably could not be obtained. He himself felt guilty in that the United States had in Russia insufficient forces, but it was not possible to increase them. It was certainly a cruel dilemma. At present our soldiers were being killed in Russia, if they were removed many Russians might lose their lives. But some day or other the Allied troops would be withdrawn; they could not be maintained there for ever and the consequences to the Russians would only be deferred.

Churchill then explored another possibility. If Prinkipo failed, he asked, would the Council approve 'of arming the anti-Bolshevik forces in Russia'? President Wilson replied 'that he hesitated to express any definite opinion', but that whatever the Council decided, he would 'cast in his lot with the rest'. The meeting then adjourned until the following afternoon. A few hours later, President Wilson left Paris by train for Cherbourg, and the United States.

That night, Churchill, Sir Henry Wilson and Philip Kerr dined together to discuss the Russian impasse. According to a letter which Kerr sent to Lloyd George on February 15, Churchill proposed that the Council of Ten should be asked to reach two decisions: first, that an Allied Commission would go to Prinkipo provided hostilities were stopped throughout Russia 'within, say, ten days'; and second, that an Inter-Allied Commission should be set up at once to decide what military and economic action the Allies should take, in conjunction with Russia's neighbours, 'to bring the Bolshevik regime to an end'.

On the morning of February 15, Churchill, Sir Henry Wilson and Kerr met again, to discuss the drafts which they had prepared: Wilson's about the Inter-Allied Commission, Churchill's and Kerr's about the invitation to the Bolsheviks to come to Prinkipo. 'Mr Churchill's draft,' Kerr wrote to Lloyd George in his letter of February 15, '. . . made it a condition of coming to Prinkipo that the Soviet Government should notify the Peace Conference that it had ceased hostilities and withdrawn its troops for a distance of five miles within a stated period, in which case the Allied Governments would invite pro-Ally forces to do the same.' Kerr himself had prepared a more general draft, which, Kerr explained to Lloyd George, 'was addressed impartially to both sides'. But Kerr went on to say that Balfour, to whom the drafts were shown that morning, 'preferred Mr Churchill's', and that it was therefore Churchill's draft that would be put before the Council of Ten when it reconvened that afternoon.

In his letter to Lloyd George, Kerr wrote that he was 'inclined to think' Churchill's attitude towards Prinkipo 'the right one', provided it were drafted in such a form as to give the Bolsheviks 'every inducement' to accept a cease-fire. Kerr's letter ended, however, with a warning:

. . . I cannot conceal from you that in my opinion Mr Churchill is bent on forcing a campaign against Bolshevik Russia by using Allied volunteers, Polish and Finnish and any other conscripts that can be got hold of, financed and equipped by the Allies. He is perfectly logical in his policy, because he declares that the Bolsheviks are the enemies of the human race and must be put down at any cost.

Kerr urged Lloyd George 'to watch the situation very carefully, if you do not wish to be rushed into the policy of a volunteer war against the Bolsheviks in the near future'.

On Saturday February 15, Churchill lunched with Balfour, and sought his support for his proposal that, if the Bolsheviks refused to come to Prinkipo, the Allies should offer immediate, extra and substantial aid to all anti-Bolshevik forces. Sir Henry Wilson, who was present at the lunch, noted in his diary that Balfour was 'generally favourable' to Churchill's plan.

The Council of Ten reconvened to discuss Russia at three that afternoon, in Pichon's room at the Quai d'Orsay. Clemenceau was in the chair. Churchill proposed that the Allies inform the Bolsheviks that negotiations for a Russian settlement could only begin when the Bolsheviks agreed to call a cease-fire and make a token troop withdrawal on all fronts. He also asked for the immediate setting up of an Allied Council for Russian Affairs, which would have powers of executive action within the limits of the policy laid down by the Allied Governments, and would begin its work at once. This Allied Council, Churchill explained to Lloyd George in a telegram that evening, would draw up 'a complete military plan', and also give its opinion as to whether 'there is a reasonable prospect of success'.

After Churchill had set out his proposals, Clemenceau argued that the Prinkipo proposals should be regarded as already having broken down, and urged an immediate examination of the military problems of intervention. He was supported, 'very effectively', as Churchill later telegraphed to Lloyd George, by the Italian Foreign Minister, Baron Sonnino, and by the Japanese Foreign Minister, Count Makino,[1] all three of whom 'expatiated' on the harm done to the military position by the continual delay. But Churchill and Balfour then joined forces to deprecate premature action. As Churchill informed Lloyd George:

Balfour and I pointed out the advantages to British public opinion of having made it clear to the whole world that we were doing our utmost to seek a termination of the bloodshed in Russia and to promote a peaceful solution, and that we should not make a sharp turn which would appear to be breaking off negotiations abruptly. . . .

Churchill and Balfour were supported by the two Americans present,

[1] Nobuaki, Count Makino, 1861–1949. Educated at Tokyo University and in England. Japanese Minister in Rome and Vienna. Subsequently Minister of Agriculture, Commerce and Foreign Affairs. One of the Japanese representatives at the Paris Peace Conference, 1919. Grand Keeper of the Imperial Seals.

Lansing[1] and Colonel House.[2] But Baron Sonnino brought these arguments to a close by pointing out that the original Allied invitation to the Bolsheviks had given that very day, February 15, as the date by which all fighting should have stopped, and the Russian representatives should actually have arrived at Prinkipo. As a result of the emergence of this fact, 'everyone felt very strongly', Churchill told Lloyd George, 'that a perfectly fair and reasonable breaking-off point had been reached, that the Bolsheviks had spent the month in attacking us and were advancing with success on all fronts, and that they had sent us a baffling and in some ways an insulting reply, that they had not made any attempt to come themselves and that none of the pro-Allied Russian Governments would meet them'.

The only decision reached was to adjourn yet again, until Monday February 17. 'I have made it perfectly clear throughout,' Churchill told Lloyd George, 'that we can in no circumstances send men by compulsion to Russia.'

While Churchill was in Paris, he and his advisers ordered an important initiative in North Russia. 'As question of Russia is still under discussion at Paris,' General Harington telegraphed to General Ironside on February 15, 'we cannot give you definite statement of policy. You should therefore make preparations for an active defensive on the Dvina River pending further instructions. . . .' On February 16 a War Office memorandum, prepared by Major-General Radcliffe[3] and the Operations section of the General Staff, noted that even if it was decided to withdraw from North Russia, this would be a dangerous manoeuvre, requiring reinforcements to protect it, and that while the withdrawal was taking place an extra force of some 3,000 would be needed 'in order to take the offensive and deal the Bolsheviks a really

---

[1] Robert Lansing, 1864–1928. Admitted to the American Bar, 1889. Specialist in international law and arbitration. Counsellor for the Department of State, 1914–15. Secretary of State, 1915–20. A Commissioner to the Paris Peace Conference, 1919. He published two books, *The Peace Negotiations* and *The Big Four at the Peace Conference* (both in 1921).

[2] Edward Mandell House, 1858–1938. Born in Houston, Texas. Personal Representative of President Wilson to the European Governments, 1914, 1915 and 1916. Special Representative of the United States at the Inter-Allied Conference, Paris, 29 November 1917; at the Supreme War Council, Versailles, 1 December 1917; and during the Armistice negotiations, 1918. United States Peace Commissioner, Paris, 1919. Member of the Mandates Commission, 1919.

[3] Percy Pollexfen de Blaquiere Radcliffe, 1874–1934. 2nd Lieutenant, Royal Artillery, 1893; Captain, 1900. On active service in South Africa, 1899–1900. Major, 1910. Brigadier-General, General Staff, 1915. Major-General, 1918. Director of Military Operations, War Office, 1918–22. Knighted, 1919. Mission to Poland, 1919, when he assisted General Weygand in the reorganization of the Polish Army. General Officer Commanding the 48th Division, 1923–6; the 23rd Division, 1926–7; Scottish Command, 1930–3. Lieutenant-General, 1927; General, 1933. General Officer Commanding-in-Chief, Southern Command, 1933–4.

heavy blow'. Thus was initiated the policy of the forward defensive movement.

In his telegram to Lloyd George on February 15, reporting on the meeting of the Council of Ten, Churchill had added his personal opinion of what should happen if Prinkipo failed. The Allies, he wrote, should decide on the basis of 'a complete military plan' from 'the highest military authorities' whether there was 'a reasonable prospect of success' against the Bolsheviks. They would then be in a position 'to take a definite decision whether to clear out altogether or adopt the plan'. Churchill also proposed a wireless message to the Bolsheviks, repeating the Prinkipo invitation, on condition that 'the fighting should stop, and stop forthwith', and giving the Bolsheviks a further ten days, until February 25, to call a cease-fire and to withdraw at least five miles from the anti-Bolshevik front line. Lloyd George replied on February 16, in a telegram to Philip Kerr, approving this wireless message, but asking that, in the event of the Bolsheviks refusing these conditions, Churchill 'will not commit us to any costly operations which would involve any large contribution either of men or of money'. Lloyd George's telegram continued:

The main idea ought to be to enable Russia to save herself if she desires to do so, and if she does not take advantage of the opportunity then it means either that she does not wish to be saved from Bolsheviks or that she is beyond saving. There is only one justification for interfering in Russia, that Russia wants it. If she does then Kolchak, Krasnoff and Denikin ought to be able to raise a much larger force than the Bolsheviks. This force we could equip and a well equipped force of willing men would soon overthrow the Bolshevik army of unwilling conscripts especially if the whole population is against them.

If on the other hand Russia is not behind Krasnoff and his coadjutors it is an outrage of every British principle of freedom that we should use foreign armies to force upon Russia a Government which is repugnant to its people.

On the morning of Sunday February 16, before Lloyd George's reply reached him, Churchill sought to enlist Balfour's support for a rapid decision on Russia. Writing to Balfour that morning, he warned him that unless February 15 were accepted as the date when the Prinkipo offer 'definitely lapsed', there would be a danger of 'further overtures involving further delays', and the Allies might then 'destroy the last remaining chances of military action'. Churchill wanted Balfour to telegraph to Lloyd George to say that 'we do not feel that Prinkipo can be kept alive after tomorrow's meeting'. Churchill then outlined to Balfour another scheme he had in mind:

I have been asking myself whether the Bulgarians might not be given a chance to relieve their past misdeeds, placing an army at our disposal to undo some of the harm they did to Russia by their ingratitude. Such an army of, say, three Bulgarian double divisions could be brought into action across the Black Sea in conjunction with Denikin's troops and far removed from any contact with the Greeks or Roumanians. The Enos-Adrianople-Midia line might be their reward. . . .

'I only set these ideas down,' Churchill added, 'to show how many pieces there are on the board, which, if all set in motion effectively and in concert, might very speedily alter the present disastrous situation.' It was essential, he concluded, for the Allies to agree at their meeting on February 17 to set up 'without delay' the special 'Military Commission for Russian Affairs' for which he had argued on the previous day.

Balfour did not respond to Churchill's appeal as Churchill had hoped. That same day he replied:

I am most ready and anxious to back you up in any policy which you may decide upon in regard to Prinkipo; but I am reluctant to take the lead. The policy to be pursued is difficult, and must be determined largely by political instinct. I see great merits in the Prinkipo scheme from the point of view of English and American Public Opinion, but I am not the inventor of it, and never felt as enthusiastic about it as the Prime Minister, who was its author and to whom all the credit of initiating it is due. He has sent you over here because, having been present at the Cabinet Meetings where the whole subject was discussed at length, you are not merely acquainted with the paper arguments on either side but are bathed in the atmosphere which prevails in Downing Street, and have received directions immediately from there. I will of course, give you all the assistance in my power; but I think in the circumstances detailed above, you have no choice but to take the lead.

Churchill received Balfour's letter at noon that Sunday. He immediately sent a second telegram to Lloyd George, outlining the course he intended to take at the Monday meeting. First, he said, he would not propose to make any public reference to the Prinkipo time-limit having expired; then he would, as the 'more prudent course', seek Allied agreement to the immediate formation of a Military Commission 'to prepare, out of the resources which are available, a plan of war against the Bolsheviks' and to submit the plan to the Allied Powers 'together with an expression of authoritative military opinion, as to whether it has reasonable chances of succeeding or not'. If the chances of defeating the Bolsheviks were found to be good, 'then will be the moment to proclaim that Prinkipo has already lapsed as from February 15th and hearten up our allies by every means we can employ'.

Unless he were to hear from Lloyd George 'to the contrary', Churchill proposed to act at Monday's meeting as he had outlined in his telegram. The telegram was despatched from Paris, at 2.18 p.m., with the priority prefix: 'Clear the line.'

That night Lloyd George dined with Sir George Riddell at Walton Heath. Riddell recorded Lloyd George's remarks in his *Intimate Diary of the Peace Conference and After*. 'Winston is in Paris,' Lloyd George told him. 'He wants to conduct a war against the Bolsheviks. That would cause a revolution. Our people would not permit it.'

Lloyd George's reply to both Churchill's telegrams arrived in Paris on Monday February 17. 'Peevish wire in early from LG to Winston,' Sir Henry Wilson wrote in his diary, 'saying that country was in dangerous state, that war against the Bolsheviks was impossible etc etc. Winston quite calm.' Lloyd George's telegram was indeed blunt. He was, he said, 'very much alarmed' at Churchill's second telegram 'about planning war against the Bolsheviks'; and he proceeded to set out British policy as he saw it. The Cabinet, he insisted, had 'never contemplated anything beyond supplying arms in anti-Bolshevik areas in Russia with necessary equipment to enable them to hold their own'. Even this policy was to be pursued 'only in the event of every effort at peaceable solution failing'. There was also the danger, Lloyd George went on, of 'driving the anti-Bolshevik parties in Russia into the ranks of the Bolsheviks'; the War Office itself had warned about this danger. Lloyd George then repeated his reasons for opposing armed Allied intervention in Russia:

If Russia is really anti-Bolshevik, then a supply of equipment would enable it to redeem itself. If Russia is pro-Bolshevik, not merely is it none of our business to interfere with its internal affairs, it would be positively mischievous: it would strengthen & consolidate Bolshevik opinion. An expensive war of aggression against Russia is a way to strengthen Bolshevism in Russia & create it at home. We cannot afford the burden. Chamberlain says we can hardly make both ends meet on a peace basis, even at the present crushing rate of taxation; and if we are committed to a war against a continent like Russia, it is the road to bankruptcy and Bolshevism in these islands.

The French are not safe guides in this matter. Their opinion is largely biased by the enormous number of small investors who put their money into Russian loans and who now see no prospect of ever recovering it. I urge you therefore not to pay too much heed to their incitements. There is nothing they would like better than to see us pulling the chestnuts out of the fire for them.

I also want you to bear in mind the very grave labour position in this country. Were it known that you had gone over to Paris to prepare a plan of war against the Bolsheviks it would do more to incense organised labour than anything I can think of; and what is still worse, it would throw into the ranks of the extremists a very large number of thinking people who now abhor their methods. . . .

Lloyd George asked Churchill to show his two telegrams to Balfour. He also made sure that as many people as possible knew of his embargo on Churchill's proposals. 'Later in the day,' Sir Henry Wilson wrote in his diary, 'Winston & I found that LG had wired to Philip Kerr to send copies of these telegrams to Colonel House. This was a low down trick, as this general tenor showed that LG did not trust Winston. Winston very angry.' Kerr himself wrote to Lloyd George later that day:

Mr Churchill was very indignant at this on the ground that it revealed to the Americans the internal disagreement of the British Government and made it seem as if you had not confidence that he would represent your views. I told him that I was certain that there was no such idea in your mind, that you regarded Colonel House as a friendly member of a body which was responsible for working out the peace of the world and that you habitually communicated documents to the other members of the Conference. I said that I was certain that you had no idea of showing the slightest want of confidence in him. . . .

Sir Henry Wilson had himself become uncertain of the wisdom of direct allied intervention. Throughout the morning of Sunday February 16, he had discussed the possibility of sending British troops to Russia at a meeting with Sackville-West and General Radcliffe. 'It looks as though our extremest action,' he wrote, 'will consist of defending Finland, Esthonia, Poland etc'; and at lunch on the Monday, after again discussing Russia with Sackville-West, he wrote in his diary: 'I really believe we shall be unwise to march in against the Bolsheviks.'

Churchill could not go against Lloyd George's veto on further intervention in Russia. 'Have consulted with my colleagues,' Lloyd George telegraphed him on February 17. 'They approve of my telegram. They urge you not to commit this country to anything beyond what is contained therein.' But Churchill still tried to defend his position, telegraphing to Lloyd George on the morning of February 17 that his proposals were not a drastic departure from existing policy, but still tended towards moderation and caution:

There is no difference at all between my second telegram and my first so far as the military enquiry is concerned. The limited character of our assistance will be clearly stated in accordance with your views, which I perfectly understand on this point. Other Powers will presumably say what they can do.

Perhaps the Japanese can do much more than any of us. When all the available information has been sifted and weighed by the military authorities, we shall have their recommendation as to whether there is or is not a reasonable military hope. It is with this recommendation clearly before them that the Supreme War Council, probably a week hence, will have to make up its mind whether to go on or quit.

On reflection it seemed to me more prudent not to send the telegram which in all probability finally disposes of Prinkipo until we knew what the result of the military enquiry was. Otherwise we might be in the position of being unable either to fight or parley. My second telegram is really more tender towards Prinkipo than the first, because I am afraid to shut that door without being sure that there is another one open.

You need not be alarmed about the phrase 'planning war against the Bolsheviks'. As you pointed out at the Cabinet, we are actually making war on them at the present moment. All that is intended is to assemble in a comprehensive form possible means and resources for action, and to submit this report to the Supreme War Council.

Believe me I realize perfectly all your difficulties. I only wish I could see a solution of them.

Churchill had yet to put his proposals before the Council of Ten. But Lloyd George's telegram of protest, a copy of which had been sent to the American negotiators, undermined Churchill's position, for it seemed to his fellow-negotiators, both British and Allied, that he had exceeded his instructions, and been disowned by his Prime Minister. Angered at having his authority undermined, Churchill drafted a long letter to Lloyd George, which he intended to send on February 17, but finally decided to hold back. It was a clear expression of his feelings:

I understand perfectly your view as conveyed in your two telegrams, and nothing which I am doing or going to do will commit you to anything inconsistent with it or beyond it. But I do hope you realise that, as soon as the Military Commission has reported (which ought not be to more than a week) you will have to take a definite decision one way or the other.

As Secretary of State for War under the present arrangements, I am not responsible for anything beyond carrying out the policy you settle and providing you with the means for carrying out such a policy. If after receiving the military report you decide to clear out of Russia with or without your allies, orders will immediately be issued and action will follow as fast as is physically possible.

Churchill went on to give Lloyd George his pessimistic view of the future, if Britain were to disinterest herself in Russian affairs:

I will not dwell on the odious character of the events which will follow, because it is obvious. There will be no peace in Europe until Russia is restored.

There can be no League of Nations without Russia. If we abandon Russia, Germany and Japan will not. The new States which it is hoped to call into being in the East of Europe will be crushed between Russian Bolshevism and Germany. Germany will regain by her influence over Russia far more than she has lost in colonies overseas or provinces in the West. Japan will no doubt arrive at a somewhat similar solution at the other end of the Trans-Siberian Railway. In five years, or even less, it will be apparent that the whole fruits of our victories have been lost at the Peace Conference, that the League of Nations is an impotent mockery, that Germany is stronger than ever, and that British interests in India are perilously affected. After all our victories we shall have quitted the field in humiliation and defeat.

Above all, Churchill wrote, Lloyd George should try to act on the basis of the actual military situation:

This is an unpleasant prospect, and before embracing it I think you should be fortified by the strongest military opinion showing that no other course is open, that the situation is hopeless, that the Russian armies are quite useless and that there are no means at our disposal of animating and sustaining them—that there is nothing for it but to let things rip and take the consequences.

I think it quite possible that the military report will be to this effect, and that it will be clear that, as the great nations will not fight with large national armies to restore Russia, it is not worth while keeping alive the embers of Russian resistance. To do that would only be to prolong the agony.

On the other hand, the military report may show that there is a reasonable possibility of success. But still, in spite of that report, you may decide to quit. This would be, in my opinion, a decision more difficult to defend before history, but still it would be a decision quite open for you to take and which only you can take. What would be utterly indefensible would be to come to this truly awful decision without accurate, comprehensive and authoritative military advice. That I am sure you will not wish to do.

There is also a minor point on which the War Office is bound to have a direct responsibility, viz., if it is decided not to support John Ward and Co actively by every means in our power, they have got to come away at once. I could not take the responsibility of leaving these men unsupported to their fate after the policy which sent them there had been definitely abandoned. Therefore, there seems to me to be no escape from the dilemma—fight or quit; get on or get out.

Churchill did not believe that he was in any way taking an extreme position, or trying to force Lloyd George's hand in any way. His letter ended:

I think you will see that I am taking a level and detached view of the position. I am carefully avoiding forming any opinion on the military aspect, and I have told Henry Wilson to be on his guard not to let the wish be father to the thought. I have also, in order that your hands may be absolutely free, tried to keep Prinkipo from being finally ruled out until the result of the military enquiry is known. If we cannot fight, I suppose we ought to parley. Perhaps if we gave the Bolsheviks boots, clothing, food and money they might be willing to show mercy to Koltchak, Denikin and Co. I am not at all sure, however, whether the House of Commons would approve of this. It seems to me very probable that they will neither supply the means to fight nor the authority to negotiate.

I have also been doing my best to maintain a consistent line on your Prinkipo policy. It has no friends here now that President Wilson has gone, and Colonel House announced himself opposed to it. Sonnino and Clemenceau are infuriated with it. Makino deposed that it had prejudiced the military situation in Siberia. Balfour, in private, disowns it. All the military men without exception condemn it. But if we cannot fight or will not fight, it is no doubt logical that we should sue for peace on the best terms that we can get for ourselves and those we have brought into the field.

You must forgive me putting these cruel facts before you when you have so many anxieties and burdens to bear. I am sure your courage will not shrink from facing them in their ugliest aspect.

At noon on February 17 there was a meeting in Paris of the Imperial Cabinet, with Balfour in the chair. 'Much talk about Russia,' Henry Wilson noted in his diary, '& of course nothing settled. Borden plainly said that he was going to withdraw his Canadians from Vladivostock leaving our 2 poor Batt^{ns} in the lurch at Omsk.'

The Council of Ten convened at three o'clock that afternoon. The meeting was a stormy one. When Churchill put forward his proposal that the military aspects of intervention should be studied by a special committee of allied military representatives, Colonel House protested. To Churchill's chagrin, Balfour supported House. Clemenceau and Sonnino supported Churchill. Henry Wilson recorded in his diary: 'House said neither American men nor material would be allowed to go to Russia. Tiger said, that being so, the other Powers would discuss Russia without America. He said it was a pitiful thing to see the victors of the Boches afraid to refer the Russian problem to Versailles. . . . Winston spoke a little & well.' It was decided, on American insistence, that no joint Allied note should be issued, but that each country should first seek the separate advice of its own military advisers. Henry Wilson commented in his diary: 'I think this is the greatest depth of impotence I have ever seen the Frocks fall to. I advised Winston to go home as he was doing no good here & would get tarred. . . .'

In his diary, Colonel House gave his impression of the meeting.

'Although Churchill had received his instructions from Lloyd George,' he wrote, 'he was persistent in pushing his plan for a military committee to examine the question as to how Russia could best be invaded in the event it was necessary to do so. I opposed this plan with some vehemence. . . .'

As soon as the meeting was over, Churchill telegraphed an account of it to Lloyd George. His telegram was terse and bitter:

This afternoon I proposed the formation of a military commission to enquire into what measures were possible to sustain the Russian armies we had called into being during the war with Germany and to protect the independence of the border States.

The Americans who had had the advantage of reading your telegrams to me made difficulties even in this, expressing fears that even setting up a commission to enquire into the military situation might leak out and cause alarm.

Mr Balfour therefore proposed that no formal commission should be set up but that the military authorities might be allowed informally to talk together and, instead of presenting a report to the Conference as a whole, might individually hand to their respective representatives on the Conference a copy of the results of their informal and unofficial conversations.

After Clemenceau had commented on the strange spectacle of the victorious nations in this great struggle being afraid even to remit to the study of their military advisers at Versailles a matter admittedly of vital importance to Europe, this project was agreed to.

You are therefore committed at some date in the near future to receiving an informal document embodying certain military opinions bearing upon Russia. You are committed to nothing else.

Churchill's desire to get a united Allied plan in the event of negotiations failing had been frustrated. Disappointed and angry, he accepted Sir Henry Wilson's advice and returned to London. Before leaving, he had a long talk with Sir Douglas Haig, who was sympathetic. 'The whole proceedings of the council,' Haig wrote in his diary that night, 'are feeble to a degree. Nothing but talk, talk, talk, and no decision to act is ever taken. It is a bad show, and it is desirable that Winston should keep clear of it, otherwise he will be associated with the failure which is bound to come in time.'

14

'I know of no Russian policy'

O N February 17 Churchill took the night train to Boulogne, reaching London shortly after midday on February 18. He went at once to Downing Street, to express his anger that the Prime Minister should have undermined his authority in Paris. Lloyd George did not defend the arguments in his two telegrams, but began instead to moderate them, and to declare himself in favour of indirect intervention. 'He does not wish to make war on the Bolsheviks,' Churchill telegraphed to Sir Henry Wilson on February 19. 'He is, however, quite willing to help the Russian armies on the lines specified provided that it is not too costly. On this point he wishes to be particularly informed. He was entirely in opposition to the cutting off of supplies from Kolchak, Denikin and Co as he considered that since we called them into the field for our own purposes in the German war we were bound to help them in this way. . . .'

At noon on February 19 Churchill was the principal guest at a luncheon at the Mansion House. During his speech he declared:

If Russia is to be saved, as I pray she may be saved, she must be saved by Russians. It must be by Russian manhood and Russian courage and Russian virtue that the rescue and regeneration of this once mighty nation and famous branch of the European family can alone be achieved. The aid which we can give to these Russian Armies—who we do not forget were called into the field originally during the German war to some extent by our inspiration and who are now engaged in fighting against the foul baboonery of Bolshevism—can be given by arms, munitions, equipment, and technical services raised upon a voluntary basis. But Russia must be saved by Russian exertions, and it must be from the heart of the Russian people and with their strong arm that the conflict against Bolshevism in Russia must be mainly waged.

Churchill and Lloyd George seemed, at last, to be in agreement; Britain would not intervene against Bolshevism directly, but would be

257

willing to give aid and advice to anti-Bolshevik forces. But it still
remained to work out a plan of withdrawal for the British troops in
North Russia and Siberia, to decide what support to give to the anti-
Bolshevik armies of Denikin and Kolchak, and to estimate how far
Britain was prepared to go in helping to defend the peripheral states of
the Baltic and Caucasus. Churchill wanted these decisions reached
without delay; once he knew what the Cabinet's Russian policy was, he
would carry it out. His colleagues wanted to know what his views were,
now that Lloyd George had ruled out direct intervention. On February
20 Edwin Montagu wrote to Churchill from the India Office: 'Am I to
understand that the only volunteer army you wish to raise for Russia is
for technical services, artillery, tanks and air?' To which Churchill
replied, at the foot of Montagu's letter: 'I am raising no army for
Russia. But if it is decided to go on helping Denikin, Kolchak & Co I
shd organise certain volunteer units specially to help in the technical
services you mention.'

On February 20 Lloyd George complained to Churchill that the War
Office had consistently failed to provide the Cabinet with a proper
estimate of the cost of indirect intervention, and that without such an
estimate, no decisions could be reached. Why, he wrote, had the War
Office not prepared detailed estimates of the men and material needed?
His letter continued:

As to the cost of the suggestions put forward, it is no use ignoring this all-
important element in policy. The Treasury is experiencing the greatest
difficulty in meeting essential demands for housing and land settlement for
soldiers, and the burden of annual expenditure even on a peace footing will
tax the resources of this country to the utmost. And the question of whether
any given policy means millions or tens of millions or hundreds of millions
ought to weigh in our decision. I have tried for weeks to get from the W.O.
some estimate which would afford me any guidance. The Cabinet have urged
the same consideration. It is no use clamouring for policy until the War
Office, which alone is in possession of the facts and the technical experience,
can supply us with this information.

Lloyd George went on to ask Churchill why no decision had been
reached in Paris:

May I also point out that in so far as a policy is possible without this
information, very definite instructions in writing were given you when you
went to Paris to represent the Cabinet at the Allied Conference on Russia. I
understand that Mr Balfour left the matter entirely in your hands. You do
not seem to have succeeded in securing any decision. I certainly suggest no
blame to you. I am not even criticising the Allies. They also want facts &

estimates of cost and it seems that they have so far been as unsuccessful in obtaining guidance from their military men as we have been with ours.

Churchill was angered by the various charges in Lloyd George's letter, and on February 21 he drafted a full reply which, on reflection, he decided not to send. In it, he wrote, in exasperation:

With regard to Russia, you speak of my 'Russian policy'. I have no Russian policy. I know of no Russian policy. I went to Paris to look for a Russian policy. I deplore the lack of a Russian policy, which lack may well keep the world at war for an indefinite period and involve the Peace Conference and the League of Nations in a common failure.

All I am doing is carrying on from day to day, guided by such indications as I receive from the War Cabinet, for whose decisions I naturally have no responsibility beyond my departmental duty.

All the British troops in Russia, Churchill continued, had been sent there before he had been appointed Secretary of State for War. Those in northern Russia could not be evacuated until the ice had melted, in July. Those at Omsk, in Siberia, could not be withdrawn 'without grave risk of breaking up the Russian armies with whom they are serving and which were called into the field by us for our own purposes during the war with Germany'. In the Caucasus, he continued, there were four brigades, mostly of Indian troops, holding the Batum–Baku railway, and on the Caspian Sea there were small armed ships, controlled by the Admiralty, 'which it is believed secure the command of that great inland puddle'. The troops in the Caucasus, he added, although not in direct contact with the Bolsheviks, did provide 'a certain support' for Denikin's army, which, he reminded Lloyd George, 'has recently gained an important victory, taking 31,000 prisoners. . . .' Churchill's letter continued:

Until I receive instructions to withdraw these various troops and let the Russian situation crash to the ground, I must do my best to nourish them and sustain them. But it is very difficult, in view of the indecision of the Cabinet and the ignorance of the public; and so far I am not responsible for sending a single man to Russia.

If it is decided that we are to go on helping Denikin, Koltchak and Co, I shall organise specially certain volunteer units to help the Russian armies with the technical services you mention, and I shall try to replace the conscript troops now in Russia by these technical volunteer units gradually and so as to avoid a sudden collapse.

Churchill ended his letter with a direct rebuke to Lloyd George:

I may add that it is clear to me that you are altogether failing to address your mind to the real dangers which are before us. . . .

Russia will certainly rise again, perhaps very swiftly, as a great united empire determined to maintain the integrity of her dominions and to recover everything that has been taken away from her. While this process is going on Europe will be in a perpetual state of ferment. The belt of little States we are now calling into being will be quaking with terror and no doubt misconducting themselves in every possible way. Germany and Russia will have miseries and ambitions in common and their mighty national interests will be struggling for expression and restoration.

When we have abandoned Russia, she will be restored by Germany and Japan, and these three Powers together will constitute a menace for Britain, France and the United States very similar to that which existed before the present war. The position of India in face of such developments is not an enviable one, and I wonder that with your vision you have not perceived the danger.

Although Churchill did not send this letter, he was still determined to help the anti-Bolsheviks. But on February 21 Sir Henry Wilson presented him with proposals for a complete British withdrawal from Russia at the soonest possible moment. 'I gave Winston my proposals,' Wilson recorded in his diary, 'which, he said, were most cold-blooded. He talked much wild nonsense about sending 6000 men each to Denikin & Kolchak.' Despite Wilson's advice, Churchill insisted that the War Office play an active part in examining the possibilities of anti-Bolshevik action even if the Government's policy were still undecided. On February 22 he wrote to General Harington: 'It is the business of the general staff to continually be exposing all the possibilities of a military situation without regard to the political limitations which Governments may find it necessary to impose on military action. . . .' Churchill ended his letter to Harington: 'We may live to regret bitterly the opportunities and resources we are losing through the present indecision.'

At the War Cabinet meeting on Monday February 24, there was only a brief discussion about Russia. Lloyd George declared that it was 'not the fault of the British delegates' that no decision had been reached in Paris. Any decision must now await his return to Paris; the views of five different Governments had to be taken into account. But Churchill insisted on the need for a swift decision. 'There might be a serious disaster at Archangel in the coming spring,' he warned, 'unless an early decision were come to.' Lloyd George refused to commit himself. 'The question of our policy in Russia,' he replied, 'was one which could only be usefully discussed in conjunction with our Allies.'

During the last week of February the military news discouraged those who believed in the success of the intervention in North Russia. On February 23 General Ironside had telegraphed from Archangel that one of his British battalions, the 13th Yorks, had 'refused to go in support and relief of Russian and British troops' on the Archangel front. The morale of his troops, Ironside added, had probably been aggravated 'by an official announcement in America . . . that American troops in Russia are to be relieved at an early date'. On February 26 Ironside went to the front to see the position for himself, telegraphing to Churchill on the following day that he had found a 'quite serious situation', in which the mutinous fighting troops had been joined by Army Service Corps and Royal Army Medical Corps personnel, and had been 'very obstinate and persistent'. Ironside had selected three non-commissioned officers, and 30 men, for court martial. If the Allies did not send out relief troops at once, he added, 'I should have renewal of trouble of this kind'. The sense of isolation in North Russia, Ironside warned, 'upsets even the best of men'.

On February 27 Churchill sent Lloyd George the details of British expenditure in Russia, which Lloyd George had asked for on February 20. With the details, he also sent Lloyd George an anguished letter pleading for a firm Allied decision about Russia:

There is no 'will to win' behind any of these ventures. At every point we fall short of what is necessary to obtain real success. The lack of any 'will to win' communicates itself to our troops and affects their morale: it communicates itself to our Russian allies and retards their organisation, and to our enemies and encourages their efforts . . . the Allied Powers in Paris have not decided whether they wish to make war upon the Bolsheviks or to make peace with them. They are pausing midway between these two courses with equal dislike of either.

His own advisers, Churchill went on, 'are unable to deal with this Russian problem without the clearest political guidance'. Churchill ended his letter:

. . . I must quote the decision of the War Cabinet (515) of 10 January in which it is clearly shown that you conceived yourselves to be fully equipped to obtain at Paris the main decisions from the allies on Russian policy, and that you realised that this was the first matter that should be dealt with. Since then nothing whatever has been decided. I recognize the necessary difficulties of the problem & the minimum pressure of events: but I do not feel that the War Office is to blame.

It is necessary in my opinion that you shd go to Paris & with the necessary War Office assistance hammer out a policy & force by yr personal authority

the Allies or some of them to come to an agreement on the critical political &
military aspects. No one below you can do it. . . .

Not having received a reply to his letter, Churchill wrote to Lloyd
George again three days later, on March 2, to say that all British troops
should leave the Caucasus 'as soon as possible', and that all British warships should be withdrawn from the Caspian Sea once Denikin had
captured Astrakhan and gained control of the mouth of the Volga. If
Britain withdrew from the Caucasus and the Caspian, Churchill added,
'we ought to make it up to Denikin' by sending him an advisory mission
of officers and sergeants. 'This is the policy,' he wrote, 'which I should
enforce if the matter were left in my hands. . . .'

The War Cabinet met on March 4. It had many other matters to
discuss. H. A. L. Fisher recorded in his diary that most of the discussion
was of housing and Sinn Fein prisoners, and that Lloyd George, who was
about to go to Paris, was 'in a great hurry'. Henry Wilson also wrote an
account of the discussion in his diary, ending with a brief but decisive
reference to Russia:

Cabinet harmonious about clearing out of Archangel & Murmansk, & also
Caucasus.

The War Cabinet having decided that the War Office should at once
prepare to evacuate all British troops from North Russia by the end of
June, Churchill wrote at once to Wilson:

I am expecting to receive from you a statement of the forces you require to
cover a withdrawal from Archangel & Murmansk & to maintain the full
security of our troops there till we decide to go. Will you consult with A.G.
[General Macdonogh] & let me have definite proposals together with a
time table. I will then do my utmost to meet yr requirements.

Lloyd George left London for Paris on March 5. While he was en
route, Churchill took steps to implement the War Cabinet's decision,
writing that day to General Harington and General Radcliffe:

In view of the Cabinet's decision yesterday that we are to prepare for
evacuation in June, I wish to receive at the earliest date definite plans for
such an operation prepared by the Generals on the spot and carrying with
them the approval of the General Staff.

I wish the Generals on the spot to know that they are free to claim reinforcements, etc., for the purpose of covering the operation of withdrawal. . . .

I wish to see a definite time table for this operation prepared with the
necessary latitude. . . .

I am extremely anxious about this position, and from day to day my anxieties increase. We have now got our authority from the War Cabinet to go ahead making preparations, and I have announced to Parliament and pledged the War Office to leave no stone unturned, and therefore I wish that a most intense effort shall be made and pressed forward, having as it were a first charge on all our interests and resources, in order to secure the effective execution of the Government policy in a manner not incompatible with the honour of our army.

I should like also to be able to raise the morale of our men out there by promising them definitely in a message direct from me that they will either be relieved by volunteers from England or withdrawn altogether as soon as Archangel is open. . . .

Churchill then set out his own proposals to cover the withdrawal. They involved a large reinforcement of the troops already in Russia:

It seems to me that we ought to be preparing without delay a force of 5,000 or 6,000 men who could be sent if necessary to extricate these North Russian expeditions. What sort of force would be most useful? How would it be organised? Clearly it must be a first charge on the men who are now volunteering for general service in the volunteer armies.

The AG should submit a scheme, prepared in conjunction with the General Staff, which would enable the assembly of such a force to be begun without the slightest delay. It is not necessary even to wait for the reports of General Ironside and Maynard. I obtained the authority of the Cabinet yesterday to embark at once on the preparation of this force. If it is not needed subsequently, all the better. Having regard to the fact that men volunteering are entitled to leave, I wish to know whether we have as many as 5,000 or 6,000 now available. There is no need to tell these men where they are going at this stage. The thing is to form them into these special battalions and see that they are kept in the best of order and good spirits.

When would the first battalion be ready? I want a time table showing the dates at which these units will be respectively completed. . . .

On the morning of March 6 Lord Curzon summoned an interdepartmental conference to the Foreign Office, to discuss British intervention in the Caucasus and South Russia. Churchill was the only other Minister present.[1] Curzon opened the meeting by explaining that Lloyd George was keen to see British forces withdrawn as soon as possible from the Caucasus, and had been 'dismayed' when Curzon had told him that any withdrawal would probably take at least six months to complete. Curzon feared that a precipitate British withdrawal would lead to the

---

[1] The Admiralty were represented by Admiral Sir Sydney Fremantle (Deputy Chief of the Naval Staff) and Captain Coode (Director of the Operations Division). The Treasury sent S. D. Waley; the India Office sent J. E. Shuckburgh. Curzon was accompanied by Professor Simpson and George Kidston; Churchill by General Radcliffe.

immediate occupation of the Caucasus by General Denikin. 'It must not be forgotten,' he warned, 'that the only place where a renascent Russia had any real chance of early success was the Caucasus. Denikin was an Old Russian, an Imperialist and a Monarchist.'

Churchill did not press for any particular policy. 'It was for the Government to say what the War Office was to do,' he remarked, 'and it was for the War Office to carry out the Government's policy in ship-shape fashion.' He himself, he added, 'was interested in fighting the Bolsheviks' through Denikin. He therefore favoured 'the quickest possible evacuation of our troops from the Caucasus'. It was to Denikin, he said, that 'munitions and arms' should be sent.

Churchill advised making it a condition of British help to Denikin, that he promise not to turn against the Caucasus. He added that Denikin 'would be likely to accept the conditions laid down by us because, without our help in arms and ammunition, and without our military mission, he was bound to fail.' But he went on to declare:

As to Georgia, Azerbaijan, Daghestan, and the other small States, he really did not see what British interests were involved. There seemed to be no doubt that as soon as Russia revived they would be reconquered, and once more form a part of the Russian Empire; what happened in the interval did not affect us, for we had no interests there.

Curzon rebuked Churchill for being 'indifferent to the New Republics of the Caucasus', but Churchill replied that he feared that if Britain gave the Caucasian States any further help, 'we should find ourselves still more deeply involved', and unable to get out 'in style'. It was 'quite obvious', Churchill added, 'that the longer we stayed the deeper our claws would stick in'.

Curzon spoke of his fears for Persia, if the Bolsheviks controlled the Caucasus, and Churchill went so far as to say that he would 'personally like very much to annex the Caspian', if there was 'any prospect of our keeping it permanently'. But he was certain, he said, that 'we could not keep it, and if we did it would only bring us into collision with Russia'.

After further discussion between Churchill and Curzon, it was decided to set plans in motion to evacuate British troops from the Caucasus, but, before this was done, to establish an advance British air base in the Caucasus from which to bomb the Bolshevik fleet at Astrakhan. It was also agreed to offer Denikin arms, ammunition and a military mission; to give him British naval support to capture Astrakhan; and to make all this help 'conditional on his giving an undertaking to respect a stated frontier with regard to the Caucasian States'.

The War Cabinet met that afternoon. In Lloyd George's absence, Bonar Law acted as chairman. The Ministers had before them the proposal about British policy in the Caucasus and South Russia recommended to them by that morning's inter-departmental conference. The conference's formal recommendation was threefold:

(i) To make preparations to withdraw;
(ii) To compensate General Denikin for our withdrawal by supplying him with material and munitions of war, and with a military mission as proposed;
(iii) To make it a condition of such support that General Denikin should not interfere with the Georgians and other independent States in the Caucasus.

The War Cabinet accepted these recommendations. Churchill pointed out that the supply of arms to Denikin would act as a lever, 'on the one hand, to enable him to fight the Bolsheviks, and, on the other, to prevent him from maltreating the Southern States'. The supply of military aid to Denikin, he added, 'was an essential part of the scheme for removing our troops as quickly as possible'. Britain, he said, should provide the ships necessary to transport the arms to South Russia. It was 'useless' to ask either France or the United States to participate, as 'General Denikin came solely within the British sphere'.

Churchill crossed over to France on March 8, reaching Paris late that night. On the following morning he discussed Russia with Lloyd George over breakfast. At their discussion, Lloyd George recapitulated the War Cabinet's decisions on British policy towards Russia. Later that day, in a letter to Lloyd George, Churchill set out his comments on what had been decided:

My dear Prime Minister,
    I send you the following notes on our conversation this morning.
(1) It is your decision and the decision of the War Cabinet that we are to evacuate Murmansk and Archangel as soon as the ice melts in the White Sea. Russians (including women and children) who have compromised themselves through working with us are to be transported, if they desire it, to a place of refuge.
    If reinforcements are required to cover the extrication of our forces and the withdrawal of the aforesaid Russians, they may be taken for this purpose from the volunteers now re-engaging for service in the army. It will be made clear

to these men that they are only going to extricate their comrades and not for a long occupation of Northern Russia.

Subject to the above, I am to make whatever military arrangements are necessary to carry out your policy.

(2) It is also decided by you and the War Cabinet that we are to withdraw our army from the Caucasus as quickly as possible. This will certainly take 3 or 4 months, as the detachments which have been thrown out as far as Kars to the Southward and the troops on the other side of the Caspian have also to be withdrawn, and our lines of communication from Hamadan to Enzeli have to be wound up.

Denikin will be compensated for the loss of the support of this army (a) by arms and munitions and (b) by a military mission, which may if necessary amount to 2,000 in all of technical assistants and instructors. This military mission is to be formed of officers and men who volunteer specially for service in Russia and not by men of the regular volunteer army ordered to proceed there. In return for this support, we should secure from Denikin undertakings not to attack the Georgians and others South of a certain line which the Foreign Office are tracing; and later instalments of arms and munitions will be dealt out to him as he conforms to this agreement. If he fails to conform to this agreement, it will be open to us to withdraw our mission. The limits of our assistance to Denikin will be clearly stated to him, and it will be open to him to accept or reject our conditions and our help.

(3) You have also decided that Colonel John Ward and the two British battalions at Omsk are to be withdrawn (less any who volunteer to stay) as soon as they can be replaced by a military mission, similar to that to Denikin, composed of men who volunteer specifically for service in Russia.

(4) On these lines and within these limits, I should be prepared to be responsible for carrying out the policy on which you and the War Cabinet have decided. It will be necessary to inform the allies of our intention, and this I presume will be done by yourself or Mr Balfour.

If, however, I have wrongly interpreted your decisions in any respect, I hope you will let me know what you really wish, in order that I may see whether it can be done.

Yours very sincerely
Winston S. Churchill

Churchill accepted the policy which Lloyd George had outlined. In the event of the Prinkipo negotiations failing, he had wanted a more active intervention, joint military action by all the Allies, and a positive British commitment to destroy Bolshevism. After March 8, despite his personal distaste for the policy, he had no alternative, except resignation, than to supervise the withdrawal of British troops from every

Russian war zone, and the limitation of British involvement to the despatch of arms, and a small military mission, to Denikin. Here at last was a clear policy, such as he had been demanding for over eight weeks. Much as he disliked this policy, he had accepted it; he had now to carry it out.

15

'The Bolshevik Tyranny is the Worst. . . .'

THE anti-Bolshevik leaders had hoped for substantial British aid, including troops. On March 14, Churchill wrote bitterly to Lloyd George about the Allied decision to dissociate itself from these developments, which, he wrote, 'cause me increasing anxiety'. And he continued:

You and President Wilson have, I fear, definitely closed your minds on this subject and appear resolved to let Russian affairs take their course. You are the masters and you may, of course, be right in thinking that no other course is possible. It is my duty, however, to warn you of the profound misgivings with which I watch the steady degeneration of so many resources and powers which, vigorously used, might entirely have altered the course of events.

It was 'vain to suppose', Churchill went on, that Europe could have peace or prosperity while Russia was in anarchy:

I apprehend that after enormous possibilities and opportunities have been lost and great potential resources have been dissipated, we shall nevertheless be drawn, in spite of all your intentions, into the clutches of the Russian problem in some way or another, and we shall then bewail the loss of much that is now slipping through our fingers unheeded. This was the fate of Mr Pitt in regard to France.

Churchill ended his letter with a grave forecast of what he believed was yet to come:

When the Bolshevik frontier in Siberia is limited only by whatever line the Japanese choose to keep for themselves, when the whole of the Caucasus and Trans-Caspia have fallen into Bolshevik power, when their armies are menacing Persia and Afghanistan and their missionaries are at the gates of

India, when one after another the Border States in the West have been undermined by want and propaganda or overborne by criminal violence, not only the League of Nations but the British Empire, with which we are particularly concerned, will wake up to the fact that Russia is not a negligible factor in world politics.

Churchill reiterated his warning at a meeting of the War Cabinet on March 17 at which, in Lloyd George's absence, Bonar Law took the chair. 'Everything was going wrong,' Churchill declared. The Russian forces were disheartened, the Ukraine 'rich in food' was in Bolshevik hands; for four months the Allies had pursued 'a policy of drift'. And he went on:

It was idle to think we should escape by sitting still and doing nothing. Bolshevism was not sitting still. It was advancing, and unless the tide were resisted it would roll over Siberia until it reached the Japanese, and perhaps drive Denikin into the mountains, while the border Baltic States would be attacked and submerged. No doubt when all the resources friendly to us had been scattered, and when India was threatened, the Western Powers would bestir themselves and would be prepared to put forth ten times the effort that at an earlier stage would have sufficed to save the situation. He could only express the profound apprehension with which he awaited what was coming.

On March 23, only four days after Churchill's warning, the Communists seized power in Budapest, and their leader, Bela Kun,[1] at once set about trying to establish a Hungarian Bolshevik bastion in central Europe. Three dangers at once presented themselves to the Allies: that Bela Kun would refuse to accept the Hungarian frontiers being worked out by the Paris Peace Conference; that he would link forces with the Russian Bolsheviks to the east; and that with its base now in Budapest instead of Moscow, Bolshevism would spread rapidly northwards to Vienna, and thence into Germany.

The War Cabinet met on March 24 to discuss the Communist success. At one point, as Thomas Jones wrote to Sir Maurice Hankey after the meeting, the Cabinet baulked at the idea of equipping the Rumanian army for use either against the Russian or against the Hungarian

[1] Bela Kun, 1886–1936. A Hungarian Jew, he worked before 1914 as a journalist on a Socialist newspaper in Budapest. Served as the Lieutenant-Commander of an ammunition supply column, 1914. Captured by the Russians on the eastern front and imprisoned in Russia, 1915–17. He supported the Bolsheviks in 1917; in October 1918 he returned to Hungary as leader of a revolutionary party. Prime Minister of Hungary, March–August 1919, when he instituted a communist regime. In July 1919 the Allies halted his invasion of Slovakia. He fled to Vienna in August 1919, and was interned in a lunatic asylum. Allowed by the Allies to go to Russia, 1920, he became a leading figure of the Comintern. Eventually he was imprisoned, then murdered on Stalin's orders.

Bolsheviks. As a result, Jones wrote: 'Churchill grew very hot and prophesied vast and immediate disaster as the result of the dilatoriness of the Peace Conference.'

On March 26 a further British withdrawal was put into operation. That morning the War Office and the Admiralty arranged, as Sir Henry Wilson recorded in his diary, 'that the Italians should take over the Caspian from our sailors at the same time that they take over the Caucasus from us'. During the morning Wilson saw Churchill at the War Office. Churchill told him that the French ought now to make an alliance with Germany, as a protection against Bolshevism.

That night Churchill spoke in the House of Commons, warning of the evils of Bolshevism. The Bolsheviks, he declared, 'destroy wherever they exist', but at the same time 'by rolling forward into fertile areas, like the vampire which sucks the blood from his victims, they gain the means of prolonging their own baleful existence'. Later in his speech, however, Churchill spoke critically of the French and Greek intervention in southern Russia, warning the House of Commons of the danger 'of rash interference or meddling'. Such action, he felt, 'would enable the Bolsheviks to rally to themselves perhaps even a patriotic movement'.

A further cause for pessimism reached Churchill on March 27, in the form of a memorandum from the Director of Military Operations, Major-General Radcliffe, who warned of the dangerous military situation in North Russia. The chief cause of anxiety, he wrote, 'is not so much the actual military offensive power of the Bolshevik forces opposing us, as the unreliable state of the troops composing the forces under the command of Generals Ironside and Maynard. . . .' These troops, Radcliffe pointed out, 'are a heterogeneous assortment of all nationalities and were never of high quality. They are now tired, dispirited, home-sick and inclined to be mutinous; their morale is undoubtedly so low as to render them a prey to the very active and insidious Bolshevik propaganda which the enemy are carrying out with increasing energy and skill.'

General Radcliffe advised sending to North Russia at once 'selected officers of the highest stamp', and announcing at the same time that all British troops in North Russia who were entitled to demobilization would be replaced 'at the earliest possible moment by fresh personnel'. Radcliffe also wanted an active interventionist policy on the other anti-Bolshevik fronts; the continuing presence of British troops—the 9th Battalion, Hampshire Regiment—with Kolchak at Omsk, encouragement for the Japanese to send troops to the Ural front, and British help in equipping, training and organizing the Siberian Army. 'Lastly,' he wrote, 'we should encourage a Finnish offensive on Petrograd in conjunction with that of the Germans and Esthonians, with the same object, viz. of forcing the Bolsheviks to detach troops from Archangel. . . .'

Churchill was convinced that public hostility to the Bolsheviks would increase when it was made clear that the Bolshevik forces, and their political commissars, carried out atrocities on a massive scale. As early as November 1918 the War Cabinet had decided to collect material on these atrocities with the intention of 'full and speedy publication'. But although a vast mass of material had been collected, some from Foreign Office reports and some from informers, during January and February, nothing had yet been published. 'Surely the moment has come to publish the Bolshevik atrocity blue-book,' Churchill wrote to Curzon on March 28. And he added: 'We really have no right to keep Parliament in the dark any longer.' Churchill went on to give his reason for wanting a speedy publication. 'In the absence of a true view about the Russian situation,' he told Curzon, 'I find it a difficulty in supplying the necessary reinforcements for Archangel and Murmansk; public opinion is not sufficiently instructed.'

That night Curzon told Churchill that he was 'pushing on' the Blue Book 'as hard as I can'. But before the Blue Book could be presented to Parliament, a further decision by the French Government weakened the inter-allied nature of the anti-Bolshevik front. On March 27, Marshal Foch had told Lloyd George that as he saw little hope of Denikin's army being successful, the French had no intention of remaining in Odessa.

On being told of Foch's decision, Churchill wrote at once in protest. 'The facts at our disposal,' he telegraphed direct to Foch on March 28, 'do not confirm the adverse views you have formed.' It was essential, Churchill continued, for all those who were trying 'to sustain the forces of civilisation against the Bolsheviks' to act in unison. And he went on: 'There are so many opponents of action in any form at the present time, that those who are agreed on its importance should be especially careful to speak with a united voice.'

The War Cabinet met on March 31. Churchill was not present. Lord Curzon argued against an early British evacuation of Archangel and Murmansk, declaring that too early an evacuation would have a 'disastrous effect . . . upon the various States who were cooperating with us in fighting the Bolsheviks'. Austen Chamberlain spoke against any further delay in withdrawing British troops from Russia. There should be 'some arrangement with the Bolshevik Government', he said, to ensure a safe and speedy withdrawal. Curzon was indignant at this suggestion. 'Any recognition of, or negotiations with, even a provincial Bolshevik Government,' he said, 'would give considerable impetus to Bolshevik prestige throughout Russia.' At the end of the discussion Churchill arrived. He spoke bitterly of the French decision to evacuate Odessa. This decision, he said, 'completely compromised our position in North Russia, and might gravely endanger the lives of our soldiers, of whom there were some 13,000 in that theatre'.

On April 1 Churchill sent a 'private and secret' letter to Clemenceau, appealing against the French intention to withdraw from Northern Russia, and protesting about a declaration by Léon Abrami[1] 'that not another single man would be sent to the aid of this small force'. Even worse, he said, Pichon had given the Chamber of Deputies the exact figure of Allied military strength in North Russia, 'and thus let the enemy see how very weak we are'. Churchill told Clemenceau:

I have waited all these months in the vain hope of receiving from the League of Nations, so far as that body is at present in existence, some indication of the policy we should pursue towards Russia. I have received no indication. But at Archangel and Murmansk the problem is not one of policy, but of keeping our troops alive throughout this treacherous and dangerous Spring and of extricating them, and those loyal Russians dependent on them, at the earliest possible moment. This may and probably will require reinforcements to be sent, even for the purpose of evacuation. I am therefore preparing a strong brigade of volunteers and holding ships in readiness to press through as soon as it is possible, in order either to relieve the troops who are there or to cover their evacuation and that of the compromised civil population.

I hope you will be able to have language used by your Ministers which is not inconsistent with a firm posture in the face of an aggressive enemy. In the House of Commons, where of course they are very much opposed to Russian expeditions, everyone, even the most extreme opponents of the Government like Mr Hogge,[2] have declared that if the question arises of rescuing and extricating our troops and those of our allies in North Russia, they would support the despatch of the necessary reinforcements there. I should have

[1] Léon Pierre Abrami, 1879–1939. Born in Constantinople, of Italian-Jewish parents. Naturalized as a Frenchman at the age of one. Studied law, political science and oriental languages in Paris. Barrister. Private Secretary to the Minister of Marine, 1913. Elected to the Chamber of Deputies, 1914, as a left-republican. On active service in Lorraine and the Argonne, 1915–16. Senior Staff Officer on the staff of General Sarrail, Commander of the Army of the East, 1916–17. Appointed by Clemenceau as Under-Secretary of State for War (with special responsibility for pensions), 1917–20. Served as a Deputy until 1936.

[2] James Myles Hogge, 1873–1928. Liberal MP for East Edinburgh, 1912–24. President of the Edinburgh University Liberal Association. A persistent back-bench advocate of Scottish interests. Chief Whip of the Asquithian Liberals (the Wee Frees), 1922.

thought you would meet with similar support as long as the operation was clearly defined as one of succour and extrication. . . .

Churchill also asked Clemenceau to replace the French troops at Archangel, 'who are tired out with all they have gone through and have to a large extent lost heart and discipline' by 'fresh, trustworthy men'.[1]

Churchill wanted a direct statement from Lloyd George that no barrier would be put in the way of sending extra troops to Northern Russia in order to cover the evacuation of the troops already there. 'It may not be necessary to send these reinforcements,' Churchill telegraphed to Lloyd George on April 2, 'but if the safety of our men and their efficient withdrawal requires it at any moment I am sure you would wish them to go and I must have them ready to go. We cannot abandon our own men and a certain number of Russians who have compromised themselves will have to be brought off too.' Churchill pointed out that in only two days the Admiralty had been able to find 900 volunteers willing to go to North Russia. 'It was shameful of the French,' Churchill added, 'to disclose our weakness and intention to withdraw to the enemy'; Abrami's statement to the Chamber of Deputies, he warned, 'might easily lead to the destruction of our whole force while it is still cut off by ice'.

Lloyd George was willing to give Churchill the authority for which he had asked. On April 3 he sent Churchill a brief but incisive telephone message, stating:

I regret Abrami's statement as much as you do. The first I heard of the matter was when I read the speech in the papers next day. I do not wish any interference with any arrangements you may have made for making evacuation of troops and those associated with them in Northern Russia, perfectly safe.

Churchill acted at once on receipt of this message. It no longer worried him that the French were pulling out in haste, or that the Canadians, as Sir Henry Wilson wrote from Paris that same day, 'propose to withdraw certain men from their two batteries at Archangel at once and without relief'. Lloyd George's telephone message gave Churchill the clear authority to take what steps were needed to relieve

---

[1] Clemenceau did not reply until April 9, when he wrote: 'Comme vous le savez, le Parlement et l'opinion publique sont, en France comme en Angleterre, résolument opposés à toute expédition en Russie.' It was this fact, Clemenceau added, which had led to Abrami's statement. But he agreed to send one battalion of infantry, and the personnel of 3 artillery batteries, from France, to replace the troops who were being withdrawn. The withdrawal itself was necessary, Clemenceau explained, because his troops were 'fatigué physiquement et moralement'.

the British troops in North Russia. 'Very many thanks for your message,' he telephoned in reply on April 4. 'I was sure that would be your view'; and he wrote at once to General Harington with suggestions for prompt and vigorous action:

The telephone message I have received from the Prime Minister fully empowers me to take all necessary measures for the relief and rescue of our troops in North Russia.

I am ready, therefore, to receive proposals for strong action. I consider the force we are forming should be known as 'The Rescue Force', which will in every way shield it from criticism and gain it support.

I do not see why we should not call for volunteers in addition to those we have already selected. It would be interesting to see what response we got.

Let me know what happened to the Admiralty scheme for getting men. Apparently they got their 900 men almost immediately.

The terms of engagement should be for 9 months and carry with them, say, a £30 bounty. We might quite easily find ourselves tapping a new source of re-enlisting men.

Speak to me to-day about this after you have discussed it among yourselves.

General Harington shared Churchill's desire for vigorous action in North Russia 'for the relief and rescue' of British troops. He proposed that Ironside should be sent some of the new poison gas that had been developed in the final months of the war, but never used in action. Churchill did not entirely favour Harington's proposal. 'Are you sure,' he wrote to him on April 4, 'that it is wise to give away the secret of our new gas for the sake of such a small application as would be possible in North Russia?' Harington replied, on April 4, that the gas 'experts' in the War Office favoured its use. 'Of course,' Churchill wrote five days later, 'I shd vy much like the Bolsheviks to have it, if we can afford the disclosure as proposed.'

General Ironside had already, on April 2, informed the War Office that he would like to use gas, and on April 11 he was told by the War Office that 24 gas officers, with supplies, would be sent out to him as quickly as possible. On April 24 a War Office minute proposed sending out the gas 'as early as possible' after May 1, and to this Churchill gave his immediate approval.

Churchill feared a breakdown of troop morale in North Russia before the reinforcements could arrive. On April 3 he drafted a personal appeal to all soldiers, telling them: 'you are not forgotten. Your safety and well-being, on the contrary, is one of the main anxieties of the War Office, and we are determined to do everything in our power to bring you safely home.' His appeal continued:

Whatever may be the plan of action towards Russia decided on by the League of Nations, *we intend to relieve you at the earliest possible moment*, and either bring the whole force away or replace you by fresh men. These reliefs are being prepared now, and will come through the ice to your aid at the earliest moment when the ships can break through. Meanwhile, your lives and your chance of again seeing your home and friends and your fellow-countrymen, who are looking forward to give you a hearty welcome, depend absolutely upon your discipline and dogged British fighting qualities. . . .

Only a few more months of resolute and faithful service against this ferocious enemy and your task will have been discharged. Carry on like Britons fighting for dear life and dearer honour, and set an example in these difficult circumstances to the troops of every other country. Reinforcement and relief are on the way. We send you this personal message with the most heartfelt wishes for your speedy, safe and honourable return.

This message was ready to send to Archangel and Murmansk on April 4. Churchill telegraphed a copy to Sir Henry Wilson, in Paris, telling him to show it to Lloyd George. Lloyd George gave his approval, on condition that Churchill made it a War Office message, not a personal one. On April 6 Churchill telegraphed to Lloyd George, agreeing to make the message an impersonal one; and he added: 'It is true that the operations in North Russia are tiny compared with the great war in Europe, but from the point of view of the 13,000 British troops, who think themselves forgotten there, they seem quite important.'

On April 5 the last French ship sailed from Odessa harbour, thereby completing the evacuation of 30,000 Russian civilians and 10,000 anti-Bolshevik soldiers from the Volunteer Army. In leaving Odessa, the French destroyed much equipment that would have been of value to Denikin's forces. But Denikin had not even been informed in advance that the French were leaving. Churchill was angered by the French action. He was also bitter that he had no means of reversing the Cabinet's decision of March 4 to leave North Russia at once. On April 8, he spoke privately about the Russian situation to H. A. L. Fisher, who recorded in his diary: 'Winston says he will seriously consider resignation before submitting to ignominious withdrawal from Russia.' Fisher also recorded Churchill's sharp comment: 'After conquering all the huns—tigers of the world—I will not submit to be beaten by the baboons!'

On April 9 the House of Commons debated the Government's White Paper on Bolshevik atrocities. Many MPs expressed their fears that the Allies were about to open negotiations with the Bolsheviks. When Churchill's friend Josiah Wedgwood[1] protested that the atrocity stories were 'anonymous tittle-tattle', there were widespread shouts of 'Shame!' The debate had shown, Churchill informed Lloyd George on April 10, 'a practical unanimity against any negotiations with the Bolsheviks or any recognition of Lenin and Trotsky'. The Labour Party supporters of the Coalition, he added, had a most 'anti-Bolshevik element', and the general view opposed a compromise with Moscow. 'I do trust President Wilson will not be allowed to weaken our policy against them in any way,' he wrote. 'His negotiations have become widely known and are much resented.'[2]

In the public mind, Churchill was becoming identified with a vigorous anti-Bolshevik policy. Lloyd George himself was suspicious of Churchill's intentions, telling J. E. B. Seely that he believed Churchill was the inspiration behind an article in the *Daily Mail* advocating an attack on Petrograd by anti-Bolshevik forces, led by General Yudenitch.[3] Seely told Churchill of this charge. 'I have never done anything of the sort,' Churchill protested to Lloyd George in a letter of April 9. 'My advisers are very doubtful about the Petrograd plan, and the only step I have ever taken in connection with it is to forward to you a letter from Master Sutherland, who seems to have been bitten with it. Disabuse your mind I beg you, therefore, of this impression. . . .' In his letter Churchill noted that all his advisers at the War Office were agreed that the most urgent problem was 'to feed Germany', in order to prevent the

---

[1] Josiah Clement Wedgwood, 1872–1943. Liberal MP, 1906–19. Commanded armoured cars in France, Antwerp, Gallipoli and East Africa, 1914–17. Assistant Director, Trench Warfare Department, Ministry of Munitions, 1917. War Office Mission to Siberia, 1918. Labour MP, 1919–42. Vice-Chairman of the Labour Party, 1921–4. Chancellor of the Duchy of Lancaster, 1924. Created Baron, 1942.

[2] On 22 February 1919 a young American diplomat, William C. Bullitt, had been sent by Woodrow Wilson direct to Moscow from Paris to negotiate with the Bolsheviks. On March 8 he had begun five days of discussions with Lenin, Chicherin and Litvinov, and in the first week of April he brought several Soviet peace proposals to both Wilson and Lloyd George; but these were rejected.

[3] Nikolai Nikolaevich Yudenitch, 1862–1933. Entered the Russian Army, 1879. Served as an infantry officer in the Russo-Japanese War, 1904–5, and in the punitive expedition against Armenia, 1905–6. Chief of Staff, 1913. Commanded the Russian Forces in the Caucasus, 1915 and 1917. Commanded the anti-Bolshevik North-Western Army against Petrograd, 1919. After his offensive failed, he was arrested by a fellow General, but on British insistance was released, and emigrated to Britain. He himself anglicized his name as 'Youdenitch'.

Germans seeking to 'escape the consequences of the war' by 'taking refuge into Bolshevism'. Churchill continued, with bitterness:

Once you are a Bolshevist you are apparently immune. All past crimes are forgiven and forgotten; all past sentences are remitted and all debts are forgiven; all territory that you want to have is restored to you. You may fight anybody you like and nobody may fight against you. The mighty armies of the victorious allies are impotent against you. You boot the French into the Black Sea, or the British into the White Sea, and everybody else (except the Japanese) into the Yellow Sea. Altogether you have a splendid time and incidentally you deal with the domestic capitalist and landlord. Can one wonder that the creed should be so popular? . . .

Churchill then told Lloyd George of his fears that the Russian revolution would develop as the French revolution had done, and that 'all civil society being destroyed', the structure of the country would only be restored by a military regime:

It seems to me very likely that the purely military phase will soon be reached. I am told that on the Southern Front there are good Bolshevik Generals and disciplined troops and that the atrocities there have gradually diminished, while all the time the military attacks become more formidable. On the other hand, Denikin is still alive, little though he has been helped, and his army is still a real factor. Koltchak has done very well, though apparently because the forces on his front have been greatly weakened for the sake of the Southern attack. Some of the new divisions he is raising will soon be ready to strengthen his fighting front. His right hand is gradually stretching out towards the Archangel region.

My view of the future is therefore rather inclining in the direction of a purely military Russia in one form or another coming to the aid of a Bolshevist Germany and Austria and Hungary, and thus confronting us after a few years with a situation very formidable to France and Britain, and to the United States as well unless she keeps out of it. It seems to me that Japan will certainly be drawn to act with Germany and Russia in this eventuality. . . . So you may have two Leagues of Nations instead of one, and the beaten ones re-arming while the victorious ones are disarming.

Churchill ended his letter by suggesting that the policy which could be supported by 'an enormous body of educated opinion' was a simple one: 'Feed Germany; fight Bolshevism; make Germany fight Bolshevism.' But, he added: 'It may well be that it is too late for this. It may well be that even if time remained you could never get the allies to agree.'

Fifty years later, Asquith's daughter Violet[1] recalled having asked

[1] Violet Asquith, 1887–1969. Asquith's eldest daughter, by his first wife. In November 1915 she married Asquith's Private Secretary, Maurice Bonham Carter. Active in Liberal politics throughout her life. Created Baroness Asquith of Yarnbury, 1964.

Churchill: 'What is your Russian policy,' to which he had replied, simply: 'Kill the Bolshie, Kiss the Hun.'

On April 11, Churchill spoke in the Connaught Rooms, London, as a guest of the Aldwych Club. He was enthusiastic about the activities of the anti-Bolshevik armies, but stated without qualification that if Bolshevism were to be destroyed, it must be destroyed by the Russians themselves:

There are still Russian armies in the field under Admiral Kolchak and General Denikin, who have never wavered in their faith and loyalty to the Allied cause, and who are fighting valiantly and by no means unsuccessfully against that foul combination of criminality and animalism which constitutes the Bolshevik regime. We are helping these men, within the limits of our ability. We are helping them with arms and munitions, with instructors and technical experts, who volunteered for service.

It would not be right for us to send out armies raised on a compulsory basis to Russia. If Russia is to be saved, it must be by Russian manhood, but all our hearts are with these men who are true to the Allied cause in their splendid struggle to restore the honour of muted Russia, and to rebuild on a modern and democratic basis the freedom, prosperity, and happiness of its trusted and good-hearted people.

In his speech, Churchill dwelt on Bolshevik atrocities. 'Of all tyrannies in history,' he said, 'the Bolshevik tyranny is the worst, the most destructive, the most degrading.' The atrocities committed under Lenin and Trotsky were 'incomparably more hideous, on a larger scale, and more numerous than any for which the Kaiser is responsible'. The decision of Russia to leave the war was a betrayal of honour and an act of murder. 'Every British and French soldier killed last year,' Churchill declared, 'was really done to death by Lenin and Trotsky, not in fair war, but by the treacherous desertion of an ally without parallel in the history of the world.'

Although Churchill was now only committed to limited British activity in Russia, he was increasingly anxious about Bolshevism's possible effect on Europe, and regretted what he believed were wasted opportunities for a more active intervention. On April 16 he learnt that all those Russian prisoners-of-war in Germany who had been captured before the revolution were to be repatriated to Bolshevik Russia. Although they were to be repatriated only in small groups, Churchill was angered, writing that day to General Harington, General Thwaites, General Macdonogh and General Radcliffe:

Whereas we could have made out of these an army of loyal men who would have been available to sustain the defence of Archangel and Murmansk or to aid General Denikin and Kolchak, we are now I presume simply sending a reinforcement of 500,000 trained men to join the armies of Lenin and Trotsky. This appears to me to be one of the capital blunders in the history of the world.

16

'Now Is the Time to Help'

O N April 15 the War Office General Staff completed its survey of the position in Russia, for which the War Cabinet had asked. On the following day Sir Henry Wilson sent the survey to Churchill for his approval. It had been worked out within the clear framework of eventual British evacuation from North Russia. But it included a plan for a distinct forward movement by British troops, before the evacuation was finally carried out.

The General Staff proposed three principal actions by Britain, if the 'stability' of the anti-Bolshevik Government at Archangel were to be made 'quite certain':

(i) Strike a sharp and successful blow at the Bolshevik forces.
(ii) Effect a real and permanent junction between the North Russian forces and the right wing of Kolchak's Siberian Army.
(iii) Provide a cadre of British officers and non-commissioned officers to organize, instruct and lead Russian units.

In justifying its proposals for a temporarily forward policy, the General Staff asserted that unless such action were taken, 'the fall of the Archangel Government and the disintegration of the anti-Bolshevik forces may be reckoned on as certain'. To bring the North Russian and Siberian armies together, it was essential to control the railway line from Viatka to Kotlas; but this would mean further advances by the anti-Bolshevik forces in North Russia. It was also necessary, the General Staff declared, for Kolchak's Siberian forces to be given every possible help.

In their conclusion, the General Staff asked for two immediate decisions by the War Cabinet, that British units in North Russia be authorized to advance on Kotlas, and that British soldiers be allowed to volunteer for employment in Russian units.

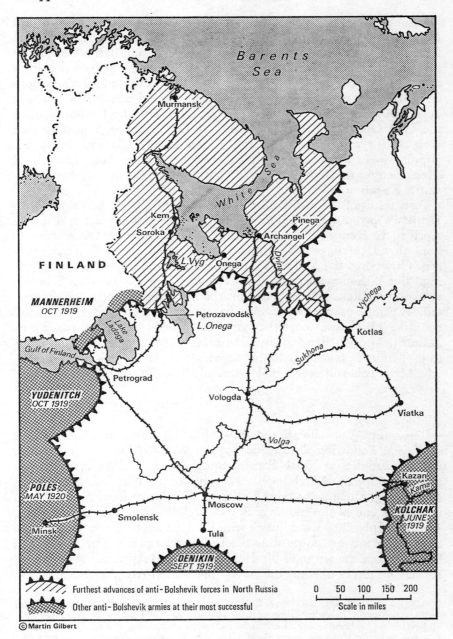

THE INTERVENTION IN NORTH RUSSIA, 1919

Churchill supported these proposals. In North Russia itself, General Maynard telegraphed to the War Office on April 17, the anti-Bolshevik forces had gained complete control of Lake Vyg, and had taken 'a considerable number' of Bolshevik prisoners. Maynard proposed a joint attack on Petrozavodsk by his forces from the north and Finnish troops from the west; a plan which, he believed, would provide 'a splendid opportunity for concerted action'. Four days later a telegram reached the War Office from General Knox at Ekaterinburg, reporting that Kolchak's army had crossed the Kama River, was mobilizing the population in the newly occupied areas, and after reorganizing and strengthening its Divisions, would continue its offensive westwards towards Kazan and Viatka.

As a result of the anti-Bolshevik successes in Siberia and the North, Denikin's prospects in South Russia also seemed more hopeful. On April 19 Sir Henry Wilson telegraphed to General Briggs[1] to express the hope that Denikin would be able to take advantage of Kolchak's successes 'to reorganize and make effective use of the stores we are supplying.' But Wilson went on to warn Briggs: 'That Denikin has been led to expect assistance in the shape of Allied troops is greatly to be regretted, as public opinion is absolutely opposed to such a measure in this country. There are, too, other grave objections to this course. Many authorities on the Russian situation hold that the effort must be made from within if Russia is to be regenerated. It is very questionable, whether Russia will ever be able to stand alone if it comes from without.'

The military activities of the anti-Bolsheviks gave Churchill cause for optimism. Following the decision of the War Cabinet to send British military supplies to North Russia, equipment and clothing for 50,000 men was shipped to Archangel. As a result of the War Cabinet decision of March 4, all British troops had to be withdrawn from North Russia before the end of the summer. But Churchill hoped that during May, June and July, they would work with the Russian troops in pushing the front as far forward as possible before the evacuation. The presence of British troops, he wrote to Sir Henry Wilson on April 22, 'may enable Koltchak's forces to come into touch on our left Archangel front'.

---

[1] Charles James Briggs, 1865–1941. Entered the Army, 1886. On active service in South Africa, 1899–1902. Brigadier-General, commanding the 1st Cavalry Brigade, 1913–14. Major-General, February 1915. Lieutenant-General, commanding the 16 Army Corps at Salonika, 1916–18. Knighted, 1917. Head of the British Mission to South Russia, 1918–19.

During the third week of April the Treasury proposed ending the British subsidy for the Russian Military Mission in London. Churchill was outraged. The anti-Bolshevik forces, he wrote to Austen Chamberlain on April 22, 'have exhibited a continual increase of fighting strength and efficiency'. It was essential for the Russian Military Mission to be 'properly sustained'. And he continued: 'It may well be that before a year is out they will be the representatives of a Government speaking in the name of a united Russia. How shortsighted it would be for us to cripple them!'

On April 23, when Sir Henry Wilson had returned from Paris, he and Churchill discussed the Russian situation. Over 3,500 men had already volunteered for service in North Russia, a smaller number than they had hoped for, but sufficient, they believed, to make the General Staff plan a practical proposition. 'Winston & I,' Wilson wrote in his diary that evening, 'discussed a good punch towards Viatka to join with Kolchak before we cleared out.' On April 25, a telegram reached the War Office from General Knox in Ekaterinburg, in which Knox reported General Gaida's[1] opinion 'that by the end of May he would occupy Kotlas and Viatka with his own forces without British assistance'. If the North Russian and Siberian armies could join, Knox believed that the 'best avenue for British trade will by this means be opened up'.

The news from North Russia confirmed Churchill's optimism. In a telegram sent from Murmansk on April 25, General Maynard outlined his plans to advance, with British, Russian and Serbian troops, to the northern tip of Lake Onega. 'Russian leaders are urging me very strongly to press forward,' Maynard wrote, 'stating that unless they are permitted to follow up recent successes the morale of the troops will suffer. They affirm too that the advance will open up the most hopeful of all recruiting areas, and do more than anything else to stop Bolshevik agitation throughout the occupied areas.' At Kem and Soroka, Maynard

---

[1] Rudolf Gaida, 1892–1948. Born in Montenegro (then a part of Austria-Hungary). Trained as a pharmacist in Bohemia. Conscripted into the army medical corps, July 1914. Deserted to a Montenegrin regiment, pretending to be an officer, 1915. Captured by the Russians, 1917. In May 1918, with the rank of Captain, he served in the Czechoslovak Corps, and favoured fighting the Bolsheviks. Colonel commanding the Czech forces in Central Siberia, July–October 1918. Supported Admiral Kolchak's seizure of power at Omsk, November 1918. Promoted Major-General by Kolchak, November 1918. Commanded Kolchak's Nothern Army, June–July 1919, with the rank of Lieutenant-General. Dismissed by Kolchak, July 1919. Attempted unsuccessfully to seize power at Vladivostok, November 1919. Returned to Czechoslovakia, 1920. Chief of the Czech General Staff, 1926. Cashiered for trying to take part in a fascist putsch. Imprisoned for 'banditry', 1931. Headed the Czech Fascist organization, 1939–45. Arrested as a collaborator, 1945, and subsequently shot.

reported, 'leading men, who have been plotting against us, had been removed'; at Murmansk, 'a considerable number of undesirables' had been deported. 'I feel justified,' Maynard explained, 'under these circumstances, in further aggressive action, providing really good results are promised.'

During the third week of April, General Radcliffe and General Harington pressed Churchill to secure Allied recognition for Admiral Kolchak. Churchill approved their advice, and on April 26, in a letter to Lloyd George, he set out the reasons for recognition. Kolchak, he wrote, had already achieved 'a very remarkable measure of success', and had 'a very good chance' of reaching the Volga, and even of continuing his advance westwards towards Moscow. There was also, Churchill added, a possibility of a link between Kolchak's forces and the anti-Bolsheviks at Archangel; indeed, small patrols from both forces had already established contact near Viatka, less than 500 miles from Moscow. If Britain were to recognize Kolchak as 'Supreme Ruler of All Russia', and give him material help, it would then be possible, Churchill argued, to withdraw all British troops from Russia 'without either having to carry away many thousands of the local inhabitants who have compromised themselves with us, or leaving them to be massacred by the Bolsheviks'. The Northern Russian Government, led by Nikolai Tchaikowsky,[1] was, Churchill pointed out, 'the most democratic Government in the field against the Bolsheviks'; Kolchak himself, Churchill suggested, should only be recognized after he had agreed to set up a constitutional regime. In his letter, Churchill stressed the significance of Kolchak's successes, and the part played by British aid:

The advance of Koltchak's armies is the more remarkable in view of the fact that it is being conducted exclusively with Russian troops. The Czechos, who were formerly the only other troops on this front, are now employed simply on guarding the railway a long way back. The whole credit of regaining this really enormous stretch of country rests with a purely Russian army of about 100,000 men. There is, however, as you know, a Russian army of

[1] Nikolai Vasilievich Tchaikowsky, 1850–1926. Active in the first revolutionary Populist organization in St Petersburg, in the 1870s (known as the Tchaikowsky circle). In the 1880s he left Russia for the United States, where he tried to establish a religious commune. He returned to Russia during the 1905 revolution and was a leading member of the Popular Socialist Party. Strongly opposed the Bolsheviks in 1917. Head of the Provisional Government of North Russia (at Archangel), 1918–19. Went to Paris to plead the anti-Bolshevik cause at the Paris Peace Conference, 1919. He died in exile in England.

100,000 in an advanced state of formation in Siberia, and five divisions from this army are expected to reach Admiral Koltchak during the course of the next three months. As the front has advanced Westward, districts containing large numbers of men have been recovered, and these men are already being used to fill up the divisions at the front. Apparently wherever Bolshevism has been tried it is loathed. It is only popular where it has not been felt, and Koltchak's armies have been well received by the population on their onward march.

We can, I think, claim to have given more effective support to Koltchak than any of the other great Powers, as we have supplied him with nearly 12 million pounds' worth of our surplus munitions, and by the labours of our officers and agents this great mass of stuff has been filtered along the Siberian railway. In fact, the Russian forces in which we are interested, whether in North Russia, Siberia, or those of Denikin, have received from us assistance which has already been substantial and may shortly prove effective. . . .

Lloyd George discussed Churchill's letter with Sir Henry Wilson, after they had dined together in Paris on April 27. The two men had a further discussion about it at breakfast on April 28. Later that morning, Wilson sent Churchill an account of Lloyd George's response, which was not entirely favourable:

He wants to know exactly what it is you mean by recognising the Government of Kolchak. He says that he cannot find in your letter a clear definition of your proposal, and he wants to know whether you think Kolchak ought to be recognised as the *de facto* Governor of Siberia, in which case he thinks we may clash both with Kolchak and with Sazonov,[1] who claim that Kolchak represents the Government of all Russia; or whether you wish to recognise Kolchak as the Governor of all Russia, i.e. European Russia and Siberia?

I told him that I thought it would be sufficient if Kolchak was recognised up to the limit of those parts of Siberia and European Russia where his writ ran, and that similarly we could recognize Tchaikowsky as the *de facto* Governor for the country in which his writ runs. I pressed strongly the view that without unnecessarily delaying our own departure from Archangel and Murmansk we ought to do all in our power to stretch out a hand to Kolchak's people so that before we went the Tchaikowsky Government and the Kolchak Government would be in immediate touch. I did not find the Prime Minister opposed to this idea although he was not as enthusiastic about it as we are. . . .

Churchill received Wilson's letter later that same day. He wrote at once to Lloyd George: 'Don't be vexed with me about my Kolchak.

[1] Sergei Dmitrievich Sazonov, 1866–1927. Russian Minister of Foreign Affairs, 1910–15. Dismissed by the Tsar in November 1915 following his advocacy of Home Rule for Poland. Chief representative abroad of Admiral Kolchak, 1919–20. Nominated Foreign Minister of Russia by both Kolchak and Denikin, with headquarters in Paris. Died in exile in France.

There really is a good chance of his pulling the chestnuts out of the fire for us all.'

To the British officers serving in Siberia, Kolchak's confidence was evident. 'The news from the front now is very good,' Captain Savory[1] wrote to his mother from Vladivostok on April 26, '& the Bolsheviks seem to be retiring at a good pace. The Powers that be, here, take a very optimistic view of the show, & say that if things go on as they are at present, we should be in Moscow before the year is up.'

At a meeting of the War Cabinet on April 29, Churchill argued in favour of recognizing Kolchak's Government as soon as possible, pointing out that Kolchak expected to reach Kotlas by the beginning of June. But before Kolchak were recognized, Churchill again stressed, he should be made to issue a public declaration in favour of a 'democratic policy' on land and constitutional questions. 'The people of this country,' Churchill said, 'should be reassured that we were not endeavouring to reinstate a Czarist regime.' That same day Lloyd George saw Tchaikowsky in Paris, and asked him whether he intended to set up a Tsarist regime, or 'a more democratic institution', as Henry Wilson reported to Churchill on the following day. All Tchaikowsky could reply was that he would 'obtain some information from Kolchak' on the subject. Churchill was impatient at the delay which such enquiries would create. On May 1 he wrote to Lord Curzon:

Is it not possible to recognise Kolchak as 'The Russian Government' without defining its actual territorial scope either as against the Bolsheviks or as between united Russia and the Allies? The French expression that Kolchak's Government represents 'Le Principe Russe' is a very convenient one. In harmony with this, could we not perhaps recognise the Omsk Government as the 'Russian National Government' as opposed to the International conceptions of Lenin and Trotsky? . . .

Curzon did not share Churchill's enthusiasm for Kolchak. 'There is as you know,' he wrote to Churchill on May 2, 'great suspicion of Kolchak's imperialistic indiscretions in many Russian quarters, and any too ambitious designation wd be quite as likely to bring about his downfall as to give him help.' The widest title Curzon would recommend for

---

[1] Reginald Arthur Savory, 1894–   . Educated at Uppingham School. 2nd Lieutenant, January 1914. On active service at Gallipoli, 1915 (where he was wounded and awarded the Military Cross), in Mesopotamia, Siberia (1919), Kurdistan (1923), the north-west frontier of India (1930) and Waziristan (1937). Commanded the 11th Indian Infantry Brigade in the Middle-East, 1940–1. General Officer Commanding, Eritrea, 1941. Commanded the 23rd Indian Division, 1942–3. Director of Infantry, India, 1943–5. General Officer Commanding, Persia and Iraq, 1945–6. Adjutant-General, India, 1946–7. Knighted, 1947. In 1969 he married Marie Nikolaevna Zurabova, whom he had first met in Siberia in 1919.

Kolchak's regime was 'The Provisional Government of Siberia'. Churchill himself preferred the term 'Russian National Government', to distinguish it, he explained to Henry Wilson on May 3, 'from the Inter-National or Soviet Government'. But he accepted Curzon's more restrictive title.

In Paris, Henry Wilson had himself explained the military situation to Bonar Law and Lloyd George. 'After great struggles,' he wrote in his diary on May 1, 'LG agreed to my proposals to let Ironside join Gaida at Kotlas.' The three men had discussed the possibility of Kolchak's forces linking up with those at Archangel, and of a joint attack on Petrograd by the Russian General, Yudenitch, and the Finnish General, Mannerheim.[1] That afternoon Wilson had sent Churchill an account of his discussions with Lloyd George, together with his own thoughts:

My own opinion is that we should ascertain from Kolchak how he would view an occupation of Petrograd by a mixture of Mannerheim and Yudenitch before we commit ourselves to approving and possibly supporting such an operation.

As regards Gaida's move on Viatka and Kotlas, Prime Minister would not go further than to say that if Gaida reaches Viatka and establishes himself there firmly and if he moves up the railway to Kotlas there would be no objection to Ironside having everything prepared for a blow up the Dwina on Kotlas but that Cabinet would have to be consulted before such a move were actually carried out. . . .

On May 4, following Lloyd George's approval, the War Office telegraphed to General Ironside at Archangel, authorizing him to make all preparations, with the resources at his disposal, 'to strike a heavy blow against the Bolsheviks in the direction of Kotlas', with the intention of 'effecting a junction' with General Gaida, on the right flank of Kolchak's forces. Churchill himself continued to press the French and British leaders to recognize Kolchak, if only as head of a Siberian Government. 'The important thing to do is to recognise them at the earliest possible moment,' he telegraphed to Sir Henry Wilson in Paris on the afternoon of May 5. 'Now is the time to help them. More than a fortnight has already passed since War Office and Foreign Office papers were written and we are still paralysed.' An hour and a half later

[1] Carl Gustav Emil Mannerheim, 1867–1951. Member of a distinguished Finnish noble family. Served for thirty years as an officer in the Imperial Russian Army. Commanded a joint Rumanian and Russian Army Group in the Carpathians, 1916–17. Returned to Helsinki after Finland proclaimed its independence from Russia, 1917. Commander-in-Chief of the Finnish Army, 1918. Fought against the Russians, and against the Red Finns, 1918. Entered Helsinki at the head of 16,000 men, May 1918. Regent of Finland, 1919. Recalled as Commander-in-Chief during the Russo-Finnish War, 1939–40. President of Finland, 1944.

Churchill telegraphed to Lloyd George: 'If Kolchak continues to advance successfully there is a good chance of securing at no distant date a civilized Government for a united Russia more friendly to Britain than to any other power.'

That night Churchill telegraphed once more to Sir Henry Wilson, urging him to press upon the statesmen in Paris the need to recognize Kolchak. 'Recognition,' he explained, 'is taking sides formally, and once committed to this, wider forms of recognition must follow.'

In this second telegram to Sir Henry Wilson, Churchill dwelt at some length upon Yudenitch's proposed attack on Petrograd. 'We have no means of knowing whether the operation is feasible,' he warned, 'and certainly we should commit a grave imprudence to mix ourselves up with what may possibly be a hopeless failure.' But Churchill was anxious to give Yudenitch British support in the event of an attack on Petrograd by Mannerheim and the Finns, so that the enterprise should 'cease to be a purely Finnish show', and thereby please both Kolchak and Denikin.

Churchill's enthusiasm for Kolchak and Denikin was not shared by Lloyd George. In Paris, the Prime Minister had spoken at length to Tchaikowsky, and also to the Polish leader, Paderewski.[1] 'Neither of them,' he telegraphed to Churchill on May 6, 'take your views as to Kolchak and Denikin and their entourage: on the contrary they are genuinely alarmed lest their success should result in the triumph of reaction.' Lloyd George went on to declare that if British efforts 'simply ended in establishing a reactionary military regime in Russia, British democracy would never forgive us'.

Churchill believed that the recognition of Kolchak was both necessary and urgent. On May 7 he telegraphed his reply to Lloyd George:

I feel convinced that now is the time and that if the opportunity is lost Kolchak may either become too weak to be of any use or too strong to require our advice. It seems to me we have a tremendous chance of securing the future of Russia as a civilized democratic state friendly above all to us and that an event of this kind is indispensable to the completion of the main work in which you are engaged. Such a policy whole-heartedly carried through would secure overwhelming approval here. . . .

[1] Ignacy Jan Paderewski, 1860–1941. Pianist and Composer. A leading propagandist for Polish independence, 1914–17, based in Switzerland. Organized, in the United States, a Polish army to fight in France, 1917. Representative of the Polish National Committee in the United States, 1917–18. Prime Minister of Poland, and also Foreign Minister, January–November 1919. One of the two Polish signatories of the Versailles Treaty, June 1919. Polish Representative at the League of Nations, Geneva, 1920–1. An opponent of Pilsudski's regime, he lived in Switzerland, and on his estate in California, 1921–39. Chairman, Polish National Council (in exile), 1939–41. He died in New York.

The Foreign Office rejected this policy. 'It was safer,' Curzon minuted on May 9, 'to confine recognition of Kolchak at present to areas of which he is in more or less effective control.' Any wider recognition, he added, 'is certainly unjustified—it may be extremely unwise and it might commit us to results which we should afterwards deplore'.

In South Russia, British aid to the anti-Bolshevik forces had continued throughout April and May, despite the political and diplomatic uncertainties. On April 15 the first British ship bringing supplies to General Denikin had completed discharging its cargo at Novorossisk.[1] But in a telegram to Churchill on April 28, the head of the British Military Mission to Denikin, General Briggs, was pessimistic as to the fighting abilities of Denikin's Volunteer Army.

Churchill decided to replace Briggs by another General, Herbert Holman.[2] The War Cabinet had authorized Churchill to send a total of 2,000 British soldiers to South Russia as advisers to Denikin's forces; Churchill wanted Holman to command this enlarged Mission. On May 12, while the War Office was drawing up lists of supplies to be sent out to Russia with Holman, Churchill wrote to General Harington: 'We must act up to the full limit of the authority which has been granted to us.' And he went on:

I do not consider that the stores and equipments, either for Kolchak or Denikin, are necessarily limited by the amounts which have been agreed upon. If more can be used, every effort should be made to provide them and to secure the necessary authority.

I hope General Holman is asking for everything he requires and will go out with the feeling that his mission is being well provided for.

On May 14, in London, the War Cabinet discussed the state of British aid to the anti-Bolshevik forces. Churchill was not present at the meeting, but at Austen Chamberlain's request, the Cabinet approved a £9,000,000 loan by the British banking firm of Barings, to Kolchak's Government in Siberia. That morning, Churchill had arrived in his constituency to speak during the presentation of the freedom of Dundee

[1] Its cargo consisted of 18 heavy guns, 5,000 tons of ammunition and 480 tons of stores. By May 12 a total of nine ships had arrived, some from London, some from Salonica and some from Alexandria, bringing in all 452 heavy guns, over 10,000 tons of ammunition and 9,000 tons of supplies.

[2] Herbert Campbell Holman, 1869–1949. Entered Army, 1889. On active service in Burma, 1891 (wounded). Served in China as an interpreter, 1900. Attaché with the Russian Forces in Manchuria, 1905. Lieutenant–Colonel, 1914. Served on the Western Front, 1914–19. Brigadier-General, in charge of Q services, 4th Army, 1918. Major-General, 1919. Chief of the Military Mission to South Russia, 1919–20. Knighted, 1920. Deputy Quartermaster General, India, 1921–2. Lieutenant-General Commanding the 4th Indian Division, 1924–7.

to Sir Douglas Haig. At one point in his speech he spoke of the difficulties of bringing troops home from the distant theatres of war. At that moment a heckler called out: 'What about Russia?' Churchill took up the challenge. 'I got more volunteers in three weeks to go to the north of Russia,' he said, 'than came forward to fill the whole of the rest of the Army. Our soldiers are not nearly so much in love with the Bolshevists as some people think. . . .' Later in his speech Churchill criticized another heckler who wanted self-determination for India and Egypt. Once again he spoke of Russia:

> What has self-determination done for Russia? (Cheers.) Self-determination does not mean the right of every half-wit to order great communities about. (Loud cheers).
>
> Self-determination is one of those ridiculous expressions which were coined by the Bolshevists in the early days of the attack upon the prosperity and freedom of the Russian people. (Oh, oh.)
>
> I know they have got a few friends here, but it is very lucky for those people that the great mass of the British nation is sensible, solid and sound, because when it comes to revolutions the revolutionaries are the first to suffer, and when the revolution has come to an end all the most excitable people have been put out of the way, and you have got a great period of reaction, with probably a military dictator at the head of the State. . . .

In North Russia, military events still seemed to favour the anti-Bolshevik cause. On May 13 a British river flotilla left Archangel to sail up the now ice-free Dvina river, and bombard the Bolshevik shore positions. On May 18 General Maynard's force captured the northernmost end of Lake Onega, and continued its advance. As well as Russian and Serbian troops, two British infantry companies, and a detachment of Royal Marines, took part in the action. But success on the Murmansk front was offset by a severe setback at Archangel. That same day General Ironside telegraphed to Churchill from Archangel with news of a further mutiny among the Russian troops under his command. At Pinega two companies of Russians had mutinied, killing two of their officers. 'I regret to report,' Ironside wrote, 'I had to shoot fifteen but the companies are back at duty. . . .'

On May 20 Churchill was in Paris, trying to persuade Lloyd George to recognize Kolchak's Government, and to give Kolchak's forces more active support. Of all the anti-Bolshevik armies, Kolchak's controlled the largest territory, and seemed capable of the most decisive action. On May 6 General Knox had sent the War Office an account of Kolchak's military plans. On his right flank, with his Siberian Army, he intended to occupy Kotlas and link up with Archangel; on his left flank, with his Western Army, he intended to occupy the eastern bank of the Volga from opposite Kazan to Samara, and then open up direct communications with Denikin; this done, his plan was for both armies to advance on Moscow. These objectives were ambitious, and Knox was sceptical of their chance of success. 'It is useless for me,' he wrote, 'to telegraph academic criticisms of the rashness of the general plan reminding you that it is part of the Russian character to draw up plans without estimating the means to carry them out. We have to go on.'

Churchill agreed with Knox's conclusions, and was convinced that, with Allied recognition, Kolchak's morale and status would be perceptively enhanced. On May 21, while still in Paris, he sent Lloyd George a long appeal. The anti-Bolsheviks, he wrote, 'should be treated with proper consideration and not treated simply as a pack of worthless emigrants. In a very little while the wheel of fortune may place these men—some of whom are experienced statesmen with whom we have worked for many years—in positions of authority, and it is only prudent to preserve civil and considerate relations with them.' But Churchill also wanted the Allies to secure, from Kolchak, 'definite guarantees for the democratic government of Russia'. In his letter he listed four principles to which Kolchak must agree before recognition was granted:

(a) a constituent assembly on a democratic franchise to decide the future form of Russian Government,
(b) a bold agrarian policy,
(c) the acceptance of the independence of Poland and of the autonomous existence of Finland, and
(d) the acceptance of the fact that the provisional arrangements which the allies have made in regard to Esthonia, Livonia, Latvia, Lithuania, Georgia and Azerbaijan shall be dealt with only in accordance with the agreements reached between the new Russia and the League of Nations.

Churchill opposed the suggestion, which had been made by Lord Hardinge,[1] that the Allies should invite 'both parties in Russia' to cease

---

[1] Charles Hardinge, 1858–1944. Entered Foreign Office, 1880. Knighted, 1904. Ambassador at Petrograd, 1904–6. Permanent Under-Secretary of State for Foreign Affairs, 1906–10. Created Baron Hardinge of Penshurst, 1910. Viceroy of India, 1910–16. Permanent Under-Secretary of State for Foreign Affairs, 1916–20. Ambassador to Paris, 1920–3.

fighting: 'There can be no question of Kolchak's Government ceasing fighting at the present time,' Churchill wrote in his letter to Lloyd George. 'If their armies stopped fighting,' he explained, 'they would disintegrate, and Bolshevik propaganda is more dangerous in a truce than when actual fighting is taking place.' Churchill derided Hardinge's further proposal, that unless Kolchak ceased fighting his supplies should be halted. 'It betrays,' he wrote, 'most complete want of comprehension of the issues which are at stake in Russia. You might as well ask fire and water to cease their conflict.'

On May 25 General Gough,[1] who had arrived in Helsingfors to report on the military situation in the Baltic, telegraphed to the War Office that Yudenitch would be able to capture Petrograd 'if given immediately 2,000 tons of food and supplies and a sufficient quantity of arms and munitions to equip existing reserve of 5,000 men'. On May 26 representatives of the War Office, the Foreign Office, the Admiralty and the Ministry of Shipping met at the War Office to discuss Gough's request. General Harington presided over the meeting, which decided to send Yudenitch, 'in the first instance':

a) Rifles, small arm ammunitions, clothing and equipment for 7,500 men.
b) Boots for 10,000 men.
c) 18 pr. guns, 16, with 2,000 rounds per gun.
d) 6 inch howitzers, 8, (tractor drawn) with 1,000 rounds per gun.
e) Lorries, 20, with petrol, oil and spares.
f) Medical stores for 10,000 troops.

When Churchill saw these proposals, he at once showed them to Lloyd George, noting in the margin: 'Prime Minister has no objection to this.'

There was much speculation as to the effect of the possible capture of Petrograd. On May 30 the British Minister in Stockholm, Robert Clive,[2] spoke to a Russian exile, N. I. Tereschenko,[3] whose views he re-

[1] Hubert de la Poer Gough, 1870–1963. Entered Army, 1889. On active service in the Tirah, 1897–8 and South Africa, 1899–1902 (severely wounded). Professor, Staff College, 1904–6. Major-General, 1914. Lieutenant-General, 1915. Knighted, 1916. Commanded the 3rd Cavalry Brigade, 1914; the 2nd Cavalry Division, 1915; the 1st Army Corps, 1916; the Fifth Army, 1916–18. Removed from his command after the German breakthrough of March 1918. Chief, Allied Mission to the Baltic, 1919.

[2] Robert Henry Clive, 1877–1948. Grandson of the 8th Earl of Denbigh. Entered the Diplomatic Service, 1902. Served in Stockholm, 1915–19. Minister to Teheran, 1926–31; at the Vatican, 1933–4. Knighted, 1927. Ambassador in Brussels, 1937–9.

[3] Nikolai Ivanovich Tereschenko, 1888–1958. A millionaire sugar refiner in the Ukraine, known as the 'Sugar King'. Chairman, Kiev War Industries Committee, 1914. Vice-Chairman, Central War Industries Committee, 1916–17. Minister of Finance in the Provisional Government, March–May 1917; Minister of Communications, May–July 1917; Minister for Foreign Affairs, July–November 1917. Emigrated, 1918; died in exile.

ported back to London on the following day: 'He said that he believed
Petrograd would certainly be taken and before long, and that there
would be very grave excesses when it was. But he added the world
must be prepared for this. Bolshevik leaders would have to pay the
penalty. . . .'

When Churchill saw this telegram, he underlined the words 'grave
excesses'. And on June 2 he wrote to General Harington: 'Any force wh
we support even indirectly must proceed according to the recognized
laws & customs of war & be guided by humane considerations.' He
added that the message from Tereschenko would 'do us harm in our
own counsels if it is left unchallenged. . . . Wholesale executions are
unpardonable on political as well as on moral grounds.'

Churchill was determined to warn Yudenitch against all forms of
brutality and revenge, including the murder of Jews. He therefore telegraphed on June 6 to General Gough, sending details of what Tereschenko had said, and adding:

> Excesses by anti-Bolsheviks if they are victorious will alienate sympathies
> British nation and render continuance of support most difficult. This should
> be represented tactfully but strongly to Yudenitch, and other leading Rus-
> sians with whom you come in contact. You should press for fair public trial of
> all culprits and stringent orders against terrorism and indiscriminate shoot-
> ing. In view of prominent part taken by Jews in Red terror and regime
> there is special danger of Jew pogroms and this danger must be combatted
> strongly.

On May 29 in the House of Commons Churchill's friend, Josiah
Wedgwood, who had joined the Labour party in 1918, spoke scathingly
of the atrocities committed by Denikin's troops in South Russia. 'At
Ekaterinoslav,' he said, 'Denikin ordered every Red Russian found in
possession of Red literature to be shot forthwith. At Bataisk, in the Don
district, every man with a son in the Red Guard was killed. In one place
every tenth workman was shot as an example to the rest.' Churchill did
not attempt to answer Wedgwood's specific charges. But he spoke with
enthusiasm of Denikin's successes. 'He has advanced his whole front, in
some places, to a distance of eighty miles,' Churchill said, 'and in this he
has been aided by rebellions which have broken out among the people
who are enjoying what my hon. and gallant friend Colonel Wedgwood
would no doubt call the blessings of Bolshevik rule.' Churchill went on
to say that the effect of British munitions 'with which we have been

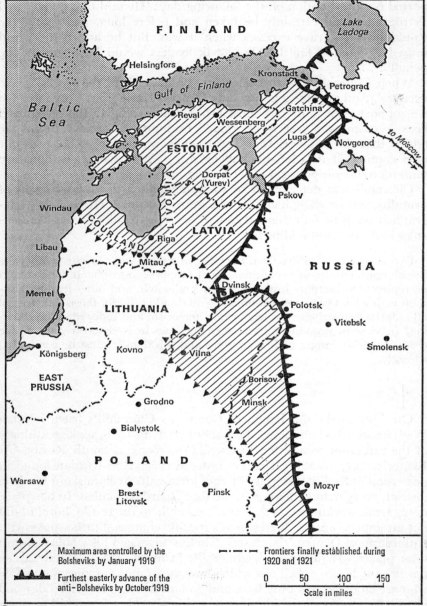

THE BALTIC, 1919–1920

supplying him, and with which we propose to continue to supply him, is only now beginning to be felt'.

On the whole western frontier of Russia, Churchill told the House of Commons, from Finland to Rumania, the anti-Bolshevik forces were standing firm. A strong force of British volunteers had begun to land at Archangel. A strong naval flotilla was ascending the River Dvina, 'well armed with guns'. In Siberia, Kolchak's troops were fighting 'with British ammunition and rifles'.

Churchill's speech pleased many Conservatives. On May 31 a Conservative MP, Sir Samuel Hoare,[1] wrote to him:

You must allow me to write these two or three lines of most sincere congratulations and gratitude for all that you have done in the matter of Russia. For the last six months I have been convinced that the whole future of Europe, and indeed of the world, depends upon a Russian settlement and the destruction of Bolshevism. If I may say so, you alone of the Allied Ministers have consistently held and expressed the same view. Whilst however there was little that I or the group of Members with whom I work could accomplish, you fortunately were in a position to carry your convictions into effect. . . .

The Labour Party reacted strongly against Churchill's speech. In a leading article on May 30 the *Daily Herald* declared:

The gambler of Gallipoli, Winston Churchill, stood in his place in the House of Commons last night and expounded the policy of the 'second throw', in the midst of a storm of interruptions that recalled his recent fiasco at Dundee, when, be it carefully remembered, he assured his constituents that the object of his and our policy in Russia was only and 'honourably' to extract our troops from the adventure into which he has now deliberately plunged us.

The gambler's first throw was Gallipoli, which, as Lord French has just told the world, led to the early shell-starvation, misery, and needless slaughter of our troops in France. His second throw is the new war in Russia, to back reaction in the persons of Kolchak and Denikin.

During his speech of May 29, Churchill had admitted that Kolchak's forces had suffered a 'considerable setback'. They had, in fact, been struggling for nearly a month to maintain their line of advance. The

---

[1] Samuel John Gurney Hoare, 1880–1959. Conservative MP for Chelsea, 1910–44. Succeeded his father as 2nd Baronet, 1915. Lieutenant-Colonel, British Military Mission to Russia, 1916–17 and to Italy, 1917–18. Deputy High Commissioner, League of Nations, for care of Russian refugees, 1921. Secretary of State for Air, October 1922–January 1924 and 1924–9. Secretary of State for India, 1931–5; for Foreign Affairs, 1935. First Lord of the Admiralty, 1936–7; Home Secretary, 1937–9; Lord Privy Seal, 1939–40; Secretary of State for Air, April–May 1940. Ambassador to Spain, 1940–4. Created Viscount Templewood, 1944.

Bolsheviks had won their first, small, counter-attack on May 4. Thenceforth, slowly, but with a steadily increasing momentum, they pushed Kolchak's armies further and further eastwards. Lenin was determined to drive Kolchak back across the Urals. 'If we do not conquer the Urals by winter,' he telegraphed on May 29 to the Military Revolutionary Council on the Eastern Front, 'I consider disaster to be inevitable for the Revolution.' Trotsky shared Lenin's belief. 'The offensive on the Eastern Front must proceed without halt,' he telegraphed to Ephraim Sklianksi[1] on June 1. Any hesitation, he warned, 'let alone withdrawal on our part . . . would create conditions favourable to the recognition of Kolchak. Once committed, the Entente would go on and on.'

During the first week in June, Kolchak's forces were driven back on all fronts. 'General situation is not satisfactory,' the British Consul at Omsk, Robert Hodgson,[2] telegraphed to the Foreign Office on June 3. 'Situation was aggravated by treachery of Ukrainian Regiment going over to the enemy after murdering its officers.'

On June 4 Kolchak replied to an Allied note of May 26, refusing the Allied demand to summon the Constituent Assembly of 1917, and giving an evasive answer about the future sovereignty of Finland and the Baltic States, both of which had been Russian before the revolution. Nor did his advance towards Moscow go as smoothly as his supporters hoped. On June 6 Churchill told the House of Commons that in the previous week Kolchak's forces had been driven back 120 miles. He went on to describe the nature of the fighting east of Moscow, and to warn against undue optimism:

The House will realise that this is an extremely attenuated form of warfare. A few thousand men are spread over twenty miles of front. The railways are few and far between. The rolling stock is limited and defective on both sides. Occasionally local concentrations are arranged which produce these changes. This line sways backwards and forwards. It is often a case of easy come and easy go with accessions of land in this kind of warfare. But, as I say, I have not at all attempted to encourage the extravagant hopes being based upon the advance of Admiral Kolchak, and I very much deprecate the kind of suggestion that I see in some of the newspapers that he is likely to be at the gates

[1] Ephraim Markovich Sklianski, 1892–1925. A doctor. Joined the Bolsheviks in 1913. Chairman of the Army Committee of the Fifth Army (Dvinsk), November 1917. Supreme Commissar of the Field Staff, 1918. Deputy Commissar for War, 1918–19. Trotsky's most trusted helper and deputy, 1918–24. Drowned accidentally while visiting the United States.

[2] Robert MacLeod Hodgson, 1874–1956. Vice-Consul, Marseille, 1901–6; Vladivostok, 1906–11. Consul, Vladivostok, 1911–19. Acting British High Commissioner in Siberia, 1919–21. British Agent to the Soviet Government, 1921–4. Chargé D'Affaires, Moscow, 1924–7. Knighted, 1925. Minister to Albania, 1928–36. British Agent to Nationalist Spain, 1937–9; Chargé d'Affaires, Burgos, 1939. Foreign Office Adviser to the Censorship, 1942–4.

of Moscow within a short time. He is hundreds of miles from the gates of Moscow, and no such expectation would be at all reasonable.

The *Daily Herald* exulted in Kolchak's imminent demise. But it had harsh words for Churchill, declaring in its leading article on June 7:

We have, on Mr Churchill's own showing, sent to Russia munitions which cost us over twenty millions pounds sterling to produce. And even so the Bolsheviks would seem to be winning. It is all very sad for Mr Churchill. Only last week he drew a picture for us of 'the inherent vice of Bolshevism rotting every part of the social structure of Russia'—'even the military tyranny on which alone the Soviet power depends'. And now it is Kolchak's power, Kolchak's military tyranny, that is rotting! . . .

On June 7 Josiah Wedgwood, one of the strongest Parliamentary critics of Churchill's Russian policy, wrote to ask him a personal favour. Could he go to Vienna at the end of June, he asked, for his daughter's wedding, 'in uniform', possibly with 'some nominal mission'. All he wanted was to be able to wear his Naval Commander's uniform at the ceremony. And he added: 'Sealed instructions to execute the bearer at sight I will risk.' Churchill was not amused, replying on June 13:

I am afraid it is quite impossible for me to do what you wish at the present time. You have insisted on painting yourself an extreme revolutionary Bolshevik eager to take up arms in the class war. For you to go out in uniform or on a mission to Vienna in the present circumstances would give rise to far-reaching misunderstandings which I could not dispel by any explanation that would be believed.

I deeply regret therefore that it is not in my power to help you as I should always wish to do on personal grounds without compromising graver issues.

In his postscript Churchill added: 'Come & see me any time.' But on the question of the uniform he was inflexible.

On June 8, Knox telegraphed from Omsk to the War Office: 'general situation from military point of view most unsatisfactory and uncertain, largely due to panic . . . and also to quarrels between the chiefs. . . .' But despite this warning, and despite Kolchak's refusal to accept the Allies' democratic demands, both Churchill and his War Office advisers continued with the Kotlas plan to link Kolchak's forces with those in North Russia. On June 6 Ironside had telegraphed from Archangel that he could begin operations towards Kotlas in the first week of July. Bolshevik morale, he reported, was bad; they were short of both food and equipment. 'A strong push will upset everything,' Ironside declared. He then outlined his plan in detail. Churchill at once sent Ironside's proposals to Sir Henry Wilson in Paris, and asked Wilson to find out if Lloyd George approved. 'I lunched with LG,' Wilson wrote in his diary on June 10, '& afterwards explained Ironside's proposals to him & to Bonar on the map & he made no objection. His mind was full of Fiume[1] & terms for the Boche & against the Roumanians & anger against Winston for giving Gough a GCMG!' That night Wilson telegraphed to Churchill: 'I have received your letter regarding Ironside's proposals and have explained the whole situation to Prime Minister who raises no objection. I cross tonight and hope to see you tomorrow afternoon.'

Lloyd George having raised no objection to the Kotlas plan, the War Office, on June 10, telegraphed to General Knox to ask if the Czech troops still in Siberia might not be asked to advance on Kotlas from the south east. 'It is possible,' the War Office telegram read, 'that they might welcome the prospect of cutting their way through to Archangel, and their eventual repatriation by this route, as this would be shorter and quicker than via Vladivostock.'

The War Cabinet met to discuss General Ironside's plan at half past six on the evening of June 11. 'I explained our proposals for Ironside's attack on Kotlas & joining hands with Kolchak via Kotlas and Viatka,' Sir Henry Wilson noted in his diary. 'They all agreed to my proposals.' According to the Minutes of the meeting, Wilson had told the Cabinet: 'Our object was twofold; (i) to hit the enemy hard, and (ii) to join up with the friendly forces in the South.' Once this latter aim was achieved, 'we would hand over control of the operation to Admiral Kolchak and proceed ourselves to withdraw from North Russia'. The whole intention of the plan, Wilson reiterated, 'was to facilitate that withdrawal'. 'Whatever pressure Kolchak might exert,' he added, 'we did not intend to remain in North Russia another winter.' In answer to questions by both Curzon and Montagu, as to whether the Kotlas advance fitted in with Churchill's promise to Parliament that British troops were leaving North Russia, Churchill himself remarked that he 'did not think that there was anything in the operations now projected which was incon-

---

[1] On the eastern Adriatic coast, the only port of Hungary before 1914. Promised to Croatia by the Treaty of London, 1915. Demanded by Italy, 1918. Seized by Croat troops, 23 October 1918. Claimed by Italy throughout the summer of 1919, when Italian ships entered the harbour, but were later replaced by American naval forces, pending a decision on the future of Fiume by the Peace Conference. On 12 September 1919, before any decision was reached, the port was occupied by the Italian poet and soldier-of-fortune, Gabriele D'Annunzio, and the Italians remained in control until 1945, when Fiume was transferred to Yugoslavia.

sistent, or could not easily be reconciled, with what he had stated in Parliament'. Churchill went on to speak optimistically of the operation's chance of success.

Five days later, having returned to Paris, Wilson found that Lloyd George had developed doubts about the proposed advance. 'Breakfast with LG,' he wrote in his diary on June 16. 'Lindley[1] from Archangel also there. A long talk about Ironside's Kotlas expedition. LG is afraid of Ironside getting committed & then having to be pulled out & he wants me to send him a wire pointing out that no further reinforcements can be sent, & he *must* get out before the winter.'

On June 17 a telegram reached the Foreign Office from Siberia, recording a serious setback in Kolchak's position: his western army, led by General Gaida, had been defeated by a Bolshevik force much smaller than his own. Curzon, Austen Chamberlain and Milner at once decided to call a special meeting of the War Cabinet, to question the wisdom of proceeding with the Kotlas campaign. The meeting was convened at 10 Downing Street at noon on June 18. Curzon opened the proceedings by stating that he was 'much disturbed at the possibility of our undertaking a venture which would prove unsuccessful'. The position, Churchill admitted, 'was not quite a happy one' on Kolchak's front, but he still believed that the Kotlas advance should be tried. He had no doubt, he said, 'that the military experts would be able to make a case for our advance, even though the plan for joining hands with Admiral Kolchak was no longer feasible'. Austen Chamberlain spoke strongly against proceeding with the advance, and Curzon supported him. After a lengthy discussion, the only agreement reached was to discuss the matter again in ten days time, on June 27. In the meantime, it was decided that General Ironside 'should not undertake a definite advance until the War Cabinet had finally decided upon the course of action'.

At one point during the War Cabinet's discussion, General Radcliffe declared, on behalf of the War Office, that it had always been Sir Henry Wilson's intention 'to strike a blow at the Bolsheviks in the direction of Kotlas, in order to ensure the withdrawal of Allied troops in a satisfactory manner. . . .' Explaining this statement in a minute to Churchill after the War Cabinet had ended, Radcliffe pointed out that the

---

[1] Francis Oswald Lindley, 1872–1950. 4th son of Baron Lindley. Entered Diplomatic Service, 1897. 3rd Secretary at Vienna, 1899. 2nd Secretary, Cairo, 1904–6. Counsellor of Embassy, Petrograd, 1915–17. Commissioner in Russia, 1918; Consul-General, Russia, 1919; High Commissioner Vienna, 1919–20. Minister to Athens, 1922–3; to Oslo, 1923–9. Knighted, 1926. Ambassador to Portugal, 1929–31; to Japan, 1931–4. Member of the Home Office Advisory Committee on Interned Aliens, 1939–45.

General Staff paper of April 15, approved by Henry Wilson and transmitted to Ironside, had specifically instructed him 'to make all necessary
preparations to strike as effective a blow as possible at the hostile forces,
with the object of facilitating the ultimate withdrawal of the Allied
forces. . . .' On June 20 Churchill sent the paper of April 15 to Bonar
Law, Curzon and Austen Chamberlain, with the covering note: 'You
shd glance at this. The military view has always favoured this operation
even if isolated. There is no change of view.'

Curzon was not mollified by this explanation. The point under discussion, he replied, was 'whether it would do more good or harm to
advance and then retire'. General Ironside, however, tried to set the
Cabinet's worries at rest. He had no plans to go beyond the instructions
of April 15, he telegraphed to the War Office on June 19, or 'of allowing
British forces to get into such a position that they would require relief or
that they could not withdraw'. And he gave as his personal opinion that
it would not be advisable even 'to continue an advance against Kotlas
if the enemy really puts up a stubborn resistance'.

On June 20 Austen Chamberlain wrote to Churchill, Curzon and
Bonar Law, warning that the whole Kotlas plan was 'incapable of
realisation' unless 'Kolchak can effect a junction with them', and that
any territory won by Ironside would be lost once the British withdrew.
The Archangel Government, he declared, would quickly be overthrown, or fall a victim 'of its own inherent weakness'. When left alone
the anti-Bolshevik Russians 'had not fought and would not fight'.
Churchill replied on the following day in a note to General Harington:

> I understand that the General Staff considers that the advance will not
> involve serious fighting by the British troops; & that the Russian troops will
> be strong enough to hold Kotlas after it has been taken while the British
> withdraw: & that the destruction of the Kotlas base, flotilla etc will protect
> Archangel from any speedy attack.

The preliminaries of the Kotlas plan had already been put into
operation. On June 20, a detachment of British and Russian troops had
advanced southwards along the Dvina river, supported by a Royal
Naval flotilla and some Royal Air Force planes. During the day the
British captured 400 Bolshevik soldiers and 3 field guns.

At the War Cabinet meeting on June 27 it was agreed 'to sanction
General Ironside's proposed operations'. The operations themselves,
however, went badly. On July 7 a mutiny broke out among a battalion
of Russian troops being held in reserve on the right bank of the Dvina.
The mutineers murdered three British and four Russian officers. The

ringleaders, taking a number of men with them, escaped to the Bolsheviks.

On the day of the Dvina mutiny Churchill and Sir Henry Wilson were driving to North Wales, for a series of discussions with Lloyd George at his home. 'Both arrived depressed,' Sir Maurice Hankey recorded in his diary, 'presumably by the failure of Kolchak in Russia.' Lloyd George, Hankey added, 'was always opposed to Winston's operations for Archangel and was only persuaded with great difficulty to assent to them, so he was in rather a "I told you so" mood & twitted Winston a great deal. . . .' Lloyd George made no secret of his attitude to the anti-Bolshevik movement. 'It is clear,' Wilson wrote in his diary, 'LG wants to cut our connection with it altogether, even to stopping supplies & missions to Denikin & Kolchak.'

Throughout the first week of July, the water level of the Dvina, no longer swollen by melting snows or spring rains, had been falling daily. On July 9 it fell to only two feet six inches—well below the level needed by the Royal Navy flotilla to remain in operation. The flotilla, an indispensable part of the Kotlas forces, at once withdrew down river in order to avoid being stranded, and captured. All chance of linking up the Archangel army with the anti-Bolsheviks in Siberia was ended. The War Cabinet met that day to discuss the new situation. It was clear that the Kotlas plan would not now be put into operation, despite all the hopes that had been vested in it. Churchill told his colleagues that the War Office 'had not interfered in any way with General Ironside's judgement, and he (General Ironside) had come independently to the conclusion that the suggested attack would be unwise, at any rate during the present month'. Churchill pointed out, in support of Ironside's decision, that not only was the river level 'abnormally low', but that the morale of the Bolsheviks 'was better than had been anticipated', and that the Bolshevik artillery 'was of longer range than our own'.

Curzon was worried lest the abandonment of the Kotlas plan would jeopardize the final withdrawal of the British force. The 'whole argument in support of the attack', he pointed out, 'had been that it was necessary in order to secure the evacuation of our troops'. In reply, Churchill agreed that as the Kotlas expedition 'had now been abandoned', the evacuation would be more difficult. Nevertheless, 'he still believed that it would be possible to evacuate on the date named, and he expected that the last remaining British units would leave on or before November 10. . . .' Only a small British Mission of 2,000 men would remain, to advise the North Russian Government in matters of defence, and to supervise that Government's own evacuation.

On July 19 the Italian contingent in North Russia was withdrawn from the line. On July 22 there was a mutiny on General Maynard's sector of the Onega front, where a regiment of Russian troops handed over the front line to the Bolsheviks. That same day, on the Archangel–Vologda railway, British and Polish officers forestalled yet another mutiny. The last 700 American troops in North Russia were evacuated on July 28. On the following day, in the House of Commons, Churchill announced that all British troops would be withdrawn from North Russia before the date originally set, October 15. 'It is a matter of very great and painful difficulty,' he said, 'to sever the ties and quit the scene.' During the course of his speech, Churchill defended his personal role in the intervention:

I should like to point out, if I may do so parenthetically, as I am known to hold strong views on this subject, that I have not committed this country to any commitments or to any obligations of any sort or kind with regard to Russia to which we were not committed, and as I think properly committed, before I had anything to do with the affair at all.

All I have been labouring to do is to discharge faithfully, honourably and efficiently the obligations into which we had entered in the days of the German War and into which I hold we had rightly and properly entered. I think that should be recorded if it is not challenged in any quarter of the House.

I defy anyone to show a single commitment or obligation which I have been personally responsible for creating on behalf of this country in regard to intervention or interference or intercourse with Russia during the present period of war.

17

'The Whole Fate of Russia'

====

CHURCHILL had been disappointed at the failure of the anti-Bolshevik forces in North Russia and Western Siberia. But there still remained, in South Russia, one army which seemed capable of reaching Moscow, that of General Denikin. On May 29, when the War Cabinet had met in London to discuss an appeal from General Denikin for financial help to improve the condition of the railways in the territory under his control, Churchill pointed out to his colleagues that as the Supreme Economic Council in Paris had refused to help maintain Denikin's railway system, it was up to Britain to assist him.

The 'minimum value' of the railway stores and equipment needed by Denikin was calculated by the War Office at £1,000,000. Churchill wanted this sum allocated at once. But Austen Chamberlain protested that the 'whole burden of fighting the Bolshevists in Russia was now being borne by Great Britain alone', and that the situation 'was becoming intolerable'. Britain herself, he pointed out, was 'exceedingly short' of railway material. The War Cabinet finally agreed that Denikin could only receive the supplies he needed if they could be sent 'without any sacrifice of the essential interests of this country'.

Throughout the summer of 1919, Denikin's policy in the Caucasus added to Churchill's anxieties. Since the revolution of November 1917, four independent Republics had been declared in the Caucasus: Georgia, Azerbaijan, Armenia and Daghestan. Denikin opposed the independence of these Republics; for him, this area, most of which had been under Russian rule for nearly a century, was an intrinsic part of Greater Russia. In the second week of June Churchill drafted a telegram to General Milne,[1] instructing him to give his support to Denikin's view

[1] George Francis Milne, 1866–1948. Entered the Royal Artillery, 1885. Commanded a battery at Omdurman, 1898. Served on Kitchener's Intelligence Staff in South Africa, 1900–2. Brigadier-General, commanding the 4th Division artillery, 1913–14. He took part in the

of the matter. But, as Lord Curzon wrote to Churchill on June 10, it was not simply a matter of taking sides:

> As regards Georgia I do not know if you are aware that Balfour definitely recognized its independence & pledged our support to its cause at the Peace Conference.
>
> Further at the very moment when you propose to telegraph to Milne telling him & his officers not to show too much sympathy with the Republicans, *your own office* is telegraphing a strong warning to Denikin not to overstep a given line separating him from the Republicans on pain of the severe displeasure of HMG.
>
> Should General Milne therefore receive your proposed instructions, I think he would find no small difficulty in deciding on which leg he was expected to stand.
>
> Finally I submit that the only way in which to secure Denikin's success is to keep the Caucasus quiet behind him. This can only be done by recognizing the 'Separatist interests of the Republics'.
>
> They cordially dislike & distrust Denikin & would sooner become Bolsheviks than accept his dispensation. The worst thing that could happen to Denikin would therefore be in my judgement that the Republics should be snubbed, for it is on Denikin that they would take it out. . . .

Churchill replied to Curzon on the following day, pointing out that the question of British support for the Caucasian republics would be determined by the fact that British troops were in the process of a complete withdrawal, and were about to be replaced by an Italian occupation force:

> I think you underrate the extent to which the original instructions given to our officers have become obsolete in view of our impending abandonment of this whole theatre. We should have actually cleared out on Sunday next, but for the interests of Denikin's operations. Our present date is July 15th; after which the Italians or chaos or both!
>
> Let me have my telegram back. I continually meet soldiers who seem to be toiling to build up 'strong independent Republics'; and who think we have a policy in that direction for which we are going to make exertions and sacrifices. Surely they should be undeceived.

Curzon still believed that it was a major British interest to support the Caucasian republics. In a draft telegram to Balfour early in June he had

---

battles of Le Cateau, Marne, and Aisne, 1914. Lieutenant-General Commanding the British forces at Salonika, 1916–18. Knighted, 1918. Commanded the British Forces at Constantinople (Army of the Black Sea), 1919–20. General, 1920. Chief of the Imperial General Staff, 1926–33. Field-Marshal, 1928. Created Baron, 1933.

warned of the wide ranging dangers of a British withdrawal. The rich oil resources of Baku, he wrote, 'must almost inevitably fall into the hands of the Bolsheviks'; the independent Republic of Azerbaijan 'will disappear'; the vast resources of the whole region 'will be at the mercy of a horde of savages who know no restraint and are resolved to destroy all law'. Britain, he added, 'apparently proposed to surrender without lifting a finger the key to the whole of the vast territory which stretches from the Black Sea to the borders of the Indian Empire'.

The conflict between Britain's support for the Caucasian republics, and her support for Denikin, was resolved on June 11 by the Cabinet's decision to withdraw all British troops from the Caucasus, and by the rapid strengthening of links with Denikin. During June, eight merchant ships completed the unloading of British stores at Novorossisk, providing a total of over 9,000 tons of ammunition, as well as rifles and equipment.

Churchill's public utterances on Bolshevism became stronger during June and July. On June 22 he published a fierce article in the *Weekly Dispatch*, on the need to rescue Russia from Bolshevism. Bolshevism, he wrote, 'means in every country a civil war of the most merciless kind between the discontented, criminal and mutinous classes on the one hand and the contented or law abiding on the other'. He went on to write: 'Bolshevism, wherever it manifests itself openly and in concrete form, means war of the most ruthless character, the slaughter of men, women and children, the burning of homes, and the inviting in of tyranny, pestilence, and famine.'

Churchill's outspokenness, and the Government's policy of sending aid to Denikin, provoked an upsurge of popular dissatisfaction with the Government's Russian policy. On June 27, at the Labour Party Conference at Southport, delegates voted unanimously in favour of a motion condemning the intervention in Russia 'whether by force of arms, by supply of munitions, by financial subsidies, or by commercial blockade'. That same day, the War Cabinet met to discuss the future of the intervention. The campaigns taking place in Russia, Churchill declared, 'were on both sides wars of the weak'. It would be 'a great mistake', he said, 'for us to break our political necks for Russia by maintaining indefinitely a kind of equipoise warfare', and he supported Lloyd George's view 'that next year our policy generally would require reconsideration'. He did not believe, he added, 'in an early collapse of the Bolshevists' power', but he did hope that the Russian anti-Bolshevik armies 'would be self-supporting in 1920'.

During the War Cabinet meeting on June 27, the Permanent Secretary at the Ministry of Labour, Sir David Shackleton,[1] warned that the growing labour unrest in Britain arose mainly because of the intervention. 'He himself had been surprised,' the Minutes recorded, 'at the extent to which men of all classes were now coming round to supporting the Labour view that the Soviet Government ought to be given a fair chance.' There was no doubt, he added, that this feeling was spreading 'and he was afraid that the agitation might assume formidable proportions'. Churchill replied that he was 'quite prepared' to defend British policy in Parliament. 'The evacuation of troops in every part of Russia,' he pointed out, 'from Archangel to the Caucasus was proceeding day by day. . . .'

By the end of June, Denikin's armies were making considerable advances each day. On June 30 Sir Henry Wilson, after seeing Churchill, noted in his diary: 'good news from Denikin who has taken Kharkof'. So swift were Denikin's successes, that General Holman went so far as to warn him not to advance too quickly, but to consolidate his position and strengthen his supply lines. But Denikin was determined to continue northwards. A member of the British Mission, Lieutenant Roberts,[2] later recalled: 'Denikin seemed obsessed by one thought: "I must get to Moscow. When we get to Moscow we will put our house in order." '

On July 2, on Churchill's instructions, Henry Wilson summoned a conference at the War Office to discuss the possibilities of British trade in the areas controlled by Denikin. Churchill himself presided. On the previous day, he had set out for Henry Wilson the case which he wanted the War Office to make:

(a) that the permanency of Denikin's gains depend upon good trading conditions springing up behind his front, and

[1] David James Shackleton, 1863–1938. Worked in a cotton mill, 1880–1900. Secretary, Darwen Weavers' Association, 1894–1907. Labour MP, 1902–10. President of the Trade Union Congress, 1904–10. Chairman of the National Labour Party, 1905. A leading advocate of votes for women, 1910. Senior Labour Adviser (to Churchill) at the Home Office, 1910–11. National Health Commissioner, 1911–16. Knighted, 1917. Permanent Secretary, Ministry of Labour, 1918–21. Chief Labour Adviser to the Government, 1921–5.
[2] Charles Douglas Roberts, 1897–   . Born in Odessa of British parents. Educated in England. Enlisted, Royal Artillery, 1917; 2nd Lieutenant, 1918. Served in South Russia, first as Artillery Instructor, British Mission, then as ADC to General Holman, 1919–20. Acting Captain, 1919; demobilized, 1920. Worked on Famine Relief in Russia, Nansen Organization and Save the Children Fund, 1921–3. In the mining business, Caucasus and Eastern Siberia, 1924–30. Rejoined Army (intelligence), 1939. Served in the Middle East, 1940–6; Brigadier, 1944; retired, 1947.

(b) that if this opportunity is seized British manufacturers may obtain a market in South Russia of great and lasting importance.

According to the Minutes of the conference, Churchill opened the discussion by pointing out that British traders were already 'very much to the fore out there, and so there was a tremendous opportunity for places like Manchester, Sheffield, Leicester and so on to gain an entirely new market'. There were, he said, 'millions of people to be held for generations to come' in South Russia. The present was the time 'to act and gain the trade'.

At one point in the discussion, when General Briggs said that what Denikin wanted was to regulate trade and be 'independent of the profiteer', Churchill remarked that he was 'rather in favour of the profiteer at this stage'.

Denikin's success in driving the Bolsheviks from Kharkov had not been matched by any similar successes on the other fronts. Yudenitch's long awaited advance on Petrograd had failed to cut the railway line bringing Bolshevik troops and supplies from Moscow. At the War Cabinet on July 4 the discussion turned to the possibility of a joint attack on Petrograd by Finnish troops, and the North Russian Corps commanded by Yudenitch. The Cabinet had before it a report from General Gough, who had been unable to persuade the Finnish leader, General Mannerheim, to co-operate with Yudenitch. Churchill told the War Cabinet that he would take 'no responsibility at all' in respect of the projects for Petrograd's capture. 'We had, indeed,' he said, 'given a few guns and a certain amount of ammunition to the North Russian Corps, but that was all.' Churchill told his colleagues that he had already telegraphed to General Gough 'that we could not in any circumstances, take the responsibility of initiating this project of getting the Finns into Russia, which was an enterprise of a highly speculative character'. British 'diffidence' in this area might be adversely criticized he said, 'but undoubtedly it was the best policy. . . .'

The only British activity in the Baltic was naval, not military; the responsibility, not of Churchill, but of the First Lord of the Admiralty, Walter Long. During 1919 ninety-four million pounds were spent maintaining British naval strength in the Baltic Sea and the Gulf of Finland, and blockading the Russian Baltic ports. There were 200 British warships involved in the blockade, of which 17 were sunk.

When the question of further naval activity was raised at the War

Cabinet meeting on July 4, Lloyd George said that although Britain was 'at war with the Bolsheviks', she had nevertheless decided 'not to make war', and that he opposed any naval action against Petrograd. Curzon supported Lloyd George. Britain, he said, must 'proceed with caution', as there was 'a strong element in the House of Commons that was opposed to intervention'. Walter Long pressed for a decision on the naval question, and was supported by Bonar Law. Churchill said nothing. The War Cabinet finally decided that:

(a) In fact, a state of war did exist as between Great Britain and the Bolshevist Government of Russia.

(b) In consequence of (a), our Naval forces in Russian waters should be authorized to engage enemy forces by land and sea, when necessary.[1]

On July 9, Churchill received a memorandum from General Briggs, setting out the argument in favour of massive British help to Denikin. 'As starvation means Bolshevism,' Briggs wrote, 'it is very necessary that this subject should be taken into full consideration . . . in the Donetz basin three months ago all the labourers were Bolsheviks, but when given half rations they at once became loyal subjects'. Unless Britain was at once to send Denikin arms, clothing and equipment for 250,000 men, Briggs declared, 'he will lose the ground already won, and further progress in his march on Moscow will cease. His troops will commence retiring, and the whole country under his regime will relapse to Bolshevism.'

Churchill supported Briggs' proposals. He also persevered in his public efforts to arouse influential opinion against the Bolsheviks. On July 15, at a private dinner given by a group of young Coalition MPs at the Criterion Restaurant in London, he insisted on the need for continued Liberal and Conservative co-operation 'to fight Bolshevism'. On July 17 he was the chief guest of the British-Russia Club at the Connaught Rooms in London, where he warned of the danger to the 'old and feeble Powers' of eastern Europe if Bolshevism were to succeed in Russia.

When the War Cabinet met in London on July 25, it was clear that Denikin's successes had not won him any political advantage in Britain. 'Austen was very critical of my proposal to concentrate all our efforts on Denikin,' Sir Henry Wilson wrote in his diary. 'Fisher, Auckland

---

[1] Two weeks before the Cabinet decision, on June 17, the most spectacular of all the British naval exploits against the Bolsheviks had taken place when Lt. Agar penetrated the Bolshevik naval defences outside Kronstadt in a coastal motor-boat and torpedoed a 6,600-ton Bolshevik cruiser. For this act he was awarded the Victoria Cross.

Geddes,[1] Addison, Walter Long & Barnes were in favour of clearing out of Russia altogether.' The Minutes of the meeting recorded Churchill's strong appeal in favour of a commercial loan to Denikin: 'In his opinion, such a loan was indispensable to the success of General Denikin's operations, in order to make independent the territory which he was administering and to start trade again. It was necessary to have articles to barter for grain in the regions in question. The country was very big, and was really capable of paying for everything. . . .' Churchill added a few remarks about North Russia: 'He regretted profoundly that it had not been possible to give the Bolsheviks a severe blow.' Lloyd George, who had returned to London from Paris, spoke critically of Denikin, and deprecated any increased British activity in South Russia. According to Lloyd George:

Everything indicated that General Denikin was surrounded by persons of reactionary tendencies and it was quite possible that he might be beaten— not by the Bolshevist army in front of him, but by the forces behind him. It was very desirable to have effective guarantees that General Denikin and the officers with him were going to play the game. . . . One telegram which he had seen had stated that some of these officers had openly said that they were not in favour of a National Assembly, and that, as soon as they reached Moscow, stern measures would be resorted to and a Czarist *regime*, though milder than the former one, set up.

Churchill defended Denikin's political intentions. Both Denikin, he said, and 'everyone with him', was pledged to a 'Universal Suffrage Assembly' as Russia's future form of Government. But, as Sir Henry Wilson had noted, successive Ministers spoke strongly against any further British attempt to destroy Bolshevism, directly or indirectly. The Minister of Education, H. A. L. Fisher, spoke of the effect of the intervention on the Russians. The Bolsheviks, he said, 'had been able to say that the sacred soil of Russia had been polluted by the English, Americans and Japanese. Having begun as doctrinaire internationalists, they were now able to appeal to the strong national sentiment which prevailed in Russia. In the circumstances, he thought it would be more

[1] Auckland Campbell Geddes, 1879–1954. A distant relative of Lord Haldane. On active service in South Africa, 1901–2. Doctor of Medicine, Edinburgh, 1908. Professor of Anatomy, Royal College of Surgeons, Dublin, 1909–13. Professor of Anatomy, McGill University, Canada, 1913–14. Major, Northumberland Fusiliers, 1914. Assistant Adjutant-General, GHQ, France, 1915–16. Director of Recruiting, War Office, with the rank of Brigadier-General, 1916–17. Knighted, 1917. Conservative MP, 1917–20. Minister of National Service, 1917, 1918 and 1919. President of the Local Government Board, 1918. Minister of Reconstruction, 1919. President of the Board of Trade, 1919–20. Ambassador to Washington, 1920–24. Chairman of the Rio Tinto Company, 1925–47. Created Baron, 1942.

in our interests to withdraw than to persist in actively helping the anti-Bolshevist forces. . . .'

Fisher had a new suggestion to make, as the Minutes recorded: 'It was scarcity of food which caused Bolshevism,' he asserted. The 'best offensive' against the Bolsheviks would be 'the tackling of the food question, and that, when the winter came, provided our Allies were prepared to co-operate, we should inform the Bolshevist Government that we were prepared to send food to Petrograd, provided that we controlled the administration.'

The President of the Board of Trade, Sir Auckland Geddes, challenged a suggestion which Churchill had made, that South Russia offered a fertile field for British trade. 'He did not believe,' the Minutes recorded, 'that the United Kingdom was in a position to develop trade in the territories occupied by General Denikin.' Geddes went on to warn that there was little chance of preventing 'the whole social organisation' of the areas occupied by Denikin from 'crumbling to pieces next winter', and urged his colleagues to consider carefully 'if it was desirable to throw good money after bad'.

Nowhere in the detailed Minutes of the meeting was anyone recorded as having suggested further aid to Denikin, either of men, arms, stores or money. Towards the end of the meeting, Churchill declared bitterly 'that the anti-Bolshevik movement might collapse within the next few months, and then the Lenin or Trotsky empire would be complete'.

The War Cabinet made no decision about Denikin, but confirmed, as its Minutes recorded, that:

(a) All British troops, both from Archangel and Murmansk, should be evacuated.
(b) No British Mission should be left at Archangel.
(c) The 9th Battalion, Hampshire Regiment, and 25th Middlesex Regiment should be withdrawn from Siberia as soon as transportation and shipping facilities allow.
(d) To take note of the fact that the War Office hoped to begin the evacuation of the British troops from the Caucasus on the 13th August.

On July 26 Sir Henry Wilson had appealed to Churchill to appoint a senior General to supervise the Murmansk and Archangel evacuations. 'I am no longer satisfied,' he wrote, 'that we in the War Office can exercise sufficient supervision and command over these two simultaneous and almost interdependent operations.' In his letter Wilson asked Churchill's permission to appoint Sir Henry Rawlinson to the 'supreme command' of the withdrawal from North Russia. On Sunday July 27 Wilson met Rawlinson at the Travellers' Club in Pall Mall, and

offered him the command. Two days later Churchill gave the appointment his approval. General Ironside and General Maynard were both
knighted, as proof that the appointment involved no criticism of
them.

Churchill spent Sunday July 27 at Taplow Court, near Maidenhead.
During the afternoon he walked around the grounds with H. A. L.
Fisher. 'He is very vehement about Russia,' Fisher noted in his diary.
'Won't see that the Expedition is unpopular. Feels the humiliation of
withdrawal from Archangel. Won't contemplate treating with Bolsheviks. Says the Gov. stands for resistance to Bolshevism.' Fisher's
private comment on Churchill's views was: 'Very unsound.'

On July 28 Churchill joined Lloyd George at Chequers. 'Winston and
I had a long talk about Russia,' Sir Henry Wilson recorded in his diary
that night. 'Winston very excited & talked of resigning!' On the morning of July 29 the *Daily Express* declared: 'The country is absolutely
unwilling to make a great war in Russia. . . . Let us have done with the
megalomania of Mr Winston Churchill, the military gamester. Let us
bring our men back—if we can.'

The War Cabinet met on the morning of July 29. During the discussion, Churchill was contemptuous of the policy which he had been
instructed to carry out. 'An evacuation was an easy thing to order,' he
said, 'but terribly difficult to carry out.' He was very sorry, he added, 'to
be associated with such an operation. It would be repugnant to everyone
to feel that we were leaving a small Government to fall to pieces, some of
whom had stood by us and some of whom had not, and to be at the
mercy of the Bolsheviks. . . .' Bitterly he declared: 'It would give the
greatest satisfaction to the Germans and to the Bolshevist sympathisers
throughout the world to know that we were evacuating Archangel.'
Churchill then explained what he hoped might still be decided:

The one place where there was a chance of doing something was in the area
occupied by General Denikin and he thought it ought to be made clear that
we would assist him by opening up trade and supplying the people with food
and munitions of war. He suggested that we should do this for a fixed time,
possibly six months, and that it should be made clear to General Denikin that
we only bound ourselves for that time, at the end of which the situation would
be reviewed. . . .

What he specially wished to avoid was a decision to evacuate North Russia
without any definite policy as regards South Russia. He thought if it was
decided not only to evacuate North Russia but also to throw over General
Denikin and the anti-Bolsheviks in Siberia, our policy would be very difficult
to defend in this country.

Lloyd George intervened to say that Britain could not 'bind itself indefinitely' to help Russia, and that the Government 'must not give any pledges as to the future'.

The discussion then returned to North Russia. When the question arose of the possibility of arranging an armistice at Archangel between the Bolsheviks and the anti-Bolsheviks, Churchill declared, as the Minutes recorded, that in his opinion, 'it would be most disastrous for any British Government to ask the Bolsheviks to grant an armistice. He could not conceive that we could sink so low. It would be very much better to evacuate North Russia in our own time. . . .' Surprisingly, Lloyd George supported Churchill, telling the War Cabinet that he did not think an armistice would be of any use, 'as we could not trust the Bolsheviks not to indulge in massacres, and, apart from our honour, it might be ruled out'. To this the War Cabinet agreed.

Lord Curzon then gave his colleagues a lengthy and pessimistic account of the intervention as a whole. 'All round,' he said, 'the situation appeared to be one of complete failure.'

There was a brief adjournment, after which Curzon spoke again, arguing the case in favour of the Caucasian republics, and against Denikin. 'General Denikin,' he said, 'represented the old Russian party, and would like to crush the small republics we had been supporting.' Curzon pointed out that Britain had already suggested 'lines of demarcation' across which Denikin's forces had been told not to move. But, he warned, when Britain withdrew, Denikin 'would move north, south or west as he liked, and all our good work in the smaller republics would collapse'.

When George Barnes remarked that the policy of intervention had shown small results for its high cost, Churchill defended what had been done. The results of Britain's involvement had been 'enormous', he said, and he went on to explain what he believed had already been achieved:

Although the forces of Admiral Kolchak and General Denikin did not exist a year ago, they were now holding between them about three-quarters of the whole Bolshevist army. He thought that when one considered the weak elements which had been available it was extraordinary what had been done. If we had not intervened in Russia the little States in which the League of Nations took so much interest would have been overpowered by now, and we should certainly have been forced to support the *cordon sanitaire*. The situation at present was that everyone was demobilising except our most deadly enemies.

Some people said that we should have been better off if we had never given any rifles. With this view he did not agree. What had been wanted was the resolute will to win, and had this existed the results would have been quite different. The results of the operations of the next three months might decide the whole fate of Russia.

He thought personally, it was quite possible that Admiral Kolchak might retrieve his position. General Denikin was confident of his ability to attain successful results.

Churchill's colleagues did not share his confidence in the anti-Bolsheviks. Sir Auckland Geddes was worried that the further Denikin advanced, 'the greater our responsibilities and obligations would become'. The areas of Russia under anti-Bolshevik control were 'huge', Geddes warned, 'and it appeared to him that there was no end to the extent to which we might commit ourselves. . . .' Denikin appeared to have 'a fascination for going on'.

During the discussion Lloyd George disassociated himself from Churchill's policy. 'If the Allies had decided to defeat Bolshevism,' he said, 'great armies would have been required. The small British force in Russia had not been sent there for this purpose. It was true that one member of the Cabinet had always urged this policy, but he himself had always protested against it.' The War Cabinet, Lloyd George added, 'had accepted the view that it was not our business to interfere in the internal affairs of Russia'. He went on:

If Russia preferred a Czarist Government, or an Octobrist Government, it was her business, and the same applied to the Bolshevist Government. Personally he did not admire any of the Russian Governments. The Government of the Czar was thoroughly bad, and there had been many massacres of Jews as bad as those of the Bolsheviks. Hence he objected to the operations being considered as war against Bolshevism. . . .

The northern expeditions had been undertaken as part of our operation of the Great War. We had not gone to Archangel to attack Bolshevism, and no one would choose to attack Bolshevism from that direction if that were their object. Now the War was over. We had said to Kolchak and Denikin and the Archangel Government: 'You say that the Russian people are opposed to the Bolsheviks, who are tyrannising over them by the aid of Lettish and Chinese soldiers, and using them to cut the throat of every respectable Russian.' Then the British Government replied: 'In that case we will help you.'

We had helped them, and for a year we had supplied them with everything they required—guns, rifles, machine-guns, ammunition, tanks, uniforms, boots, &c. . . .

Lloyd George told his ministers that if Denikin 'really had the people behind him', the Bolsheviks could never overcome him; but he must help himself, not expect endless help from Britain. It was finally decided that all assistance to Denikin 'should be continued on the same lines as hitherto'.

That evening Churchill spoke in the House of Commons on the Russian situation. The British troops in North Russia would be withdrawn, he said, 'before another winter set in'. Other nations would try to contain the anti-Bolsheviks elsewhere: the Japanese and Americans by means of their troops in Siberia, the French by their support for the independence of Czechoslovakia, Poland and Rumania. 'We are not taking or contemplating isolated British action,' Churchill declared. 'Any action we take will be inter-Allied and international.' The British Military Mission would remain with Denikin. He 'did not disguise from the House' that he had hoped to see Kolchak's troops link up with the men at Archangel. But it was impossible to 'indulge that hope any longer'. In his conclusion, Churchill said:

I can never clear my mind from a sense of anxiety regarding the danger of a hostile Russia and a revengeful Germany. We should make a fatal mistake if we assume that the great victory which has been won can now be safely left to take care of itself, that we should not interest ourselves in the affairs of Russia, and that we should leave the Russian people to stew in their own juice.

Denikin's military successes continued, and, on July 31, his troops entered Poltava. But when the War Cabinet met on August 1, George Barnes challenged the conclusion of their previous meeting to continue supporting Denikin. 'Up to date,' he said, 'General Denikin had been given men, munitions, and food', and he thought 'very strongly that General Denikin should be given no more men, for if casualties occurred a difficult situation would be created'.

Churchill defended the policy which the War Cabinet had approved. The British Mission in South Russia, he explained, would not exceed 2,000 men. They were not intended to be fighting men, but, he explained, 'if in the front line they might have to take part in the fighting. These men were really there in order to supervise the transport and distribution of the stores which we were giving to General Denikin, and at the same time to explain to the Russians the working of tanks and machine guns. There were also a certain number of aviators who were teaching the Russians to fly.' All munitions sent to Denikin, Churchill continued, were 'surplus to our own requirements'. All the men were volunteers.

Lloyd George sought to dampen Churchill's appeal. 'Was it right,' he asked, 'to encourage General Denikin to believe that we would go on helping him with munitions for an indefinite time—that is, if his operations lasted for another year or two?' As to food, he said, 'it must be remembered that any food sent to General Denikin would have to be taken away from the people of this country'. Churchill proposed six months as the time-limit for economic aid. Later in the discussion, at his request, the War Cabinet authorized a sum 'not exceeding' £100,000 to be given to the War Office as 'petty cash' for interventionist purposes. But it was decided to postpone the question of future assistance to Denikin until Lord Curzon had prepared a memorandum showing what money had already been spent by all Departments.

On the night of July 31 the War Office announced that Sir Henry Rawlinson would leave at once 'to co-ordinate the difficult military operation of the withdrawal of the Archangel and Murmansk forces'. Rawlinson gave his own assessment of the situation in his diary that same day:

North Russia is a nasty job, but I have decided to accept it. The Government is in a hole, and I consider it my duty to go and try to help them out of it. There are, no doubt, risks, but there are risks in most things that are worth undertaking, and the problem is desperately interesting. I accepted on condition that they sent me reinforcements and some tanks, and this both H. Wilson and Winston promised to do. Winston thanked me profusely for going, saying it was a very sporting thing to do. . . .

I explained to Winston that in order to cover the withdrawal it would almost certainly be necessary to make an attack, probably both at Archangel and at Murmansk. He has agreed to that.

The public announcement of Rawlinson's mission was greeted with alarm by Press critics of the intervention, who saw it as a new and sinister initiative. The *Daily Express* described it on August 1 as 'sensational', and continued:

This will open the eyes of the British public to the grave consequences of Mr Churchill's gamble in North Russia. . . .

There will be a combined naval and military operation and the choice of one of the most experienced British generals to direct it suggests that it will be on a large scale. We are, in fact, in peril of drifting into a new war.

When Rawlinson sailed for North Russia on August 4, however, his sole instruction was that given to him by Churchill on August 2, to organize the final British withdrawal, and to complete it before the winter. The evacuation from North Russia continued throughout

August. It was accompanied by several successful rearguard actions; brief victories in the course of an ordered and irreversible retreat. On August 9 General Rawlinson reached Archangel, where Ironside met him at the quayside. The situation, he wrote in his diary, 'is far more satisfactory than I had dared to expect'. But Rawlinson had no illusions about the fighting potential of the Russian anti-Bolsheviks. 'Their troops won't fight alone,' he wrote, 'and their officers are hopeless.'

There were still 53,000 Allied troops in North Russia, under Rawlinson's command, of whom 18,000 were British. Other than the British troops, Rawlinson wrote in his diary on August 11, 'the rest was a job-lot —good, bad and indifferent—mostly'. On August 12 Rawlinson made his plans. Ironside was to withdraw from Archangel by the end of September, Maynard from Murmansk by mid-October. The Russian leader, General Miller,[1] could not decide whether to try to hold on to Archangel alone, or to seek the comparative safety of Murmansk. 'The trouble with the White Russians,' Rawlinson wrote in his diary on August 12, 'is that they have no real leaders of character and determination, and their subordinates are a hopeless lot. . . . The Bolos, on the other hand, know what they want, and are working hard to get it.' Many Russians had decided not to make a last-ditch defence. On August 17, over a thousand Russian civilians were taken from Archangel into exile on board a British ship.

The War Cabinet met at 11.30 on the morning of August 12 to formulate its policy towards Denikin. Churchill described Denikin as 'the one bright spot in Russia', and went on to report General Holman's impressions of Denikin's army. Holman, he said, 'had been up to see the recent fighting, and had been much impressed by the powers of quick movement and fighting qualities of Denikin's volunteer troops. Denikin seemed to be welcomed everywhere, and many volunteers were coming forward to join him. . . .'

[1] Yevgenii Karlovich Miller, born 1867. Commissioned in the Imperial Russian Cavalry, 1886. Major-General, Chief of Staff, 5th Army, 1914. Lieutenant-General, Corps Commander, XXVI Army Corps, 1915–16. General, Army Commander, March 1917. Emigrated to Italy, November 1918. At the request of the Government of the Northern Region, he returned to Russia in January 1919, and was appointed, first Governor-General of Archangel, and second, Commander-in-Chief of the North Russian Army. Became de facto head of the Northern Region Government on the withdrawal of Tchaikowsky to Paris. Evacuated Archangel, February 1920, and emigrated to Paris. Succeeded General Kutepov as Leader of the White Officers' Emigré Organization (ROVS) in Paris, 1930. Kidnapped in Paris by Soviet agents, September 1937, and disappeared.

Curzon disagreed with Churchill's prognosis. Denikin's ambitions, he believed, 'lay not in the direction of Moscow but towards the Caucasus'. And he went on to warn that 'he doubted whether Denikin would achieve any great success, and it was possible that he might fail like Kolchak. . . .' Austen Chamberlain commented that Curzon's fears about Denikin 'applied to all the Russians we had helped. He doubted whether any of them would ever listen to our advice or give us the guarantees we wanted, and accept our direction of policy.'

Lloyd George pressed Sir Henry Wilson to say whether Denikin had any chance of success. Wilson replied that if Denikin were well supported with arms and equipment, and could 'keep the population he was at present absorbing in a good temper', there was no reason why he should not reach Moscow, and also drive the Bolsheviks from the Black Sea Coast.

Churchill then set out what he wanted British policy to be:

. . . all he had suggested was that we should continue to send to Denikin our surplus non-marketable ammunitions; that we should maintain our handful of British officers and non-commissioned officers; that we should send a certain amount of marketable stuff, which Denikin had asked for; that the War Office should fix the sum to be spent on the latter; and that we should settle now an interim policy to be pursued for the next six months, at the end of which the whole situation should be reviewed. We should also reserve to ourselves complete freedom to reverse our policy if we choose.

H. A. L. Fisher appealed for an end to intervention. 'If,' he said, 'the Russians thought that the *Entente* meant to set up separate provincial governments at Reval, Moscow or elsewhere, they would throw themselves into the arms of Germany.' Denikin 'had shot his bolt'. No matter what government was set up in Russia, he added, 'what was really important was that trade should be set going and production started afresh'.

George Barnes declared that Britain was 'always backing the wrong horse'. And he went on to say: 'The real governing force in Russia was the Soviet Government. . . .' Dr Addison felt that 'the warring elements today in Russia should be left to settle their own squabbles themselves. . . .' When Churchill asked him whether Britain ought not to support countries like Estonia, who had newly won their independence from Russia, Addison replied that, in his view, the Estonians ought to be encouraged to open negotiations with the Bolsheviks. 'It was out of the question,' he said, 'that Estonia could exist as a separate State unaided.'

Churchill then told his colleagues what he believed should be the limit of British help to Denikin. 'If his movement succeeded,' he declared, 'well and good. If, on the other hand, an equipoise was maintained between the conflicting forces, he thought we should try and get Lenin's Government and the anti-Bolsheviks to come to terms.'

Bonar Law supported Churchill's proposal. Britain, he added, should help Denikin 'until the end of the year and tell him that after that period our support must be withdrawn'.

Later in the discussion Churchill pointed out that if Britain had been willing to put 'thirty divisions' into the field, 'the attitude of the various elements in Russia might be very different', and he reminded his colleagues that Kolchak, Denikin and their followers 'had been engaged many months in fighting the most horrible tyranny and brutality the world had ever seen'.

Before the War Cabinet meeting ended, Lloyd George explained his own feelings. In May, he said, when Kolchak's chances had been good, it had been 'quite a legitimate risk' to support him. But he felt that there was 'hardly an even chance' of Denikin ever reaching Moscow, and that Britain must 'look at probabilities', and frame its policy accordingly. 'He inclined,' he said, 'to the policy suggested by Mr Churchill.' His hope was that, if Britain sent Denikin supplies, but not soldiers, a balance would be established between the Bolshevik and anti-Bolshevik forces, and a compromise peace established. Lloyd George told his ministers that if peace were established 'the Bolsheviks would not wish to maintain an army, as their creed was fundamentally anti-militarist'. And he continued:

He himself would give Denikin one last 'packet', so to speak, and he suggested that the Secretary of State for War should state what the contents of the 'packet' should be, and estimate its cost. We should say to Denikin: 'You must make the most of it. You have all the coal of Russia, you will get plentiful supplies of oil, and you will soon be in possession of the main food supplies. We have carried you up to a point where you are self-supporting; we cannot give you gratis any more supplies, though we are prepared to trade with you on the usual lines.' Then, when he was firmly established, we should aim at making peace in Russia.

The War Cabinet concluded, as Lloyd George had asked, that Churchill should prepare a statement showing the amount of stores he proposed to send to Denikin 'as a final contribution from His Majesty's Government'.

Churchill still hoped that the anti-Bolshevik forces would, by their own efforts, win more than the mere stalemate which both he and

Lloyd George envisaged. Two days later, on August 14, he set out his hopes in a letter to Lord Curzon:

The Kolchak and Denikin operations, taken as a whole, are still approaching their climax, which I think will be reached in the next three months, or at any rate by Christmas. I do not believe the Siberian army is finished. At any rate, it is drawing 120,000 Bolsheviks ($\frac{1}{4}$ of their whole force) into a very unsound strategic situation. The Siberian forces can retreat to Omsk, or if necessary to Irkutsk, & if at any time their pursuers cease to totter after them they will be able to totter back in their turn. It is more than likely that both America and Japan will make exertions to save the situation in this part of the world.

Meanwhile Denikin's successes continue, & his left is advancing very rapidly towards the Roumanian front. The Roumanians, Poles & North West Russians are all holding their own or advancing. The Bolsheviks are showing great military weakness; & at the present moment it is anybody's fight. It is further very unlikely that even in the event of a draw on present lines in the campaign, the Bolsheviks can survive a winter in which they will be cut off from fuel & food, with paralysed communications & dwindling ammunition. . . .

At the War Cabinet on August 12 Curzon had appealed to Churchill to support the maintenance of a British force in the Caucasus. Churchill had been unable to do so. In his letter to Curzon he explained why, not without a touch of bitterness. 'I am very sorry about the Caucasus,' he wrote: 'I would gladly have remained there another month or 6 weeks had you come to me in time, but the pressure upon me is too strong, & any help I get so exiguous & so uncertain, that the W.O. have to concentrate what little strength they have upon the most promising & important theatre. . . .'

18

'Mr Churchill's Private War'

O N August 16 Churchill left England for a five-day visit to the British Army on the Rhine. Clementine Churchill accompanied her husband, who inspected many of the British units in the occupied zone.

While Churchill was in Germany Lloyd George decided upon a major economy in Government spending. As Sir Maurice Hankey noted in his diary on August 17, the War Office, the Admiralty and the Air Ministry were to base all future estimates 'on the following assumption:—no great war for ten years, no increase to the naval shipbuilding, ships of no mercantile value not to be completed; the army to be organised only for the maintenance of order in India, Egypt, Palestine & Mesopotamia & for support of the civil power in Great Britain & Ireland. . . .' Hankey noted that Walter Long accepted the proposal, but not Churchill, who 'made out that he could never cut down to these limits'. Hankey added a personal comment: 'Churchill obviously does not care to be a War Minister without a war in prospect, and finds the task of curtailing expenditure distasteful.'

In South Russia the military situation continued to improve for the anti-Bolsheviks. On August 18 Denikin's forces drove the Bolsheviks from two important naval bases, Kherson and Nikolaev, leaving only one Black Sea port, Odessa, under Bolshevik control. On August 19 Churchill telegraphed directly to Clemenceau, from Germany, hoping to prevent some 50,000 Russian soldiers then in France from being repatriated to Odessa. 'I am assured,' Churchill stated, 'that a regular Bolshevik organization is in existence at Odessa which will at once incorporate all men repatriated there or in that neighbourhood in the ranks of the Bolshevik Army under practical pain of death by shooting or starvation.' Denikin's operations, he wrote, 'are about the only hope of a satisfactory solution of the Russian question in the next few years'.

No steps should be taken, he added, 'to compromise the possibilities of General Denikin's success. . . .'

On August 23 the anti-Bolshevik forces entered Odessa. Denikin was now in occupation of the Black Sea shore from the Rumanian border to Novorossisk. 'The thing is getting bigger every day,' Churchill wrote to Lloyd George on the day of Odessa's capture, 'and may be either cast away or turned to permanent advantage.' During the same week the prospect of successful anti-Bolshevik action also presented itself in North-West Russia, where General Yudenitch, having recovered from his defeat in the spring, was preparing to advance once more on Petrograd. German troops in the Baltic States were eager to join this anti-Bolshevik action. Churchill supported such a plan, and on August 23 he wrote to A. J. Balfour to suggest that the Germans in the Baltic 'should equip a corps of Russians collected from their Russian prisoners', and use them to join in the attack on the Bolsheviks in the Petrograd region. No doubt, Churchill added, such a plan would lead to increased German influence in the Baltic States, but, he asked, 'is it not worth while letting them do this if in fact the Lenin–Trotsky régime is struck at effectively'. Churchill was anxious to see Britain support Yudenitch as well as Denikin. His letter to Balfour continued:

The ruin of Lenin and Trotsky and the system they embody is indispensable to the peace and revival of the world. Whether it will be achieved or not I cannot tell; but we are not far from it at the present moment, and any concentration of anti-Bolshevik forces in the Baltic States, or the dethronement of Bela Kun at Budapest, or a junction between the Roumanian armies and Denikin's forces advancing into the Ukraine, are all in their way extremely important and hopeful factors towards the decision we are seeking.

News of Yudenitch's impending advance on Petrograd stimulated Labour suspicions of Churchill's policy. On August 21 the *Daily Herald* warned its readers: 'The Russian crusade is not ending. It may be only beginning. . . . Utterly out of touch with public opinion, here as everywhere else, Churchill cannot see that the revolt against far-off costly and reactionary adventures grows into "turbulence" at home. . . .' *The Times*, however, approved of Yudenitch, and advocated British support for him, in order 'to strike the Bolshevik enemy so resounding a blow as to shatter his prestige'.

With Denikin's forces in occupation of all the Black Sea ports formerly controlled by the Bolsheviks, Churchill considered that an attack on Petrograd might be the decisive step in destroying Lenin's regime. On August 24 he wrote to Lloyd George, Balfour and Curzon:

The position of the anti-Bolshevik forces in the Baltic theatre ought to be considered as part of the general situation. Very little help, apart from that of the Navy, has been given by the British either to Yudenitch or to the Esthonians. Practically none has been given by anyone else. . . . We have not thought it right to take any responsibility for encouraging the Finns to attack Petrograd, and meanwhile Mannerheim has disappeared. We have only given a few shiploads of munitions to the Esthonians and the North-West Russian Corps. . . .

There has been no concert, no direction and no decisive policy. As the result, all through the Spring and Summer great opportunities of liberating Petrograd from the most appalling conditions of misery and cleaning up this part of the world without the need of using British troops have remained dangling at our finger tips and we have never grasped them. . . .

Simply to throw away this situation would appear to me to be disastrous and wrong. Our representatives on the spot are entitled to sympathy, for they have been facing the most unsatisfactory and painful situation where nothing is decided one way or another, where no clear policy exists which they can understand, and where resources are being frittered away, opportunities are being missed, and men are being killed.

I ask, therefore, that advantage should be taken of the Prime Minister's presence in Paris on or after the 8th September to have a full conference and discussion of the North-West Russian position. . . .

To Sir Henry Wilson, Churchill wrote on August 24: 'There is no reason why further arms and munitions should not be sent to Yudenitch in the small quantities which have hitherto been sufficient for that region. . . .' On the same day, Churchill suggested to Wilson that General Milne should 'remain in temporary occupation of the Caucasus' with a brigade of British troops. Both these suggestions were contrary to the War Cabinet's decisions, and to Churchill's own reservations of August 12.

Wilson was convinced that Churchill exaggerated the potential success of the anti-Bolsheviks. On August 29 he sent Churchill an account of his conversation that morning with General Gough, who had recently returned from the Baltic. 'Gough tells me that he thinks it is really a waste of time and money to help the Russians under Yudenitch,' Wilson told Churchill, 'and that with very few exceptions these Russians are much more pro-German than pro-English, and directly we finish sending them stores they will turn to the Boches; he includes Yudenitch in this category.'

Wilson also warned Churchill that by encouraging the Baltic Germans to co-operate with Yudenitch, Britain was in danger of greatly increasing German influence both in the Baltic, and in non-Bolshevik

Russia. Churchill rejected Wilson's warning, writing to him on August 31:

> With regard to Yudenitch and the North-West Russian frontier, there are the proverbial three policies—(a) to give as much help as we can ourselves to the anti-Bolsheviks and allow the Germans to help too; (b) to give as much help as we can ourselves and forbid the Germans to help; and (c) to disinterest ourselves in the whole concern and let the Germans fill the gap if they choose. My policy would be (a). The policy we have been following is (b). If, as seems likely, this policy (b) breaks down, we must reconcile ourselves to (c). Many high authorities think it inevitable that Germany should get hold of Russia and that all efforts to avert it are vain. What I do not think we can do is to clear out ourselves and then abuse the Russians for seeking help from the Germans, or abuse the Germans for giving help in a theatre in which they are so vitally interested and in which we have decided to let things rip. . . .

In his letter to Wilson, Churchill commented on 'the lack of support or of any concerted plan towards Yudenitch', and he continued:

> The policy I am trying to pursue in Russia is a very simple one. It is to avoid as far as possible a complete collapse at any point on the anti-Bolshevik front until the climax of the Kolchak–Denikin operations has been reached one way or the other. This I think must happen before the Winter. And then, according to results, we must take a new view. . . .

Henry Wilson continued to argue against supporting the Baltic Germans, even in a concerted attack on Petrograd. 'Do we want the Germans to absorb the Baltic States or do we not?' he wrote to Churchill on September 5. 'Do we want German troops to enlist under Baltic flags,' he asked, 'and seize the power in the Baltic States even if by so doing they may keep out the Bolsheviks?' Churchill reiterated his earlier view, replying to Wilson on September 6: 'I do not want a complete collapse in this part to take place while the issue of the Kolchak–Denikin campaign hangs in the balance. Action must be considered in this light.'

Lloyd George had been angered by what he saw as Churchill's revived enthusiasm for intervention. From Deauville, where he was spending a few days, he replied on August 30 to Churchill's memorandum of August 24. His reply took the form of a memorandum addressed to Balfour, Churchill and Curzon:

> I earnestly trust the Cabinet will not consent to committing British resources to any fresh military enterprises in Russia. They have decided to withdraw from Siberia, from Archangel, from the Baltic, and after furnishing General Denikin with one more packet, to let the Russians fight out their own

quarrels at their own expense. I hope nothing will induce the Ministry to deviate from this decision.

As to the 'great opportunities' for capturing Petrograd which we are told were 'dangling at our finger tips', and which we never grasped, we have heard this so often of other 'great opportunities' in Russia which have never materialised in spite of lavish expenditure on their prosecution. We have already this year spent over 100 millions in Russia. We have sent some excellent troops there. Early in the year there were 'great opportunities' of liberating Moscow, and we were assured it was within our grasp. We sent every assistance in our power to Admiral Kolchak to exploit these opportunities, not merely by helping him to equip his forces but by sanctioning a military expedition which was to penetrate far into Russia in order to join hands with him. The liberating army—or at least what is left of it—is now running as hard as it can back to Omsk, and is meditating a further retreat to Irkutsk. The failure was certainly not due to any default on our part. It is due to facts which are none the less stubborn because some of our advisers have habitually refused to take cognisance of them.

Lloyd George was particularly scathing about Churchill's enthusiasm for Yudenitch:

General Yudenitch never had a chance of taking Petrograd. The Esthonians, so far from co-operating with him, distrusted him as much as the Bolsheviks, and the result of his operations up till now has been to drive the Esthonian Republic to make a separate treaty with the Bolsheviks. He is a notorious reactionary, as much distrusted by the Esthonians as by the Russian people. He is not a man of any military distinction, and there is no proof that he is capable of leading such an enterprise as he meditated. If North Russia were groaning under Bolshevik tyranny and the Esthonians and Latvians were eager to join in a war of liberation, there would now have been an army numbering hundreds of thousands sweeping over North West Russia. The fact that out of a population of several millions the anti-Bolsheviks have only mustered 20 or 30,000 men is another indication of the complete misreading of the Russian situation, upon which the military policy has been based. . . .

In conclusion, Lloyd George deprecated any further British involvement in Russia:

If Russia were anxious to overthrow Bolshevik rule, the help we have given her would have provided her with a full opportunity. We have discharged faithfully our honourable obligations to Denikin and to Kolchak. We have never entered into any with Yudenitch and I hope we shall not do so. The British public will not tolerate the throwing away of more millions on foolish military enterprises.

I am anxious for another reason to have done with these military ventures in Russia as soon as possible. I cannot help thinking that they have taken away the mind of the War Office from important administrative tasks which urgently needed attention. If the amount of intense and concentrated attention which has been devoted to the running of these Russians wars had been given to reducing our expenditure, I feel certain that scores of millions would have been saved. Russia does not want to be liberated. Whatever she may think of the Bolsheviks she does not think it worth while sacrificing any more blood to substitute for them men of the Yudenitch type. Let us therefore attend to our own business and leave Russia to look after hers.

On August 31, the day after Lloyd George had sent Churchill this scathing criticism of intervention, Denikin's forces won a major victory, entering Kiev, the capital city of the Ukraine. Denikin now controlled all of South Russia. His hopes of reaching Moscow before the end of the year no longer seemed, to his supporters, to be an impossibility. Even his enemies feared for the future. On August 9 Lenin had telegraphed to Trotsky that Odessa and Kiev must be defended 'to the last drop of blood', and he had added: 'the fate of the entire Revolution is in question'. Now, less than a month later, both Odessa and Kiev were controlled by Denikin. On the north-east of Denikin's line, a force of 9,000 anti-Bolsheviks, including 7,000 cavalry, commanded by General Mamontov,[1] had broken through the Bolshevik defences on August 10, and for over a month caused havoc behind the lines. On September 6 Trotsky telegraphed to Lenin that the attempt to suppress the marauding 'has up to now yielded almost no result'. The motorized machine gun detachments which Trotsky had wanted to send into action against Mamontov had not received their machine guns.

Churchill was elated by these events. At the end of August, when he had received a delegation of North Russians at the War Office, he spoke of his deep sympathy for Russia 'struggling in its torment at the present time', and was optimistic about the anti-Bolshevik cause:

I firmly believe that with the weapons that will be available and the stores and munitions which will be at your disposal, with the strong defences that are in existence, and with the numbers you have, you will be able, if you stand together, to succeed in maintaining yourselves. I do not myself think that the Bolsheviks will have many men to spare from other fronts to attack you. They are very hard pressed—in the South by General Denikin, who has been advancing daily and on the West they are confronted by the armies of the Poles and other forces. Therefore I trust that if you face these difficulties in a manful and self-reliant spirit you will succeed in defending yourselves completely.

[1] Konstantin Konstantinovich Mamontov, 1869–1919. A Tsarist Cavalry officer and Colonel in the Tsarist Army, 1917. Appointed General by Denikin, 1919, Commander of one of Denikin's Cavalry Corps, 1919.

So far as we are concerned, we have remained longer than it was our intention to do in order to give you time to organise your own self-defence, and we hope and believe that you have been able to do this. In any case I would most strongly advise you to follow the guidance which will be given you by General Lord Rawlinson. I do not myself think that this time of trial will go on indefinitely. I think that the end may come sooner than many people expect, and if you can keep the Russian Flag flying in the North of Russia, either at Archangel, or if not at Archangel at Murmansk, then you will have perhaps not too long to wait before a complete victory and a general peace ends the present troubled state.

In North-West Russia, Yudenitch was preparing to launch his attack on Petrograd. On September 6, when Churchill replied to Lloyd George's memorandum of August 30, he defended his earlier support for Yudenitch, but did not underestimate the difficulties which still confronted the anti-Bolshevik forces:

I am sorry you did not like my note on the North West Russian position. The crisis of the whole Anti-Bolshevik campaign seems to me to be approaching steadily—in a month or two the result shd be apparent. It is a pity by letting down suddenly this or that sector of the front to compromise the chances of success which exist. Like you I am not vy hopeful of a favourable result. Kolchak shd be fighting his decisive battle now, & if he loses the Siberian front may well disappear altogether. . . .
We are evacuating in the North & the collapse in the North West seems also imminent. On the other hand the course of events on Denikin & Kolchak's front may be different. They may beat the armies opposite to them. It all hangs in the balance.

Churchill went on to defend himself against Lloyd George's more personal complaints:

In yr memo you write as if I was responsible for bringing things to such a pass. But I have made no commitments in Russia of any kind. All without exception were made before I went to the War Office. Our troops were already marooned in Archangel & deeply involved with the local population.
The British fleet was already in the Baltic & the Black Sea. The Caucasus had already been occupied. The Hampshire regiment was already in Siberia. Even the munitions to Kolchak & Denikin had already been promised & definitely ordered before I was in any way brought in contact with these events. I have simply tried to discharge honourably and efficiently the obligations entered into by my predecessor & by the Cabinet within the limitations imposed.
You are right when you say they have occupied a good deal of my thoughts. They have indeed caused me a great deal of distress. To see gt matters go so ill & to be powerless to avert the disasters is always painful. But I shd have

been much more distressed if I had had the slightest responsibility for the general course of affairs. My part has been limited to carrying out yr orders to evacuate Siberia, N. Russia & the Caucasus & to wind up our affairs in all these theatres—& secondly to sending Denikin & Kolchak the arms wh they had been assured they were going to get in Milner's time; & to minor action in connection with the above such as was required from day to day. I shd have been vy wrong if I had not given most careful attention to this seeing the extent to wh British troops & treasures were involved. . . .

As Denikin's advance in South Russia gathered momentum, the evacuation of Allied forces both from North Russia and Siberia continued without respite. On August 31 over a thousand troops of the Finnish Legion sailed from Archangel. 43 Korean troops and 262 Chinese labourers were evacuated on September 4. On September 7 the 25th Battalion of the Middlesex Regiment sailed from Vladivostok. Three days later Churchill wrote to Lord Curzon to warn him of the dangers of a Bolshevik advance into Central Asia. It was quite possible, he wrote, that Bolshevism 'may over-run the whole of those enormous regions from the Caspian to the Indian frontier' and that the British Empire 'will have the pleasure of seeing all their interests in Persia and Afghanistan directly attacked and jeopardised'. Churchill told Curzon that he would like to see much greater anti-Bolshevik activity in the Baltic and North Russia to prevent 'the collapses which are dominant in those theatres from reacting upon the climax of the main operations'. 'Unhappily,' he added, 'the resources of which I dispose are very feeble.'[1]

On September 9, Churchill sent Sir Henry Wilson an appreciation of the Russian situation. His conclusion was that it was 'anybody's victory at the present time'. But Denikin's control of the Ukraine, he wrote, and his occupation of Kiev and Odessa were 'events of the highest magnitude'. On the western frontier, the Poles had advanced into 'Russia proper'. Even Kolchak might be able to maintain an anti-Bolshevik front 'at Omsk or at Irkutsk or somewhere on the Siberian line'. The Bolsheviks had failed to capture Tsaritsyn. Yudenitch's force 'staggers and struggles on on a basis wholly of bluff and rumour, and its value is to be measured entirely by the number of enemy troops retained on this Baltic front'. Events were tending 'steadily towards the climax'; September and October would be the decisive months. Churchill's letter to Wilson concluded:

[1] Churchill had begun to feel the strain of the prolonged Russian crisis. 'I hope you have had some rest,' he wrote in his letter to Curzon on September 10. 'I have had *change* & *diversion* but no rest. Nor am I likely to get any.' To his mother, Churchill wrote six days later: 'I am afraid you found me preoccupied with business. These are vy difficult times.'

Everything should therefore be done to keep up morale in this interval, when the fruits for which we have paid so much and in which we have such great interests will either be gained or lost.

What of the Winter? Will not the Bolshevik position in the Winter, deprived of the fuel and food of the Ukraine and not yet able to exploit to any great extent the new territory they have recovered in the Urals, be a very terrible one?

It seems to me that if we are able to keep everything going as much as possible for the next two months, say till the middle of November, either (a) the Bolsheviks will be definitely beaten and lose their political credentials with their own people, or (b) that kind of equipoise and division of Russia between Bolshevik and anti-Bolshevik populations will be established, which the Prime Minister favours and believes is for the interest of Britain; and in that case it may become our policy to stabilise such a situation by some general arrangement while the fear of the Winter is still hanging over the enemy. . . .

Sir Henry Wilson replied on September 11. The more Britain could support the Baltic States, he wrote, 'the better for North Russia, for the Baltic States, for Denikin, and Kolchak'. But he agreed with Churchill that 'the only place where we really have a chance to help the Russians —our Russians—is in Denikin's theatre'. On September 13 Churchill was in Paris, trying, as he wrote to Wilson that day, 'to get some better arrangements in regard to the Baltic States'. But Lloyd George's motive in inviting him was to discuss the general reduction of military expenditure. On September 14 Clementine Churchill wrote to her husband from Lullenden: 'I hope you are having an interesting time in Paris & that the PM is not going to let you down over this Russian business.'

On September 16 Sir Henry Wilson wrote to Churchill to warn him that the Baltic States would have to come 'to some agreement with the Bolsheviks' as soon as Britain stopped supplying them 'with material and moral assistance'. Unless the Baltic States were to combine with Finland and Poland, Wilson wrote, they would be conquered 'one by one'. On September 17 Churchill wrote to Lord Curzon, approving a Foreign Office telegram to Estonia, urging her not to make a separate peace, and adding: 'I can easily give them a consignment of weapons, if that makes the difference to their carrying on. . . .' But he felt that the French should be encouraged 'to take the lead' in the Baltic. His greatest hope for an anti-Bolshevik victory, and his principal concern, remained South Russia. In his letter to Curzon he declared:

Denikin is doing better and better. He has heavily repulsed the enemy at Tsaritzin without the need of bringing troops from other parts of his front. He has completely repulsed the Bolshevik counter-attack on the Donetz coal basin. He has enormously extended his gains in the Ukraine. Mamontov, the cavalry General who is operating behind the Bolshevik front, has had remarkable successes and proves great interior weakness of the Bolshevik organisation. If only we can keep the general front steady without letting sections fall away at this most crucial time, we may be in a position before the end of the year to secure a general pacification.

Churchill again envisaged a compromise peace, as he had done on August 12, in which the Bolsheviks would accept the permanent existence of a non-Bolshevik South Russia, with Kiev as its capital, and the Black Sea as its southern frontier. Once a secure dividing line were reached, Britain could sponsor negotiations between Lenin and Denikin.

During the third week in September, the Polish Prime Minister, Paderewski, tried to persuade the Allied Powers, in Paris, to authorize an advance on Moscow by 500,000 Polish troops, financed by the Allies. Churchill disapproved of such a plan, as did Sir Henry Wilson. 'I quite agree with you,' Wilson wrote to Churchill on September 18, 'that it would be madness for us to advise Paderewski, and to support him, in any attempt to occupy Moscow. If anything could combine all Russia into one whole, it would be a march of the Poles on Moscow. I can almost conceive Denikin and Lenin joining hands to defeat such an object.'

The War Cabinet met during the afternoon of September 18. 'Churchill expatiates on Denikin's recent successes in Russia,' H. A. L. Fisher noted in his diary, 'Radcliffe demonstrating from map.' Henry Wilson had himself drawn encouragement from the Siberian situation, where Kolchak had succeeded in halting the Bolshevik advance, and in pushing back the Bolsheviks westwards across the Tobol River, less than three hundred miles west of Omsk. In his letter to Churchill of September 18 Wilson wrote:

Kolchak appears to be doing well and as I have often said, in that amazing country, I will not be the least bit surprised in the course of the next six months to find Kolchak moving on Moscow and Denikin falling back into the Caucasus! But I am entirely with you in continuing our help to Denikin so long as the Cabinet will allow us. It is the one bright spot in all this Russian fog, round which the Kolchaks, and the Baltics, and even Murmansk may possibly rally.

The War Cabinet authorized Churchill to submit proposals for assistance to Denikin 'in personnel, material and stores' as the 'final contribution to his cause in the struggle against the Soviet Government'. Churchill did not try to exceed this instruction. But he tried to do all in his power to help make Denikin's advance easier. Shortly after the Cabinet of September 18 he telegraphed to General Holman, asking him to urge Denikin not only 'to do everything in his power to prevent a massacre of the Jews in the liberated districts' but also to issue 'a proclamation against anti-Semitism'. The reason for this advice was, he explained, that 'the Jews are very powerful in England, and if it could be shown that Denikin was protecting them as his army advanced, it would make my task easier'.

There were limits to the help which Churchill was prepared to give Denikin. On September 20 he telegraphed to General Holman: 'I think it inadvisable that British airmen should be used in present circumstances to bomb Moscow.' That same day, Denikin's forces entered Kursk, an important town only 300 miles south of Moscow. Encouraged by Denikin's renewed progress, Churchill again sought to influence Lloyd George, writing to him on September 20:

Nothing can preserve either the Bolshevik system or the B. regime. By mistakes on our part the agony of the Russian people may be prolonged. But their relief is sure. The only question open is whether we shall desert them in the crisis of their fate; and so lose all that we have worked so hard to win. . . .

I do hope and trust that you will not brush away lightly the convictions of one who wishes to remain your faithful lieutenant and looks forward to a fruitful and active co-operation.

Two days later Churchill sent Lloyd George another letter, four pages long, suggesting that Britain should urge the Baltic States not to enter into individual agreements with the Bolsheviks, but to continue to 'maintain their security' against the Bolsheviks. He also wanted Lloyd George to offer the Baltic States a further supply of arms and munitions. On the same day he sent Lloyd George a five-page memorandum entitled 'Final Contribution to General Denikin', in which he proposed sending Denikin, on credit, all British surplus military stores, many of which were in Egypt or at Salonika, involving a cost to Britain of £4,000,000, and granting Denikin a loan to purchase a further £14,000,000 of British stores. For his part, Denikin must agree that the repayment of all costs incurred by Britain 'during the war of liberation' should take precedence over all other debts incurred by the anti-Bolsheviks.

On September 16, while he was in Paris, Churchill had written a

five-thousand-word memorandum entitled 'Russian Policy'. This he
circulated to the Cabinet on September 22, sending a copy to Lloyd
George. In it he stressed that Denikin's position was one 'of great
strength', and that he had under his control a region containing thirty
million people. To desert Denikin now, Churchill declared, 'is to make
certain that whatever else may be the outcome, we have a hostile
Russia to face'.

Churchill asked his colleagues to continue to support the anti-
Bolshevik Russians 'by all means in our power', and thereby 'to keep a
firm hold on them'. He also wanted Britain to make 'whatever use is
possible' of the anti-Bolshevik Germans in the Baltic States. But Lloyd
George was no longer receptive to such arguments. For nearly a month
the newspapers had been attacking the Government with venom about
the continuing intervention, and had singled out Churchill as the
principal villain, whom Lloyd George could not control. In the public
mind, Churchill seemed to have led the Government's Russian policy
into disaster.

On September 22, as soon as Lloyd George received Churchill's
letter and memorandum, he set out his feelings in a blunt and angry
reply:

My dear Winston,
    Your letter distressed me. You know that I have been doing my best for the
last few weeks to comply with the legitimate demand which comes from all
classes of the country to cut down the enormous expenditure which is
devouring the resources of the country at a prodigious rate.
    I have repeatedly begged you to apply your mind to the problem. I made
this appeal to all departments, but I urged it specially upon you for three
reasons. The first is that the highest expenditure is still military; the second
that the largest immediate reductions which could be effected without damage
to the public welfare are foreseeable in the activities controlled by your
Department. The third is that I have found your mind so obsessed by Russia
that I felt I had good ground for the apprehension that your great abilities,
energy, and courage were not devoted to the reduction of expenditure.
    I regret that all my appeals have been in vain. At each interview you
promised me to give your mind to this very important problem. Nevertheless the first communication I have always received from you after these
interviews related to Russia. I invited you to Paris to help me to reduce our
commitments in the East. You then produce a lengthy and carefully prepared
memorandum on Russia. I entreated you on Friday to let Russia be for at
least 48 hours; and to devote your weekend to preparing for the Finance
Committee this afternoon. You promised faithfully to do so.
    Your reply is to send me a four-page letter on Russia, and a closely printed

memorandum of several pages—all on Russia. I am frankly in despair. Yesterday and today I have gone carefully through such details as have been supplied about the military expenditure, and I am more convinced than ever that Russia has cost us not merely the sum spent directly upon that unfortunate country, but indirectly scores of millions in the failure to attend to the costly details of expenditure in other spheres.

You confidently predict in your memorandum that Denikin is on the eve of some great and striking success. I looked up some of your memoranda and your statements made earlier in the year about Kolchak, and I find that you use exactly the same language in reference to Kolchak's successes.

The Cabinet have given you every support in the policy which they have laid down, and which you have accepted. I am not sure that they have not once or twice strained that policy in the direction of your wishes. The expedition to Kotlas was hardly a covering one to protect the retirement of Ironside's troops. The sequel has shown that it was quite unnecessary from that point of view. It was in the nature of an attempt to cut through in order to join hands with Kolchak. Nevertheless you received all support in your effort. That failed, but it was not the fault of the Cabinet that it did not succeed.

You proposed that the Czecho-Slovaks should be encouraged to break through the Bolshevik armies and proceed to Archangel. Everything was done to support your proposal. Ships were promised for Archangel if they succeeded. Denikin has been supplied with all the munitions and equipment that he needed. Still you vaguely suggest that something more could have been done and ought to have been done.

I abide by the agreed policy. We have kept faith with all these men. But not a member of the Cabinet is prepared to go further. The various Russian enterprises have cost us this year between 100 and 150 millions, when Army, Navy and Shipping are taken into account. Neither this Government nor any other Government that this country is likely to see will do more. We cannot afford it. The French have talked a good deal about Anti-Bolshevism, but they have left it to us to carry out the Allied policy. Clemenceau told me distinctly that he was not prepared to do any more. Foch is distinctly and definitely opposed to these ventures at the allied expense. Their view is that our first duty is to clear up the German situation. I agree with them.

I wonder whether it is any use my making one last effort to induce you to throw off this obsession which, if you will forgive me for saying so, is upsetting your balance. I again ask you to let Russia be, at any rate for a few days, and to concentrate your mind on the quite unjustifiable expenditure in France, at home and in the East, incurred by both the War Office and the Air Department. Some of the items could not possibly have been tolerated by you if you had given one-fifth of the thought to these matters which you devoted to Russia.

I would only add one word about the Baltic States. You want their independence recognised by the Allies in return for an undertaking by them to attack the Bolsheviks. It is quite clear from their communications that that would not satisfy them in the least, and that they would ask (1) that we should guarantee that independence (2) that we should supply them with the necessary equipment and cash to enable them to maintain their armies. Are you prepared to comply with these two requests? There is no other member of the Cabinet who would. It would be the height of recklessness to do so. Whether the Bolsheviks or the anti-Bolsheviks get the upper hand, they would not recognise the independence of these States as it would involve the permanent exclusion of Russia from the Baltic. Would you be prepared to make war with an Anti-Bolshevik regime if they attempted to reconquer these States and to secure the old Russian ports of Riga and Reval? If not, it would be a disgraceful piece of deception on our part to give a guarantee. In the second place, do you wish this country to maintain armies in the field of Esthonians, Latvians and Lithuanians to invade Russia? Unless you do, it is idle to hurl vague reproaches at your colleagues. The reconquest of Russia would cost hundreds of millions. It would cost hundreds of millions more to maintain the new Government until it had established itself. You are prepared to spend all that money, and I know perfectly well that is what you really desire. But as you know that you won't find another responsible person in the whole land who will take your view, why waste your energy and your usefulness on this vain fretting which completely paralyses you for other work?

I have worked with you now for longer than I have probably cooperated with any other man in public life: and I think I have given you tangible proof that I wish you well. It is for that reason that I write frankly to you.

Ever sincerely
D. Lloyd George

Churchill replied to Lloyd George's letter that same day, from the Turf Club in Piccadilly:

My dear Prime Minister,

I find the suggestions of yr letter vy unkind & I think also unjust. I have done my vy best to serve you in circumstances of exceptional difficulty. All my work has been explained to Parliament at every stage & I am quite ready at any time to give a clear account of it there. I will not burden you with argument, because if you have formed an adverse opinion I certainly shd not feel disposed to contest it. I only hope you will take what you think is the best course in the public interest. It is a disappointment to me to find you so unappreciative of such efforts as I have been able to make. If you had not been so pressed with other business you wd I hope have understood better what the difficulties of this year of Army Administration have been when we have had to restore an army from mutiny to contentment, to dissolve an immense army, to create a new voluntary army, & all the time to meet the many and varying demands for disciplined troops at home & in foreign

theatres. I am sure you wd have some better means of recognising what has
been achieved than you used this afternoon.

Even now what you are asking will butt up against the impossible at many
points. You will not be able to reduce the garrison of Ireland to its prewar
figure without an Irish policy. You will have to maintain exceptional forces
in Palestine, Egypt & Mesopotamia till you have settled with Turkey & till
the provocation of Turkey by the Greeks has come to an end. You will not be
able to dispense with a certain solid force in this country in aid of the civil
power. You will not be able to catch up the delay in demobilisation caused by
the delay in making peace in time to remedy the excess on this year's Estimates. Of course in a gigantic sphere like that of our dissolving armies with all
their litter scattered about the globe, there are many things wh may serve the
purposes of unfriendly or captious criticisms. I can hardly bring myself to
believe that you wd try to throw the blame on me. But I shd not shrink from
the debate if it arose.

Then about Russia: there the difficulty has been that you have had one
policy in yr heart & have carried out another. I have publicly asked to be
told what commitment in Russia is due to me. No one has been able to reply.
When I went to the War Office the Archangel force was already marooned on
that Arctic coast: the promises of arms & munitions to Kolchak & Denikin
had already been made. The Caucasus was already occupied. The Hampshire
regiment was at Omsk, the British Fleet was in the Baltic. Not I assuredly had
sent them there.

My part has been to wind up these commitments if possible without dishonour: & in this I have made no proposal for military operations to you or
to the Cabinet except those wh the General Staff recommended as essential to
the safe withdrawal of the troops. The Chief of the Staff has been at yr side
not at mine during the greater part of these anxious months.

It is not correct to say Kotlas 'has failed'. It was never attempted. Not that
it is now proved to have been unnecessary. Instead we have had to send large
reinforcements of troops to come out safely—as thank God I think we are
going to do in the next few days. But anyhow these are military matters in
regard to wh you have had more access to the experts than I have, & plenary
power of decision. I do not think it is fair to represent operations thus
demanded by military men of yr own choosing, as if they were so many sugar
plums given to please me.

It was however the purpose of my letter to wh you have so fully & patiently
replied to try to impress upon you the realisation I have of the intense &
horrible situation in Russia & of its profound influence upon all our affairs. I
may get rid of my 'obsession' or you may get rid of me: but you will not get
rid of Russia: nor of the consequences of a policy wh for nearly a year it has
been impossible to define. I must confess I cannot feel a sense of detachment
from their tragical scene. I hear you give directions in Cabinet as the result of
wh the Navy dash into Kronstadt harbour at deadly risk, with heavy loss—
for what? And then almost simultaneously the whole anti-Bolshevik front in

the Baltic States is treated as if it were a matter of indifference to Britain, about wh I have no business to worry. I see millions of money spent on Denikin or Kolchak to carry them to a certain point & then just perhaps when something is going to be achieved—another vital sector of the front— wh in yr own doctrine is 'all one'—is left to tumble down or stand up as it chances. Treasure has been spent, men are being killed & behind such things there ought to be a clear resolute policy pushed within the limits that are open to its full conclusion.

With half the world in disorder and its problems on yr shoulders I can understand that it all seems fairly small to you. But right up against it as I am —as I have been put by you—I cannot help feeling a most dreadful & ever present sense of responsibility. Am I wrong? How easy for me to shrug my shoulders & say it is on the Cabinet, or on the Paris Conference. I cannot do it. I feel an earnest desire to appeal to the nation regardless of the unthinking opinion. And surely I am not wrong in writing earnestly & sincerely to my chief & oldest political friend to let him know that things are not all right & are not going to get all right along this road. Surely I was bound to do this.

Ever sincerely
Winston S.C.

Lloyd George's letter of September 22 made it clear that Churchill could no longer hope for any increase in British aid to Russia, however successful Denikin's forces might be from day to day. On the other fronts, the policy of withdrawal continued. On the day of Lloyd George's letter, over four hundred Polish troops were evacuated from Archangel. On September 23 all British troops were withdrawn to the inner defences of the city.

Lloyd George spent most of September 23 at Cobham, in the company of Dr Addison, H. A. L. Fisher and Captain William Edge.[1] 'We discuss the unpopularity of the Russian policy,' Fisher recorded in his diary. 'LG thinks Winston is a greater source of weakness than of strength to the Gov.' Lloyd George went on to describe Churchill as like the counsel employed by a solicitor, not because he is the best man, but because 'he would be dangerous on the other side'.

The War Cabinet discussed Russia for two hours on the afternoon of September 24. Curzon explained that on the previous day the Foreign Office had telegraphed to the provisional Government of Lithuania,

[1] William Edge, 1880–1948. Liberal MP, 1916–23 and 1927–31. National Liberal MP, 1931–45. A Junior Lord of the Treasury, August 1919–February 1920. A National Liberal Whip, 1922–3. Knighted, 1922. A Charity Commissioner, 1932–5. Created Baronet, 1937.

recognizing it as a '*de facto* independent body'. But after what the
Minutes describe as a 'prolonged discussion', the War Cabinet rejected
any further British commitment to the Baltic States. Fisher, who was
present, recorded in his diary: 'Decided that we cannot urge them to
continue war with the Bolsheviks, or give them supplies or a loan. They
are to be free to make peace. Winston doesn't like that & argues that the
front is one.'

It was too late for Churchill to reverse the policy of withdrawal and
disassociation which the War Cabinet had now adopted towards North
Russia, Siberia and the Baltic States. Only Denikin and Yudenitch were
still in receipt of official British encouragement. Denikin could expect
nothing more direct than the training of his forces by British officers,
while in North-West Russia, the last British munitions and stores had
reached Yudenitch. On September 24, Yudenitch wrote to Churchill
from Reval, where he was preparing his assault on Petrograd:

Dear Sir,

On behalf of the Russian people, struggling to throw off the yoke of the
Bolsheviki, I tender you the sincerest thanks for the timely assistance the
munitions and supplies afforded to our army.

They have removed from us the fear of cold that threatened us during the
approaching winter and greatly raised the morale of our troops.

In our efforts to combat the common enemy, we hope to continue to
receive the moral and material support that a generous England has always
given to those fighting against oppression.

I am, Dear Sir,

Yours faithfully
General Youdenitch

On September 25 Churchill circulated a morose memorandum to the
War Cabinet about the fate of the Baltic States:

I—We are to tell them that we will send them no more supplies.
II—We are to tell them that we cannot encourage their hopes of inde-
pendence.
III—We are to tell them that we cannot assist them with a loan.
IV—In these circumstances we have no right to press them to continue
their struggle with the Bolshevists.
V—We are to tell them that we have ordered the Germans to leave
Courland, and will take steps to make them do so.

It is worth noting that every one of these steps, necessary as some of them
are, helps the Bolshevists, with whom on other parts of the front we are at war.
The following consequences may arise therefrom:—

1. The Baltic States may make peace with the Bolshevists.

15. Sir Henry Wilson and Churchill in Paris, March 1919

16. British Ministers in Paris, June 1919: from left to right: George Barnes (far left), A. J. Balfour, Edwin Montagu, Lloyd George, Austen Chamberlain (with monocle), William Hughes (Prime Minister of Australia), H. A. L. Fisher, Lord Birkenhead, Lord Robert Cecil (immediately behind Birkenhead), Churchill, Sir Maurice Hankey (behind Churchill) and Sir Henry Wilson (far right)

17. A. J. Balfour

18. Lord Curzon

19. Andrew Bonar Law

20. H. A. L. Fisher

21. Admiral Kolchak

22. General Denikin

Генералъ-Лейтенантъ
П. Н. БАРОНЪ ВРАНГЕЛЬ.

23. General Wrangel, a contemporary postcard, 1920

24. Leonid Krassin

25. 'Into Russia, Out of Russia': a cartoon by Strube, *Daily Express*, 8 September 1919

26. 'Winstonsky': a cartoon by Low, the *Star*, 12 August 1920

27. Churchill addressing British troops at Cologne, August 1919

28. Churchill inspecting troops at Cologne, August 1919

29. At Cologne, August 1919: to the right of Clementine Churchill sit Sir William Robertson, Churchill, Lady Robertson and Sir Henry Wilson. Sir Archibald Sinclair is in the second row behind Sir Henry Wilson

30. Lord Londonderry and Churchill in 1919, walk-ing away from the War Office

2. The North-West Russian army may, in consequence of such peace, be annihilated.
3. Finland probably, and Poland possibly, may follow the example of the Baltic States or join with them in making a peace.
4. 97,000 Bolsheviks on these fronts will be liberated, and will immediately be hurled upon the armies of General Denikin.
5. The effect of any of these peace settlements, particularly a peace settlement by Finland, upon the fortunes of the North Russians, whom we have left to fight it out alone at Archangel and Murmansk, will probable be fatal.
6. Petrograd, whose hopes of deliverance and food have been encouraged all this year by the operations of the British Navy, will be reduced tc despair.
7. If the Germans in Courland do not obey our orders to quit, all the Russians in this North-Western region will have no hope but to turn to them and try to make common cause with them.
8. The death-knell will have been struck of British influence in these regions, and the episode will be, rightly or wrongly, regarded by Russia as a supreme act of indifference and abandonment.

In these circumstances, the final decision which the War Cabinet have to take is one of far-reaching importance. . . .

Churchill went on to argue that the simplest, safest course would be 'to make war upon the Bolshevists by every means in our power . . . with a coherent plan on all fronts at once', until either the Bolsheviks were defeated, or a 'general peace' negotiated 'in which all parties would be included'. On October 5 he wrote personally to Kolchak that, as far as Britain was concerned, 'the shortest way to win' was to support Denikin, whose armies were so near to Moscow, and who possessed 'the food and fuel areas of Russia'.

On October 4 Denikin's armies began to advance on a broad front, capturing over 2,500 prisoners within twenty-four hours. On the Volga front, British airmen continued to support the anti-Bolshevik attack. South of Voronezh, Denikin's cavalry drove the Bolsheviks to the outskirts of the city, capturing 5,000 prisoners and 25 machine guns. Churchill was convinced that the defeat of the Bolsheviks was near. On October 5, before he had learned of Denikin's most recent advances, he wrote to Lord Curzon, almost in triumph:

Out of all this Russian tangle it is, I think, now possible to see very definite decisions emerging. The Bolsheviks are falling and perhaps the end is not distant. Not only their system but their regime is doomed. Their military effort is collapsing at almost every point on the whole immense circle of their front, while communications, food, fuel, and popular support, are all falling within that circle. In March they had 430,000 troops on the fighting front against 320,000 anti-Bolshevik Armies: today the numbers are 460,000 Bolsheviks to 630,000 anti-Bolshevik Armies. In other words, a situation and a preponderance of force is being created very similar to that which preceded the German debacle of last October. It by no means follows that the closing stages of this process will continue to be gradual. As Mr Bagge[1] of Odessa expressively says—'they may pass like a heap of snow melts under a hot sun, leaving behind only the dirt which it had gathered'.

Kolchak has advanced nearly 100 miles on a 300 mile front during the last month. Denikin is master of regions which cannot contain much less than 35,000,000 persons, including the food and the fuel of Russia. His army is nearly double the strength of the Bolsheviks opposing him. Except Moscow and Petrograd, all the greatest cities of Russia are in his hands and all her open ports. It is by no means impossible that he will enter Moscow before the end of the year. It seems quite certain, even at the worst, that he will hold and consolidate his gains. At any moment, therefore, in the near future, Russia may resume her position as a Great Power restored to sanity and civilisation and on our attitude in these fateful months depends the vital question whether it is to Germany or to Great Britain that her new rulers will turn.

In spite of the very slender and grudged resources which have been at our disposal to help the Russian National Cause and preserve a continuity of our alliance of 1914, there is no doubt that we stand today with the probable victors among the Russians in a position far superior to that occupied by any other country, and the advantages which may be reaped by us, certainly in the next few years and possibly for a much longer period, by a successful development of our strong position are incalculable but certainly enormous.

I do suggest to you most earnestly that the possibility of the advance of Denikin to Moscow and the fall or flight of the Bolshevik regime, and of the reconstitution of a National Russia, should be our main preoccupation at this moment. I do not think we could any longer stop it if we chose. All we can do is, by quarrelling with Denikin in the moment of success, harassing his flanks and cutting off his supplies, to exclude ourselves from any share in the fruits of a victory which our past exertions have helped to gain. I hope that a true proportion of events will be preserved and that the gigantic issues involved will not suffer on account of very small passing interests of a subsidiary character.

Let us do everything in our power to help Denikin in his advance towards Moscow. . . .

---

[1] John Picton Bagge, 1877–1967. Entered the Consular Service, 1905; served in Russia, 1905–18. Commercial Secretary, Russia (at Odessa), 1918–20. British mediator between General Wrangel and the Bolsheviks, 1920. Transferred to Switzerland, 1921; to Belgium, 1922. Director of the Foreign Trade Division, Department of Overseas Trade, 1928–37. Succeeded his brother as 5th Baronet, 1939.

Churchill then listed eight things which would, he believed, help
Denikin reach Moscow: the continuation of supplies to South Russia;
pressure on the Caucasian republics not to attack Denikin from behind;
pressure on the Rumanians to abandon their support for the Ukrainian
separatist army of Petliura;[1] pressure on the Poles to attack the Bolsheviks from the west, in the direction of Smolensk; prevention for as
long as possible of a peace between the Baltic States and the Bolsheviks;
renewed help, 'in minor ways', to the anti-Bolsheviks in North Russia
'who are now making a brave effort to carry on alone'; pressure on the
United States to supply equipment and winter clothing to Kolchak;
and, finally, a British initiative in favour of a 'union of Russian and
British financial interests . . . in order to establish good conditions of
credit and trade in the enormous areas newly liberated from Bolshevik
rule by Denikin'.

On October 6, when details of Denikin's advance reached the War
Office, Churchill sent them by messenger to 10 Downing Street. His
covering note was optimistic:

Prime Minister,
    Denikin having got his wireless working at last has now started to bark on
his own.
    I hope his estimates of prisoners are not too sanguine. I am cautioning him
agst over-optimism in counting them & generally in his wireless.
    I see both sides agree the Bols. are out of Dimitriev. Orel is only 20 miles
away. Voronej nearly surrounded. Many thanks for yr 'packet'.

                                                                    WSC

Lloyd George's 'packet' was a further British expenditure in South
Russia of £3,000,000, which was approved by the War Cabinet on
October 7. The terms of the War Cabinet's decision laid down that as
much of the material as possible should come out of existing War Office
stocks, and that any new purchases should be made 'within the narrow-
est possible limit'. Churchill was also instructed to notify Denikin that a
date would soon be fixed for the return of the British Mission. This was
not the 'packet' Churchill would have liked. But it was better than
nothing; nor had any specific date been set for the recall of the British
Mission.

---

[1] Simon Vasilievich Petliura, 1877–1926. A Social Democrat, active in the Ukraine, before
1917. Secretary General for Military Affairs, in the Ukrainian Government, June 1917. He
acquired notoriety on account of the anti-semitic pogroms carried out by his troops. He
captured Kiev in the summer of 1919, and fought against Denikin, 1919–20. In 1920 he
allied himself with the Poles against the Bolsheviks. Tried to organize anti-Bolshevik uprisings
in Ukraine, 1920–2. Killed in Paris by a Jew.

On October 6, Denikin's troops entered the city of Voronezh, and prepared for their final assault on Moscow. Two days later, on October 8, the last British troops sailed from Murmansk. On October 9, the day after the Murmansk evacuation had been completed, Lloyd George received a deputation from the Trades Union Congress, demanding that all British troops leave Russia at once. Lloyd George asked Churchill to give him a statement showing the exact position of all British forces remaining in Russia. On October 9 Churchill sent Lloyd George the facts he had asked for, together with some advice on how these facts should be presented to the trades unionists:

All British troops, officers and men, with the exception of a small Intelligence Mission about 12 strong, will have left North Russia (both Archangel and Murmansk) by October 15th.

It is desirable to point out that this evacuation was not effected as a result of newspaper or other agitation in this country, but that it followed upon a policy decided on by the Cabinet in February upon the advice of the General Staff. According to the latest accounts, the Russians left behind are holding their own well both at Archangel and at Murmansk, and the prospects of a massacre being avoided are much brighter than could have been expected at any time this year.

A lot of nonsense is talked about British Brigades and forces in the Baltic States. Actually there is a Military Mission of 46 Officers and 47 Other Ranks, including Cipher and Intelligence Officers, Interpreters and Clerks. In addition there are 22 Officers and 29 Men of the Tank Corps. These latter will be back in the United Kingdom before the end of November. It is probable that the whole of the British Mission will be back before the end of the year.

Churchill's advice to Lloyd George continued:

It would be well here to refer to the importance of our keeping an eye on what the Germans are doing in these countries and not losing touch altogether with the small Baltic States whose future prosperity must be a matter of some interest to us.

The Middlesex Regiment is already home from Siberia, and the Hampshire Regiment will have left by the 15th October. By that date all British units will have embarked. There are at present about 550 Officers and Other Ranks with the British Mission in Siberia. All non-volunteers are being sent home at once. Orders have been issued to reduce this Mission to 46 Officers and Other Ranks—all volunteers.

It was about South Russia that Churchill wanted Lloyd George to speak most firmly, for it was here that victory seemed near, and British help most justifiable:

There are no British fighting troops with Denikin except a few aviators and only one man has been wounded on this front during the whole of the year. Authority was given by the Cabinet in January for a Mission of Volunteer Officers and Sergeants to supervise the distribution of stores to Denikin and to help the formation and training of his armies. This number has never been exceeded, and it is not intended that it shall be. All these, of course, are men who have volunteered specially and who can apply for return at any time.

In consequence of the assistance we have given to Denikin, an enormous wedge including the fertile part of Russia has been liberated from the Bolsheviks. There is no doubt whatever that the bulk of the people living in this area, including particularly the peasants and smallholders, are entirely opposed to being put back under the Bolshevik oligarchy. Considering that the Bolsheviks armed themselves with a very great part of the weapons and munitions sent to Russia by the Allies to be used against the Germans and have been using these weapons to hold down the population even of those districts which most disliked their rule, it would have been very unfair to have left those populations entirely unarmed and without means of self-defence of any kind.

I strongly deprecate an apologetic tone in regard to the help we have given to Denikin as his success is increasing every day and no-one can say how far he will go. Our influence with him is very great and it is all exercised and will be exercised to secure moderation in victory and the summoning of a Constituent Assembly on a democratic basis for all Russia as soon as success is obtained. . . .

On October 8 the War Cabinet had discussed yet further economic support to Denikin. In addition to the £3,000,000 of surplus War Office supplies which they had authorized on October 7, they now agreed to send Denikin further munitions and supplies to a total value of £14,500,000. 'These munitions and supplies,' Churchill telegraphed to Denikin on October 9, had been granted by the War Cabinet, 'on the condition that it would be the last', and that from March 1920 'your Excellency's armies would be self supporting; purchasing any further supplies by export and taking into the Russian service any officers and sergeants of the British Military Mission whom you may wish thereafter to remain and who volunteer to stay'.

The anti-semitism of many of Denikin's supporters had led to anti-Jewish outrages throughout South Russia. Churchill had already tried, in vain, to persuade Denikin to moderate the violence of his subordinates. The Jews of England were outraged by the anti-semitism of those to whom Britain was giving military support. On October 7, Sir Alfred Mond[1] had sent Lloyd George details of anti-Jewish atrocities in South

---

[1] Alfred Moritz Mond, 1868–1930. Son of a Jewish chemist who had come to England from Germany in 1862. Called to the Bar, 1894, and practised for a while as a barrister. Became

Russia. Lloyd George sent Mond's letter to Churchill with a stern covering note:

I wish you would make some enquiries about this treatment of the Jews by your friends. Now that we are subsidising the volunteer army and providing them with weapons we certainly have a right to protest against outrages of this character being perpetrated. You may depend upon it that sooner or later a discussion will be raised on the subject and I do not wish to see the British Government placed in the same position as the Kaiser when he kissed the cheek of Abdul Hamid[1] shortly after he had massacred the Armenians. Apart from the iniquity of the proceeding and one's natural repugnance to be associated with it, it provides material for a most disagreeable debate in the House of Commons.

Churchill replied to Lloyd George on October 10, describing his efforts to persuade Denikin 'to restrain his troops' from anti-semitic action. By continuing to supply arms to Denikin, Churchill argued, Britain would be 'constantly in a position to exercise a modifying influence'. On the other hand, by 'cutting ourselves adrift from National Russia on the eve of its restoration', Britain would lose all power to influence events, 'either in the direction of mercy or democracy', and would make it impossible for Denikin and his generals 'to stand against the tide of popular vengeance'. The anti-Jewish violence, Churchill explained, did have a cause:

1. There is a very bitter feeling throughout Russia against the Jews, who are regarded as being the main instigators of the ruin of the Empire, and who, certainly have played a leading part in Bolshevik atrocities.[2]
2. This feeling is shared by the Volunteer Army and the Army of the Don under General Denikin. . . .

In his letter, Churchill wrote of 'particularly fearful massacres of Jews' that had been carried out by some of the anti-Bolshevik forces. That same day, he sent Denikin a further word of warning:

---

a Director of Brunner, Mond & Co., 1895. By brilliant management and skilful amalgamation, he created, by 1926, the Imperial Chemical Industries (ICI), with a capital of £95,000,000. Liberal MP, 1906–10, 1910–23 and 1924–8. Created Baronet, 1910. First Commissioner of Works, 1916–21. Minister of Health, 1921–2. An enthusiastic Zionist, in 1921 he gave £100,000 to the Jewish Colonization Corporation for Palestine. Joined the Conservative Party, 1926. Created Baron Melchett, 1928.

[1] Abdul Hamid, 1842–1918. Sultan of Turkey, 1876–1909. Prorogued Parliament, 1878; ruled autocratically for thirty years. Forced to restore the Constitution by the Young Turks, 1908. Deposed, 1909. The Kaiser visited him at Constantinople in 1899.

[2] Churchill blamed, not Denikin's armies, but those of Petliura, Makhno and Gregorieff, the last two of whom he described as 'ex-Bolshevik guerilla leaders of criminal anticedents'. During 1919, more than 100,000 Jews were murdered in South Russia.

Your Excellency, I know, will realise the vital importance at this time, when such brilliant results are being secured, of preventing by every possible means the ill-treatment of the innocent Jewish population. My task in winning support in Parliament for the Russian National Cause will be infinitely harder if well-authenticated complaints continue to be received from Jews in the zone of the Volunteer Armies.

Prime Minister has today sent me a letter on this subject enclosing allegations which I am referring to your Excellency by mail. I know the efforts you have already made and the difficulty of restraining anti-semitic feeling. But I beg you, as a sincere well-wisher, to redouble these efforts and place me in a strong position to vindicate the honour of the Volunteer Army. . . .

Churchill ended his telegram to Denikin with words of encouragement. 'I have been overjoyed,' he declared, 'at the wonderful succession of victories which your armies have gained and by their steady advance towards the goal.'

As Denikin prepared his final attack on Moscow, Churchill did everything within his power to help him. On October 9 he protested to Lord Curzon about the activities of the British representative in the Caucasus, John Wardrop,[1] who supported the consolidation of Georgian power in Baku and Batum. 'Denikin's advance is more remarkable each day,' Churchill wrote. 'It is very hard he should be hampered and harassed by these attacks upon his rear. Can you do nothing to assist? Wardrop and Holman are absolutely split. They might be on opposite sides.' Curzon was angered by Churchill's lack of concern for the Caucasian republics, minuting on October 10: 'We shall never satisfy WO. Anyone who does not bend the knee to Denikin & Kolchak is looked upon as a double-eyed traitor.'

On October 10 Churchill wrote to Curzon again, this time to protest about the reports sent to the Foreign Office from Vladivostok by the acting British High Commissioner, William O'Reilly,[2] who had been highly critical of Kolchak's autocratic behaviour, and had received a deputation of Kolchak's Russian critics. Churchill did not mince his words:

[1] John Oliver Wardrop, 1864–1948. Educated at Balliol College, Oxford. Published *The Kingdom of Georgia*, 1888. Entered the Army, 1890; Army interpreter for Russian. Transferred to the Diplomatic Service, 1892. Vice-Consul, Kertch, 1895–1902. Sebastopol, 1899. Consul, St Petersburg, 1903–6; Bucharest, 1906–10. Consul-General, Moscow, November 1917. Political Intelligence Department, Foreign Office (London), 1919. Chief British Commissioner, Georgia, Armenia and Azerbaijan, 1919–20. Consul-General, Strasbourg, 1920–7. Knighted, 1922.

[2] William Edmund O'Reilly, 1873–1934. Entered the Foreign Office, 1896. Acting High Commissioner, Vladivostok, 1919. Minister to Bolivia, 1919–24; to Guatemala, 1924–6; to Albania, 1926; to Venezuela, 1926–32.

I cannot understand this man. His ignorance of the Russian situation, his want of conviction as to policy, his fatuous verbosity—are really the limit. Why should he be allowed to choke the wires with unending telegrams about the gossip and intrigue of the port of Vladivostock and unending abuse and detraction of Kolchak. All this stuff circulating about the Cabinet does harm. People who are not closely informed on the Russian situation fasten on this or that phrase. If you throw enough mud some sticks. And people forget that O'Reilly is 4,000 miles from the battle front where Kolchak's men have overcome so many heartbreaking difficulties. At least Kolchak might be judged by those who are near him and share his difficulties and dangers, and not by this muddle headed tittletatler at the base.

Forgive this fury. We are so near to immense events. And yet there is time to baulk them.

Curzon accepted Churchill's protest, and O'Reilly was recalled.

Now that he believed success was near, Churchill was more anxious than ever to co-ordinate all anti-Bolshevik activity. During October a serious conflict had arisen between those who wished to contain Bolshevism by supporting the anti-Bolshevik Russians, and those who believed that it was only by the creation of a strong, independent Poland that any reliable barrier could be erected between Bolshevism and the west. Churchill himself tried to reconcile the two groups. On October 10, in an interview with Paderewski, he suggested that Poland's wisest course would be to come to a friendly agreement with Denikin. For his part, he said, he was willing to use his influence to persuade the anti-Bolshevik Russians to accept Poland's independence, and indeed to welcome it. Later that day Churchill explained his hopes in a letter to Lloyd George:

Kolchak & Denikin are quite ready to come to terms with an Independent Poland, & now is the time to seal the bargain. . . . It seems to me that the right policy for us to pursue now is to promote the accord & concerted action between Poland & Denikin. Poland is bound to be anti-Bosch as well as anti-Bolshevik. Properly guided now Denikin & K may be made to be anti-German as well as anti-Bol. In arming Poland we build up the barrier between Germany & Russia. In attaching Poland to New Russia we confirm the anti-German development of Russia (as far as it is in our power to influence events).

Churchill went on to suggest to Lloyd George that, if Poland and the new Russia of Denikin were willing to work together, Britain should offer to arm Poland 'with surplus munitions in conjunction with the French'.

The Press had nothing to say in favour of the anti-Bolsheviks. Denikin, despite his military successes, was portrayed as a double villain; he allowed anti-semitic violence to flourish behind his lines, and he was as keen to destroy Polish—or Caucasian—independence as he was to defeat the Bolsheviks. On October 10 the editor of the *Westminster Gazette*, J. A. Spender,[1] published a strong attack on the anti-Bolsheviks, and on those who supported them. Behind Denikin, Kolchak and Yudenitch, he asserted, were Russians of a most undesirable type, seeking to win back their old positions of power and privilege; the 'White' massacres were quite as revolting, and even more indiscriminate than the 'Red' massacres; Kolchak would restore the anti-democratic, centralized beaurocracy of Tsarist times; and above all, Denikin would seek to subvert the independence of Poland.

As soon as Churchill read Spender's article, he sought to rebut it, writing to him on October 10:

> Your article to-day is not in accordance with facts. So far from trying to break up the Polish settlement, General Denikin is endeavouring to come to a working understanding with the Poles. The advantages of this from his point of view, and I think from everybody's, are very great. Poland must in the nature of things be anti-Bosch and anti-Bolshevik. Recognition by National Russia of Poland's claims throws these two countries together and works solidly against a Russo-German arrangement. . . .
>
> Considering the kind of line that is taken up by so many of the English newspapers in favour of leaving Russia to 'stew in her own juice' and to 'work out her own salvation', it would really not be surprising if the National Russians had turned to Germany as their sole means of future recovery. I am sure they would do so, and I am sure they would be right from their point of view to do so, if the kind of policies which are advocated were carried out. I cannot think of anything more perilous to the general results we have secured from the war or particularly to our own British position. . . .

Churchill ended his letter to Spender on a personal note:

> I have had so many bitter experiences in the last five years, and seen so many fine chances thrown away or hopelessly delayed, that I refrain from making predictions about the future. Still, when I look back over the events of the last six months, I am amazed at the wonderful progress that has been made with such small resources, through such baffling counsels and over such

[1] John Alfred Spender, 1862–1942. Entered journalism, 1886. Editor of the *Westminster Gazette*, 1896–1922. A friend of Asquith's, and a staunch Asquithian Liberal. Co-author of *The Life of Lord Oxford and Asquith* (1932), and author of seventeen other volumes.

fearful difficulties towards the restoration and liberation of the Russian people; and I see no reason why, in spite of everything, a favourable evolution of affairs should not continue.

Churchill's advisers were still convinced that the Bolsheviks were doomed. On October 10 he received a General Staff memorandum which declared emphatically:

1. The combined operations of the anti-Bolshevik forces in all quarters of Russia have now reached a critical stage. Victory is in sight. The Bolshevik power is showing unmistakable signs of complete collapse at an early date . . . only in the Baltic States and North Russia is the situation still unsatisfactory.
2. The history of the past year shows that is has been lack of concerted effort on the part of the supporters of the anti-Bolshevik cause which has given the Soviet Government breathing space and enabled it to hold out so long. . . .

On October 12 Denikin's forces entered Chernigov, and on October 13 they drove the Bolsheviks from Orel, only 250 miles from Moscow. 'When we entered Orel,' Lieutenant Roberts later recalled, 'we were deciding which horses we should ride during the triumphal entry into Moscow.' In the north, Yudenitch succeeded in cutting the Pskov–Petrograd railway at Luga on October 13, and by nightfall on October 14 was less than 35 miles from Petrograd. East of the Urals, Kolchak had again begun to advance, and in less than two weeks had recovered 100 miles of lost territory. On October 14 Churchill circulated a triumphant, six-page memorandum to the Cabinet. 'The Bolshevik system,' it began, 'was from the beginning doomed to perish in consequence of its antagonism to the fundamental principles of civilised society.' Sooner or later, he added, 'the system and the regime must perish beneath the vengeance of the Russian nation', nor was it ever possible for any civilized Government 'to establish normal peaceful relations with the Bolshevik Government'. Even had it been possible, he concluded, the Bolshevik Government 'carried within it the seeds of its own destruction, so that the arrangement could only have been temporary and we should have been building on a perishing foundation'.

On October 15 Denikin's troops prepared to advance north of Orel, in the direction of Tula, while Yudenitch prepared his troops for their final 35-mile march to Petrograd. In Moscow, the Politburo of the Central Committee of the Communist Party met to discuss the worsening situation. The minutes of the meeting recorded: 'In recognition of the presence of a military threat of the utmost danger it is decided to bring about the actual conversion of Soviet Russia into a military camp.'

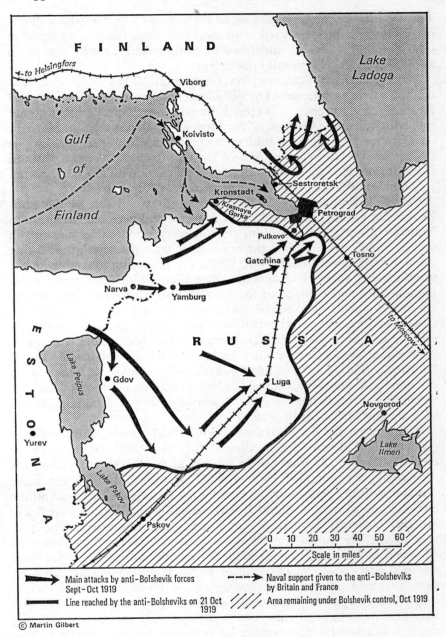

GENERAL YUDENITCH'S ADVANCE, OCTOBER 1919

There was to be 'no surrendering of Petrograd'. The Moscow military district was to be organized with stocks of food, fodder and straw so that it could exist 'as an independent entity'. And Trotsky was to go at once to Petrograd to rally the defence.

Trotsky reached Petrograd on October 16. That same day, Yudenitch's troops approached to within twenty-five miles of the city, and Denikin's army prepared to launch its attack on Tula. 'I had another talk with Winston after lunch,' Sir Henry Wilson recorded in his diary on October 16, 'when he told me that if Denikin got to Moscow he [Winston] wanted to go out & help Denikin to mould the new Russian Constitution. He said he had talked over this idea with LG who was not ag^t the idea. Winston would go out as a sort of Ambassador.'

Churchill had confidence that Petrograd would fall to the anti-Bolsheviks. On October 17, he sent a 'secret and personal' telegram to Yudenitch, congratulating him on 'the very remarkable measure of success which has attended the opening of your offensive', and listing the war materials which the War Office was preparing to send 'with the utmost speed' to assist his attack. These supplies included tanks, aeroplanes, rifles and equipment for 20,000 men, winter clothing, twenty 18-pounders with 3,000 rounds per gun, twelve 4·5-inch howitzers with 2,000 rounds per gun and four 6-inch howitzers with 1,000 rounds per gun. In addition, 400 Russian officers who had been under training at Newmarket would leave at once on board the British steamship *Cassell* for Reval. 'This ship,' Churchill added, 'will also carry a large part of the munitions above-mentioned.' If Petrograd were captured, Churchill wrote to Curzon that same day, 'it will be with British munitions and with the aid of the British Fleet'.

Victory over the Bolsheviks seemed near and certain. Outside Petrograd, south of Moscow and in Siberia, three anti-Bolshevik armies were on the offensive. On October 12 the last of the British troops had left Archangel, accompanied by 700 Siberian troops; but on the three remaining fronts British advisers continued to give their support to the anti-Bolshevik forces. General Knox was still with Kolchak's armies in Siberia; General Holman was at Denikin's headquarters. The 47th Squadron of the Royal Air Force was actively assisting the advance on Moscow. As Yudenitch marched on Petrograd, units of the Royal Navy dominated the coast of the Gulf of Finland, supporting his advance. British-trained officers were fighting on all three fronts, with British arms and equipment. Churchill believed that the defeat of the Bolsheviks would vindicate these wide-ranging involvements, and give him the justification he was certain he deserved for his persistence and initiative in the anti-Bolshevik cause. On the eve of victory, Churchill was wary of too much optimism, and yet unable to shake off the hope of triumph. 'I make no predictions,' he wrote to Curzon in his letter of October 17, 'having suffered too much. Anything, however, may happen, and may happen straight away.'

Churchill's enthusiasm for the anti-Bolshevik cause, and his persistent support for Denikin, had convinced many observers that he was acting alone, in defiance of Lloyd George, and without regard for the mounting Press and public hostility. Among the headlines with which his speeches were being greeted was one which reoccurred throughout the summer: 'Mr Churchill's Private War'. Neither the arguments that he used, nor the sincerity of his convictions, but this hostile image of him, lodged in the public mind, even when victory seemed near for the anti-Bolshevik cause.

19

General Denikin's Retreat

OCTOBER 18 was the first black day for the anti-Bolshevik forces in southern Russia. At Orenburg, several units of Cossacks transferred their allegiance from the Whites to the Reds. They were at once, on Lenin's orders, granted an amnesty and redrafted into the Bolshevik army. That same day news reached London of an uprising in the Caucasus, where the people of Daghestan rose in revolt against Denikin's overlordship, and forced him, at the testing time of his advance on Moscow, to divert 15,000 of his troops to the south.

Churchill was still exhilarated by the prospect of an anti-Bolshevik victory. During the day he sent Sir George Ritchie, the chairman of the Dundee Liberal Association, an open letter in which he declared: 'There are now good reasons for believing that the tyranny of Bolshevism will soon be overthrown by the Russian nation.' Britain would use her influence, he added, 'in building up a New Russia on the broad foundation of democracy and Parliamentary institutions'.

General Yudenitch's advance continued throughout October 19. By nightfall his forward units were only twelve miles from Petrograd. On October 20 Churchill and Sir Henry Wilson debated the wisdom of sending a senior British general to Yudenitch. Their choice fell on Sir Richard Haking,[1] who had commanded the Eleventh Corps on the western front. Wilson recorded in his diary how he and Churchill discussed sending Haking to Russia 'for the entry into Petrograd'.[2]

That night Trotsky ordered the first Bolshevik counter-attack. But

---

[1] Richard Cyril Byrne Haking, 1862–1945. Entered Army, 1881. Lieutenant-General commanding the XI Corps, 1915–18. Knighted, 1916. Commanded British Military Mission to Russia and the Baltic Provinces, 1919. High Commissioner, League of Nations, Danzig, 1921–3. General Officer commanding the British troops in Egypt, 1923–7.

[2] Within the Foreign Office there was a certain scepticism about these plans. During the day J. D. Gregory minuted: 'it may be that even if Yudenitch and Denikin take Petrograd and Moscow respectively, their tenure may not be long-lived'.

still Yudenitch advanced, and by the evening of October 21 one of his units reached within two miles of the Moscow–Petrograd railway. That day Churchill wrote to Lord Curzon to say that Sir Richard Haking would leave for Russia on October 23, and that Britain must use her influence 'to prevent excesses in the event of victory'. The officers of the War Office General Staff, he added, 'continue confident that the overthrow of the Bolsheviks is certain, taking the situation as a whole'. There was, he reported, hard fighting 'not only around Petrograd but on the whole of Denikin's long front'.

On October 21 Churchill drafted a comprehensive 'Outline of Instructions' for Sir Richard Haking. The principal paragraph began: 'On the assumption that Petrograd is captured . . .' and instructed Haking to warn Yudenitch not to establish 'a military dictatorship'. He must, Churchill wrote, 'clothe his action with as great an appearance of constitutional support as possible'. As for the future relations of 'the small Baltic States with the New Russia', these must be left to negotiation by the Council of the League of Nations, but Haking was reminded that Britain had 'declined to guarantee them their independence'. It was essential, Churchill added, that the Baltic States 'must not open their mouths too wide or be led by us into a position which Russia will never endure as a permanent settlement'. Haking's 'chief care', according to his instructions, was to be the establishment in Petrograd of a 'decent, enlightened and humane administration'. There must be no 'indiscriminate or wholesale executions'; even the worst criminals were 'entitled to a trial'; full public trials 'where the misdeeds of these men can be brought to full light' would be of 'more lasting service' to the anti-Bolshevik cause than summary execution; above all, 'anything in the nature of a Jewish pogrom would do immense harm to the Russian cause'.

Churchill sent a copy of Haking's instructions to Lord Curzon, commenting in his covering note: 'He will go on a special mission of a purely departmental character in order to be at Yudenitch's side in the event of his entry into Petrograd.' The officers at the War Office, Churchill added, 'continue confident that the overthrow of the Bolsheviks is certain, taking the situation as a whole'.

In South Russia, behind Denikin's lines there appeared an even worse disaster than the Caucasian revolt. On October 11 the anarchist leader Nestor Makhno[1] had seized the port of Berdiansk on the Sea of Azov.

---

[1] Nestor Ivanovich Makhno, 1884–1934. A shepherd, of peasant origin, he took part in the revolution of 1905 and became an anarchist. Sentenced to life imprisonment, 1908; released during the February revolution of 1917. Formed an anti-German partisan group in the

Taking advantage of Denikin's now desperate struggle between Orel and Tula, Makhno's bands entered Mariupol, Nikopol and Alexandrovsk, seizing guns, shells, ammunition and vehicles. On October 22, as the Bolsheviks drove southwards, forcing Denikin to abandon Orel, Makhno took temporary charge of two important railway junctions, Lozovaya and Sinelnikovo. In their moment of need, Denikin's troops were cut off from their supply bases. After threatening Denikin's own headquarters at Taganrog, Makhno and his men entered Ekaterinoslav, one of the largest towns of the south Ukraine, and declared the inauguration of a regime of anarchy.

While Makhno disrupted Denikin's lines of communication in South Russia, the Red Army was preparing to take the offensive against Yudenitch's troops outside Petrograd. On October 22 Lenin telegraphed to Trotsky from Moscow: 'It is *damnably* important for us to finish off Yudenitch (just that—finish him off: dispatch him). If the offensive is to be launched cannot a further 20 thousand or so Petrograd workers be mobilized, plus 10 thousand or so of the bourgeoisie, machine guns to be posted to the rear of them, a few hundred shot and a real mass assault on Yudenitch assured?' Yudenitch, he added, 'must be finished off *swiftly*; then we will switch *everything* against Denikin'.

At Yurev, behind Yudenitch's lines, the Bolsheviks opened negotiations with Estonia, determined to cut Yudenitch off from further support or future asylum. The Estonians welcomed the chance of making peace.

On October 22, at a Cabinet Finance Committee meeting in London, Lloyd George complained to his colleagues that the 'Russian campaign' had accounted for an expenditure of £100,000,000. Churchill at once challenged this figure. £60,000,000 of the total, he explained, had not been taxpayers' money at all, but 'surplus non-marketable munitions' which, had Denikin not taken them, would have been discarded or destroyed. Churchill also pointed out that when he had taken office nine months earlier it had been assumed, for financial purposes, that the Archangel expedition would last all year, 'although', as he noted, 'it was now over', and the burden to the Exchequer from that source had ended.[1]

Ukraine, early 1918. In March 1919 he commanded an independent force of 15,000 men. He challenged successively Denikin, Wrangel and then the Bolsheviks. Fled to Rumania, 1921; then to Paris, where he died.

[1] Among those present at the Finance Committee were Bonar Law, Lord Milner, Sir Auckland Geddes and Stanley Baldwin. Two days later, on October 24, at a further meeting of the Committee, Churchill reiterated that £60,000,000 of the stores sent to Denikin had no real market value, and he added: 'the pay of soldiers engaged in Russia would have been incurred in any event, owing to the impossibility of demobilising at a more rapid rate'.

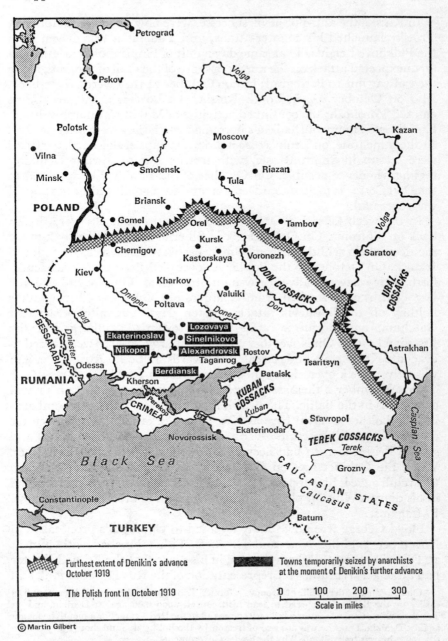

GENERAL DENIKIN'S DEFEAT, OCTOBER—DECEMBER 1919

In Russia, the anti-Bolshevik successes were now over. On October 23 Trotsky launched his counter-attack, and Yudenitch was driven from the Pulkhovo heights. That same day a unit of Finnish soldiers launched an unexpected attack on the northern shore of the Gulf of Finland, along the railway line to Petrograd; but on October 24 they were driven back. Also on October 24, in South Russia, the Bolshevik Cavalry Corps entered Voronezh; the continued activities of Makhno's anarchist bands had diverted many of Denikin's horsemen when they were most needed. At the same time, on Lenin's direct orders, groups of Bolshevik partisans were set up in South Russia, with instructions to disrupt Denikin's regime whenever possible. On October 26, the Bolsheviks appealed to the Don Cossacks to abandon Denikin, and turn against him; the appeal was successful.[1]

In the week following October 26, the anti-Bolsheviks were driven back on all fronts. On October 28, in Siberia, Admiral Kolchak made the decision to withdraw from Omsk, eastwards nearly 1,500 miles to Irkutsk. On October 30 the Bolsheviks occupied Petropavlovsk. Henceforth their eastward advance was uninterrupted. On November 1 the last British troops sailed from Vladivostok. On November 3, after holding off the Bolshevik attacks for ten days, Yudenitch evacuated Gatchina, and began a rapid retreat towards Yamburg and the Estonian border. On November 4 the Orenburg Cossacks were forced to evacuate Kokchetav, and retreated eastwards. In South Russia, Denikin was driven back over eighty miles from Orel to Kursk.

On November 2 the *Sunday Express* drew attention to Britain's naval operations in the Baltic. The British monitor *Erebus* had been bombarding the Bolshevik naval base at Krasnaya Gorka for three consecutive days, with no visible result. Over a hundred sailors had been killed, and several British airmen had been shot down behind the Bolshevik lines. When the Cabinet met on October 31 to discuss the Navy's action, Churchill gave it his support. H. A. L. Fisher, who was present, recorded in his diary: 'Winston pleads that it may go on bombarding till the ice. PM against.'

Lloyd George was now totally opposed to Churchill's proposals. On November 3 Philip Kerr and H. A. L. Fisher lunched with him at 10 Downing Street. Fisher recorded in his diary that the Prime Minister had attacked 'Winston's misrepresentation of the Russian situation', and

---

[1] One Cossack leader, Philip Mironov, a former Tsarist general who had been captured earlier by the Bolsheviks, agreed to lead his troop of 5,000 men against Denikin, and, at Trotsky's suggestion, was given a military command in the Red Army. For a month he fought against Denikin. Later he was accused of treason by the Bolsheviks, and shot (1921); but in the 1960s he was 'rehabilitated' by the Soviet Government.

he added: 'LG does not want Denikin to win.' During their discussion, Lloyd George asked Fisher to raise the Russian issue when the Cabinet met on the following day. This Fisher agreed to do. 'Debate on Russian policy,' he wrote in his diary on November 4. 'Addison and I urge peace as soon as possible.'

On November 6 the House of Commons debated the Russian situation. Colonel Malone[1] spoke bitterly of Denikin's anti-semitism. There were, he said, over six million Jews in Russia. 'I wonder how many of those Jews will be alive,' he asked, 'if Denikin or Kolchak wins.' Josiah Wedgwood, who had, like Malone, fought at Gallipoli, also denounced Kolchak and Denikin as 'reactionary'. Their aim, he said, was the restoration of autocracy and Tsardom. By contrast, the Bolsheviks, he believed, were restoring the 'democratic process' to Russia. Colonel Ward, who had returned from Siberia, challenged Wedgwood's analysis; the Bolsheviks, he declared, were murderers. He himself had examined the bodies of Bolshevik victims who had been thrown through a hole in the ice on the River Kama. According to Ward, those who had been murdered included women and children, 'and, what was remarkable, you could tell by the blackened marks on the hands of some of the old workmen—the proletariat that we are supposed to defend—what some of the other victims were. They were all mixed up in hopeless confusion'. The Bolsheviks, Ward added, were murdering 'every Social Democrat they could get hold of'.

Churchill then defended his policy. The Bolshevik 'ideal', he said, was no less than world-wide revolution. He went on to denounce Lenin as a tool of the Germans, and to describe Bolshevism as a disease:

Lenin was sent into Russia by the Germans in the same way that you might send a phial containing a culture of typhoid or of cholera to be poured into the water supply of a great city, and it worked with amazing accuracy. No sooner did Lenin arrive than he began beckoning a finger here and a finger there to obscure persons in sheltered retreats in New York, in Glasgow, in Berne, and other countries, and he gathered together the leading spirits of a formidable sect, the most formidable sect in the world, of which he was the high priest and chief. With these spirits around him he set to work with

[1] Cecil J. L'Estrange Malone, 1890–1965. Entered the Royal Navy, 1905. Learnt to fly at Eastchurch, 1911–12. Assistant Director of the Air Department, Admiralty, 1912–14. Squadron-Commander, 1914. Commanded the Royal Naval Air Service raid on Cuxhaven, 25 December 1914. Served at the Dardanelles in command of the aircraft carrier *Ben-my-Chree*, March 1915–January 1916. Commanded the Egypt Seaplane Squadron, 1916–18. Lieutenant-Colonel, 1918. Air Attaché, Paris, 1918. Air Representative, Supreme War Council, Versailles, 1918. Coalition Liberal MP, 1918–22. Labour MP, 1928–31. Parliamentary Private Secretary, Ministry of Pensions, 1931.

demoniacal ability to tear to pieces every institution on which the Russian State and nation depended. Russia was laid low to the dust. . . .

H. A. L. Fisher, who was present during the debate, recorded in his diary: 'Winston brilliant.' And he added that when the debate was over, A. J. Balfour had gone up to Churchill and remarked: 'I admire the exaggerated way you tell the truth.'

In Russia itself, the Bolsheviks continued to advance on all fronts. 'Winston very lonesome about Russia,' Sir Henry Wilson noted in his diary on November 7, 'as Kolchak is going to lose Omsk & Yudenitch is falling back. . . .' That same day Churchill wrote despairingly to Lloyd George:

Prime Minister,
    This increasingly grave situation wd appear to require Cabinet consideration. Is there no means of obtaining Japanese or American assistance.
    If the whole of Siberia goes up to Lake Baikal the consequences will be far-reaching & long lasting.

                                                                    WSC

Lloyd George understood at once the seriousness, and significance, of the Bolshevik successes. On November 8, when he was the guest of honour at the Guildhall, he spoke of how he dreaded 'an interminable series of swaying contests, laying waste to some of the most fertile land in the world, devastating a country the welfare of which is essential to the prosperity of the world'. Bolshevism, he said, 'could not be suppressed with the sword'. And he went on:

We cannot, of course, afford to continue so costly an intervention in an interminable civil war. Our troops are all out of Russia. Frankly, I am glad. Russia is a quicksand. Victories are usually won in Russia, but you sink in victories: and great armies and great empires in the past have been overwhelmed in the sands of barren victories. . . .

Churchill was present while Lloyd George spoke. Another guest, the American Ambassador, John W. Davis,[1] noted a startled expression on his face at Lloyd George's remarks.

When the Cabinet met at 10 Downing Street on November 9,

    [1] John William Davis, 1873–1955. Member of the Democratic National Convention, 1904–32. Solicitor-General, USA, 1913–18. Ambassador to London, 1918–21. Unsuccessful Democratic nominee for President, 1924. Honorary knighthood, 1953.

Churchill made a strong defence of Denikin against his critics. Denikin was quite willing, he said, to pay for all the British supplies he needed, and after March 31 he would only be able to obtain such supplies 'by purchase'. It was 'unjustifiable' to call Denikin an adventurer, as Asquith had done at Aberystwyth on October 31. 'He had remained loyal to the Allies all through, and at the moment of his greatest success had placed himself under Admiral Kolchak at a time when the latter was losing.'

The discussion turned to the Caucasus. There was 'general agreement' that if Denikin 'had designs on the independence of the new-formed States in the Caucasus, the despatch of supplies to him should be stopped'.

Churchill still pressed for greater action. Before the Cabinet met on November 12, he circulated his colleagues with a lengthy memorandum, pointing out that whereas Britain was supporting Denikin in South Russia, she was showing towards North-West Russia and Siberia 'a helpless indifference to the course of events'. Churchill wanted his colleagues to agree to several positive actions; to send a warship to Murmansk with food and supplies in order to 'encourage the resistance of the North Russian Government'; to inform Finland 'that we earnestly desire her to take Petrograd'; to urge the Rumanian Government to come to terms with Denikin and give active support to the anti-Bolshevik forces; and to appeal to both Japan and the United States 'to exert themselves to avert the collapse of the Siberian front'. A single Japanese division, Churchill added, 'would restore the whole situation' in Siberia.

Churchill ended his memorandum with a warning: 'If we do not use these anti-Bolshevik forces to crush the Bolshevik movement,' he wrote, 'the danger will present itself to us alone after all these forces have been dispersed or squandered, and we shall have to use our own flesh and blood, and spend far greater quantities of our own money, without any of the hopes of a satisfactory solution which are now within our reach.'

After the Cabinet meeting, H. A. L. Fisher recorded in his diary: 'Winston wants more vigorous support all round: difficulty, neither Denikin nor Kolchak will consent to independence of Baltic States.'

Unknown to Churchill, the Bolsheviks had been negotiating secretly with the Poles for over a month, in order to help secure their western frontier. On October 11, shortly after Denikin had entered Orel, a Soviet and a Polish Red Cross Mission had begun talks at a small railway halt sixty miles east of Pinsk. By November 2 the two sides had reached agreement on the return of Polish hostages held by the Bolsheviks. On November 9 they signed an agreement for the mutual exchange of civilian prisoners. They had also discussed the possibility of a full-scale military truce. On November 14 Trotsky told the Politburo of the Central Committee of the Communist Party, meeting secretly in Moscow, that these discussions had been taking place. The Politburo decided that Trotsky and Chicherin[1] should work out, in detail, 'the terms of a truce with the Poles'.

The skill of Bolshevik diplomacy was matched by their success in the field. On November 14 Kolchak left Omsk; that same day, Yudenitch returned to Yamburg, from where he had begun his Petrograd expedition. As a result of the Bolsheviks' negotiations with the Estonians, Yudenitch's army was immediately disarmed, interned and soon disbanded. On November 15, in South Russia, Denikin was defeated at Kastorskaya, an important railway junction between Kursk and Voronezh, and two days later, on November 17, the Bolsheviks entered Kursk itself. The capture of Kastorskaya enabled the Bolshevik Cavalry Corps to drive a deep wedge between Denikin's Volunteer Army and the Don Cossacks to the east, and was the final blow to the morale of Mamontov's cavalrymen.

On the day that Kursk fell to the Bolsheviks, ten British tanks were landed at Novorossisk. For several weeks they were parked on the breakwater, waiting for the arrival of railway trucks on which they would be sent to the front. A member of the British Mission in South Russia, Captain Wood[2] later recalled the fate of the tanks. 'The town had its own special wind,' he said. 'One day, while I was watching, tank after tank was washed off the breakwater and into the sea.'

On November 19 Churchill telegraphed to General Holman, asking whether the Bolshevik advance was 'a desperate effort which cannot last long, or is it evidence of really superior power on their side?' His telegram continued:

[1] Georghy Valentinovich Chicherin, 1872–1936. A Russian diplomat and landowner, he resigned from the Tsarist Diplomatic Service in 1905, renounced his estates and joined the Social Democratic Movement. Arrested near Berlin, 1908, and expelled from Germany. Lived in Paris and London, 1908–17. Imprisoned in Brixton Gaol, November 1917; expelled from England, January 1918 (in exchange for the British Ambassador in Petrograd, Sir George Buchanan). People's Commissar for Foreign Affairs, 1918–30.

[2] George Neville Wood, 1898–1900. Educated at Sandhurst; commissioned into the Dorset Regiment, January 1916. On active service in France, 1916–17, when he was badly wounded. Served in South Russia, 1919–20, and in Turkey (Ismid), 1920–1, when he was awarded the Military Cross. Lieutenant-Colonel, 1938. Commanded the Oxford University Officers' Training Corps, 1938–9; the 2nd Battalion Dorset Regiment, 1941–2; the 4th Infantry Brigade, 1943. On active service in Assam and Burma, 1943–4. Commanded the 25th Indian Division, Arakan and Malaya, 1944–6. Major-General, 1946. Commanded 3rd Division, Southern Palestine, 1947. Director of Quartering, War Office, 1950–2.

We do not want to see Denikin broken up as Kolchak was. If he has no good chance of winning or of getting to Moscow, you should carefully consider whether we ought not to advise negotiations having as their object the maintenance and consolidation of the territories now held by the anti-Bolshevik forces. It is possible that I might be able to get much more powerful support on the basis of holding on to the liberated areas and preventing the Bolsheviks from invading them than for a general attempt to reconquer the whole country. Examine carefully the proposition that we may go further in the struggle and fare worse. Denikin has an enormous area of immense value, and if that were consolidated after a suspension of hostilities it would be much better than the complete triumph of the Bolshevik Empire after Denikin had lost back all his winnings again. . . .

Churchill now grasped at a temporary compromise solution. 'It is no good fighting on blandly after all chance of success has departed,' he told Holman, 'if it is possible to make terms which enable at any rate a large portion of Russia to be saved from ruin.' Churchill deleted the words: 'which perhaps enable the struggle to be resumed under better conditions at a later stage'.

Churchill had wanted both the Foreign Office and the Treasury to support a French proposal for the formation of a special Russian Corps to be attached to General Yudenitch. On November 20 he wrote bitterly to Henry Wilson: 'No doubt the Treasury will refuse the request: most probably the Cabinet will endorse this refusal. But that is no reason why the War Office should not very clearly point out the futility of the proceedings and dissociate themselves from any responsibility in the matter.' Churchill confided to Wilson his hopes for the future. 'I anticipate a very considerable revirement,' he wrote, 'both in England and France, of the present policy of indifference as the Bolshevik military and political menace steadily develops. I do not want the War Office to stultify itself.'

Churchill's hopes were dashed on November 21, when Lloyd George told him that the French Government had decided to cut off all financial and military aid to the anti-Bolsheviks. 'I must say quite frankly,' Churchill wrote later that day to Louis Loucheur, 'that this appears to me to be a suicidal policy for France,' and he continued:

If the Russian National forces get the upper hand and overthrow the Bolshevik regime after France has abandoned them, they will undoubtedly be animated by sentiments of lasting resentment towards the Entente Powers, in whose cause they lost more than three million men. If, on the other hand, they are beaten, as is very likely, Europe will have to reckon with a mighty Jacobin military Empire rallying the National Russian spirit to recover Russian lopped-off provinces, and dividing the populations of the Entente countries by revolutionary propaganda fed by the financial resources of a powerful State. In either event these hostile Russian forces will look to Germany, where alone she can get the instructors and organisers to develop their military life and to rebuild their economic power. In Germany, on the other hand, there can only be one policy—to unite with Russia, either Bolshevik or anti-Bolshevik which- ever comes uppermost. Russia can give back Germany everything she has lost. Munitions, man-power, raw material, markets, expansion; all can be found by Germany in Russia. . . .

Churchill went on to warn Loucheur that France and Britain 'could never indefinitely maintain a war on land' against a Russo-German combination. On November 29 he wrote to Lord Reading: 'The outlook is gloomy, but I still have strong hopes of Denikin. . . .' But these hopes were ill-founded. 'Poor Denikin is falling back in an awkward way,' Sir Henry Wilson wrote in his diary on December 2; and during December, Denikin's army collapsed utterly.

Churchill had always made it clear, in his telegrams to Denikin, that the Caucasian States must in no way be interfered with. On December 3, hearing a rumour, sent to London by Wardrop, that Denikin was about to attack Baku, Churchill at once telegraphed to Holman:

As long as we are supplying vital munitions Denikin must respect our wishes in a matter of this kind. If he is in difficulties about his oil supply we will put pressure on the Georgians to assist him in this. Tell him from me that violent action as alleged will destroy my last few chances of getting him properly supported. . . .

Churchill ended his telegram by telling Holman: 'I have not yet despaired of getting a definite allied policy adopted against the Bol- sheviks. . . .' That same day, however, he learnt that the Poles were still advancing eastwards, deep into Denikin's 'territory'. Bitterly, he wrote at once to Lloyd George, Bonar Law and Curzon:

The last chances of saving the situation are passing away. No action what- ever is being taken by us to induce Poland to make her weight tell on the front, or to arrange matters between Denikin and Poland. Very soon there will be nothing left but Lenin and Trotsky, our vanished 100 millions, and mutual reproaches.

In the first week of December Kolchak's main defences collapsed, and the Bolsheviks took an enormous toll of his forces, capturing a million rounds of mostly British ammunition. While Kolchak fled eastwards into

Siberia, Denikin was being driven southwards towards the Black Sea. But on December 8 General Holman telegraphed to say that Denikin was about to launch a strong counter-attack, supported by six fresh cavalry divisions, which might restore his fortunes. For three days Churchill waited; but he heard no more, and on December 11 he telegraphed anxiously to General Holman: 'Has the important decisive battle of which you spoke yet taken place? Have the six cavalry divisions concentrated at and north of Valuiki been thrown in, or has Valuiki been abandoned without a struggle?' He was apprehensive, he said, 'that the effort has been made and has miscarried'. Churchill's fears were well-founded. Throughout the second week of December, Denikin's forces were in constant, and at times chaotic, retreat.

Unwilling to accept that Denikin was really defeated, Churchill continued to seek means to help or to encourage him. On December 11 he had sent him a thousand-word telegram of advice and exhortation. The 'very large quantities of military material' on their way to Russia should serve for three or four months, he said. After that, although there could be no more direct aid, Denikin could 'buy from me further munitions at the very low prices which they would fetch here if sold or broken up for scrap purposes'. Churchill urged Denikin to 'try to collect some commodities which would afford a basis of exchange, and thus avoid my making demands upon the Treasury which raise political issues of great difficulty'. The French, Churchill went on, had become more anti-Bolshevik, and might do more to help. 'Monsieur Clemenceau is in London today,' Churchill explained, 'and I am trying to secure an agreement between him and Mr Lloyd George in a concerted policy against the Bolsheviks.' But, Churchill warned, such a policy could only be a limited one, 'as both England and France are weary of war and deeply burdened by debt'. Denikin's principal aim, Churchill advised, should be agreements with Poland, Finland and the Baltic States. Churchill begged Denikin not to reject this advice:

Believe me, my friend, I understand your difficulties, and I pursue only one object, namely, the destruction of the Bolshevik tyrannies which menace the ignorant, thoughtless and tired-out nations.

Churchill went on to ask Denikin to take seriously the views and plans of Boris Savinkov,[1] who had pleaded for an anti-Bolshevik alliance between Denikin, Poland and the Baltic States:

[1] Boris Viktorovitch Savinkov, 1877–1925. Russian nihilist. Exiled to Siberia as a student, for revolutionary activity. Escaped to Switzerland. Returned to Russia, 1905; and took part in the assassination of Archduke Serge. Condemned to death. Escaped to Switzerland for a second time. Political commissar for the Provisional Government, charged with restoring

I am much impressed with Monsieur Savinkov, with whom I have had many long talks. He came with me to Mr Lloyd George and made a most powerful appeal on behalf of Russia, which affected the Prime Minister greatly. Do not let this man's past prejudice you against him. He has the root of the matter in him, and I think he is right in believing that Russia can only be reconstructed on the basis of Left-Centre, as we should say in parliamentary language.

Churchill ended his telegram to Denikin with words of encouragement. The Bolsheviks, he said, were 'anxious for peace . . . in spite of their military successes, they fear terribly the winter. For you, it seems to me, the main thing is to remain an effective power and consolidate yourself. . . .' But no such consolidation was possible. On December 12 the Bolsheviks entered Kharkov, and Denikin's forces fled in disorder towards the south. Churchill at once cancelled his telegram.

On the day that Kharkov fell, Lloyd George and Clemenceau met at 10 Downing Street to discuss Churchill's request for further help to Denikin. But the two Prime Ministers were unanimous in their conclusions, agreeing: 'Not to enter into any further commitments as to furnishing assistance to the anti-Bolshevik elements in Russia, whether in the form of troops, war material or financial aid. . . .' As a warning to Denikin, it was also agreed 'that a strong Poland was in the interests of the Entente Powers'.

When the Cabinet met later that day, Churchill protested that he was not in agreement 'with the policy as set forth . . . which involved the abandonment of the anti-Bolshevik forces in Russia which we had supported up till now'. He told his Cabinet colleagues that when he had 'paid his respects' to Clemenceau that morning, he had found him in favour of 'mediation between Poland and Denikin, with a view to the establishment of a common front from the Baltic to the Caspian', and also willing to support joint Anglo-French pressure on Estonia, 'not to enforce the disbandment of General Yudenitch's forces'. Churchill also wanted a public announcement that the anti-Bolshevik forces would be allowed to purchase British 'warlike stores' at their disposal value, and that the Russian war material captured by Germany between 1914 and 1917, and at present in Germany, would be 'handed over to the anti-Bolshevist forces in Russia'. But the Minutes of the Cabinet meeting

discipline on the eastern front, July 1917. Deputy Minister of War in the Provisional Government, August 1917. An opponent of Bolshevism, he joined General Alexeiev's forces on the Don, November 1917. Accredited Agent in Paris, first of Alexeiev, then of Kolchak and finally of Denikin, 1918–20. Organized an anti-Bolshevik army in Poland, 1920. Returned to the Soviet Union voluntarily, 1924. Tried, condemned to death, and given a commuted sentence of ten years in prison, 1924. Died in prison.

recorded that the 'general view of the Cabinet in regard to any announcement of Russian policy was that the less said the better. . . .'

On December 13, Denikin's forces were driven from Poltava. But still Churchill did not despair of a revival of anti-Bolshevik fortunes. On December 15, when General Briggs returned to London from a brief mission to South Russia, he reported to the War Office and gave his opinion of Denikin's prospects. 'He is *sure* of Denikin's ultimate victory,' Sir Henry Wilson noted in his diary. That same day, Churchill drafted a 1,400-word memorandum, 'Inter-Allied Russian Policy', in which he wrote bitterly of the failure of the Allies 'throughout the whole of the present year . . . to pursue any consistent policy against the Bolsheviks'. His memorandum ended:

It is a delusion to suppose that all this year we have been fighting the battles of the anti-Bolshevik Russians. On the contrary, they have been fighting ours; and this truth will become painfully apparent from the moment that they are exterminated and the Bolshevik armies are supreme over the whole vast territories of the Russian Empire.

Churchill's memorandum was printed for circulation to the Cabinet on December 15. But it was never circulated. On December 16 the Bolsheviks re-entered Kiev. Four days later Churchill and Sir Henry Wilson discussed the Russian situation with General Mannerheim, who had himself just returned from Warsaw. Mannerheim was convinced, Wilson wrote in his diary, 'that Denikin was going to be beaten out of the field'.

By the end of the year, all hopes of an anti-Bolshevik revival were at an end. On December 24, in Irkutsk, the Bolsheviks seized the main railway station while Admiral Kolchak held the town centre. Protected by Japanese troops, the Allied Missions retired at once to Vladivostok. But Kolchak was captured by the Czech Legion, and kept in Irkutsk as a prisoner. General Knox, Kolchak's principal ally, sailed from Vladivostok for England on December 26. That same day, General Holman telegraphed to the War Office from South Russia, asking, as a matter of urgency, for sufficient shipping to evacuate 800 members of the British Mission from Taganrog.

On December 27, a telegram from Denikin reached the War Office. 'Poor Denikin,' Sir Henry Wilson wrote in his diary on the following day, 'wires to Winston to say he *must* have Allied troops to help him even "if only 1 or 2 Corps". Denikin claims to be fighting our battles which is true.' But Churchill now accepted that the anti-Bolshevik cause was lost, writing to Wilson on December 31:

There seems to be very little doubt of the complete victory of the Bolsheviks in the near future. The Japanese will no doubt hold up to Lake Baikal, and I suppose a remnant of the Volunteer Army will maintain for some time a guerilla resistance in the mountains of the Kuban. Everywhere else we must look for a complete smash up. . . . As soon as Denikin's fate is settled, we ought to withdraw our troops from Batoum. There can be no use keeping this Brigade in this dangerously isolated position once Denikin has ceased to be an effective military factor. . . .

Churchill ended his letter to Wilson on a pessimistic note:

I am convinced that very great evils will come upon the world, and particularly upon Great Britain, as a consequence of the neglect and divided policies of this year on the part of the Allies and of ourselves. We shall find ourselves confronted almost immediately with a united Bolshevik Russia highly militarised and building itself up on victories easily won over opponents in disarray.

20

The Triumph of the Bolsheviks

SPEAKING to a large and enthusiastic audience at Sunderland on
2 January 1920, Churchill drew a lurid picture of life under the
Bolsheviks:

Was there ever a more awful spectacle in the whole history of the world
than is unfolded by the agony of Russia? This vast country, this mighty
branch of the human family, not only produced enough food for itself, but
before the war, it was one of the great granaries of the world, from which food
was exported to every country. It is now reduced to famine of the most
terrible kind, not because there is no food—there is plenty of food—but
because the theories of Lenin and Trotsky have fatally, and it may be finally,
ruptured the means of intercourse between man and man, between workman
and peasant, between town and country; because they have scattered the
systems of scientific communication by rail and river on which the life of great
cities depends; because they have raised class against class and race against
race in fratricidal war; because they have given vast regions where a little
while ago were smiling villages or prosperous townships back to the wolves
and the bears; because they have driven man from civilization to a barbarism
worse than the Stone Age, and have left him the most awful and pitiable
spectacle in human experience, devoured by vermin, racked by pestilence,
and deprived of hope.
  And this is progress, this is liberty. This is Utopia! What a monstrous
absurdity and perversion of the truth it is to represent the communistic
theory as a form of progress, when, at every step and at every stage, it is
simply marching back into the dark ages. . . .

  The purpose of Churchill's speech at Sunderland was to warn, not
only of the wickedness of Bolshevism abroad, but of the dangers of Bolshevism at home. In the course of his remarks he denounced 'the
would-be initiators in this country of the Bolsheviks', and spoke scathingly of the British Labour Party, which was, he declared, 'quite un-

365

fitted for the responsibility of Government'. As for actual 'Bolsheviks' in Britain, he said, 'if they had their way they would destroy the democratic Parliaments on which the liberties of free peoples depend, and would also shatter the economic and scientific apparatus by which alone the great millions of modern populations can be maintained alive'.

Churchill still hoped that some further Allied action might be co-ordinated to unite the states on Russia's borders. 'I apprehend,' he wrote to Sir Henry Wilson on January 5, 'that the alarm of Poland and the danger to Persia, Afghanistan etc may lead to an eleventh hour effort to take effective steps.' He instructed Wilson that the War Office should 'keep constantly surveying the possibilities of action in case we are empowered to move'.

On January 5 Churchill had read a telegram from Lord Curzon about the final collapse of Yudenitch's North Western Army; a telegram in which Curzon had stated that the Government 'welcome its disappearance'. Churchill was stung to an angry reply:

I should like to point out that this army, whatever its defects, has at practically no cost to the Allies beyond one or two shipments of munitions kept during the whole of the present year anything from thirty to fifty thousand Bolsheviks on the Petrograd front.

Had the North West Russian army not existed, these Bolshevik forces would have been transferred to the Southern Front against General Denikin and would have accelerated and aggravated his reverses. The disappearance of the North West Russian Army which you welcome will undoubtedly achieve that result now.

Considering that we have spent large sums of money and are employing 2,000 officers and men in aiding General Denikin, and that hitherto this policy has commanded your full approval, I do not understand how it is that you can at the same time consistently welcome the disappearance of a force which, although operating in a different geographical theatre, is in fact an integral part of the anti-Bolshevik Russian forces.

'It is just this idea of war in compartments,' Churchill continued, 'that has been fatal to the military situation. The whole front is one, and the withdrawal of pressure from any part increases the difficulties of every other part.' Churchill ended his letter on a caustic note. 'It seems to me,' he wrote, 'that you are likely in the near future to have further causes of satisfaction of this character afforded you.'

On January 8, General Holman sent Churchill a personal telegram from Ekaterinodar. In it he warned Churchill of the demoralization of Denikin's armies, which had, he said, been increased by Lloyd George's speeches advocating a settlement with the Bolsheviks. And he added:

Denikin has been badly served by his own Headquarters Staff who have failed to appreciate situation owing to incompetence and lack of personal acquaintance with front line conditions. Some Commanders have failed in their plain duty. Clever and persistent German and Bolshevik propaganda has derived immense advantage from Premier's speeches and there is grave danger of split amongst Denikin's officers. About 25 per cent are staunch gallant patriots and see danger to their country of German-aided Bolshevik regime. I believe that 75% are weary of fighting and of constant danger and discomfort surrounding their families and relatives, and believe only salvation liberation in understanding with Germany. . . .

Holman then appealed to Churchill for some concerted Allied action:

In my opinion the greatest danger of this situation is the uncertainty of the Allied policy which may entail a complete collapse, if immediate steps are not taken to guarantee to Denikin all necessary assistance until Bolshevists are beaten and to enable Denikin to communicate to all his officers an assurance that their families will not be abandoned by us if the Bolsheviks drive them to the sea. Moral support in present stagnation of nerves is imperative. . . .

At midday on January 9, General Holman telegraphed to Churchill again. He was, he insisted, 'optimistic' about Denikin's chances. But, he declared, 'ultimate result depends upon immediate adequate and determined action by allies'. Holman went on to warn Churchill that 'Russia will become a German colony sooner or later if we miss this golden opportunity of saving the best elements of a country of vast potentialities from a German-engineered regime of crime and brutality. . . .' The brutality did not affect only the Russians. On the day of Holman's telegram, a young British officer, Captain Frenchville,[1] disappeared, and, as his friend Captain Wood later recalled, 'was alleged to have been killed publicly—captured, then killed unpleasantly'. Wood remembered his reaction. 'One didn't want to get caught by the Reds,' he recalled, 'one didn't want to lay down one's life for Holy Russia.'

The news from the other anti-Bolshevik fronts held out no hope for an advance elsewhere. On January 10 General Yudenitch wrote direct to Churchill to say that, as a result of the armistice concluded at Dorpat between the Bolsheviks and Estonia, he could no longer maintain his forces on Estonian soil, and that it would therefore be impossible 'to establish a new Russian front-line in the Petrograd direction'. Yudenitch

[1] William Ralph Frenchville, 1895–1920. Son of William Frenchville, Professor of Mining at the Imperial College of Science and Technology, London. Educated at Rugby School. 2nd Lieutenant, Royal Engineers, November 1914: Lieutenant, 1916; Captain, 1917. Volunteered for service in South Russia, 1919. Captured by the Bolsheviks near Rostov, 9 January 1920. Presumed to have been killed by the Bolsheviks shortly after his capture.

offered to transfer his army to Denikin's front, and sought shipping for this purpose from Britain. 'During the whole time of our unequal fight with the Bolsheviks,' Yudenitch added, 'you proved to be a true and open friend to White Russia.' But Churchill had no means of persuading the Cabinet to use British shipping to transfer Yudenitch's troops from the Baltic to the Black Sea. 'I do not see what action is possible,' he noted at the bottom of Yudenitch's letter.

On January 11, the day after Yudenitch's appeal, Churchill learnt that yet another bastion of the intervention had fallen, for on that day the final evacuation of United States troops was begun from Vladivostok. It seemed to Churchill that General Holman's optimism had been misplaced. In a 'Personal & Secret' telegram to Holman on January 11, he set out his feelings with frankness, and advised Denikin to appeal for an armistice:

I do not see what possible chance there is of victory. Kolchak and Yudenitch are finished. The Esthonians will not fight any more. America does nothing. France is completely indifferent. The British Government will not do any more. Poland and the Letts are the only possible allies and Poland cannot move until the Spring. Even if Denikin can hold out for a few more months, what good can that do? The Bolsheviks will continue to concentrate their strength against him and a complete massacre will be the only result. They have now got corn & coal.

Meanwhile, there is no doubt the Bolshevik regime at the centre has greatly altered its character. Many respectable people are helping them. Many Czarist Generals and officers are commanding their armies. Constantine Benckendorff,[1] son of the late Russian Ambassador here, is the Bolshevik naval delegate at the Dorpat Conference. I have sure information that the Bolsheviks wish for peace, especially with England. If Denikin, in these circumstances, appealed for British mediation, I believe the Prime Minister would go a long way to try to save as much as possible from the wreck. The fighting might be stopped by an armistice and we might try by negotiation to secure the autonomy of Cossack regions.

I am only giving you my personal opinion as I have not consulted anyone else. You should not show this telegram to anyone, but without committing me or saying you have heard this from me you should now find out from Denikin what his view is. If a portion of Southern Russia were autonomous, there would at any rate be an asylum for the refugees, for the families of Denikin's army and for his soldiers. If Denikin contemplates any step of this

---

[1] Constantine Benckendorff. Elder son of Count Benckendorff (Russian Ambassador to London). An officer in the Russian Imperial Navy; Senior Naval Officer at Murmansk, 1916–17. Bolshevik Naval Delegate, Dorpat Conference, 1920. Disillusioned with the Bolsheviks, he emigrated to England, where he lived until his death. His younger brother Pierre had been killed in action early in the First World War.

kind, he had better take it before he gets too weak. Negotiations are sure to take a fortnight or three weeks, during which time he would have to hold his front or be broken up anyhow.

Churchill saw no hope in any further anti-Bolshevik initiative. His thoughts had turned towards the defensive. On January 11, he instructed Sir Henry Wilson to despatch Britain's 'final packet' of war supplies to Denikin. 'The Crimea will probably be the last place of refuge for all these miserable people,' Churchill wrote, 'and the least we can do is to help them to hold the Isthmus while some general arrangement is made about their fate. . . . Every day must be vital now.'

During the morning of January 14, Churchill and Wilson discussed Denikin's continued retreat. 'As a result of our talk,' Wilson recorded in his diary, 'I sent 2 telegrams over to Holman telling him to collect at ports & stand ready for embarkation. . . .' At noon, Churchill and Wilson described to the Cabinet the instructions which Holman had been given. 'Winston announces impending defeat of Denikin,' H. A. L. Fisher noted in his diary.

The Cabinet instructed Walter Long that 'not less than two warships' should be sent to Novorossisk 'to cover the embarkation of the British Mission, and any friendly refugees whom it might be possible to assist to escape'. It was also agreed to withdraw the British troops from Batum 'at the earliest moment'. In telegraphing a summary of the Cabinet's decisions to Lloyd George, Churchill warned that the collapse of Denikin 'will probably be followed, or perhaps preceded, by outbreaks of Bolshevism in Georgia', and he ended his telegram:

> You will doubtless appreciate the facts of the situation, which imply our complete loss of control and influence upon events throughout the Caucasus, on the Caspian Sea and in Trans-Caspia. If Denikin can continue to hold out and maintain any kind of fighting front, this result will be deferred and the Allied Powers may have further time to consider the situation. The withdrawals of the Mission and of the Batoum garrison will so far as possible be timed so as not to destroy what slender prospects yet remain.

On January 15, at Irkutsk, the Czech Legion handed Admiral Kolchak to the local Bolshevik authorities. All Siberia, from the Volga to Lake Baikal, was now under Bolshevik control. Only in eastern Siberia, around Vladivostok, were anti-Bolshevik Russians and Japanese troops still in control. But they no longer possessed any offensive power. In Russian Central Asia, the Bolsheviks had, by mid-February, estab-

lished their rule from Tashkent to Ashkabad, and from the Urals to the
Aral Sea. With both the Ural and Orenburg Cossacks in final retreat,
all Trans-Caspia was under Lenin's authority.

Fear of Bolshevik movements inside Britain itself roused the alarm of
several Ministers. At a meeting of the Transport sub-committee of the
Cabinet on January 15 all the Ministers present spoke of the imminent
danger of strikes and civil violence. Sir Eric Geddes took the chair.
Walter Long, Churchill, Sir Robert Horne, George Roberts and Sir
Joseph Maclay were among those Ministers present. 'An amazing meeting,' Sir Henry Wilson recorded in his diary. 'One after another got up
& said that we were going to have the Triple Red Revolution strike. . . .
It is a truly terrifying state of affairs, & not one of them except Walter
Long & Winston seemed prepared to put up a fight.' Later that day he
noted in his diary: 'Frankie Lloyd[1] came to see me to report that there
is a considerable amount of revolutionary talk going on in the Bde of
Guards.'

On January 15, in view of the fears expressed by his Ministers, Lloyd
George summoned them and their senior advisers to Paris. At 8.20 that
evening Churchill left Waterloo by train. With him were Walter Long,
Sir Henry Wilson and Sir David Beatty. On the following day Hankey
wrote from Paris to Thomas Jones:

The Ministers who have come over here seem to have 'the wind-up' to the
most extraordinary extent about the industrial situation. CIGS also is positively in a state of dreadful nerves on the subject. Churchill is the only one
who is sane on the subject. . . .

From a meeting yesterday evening I came away with my head fairly
reeling. I felt I had been in Bedlam. Red revolution and blood and war at
home and abroad!

It seems to be Horne who has upset them all.

At five o'clock on the afternoon of January 16 Lloyd George summoned a Cabinet meeting in a Paris Hotel. Six ministers were present:
Bonar Law, Curzon, Birkenhead, Montagu, Long and Churchill. The
discussion opened with a survey by Sir Henry Wilson of 'the state of
unrest in England'. Walter Long then described the previous day's

[1] Francis Lloyd, 1853–1926. Entered the Army, 1874. Served in the Sudan campaigns of
1885 and 1898, and in South Africa, 1900–2, where he was severely wounded. Brigadier-
General Commanding the 1st Guards Brigade, 1904–8. Major-General, 1909. Knighted,
1911. Commanded London District, 1913–19. Lieutenant-General, 1917.

meeting of ministers in London, when Churchill had stressed that he could not provide troops to protect factories during a major strike.

The discussion then turned to Russia. Curzon argued strongly in favour of British troops holding Batum and Baku. Montagu supported Curzon. Strong words followed, as Wilson recorded:

> Winston very heated at idea of not supporting Denikin. Curzon argued for holding the line Batum–Baku & the Caspian. Beatty said if he could get Denikin's ships he could hold the Caspian with 1,200 sailors, but of course must have a secure base at Batoum.
> Montagu agreed with Winston, LG & BL with Curzon, when I weighed in & said I was not prepared to hold a passive line: Batoum–Baku with less than 2 Divs with a reinforcing Div at C'ple or Egypt. This completely wrecked Curzon's ridiculous project.
> We broke up—nothing settled.

At midnight on January 16, before going to bed, Wilson had a long talk with Lloyd George about Russia, recording in his diary: 'He thinks Winston has gone mad. . . .' A week later, Lloyd George told Lord Riddell:[1] 'While we were in Paris Winston was very excited about Russia. I had to handle him very firmly. He was most insistent and prepared to sacrifice both men and money.'

At lunch on January 17, Churchill discussed Russia with Lloyd George. It was Lloyd George's fifty-seventh birthday, and Frances Stevenson, who was present, recorded the conversation in her diary:

> A most amusing meal, at which Winston waxed very eloquent on the subject of the old world & the new, taking arms in defence of the former. He has arrived simply *raving* because of the decision of the Peace Conference with regard to trading with Russia, which absolutely & finally ruins his hopes of a possible war in the East. At times he became almost like a madman. Sir George Riddell happened to ask him who it was at the War Office that has issued a communiqué of an alarmist character, bidding people prepare for a new war. Winston glared at him, & almost shouted 'You are trying to make mischief'. Someone happily turned the conversation to other matters or it looked as though there might have been bloodshed.

That afternoon Sir Henry Wilson recorded in his diary: 'Then a talk with Winston who is in very uncertain mood & is balancing about resigning.' At five o'clock he and Churchill went to see Lloyd George, to discuss Russia once more, but the Prime Minister, having played a round of golf after luncheon, was asleep.

That evening Churchill and Lloyd George were among Edwin

---

[1] Sir George Riddell had been created Baron Riddell on 1 January 1920.

Montagu's guests at Ciro's. Churchill again raised the spectre of Bolshevism triumphant. 'Winston still raving on the subject of the Bolsheviks,' Frances Stevenson noted in her diary, '& ragging D about the New World. "Don't you make any mistake," he said to D. "You're not going to get your new world. The old world is a good enough place for me, & there's life in the old dog yet. It's going to sit up & wag its tail." ' Lloyd George replied that Churchill was now 'the only remaining specimen of a real Tory'.

At five o'clock on the afternoon of January 18 Lloyd George summoned his second Paris Cabinet. Sir Robert Horne had arrived, to join the Ministers already in the city. The Caucasus was the first item on the agenda. Walter Long argued strongly in favour of Britain taking over the naval control of the Caspian, and Sir David Beatty spoke of the value to Britain of the oilfields of Baku. Lord Curzon then pressed for the military occupation, by British troops, of the Batum–Baku line. But Sir Henry Wilson repeated that none of the States on Russia's border, whether on the west or south, would make reliable allies, and declared that only a full scale British occupation, entirely self-reliant, could be effective. For this, he argued, there were not sufficient troops available. Churchill gave his support to Marshal Foch's plan for the combination of all the States on Russia's western border in a *cordon sanitaire*, sealing off the Bolsheviks from the rest of Europe. Such a scheme depended upon six States, Finland, Estonia, Latvia, Lithuania, Poland and Rumania, working in harmony. The Poles were keen on it; but the Estonians were already engaged in peace negotiations with Moscow.

Lloyd George deprecated an active British policy in the Caucasus, telling his Ministers, as Sir Henry Wilson recorded, 'that in his opinion if we leave Lenin alone he will not attack Georgia or Azerbaijan or Poland or Roumania or anywhere'. Nor did Churchill's plan of a *cordon sanitaire* appeal to him. 'There is not the least doubt,' Wilson noted, 'that if Lenin does attack Poland she won't get any assistance from us. . . .'

The Allied Supreme Council met at the Quai D'Orsay at half past ten on the morning of Monday January 19. Clemenceau was in the Chair; Lloyd George, Curzon, Walter Long and Churchill represented Britain; the Italian Prime Minister, Signor Nitti,[1] was also present. The sole

---

[1] Francesco Saverio Nitti, 1868–1952. Italian journalist and political economist. Minister of Agriculture, Industry and Commerce, 1911–14; a Minister at the Treasury, 1917–19. Prime Minister, June 1919–June 1920. His son was a prisoner-of-war in Germany, 1917–18; he himself was arrested by the Germans, August 1943, and deported to Germany, 1943–5. Founded the Unione Democratica Nazionale, 1946. Author of *Peaceless Europe* (1922) and *The Decadence of Europe* (1923).

topic was whether or not the Allies should intervene directly in the Caucasus. To his chagrin, Sir Henry Wilson's plea against such a plan did not influence the politicians, or 'frocks', as he recorded in his diary:

I was asked my opinion about arming Georgia & Azerbaijan. I said I was wholly opposed to it unless we had command of the Caspian, & that as command of the Caspian meant the employment of 2 Div^s & was therefore impossible I was opposed to arming these people, since if Denikin fell down the Bolsheviks would certainly take Baku & all the arms would become a present to the Bolsheviks. Foch agreed.

The frocks then sent for the Georgian & Azerbaijanese representatives who told the Frocks the same ridiculous cock & bull stories they had told me & Beatty the day before yesterday, &, for LG's benefit & Winston's anger they added that they feared & hated Denikin who was a Tsarist.

After the dagos had withdrawn Foch laid out his plans for trying to get a combination of all the states from Finland to Odessa which was my plan of a year ago but which in my opinion is no longer practical. We (military & naval gentlemen) were then dismissed, & the Frocks decided to arm, equip & feed the Georgians, Azerbaijanese & Armenians & Foch & I are to advise on the amount etc. . . .

Lloyd George convened his third Paris Cabinet in his hotel room at half past five that afternoon. The decision of the Allied Supreme Council, to arm and feed the Caucasian republics, was approved. Churchill was worried that this would adversely affect Denikin, as the official notes of the meeting recorded:

Mr Churchill asked if we were going to take away from Denikin the war material promised to him and to hand it over to the Caucasian States while Denikin was still fighting. He himself did not oppose the new policy in view of the pass to which things had come, but he asked for fair treatment to Denikin so long as he maintained his front.

The Prime Minister agreed, so long as the General Staff was convinced that Denikin was putting up a real fight.

As soon as the Cabinet was over, Lloyd George and his Ministers hurried to the Quai d'Orsay, for a further meeting of the Allied Supreme Council. Clemenceau again presided, but for the last time, as he was being superseded as Prime Minister by Alexandre Millerand,[1] who was also present at the meeting. It was agreed to ask the Georgians, Armen-

---

[1] Alexandre Millerand, 1859–1943. Elected to the French Chamber of Deputies as a Radical Socialist, 1885. Minister of War, January 1912–January 1913; and again from January 1914 to October 1915. He resigned following accusations that he had failed to find sufficient heavy artillery. Commissar-General for Alsace and Lorraine, 1919–20. Minister for Foreign Affairs, January 1920. Prime Minister, 1920. President of the Republic, 1920–4.

ians and Azerbaijanis what arms and equipment they would need to protect themselves against Bolshevik attack.

Churchill was isolated and angry. But he accepted his defeat. On January 19 he said to Lloyd George, as Frances Stevenson recalled on the following day:

Well, you have downed me & my policy, but I can't help admiring you for the way you have gone about it. Your strategy is masterly. You saw me going in one direction & you blocked the way. I tried another & found it blocked too. You have gone on consistently, never varying, but always with the same fixed idea. I fought you, & you have beaten me, yet I cannot help admiring you for it.

'The worst feature of Winston,' Lloyd George told Frances Stevenson, 'is his vanity! Everything that he does points to one thing—self.' On the following day Churchill wrote to his wife:

Needless to say no policy of any scope & clearness has been settled in regard to Russia: & the present state of drift is to continue. The dangers & losses of this will be acutely felt in coming months & will much reflect on the credit of the Government. . . .

Churchill ended his letter on a personal note:

Darling one, today I am telephoning to you to ask what you wd like me to bring you back from Paris. Is there anything you want for yr trousseau? . . .

My sweet Clemmie, I wd so much rather have spent these days in the basket instead of loafing around here. I look forward vy much indeed to getting home. You are vy good to me & put up with many shortcomings on the part of yr nevertheless always devoted & loving

W

On January 22 there was a strong attack on the intervention in the *British Weekly*, a paper sympathetic to Lloyd George. Churchill believed the article was 'vy damaging & unfair', as he wrote to Lloyd George six days later. But Lloyd George dissuaded him from sending a strongly worded reply. In the article, the *British Weekly* declared:

It has been a tolerably open secret that for many months the Prime Minister has been in conflict with Mr Winston Churchill on the subject of our duty and obligations to Russia in her present conflict. Up to a certain point Mr Churchill was the winner. He was allowed to spend a hundred millions, in one way or another, and to expose British troops to perils which in many cases led to death or permanent disablement.

Churchill decided to defend his views publicly. On Sunday January 25, he published a full page article in the *Illustrated Sunday Herald*, entitled 'The Red Fever'. In it he wrote:

The Bolshevist is not an idealist who is content to promote his cause by argument or example. At the first favourable opportunity he helps it forward by the bullet or the bomb. The essence of Bolshevism as opposed to many other forms of visionary political thought, is that it can only be propagated and maintained by violence.

No contempt has equalled that with which Lenin has saluted every group of philosophical Socialists, who base their hopes of establishing Utopia upon the processes of reason, free speech and fair play. . . .

Of Lenin, Churchill wrote: 'He had a conscious purpose. He has pursued it all his life; and it is plainly diabolical.' The lesson to be drawn, he went on, was a clear one: 'All tyrants are the enemies of the human race. All tyrannies should be overthrown.'

Churchill went on to declare that the 'disdain' which Lenin and Trotsky felt for the masses of Russia was far greater than that felt by any of the Tsars. Both the United States and the Swiss Government had expelled the Bolsheviks in their midst; this, Churchill believed, was a measure of the utmost prudence. If Bolsheviks were allowed to 'circulate freely' among ordinary citizens, there was a danger, under certain conditions of 'an outbreak of pestilence more destructive of human life to the Black Death or the Spotted Typhus'.

Churchill continued with a specific, if caustic, proposal:

Instead of wrecking a score of great States and squandering in a single convulsion the capital which mankind has acquired in long, blind ages of slow improvement, the Bolsheviks should be collected and segregated into a country—we beg their pardon, into an area of the earth's surface—which they can really call their own.

In some region sufficiently wide to accommodate their numbers, and sufficiently productive to support their existence, the devotees of Jacobinism (or Bolshevism as it is now called) should be given their chance to put their theories into the fullest application *against one another*. There, with no peasants or workmen to mislead or oppress, with no middle classes to starve, or princes to butcher, with no toiling millions to exploit, and with no glittering civilisation to pillage, the apostles of Lenin and Liebknecht, the successors of Robespierre and Marat, might enjoy themselves among the massacres of a bloodier September and the rigours of an unnatural equality. . . .

On January 29 the Cabinet met to discuss a proposal by Sir Halford Mackinder[1] for a final British effort to bring together all the anti-

---

[1] Halford John Mackinder, 1861–1947. Reader in Geography, Oxford University, 1887–1905. Principal of University College Reading, 1892–1903. Made the first ascent of Mount Kenya, 1899. Director of the London School of Economics, 1903–8. Conservative MP, 1910–22. Active in organizing recruiting in Scotland, 1914–18. British High Commissioner for South Russia, 1919–20. Knighted, 1920. Chairman of the Imperial Shipping Committee, 1920–45.

Bolshevik forces in Russia, Poland, the Caucasus and the Baltic. General Milne believed that Britain should take an active part in any such plan, and recommended landing two battalions of British troops at Novorossisk, and further battalions at Odessa and in the Crimea. But the Cabinet had no intention of following such advice. Its conclusions were clear. Intervention would not be started up again. The Minutes recorded:

(a) There can be no question of making active war on the Bolsheviks, for the reason that we have neither the men, the money, nor the credit, and public opinion is altogether opposed to such a course.
(b) There can be no question of entering into Peace negotiations with the Bolsheviks until they have demonstrated their capacity to conduct an orderly, decent administration in their own country and their intention not to interfere, by propaganda or otherwise, in the affairs of their neighbours, nor until they can show that they represent the governing authority of the areas for which they claim to speak. . . .
(c) The Border States surrounding Russia must themselves take the full responsibility for deciding as between peace and war. Not the slightest encouragement, however, should be given them to pursue the policy of war, because if we were to give that advice we should incur responsibilities which we could not discharge.

The Cabinet then 'approved' Lloyd George's statement of January 25 to the Polish Government, that Britain could give no military aid to Poland for the purpose of an attack on Russia. The final Cabinet conclusion set a clear limit to future British aid. 'We should continue our policy of giving material support,' it read, 'to enable the Border States to defend themselves if attacked by the Bolsheviks.' But in reply to General Milne's request for British military landings, the Cabinet of January 29 specifically concluded: 'that no British troops should be moved to defend any Russian ports or territory'.

On February 3 the Cabinet discussed what the British attitude should be towards General Denikin, and his rapidly disintegrating army. It was decided to warn Denikin that Britain could no longer support any anti-Bolshevik combination. As soon as the Cabinet was over Churchill telegraphed to General Holman:

It is necessary that you should put the facts of the situation plainly before General Denikin and you are authorised, if you think fit, to show him this telegram.
I cannot hold out any expectation that the British Government will give any further aid beyond what has been already promised in the final packet, neither will they use their influence to make an aggressive combination

between the Poles, Baltic States, Finland, etc., with Denikin against Soviet Russia. Their reason is that they do not possess the resources in men or money sufficient to carry any such enterprise to success, and they do not wish to encourage others without having the power to sustain them. . . .

Denikin is fighting for the control of Russia. We cannot undertake to make further exertions in support of this last objective, although we sympathise with it. We do not think it is in our power to achieve it in the immediate future.

The question which must now be faced is how to save as much as possible from the wreck and how to find some area in which the forces of Denikin and the refugees dependent upon him can live. . . .

Churchill advised a compromise whereby the Cossack, Crimean and Odessa regions should 'proclaim their independence', and then appeal for aid to the Great Powers. This would test the Bolshevik declaration that they were ready to respect the frontiers 'of any independent state'. If they then invaded these States, it would place them, he wrote, 'at an immense disadvantage with the British democracy'. But Churchill's main mood was one of gloomy realism, as his telegram made clear.

. . . if Denikin is determined to fight on, I will do nothing to minimise his chances. But it seems to me—as I telegraphed to you over two months ago—that no solution can be so bad as driving into the sea and completely wiping out all those loyal elements in Russian national life which are embodied in the Volunteer, Don and Caucasian Armies.

In his message to Denikin, Churchill declared:

Great changes are taking place in the character and organisation of the Bolshevik Government. In spite of the hellish wickedness in which it was founded and has been developed, it nevertheless represents a force of order: the men at the head are no longer merely revolutionaries but persons who having seized power are anxious to retain it and enjoy it for a time. They are believed earnestly to desire peace, fearing no doubt if war continues to be devoured later on by their own armies. A period of peace coupled with commercial reorganisation may well prepare the way for the unity of Russia through a political evolution.

Shortly before dawn on February 7, Admiral Kolchak was taken from his prison cell at Irkutsk by the Bolsheviks, and shot on the bank of a nearby river. The official Soviet account of his execution recorded that he had borne himself 'like an Englishman'. His body was pushed down the river bank, and disappeared under the ice. That same day, the Bolsheviks entered Odessa in triumph, and established themselves once more on the Black Sea coast. Thousands of Denikin's followers were shot. The remnant escaped by sea to the Crimea.

The Cabinet met on February 9. 'Churchill bumbles about Russia,' H. A. L. Fisher noted in his diary. And Thomas Jones wrote in his diary:

At the Cabinet this morning the PM gave Winston a dressing down about Russia. Winston had been complaining that we had no policy. This the PM described as ridiculous. Our policy was to try to escape the results of the evil policy which Winston had persuaded the Cabinet to adopt.

21

'Everybody Wishing to Make Their Peace'

A T the opening of Parliament on 10 February 1920 Lloyd George made a strong appeal for peace and trade with the Bolsheviks. It was true, he said, that 'the horrors of Bolshevism have revolted the consciences of mankind', and that the 'rapine and plunder which are essential parts of their policy' were condemned in 'every civilised land'. It was equally true that Bolshevism was not a democracy, and that if Russia could have been 'restored' by an anti-Bolshevik regime, all democratic countries in the world would have preferred it. But, he continued, it had become 'perfectly clear now to every unprejudiced observer that you cannot crush Bolshevism by force of arms'.

Lloyd George then referred to the solution which Churchill had so strongly pressed upon him in the past:

Take another suggestion which has been put forward—that you should organise an advancing ring of fire—Finland, the Baltic States, Poland, Rumania, Denikin's Forces and the Japanese—encircle Soviet Russia, and march right into it and scorch Bolshevism out. The first question I put there is this. Is there anyone here or anywhere else who will do it? Will Finland do it? General Mannerheim may be a very influential man, but he is not Finland. The Baltic States are making peace. Rumania has as much as she can do to watch her Hungarian frontier. The Japanese certainly will not advance.

Lloyd George insisted that there was no Bolshevik threat to Poland, to Central Europe or to the Middle East; all areas in which Churchill feared Bolshevik activity. 'It is no use preparing for dangers that are not imminent,' he declared. But there were, he continued, benefits to be gained by a friendly policy: 'Trade, in my opinion, will bring an end to the ferocity, the rapine, and the crudities of Bolshevism surer than any

379

other method. Europe needs what Russia can give. . . . The corn bins of Russia are bulging with grain. . . .' Europe needed Russian grain, he declared. But as long as 'contending armies roll across the borders', the grain would not come. 'When people are hungry,' he insisted, 'you cannot refuse to buy corn in Egypt because there is a Pharoah on the throne.' It was not Bolshevism that frightened him, he said. 'The dangers are not in Russia, but here at home. . . . We must fight anarchy with abundance.'

In South Russia, British aid was being brought to an end. On February 13, on Trenchard's insistence, a telegram was sent to General Holman informing him that the Royal Air Force Mission in South Russia was to be withdrawn. Three days later Holman himself sent a stern note to Denikin, pointing out that if he had not given orders to stop the use of British coal to enable his warships 'to bombard Georgian ports and troops', it would have 'compelled the British Government to withdraw all support from you at once'.

'The conviction is gaining ground daily in Europe,' Holman added, 'that the Soviet Government is developing the sense of the responsibilities of a Government and there is a danger that those who do not understand or believe in the perpetration of the hellish crimes of the Bolsheviks may force their governments into negotiations with these criminals.'

Churchill could do no more than watch over the collapse of the anti-Bolsheviks, and seek to prolong Denikin's resistance, despite the continual retreat. When he learnt that Trenchard had ordered the Royal Air Force detachment to leave South Russia he wrote to Sir Henry Wilson, on February 21: 'I must be sure we do not pull Denikin down.'

While in Paris on February 24, Lloyd George persuaded the French and Italian Prime Ministers, Millerand and Nitti, to make a public statement on Russia along the lines of his own evolving policy. On the following day, the Supreme Allied Council announced that the Allied Powers could no longer accept the responsibility of advising the border states 'to continue war which may be injurious to their own interests. Still less would they advise them to adopt a policy of aggression towards Russia.' In their next paragraph the Allies set out their new policy of conciliation with the Bolsheviks. 'Commerce between Russia and the rest of Europe,' they declared, 'which is so essential for the improvement of the economic conditions, not only in Russia, but in the rest of the world, will be encouraged to the utmost degree possible without relaxation of the attitude described above.'

The decision of the Supreme Allied Council was announced in Parlia-

ment on the morning of February 25. Churchill had to communicate it
to Denikin, whose fate it sealed. At two o'clock on the afternoon of
February 25 his telegram was despatched from the War Office to
General Holman. The first part of the telegram consisted of the text of
the Allied declaration. This was followed by a warning from Churchill
that the announcement 'would exclude territories held by Denikin from
the list of States whose independence or *de facto* existence has been
recognized by the Allied Powers'. That is to say, the Allies would not
consider Denikin eligible for the Allied promise to defend border states
against a Bolshevik attack. 'If everyone else makes peace,' Churchill
continued—and this was the advice now given them by the Allies—
'surely Denikin must be crushed, and the territories occupied conquered.'

In his telegram, Churchill gave Denikin his advice on how to try to
avoid the full consequences of the Allied decision, suggesting that: 'a
declaration of independence on the part of the Crimea, Don, Kuban
and Terek Cossack territories now in Denikin's control would seem to
place these territories in the same position as Esthonia, Georgia, Azerbaijan etc.' His telegram continued: 'Surely Denikin would be well
advised now to secure the independence of these Cossack States which
alone can afford an asylum for him and his armies.'

Nothing came of Churchill's proposal. On February 28, the Red
Army entered Stavropol, the principal town of the northern Caucasus,
and an important grain centre.

The War Office were determined to withdraw the British Mission
from South Russia as quickly as possible. 'Repugnant as it is to abandon
a brave man in trouble,' General Radcliffe wrote to Henry Wilson on
March 1, 'I feel that we ought to withdraw the whole of Holman's
mission now before the situation gets even worse.' Henry Wilson approved Radcliffe's proposal, writing to Churchill that same day for
permission to withdraw the whole of Holman's mission to Constantinople. 'I feel very strongly,' he wrote, 'that loyalty to our men should
over-ride all sentimental feelings for the Russian.' Wilson wanted
General Milne to be given overall command of Holman's mission, in
order to organize the withdrawal as quickly and efficiently as possible.
Churchill noted on Wilson's letter: 'Do proceed.' It was his sole comment. On March 5 he telegraphed personally to General Holman: 'You
have shown throughout this difficult and melancholy task the greatest
courage and loyalty. . . .'

Churchill tried to take one final initiative to sustain the anti-Bolshevik
cause. The idea was not his own, but came from Germany. The British

occupation authorities reported from Berlin that General Ludendorff[1] was anxious to have a private talk with Churchill, to discuss the dangers of Bolshevism. When Ludendorff's proposal was raised in Cabinet, the reaction was hostile. H. A. L. Fisher wrote to Lloyd George on March 13:

I am alarmed by the suggestion that Winston should meet Ludendorff (*incognito*) in Germany for the triple purpose of
1. Establishing a military dictatorship in Germany.
2. Organizing an Anglo-German army against Russia.
3. Tearing up the Peace settlement with regard to Poland.
Really these Huns are very impudent.

Five days later Churchill reflected on the German approach in a minute to General Harington. 'In my view,' he wrote, 'the objective wh we shd pursue at the present time is the building up of a strong but peaceful Germany wh will not attack our French allies, but will at the same time act as a moral bulwark against the Bolshevism of Russia.' On every foreign policy question, Churchill added—Russia, Germany and Turkey—'the advice of the WO throughout the last 15 months has constantly tended to that recovery, stability & tranquilisation of Europe, wh wd enable Britain to enjoy the fruits of victory. It is a pity it has fallen on deaf ears.'

Nothing more was heard of the German scheme. Churchill continued to supervise, without interruption, the withdrawal of the British Mission from Russia. He saw no future for Denikin or his army, writing to General Harington on March 15: 'We ought to make Denikin retire forthwith to the Crimea (if it still holds out), & there he & his people can find asylum till a convention has been made with the Bolsheviks about them.'

On March 17 the Bolsheviks drove Denikin from Ekaterinodar, the centre of the Kuban, and principal town of the Kuban Cossacks, whose chances of maintaining their independence Churchill had written of only three weeks before. Further to the east, the Bolshevik forces advanced towards the town of Grozny, the centre of a rich oil region, and of the Terek Cossacks, whose independence Churchill had also hoped would be maintained. On March 18 Churchill wrote to Lloyd

[1] Erich von Ludendorff, 1865–1937. Entered the Prussian Army, 1883. Served on the German General Staff, 1894–1913. Quartermaster General of the 2nd Army, August 1914. In command of the 14th Brigade of Infantry, which captured Liège. Chief of Staff to Hindenburg in East Prussia, 1914–15; First Quartermaster General of the German armies, 1916–18. Fled to Sweden, November 1918. Returned to Germany, April 1919. Joined Hitler's unsuccessful attempt to seize power in Munich, November 1923. Entered the Reichstag as a National Socialist, 1924.

George, asking if he could take 'a short holiday in the South of France', adding, 'I have need of a change'. Lloyd George agreed to let him go.

During the fourth week of March, while still in London, Churchill gave instructions to General Holman to help Denikin's army escape from Novorossisk to the Crimea. But in a telegram to Holman on March 22, he asked the General to 'make it clear' to Denikin 'that we cannot undertake to do rear-guard for his fighting men'. On March 23, Churchill read General Rawlinson's report of the efforts made in North Russia by the anti-Bolsheviks, after the British force had withdrawn. He asked that the report should be amended, so that critical references to General Miller's refusal to withdraw from Archangel to Murmansk should have 'at least . . . a neutral tint'. And he added: 'I think they did all that men could do, holding on month after month with no hope in the world and everybody wishing to make their peace with the Bolsheviks.'

On March 27 the last of Denikin's troops were evacuated from Novorossisk. Later that day the Bolsheviks entered the town, seizing a vast quantity of British stores. Thus most of Britain's 'final packet' to Denikin became the property of those whose defeat it was intended to bring about.[1]

Over two thousand British officers and men had served on the British Mission in South Russia during 1919 and in the first three months of 1920. Only six members of the Mission had been killed in action, of whom at least two had died at the hands of the Bolsheviks after they had been captured. Twenty-nine members of the Mission died of disease and nine had been killed accidentally; a total of deaths from all causes of forty-four. In North Russia 194 British troops had been killed in action; in the Baltic 129; in South Russia 6: a total in all theatres of 329.

On March 29, the War Office received a telegram from General Milne, reporting that all Holman's Mission had been safely shipped from Novorossisk, and that Denikin had reached the Crimea with more than 35,000 troops. That evening Sir Henry Wilson wrote in his diary:

So ends in practical disaster another of Winston's military attempts. Antwerp, Dardanelles, Denikin. His judgement is always at fault, & he is hopeless when in power.

---

[1] These stores included over 80 heavy guns, 25 aeroplane engines and a large collection of aeroplane parts; over a million pairs of socks, vast quantities of winter clothing, 85,000 pairs of trousers, 22,000 horse shoes and an enormous quantity of miscellaneous stores. The last ship bearing these stores to Novorossisk had only completed discharging its cargo at the end of December, three months earlier.

22

'The Hairy Paw of the Baboon'

O N 24 March 1920 Churchill left London for his holiday in
France. Accompanied by General Rawlinson, he planned to
spend two weeks on the Duke of Westminster's estate at Mimizan, south
of Bordeaux. During the Channel crossing, he sent Lloyd George his
thoughts on the European situation:

Private & Secret
My dear PM,

I write this as I am crossing the Channel to tell you what is in my mind.

Since the armistice my policy wd have been 'Peace with the German
people, war on the Bolshevik tyranny'. Willingly or unavoidably, you have
followed something vy near the reverse. Knowing the difficulties, & also yr
great skill & personal force—so much greater than mine—I do not judge yr
policy & action as if I cd have done better, or as if anyone cd have done
better. But we are now face to face with the results. They are terrible. We
may well be within measurable distance of universal collapse & anarchy
throughout Europe & Asia. Russia has gone into ruin. But Germany may
perhaps still be saved. I have felt with a great sense of relief that we may be
able to think & act together in harmony abt Germany: That you are inclined
to make an effort to rescue Germany from her frightful fate—wh if it over-
takes her may well overtake others. If so, time is short & action must be
simple. You ought to tell France that we will make a defensive alliance with
her against Germany if *and only if* she entirely alters her treatment of Germany
& loyally accepts a British policy of help & friendship towards Germany.
Next you shd send a great man to Berlin to help consolidate the anti-
Sparticist anti-Ludendorff elements into a strong left centre block. For this
task you have two levers 1. Food & credit, wh must be generously accorded
in spite of our own difficulties (wh otherwise will worsen) 2ndly Early revision
of the Peace Treaty by a Conference to wh New Germany shall be invited as
an equal partner in the rebuilding of Europe. Using these levers it ought to be
possible to rally all that is good & stable in the German nation to their own

redemption & to the salvation of Europe. I pray that we may not be 'too late'.

Surely this is a matter far more worth while taking yr political life in yr hands for than our party combinations at home, important tho' they be. Surely also it is a matter wh once on the move wd dominate the whole world situation at home & abroad. My suggestion involves open resolute action by Britain under yr guidance, & if necessary *independent* action. In such a course I wd gladly at yr side face political misfortune. But I believe there wd be no misfortune, & that for a few months longer Britain still holds the title-deeds of Europe.

As part of such a policy I shd be prepared to make peace with Soviet Russia on the best terms available to appease the general situation, while safe-guarding us from being poisoned by them. I do not of course believe that any real harmony is possible between Bolshevism & present civilisation. But in view of the existing facts a cessation of arms & a promotion of material prosperity are inevitable: & we must trust for better or for worse to peaceful influences to bring about the disappearance of this awful tyranny & peril. . . .

I have felt bound to write you these convictions of mine derived from a study of all the information at our disposal. Do not take them in ill part. I am most sincerely desirous of continuing to work with you. I am all with you in our home affairs. My interests as well as my inclinations march with yours, & in addition there is our long friendship wh I so greatly value.

Yours ever sincerely
WSC

Churchill reached Paris on March 25. That afternoon he had a long talk with the French Minister of War, André Lefevre.[1] On the following day he sent his wife an account of their conversation:

His principal demand was to march into Germany and seize Frankfurt and Darmstadt and hold them as further guarantees; for charbon, an indemnity, etc. I explained to him that we thought in England that the French ought to try now to live on the fruits of their own labours for a bit—dig their own coal or buy it from others; tax themselves in the same sort of way as the English and the Americans had done; do a little hard work like the Belgians were doing, and so on. And I warned him very plainly that we would have nothing to do with a policy of crushing Germany. He seemed a very foolish inexperienced man; spoke with great scorn of Clemenceau, as much as to say how much better he was doing—I don't think!

That night Churchill and Rawlinson set off by train to Bordeaux. General Spears had persuaded the French War Office to attach a special sleeping car to the end of the train. 'But,' Churchill told his wife, 'it proved a snare, for there were no blankets for the bed and only mat-

---

[1] André Joseph Lefevre, 1864–1929. Vice-President of the Paris Town Council before 1914. Member of the Chamber of Deputies, 1919–24. Minister of War, January–December 1920.

tress covers. We therefore had to pass the night in our clothes, which made me furious till at last I got to sleep.'

Churchill and Rawlinson reached Mimizan on the morning of March 26. During the day they hunted for more than five hours, in search of wild boar, returning to Mimizan in time for Churchill to paint a picture. 'There are some lovely views here,' Churchill wrote to his wife, 'now that the gorse is out, the whole of these dark pine-woods have an underwing of the most brilliant yellow. . . .' On March 27 he sent his wife a full account of the second day of his holiday:

The General and I are entirely alone here and we lead a very simple life divided entirely between riding, painting and eating! The weather to-day has been delicious: although it threatened to blow in the morning—and was in fact blowing hard on the sea front—the afternoon was gentle and glorious.

As the hounds will not be fit for hunting till Monday, we went out for a long ride this morning down to the sea; over two hours at a pretty good pace. I had a splendid horse—a different one to the one I hunted yesterday: an enormous black English hunter with a head and shoulder which made you feel as if you were on the bridge of a battle-cruiser. He climbed up and down these extraordinary banks—which you will remember—as if they were nothing. It is wonderful the places that horses can negotiate. You ride up and down the most astonishing precipices of sand.

Three quarters of an hour's ride brought us to the sea. Most lovely sands are spread for miles. There was, as is usual here, a fine display of breakers; seven or eight great walls of foam advancing, one on top of the other, at almost any moment, and sweeping over the smooth sand for a hundred yards or more in their stride. We rode our horses into the surf up to their backs, and so for a couple of miles along the beach and then back to lunch. . . .

To-night we painted by the lake at a new place, from which we returned by water. The General paints in water colours and does it very well. With all my enormous paraphernalia, I have so far produced very indifferent results here. The trees are very difficult to do and there is great monotony in their foliage also, water has many traps of its own. How I wish Lavery[1] were here to give me a few hints; it would bring me on like one o'clock. . . .

March 28 was overcast. But in the evening the sun shone for a few hours, and Churchill painted two more pictures. 'The cloudy weather is bad for painting,' he wrote to his wife on the following day, 'but good for hunting—especially a little rain.' On March 29 he hunted

---

[1] John Lavery, 1856–1931. Painter. Born in Belfast. A Roman Catholic. Exhibited his first oil painting at Glasgow, 1879. Vice-President of the International Society of Sculptors, Painters and Gravers, 1897. Knighted, 1918. President of the Royal Society of Portrait Painters from 1932 until his death. Some of Churchill's earliest paintings had been done in Lavery's London studio.

wild boar again. There was no post, and therefore no official pouches with War Office or Cabinet papers. 'The general & I,' he wrote to his wife, 'discuss the various battles of the war without cessation in the intervals of painting and riding.' In his postscript he added: 'I have not done one scrap of work or thought about anything. This is the first time such a thing has happened to me. I am evidently "growing up" at last.'

On March 30, while still at Mimizan, Churchill sent his wife a letter which he hoped would reach her on her birthday on April 1:

My darling one,
    This is a line & only a line (as the sun is shining bright) to wish you many happy returns of the day. Twelve times now I have seen yr birthday come, & each time yr gracious beauty & loving charm have made a deeper impression on my heart. God bless you my darling in the year that now opens & give you happiness wh fills yr life. Always yr devoted loving husband

W

Clementine Churchill kept her husband informed of family news. 'This week,' she wrote on March 31, 'has been occupied in taking Randolph to have his school clothes fitted. He looks such a thin shrimp in trousers & an Eton collar!' She hoped Churchill would succeed in catching some wild boar. 'Please bring me back their gleaming tusks.' That same day, Churchill sent an account of his activities to his wife.

I have had a swollen face myself; I do not know why. And so last night I took ten grains of aspirin[1] and did not wake up finally till ten o'clock this morning, when in comes the General with the news that a very large pig had been located within three miles of the house. We had not intended to hunt till to-morrow, but on this news we all sallied forth.

The pig was found exactly where he had been marked down, and I had a splendid view of him galloping away. He was a good size pig—very fat and very dark coloured. Usually you have a good chance of killing a pig if you start off right on his tail as we did, and our hopes were very high after we had galloped without stopping for an hour and a quarter as fast as we could go through the sunlit woods with all the hounds chiming in frantic chorus. But, alas, instead of losing his wind and sitting down to fight, this obstinate animal continued his career, made for the river and swam as if followed by all the hounds. We had to break off and go a mile up to a bridge, with the result that we never saw pig nor hounds again, except a number of stragglers; and after making many casts, now in this direction, now in that, we rode off home. We had been out five hours, most of it at the gallop, and personally I was quite content. It will be two days before the hounds are sufficiently recovered for another hunt. But as long as it is sunshiny I can find plenty to do with my

---

[1] The equivalent of two modern aspirin tablets.

paint box. I have painted rather a good picture this evening; the best I have done since coming here—in fact, the only one that is tolerable. . . .

The Cabinet met in London on the evening of March 31. In Churchill's absence, the Director of Military Intelligence, General Thwaites, represented the War Office. 'We decided,' H. A. L. Fisher wrote in his diary, 'Curzon leading, finally to tell Denikin to wind up affairs & come to terms with Soviet Govt. Great joy. Winston fortunately abroad. Beatty relieved at decision.' It was formally agreed, according to the Cabinet Conclusions, 'to invite General Denikin to give up the struggle; to urge upon him that Russian interests would best be served by making Peace at once; and to offer our services as intermediaries with the Soviet Government, with whom we would endeavour to arrange an amnesty and terms of capitulation'. At the same time, Admiral de Robeck[1] was instructed 'to abstain from further belligerent action in support of General Denikin'.

Churchill remained at Mimizan, hunting, riding and painting. He made no effort to influence, or to challenge, the Cabinet's decision. On April 1, General Thwaites informed Sir Henry Wilson by Minute that it had been decided 'that no further help should be given to Denikin, that the packet should now stop and that he should be advised to make terms'. Wilson noted that same day: 'Thank goodness.' On the previous day Churchill had written to Lloyd George: 'I have been having a *complete* holiday and trying to forget about all the disagreeable things that are going on.'

Although Churchill accepted the Cabinet's decision of March 31, whereby Denikin could no longer receive either men or supplies from Britain, he still tried to mitigate its consequences. 'It seems to me essential,' he wrote to Sir Henry Wilson from France on April 9, 'that we should press for aid to be given, as far as General Milne and Admiral de Robeck can find, to help maintain the Crimea until such time as some arrangement has been made for the disposal of the refugees there.'

---

[1] John Michael de Robeck, 1862–1928. Entered Navy, 1875. Rear-Admiral, 1911. Commanded the 9th Cruiser Squadron, charged with protecting British merchant ships in the mid-Atlantic, 1914–15. Second in command of the Allied naval forces at the Dardanelles, February–March 1916. Vice-Admiral commanding the Allied naval forces at the Dardanelles, March 1915–January 1916. Knighted, 1916. Commanded the 2nd Battle Squadron in the North Sea, 1916–18. Created Baronet, 1919. Commander-in-Chief of the Mediterranean Fleet, and High Commissioner at Constantinople, 1919–21. Admiral, 1920. Commander-in-Chief of the Atlantic Fleet, 1922–4. Admiral of the Fleet, 1925.

Churchill realized that the Cabinet decision would not be reversed. 'I should be quite willing,' he told Wilson, 'to agree to negotiations with the Soviet Government to respect the Crimea pending some settlement. . . .'

On April 4, while Churchill was still in France, General Denikin had resigned as Commander-in-Chief of the Armed Forces of South Russia. He was succeeded by one of his more successful commanders, Baron Wrangel,[1] and at once left for Constantinople on a British destroyer.

Before returning to England, Churchill spent a few days in Paris. In the week since he had passed through the city on his way south, a major crisis had broken. On April 3 the German Government, in order to suppress a revolutionary uprising in the Ruhr, had sent troops in to restore order. Britain, Italy and the United States had approved the German action, as being a safeguard against the westward march of Bolshevism. But France, furious at this German occupation of the 'neutral' Ruhr, marched her troops into four German towns, Darmstadt, Frankfurt, Hanau and Hamburg, angering the Germans, not only because of her action, but because among the French troops were negroes from Senegal.

While in Paris on April 9, Churchill discussed the crisis with André Lefevre. The two Ministers lunched together privately, Lefevre being accompanied by the Chief of the General Staff, General Buat.[2] Later that day Churchill sent Lloyd George a long account of the conversation. Lefevre, he wrote, was animated 'by a thoroughly chauvinistic spirit'. He did not seem to mind if France alienated Britain by her action in occupying the four towns, and was prepared in the future to face Germany alone. Lefevre then spoke of French fears that the Germans had planned an actual invasion of France and General Buat supported him. But under pressure from Churchill, they did not attempt to maintain this argument, 'and fell back on infractions of the Treaty.

[1] Peter Nikolaevich Wrangel, 1878–1928. Served in the Russo-Japanese and First World Wars. Joined the anti-Bolshevik forces of General Denikin, 1918. Assumed command of the anti-Bolshevik forces in southern Russia, April 1920. Launched an offensive against the Bolsheviks, June 1920, whereupon the British at once withdrew their support for his actions. Evacuated his forces from the Crimea, November 1920. In exile in Belgium.

[2] Edmond Alphonse Leon Buat, 1868–1923. Entered the French Army, 1889. Chef du Cabinet of the Minister of War, 1914–15. Colonel commanding the 245th Infantry Brigade, 1915–16. Général de Brigade, 1916. Général de Division, commanding the Artillery Reserve, 1917–18. Commanded the 33rd Infantry Division, February 1918: the 17th Army Corps, March 1918; the 5th Army, June 1918. Chief of the General Staff, 1920–3.

Where was it going to stop, and so on?' Churchill's letter to Lloyd George continued:

I then explained that the British Government, and I believed the British people, would be roused immediately by an unprovoked attack by Germany upon France, and that their wish would be to come to her aid in a righteous quarrel such as had broken out in August, 1914. But I was sure that they would be increasingly alienated by an attitude of military triumph and arrogance over a beaten foe, especially of denying a nation like Germany an opportunity of re-establishing order and prosperity within her own bounds.

They replied by quoting the 'Times' and the 'Daily Mail' to show that the British people were already roused. I said that they must not deceive themselves by the Northcliffe press. The Government existed in spite of the Northcliffe press, which was persistently hostile and which consequently was discounted. It was folly to suppose that the British Cabinet would not command the continuous support, in a matter of this kind, of Parliament and of all the necessary national forces of opinion. . . .

Churchill tried to reassure Lefevre that Britain would 'press perseveringly and unswervingly for the strict execution of the disarmament policy'. But he warned that, in occupying the four German towns against the advice of their former Allies, France 'had committed a grave error in tactics and had lost far more in prestige and authority than they had gained'. Churchill's account of the conversation continued:

I then spoke of the future, the past being beyond recall, and I asked pointedly, Did they intend to attach other conditions to their evacuation of the towns than the corresponding evacuation of the Ruhr by the Germans? Were they going to mix it up with questions of other infractions of the Treaty? On this point, he seemed very decided, although, as he said, he spoke, as I did, as an individual. He repeated that if they were given a measure of sympathy by their allies, the instant that the Germans withdrew from the Ruhr, they would similarly evacuate the towns. If they were left alone to face the situation by themselves, they would of course take whatever action they thought fit.

Within a few days of Churchill's talk with Lefevre, the French Government agreed not to act in future over alleged Treaty violations without consulting its Allies. The British Government formally announced that for its part, it would insist that the Germans respected the terms of the Treaty. In mid-May, after the German Government had suppressed the Ruhr uprising, both the German and French troops were withdrawn without further incident.

The Supreme Allied Council had set up, as a result of the San Remo discussions, a 'Permanent Committee on the Resumption of Trade with Russia'. Lloyd George had played an active part in bringing about this decision, and had welcomed the proposal to invite a leading Bolshevik, Leonid Krassin,[1] to discuss with the Allies the possibility of Anglo-Soviet trade. Churchill was not sent a copy of the San Remo discussions, and was much annoyed. On May 13 he protested about this to Sir Maurice Hankey, explaining that when he had been at Windsor in the last week of April the King had wanted to discuss the reports of the discussions with him. 'I had to explain,' Churchill wrote to Hankey, 'that I had not been kept informed.' 'I do not see,' he continued, 'how Ministers can be expected to take interest in or assume responsibility for what is going on at these Conferences, if no account of what takes place is given to them till about three weeks after they are all over, when the passage of time has sensibly affected the importance of the conclusions.' Hankey replied on the same day to say that Lloyd George had specifically restricted the daily reports to himself, the King, Bonar Law and Curzon. 'It would be very much easier,' Hankey added in self-defence, 'if I had a free hand in circulating these documents to the Cabinet. . . .'

Churchill was angered by the imminent talks between the Allies and the Bolsheviks. But he did not allow the talks to undermine his determination to give Denikin's successor, General Wrangel, the full support of the British Mission, as well as naval protection. When Henry Wilson asked Churchill to authorize the immediate withdrawal of the British Mission from the Crimea, Churchill resisted Wilson's advice. 'Surely this will bring Wrangel down with a run,' he wrote to Wilson on May 1. 'The Navy have now been definitely ordered to help hold the Perekop approaches pending negotiations,' he added. 'I cannot consent to the withdrawal of the reduced mission at this moment.'

Churchill expected General Wrangel to negotiate with the Bolsheviks within a number of weeks, after which the British Mission could be withdrawn. He made no attempt to enter into direct communication

[1] Leonid Borisovich Krassin, 1870–1926. Born at Kurgan, in Siberia, the son of a civil servant. Joined the revolutionary movement while a student at St Petersburg, 1890; expelled from the capital, 1891. Became a close friend of Lenin in the 1890s. Russian representative of the German industrial firm of Siemens. Active in organizing revolutionary activity in Russia, 1914–17. Appointed by Lenin, Commissar for Commerce and Industry, 1918. Commissar for Foreign Trade, 1918–22. Sent by Lenin to open trade relations with Britain, May 1920. Soviet Ambassador to Berlin, 1922; to Paris, 1924. Appointed Soviet Chargé d'Affaires in London, October 1925; he died in London in November of the following year. On 13 June 1920 Lord Riddell recorded in his diary Lloyd George's description of Krassin: 'He is always looking over his shoulder as if he expected to be shot!'

with Wrangel, as he had done with Denikin, or to encourage him to fight on. On May 1, when Lord Curzon objected to allowing Maxim Litvinov[1] to take part in the Allied discussions with the Bolsheviks, Churchill circulated the following memorandum to the Cabinet:

I am afraid I cannot follow the reasoning which has led the Government, while negotiating with the Bolsheviks, to boggle at receiving Litvinoff. Litvinoff is no doubt a mischievous crank, but certainly not one of the most sinister or bloodstained of the Bolshevik leaders.

The Bolsheviks deserted the Allied cause and let loose a million Germans on our front. They have repudiated their obligations in every direction and torn up every treaty. They murdered Commander Cromie, the British Naval Attaché in Petrograd, at the door of the British Embassy, which they sacked. The essence of their policy is to produce world-wide revolution, and that is their only chance of permanent life. They are engaged in wholesale extermination in their own country of the upper and middle classes and to a very large extent of the educated class. They have committed, and are committing, unspeakable atrocities and are maintaining themselves in power by terrorism on an unprecedented scale and by a denial of the most elementary rights of citizenship and freedom.

If we are prepared to swallow all this, negotiate with them, traffic with them, parley with them, invite them to London, endeavour to get on friendly terms with them, seek commercial advantages from them, &c., surely it is straining at a gnat to refuse to meet, and to exert ourselves to persuade the entire Supreme Council of the victorious Allies to refuse to meet, a feather-headed agitator like himself. No doubt one must draw the line somewhere, but I should have thought it hardly worthwhile drawing it here. . . .

In his memorandum, Churchill also gave his opinion on the Soviet request for the release of the defeated and exiled Hungarian Bolshevik leader, Bela Kun, who had fled from Budapest to Vienna, and had been interned:

It seems to me also that there would be no harm in our using our good offices with the Austrians to secure the release of Bela Kun and his associates to Soviet Russia. There is no place where these creatures can do less mischief, than in Sovdepia. A few additional serpents in that nest will make no appreciable difference to its poisonous character. They can bite each other if they like.

[1] Maxsim Maxsimovich Litvinov, 1876–1951. Jewish. Born Meyer Wallach; educated in Bialystok. Became a Bolshevik on the formation of the Party in 1903. Lived for many years in London, where he married an English Jewess, Ivy Low, in 1916. In London at the time of the revolution. In Stockholm, 1918–19. Deputy Foreign Minister, 1921–30. Foreign Minister, 1930–9. Full member of the Central Committee of the Communist Party, 1934–41. Ambassador to Washington, 1941–3. Deputy Foreign Minister, 1943–6.

Bela Kun returned to Soviet Russia; but the Allies agreed to Curzon's demand that Litvinov should be excluded from their negotiations with the Bolsheviks.

On May 5, the Cabinet met to discuss the withdrawal of British troops from Batum. As Lloyd George was ill, Bonar Law took the chair. 'We discussed Batum,' Henry Wilson wrote in his diary, '& to my disgust Curzon by a long-winded jaw persuaded the Cabinet to allow over 2 Batt[ns] to remain on for the present. Winston didn't fight. I did but was over-ruled.' Churchill did try to insist on the withdrawal of the British garrison at Enzeli, on the Caspian Sea, which, he said, was costing the War Office two million pounds a year. But Curzon protested against this also, and, as a result of his insistence, British troops remained both at Batum and at Enzeli.

During the first week of May the events in the Crimea and the Caucasus, and the fears of a Bolshevik descent on Persia, India or Mesopotamia, were overshadowed by the news from the Russo-Polish borderlands. Since February 1919, the Polish and Bolshevik forces had been at war; but it had been a war of cavalry skirmishes, brief advances and quick retreats which did not attract serious attention in the west while the struggle between the Bolshevik and anti-Bolshevik armies was at its height inside Russia itself. But on April 25 the Chief of the Polish State, Marshal Pilsudski,[1] had launched a major offensive against the Bolsheviks, and the British Government found itself confronted with a new crisis. The Polish advance was rapid and sustained. On May 6 the Bolsheviks evacuated Kiev, and on the morning of May 7 the Polish forces occupied the city. In a 'Proclamation to the Citizens of the Ukraine', Pilsudski declared that his aim was the establishment, not of an enlarged Polish state, but of an independent Ukraine, after which the Poles would withdraw.

Lloyd George was alarmed and angered by the Polish advance.

[1] Joseph Clemens Pilsudski, 1867–1935. Born in the Vilna Province of Russian Poland. Involved in an anti-Tsarist plot and deported to Siberia, 1887–92. Edited, printed and distributed a secret Radical paper, *Robotnik*, 1894–1900. Imprisoned, 1900. Escaped from prison, 1901. In exile in London, 1901–2. Established a Polish army in Austrian Poland, 1908–14; in 1914 his 10,000 men fought in the Austro-Hungarian Army. Minister of War in the Council of State, Warsaw (under Central Power auspices), 1916–17. His army refused to support the Germans, July 1917. Imprisoned by the Germans, July 1917–November 1918. Chief of the Polish State, November 1918–December 1922. Chief of the General Staff, 1923. Retired from public life, July 1923. Occupied Warsaw, May 1926. Minister of War from 1926 until his death. Prime Minister, 1927–8 and 1930.

THE RUSSO-POLISH WAR, 1920

Legend:

Poland's established frontiers, June 1920

Furthest eastward advance of the Polish armies, May – June 1920

Principal towns captured by the Red Army, July – August 1920

Furthest westward advance of the Red Army, August 1920

Seized by Poland from Lithuania, Oct. 1920

Poland's eastern frontier, March 1921 (Polish-Soviet Treaty of Riga)

© Martin Gilbert

'Unless the Poles are careful,' he told Lord Riddell on May 9, 'they will revive the intensity and the spirit of Russian nationality.' And he added: 'The Poles are inclined to be arrogant and they will have to take care that they don't get their heads punched.'

Churchill hoped that the Polish attack, although unaided by Britain, would drive the Bolsheviks from the Ukraine. On May 11, in a Cabinet memorandum arguing against the resumption of trade with Soviet Russia, he asked: 'would it not be better to wait and see what Government is likely to be in control at the end of the next harvest of the principal granary of Russia—the Ukraine?' Surely, he added, if the Bolsheviks only controlled Moscow 'and the starving Northern Provinces' by September 1920, and anti-Bolshevik forces were in control of the Ukraine, Odessa, 'and the railways leading straight into Poland, Czecho-Slovakia and Austria', it would be better for Britain's 'economic purpose' to deal with the anti-Bolsheviks.

Later that day, in the House o1 Commons, a Liberal MP, George Lambert,[1] asked whether the War Office was giving 'any encouragement or military assistance to the Poles in this adventure'. 'No, Sir,' Churchill replied. The War Office, he went on to explain, had given 'no assistance to the Poles in this enterprise', although both Britain and France had, 'last year and so on', helped to 'strengthen and equip' the Polish Army.

Munitions were, in fact, being sent to Poland even while Churchill was speaking. A ship, the *Jolly George*, was at the London Docks, ready to be loaded. The dockers, on learning that the munitions were to be used against the Bolsheviks, refused to continue loading the ship. The Labour Party supported their stand. On May 14 Churchill spent the day with Lloyd George at Lympne, near the Channel Coast. Lloyd George said that he was prepared to stop the *Jolly George* sailing. But on his return to the War Office Churchill wrote to protest against giving way to public pressure:

I think you shd see the history of the consignments of arms wh were being sent to Poland by the 'Jolly George'. I naturally had assumed that anything settled as far back as October last year wd long ago have been sent. However it appears that the financial arrangement, packing-cases etc, have only just allowed the actual movement of stores to begin.

I do not think it wd be right to hold up these stores now, still less to allow them to be held up by a violent act of this kind. They are the property of the

---

[1] George Lambert, 1866–1958. Liberal MP, 1891–1924; 1929–31. Civil Lord of Admiralty, 1905–15. Chairman of the Liberal Parliamentary Party, 1919–21. Liberal National MP, 1931–45. Created Viscount, 1945.

Polish Govt. & we are definitely bound by our agreement with them. The policy of Poland is no doubt a matter for the Supreme Council, & should be talked out there. Of course, for all we knew the Poles wd by now have been defending themselves against an overwhelming Bolshevik attack, & they may be again in the near future in that position.

You will see I have acted entirely in accordance with Cabinet decisions, & I do not think those decisions ought lightly to be set aside, once definite international agreements have been made upon them.

Neither Churchill nor Lloyd George could assuage the anger of the dockers, and the *Jolly George* did not leave the East India Dock until the munitions had been set aside.

On May 19 Churchill sent his thoughts on Poland to General Radcliffe and General Thwaites. Any military truce between Poland and the Bolsheviks would not, he believed, be of any value to Poland. Once fighting ceased between the Bolsheviks and an enemy, he wrote, 'instead of being attacked by soldiers on the frontier, one is poisoned internally'. Denikin's defeat would enable the Bolsheviks to use a much increased military force against the Poles than they had deployed hitherto. Any profession of a 'desire for peace' would be false. The Poles, however, were in a strong position, especially politically. While Denikin was active, he had always refused to contemplate an independent Ukraine; now there was no reason why one should not be set up, as Pilsudski urged. Churchill favoured such a policy:

There could be no greater advantage to the famine areas of Central Europe than the re-establishment of a peaceful state in the Ukraine on the basis which permitted economic and commercial transactions to take place. It is there in the Ukraine, and not in the starving regions of Russia reduced to destitution under Bolshevik rule, that an addition to the food supply may be hoped for.

Churchill's memorandum continued:

It is not possible to say yet what the outcome will be. The Bolsheviks will no doubt make an effort to overwhelm the Poles, and they will certainly get any assistance from the Germans which can be given unofficially. It will be very difficult for the Ukranians to establish order in their own country. But on the assumption that the Ukraine manages to set up and maintain a separate Government of a civilised type capable of liberating the corn supplies of the Ukraine, and that she is sheltered and assisted in this task by a strong Poland, it ought not to be impossible to arrive at satisfactory conditions of a general peace in the East in the course of the present Summer. If, on the other hand, Poland succumbs to Bolshevik attacks and the Ukraine is again over-run, anarchy in Russia will prevent all effective export of grain, and the downfall of Poland will directly involve the vital interests of France and, in a lesser degree, of Great Britain.

On May 20 the House of Commons debated the Polish and Russian situations. George Lambert attacked Sir Henry Wilson for having stated publicly, three days before, that 'except in August 1914, our country and our Empire has never wanted you more'. Churchill replied that Wilson was referring to the 'enormous numbers of obligations at the present time'—Cologne, Constantinople, Ireland, Mesopotamia, Egypt and India. He made no mention of Poland or Russia. Wilson's remarks, he said, did not imply 'that we are on the verge of some great explosion or of cataclysm. That is over. We are in a period of great disturbance and of increasing degeneration in many parts of the world, but anything similar to the onrush of the organised legions of Germany upon the world need not be expected again.'

At half past six on the afternoon of May 19 a telegram reached the War Office from Teheran to say that the British garrison at Enzeli, on the Caspian Sea, had been surrounded by the Bolsheviks and taken prisoner. 'A nice state of affairs,' Henry Wilson wrote in his diary, 'which will have a *bad* effect in the East. For months I have been begging the Cabinet to allow me to withdraw from Persia & from the Caucasus. Now perhaps they will.' At half past seven Wilson and Churchill went to the House of Commons to see Bonar Law, and to press upon him the urgent need for a Cabinet decision to withdraw all remaining troops from Batum and the Caspian.

On May 20 Churchill wrote to Curzon, pressing for an immediate withdrawal of all British troops who were still in Persia, as well as the troops at Batum. During the course of his letter Churchill declared:

There is something to be said for making peace with the Bolsheviks. There is also something to be said for making war upon them. There is nothing to be said for a policy of doing all we can to help to strengthen them, to add to their influence and prestige, to weaken those who are fighting against them, and at the same time leaving weak British forces tethered in dangerous places, where they can be easily and suddenly overwhelmed.

I do not see that anything we can do now within the present limits of our policy can possibly avert the complete loss of British influence throughout the Caucasus, Trans-Caspia and Persia. If we are not able to resist the Bolsheviks in these areas, it is much better by timely withdrawals to keep out of harm's way and avoid disaster and shameful incidents such as that which has just occurred.

I should have been only too ready to have helped you with a different policy which, properly supported, would ere now have ended this criminal regime in Russia. But in view of the decisions which were taken six months and eight months ago, and in view of the uninstructed state of public opinion, I think that it is impossible. It only remains to accept the consequences and withdraw our forces everywhere to defensive positions in close proximity with their railheads, where they can be cheaply maintained and where they can operate effectively against an aggressive enemy. I must absolutely decline to continue to share responsibility for a policy of mere bluff.

The Cabinet met twice on May 21, at noon, and again after lunch. At both sessions Curzon insisted that Batum should be held, and that the British garrison there was in no danger. Lord Milner warned that if Persia were lost, 'we should lose Mesopotamia & then India was in danger'. But, as H. A. L. Fisher recorded in his diary: 'Winston and I protest that we are not committed to military defence of Persia,' and Lloyd George agreed with them. The Cabinet finally decided to withdraw all the British troops from northern Persia, and to instruct General Milne to order the withdrawal from Batum as soon as he considered that the force there was in danger.

On the day after the Cabinet meeting Churchill sent Curzon a private, handwritten letter, regretting their failure to work out a joint plan of action towards Russia. 'It is a gt pity,' he wrote, 'that we have not been able to develop any common policy between W.O. & F.O. I have to bear the abuse of F.O. policy & to find the money for it. Yet there is no effective cooperation or mutual support.' And he went on bitterly to tell Curzon:

You have willingly acquiesced in the destruction of the Volunteer armies, because of their friction with your Georgians & Azerbaijanis. Now you expect me with the vy slender weak & raw forces at my disposal to carry out the military side of a policy wh required for its success strong friendly Russian armies.

I see no alternative but a retirement to the Mesopotamian railheads. There and on the Indian frontier we can maintain ourselves against all comers. But if we continue scattered about far from our railways, a series of humiliations & disasters to ourselves & those to whom we commit ourselves are all that the future has in store.

At noon on May 28 the Conference of Ministers met at 10 Downing Street under Lloyd George's chairmanship to discuss the now imminent negotiations with the Bolsheviks. Sir Robert Horne, who had been appointed President of the Board of Trade in March, and Sir Laming Worthington-Evans, Minister without Portfolio, were put in charge of the negotiations. Curzon asked that they should not restrict their discussions to trade, but that the opportunity of Krassin's visit 'should be seized in order to come to an understanding concerning the many points on which the British Government were at issue with the Soviet Government in different parts of Europe and the East'. Churchill declared that Britain was in a strong bargaining position. The official Minutes recorded him as saying:

In Poland, while there are indications that at the moment the Bolsheviks were enjoying some success against the Polish armies and that the Poles would be unable to maintain hostilities later than July, the Polish army is a strong military force.

In the Crimea, General Wrangel had succeeded in re-organising his Army and instilling discipline into it. He had also conciliated the other political parties opposed to the Bolsheviks, and his force was one which now had to be reckoned with. It seemed very likely that he would be able to hold the Crimea against all attacks.

In the Ukraine there was strong anti-Bolshevik feeling, and the peasantry were well-armed and capable of offering a strong resistance to the Bolsheviks. All these facts must be borne in mind in negotiating with M. Krassin.

Churchill then suggested:

. . . that the British Government should offer to the Soviet Government their whole-hearted co-operation in concerting a Peace between the Soviet Government, on the one hand, and General Wrangel and the Polish Government on the other. The agreement in regard to General Wrangel should provide that the Crimea should form an Asylum for the remnants of the classes opposed to the Bolsheviks, and that immunity from Bolshevist advances should be granted to the Crimea for at least a year. If such an arrangement was come to it was thought that the situation in Russia would be greatly improved and would permit of the Russian refugees now in the Crimea returning under amnesty to Russia.

In return, the British Government should insist on a comprehensive agreement which should cover the various points at issue between the Soviet Government and this country, namely, the return of prisoners from Russia, and Bolshevist interference in Afghanistan, Persia and the Caucasus. The agreement should also cover Bolshevist propaganda in the United Kingdom, Allied countries and Central Europe. . . .

The Conference of Ministers agreed to Lord Curzon's suggestion that the negotiations should aim at 'comprehensive political agreement with the Soviet Government'. But they did not take up Churchill's suggestion that Britain should insist on the immunity of the Crimea against attack for at least a year.

On May 31 Lloyd George and Leonid Krassin held their first meeting. Lloyd George was accompanied by Lord Curzon, Bonar Law, Sir Robert Horne and Sir Maurice Hankey. That evening Hankey wrote in his diary: ' "I grasped the hairy paw of the baboon" to use Winston Churchill's picturesque phrase.'

23

The Amritsar Debate

===

A T the beginning of July Churchill was called upon to defend the Government in a controversial debate in the House of Commons. More than a year earlier, during a week of anti-British violence in the Punjab, a senior British officer, General Dyer,[1] had ordered his troops to fire on an unarmed Indian mob in the Jallianwalla Bagh at Amritsar. As many as 300 Indians had been killed, and over 2,000 wounded. A Government Commission, the Hunter Commission, had condemned General Dyer's action, and the Army Council, on Churchill's insistence, had refused him any further military employment. The Conservative majority in the House of Commons was outraged that a British General had been publicly condemned, while acting, as he saw it, to protect British life and to uphold British imperial authority. A further reason for Conservative anger was that the Commission which condemned the General had been set up by the Secretary of State for India, Edwin Montagu, a Jew.

The Amritsar debate began at four in the afternoon on Thursday July 8. With Lloyd George's approval, Bonar Law had arranged for Montagu to speak first, and to make, as he wrote to Churchill on the previous day, 'a short speech'. Churchill was to speak later, either before dinner or at the end of the debate, 'as we judge best by the early course of the debate', Bonar Law explained.

From the moment Montagu began to speak, the debate went badly

[1] Reginald Edward Harry Dyer, 1864–1927. Born in India; educated in Ireland. Entered Sandhurst, 1884. 2nd Lieutenant, Queen's Royal West Surrey Regiment, 1885; on active service with the Burma Field Force, 1886–7. Transferred to the 39th Bengal Infantry, 1887; to the 29th Punjab Infantry, 1888. Promoted Captain, 1893. At the Staff College, Camberley, 1896–7. Took part in the Waziristan Expedition, 1901–2. Deputy Assistant Adjutant General for Instruction, Chakrata Garrison School, 1901–5. Major, 1903. Musketry Instructor, Rawalpindi, 1906–8. Colonel, 1910. Commanded the British Military Operations in South-East Persia, 1916. Temporary Brigadier-General, 1916. Commanded the Jullundur Brigade, 1917–19; the 5th Brigade, 1919–20. Relieved of his command, 1920.

for the Government. Although he had intended to make only a short speech, his outspoken manner alienated his critics from the outset. Montagu insisted, in the clearest way possible, that the Amritsar shooting could not be condoned, and must not be repeated. He derided General Dyer's remark to the Hunter Commission that his motive was a desire 'to teach a moral lesson to the Punjab'. This, Montagu declared, was 'the doctrine of terrorism'. And he continued: 'Once you are entitled to have regard neither to the intentions nor to the conduct of a particular gathering, and to shoot and to go on shooting with all the horrors that were here involved, in order to teach somebody else a lesson, you are embarking on terrorism, to which there is no end.'

To the accompaniment of fierce protests from several Conservative MPs, Montagu went on to condemn both the whipping punishment which Dyer had imposed in the subsequent weeks, and the order that all Indians passing through the street in which an English woman missionary[1] had been attacked must do so on their hands and knees. 'Are you going to keep hold of India,' Montagu asked, 'by terrorism, racial humiliation and subordination, and frightfulness, or are you going to rest it upon the goodwill, and the growing goodwill of the people of your Indian Empire?'

As Montagu's speech continued, his remarks provoked increasing dissent from the Conservatives. But he was determined to discuss the broader issue of British rule in India, and denounced 'the ascendancy of one race over another'. Were such to be the basis of British rule, he warned, Britain would be driven out of India 'by the united opinion of the civilised world'. He ended his speech with a forceful challenge. 'I invite this House to choose,' he said, 'and I believe that the choice they make is fundamental to a continuance of the British Empire, and vital to the continuation, permanent as I believe it can be, of the connection between this country and India.'

The House of Commons reacted with fierce hostility to Montagu's speech. 'Montagu far too provocative & violent,' H. A. L. Fisher wrote in his diary. 'Everyone disturbed about it.' And on the following day Sir William Sutherland sent an account of the debate to Lloyd George:

Montagu thoroughly roused most of the latent passions of the stodgy Tories and many of them could have assaulted him physically, they were so angry. It was not so much what Montagu said as the way he said it that roused them. Under interruption, Montagu got excited when making his

---

[1] Frances Marcella Sherwood,   –1966. Went to India as a missionary teacher, 1904. In Amritsar, 1915-19. Returned to England immediately after the Amritsar riots. Served in Singapore, 1921-6. Returned to India, 1926; retired from missionary teaching, 1956.

speech and became more racial and more Yiddish in screaming tone and gesture, and a strong anti-Jewish sentiment was shown by shouts and excitement among normally placid Tories of the back Bench category. A critic sees of course that Montagu should have been quiet and judicial, and argued more on the merits of the Dyer case itself than on general principles. . . .

Sir Edward Carson spoke immediately after Montagu, defending what General Dyer had done, and condemning the Government for not supporting his action. At one point in his speech, when he described Dyer as 'a gallant officer of 34 years' service', Josiah Wedgwood interrupted: 'Five hundred people were shot.' But Carson persevered in his argument. Dyer was, he said, 'without a blemish upon his record'. And he continued:

You talk of the great principles of liberty which you have laid down. General Dyer has a right to be brought within those principles of liberty. He has no right to be broken on the *ipse dixit* of any Commission or Committee, however great, unless he has been fairly tried—and he has not been tried. Do look upon the position in which you have put an officer of this kind. . . .
On the 11th and the 12th murders of officials and bank managers were rife. The civil power had to abandon their entire functions, and what did you ask this officer to do? To make up his mind as best he could how to deal with the situation, and now you break him because you say he made up his mind wrongly. . . .

Carson went on to point out that Dyer's action had been approved by his Divisional Commander, General Beynon,[1] and by the Lieutenant-Governor of the Province in which he served, Sir Michael O'Dwyer.[2] Despite the shootings, Dyer had been promoted. He had been appointed to command a difficult military mission. For eight months no one had given him any indication that he would not be employed again. Now he was being condemned for inhumanity and an error of judgement. 'We all know perfectly well,' Carson said, 'how differently everybody views the situation when the whole atmosphere is different, and when the whole danger has passed away.'
Carson ended his speech with the words: 'I say, to break a man under

---

[1] William George Lawrence Beynon, 1866–1955. 2nd Lieutenant, Royal Sussex Regiment, 1887. Lieutenant, Indian Staff Corps, 1889. On active service at Chitral, 1895; on the North-West Frontier, 1897–8; in Somaliland, 1901, and in Tibet, 1904. Served with the Waziristan Field Force, 1916–17. Major-General, 1917. Knighted, 1917. General Officer Commanding the 16th (Indian) Division, Northern Army, India, 1918–19.
[2] Michael Francis O'Dwyer, 1864–1940. Born in County Tipperary. Entered the Indian Civil Service, 1885. Revenue Commissioner, North-West Frontier, 1901–8. Acting Resident, Hyderabad, 1908–9. Viceroy's Agent in Central India, 1910–12. Knighted, 1913. Lieutenant-Governor of the Punjab, 1913–19. He published *India as I knew It* in 1925.

the circumstances of this case is un-English.' This was a clear allusion to the fact that Montagu was a Jew. Writing to Lloyd George on the following day, Sir William Sutherland noted that Carson's 'cleverest thing' during his speech 'was his quiet tone so apparently traditional and British which made Montagu's excitement look all the worse: and Carson rubbed this in by innuendo'.

Bonar Law had not intended to call on Churchill until the debate had developed further. But the situation had become so serious for the Government that he asked Churchill to speak at once.

Churchill's speech transformed the debate. It was essential, he said, 'to approach this subject in a calm spirit, avoiding passion and avoiding attempts to excite prejudice'. He then spoke at some length of the legal position of an officer who was to be removed from his command. 'He began so haltingly,' *The Times* noted, 'as to get the patient ear of the House. He avoided at first expressing an opinion on the merits and entered on an elaborate, not to say dry discourse on the law of master and servant in the Army.' Churchill pointed out that under the Army Act, when an Officer was removed from his employment and relegated to half pay, he had 'no redress . . . no claim to a court of inquiry or a court martial . . . no protection of any kind against being deprived of his appointment'. This might be a 'harsh' procedure, Churchill added, but it was inevitable, and it was 'well understood'. Dyer had not been treated differently to 'hundreds, and probably thousands, of officers'; he had simply been informed, according to the correct and well-established military procedure, 'that there was no prospect of further employment for him under the Government of India'. Churchill added:

The conclusions of the Hunter Committee might furnish the fullest justification for removing him from his appointment——
Commander BELLAIRS:[1] No, no!
Mr CHURCHILL: I am expressing my opinion. When my hon. and gallant Friend is called, he will express his opinion. That is the process which we call Debate. . . .

Churchill went on to tell the House of Commons that the Army Council had been unanimous in its decision to uphold Dyer's dismissal. But he added that he made it 'perfectly clear' to his colleagues on the Army Council that whatever their decision might be, 'I held myself

---

[1] Carlyon Bellairs, 1871–1955. Entered the Royal Navy, 1884; Lieutenant, 1891. Retired from the Navy on the failure of his eyesight, 1902, with the rank of Commander. Liberal MP, 1906–9. Conservative MP, 1909–10, 1915–18 and 1918–31. An opponent of political honours, he declined a baronetcy in 1927. Founded and endowed the Biological Institute, McGill University, Canada, 1954.

perfectly free if I thought it right, and if the Cabinet so decided, to make a further submission to the Crown for the retirement of General Dyer from the Army'.

Churchill then turned to what he described as 'the merits of the case'. He had no hesitation in condemning the Amritsar shooting:

> However we may dwell upon the difficulties of General Dyer during the Amritsar riots, upon the anxious and critical situation in the Punjab, upon the danger to Europeans throughout that province, upon the long delays which have taken place in reaching a decision about this officer, upon the procedure that was at this point or at that point adopted, however we may dwell upon all this, one tremendous fact stands out—I mean the slaughter of nearly 400 persons and the wounding of probably three or four times as many, at the Jallian Wallah Bagh on 13th April.
>
> That is an episode which appears to me to be without precedent or parallel in the modern history of the British Empire. It is an event of an entirely different order from any of those tragical occurrences which take place when troops are brought into collision with the civil population. It is an extraordinary event, a monstrous event, an event which stands in singular and sinister isolation.

The words 'and sinister' were not in Churchill's notes; he added them as he spoke.

Churchill went on to speak of the fact that there had been '36 or 37 cases' of officers firing on Indian crowds during the Punjab disturbances of April 1919. Each of these actions, he said, had involved the British officer concerned in a 'distasteful, painful, embarrassing, torturing situation, mental and moral'. No words of his, he said, 'could exaggerate those difficulties'. But there were 'certain broad lines', he insisted, which every officer had to follow, certain questions he had to ask, and on these Dyer had failed:

> First of all, I think he may ask himself, Is the crowd attacking anything or anybody? Surely that is the first question. Are they trying to force their way forward to the attack of some building, or some cordon of troops or police, or are they attempting to attack some band of persons or some individual who has excited their hostility? Is the crowd attacking? That is the first question which would naturally arise. The second question is this: Is the crowd armed? That is surely another great simple fundamental question. By armed I mean armed with lethal weapons.

Sir W. JOYNSON-HICKS:[1] How could they be in India?

---

[1] William Joynson-Hicks, 1865–1932. Known as 'Jix'. Solicitor. Conservative MP, 1906–29. Chairman of the Parliamentary Air Committee, in 1916 he published *The Command of the Air*. Created Baronet, 1919. Parliamentary Secretary, Department of Overseas Trade,

Mr CHURCHILL: Men who take up arms against the State must expect at any moment to be fired upon. Men who take up arms unlawfully cannot expect that the troops will wait until they are quite ready to begin the conflict. . . . Armed men are in a category absolutely different from unarmed men. An unarmed crowd stands in a totally different position from an armed crowd. At Amritsar the crowd was neither armed nor attacking. [*Interruption.*] I carefully said that when I used the word 'armed' I meant armed with lethal weapons, or with firearms. There is no dispute between us on that point. 'I was confronted,' says General Dyer, 'by a revolutionary army.' What is the chief characteristic of an army? Surely it is that it is armed. This crowd was unarmed. These are simple tests which it is not too much to expect officers in these difficult situations to apply.

Churchill outlined the other considerations which he believed should guide an officer's behaviour, before opening fire on a crowd. One 'good guide', he said, was the doctrine 'that no more force should be used than is necessary to secure compliance with the law'. Another consideration was the need of an officer to 'confine himself to a limited and definite objective, that is to say to preventing a crowd doing something they ought not to do. . . .', and not acting with the intention of influencing events elsewhere. He continued:

My right hon. Friend (Sir E. Carson) will say it is easy enough to talk like this, and to lay down these principles here in safe and comfortable England, in the calm atmosphere of the House of Commons or in your armchairs in Downing Street or Whitehall, but it is quite a different business on the spot, in a great emergency, confronted with a howling mob, with a great city or a whole province quivering all around with excitement. I quite agree.

Still these are good guides and sound, simple tests, and I believe it is not too much to ask of our officers to observe and to consider them. After all, they are accustomed to accomplish more difficult tasks than that.

Over and over again we have seen British officers and soldiers storm entrenchments under the heaviest fire, with half their number shot down before they entered the position of the enemy, the certainty of a long, bloody day before them, a tremendous bombardment crashing all around—we have seen them in these circumstances taking out their maps and watches, and adjusting their calculations with the most minute detail, and we have seen them show, not merely mercy, but kindness, to prisoners, observing restraint in the treatment of them, punishing those who deserved to be punished by the

1922–3. Postmaster General and Paymaster General, 1923. Entered the Cabinet as Financial Secretary to the Treasury, 1923. Minister of Health, 1923–4. Home Secretary, 1924–9. Created Viscount Brentford, 1929. Chairman of the Automobile Association. Vice-President of the Safety First Council and the Institute of Transport. President of the National Church League.

hard laws of war, and sparing those who might claim to be admitted to the clemency of the conqueror.

We have seen them exerting themselves to show pity and to help, even at their own peril, the wounded. They have done it thousands of times, and in requiring them, in moments of crisis, dealing with civil riots, when the danger is incomparably less, to consider these broad, simple guides, really I do not think we are taxing them beyond their proved strength.

Any British officer, Churchill declared, finding himself in 'this painful, agonizing position', ought still to be able 'to pause and consider these broad simple guides—I do not even call them rules—before he decides upon his course of conduct'. There were many examples, he believed, in which officers caught in 'infinitely more trying' circumstances than General Dyer, had shown themselves 'capable of arriving at the right decision'. That decision was not only based, he asserted, on positive guidelines. There was one guide 'of a negative character' of which he wished to speak:

There is surely one general prohibition which we can make. I mean a prohibition against what is called 'frightfulness'. What I mean by frightfulness is the inflicting of great slaughter or massacre upon a particular crowd of people, with the intention of terrorising not merely the rest of the crowd, but the whole district or the whole country.

A Conservative MP, General Page Croft,[1] interrupted with the question: 'Was not the frightfulness started three days before? Was not the frightfulness on the other side?' But Churchill ignored Page Croft's question, and continued with his speech:

We cannot admit this doctrine in any form. Frightfulness is not a remedy known to the British pharmacopoeia.

I yield to no one in my detestation of Bolshevism, and of the revolutionary violence which precedes it. I share with my right hon. and learned Friend (Sir E. Carson) many of his sentiments as to the world-wide character of the seditious and revolutionary movement with which we are confronted. But my hatred of Bolshevism and Bolsheviks is not founded on their silly system of economics, or their absurd doctrine of an impossible equality. It arises from the bloody and devastating terrorism which they practise in every land into which they have broken, and by which alone their criminal regime can be maintained.

[1] Henry Page Croft, 1881–1947. Conservative MP for Christchurch, 1910–18; for Bournemouth, 1918–40. Served in the Great War, 1914–16; Brigadier-General, 1916. Member of the Speaker's Conference on the Franchise, 1918; Civil List Committee, 1936; Committee of Privileges, 1939. Created Baron, 1940. Parliamentary Under-Secretary of State for War, 1940–5. His memoirs, *My Life of Strife* were published posthumously, in 1949.

I have heard the hon. Member for Hull (Lieut-Commander Kenworthy)[1] speak on this subject. His doctrine and his policy is to support and palliate every form of terrorism as long as it is the terrorism of revolutionaries against the forces of law, loyalty and order.

Governments who have seized upon power by violence and by usurpation have often resorted to terrorism in their desperate efforts to keep what they have stolen, but the august and venerable structure of the British Empire, where lawful authority descends from hand to hand and generation after generation, does not need such aid. Such ideas are absolutely foreign to the British way of doing things.

Churchill then spoke of the shooting in the Jallianwalla Bagh. It was, he said, a violation of all the guidelines he had set out, and was an exhibition of the very frightfulness which he had condemned:

Let me marshal the facts. The crowd was unarmed, except with bludgeons. It was not attacking anybody or anything. It was holding a seditious meeting. When fire had been opened upon it to disperse it, it tried to run away.

Pinned up in a narrow place considerably smaller than Trafalgar Square, with hardly any exits, and packed together so that one bullet would drive through three or four bodies, the people ran madly this way and the other. When the fire was directed upon the centre, they ran to the sides. The fire was then directed upon the sides. Many threw themselves down on the ground, and the fire was then directed on the ground. This was continued for 8 or 10 minutes, and it stopped only when the ammunition had reached the point of exhaustion.

Commander BELLAIRS: This is absolutely denied by General Dyer.

Mr CHURCHILL: It stopped only when it was on the point of exhaustion, enough ammunition being retained to provide for the safety of the force on its return journey. If more troops had been available, says this officer, the casualties would have been greater in proportion. If the road had not been so narrow, the machine guns and the armoured cars would have joined in. Finally when the ammunition had reached the point that only enough remained to allow for the safe return of the troops, and after 379 persons, which is about the number gathered together in this Chamber to-day, had been killed, and when most certainly 1,200 or more had been wounded, the troops, at whom not even a stone had been thrown, swung round and marched away.

Churchill regretted that his attitude to the Amritsar shootings should have put him in opposition to many of those with whom 'on the general

---

[1] Joseph Montague Kenworthy, 1886–1953. Entered Royal Navy, 1902. Commanded HMS *Bullfinch*, 1914; HMS *Commonwealth*, 1916. Lieutenant Commander, 1916. Admiralty War Staff, 1917. Assistant Chief of Staff, Gibraltar, 1918. Retired from the Navy, 1920. Liberal MP, 1919–26. Labour MP, 1926–31. Succeeded his father as 10th Baron Strabolgi, 1934. Opposition Chief Whip, House of Lords, 1938–42. President of the United Kingdom Pilots Association, 1922–5. Chairman of the Advisory Committee on Sea Fisheries, 1926–32.

drift of the world's affairs at the present time', he found himself in full agreement. But he felt that it was essential to condemn Dyer's action. 'I do not think that it is in the interests of the British Empire or of the British Army,' he said, 'for us to take a load of that sort for all time upon our backs. We have to make it absolutely clear, some way or other, that this is not the British way of doing business.'

General Dyer's supporters were convinced, and Carson himself had stressed, that the Amritsar shootings had averted a major revolt, on a scale unprecedented since the Indian Mutiny sixty-three years before. Churchill challenged this assertion that Dyer's use of force had saved India. Since the Mutiny, he pointed out, British military power in India had increased enormously, not only its manpower, but its mastery of all the inventions of mechanical warfare: machine guns, the magazine rifle, and even air power. And he continued:

When one contemplates these solid, material facts, there is no need for foolish panic, or talk of its being necessary to produce a situation like that at Jallianwalah Bagh in order to save India. On the contrary, as we contemplate the great physical forces and the power at the disposal of the British Government in their relations with the native population of India, we ought to remember the words of Macaulay—'and then was seen what we believe to be the most frightful of all spectacles, the strength of civilisation without its mercy.'

Our reign in India or anywhere else has never stood on the basis of physical force alone, and it would be fatal to the British Empire if we were to try to base ourselves only upon it. The British way of doing things, as my right hon. Friend the Secretary of State for India, who feels intensely upon this subject, has pointed out, has always meant and implied close and effectual co-operation with the people of the country. In every part of the British Empire that has been our aim, and in no part have we arrived at such success as in India, whose princes spent their treasure in our cause, whose brave soldiers fought side by side with our own men, whose intelligent and gifted people are co-operating at the present moment with us in every sphere of government and of industry.

Churchill then spoke about Montagu, praising his great 'personal contribution' to the task of preventing a breakdown between the people of India and the Government of India by his policy of 'co-operation and goodwill'. He had been astonished, he said, when, 'in the supreme crisis of the War', Montagu had 'calmly journeyed to India, and remained for many months absorbed in Indian affairs'. Now he understood what Montagu had achieved 'from the point of view of the national interests of the British Empire', in helping to keep alive 'that spirit of comradeship, that sense of unity and of progress in co-operation, which must ever ally and bind together the British and Indian peoples'.

Churchill ended his speech by telling the House of Commons that he himself believed that Dyer should have been censured more severely than by 'the loss of employment from which so many officers are suffering at the present time'; he had hoped to see him 'placed compulsorily upon the retired list'. But this was impossible, he said, because of the 'virtual condonation' of the Amritsar shooting by both Sir Michael O'Dwyer and General Beynon. For this reason, he explained, the Cabinet had accepted the Army Council's request that no further punishment should be meted out, 'and to those moderate and considered conclusions we confidently invite the assent of the House'.

Churchill's speech was a personal triumph, and seemed to all who listened to have saved the Government from the danger of a serious setback. *The Times* described it as 'amazingly skilful', and believed that it had 'turned the House (or so it seemed) completely round. . . . It was not only a brilliant speech, but one that persuaded and made the result certain.' *The Times* added that Churchill had 'never been heard to greater advantage'. H. A. L. Fisher described the speech in his diary as 'excellent—cool, but with imaginative touches'. Sir William Sutherland likewise described it as 'an excellent speech' when he wrote to Lloyd George on the following day. 'He really did very well,' Sutherland wrote, 'and showed an expert knowledge of the House.'

The rest of the debate was an anti-climax, justifying Bonar Law's decision to put Churchill in early. Asquith, who spoke immediately after Churchill, told the House that he 'deplored and reprehended that the civil authority abdicated their function, and handed over something very much in the nature of a *carte blanche* to the General in command'. The pro-Dyer lobby found no comfort in these words. The Labour Party's argument, in favour of a sterner punishment for Dyer was put by Benjamin Spoor.[1] The desire of the Labour movement, he said, was for the recall of the Viceroy, for the impeachment of Sir Michael O'Dwyer, for the trial 'before the Courts of Justice of all those officers against whom allegations had been made. . . .'

The debate continued for five more hours. In his letter to Lloyd George, Sutherland described the atmosphere as the debate progressed:

The House was as excited as in an old land debate in the pre-war days. The interruptions were continuous and also the shouts. I was on the door before

[1] Benjamin Charles Spoor, 1878–1928. Labour MP from 1918 until his death. A member of the Executive Council of the Labour Party, 1919. Parliamentary Secretary to the Treasury in the first Labour Government, 1924. Chief Whip of the Labour Party, 1924–5.

dinner and quite a number of Tories consulted me on the point whether if they carried the resolution against the Government it would only mean Montagu's going. The Unionist Army Committee at its meeting the day before the Debate, agreed to support the Government, but after Montagu's speech they called another meeting and decided to vote against the Government.

Altogether it was a very astonishing exhibition of anti-Jewish feeling. It put everything else in the shade yesterday.

The anti-Montagu feeling had still not entirely subsided in this closing stage of the debate. 'Great excitement in the House,' H. A. L. Fisher wrote in his diary. 'B. Law speaking amongst interruptions. In lobbies they say M's speech will lose us 100 votes.' But when the Labour Party's motion to reduce Montagu's salary was put, at 10.49 p.m., only 37 MPs voted in favour, while 247 MPs voted for the Government. Sir Edward Carson's motion, also for reducing the vote, did slightly better, but was likewise defeated, by 230 votes to 129. General Dyer himself was in a seat under the Gallery when the figures were announced. A week later, on July 17, the Archbishop of Canterbury, Randall Davidson,[1] wrote to Lord Curzon describing Churchill's speech as 'unanswerable'.

[1] Randall Thomas Davidson, 1848–1930. Dean of Windsor and Domestic Chaplain to Queen Victoria, 1883–91. Bishop of Rochester, 1891–95. Bishop of Winchester, 1895–1903. Archbishop of Canterbury, 1903–28. Created Baron, 1928.

24

'The Poison Peril from the East'

NEGOTIATIONS between Britain and the Bolsheviks opened
in London on 31 May 1920. Although General Wrangel still
commanded a substantial anti-Bolshevik army in the Crimea, all Allied
help to him was withdrawn. On June 3 he was handed a brief but
decisive communication, informing him that if his troops attacked the
Bolsheviks, 'His Majesty's Government will be unable to concern
themselves any further with the fate of your army.'

The Cabinet met that same evening. Their discussions, which were
lengthy, were devoted to the forthcoming trade negotiations between
Lloyd George and Krassin, and how Bolshevik Russia was to pay for
British goods. The Cabinet concluded that, whatever the technical or
financial difficulties, 'it was highly important for the British Empire
that trade with Russia should be resumed with as little delay as
possible'.

Lloyd George's negotiations with Krassin continued throughout
June. Krassin agreed that, as part of any trade agreement, the Bolsheviks would halt their anti-British propaganda. Lloyd George
promised that at no stage would Britain support any anti-Bolshevik
action by General Wrangel, but would use her influence to try to persuade Wrangel to enter into negotiations with the Soviet Government.

In the second week of June, General Wrangel launched an attack on
Bolshevik positions north of the Crimea. Lloyd George adhered to his
promise to Krassin, and refused Wrangel any support. When the
Cabinet met on the evening of June 11, it was 'generally agreed',
according to the Minutes of the meeting, that Wrangel's action 'relieved
us of all further responsibility', and should be made the reason for the
immediate withdrawal of the former British Mission to South Russia.
Churchill was instructed to telegraph at once to General Milne:

Cabinet consider that Wrangel's assumption of the offensive must be taken as a final release for us from our responsibilities in regard to all forces under his command. No member of the Military Mission is on any account to take part either in directing, in organising, or in any way participating in the present operation. They are to wind up their work without delay, and should be withdrawn from the Peninsula as soon as they can be collected and shipping is available.

Lloyd George's negotiations with Krassin continued. On June 11 Krassin agreed to the withdrawal of all Soviet troops from the Persian port of Enzeli. Churchill was upset by the progress of the talks. On June 12 he lunched with Lord Riddell, who recorded in his diary:

As usual he was violent against the Bolsheviks. He described the Prime Minister as a wonderful man. He said: 'It is extraordinary that we have been able to work together on such terms of personal friendship notwithstanding the divergence of our views regarding Russia. . . . The difference is so marked that I know exactly which foreign telegrams will please him and which will please me. I could mark them with red and blue before he sees them, and I should be right in every case.'

Churchill refused to believe that the Bolsheviks were willing to abandon either their internationalist aims or their aggressive methods. On June 21, in a memorandum for the Cabinet, he asked:

Are we looking ahead at all and making up our minds what we shall do if there is a complete Polish collapse and if Poland is over-run by the Bolshevik armies or its government overturned by an internal Bolshevik uprising? Would it be the policy of the British Government to remain impassive in the face of such an event, which may be conceivably near? If so, what would be the policy of the French Government? In the event of the collapse of Poland, what reaction would this situation entail upon the German position? It would clearly not be possible to disarm Germany if her eastern frontiers were in contact with a Bolshevised area. . . .

On June 25 the Bolsheviks drove the Poles from Kiev, and began to advance westwards on a broad front. Churchill feared that this attack would develop into a serious threat, not only to Poland, but to Germany. The Cabinet met on July 1 to discuss the new Polish reverses, and in particular the implications of the loss of Kiev. 'LG condemns rashness of Poles,' H. A. L. Fisher noted in his diary. 'Pilsudski should have held on to Kieff. . . . LG says Poles are lunatics.'

Churchill was angered by what he regarded as a cynical lack of policy, writing to Lloyd George, Bonar Law and Balfour on July 1:

Naturally it is very painful to me to see all these rods preparing for us, while all the time we are deliberately throwing away *piecemeal* the friends who could have helped us.

Half hearted war is being followed by half hearted peace. We are going I fear to lose both: & be left quite alone. There is much to be said for a comprehensive arrangement providing for all interests: viz Poles, Wrangel, Russians, our Eastern interests simultaneously. But we are just crumbling our powers away. Before long we shall not have a single card in our hands.

The Bolshevik advance continued. On July 7 the Poles were driven out of Tarnopol, and on July 8 a Galician Revolutionary Committee announced the establishment of an independent Galician Soviet Republic. Three days later the Bolsheviks entered Minsk and on July 14 the Poles were forced to evacuate Vilna. Churchill wanted immediate action against this new Bolshevik advance, writing to Bonar Law on July 16: 'All my experience goes to show the advantage of attacking these people. They become vy dangerous the moment they think you fear them. It is like taming a tiger—or rather a mangy hyaena!'

On July 19 General Percy[1] arrived in London from the Crimea, and went at once to the War Office to report on his Mission to General Wrangel. The news he brought added to the evidence of Bolshevik atrocities and to the alarm over Polish weakness. Henry Wilson recorded Percy's statement in his diary: 'He says that when the Bolsheviks have finished with the Poles & go & fall on Wrangel he will be destroyed, & that there will be the most appalling massacres in the Crimea which is full of Russian aristocrats. He says the Bolsheviks are cutting off the feet of Russian officers & cutting shoulder straps out of their skins to give them "permanent commissions".'

Lloyd George had already begun to put his policy of conciliation into effect. On July 16 he had telegraphed to the Bolshevik leaders from Spa, urging them to enter into negotiations for an armistice with both the Poles and General Wrangel. On July 20 he returned to London to discuss the Bolshevik reply with his Cabinet. 'A very insolent document,' H. A. L. Fisher described it in his diary. The Cabinet Minutes recorded that, on a 'general review' of the situation, 'it was pointed out

[1] John Samuel Jocelyn Baumgartner, 1871–1952. 2nd Lieutenant, East Lancashire Regiment, 1891. Served on the North-West frontier India, 1894–95, in South Africa, 1899–1902. General Staff Officer, India, 1908–12. Lieutenant Colonel, 1915. Assumed the surname of Percy, 1917. Served on the General Staff of the 5th and 7th Armies, France, 1917–18. Commanded the 3rd London Brigade, Army of the Rhine, 1919. Brigade-Commander, South Russia, 1919–20. Knighted, 1920. Commanded the British Military Mission to General Wrangel, 1920. Retired from the Army, 1920. Inspector-General of the Albanian Gendarmerie, 1926–38. His only son was killed in action, 1941, while in the Royal Air Force.

that while Poland had probably brought upon herself her present desperate situation by ill-advised attacks directly contrary to the advice of the Allies, nevertheless this did not alter the fact that, if nothing were done, Polish independence was threatened with extinction. The Cabinet were agreed that if Poland 'disappeared', and were 'absorbed in Soviet Russia', this might be a prelude to the union of Russia 'with the Bolshevist elements in Germany'. It was decided to continue to try to persuade the Bolsheviks to agree to an armistice, and to send Lord D'Abernon[1] to Warsaw, with General Radcliffe, to see what prospects there were of persuading the Poles to agree to make peace with the Bolsheviks.

Churchill believed that if the Bolsheviks continued to advance towards Warsaw, the moment would come when both Britain and France would be forced to offer Poland armed assistance. As Secretary of State for War he saw his task as having to ensure that the War Office was not caught unawares. On July 20 he wrote to Sir Henry Wilson, General Harington and General Macdonogh:

You should meet together this afternoon and consider what steps could be taken if it were decided by the Cabinet to assist Poland in defending her native soil and capital against the Bolshevik invasion which is now threatened. It is understood that the French would co-operate actively in this. Even if Warsaw is taken, the defence of the Polish State would also have to be maintained. It is late in the day to consider all these matters after so many opportunities and resources have been thrown away with both hands through all these disastrous months. However, the issue now presents itself in a form in which decided action may be taken by the British and French Governments.

In his letter, Churchill listed the resources which he believed Britain could provide for Poland. These included British aeroplanes and guns, captured German munitions, and British technical advisers. Finland, Rumania and Serbia, he added, could also be sent arms, to encourage them to intervene. Even the British air squadron at Cologne, he believed, might be of value if sent at once to Warsaw.

On July 21 Lloyd George made his first public statement about the Polish situation. 'We British,' he told the House of Commons, 'cannot disinterest ourselves in the fate of Poland.' He went on: 'If the Bol-

---

[1] Edgar Vincent, 1857–1941. Served in the Coldstream Guards, 1877–82. Financial Adviser to the Egyptian Government, 1883–89. Knighted, 1887 (at the age of thirty). Governor of the Imperial Ottoman Bank, 1889–97. Conservative MP, 1899–1906. Created Baron D'Abernon, 1914. Chairman, Central Control Board (Liquor Traffic), 1915–20. Mission to Poland, 1920. Ambassador to Berlin, 1920–6. Created Viscount, 1926. Chairman, Medical Research Council, 1929–33. In 1931 he published an account of the battle of Warsaw, *The Eighteenth Decisive Battle of the World*.

sheviks over-ran Poland, they march right up to the frontiers of
Germany, and Sovietland, after destroying the independence and
existence of a free people, extends as a great aggressive, imperialist
power right up to the borders of Germany. . . .' Lloyd George ended
his speech with a stern declaration: 'It is to the British interest,' he said,
'it is to the European interest, that Poland should not be wiped out. It
would be fatal to the peace of Europe and the consequences would be
disastrous beyond measure.'

On July 23 Churchill was one of the guests at a dinner given by Lord
Birkenhead in the House of Lords. The King was the guest of honour.
At the dinner, Churchill sat next to Lord Riddell, who recorded in his
diary:

> He dilated at length on the Bolshevist danger to civilisation. He said, 'What
> I foresaw has come to pass. Now they are invading Poland, which they mean
> to make a jumping-off ground for propaganda in the rest of Europe. They
> will make peace with the Poles and endeavour to form a Soviet Government
> in Poland. The Bolsheviks are fanatics. Nothing will turn a fanatic from his
> purpose. LG thinks he can talk them over and that they will see the error of
> their ways and the impracticability of their schemes. Nothing of the sort!
> Their view is that their system has not been successful because it has not been
> tried on a large enough scale, and that in order to secure success they must
> make it world-wide.'

During the last week of July, the Bolsheviks continued to advance
into Poland. On July 24, speaking in Moscow, Trotsky declared that
Poland would soon cease to exist. That same day a Provisional Polish
Revolutionary Committee[1] was set up in a railway siding in the Russian
town of Smolensk. Working from a train which carried a printing shop
and a command carriage, this embryo Government moved forward
behind the advancing army; on July 25 it was at Minsk, poised for a
further westward advance.

A confrontation between Britain and the Bolsheviks appeared inevitable. On the day the Polish Revolutionary Committee reached
Minsk, Lord D'Abernon's Mission reached Warsaw. That same day the
Dutch steamship *Triton* reached Danzig with 150,000 Allied rifles, en
route to the Polish Army. On July 26 the United States Government
promised the Poles that America would be willing to equip and maintain ten Polish infantry divisions for the duration of the war.

Lloyd George still hoped to avoid a direct Allied clash with the Bolsheviks, and to persuade both sides to agree to an armistice. On July 26,

---

[1] Its two senior members were Julian Marchlewski and Felix Dzerzhinski, both friends of
Trotsky, and both in direct personal contact with Lenin.

the Soviet Government agreed to his request for a conference between it and the Allied Powers. That same day the Poles also accepted Lloyd George's mediation. But still the Bolsheviks advanced. On July 27 the Red Army occupied Pinsk, while on the same day the train carrying the Polish Revolutionary Committee entered Vilna. On July 28 Churchill published an article in the *Evening News* warning of the dangers of a Bolshevik victory over Poland. The article was entitled 'The Poison Peril from the East'. In it, Churchill stressed Britain's overwhelming desire for peace, but warned that there were still 'formidable dangers' in the world, which, 'foolishly handled or supinely disregarded', would ruin all prospect of a peaceful future. The survival of Poland, he argued, was a vital British interest:

Poland is the lynch-pin of the Treaty of Versailles. This ancient State, torn into three pieces by Austria, Prussia and Russia has been liberated from its oppressors and reunited in its integrity after 150 years of bondage and partition.

We ask ourselves, How has the Polish national character and spirit been affected by this prolonged and melancholy experience? What has Poland learnt from her vicissitudes? What has she lost in her captivity?

As far as we can judge by what has happened in the last eighteen months, 150 years of adversity have neither broken the spirit of Poland nor taught her wisdom. . . .

'Justice to Poland,' Churchill added, 'requires a fair recognition of her extraordinary difficulties'; and these he then proceeded to explain, beginning with the situation in January 1919:

To the westward lay terrific Germany, half stunned, half chained, but still endowed with those tremendous faculties and qualities which had enabled her almost single-handed to wage an obstinate war against nearly the whole world at once.

Eastward, also prostrate, also in dire confusion, lay the huge mass of Russia—not a wounded Russia only, but a poisoned Russia, an infected Russia, a plague-bearing Russia, a Russia of armed hordes smiting not only with bayonet and with cannon, but accompanied and preceded by the swarms of typhus bearing vermin which slay the bodies of men, and political doctrines which destroy the health and even the soul of nations.

And between these two agonised Empires, reacted upon continually by their convulsions, stood Poland, comparatively weak, comparatively small, quite inexperienced, without organisation, without structure, short of food, short of weapons, short of money, brandishing her indisputable and newly reaffirmed title deeds to freedom and independence. A reasonable comprehension of Poland's difficulties is indispensable to a true view of Poland's peril.

Churchill was convinced that the Bolshevik threat to Poland was one which concerned Britain directly. In his article he explained why:

It is easy for those who live a long way from the Russian Bolshevists,—especially those who are protected by a good strip of salt water, and who stand on the firm rock of an active political democracy—to adopt a cool and airy view of their Communist doctrines and machinations.

But a new, weak, impoverished, famishing State like Poland, itself quaking internally, is placed in hourly jeopardy by close and continuous contact with such neighbours.

The Bolshevik aim of world revolution can be pursued equally in peace or war. In fact, a Bolshevist peace is only another form of war.

If they do not for the moment overwhelm with armies, they can undermine with propaganda.

Not a shot may be fired along the whole front, not a bayonet may be fixed, not a battalion may move, and yet invasion may be proceeding swiftly and relentlessly. The peasants are roused against the landlords, the workmen against their employers, the railways and public services are induced to strike, the soldiers are incited to mutiny and kill their officers, the mob are raised against the middle classes to murder them, to plunder their houses, to steal their belongings, to debauch their wives and carry off their children; an elaborate network of secret societies entangles honest political action; the Press is bought wherever possible.

This was what Poland dreaded and will now have reason to dread still more; and this was the cause, even more than the gathering of the Russian armies on the Polish front, continuous for nearly a year, that led the Poles to make that desperate military sally or counter-stroke which English Liberal opinion has so largely misunderstood, and which Socialist opinion has so successfully misrepresented.

Churchill ended his article with an appeal to the Germans to take their place at the side of the Allies:

It will be open to the Germans either to sink their own social structure in the general Bolshevist welter and spread the reign of chaos far and wide throughout the Continent; or, on the other hand, by a supreme effort of sobriety, of firmness, of self-restraint and of courage—undertaken, as most great exploits have to be, under conditions of peculiar difficulty and discouragement—to build a dyke of peaceful, lawful, patient strength and virtue against the flood of red barbarism flowing from the East, and thus safeguard their own interests and the interests of their principal antagonists in the West.

Churchill's article provoked strong criticism. 'Mr Churchill,' *The Times* declared on August 5, 'clearly ought not to remain a member of the Government of whose peace policy he disapproves.' And on August 6, Lord Derby wrote to Lloyd George from France: 'What a mess this Polish affair is. Winston's hint of an alliance with Germany to fight the Bolshevists has made the French mad!'

On July 30 the Polish Revolutionary Committee reached Bialystok, a predominantly Polish town only one hundred miles from Warsaw, and on August 4 the Red Army prepared for its final assault on the Polish capital. On learning of this imminent danger, Churchill hurried to see Lloyd George at 10 Downing Street. The Prime Minister was already in conference with Krassin and Kamenev,[1] and could not see him. But Lloyd George was himself in a stern mood, and delivered an ultimatum to the two Russians. While Churchill waited outside the Cabinet room, Lloyd George sent him a note of what he had said:

I told Kameneff & Krassin that the British fleet would start for the Baltic in 3 days unless they stopped their advance.

As soon as Krassin and Kamenev had gone, the Cabinet met to discuss Lloyd George's ultimatum. Every Minister was aware that it was the sixth anniversary of the outbreak of war in 1914. Nine years later, in *The World Crisis*, Churchill recalled his own mood:

On that famous anniversary, as we sat in the Cabinet room upon this serious communication, my mind's eye roamed back over the six years of carnage and horror through which we had struggled. Was there never to be an end? Was even the most absolute victory to afford no basis for just and lasting peace? Out of the unknown there seemed to march a measureless array of toils and perils. Again it was August 4, and this time we were impotent. Public opinion in England and France was prostrate. All forms of military intervention were impossible. There was nothing left but words and gestures.

On August 6 the Red Army continued its advance. Lloyd George's ultimatum had only twenty-four hours to run. 'Britain Plunging into War with Soviet Russia,' declared the *Daily Herald*, and *The Times* demanded of the nation 'the same unanimity and the same courage with which we faced the crisis of 1914'. At a meeting of the Cabinet Finance Committee on the morning of August 6, Churchill warned of the actual danger to British forces if the Russians rejected the British ultimatum. Within 48 hours, he said, 'we might conceivably find our-

[1] Lev Borisovich Rosenfeld, 1883–1936. Of Jewish parentage. Joined the Social Democratic Party, 1901. Known as 'Kamenev'. In exile with Lenin, 1909–14, he helped to direct Bolshevik activity from outside Russia. Returned to Russia, 1914; banished to Siberia. Returned to Petrograd, 1917. Opposed Lenin's intention to seize power, and advocated a coalition of all socialist parties. Reconciled to Lenin, he became Chairman of the Moscow Soviet, and of the Central Executive Committee of the Soviets, 1918. Member of the Politburo, 1919–25. Soviet Ambassador to Italy, 1926–7. Supported Stalin against Trotsky; subsequently led the opposition to Stalin. Sentenced to death, 1936, and shot.

selves at war with the Bolsheviks, in which event Bolshevist forces would attack us wherever possible, and in particular in Northern Persia, where the smallness and isolation of the troops rendered them a tempting bait'.

Churchill believed that in the event of war with Russia, General Wrangel, as well as the Poles, would have to be given British aid. He therefore telegraphed to General Milne in Constantinople:

> Political situation with Bolshevik Russia has become very critical on account of invasion of Poland, and a definite rupture from both Britain and France may take place next week. In that event we should probably resume our help to Wrangel in an energetic way. Prime Minister has already asked Admiralty to state what they could do to help him. You should make similar preparations, including organisation of a mission, despatch of arms, munitions and stores, but excluding employment of British or India units. It is possible sanction would be given for British Air Force to assist Wrangel. Air Ministry have been instructed to communicate directly with Officer Commanding Air Force. You should confer with him as to whether you could spare the new squadron from Egypt and how long it would take to bring it into action in Wrangel's area.

> Telegraph in reply what is possible in all these respects, but do not take any action until you receive official instructions.

At noon on August 6 Lord D'Abernon telegraphed to Lord Curzon from Warsaw, urging the immediate despatch of a Franco-British Expeditionary Force of at least 20,000 men. 'This force,' he added, 'should rigorously exclude any elements liable to be affected by Bolshevik or Sinn Fein propaganda.' But Lloyd George hoped to resolve the crisis without war. At midday he summoned Krassin and Kamenev to meet him and Bonar Law at 10 Downing Street.

When H. A. L. Fisher went to 10 Downing Street on August 7, Philip Kerr told him what had happened on the previous day. 'The PM & Bonar had a six hours talk with Kameneff & Krassin yesterday,' Fisher recorded in his diary. 'Result, terms of the armistice agreed on. The PM is in his best form: handles them admirably. Kamenev excellent. . . . K & K both want Peace.'

Lloyd George's ultimatum to the Bolsheviks expired that same day. But nothing was done and, on August 8, when he discussed the crisis with Millerand and Foch at Lympne, all that was decided was that in the event of an Anglo-French decision to come to Poland's assistance, Britain should provide 'boots, clothes and saddlery', France 'arms, munitions etc'.

On the afternoon of August 10 Lloyd George went to the House of Commons, where he explained the Government's Polish policy to what

H. A. L. Fisher described as 'a breathless House'. The Soviet Government, he said, had been right to react against the Polish attack in June, an attack which had been delivered, he pointed out, 'in spite of the warnings of the Allies'. But, he continued, 'Whatever the mistakes may be which are committed by a Government in an act of aggression against another nation, nothing justifies a retaliation or a reprisal or a punishment which goes to the extent of wiping out national existence.' Were Russia to destroy Poland, he said, it would 'not merely be a crime, it would be a peril. . . .' If Poland's independence were in danger, Britain would give 'such support as it was in our power to give'.

Lloyd George went on to tell the House that no British troops would be sent to Poland, but that if Russia tried to destroy Polish independence, Britain would send military stores and advisers, and would 'exercise an economic pressure upon Soviet Russia to release her stranglehold on the life of the Poles'.

Churchill was present throughout Lloyd George's speech. At six o'clock that evening he was among the Ministers summoned by Lloyd George to Bonar Law's room in the House of Commons, and was told that the Russians had just produced their peace proposals. These were hard on the Poles: the Polish army to be reduced to 50,000 men, all other arms to be given up, a special Citizen's Militia established, free grants of land to all wounded Polish soldiers and to all soldiers' widows, and free transit of all Russian commerce across Poland. For their part, the Russians agreed to withdraw to Poland's ethnographic border, as defined by Lord Curzon.

Lloyd George gave the Poles twenty-four hours in which to accept the Soviet terms. At eight o'clock on the evening of August 11 senior Ministers met again at the House of Commons. H. A. L. Fisher recorded in his diary: 'Winston vehement agst 24 hours time scheme.'

On August 4 Lloyd George had given the Russians a three-day ultimatum to cease hostilities against Poland. But hostilities had continued, and the ultimatum had lapsed. On August 10 he had given the Poles a twenty-four hour ultimatum to accept the Russian peace terms. Now it was the Poles who ignored his ultimatum, preferring to continue to resist the Russian advance. 'Poland will not agree to any humiliating terms,' Prince Sapieha[1] telegraphed direct to Lord Curzon on August 13. 'There can be no question of demobilisation and disarmament.'

---

[1] Eustace Sapieha, 1881–1963. Educated in Britain before 1900, he returned to Russian Poland and became a Russian subject. Polish Minister to London, 1919–20. Foreign Minister, 1920–1. Member of the Polish Parliament, 1928–30. Left Poland during the German occupation, 1944, and settled in Kenya, where he died.

On August 13 troops of the Red Army entered the village of Radzy-min, only twelve miles north-east of Warsaw. That same day the Poles rejected the British ultimatum. By August 14, Soviets had been established in Bialystok, Tarnopol, Lomza and Brest-Litovsk. The Polish Revolutionary Committee saw total victory in their grasp. But on August 15 the Poles counter-attacked, and Radzymin was recovered. For five days the Russians tried to hold the positions they had won. But with each day they were pushed further eastwards.

After August 13, Lloyd George and his Cabinet had ceased to try to influence events in Poland. During the climax of the Battle for Warsaw, Churchill was not even in London. On August 13 he went to Rugby to play polo, only returning to London on August 16, after the Battle of Warsaw had finally ensured Poland's survival.

The negotiations between Lloyd George and Krassin continued. All British military action in Russia had ended. No British troops remained at Batum; General Wrangel had been left to his own devices; the Poles had pushed the Bolsheviks back from Warsaw by their own efforts. Churchill had no authority to commit Britain to any further, or new, involvement. On August 19, Edward Marsh informed him that Boris Savinkov wanted permission for sixteen wagons of British war material, which had been sent to Libau 'long ago' for Yudenitch, to be transferred to a small Russian force under Savinkov's command. This force, Savin-kov explained, intended to cross the Soviet frontier near Pskov and 'push forward into Soviet territory collecting a huge snowball of Anti-Bolshies'. But on August 20 Churchill instructed Marsh to reply:

> I cannot help in this matter at all, owing to the decisions of policy which have been taken by my Government. But Monsieur Savinkov must not suppose that my personal feelings towards him are any the less cordial or that my interest in his cause has in any way weakened. I am bound, however, by the decisions of my Government, to which I am a party.

On August 17 the Cabinet had been informed that evidence existed proving that Krassin and Kamenev 'during their present mission to London' had indulged in Bolshevik propaganda, and had 'generally been guilty of conduct which was not compatible with the conditions under which their Mission had been permitted to proceed to England'. Churchill was outraged, and wanted Krassin's activities to be exposed publicly. But the Cabinet rejected his suggestion, and decided instead to ask Krassin and Kamenev for 'an explanation' of their conduct.

Churchill's anger was based upon the telegrams which had been exchanged between Chicherin in Moscow, and Kamenev in London; telegrams which the British had been able to intercept. Twice on August 18 he discussed these 'intercepts' with Henry Wilson. The two men were of like mind in wanting Krassin and Kamenev expelled without delay. Wilson made a note of their conversation in his diary:

Winston was much excited. He said it was quite true that LG was dragging the Cabinet step by step towards Bolshevism & he enumerated the different steps from Prinkipo to to-day when although pretending to uphold the integrity of Poland we did *nothing* to ensure it & even prevented arms & stores passing through Danzig. He asked me to write him a note on the subject & I said I would. . . . he said he would circulate with a covering note of his own to the Cabinet.

During August 18 Churchill assembled a set of the intercepted telegrams and sent them at once to Lloyd George, Bonar Law and Balfour. In his covering note he declared: 'The proofs of *mala fides* on the part of the Krassin Kameneff mission, & of their breach of their understanding about propaganda are now becoming so serious that I feel compelled to address a memorandum to the Cabinet on the subject.' And he added: 'A veritable plot is being hatched against England & France.'

Among the intercepted telegrams which Churchill sent to Lloyd George were several sentences which Churchill had specially marked, as indications of the Soviet plot against England. On August 12 Kamenev had telegraphed to Chicherin and Litvinov that he was continuing efforts to 'increase the tension and drive in still further the wedge between England and France. . . .'; on August 13 he had telegraphed to Chicherin of the need to buy arms 'over and above those that are required for the army of 50,000 and distribute them to the workmen'; later that same day Litvinov (in Copenhagen) had telegraphed to Chicherin (in Moscow): 'We must now aim at isolating France and coming to a separate agreement with Britain and also with Germany'; and on August 14 Kamenev had telegraphed to Litvinov and Lenin: 'We must not allow the ferment created among the workmen to subside.'

On August 19 Churchill returned to Rugby for a few days' holiday, and polo. On the following day he wrote to General Thwaites from Rugby: 'The more evidence you can secure to compromise Kameneff and Krassin the better. Pray keep me constantly informed.'

On August 20 a further telegram sent by Kameneff from London was decyphered, and shown to Churchill. The telegram referred to Russian financial support for the *Daily Herald*, and had been addressed to Lenin personally. It read:

We have sold some of the stones which we brought with us. £40,000 of the money realised was paid over to the newspaper as decided by the Central Committee of the Russian Communist Party. We shortly hope to realise on the white metal, which together with the money which is still being realised on the stones will give us over and above the money paid to the newspaper a further sum of about £60,000. Out of that sum we will pay another £10,000 to the newspaper, thus completing the amount. . . .

While General Thwaites was assembling these telegrams, Churchill drafted a covering note of his own:

There is no doubt that Kameneff and Krassin are actively interfering in our internal affairs as well as in our relations with France. They are 'the authorities responsible for organising Soviet institutions abroad'. They disburse the funds for revolutionary propaganda. We know what they have done with the 'Herald'. We do not know what other money they have spent and to what other sources it goes. No one can doubt that they are a fountain of conspiracy and corruption, having ceaselessly the purpose of paralysing and overturning this country and isolating it from its allies.

We know furthermore from the telegrams which have been passing that they are not trying to get better terms for Poland and so bring about a peaceful settlement. What they are trying to do is, as they plainly avow, to make sure that terms which will effectively sovietise Poland are stated in language which will deceive British working men and Labour leaders. We know that they are actuated by a spirit of absolute treachery and bad faith. We know that they have repeatedly and flagrantly broken their undertaking to abstain from propaganda while in this country. . . .

Churchill went on to point out that General Thwaites had 'secured evidence' which proved that Kamenev himself had been at the original meeting of Trade Union leaders at which the Council of Action had been set up, and that he had 'guided the proceedings'. His covering note continued:

I feel bound to bring to the notice of my colleagues the perturbation which is caused to the British officers who are concerned with this intelligence work when they see what they cannot but regard as a deliberate and dangerous conspiracy aimed at the main security of the State unfolding itself before their eyes and before the eyes of the executive Government without any steps being taken to interfere with it. . . .

Are we really going to sit still until we see the combination of the money from Moscow, the Kameneff–Krassin propaganda, the Council of Action, and something very like a general strike all acting and reacting on one another, while at the same time our military forces are at their very weakest.

Henry Wilson saw a copy of Churchill's note on August 23. He was pleased with it, but noted in his diary: 'He does not mention that *he* had thought of resigning.' Churchill returned to London from Rugby for the day on August 23. General Thwaites gave him the set of 'intercepts' for which he had asked. Henry Wilson recorded in his diary:

I told Winston it was the chance of his life to come out as an Englishman & that in one bound he would recover his lost position & be hailed as saviour by all that is best in England. I think I have got him pretty well fixed.

I warned him that we soldiers might have to take action if he did not & in that case his position would be impossible. He agreed. He said he was 'much worried' about LG's attitude and so am I, and it will take some explaining to ease my mind of the suspicion that LG is a traitor. . . .

On August 24 General Radcliffe telegraphed to the War Office from Warsaw to report that the Poles had captured 63,000 Russian prisoners, 200 heavy guns and 1,000 machine guns. Henry Wilson was excited, noting in his diary: 'As I said to Winston, what a good moment for kicking out Kameneff & Krassin.' On August 25 Churchill finally sent off his note, together with the selected intercepts, to Lloyd George and the six Ministers. On August 26 he returned to Rugby to continue his holiday. Before leaving the War Office, he wrote to Lloyd George:

I am quite clear that Kameneff and Krassin ought to be given their pass-ports, and I sent you last night a memorandum on this point. I do beg you to give it most serious consideration. It is far from my wish to add to your diffi-culties, but we are confronted with a treasonable conspiracy and our duty is clear. I have reason to believe that the military and naval personnel engaged in the secret telegrams, including the Directors of Military and Naval Intelli-gence, consider that the advantages of publishing the telegrams far exceed the disadvantages; and certainly they are an absolutely blasting record not only of the way we have been trifled with and intrigued against by the Bolsheviks but of the manner in which the Council of Action itself has been fooled. No more deadly propaganda has ever come before me than this publication will make. . . .

Churchill told Lloyd George that he could see no reason to negotiate a trade agreement with the Bolsheviks. All that was needed to open up trade with Russia, he wrote, was to 'lift the Blockade and authorise British subjects to trade freely if they choose and if they can'. He went on:

Why have we, a monarchical country with a large Conservative majority in the House of Commons, got to undertake the role of being the official bear-leaders to these ruffianly conspirators and revolutionaries. A policy of detachment should surely free us from this odious function. All the time they have been here they have been trying to foment a revolutionary movement and intriguing or bribing on every side. They had done much to render the Labour situation more dangerous, while so far as the Tory Party is concerned the harm done to our political and party interests is progressive and continuous. Moreover, there is neither food nor trade to be expected from the Russia which the Bolsheviks control. Wrangel and the Cossacks may very soon be in control of the coal, oil and food of the South, and the Ukrainians, who have the other great granary, are never going to let their corn be stolen by the Bolsheviks when they can trade it out in a Westerly direction to a civilised and victorious Poland.

From a national point of view their presence is most dangerous. From a party point of view it is simply estranging day after day the strong and dominant forces in our national life which you were so proud to lead in the war and which gave you their confidence at its close. I am very deeply distressed about the position because it is ever my desire to be a help and not a hindrance to you. . . .

Neither Churchill's letter, nor Wilson's memoranda, nor the intercepted telegrams, were able to persuade Lloyd George to expel the two negotiators. On August 29 Churchill had begun to draft yet another memorandum. 'Nothing can now save Poland,' he wrote:

Possibly in two stages, under some camouflage or other, the Russian part of her will be re-absorbed in the Russian system. I apprehend that the same fate will speedily overtake Lithuania, Latvia and Esthonia. These Baltic Provinces of Russia, the conquests of Peter the Great, will never be suffered to remain outside Russian Bolshevik control. As for Finland, partly by revolution from within, partly by attack from without, her turn will come.

But, after all, the reincorporation within the limits of the Russian Empire of these former Russian States that had not the wit to defend themselves in common, though a melancholy event, is not in itself a decisive event in European history. I have always believed that Russia would regain her 1914 frontiers and would never rest till she had done so. I had hoped, however, that she would have regained them under a Government friendly to the Allies, loyal to them in the War, and hostile to Germany. The disastrous fact for France, & also for us, is that they will be regained by a Russian Government fundamentally hostile to France and, indeed, to all the Allies. . . .

In his memorandum Churchill forecast, not only Russia's return to the imperial frontiers of 1914, but also 'a combination of interest and of policy' between Russia and Germany. Such a combination, he wrote, 'would create a mass against which the Western Powers will be quite unable to assert themselves and even, possibly in a few years to defend themselves'. And he continued:

There is, however, one method and one method alone by which the degeneration of the European situation could perhaps be arrested. To that method the French will, I fear, be unalterably opposed until it is again 'too late'. It seems to me that the immediate co-operation of Germany on loyal and equal terms is indispensable, if the position is to be saved. . . .

Churchill went on to explain that co-operation with Germany did not mean 'a war by Germany as mandatory for the Allies against Soviet Russia'. What it did mean, as he saw it, was 'a working agreement between Britain, France and Germany in regard to the arrangements for the pacification and reconstruction of Europe'. Churchill recognized that France did not want to bring Germany back into any position of authority in Europe. But, he went on:

France is unreasonable because she is terrified. She sees the forces massing up against her in the East. She sees herself abandoned by the United States. She is convinced that Britain means to detach herself. The best chance of making France reasonable is to reassure her. Reassurance can only be given in the form of a binding alliance between Great Britain, France and Germany to defend the Western Front in the event of an unprovoked attack by Russia. That is what we ought to offer now. What ought we to demand in exchange? Clearly a tripartite arrangement between Great Britain, France and Germany for the re-construction of Europe and the pacification of its Eastern regions. This implies a profound revision of the Treaty of Versailles and the acceptance of Germany as an equal partner in the future guidance of Europe. . . .

Churchill had been prompted to write his memorandum because of the danger of a Russian conquest of Poland. Even as he wrote it, the Poles were following up their successes. On August 20 the Red Army had been forced to abandon the siege of Lvov; henceforth, it was in continual retreat. By the end of September the Poles had reoccupied all of ethnographic Poland, from the Lithuanian border to the Pripet Marshes. The Polish Revolutionary Committee had fled from Bialystok on August 20, and returned to Soviet Russia. The leaders of the Galician Soviet Republic abandoned Tarnopol on September 21. On the top of his draft memorandum of August 29, Churchill noted:

Happily superseded by events. 'Poland has saved herself by her exertions & will I trust save Europe by her example.'

Churchill was still determined to persuade Lloyd George of the need for the expulsion of Kamenev and Krassin. On the evening of August 31 he summoned Sir Henry Wilson, General Thwaites, Sir Basil Thomson[1] and Captain Sinclair[2] to his room at the War Office. Churchill asked both Thomson and Sinclair to draw up papers giving reasons to show why Kamenev and Krassin should be expelled. Both papers were completed by noon on September 1. Thomson's paper stressed the connection between Kamenev and the Labour Party, as shown by the Russian subsidy for the *Daily Herald*. Sinclair's paper pointed out the danger of Bolshevik agitation in the Navy, as shown by Kamenev's encouragement for the establishment of 'Soviets' in the ports. Henry Wilson sent both these papers to Churchill at Lympne as soon as they were ready.

Churchill returned from Lympne that same night, and at one o'clock in the morning held a meeting of two of the Ministers who supported his demand for expulsion, Sir Robert Horne and Sir Eric Geddes. Henry Wilson, who was present, recorded in his diary that it was decided 'to get Bonar (who returns from Dinard tomorrow) to hold a Cabinet tomorrow afternoon & then if all agreed he is to write to LG & call for the expulsion of Kameneff etc'. Wilson also noted that Horne and Geddes were 'as strong as Winston & I for expulsion'.

Churchill left London on the morning of September 2 for a two-week holiday at Mimizan, the Duke of Westminster's estate south of Bordeaux. That same morning Bonar Law returned to London. He at once summoned Balfour and Horne to a 'Conference of Ministers' at 10 Downing Street. They met at eleven o'clock that morning. Sir Basil Thomson was present throughout their discussion, and showed them the intercepted telegrams which had so outraged Churchill and Wilson. Sir Robert Horne then declared 'that the damage which was being done by the Russian agitators was of so grave a nature that it was most important to get them out of the country immediately' and also, by publishing the intercepted telegrams, 'to make a complete exposure of their trickery'. Balfour and Bonar Law agreed, and the three Ministers then

---

[1] Basil Home Thomson, 1861–1939. Entered the Colonial Service, 1881. Acting Prime Minister of Tonga, 1890. Transferred to the Home Office (Prison Service), 1896. Governor of Dartmoor Prison, 1901–7; of Wormwood Scrubs Prison, 1907–8. Secretary to the Prison Commission, 1908. Assistant Commissioner, Metropolitan Police, 1913–19; in charge of intelligence operations against German agents in Britain, 1914–18. Knighted, 1919. Director of Intelligence, Home Office, 1919–21.

[2] Hugh Francis Paget Sinclair, 1873–1939. Entered the Navy, 1886; specialized in torpedo work. Assistant Director, Mobilization Division, Admiralty War Staff, 1914–16. Commanded HMS *Renown*, 1916–17. Chief of Staff, Battle Cruiser Force, 1917–19. Director of Naval Intelligence, 1919–21. Chief of the Submarine Service, 1921–3. Knighted, 1935.

formally agreed that 'the time had now come to request the Russian Trade Delegation to leave this country. . . .' But when they wrote to Lloyd George for an immediate decision, he replied, on September 4, that they must await his return to London.

Lloyd George was back in London on September 9, and summoned a Cabinet, in the absence of both Churchill and Walter Long, to discuss the expulsions. His mood was clearly going to be cautious and conciliatory. At noon on September 9 he spoke to H. A. L. Fisher, who wrote in his diary: 'He gives me the K & K intercepts to read and asks me what I think of them. I am against publication. . . . PM agrees. If *we* break with Russia, what advice can we give to Roumania and Poland. . . . The trickery of the Russians not worse than that of the French etc.'

The Cabinet met at three that afternoon. It was decided, Fisher noted in his diary, 'to postpone considerations of expulsion. PM very brilliant against breaking off with Russia. Cites duplicity of French.' Sir Robert Horne was emphatic that Kamenev had helped to strengthen 'the revolutionary party' in Britain by his money and advice.

The Cabinet met again on the morning of September 10, and decided not to order the expulsion either of Kamenev or of Krassin. It was agreed instead that Lloyd George should see Kamenev personally 'and warn him that his conduct had given rise to suspicion. . . .' Kamenev saw Lloyd George that evening, and on the following morning returned to Russia, leaving Krassin in charge of the Mission.

From France, Churchill initiated a final move to expel Krassin from England, writing to General Thwaites on September 17:

I see everywhere in the papers mention of this large contract for cloth placed by Krassin in Yorkshire. I remember a recent telegram in which Krassin was urged vehemently to secure a very large quantity of cloth for military uniforms. Probably this is the cloth. Let immediate enquiries be made as to the texture and quality; whether it is particularly suited for military uniform, and, if so, how many soldiers could be clothed with it. Is it for making great coats or ordinary uniforms? Look up the telegrams referring to this. Let me have all the information you can upon a file. It seems to me that if munitions are to be prevented from going to Poland, the least we can do is to refrain from facilitating the formation of a large Bolshevik army to attack Poland in the Spring. . . .

'As long as any portion of this nest of vipers is left intact,' Churchill added, 'it will continue to breed and swarm.'

The Cabinet met at noon on September 21 to discuss the question of

Bolshevik cloth. Churchill had returned from France that morning, and had circulated a memorandum demanding 'the dismissal of the Bolshevik Delegation'. According to the Cabinet Minutes: 'Authentic information was adduced to show that this cloth was required for the manufacture of military uniforms for the Bolshevik Army,' and comment was made 'on the undesirability of opening trade relations with the Bolshevik Government by supplying uniforms for troops, who might even be employed against British troops in Persia or elsewhere'. But later in the discussion, as the Minutes recorded, someone reminded the Cabinet 'that before the war the practice had been to permit the sale of goods, including even war material, to anyone who would pay, whether belligerent or not'. No further action was taken.

Kamenev having returned to Russia, Krassin remained in England as head of the Soviet Mission. Trade negotiations soon resumed. On September 24 H. A. L. Fisher recorded in his diary: 'I go to Nº 10 & find B. Law, LG and Winston—Winston complaining of LG's "tame cobras".'

The end of intervention left Churchill personally embittered, and even more widely distrusted than before. He had roused against himself the accumulated hostility of the Labour Party and its Press. His fierce, public determination to see Bolshevism destroyed, or at least isolated, alienated many of his colleagues. It caused a break in his intimacy with Lloyd George. And in the public mind it was yet further proof that he was a man who delighted in war. As Sir William Sutherland had written to Lloyd George on 6 July 1920: 'Winston has a reputation as a buccaneer. The country regard him as a bold, bad man.'

25

Russia's 'Bloodstained Gold'

CHURCHILL'S hostility towards Bolshevism did not abate with the defeat of the intervention in the autumn of 1920. Nor did he give up hope that the two armies still fighting the Bolsheviks—the Polish Army on Russia's western border and General Wrangel's Army in the Crimea—might have some measure of success. In Cabinet, he acted as a private watchdog over the fortunes of these two Armies, and continued to resist Lloyd George's plans for trade and reconciliation with Soviet Russia.

Churchill's advisers continued to warn him of the dangers of Bolshevism. On 13 October 1920 he was sent a report drawn up by the War Office General Staff, about Bolshevik activity in Persia. The report was based on intercepted Soviet telegrams. It showed, according to its introduction, that it was the British Empire which constituted 'the main stumbling block in the way of the expansion of Communism', and that the Empire would therefore be attacked 'at every vulnerable point, one of the most vulnerable being British Interests in the East'.

In Warsaw, Boris Savinkov pleaded the anti-Bolshevik cause with the Allied Ministers. But Lord Curzon instructed the British Minister, Sir Horace Rumbold,[1] to inform Savinkov that the anti-Bolshevist forces could expect no further British aid of any sort. When Churchill saw a copy of Curzon's telegram to Rumbold he was much angered, writing direct to Lloyd George on October 17: 'There is a deep insight behind

---

[1] Horace George Montague Rumbold, 1869–1941. Entered the Diplomatic Service, 1891. Succeeded his father as 9th Baronet, 1913. Chargé D'Affaires, Berlin, July 1914. Minister in Berne, 1916–19; in Warsaw, 1919–20. High Commissioner, Constantinople, 1920–4. Signed the Lausanne Treaty with Turkey on behalf of the British Empire, 24 July 1923. Ambassador in Madrid, 1924–8; in Berlin, 1928–33. Vice-Chairman of the Royal Commission on Palestine, 1936–7.

Savinkoff's affairs. It is a shame we are putting a spoke in his wheel. I never thought you would allow it.'

In the third week of October the Foreign Office learned that over ten thousand rifles, and eight million rounds of ammunition, were being loaded at Varna, for despatch to General Wrangel in the Crimea. The ship which was to carry the arms to Wrangel had, it seemed, been requisitioned by the French military authorities in Bulgaria. In a telegram to Lord Derby on October 25, Curzon instructed Derby to protest to the French Government about the despatch of weapons to Wrangel, and to insist on an immediate halt to the movement of arms. As soon as Churchill saw Curzon's telegram, he again protested. 'Here we are seen actually taking sides against the Anti-Bolshevists,' he wrote to Lloyd George on October 26. 'Surely this was not yr intention: less is it in any way required by the engagements wh we have entered into.'

This incident stimulated Churchill to look again at Britain's eastern policy. On October 27 he wrote a four-page memorandum on Russia for the Cabinet, pointing out that as a result of the Polish victory and General Wrangel's 'increasing power and successes in the Crimea', the immediate Bolshevik threat to the British forces at Kazvin, in Persia, had been much reduced. The victories of the Poles and of Wrangel had therefore been, he wrote, 'of the greatest service to us'. But, he added:

We cannot, however, take much credit to ourselves for them, because we advised the Poles to accept the Bolshevik terms of surrender before the Battle of Warsaw was fought, and we have rigorously abstained from supplying Wrangel with any assistance—even chloroform and antiseptics were denied to his wounded. Therefore we must look upon these victories in the light of a most happy windfall which we have not deserved. . . .

Churchill warned that the advantages gained by the Polish and Crimean successes would be 'fleeting'. The Bolsheviks had opened negotiations with Britain for the purchase of military greatcoats and cloth. They had also signed an armistice with the Poles on October 12, thus ending their two-year war on their western borderlands. This would enable the Red Army, Churchill wrote, 'to concentrate upon Wrangel and, to some extent, upon Armenia'. If they destroyed Wrangel's army, 'as they may', they would then be able 'to increase their pressure upon our troops in North Persia and generally in the East'. Churchill went on:

Last year at this time I warned the Cabinet that if Denikin was destroyed the blow would fall on Poland in the Spring. It fell, and we well know the shocking dangers from which we were miraculously rescued by the Battle of

Warsaw. If this Autumn witnesses the destruction of Wrangel, it seems almost certain that the Spring will witness a great recrudescence of Bolshevik pressure in the East, upon Persia and towards Afghanistan. This is the moment when we are busily engaged in stopping the French sending aid to Wrangel and ourselves making the Great Coats and equipment on which the Bolshevik military power depends.

Churchill was angered by the British failure to help Wrangel, and by the trade negotiations with the Bolsheviks. 'It is no longer possible,' he wrote in his memorandum, 'to pose the question, "Which side are we on?" It is clear that we are on both sides at the same time.'

When Curzon wrote to Churchill on October 29 to explain that the arms at Varna were not intended for Wrangel at all, but for the Caucasus, Churchill replied by setting out his unhappiness about the Russian policy being pursued by the Foreign Office:

Thank you for your letter enclosing the telegram which shows that these arms were not after all intended for the wicked Wrangel but only for the good Armenians and Georgians.

There is another point which I have been meaning to mention to you. A few weeks ago I saw a telegram suggesting to our representative at Warsaw that he should put a spoke in Savinkov's wheel, and several other telegrams have passed in that sense. I was very sorry to see this, because although we cannot help him we ought not to hamper him. The Prime Minister thinks more of Savinkov than of any other anti-Bolshevik Russian or than all the other anti-Bolshevik Russians put together, and we have had several long confabulations and lunches at 10 Downing Street, with Savinkov. When I reproached him with not merely throwing him over but actively taking sides against Savinkov, he denied it altogether and seemed greatly surprised to read the telegrams. I am sure his view would be that we should keep out of it, neither helping nor hindering; and that is all I ask. I am sure the failure of a pro-Bolshevik policy will become more pronounced with every month that passes.

Churchill continued to speak out against the Bolsheviks whenever an occasion presented itself. At the Cannon Street Hotel in London on November 4, he warned his audience that there was 'a worldwide conspiracy' to overthrow the British Empire, in which Bolshevism played a leading part. But his speech provoked an immediate reaction. Three days later, on the occasion of the third anniversary of the Russian revolution, Colonel L'Estrange Malone spoke in the Albert Hall of the Bolsheviks' achievements, and urged his audience to leave no stone unturned in preparing for revolution in Britain itself. 'What are a few Churchills or Curzons on lamp-posts,' he asked, 'compared to the massacre of thousands of human beings?' Malone was arrested two days after his speech, charged with inciting revolution, and sentenced to six months' imprisonment.

On November 8 the Red Army launched a major offensive against General Wrangel's forces in the Crimea. Realizing that the end was near, Wrangel issued instructions for the evacuation of his troops to Constantinople. On November 11 he ordered his troops to begin embarking from the Crimea. Their heavy transport, he told them, must be abandoned. At a Cabinet meeting that morning at 10 Downing Street, Lloyd George read out a telegram which had reached the Admiralty from Sir John de Robeck, the Naval Commander-in-Chief in the Mediterranean, reporting a French request for British help in evacuating some 80,000 anti-Bolshevik Russians from the Crimea. According to the Cabinet Minutes, it was agreed that the British Government 'should not undertake any action for the evacuation of refugees other than those of British nationality or for the removal of ships under General Wrangel in Black Sea ports'. The Cabinet Minutes recorded that 'The Secretary of State for War (Mr Churchill) asked that his protest might be recorded against this decision, which, in his view, might probably result in a massacre of the civilians in the Crimea.'

While the Cabinet was meeting at 10 Downing Street, a telegram from de Robeck was being decyphered at the Foreign Office. 'General Wrangel's situation is reported to be critical,' de Robeck reported, 'and he has telegraphed begging for our assistance in evacuating all women and children from Crimea. I should be glad of immediate instructions as to what attitude His Majesty's Government wish me to adopt with regard to assisting in humanitarian work of saving these people from Bolshevik excesses.' Churchill saw this telegram after the Cabinet had ended. He sent it at once to Lloyd George, with a covering note:

This is what I told you to day was to be repeated.

We ought not to be guilty of inhumanity; & anyhow we shall have a burden thrust upon us.

On November 14 the Bolsheviks captured Sebastopol. Tens of thousands of anti-Bolshevik Russians made their way, as best they could, on Russian and French ships, to Constantinople, and exile.

In refusing further British help to both Denikin and Wrangel, the Cabinet had made it clear that no help could be given to any other anti-Bolshevik forces. Churchill's one remaining hope was to prevent Lloyd George from opening trade negotiations with the Bolsheviks. On November 16 he circulated to the Cabinet a two-thousand-word memorandum on the subject, reminding his colleagues that their original decision to trade with Russia had been made on the assumption 'that we would not trade with the Bolsheviks at all but only with the Russian co-operators'—the peasants and tradesmen organized into local trade associations. This attitude, Churchill continued, had been 'insensibly abandoned' after the British Government came to realize 'that the Bolshevik Government has devoured the co-operators as well as all forms of individual trading in Russia'. It had earlier been believed that the Bolsheviks would export large quantities of surplus food, and particularly corn. This argument had been put forward with conviction by Lloyd George on February 10 in the House of Commons, but, as Churchill pointed out:

So far from Russia having large surpluses of foodstuffs to export, the Bolshevik Government is confronted with a general scarcity steadily developing into a terrible famine. There is no prospect within any measurable period of any relief being derived by Great Britain or by Europe by large exportations of food and raw materials from Russia.

It had become clear, during the previous weeks, that the Russians intended to pay for British goods, not by foodstuffs or raw materials, but by gold and precious stones. It was this fact which Churchill found repellent. 'This treasure does not belong to the Russian Bolshevik Government,' he wrote. 'It has been forcibly seized by these usurpers. Part has been stolen from the Roumanian State treasure which fell into Russian hands when the Roumanian Government was forced to take refuge on Russian soil. The jewels have been stolen from their owners in Russia and in many cases from their corpses.' Churchill's argument continued:

. . . We are now asked to give the Bolsheviks a special title to this plundered gold in order that with it they may make purchases in the British market. It seems to me that this is a very serious step for us to take. We shall be condoning as a Government the wholesale repudiation of contracts in order to obtain for the benefit of this country the proceeds of piracy. I do not consider that the amount of gold in question, which does not I believe exceed 20 or 30 millions, will make a material difference to the economic well-being of Great Britain. It is not gold we want from Russia but goods.

The transference of this stolen gold from Russia to England stands on an entirely different basis in my view to the transference of corn, flax or other raw materials. One can easily understand that, in view of the financial chaos in Russia, it will be necessary to start a system of barter if ever trade is to be resumed, and the newly created wealth of each year in the shape of crops might well be accorded a temporary relief from the claims of past creditors. But this bloodstained gold is not the product of new and honest labour but purely stolen property.

The 'Russian nation as a whole', Churchill added, would gain nothing from trade with Britain. The only people to benefit would be 'the gang of criminals who have usurped power and now rule with tyranny'. The goods brought from Britain—locomotives, clothing, boots —would not be in sufficient quantity 'to effect the economic construction of the country', but would serve only to help the Bolshevik regime 'in maintaining itself in power, in clothing and equipping its armies and in transporting them from one part of its frontier to another'. Churchill was emphatic in his denunciation of the effects of British trade with Russia:

We shall simply fortify the existing evil regime without effecting any amelioration in general conditions. . . . I fear that the steps we are asked to take in the hopes of mitigating the sufferings of the Russian people will, therefore, only rivet the chains of the communist tyrants more firmly on their necks, and that no relief will reach the masses. . . . I do not see why a monarchial country like ours and a Government based on a large conservative majority in both Houses of the Legislature should go out of its way to condone what has happened in Russia and should put itself in a position before all the world of giving special countenance to this criminal regime.

On November 16 the last units of General Wrangel's anti-Bolshevik army was evacuated from the Crimea, and sailed to Constantinople.[1] At half past eleven on the morning of November 17 the Cabinet met at 10 Downing Street to discuss the opening of trade with the Bolsheviks. Churchill's memorandum of November 16 was among the documents circulated to all Ministers in advance of the meeting.

The discussion was opened by the President of the Board of Trade, Sir Robert Horne. He pointed out that nearly five months earlier, on June 30, the British Government had telegraphed to Chicherin, setting

---

[1] The British authorities took immediate steps to receive as many Russian refugees as possible in Constantinople. Sir Horace Rumbold, who had arrived in the city, as British High Commissioner, in the second week of November, set up a British Emergency Committee to help with the feeding, bathing and clothing of ten thousand Russian women and children. The problem was a massive one. By the end of November there were 120,000 Russians crowded on sixty ships in the Sea of Marmara, and a further 20,000 in Constantinople itself.

out the conditions under which Britain would trade with Russia. These
were that the Russians would agree to end all revolutionary propaganda
in Britain, and would return all British soldiers captured during the
intervention. The Russians had agreed to both these conditions. Britain
would be 'guilty of bad faith', Horne insisted, if she did not now agree to
Anglo-Soviet trade. 'The Russians are prepared to put large orders in
this country,' he added, 'and many of the contracts are in an advanced
state.' Such orders, he declared, would help to avert 'the menace of unemployment' in Britain. Horne then widened the scope of his arguments.
'I feel strongly,' he said, 'the only way we shall fight Bolshevism is by
trade. It thrives best in uncivilised conditions. The longer Trotsky
keeps the terror up the longer he keeps up Bolshevism.' In his concluding remarks Horne stated emphatically: 'Our trading community
as a whole want to resume trade. . . .'

Lord Curzon spoke next. He was unconvinced that the Russians
would really end their 'hostile propaganda', and warned his colleagues:
'The Russian menace in the East is incomparably greater than anything
else that has happened in any time to the British Empire.' He feared
'conspiracies worked by Bolshevik agents and paid for by Bolshevik
gold' throughout Asia.

Curzon's arguments did not influence Bonar Law, who spoke strongly
in favour of trade with the Bolsheviks. 'I agree with Horne,' he said, 'we
have been playing with this Russian situation too long.' If Britain did
not trade with the Bolsheviks, he said, she would 'lose the chance of
political influence'.

Lloyd George spoke after Bonar Law. Each of his arguments was in
favour of immediate negotiations with Soviet Russia. The verbatim
Cabinet Minutes recorded his remarks:

The Russians are prepared to pay in gold and you won't buy. We trade
with cannibals in the Solomon Islands. Within the last few days an offer has
been made to the British Government for £10 million worth on condition that
the order shall be put in this country, but I must not give details. . . . If we
refuse it, it will leak out that we turned it down because of Persia and Tashkent and because we hate the Bolsheviks at a time when we are voting £4 or
£5 millions for the unemployed. Of the £10 million, half of it would be
wages. This will be said over and over again and will add to the public
discontent.

As to propaganda, Curzon says we must have an undertaking that propaganda has ceased. Even with the best will in the world with Bolshevik outbreaks, you will not be able to restrain it. As long as there is a pamphlet
published in India our officials, who are violently anti-Bolshevik, will hold

that the conditions have not been fulfilled. . . . It is no use saying that if six months hence there is no propaganda you will enter into an agreement. By that time you will be in the depths of trade depression, and you will be forced to make a trade agreement.

In spite of a lot of newspaper propaganda here there has been no response to the campaign to prevent trade with Russia. . . . When I mentioned the possibility of our going to war to support Poland a shudder passed through the House, and those who were clamouring against Bolshevism immediately shewed the white feather. . . .

I have heard predictions about the fall of the Soviet government for the last two years. Denikin, Yudenich, Wrangel, all have collapsed, but I cannot see any immediate prospect of the collapse of the Soviet government.

The general inclination of the Cabinet was in favour of Anglo-Soviet trade. Churchill was extremely angry at the failure of his memorandum to influence his colleagues. A few moments before the meeting adjourned, he handed a note to Lord Birkenhead, announcing that if the Cabinet decided to trade with Russia, he would resign. That afternoon Birkenhead wrote to Churchill, seeking to dissuade him from so rash a course:

My dear Winston

I have been considering very carefully the most important note which you handed me at the Cabinet this morning. I am most clearly of opinion that if the decision goes against you tomorrow, you would be making a mistake of a magnitude which shocks me, if you carried out any such intention. You would find yourself the hero of the 'Morning Post' and the leader of some thirty Tories in the House of Commons, who would disagree with you on 90% of all the subjects about which you feel really deeply. Moreover, you would cut yourself adrift perhaps permanently, certainly for a very long time, from the Coalition, which on every other point you support, in the necessity of which you believe, and of which in my judgment you are an indispensible member. I do not deal, because such a point is of relatively small account, upon the pain and sorrow with which I should contemplate the dissolution of an Association which has been so great a source of pleasure to both of us, and has not, I think, been without public advantage in a very critical period. . . .

Two other points seem to me of importance.

1. I do not believe that Public Opinion in this country is wholly adverse to the resumption of trade with Russia. Indeed I believe the contrary, provided that such a resumption involves no acquiescence in the Bolshevic repudiation of their public, and private debt. The London Bankers according to my information, which I have carefully checked from Liverpool Traders, speak for themselves and themselves alone.

2. I think you overrate the amount of support you are likely to meet with in the Cabinet. Certainly I am convinced that it will occur to nobody else to

resign upon such an issue, or even to feel that a surrender of their standpoint involves more than the concession to a Cabinet decision, which we all of us, however, unwilling, are commonly constrained to make. And I am quite sure that after the very plain and repeated indications made by the last speaker (L.G.) at the Cabinet meeting this morning, there are very few who would be prepared to carry the matter to a conclusion adverse to his opinion.

I have only to add that I am persuaded that this is not one of those great occasions on which a Member of a Government is faced with a decision so vital upon a point of principle (which his countrymen will recognise as adequate) as to justify him in separating from his colleagues with whom he is otherwise in general agreement, and in withdrawing his services from a country which very greatly needs him in the constructive work of reorganisation.

Yours as ever
F.E.

In his postscript Lord Birkenhead wrote: 'This is rather pomposo but I had to dictate.' Birkenhead's arguments could not lightly be dismissed. He was Churchill's closest and most trusted friend.

The Cabinet met again at half past eleven on the morning of Thursday November 18, and at once resumed their discussion. 'A frantic appeal from Churchill against the agreement,' Sir Maurice Hankey wrote in his diary. 'He said the diamonds were all stolen, many from the dead bodies of the Russian aristocracy.' There was, he added, according to the Minutes of the meeting, 'no corn in view'. One by one Churchill reiterated the arguments in his memorandum of November 16. Lloyd George replied at once, telling the Cabinet:

. . . the difference between my view and Mr Churchill's is on the question whether you make it a condition precedent of the agreement that all abuses should stop. I say 'Here is the agreement and conditions of trade—you break them and trade stops'. I do not challenge that the proportion of trade is small but the public will exaggerate what you will get if you stop it.

The discussion turned to Bolshevik actions in the East. 'If you are going to wait for all abuses to be removed,' A. J. Balfour commented, 'it is hopeless.' But he was willing to ask the Russians to 'show good faith' by offering, for example, to suspend all activity in Persia. Lloyd George replied that there were Bolsheviks in Persia 'for whom the Soviets are not responsible'. When Curzon said that there were as many as five thousand Bolsheviks 'in occupation of the ports' of the Persian end of the Caspian, Lloyd George described this, not as an external aggression, but as 'a rising tide of Bolshevism within the countries'. If trade were delayed, he added, 'until you get all this put right, you will get endless arguments. I would enter into the trade agreement, take the risk and say if you break this the trade is gone and the burden rests with you.'

The discussion became diffuse. Edwin Montagu spoke of the desire of Moscow 'to stir up action on the Afghan borders', by means of agents in Kabul. Lloyd George retorted: 'I am not here as an advocate of Bolshevism. I am trying to prevent Bolshevism in this country.' Austen Chamberlain spoke as someone whose position 'is very close to Curzon's and Churchill's'; but when he had finished speaking he had adopted Bonar Law's position, telling his colleagues: 'We must therefore have an agreement.'

Lloyd George was prompted by Austen Chamberlain's change of heart to ask: 'May we take it that the principle of concluding an agreement is accepted?' Lord Birkenhead was the first to reply. 'Yes,' he said, 'with great difficulty, I agree.' According to Hankey's diary the decision was then taken, by vote, 'in favour of continuing the negotiations'. Curzon, Churchill and Milner voted against. Walter Long, who was ill, had sent word that he was also against. All other Ministers gave the negotiations their support.

Hankey noted in his diary that Churchill had been 'so upset by the decision that he declared himself unequal to discussing other items on the Agenda affecting the army. He was quite pale and did not speak again during the meeting.'

At the end of the meeting Churchill asked if it might be recorded in the Cabinet Minutes that no Cabinet Minister would be 'fettered' as regards making anti-Bolshevik speeches. His request was granted. That evening he went to Oxford, where he delivered a violently anti-Bolshevik speech to the Oxford Union. It was his view, he declared, 'that all the harm and misery in Russia has arisen out of the wickedness and folly of the Bolshevists, and that there will be no recovery of any kind in Russia or in eastern Europe while these wicked men, this vile group of cosmopolitan fanatics, hold the Russian nation by the hair of its head and tyranizes over its great population'. He continued: 'The policy I will always advocate is the overthrow and destruction of that criminal regime.'

Lloyd George was worried that Churchill and the other Ministers opposed to trade with Russia would insist, despite the Cabinet decision, on certain conditions being included in any trade agreement, particularly conditions regarding Bolshevik propaganda in the East. On

November 19 he asked Hankey to see Sir Robert Horne, who was to conduct the negotiations, 'and to rub into him that, if Curzon and Churchill are obstructive', he must bring the matter to Lloyd George himself. Hankey noted in his diary that the Prime Minister 'is determined to push the agreement through'.

The negotiations began in December between Horne and Krassin. On December 5, Churchill reiterated his loathing of Bolshevism in a long article in the *Sunday Express*. The article took the form of an answer to an earlier one by H. G. Wells,[1] who had just returned from a visit to Russia, and who had argued in favour of British and American help to the Bolsheviks in order to enable them to 'establish a new social order'. Wells had described the Bolsheviks as the only Government that could prevent 'a final collapse of Russia'. Churchill rejected this contention, declaring, in the course of a bitter reply:

We see the Bolshevik cancer eating into the flesh of the wretched being; we see the monstrous growth swelling and thriving upon the emaciated body of its victim. And now Mr Wells, that philosophical romancer, comes forward with the proposition that the cancer is the only thing that can pull the body round; that we must feed that and cultivate that. After all, it is another form of life. It is 'a new social order'. Why be so narrow-minded as to draw the line between health and disease, still less between right and wrong? Adopt an impartial attitude. Put your money on the disease if you think it is going to win.

Churchill refused to accept H. G. Wells' argument that the starvation and dislocation of life in Russia had in part been caused by the Allied intervention and blockade. He believed that famine conditions had been created as a result of Bolshevik policy itself. 'There has never been any work more diabolical in the whole history of the world than that which the Bolsheviks have wrought in Russia,' he wrote. 'Consciously, deliberately, confidently, ruthlessly—honestly, if you will, in the sense that their wickedness has been the true expression of their nature—they have enforced their theory upon the Russian towns and cities; and these are going to die. . . .'

H. G. Wells replied to Churchill on December 12. His article, published in the *Sunday Express*, contained a personal portrait of severity and scorn:

[1] Herbert George Wells, 1866–1946. Author and novelist. Among his earliest works were *The Time Machine* (1895), *The War of the Worlds* (1898) and *The First Men in the Moon* (1901). On his return from a visit to Russia in 1920 he published *Russia in the Shadows*. He parodied Churchill in his novel *Men Like Gods* (1923), where he wrote, of 'Rupert Catskill', that 'his wild imaginings have led to the deaths of thousands of people'.

I cannot call myself Anti-Churchill. I have known Mr Churchill for a dozen years perhaps, and there is much to like in him. He has an imaginative liveliness rare in politicians, and his personality is unusually amusing.

But I will confess that it distresses me that he should hold any public office at the present time. These are years of great scarcity, and Mr Churchill is temperamentally a waster; there are dangerous corners ahead, and for two years Mr Churchill has—if I may use the most expressive word—monkeyed with our Eastern policy.

I want to see him out of any position of public responsibility whatever. . . . The Government would look more serious and statesmanlike without him.

Churchill's retirement, Wells added, 'would not be a tragic fall'. After all, he explained, 'Mr Churchill has many resources. He would, for instance, be a brilliant painter'.

26

Ireland 1919–1920:
'Let Murder Stop'

THROUGHOUT 1919 and 1920 Churchill had been concerned with the worsening situation in Ireland. During his two years as Secretary of State for War, he was responsible for the actions and safety of the increasing number of British troops called in to halt the drift to civil war. At the British General Election of December 1918 seventy-six Irish constituencies had returned candidates of the Sinn Fein party. The old Irish Nationalist party, which was pledged to work within the British Constitution, won only seven seats. Sinn Fein—'ourselves alone' —totally rejected the Nationalist Party's argument that Ireland's future would be best secured inside the United Kingdom. They also rejected the Liberal Party's pledge of Home Rule for Ireland, believing that such a pledge did not give Ireland the independence that was her right.

The result of the election was announced on 28 December 1918. Less than three weeks later, on 15 January 1919, a Sinn Fein Congress met in Dublin, and formally decided that its seventy-six MPs would boycott the British parliament. They then announced their intention of setting up a Parliament of their own in Dublin. They were fiercely determined both to force Britain to abandon her control of Irish affairs, and to ensure that the interests of the Protestants of Ulster did not stand in the way of independence for all Ireland.

Since May 1918, Viscount French of Ypres, the former Commander-in-Chief of the British Expeditionary Force in France, had been Lord Lieutenant—or Viceroy—of Ireland. French was determined to crush any Sinn Fein violence before it could develop into full rebellion. On 17 January 1919 he telegraphed to the War Office from Dublin, asking for substantial reinforcements of equipment and arms. Churchill had

Lough Swilly

Londonderry

ANTRIM

DONEGAL LONDON-
DERRY

Carrickfergus

Strabane

Antrim

TYRONE

Belfast

Ballyshannon Pettigo Lisburn

Belleek Inniskillen

Sligo FERMAN-
AGH ARMAGH DOWN

LEITRIM CAVAN MON-
AGHAN Clones

SLIGO LOUTH

Dundalk

MAYO

Castlebar LONGFORD

ROSCOMMON WESTMEATH MEATH

Balbriggan

Tuam Athlone

GALWAY

Galway OFFALY DUBLIN

Dublin

KILDARE

CLARE LAOIGHIS WICKLOW

Ennis CARLOW

Thurles KILKENNY

Limerick TIPPERARY WEXFORD

LIMERICK

WATERFORD

Fermoy KERRY

Killarney CORK

Cork

Macroom

Bandon Queenstown

Bear
Island

The boundary of the six counties of Ulster (approved by
both Belfast and Dublin on 30 March 1922)

0 10 20 30 40 50

Scale in miles

© Martin Gilbert

IRELAND, 1919–1920

been at the War Office for only four days when French's request arrived, and it was dealt with primarily by Sir Henry Wilson, who was an Ulsterman with a deep hatred of Irish Catholic extremism. On January 18 Wilson wrote in his diary: 'We are sending over to Ireland *at once* the armoured cars, Tanks and the M-Guns they telegraphed for last night.'

The reinforcements for which Lord French had asked were despatched to Ireland in the third week of January. But neither weapons nor men were able to weaken the rapidly growing nationalism in the South. On January 21 two policemen were shot dead by gunmen in County Tipperary. On January 22, Sinn Fein summoned a Parliament, or Dail, in Dublin. The Dail, meeting at the Dublin Mansion House, ratified the Republic which had been declared at the time of the Easter Rising, and elected a 'Cabinet'.

On February 2 the Secretary to the Army Council, Sir Reginald Brade,[1] sent Churchill a note to explain the position of the War Office in relation to these events. The Army, he wrote, was empowered to carry out the policy of the Chief Secretary for Ireland, but had no independent powers. In fact, Brade wrote, 'the initiative comes from the Irish Government and the responsibility rests with them. The Army Council have only acted as their agents, and this has always been understood.' Even the decision to impose martial law, Brade explained, would have to come from the Lord Lieutenant in Dublin and the Chief Secretary in London.

On February 4, when the newly-elected House of Commons met at Westminster, not one Sinn Fein MP took his—or her—seat, and Ireland was represented only by the seven National Party MPs and twenty-four Ulster Unionists. In Ireland, Sinn Fein appealed for volunteers, and built up their own armed force, the Irish Republican Army, or IRA. The Sinn Fein leaders, in their Dublin Cabinet, took on the full functions of independent Cabinet Ministers. The Finance Minister, Michael Collins[2]—who was also the Adjutant-General of the IRA—secretly raised a loan within Ireland from those sympathetic to the Republican

[1] Reginald Herbert Brade, 1864–1933. Entered the War Office as a Clerk, 1884. Assistant Secretary, War Office, 1904–14. Knighted, 1914. Secretary, War Office, 1914–20.

[2] Michael Collins, 1890–1922. Born in County Cork, the son of a Catholic farmer. Worked first as a Post Office employee, then as a bank clerk in London, 1906–16. Took part in the Easter rebellion in Dublin, 1916. Imprisoned for eight months, 1916. Adjutant-General of the Irish Republican Army, 1917–18. Imprisoned for a second time, 1918. Minister of Home Affairs, and Finance Minister, in the Sinn Fein Government, 1919–21. One of the Delegates who negotiated the Irish Treaty with Britain, 1921–2. Chairman of the Provisional Free State Government, and Minister of Finance, 1922. Commanded the Irish Free State army against the opponents of the Treaty, June 1922; ambushed and killed, August 1922.

446 'LET MURDER STOP' 1919

cause. The President of the Dail, Eamon De Valera,[1] visited the United States and raised five million dollars for an Irish National Loan.

The situation worsened during March. Several policemen were killed, moderate Home Rulers were threatened and British rule was challenged throughout Ireland. On April 3 the Government's policy was set out by the new Chief Secretary for Ireland, Ian Macpherson,[2] who, speaking in the House of Commons, emphasized that large military force had to be kept in Ireland for as long as murders and outrages 'of the most cruel and unpardonable kind continue to darken Irish life'.

On April 10 Lord French appealed direct to Churchill for more troops, weapons and equipment. Nine extra battalions, he insisted, were needed at once if the Republican outrages were to be prevented. Churchill accepted the validity of French's request, but did not agree to send as many troops as French had asked for, telegraphing on April 11: 'Priority. Personal and Secret. We are doing our utmost to help you with troops. One battalion goes tonight. MG btn tomorrow & 4 more as soon as the ships have turned round. You ought to have the 6 in 6 days. The other 3 requires further study.'

During the summer the Ulster leaders warned that any attempt to impose Home Rule would only stimulate the Catholics to demand the total end to British rule. The Protestants of Ulster were prepared to resist Home Rule by force. Their determination was challenged by two months of Sinn Fein and IRA violence, which reached a climax on September 7 when a party of British soldiers was fired on in the predominantly Catholic town of Fermoy, and one was shot dead. On the following day, a mob of nearly two hundred soldiers, incensed by the death of their colleague, appeared in the streets of Fermoy armed with hammers and pieces of iron, and proceeded in reprisal to smash windows and loot shops.

On September 10 Lord French issued proclamations outlawing Sinn Fein in several counties, and in the County Borough of Dublin. On

---

[1] Eamon De Valera. Born, 1882, in New York. A leading figure in the Easter Rebellion, 1916. Sentenced to death; sentence commuted to life penal servitude on account of his American birth. Released under the general amnesty, June 1917. President of the Sinn Fein, 1917–26. Elected to Parliament as a Sinn Fein MP, 1918. Imprisoned, 1918; escaped from Lincoln Jail, February 1919. 'President' of the Irish Republic, 1919–22. Rejected the Irish Treaty and fought against the Free State Army, 1922–3. Leader of the Opposition in the Free State Parliament, 1927–32. Minister for External Affairs, 1932–48. Head of the Government of Eire (Taoiseach), 1937–48, 1951–4 and 1957–9. President of the Republic of Ireland, 1959–73.

[2] James Ian Macpherson, 1880–1937. Barrister. Liberal MP, 1911–18; Coalition Liberal, 1918–31; Liberal National, 1931–5. Under-Secretary of State for War, 1914–16. Vice-President of the Army Council, 1918. Chief Secretary for Ireland, 1919–20. Minister of Pensions, 1920–2. Created Baronet, 1933. Created Baron Strathcarron, 1936.

September 12 he issued a further proclamation, prohibiting and suppressing the Sinn Fein Parliament. But the violence and the terror continued. On September 12 a police constable was shot dead in one of the busiest streets of Dublin. There followed the arrest of two Sinn Fein MPs, and the suppression of newspapers favourable to the Sinn Fein cause.

The Republicans were determined to be rid of Britain altogether. On December 15 yet another policeman was shot dead, in County Cork. In an attempt to halt the killings, Lord French appealed for a citizen volunteer force to assist the police. On December 19 an attempt was made to kill French himself. Several bombs were thrown at his car as he was driving to Viceregal Lodge, but he escaped unhurt. One of the attackers was killed. On December 22 Henry Wilson wrote in his diary: 'Winston told me this evening that Macpherson had warned him today that Ireland might have to be seriously reinforced in the next fortnight.'

Eighteen Government servants—mostly policemen and soldiers—had been murdered in Ireland during 1919.

On 23 February 1920 Churchill introduced the Army Estimates in the House of Commons. In the course of the debate the Nationalist Party MP for West Belfast, Joseph Devlin,[1] declared that Ireland's right 'to manage its own affairs and determine its own destinies' had been taken away. He went on to criticize the presence of over 40,000 British troops in Ireland. Commenting on Devlin's speech, Churchill remarked: 'We saw the flames of orange and green flash out from the Irish furnace.'

Churchill told the House of Commons that the War Office was not responsible for the Government of Ireland. 'The Irish Secretary,' he insisted, 'conducts the Government of Ireland. The responsibility of the War Office is limited to providing the necessary troops.' These troops, however, had been attacked during the debate for undue violence, and for harsh measures in keeping down Catholic unrest. Churchill went on to tell the House of Commons:

. . . the military have a very difficult task in Ireland. They have a terrible task. I believe they have far more often erred on the side of weakness, even

[1] Joseph Devlin, 1872–1934. Irish Nationalist MP for Kilkenny North, 1902–6; for West Belfast, 1906–18; for the Falls Division of Belfast, 1918–22 and for Fermanagh and Tyrone, 1929–34.

though it placed them in a foolish position, than on the side of violence. I think we will be agreed upon that.

My hon. Friend spoke of the number of troops we had to keep in Ireland as a great evil which had arisen because in some way or other we had departed from the true line of policy towards Ireland. I do not think that is true. For many years I have been associated with the hon. Members and others in this House seeking to solve the Irish problem by a measure of self-government.

We are endeavouring to solve the Irish problem by a measure of self-government. Before the War the Liberals of those days extorted from the Irish Nationalist leaders a definite agreement that Ulster was not to be compelled against her will to join a Home Rule Parliament until two successive General Elections had taken place, which everybody knew was tantamount to saying that she could never join a Dublin Parliament. That is the position the Government take up now.

Churchill then appealed to the Irish Catholics to accept Lloyd George's proposal that, for the time being, the six counties of Ulster should be excluded from the largely autonomous Southern Ireland which the Coalition Government wished to create. Addressing himself directly to Joseph Devlin, whose constituency was in the area to be excluded initially from Home Rule, Churchill said:

If my right hon. Friend could lead his fellow countrymen to accept the measures now proposed in the name of all Britain for the first time, and make a genuine effort to work the constitution which will arise from this measure, the day would soon come when this military force to which he objects and which is no doubt a burden, and whose administration necessarily must be clumsy and galling would be withdrawn. The day would also come when after a few years of successful administration by an Irish Parliament on College Green dealing with the affairs of three parts of Ireland, the fourth part of her own free will would come in and associate herself with you. . . .

On February 25 a Home Rule Bill was introduced into Parliament. It proposed a Northern Irish Parliament of 52 members and a Southern Irish Parliament of 128 members; a further 42 MPs were to be elected by Irish voters to the Westminster Parliament. There was to be a Council of Ireland consisting of twenty members of each of the two Irish Parliaments. Under the Bill, the Westminster Parliament was to retain control of all matters relating to peace and war, foreign affairs, customs and excise, Army and Navy, land and agricultural policy, and the machinery for maintaining law and order. Sinn Fein denounced the Bill as a betrayal of Irish national rights; a scheme, declared the *Freeman's Journal*, for the 'plunder and partition of Ireland'.

On March 23, during the final stage of the Army Estimates debate,

Lieutenant-Commander Kenworthy complained bitterly of the Army's conduct in Ireland. There were, he said, at least 500 or 600 raids carried out by soldiers every week on private homes in Ireland. 'Complaints are made,' he said, 'of ornaments, pictures and so on being deliberately smashed, and also furniture.' The conduct of many of the troops was, he alleged, 'scandalous and dishonouring to His Majesty's Army, to the whole country, and to this House'.

Churchill's own sympathies were with the soldiers. 'It is not only a very wrong thing,' he said, 'but a very dangerous thing to shoot soldiers who fought in the War, who have come home from the War expecting to have a period of rest and peace, and who do not expect to be murdered from behind hedgerows in a civilised country by a population for whose defence they risked their lives during the War.' To strengthen the Army in Ireland, Churchill appointed Sir Nevil Macready[1] to command; Macready took up his post on March 26. That same morning, the Resident Magistrate in Dublin, Alan Bell,[2] was dragged from a tram and shot dead. 'This new Irish murder is very horrible,' Clementine Churchill wrote to her husband on March 27. Four days later he replied:

The Irish murders are really getting very serious. The only thing to be thankful for is that apparently they are concentrating their attention on one another. I should take a still graver view if they started serving us out with any of it. What a diabolical streak they have in their character! I expect it is that treacherous, assassinating, conspiring trait which has done them in in the bygone ages of history and prevented them from being a great responsible nation with stability and prosperity.

It is shocking that we have not been able to bring the murderers to justice. If we could get one or two of them we might secure a confession on the steps of the scaffold which would enable us to break up the whole organisation of this murder club. In this, as in so many other things, it is the first step that counts.

Churchill himself was in the South of France at the end of March, when the Home Rule Bill passed its second reading in the House of

---

[1] Cecil Frederick Nevil Macready, 1862–1946. Entered Army, 1881. Major-General, 1910. Knighted, 1912. General Officer Commanding, Belfast, 1914. Adjutant-General, British Expeditionary Force, 1914–16. Member of the Army Council, 1916. Lieutenant-General, 1916. Adjutant-General to the Forces, 1916–18. General, 1918. Commissioner of the Metropolitan Police, 1918–19. Commanded the Forces in Ireland, 1919–22. Created Baronet, 1923.

[2] Alan Bell, the son of a Church of Ireland clergyman, he joined the Royal Irish Constabulary in 1879. Appointed a Resident Magistrate, 1898. Presided over an enquiry into the relations between Irish banks and the Sinn Fein, 1919. At the time of his murder he was engaged in investigating the assassination attempt on Lord French.

Commons. The outrages in Ireland continued. Daily during the first two weeks in April several policemen were murdered in broad daylight. Churchill returned to the War Office from France on April 14. 'I told him,' Henry Wilson wrote in his diary, 'I was sending over 2 Cav: Regts (17th & 10th Royals) to Ireland & the 9th were under short notice.' Churchill approved Wilson's decision.

The strain of being responsible for Irish policy had been too much for Ian Macpherson. On April 2, at his own request, he relinquished the post of Chief Secretary. The situation in Ireland worsened. On May 3 a policeman was murdered in County Kerry, and another four policemen were killed on May 10.

Lloyd George was alarmed by the growing violence. On May 10 he decided to enlist Churchill's support:

My dear Winston,

I am very anxious about Ireland, and I want you to help. We cannot leave things as they are. De Valera has practically challenged the British Empire, and unless he is put down the Empire will look silly. I know how difficult it is to spare men and material, but this seems to me to be the urgent problem for us.

I understand from Bonar that there will be an important Conference tomorrow morning to discuss the situation.

Macready has certain proposals which he is bringing over from Ireland. I am very anxious you should see him before the Conference. Do your best to put them through without any loss of time.

Churchill responded to Lloyd George's appeal. The proposals which General Macready had brought from Ireland, and which Lloyd George so strongly supported, were for a substantial reinforcement of the troops in Ireland. Macready wanted 8 new Battalions—of approximately 8,000 men in all—and over 600 expert personnel for wireless and telegraph installations. He asked also for a further 234 lorries and cars, and a large Intelligence Staff.

On the morning of Tuesday May 11 Churchill was present at the Conference of Ministers which Lloyd George had asked to look into Irish affairs. Lloyd George himself was unwell, and did not attend—he was staying at Lympne as the guest of Sir Philip Sassoon. Churchill took Henry Wilson with him to the Conference, which was presided over by Bonar Law. General Macready explained to the Conference why he had asked for such substantial reinforcements. 'The Cabinet were frankly frightened,' Henry Wilson noted in his diary, '& agreed that all Macready's proposals must be acceded to.' Wilson himself opposed Macready's request on practical grounds. There were, he explained, only forty-six Battalions on which to draw. But ten of these were Guards Battalions which 'it was not wise to remove' from England in view of the general industrial unrest, and eight were Irish Battalions which could not be sent to police Ireland. This left only twenty-eight Battalions from which to select the eight for which Macready had asked. 'If 8 Batt^{ns} were sent to Ireland,' Wilson wrote, 'we should have very little for our own internal troubles & *nothing* for India, Egypt, C-ople etc.'

As a result of Henry Wilson's arguments, the Conference agreed that Macready was to delay calling for the eight Battalions for as long as possible. It was Churchill who then proposed a solution which, he believed, would strengthen the Royal Irish Constabulary without putting any pressure on the British Army. 'Winston suggested,' Wilson wrote in his diary, 'that a special force of 8000 old soldiers be raised at once to reinforce the RIC. This, in principle was also agreed to.'[1]

Throughout May 13 the Army Council discussed the new scheme. A 'panic measure', Wilson wrote in his diary, 'of raising 8000 scallywags would, for some months anyhow, give us no military value but great anxieties'. But Wilson was convinced that, as a minimum, Macready must receive eight thousand reinforcements, however difficult it might be to train them in time. On May 14 he saw Bonar Law, who promised to bring to the Cabinet the question of raising eight thousand recruits, and to stress the urgency. Bonar Law raised the matter in Cabinet on Friday May 21. But the subject of Ireland was only reached after a long discussion about Russia, Persia, the Caspian Sea and the Caucasus, nor was Wilson satisfied by the way in which it was treated, writing in his diary:

Then we discussed the A.C.^{s} proposals to raise 8 Garr: Batt^{ns} for Ireland. This was received with languid interest & even with boredom, LG especially taking no interest. I urged that the thing would be a frost unless L.G. himself made a stirring appeal to the country for help. This also was agreed to as a bore! L.G. saying he did not think it was any good going on with the H.R. bill until law & order had been established in Ireland. . . .

On Monday May 31, the Cabinet Committee on Ireland met at 10 Downing Street to discuss the Irish situation. Lloyd George presided over their deliberations. Henry Wilson was not asked to attend. Sir

[1] The gist of Sir Henry Wilson's detailed account of the Cabinet Conference of May 11 is confirmed by the much shorter official Cabinet record. But this latter gives only the conclusions of the Conference, and not the actual course of the discussion. The official record notes that Churchill 'undertook to submit to the Cabinet a scheme for raising a Special Emergency Gendarmerie, which would become a branch of the Royal Irish Constabulary'.

Nevil Macready was the only General present; Field Marshal French attended in his capacity of Viceroy.

The first task of the Committee was to hear the report of the new Chief Secretary, Sir Hamar Greenwood,[1] who had just returned from a visit to Ireland. According to the account kept by Thomas Jones, Greenwood stated emphatically that 'the real difficulty in Ireland is not so much the big issue of putting down crime as the inadequacy and sloppiness of the instruments of Government'. Only the Army, the Navy and the Royal Irish Constabulary were reliable, he said, and he added: 'The Dublin police cannot be relied on, nor the Post Office, nor the Civil Service.'

Greenwood recommended to the Committee that, in order to try to end terrorism, all General Macready's military requests should be agreed to. Churchill then proposed 'a special tribunal for trying murderers'. 'It is monstrous that we have some two hundred murders and no one hung,' he said. When Greenwood pointed out that a few cases would come up at the July Assizes, Churchill protested:

Mr Churchill: What strikes me is the feebleness of the local machinery. After a person is caught he should pay the penalty within a week. Look at the tribunals which the Russian Government have devised. You should get three or four judges whose scope should be universal and they should move quickly over the country and do summary justice.

Mr Denis Henry:[2] When that was put to the judges some months ago they did not want to touch it.

Mr Churchill: Shows all the more the need for extraordinary action. Get three generals if you cannot get three judges.

Mr Fisher: How many men have you strong evidence against?

Sir Hamar Greenwood: Six in jail with good cases against them.

Mr Denis Henry: We can use courts martial for raiding for arms but murder was exempted under D.O.R.A. regulations.

Mr Churchill (to the P.M.): You agreed six or seven months ago that there should be hanging.

---

[1] Hamar Greenwood, 1870–1948. Born in Canada. Served in the Department of Agriculture, Ontario. Liberal MP (at Westminster), 1906–22. Parliamentary Secretary to Churchill at the Colonial Office and Board of Trade, 1906–10. Baronet, 1915. On active service with the British Expeditionary Force in France, as a Lieutenant-Colonel, 1915–16. Deputy Assistant Adjutant-General, War Office, 1916. Under-Secretary of State, Home Office, 1919. Secretary, Department of Overseas Trade, 1919–20. Chief Secretary, Ireland, 1920–2. Joined the Conservative Party, 1922. Conservative MP, 1924–9. Created Baron, 1929. Treasurer of the Conservative Party, 1933–8. Created Viscount, 1937.

[2] Denis Stanislaus Henry, 1864–1925. Called to the Irish Bar, 1885. Commissioner of Charitable Bequests, 1912. Unionist MP for South Derry, 1916–21. Solicitor-General for Ireland, 1917–18. Attorney-General for Ireland, 1919–21. Lord Chief Justice of Northern Ireland, 1921–5. Created Baronet, 1922.

The P.M.: I feel certain you must hang. Can you get convictions from Catholics?

Mr Denis Henry: Substantially, no.

The discussion focussed on the difficulties of bringing the gunmen to justice. Lloyd George wanted to increase the 'pecuniary burdens' of any farmers harbouring gunmen, or not willing to give evidence about murders. 'Can we not multiply burdens and inconveniences?' he asked. 'Why not make life intolerable in a particular area?' Churchill added. This, Denis Henry said, had already been tried. 'We made ten thousand raids in six months,' he explained. 'We did not get hold of the revolvers. They bury them in bogs. . . .'

The discussion turned finally to the eight thousand special volunteers whose recruitment had been accepted in principal by the Cabinet nearly three weeks before, on May 11. Churchill told his colleagues that in his view it was 'rather a gamble' to appeal for volunteers. Only two thousand might come forward. H. A. L. Fisher thought the idea of a special force of volunteers a 'most unappetising prospect'. 'You may be driven to it,' Churchill replied.

The Cabinet Committee came to no firm conclusions, despite the determination of all those present not to give way to Sinn Fein. In Ireland the murders and reprisals continued. When the full Cabinet met on the morning of June 2, Austen Chamberlain suggested that the Government should open negotiations with the Sinn Fein leaders, in the hope of being able to reach agreement with them. Churchill told Henry Wilson of this proposal that same afternoon, and Wilson wrote in his diary: 'LG said this would be making peace after a defeat.[1] Winston & Walter Long spoke agᵗ Austen & in the end the proposal was turned down. But, as Winston said, it was symptomatic that such a rotten proposal could be made.' The desire for firmness was, however, widespread. On May 28, Sir Maurice Hankey had written in his diary: 'My view is that terror must be met by greater terror,' and at the Cabinet meeting on May 31 Hamar Greenwood had described Britain's 'great task' as 'to crush out murder and arson'.

On June 13 Churchill gave his general view of the situation in an article in the *Illustrated Sunday Herald*, in the course of which he wrote:

No nation has ever established its title-deeds by a campaign of assassination. The British nation, having come grimly through the slaughter of Armageddon, are certainly not going to be scared by the squalid scenes of

[1] And yet H. A. L. Fisher noted in his diary later that day: 'See Philip Kerr who says PM is quite ready for a chat with Sinn Fein when the time comes.'

sporadic warfare which are being enacted across the Irish Channel. They may be alienated, they may be irritated; but they will certainly not be terrorised by such proceedings. The sense of exhaustion, the intense desire for repose and relaxation following on the long stresses of war, have produced at the present time a phase of political apathy and indifference in Britain which may well last for a considerable period.

The ordinary Englishman or Scotsman does not want to be bothered about Ireland or anything else. He wants to build his house, to cultivate his garden, to resume his family life, to reorganise his business, to get prices down and taxes reduced, to have some rest, to have some pleasure. But while engaged in these modest pursuits, he has not forgotten that he is a conqueror, and that the greatest States and Empires in the world have been shattered beneath his blows. And if his lassitude is broken by intolerable provocation, it will not be in any mood of sentimental sympathy, still less of panic, that he will rouse himself to action.

Meanwhile, no course is open to the Government but to take every possible measure to break the murder campaign and to enforce the authority of the law, while at the same time pressing forward the Home Rule Bill.

Churchill went on to try to impress on the Irish the serious nature of the alternatives confronting them:

This dual policy will continually confront Irishmen with the fact that along the path of violence there will be found nothing but increasing resistances by superior power, and that all the time another path is open by which they may constitutionally, prosperously and speedily obtain the effective self-government of their country. On the one hand, nothing but barbed wire and unscalable walls; on the other, an open door—that is the picture which by every act of policy we should endeavour to imprint upon the Irish imagination.

On June 14 Walter Long wrote to Churchill: 'Thank you for a most admirable & very helpful article on Ireland.' But it did not satisfy Henry Wilson, who wanted the Government to declare full-scale war on Sinn Fein, and pressed Churchill to take the initiative. On June 25 Wilson recorded in his diary that he had told Churchill 'that the present procedure would never solve the problem & that our small detachments would continue to be disarmed by the rebels as long as the rebels were at war with us & we were at peace with them'. Churchill was not convinced by Wilson's argument, writing to him on June 25:

I do not think it is any use simply saying that the Government should declare war on Sinn Fein and act accordingly, unless you show by a series of definite illustrations the kind of measures you think should be adopted. It is in this field of practical suggestions that your military knowledge would be of the utmost advantage, whereas, as long as you confine yourself to generalities, it is impossible for me to carry the matter any further. . . .

I have now become a member of a Cabinet Committee specially charged with the duty of watching over Irish affairs and suppression of crime and disorder in Ireland. Therefore, I shall be in a position to bring any recommendation you may make to the notice of this Committee at the earliest moment. It is no use, for instance, answering the question, 'What would you do in Ireland', by saying 'I should shoot', or 'I should shoot without hesitation', or 'I should shoot without mercy'. The enquiry immediately arises, 'Whom would you shoot.' And shortly after that, 'Where are they.' 'How are you going to recognise them.' If by acting as if a state of war existed you mean that an incident such as that which occurred at Ennis should be followed by burning down a dozen houses or by shooting a certain number of the inhabitants, drawn by lot or otherwise, you should say so plainly so that the matter may be considered.[1] Then if your suggestions are not adopted by superior authority, you will at any rate have left them in no doubt of what your views are. Everyone knows that the situation in Ireland is unsatisfactory, that it is bad for the troops and full of potential dangers for this country. I do not myself believe it would be better by the kind of methods the Prussians adopted in Belgium. . . .

The Cabinet Committee to which Churchill had referred in his letter to Wilson held its first meeting four days later. Churchill was Chairman; the other members were Balfour, Birkenhead, Fisher, Greenwood, Walter Long and Sir James Craig.[2] Their task was to make suggestions for action. On July 1 Churchill set out his first proposal in a letter to General Harinton and Sir Hugh Trenchard:

Suppose information is received that Sinn Feiners are accustomed to drill in considerable numbers at any particular place, with or without arms. They must be regarded as a rebel gathering. If they can be definitely located and identified from the air, I see no objection from a military point of view, and subject of course to the discretion of the Irish Government and of the authorities on the spot, to aeroplanes being despatched with definite orders in each particular case to disperse them by machine gun fire or bombs, using of course no more force than is necessary to scatter and stampede them.[3]

[1] On June 16 a band of Catholics had besieged a Protestant Club, and demanded the 'surrender' of the Protestants inside it. In the ensuing riots seventeen people had been killed.

[2] James Craig, 1871–1940. Born in Dublin, the son of a wealthy distiller. A stockbroker by profession. Served in the South African War, 1899–1902. Unionist MP, 1906–21. A leading opponent of Home Rule before 1914. Fought against the Germans in South-west Africa, 1914–15. Created Baronet, 1918. Parliamentary Secretary, Ministry of Pensions, 1919–20. Financial Secretary, Admiralty, 1920–1. Prime Minister of Northern Ireland (under the Government of Ireland Act), from June 1921 until his death. Created Viscount Craigavon, 1927.

[3] Lord French had already obtained aircraft for reconnaissance purposes. He had wanted the aircraft armed with bombs and machine-guns, but this had not been agreed to. In

On the evening of July 12 Henry Wilson told Churchill of General Tudor's plan to set up an anti-Sinn Fein organization which would use the same methods as the IRA. At Spa, Lloyd George had approved Tudor's plan. Wilson was not so certain of its wisdom. In his diary he recorded his conversation with Churchill:

I told him of LGs amazing belief & faith in Tudor getting up a counter-murder Ass^n & what an amazing thing this was.

Winston agreed, but he evidently had some lingering hopes of our 'rough handling' of the Sinn Feins. . . .

In Ireland, the violence continued. On July 17 a Divisional Commissioner of Constabulary for Munster, Colonel G. F. Smyth,[1] who had lost his left arm in the war, was shot dead by a band of thirteen or fourteen men who burst into the County Club, Cork.

The murder of Colonel Smyth provoked riots in Belfast and Londonderry, where Protestants and Catholics confronted each other in large numbers. By July 23, only four days after the Colonel's death, at least thirteen people had been killed, and over a hundred injured.

The Cabinet met at 10 Downing Street on July 23. General Macready proposed four measures which were needed if Ireland 'was to be compelled to be quiet'. These were: martial law with the power of inflicting the death penalty; the army and police to have the right to seize members of the IRA; strict press censorship to prevent inflammatory appeals; and measures 'to deal with persons coming into Ireland from the United States'.

As the discussion developed, it was clear that all efforts to enforce law and order would be hard to carry out. Greenwood pointed out that the position in Ireland was 'very different from the old days. Now every man carried arms and Civil Servants went in danger of their lives'. Churchill believed that a stronger policy had the best chance of leading to a settlement, as Thomas Jones recorded:

September 1920 Sir Nevil Macready again asked for armed aircraft, but his request was not granted until March 1921, when Churchill was no longer Secretary of State for War and Air.

[1] Gerald B. Ferguson Smyth, 1882–1920. 2nd Lieutenant, Royal Engineers, 1906. Crossed to France with the Expeditionary Force, 1914. Served on the Western Front from 1914 to 1918, being wounded six times and losing his left arm at Le Cateau in 1914, after which he was awarded the DSO for 'consistent skill, daring and hard work' while severely wounded. Major, 1916. Awarded a bar to his DSO, 1917, for 'conspicuous gallantry and devotion to duty'. Brigadier-General, 1918. Divisional Commissioner, Royal Irish Constabulary, and Police Commissioner for Munster, 1920. Four of his first cousins had been killed in action on the western front.

Mr Churchill thought it was the prolonged strain which was breaking down the officials in Ireland. It was necessary to raise the temperature of the conflict to a real issue and shock, and trial of strength. He would do that in the hope that there would then be a chance of settlement on wider lines.

Before a settlement was reached, Churchill added, the Government ought to recruit a force of some 30,000 Ulstermen, to uphold 'the authority of the Crown', not only in Ulster, but throughout Ireland.

On August 2 Hamar Greenwood introduced a Bill into the House of Commons providing for the suspension of trial by jury in the disturbed areas, and setting up courts martial in its place. During the debate Lloyd George declared that Britain would never allow the Irish to secede from the United Kingdom. The Committee stage of the Bill was taken on August 3, and six days later it received the royal assent.

On August 16 Lloyd George announced that he would be glad to discuss a Home Rule settlement with any 'responsible' body. But he specifically excluded Sinn Fein from the ranks of the responsible. During the following week six more Irish policemen were killed, one while he was leaving church. On August 22 there were reprisals at Lisburn, when a large number of buildings belonging to Republican supporters were burnt down.

On August 25 three Cabinet Ministers—Churchill, Balfour and Edward Shortt[1]—met at 10 Downing Street to discuss what policy to adopt towards the Lord Mayor of Cork, Terence McSwiney,[2] who had been imprisoned in Brixton Gaol, and was on hunger strike. There had been an outcry in Ireland in favour of McSwiney, and in England the Labour Party were urging his release, on the grounds that he was not a criminal, but a political prisoner. 'Considerable discussion took place,' the notes of the meeting recorded, 'with regard to the effect on the country of the apparent climb down of the Government if he were released. . . .' It was finally decided to ask General Macready's opinion 'as to the effect in Ireland' of McSwiney's release. Macready advised against it; McSwiney remained at Brixton and continued his hunger

[1] Edward Shortt, 1862–1935. Barrister, 1890. Recorder of Sunderland, 1907–18. King's Counsel, 1910. Liberal MP, 1910–22. A frequent and persuasive speaker at the time of the passing of the Home Rule Bill, 1912. Chairman of the Select Committee which reviewed the administration of the Military Service Acts. Chief Secretary for Ireland, May 1918–January 1919. Home Secretary, January 1919–October 1922. President of the British Board of Film Censors, 1929. His only son was killed in action in 1917.

[2] Terence McSwiney, 1880–1920. Schoolmaster. Commander of an IRA brigade. Elected to Parliament for Mid Cork, 1918, but, like all Sinn Fein, MPs, refused to take his seat at Westminster. Elected Lord Mayor of Cork, March 1920. Arrested, August 1920. Died in Brixton prison after a hunger-strike of seventy-four days.

strike. After refusing to eat for a further two months, he died on October 25.

In Ireland, the murders and the reprisals continued. General Tudor's newly created force acted with alacrity in reply to every outrage. Owing to a shortage of Royal Irish Constabulary Uniforms, these troops wore a mixture of regular Army khaki uniforms, and Royal Irish Constabulary belts—which were black—and caps—which were dark green. As a result of this amalgam, they quickly became known as the 'Black and Tans'. On August 30 Henry Wilson discussed the new force with Churchill, recording in his diary:

In a letter from Macready this morning he refers to Tudor's 'Black & Tans' carrying out wild reprisals & deprecating their policy. This was the first I have heard of this body & its activities.

I told Winston that I thought this a scandal & Winston was very angry. He said these 'Black & Tans' were honourable & gallant officers, etc. etc, & talked much nonsense.

This undoubtedly is the scheme which LG referred to in Spa when talking to me and later to Derby. It is an amazing & scandalous thing.

On September 1 Macready sent Churchill a full description of the work and status of the 'Black and Tans'. He was particularly worried that their activity was creating ill-feeling among the regular soldiers in Ireland. In his letter he stressed that 'the human endurance of the troops is rapidly reaching a point where restraint will be impossible'. It was not only the 'Black and Tans' who carried out reprisals; indeed, the first reprisals had been committed by soldiers some months before. Macready explained to Churchill why the soldiers acted as they did:

As regards the troops themselves, they are the object of daily attacks in towns, and while moving about the country, by persons whom it is impossible to distinguish from ordinary civilians, and often the very nature of a duty necessitates guards and sentries being posted where crowds of civilians are apparently pursuing their ordinary avocations, but who suddenly, turn upon and attack the soldiers.

The result of this state of affairs is that the troops are gradually getting—to use a slang expression—'fed up' with the unsatisfactory situation in which they find themselves, and retaliation for the wounding and murder of their officers and comrades is prevalent. . . .

Last week an officer of the Cameron Highlanders was very seriously wounded, and the men of the Battalion incensed at the outrage, broke out and wrecked a large number of houses and shops in Queenstown.

During the second and third weeks of September, Churchill was in France with his wife. Using the Duke of Westminster's house at Mimizan as their base, they drove about in the region between Bordeaux and the Spanish frontier. 'It is delightful,' Churchill wrote to his friend Evan Charteris[1] from Mimizan on September 13, 'and I have painted a lot of pictures which give pleasure to me if to no one else.' That same day, General Tudor returned to England from Ireland, and was summoned to the War Office to report on the Irish situation. At Churchill's request, he saw Henry Wilson, who recorded in his diary:

Tudor came to see me & had a long talk about the RIC & his Black & Tans & cadets. He says that all that is really happening is that when the police carry out reprisals the authorities look the other way. For instance when he was in Galway last Wed, he had just gone to bed when he heard a few shots, & a policeman was murdered. On that the other policeman saw red went straight to the houses of 3 notorious SF[s], pulled them out of bed, put them up against a wall & shot them.

He quoted other cases where these reprisals had a most salutary effect but he agreed with me that this procedure would never solve the Irish question & that the only chance was for the Cabinet to rouse England & then exterminate or transport the rebels. . . .

Churchill returned briefly to England on September 17; five days later he set off again to continue his holiday at Amalfi in Italy. But while he was in London Henry Wilson appealed to him to act against the 'Black and Tans', and openly to condemn reprisals by troops or police. Churchill would not do so, nor did he agree with Wilson that the spread of reprisals indicated a disintegration of the Irish situation. On September 18 he set out his views in a memorandum which he sent to both Wilson and Macdonogh. In the course of his memorandum Churchill declared:

Naturally everything will be done to prevent violent, harsh or inhumane action by the troops; but the greatest help in this respect will be given by the Irish population of towns where troops are quartered if they not only abstain from murdering the soldiers and their officers by treacherous means but also render the assistance which it is easily in their power to give for the detection of the actual criminals.

I do not think the state of things is going from bad to worse in Ireland. On the contrary, the impression I have formed is that we have held our own very

[1] The Hon. Evan Edward Wemyss Charteris, 1864–1940. Sixth son of the 10th Earl of Wemyss. Lieutenant, Coldstream Guards, 1885. Barrister, 1891. A trustee of the National Portrait Gallery, 1913 (Chairman, 1928). Staff Captain, Royal Flying Corps, 1916; Royal Tank Corps, 1916–18. A trustee of the National Gallery, 1932–9. Chairman of the Tate Gallery, 1934–40. Chairman of the Standing Commission on Museums and Galleries, 1937.

well. I see no reason why, with patience and firmness, we may not wear the
trouble down in the course of a few years and secure the re-establishment of
order together with the acceptance by the Irish people of the responsibility of
their own internal government. I do not believe that the discipline of the
army has deteriorated in any fundamental sense, and the increasing success
of the troops in dealing with treacherous attacks upon them, and the increasing losses by those who have made these attacks, confirm this view. Care must
be taken not to discourage the loyalty and zeal of the troops in defending
themselves from cowardly and treacherous attacks.

Churchill went on to point out that it was at his suggestion that Henry
Wilson had seen General Tudor on September 13 to discuss 'the alleged
action of the cadets of the RIC'. 'I do not believe,' Churchill wrote,
'that their conduct in any way merits the strictures which General
Macready has passed upon them.' And he added: 'It must be in all
circumstances understood and impressed on every military officer
serving under the War Office that the resolve of the Government to
resist the establishment of an Irish Republic is inflexible.'

In Ireland, shootings and reprisals continued unabated. Between
August 30 and September 20, more than forty people were killed, some
by Republicans, some by soldiers, some by the new recruits to the Royal
Irish Constabulary. On September 21, Churchill discussed the Irish
reprisals with Henry Wilson at the War Office. 'I warned him again,'
Wilson noted in his diary, 'that those "Black & Tans" of Tudor who are
carrying out very indiscriminate reprisals will play the devil in Ireland,
but he won't listen or agree.'

On September 22, after five policemen had been ambushed and
murdered in County Galway, further reprisals were carried out by
uniformed 'Black and Tans'; three young men were shot dead and
several houses were burnt down in three nearby villages. On the following day, before leaving for Italy, Churchill discussed this new incident
not only with Henry Wilson, but also with General Tudor himself.
Wilson recorded the discussion in his diary:

Tudor made it very clear that the Police & the Black & Tans & the 100
Intell: officers are all carrying out reprisal murders.

At Balbriggan, Thurles & Galway yesterday the local police marked down
certain SFs as in their opinion actual murderers or instigators & then coolly
went & shot them without question or trial.

Winston saw very little harm in this but it horrifies me.

During the day, Churchill went with General Tudor to see Lloyd
George at 10 Downing Street, 'Winston told me tonight,' Wilson wrote
in his diary, 'that LG told Tudor that he would back him in this course

through thick & thin.' The War Office General Staff were also coming to feel that reprisals were necessary. On September 23 General Radcliffe wrote to Henry Wilson:

I think the only solution of this problem is to institute the system of *official* reprisals and to impress on the troops that by taking the law into their own hands they damage the cause instead of furthering it.

If there is any definite scheme of reprisals in force, & made known beforehand, it should be easy to get the troops to restrain their unofficial efforts, while the deterrent effect on the Sinn Fein cannot fail to be considerable.

Wilson shared Radcliffe's opinion. 'I am all in favour of reprisals,' he wrote in his diary that night, 'but these shd be done on the Gvt's authority & shooting should be done by a roster drawn up officially & publicly posted.'

On September 24 Churchill discussed the problem of reprisals with Lloyd George, at 10 Downing Street. Bonar Law and H. A. L. Fisher were also present. The latter noted in his diary Lloyd George's comment 'that you cannot in the excited state of Ireland punish a policeman who shoots a man whom he has every reason to suspect is connected with the police murders'. 'This kind of thing,' Lloyd George insisted, '*can* only be met by reprisals.'

At the end of September Churchill discussed the Irish situation with his cousin Shane Leslie,[1] who was eager to see a reconciliation between all Irish factions. On October 2 Churchill wrote to Leslie from the War Office:

My dear Shane,

You asked me what advice I would give to the Sinn Feiners, and I replied 'Quit murdering and start arguing'. This is in no sense an offer of negotiation and could not be represented as such; but I am quite sure that the moment the murders cease the Irish question will enter upon a new phase, and I shall not be behindhand in doing my utmost to secure a good settlement. As long as the murder conspiracy goes on things will go from bad to worse: the military power of the British Government in Ireland will continually increase, and the whole prosperity of the country is sure to be affected by the continuance of these troubles.

Yours ever
W

Sinn Fein had no intention of halting its military activities, and Lloyd George continued to support General Tudor's policy of un-

[1] John Randolph Shane Leslie, 1885–1971. Son of Sir John Leslie and Leonie Jerome. Author and lecturer. Contested Derry City as an Irish Nationalist, 1910, but defeated. Served in British Intelligence in the USA, 1915–16. Succeeded his father as 3rd Baronet, 1944.

planned reprisals. Speaking at Carnarvon on October 9, he strongly defended the action of the police in retaliating as they did.

Churchill returned to England from his holiday on October 11. That night he dined with Lloyd George, and on October 12 he discussed Lloyd George's speech with Henry Wilson, who recorded in his diary:

He was full of admiration for LG's speech at Carnarvon & for its bravery. LG had told him last night that during the war he had hated being up near the front & was frightened of shells & he supposed this was because it was not his business & his duty to so get killed. Whereas he had no fear of denouncing the SFs as assassins etc. although he knew it sensibly increased his own chance of being murdered. In this case he conceived it to be his duty; and Winston asked me to say something to LG which I will. Winston said: 'You have been right all along C.I.G.S. & the Gov' must shoulder the responsibility of their reprisals.'

Winston is going to repeat, at Dundee, all LG said & go still further towards responsibility. As I said to him once the Gov' shoulder the responsibility the reprisals can start in a mild form & go on to crescendo if necessary.

Churchill was opposed to any measure of Home Rule while the killings in Ireland continued. Speaking to his constituents at Dundee on Sunday October 16 he declared that it was the Government's firm intention 'to break up the murder gang in Ireland'. Churchill told his audience that while he favoured a permanent settlement in Ireland on the basis of Home Rule, no such settlement could be achieved on the basis of 'surrender to treacherous murder, but only on the basis of justice and generosity'.

While the murders and counter-murders continued in Ireland itself, Lloyd George persevered with his Government of Ireland Bill, designed to give an equal measure of Home Rule to both North and South. The Bill passed the Committee Stage in the House of Commons on October 29. Lloyd George believed that the firm offer of Home Rule to Southern Ireland, even within the overall framework of British sovereignty, would abate the fierce passion of Republicanism, and be accepted by a majority of Irish Catholics. In the North, after much protest, the Protestants accepted Home Rule for Ulster as a guarantee that they would never be abandoned by Westminster to the mercy of the Catholic South. On November 9, in a speech at the London Guildhall, Lloyd George declared: 'We have murder by the throat.'

Henry Wilson believed that stronger measures were needed if the Sinn Fein were to be silenced. 'I had a long talk with Winston,' he wrote in his diary on November 2, 'and for the 100th time I urged him to take over the Gov' of Ireland and not leave it to the Black & Tans &

the soldiers.' General Macready was quite willing, Wilson told Churchill, 'to take more severe disciplinary action even to removing COs if the men took reprisals on their own'. But Churchill rejected Wilson's appeal, as Wilson recorded:

Winston wants us to go on shouldering the onus for reprisals for some time longer. . . . But I told Winston to hurry it up as it was not fair on the soldiers & if the present regime was continued much longer the P.M. would have the Army against him or else have a mob instead of an army & I asked Winston to remember that in the end the authority of the Cabinet rested on the bayonets of the soldiers.

Churchill was determined to support the actions of the British troops. On November 3 he gave instructions that all Macready's court martial verdicts on soldiers accused of unauthorized reprisals were to be submitted to him at the War Office before being confirmed by Macready in Dublin. 'This of course is inadmissable,' Wilson wrote in his diary on November 3, 'for Macready alone is responsible for the discipline & morale of his command.'

On November 3, in a letter to Lloyd George, Churchill explained why he supported the institution of official reprisals:

Very strong representations are being made to me by the military authorities that reprisals within certain strictly defined limits should be authorised by the Government and regulated by responsible officers of not less than Divisional rank. Complaint is made that the troops are getting out of control, taking the law into their own hands, and that apart from clumsy and indiscriminate destruction, actual looting and thieving as well as drunkenness and gross disorder are occurring. In consequence of this a number of Courts-Martial are being held, yet the position of the troops, always liable to be murdered by Sinn Feiners, is such that it will not be possible to restrain their anger when outrages occur in their neighbourhood.

I do not consider that the present Government attitude on reprisals can be maintained much longer. It is not fair on the troops it is not fair on the officers who command them. Although the spirit of the Army is absolutely loyal and very hostile to the Irish rebels, there is no doubt that service in Ireland is intensely unpopular. I have repeated requests from officers of middle and senior rank to be allowed to retire or to be transferred. When a post is vacant in Ireland, sometimes six or seven officers refuse it in turn. This is not because these men are not resolute and loyal, but because they feel themselves to be in a false position.

I am prepared to support and to defend in Parliament a policy of reprisals within strict limits and under strict control in certain districts in which it should be declared that conditions approximating to a state of war exist. I believe that such a policy would be less discreditable and more effective than what is now going on. The recent formidable increase in outrages in particular districts affords an opportunity for a review of the position. I cannot feel it right to punish the troops when, goaded in the most brutal manner and finding no redress, they take action on their own account. If they were to remain absolutely passive, they would become completely demoralised and the effectiveness of the military force would be destroyed. On the other hand, when these responsibilities are thrown upon privates, sergeants and lieutenants, many foolish and wrong things will be done which cannot be passed over by higher authority.

Churchill asked Lloyd George to summon a special cabinet to consider his proposals, 'in order that the excesses of the troops may be controlled and the discipline of the army maintained'. Churchill also wanted 'every male in Ireland' to be made to carry an identity card, after which a system of 'sweeps and roundings up in large areas' would reveal those who had not dared to come forward to ask for identity cards. A further safeguard, Churchill wrote, was for a system of passports for all people travelling between Great Britain and Ireland. 'There is no reason,' he explained, 'why the Irish desperadoes should be permitted to transfer their operations over here at any moment they think fit, or come over here for rest and peace whenever the hunt gets too hot for them in Ireland.'

On November 4 Churchill spoke to a meeting held in the Cannon Street Hotel, London. His speech was reported in the *Daily Telegraph* on the following day. The 'Irish murder gang', he told his audience, were part of 'a world-wide conspiracy against our country', a conspiracy which, in Ireland, in India, in Egypt, and in Britain itself, was 'designed to deprive us of our place in the world and rob us of victory'. But Britain, he insisted, would not allow itself 'to be pulled down and have our Empire disrupted by a malevolent and subversive force, the rascals and rapscallions of the world who were now on the move against us'.

On November 9 it seemed as if some such conspiracy might threaten Churchill personally. During the day the Director of Intelligence at Scotland Yard, Sir Basil Thomson, wrote to Churchill of how, 'At a Sinn Fein meeting in a private house in Glasgow last Saturday night it was decided that the best form of reprisals upon the British Government would be the kidnapping of any of the following Ministers:—the Prime Minister, Mr Bonar Law, Lord French, Mr Winston Churchill, Sir Hamar Greenwood.' Thomson added that six members of the Sinn Fein Executive had been appointed to carry out the kidnapping, and allocated £250 for their task. Thomson warned Ministers not to go to

31. 'Winston's Bag': a cartoon by Low, the *Star*, 21 January 1920

32. At Hendon Aerial Pageant, 3 July 1920: on the left, Churchill and Sir Frederick Sykes (both with top hats); centre, one of Churchill's pilots, Captain Scott (with sticks); far right, Lord Birkenhead

33. With Sir Hugh Trenchard at Hendon, 3 July 1920

34. General Sir Charles Harington, a photograph taken in Constantinople, 1922

35. Churchill, Balfour, Poincaré, Lloyd George and Pétain.

36. 'A Little War Coming in the East': a cartoon by Strube, *Daily Express*, 23 January 1920

37. Eamon De Valera and Arthur Griffith, July 1921

38. Sir James Craig

39. Michael Collins, March 1922

40. Churchill on his way to the Irish Conference, October 1921

41. Churchill and General Macready at the Inverness Cabinet, 7 September 1921

42. 'Dr Winston's Insulting Room': a cartoon by Poy, *Daily Mail*, 17 February 1920

43. Churchill, and his cousin, Frederick Guest, 11 April 1921

44. 'Socialism Bogey': a cartoon by Low, the *Star*, 10 May 1922

45. Churchill on his polo pony, 11 May 1921

46. 'Strenuous Lives': a cartoon by David Wilson, *Passing Show*, 14 February 1920

Scotland 'for the next few days or weeks'. He also arranged for Churchill himself to have a personal bodyguard, and one of Lloyd George's former bodyguards, Detective Sergeant W. H. Thompson,[1] was selected for the task. Henceforth, wherever Churchill travelled—whether by car or by train—Thompson accompanied him, not only on his official journeys, but on all private journeys as well.

On November 15 four British Staff Officers, who were in plain clothes, were seized by armed men while travelling by train from Cork to Bandon. They were then driven off, and were never seen again. Henry Wilson discussed the disappearance of the officers with Churchill on the evening of November 16, noting in his diary: 'He thinks we have nearly won in Ireland!' On the night of November 17, the Black and Tans carried out reprisals in Cork, entering several houses, and killing three men. In the early hours of November 21 several groups of Republicans raided houses and hotels throughout Dublin, killing fourteen men, including six British officers. Some of the officers were pulled out of bed, and shot in front of their wives. Later that day, at a football ground in the city, soldiers opened fire on a crowd which included several gunmen, and nine people were killed.

The first news of the death of the British officers reached London on the morning of November 22. 'This ought to be sufficient,' Henry Wilson noted in his diary, 'to ease the conscience of the Cabinet about taking strong *Gov*^{t} measures instead of leaving the Government of Ireland to the Black & Tans.' That same day the House of Commons debated the new murders. Lloyd George declared that the authorities in Ireland were gradually succeeding in breaking up the murder gangs. That evening Henry Wilson discussed the situation with Churchill, noting in his diary:

Tonight Winston insinuated that the murdered officers were careless, useless fellows & ought to have taken precautions. This fairly roused me & I let fly about the Cabinet being cowards and not *governing* Ireland but leaving it to Black & Tans etc.

No Cabinet meeting as the Cabinet do not seem to think anything out of the way has happened!

[1] Walter H. Thompson. Detective Constable, Special Branch, Scotland Yard, 1913. Bodyguard to Lloyd George, 1917–20. Bodyguard to Churchill, 1920–32. Retired from the police force with the rank of Detective Inspector, 1936. Worked as a grocer, 1936–9. Recalled to the police force, 1939, and served as Churchill's personal bodyguard until 1945.

On November 26 the six murdered officers were buried in London with full military honours. Henry Wilson was present at Westminster Abbey for their memorial service. 'LG, Winston & Hamar Greenwood walked up the aisle behind the coffins,' Wilson recorded in his diary. 'I wonder they did not hide their heads in *shame*.'

On November 27, on the advice of Sir Basil Thomson, all the approaches to Downing Street were boarded up, in order to forestall a possible attempt by Irish Republicans to kill Lloyd George. On the following day over fifteen fires were started simultaneously in Liverpool, and at least one person was murdered. Also on November 28, seventeen Black and Tans, each of them a former British Army officer who had shown conspicuous merit in battle during the war, were ambushed near Macroom. Fifteen of the seventeen were killed immediately, one was wounded and died later, and one disappeared.

The Cabinet met on Wednesday December 1. The Macroom murders had considerably reduced Lloyd George's optimism of the previous week. According to Thomas Jones' account of the meeting, Lloyd George declared at the outset that the murders seemed to him, to Bonar Law and to Hamar Greenwood to be something different to assassinations. They were, instead, 'a military operation', and there was therefore 'a good deal to be said for declaring a state of siege or promulgating martial law in that corner of Ireland'. All those found with arms, and not having a permit he added, 'should be treated as rebels'. The discussion turned on which areas should be included in the Martial Law proclamation. Henry Wilson had wanted all Ireland to be covered. But Churchill's scheme was different, as he told the Cabinet:

> We should select areas and concentrate our forces there. The Chief of the Staff is going to ask General Jeudwine[1] if he has the necessary forces. The area would have to be confined to these limits but I will hold 10 additional battalions at his disposal for this area and 10 in reserve. It is for me to take the responsibility of sending them. They can be ferried back here if required by any nasty trouble here. I will only send them if he asks for them, not otherwise.

Austen Chamberlain wanted reassurance that the powers of Martial Law would not be exercised 'by junior officers without control', as had

[1] Hugh Sandham Jeudwine, 1862–1942. Entered the Army, 1882. On active service in South Africa, 1899–1901. Colonel, 1912. Brigadier-General, General Staff, Fifth Corps, 1915. Commanded the 41st Infantry Brigade, 1915–16. Major-General Commanding the 55th Division, 1916–19. Knighted, 1918. Commanded the 5th Division in Ireland, 1919–22. Temporarily in command of all British troops in Ireland, November–December 1920. Lieutenant-General, 1920. Director-General of the Territorial Army, 1923–7.

happened in South Africa during the Boer War. Churchill pointed out that it would be easier to control Martial Law in Ireland 'because the country is smaller'. The 'real danger' in Ireland, Lloyd George remarked, 'is drink'. It was, said Churchill, smiling, 'a very moist climate!' Later in the discussion Churchill put forward another suggestion:

Has the Home Secretary thought of offering large rewards for the capture of Sinn Feiners in this country? It would be useful before Sinn Fein got installed here. If these rewards are out early people will have their eyes open for suspicious strangers. I would pay up to £5,000 for a hanging case (Laughter) and proportionally for the others.

On December 9 the Cabinet agreed to proclaim Martial Law in four Irish counties—Cork, Kerry, Limerick and Killkenny—beginning in three weeks' time.[1] On December 10 Lloyd George told the House of Commons that a proclamation would be issued in four counties calling for the surrender of all arms. After December 27 anyone found with arms would be tried by court martial. The penalty for carrying arms would be death.

On the day after Lloyd George's declaration, a member of the Black and Tans was killed in the city of Cork. The murder was followed by immediate and severe reprisals. Over three hundred buildings in the commercial centre of the city were burnt down, and over three million pounds' worth of damage done to private property. When the Cabinet met on the evening of December 13, Lloyd George referred to the desire of 'the decent public in Ireland' for a truce. Churchill suggested that if the Sinn Fein MPs were to meet 'and showed an attitude bent on peace', Britain should be prepared to offer a month's truce. 'I believe that if murder once stops it would light up again,' he said, 'and it would give a chance for the murderers to go off to America.' On December 14 Churchill explained his opinions to the Archbishop of Tuam:[2]

No one desires more than I do a cessation of the conditions of strife which are ruining the happiness and the prosperity of the Irish people. It is my earnest hope that better days may come. It is in that sense I have acted throughout; but the murders of the police and military must stop. Until they

[1] According to Henry Wilson's diary Lloyd George's reasons for delaying Martial Law for two weekends was 'to have 2 Sundays during which the priests are to be exhorted to get the rebels to hand over their arms to them—the priests—to be passed on to the military authories'. Wilson commented: 'These are the sort of puerile tricks that LG loves.'

[2] Thomas P. Gilmartin, 1861–1939. Born in County Mayo, the son of a farmer. Vice-President, Maynooth, 1904. Roman Catholic Bishop of Clonfert, 1910–18; Archbishop of Tuam from 1918 until his death.

stop there can be no recovery and things will go from bad to worse. As soon as they stop the Irish people will be able to take up the constitutional discussion of their relations with Great Britain; and surely the fact that the present Home Rule is passing into law not upon the authority of a single Party dependent on the Irish vote, but with the assent of the overwhelming majority of the Unionist Party, is a great fact to which none should blind themselves.

On December 15 the House of Commons discussed the supplementary Army Estimates. Churchill's speech was devoted almost entirely to the increase in military needs abroad. He made only a brief reference to Ireland:

It seems to me a very remarkable thing that the expenditure we have been put to in Ireland, compared with the expenditure we have been put to in the more distant regions of the Middle East should be so remarkably small. Ireland bulks very largely in our minds because it is the heart's centre of the British Empire. Any disturbance or movement there produces vibrations, almost convulsions, throughout the whole of our system of society. There is far larger skill involved; a far greater loss of life, I am sorry to say, and a far greater expenditure of money takes place in the more distant but much more loosely connected parts of the British Empire which do not seem to us to raise problems nearly so formidable.

Later in the debate, Joseph Devlin spoke bitterly of the money spent by the Army in Ireland. 'There are at present unemployed in the Great Britain over 1,000,000 men,' he said. 'Look what that money could do for them.' The form of military Government in Ireland, he declared, 'has been one of the most horrible things in history . . . the men mainly responsible for all the terrible mischief and horrible things going on in Ireland are men who sometimes describe themselves as "Tudor's Toughs". Someone suggests that they should be called "Churchill's Lambs". I do not suggest that at all.' Were Churchill not a member of the Government, Devlin declared, 'and had not to support everything going on in Ireland', his humanity was such as to have 'his whole nature stirred by these events, just as deeply as mine is'.

Churchill insisted that the money for the Black and Tans, whom Devlin was attacking, came, not from the Army Estimates, but from the Irish Office vote. But Devlin continued to attack the Black and Tans:

These men travel all over the country, firing shots in the air, frightening innocent people, terrorising women, and even shooting women, on motor lorries, for which this Committee is asked to give a Vote to-day, and on motor lorries, which go through peaceful agricultural districts, where there is neither crime nor even agitation, terrorising these people who are guilty of no offence. . . .

You have fanned the flames of hatred, you have impregnated into a healthy community fresh poison, you have gone on from bad to worse, and things are now so bad that I do not think they can be worse; and you are flattered to-day with the prospect that it is all going to end. A month ago it was all ending. A month ago murder had been brought to a termination, reprisals were not to occur again. There have been twenty times more murders since that prophecy was made, and there have been more infamous reprisals every day. . . .

Devlin then appealed direct to Churchill:

If the right hon. Gentleman has any regard for the honour of the Forces which he controls, let him put an end to these things. You have been preaching peace, and you are anxious for peace. Is it upon these grim foundations that the fabric of peace is to be built. . . .

Devlin's speech made it necessary for Churchill to defend the Army's action in Ireland, and this he did:

I have a great measure of sympathy with my hon. Friend (Mr Devlin) because he is fighting as well as he can, with all his might and main, for the cause of his country and he is fighting for it by constitutional methods. In my opinion it takes a great deal more pluck to stand up day after day against a necessarily hostile House of Commons than it does to lie behind a hedge waiting to shoot some poor Irish constable when he is on the way home to his wife and children after his day's work is done. . . .

So far as Ireland is concerned, who began the new strife? We did not begin it. Until about 150 policemen and soldiers had been shot dead, there was no disturbance and disorder in Ireland of the kind my hon. Friend has made such great complaint. . . .

Let murder stop, let constitutional dominion begin, let the Irish people carry the Debate from the squalid conditions in which it is now being pushed forward by the Irish murder gang——

Mr J. DAVISON:[1] And by the Government.

Mr CHURCHILL: Let them carry this Debate into the field of fair discussion. Let them press their constitutional claims, as all the people of the British Isles have a right to do, in the great constitutional Parliamentary assemblies of the Nation, and they will find that instantly there will be a release of all those harsh and lamentable conditions which are bringing misery upon Ireland, and undoubtedly bringing discredit upon the whole of the British Empire.

Churchill's arguments did not impress the Irish themselves. When the Archbishop of Tuam wrote to him on December 17, it was to say that unless Churchill would suspend 'all military operations and extra-police

[1] John Emanuel Davison, 1870–1927. An official of the Ironfounders' Society. Labour MP for Smethwick, 1918–27. A Labour Whip, 1924–7. Vice-Chamberlain of the King's Household, 1924.

operations, for a given time—say a month or six months', there could be no truce on the Irish side. 'You have no idea of the state of things here at present,' the Archbishop went on, 'even in peaceful districts like Galway. The auxiliary Police are exercising terror & torture unchecked & still the spirit of Sinn Fein is as strong as ever.' Nobody, the Archbishop added, took the Home Rule Bill seriously for it did not represent 'the just demands of the great majority of the Irish people'.

On December 27 Martial Law was proclaimed in four Irish counties, Cork, Kerry, Limerick and Kilkenny. But Churchill believed that the Irish could still be persuaded to denounce violence and that there was a mass of moderate people who would welcome a truce. That same day he set out his feelings in a letter to the Archbishop of Tuam:

I need scarcely tell you how intensely I feel the desire and need for a truce and an appeasement in Ireland. The difficulty which we encounter is that no body is in corporate and continuous existence which has the power or even the constitutional right to speak for Ireland. Meanwhile the efforts and wishes of well-meaning individuals and, as I believe, the general desire of the Irish people are both paralysed by the terroristic action of a violent and desperate body of men and the inevitable consequences in quasi-war conditions which such action produces.

The first necessity is therefore that the Irish people and their natural leaders should make their voices heard in language of far-reaching courage and of ultimate goodwill. This is a matter in which Irishmen must take the lead. Naturally the British Government, although quite able to cope with violence, would be bound to meet every such advance step by step. From this point of view you must not undervalue the present Home Rule Act now on the Statute Book with the assent of all parties and the full authority of the Crown. Action will follow on this measure. You say, 'It does not represent the just demands of the great majority of the Irish people.' No one has ever said that it is the last word in the relations between the two islands. On the contrary, it is the first word. But spoken as it is, not under duress but from conviction, it is a great word; and your countrymen will be most unwise if they do not meditate profoundly upon it.

Britain will never consent, while life and strength remain, to the destruction of the integrity of the British Empire. Was it not Grattan who said 'The Channel forbids union; the ocean forbids separation.'?

On December 29 Lloyd George summoned a special Cabinet meeting to discuss Ireland, and proposed a one or two months' truce. 'He was backed by Winston,' Henry Wilson recorded in his diary, 'who, to my disgust, was all in favour of it.' H. A. L. Fisher and Austen Chamberlain also supported a truce. Edward Shortt opposed it. Wilson noted: 'Hamar gave no opinion. Macready not nearly strong enough against, but Tudor, Strickland[1] & Boyd[2] very good. I finished up in a very strong statement *against* so fatuous and fatal a policy which would immeasurably strengthen the enemy & incalculably weaken our friends, as also that great central body of peasants who always sided with the stronger man.' Wilson asked the Cabinet to extend Martial Law to all Ireland. Macready suggested extending it to at least four more counties, Clare, Tipperary, Wexford and Waterfo d. Fisher noted in his diary that the soldiers who had come to the Cabinet 'think they can control the situation in four months'.

The advice of the soldiers for further Martial Law over-rode the instinct of the politicians for a truce. When the Cabinet met again on December 30 it was decided to extend Martial Law to the four extra counties requested by General Macready. The extension came into force on 4 January 1921. The policy of coercion had prevailed. A month later, Churchill left the War Office, and the problems of Ireland passed, temporarily, to others. But his wife, who had throughout 1920 been critical of the policy of reprisals, urged him to continue to take both an active and more positive part in Irish affairs, writing to him on 18 February 1921:

Do my darling use your influence *now* for some sort of moderation or at any rate justice in Ireland.

Put yourself in the place of the Irish. If you were ever leader you would not be cowed by severity & certainly not by reprisals which fall like the rain from Heaven upon the Just & upon the Unjust. . . .

It always makes me unhappy & disappointed when I see you *inclined* to take for granted that the rough, iron-fisted 'Hunnish' way will prevail.

[1] Edward Peter Strickland, 1869–1951. 2nd Lieutenant, 1888. On active service in Burma, 1888–9, the Sudan, 1897–8 and Nigeria, 1906. Colonel, Northern Nigeria Regiment, 1909. Brigadier-General, 1915. On active service on the western front, 1915–18. Major-General, 1918. Knighted, 1919. Commanded the 6th Division in Ireland, 1919–22. Narrowly escaped death when his car was fired on by Sinn Fein gunmen, September 1920. Lieutenant-General, 1926. General Officer Commanding the British Troops in Egypt, 1927–31. General, 1931.

[2] Gerald Farrell Boyd, 1877–1930. Entered the Army as a Private, 1895; Sergeant, 1899; 2nd Lieutenant, 1900. Awarded the DSO in the South African War, 1899–1902. Major, Royal Irish Regiment, 1915. Brigadier-General, General Staff, 5th Army Corps, and Brigade Commander, 170th Infantry Brigade, 1916–18 (severely wounded). Major-General, 1919. Commanded the 46th (Midland) Division, 1919. Knighted, 1923. Commandant, Staff College, Quetta, 1923–7. Military Secretary to the Secretary of State for War, 1927–30.

27

Turkey in Defeat

A S Secretary of State for War in 1919, Churchill was responsible for the British armies of occupation in Turkey. On 30 October 1918, when the Turkish Empire had surrendered to the Allies, British troops were already in occupation of large areas of the Turkish Empire in the Middle East, including Palestine and Mesopotamia. The occupation of these territories provided a direct overland link between the British Empire in Egypt and the Persian Gulf, while the occupation of Constantinople and the Straits also gave Britain control over Russia's access to the Mediterranean.

During April 1919 Austen Chamberlain tried to set an upper limit on British military expenditure of £110 million for the first peace-time year. Churchill protested at this limitation. 'The responsibilities of the Army will have been increased by the war,' he wrote to Lloyd George on May 1. 'The whole East is unsettled by the disintegration of Turkey, and we shall have large additions of territory in Palestine and Mesopotamia to maintain.'

On May 15, with the approval of the Allied Powers, 20,000 Greek troops landed in Asia Minor, and occupied the Turkish port of Smyrna. The occupation of Smyrna by Greece was part of the wider Allied policy of breaking up the Turkish Empire, according to divisions secretly agreed upon during the war, and was carried out with great brutality.

On May 16 one of the heroes of the Gallipoli Campaign, Mustafa Kemal,[1] left Constantinople for Sivas and Erzerum, where he demanded the complete evacuation both of Anatolia and of Turkey-in-Europe by all non-Turkish powers. For the Turks, Kemal's appeal came at a time

---

[1] Mustafa Kemal, 1881–1938. Served in the Libyan and Balkan campaigns, 1911–13. Turkish Military Attaché in Sofia, 1913–14. Served at Gallipoli, 1915, in the Caucasus, 1916, and in Syria, 1917–18. Assumed command of the Turkish National Movement, 1919. First President of the Turkish Republic from 1922 until his death. Known as Atatürk.

of growing fears for their future. Throughout June and July the Greeks strengthened their position at Smyrna and seized control of a substantial hinterland; the Italians occupied the Cilician province in south-western Anatolia; and British, French and Italian forces remained in occupation of Constantinople and the Straits.

Churchill was convinced that Britain must make peace with Turkey. He saw no merit either in supporting Greek territorial ambitions, or in maintaining British control over Constantinople itself. On August 12 he wrote to Balfour, who was in Paris at the Peace Conference:

. . . could you give me any indication of how long we are expected to maintain an army at Constantinople? We have maintained a force of some 40,000 men in Constantinople and on the Black Sea shores ever since the 11th November. The strain of this upon our melting military resources is becoming insupportable. I hope, therefore, that it will be possible to arrange Peace with Turkey of a kind which will enable us to close down and bring home all British military establishments in Constantinople by the end of October at the latest, and that the peace negotiations with Turkey will be conducted in the light of this fact. I know how great your difficulties are, but I trust you will realise that the length of time which we can hold a sufficient force at your disposal to overawe Turkey is limited, and that I have not the legal power, nor the financial means, nor the political support necessary to extend those limits.

'With regard to Turkey,' Churchill wrote again to Balfour on August 23, 'we must either quit or stay. If we stay we must stay in sufficient strength to be safe. Both you and the Prime Minister say that we have no alternative but to keep an effective army at Constantinople for the present. It must be costing at least £50,000 a day. . . .'

Because both Lloyd George and Balfour insisted that Britain should maintain her garrison at Constantinople, it seemed to Churchill that it was in Mesopotamia that the principal troop reduction would have to be made. On August 30 he telegraphed to the General Officer Commanding-In-Chief, Mesopotamia, Sir George MacMunn,[1] that of the 25,000 British troops under his command, 13,000 must be sent home 'within the next three months'. He must also send back to India 45,000 of the 80,000 native Indian troops, and 100,000 of the 130,000 camp followers. Churchill's telegram ended: 'There can be absolutely no

---

[1] George Fletcher MacMunn, 1869–1952. 2nd Lieutenant, Royal Artillery, 1888. On active service in Burma, 1892, Kohat, 1897, Tirah, 1897–8 and South Africa, 1899–1902. Colonel, 1915. Served at Gallipoli, 1915 and in Mesopotamia, 1917–18. Knighted, 1917. Major-General, 1917. Commander-in-Chief, Mesopotamia, April 1919–January 1920. Quartermaster-General, India, 1920–4.

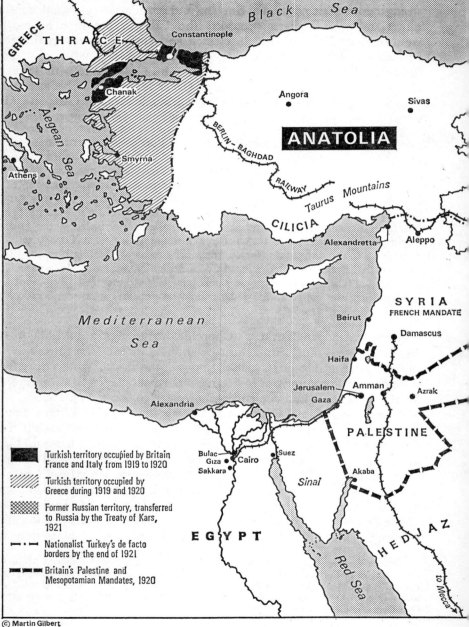

Turkish territory occupied by Britain France and Italy from 1919 to 1920

Turkish territory occupied by Greece during 1919 and 1920

Former Russian territory, transferred to Russia by the Treaty of Kars, 1921

Nationalist Turkey's de facto borders by the end of 1921

Britain's Palestine and Mesopotamian Mandates, 1920

© Martin Gilbert

TURKEY, PERSIA AND THE

MIDDLE EAST, 1919–1922

question of holding the present enormous forces at your disposal, and you must make the best military plan you can in the circumstances. I would remind you that under the Turks Mesopotamia not only paid its way but supplied a revenue to the Central Government.' Churchill's telegram ended: 'The military establishment you are maintaining at the present time would simply crush the province and possibly prove fatal to its retention by Great Britain.'

Lloyd George persevered in his demand for economy. On August 20 he had written to Churchill urging the War Office to play its part in the reduction of departmental spending to which all departmental Ministers had been asked to contribute. After making enquiries of his subordinates, Churchill replied on September 1 that he was satisfied 'that the whole of the administrative branches of the War Office is concentrated upon the problem of demobilizing the army in all parts of the world and reducing it down to the lowest levels compatible with the safe and efficient discharge of the obligations laid upon us by State policy'. One of the main barriers to further economy, he added, was 'the uncertainty of the political as well as the military policy in Palestine, Mesopotamia and generally towards the Turkish Empire'.

On September 22 Churchill wrote to Lloyd George to reiterate his plea for an early peace with Turkey. 'You will have to maintain exceptional forces in Palestine, Egypt & Mesopotamia,' he argued, 'till you have settled with Turkey & till the provocation of Turkey by the Greeks has come to an end.' But Lloyd George was still sympathetic towards Greek claims to sovereignty on the eastern borderlands of the Aegean. Churchill therefore continued his attempts to reduce military expenditure without impairing Britain's struggle to resist, if necessary, a Turkish attack.

On October 20 the Commander-in-Chief of the Army of the Black Sea, General Milne, sent Churchill an account of the strength and aims of the Turkish Nationalists, which made it clear that it was not the Turkish Government in Constantinople, under Allied control, but Mustafa Kemal in Anatolia, to whom the Turks would look for leadership, and with whom the Allies must deal. According to Milne, the Nationalist Movement 'has consolidated public opinion in Turkey, and, now that its supporters hold the reins of power, will do so still more'.

There were three main areas, Milne asserted, which Mustafa Kemal and his followers would fight to regain: Constantinople, Armenia and Thrace. Nor would they ever abandon their claim to Smyrna. 'The events of Smyrna have affected the position so greatly,' Milne wrote, 'that it is inevitable that its evacuation and return to Turkey will be one of the foremost demands of every Turk.' In Thrace, however, he believed that even the Nationalists would be willing to accept 'some adjustments'. Above all, Milne warned:

If the decisions of the Peace Conference are so drastic in the treatment of Turkey that the older men, who have the spirit of compromise, are unable to keep the wilder spirits in check, then it will turn out that the National Movement has very greatly prejudiced the military position of the Allies. The population is armed, and now united for the first time; and it is difficult to calculate the force which might be available in the event of a national rising.

Within the War Office, Churchill's senior advisers discussed the merits of a pro-Turkish policy. 'I am convinced,' Henry Wilson wrote in his diary on November 7, 'that if our FO goes on backing Greece against Turkey we shall be in trouble all over the East. I said this to Curzon on Wed.' General Radcliffe was likewise unwilling to provoke the Turks. It was in Britain's interest, he minuted on November 12, 'to ameliorate & not to exasperate the Turks by appearing to assist the Greeks in stripping them of their few remaining possessions'. Wilson approved Radcliffe's remarks, writing to Churchill on November 13: 'If we antagonize the Turks we lay up an uncomfortable military future for ourselves.'

During the first week of 1920 Churchill took a lead in the Cabinet in urging Lloyd George to end the British occupation of Constantinople. But Lloyd George sought his Cabinet's approval to allow the Greeks to control the city, under British military protection. When the Cabinet met on January 6 Churchill linked his fear of Bolshevik expansion with the need to retain a Turkish Government at Constantinople. In a Note which he took to the Cabinet, he argued that:

(1) Constantinople is the best place to control Turkey from. We shall be in a far better position to exercise control over the Sultan,[1] and through him over Turkey, if we have got him actually in our hands.

(2) I must bow to the overwhelming evidence, supplied by the Secretary of State for India, of the resentment that would be excited in India and throughout the Mohammedan world by the expulsion of the Turks from Constantinople. All our limited means of getting the Middle East to settle down quietly are comprised in the use of Indian troops. We must not do anything

---

[1] Mehmed Vahid-en-Din. Became Sultan, as Mehmed VI, in July 1918. Fled from Constantinople, 17 November 1922. Lived in exile at San Remo from 1922 until his death. The Nationalists abolished the Sultanate shortly after his flight from Turkey.

that will raise Indian sentiment against the use of these troops or affect their own loyalty.

(3) I expect to see a united militarist Russia in the near future. I fear it will not now be a friendly united militarist Russia but a hostile united militarist Russia. If the Turk is in Constantinople, the manhood of the Turkish Empire can be used to prevent the forcible acquisition by Russia of Constantinople and the Straits. If the Turk is gone, there will be nobody to defend Constantinople except the international force, which of course would be valueless against a great Power unless all the countries involved are prepared to take up arms. Once the Turk is out of Constantinople there will be no reason why Turkish Mohammedans and Russian Bolsheviks should not make common cause.

On February 7 Churchill circulated the Cabinet with an outline of his 'Army Estimates, 1920–21'. The Middle East was by far the largest drain on military manpower, with 9,500 British troops at Constantinople and the Straits, 6,000 in Egypt, 9,000 in Palestine and 14,000 in Mesopotamia. Each of these garrisons was, in Churchill's view, excessive: the Constantinople garrison could be terminated 'by a decision of policy'; the Palestine garrison cost 'far beyond anything which Palestine can ever yield in return'—nine million pounds a year. The cost of the garrison in Mesopotamia was more than twice that of Palestine, and was, Churchill wrote, 'out of all proportion to any advantage we can ever expect to reap from that country'. Yet Churchill no longer drew the conclusion that these expenditures could be reduced if Britain made peace with Turkey. Instead he saw a new danger in the Turkish Nationalist movement. 'I must further point out,' he wrote, 'that the Bolshevik and Turkish Nationalist menace, together with the Arab disturbances consequent upon the French seizure of Syria, will expose our troops in Mesopotamia to continued and increasing danger.'

Churchill feared the spread of Bolshevism as a destructive force in the Middle East. On February 10 Edwin Montagu stimulated these fears. 'I wish to draw your attention,' he wrote, 'to the latest news from Switzerland of Bolshevik intrigue with the Turks and Feisal.'[1] Churchill sent Montagu's enclosures to Lloyd George and Bonar Law on February 12, adding in his covering note: 'This is only one of many indications.' Speaking of Turkey in the House of Commons on February 23, Churchill

[1] Feisal Ibn Hussein, 1885–1933. Third son of Hussein, Sherif of Mecca. Accompanied his father as an exile to Constantinople, 1891. A Member of the Turkish Parliament, 1913. Leader of the Arab revolt against the Turks, 1916–18. Proclaimed himself King of Syria and Palestine, 10 March 1920. Deposed by the French, and fled from Damascus, 25 July 1920. Elected to the throne of Mesopotamia (Iraq), 1921, where he ruled until his death.

declared: 'We do not know what aggressive action the Russian Bolsheviks may take in this sphere.' But he went on to warn against a harsh Peace Treaty with Turkey. 'We have lost ground steadily through the whole of last year,' he declared, 'and I trust that, having dispersed our armies, we shall not now take steps which will drive the Turkish people to despair, or undertake any new obligation, because our resources are not equal to the discharge.'

On March 5, at an Allied Conference in London, it was decided to declare an official Allied occupation of Constantinople and the Straits. Churchill approved this decision, and on March 17 he authorized General Milne to take overall command of the Allied troops stationed there. Fearing disagreement between the British and French forces in the City, Churchill added: 'You will, of course, do what you can to humour Allied susceptibilities, and be careful to show a solid Allied front to the Turks.'

During March the Allied Prime Ministers prepared to assemble, in order to work out a Turkish Peace Treaty. But on March 10 the Emir Feisal proclaimed himself 'King of Syria', and made it clear that by 'Syria' he included both Palestine and Mesopotamia, which Britain had assumed would be given to her as League of Nations' Mandates. On March 19 Lloyd George, Churchill and Curzon met at 10 Downing Street. Henry Wilson, who was present, recorded in his diary that they discussed Feisal's proclamation, 'which of course is inadmissible, though LG rather favoured it'.

The imminence of a Turkish peace treaty stimulated the Greeks as much as the Arabs. In the second week of March the Greek Prime Minister, Eleutherios Venizelos,[1] was in London, asserting Greek claims to both Smyrna and Thrace. On the afternoon of March 19 he went to the War Office, and put his points to Churchill. Henry Wilson was also present. According to the official War Office notes of the conversation, Churchill, at the outset, made it 'quite clear' to Venizelos that England 'could not help him with troops, either in Thrace or in Asia Minor', but would be willing to 'render such assistance as she could in arms and munitions'. Henry Wilson then said that if the Greeks insisted on occupying Thrace and Smyrna, they would be engaged 'for 10 or 15 years in hostilities with the Turks and that although the Greeks had ample troops the cost in money might become prohibitive'. Venizelos disagreed strongly. 'He was confident,' the Minutes recorded, 'that in

[1] Eleutherios Venizelos, 1864–1936. Prime Minister of Greece, 1910–15. Forced to resign by King Constantine, May 1915. Prime Minister for the second time, August to October 1915. Subsequently Prime Minister, 1917–20, 1928–32 and 1933.

taking over Smyrna Vilayet and Thrace he was not proposing to do anything outside the power of Greece, either in men or money. . . .'

While in London, Venizelos succeeded in persuading Lloyd George to accept permanent Greek control of the coast of Asia Minor, and sovereignty over all Turkey-in-Europe as far east as the Chatalja lines. Even Lord Curzon was surprised by Lloyd George's acceptance of Greek sovereignty over Smyrna. 'I am the last man to wish to do a good turn to the Turks,' he wrote to Lloyd George on April 9, '. . . but I do want to get something like peace in Asia Minor, and with the Greeks in Smyrna, and Greek divisions carrying out Venizelos's orders and marching about Asia Minor, I know this to be impossible.'

Churchill still believed that Turkish nationalism was a force to be won over, not provoked. On March 24, while on his way to France for a short holiday, he wrote to Lloyd George of how he was 'vy anxious about yr policy towards Turkey'. He could not approve of a peace treaty based upon the partition and occupation of Turkey, and explained why:

With military resources wh the Cabinet have cut to the most weak & slender proportions, we are leading the Allies in an attempt to enforce a peace on Turkey wh wd require gt & powerful armies & long costly operations & occupations. On this world so torn with strife I dread to see you let loose the Greek armies—for all sakes & certainly for their sakes. Yet the Greek armies are yr only effective fighting force. How are you going to feed C'ple if the railways in Asia Minor are cut & supplies do not arrive? Who is going to pay? From what denuded market is the food to come? I fear you will have this gt city lolling helplessly in yr hands, while all around will be guerilla & blockade. Here again I counsel prudence & appeasement. Try to secure a really representative Turkish governing authority, & come to terms with it. As at present couched the Turkish Treaty means indefinite anarchy.

Lloyd George made no reply to Churchill's criticisms. For his part Churchill continued to seek to reduce Britain's military expenditure in the Middle East. On April 1 he wrote to General MacMunn's successor in Mesopotamia, Sir Aylmer Haldane,[1] urging him to devise 'a reasonable scheme for maintaining order . . . at a cost which is not ruinous'.

---

[1] J. Aylmer Lowthorpe Haldane, 1862–1950. Entered Army, 1882. On active service, Chitral, 1895, the Tirah, 1897–8, and South Africa, 1899–1900. Imprisoned (with Churchill) in Pretoria, 1900, (having commanded the armoured train in which they were both captured). Military Attaché with the Japanese Army, Far East, 1904–5. Served throughout the Great War; commanded the 10th Infantry Brigade (retreat from Mons), 1914; the 3rd Division, 1914–18. Lieutenant-General, 1918. Knighted, 1918. Commander-in-Chief, Mesopotamia, 1920–2. General, 1925. He published his memoirs, A Soldier's Saga, in 1945.

The 'fate of the province', he added, would depend upon a cheap scheme being possible.

A month later, on May 1, Churchill elaborated his views in a two-thousand-word memorandum entitled 'Mesopotamian Expenditure', writing bluntly of 'the waste of money entailed by our present military and administrative policy. . . .' There were, he said, over 60,000 British and Indian troops in Mesopotamia, 'scattered over an enormous area', and costing over £18,000,000 a year. Yet the War Office had no say in the distribution of these troops, which was a political matter over which the Foreign Office 'gives the directing impulse'. Churchill wrote critically of the effect of the Foreign Office's decisions—'this vicious system', he described it—whereby remote garrisons were set up, and had then to be made strong enough 'to resist every conceivable attack'. The result, he said, was that 'a score of mud villages, sandwiched in between a swampy river and a blistering desert, inhabited by a few hundred half naked native families, usually starving' were now occupied by garrisons 'on a scale which in India would maintain order in wealthy provinces of millions of people'. Churchill warned that as a result of trying to hold 'these worthless villages', the troops had been widely dispersed, ill-health was rampant, and discontent growing. 'How long,' he asked, 'is this state of affairs to continue?' And he answered: 'It will continue as long as the department calling the tune has no responsibility for paying the piper.'

Churchill proposed handing over Mesopotamia to the Colonial Office, and making the Colonial Office responsible for both policy and expenditure. The transfer, he said, should be made 'immediately'; the amount to be spent annually should then be fixed; and a policy should be worked out 'within those limits'—all by a single Department, responsible to a single Minister. If the financial liabilities were carefully worked out, the War Office could then provide the necessary troops. But his Department no longer wanted to be presented with 'a blank cheque upon our resources in money and men'.

In his memorandum of May 1, Churchill also proposed transferring all the military responsibilities in Mesopotamia from the Army to the Air Force. The first advantage of aerial control, he explained, was the avoidance of long, costly and vulnerable lines of communication. 'From a central position at Baghdad . . .' he pointed out, 'air forces can in a few hours reach almost any point in the area which it is reasonable for us to attempt to occupy in the first instance.' Small, sedentary garrisons could be 'fed or reinforced or relieved by aeroplanes from Baghdad at any time'. Were Mesopotamia to be garrisoned by the Royal Air

Force, Churchill asserted, 'substantial' economies could be made 'in the near future'.

At the end of April the Allied Prime Ministers met at San Remo to draw up the Turkish peace treaty. As a result of their deliberations it was finally decided to allow the Greeks to control both Smyrna and Thrace. The Allies also upheld the general plan of the wartime secret treaties, which destroyed Turkey as an imperial power. Palestine became a League of Nations Mandate, under British control, and with the proviso that it become the site of the 'Jewish National Home'. Syria became a French Mandate. Arabia was to be left to the Arabs. Mesopotamia became a British Mandate. Armenia was given its independence. The Turkish Army was reduced to a maximum of fifty thousand men, and compulsory military service abolished. The Turkish Navy and Air Force were to be disbanded altogether. The power of imposing taxes was withdrawn from the Turkish Government, and transferred to a Finance Commission composed of British, French and Italian representatives. A neutral 'Zone of the Straits' was established, in which no Turkish troops were allowed, and in which Allied garrisons were to remain in permanent occupation.[1]

The decisions of the San Remo conference were put to the Turks at Sèvres, near Paris, at the beginning of May. On May 11 the completed 'Treaty of Sèvres' was presented to the Turkish delegates, who reacted with dismay and hostility. Although the Turkish Government at Constantinople were prepared, under pressure, to sign it, the Nationalists, who had established their capital at Angora, denounced it as a betrayal of Turkish national rights, and pledged themselves to the total restoration of Turkish sovereignty in Asia Minor and Turkey-in-Europe. But even the Nationalists, guided by Mustafa Kemal, accepted the loss of Syria, Palestine and Mesopotamia.

As Constantinople and the Straits were to continue to be garrisoned by Britain, Churchill took steps to ensure that they were adequately manned and supplied. As Palestine was to become a British Mandate, he continued to supervise its military administration until such time as the Mandate was in force, and the administration transferred to the Colonial Office. In Mesopotamia he continued to carry out the policy on which Lloyd George insisted, of reducing military expenditure to a minimum. But he was not always helped by the attitude of his principal

[1] See map on page 822.

advisers. Henry Wilson did not approve of the search for economy, writing in his diary on May 1: 'Winston, regardless of safety & hoping that any disasters may come after he has left office, is trying to gain credit & make a name by saving money. He certainly won't do so with my approval nor without a very clear definition from the Cabinet of those who will bear the responsibility.'

On May 10 Churchill wrote to Austen Chamberlain, to explain the economies which he was making:

. . . I am proposing to transfer the military security of Mesopotamia from the Army to the Air Force as from the end of the financial year, with a consequent agreed reduction from over eighteen millions a year to between five and six millions. I am proposing in the meanwhile, if the Cabinet will support me, to effect an immediate drastic reduction of the Mesopotamian garrison by withdrawing all outlying forces to the heads of the different railway lines in Mesopotamia. This should enable a large proportion of the garrison to be sent away in the next few months, and a still larger proportion of the expense to be saved. I am dealing with the question of Palestine in a similar spirit.

In his letter Churchill also informed Austen Chamberlain of some of the difficulties with which he was confronted in the Middle East, arising from the attitude of his own subordinates towards economy:

Needless to say, in these matters I am getting little help from the General Staff and none from the commanders on the spot, and you have probably no idea of what the difficulties are in enforcing a policy of this kind on reluctant or apathetic professional men to whom the flowing out of expenditure month by month is no cause of anxiety, and who consider that they have done their duty when they have demanded whatever forces they consider are necessary to make themselves absolutely safe.

Churchill's policy continued to be one of caution and economy. At a meeting of nine senior Ministers on June 18 both he and Sir Henry Wilson made it clear, as the official notes of the meeting recorded, 'that the military forces at the disposal of Great Britain were insufficient to meet the requirements of the policies now being pursued in the various theatres'. An immediate curtailment of British responsibilities was, they urged, 'indispensable if grave risk of disaster was not to be incurred'. Indeed, they added, if Britain tried to maintain simultaneously her commitments in Palestine, Persia and Mesopotamia, as well as at Constantinople, 'the possibility of disaster occurring in any or all of these theatres must be faced, and the likelihood of this will increase every day'.

In Palestine the problem of administration was made more difficult because of growing Arab–Jewish friction. On April 4, during a Muslim pilgrimage, anti-Jewish riots had broken out in Jerusalem. The Jews had retaliated in self-defence, and the British Army had acted to restore order.

Churchill had long been interested in Zionism. As early as 1908 he had written, in the draft of a letter intended for a constituent[1] who had argued in favour of Jewish settlement in East Africa: 'Jerusalem must be the only ultimate goal. When it will be achieved it is vain to prophesy: but that it will some day be achieved is one of the few certainties of the future.' Twelve years later, in an article published in the *Illustrated Sunday Herald* on 8 February 1920, Churchill had reiterated this opinion, while contrasting the 'absolutely destructive' influence of the Bolshevik Jews of Russia with the 'inspiring movement' led by Dr Chaim Weizmann.[2] Under the protection of the British Crown, he wrote, the Jews could establish 'by the banks of the Jordan' a Jewish state of three to four million inhabitants. Successful Zionism, he added, would thwart all Trotsky's schemes 'of a world wide communistic state under Jewish domination'; Zionism itself was a 'simpler, a truer, and a far more attainable goal'. Only once had Churchill been critical of what he believed were Zionist aspirations when, on 25 October 1919, he had written—in a survey of those who stood to gain from the partition of the Turkish Empire—'Lastly there are the Jews, whom we are pledged to introduce into Palestine, and who take it for granted that the local population will be cleared out to suit their convenience.'

Despite Churchill's enthusiastic outburst in favour of Zionism in the *Illustrated Sunday Herald*, he did not consider Palestine a region in which Britain should become involved; indeed, he saw clearly the complexities which the Arab–Jewish conflict would create. On June 13 he wrote to Lloyd George:

. . . Palestine is costing us 6 millions a year to hold. The Zionist movement will cause continued friction with the Arabs. The French ensconced in Syria with *4 divisions* (paid for by not paying us what they owe us) are opposed to the Zionist movement & will try to cushion the Arabs off on to us as the real

---

[1] The constituent was Alderman Moser, of Manchester; the letter was dated 30 January 1908; but the paragraph quoted was deleted in the final draft.

[2] Chaim Weizmann, 1874–1952. Born in Russia. Educated in Germany. Reader in Biochemistry, University of Manchester, 1906. Naturalized as a British subject, 1910. Director Admiralty Laboratories, 1916–19. President of the World Zionist Organization, and of the Jewish Agency for Palestine, 1921–31 and 1935–46. Chairman, Board of Governors, Hebrew University of Jerusalem, 1932–50. Adviser to the Ministry of Supply, London, 1939–45. First President of the State of Israel from 1949 until his death. His eldest son, Flight-Lieutenant, Michael Weizmann, RAF, was killed in action in 1942.

enemy. The Palestine venture is the most difficult to withdraw from & the one wh certainly will never yield any profit of a material kind.

Lloyd George saw Churchill on June 15, and discussed his letter with him. They decided to try to keep the Palestine expenditure to a minimum, and to put their faith in the High Commissioner designate, Sir Herbert Samuel. On the following day Churchill told Henry Wilson what the Prime Minister had said. 'LG is in favour,' Wilson wrote in his diary, 'of getting Samuel to keep order in Palestine with Jew & Arab police. . . .'

Sir Herbert Samuel reached Palestine on June 30, and was at once installed as High Commissioner. With Samuel's arrival, the administration of Palestine became the direct responsibility of Lord Milner and the Colonial Office.

Churchill remained convinced that there could not be peace in the Middle East until Turkey had been offered a moderate and acceptable Peace Treaty. On June 7 he had circulated to the Cabinet a memorandum entitled 'Turkey', in which he criticized the as yet unsigned Treaty of Sèvres as being neither just nor enforceable. Meanwhile, he wrote, the British troops in and around Constantinople were costing six million pounds a year. The French, who were trying to conquer Syria by force, would not have sufficient troops to spare 'to enforce the Peace Treaty on other parts of Turkey'. The British could not undertake to enforce a Treaty which was so clearly repellent to the majority of Turks. A further problem arose in the Smyrna and Thrace regions. There, the Greeks 'have been authorized to begin a new war with the Turks'. He would not try to predict its outcome, but it might well be 'very lengthy'. Britain could not afford to become involved in yet another conflict. Even the occupation of Constantinople was an expensive burden. This was a situation which France, Britain's ally, did not hesitate to exploit. Churchill asked his colleagues: 'Is it the intention to settle down in Constantinople as we have settled down in Egypt, and retain permanently for Britain a predominance there?' This, he warned, would be 'a very dangerous policy; it would be an unscrupulous policy. . . . It would draw upon this country the combined animosities over a long period of years of France, Russia and Turkey.'

At the end of his memorandum, Churchill returned to the proposed Treaty of Sèvres. It was not only a Treaty, he wrote, which the Allies had no power to enforce, but it would condemn the greater part of the Turkish Empire 'to anarchy and barbarism for an indefinite period. . . .'

The first proof of Churchill's fears came in the second week of June when Nationalist troops, under direct orders from Mustafa Kemal, advanced towards Ismid, on the edge of the designated neutral 'Zone of the Straits'. On June 13 Churchill wrote to Lloyd George, reiterating the arguments of his memorandum on June 7, and warning of the imminent dangers if Britain persisted in trying to hold Constantinople:

Are we to go on bearing the main burden of holding Cple or are we to reduce our forces to the quota to be borne by France & Italy. . . . At present with the integrity of command held by the British Fleet & Army we can probably hold the city & defend its approaches. Fighting is however likely in the vy near future, & if the troops on the spot are not sufficient, *we have no reserves anywhere.*

Lloyd George was not convinced by Churchill's arguments, and believed that the Turks would not find the strength to regain their lost dominions. On June 14 Churchill spoke to him about Turkey, and on the following day Churchill told Henry Wilson what Lloyd George had said. 'LG is in favour,' Wilson noted in his diary '. . . of occupying C-ople with British & Greeks if the French & Italians turn crusty.' The Prime Minister was also convinced, Wilson added, 'that the Greeks are the coming power in the Mediterranean both on land & sea & wants to befriend them'.

On June 16 two telegrams reached the War Office from General Milne, reporting, as Henry Wilson recorded in his diary, that 'the Turkish Govt troops had been defeated by the Nationalists & now the Nationalists under Kemal were attacking us on the Ismid line'. Milne added that he did not have 'sufficient forces to hold C-ople & Ismid, & he asks for orders as to what he is to do. . . .'

At eleven o'clock on the morning of June 17 the seven senior Ministers concerned with Eastern Affairs, Bonar Law, Walter Long, Curzon, Austen Chamberlain, Montagu and Churchill, met in Lloyd George's room in the House of Commons. For nearly six hours, under Lloyd George's chairmanship, they discussed what should be done to defend Constantinople against Mustafa Kemal. Henry Wilson recorded the course of the discussion in his diary:

LG called on me for my statement. I made, for me, a long & full statement amounting to this:—that I had not enough troops to carry out the Cabinet Policy in Ireland, C-ople, Palestine, Mesopot: & Persia not to mention England, Egypt & India.

I said I must have, at least, another Division in C-ople & another in
Mesopotamia: I proposed a Greek Div: for C-ople since I gathered that
neither France nor Italy would help. . . .

As I was speaking, a telegram came in from Milne calling for a Division,
2 Cav Regts. etc. & a lot of guns. This fitted in exactly with what I had just
said & was most opportune.

Venizelos was sent for & asked if he could give me a Division. He said I
could have 1 of the 3 Div^s lining up on the Maritza & he would temporarily
postpone his advance into Eastern Thrace.[1]

The Cabinet concluded, according to the official Minutes: '. . . that
having regard to the very strong and even dramatic line of policy taken
by the British plenipotentiaries in regard to the Treaty of Peace with
Turkey, to retire from Constantinople before a bandit like Mustapha
Kemal would deal a shattering blow to our prestige in the East'.

In his memorandum of June 7, and his letter of June 13, Churchill
had warned of the dangers of pursuing an anti-Turkish policy. But the
appearance of Venizelos at the meeting of Ministers, and his offer of
troops, confirmed Lloyd George in his policy, and convinced a majority
of Ministers that it was a sound one. Venizelos had spoken of a new
Greek offensive, both at Smyrna and in Thrace. He had offered to send
Greek troops to the Ismid peninsula to help General Milne defend
Constantinople. His offers, and his confidence, were decisive. Even
Churchill seemed unwilling to allow Mustafa Kemal actually to
threaten British troops. 'Long talks with Winston,' Wilson wrote in his
diary on June 19, 'who is already excited & rattled. He wants to send
out to C-ople the 4 Batt^{ns} I earmarked for foreign service.' But Wilson
had warned Churchill that if Greek troops could not hold the Ismid
peninsula 'then the sooner we come to terms with Kemal the better'.

On Sunday June 20, at Sir Philip Sassoon's house at Lympne, Lloyd
George discussed the Turkish crisis with Alexander Millerand and
Marshal Foch. Churchill was not present. During the discussions,
Lloyd George persuaded Millerand to agree to an immediate occupa-
tion of Thrace by Greece. Hitherto Thrace had been garrisoned by a
predominantly French force. Millerand also agreed to allow the Greeks
to advance northwards and eastwards from Smyrna, to the shore of the
Sea of Marmara. This they proceeded to do, driving the Turks from
Panderma and Brusa, and occupying all of Eastern Thrace as far as the
Chatalja lines. Speaking to Lord Riddell on June 26, Lloyd George
defended his support for the Greeks. Riddell recorded Lloyd George's
remarks in his diary:

[1] See map on page 822.

The Turks nearly brought about our defeat in the war. It was a near thing. You cannot trust them and they are a decadent race. The Greeks, on the other hand, are our friends, and they are a rising people. We want to be on good terms with the Greeks and Italians.

We must secure Constantinople and the Dardanelles. You cannot do that effectively without crushing the Turkish power. Of course the military are against the Greeks. They always have been. They favour the Turks. The military are confirmed Tories. It is the Tory policy to support the Turks. They hate the Greeks. That is why Henry Wilson, who is a Tory of the most crusted kind, is so much opposed to what we have done.

Lloyd George's policy succeeded. The Kemalist forces halted outside the British occupied zones. Both Ismid and Chanak remained under British control. The Greeks, acting as Britain's allies, drove the Kemalists from the southern shore of the Sea of Marmara, and consolidated their position throughout western Anatolia. Within a month, on July 21, Lloyd George felt able to tell the House of Commons, in triumph: 'Turkey is no more.'

On August 10 the representatives of the Constantinople Government finally signed the Treaty of Sèvres, accepting, on Turkey's behalf, the partition of their country. But the authority of the Constantinople Government extended no further than the area occupied by British troops: Constantinople itself, and the neutral zones protecting the Bosphorus and the Dardanelles. At Angora, in defiance, Mustafa Kemal summoned a Grand National Assembly, and declared that the Treaty of Sèvres was a direct act of aggression on Turkey by Britain, France, Italy and Greece. Henceforth, he declared, the Angora Government was at war with the Allies, and would drive them from Turkish soil.

For eight months Churchill's main concern in the Middle East had been to secure peace with Turkey: a peace which would check Greek ambitions, and enable Britain to have friendly relations with the Turkish Nationalists. His views had not prevailed. Guided by Lloyd George, the British Cabinet had committed Britain to the Greek cause, and roused intense Turkish hostility. This hostility threatened to bring war to Britain's new Arab territory, Mesopotamia, and to antagonize Muslim feeling both in Mesopotamia and in Palestine. Concerned above all with economy, Churchill feared Muslim antagonism, and warned that the policing of these two territories could become extremely expensive unless Turkey were appeased. Unwilling to see his War Office budget drained away in Middle Eastern conflicts, he had taken a lead in urging a policy of withdrawal and disengagement. But just as Lloyd George supported the Greeks against the Turks, he was also eager to see

British power retained in Palestine and Mesopotamia. Churchill therefore persevered in a joint policy of control and economy, but remained sceptical that either could really succeed if they were forced to run together.

28

'These Thankless Deserts'

IN the third week of March 1920 General Haldane reached Mesopotamia, and took command of 4,200 British and 30,000 Indian troops.
Among his responsibilities was the guarding of 14,000 Turkish prisoners-
of-war; 50,000 Armenian and Assyrian refugees mostly encamped at
Baquba; and two thousand miles of road, rail and river communications. Towards the end of May the Bolsheviks occupied the Persian port
of Enzeli, on the Caspian Sea, and this threat to Persia forced Haldane
to send 2,000 of his British troops to Kazvin. It was at this moment, on
May 26, that an Arab rebellion broke out at Tel Afar, near Mosul, following the arrest of a local sheikh for debt, an act which General
Haldane later described as 'injudicious'. The Arabs reacted fiercely,
killing four British soldiers. Two armoured cars were at once sent from
Mosul to Tel Afar. Both of them were ambushed on arrival, and their
crews, two officers and fourteen men, were killed.

A punitive expedition was at once mounted from Mosul, and on
June 9, having destroyed en route most of the harvest on which the
Mosul garrison depended, the expedition drove the entire population of
Tel Afar into the desert. The murderers themselves were never caught.
The rebellion spread quickly. In the first week of July there was fierce
fighting at Samawa and Rumaitha. At Rumaitha the Royal Air Force
dropped food and ammunition for the besieged garrison, and attacked
the Arabs who were investing the town. 'The fighting was severe,'
Churchill told the Cabinet on July 7, 'but our attack was successful.
. . . The enemy were bombed and machine-gunned with effect by aeroplanes which cooperated with the troops.'

On July 15 Henry Wilson, who was at the Spa Conference with
Lloyd George, received a telegram from General Haldane describing
the growing strength of the rebellion. 'At midnight,' he wrote in his
diary, 'just before going to bed, I wired Winston that in view of reports

490

from Mesopot: I urged the despatch of the whole Div: from India & not only a Brigade for it was essential to give these Arabs on the Lower Euphrates a good lesson.' But Churchill was more concerned with the problem of economy. 'A wild wire from Winston,' Wilson wrote in his diary on July 16, 'about Mesopotamia & the expense! I showed it to LG & he agreed to have an early Cabinet next week.' But before the Cabinet could meet, the news from Mesopotamia worsened. On July 20 a force under Brigadier-General Coningham[1] reached Rumaitha and raised the siege, but during the battle five British officers and thirty Indian soldiers were killed. That same day the Arabs seized the town of Kifl. On July 21 Wilson again urged Churchill to send a whole Division of troops from India as reinforcements. But Churchill still hesitated to commit so large and costly a force.

On July 21 Major-General Leslie[2] set out from Hilla to recapture Kifl with 800 men of the Manchester Regiment. But on July 24, before he had reached the town, his camp was attacked, and he ordered an immediate retreat. During the retreat 180 of his men were killed and 160 captured.

The Cabinet met on the morning of July 26 to discuss the Mesopotamian defeats. Henry Wilson was summoned to attend, 'but', he noted in his diary, 'it was turned into a Cabinet on Ireland'. It was decided to discuss Mesopotamia in four days time, but again the discussion did not take place. 'LG is sick,' Henry Wilson wrote in his diary on July 30, 'so the Cabinet is again postponed & nothing settled about Mespot. . . .' That same day, on Wilson's insistence, Churchill finally agreed to the despatch of a whole Division from India to Mesopotamia.

Churchill wanted the Cabinet to decide officially on a policy towards the Arab revolt in Mesopotamia. He also wanted a decision as to whether British troops in Persia were to halt any Bolshevik advance, in which case they must be reinforced; or be withdrawn, in which case the sooner they could be returned to General Haldane's command the better. 'Mr Churchill is dismayed,' Thomas Jones wrote to Lloyd George on July 30, 'at the delay in dealing with these subjects and has personally made several vigorous protests over the telephone. . . . He

---

[1] Frank Evelyn Coningham, 1870–1934. Entered the Army, 1890; Captain, Indian Army, 1901. On active service in Waziristan, 1894; the Tirah, 1897, Tibet, 1904, and Mesopotamia, 1916–18. Colonel, 1918. Commanded the 10th Gurkha Rifles, during the Arab Rising, Mesopotamia, 1920. Brigadier-General, 1920. Commanded the Razmak Field Force, 1922–3. Major-General retired, 1932.

[2] George Arthur James Leslie, 1867–1936. Entered the Army, 1887. On active service in the Tirah, 1897; Chitral, 1900; and in the Great War. Major-General Commanding the 17th Indian Division, Mesopotamia, 1918–20. Retired, 1923.

has telegraphed to India that the embarkation of troops there for Mesopotamia is to continue pending further instructions. I have told him that these subjects shall be taken on Tuesday morning. I hope you will agree to this.'

On August 2 a telegram reached the War Office from General Haldane, declaring that the position in Baghdad itself was insecure. On the following day the Finance Committee of the Cabinet met to discuss what should be done. The first suggestion was put forward by the former Acting Commissioner for Mesopotamia, Colonel Wilson,[1] who was convinced that the unrest in Mesopotamia could be allayed if Britain agreed to set up an entirely Arab Administration, with the Emir Feisal at its head.

It seemed an opportune moment for Britain to offer to set up an Arab Kingdom in Mesopotamia. Eight days earlier, on July 25, the French had occupied Damascus and Aleppo, thereby destroying Arab hopes of a Kingdom in Syria, and leaving Feisal in search of a kingdom. The suppression of Arab aspirations would be costly in both life and money. But if Feisal were made king, the burden of maintaining law and order would fall on him.

In the discussion that followed, 'the opinion was expressed', according to the Minutes, 'that concessions made in the moment of defeat never improved any situation'. It was therefore decided, as a first step, to concentrate strong British forces on the Lower Euphrates 'and teach the turbulent tribes a sharp lesson'. Only when the rebellion had been crushed, 'in two or three months' time', would the question of Feisal's appointment as King of Mesopotamia 'be revived'.

On August 5 Churchill wrote to Lloyd George to warn him of the dangers of a divided policy which sought to combine economy with the suppression of rebellion. Matters had reached a point, he warned, 'where my responsibility to prevent a great disaster had become a very real one'. He urged Lloyd George to take into account both his warnings in June of the need to provide adequate forces in Mesopotamia, and

[1] Arnold Talbot Wilson, 1884–1940. Entered the Army, from Sandhurst, 1903. On duty in Persia, guarding the Ahwaz oilfields, 1907–9. Transferred to the Indian Political Department, 1909. Consul at Mohammerah, 1909–11. Deputy Chief Political Officer, Mesopotamia Expeditionary Force, 1915; Deputy Civil Commissioner, 1916. Acting Commissioner, Mesopotamia and Political Resident, Persian Gulf, 1918–20. Knighted, 1920. Adviser to the Anglo-Persian Oil Company, 1921–32. Author of several works about Mesopotamia and the Persian Gulf, including *Loyalties* (1930) and *A Clash of Loyalties* (1931). Conservative MP, 1933–40. A leading advocate of Anglo-German reconciliation after Hitler came to power in 1933. Chairman, Home Office Committee on Structural Precautions against Air Attack, 1936–8. Pilot Officer (Air Gunner), 1939–40. Killed in action over France, 31 May 1940, when his plane crashed behind German lines.

'the imperative decision taken by the Cabinet in January to reduce the forces in Mesopotamia to half their strength in the current financial year, on which decision I was bound to take action. . . .' Churchill also sent Lloyd George a memorandum by Henry Wilson, warning of the dangers to Britain's position in Mesopotamia if General Haldane did not receive sufficient reinforcements. But when the Cabinet met on August 6, no decision was reached, as Wilson recorded in his diary:

No decision except to send Sir Percy Cox[1] back to report. He had just come home to report, now he is going out to report. I spoke very strongly in the sense of my paper last night but it was no use. Milner & Curzon made it clear they would resign if we came out of Persia & LG *funked*. So although Winston spoke up, no decision was reached. . . .

The Cabinet met again on August 12. During the discussion Sir Percy Cox spoke of the need for a 'separate Department' to administer all the affairs of the Middle East and to bring an end to the overlapping and at times conflicting policies of the War Office, the Foreign Office, the India Office and the Colonial Office. Cox insisted 'that no existing Department of State could properly do the work'. Five days later, at a Cabinet on August 17, Lord Curzon circulated a memorandum strongly critical of Cox's suggestion. But in the ensuing discussion several Ministers, including Churchill, spoke in support of a special Middle East Department.

As August progressed, the situation in Mesopotamia worsened. After the railway line had been cut north of Baquba on August 9, all British communications with Persia were severed, and Baquba itself had to be abandoned three days later. On August 13 the Arabs at Shahraban rose in revolt, killing five of the six English officials in the town. On August 26 Churchill wrote to Lloyd George:

With regard to Mesopotamia, I have told Henry Wilson that now that the Cabinet have definitely decided that we are to plough through in that dismal country every effort must be made to procure vigorous action and decisive results. You will see that Haldane thinks that with the reinforcements we are sending he should be able to quell the revolt by the end of November. . . .

There are only two air squadrons at present working there, but the third

[1] Percy Zachariah Cox, 1864–1937. Entered the Army, 1884. Served in India, 1884-93. Captain, 1892. Assistant Political Resident, Zeila, British Somaliland, 1893. Led an expedition which defeated a tribal uprising at Berbera, 1895. Political Agent and Consul at Muscat, 1899–1904. Political Resident in the Persian Gulf, 1909–14. Knighted, 1911. Accompanied the Indian Expeditionary Force to Mesopotamia, as Chief Political Officer, 1914–17. Major-General, 1917. Acting Minister to Teheran, 1918–20. High Commissioner, Mesopotamia, 1920–3. His only son, an air force pilot, was killed in action over France in 1917.

should be in action early next month, and I have now ordered a fourth
squadron (the one we brought to Constantinople when the Ismid Peninsula
was threatened) to proceed at once to Mesopotamia, where it should come
into action before the end of October. We are also sending out fresh machines
from this country. . . .

Churchill also telegraphed that day to General Haldane, informing
him that the Cabinet 'have decided that the rebels must be quelled
effectively', and listing the reinforcements that he was to receive. By the
end of October, Churchill wrote, 'you should be possessed of effective
striking forces, and a vigorous use of these to put down and punish disaffection, combined with the policy of setting up an Arab State should
bring about a better situation'.

In an effort to make air power more effective in the Middle East,
Churchill wanted the Royal Air Force experts to proceed with experimental work on gas bombs; 'especially mustard gas', he wrote to
Trenchard on August 29, 'which would inflict punishment upon recalcitrant natives without inflicting grave injury upon them'. The news
from Mesopotamia seemed to bear out the need for new and drastic
measures. On August 26 the town of Kifri had been attacked and
pillaged, and its Political Officer, Captain Salmon,[1] had been imprisoned. Two days later, while still in prison, Salmon was murdered.
'Long talk with Winston,' Henry Wilson wrote in his diary on August
30. 'The news from Mesopot: is very serious & Haldane in a long
telegram talks of wanting 2 more Div[s] over & above the 19 Batt[ns] we are
sending him from India. The real fact being that the whole country is
"up" & we are going to have difficult times.'

That afternoon Churchill telegraphed to Haldane, pointing out that
it was 'very difficult to see how or to what extent' his demands for extra
troops would be met:

First, although you make requests for very large numbers of troops and
have a large army at your disposal at present time there seems to be very
little fighting and, apart from disaster to Manchester Regiment, no serious
fighting. Is this due to great heat making aggressive movements impossible? Is it due to elusive and non-aggressive tactics on part of enemy? In
various telegrams you describe small brushes with enemy in which their losses
are always much heavier than ours. What happens when troops meet
rebels? Who is the stronger man for man, taking everything into consideration? Could a mixed force of three or four thousand men with adequate

[1] G. H. Salmon, 1894–1920. Captain, 6th Devon Regiment. Appointed Assistant Political
Officer, Kirkuk, June 1919; transferred to Kifri, January 1920; murdered by tribesmen,
August 1920.

transport make their way effectively through the country? Or would they meet concentrations of the enemy sufficient to round up, immobilise and destroy a British-India force of such dimensions? Am I right in assuming that the troops when concentrated into bodies of this size can hold their own against any attack? I observe also that no fortified posts have been successfully assaulted by the enemy. Please try and answer these questions so as to convey a true picture, as you see it, to my mind.

These questions, Churchill explained, 'are not put to dictate your action but to secure me indispensable information'. Finally, Churchill asked, would it be possible, if the rebellion grew even fiercer, 'to draw in your troops to Baghdad and retire to Basra? How would you do it if you had to.' Naturally, Churchill added, 'everything in human power must be done to avert such a withdrawal. . . .'

The danger of disaster in Mesopotamia forced Britain to rely still further upon the Greeks. On August 31 Churchill telegraphed direct to Venizelos, in Athens, that it would be necessary to withdraw a substantial number of British troops from Constantinople 'in the near future'. He pressed Venizelos 'to accelerate the arrival of remainder of the Greek Division which you promised Chief of the Imperial General Staff you would send', adding: 'Matter is urgent and serious as we are counting on this Division in our general arrangements.'

On August 31 Churchill wrote to Lord Curzon: 'We are at our wits' end to find a single soldier.' That same day he drafted a letter to Lloyd George, setting out his feelings of exasperation. The situation in Mesopotamia, he wrote, was becoming 'increasingly formidable'. Haldane had asked for extra reinforcements to work up from Basra along both the Tigris and the Euphrates, a 'demand', Churchill added, 'that it is impossible to meet'. Extra troops were already being drawn from India, Palestine, Constantinople, Egypt and the Rhine. 'You will readily appreciate the danger and disadvantages of all these moves,' Churchill wrote. 'We shall be left with only two British battalions in Constantinople. . . . India has sent us privately as well as officially the most earnest warnings against removing either British or Gurkha troops from India. . . . On the other hand, so great is the strain in Ireland that we cannot keep up our drafts to India this year. . . .'

Churchill then set out his deeper fears. On reflection, he decided not to send the letter, which expressed his feelings so bluntly:

There is something very sinister to my mind in this Mesopotamian entanglement, coming as it does when Ireland is so great a menace. It seems to me so gratuitous that after all the struggles of the war, just when we want to get together our slender military resources and re-establish our finances and have a little in hand in case of danger here or there, we should be compelled to go on pouring armies and treasure into these thankless deserts. We have not got a single friend in the press upon the subject, and there is no point of which they make more effective use to injure the Government. Week after week and month after month for a long time to come we shall have a continuance of this miserable, wasteful, sporadic warfare, marked from time to time certainly by minor disasters and cuttings off of troops and agents, and very possibly attended by some very grave occurrence. Meanwhile the military expense of this year alone will probably amount to something like fifty millions, thus by this capital expenditure knocking all the bloom off any commercial possibilities which may have existed.

It is an extraordinary thing that the British civil administration should have succeeded in such a short time in alienating the whole country to such an extent that the Arabs have laid aside the blood feuds they have nursed for centuries and that the Suni and Shiah tribes are working together. We have been advised locally that the best way to get our supplies up the river would be to fly the Turkish flag, which would be respected by the tribesmen. I hope Percy Cox will be able to get things on to better lines, but I must confess that I do not feel any complete sense of confidence in him. His personality did not impress me, and all his recent prognostications have been falsified.

I am carrying out the Cabinet directions to the best of my ability. Every possible soldier that we can find is being set in motion for reinforcement to the utmost limits of our available transport. This is equally necessary whether we decide to stay or to quit. There is nothing else to do but this and it will take some time.

On September 1 Churchill left England for a two-week holiday in the South of France. 'I am having here a little sunshine and change,' he wrote to Sir George Ritchie from Mimizan on September 7, 'which I badly needed after all these years of increasing racket and worry, and after the chilling July and August which we suffered in England.' Churchill was back in England, briefly, on September 20. 'I got him to agree,' Henry Wilson noted in his diary, 'to a Br: Batt^n being sent from C-ople to Mesopot. . . .' Churchill also decided that General Harington was the best officer available to succeed General Milne at Constantinople, and this was finally agreed by the Army Council on September 21.

On September 25 Churchill again left for France. While he was away, the war in Mesopotamia drew to an end, and Haldane began the long and stern process of punishment and retribution. During the next three and a half months punitive expeditions set out to all the centres of revolt. Villages were burned. Fines were collected. Over sixty thousand rifles were taken from individual Arabs, and three million rounds of small-arms ammunition were surrendered to the Government. Communications were restored, and blockhouses established at all important road and rail centres. From October 11, the day on which Sir Percy Cox reached Baghdad, and took over as Civil Commissioner from Colonel Wilson, the administration of Mesopotamia reverted to a predominantly peace-time basis, under the ultimate Ministerial authority of the India Office, and of Edwin Montagu. When Churchill returned from his holiday on October 12, the Mesopotamian crisis had passed.

No sooner had the Mesopotamian uprising been suppressed, than the Turkish problem reasserted itself. In the second week of October, Venizelos, determined to exploit Britain's support to the full, proposed to attack the Nationalist capital, Angora, and to seize the Black Sea port of Trebizond. The Cabinet met to discuss Venizelos' proposal on the morning of October 12. 'Curzon says it will mean the break off of the Turkish Treaty,' H. A. L. Fisher wrote in his diary. 'PM observes we shall have to give Constantinople *either* to Greece or Russia in the end.' The Cabinet reached no decision.

On November 14 Venizelos was defeated at the polls, and at once resigned as Prime Minister. This unexpected turn of events was a blow to Lloyd George, who had worked so closely in concerting an anti-Turkish policy. Venizelos' defeat presented an opportunity to the Allies for reconciliation with the Angora Government. The need for such a reconciliation was underlined on November 17, when the Nationalists won a further territorial success, driving the Armenians from the eastern city of Kars.[1] On November 23 Churchill circulated a memorandum to his Cabinet colleagues in which he wrote:

An opportunity now presents itself of securing an effective abatement of the strain and pressure put upon our troops and interests in the East and Middle East. We ought to come to terms with Mustapha Kemal and arrive at a good peace with Turkey which will secure our position and interests at Constantinople and ease the position in Egypt, Mesopotamia, Persia and India.

Now is the time to abandon the policy of relying on the weak and fickle Greeks and by so doing estranging the far more powerful, durable and

[1] The capture of Kars by the Turks effectively brought to an end all chance of the independent state of Armenia as 'established' in the Treaty of Sèvres. Between 1915 and 1922 more than a million Armenians were murdered by the Turks.

necessary Turkish and Mohammedan forces. We should thus recreate that Turkish barrier to Russian ambitions which has always been of the utmost importance to us.

By regaining our influence over the Turks we should be able to do something to save the Armenians and enable Georgia to withstand Bolshevik influences. We have always hitherto had either Turkey or Russia on our side. Our policy since the peace has brought about to a very large extent an extraordinarily unnatural union between these opposite forces.

In our present state of military weakness and financial stringency we cannot afford to go on estranging the Mohammedan world in order to hand over a greater Greece to King Constantine.[1] The Greek nation themselves evidently feel unequal to the strain and burden which Venizelos was prepared to accept on their behalf. A little weak people like this kept all these years at full tension are definitely bound to break down under the load. Let us therefore, without delay and in conjunction with the French, establish a just and lasting peace with the real leaders in Turkey.

Within the War Office, both Henry Wilson and General Thwaites wanted Britain to open negotiations with the Nationalists, and to avoid the expense and dangers of supporting Greek ambition in Asia Minor. On November 30 Thwaites wrote to Churchill: 'CIGS asked me to give you all we have got tending to show that Mustapha Kemal is willing to negotiate. I have put all the papers together and given you the gist of their contents in a short précis.' At the India Office, Edwin Montagu was likewise eager for Britain to open negotiations with Kemal. He feared that India's Muslims would eventually revolt if Britain set herself up as the enemy of Islam in Turkey. On December 2 the Aga Khan[2] sent Montagu a long appeal. 'As long as the terrible Treaty with Turkey remains, in form,' the Aga Khan wrote, 'as long as Great Britain is the centre of opposition towards revision that broke the heart of every sincere Muslim, I fear, and I beg you to believe me, we will never have real peace and goodwill or moral quiet in the Islamic world or in India.' Montagu sent the Aga Khan's letter to Churchill. But even Venizelos' defeat had not weakened Lloyd George's championship of the Greeks, or of Greece's desire to oust the Turks from Thrace, the Pontus and

---

[1] Constantine, 1868–1923. Became King of Greece in 1913, when he was created a Field-Marshal in the German Army. Vetoed Greek co-operation at the Dardanelles, 1915. Refused to help the Allied Army at Salonika, 1916–17. Forced to leave Greece by the Allies, 1917. In exile, 1917–20. Returned as King, 1920. Abdicated after a military revolt, 1922.

[2] Aga Sultan Mahomed Shah, the Aga Khan, 1877–1957. Head of the Ismaili Muslims. Knighted, 1898. Member of the Viceroy's Council, 1902–4. Founded the Muslim University of Aligarh, 1910. On the outbreak of war with Turkey, he appealed to India's Muslims to remain loyal to Britain. Chairman of the Indian Delegation to the Round Table Conference, Geneva, 1932. President of the League of Nations Assembly, Geneva, 1937. His horses won the Derby five times.

western Anatolia. On December 4 Churchill sent Lloyd George a long and emotional appeal, begging him to change his policy:

My dear Prime Minister,

I am vy sorry to see how far we are drifting apart on foreign policy. No doubt my opinions seem a vy unimportant thing. But are you sure that about Turkey the line wh you are forcing us to pursue wd commend itself to the present H. of C? I feel vy deeply that it is most injurious to the interests we have specially to guard in India & the Middle East. I think—tho' I have not consulted them except in casual conversation—that most of the Ministers who are concerned in this sphere feel serious misgivings. . . .

In the military circles whose opn it is my duty to understand, there is universal disagreement & protest. These circles exercise much influence in the Conservative party. Altho' while Ireland holds the field all other topics are in suspense, there is a strong & steady undercurrent of disapproval among people who have been & still wish to be yr most ardent supporters.

It wd be quite easy for you to be vexed with me & to override any counsels I may offer in all good will & sincerity. It wd be vy easy for me to sit still & let events take their course. I do not often trouble you with letters; but I feel I owe it to you & to yr long friendship & many kindnesses to send a solemn warning of the harm wh yr policy—so largely a personal policy—is doing to the unity & cohesion of several important elements of opinion on wh you have hitherto been able to rely.

Moreover it seems to me a most injurious thing that we, the greatest Mohammedan Empire in the world, shd be the leading Anti-Turk power. The desire you have to retain Mosul—& indeed Mesopotamia—is directly frustrated by this vendetta against the Turks. The terrible waste & expense wh the Middle East is involving us in brings the subject forward in a practical & urgent form. I deeply regret & *resent* being forced to ask Parlt for these appalling sums of money for new Provinces—all the more when the pursuance of the Anti Turk policy complicates & aggravates the situation in every one of them, & renders cheaper solutions impossible.

I had a feeling at our last discussion that nothing I said wd ever make any difference; . . . We seem to be becoming the most Anti Turk & the most pro-Bolshevik power in the world: whereas in my judgement we ought to be the exact opposite. Our interests in the East require the amity of the Turk: the character of the political structure wh supports us wd benefit by a marked aloofness from Leninism. All yr great success & overwhelming personal power have come from a junction between yr Liberal followers & the Conservative party. It was on that basis that you were able to carry through the war. But surely at this time—when we Coalition Liberals are vy weak in the Constituencies—it is adding to our difficulties to pursue policies towards the Turks & the Bolsheviks both of wh are fundamentally opposed to Conservative instincts & traditions.

When we sat in the treetops at Fontainbleau you said I was a branch that cracked before it broke. So don't complain of this frank letter wh I send in a spirit utterly free from personal feeling or from any cons [considerations] of my personal interests.

In his letter, Churchill warned Lloyd George of the dangers of excessive personal power:

When one has reached the summit of power & surmounted so many obstacles, there is danger of becoming convinced that one can do anything one likes, & that any strong personal view is necessarily acceptable to the nation & can be enforced upon one's subordinates. No doubt I in my time of important affairs was led astray like this. I suddenly found a vy different world around me: though of course all my fortunes were on a petty scale compared to yours. Venizelos too under-rated the deep detachment of some of the most powerful forces in Greece from his policy—brilliantly successful tho' it was.

But is yr policy going to be successful? I fear it is going wrong. First you are up against a shocking bill for Mesopotm., Palestine & Persia. More will have to be spent in these countries next year than the Navy is demanding to save our sea supremacy. The two cannot be compared from a National point of view. Second, one of the main causes of the trouble throughout the Middle East is *your* quarrel with the remnants of Turkey—not for the sake of the Armenians either (wh at any rate was a Liberal cry). Third, all the soldiers continually say they disapprove of the policy against Turkey & do not care abt Mesopa or Palestine; & that all the extra expense of Army Estimates arises from this evil combination. This soaks in. Fourth, Conservatism is getting stronger all over the world, & in this country you will find a continually stiffer line taken by the Tory Party in its relations to us. Fifth. Nothing but discredit & political loss will come out of the Russian negotiations; tho I admit that there wd be difficulties in refusing to trade with Soviet Russia at this time. Sixth. All Indian opinion is upset both by the pro-Bolshevik & the Anti-Turk line. The India circles are also vy powerful in this country. . . .

Churchill ended his letter on a personal note:

Well there I have written what I have in my mind—& if you resent it so much the worse for all of us. I can never forget the service you did me in bringing me a fresh horse when I was dismounted in the war, & intensely longing to take a real part in the struggle. Office has not now the same attraction for me, & I have other new interests on wh I cd fall back. Therefore the counsels I offer are those of a friend & of a sincere friend—but of a friend who cannot part with his independence.

On December 16 Churchill elaborated his views in a thousand-word memorandum for the Cabinet. It was essential, he argued, for Britain to have at least 'some friends' in the Middle East. This, he said, had been an historic policy. 'When Russia was our enemy,' he pointed out, 'the Turk was our friend: when Turkey was our enemy Russia was our friend. We have utilised to the full the division between the Arab and the Turk. When everything else had been let go, we had at least the Greeks. Now we are out of joint with the whole lot at once.'

At the end of his memorandum, Churchill appealed for peace to be made with Turkey before the Greeks were defeated by the Turks, and the Turks stimulated by victory to turn on the British forces at Constantinople. As he explained it:

> The collapse or withdrawal of the Greek division covering Constantinople would destroy a great part of our bargaining power with the Turk. His strength would be greatly increased and our position dangerously laid open. Similarly, to let the Greeks collapse at Smyrna will leave us confronted with a Turkish triumph and the Turks will have got back Smyrna by their own efforts instead of as the result of a bargain with us which might well safeguard Greek Christians there as well as our own general interests in the Middle East.
>
> If we are to make a satisfactory peace with Turkey, surely we should do it before the Greek armies in the field have crumbled away or been withdrawn.
>
> We are already immensely weaker than we were, and if we allow the present situation to drift on for a few more weeks or months we shall find ourselves in a position where we are universally disliked and extremely weak. In addition we may either have to evacuate Constantinople or send a considerable army to reinforce it. I do not know where this army can be found.

In this Cabinet memorandum, as in his letter to Lloyd George of December 4, Churchill wrote with a sense of urgency and alarm. But Lloyd George tenaciously clung to his pro-Greek policy, and was supported by Curzon. On November 22 Curzon wrote to Lord Derby that any modification of the Treaty of Sèvres would constitute a 'humiliating' concession to the Turks. But Derby supported Churchill, and on December 21 Churchill wrote to him direct: 'I think we should use Mustapha Kemal and a reconciled Turkey as a barrier against the Bolsheviks and to smooth down all our affairs on the Middle East and in India.' Replying two days later, Derby described the Treaty of Sèvres as 'to put it mildly, a rotten bad one'. Kemal, he believed, was 'in his way a patriot, and did what a great many of us would have done if it had been our own country that was being divided up'. Derby's letter continued: 'I believe you are quite right in saying that we ought to try and come to some terms with him, and strictly between you and me, although they denied it, I am practically certain the French, and absolutely certain the Italians have made advances to him behind our back.'

Determined to end speculation, to curb opposition and to assert his own authority, Lloyd George told the House of Commons on December 22 that it was impossible to alter Britain's policy to Greece merely because of a Greek election. Greek friendship in the Mediterranean was, he asserted, essential for Britain, nor was he willing 'to purchase a way out of our difficulties by betraying others'. The Treaty of Sèvres would stand. Greece, even under Britain's former enemy King Constantine, would be allowed to control large areas of former Turkish soil, and the Turkish Nationalist leader, Mustafa Kemal, was to continue to be regarded as a rebel and an outcast.

Early in November a new and serious problem arose about the Palestine Mandate. Under the scheme proposed at the San Remo Conference, 'Palestine', as allocated to Britain, included the lands east of the Jordan known as 'Transjordan'. This eastern portion of the Mandate was far larger than the western one. It was inhabited by over 300,000 Arabs, was largely desert and had almost no Jewish settlers. During the Emir Feisal's brief period as 'King of Syria', Transjordan had been included among his dominions. After he had been driven from Damascus by the French, one of his brothers, the Emir Abdullah,[1] had sought to establish control over Transjordan.

The Commander of the Egyptian Expeditionary Force, Lieutenant-General Congreve,[2] in whose command Palestine was included, did not feel confident that he could control Transjordan. On November 15 he wrote to Churchill from Cairo that without British troops in Transjordan the British advisers there were 'powerless to enforce their orders or give advice to the local governments, or to maintain internal order, as the Gendarmerie, who are locally recruited, are practically useless, and refuse to fire, from fear of starting blood feuds'. To send a detachment of troops into Transjordan would, Congreve warned, require an

[1] Abdullah Ibn Hussein. 1882–1951. Son of Hussein, Sherif of Mecca. One of the leaders of the Arab revolt against Turkey, 1915–18. Emir of Transjordan, 1921–46. Knighted, 1927. Air Commodore, Royal Air Force. King of Transjordan from 1946 until his assassination on 20 July 1951. His *Memoirs of King Abdullah of Transjordan* were published in 1950.

[2] Walter Norris Congreve, 1862–1927. 2nd Lieutenant, Rifle Brigade, 1885; Major, 1901. Served in South Africa, 1899–1902, when he won the Victoria Cross. Major-General, 1915. Knighted, 1917; Lieutenant-General, 1918. General Officer Commanding the Troops in Egypt and Palestine, 1921–3. C-in-C, Southern Command, 1923–4. Governor and C-in-C, Malta, 1924–7.

increase in the number of troops under his command. Congreve's solution was to give up the Palestine Mandate altogether east of the river Jordan, arguing that if this were done, troop costs could actually be reduced.

On December 1 a special Conference of Ministers, presided over by Lloyd George, discussed at length the problems of British military expenditure in the Middle East. According to the official minutes of the meeting, it was 'generally accepted' that the House of Commons would only grant a further sum of money 'on receiving an assurance that this represented the end of the heavy military expenditure. . . .' The minutes went on to record: 'Criticism of the Government's expenditure was becoming every day more insistent, particularly from the Government's own supporters, and it was clear that the country would demand that the permanent military expenditure of the future should be vigorously reduced.' General Congreve's suggestion that Transjordan should be transferred to an Arab ruler fitted well into this call for economy.

The Conference of Ministers met again on December 2, to discuss the suggestion of peace negotiations with the Turks. According to the Minutes of the meeting, the proposal met with relatively little enthusiasm, while the pro-Greek feeling of the meeting was manifest by the 'unanimous agreement' of all those present not to allow Smyrna to return to Turkey. Churchill only saw the Minutes of the meeting on December 10, and was exceedingly angry at what he regarded as a complete misrepresentation of his views, and those of his colleagues. He wrote at once to Sir Maurice Hankey, who had drafted the Minutes:

I consider that the account of the discussion on this subject does not fairly represent the opinions expressed. I stated my own views and those of the General Staff, but I thought that they were in the main in accordance with those of the Lord Privy Seal, the Chancellor of the Exchequer and the Secretaries of State for India and the Colonies. Those views were that we should make a definite change in our policy in the direction of procuring a real peace with the Moslem world and so relieving ourselves of the disastrous reaction both military and financial to which our anti-Turk policy has exposed us in the Middle East and in India.

However, speaking only for myself, I repudiate the suggestion in the third paragraph that 'there was unanimous agreement with the view that the possibility of handing back Smyrna to the Turks by the Allies could not be entertained'. On the contrary, I am convinced that the restoration of Turkish sovereignty or suzerainty over the Smyrna Province is an indispensable step to the pacification of the Middle East. It is quite true that like others I hold that effective administrative protection must be secured to the Christian population; and I am sure that there are several ways in which this could be afforded without depriving the Turks of the Suzerainty. . . .

The sentence 'It was felt that sooner or later it might possibly be desirable to enter into direct negotiations with Mustapha Kemal' is, in my opinion, a complete understatement of the general view. The Prime Minister himself said he was in favour of entering into negotiations with Mustapha Kemal, and the Foreign Secretary declared that efforts were now actually being made to open such negotiations. Certainly the general conclusion was that they were necessary and desirable.

It would appear to be very injurious that such an incomplete account should be circulated to Members of the Cabinet who did not hear the discussion; and I request that this Memorandum may be sent to any Ministers who have received it.

The Cabinet met again to discuss the future of Mesopotamia on the morning of December 13. Churchill suggested withdrawing altogether from the Mosul and Baghdad Vilayets, to a line covering only Basra and the Persian oilfields on the Karun river. By taking only this southern portion of Mesopotamia, he told his colleagues, Britain would save fifty million pounds a year. But Churchill's proposal was rejected. According to the Cabinet minutes, an unnamed Minister had opposed Churchill's arguments for a withdrawal, by claiming that, were this done, 'the Turks, possibly in collusion with the Bolsheviks, would enter into the vacuum thus created'. The Cabinet reconvened that same afternoon. If Britain withdrew, it was argued, the Turks—if not the Bolsheviks— would certainly gain the advantage. It was generally felt, the Cabinet minutes recorded, 'that the re-establishment of Turkish rule would be a most deplorable sequel to our great and successful campaign in this area'. 'They have accepted the Mandate for Mesopot!' Henry Wilson wrote in his diary that evening.

On December 15 Churchill introduced the supplementary Army Estimates to Parliament. In asking for an additional £40 million, of which £9 million was to cover the cost of the war in Mesopotamia, he told the House of Commons that he was worried lest 'these enormous charges . . . swamping any economies which may be made departmentally, may not discourage and dishearten the Military and Air Force officers, and the officials of those Departments who are labouring to save small sums of money by thrifty administration from day to day. . . .' Churchill insisted that there had been no extravagance in the Mesopotamian campaign, but he went on to warn:

This is not a case in which there is any use in becoming excited or angry. We have to face real responsibility and real difficulties, and we have to face them not with hysteria or irritation, but with firmness and courage.

If the House at this moment were to say, 'We refuse to vote another penny for Mesopotamia', they might dismiss the Government from power, but they would not alter the difficulty which exists in that country, nor would they diminish the expenditure which we shall have to incur on account of it. If at this moment we were to order the troops in Mesopotamia to begin evacuation it seems very probable we would be involved in general heavy fighting in many parts of that region which would last well into the next financial year.

Let me add this word of caution at the end of my remarks: I am quite certain that the loose talk indulged in in the newspapers about the speedy evacuation of Mesopotamia earlier in the year was a factor which provoked and promoted the rebellion.

Whatever your policy might be, it would certainly be in the highest degree imprudent to let it be thought that this country, having accepted the mandate, having entered into territory of that kind, having incurred, accepted, and shouldered responsibilities towards every class inhabiting it, was in a moment of irritation or weakness going to cast down those responsibilities, to leave its obligations wholly undischarged, and to scuttle from the country regardless of what might occur. Such a course would bring ruin on the province of Mesopotamia, and it would also impose a heavier expense on the British taxpayer than I believe would be incurred if we actually and firmly resumed the policy of reducing our garrisons, of contracting our commitments, and of setting up a local government congenial to the wishes of the masses of the people. . . .

By the end of 1920 Churchill wanted to leave the War Office. His two years as Secretary of State for War had disappointed him. He had failed to convince his colleagues that Bolshevism was an evil that must be destroyed. He had failed to persuade the Government to enter into negotiations with Mustafa Kemal. He had even failed to secure the military economies to which he was pledged in Mesopotamia. For over a year his attempts to influence British policy in the Middle East had been frustrated. Ministerial responsibility had been so arranged as to divide up the area between four Departments of State—his own, the India Office, the Colonial Office and the Foreign Office. Under such a system, it had proved impossible to secure the clear decisions and bold policies which he wanted. The rivalries and conflicting interests of himself, Edwin Montagu, Lord Milner and Lord Curzon had paralysed initiative over a wide area of Government policy.

The overthrow of Bolshevism, to which Churchill had devoted so large a part of his time and energies, had proved impossible for other reasons. Despite their many successes, none of the anti-Bolshevik armies had reached Moscow. The Allied intervention had not only failed to tilt the balance against the Bolsheviks, it had also helped to rouse Russian patriotism and rally many non-Bolsheviks to the Bolshevik cause. By the end of 1920 the last anti-Bolshevik armies had been defeated. The Bolsheviks, on the other hand, had begun to reassert their authority in the Caucasus, Central Asia and Western Siberia. They had entered into diplomatic agreements of a friendly nature with the Baltic States, Turkey and Afghanistan. All Churchill's hopes of mobilizing the resources of the British War Office to aid and stimulate a ring of anti-Bolshevik armies had been frustrated. During the last months of 1920 he had failed to prevent negotiations between Britain herself and the Bolsheviks, abhorrent though these negotiations were to him.

Churchill's stance as the enemy of Bolshevism left him politically isolated and personally discontented. He had frequently been attacked, both in Parliament and in the newspapers, for policies which were not his own, or to which he was in fact opposed. To the Labour Party he had become a hated figure by the end of 1920. Most Conservatives still distrusted him as an unprincipled adventurer. His attempts to encourage the creation of a National Party had failed. The demobilization of the armies at the beginning of 1919 had been almost his only constructive success. As Secretary of State for Air, Churchill had upheld the claims of an independent Air Force; but he had not been able to find the time to make air matters his cardinal concern.

By the beginning of 1921 Churchill found himself in charge of a War Office without a war, committed to economies, withdrawals and, in Ireland, reprisals. His constructive talents seemed to have no outlet; his administrative skills no challenge. He wanted a greater sphere of action and a wider range of responsibilities. Foreign affairs had always interested him intensely; the Treasury was a department he believed he could control; responsibility for Britain's overseas interests, whether in India or in the wide circle of Colonial affairs, was something that might bring out more fully the talents he knew he possessed. Above all, he did not wish to remain responsible for policies where his judgement was in conflict with that of Lloyd George; indeed, on 23 January 1921 he went so far as to tell Henry Wilson that his main reason for wanting a new Ministry was that he 'would not have lasted much longer in the W.O. owing to differences with L.G.'.

29

Creating the Middle East Department

AT a meeting of the Cabinet Finance Committee on 20 August 1920, Churchill had emphasized the importance of setting up a special Department for Middle Eastern Affairs, to co-ordinate Government policy in Palestine, Mesopotamia and Arabia, and to effect substantial cuts in military expenditure throughout the Middle East. He had repeated this request at a Finance Committee meeting on December 7, and, two weeks later, he had again pointed out, to the Finance Committee of December 21, that Mesopotamia, Egypt and Palestine 'together accounted for a large force, involving an excess cost of £37,000,000'. According to the minutes of the meeting, the discussion of this expenditure had led 'to a further suggestion, that the mandated territories ought to be administered as a whole'.

When the full Cabinet met on December 31, it was finally decided, at Churchill's suggestion, to set up a special Middle East Department, within the general aegis of the Colonial Office. This plan, the minutes recorded, would enable the existing divided responsibilities of the War Office, the India Office, the Colonial Office and the Foreign Office, 'to be concentrated in a single Department', under a single Minister. But the Colonial Secretary, Lord Milner, wanted no part of these new and heavy responsibilities, and had already told Lloyd George that he wished to leave the Government altogether.

Churchill spent New Year's eve with Lloyd George as one of Sir Philip Sassoon's guests at Lympne. On the following morning Lloyd George asked Churchill if he would be willing to succeed Lord Milner as Colonial Secretary.

Churchill hesitated. The New Year's festivities continued. Lord

Riddell recorded their progress in his diary, and gave a glimpse of the friendship between Churchill and Lloyd George:

LG and Winston in great form. Sutherland brought with him gramophone records of speeches made by Harding,[1] the American President-Elect, and other American politicians. We all sat round and listened to platitudes delivered through the gramophone horn. The interjections of the P.M. and Winston, shouted into the horn as the speeches progressed, most amusing.

Winston said that American politicians have to confine themselves to platitudes because the politician usually represents a compromise. It is not safe to go far beyond, 'The sun shone yesterday upon this great and glorious country. It shines to-day and will shine to-morrow.' . . .

On the Saturday and Sunday evenings after dinner we had some lusty singing, everyone joining in the choruses. L.G. sang 'Cockles and Mussels' and two or three other songs with great effect. He would have made a fortune on the music-hall stage. Winston sat watching him with the keenest admiration and the eye of an artist. He said, referring to L.G., 'What a wonderful man he is! What an actor he would have made!' The great success of the performance was 'Rule Britannia!' which we all sang with special reference to the American Fleet. Winston read the words out to us several times and insisted upon their beauty and patriotic fervour. He remarked, 'The last two verses would make a splendid peroration.'

Sutherland described Winston as an artist in words—not a bad description. He has a wonderful verbal memory, and with much gusto regaled us by reciting numerous music-hall songs and other verses, which he remembered with little effort, although he had not heard many of them for years. His painting has greatly improved and it is interesting to hear him descant as an artist upon the allegorical scenes depicted on the walls and ceilings of Sassoon's drawing-room.

On Saturday afternoon L.G. went off to rest with a bundle of official papers. Winston remarked on the tireless industry of the P.M.

While at Lympne, Churchill gave Lloyd George a set of notes about his possible transfer to the Colonial Office. In them he asked for the widest possible powers to reduce British expenditure throughout the Middle East. He also asked that his control of Mesopotamia should start at once, covering even his remaining weeks as Secretary of State for War. On January 4, having returned to London, he sent Lloyd George a fuller version of his notes, together with a covering letter, accepting the Colonial Office, but upon precise terms:

[1] Warren Gamaliel Harding, 1865–1923. Born in Ohio; a Baptist. Member of the US Senate from Ohio, 1915–21. Twenty-ninth President of the United States, from March 1921 until his death in August 1923.

My Dear Prime Minister,

I have carefully considered the task which you wish me to undertake; & in view of all the circumstances I feel it is my duty to comply with your wish. I must however ask for the power & the means of coping with the vy difficult situation in the Middle East, & of dealing effectively with the Parliamentary aspects.

The paper which I enclose is an amplification of that wh I gave you on Sunday. I have thought out carefully every point in it, & I hope you will be able to give me the aid & authority I shall require. If you disagree with or see an obstacle in any of my requests, perhaps you will discuss the particular point with me, & let me explain my reasons.

While I feel some misgivings about the political consequence to myself of taking on my shoulders the burden & the odium of the Mesopotamia entanglement, I am deeply sensible of the greatness of the sphere you are confiding to my charge, of the honour which you have done me in choosing me for such critical employment, and also of the many acts of personal kindness by which you have marked our long friendship & political association.

Yours ever sincerely,
Winston S. Churchill

In his notes to Lloyd George, Churchill asked to be given the authority to set up this Department 'forthwith under my supervision'. He also asked that 'an announcement of the impending transfer and appointment' should be made as soon as possible. 'Otherwise,' he wrote, 'it is sure to leak out.' He also wanted an immediate announcement 'that the title of the Colonial Office must be altered to suit its new responsibilities for the mandated territories' and that the exchange of seals should take place 'early in February before the meeting of Parliament'.

On January 7 Churchill discussed his various conditions with Lloyd George, while they were again at Lympne as the guests of Philip Sassoon. Lloyd George agreed that Churchill's responsibilities as Colonial Secretary should include both the civil and the military administration of Palestine and Mesopotamia, and that he could set up the Middle East Department at once.

While he was at Lympne on January 7, Churchill telephoned to Sir Maurice Hankey, who wrote in his diary of how Churchill told him, 'in cryptic language', that he was to become Colonial Secretary. Churchill asked Hankey to advise him on his new responsibilities. He was 'so nice and complimentary', Hankey noted, that he agreed to go specially to London on January 8, a Saturday, to give Churchill the guidance he sought. While speaking on the telephone, Churchill also put to Hankey an idea which he had been thinking about since the Colonial Office post had first been mooted five days before—a personal visit to Mesopotamia, to examine the problem at first hand. Hankey sought to dissuade Churchill from such a visit, having, as he wrote in his diary, 'memories of Antwerp' in mind.

Churchill returned to London on the afternoon of January 7. On the following day he was busy at the War Office working out how to organize his new Department. During the day, Edward Marsh brought T. E. Lawrence[1] to see him and Lawrence agreed to become his adviser on Arabian affairs. Churchill knew that Lord Curzon's goodwill and co-operation was essential if the Middle East Department was to be allowed to function unimpeded, and wrote to him on January 8:

I am sure I can count upon yr help in the difficult & embarrassing task I have undertaken. It has been imposed upon me by circumstances & the Prime Minister after I had more than once declined them.

I look forward only to toil & abuse. But I hope at least to have some measure of control.

I shall greatly value any advice that you may be willing to give me, & also the aid—indispensable at so many points—of the Foreign Office. . . .

Churchill went on to refer to the help which he hoped Curzon would give him in the area of foreign affairs. 'In yr gt sphere,' he wrote, 'you hold the controls wh alone can make the local solution of the Middle Eastern problem possible. If you can make friends with the Turks & persuade the French not to quarrel with the Syrians, it will not be impossible to arrive at satisfactory results.'

During January 8 Churchill sent Lloyd George a brief progress report. 'My dear P.M.,' he wrote, 'I have put all matters in train. The question of my journey & its date requires further reflection. A little more time & consideration are needed before definitely launching Feisal. I must feel my way & feel sure of my way.'

Also on January 8, Churchill telegraphed to the High Commissioner in Mesopotamia, Sir Percy Cox, and to the Commander-in-Chief, General Haldane, to tell them that he had been 'entrusted with the

[1] Thomas Edward Lawrence, 1888–1935. Travelled in Syria and Palestine while an undergraduate at Oxford. Obtained a first class degree in history, 1910. On archaeological work at Carchemish, 1911–14. Explored the Negev desert south of Beersheba, 1914. Served in the Geographical Section, General Staff, War Office, 1914–15; military intelligence, Egypt, 1915–16. Accompanied Ronald Storrs to Jidda, 1916, at the start of the Arab revolt against the Turks. Liaison officer and adviser to the Emir Feisal, 1917–18. Took part in the capture of Akaba from the Turks, August 1917, and the capture of Damascus, October 1918. Accompanied Feisal to the Paris Peace Conference, 1919. Joined the Middle East Department of the Colonial Office, 1921; resigned, 1922. Enlisted in the Royal Air Force (as J. H. Ross), 1922 and again (as T. E. Shaw), 1923. Served on the North West Frontier of India, 1926–8. Retired from the RAF, 1935. Killed in a motor cycle accident.

general direction of the Cabinet policy in Mesopotamia', and to inform them of what that policy was to be. 'It is impossible,' Churchill explained, 'for us to throw upon the British taxpayer the burdens for military expenditure which are entailed by your present schemes for holding the country.' Unless Mesopotamia could be governed more cheaply, Churchill warned, 'retirement and contraction to the coastal zone is inevitable', and would have to be carried out 'as rapidly as possible'.

In his telegram to Cox and Haldane, Churchill outlined the solution as he saw it. Britain would have to set up 'an Arab Government' at Baghdad, which would develop the country peacefully, 'without undue demands upon Great Britain'. The peace of the country would be maintained, he added, by a British Police Force 'of exceptional individual quality', by Indian troops 'specially recruited from India', and by the wide application 'of the system of air control' already in embryo. It was his 'earnest wish', Churchill concluded, 'to collaborate with you on this task and thus to avoid the melancholy consequences attendant upon its failure'.

Churchill spent January 9 at the War Office. During the day Lord Curzon wrote to him about the future ruler of Mesopotamia, a subject which had hitherto been handled by the Foreign Office. At the Cabinet of December 31, Curzon had been specifically instructed to open secret negotiations with the Emir Feisal, to find out whether he would be willing to be a candidate for the Mesopotamian throne. In his letter to Churchill, Curzon explained that Feisal, who was then in London, had been told of the Mesopotamian prospect, and had 'behaved like a real gentleman & with a fine sense of honour & loyalty'; that is, he was not only willing to be considered as a possible ruler, but he was also willing to leave the decision to the British Government. Curzon ended his letter: 'I do not know whether to congratulate or commiserate with you on taking over these ventures. Anyhow I wish you a better return for heavy but thankless labours than I have received.'

On January 10 Churchill drafted a lengthy telegram to Sir Percy Cox, which was despatched that evening. The telegram took the form of a series of questions and observations, and began:

Do you think that Feisal is the right man and the best man? Failing him, do you prefer Abdullah to any local man? Have you put forward Feisal because you consider taking a long view he is the best man or as a desperate expedient in the hopes of reducing the garrisons quickly? If you are really convinced that Feisal is necessary, can you make sure he is chosen locally? Once I know your true mind on these points decision can be taken here immediately. We can then consider method of bringing about what we have decided on in a most favourable and diplomatic manner. I do not think Cabinet would allow French objection to debar us from taking the best course. I do not think it would be impossible to placate the French provided matters are handled with them candidly and courteously. Anyhow, do not let us slip into taking the wrong man against our better judgment.

As to the actual appointment of a ruler, Churchill added: 'Western political methods are not necessarily applicable to the East and basis of election should be framed.'

Churchill had been busy since January 2 collecting facts and figures about the Middle East. His principal source of information was the Permanent Under-Secretary of State at the India Office, Sir Arthur Hirtzel.[1] On January 10 Hirtzel sent him a substantial summary of the situation in Mesopotamia, drawn up by a senior official at the India Office, John Shuckburgh.[2] In his notes, Shuckburgh explained that under the terms of the League of Nations mandate, Britain was pledged —as Lloyd George had told the House of Commons on 3 June 1920—to create in Mesopotamia 'an independent nation subject to the rendering of administrative advice and assistance by a mandatory until such time as she is able to stand alone'. Later that month, on June 28, Lloyd George had added that it was Britain's intention 'to withdraw troops from Mesopotamia as soon as the conditions of the country permit'.

During January 10, Lloyd George completed the appointment of a special Committee to determine the precise nature of Churchill's new Middle East responsibilities. The Committee consisted of six members, with Sir James Masterton Smith as Chairman, and was asked to report direct to Churchill by February 1.[3] Churchill himself, meanwhile, was making preparations to visit the new areas that were to come under his control. As he explained in a telegram to Sir Percy Cox on January 10:

Prime Minister is anxious that I should visit Mesopotamia in March and take necessary decisions on the spot. A light cruiser would bring me from

---

[1] Arthur Hirtzel, 1870–1937. Entered the India Office, 1894. Secretary to the Political Department, 1909–17. Knighted, 1911. Assistant Under-Secretary of State for India, 1917–21; Deputy Under-Secretary, 1921–4; Permanent Under-Secretary, 1924–30.

[2] John Evelyn Shuckburgh, 1877–1953. Entered the India Office, 1900. Secretary, Political Department, India Office, 1917–21. Appointed by Churchill to be Assistant Under-Secretary of State, Colonial Office, 1921. Knighted, 1922. Remained Assistant Under-Secretary of State until 1931; Deputy Under-Secretary of State, 1931–42. Appointed Governor of Nigeria, 1939, but did not assume office owing to the outbreak of war. Worked in the historical section of the Cabinet Office, 1942–8.

[3] The War Office was represented on the Masterton Smith Committee by Sir Herbert Creedy, the India Office by John Shuckburgh, the Foreign Office by Major Hubert Young, the Colonial Office by Sir Herbert Read and the Treasury by Russell Scott.

Suez to Basra in seven days. Responsibility for deciding will rest with me, but I should like to know your view together with itinerary of one month's duration in the country, and any advice about climate, etc.

This telegram was despatched from London late on the afternoon of January 10. Churchill had already left London for Paris, where he was the guest of honour at a dinner party given by Louis Loucheur, and on the following morning he spent an hour with the new French President, Alexandre Millerand, with whom he discussed Germany, Eastern Europe and the Middle East. On the following day, after he had reached the South of France, Churchill sent Lloyd George and Curzon a long letter outlining the conversation with Millerand. In his letter he explained that he had told Millerand 'in secrecy' that he would shortly be responsible 'for the administration of the British Mandates in the Middle East'. The French, he added, 'are very ready to be conciliatory and accommodating to us'. And he went on to point out that the French were 'pretty nearly in the same position' in Syria as Britain was in Mesopotamia, 'namely, utterly sick of pouring out money and men on these newly acquired territories when all their great interests in Africa are denied the funds necessary to develop them'.

During the discussion, Churchill had told Millerand that Britain and France had 'a common interest in the appeasement of the Middle East'. Millerand, in reply, had insisted upon the need to make peace with Turkey, in order to forestall a Turkish attack on Syria. Churchill had assured Millerand that Britain would favour any agreement with Turkey 'which resulted in the Turks calming down and not disturbing or threatening us any further'. Churchill's account of the conversation continued: 'I pointed out the absolute need from both British and French points of view of appeasing Arab sentiment and arriving at good arrangements with them. Otherwise we should certainly be forced by the expense of the garrisons to evacuate the territories which each country had gained in the war.'

During their discussion, Millerand criticized Britain's wartime declaration in favour of a Jewish National Home in Palestine; a promise made by A. J. Balfour in November 1917, and subsequently embodied by the League of Nations as an integral part of the Palestine mandate. According to Churchill's account Millerand 'instanced Zionism in Palestine as a cause of disturbing the Arab world', and told Churchill that 'he feared that the Jews would be very high-handed when they got together there'. Churchill defended British policy towards the Jews. 'I expatiated on the virtues and experience of Sir Herbert Samuel,' he wrote, 'and pointed out how evenly he was holding the balance between Arabs and Jews and how effectively he was restraining his own people, as perhaps only a Jewish administrator could do.'

In a further letter to Lloyd George alone on January 12, Churchill repeated his request that his new department should be as comprehensive as possible. 'The more I study the Middle Eastern problem,' he wrote, 'the more convinced I am that it is impossible to deal with it unless the conduct of British affairs in the whole of the Arabian peninsula is vested in the Middle East Department. The Arab problem is all one, and any attempt to divide it will only reintroduce the same paralysis and confusion which has done so much harm during the last two years.' And he continued:

It will be fatal to all prospects of success to introduce conflicting or divergent policies—Feisal or Abdullah, whether in Mesopotamia or Mecca; King Hussein [1] when at Mecca; Bin Saud [2] at Nejd; Bin Saud at Hail; the Sheikh of Kuweit; [3] and King Samuel at Jerusalem are all inextricably interwoven, and no conceivable policy can have any chance which does not pull all the strings affecting them.

'To exclude Arabian relations,' Churchill warned, 'would be to disembowel the Middle Eastern Department. If you have any doubt about this, you should talk to Montagu or to Milner or to Hirtzel or to Lawrence.' Churchill added that he had every hope that when the Masterton Smith Committee completed its report, it would 'demonstrate the impossibility of any divided control. . . .' And he went on to insist: 'I must have control of everything in the ringed fence.' 'I am just arriving in the sunshine,' Churchill wrote at the end of his letter, 'and wish that out of my abundance I could send some gleams to light on you.'

On January 13 Churchill's Mesopotamian proposals found their first critic, General Haldane. In a telegram to Churchill on January 13 he warned that 'if chaos is to be avoided' there could be no reduction in his forces. He added that the use of air power as the main instrument of

---

[1] Hussein, c. 1854–1931. Amir of Mecca, 1908–16. King of the Hejaz, 1916–24 (he had proclaimed himself 'King of the Arab Countries'). Defeated by Ibn Saud, 1924, and abdicated. In exile in Cyprus (under British protection), 1925–30, and awarded an honorary knighthood. He died in Transjordan (which was then ruled by his son Abdullah).

[2] Ibn Saud, c. 1880–1953. Began the reconquest of Saudi lands in Arabia, 1902. Received a subsidy from the British in return for fighting the pro-Turkish forces of Ibn Rashid, 1916. Sultan of Nejd, 1921–2. Invaded the Hejaz and besieged Jedda, 1924. King of the Hejaz, 1926, and King of Nejd, 1927. United the Hejaz and Nejd as 'Saudi Arabia', of which he became both King and Imam, 1932. Granted the first Arab oil concession to an American oil company, 1933. Defeated the army of the Yemen, 1934.

[3] The Sheikh of Kuwait in January 1921 was Salim ben Mubarak. He died a month later, and was succeeded by Ahmad al-Jabir, who remained as ruler of Kuwait until 1950.

control would not work. The same day an even more outspoken telegram was despatched from Baghdad by Sir Percy Cox, who stated bluntly that if Churchill's outline of policy and plans was intended simply as a basis of discussion only, all would be well, but that if it was an order, then Cox wished Churchill to know at once 'that I am not prepared to associate myself with one or the other, and if pressed to do so, must, with deep regret, ask His Majesty's Government to accept my resignation'. On January 15 Cox telegraphed again, this time to state that he supported Haldane's fears that any substantial reduction of troops would be a mistake, and that the Royal Air Force could be 'nothing more' than a 'valuable auxiliary'.

Before leaving Paris, Churchill had gone with Major Geiger[1] to an art gallery to see the paintings of a newly exhibited artist, Charles Morin. As Geiger wrote to Sinclair a few days later: 'The works of this artist were produced and criticized for forty minutes . . . and the S of S was very interested.' Charles Morin was in fact Churchill himself; it was the first public exhibition of his paintings.

While Churchill was in the South of France, Sir Arthur Hirtzel sent him copies of all Middle East telegrams, and Churchill sent Hirtzel his draft replies. On January 14 Hirtzel wrote to Churchill about the negotiations being carried on between Feisal and the Foreign Office. Feisal's willingness to accept Mesopotamia was, he wrote, 'a surprise— & does him credit, if he has no arrière-pensée'.

In his letter to Churchill of January 14 Hirtzel added: 'You will, I suppose, await Lawrence's report before doing anything.' Lawrence sent Churchill his report three days later, on Monday January 17. It was addressed to Edward Marsh:

Concerning Feisal this is how it stands:
    He has agreed to make no reference to the French-occupied area of Syria in his talks with H.M.G.
    He has agreed to abandon all claims of his father to Palestine. This leaves four questions:
    (a) Mesopotamia: for which he claims a watching brief in respect of the McMahon papers.
    (b) Trans-Jordan: where he hopes to have a recognized Arab State with British advice.
    (c) Nejd: where he wants the Hussein–Ibn Saud question regulated.
    (d) Yemen: on which he has a suggestion to make.

[1] Gerald John Percival Geiger, 1876–1958. A contemporary of Churchill's at Harrow and Sandhurst. Entered the Army, 1896. Served in Crete, 1897–8. Major, 1915. Awarded the Croix de Guerre (twice), 1917, 1918 and the Legion d'Honneur, 1918. Head of the British Military Mission to Paris (in succession to General Spears), 1920–2. OBE, 1921.

The advantage of his taking this new ground of discussion is that all question of pledges & promises, fulfilled or broken, are set aside. You begin a new discussion on the actual positions today & the best way of doing something constructive with them. It's so much more useful than splitting hairs. Feisal can help very much towards a rapid settlement of these countries, if he wants to: and if we can only get them working like a team they will be a surprising big thing in two or three years. . . .

In his postscript Lawrence wrote: 'I think all he asks in a.b.c.d. can be made useful to ourselves. They tend towards cheapness & speed of settlement.'

On January 15 Sir Percy Cox had telegraphed angrily to Churchill from Baghdad that 'premature evacuation, or even talk of evacuation . . . will inevitably be cause of the collapse not only of the present provisional Government but of whole machinery of administration in Baghdad and Mosul. . . .' Sir Arthur Hirtzel forwarded Cox's telegram to the South of France. On January 16 Churchill replied, from Nice, to Cox's earlier telegram, in which the High Commissioner had threatened resignation. 'I am sorry to receive your telegram . . .' he wrote, 'but I hope that its tone is due to a misunderstanding.' The search for economies, Churchill went on to explain, was not intended to lead to loss of political or military control in Mesopotamia. 'No province in the British Empire,' Churchill added, 'has ever been acquired by marching in and maintaining a large regular army at the cost of the British Exchequer, but always by skilful and careful improvisations adapted to its special needs.' Churchill's telegram continued:

I quite understand your difficulties, and you in your turn ought to try to realise the difficulties which exist at home and face the inexorable facts. For instance, we have spent nearly 30 millions on military expenditure in Mesopotamia in 1920–21. We are inevitably committed to a further 20 millions in 1921–22.

You now propose for several years after 1921–22 a garrison of one division, one brigade and line of communication troops which, with the Air Force, would not cost less than 12 or 14 millions a year. I do not think there is the slightest chance of the Cabinet or Parliament agreeing to expenditure on such a scale for a country which we only hold under the League of Nations and are pledged to return to the Arabs at the earliest possible moment. . . .

The Chancellor of the Exchequer does not know which way to turn for money, and the whole country is furious at the present rate of expenditure, no part of which is more assailed than money spent in Mesopotamia.

Churchill then made a personal appeal to Cox:

I have undertaken very reluctantly to face this storm and difficulty in the hopes that all British work and sacrifice in Mesopotamia may not be cast away, and I have a right to loyal aid and support from the men on the spot. I am not committed to any particular alternative method of providing the force necessary to sustain the Arab Government, but I am determined that every avenue shall be promptly and thoroughly explored. . . .

Churchill ended his telegram by warning Cox that he would 'take a great responsibility if, before any such decision has been taken, you deprived His Majesty's Government of your local knowledge and influence, and thus diminished gravely the chances of a satisfactory solution'.

On January 17 Lord Curzon wrote to Churchill about the Middle East. His tone was conciliatory and helpful. 'I wish I saw more light about Turkey,' he wrote, and he went on:

I will of course render any help I can about Palestine & Mesopotamia & will look after the former for the present.

PM says he is going to send you out to Mesopotamia; & in the atmosphere that produced Nebuchadnezzar, Darius, Xerxes & other military heroes of the past I am hopeful that you will institute sound ideas about the importance of the Middle East. Whatever you do, do not follow the example of Alexander who found Babylon too much for him.

The spheres of CO and FO will overlap at points in the future and we shall need careful adjustment & close cooperation.

While he was at Nice, Churchill telegraphed every day to Sir Arthur Hirtzel with instructions and queries. For his part, Hirtzel kept Churchill informed of all the Mesopotamian telegrams reaching London. On January 19 Churchill sent Hirtzel a draft telegram for General Haldane, for immediate despatch to Baghdad, setting out his desire for good relations with Turkey. 'I am naturally doing my utmost,' Churchill declared, 'to procure a settlement with the Turks which will ease our position throughout the Middle East.' That same day Haldane telegraphed to Churchill about his proposed visit to Mesopotamia. 'Sir Percy and I will meet you at Basrah,' he wrote, 'where you would see local notables.' The proposed tour, Hirtzel minuted on January 21, 'wd take about three weeks'. In a second telegram on January 19, Haldane sent further details of the route of the tour, and added: 'Climate may be variable. Bedding, summer and winter clothing and sun hat preferably Cawnpore Tent Club pattern should be brought.'

On January 21 Churchill left Nice for Paris, where Lloyd George had gone for talks with the new French Prime Minister, Aristide Briand.[1] On January 22, while still in Paris, he received a letter from Masterton Smith about the progress of his Committee. The India Office and the Foreign Office had agreed, he wrote, to transfer the whole Arabian 'triangle' to the new Department. As for the date of the setting up of the Department, 'the sooner the better' was the Committee's view. They hoped to have their report ready by the end of January. Masterton Smith advised Churchill to enlist the help of an India Office official, Major Young,[2] who was, he wrote, 'an exceptionally able man, knows the Middle Eastern problem well from both ends (F.O. & Arabia), and carries plenty of F.O. and I.O. goodwill. He has helped me enormously.' In a covering note, Masterton Smith advised Churchill against going to Mesopotamia. 'I am sure your hands will be very full at the C.O. at first,' he warned, and it would not be wise to go away so early 'with no-one in effective or experienced charge . . . to safeguard your interests'.

On January 23, while still in Paris, Churchill sent Sir Arthur Hirtzel a further set of queries about the Middle East. He was particularly concerned to know about the relative strength of King Hussein within the Sherifian family. 'Write me a brief opinion on this,' Churchill asked. 'You might set the facts out in a genealogical tree. . . .' Hirtzel did as he was asked. So long as Britain supported Hussein and his family, he replied, 'it seems improbable that any other wd think it worth while to put itself forward'. Even if the Sherifians were ejected from the Hedjaz, Hirtzel wrote, 'the influence of the sons outside it wd not *necessarily* be weakened'. Hirtzel's answers gave credibility to Churchill's hopes that, from an Arabian point of view, Hussein's two sons, Feisal and Abdullah, could safely be installed in Mesopotamia and Transjordan respectively.

[1] Aristide Briand, 1862–1932. French politician. Minister of Public Instruction and Worship, 1906–9. Prime Minister, 1909–10. Minister of Justice, 1912–13. Prime Minister, January–March 1913. Minister of Justice, 1914. Prime Minister, October 1915–March 1917. Prime Minister and Minister of Foreign Affairs, January 1921–January 1922. Minister of Foreign Affairs, 1925. Prime Minister, November 1925–July 1926. Minister of Foreign Affairs, 1926. Awarded the Nobel Peace Prize for his part in the Locarno Agreements, 1926. Prime Minister for the sixth time, July–October 1929.

[2] Hubert Winthrop Young, 1885–1950. 2nd Lieutenant, Royal Artillery, 1904. Transferred to the Indian Army, 1908. Assistant Political Officer, Mesopotamia, 1915. Deputy Director, Local Resources Department, Mesopotamia, 1917. Transferred to the Hedjaz operations, March 1918, where he organized transport and supplies for the Arab forces. President of the Local Resources Board, Damascus, 1918. Member of the Eastern Department of the Foreign Office, 1919–21. Assistant Secretary, Middle East Department, Colonial Office, 1921–6. Colonial Secretary, Gibraltar, 1926–9. Counsellor for the High Commissioner, Iraq, 1929–32. Knighted, 1932. Minister to Baghdad, 1932. Governor and Commander-in-Chief, Nyasaland, 1932–4; Northern Rhodesia, 1934–8; Trinidad and Tobago, 1938–42.

Churchill returned to London from Paris on January 24. He was still worried by Lloyd George's hostility towards Turkey. That day he dictated a letter of protest. But when it was given to him to sign he decided to hold it back. 'The present misfortunes from which we are suffering throughout the Middle East,' he had written, 'are in my opinion the direct outcome of the invasion of Smyrna by the Greeks.' Churchill forecast a disaster for British interests if Lloyd George insisted upon ratifying the Treaty of Sèvres which, he warned, 'contains clauses which the Turks would never accept and which we have no power to enforce'.

At the end of his letter to Lloyd George, Churchill had intended to hint at resignation. 'If in your superior knowledge and experience you should come to such a decision,' he had written, 'I fear it would raise the gravest political issues for me, and in the work which you have done me the honour to ask me to undertake in the Middle East I should be so hopelessly compromised from the outset that I should not be able to undertake it with any prospects of success.'

On January 25 Major Young sent Churchill a memorandum, warning of the dangers of anti-French activity by Feisal and Abdullah. Abdullah's aim, he believed, was to try to get Feisal back to Damascus, and if Britain were to appear in any way to countenance such activity, Anglo-French relations would be gravely endangered. But, Young stressed, if Feisal could be contented with authority over Mesopotamia, and Abdullah with a kingdom in Transjordan, friction with France might be avoided. Indeed, the brothers could be told that their two kingdoms would not be granted unless they specifically agreed not to attack the French. Confident that such an outcome would enable major economies to be made, on January 27 Churchill telegraphed to General Haldane, instructing him to make preparations to complete the total evacuation of British troops from Mesopotamia by the end of the year, 'so that by December 31st we shall be responsible for nothing outside Basra'.

On his return from France, Churchill became aware of strong War Office hostility both to the evacuation of all British troops from Mesopotamia, and to the use of the Royal Air Force in their place. On January 25 Sir Arthur Hirtzel wrote to him about General Haldane's 'obstructiveness' and pointed out that answers to important questions had been 'delayed for over a fortnight'. Two days later Churchill wrote to the Under-Secretary of State for War, Sir Laming Worthington-Evans, to protest at the War Office attitude. 'I am quite willing,' he wrote, 'that the Cabinet shd decide whether we shd stay there or quit. But if the decision is that we shd stay, and you bow to it, then I am entitled to yr loyal comradeship and aid, & to yr sharing in a general sense the risks . . . you must do yr part in good will & in good faith. At present the attitude of yr Dept is inveterate hostility and obstruction to a policy to wh you are a party.' It was now his own responsibility, Churchill added, as Colonial Secretary, to assemble all the facts and figures needed, if reductions were to be made in military expenditure. And yet, he went on, 'sixteen separate Inter Departmental conferences between officials have failed to elicit any detail or explanation of the estimates we have to present to Parliament in the next few weeks! It is a form of warfare of wh I have never seen the like in all my (now long) experience.'

On reflection, Churchill held back his protest. On January 29 he was one of Sir Philip Sassoon's guests at Lympne. Lloyd George and Lord Birkenhead were among the other guests. 'We had the usual pleasant weekend. . . .' Churchill wrote to his wife on January 31, after his return to London. 'We picnicked on the slope of that big hill by the chalk pit amid the sunshine wh heralded spring, & the popping of Champagne corks wh heralded a sumptuous repast.'

On February 5 Lord Milner wrote to the High Commissioner in Palestine, Sir Herbert Samuel, to inform him that Churchill was to become Colonial Secretary. 'Churchill seems inclined to go out & see for himself immediately,' Milner wrote, '& I am strongly encouraging this idea. He is very keen, able & broad minded & I am sure, if he only gives himself time to thoroughly understand the situation, he will take sound views & you will find him a powerful backer.' But Milner went on to warn Samuel of Churchill's 'weakness'. He was, he said, 'too apt to make up his mind without sufficient knowledge'.

On Sunday February 6 Churchill was again with Lloyd George, as his guest at Chequers.[1] That evening he sent his wife an account of the place, and of his host:

My Darling,
    Here I am. You wd like to see this place. Perhaps you will some day! It is just the kind of house you admire—a panelled museum full of history, full of treasures—but insufficiently warmed—Anyhow a wonderful possession. . . .

---

[1] In 1920 Lord Lee of Fareham had offered his country house, Chequers, as a gift for the Prime Minister of the day. Lloyd George had first taken up residence on 8 January 1921, the day on which the deed of gift was signed.

I have not yet received reports about the Broadstairs party—except that they are all right. Nor any news from Randolph.

The P.M. has been as agreeable, evasive, elusive & indefinite as usual. He has not yet made up his mind about any of the detailed points of Gvt construction—all of wh affect my affairs in the second degree. I have served him with my letter wh is at any rate precise & this he is now studying.

I am to take over the Colonial Office seals tomorrow at 7. Thus for a week I shall hold the seals of three separate Secretaryships of State—I expect a record.

Churchill sent his wife news of their daughter Marigold, who had just celebrated her third birthday, and was with him at Chequers. 'The so-called Duckadilly,' he wrote, 'marched into my room this morning, apparently in blooming health. It was a formal visit & she had no special communication to make. But the feeling was good.'

Churchill ended his letter with two pieces of financial news, one concerning an article he had written about his own paintings, the other concerning his mother's good fortune:

The Strand magazine accept my terms & will pay £1000 for two articles with pictures reproduced in colour. As this will not be subject to Income Tax, it is really worth £1,600 so the painting has paid for itself, & a handsome profit over.

Great news (*but not for circulation*) from the Berkeley Square front. My mother has sold her house for £35,000—a clear profit of £15,000. She has already taken a little house in Charles St. No need to go abroad. All is well. I am so glad.

Churchill's own financial position had been further enhanced by a legacy which he received at the beginning of 1921. On the death of his cousin, Lord Henry Vane-Tempest,[1] he inherited the Garron Towers Estate, in County Antrim, northern Ireland, from which he stood to obtain an income of at least £4,000 a year.

On February 6, while he was at Chequers with Lloyd George, Churchill decided to abandon his plan to visit Mesopotamia, and to go instead to Cairo, and summon there a meeting of all the leading Middle East authorities. On his return to London on February 7, from his old room at the War Office, he asked his five closest advisers—Edward

---

[1] Lord Herbert Lionel Henry Vane-Tempest, 1862–1921. Third son of the 5th Marquess of Londonderry. Major, Durham Artillery Volunteers. High Sheriff of Montgomery, 1910. Knighted, 1911. Killed in a railway accident in Wales, 25 January 1921. Unmarried.

Marsh, Sir James Masterton Smith, Sir Herbert Creedy and Sir Arthur Hirtzel—to help him on the details of his visit. 'I should of course take advantage of being in Egypt,' he wrote to them, 'to confer with Allenby and also to spend a few days at Jerusalem with Sir Herbert Samuel.' To Sir Percy Cox he telegraphed that same day: 'The questions at issue cannot be settled by interchange of telegrams. . . . I propose therefore a Conference in Egypt beginning during the first or second week of March. A light cruiser can bring you from Basra to Suez in approximately seven days.'

In his telegram to Cox, Churchill explained the decisions about Mesopotamia which he hoped to reach during the Cairo Conference: 'First, the new ruler. Second, future size, character and organisation of the future garrison. Third, the time-table of reduction from present strength to that garrison. Fourth, total amount of the grant-in-aid. Fifth, arising out of above the extent of territory to be held and administered.' After the Conference, Churchill added, 'I shall be in a position to make definite recommendations to the Cabinet for action.'

While making his plans to confer with his Mesopotamian officials in Cairo, Churchill continued to press them to make drastic economies. On February 7 he telegraphed to General Haldane to protest against the maintenance of a cavalry regiment, at £100,000 a year, on the Upper Euphrates north-west of Mosul. It was clear from Haldane's own report, Churchill declared, 'that we are maintaining this regiment in region named for purpose of gathering taxes, and that the taxes gathered do not exceed one quarter of the cost of their collection'. Churchill added, somewhat curtly: 'I expect this is typical of a great deal of the waste of force and of money which is going on in Mesopotamia.' On February 8 Churchill protested again, this time through Sir Arthur Hirtzel, about General Haldane's expenditure of £300,000 a year for barracks near Baghdad. 'Why is this enormous expenditure necessary,' Churchill asked, 'in view of the approaching evacuation of the Army. Why have we got to pay £300,000 a year for wretched shanties in Baghdad?'

In one area of expenditure, however, Churchill was unwilling to make reductions. This was in the annual payment of cash subsidies to the Arab rulers of Arabia. When the Treasury opposed Sir Percy Cox's suggestion of paying £100,000 a year to Ibn Saud, Churchill supported Cox, writing to Hirtzel on February 7 of the dangers 'if this penny wise pound foolish policy is persisted in', and on the following day he wrote to him again: 'My view is that in this critical year, while the withdrawal from Mesopotamia is in progress, we should be generous with subsidies to the Arab chiefs.'

On January 31 Masterton Smith had handed Churchill a copy of his Committee's Report on the Middle East. On February 7 Churchill circulated the Report to the Cabinet, asking for an early decision. The Committee's conclusions were what Churchill wanted: that a special Middle East Department was not only necessary, but should be given wide powers covering Mesopotamia, Palestine, Transjordan and Aden. These powers, the Committee believed, should cover the question of frontiers, internal administration, civilian personnel, military control, internal policing and all expenditure 'whether civil or military'. It also urged the setting up of the new Department by March 1.[1]

Churchill had sent an advance copy of the Committee's Report to Lord Curzon. In a series of undated notes written at 10 Downing Street during a Cabinet meeting—probably on February 10—the two men discussed the Committee's conclusions. Curzon was worried that Churchill's proposed powers would deprive the Foreign Office of its negotiating authority with King Hussein in the Hedjaz. Curzon offered Churchill 'a concrete case' to consider:

The Hejaz is independent. Hussein deals with me. He comes to me and says—I am being attacked by Ibn Saud. Stop him. I reply—'He is not my man. He is Churchill's.' That will not convince him. Then I come to you. But your policy may be to run Ibn Saud rather than Hussein. There are all sorts of difficulties that will arise.

Churchill sought to put Curzon's mind at rest, passing Curzon's note back with the comment that his policy would be to 'run' both Ibn Saud and Hussein—'To dole out benefits of various kinds to each on condition that they play our game & don't bite each other.' A few moments later Churchill sent Curzon another note about the extent of his proposed authority:

There is a gt difficulty. The Cte's solution is not mine. My wish is to have direct control of the *internal* affairs of the Arabian triangle, & to recur to FO

---

[1] Churchill had made the setting up of this Committee a condition of his accepting the Colonial Office. On 16 March 1921 Sir Herbert Creedy explained the Committee's origins to Sir Laming Worthington-Evans. 'Mr Churchill's original idea,' Creedy wrote, 'was to have a sort of a War Office of his own with military and military-finance departments. With characteristic thoroughness he wished to be completely master in his own household. He took a great personal interest in the deliberations of the Committee and did not conceal from them the lines on which he expected their recommendations would be framed. . . .' Creedy went on to defend Churchill against any charge of having sought to bypass the War Office or usurp its authority. 'It was certainly Mr Churchill's intention,' he informed Worthington-Evans, 'as expressed to me, only to work in consultation with the War Office. . . .'

only whenever French or other foreign interests are affected. But I am ready to try to work the system proposed by the Cte, because I don't suppose we shall really disagree vy much.

In a final exchange of notes during this Cabinet, Curzon expressed his anxiety that either Feisal or Abdullah might use their British-given kingdoms to mount attacks upon the French in Syria. Churchill replied that he would try to devise a policy whereby Britain would be in a position 'to promise the French no attack through Trans Jordania upon them in consequence of the friendly relations we are establishing with Hussein & Sons Ltd.'.

The time had come for Churchill to decide upon his senior adviser in the new Department. On February 8 he asked Sir Arthur Hirtzel if he was willing to leave the India Office to become head of the Middle East Department. But Hirtzel declined. His ambitions were centred on the India Office, in which he had served all his life. On February 9 Hirtzel wrote to Churchill to advise that John Shuckburgh be given the post. 'I am sure you would find in him a most valuable head . . .' Hirtzel wrote. 'He is really first rate—level headed, always cool, very accurate & unsparing of himself: his only fault perhaps a tendency to excessive caution. . . .' But even this, Hirtzel believed, might prove a virtue 'in dealing with regions where pressure will come from various quarters to go too fast'. Churchill decided to accept Hirtzel's advice, and to offer the post to Shuckburgh. As his Under-Secretary in the House of Lords, Churchill appointed his friend the Duke of Sutherland.[1]

While Churchill was working in London, his wife was still in the South of France, staying at St Jean Cap-Ferrat. On February 7 she wrote to her husband:

My Darling Winston,
 . . . I can imagine that all the various things which are filling your mind, i.e. your new post, your inheritance, the painting, Chequers, the P.M., the re-arrangement of the Government . . . the poor old worn out War Office— make this little peninsula seem a pin point in the sea, while you are soaring in an aeroplane above the great Corniche of life.
 You once told me that Sir William Harcourt[2] said 'that nothing ever

[1] George Granville Sutherland-Leveson-Gower, 1888–1963. Known as 'Geordie'. Succeeded his father as 5th Duke of Sutherland, 1913. Served with the British Military Mission to Belgium, 1914–15. Commanded Motor Boat Flotillas, Egypt and Adriatic, 1915–17. Represented the Colonial Office in the House of Lords, 1921–2. Under-Secretary, Air Ministry, 1922–4. Paymaster-General, 1925–8. Parliamentary Under-Secretary of State for War, 1928–9. Lord Steward of the Household, 1936–7.
[2] William George Granville Vernon Harcourt, 1827–1904. Liberal stateman and friend of Gladstone. Home Secretary, 1880–5. Chancellor of the Exchequer, 1886 and 1892–5.

happens' but really this last month so many things have happened to us that it makes me quite dizzy. And strangely enough the change of office, which when it has happened before has always been of intense interest & sometimes thrilling excitement—takes rather a back seat. But this won't be for long becos I do think it is the best office just now & if you are able to 'feature' the Empire once more it will make all English people happy, at peace with each other (more or less) & able to resume our lofty but unconscious contempt of the Foreigner.

I wish I were with you spinning round & round instead of sitting lazily here in the sun.

Churchill received his wife's letter on February 9, replying at once with news of Lord Birkenhead, who had decided to give up drink to spare his health: 'He drinks cider & ginger pop & looks ten years younger. Don't make a mock of this, as he is quite sensitive about it. He looks sad.' Churchill added, with a reference to himself: 'Not for Pig.'

In his letter, Churchill gave his wife a description of his social life. At one dance, he wrote, 'I trod with my heel upon the P of W's[1] toe & made him yelp. But he bore it vy well—& no malice. . . . I am booked almost every night for one of these tiny parties.' The encounter with the Prince of Wales stirred Churchill's imagination in another way. 'Last night,' he told his wife, 'my artist's eye saw a wonderful resemblance to Henry VIII by Holbein at Hampton Court in the youthful lineaments of the Prince. . . . What a strange thing heredity is. We are really only variants of what has gone before.'

In the second week of February Churchill took two further steps to strengthen his powers as Colonial Secretary. On February 8 he wrote to Walter Long to ask for permission to continue to see the intercepted naval telegrams, 'of which I am accustomed to make a special study'. And he added: 'As you know . . . I rely upon this series of telegrams as an essential factor in my judgement of foreign affairs.' On the following day he wrote to Lord Curzon, asking to receive 'the same series of Secret Service reports as I have been accustomed to do at the War Office'. And he added: 'I have for years made a very close study of all these documents, and I regard them as essential to forming an instructed view.' Both Long and Curzon agreed to Churchill's request.

On February 10 Lord Rawlinson wrote to Churchill from Delhi, where he had gone as Commander-in-Chief, India:

[1] Edward Albert Christian George Andrew Patrick David, 1894–1972. Entered Royal Navy as a Cadet, 1907. Prince of Wales, 1910–36. 2nd Lieutenant, Grenadier Guards, August 1914. Served on the Staff in France and Italy, 1914–18. Major, 1918. Succeeded his father as King, January 1936. Abdicated, December 1936. Duke of Windsor, 1936.

I must send you a line of congratulations on your new appointment to the Colonial Office, and, at the same time, express regret that we are losing you in the conduct of our military affairs; but all of us out here, who are watching with considerable anxiety the situation in the Middle East and in Central Asia, welcome with acclamation the passing of the control of our mandatory areas and the Middle East into the hands of the Colonial Office under your direction.

At the beginning of February Churchill had pressed Lord Curzon to allow William Ormsby-Gore[1] to become an Additional Under-Secretary of State for Foreign Affairs, with special responsibility for the Middle East. Such an appointment would, Churchill believed, ease the burden of his work, and bring the Foreign Office into a closer and more sympathetic relationship with the Colonial Office. But Curzon resisted the appointment. He did not like Ormsby-Gore, and he did not want a second Under-Secretary of State. On February 10 Churchill appealed to Bonar Law. He was willing, he said, to accept Leopold Amery instead of Ormsby-Gore, if the latter were barred. And he continued:

I have not sought this odious Mesoptn. embarrassment; & have only undertaken it from a desire to give a hand where one is needed. I certainly expected—& indeed asked in writing before acceptance—for an U.S. in the Commons who cd be a real assistance. There are *millions* to be saved in the Middle East & it wd be vy unwise to grudge the proper Parliamentary Staff. I do hope that with yr usual gt kindness to me you will consider my difficulties.

Curzon continued to protest about Ormsby-Gore, regarding him, as he wrote to Churchill on February 15, 'with the most profound distrust', and not wishing to have 'any dealings with him'. To this Churchill replied on the following day:

Considering your great position are you not a little too severe on a young man making his way in Parliament? Sometimes they can be caught & trained, at other times they are made into disagreeable enemies forever. Personally I always forgive political attacks or ill-treatment not directed at private life. However do not think from this that I am set on O.G. My own inclination

[1] William George Arthur Ormsby-Gore, 1885–1965. Conservative MP, 1910–38. Intelligence Officer, Arab Bureau, Cairo, 1916. Assistant Secretary, War Cabinet, 1917–18. Assistant Political Officer, Palestine, 1918. Member of the British Delegation (Middle East Section) to the Paris Peace Conference, 1919. British Official Representative on the Permanent Mandates Commission of the League of Nations, 1920. Under-Secretary of State for the Colonies, 1922–4, and 1924–9; Secretary of State, 1936–8. Succeeded his father as 4th Baron Harlech, 1938. High Commissioner, South Africa, 1941–4.

will be much more towards Winterton.[1] But there is no doubt who is the best speaker & under a system of Parliamentary Government this aspect is not immaterial.

The final decision was a victory for Curzon: no additional Under-Secretary of State was appointed in the Foreign Office.

On February 12, two days before Churchill was formally to move from the War Office to the Colonial Office, he wrote to Lloyd George, setting out the extent of the authority he required in his new position:

On the 8th January you placed in my charge, subject to Cabinet approval, the entire conduct of Mesopotamian affairs, both military and civil; and I accordingly assumed responsibility as from the 10th. Mr Montagu thereupon placed the machinery of the India Office at my disposal and I have been using it with much convenience ever since.

Now that I am leaving the War Office for the Colonial Office it is essential that there should be a similarly clear understanding about the military aspect. It is absolutely necessary for me to have effective control of the general policy and to be able to communicate directly with the Commander-in-Chief in Mesopotamia, and to move the Secretary of State for War to change the Commander-in-Chief at the time I consider convenient. It will be convenient for me to send all my communications to the G.O.C., Mesopotamia, through the War Office in the same way as I have been communicating with Sir Percy Cox through the India Office. All actual operative orders should be sent as at present by the War Office but in general accordance with the policy I am pursuing subject to Cabinet approval. Unless in this way I secure the effective initiation and control of the whole policy, I could not undertake the task with any prospects of success.

Lloyd George made no objection to Churchill's delimitation of his authority, and on February 13 Churchill asked Masterton Smith for his final advice about the personnel of his new Department. Replying that same day, Masterton Smith confirmed that John Shuckburgh was 'the best man' to head the Department, while Hubert Young's services would be 'essential' if the Department were to flourish. As for Churchill's desire to have T. E. Lawrence as an adviser on Arab affairs, Masterton Smith sounded a note of caution. 'He is not the kind of man to fit easily into any official machine,' he wrote, 'and I consider it important that Mr Shuckburgh and Major Young should have their position as your responsible Departmental advisers clearly beyond challenge.' Masterton

[1] Edward Turnour, 1883–1962. Conservative MP, 1904–18, 1918–40 and 1940–51. Succeeded his father as 6th Earl Winterton, 1907. As an Irish peer, he continued to sit in the House of Commons. Served at Gallipoli, in Palestine and in Arabia, 1915–18. Under-Secretary of State for India, 1922–4; 1924–9. Chancellor of the Duchy of Lancaster, 1937–9. Paymaster-General, 1939. Chairman, Inter-Governmental Committee for Refugees, 1938–45.

Smith added: 'I gather that Col. Lawrence has got used to dealing with Ministers—and Ministers only—and I see trouble ahead if he is allowed too free a hand.' [1]

On February 14 the Cabinet met to consider the report of the Masterton Smith Committee. The Committee had recommended the establishment of a Middle East Department on precisely the lines that Churchill had hoped, with wide powers which would enable it to administer both Mesopotamia and Palestine direct from the Colonial Office, and independently of the four other Departments which had handled them hitherto.

The Cabinet's discussion centred entirely upon the Mesopotamian aspects of the Committee's report. Having undertaken the 'burden' of the Mesopotamian Mandate, Churchill told his colleagues, 'it would be shameful if Great Britain threw the Mandate aside without making an effort to set up an Arab Administration in the place of the Turkish Government which she had destroyed'. Later in the discussion Curzon challenged Churchill's right to be responsible for questions such as the choice of the ruler of Mesopotamia; questions which he described as 'of the first magnitude'. Lloyd George expressed his support for Curzon's fears that the Middle East Department might usurp the authority of the Foreign Office, but, after what H. A. L. Fisher described in his diary as 'a long wrangle', the Cabinet finally accepted the Masterton Smith Committee's recommendations.

That same day Lord Curzon wrote to his wife [2] of how, during the Cabinet, there had been 'rather a long and worrying controversy between Winston & myself over the Middle East. He wants to grab everything in his new Dept & to be a sort of Asiatic Foreign Secretary. I absolutely declined to agree to this, & the PM took my side. But it was hot fighting while it lasted.' Churchill also wrote to his wife after the Cabinet meeting. But he was more concerned to tell her about their

---

[1] On February 16 Churchill informed Lord Curzon of his choice of staff. 'You are fortunate in getting Shuckburgh,' Curzon replied that same day, 'a man of excellent judgments & the best drafter of an official telegram I have ever known.' As for Hubert Young, Curzon wrote, he was 'an able young fellow, with ideas, and an obstinacy that is not perilous because in the main superficial'. As for Lawrence, Curzon added, he would be 'very useful, if he will cease to intrigue'.

[2] Grace Elvina Hinds. Daughter of J. Monroe Hinds (one time United States Minister to Brazil) and widow of Alfred Duggan of Buenos Aires. She married Curzon (as his second wife) in January 1917. On learning of Curzon's wedding, Churchill had written to him, on New Year's Day 1917: 'Some—probably most—people's lives maintain an ordinary daylight of fortune. But yours comes like sunshine on a cloudy day. When I first knew you you were about to enter upon a brilliant period, and now after many years I earnestly hope you are about to enjoy another sunblaze both in public and private life.'

children, and to defend his decision to publish an article on painting, than to describe the political events of the day:

My Darling,

I went to see Randolph yesterday at Sandroyd and found him very sprightly. The Headmaster[1] described him as very combative and said that on any pretext or excuse he mixes himself up in fights and quarrels; but they seemed quite pleased with him all the same.

He was much excited about our inheritance and wanted to know all about the house and the lands, etc. I did not gratify his curiosity except in very general terms. He was also anxious to know whether my move to the Colonial Office was promotion or otherwise.

He declared himself perfectly happy and said he did not want anything. Most of the boys have got colds, and he is a happy exception.

The Broadstairs party are going on all right and I think they had better come back at the end of their third week. Marigold has a little cough again to-day, but otherwise she seems all right. She pays me a visit every morning and takes great interest in everything that is said to her or shown her.

All that you say about the article on painting I will carefully consider. There is nearly a year before it will appear and it will be the only article I shall write. It is quite unconnected with politics and therefore not open to any of the objections which have been urged against others. An article by Mr Balfour on golf or philosophy or by Mr Bonar Law on chess would be considered entirely proper. I think I can make it very light and amusing without in any way offending the professional painters. On the contrary, I hope to encourage other people to make an effort and experiment with the brush and see whether they cannot derive some portion of the pleasure which I have gained in amateur painting. . . .

You will see from the papers that it has been decided that Worthington Evans shall follow me at the War Office and Lord Lee[2] shall go to the Admiralty. The new Secretary of State for War will not have the Air, which will be an independent office. I much regret I cannot keep it in my hands and protect it. I shall certainly not hand over the seals if I can help it until my successor is definitely appointed. To-night I give up the War Office seals and take those of the Colonies.

You will see that I delivered an oration at the banquet of the English

[1] William Meysey Hornby, 1870–1955. One of the founders of Sandroyd, he was headmaster from 1898 to 1931.

[2] Arthur Hamilton Lee, 1868–1947. Entered the Royal Artillery, 1888; retired with the rank of Lieutenant-Colonel, 1900. Special Correspondent for the *Daily Chronicle* in the Klondyke Gold Rush, 1896. Military Attaché, Washington, 1899. Conservative MP for Fareham, 1900–18. Civil Lord of Admiralty, 1903–5. On special service with the British Expeditionary Force, 1914. Personal Military Secretary to Lloyd George (at the War Office), 1916. Knighted, 1916. Director-General of Food Production, 1917–18. Created Baron Lee of Fareham, 1918. Minister of Agriculture and Fisheries, 1919–21. First Lord of the Admiralty, February 1921–October 1922. Created Viscount, 1922. Member of the Royal Fine Art Commission, 1926–47.

Speaking Union to Lord Reading which has been well reported in the
'Times'. I have been elected the new President of the English Speaking
Union. It was uphill work to make an enthusiastic speech about the United
States at a time when so many hard things are said about us over there and
when they are wringing the last penny out of their unfortunate allies. All the
same there is only one road for us to tread, and that is to keep as friendly with
them as possible, to be overwhelmingly patient and to wait for the growth of
better feelings which will certainly come when the Irish question ceases to be
in its present terrible condition. If anything it has been getting more grave in
the last few weeks and the confident assertions of Hamar and the military do
not seem to be borne out by events. I am feeling my way for a plan for submitting the cases both of Ireland and Egypt to the Imperial Cabinet, which
meets in June, where all the Prime Ministers will be assembled.

It has now been settled that I remain S. of S for Air for the next few weeks
at any rate as well as Colonies.

A day of intense bustle & pressure. I will write again tomorrow. Tender
love. Let me know how much more money if any you want.

Yr devoted & loving
W

That night Churchill received the Seals of his new office, and was
formally appointed Colonial Secretary. He had begun his Ministerial
career as Under-Secretary of State at the Colonial Office fifteen years
before, in December 1905. Since then he had held six offices of Cabinet
rank. Yet he was still one of the youngest members of Lloyd George's
Cabinet. He was only forty-six years old; the age at which his father had
died.

On February 15 Churchill moved into his new room at the Colonial
Office. 'It is very fine and sedate,' he wrote to his wife a day later. 'My
new room is at least twice as big as the old one—an enormous square,
but well warmed. It is like working in the saloon at Blenheim. . . . I
cannot tell you how busy I have been with farewells at WO & saluta-
tions at CO, two speeches, perpetual Cabinets & Committees—the
Middle East, Air Estimates, etc. But I shall soon get into calmer
waters.'

30

'I am determined to save you millions'

CHURCHILL began work at the Colonial Office on the morning of February 15, and planned to leave London for Egypt on the evening of March 1. This gave him only two weeks to prepare for the Cairo Conference before leaving. He had also to introduce the Air Estimates to Parliament, in his capacity as outgoing Secretary of State for Air. Throughout February 15 he was busy, as he wrote to his wife on the following day, 'forming my new Middle Eastern department'. But he was still worried that Curzon would try to overrule him in his new work. 'Curzon will give me lots of trouble,' he wrote '& will have to be half flattered & half overborne. We overlap horribly. I do not think he is much good. Anyhow I have the burden on my back. We are on quite good terms personally. I shall take lots of trouble to bring him along.' During the day Churchill sent a progress report to Austen Chamberlain: 'I am settling all the details of my new Middle Eastern Department with Warren Fisher,[1] who has apparently received your instructions to help in every way. I am very grateful for this. I hope to have the principal work of formation completed to-day. At present I am quite without a machine.' And he added: 'I am determined to save you millions in this field.'

In trying to make the Middle East an area which would be cheap to administer and free from political unrest, Churchill was determined to ensure that no Arab action would bring Britain into conflict with France. In a letter to Curzon on February 16 he stressed the need to

---

[1] Norman Fenwick Warren Fisher, 1879–1948. Entered the Inland Revenue Department, 1903. Seconded to the National Health Insurance Commission, 1912–13. Deputy Chairman, Board of Inland Revenue, 1914–18; Chairman, 1918–19. Knighted, 1919. Permanent Secretary of the Treasury, and Official Head of the Civil Service, 1919–39.

reach 'a certain definite and clear understanding with the French' within the shortest possible time. He had already instructed Lawrence to make it clear to the Emir Feisal that his family's territorial claims could only be supported by Britain if the Arabs ceased their anti-French activities. Churchill hoped that Lawrence could persuade Feisal to influence both his father Hussein, and his brother Abdullah, to act with moderation, and to accept a settlement organized by the British. But a peaceful settlement in the Middle East depended upon Turkish as well as Arab acceptance. Churchill still feared that if Turkey were alienated by Britain, she would stimulate anti-British feeling throughout the Muslim world, and even attack Mesopotamia, with whom she shared a common frontier, and whose Kurdish inhabitants she saw as potential allies in extending Turkish control to Mosul. But Lloyd George continued to pursue his anti-Turkish policy, and to encourage the Greeks to remain in both western Anatolia and Thrace.

Because of Lloyd George's pro-Greek policy, Churchill had to find a Middle Eastern policy which took account of possible Turkish hostility. His personal preference was still for the maximum use of air power. On February 16 Sir Arnold Wilson, who had returned from Mesopotamia after two years as acting High Commissioner, circulated a memorandum which provided important support for his arguments. Wilson stated that the Royal Air Force personnel already in Mesopotamia were, in his belief, 'better trained and more efficient than most military units in the country'. And he added: 'Hot weather conditions affected military units in Mesopotamia more catastrophically than the units of the RAF, and the RAF have learned by experience to overcome to a great extent climatic conditions. . . .' The motive power of an army, Wilson pointed out, was mostly the men themselves, always exposed to fever and exhaustion; but the motive power of an air force was, 'almost exclusively' machinery, which was not unduly affected by extremes of heat.

On February 18 Churchill drafted a seven-point outline of his proposed agenda for the Cairo Conference. The Mesopotamian question was uppermost in his mind, and the topics he wished discussed were:

(1) The new ruler. Methods of Election. The Mandate generally. Kurdistan, Bin Saud, etc.

(2) The permanent garrison for the three years 1922–23, 1923–24 and 1924–25: size, composition, location, permanent barracks; co-operation with or control by the Air Force.

(3) Critical examination of present military charges, station by station, unit by unit, category by category. After a general discussion on this, a sub-

committee will sit separately to formulate proposals for immediate economy and report before the Conference separates.

(4) The rate of reduction from the present force to the permanent garrison. My hope is that one third of the present troops can leave the country before the hot weather and another third immediately after it is over. . . .

(5) The system of taxation and the scale of the civil Government to be maintained must be reviewed in the direction of having lighter taxation and a less ambitious Government.

(6) Estimate the cost of the Grant-in-Aid for the three years 1922–23, 1923–24, 1924–25.

(7) Final review of the political situation in the light of the above and decision as to the actual territory and positions to be held.

Churchill added: 'A similar agenda *mutatis mutandis* must be worked out for Palestine.' He wanted also 'a short discussion' on the places that had been transferred from the India Office: Kuweit, Bahrein and the Aden Protectorate. These notes, he added, 'are only intended as guide'.

On February 18 Clementine Churchill wrote to her husband from Beaulieu-sur-Mer, in the South of France: 'As I am here, could I not sail with you to Egypt. The sea voyage in the *warmth* would do me good & I should love it. . . . If not suitable for me to do so on so official & serious occasion could I not go to an Hotel incognito?'

'The work is very heavy indeed,' Churchill wrote to his wife on February 19. 'Many gt thorny questions pressing for solution in Cabinet & my various departments. No time for painting or book. All work— but vy interesting.' Churchill had planned to see his wife for a few hours on his way through France. But on reflection, and before receiving her letter, he decided to ask her if she would like to go with him to Cairo itself. 'Overjoyed by your delightful plan,' she telegraphed from Beaulieu on February 20. 'Yes it really will do me good and I shall love to see all these new things with you.' On the following day he wrote from the Colonial Office:

My darling,

I am so glad you are attracted by the idea of coming to Egypt and Palestine. The 'Sphinx' is a beautiful ship and we have excellent accommodation on board her. I am travelling at the Government's expense, but I shall of course pay everything which is on account of you. I will let you know in good time when you must be at Marseilles. As soon as the ship arrives you should go on board and make yourself comfortable, or at any rate send all your luggage on board. There will probably be several hours to spare.

The people in Egypt are getting rather excited at my coming, as they seem to think it has something to do with them. This is, of course, all wrong. I have no mission to Egypt and have no authority to deal with any Egyptian question. I shall have to make this quite clear or we shall be pestered with demonstrations and delegations.

I have had a nice telegram from Herbert Samuel expressing the hope that you will be able to come too. I expect we shall stay ten days in Cairo and then go to Jerusalem. We need not yet fix definitely the date of return, as I cannot in any case get back before Parliament rises for its Easter holidays. The new Malta Constitution is to come into operation early in April, and I may take advantage of my presence in the Mediterranean to go and inaugurate it myself.

It will be above all things necessary that you should not fatigue yourself on this expedition, and I know you will let me be the judge. It would indeed be foolish if we returned without your having got quite strong and well. I shall have to work every day, either all the mornings or all the afternoons; but there is no reason why you should not see some of the temples and possibly travel a little way up the Nile. I expect there will be some lawn tennis, so do not forget your racquet. I think on an 11,000 ton ship we ought to be able to face the horrors of the sea. The 'Honour'[1] was less than 1,500 tons and even the 'Enchantress' was only 3,500.

I hope to paint a few pictures in the intervals between settling my business, and naturally I am taking all the right kinds of colours for the yellow desert, purple rocks and crimson sunsets. I shall enjoy so much showing you round: some of the places I know so well.

Let me now tell you who are coming with me. First of all, Archie. Then the famous Colonel Lawrence, who has at last consented to have a bit put in his mouth and a saddle fastened on his back; a Major Young, a very clever man who has been transferred from the Foreign Office to my new department; Mr Crosland,[2] of the Finance Branch of the War Office; and Air Marshal Trenchard, who is going to see what can be done about the air control in Mesopotamia. We shall be met by Sir Percy Cox, General Haldane, General Ironside and the principal officials of the Mesopotamian Government, who are travelling from Basra in a special Royal India Marine ship the 'Hardinge'. They will pick up on their way the Resident of Bushire,[3] who is to manage Koweit and Bahrein for me, and the Governor of Aden,[4] both these places

---

[1] A yacht belonging to Churchill's friend, the Baron de Forest. Churchill and his wife had travelled on the yacht several times before the First World War.

[2] Joseph Beardsell Crosland, 1874–1935. Entered the War Office as a Clerk (Higher Division), 1897; Principal, 1915. Director of Finance, War Office, 1918–24; Deputy Under-Secretary, 1924–34.

[3] Arthur Prescott Trevor, 1872–1930. Entered the Royal Artillery, 1891. Joined the Political Department, Government of India, 1898. Captain, India Army, 1901; Major, 1909. Political Agent, Bahrein, 1912–14. Served in the Persian Gulf and Baluchistan, 1915–20. Lieutenant-Colonel, 1917. Political Resident, Bushire and the Persian Gulf, 1920–4.

[4] Thomas Edwin Scott, 1867–1937. Entered Army, 1888. Served in Uganda, 1897–8 and at the Relief of Peking, 1900. Assistant Secretary, Committee of Imperial Defence, 1909–12. Lieutenant-Colonel, 1912. Military Secretary to the Commander-in-Chief, India, 1914–17. Brigadier-General, 1916. On special serivce, German East Africa, 1917–18. Political Resident

now coming under my responsibility. Samuel will very likely come across from Palestine and we shall travel back with him. Allenby expresses lively pleasure at our arrival. I do hope, however, that the excitement in Egypt will not make it necessary to change the rendezvous to some other place.

Tender love my darling one.

Yr devoted
W

On February 21 Churchill was shown an intercepted telegram sent from the Greek Foreign Office in Athens to the Greek Legation in London. The telegram described a conversation held between Lloyd George and Venizelos on February 16. According to Venizelos, Lloyd George had told him that 'he was happy to have succeeded in solving the Smyrna question in favour of Greece', and had added 'that he had had to contend not only against the French Premier who supported the proposals to give us only a sphere of economic influence, but also against the British Foreign Minister'. Venizelos also reported that Lloyd George had asked for 'every sort of information' dealing with the question of Thrace and Smyrna 'so that he might be in a better position' to support the Greek point of view. Much angered, Churchill showed Lloyd George this telegram on February 22, and urged him to stop encouraging the Greeks in their anti-Turkish designs. After their meeting, Churchill drafted a letter of protest. Later, he decided not to send it. 'You have the power to decide British policy,' he wrote, 'I can only wait anxiously for the result.' His letter went on:

I have yet to meet a British official personage who does not think that our Eastern & Middle Eastern affairs would be enormously eased & helped by arriving at a peace with Turkey. The alternative of the renewal of war causes me the deepest misgivings. I dare say the Greeks may scatter the Turkish Nationalists on their immediate front, & may penetrate some distance into Turkey; but the more country they hold, & the longer they remain in it, the more costly to them.

The reactions from this state of affairs fall mainly upon us, & to a lesser extent on the French. They are all unfavourable. The Turks will be thrown into the arms of the Bolsheviks; Mesopotamia will be disturbed at the critical period of the reduction of the Army there; it will probably be quite impossible to hold Mosul & Baghdad without a powerful and expensive army; the general alienation of Mohammedan sentiment from Great Britain will continue

---

and General Officer Commanding, Aden, 1920–5. Lieutenant-General, 1924. Knighted, 1925. A member of the Civil Constabulary Reserve during the General Strike, 1926.

to work evil consequences in every direction: the French & Italians will make their own explanations; and we shall be everywhere represented as the chief enemy of Islam. Further misfortunes will fall upon the Armenians.

In these circumstances it seems to me a fearful responsibility to let loose the Greeks & to reopen the war. I am deeply grieved at the prospect and at finding myself so utterly without power to influence your mind even in regard to matters with which my duties are specially concerned. All the more am I distressed because of my desire to aid you in any way open to me in the many matters in which we are agreed, & because of our long friendship & my admiration for yr genius & work.

Before leaving for Cairo, Churchill was confronted with a problem concerning Palestine. The Zionists were anxious to develop the economic potential of their 'National Home', and to this end a Jewish engineer, Pinhas Rutenberg,[1] had put forward a plan to use the waters of the Jordan and Auja rivers for electrical power. On February 23 John Shuckburgh informed Churchill that 'official opinion both in Palestine and in London' was favourable to granting Rutenberg a concession for at least his Auja river scheme, which would have the advantage of giving employment to eight hundred people, both Jews and Arabs. The Jordan scheme, Shuckburgh added, would depend on whether the Government wished to use Rutenberg's electricity to electrify the Palestine railways: 'if they are not to be electrified', Shuckburgh pointed out, 'there will be no adequate use for electric installations on the scale contemplated'.

Shuckburgh asked Churchill to grant Rutenberg's request for an expert enquiry into the Jordan scheme. To this Churchill agreed on February 24. He also instructed Shuckburgh to ask the Foreign Office 'to give me a little latitude in the matter of concession in Palestine'.

[1] Piotr (Pinhas) Rutenberg, 1879–1942. Born in the Ukraine. Graduated from St Petersburg Technological Institute. Worked in the Putilov metallurgical works. As a student, was active in revolutionary circles and imprisoned several times. Marched with Father Gapon on 'Bloody Sunday', 1905; subsequently instructed by the Social Revolutionaries to organize Gapon's execution. In exile in Italy, 1907–15, working as an irrigation engineer. Went to the United States to propagate the idea of a Jewish military force to help liberate Palestine, 1915–17. Returned to Russia, 1917. Appointed by Kerensky Deputy Governor of Petrograd, 1917. One of the defenders of the Winter Palace against the Bolsheviks, November 1917. Imprisoned by the Bolsheviks, 1917–18. Councillor for Food Supplies in the French-sponsored Odessa administration, 1918–19. Emigrated to Palestine, November 1919. Organized a survey of the water resources of Palestine, 1919–20. Helped organize the defence of Jerusalem during the Arab riots of 1920. Established the Palestine Electric Company, 1923. An active advocate of Jewish–Arab reconciliation, and friend of Abdullah. He died in Jerusalem.

On February 24 Lord Curzon wrote to Churchill to persuade him not to hold the forthcoming conference in Cairo. Curzon feared that Churchill's public criticism of Egyptian independence might lead to hostile demonstrations. 'I regard this,' he wrote, 'not as a fanciful but as a real danger.' The Conference, Curzon suggested, should be held in Jerusalem, Port Said or Ismailia.

Churchill was angered by Curzon's proposal. 'Unless Allenby spontaneously suggests that the rendezvous shd be changed,' he replied on February 25, 'I shd strongly object to a proceeding wh wd certainly produce the worst impression.' In any crisis, he added, 'I think we may leave it to Allenby to decide. I have no doubt that if he foresees difficulty he will telegraph.' Churchill's letter contained a more personal paragraph which, on reflection, he decided to cut out. 'I wish you were going to do this work,' Churchill had written. 'I greatly repent ever having allowed the consequences of the last two years in the Middle East to be thrust upon me. I shall be delighted to hand them over at any moment if the Cabinet agree.'

Churchill continued with his travel plans. His typhoid injections gave him some discomfort. 'I am drooping this afternoon under one of them,' he wrote to his wife on February 24. But he also had good news to report; their daughter Marigold had recovered from her cold, and the articles on painting which his wife had not wanted him to publish would, he pointed out, earn him £1,000 in England and £600 in the United States—'Too good to miss.' His letter ended:

Tender love my darling one. I am too tired to write more & I think I shall go home to bed. Mind you don't fail to lie up after the inoculation & don't drink alcohol for 24 hours.

A thousand kisses. I am so looking forward to seeing yr dear face again: & I pray that I may read in it a real consolation of health.

Your (temporarily battered) but always loving

W

During the last week of February the officials of the Middle East Department drew up a memorandum for the use of the Cairo Conference. It represented their collective view of what should be done, and Churchill gave it his full approval. The selection of 'an Arab ruler' for Mesopotamia was, they declared, 'an essential preliminary to the establishment of satisfactory permanent conditions in that country'. In their view, Feisal was the most suitable ruler, but Britain would retain control both of foreign relations and of 'external defence'. Both these powers had been granted to Britain under the proposed League of Nations Mandate.

The problem of reducing Britain's financial commitments in Mesopotamia would be a major theme of the Conference. The memorandum quoted a minute of Churchill's expressing the hope 'that one third of present troops can leave Mesopotamia before the hot weather, and another third immediately after it is over'. How this was to be done, and how it was to be followed up, was for the Cairo Conference to decide. The memorandum urged that the 'purely Kurdish areas' in the north of Mesopotamia should not be included in the new Arab State, but that Britain should help to promote 'the principles of Kurdish unity and nationality', sending a British Adviser to the area, and encouraging the Kurds to set up 'some form of central Kurdish organisation'.

The memorandum also dealt with Palestine. Churchill's advisers told him that there was no conflict between Britain's separate promises to the Arabs and the Jews. In 1915 the Arabs had been promised 'British recognition and support for their independence in the Turkish vilayet of Damascus', south of the area to be controlled by France. The western boundary of the vilayet had been the River Jordan. Two years later, in 1917, the Jews had been promised 'a national home for the Jewish people' in Palestine, but no specific boundaries had been mentioned. If, therefore, the land east of the Jordan were set up as the Arab State, and the lands west of the Jordan became the area of the Jewish National Home, both Britain's wartime pledges would be fulfilled. Such was the collective view of Shuckburgh, Young and Lawrence. They also believed that such a solution had high legal authority, informing Churchill that:

The Mandate itself supplies the answer. In the first place, the preamble provides that nothing shall be done which may prejudice the civil and religious rights of existing non-Jewish communities. In the second place, article 3 obliges the mandatory to encourage the widest measure of self-Government for localities consistent with the prevailing conditions. We consider that these two clauses, taken in conjunction, afford adequate justification for setting up in Trans-Jordan a political system somewhat different from that in force on the other side of the river. If British promises are to stand, this system must be Arab in character. We consider that it should preferably be centralised under an Arab ruler acceptable to His Majesty's Government and acting in important matters under their advice.

In their memorandum, Churchill's advisers pointed out that the economic development of Palestine west of the Jordan had been 'seriously hampered' by the Government's reluctance to grant industrial concessions prior to the confirmation of the Mandate by the League of

Nations. Several Jews who had sought permission to develop Palestine's industrial potential, including Pinhas Rutenberg, had been told that they must delay their applications until the Mandate was confirmed. 'We think it most undesirable,' the memorandum declared, 'that this delay should continue, and consider that cases of real urgency should be taken up forthwith.'

Churchill's advisers went on to recommend that Britain should continue to pay cash subsidies to King Hussein and Ibn Saud, provided that both rulers gave specific undertakings 'such as the maintenance of pilgrim routes, the preservation of boundaries fixed by British arbitration, abstention from hostile action in certain specified directions, and exclusion of foreign influence'. Failure to meet any of these conditions should result, they wrote, in the 'automatic stoppage' of the subsidy. And they added: 'we are strongly of opinion that His Majesty's Government should incur no new liabilities or obligations of any kind, whether military, political or financial, in the peninsula of Arabia'.

On Saturday February 26 Churchill spent a relaxing day with his children, writing to his wife on the following day:

The Broadstairs detachment arrived home yesterday. They were in the pink. I brought them home two days earlier in order to catch a glimpse of them before I left. The Duckadilly received them with joy & is quite free from cold. Indeed she is to go out today. Alas however I am the peccant one. I have a horrid cold. I do trust I have not given it to them. It is really impossible to avoid risk at one point or another.

We are going down to see Randolph today. I gave the children the choice of Randolph or the Zoo. They screamed for Randolph in most loyal and gallant fashion. So we arranged for the Zoo too. . . . Unless I have put things wrong with my cold—I shall leave a vy good state of affairs behind me. The expense of these two mites for 4 weeks is over £60. However it has done them good.

'F.E. dined last night,' Churchill added. 'Only cider! He is becoming vy fierce & calm—a formidable figure—rather morose—vy ambitious. Terrible results of intemperate self restraint.' Of their forthcoming journey to Egypt, he wrote with enthusiasm:

I am looking forward eagerly to seeing you again. We shall have a beautiful cabin together. If only it is not rough—then I shall hide in any old dog hole far from yr sight. Still I put my faith in God & in 11,000 tons. That is a fine big ship for the Mediterranean. If it is fine, it will be lovely & I shall write & paint & we will talk over all our affairs.

Before going to Cairo, Churchill made one further effort to persuade Lloyd George to enter into negotiations with the Turks. He was particularly concerned, he wrote to the Prime Minister on February 28, that the Turks should be urged not to disturb the peace in the Mosul region. Any hostile Turkish activity, he wrote, 'will fatally hamper my schemes for a more rapid withdrawal of our large army. Perhaps ten millions of money depend upon tranquility in Mosul and the absence of external pressure'. If there were to be an armistice between Greece and Turkey, he added, 'which I devoutly hope will be the case, it is of the highest importance that the tranquility of this region should be a definite part of it'. But Lloyd George had no intention of promoting a Graeco-Turkish peace, and the Greeks, encouraged by his support of their claims, continued to make plans for a major military offensive.

Tuesday March 1 was Churchill's last day in England before setting off for Egypt. He spent most of the afternoon in the House of Commons, introducing his Air Estimates and listening to the debate. 'Slowly,' he said, 'an efficient, self-respecting, well-disciplined, economically-organized Air Force' was being created. 'No more complicated service,' he added, 'has ever been brought into existence in this world.' Churchill then outlined to the House of Commons the many different aeroplanes needed to maintain an efficient service, the different types of skills required, and the establishments at which training was being carried out.

During March 1 the Political Committee of the Zionist Organisation met in London to discuss Churchill's forthcoming visit to the Middle East. According to the Minutes of the meeting, Dr Weizmann was worried about the delay in ratifying the Palestine Mandate. 'There were indications,' he said, 'that Mr Churchill might possibly desire certain changes in the Mandate. He was of a highly impressionable temperament and it was to be expected that the Arabs would organize an agitation to greet him on his arrival in the East.' But, Weizmann added: 'Mr Churchill had a low opinion of the Arab generally'.

Hoping to influence Churchill about the future boundaries of Palestine, Weizmann then sent him a thousand-word appeal, asking Churchill to extend the eastern boundary of Palestine across the Jordan river, to the line of the Hedjaz railway, or even beyond. The British, he wrote, could provide 'special safeguards for the Moslem interests in the Hedjaz Railway', and allow the whole of Transjordan to become a part of the Jewish National Home. 'It is upon these fields,' he wrote, 'now that the rich plains to the north have been taken away from Palestine and given to France, that the success of the Jewish National Home must largely rest. Trans-Jordania has from the earliest time been an integral and vital part of Palestine.' It was east of the Jordan, Weizmann added, that the tribes of Reuben, Gad and Manasseh 'first pitched their tents and pastured their flocks', and although 'Eastern Palestine', as he called it, would never have the same religious or historic significance for the Jews as Palestine west of the Jordan, it might, he said, 'bulk larger in the economic future of the Jewish National Home'. Weizmann then elaborated his argument:

The climate of Trans-Jordania is invigorating; the soil is rich; irrigation would be easy; and the hills are covered with forests. There Jewish settlement could proceed on a large scale without friction with the local population. The economic progress of Cis-Jordania itself is dependent upon the development of these Trans-Jordania plains, for they form the natural granary of all Palestine and without them Palestine can never become a self-sustaining, economic unit and a real National Home. . . .[1]

Weizmann did not ask for Transjordan alone to be included in the Palestine Mandate. He also pressed Churchill to take the southern boundary of Palestine down to the Gulf of Akaba. In his letter of March 1 he asked for both this area, and Transjordan, as compensation for Britain's agreement with France which fixed the northern boundary in such a way as to 'cut Palestine off' from the Litani River, whose waters the Zionists had hoped to harness for electrical and industrial purposes. The area between Beersheba and the Gulf of Akaba, which Weizmann claimed as part of the area of the Jewish National Home, was, he wrote, 'derelict, but potentially rich in resources essential to Palestine's future'; it ought not to be 'allotted to Egypt'. This area, known as the Negev, was, he wrote, largely 'waste' and of 'no value to any country but Palestine'.

Churchill was not influenced by Weizmann's arguments. He had already decided to separate Transjordan from Palestine. But he had also decided to allow the Negev to form part of the Palestine Mandate, and therefore to be open to eventual Jewish settlement.

That evening Churchill left London for Egypt. On the following day,

[1] Weizmann added: '. . . it is clear that apart from a small corridor along the Hedjaz Railway, there is no concession north of Maan, short of Damascus, to which Arab nationalism could attach any real or permanent value. The aspirations of Arab nationalism centre about Damascus and Baghdad and do not lie in Trans-Jordania.'

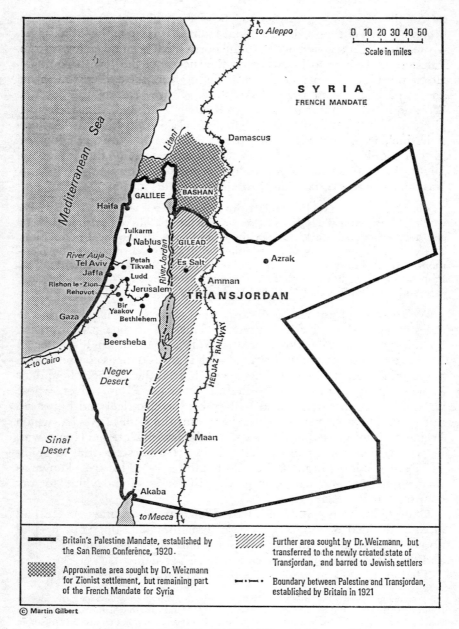

THE PALESTINE MANDATE, 1920–1922

the Executive of the Zionist Organization in London met again to discuss the policy they hoped Churchill would adopt towards Palestine. Weizmann was particularly anxious to show Churchill the full extent of Jewish colonization in Palestine, and asked Nahum Sokolow[1] to go at once to Jerusalem to organize a proper reception. Weizmann also wrote to Samuel, who was then in Jerusalem, urging him to show Churchill the constructive side of the work of the Jewish Chalutzim, or pioneers. In his letter, sent from London on March 10, he explained:

I am most anxious that should Mr Churchill visit Palestine, as it is now understood that he intends to do, he should have an opportunity of coming into contact with the Chalutzim and seeing them at work. Perhaps it would be possible for him to be accompanied, in doing so, by Mr Rutenberg. Hostile critics persistently accuse the immigrants of Bolshevik tendencies. Any prejudice that these charges may have created in Mr Churchill's mind will, I feel confident, be effectively dissipated by actual contact with the Chalutzim.

On the morning of March 3 Churchill reached Marseilles, where he was joined by his wife. Before leaving for Egypt on board the French steamship *Sphinx*, he was asked by a Press representative to explain the reason for his journey. 'I am endeavouring,' he said, 'to realise French and British unity in the East. My journey to Egypt and to Asia Minor is proof of this; we must at any price coordinate our actions to the extent of uniting them. It is by those means only that we shall be able to arrive at lasting quiet, and diminish the enormous expenditure we are both making.'

[1] Nahum Sokolow, 1859–1936. Born in Russian Poland. Popular Hebrew writer. As a journalist, attended the First Zionist Congress, 1897. Subsequently sought to reconcile Orthodox Jewry to Zionism. General Secretary of the World Zionist Organization, 1906; Member of the Zionist Executive, 1911. Sought the support of American and Canadian Jews to Zionism, 1913. Moved to London, 1914. Head of the Committee which prepared the wording of the Balfour Declaration, 1917, and active in obtaining approval for it from politicians in France and Italy. Head of the Jewish Delegation to the Paris Peace Conference, 1919. Head of the Zionist Executive, 1920. Chairman of successive Zionist Congresses, 1921–36. Chairman of the Executive of the Jewish Agency, 1929–36. President of the Zionist Organization, 1931–5. He died in London.

31

The Cairo Conference:
March 1921

FOR six days Churchill sailed eastwards from Marseilles, reaching Alexandria on the morning of Thursday March 9. That afternoon he visited Aboukir Bay, the scene of Nelson's naval victory over the French in 1798, and at midday on March 10 he left Alexandria by train for Cairo, accompanied by his wife. In protest against his reported hostility to Egyptian independence, the students of El Azhar University stopped work for the day. *The Palestine Weekly* described the scene at the main station before Churchill was due to arrive:

Some thousands of spectators gathered in Station Square, the bridge leading to the Shubra Road being packed to capacity. . . . Various notables waited patiently in the station which had been cleared of all unauthorised persons, and Bristol Fighters and huge Handley Pages circled overhead. The train steamed in to the station half an hour late and amid intense excitement disgorged five hat boxes and other baggage, the Colonial Secretary and party having got off at the suburban station of Shubra, whence they motored unseen and undisturbed to the Semiramis Hotel.

There was no demonstration of any importance though a disorderly rabble gathered outside Shepheard's crying 'Down with Churchill', but they were dispersed speedily and without casualty.

Before the Conference assembled, Churchill made further plans for the development of British air power in the Middle East. On March 11 he discussed the problem at length with Trenchard—who had just arrived in Cairo—T. E. Lawrence and Sir John Salmond, the Air Officer Commanding, Middle East Area. Churchill was eager for Salmond to take immediate steps to prepare the way for the opening of an air route from Cairo to Baghdad. Later that day Trenchard informed Churchill that 'all the machinery is available to complete this route both for cars and aeroplanes'. On the following day Trenchard informed Salmond that he could 'spend money when the word "go" is given up to the amount of £50,000', and that if he needed 'any other sanction' from either Churchill or himself, he should ask for it at once.

The Cairo Conference opened on the morning of Saturday March 12. Two Committees, one Political and one Military, were set up to discuss how to reduce expenditure in Mesopotamia. Churchill presided over the Political Committee and General Congreve over the Military Committee. The agendas for both Committees had been worked out by Churchill and his staff during the journey from Marseilles to Cairo.

Churchill opened the proceedings of the Political Committee by explaining that as Sir Percy Cox and General Haldane had 'already arrived' at an agreement on the preliminary withdrawal of troops from Mesopotamia, this item on the Agenda could be set aside. The Committee then discussed the various candidates for ruler of Mesopotamia. Cox believed that Feisal would be preferred by the Mesopotamians themselves. Churchill asked him why. Cox replied 'that he considered Feisal's previous experience during the war placed him in the best position for raising an army quickly'. Added to that, his experiences with the Allies at the Paris Peace Conference made him 'better qualified as a ruler' than Abdullah, or his other brothers. The discussion then developed in Feisal's favour, as the Minutes recorded:

Colonel Lawrence supported the candidature of Amir Faisal not only from his personal knowledge of and friendship for the individual, but also on the ground that in order to counteract the claims of rival candidates and to pull together the scattered elements of a backward and half civilised country, it was essential that the first ruler should be an active and inspiring personality. Amir Abdullah was lazy, and by no means dominating.

The Chairman pointed out that a strong argument in favour of Sherifian policy was that it enabled His Majesty's Government to bring pressure to bear on one Arab sphere in order to attain their own ends in another. If Faisal knew that not only his father's subsidy and the protection of the Holy Places from Wahabi attack, but also the position of his brother in Trans-Jordan was dependent upon his own good behaviour, he would be much easier to deal with. The same argument applied mutatis mutandis to King Hussein and Amir Abdullah. The French Government had tried to convince him that by adopting a Sherifian policy he would risk being destroyed, like Frankenstein, by a monster of his own creation.

The Military Committee also held its first meeting on March 12, to discuss the reduction of the Mesopotamian garrison. General Haldane agreed 'that all outlying detachments could be withdrawn', and the defences concentrated on the line Mosul–Baghdad–Basra. The maintenance of order outside this defended line would be the responsibility of the Civil Government and the Royal Air Force.

At the second meeting of the Military Committee on March 13, Trenchard outlined his proposals for the control of Mesopotamia by the Royal Air Force. At a third meeting that same day, General Haldane produced a detailed plan for the reduced military commitment, and the size of each garrison was discussed 'place by place'. Trenchard agreed to Haldane's request that the mobile columns of troops hitherto employed on punitive missions should be replaced by aircraft. Sir Percy Cox declared 'that he would be satisfied with such action'. The Military Committee had before them a memorandum, drawn up by Trenchard on March 12, setting out in detail his scheme for the 'Air Control of Mesopotamia'. He proposed to use eight squadrons of aircraft, including two twin-engined bombing squadrons, six armoured car companies 'maintained by RAF and manned by RAF personnel', two armoured trains and three or four river gunboats. Trenchard also wanted the construction of a main road from Egypt to Mesopotamia, through Palestine, with 'dumps of petrol' and land marks at eighty-mile intervals. 'The care of the dumps of petrol and landmarks,' he wrote, 'should be entrusted to the local Sheikhs who would be paid for the services of personnel employed on their safe keeping and efficient maintenance.'

The second meeting of the Political Committee was also held on March 13, with Churchill as Chairman. He read them a draft of telegram which he was about to send to Lloyd George, in which he stated: 'I think we shall reach unanimous conclusion among all authorities that Feisal offers hope of best and cheapest solution.' Churchill told the Committee that he felt sure 'that he could rely upon Colonel Lawrence to persuade the Sherif to act according to the suggestions', and that Feisal should reach Mesopotamia in April or May. According to the Minutes, it was 'generally agreed' that Feisal's presence in Mesopotamia 'would have such an inspiring effect upon the majority of the population that there was little fear of any opposition to his candidature'.

Later that day Churchill summoned the first meeting of the Combined Political and Military Committees. At the outset of their deliberations, he stressed the need for continued and drastic economies, to be effected 'without delay'. The modified garrison proposed by General Haldane would cost about £25,000,000 a year; Churchill hoped that this expenditure 'would eventually come down to about two-thirds of this figure'. General Haldane said that it was only a shortage of shipping that was delaying the departure of troops. But General Congreve was afraid that these reductions were proceeding too quickly. Sir Percy Cox supported Congreve. Too rapid a reduction, he declared, 'would leave him in a very difficult position'. He did not feel he could rely on Haldane's Mosul–Baghdad–Basra line; troops must, he said, be maintained elsewhere as well. Churchill then spoke strongly in favour of immediate economies, as the Minute recorded:

The Chairman, whilst agreeing that the situation was a somewhat difficult one, emphasised the fact that the British taxpayer could not be expected to continue to garrison the country at such high expense, and that rapid economies must be effected before the new financial year. He fully realised that the Military Commanders wished to refrain from placing a number of small detachments about the country involving long lines of communications, and risking the destruction of such forces in the event of hostile action, yet he thought that it must be possible to find a medium whereby the General Officer Commanding might meet the High Commissioner by slightly increasing the number of stations from the three suggested. At the same time it was essential that the training of the local forces should be accelerated as much as possible. . . .

Churchill then asked Trenchard if the Royal Air Force could take immediate control of Mesopotamian defence, but Trenchard replied that the Air Force 'was not yet in a position to do so'. Pressed as to when his men and machines would be ready he said that 'a year hence it might be possible to lend more active assistance. . . .' Searching for other means of economy, Churchill suggested that Britain might offer a subsidy to the villages on the lines of communication, 'and in return make them responsible for guarding the railway', thus reducing the number of British troops needed. But Sir Percy Cox felt that 'the time was scarcely ripe to place such a trust upon a populace which had so recently been in revolt against us'.

To emphasize the importance of the Mesopotamian expenditure, Churchill asked Joseph Crosland to give the Combined Committee a survey of comparative costs. Crosland replied that of the £30,000,000 estimated as the cost of the garrisons in both Mesopotamia and Palestine, only £3,500,000 were needed for Palestine.

After the meeting of the Combined Committee, Churchill informed Lloyd George by telegram of the immediate cuts that he intended to make in the Mesopotamian garrison. 'Incredible waste now proceeding,' he explained, '. . . can only be cured by driving large numbers of troops and followers out of country and off our pay list. . . . I am met by assertion that many thousands of men and followers could now begin to leave country if shipping were available. . . . We have to carry everybody back sooner or later, and keeping them waiting eating up our mutton is pure waste.'

Lloyd George replied on March 16:

I am in full sympathy with your desire to cure the waste and reduce troops in Mesopotamia. I have asked the Secretary of State for War and Shipping Controller to take up the matter at once.

Throughout March 14 the various Committees and Sub-Committees continued to discuss troop economies in Mesopotamia. A Sub-Committee under General Radcliffe worked out a plan to embark 5,000 troops a week from Basra, thus clearing the 20,000 troops awaiting embarkation within a month. If these troops could be got away at such speed, there would be a saving of £5,500,000 in the next financial year.

At the second meeting of the Combined Political and Military Committees, held later in the day, Churchill urged the other members to make every effort, in their calculations, to reduce military expenditure to a minimum. Wherever possible, he said, junior officers should be substituted for senior officers as the responsibility of each command was 'modified with the reduction of numbers'. In answer to a question from Churchill, Joseph Crosland calculated that the 25,000 animals being used by the Army in Mesopotamia cost £1,750,000 a year to feed. Churchill was delighted to find that if these animals were sold, there would be 'a considerable saving' in the total budget.

General Haldane then raised the question of the large accumulation of stores on which his forces were living. What would happen to these stores once the majority of the men were gone? Churchill at once saw a further chance for economy. These stores, he said, should be sold to the Civil Government. It was, he urged, 'a false economy . . . to keep a large staff to look after surplus stores, and it would be better to arrange for their immediate disposal, even if they were sold at a very low rate'. Churchill ended the meeting by telling those present that once relations with Turkey had been stabilized and local Arab forces established, he hoped to reduce the British force in Mesopotamia to about 15,000 men.

In two days the Conference had made swift progress. Feisal's Mesopotamian crown was virtually assured; Britain's military expenses were being substantially reduced with every Committee meeting.

The fourth meeting of the Political Committee was held on March 15, to discuss the question of Kurdistan. There was a lengthy debate on whether or not the Kurds could form a separate, independent state. Churchill suggested 'that it might be possible to subsidize a Kurdish chief and his more influential subordinates and to grant provisional trading facilities in consideration of an agreement that they would prevent the Turks from carrying out a policy in that area adverse to British interests. . . .'

Churchill was afraid of the actions in Kurdistan of a Mesopotamian king who might, he said, 'while outwardly accepting constitutional procedures and forming a Parliament, at the same time despise democratic and constitutional methods'. Such a king would, he warned, 'with the power of an Arab army behind him . . . ignore Kurdish sentiment and oppress the Kurdish minority'. For this reason, he favoured 'a friendly buffer State' between Mesopotamia and the Turks, and agreed with Major Young that it might be possible 'to form something in the nature of a frontier force of Kurds, under the command of British officers. . . .' But he was prepared also to defer to the views of Sir Percy Cox and Gertrude Bell,[1] who strongly favoured a 'united' Mesopotamia, with Kurdistan within its borders.

At the fourth meeting of the Military Committee on March 15, the various troop reductions already decided upon were announced by Joseph Crosland to amount in all to £5,000,000 a year, thus reducing the 1921–2 estimate by one sixth. But Churchill was not content. Such a saving, he declared in a note to the third Joint Military and Political Committee due to meet later that afternoon, was 'quite insufficient'. The Joint Committee must, he said, prepare a second stage of reductions, to come in force after October 1921, and still in time for the financial year 1921–22. These preparations, he urged, should be detailed ones, 'specifying units, arms, administrative services, civil personnel, animals &c'. By means of this second stage, he hoped for a further reduction, 'if all goes well', of £3,000,000.

On the evening of March 15 Churchill sent Lloyd George an account of the results of the first four days of the Conference. 'All authorities,' he telegraphed, 'including Cox, Generals Haldane, Congreve, Ironside, Radcliffe, Colonel Lawrence and Major Young, have reached complete agreement on all the points, both political and military.' A third of the

---

[1] Gertrude Margaret Lowthian Bell, 1868–1926. Obtained a First Class Degree in Modern History at Oxford, 1888, the first woman ever to do so. Published her own translations of two Persian books, 1894 and 1897. Settled in Jerusalem to learn Arabic, 1899. Made her name as an alpinist in Switzerland, 1901–4, when she climbed the Matterhorn. Set out from Jerusalem overland to Konya, in Asia Minor, 1905. Journeyed down the Euphrates, 1909. Travelled across Arabia, from Damascus to Hail to Baghdad, 1913–14. Served with the Red Cross at Boulogne, 1914–15; with the Arab Intelligence Bureau, Cairo, 1915–16. Attached to the Military Intelligence Staff, Mesopotamia, 1916. Oriental Secretary, Baghdad, 1916–20. Adviser to Sir Percy Cox, Mesopotamia, 1920–2. Honorary Director of Antiquities, Mesopotamia, 1918–26. She died in Baghdad.

troops budgeted for in the 1921–2 Estimates would leave Mesopotamia 'as fast as shipping becomes available'. Provided 'prompt action is taken at all points', Churchill wrote, 'Mr Crosland . . . estimates resultant saving . . . at £5,500,000'. The second stage of reductions, which would be possible if Mesopotamia were not attacked from outside, and if the Arab Government 'proves a success', would halve the remaining garrison from 23 battalions to 12, and reduce the military cost of the country to less than £6,000,000 a year.

The various Committees continued their work throughout March 16. In the morning General Congreve presided over the third meeting of the Joint Political and Military Committee, at which Sir Hugh Trenchard's scheme for the control of Mesopotamia was examined in detail. It was agreed that Royal Air Force control should also include the Armoured Car Companies 'both for purposes of unity of command and economy in upkeep', and that the river gun boats and armoured trains should also be part of air power. A major advantage of Trenchard's scheme, the Committee concluded, was Imperial rather than local, for it took into account 'the vital necessity of preparing and training an Air Force adequate to our needs in war, the importance of testing the potentialities of the Air Force, the need for giving its superior officers and staffs the experience in independent command and responsibility, and the provision of an "All Red" military and commercial air route to India'.

There followed the fourth meeting of the Combined Political and Military Committees, at which Churchill, who dominated the discussion, reiterated the need to probe every item of military expenditure. 'British troops,' he said, 'who were the backbone of the British Empire, were extremely costly, and therefore every endeavour should be made to make the best use of them.' He felt that this was not being done 'so long as they were being employed upon menial duties'. There should, he urged, be a greater reliance upon Indian troops, or local Arab forces. This suggestion brought forth a protest from General Congreve. There was 'always the danger', he said, if Indian or local troops were employed, 'of their deserting as soon as fighting commenced'. Another reason for employing British troops on menial tasks was, Congreve said, that doctors were averse 'from medical reasons' to employing Arab or Indian labour in the cookhouses. But Churchill was not to be deflected from his course. 'He was of the opinion,' the Minutes recorded, 'particularly in Mesopotamia and similar unhealthy countries' that the Government 'would do well to employ a proportion of local labour'.

During the fourth meeting of the Combined Political and Military

Committees Churchill raised the question of the use and purpose of air power. It was necessary, he said, 'to carry out a far-sighted policy of Imperial aerial development in the future'. The air route from Cairo to Karachi would shorten the sea journey from England to Australia by eight or ten days. To establish a regular civilian service 'it was essential that tranquillity should be maintained upon the route'. The civil air service could use 'the same aerodromes, sheds and pilots' as the Royal Air Force would use 'in time of war'. This amalgamation of resources 'would lead to considerable economies'.

During March 16 the fifth meeting of the Political Committee, with Churchill as Chairman, met to discuss the question of 'subsidies and commitments' in Arabia. Even in the question of subsidies to ruling chiefs, Churchill said, he was 'anxious to effect economies', though he realized that a direct subsidy did save money on the maintenance of British garrisons. Sir Percy Cox wanted the subsidy to Ibn Saud increased from its current £60,000 to £120,000 a year. Ibn Saud, he said, 'possessed considerable power to harm British policy'. The justification in paying him a subsidy, Cox added, 'lay not so much in the actual services to be expected from him, but rather in the amount of harm he would be able to cause were his policy to become hostile'. Major Young disagreed with Cox. If Britain increased its subsidy to Ibn Saud, he pointed out, 'it would be necessary similarly to augment that of King Hussein'. Young also warned of the danger of granting Ibn Saud the title of King, as he might then 'claim membership of the League of Nations', which would 'tend to remove him from British control'. This, Young insisted, was clearly 'undesirable in view of British interests in Arabia'.

Gertrude Bell wanted Ibn Saud given 'a *douceur* . . . by way of compensation', seeing that two of King Hussein's sons, Feisal and Abdullah, were to receive kingdoms from Britain. Churchill suggested that Britain should pay him his subsidy on a monthly basis, 'as we should then be able to bring more pressure to bear upon him to maintain the necessary tranquillity in Nejd'. As for the amount of the subsidy, this, he proposed, should be set at £100,000 a year.

The discussion then turned to the question of Hussein's subsidy. Churchill suggested that once again the subsidy could be raised, provided Hussein agreed 'to maintain an attitude of goodwill towards the British Government' and to 'abstain from and entirely disassociate himself from anti-French propaganda', both by himself, and by his son Abdullah in Transjordan.

On Churchill's suggestion, a special Sub-Committee was set up to examine the question of subsidies in more detail. Its four members were Sir Percy Cox, General Scott, Colonel Cornwallis[1] and Colonel Lawrence. They recommended that a total of £248,000 a year should be spent in subsidies, of which the bulk—£100,000 each—should be paid to Ibn Saud and Hussein. The Sub-Committee pointed out that Ibn Saud's subsidy would probably be as large 'as the total revenues of his Government from other sources', and would therefore act as a means of encouraging him to restrain the warlike desires of his desert followers. The subsidy to Hussein, the Sub-Committee believed, should only be granted if Hussein would promise not to allow the Muslim Holy Places at Mecca 'to become a focus for anti-British or pan-Islamic intrigue'.

On the evening of March 16 Churchill and his wife were Lord Allenby's guests at a ball. The *Palestine Weekly* reported on how Mrs Churchill danced several times, until, 'close on midnight', Sir Herbert Samuel arrived direct from Jerusalem. As soon as Samuel arrived, the newspaper continued, 'Mr Churchill at once went upstairs with him and they were seen no more. . . .' Samuel's arrival was the signal for the opening of the discussion on Palestine. On the morning of March 17 the Palestine Political and Military Committee held its first meeting, with Churchill in the chair. He began the meeting by asking Major Young to read out the memorandum prepared by the Middle East Department in London. When the reading was over Churchill pointed out that the decision to separate Transjordan from Palestine had 'been arrived at after considerable discussion'.

Samuel's first reaction to the creation of an independent Transjordan was one of hostility. The area had, he pointed out, been included by the League of Nations in the British Mandate for Palestine, and should not be regarded 'as an independent Arab State'. He feared that if Abdullah became King, he would incite the Arabs to continue fighting against the French. Samuel also warned that there was 'some probability of controversy in Palestine for some years on the question of Zionism', and that Abdullah might encourage anti-Zionist agitation 'and thus prove a danger'.

[1] Kinahan Cornwallis, 1883–1959. Member of the Sudan Civil Service, 1906–14; of the Egyptian Civil Service, 1914–24. Director of the Arab Bureau, 1916–20. A member of Ronald Storrs' delegation to Arabia which helped to inaugurate the Arab revolt, 1916. Liaison officer to the Emir Feisal, 1918. Chief Political Officer, Egyptian Expeditionary Force, 1919. Colonel, 1919. Seconded to the Foreign Office, London, 1920–1. Seconded to the Iraq Government, 1921. Adviser to the Minister of the Interior, Iraq, 1921–35. Knighted, 1929. Ambassador to Baghdad, 1934–45. His younger son was killed in action in 1945. Chairman of the Middle East Committee of the Foreign Office, 1945–6.

Churchill did not accept Samuel's arguments. The Mesopotamian solution must also be tried in Transjordan, he said. A Sherifian candidate was essential. To support Feisal in Mesopotamia, but to refuse to support his brother in Transjordan, 'would be courting trouble', especially if, by subsidizing Abdullah's father in the Hedjaz, and paying Ibn Saud not to attack the Hedjaz, 'we could obtain general peace and prosperity in Arabia'. Abdullah's rule in Transjordan, encouraged and controlled by Britain, was part of the wider scheme already decided upon. 'It seemed inevitable,' Churchill told Samuel, 'that in these circumstances we should adopt a policy elsewhere which would harmonize with our Mesopotamian policy.'

Churchill then sought to allay Samuel's fears of anti-Zionist activity conducted from Transjordan. The decisions of the Cairo Conference would, he said, place the whole Sherifian family—Hussein, Feisal and Abdullah—'under an obligation to His Majesty's Government in one sphere or another'. In order 'to guarantee that there would be no anti-Zionist disturbances' it was essential to support Abdullah either with money or troops. 'Abdullah's moral influence,' Churchill added, 'was of great importance.'

T. E. Lawrence shared Churchill's view that any anti-Zionist agitation could be kept under control. Indeed, he believed that one of the reasons why Abdullah was an ideal candidate for Transjordan was that he would be able to exert pressure on the local Arabs to refrain from anti-Zionist activity. According to the Minutes, Lawrence told the Committee that:

He trusted that in four or five years, under the influence of a just policy, the opposition to Zionism would have decreased, if it had not entirely disappeared, and it was his view that it would be preferable to use Trans-Jordania as a safety valve, by appointing a ruler on whom he could bring pressure to bear, to check anti-Zionism. The ideal would be a person who was not too powerful, and who was not an inhabitant of Trans-Jordania, but who relied upon His Majesty's Government for the retention of his office. . . .

Sherif Abdullah, by reason of his position and lineage, possessed very considerable power for good or harm over the tribesmen. This would not be the case with a local townsman who was the only other alternative. . . .

Herbert Samuel was out-argued and outmanoeuvred. His Chief Secretary, Wyndham Deedes,[1] was likewise unable to influence the

[1] Wyndham Henry Deedes, 1883–1956. 2nd Lieutenant, King's Royal Rifles, 1901. On active service in South Africa, 1901–2. Seconded to the Turkish Gendarmerie, 1910–14. Intelligence Department, War Office, 1914–15. Intelligence Officer, Gallipoli, 1915; Egypt, 1916–17; Palestine, 1917–18. Entered Jerusalem with General Allenby, 11 December 1917. Organized relief for the Jewish colonies in Palestine, 1917–18. Military Attaché,

conclusions which Churchill and the Middle East Department had reached. Deedes stated bluntly that he was 'opposed to the appointment of Sherif Abdullah'. But he then agreed that 'if the issue was prejudiced' by Abdullah's presence in Amman, 'the only course was to accept his appointment as a *fait accompli*'. Churchill at once asked Major Somerset[1] whether, if Abdullah were not appointed, Britain would be able to remove him from Amman. Somerset replied that it would be 'impossible to get rid of Abdullah in the event of his not being appointed'. He added that it would be equally impossible to remove Abdullah 'if he refused to agree to the conditions of his appointment'. Abdullah's nomination was clearly inevitable. Churchill told the Committee that he hoped, in view of the support Britain was giving his father and his brother, that Abdullah, 'with the help of a small force', would set up a stable Government, and agree to use his influence 'to prevent anti-French and anti-Zionist propaganda in Trans-Jordania'.

Later that day the Palestine Military Committee held its first meeting, presided over by General Congreve.

The Committee recommended that the troops needed for Transjordan should be taken from those allocated for Palestine, thus reducing the Palestine garrison to 7,000 men. On March 18, at the second meeting of the Palestine Military Committee, Sir Herbert Samuel spoke in favour of a Jewish force, to be employed inside Palestine in Jewish areas, which would enable the Jews 'to share in bearing the brunt of defending their National Home'. The creation of such a Defence Force would also, Samuel stressed, 'provide against the possible eventuality that British troops, at some period of difficulty for the Empire, might be wholly, or almost wholly, withdrawn'. But General Congreve said that while he would agree to a Jewish 'gendarmerie' being set up to defend Jewish settlements against local Arab attacks, he was totally opposed to the idea of a Jewish 'army' in Palestine.

On March 19, during the sixth meeting of the Combined Political and Military Committee—which had hitherto dealt only with Mesopotamia —Samuel was present when Churchill challenged the conclusion of General Congreve's Committee on the Palestine Defence Force.

Constantinople, 1918–19. Director-General of Public Security, Egypt, 1919–20. Chief Secretary to the Administration, Palestine, 1920–3. Knighted, 1921.

[1] FitzRoy Richard Somerset, 1885–1964. 2nd Lieutenant, Grenadier Guards, 1905. Employed with the Egyptian Army, 1913–19. Assistant Political Officer, Egyptian Expeditionary Force, Palestine, 1919–21. British Representative in Transjordan, 1920–1. Succeeded his father as 4th Baron Raglan, 1921. Retired from the Army, 1922. Commissioner for Boy Scouts, 1927–54. President, Royal Anthropological Institute, 1955–7. President, National Museum of Wales, 1957–62. Author of several books on religion, myth and anthropology.

Churchill realized, he said, that Congreve himself favoured the limited commitment of a Jewish gendarmerie, rather than a Jewish army. But, he added, 'bearing in mind the world-wide character of the Zionist movement, and the desire expressed by the Jews to help in their own defence, it would be better to decide upon troops'. There followed a lengthy altercation between Congreve and Samuel about what uniform the force should wear. In the event, no such force was created.

The Cairo Conference discussions on Palestine and Transjordan were at an end. In three days, two new Arab States had been created, their sovereigns chosen, and part of the Zionist case lost by default.

On March 17 it was announced in London that Bonar Law had been forced to resign from the Government on account of ill-health. The news reached Cairo on March 18. Churchill at once telegraphed to Bonar Law:

Most profoundly grieved hear your resignation and of its cause. This is very great blow to country and to Government. I feel also keen sense of personal loss on account of your unvarying kindness and comradeship to me during all these difficult years, especially when you in the teeth of much opposition enabled Prime Minister to include me in Government and thus to take responsible part in concluding stages of war.

The pages of history will often be scanned to find parallel your high self-sacrificing record which will long be cited as an example of the spirit in which British leaders encountered and surmounted the stresses of the war. My wife joins with me in expressing our very deep regret.

Bonar Law's resignation raised the immediate question of who was to succeed him as Leader of the House. 'Greatly grieved by Bonar's retirement,' Churchill telegraphed to Edward Marsh as soon as he heard the news. 'Let me know please how things are shaping.' On the afternoon of March 18 Edward Marsh replied that Austen Chamberlain was 'strong favourite' for Bonar Law's post. This meant that a new Chancellor of the Exchequer would have to be appointed. 'The newspapers very excited as to who should succeed Bonar,' Henry Wilson wrote in his diary on March 19, 'but they all seem to agree to Austen. . . . And if he gives up being Chancellor the papers think Worthington Evans or Horne will succeed him. Poor Winston, it is bad luck for him being at Cairo at this moment!'

Austen Chamberlain did become Leader of the House, and Lord Privy Seal. 'Winston must be furious,' Henry Wilson wrote in his diary on March 21, 'at being out at Cairo when all these political moves are being discussed & settled. I expect he will come back!' But Churchill remained in Cairo, and it was Sir Robert Horne who hurried home to London, from the south of France, on March 29. That night Worthington Evans told Henry Wilson that Horne would be the new Chancellor of the Exchequer, '& failing him then Baldwin,[1] a Treasury Official'. Worthington Evans told Wilson that if Baldwin succeeded Chamberlain, the appointment 'would be a scandal'. But both proposals, he added, 'are meant to keep out Winston!' On April 1, while Churchill was still in the Middle East, Sir Robert Horne was appointed Chancellor of the Exchequer, and Stanley Baldwin brought into the Cabinet as Horne's successor at the Board of Trade.

On March 19 Churchill himself took the Chair at the sixth meeting of the Combined Political and Military Committee, when he insisted that the Government of Mesopotamia must, after a few years, be prepared 'to pay a certain contribution' towards the cost of the British troops stationed there. In answer to Churchill's request, Sir Percy Cox under-undertook to 'bear in mind' the principle which this request involved. Churchill then pointed out that the formation of an Arab Army should 'in itself, provide a considerable relief to the Imperial garrison'.

On Sunday March 20 the Cairo Conference adjourned for a day, its first break since it had begun on March 12. Churchill and his wife set off with T. E. Lawrence and Gertrude Bell to see the Pyramids, and were photographed riding on camels in front of the Sphinx. Churchill also found time to set up his easel, and begin painting. The *Palestine Weekly* gave a glimpse of the day's activities. While riding on his camel, it reported, Churchill 'was thrown by his mount and grazed his hand badly, but insisted on continuing, made several sketches at Sakkara, and accompanied by Colonel Lawrence, camelled back to Mena House, the rest of the party preferring to make the return by car'.

During the day Lawrence found time to write to his brother Bob[2] from the Semiramis hotel, describing his time in Cairo as 'one of the

[1] Stanley Baldwin, 1867–1947. Conservative MP, 1908–37. Financial Secretary to the Treasury, 1917–21. President of the Board of Trade, 1921–2. Chancellor of the Exchequer (in succession to Sir Robert Horne), 1922–3. Prime Minister, 1923–4, 1924–9 and 1935–7. Created Earl, 1937.

[2] Montague Robert Lawrence, 1885–1972. Lawrence's eldest brother, he was at the Oxford High School with him, 1896–1904. Served in the Royal Army Medical Corps, in France, 1916–19. Shortly after the Cairo Conference he went as a missionary to China.

longest fortnights I ever lived'. And he continued: 'Here we live in a marble & bronze hotel, very expensive & luxurious: horrible place: makes me Bolshevik. . . . We have done a lot of work, which is almost finished. . . . We're a very happy family: agreed upon everything important: and the trifles are laughed at.'

Fifty years later Joseph Crosland's wife Jessie[1] recalled some of the less official moments of the Conference:

When things were boring in the Hotel everyone would cheer up when Winston came in, followed by an Arab carrying a pail and a bottle of wine. . . . He was unpopular with the Egyptians—many carriages had notices '*à bas Churchill*'—but he didn't care. He took his easel out and sat in the road painting—he also talked so loudly in the street that the generals got quite nervous. He was always telling people not to give up their painting. He didn't like the Arabs coming into the Hotel, not even into the garden. . . .

On March 22, in London, the Cabinet discussed Churchill's various proposals. 'Decide to invite Feisal to take over Mesopotamia,' H. A. L. Fisher wrote in his diary. Abdullah's candidature was also approved, but the proposed British military force in Transjordan met with a rougher reception. 'We discussed Winston's proposal,' Henry Wilson wrote in his diary, 'sent from Cairo, to occupy Amman & Trans-Jordania. I was opposed—& won—on the grounds of expense and further commitment.'

The Cairo Conference came to an end on March 22. That evening Churchill and his wife were driven to see the Nile Barrage, where Churchill again set up his easel and began painting. On their return, at the village of Boulac, they collided with another car. 'The fronts of both cars were damaged,' reported the *Egyptian Gazette* two days later, 'but none of the occupants sustained any injuries', and the *Palestine Weekly* added that Churchill was 'far more concerned about the safety of his painting than about himself'.

At midnight on March 23 Churchill and his wife left Cairo by train for Palestine, accompanied by Churchill's staff, and by Sir Herbert Samuel. At Cairo station Churchill told a reporter of the *Egyptian Gazette* that although he could say nothing about the discussions, 'he had enjoyed every minute of his stay in Egypt'.

[1] Jessie Raven, 1879–1973. She married J. B. Crosland in 1904. Member of the French Department of Westfield College. Author of two textbooks on medieval French literature. Her son C. A. R. Crosland was a member of Harold Wilson's Cabinets of 1964 and 1974.

32

Visit to Jerusalem

CHURCHILL's principal object in going to Jerusalem was to discuss with Abdullah the conditions on which Britain would support him as ruler of Transjordan, and to persuade Abdullah to accept them. Early on the morning of March 24, his train reached Gaza, the first large town within the south-western boundaries of the Palestine Mandate, with a population of over 15,000 Arabs, and fewer than a hundred Jews. A police guard of honour met him and Sir Herbert Samuel at the railway crossing, and a mounted escort took them to the town. One of those who accompanied Churchill, Captain Coote,[1] later recorded:

... there was a tremendous reception by a howling mob all shouting in Arabic 'Cheers for the Minister' and also for Great Britain, but their chief cry over which they waxed quite frenzied was 'Down with the Jews', 'Cut their throats'.

Mr Churchill and Sir Herbert were delighted with the enthusiasm of their reception, being not in the least aware of what was being shouted. Lawrence, of course, understood it all and told me, but we kept very quiet. He was obviously gravely anxious about the whole situation. We toured the town, surrounded by this almost fanatical mob which was becoming more and more worked up by its shouting. No one appeared to have bargained for this, but all went off without incident.

Before rejoining their train, Churchill and Samuel were given a short reception at the local Club, where a petition was presented to Churchill, signed by the leading Muslims of the town, setting out Arab aspirations for statehood, and protesting against Jewish immigration.

[1] Maxwell H. Coote, 1895– . Served with the Royal Field Artillery at Gallipoli, 1915, and in Egypt, 1916. Transferred to the Royal Flying Corps, 1917; on active service in France, 1917, and in Egypt, 1918. Captain, 1918. Orderly Officer to Churchill at the Cairo Conference, 1921.

The Arab reaction to Churchill's arrival in Palestine did not bode well for his hopes of economy and a tranquil administration. On March 25 there were Arab demonstrations in Haifa to protest against any further Jewish settlement. The Government, which had announced a ban on all public meetings during Churchill's visit, tried to break up the demonstrations. Violence followed, and the police opened fire. Two people were killed: a thirteen-year-old Christian boy and a Muslim Arab woman. Following this police action, anti-Jewish riots broke out in the city, during which ten Jews and five policemen were injured by knives and stones.

On Sunday March 27 Churchill went to the British Military Cemetery on the Mount of Olives, where he attended a service of dedication.[1] After the service he made a short speech, which was reported in the *Egyptian Gazette* two days later:

The Colonial Minister said that he spoke with a full heart, especially as he thought of the place where they stood, on the Mount of Olives, overlooking the Holy City. It was a company of many people and diverse faiths which had met to commemorate the victorious dead, who had given their lives to liberate the land and to bring about peace and amity amongst its inhabitants, but there remained the duty and responsibility on those who were present to see that the task was completed. . . .

'These veteran soldiers,' said Mr Churchill, 'lie here where rests the dust of the Khalifs and Crusaders and the Maccabees. . . . Peace to their ashes, honour to their memory and may we not fail to complete the work which they have begun'.

The ceremony ended with three volleys fired by a guard of honour, and the sounding of the last post.

That afternoon Churchill prepared for his discussions with the Emir Abdullah. In order to make sure that Abdullah knew what Britain intended, Churchill asked Lawrence to meet the Emir in advance. That Sunday, Lawrence and Abdullah met at Es Salt, east of the Jordan.

Abdullah reached Jerusalem during the afternoon of March 27. His first engagement was to have tea with Sir Herbert Samuel. That evening he dined with Samuel, and was introduced to Churchill. In his memoirs, Abdullah recalled how, during dinner, Churchill had spoken of an attack by Arab tribesmen in northern Transjordan on some French

[1] The cemetery was established at the end of 1917. It contains the graves of 2,180 British soldiers, 143 Australians, 50 South Africans, 40 men from the British West Indies, 34 from New Zealand, 65 men whose units are unknown, 16 Germans, 5 Italians and 3 Turks.

border police. 'I hear there was an attack by a band of brigands,' Churchill said, 'and murder was committed. My Government attributes this to your influence, but luckily I have two broad shoulders to carry the Government's protest for you.' Abdullah replied that he knew nothing of the incident, but added: 'I cannot ever, of course, prevent people from defending their own country.'

On Monday March 28 Churchill welcomed Abdullah to Government House in Jerusalem for their second meeting. Churchill began the discussion by saying that he wished to revert to the British policy of the war years 'of supporting Arab nationality on constructive lines, using the Sherifian family as a medium'. But, he continued, there were parts of the Arab world in which this policy could not be carried out, owing to 'the decisions of the Allies and to promises made to third parties'. These parts were Syria, which the French had decided to administer, and Palestine 'west of the Jordan', in which the Jews had been promised room for a national home. Churchill went on to say that he would like to see the Sherifian family—Hussein, Feisal and Abdullah himself— in 'a predominant position' throughout the Arab world, 'so far as this was compatible with the above exceptions'. Abdullah replied that he 'accepted the fact' that Britain was not 'free to act in Syria and in Western Palestine'.

Churchill then thanked Abdullah for supporting his brother's claims to Mesopotamia. For his part, Feisal had likewise made it clear that he would not stand in Abdullah's way in Transjordan. This attitude, Churchill remarked, 'reflected great credit on Feisal and Abdullah alike'.

The discussion turned to Transjordan. Churchill told Abdullah that while Britain 'recognized its Arab character', the country was, territorially, 'too small to stand alone'. It was Britain's belief that both economically and geographically, Transjordan 'should go with Palestine', as 'an Arab province under an Arab Governor responsible to the High Commissioner for Palestine'. Abdullah favoured a different solution, telling Churchill that if Britain would agree to an Arab Emir ruling both Palestine and Transjordan, 'he was convinced that the present difficulties between Arabs and Jews would be most easily overcome'. Churchill did not enter into the merits or difficulties of Abdullah's proposal, telling him bluntly, as the Minutes recorded: 'He did not himself think it possible for His Majesty's Government to adopt the Emir's proposal. They were already too far committed in advance to a different system.'

Abdullah repeated that, in his view, an Arab Emir in Palestine was the best solution 'to reconcile the Arabs and the Jews'. And he went on to tell Churchill of his fears:

He would very much like to know what British policy really aimed at. Did His Majesty's Government mean to establish a Jewish kingdom west of the Jordan and to turn out the non-Jewish population? If so, it would be better to tell the Arabs at once and not to keep them in suspense. Mr Churchill had referred to the decisions of the Allies; these were not, in his opinion, beyond challenge. The Allies appeared to think that men could be cut down and transplanted in the same way as trees.

At this point Sir Herbert Samuel intervened to say 'that there was no intention either to cut down or to transplant, but only to plant new ones'. Churchill then sought to put Abdullah's mind at rest:

Mr Churchill said that there was, in his opinion, a great deal of groundless apprehension among the Arabs in Palestine. They appeared to anticipate that hundreds and thousands of Jews were going to pour into the country in a very short time and dominate the existing population. This was not only not contemplated, but quite impossible. There were at present over 500,000 Moslems in Palestine and not more than 80,000 Jews. Jewish immigration would be a very slow process and the rights of the existing non-Jewish population would be strictly preserved.

Churchill went on to tell Abdullah that if he promised not to interfere with Zionist activity in Western Palestine, the British Government would promise that the Zionist clauses of the Mandate 'would not apply' in Transjordan, and that the Transjordan Government 'would not be expected to adopt any measures to promote Jewish immigration and colonization'. This promise effectively destroyed Weizmann's appeal for Jewish economic development east of the Jordan, and ended Zionist hopes of being able to extend the area of their settlement into the biblical lands of Bashan and Gilead.[1]

Churchill went on to warn Abdullah against refusing to accept the Transjordan solution:

He wished the Emir to understand that he was taking a great responsibility as the new Minister in charge of the Middle East in advising his colleagues to join hands with the Sherifian family. He had been advised by certain other people that this was a very dangerous policy. He had been told that His Majesty's Government would be better advised to split up the Arabs into distinct and separate Local Governments. This had been the policy of Rome and of Turkey in the past and appeared to be to some extent the policy of other Powers at the present time. He wished to impress upon the Emir that a

[1] See map on p. 542.

very grave choice had to be made within the next few days by His Majesty's Government, namely, whether they should divide or unite the Arab peoples with whom they had to deal.

The Emir replied that he appreciated and was much struck by the policy outlined by Mr Churchill. He still thought that his own suggestion about combining Palestine and Trans-Jordania under an Arab Emir was the best, but he was quite prepared to consider the matter in the light of the new proposals that had been made.

In a further effort to persuade Abdullah of the fairness of the British proposals, Sir Herbert Samuel explained British policy in Western Palestine to him, as far as the position of the Arabs was concerned. According to Samuel:

There was no question of setting up a Jewish Government there. The present administration would, he hoped, continue for many years—with the modification that many more local officials would gradually be employed. All religions would be equally respected. No land would be taken from any Arab, nor would the Moslem religion be touched in any way. The Mandate embodied the terms of the Balfour Declaration in which two distinct promises were made—one to the Jews and the other to the Arabs. His Majesty's Government were resolutely determined to fulfil both these promises. . . .

Abdullah was apparently impressed by Samuel's exposition, and, according to the Minutes of the conversation, thanked him 'warmly' for what he had said, adding that he had himself 'heard nothing but praise of the High Commissioner and his Administration'. The meeting then adjourned.

The Arabs of Palestine did not intend to await the outcome of Churchill's discussions with Abdullah. They had already sent a delegation to Cairo, where on March 22, Churchill had told them to see him in Jerusalem in six days time. Thus, on March 28, the Executive Committee of the Haifa Congress of Palestinian Arabs called to see Churchill, and presented him with a twelve-thousand-word memorandum, protesting bitterly against Zionist activity in Palestine. The Arab, they declared, 'is noble and large-hearted; he is also vengeful, and never forgets an ill-deed. If England does not take up the cause of the Arabs, other Powers will. From India, Mesopotamia, the Hedjaz and Palestine the cry goes up to England now. If she does not listen, then perhaps Russia will take up their call some day, or perhaps even Germany.' The voice of Russia, the Arabs declared, 'is not heard in the councils of the nations, yet the time must come when it will assert itself'.

The Arab memorandum warned that the 'unnatural partitioning' of their lands must one day disappear. Britain must befriend the Arab cause, for the Arabs 'are the key to the East. They possess its doors and passes. Arabia, on the Red Sea and the Persian Gulf, is the way to India, and Palestine, on the Mediterranean, holds today the balance between the Powers.'

In their memorandum, the Arabs sought to prove 'that Palestine belongs to the Arabs, and that the Balfour Declaration is a gross injustice'. As for the Jewish National Home, they declared:

For thousands of years Jews have been scattered over the earth, and have become nationals of the various nations amongst whom they settled. They have no separate political or lingual existence. In Germany they are Germans, in France Frenchmen, and in England Englishmen. Religion and language are their only tie. But Hebrew is a dead language and might be discarded. How then could England conclude a treaty with a religion and register it in the League of Nations? Nay, rather, how could the Jews themselves agree to this treaty? For if there exists a Jewish Power and a Jewish nation, what is the status, amongst others, of those high Jewish officials who are serving England to-day? Are they Jewish nationals or English nationals, for it is obvious they cannot be both at the same time?

The Arab memorandum went on to criticize the appointment of Sir Herbert Samuel as High Commissioner, and of Lord Reading as Viceroy. 'Now if Jew-ism is a nationality,' it asked, 'what about their English-ism. One must be sacrificed for the other, but which for which?' And the memorandum continued:

Jews have been amongst the most active advocates of destruction in many lands, especially where their influential positions have enabled them to do more harm. It is well known that the disintegration of Russia was wholly or in great part brought about by the Jews, and a large proportion of the defeat of Germany and Austria must also be put at their door. When the star of the Central Powers was in the ascendant Jews flattered them, but the moment the scale turned in favour of the Allies Jews withdrew their support from Germany, opened their coffers to the Allies, and received in return that most uncommon promise. . . .

The Jew, moreover, is clannish and unneighbourly, and cannot mix with those who live about him. He will enjoy the privileges and benefits of a country, but will give nothing in return. The Jew is a Jew all the world over. He amasses the wealth of a country and then leads its people, whom he has already impoverished, where he chooses. He encourages wars when self-interest dictates, and thus uses the armies of the nations to do his bidding.

The Arabs went on to warn Churchill of what they feared would happen to the Mandate in the years to come:

Zionists are ambitious. If to-day they accept the mandate of England they may not do so to-morrow. Their one aim is to establish a Jewish kingdom, bring back the glory of Israel in the 'Land of Promise' and gradually control the world. . . .

The Arab memorandum concluded with an appeal to Churchill to agree to five specific requests, 'in the name of justice and right'. These were:

First: The principle of a National Home for the Jews be abolished.

Second: A National Government be created, which shall be responsible to a Parliament elected by the Palestinian people who existed in Palestine before the war.

Third: A stop be put to Jewish immigration until such a time as a National Government is formed.

Fourth: Laws and regulations before the war be still carried out and all others framed after the British occupation be annulled, and no new laws be created until a National Government comes into being.

Fifth: Palestine should not be separated from her sister States.

These five requests had been circulated in the form of a mass petition before Churchill's arrival in Palestine, and several hundred signatures had been sent on to him at Cairo on March 14. The rest of the petition was now handed to Churchill by a deputation led by the President of the Haifa Congress, Musa Kazim Pasha al-Husseini.[1]

Churchill replied at once, both to the petition, and to the Arab memorandum. There were, he told the deputation, a great many 'statements of fact' in the Arab memorandum 'which we do not think are true'. It must be taken, he added, 'as a partisan statement . . . rather than as a calm judicial summing up of what is best for us all to do in the difficult circumstances in which we find ourselves'. Churchill then set out his own view of the Arab appeal:

You have asked me in the first place to repudiate the Balfour Declaration and to veto immigration of Jews into Palestine. It is not in my power to do so, nor, if it were in my power, would it be my wish. The British Government have passed their word, by the mouth of Mr Balfour, that they will view with

---

[1] Musa Kazim Pasha al-Husseini, 1847–1934. A member of one of the leading Muslim families of Jerusalem. Served the Turks as an administrator in Syria, Mesopotamia and Palestine. Governor of Jaffa, and then Mayor of Jerusalem under both the Turks and the British. A leading anti-Zionist, in 1920 he opposed the recognition of Hebrew as one of the three official languages of Palestine (with English and Arabic). Believed by the British to have been largely responsible for the anti-Jewish riots of April 1920 in Jerusalem; relieved of his position as Mayor. President of the Congress of Arab Palestinians, 1920. President of the Haifa Arab Congress, 1921. Leader of the Palestine Arab Delegation to London, 1921–2. President of the World Muslim Congress, Jerusalem, 1931.

favour the establishment of a National Home for Jews in Palestine, and that inevitably involves the immigration of Jews into the country. This declaration of Mr Balfour and of the British Government has been ratified by the Allied Powers who have been victorious in the Great War; and it was a declaration made while the war was still in progress, while victory and defeat hung in the balance. It must therefore be regarded as one of the facts definitely established by the triumphant conclusion of the Great War. . . .

Moreover, it is manifestly right that the Jews, who are scattered all over the world, should have a national centre and a National Home where some of them may be reunited. And where else could that be but in this land of Palestine, with which for more than 3,000 years they have been intimately and profoundly associated? We think it will be good for the world, good for the Jews and good for the British Empire. But we also think it will be good for the Arabs who dwell in Palestine, and we intend that it shall be good for them, and that they shall not be sufferers or supplanted in the country in which they dwell or denied their share in all that makes for its progress and prosperity. And here I would draw your attention to the second part of the Balfour Declaration, which solemnly and explicitly promises to the inhabitants of Palestine the fullest protection of their civil and political rights.

Churchill pointed out that it was not the Arabs of Palestine who had overthrown the Turks. 'It has been the armies of Britain,' he declared, 'which have liberated these regions. . . . The position of Great Britain in Palestine is one of trust, but it is also one of right. For the discharge of that trust and for the high purposes we have in view, supreme sacrifices were made by all these soldiers of the British Empire, who gave up their lives and blood.' On the road to Government House, he added, was the graveyard of over 2,000 British soldiers, 'and there are many other graveyards, some even larger, scattered about in this land'.

Churchill went on to say that the British Government were determined to give the Zionist movement 'a fair chance' in Palestine:

If a National Home for the Jews is to be established in Palestine, as we hope to see it established, it can only be by a process which at every stage wins its way on its merits and carries with it increasing benefits and prosperity and happiness to the people of the country as a whole. And why should this not be so? Why should this not be possible? You can see with your own eyes in many parts of this country the work which has already been done by Jewish colonies; how sandy wastes have been reclaimed and thriving farms and orangeries planted in their stead. It is quite true that they have been helped by money from outside, whereas your people have not had a similar advantage, but surely these funds of money largely coming from outside and being devoted to the increase of the general prosperity of Palestine is one of the very reasons which should lead you to take a wise and tolerant view of the Zionist movement.

The paper which you have just read painted a golden picture of the delight-ful state of affairs in Palestine under the Turkish rule. Every man did every-thing he pleased; taxation was light; justice was prompt and impartial; trade, commerce, education, the arts all flourished. It was a wonderful picture. But it had no relation whatever to the truth, for otherwise why did the Arab race rebel against this heavenly condition? Obviously the picture has been over-drawn. And what is the truth?

This country has been very much neglected in the past and starved and even mutilated by Turkish misgovernment. There is no reason why Palestine should not support a larger number of people than it does at present, and all of those in a higher condition of prosperity.

But you will say to me, are we to be led by the hopes of material gain into letting ourselves be dispossessed in our own house by enormous numbers of strangers brought together across the seas from all over the world? My answer is; no, that will not be, that will never be. Jewish immigration into Palestine can only come as it makes a place for itself by legitimate and honourable means; as it provides the means by which it is to be supported.

The task before the Zionists is one of extraordinary difficulty. The present form of Government will continue for many years, and step by step we shall develop representative institutions leading up to full self-government. All of us here to-day will have passed away from the earth and also our children and our children's children before it is fully achieved.

The Jews will need the help of the Arabs at every stage, and I think you would be wise to give them your help and your aid and encourage them in their difficulties. They may fail. If they are not guided by wisdom and good-will, if they do not tread the path of justice and tolerance and neighbourliness, if the class of men who come in are not worthy of the Jewish race, then they will fail and there will be an end of the experiment. But on the other hand, if they succeed, and in proportion as they do succeed year by year, such success can only be accompanied by a general diffusion of wealth and well-being among all the dwellers in Palestine and by an advance in the social, scientific and cultural life of the people as a whole.

At the end of his reply, Churchill told the Arab deputation: 'If instead of sharing miseries through quarrels you will share blessings through cooperation, a bright and tranquil future lies before your country. The earth is a generous mother. She will produce in plentiful abundance for all her children if they will but cultivate her soil in justice and in peace.'

The Arab deputation withdrew, its appeal rejected, its arguments rebutted.[1] A Jewish deputation followed in its place. They too presented

[1] The Arab reaction to Churchill's remarks was a hostile one. On April 9 a leading Arab, Mohamed Osman, described them as 'vindictive, contemptuous and disconcerting'. And he added: 'His words are the words of a dictator and not an adviser as he professes to have been.'

a memorandum, signed by the executive of the recently established Jewish National Council. The Jewish memorandum expressed gratitude to the British for helping to rebuild 'the National Home of Israel', and pointed out that the Zionist programme 'lays special stress on the establishing of sincere friendship between ourselves and the Arabs'. The Jewish people, it added, 'returning after 2,000 years of exile and persecution to its own homeland, cannot suffer the suspicion that it wishes to deny to another nation its rights'. The Jewish memorandum continued:

The Jewish people have full understanding of the aspirations of the Arabs with regard to a national revival, but we know that by our efforts to rebuild the Jewish National Home in Palestine, which is but a small area in comparison with all the Arab lands, we do not deprive them of their legitimate rights. On the contrary, we are convinced that a Jewish renaissance in this country can only have a strong and invigorating influence upon the Arab nation. Our kinship in language, race, character and history give the assurance that we shall in due course come to a complete understanding with them. . . .

The history of Jewish colonisation in Palestine is a proof of the great advantages which Jewish work has brought to the inhabitants of the country. The colonies established by Jews in the course of the last forty years have changed waste areas into flourishing gardens; sandy plains, which were not or were only to a very small degree cultivated have been turned into fertile fields and colonies, the orchards and gardens of which are now worth millions of pounds and give work and food to many people. These areas, in which formerly only the herds of the wandering Bedouins grazed, and then only during a few weeks of the year, have now become closely populated settlements with factories and industries. . . .

Through these colonies many thousands of non-Jews of the neighbourhood earn a living. Experts in all branches of science and industries are devoting their energy, their experience, and their knowledge to the development of the land, and their methods are being copied by their neighbours. Swamps which formerly bred disease and which played havoc with the first Jewish pioneers have now been changed into flourishing settlements. Industries, which were unknown in this country have been established and introduced by Jews, such as iron works, cement works, factories for building materials, furniture and joinery, machinery, mills, wine cellars, soap works, and printing houses. New towns have been built according to modern ideas and taste. The commerce of the country has been greatly developed, and its branches have

---

In his book *Palestine the Reality*, J. M. N. Jeffries wrote of how Churchill 'talked impatiently to Arab deputations, as though his hearers were boys or minors, who understood nothing and were being tiresome and perverse, and must have what was for their good told to them sharply'.

spread and widened. Parallel with the great influx of Jewish immigrants, non-Jewish production has been developed and the standard of agriculture has been raised. . . .

In his reply to the Jewish deputation, Churchill began by explaining that he had already told the Muslim deputation 'quite plainly' that there could be 'no question of our departing from the principles enunciated by Mr Balfour in his declaration'. As for his own view of the Jewish National Home, he added, 'I am myself perfectly convinced that the cause of Zionism is one which carries with it much that is good for the whole world, and not only for the Jewish people, but that it will also bring with it prosperity and contentment and advancement to the Arab population of this country. . . .'

Churchill then spoke of Arab fears; fear of being dispossessed of their lands and property, of being 'supplanted from their rights', and of being put 'under the rule of those who are now in a minority, but who will be reinforced by large numbers of strangers coming from over the seas'. The Arabs had also expressed alarm, he said, at the character of some of the new Jewish immigrants, 'whom they accuse of bringing Bolshevik doctrines'. It was the duty of the Jews, Churchill added, 'to dispel' these fears. He continued:

When I go back to London, I have no doubt I shall be told that but for the Zionist movement there would be no need to keep up such a large British garrison, at so great an expense, in this country. You must provide me with the means, and the Jewish community all over the world must provide me with the means of answering all adverse criticism.

I wish to be able to say that a great event is taking place here, a great event in the world's destiny. It is taking place without injury or injustice to anyone; it is transforming waste places into fertile; it is planting trees and developing agriculture in desert lands; it is making for an increase in wealth and of cultivation; it is making two blades of grass grow where one grew before, and the people of the country who are in a majority, are deriving great benefit, sharing in the general improvement and advancement. There is co-operation and fraternity between the religions and the races; the Jews who are being brought from Europe and elsewhere are worthy representatives of Jewry and of the cause of Zionism, and the Zionists are taking every step to secure that that shall be so.

The pioneers in a matter of this sort must be picked men, worthy in every way of the greatness of the ideal and of the cause for which they are striving, and in that way you will give me the means of answering effectively those who wish to prevent this experiment and cause from having its fair chance. . . .

I earnestly hope that your cause may be carried to success. I know how great the energy is and how serious are the difficulties at every stage and you have my warmest sympathy in the efforts you are making to overcome them. If I did not believe that you were animated by the very highest spirit of justice and idealism, and that your work would in fact confer blessings upon the whole country, I should not have the high hopes which I have that eventually your work will be accomplished.

One of the Jewish delegation, Dr Ruppin,[1] recorded in his diary that Churchill's remarks 'made a great impression on all present, as we had been afraid that he had been influenced against us by the Arabs'. That night Churchill was Ruppin's guest at a reception given in his honour by the leading Zionists in Jerusalem.

On the morning of March 29 Churchill saw Abdullah for the third time. The Emir declared that the French would fear trouble in Syria, stimulated from across the Transjordan border. But Churchill stressed in reply that Britain was determined to see 'that the French were not annoyed from Trans-Jordania'. Later that morning Churchill was present at a meeting in Government House to discuss the possibility of a Palestine Defence Force. The Cabinet, Churchill explained, 'is very averse to the idea of spending seven million on the defence of Palestine'. The Jews and Arabs must form their own militia. Samuel suggested that in any appeal for men, the Jews would come forward 'in large numbers, which cannot be said for the Arabs'. Many Jews, he added, had already had military experience, either in the British or Russian armies. General Costello[2] agreed; Jewish troops, he said, 'were quite up to the level of the Indian army', whereas militia service, he asserted, 'was not suitable to men of the Arab type, as shown by experience on the Indian frontier'. Churchill then declared bluntly: 'I want you to have a Jewish battalion which will be a credit to the Jews and to the British. . . .' He therefore favoured long service, in order to develop discipline 'and a soldierly spirit'. But Sir Herbert Samuel believed that

[1] Arthur Ruppin, 1876–1943. Born in the Posen district of Germany. Studied law and economics at Berlin and Halle universities, 1899–1902. Director of the Berlin Bureau for Jewish Statistics and Demography, 1903–7. First visited Palestine, 1907. Head of the Palestine Office of the Zionist Executive, 1908; a pioneer of Jewish agricultural settlement and land purchase. Forced by the Turks to leave Palestine, 1916, he settled in Constantinople, 1916–20. Member of the Zionist Executive, 1921–7 and 1929–31. Head of Brit Shalom, which sought to reconcile Arabs and Jews and establish a bi-national state in Palestine, 1925–9. Head of the Jewish Agency Department for the Settlement of German Immigrants, 1933–5. Director of the Institute of Economic Research, established by the Jewish Agency, 1935.

[2] Edmond William Costello, 1873–1949. A contemporary of Churchill at Sandhurst. 2nd Lieutenant, 1892. Won the Victoria Cross in the Malakand, 1897. Served in the Mohmand campaign, 1908. Major, 1910. On active service in Mesopotamia, 1915–18, and in Palestine, 1918. Brigadier-General, 1918. Commanded the Indian Contingent at the Paris Peace Celebration, 1919. Commanded the Palestine Defence Force, 1921. Subsequently Director of Military Studies, Cambridge University.

if it were a long-service force, with, say, a three-year enlistment, 'the Arabs will enlist and the Jews won't'. The Jews, he added, 'don't want to be soldiers, they want to cultivate the land. They do not come here with the idea of spending three years in the army.' Churchill was not deterred in his advocacy of long-term service: 'He thought it would be a very good thing if many of the Jews on first arriving in the country did a certain amount of service.'

No final decision was reached. But Churchill was insistent upon the need to reduce Imperial defence expenditure, and find some means of building up a local Defence Force.

At noon on March 29 Abdullah visited the Mosque of Omar. Outside the Mosque he tried to speak to a large crowd of Arabs who had gathered to see him, but was interrupted by shouts of 'Palestine for the Arabs' and 'Down with the Zionists'. The crowd then marched to the General Post Office to demonstrate against the Balfour declaration, but were dispersed by the police.

During the afternoon of March 29 Churchill visited the site of the still uncompleted Hebrew University, a project which had long been a part of Zionist aspirations. Three years earlier, on 24 July 1918, Weizmann himself had laid one of the first twelve foundation stones on Mount Scopus. Since 1918 the building and planning had continued, although, at the time of Churchill's visit, it was far from completed.

For the Jews, Churchill's visit to the site was an important landmark in the university's progress. Although the visit had only been arranged the night before, all Jewish shops in the city had closed, and shop-keepers mingled with boy scouts and girl guides in the throng. On his arrival at the site, Churchill was greeted by Nahum Sokolow, who told him: 'The Jews are not content to live on terms of peace with the Arabs, but must live on terms of cordiality and fraternity.'

Churchill was then asked to plant a tree. Before doing so, he was given a scroll of the Law. After receiving the gift he declared:

Personally, my heart is full of sympathy for Zionism. This sympathy has existed for a long time, since twelve years ago, when I was in contact with the Manchester Jews. I believe that the establishment of a Jewish National Home in Palestine will be a blessing to the whole world, a blessing to the Jewish race scattered all over the world, and a blessing to Great Britain. I firmly believe that it will be a blessing also to all the inhabitants of this country without distinction of race and religion. This last blessing depends greatly upon you. Our promise was a double one. On the one hand, we promised to give our help to Zionism, and on the other, we assured the non-Jewish inhabitants that they should not suffer in consequence. Every step you take should therefore be also for moral and material benefit of all Palestinians. If you do this, Palestine will be happy and prosperous, and peace and concord will always reign; it will turn into a paradise, and will become, as is written in the scriptures you have just presented to me, a land flowing with milk and honey, in which sufferers of all races and religions will find a rest from their sufferings. You Jews of Palestine have a very great responsibility; you are the representatives of the Jewish nation all over the world, and your conduct should provide an example for, and do honour to, Jews in all countries.

The hope of your race for so many centuries will be gradually realised here, not only for your own good, but for the good of all the world.

Once more I thank you for the present you have given me, and for the kind reception you have organised in my honour.

I am now going to plant a tree, and I hope that in its shadow peace and prosperity may return once more to Palestine.

Churchill's speech made a profound impression on all those present. But a leading English Zionist, Harry Sacher,[1] who had recently set up a law practice in Palestine, was critical of the way the tree-planting ceremony had been arranged. On March 30 he sent a report of it to a friend in England. 'It was characteristic,' Sacher wrote, 'that Churchill was asked to plant a tree on the University site. As they were handing it to him the tree broke, and there was not even a reserve. They had to hunt abt for a measly palm—wh of course won't grow there—while Churchill looked annoyed and Samuel said "Disgusting".' Sacher was worried about the implications of some of Churchill's remarks:

Churchill spoke very plainly in reaffirming the Balfour Declaration, both to the Jews and the Arabs. But he also told the Jews that they must do their bit, and he enlarged upon the pressure of the taxpayer, and the anti-Zionist critics in Parliament. The Arabs are angry, and there was a bit of trouble in Haifa, where a demonstration was dispersed by force, perhaps too much force. I am not happy about the Arab position. . . . I am still more troubled by doubts as to whether the British Government may not finish by dropping the whole thing and clearing out—for financial reasons. I really don't know whether England today can afford such a luxury as a foreign policy, with or without mandates.

[1] Harry Sacher, 1881–1971. Born in London. Educated at New College, Oxford, Berlin University and the Sorbonne. On the editorial staff of the *Manchester Guardian*, 1905–9; the *Daily News*, 1909–15 and the *Manchester Guardian*, 1915–19. Called to the Bar, 1909. Active in Zionist circles in Manchester and London, 1909–19; one of Weizmann's closest advisers in the period before the Balfour declaration. Set up a legal practice in Palestine, 1920. Lived in Palestine, 1920–31. Legal adviser for many Zionist enterprises, including the Rutenberg concession. Member of the Executive of the World Zionist Organisation, 1927–31. Returned to England, 1932. A Director of Marks and Spencer Ltd, 1932–62. Active in charitable work, especially in relation to refugees from Nazi Germany.

'Perhaps,' Sacher added, 'we ought to discover oil here quickly, and so rope in the Admiralty.'

On the morning of March 30 Churchill held his fourth meeting with Abdullah. He proposed that the Emir should remain in Transjordan for six months, with a British Political Officer as his 'chief adviser'. Abdullah and the Political Officer would, together, restore order and 'set the revenue of the country on a proper basis'. To attain this object, Churchill would be willing to give Abdullah support in both money and troops. 'In return for this support', Abdullah would guarantee to the British 'that there should be no anti-French or anti-Zionist agitation in the country'. At the end of six months, Abdullah would appoint 'an Arab Governor' to administer Transjordan 'under the High Commissioner'.

Abdullah accepted Churchill's proposal. 'He only asked,' the Minutes recorded, 'that he might be regarded as a British officer and trusted accordingly.' He added that he might not find it easy to prevent the tribes on the Transjordan side of the Syrian border from attacking tribes on the French side; attacks, he added, 'which had nothing to do with the French being there'. Lawrence suggested that Abdullah might 'direct the attention of the raiders' against their immediate neighbours on the Transjordan side of the frontier, in which case the Franco-Syrian border would be undisturbed. Abdullah said he would try to do just that. At the end of the meeting Churchill thanked Abdullah 'for his readiness to help', and assured him 'that he would be given as far as possible a free hand in the very difficult task which he had undertaken'.

Churchill had originally planned to travel north from Jerusalem, visiting the Arab town of Nablus, the Jewish settlements in the Galilee and the port of Haifa. The Zionists were particularly keen for him to see the northern settlements. But while he was still in Jerusalem, he decided to return to England as quickly as possible, hoping that there was still a chance of his being appointed Chancellor of the Exchequer in succession to Austen Chamberlain. An Italian steamship, the *Esperia,* was due to leave Alexandria for Genoa on the morning of March 31, and Churchill rearranged his itinerary in order to be on it. Instead of going north, he left Jerusalem at midday on March 30, and was driven to the coast. Before catching the evening train to Egypt, he had time to see two of the most impressive Jewish achievements in Palestine, the town of Tel-Aviv and the agricultural colony of Rishon le-Zion.

At Tel-Aviv he was met by the head of the Town Council, Meir

Dizengoff,[1] who handed him a letter of greeting, setting out the achievements of the town: In his letter Dizengoff wrote:

This small town of Tel-Aviv, which is hardly 12 years old, has been conquered by us on sand dunes, and we have built it with our work and our exertions. It is in this manner that we are determined to render fruitful the land of our ancestors by work, by knowledge and by culture. If notwithstanding the Turkish regime and notwithstanding the war, we have been able to create such a pretty oasis in the middle of the sandy desert, what cultural values shall we not create under the protection of the Government of His Britannic Majesty. . . .

'The Jewish people,' Dizengoff added, 'will still have to speak its word in the history of civilisation.' In his speech to the people of Tel-Aviv, Churchill said that he was indeed glad to have seen 'the result of the initiative of its inhabitants in so short a period during which, too the war had intervened'.

From Tel-Aviv, Churchill went to Rishon le-Zion, less than ten miles away. On his journey he stopped briefly at Bir Yaakov, a small settlement of new immigrants. Weizmann had been very keen that Churchill should be shown a pioneer settlement, and had arranged for Pinhas Rutenberg to accompany Churchill, and to interpret for him. The new immigrants, who were all from Russia, were engaged in road building. Through Rutenberg, Churchill asked the pioneers if they were Bolsheviks. They replied that they were not. Their dedication, they said, was to the ideal of labour. They wished to build up their society on the basis of self-help and physical exertion. Churchill was much impressed.

From Bir Yaakov Churchill was driven to Rishon le-Zion, where he was welcomed by the Colony's Council, and handed a letter of greeting by one of the earliest and oldest settlers, Menaché Meerovitch,[2] who had been at the settlement since its foundation nearly thirty years before. 'When we came here in the year 1882,' Meerovitch wrote, 'we

---

[1] Meir Dizengoff, 1861–1937. Born in Bessarabia (Russia). Active in anti-Tsarist revolutionary circles. Arrested, 1885. Left Russia to study chemical engineering and glass production in France, 1886. Sent to Palestine by Baron Edmond de Rothschild to establish a glass factory, 1892. Returned to Russia, 1897. Settled in Odessa. A founder of the Geulah Company, formed in 1904 to purchase land in Palestine. Settled in Jaffa, 1905. One of the founders of Tel-Aviv, 1909. Head of the Tel-Aviv Town Council, 1910–21. Expelled to Damascus by the Turks, 1915–18. Major of Tel-Aviv, 1921–5 and 1928–37.

[2] Menaché Meerovitch, 1860–1949. Born in Nikolaev, South Russia. Trained as an agronomist in Russia. Went to Constantinople in 1882 to obtain Turkish consent to Jewish settlement in Palestine. Settled in Rishon-le-Zion, 1882. Edited the first agricultural paper in Palestine, The Farmer (in Hebrew), 1893. One of the founders of the Vintners Association, 1903 and of the Judaean Settlement Association, 1913.

found the country deserted and waste serving as a dwelling for jackals, and only here and there some meagre flocks were to be seen; and now in this very place all kinds of plantations as oranges, almonds, vines, olives etc are to be found.' Meerovitch's letter ended:

Dear Minister. You will soon return to England. We beg you to transfer to His Majesty's Government all you have seen and heard here. Your kind words we were happy to hear yesterday in Jerusalem, gave us a clear idea of your opinion and they serve us as a good guarantee to enable us to reach our aim.

Churchill toured the colony, and was impressed by what he saw. In 1882 there had been only ten settlers; by 1920 the population had reached two thousand. All around him he was struck by the enthusiasm and achievements of the colonists. Ten weeks later, on June 14, he told the House of Commons of how his visit had influenced him:

Anyone who has seen the work of the Jewish colonies which have been established during the last 20 or 30 years in Palestine will be struck by the enormous productive results which they have achieved. I had the opportunity of visiting the colony of Rishon le-Zion about 12 miles from Jaffa, and there, from the most inhospitable soil, surrounded on every side by barrenness and the most miserable form of cultivation, I was driven into a fertile and thriving country estate, where the scanty soil gave place to good crops and good cultivation, and then to vineyards and finally to the most beautiful, luxurious orange groves, all created in 20 or 30 years by the exertions of the Jewish community who live there. Then as we went on we were surrounded by 50 or 60 young Jews, galloping on their horses, and with farmers from the estate who took part in the work. Finally, when we reached the centre, there were drawn up 300 or 400 of the most admirable children, of all sizes and sexes, and about an equal number of white-clothed damsels. We were invited to sample the excellent wines which the establishment produced, and to inspect the many beauties of the groves.

Churchill's experience at Rishon le-Zion increased his sympathy for the Jewish national home in Palestine. 'I defy anybody,' he said, 'after seeing work of this kind, achieved by so much labour, effort and skill, to say that the British Government, having taken up the position it has, could cast it all aside and leave it to be rudely and brutally overturned by the incursion of a fanatical attack by the Arab population from outside.' It would be 'disgraceful', he added, 'if we allowed anything of the kind to take place'. And he continued: 'I am talking of what I saw with my own eyes. All round the Jewish colony, the Arab houses were tiled instead of being built of mud, so that the culture from this centre has spread out into the surrounding district.'

Churchill had been in Palestine for only eight days. But he had been much impressed both by the enthusiasm of the Jewish settlers, and by the intensity of Arab hostility against them. The Zionists were optimistic that his visit boded well for them. It was evident, declared the magazine *Palestine*, that Churchill's 'historical imagination had been touched by the grandeur of the idea of endowing Jewry with nationhood in its old home of Palestine'. In the May issue of the *Zionist Review* Elias Epstein[1] wrote:

In a sense, the Colonial Secretary's visit marks a turning point in our movement: it indicates the passing from discussion to real practical work. He has detailed our difficulties in no uncertain manner, but with the sympathy and understanding of a friend. He has stated that his Zionism is based upon his faith in the Jewish people to make good in Palestine–it is only left to us to justify that faith.

[1] Elias Epstein, 1895–1958. Born in Liverpool, the son of a Jewish immigrant rabbi from Russia. Apprenticed to a firm of printers at the age of fourteen. Founded the Junior Zionist Society of Liverpool, 1910. A member of the Zionist Commission for Palestine, 1918. In charge of the Zionist Commission's Press Bureau, Jerusalem, 1919–20. Editor of the newly established *Palestine Weekly*, 1919–20. Arrested after the anti-Jewish riots in Jerusalem, 1920, and imprisoned for several months. Palestine Correspondent of the *London Zionist Review* and the Cairo *Egyptian Gazette*. Active in the work of the Jewish National Fund.

33

The Middle East Settlement

ON his return from the Middle East in the second week of April 1921, Churchill defended, and sought to carry out, the agreements he had reached. On April 2, while still on board ship between Alexandria and Genoa, he prepared for his Cabinet colleagues a detailed memorandum on his proposals for Transjordan. Abdullah, he wrote, had been 'moderate, friendly and statesmanlike', and would govern Transjordan 'with the assistance of a chief political officer from us'. He would have British officers for his local troops, and British money to pay his troops, whose wages were already 'three months in arrears'. No British troops, Churchill explained, would be needed in Transjordan 'at this stage'. But Abdullah would establish three aerodromes for the Royal Air Force, and would be 'constantly visited and supported' by the British air squadron at Ludd, in Palestine. Abdullah, Churchill added, 'has now returned to Amman to begin work for us'. But his position would be a difficult one, as he had been accepted throughout Transjordan 'as a deliverer who had come up to attack the French in Syria, and to protect the Moslems of Palestine from the Zionists'. Instead of this, Churchill pointed out, 'he has definitely undertaken to be our friend'.

On April 5 Churchill wrote to Lord Curzon: 'Abdullah turned round completely under our treatment of the Arab problem. I hope he won't get his throat cut by his own followers.'

At a Conference of Ministers at 10 Downing Street on the evening of April 11, Churchill defended his Transjordan proposals. The idea of employing the Royal Air Force, he explained, was to save money on a land-based garrison. Abdullah, he added, had accepted these proposals, and had returned to Amman 'on the understanding that they would be adopted'. Churchill warned his colleagues that if they refused to give Abdullah the support of British air power, 'he might fall at any time, in which case Trans-Jordania would be the scene of anarchy and a military occupation might be necessary'.

Trenchard, who was present at the Conference, then explained the Transjordan proposals in more detail. It was envisaged, he said, that aeroplanes from Palestine would fly to Transjordan 'two or three times a week'. Eventually, a 'desert route' would be established between Cairo and Baghdad which would have 'a very salutory effect upon the Arabs'. Trenchard saw little danger of Arab violence against the air installations. 'The worst that could happen,' he said, 'might be the assassination of mechanics left at aerodromes. It was not proposed, however, to leave more *personnel* in Trans-Jordania than could be removed in a crisis by the aeroplanes.'

After Trenchard had spoken, the Conference agreed to accept Churchill's proposals for a regular air patrol between Ludd and Amman. But the idea of using this patrol as part of a 'desert route' linking Egypt with Mesopotamia was looked upon with scepticism. Churchill tried to put the proposals in the wider context of his Middle East settlement, and of his pledge to Abdullah that no Zionist activity would be allowed east of the Jordan, telling his colleagues that 'his proposals really involved a diminution rather than an increase of our responsibility respecting Trans-Jordania. Further, the arrangements had been made with the express intention of excluding any extension of Zionist activity into Trans-Jordania.' Churchill went on to say that 'the establishment of the "desert route" between Mesopotamia and Egypt offered important strategical and political advantages, and, besides very materially shortening the journey to Mesopotamia, would tend to keep the desert tribes friendly to us.'

The new Secretary of State for War, Sir Laming Worthington-Evans, was not entirely satisfied by Churchill's explanation, telling his colleagues that the 'desert route' proposal might involve the 'serious risk' of fresh military commitments. The Conference therefore decided that although British air power could be used to support Abdullah, it was only agreed to on the understanding 'that the aeroplane service would be restricted to flights between Ludd and Amman and the other aerodromes to be established in Trans-Jordania'.

On April 12 Churchill asked Henry Wilson to call on him at the Colonial Office to discuss the Transjordan scheme. They also talked about the Turkish situation. 'He is delighted the Turks have whipped the Greeks,' Wilson wrote in his diary, '& hopes they may have further disasters. . . . He says the P.M. is very sore about it & advised me to walk warily & not say "I told you so".'

Despite the doubts of the Conference of Ministers on April 11 about the need for a Desert Route from Palestine to Mesopotamia, Churchill was determined to keep the scheme alive. Everyone in Cairo had approved it, yet in London it seemed doomed. On April 13 Churchill explained to Sir Maurice Hankey:

. . . The strategic and political advantages are overwhelming. The cost is practically nothing, as it simply means the employment of aeroplanes and motor cars which are now on our constant charge.

There is no question of any risk or entanglement. But the linking of Mesopotamia to Palestine and Egypt, enabling the air forces in both theatres to be available in either in a few hours, offers the prospect of very large economies in the future and is an essential part of my scheme of reduction of expenditure.

Of course it is understood that we shall feel our way with the utmost care and only proceed as tribal conditions warrant. There are hardly any human beings at all in the districts which have to be traversed.

That same day, at Churchill's request, Hankey discussed the Desert Air Route with Austen Chamberlain, but found him, as he reported to Churchill, 'absolutely obdurate about the matter'. Chamberlain refused to agree to Churchill's proposal without a Cabinet decision. 'I am sorry I was unsuccessful,' Hankey added.

Churchill persevered in his search for a quick decision. During April 13 the Colonial Office received a telegram from Sir Percy Cox, in Baghdad, seeking Churchill's approval for the immediate continuation of exploratory work on the Hit to Azraq section of the route. In an attempt to hasten the decision, Churchill wrote direct to Chamberlain on April 14:

I am very sorry to receive a note from Hankey about the Desert Survey. Do you think you are treating me quite fairly in this matter? I shd have thought it was one wh lay wholly in my discretion; unless the War Office or the Air Ministry conceivably objected. . . .

Last year the Prime Minister on more than one occasion pressed the War Office to facilitate the pipe-line and railway survey across the desert; & the only reason that I did not do this was that the desert was somewhat disturbed. Now that favourable conditions have to a vy large extent been restored, I cannot see what question of principle is raised by the survey being resumed.

It will no doubt take half an hour to explain the whole matter to the Cabinet; & how soon under the present conditions am I likely to get that half hour? I try to write very temperately on the subject, but of course if I am to be forced to bring every petty administrative action of this kind before the overburdened Cabinet, my task will become vy difficult indeed. In fact I do not see how I can possibly succeed in it unless I am given the reasonable latitude & confidence which I was promised when I undertook it.

Churchill was angered to find his scheme under attack, telling Chamberlain:

Let me also make it quite clear that I shd raise no objection whatever to being relieved of it. There is no reason why the Middle Eastern Department shd not be transferred en bloc to the Foreign Office or the War Office, or set up as a separate department under a new Minister. I wd gladly facilitate any such step, as the difficulties of working out a smooth & successful policy—albeit on a very small scale—while having to carry with me at every stage Air Ministry, Foreign Office, War Office, Treasury, & now yourself, are obviously going to be very great.

In the present instance I shall of course defer to yr wishes; but I must leave the responsibility for further action in yr hands, both as regards the Cabinet & the answer to be sent to Cox.

Chamberlain replied on April 16. He was, he said, trying to arrange a special Conference of Ministers for Monday April 18. Until then, he could not agree to any further work being done on the route. 'These questions we shall clear up at the Conference,' he wrote. 'And indeed,' he added, 'they would have been cleared up and settled at our last Conference had I received from you an inkling that such schemes were actually in progress.'

Churchill agreed to explain his proposals in greater detail at a Conference of Ministers on April 18. But a personal tragedy forced him to postpone the meeting. Three days earlier, on April 15, his brother-in-law, William Hozier,[1] committed suicide in a Paris hotel, and the funeral was fixed for the same day as the Conference. On April 18 Lord Stamfordham[2] wrote to Churchill from Buckingham Palace: 'The King is shocked and grieved to learn from the newspapers of the sad death of your brother in law and wishes me to say how deeply he feels for Mrs Churchill and you in the sorrow which has so suddenly befallen you.' On April 17 Churchill's mother-in-law, Lady Blanche Hozier,[3] wrote

[1] William Ogilvy Hozier, 1888–1921. Clementine Churchill's brother. Entered the Navy, 1904. Lieutenant, 1909. Qualified as a German interpreter, 1910. Commanded the Torpedo Boat Destroyer *Thorn*, 1914–15. First Lieutenant on board the cruiser *Edgar*, at the Dardanelles, 1915–16. Commanded the *Clematis*, 1916–18. Lieutenant-Commander, 1918.

[2] Arthur John Bigge, 1849–1931. Entered Army, 1869. Entered the Royal Household, 1880. Private Secretary to Queen Victoria, 1895–1901. Private Secretary to George V, 1910–31. Created Baron Stamfordham, 1911. His only son was killed in action, 15 May 1915.

[3] Lady Henrietta Blanche Ogilvy, 1852–1925. Daughter of the 7th Earl of Airlie. In 1873 she married Sir H. Hozier (who died in 1907). Mother of Kitty, Clementine, Nellie and William.

to him from Dieppe: 'Dear Winston I am so thankful that Clemmie has such a husband as you are.' On April 18 Churchill crossed to France for William Hozier's funeral, returning to England that same night.

The postponed Conference of Ministers met on April 19. Austen Chamberlain opened the discussion by declaring that when he and his colleagues had originally agreed to give Abdullah the 'moral support' of British air power, they had not realized 'that any further steps for the development of the desert route to Mesopotamia were in progress'. The Cabinet, he said, had 'deprecated any action which might complicate matters in Transjordania'. Flights beyond Amman, would, he warned, lead to precisely the complications which they had feared: greater involvements, the risk of local unrest and the call for military action.

Lord Curzon also spoke against Churchill's scheme. It might not be possible, he warned, to gain the support of the local tribes so easily. Two years earlier, he pointed out, 'railway reconnaisance from both ends had to return owing to hostility on the part of the tribes, and it was very questionable whether their feelings had now changed so much as to welcome our presence on this route'. Austen Chamberlain remarked that, in attempting to win the loyalty of the Arab tribes along the route, Britain 'might become entangled in complications which, at the present time, we could not afford to risk'.

Air Marshal Trenchard and Major Young were asked for their opinion. Trenchard declared that in his view 'there was no danger of the tribes molesting anyone', that the only danger was from breakdown or planes getting lost, and that although the Air Ministry would take every precaution against this, 'it must be expected in pioneer work'. Young was equally emphatic. The danger of tribal hostility was 'negligible', except at the 'Palestine end' of the line, which was precisely where Abdullah was pledged to keep the tribes in order. It was also pointed out that both Sir Percy Cox and Sir Herbert Samuel, the two High Commissioners involved, favoured the immediate inauguration of the scheme, and anticipated no danger.

Curzon and Chamberlain bowed to these arguments, and it was finally agreed that work on the Desert Air Route should proceed as Churchill had asked.

Since his return from the Middle East at the beginning of April, Churchill had been deeply dissatisfied with his political position, and convinced himself that in his absence he had been cheated of the chance to succeed Austen Chamberlain as Chancellor of the Exchequer. This sense of grievance set up a barrier between himself and Lloyd George. On April 26 Frances Stevenson wrote in her diary: 'Winston still very vexed with the PM. . . . It was the joke of the moment his being away when all the changes were made.' She added that Churchill had not been to see Lloyd George since his return, and that the two men only met 'in Cabinets & meetings of the kind'. Churchill, she noted, 'writes him "Dear Prime Minister" whereas it used to be "Dear LlG", or "My dear David" even'.

On May 8 Austen Chamberlain wrote to his sister Hilda: 'Winston has come back from the Middle East as cross as a bear with a sore head & thinks that all the world is out of joint since he is not C/E.' Four days later Lord Beaverbrook wrote to Sir Robert Borden that Churchill had 'his just grounds for his hostility'. Beaverbrook went on to point out that since Churchill's return from the Middle East, Lloyd George had left him 'to himself'.

Churchill resented his isolation, and spoke of resignation. In a note which he passed to Austen Chamberlain at a Cabinet meeting early in May he declared: 'I shd certainly expect to learn from the PM what his views were on the future of the office I now hold. . . .' Austen Chamberlain sought to mediate between the two men, sending back Churchill's note with the comment: 'You should discuss it with him. I don't think he has any fixed ideas,' and adding: '. . . don't hold aloof from him. I am very glad to be of any help I can, but I don't want you to substitute communications through me for direct talks between the PM & yourself. That would be making of me a trait de disunion instead of a trait de union.'

Churchill was not mollified, replying somewhat curtly on the same sheet of notepaper: 'It really is not for me to open up discussions on such a topic. I shall await events.'

Austen Chamberlain persevered in his efforts to assuage Churchill's discontent. 'Forgive me,' he wrote in answer, 'but I profoundly disagree. To take that line is to court misunderstanding &, on a mistaken (as I think) point of pride or honour, to curtail your own power of usefulness & opportunities of influence. I do beg you both as a friend & colleague to reconsider your decision.'

Churchill did not resign. But he adopted an openly hostile attitude to Lloyd George both privately and in Cabinet. On May 24, during a Cabinet discussion of the Coal Strike, Churchill abused Sir Robert Horne's handling of the situation and declared that had there been a proper understanding of the miners' needs 'we could have stopped the strike very much more cheaply in advance'. When Lloyd George remarked that he himself was in no hurry to settle Churchill burst out: 'That is the worst thing I have heard. I very much regret to hear that.' On the following day Frances Stevenson wrote in her diary that Churchill was trying to 'work up' the Cabinet against Lloyd George's Irish policy, and on May 31 she noted, of the Coal Strike:

Winston is going to prove troublesome, & F.E. is half inclined to back him. Horne told me on Saturday that Beaverbrook is getting hold of Churchill, & Horne thinks we ought to keep Churchill in with the P.M. But D [David] is so sick with C. I don't think he cares if he does go. Horne says Churchill is criticising the Government on Finance and Ireland in the Clubs & lobbies. H. wanted to go to Churchill & have it out with him but I advised him not to do so. I said the P.M. will give him 'one on the nose' sooner or later, & he is the best person to do it!

That evening Churchill was one of the guests at a dinner given by Philip Sassoon. During the dinner Sir Eric Geddes remarked that Lloyd George was 'the only one person that the people cared about & would listen to'. Frances Stevenson, who recorded this remark in her diary on the following day, added that when Geddes said this 'Winston could not conceal his anger & irritation & others noticed it too'.

During April Churchill appointed Colonel Meinertzhagen[1] as Military Adviser to the Middle East Department. In his diary, Meinertzhagen recorded how he had gone to see Henry Wilson about his new post, and how Wilson had said to him: 'You've got to keep Winston on the rails; he might do anything stupid and his military judgement is almost always at fault; he thinks he's the Duke of Marlborough; any trouble, come along to me; I know how to manage him.'

In the third week of April Sir Herbert Samuel decided upon the appointment of a new Mufti of Jerusalem, proposing Haj Amin el

[1] Richard Meinertzhagen, 1878–1967. Of Danish origin. Often erroneously believed to be a Jew. 2nd Lieutenant, Royal Fusiliers, 1899. Served in India, 1899–1902. Transferred to the King's African Rifles, 1902. Served in East Africa, France and Palestine, 1914–18. Colonel in charge of the Field Intelligence Section of General Allenby's Army, 1917–18. Employed at the War Office, 1918–19. A member of the British delegation at the Paris Peace Conference, 1919. Chief Political Officer in Palestine and Syria, 1919–20. Military Adviser, Middle East Department, Colonial Office, 1921–4. He published his *Middle East Diary* in 1959.

Husseini.[1] Colonel Meinertzhagen was distressed by Samuel's choice, writing in his diary on April 27 that Haj Amin had, during the riots of Easter 1920, 'delivered incendiary speeches not only against the Jews but against the British'. Indeed, the British authorities had sentenced him—after he had fled to Transjordan—to ten years' imprisonment, and Samuel had only allowed him to return to Jerusalem after strong Arab pressure. Making him Mufti, Meinertzhagen wrote, 'is sheer madness . . . sooner or later his appointment will be bitterly regretted by us'. During April 27 Meinertzhagen protested direct to Churchill, but to no avail, for Churchill, he wrote, 'did not seem to be much interested, and in any case said he could do nothing about it'. Haj Amin was formally appointed Mufti early in May.

Meinertzhagen believed that the separation of Transjordan from Palestine was a betrayal of Britain's pledge to the Jews, and decided to make his protest direct to Churchill:

I told Shuckburgh I wished to see Churchill on the question; he said it would be no good as the matter was settled; so I rang up Eddy Marsh and told him I must see the S. of S. at once and down I went foaming at the mouth with anger and indignation. Churchill heard me out; I told him it was grossly unfair to the Jews, that it was yet another promise broken and that it was a most dishonest act, that the Balfour Declaration was being torn up by degrees and that the official policy of H.M.G. to establish a Home for the Jews in Biblical Palestine was being sabotaged; that I found the Middle East Department whose business it was to implement the Mandate, almost one hundred per cent hebraphobe and could not the duration of Abdullah's Emirate in Transjordan be of a temporary nature, say for seven years, and a guarantee given that Abdullah should never be given sovereign powers over what was in fact Jewish territory. Churchill listened and said he saw the force of my argument and would consider the question. He thought it was too late to alter but a time limit to Abdullah's Emirate in Transjordan might work.

Meinertzhagen added: 'I'm thoroughly disgusted.' But on the following day, in a private conversation with Herbert Sidebotham,[2] Churchill

[1] Haj Amin el-Husseini. Born 1897. Left Palestine after the Arab riots of 1920; sentenced to fifteen years' imprisonment *in absentia* for his part in arousing the Arabs against the Jews. Appointed Mufti of Jerusalem, March 1921. Appointed (by Samuel) President of the Supreme Muslim Council of Palestine, 1922. Leader of the anti-Jewish movement among the Arabs of Palestine. Fled Palestine in disguise after the murder of Lewis Andrews in 1937. In exile in Baghdad in 1941, he helped to direct a pro-German uprising. Broadcast from Berlin, 1942; while in Berlin he protested to Hitler when some small exceptions were made to Jewish children being sent to Concentration Camps. Imprisoned in France, 1945–6. Escaped to Cairo, 1946. In 1948 he urged the total expulsion of all Jews from Palestine. Died in Beirut, 1974.
[2] Herbert Sidebotham, 1872–1940. On the editorial staff of the *Manchester Guardian*, 1895–

seemed to be willing to allow Jewish settlement in Transjordan. He also spoke lyrically of what he had seen of the Jewish colonies in Palestine. Sidebotham recorded the conversation in a note written immediately after the interview:

He has a very high opinion of Abdullah, and his idea is that Trans-Jordania should be part of Palestine, but with a special Regime under Abdullah, analogous to Kurdistan. I said this was serious and asked what about liberty of Jewish Colonisation there. There would, I understood him to say, be such liberty, but he hoped nothing would be said about it. Faire sans dire? I enquired. That would be the ideal, he said, but he recognised the difficulty the Z.O. was under. They had to make propaganda in order to get funds for their great work. Only he hoped that they would recognise *his* difficulty.

He was enthusiastic about the Jewish colonies and said that he meant to say a great deal about them in his speech. Splendid open air men, he exclaimed, beautiful women; and they have made the desert blossom like the rose.

In his note Sidebotham recorded that Churchill 'was very insistent that nothing he said should be published' and he added: 'he is very nervous about criticism; any dust up would imperil the whole business. Do consider my difficulties he said.' Sidebotham summed up the discussion: 'A little inconclusive, but he gave me the distinct impression of friendliness. He said he had always been sympathetic with Zionism ever since his N.W. Manchester days.'

While he was in Jerusalem at the end of March, Rutenberg had shown Churchill his plans for a hydro-electric scheme on the Auja river, just north of Tel-Aviv. On May 1 Samuel wrote to Churchill from Jerusalem, urging him to grant the Auja concession at once. His own departments, he said, had approved it, and the local authorities concerned had agreed to participate in the electric lighting scheme which would arise from it; 'if you concur', Samuel added, 'I am prepared to grant the concession immediately. . . .' He also informed Churchill that in order to prevent any smaller schemes being started 'which might conflict with the large undertaking', he would give Rutenberg an assurance that no other similar concession would be granted by the Government of Palestine 'without previous consultation with him'. Samuel asked for an immediate telegraphic reply to his request.

Before any reply could be sent to Samuel, either about the Rutenberg

---

1918. Military correspondent, and later Gallery correspondent, of *The Times*, 1918–21. Political adviser to the *Daily Chronicle*, 1922–3. Contributor to the *Daily Sketch* and the *Sunday Times* (Scrutator). A leading non-Jewish supporter of Zionism.

concession or the Mandate, violence broke out in Palestine. On May 1, following a fight between Jewish Communists and Jewish workers, Jews and Arabs clashed in the mixed Muslim–Jewish quarter of Jaffa. There were deaths on both sides. Three hundred troops were summoned at once from Ludd, and two armoured cars were driven down from Jerusalem. That night peace was momentarily restored.

On the morning of May 2 the riots were renewed, and more Jews and Arabs were killed. 'There has been some looting of shops,' Samuel telegraphed to Churchill that night. 'It is believed the troops did not have to fire and there were no casualties among them . . . sixty-six arrests were made and prosecution in suitable cases will follow.'

During the Jaffa riots thirty Jews and ten Arabs were killed. 'I am very sorry to hear of this regrettable event,' Churchill telegraphed to Samuel on May 3. 'I am sure you will do whatever is necessary to bring to justice persons guilty of murderous violence.' That same day, Samuel telegraphed that he had asked General Congreve 'not to remove from Palestine at present some units about to leave. . . . These measures are essential precautions against possible serious repetitions.' Churchill saw an immediate threat to his policy of economy. 'Ask what units?' he wrote to Sir Archibald Sinclair, '& what addition to expense.'

On May 3, while the riots were at their height, Samuel, in an attempt to calm Arab discontent, ordered a temporary halt to all Jewish immigration. As proof that his order was a serious one, he refused to allow two boats, carrying 162 Russian Jews, to land at Jaffa.[1] But the riots, although quelled in Jaffa, spread elsewhere. On May 5 the Jewish settlement of Petah Tikvah was attacked by an armed Arab mob. British troops intervened and there were several casualties. In a successful attempt to drive the Arabs away, bombs were dropped by Royal Air Force planes. But on the same day another Arab mob attacked the Jewish settlement at Rehovot. From both Nablus and Tulkarm the Arab population attacked small Jewish settlements nearby.

'The Jews everywhere,' Samuel telegraphed to Churchill on May 8, 'especially in the isolated colonies, are apprehensive.' And he went on to ascribe the cause of Arab unrest to the presence of the 200 Jewish Bolsheviks who had reached Palestine from Russia during the previous

---

[1] The Colonial Office were surprised by Sir Herbert Samuel having prevented these immigrants from landing. 'I am not quite convinced,' Major Young noted on May 18, 'that Sir H. Samuel could not have arranged for them to come in quietly. . . .' As a result of Samuel's order, other groups of Jewish immigrants were being held up at Constantinople, Trieste and Vienna. On May 18 Churchill himself minuted: 'I am expecting to hear from the Department what steps should be taken about the Jewish immigrants en route for Palestine. We cannot leave them in Vienna.'

twelve months. 'The Arab population,' he told Churchill, 'does not distinguish between this group and the bulk of the immigrants, and is inclined to the conclusion that Zionism must necessarily mean the importation into their country of the least desirable elements of Eastern Europe.' There was also, he said, some Arab opposition to any Jewish immigration 'no matter what might be its character, on grounds of principle, through fear of possible political consequences in a more or less distant future'.

The Arab Nationalist leaders, Samuel told Churchill in his telegram of May 8, had adopted a policy of restraint. They had 'used their best efforts', he wrote, 'to calm agitation'. It was therefore essential, he believed, not to ignore their representations, but to try to meet them, 'as far as this can be done without the abandonment of definite pledges'. Samuel therefore proposed to deport all Jewish immigrants 'who clearly belong to the revolutionary organization' and the 'temporary suspension of immigration'. In future, he added, when immigration was resumed, two conditions would have to be met. First, there must already be in existence 'enterprises on which the men are to be engaged', and second, Britain must keep 'a stricter control' over the selection of individual immigrants 'with a view to ensure the exclusion of those who are politically undesirable'.

Churchill reacted quickly to Samuel's account of the part taken by Communist Jews, telegraphing on May 12 that he must 'purge the Jewish Colonies and newcomers of Communist elements and without hesitation or delay have all those who are guilty of subversive agitation expelled from the country. . . .' That same day, Churchill asked his advisers to comment on Samuel's decision. On May 13 Major Young minuted: 'Sir H. Samuel is clearly justified in having suspended immigration and his proposed announcement will have a good effect.' Young advised Churchill to 'approve his action, concur in proposed interim announcement, and approach FO and Zionist organizations. . . .' Churchill initialled Young's suggestion on May 14. Later that day he telegraphed again to Samuel, formally approving the suspension of immigration, and instructing Samuel to announce 'that until immigrants now in the country are absorbed immigration will not be re-opened'.

But Churchill's telegram left Samuel in no doubt that the Middle East Department regarded the Arabs as the principal culprits. 'The present agitation,' Churchill declared, 'is doubtless engineered in the hope of frightening us out of our Zionist policy.' He would not, he said, allow such agitation to succeed, even if Britain had been at fault in having permitted 'more immigrants to enter the country than can be settled on the land'. The Arabs, he concluded, must not resort to force for political ends. 'We must firmly maintain law and order,' Churchill insisted, 'and make concessions on their merits and not under duress.'

On May 12 the Moslem Committee of Jaffa had sent the Colonial Office two resolutions, the first asking for 'representative elective Government', and the second for 'the annulling of the Balfour declaration and prohibition of Jewish immigration'. On May 17 Major Young sent these resolutions to Churchill, underlining the second, and noting in the margin: 'This shows clearly what the first resolution of an elected advisory Council would be.'

Evidence abounded of the violence of Arab feelings towards the Jews. On May 18 Wyndham Deedes wrote to Major Young of how the 'whole movement' of Arab discontent was 'anti-Jewish'. It was wrong to blame the presence of a few Jewish Communists, he wrote, for the Jaffa riots. And he added: 'the most incredible rumours got abroad as to what was occurring, that Jews were butchering Moslems, men, women and children, and that the Government was arming them the better to be able to do it'. As the riots spread, Deedes explained, 'the term "Jew" and "Bolshevik" became synonomous throughout the district and reason went to the winds. . . .'

T. E. Lawrence wanted Churchill to take up Samuel's proposal for talks, in London, between Zionist and Arab leaders. 'The concordat proposed between the Arab & the Jewish nationalists,' he wrote on May 19, 'is a possibility, remote in Palestine, but more feasible in London. I do not think Sir H. Samuel can do much for it in his now rather heated atmosphere: but we should be able to achieve something when the Arab delegation comes. . . .' At the same time, Lawrence added, 'we must be careful not to achieve too much, or it will be repudiated by their supporters in Palestine when they return'.

On May 30, the day before he was to explain his Middle East policy to the Cabinet, Churchill lunched with the editor of the *Daily Mail*, Thomas Marlowe.[1] Churchill was still aggrieved with Lloyd George. Later that day Marlowe sent Lord Northcliffe an account of their conversation:

[1] Thomas Marlowe, 1868–1935. Editor, *Daily Mail*, 1899–1926. Chairman, Associated Newspapers, 1918–26.

Winston is fed up with Lloyd George. He wanted to be Chancellor but Ll.G. refused to give him the job. Winston holds it is not compatible with his seniority—as a Minister of several years' standing—to have to go to Horne— a Minister of two years—when he wants a little money.

In discussing his policies, Churchill told Marlowe: 'Mesopotamia and Palestine are twin babies in his care but he is not the father. He is reducing costs as drastically as possible. He is going to make his own detached position quite clear on Thursday.'

On May 31 Churchill gave the Cabinet an account of events in the Middle East since his return from Cairo. There had been 'rapid progress', he said, in the reduction of the Mesopotamian garrison. In Transjordan, Abdullah 'had proved amenable to reason, and up to the present had kept faith'. No complaints had been received from the French. Transjordan, he explained, was not under the Palestine Government, but 'directly' under Sir Herbert Samuel. He then spoke of Palestine, and of 'the pronounced suspicions of Zionism' among the local Arabs. His own sympathies were with the Zionists, as the Minutes recorded:

The Secretary of State for the Colonies paid a high tribute to the success of the Zionist colonies of long standing, which had created a standard of living far superior to that of the indigenous Arabs. His observations had not confirmed current accounts of the inferior quality of recent Jewish immigrants, and by strict control (proportionally to the development of the country by water power, etc.) of the quality and number of the Zionists he hoped to be able to fulfil our undertaking, though this would inevitably involve the maintenance of a considerable garrison to ensure their protection. The recent rioting and loss of life at Jaffa proved the need for this. For the maintenance of order, a strong local gendarmerie was preferred to Zionist battalions.

The development of representative institutions in Palestine was at present suspended owing to the fact that any elected body would undoubtedly prohibit further immigration of Jews.

The Cabinet thanked Churchill 'for his very interesting and illuminating statement'. That evening he dined at Philip Sassoon's house in Park Lane. Lloyd George and H. A. L. Fisher were among the other guests. In his diary Fisher recorded Lloyd George's 'excursion into Arab history'. Why did the Moors in Spain retrogress, they asked; and Lloyd George replied with the suggestion 'that all their civilized work was Jewish or European. . . .'

In Jerusalem, Sir Herbert Samuel was preparing a statement about Jewish immigration and Arab representation. On June 2 Churchill approved Samuel's proposed declaration that henceforth all Jewish immigration would be limited by the 'economic capacity' of Palestine to absorb new immigrants. But he also sent Samuel, by telegram late that afternoon, some amendments and additions to the High Commissioner's original draft, warning that 'any paraphrase of the words National Home would lead to the impression that as a result of the recent disturbances the policy of His Majesty's Government had been altered'. Churchill also opposed the setting up of a specific Muslim–Christian advisory body. 'I see no adequate grounds,' he wrote, 'for providing in the Mandate for recognition of a non-Jewish agency. . . . The Mandate as a whole fully safeguards the interests of the non-Jewish elements. . . .'

Samuel made his statement on June 3. It provoked an immediate protest from the Zionists, who considered the new restriction on immigration to be a serious barrier to the establishment of a Jewish National Home. On the day of Samuel's statement, the Jewish National Council in Jerusalem telegraphed to the Zionist headquarters in London that the spirit of Samuel's remarks was 'in violent contrast with Churchill Mount Scopus pronouncement and is the result of policy of unexampled weakness'. The Jerusalem Zionists added the wider complaint that Samuel's Administration 'showed no vigour in punishing murder looting and outrage', with the result that 'neither Jewish life nor properties' were secure. On June 5 Samuel wrote to Churchill: 'The Arabs would have preferred greater definiteness, and are disappointed; the Jews regard the situation as a set-back to the Zionist idea.'

On June 5 Nahum Sokolow went to the Colonial Office to protest to Churchill personally about Samuel's restrictions on Jewish immigration. But Churchill supported Samuel's decision and was insistent that immigration could henceforth 'only go with the opportunities for work'. And he went on to warn Sokolow: 'What is exciting the Arabs is not immigration, but the speeches of the Zionists . . . that the country would become Jewish.' This, Churchill said, was clearly not the Zionist intention; he realized that they could only conduct 'propaganda for funds' by making such claims. Nevertheless, he added, 'this is the main reason for the trouble', and the cause of the new restrictions.

Although Churchill had supported Samuel's restrictions on Jewish immigration, he also told Sokolow that he had given 'new instructions for exemplary punishment' of the Arabs responsible for the Jaffa riots, and went on to say that there was no need for the Jews to send a counter-Delegation to answer what the Arab Delegation might say. The implication was that he would not allow himself to be influenced unfairly by the Arab demands.

At Cabinet on May 31 Churchill had pressed his demands for a negotiated peace with Turkey, and criticized Lloyd George's policy of support for Greece. Churchill insisted that his policy of troop withdrawals and economy both in Mesopotamia and in Palestine 'was dependent on there being no Turkish aggression'. 'Winston urged some arrangement with Kemal,' Henry Wilson recorded in his diary. 'Mond urged large reinforcement to C-ople. . . . LG is prepared to come out of C-ople but only on condition of holding Dardanelles which cannot be done. Fisher said it was far more important to hold C-ople than Ireland and we ought to send troops from Ireland to C-ople. No decision taken.'

On June 1 Churchill attended a conference of Ministers at the Foreign Office to discuss the future of Britain's Middle East Mandates. The other Ministers present were Curzon, Balfour and H. A. L. Fisher. The latter recorded in his diary: 'Winston quite anxious to get out of Mesopotamia & Palestine. Says they will cost 9 million a year for several years.' That afternoon, in Lloyd George's room at the House of Commons, Churchill told a Cabinet Committee on Constantinople that unless peace were made with the Turkish Nationalists, Britain would be unable to rule its Middle East Mandates without a heavy cost. Henry Wilson, who was present, recorded in his diary: 'Winston wanted to reinforce C-ple & make a "posture" & then try & come to terms with Kemal as otherwise he realizes that all his "hot air, aeroplanes & Arab" government will go by the Board.'

On June 2 the Constantinople Committee met again. H. A. L. Fisher recorded in his diary Lloyd George's appeal to 'see if the Greek donkey can be made to give another kick'. Later that day Churchill wrote in protest to Lloyd George:

I do not feel sure that it is not too late, whatever we do, to retrieve the position. We are drifting steadily and rapidly towards what will in fact be a defeat of England by Turkey. That is a terrible thing to happen, undoing all the fruits of the victories we have gained and exposing us to disastrous consequences through all the large Middle Eastern provinces where we are so vulnerable.

Churchill advised an immediate order to the Greeks to withdraw 'without delay' towards the Smyrna coast, and a firm warning that if no such withdrawal took place the British would 'disinterest ourselves absolutely in their future'. The Greeks must be made to agree, he said, 'within about the next ten days'. At that point, negotiations should be opened with Mustafa Kemal, based on an offer of 'British friendship and commercial assistance to Turkey'.

In his letter Churchill went on to warn Lloyd George of what would happen if his 'unpalatable' advice were ignored:

(i) The Greeks will either be driven out of Smyrna or else kept defending it at great expense so long that they will be ruined.
(ii) We shall have to leave Constantinople very quickly and in circumstances of humiliation.
(iii) The French will invite Mustapha Kemal to come into Constantinople and try to curry favour with him there. The Italians will support the French.
(iv) Mustapha Kemal will return to Constantinople or send his agents there. He will raise a considerable army out of the discontented and desperate men who throng the city. In his own time he will attack and re-conquer Thrace.
(v) We shall not be able to hold our position on the Gallipoli Peninsula. It is much too large to be held except for a very short time by the forces which we can afford to supply.
(vi) We shall be disturbed in Mosul, the reduction of troops will be arrested, and I shall have to come to Parliament for a very heavy Supplementary Estimate. We may even have a general rising there. The same applies to Palestine, where Arabs and Turks will easily make common cause against us in consequence of the Arab hatred of Zionism. Egypt you have got on your hands already. Then there is the Afghan position.

At the end of his letter, Churchill warned Lloyd George about the whole future of Britain's new Middle East responsibilities:

I now learn that the League of Nations wish to postpone the Mandates for Palestine and Mesopotamia until the Americans are satisfied, i.e., indefinite postponement. I ought to warn you that if this course is followed and if at the same time the Turkish situation degenerates in a disastrous manner, it will be impossible for us to maintain our position either in Palestine or in Mesopotamia, and that the only wise and safe course would be to take advantage of the postponement of the Mandates and resign them both and quit the two countries at the earliest possible moment, as the expense to which we shall be put will be wholly unwarrantable.

Churchill's letter was discussed that evening by the Cabinet Committee on the Future of Constantinople. According to the Minutes of the meeting it was felt that 'at the present time, it would be useless' to urge the Greeks to pull back to the Aegean coast.

On June 9 several senior Cabinet Ministers met at Chequers to discuss both the possibility of negotiations with Turkey, and the future of the Mandates. Henry Wilson, who was present, recorded in his diary that: 'In the end it was agreed, more or less, that certain terms should be offered to the Turks viz. an autonomous Smyrna, return of C-ople & Dardanelles to Turkey & no interference in Finance.'

During the course of the discussion, Lloyd George also suggested offering both Palestine and Mesopotamia to the United States. At lunch, Curzon and Churchill discussed this possibility in private conclave. That afternoon, with Curzon's approval, Churchill wrote to Lloyd George that he was 'vy much taken' with the suggestion, and would himself like to announce it publicly during the Middle East debate in the House of Commons on June 14. Lloyd George's proposal had been received by the Cabinet 'amid what I thought to be general agreement', Churchill added. But when Lloyd George replied on June 10, he not only opposed the suggestion, but dissociated himself from it:

My dear Colonial Secretary,

I have carefully thought over your suggestion regarding the mandates for Mesopotamia and Palestine, and on reflection am not in favour of any public announcement being made at this stage.

Whatever may be the merits of offering either mandate or both to the U.S.A., I am certain that a statement in this House of Commons, without previous reference to the American Government, is not the manner in which the subject should be broached. It could only suggest that we regarded these mandates as useless burdens, to be unloaded on any other power which would take them from us. To convey such an impression would, I think, be most unfortunate in its effect both on this Country and on the United States. If the U.S.A. refused—as they undoubtedly would—a formidable agitation might arise here to abandon such burdensome possessions. The American Government might also very reasonably resent our making a proposal of such importance without consultation through the public Press. If we really want them to take either mandate or both, that is not the way to set about it.

I feel, moreover, that the subject is one in which we should unquestionably consult the Dominion Prime Ministers and the representatives of India. . . .

Curzon, to whom Churchill had sent a copy of his letter to Lloyd George, was likewise opposed to any announcement of the possible transfer of Mandates. On June 10 he wrote to Lloyd George: 'For the Colonial Secy to announce such a decision (even if arrived at), in the course of a speech explaining his policy or defending his Department in the House of Commons is not to be thought of.' Churchill accepted these criticisms. 'On reflection,' he wrote to Curzon on June 11, 'I agree with what you and he say. My desire to relieve this country from these formidable Middle Eastern burdens led me to put it forward as a suggestion, but I do not press it any longer at this stage.'

As Churchill had feared, his relationship with Curzon had gone badly. On June 13 Curzon sent Churchill a four-page protest against 'your references in public speeches to foreign affairs', declaring that Churchill's remarks at Manchester in the previous week, on the urgent need for co-operation between Britain, France and Germany, 'would have been the better if the Foreign Secretary had been consulted before they were delivered'. And he added: 'I would not dream of making a speech about the Middle East (Palestine or Mesopotamia) now that you have taken them over, without prior reference to you. . . .' Curzon also wrote on June 13 to Lloyd George to say that he had for some time been 'a good deal disturbed at Winston's unauthorized and sometimes not too helpful incursions into foreign affairs which do not render my task or position any the more easy, and which as I conceive are quite contrary to the correct etiquette of Cabinet procedure'.

Churchill replied to Curzon's strictures at once, writing to him later on June 13:

My dear George,
    I always speak with very great care on these matters, and I have many years experience to guide me as to what is due to the special position of the Foreign Secretary in external affairs or the Chancellor of the Exchequer on finance. But certain broad aspects of these central problems must be treated of by Ministers in public speech from time to time if any contact is to be maintained between the Cabinet as a whole, and the constituencies. I am sure in my remarks about the European problem I was well within the limits of past precedents, and I am very glad to know that you did not disagree in general with what I said. . . .
    However, I can assure you that it is my earnest desire not to hamper you but to help you, and that if my remarks at Manchester had not been of such a very general and even obvious character, I should certainly have talked them over with you beforehand.

Curzon's anger was looked upon sympathetically by Lloyd George, who wrote to Austen Chamberlain from North Wales on June 14: 'Curzon is undoubtedly right, but I hope there will be no flare up. . . . Winston has always been in the habit of making these pronouncements on his own. He did it under the Asquith administration constantly whenever there was a chance of a real limelight effect!' That same day, Lloyd George wrote direct to Curzon, seeking to calm him. It was, he wrote, 'most improper and dangerous' for a Minister to speak on foreign policy 'not only without having had previous consultation with the Foreign Secretary, but without actually a specific request for him to do so'. An alliance between Britain, France and Germany, he added, 'is so momentous a project that it ought not to be left to any individual Minister to declare a policy upon it'. Fortified by Lloyd George's letter, Curzon wrote again to Churchill on June 15. The gist of his letter was firm and unconciliatory. 'I cannot admit,' he wrote, 'that the Minister of a Dept other than that of Foreign Affairs has any right without consultation with the FO to make speeches on Foreign Affairs, merely because he holds strong views upon them or because he thinks his views identical with the line which the Cabinet took on a particular date.' Curzon ended his letter by accepting what he described as Churchill's 'sincere desire to give help rather than to cause embarrassment'; but, he insisted, if Churchill were to transgress again, 'I shall not hesitate to bring the matter before the Cabinet in order to obtain a ruling upon it'. On receiving Curzon's letter, Churchill allowed the controversy to lapse.

On the afternoon of June 14 Churchill made his long-awaited statement to the House of Commons on the Middle East. He began by setting out the historical background of Britain's position in the area. 'During the War,' he recounted, 'our Eastern Army conquered Palestine and Mesopotamia. They overran both these provinces of the Turkish Empire. They roused the Arabs and the local inhabitants against the Turks.' The Turkish administration was uprooted, and a British military administration put in its place. In order to gain local Arab support during the advance, 'pledges were given that the Turkish rule should not be re-introduced in these regions'. Pledges were given to the Arabs 'for the reconstitution of the Arab nation, and, as far as possible, for a restoration of Arab influence and authority in the conquered provinces. . . .' A promise was also made to the Jews, a promise 'of a very important character . . . that Great Britain, if successful in the War, would use her best endeavours to establish a Jewish national home in Palestine'. These promises, Churchill continued, could not be neglected. Britain was 'at this moment in possession of these countries', having destroyed, in war, 'the only other form of Government which existed there'. And he told the House of Commons:

We cannot repudiate light-heartedly these undertakings. We cannot turn round and march our armies hastily to the coast and leave the inhabitants, for whose safety and well-being we have made ourselves responsible in the most public and solemn manner, a prey to anarchy and confusion of the worst description. We cannot, after what we have said and done, leave the Jews in

Palestine to be maltreated by the Arabs who have been inflamed against them, nor can we leave the great and historic city of Baghdad and other cities and towns in Mesopotamia to be pillaged by the wild Bedouins of the desert. Such a proceeding would not be in accordance with the view of the British Parliament has always hitherto taken of its duty, nor would it be in accordance with the reputation that our country has frequently made exertions to deserve and maintain.

It was no use, Churchill said, 'consuming time and energy' in debating whether Britain had been wise or unwise in contracting Middle Eastern responsibilities:

Moving this way and that way in the agony of the great War, struggling for our lives, striking at our enemies, now here and now there, wherever it was thought best, we eventually emerged victorious in arms and encumbered with the responsibilities which so often attach to the victor.

We are bound to make a sincere, honest, patient, resolute effort to redeem our obligations, and, whether that course be popular or unpopular, I am certain it is the only course which any British Government or British House of Commons will in the end find itself able to pursue. . . .

Churchill then told the House of Commons how, at the end of 1920, he had 'pressed most strongly' for the placing of all Middle Eastern affairs under one Minister, how the Cabinet accepted this advice, how he himself had 'no contemplation or wish at any stage' to become that Minister, and how Lloyd George had pressed him 'most strongly on several occasions to undertake this task'. He had agreed to do so, because, as he explained, 'I felt that I could hardly avoid it in view of the opinions I had been expressing'. He had accepted the responsibility for Middle Eastern affairs, he had gone to Cairo to consult with the 'authorities concerned', and he had set, 'as my paramount object', the large-scale reduction of expenditure, both military and civil. At Cairo, the principle of economy had guided their discussions, and permeated their decisions. Even before the Conference, military expenditure in Mesopotamia and Palestine had been reduced from £80,000,000 in the year 1919–20 to an estimated £40,000,000 for 1920–1. He had hoped to reduce this expenditure even further, but the rebellion in Mesopotamia in the summer of 1920 had 'frustrated this intention'. At Cairo he and his advisers had set about the task of reducing the £40,000,000 still further for the year 1921–2. Every possible economy had been examined—one economy had involved 'the wholesale destruction of great numbers of horses'—and the Estimate for which he now asked was less than £30,000,000.

Churchill then explained his settlement in detail, first as it concerned

Mesopotamia, then Palestine. It was Britain's intention 'to instal an Arab ruler in Iraq . . . and to create an Arab army for the national defence'. These matters, he said, had been left 'entirely in the hands of Sir Percy Cox', and the Government would rely upon Cox's experience to guide them. 'He is a great believer in the Arabs,' Churchill explained, 'he is devoted to the people of Iraq; he is acquainted with every aspect of Arab politics. . . .' Churchill then spoke of Britain's attitude towards the Arabs, and of the policy upon which the Government had decided:

Broadly speaking, there are two policies which can be adopted towards the Arab race. One is the policy of keeping them divided, of discouraging their national aspirations, of setting up administrations of local notables in each particular province or city, and exerting an influence through the jealousies of one tribe against another. That was largely, in many cases, the Turkish policy before the War, and cynical as it was, it undoubtedly achieved a certain measure of success.

The other policy, and the one which, I think, is alone compatible with the sincere fulfilment of the pledges we gave during the War to the Arab race and to the Arab leaders, is an attempt to build up around the ancient capital of Baghdad, in a form friendly to Britain and to her Allies, an Arab State which can revive and embody the old culture and glories of the Arab race, and which, at any rate, will have a full and fair opportunity of doing so if the Arab race shows itself capable of profiting by it. Of these two policies we have definitely chosen the latter.

Churchill then described how the decision to give 'satisfaction to Arab nationality' had led him to support a Sherifian solution; to invite the Emir Feisal to 'present himself to the people' of Mesopotamia, and to put the Emir Abdullah 'in charge' of Transjordan. At the same time the great rival chieftain, Ibn Saud, would be paid an annual subsidy of £60,000—'the cost after all of a single battalion of Indian infantry'— to keep the peace in the Nejd. In return for his subsidy, Ibn Saud had agreed to exercise 'a restraining influence' over the 'nomadic and predatory tribes' of the desert. 'We shall pay,' Churchill added, 'only in so far as good behaviour is assured. . . .'

Turning to the problems of defence, Churchill explained that the Arab army in Mesopotamia would be paid for entirely from Mesopotamian revenues, and that British control would be exercised, not by expensive land battalions, but by air power. 'It must not be supposed,' he said, 'that aeroplanes have no means of acting except by using lethal force. That, of course, is in reserve. But we hope that, by their agency, we shall be able to keep in amicable touch with the tribes and local centres, and to ward off in good time movements of unrest. . . .'

It was in Palestine, Churchill continued, that military expenditure could not easily be reduced. 'The cause of unrest in Palestine,' he said, 'and the only cause, arises from the Zionist movement, and from our promises and pledges to it.' While he was still at the War Office, he had hoped to reduce the Palestine garrison from 16,000 to 7,000 men. But with the existing unrest no reductions were possible, and it might even be necessary to send reinforcements.

Churchill then spoke of the political situation in Palestine. If the Arabs were given representative institutions, he said, they would use their powers as a majority 'to veto any further Jewish immigration'. But this could not be allowed, for it conflicted with Britain's promise 'of a national home for the Jew in Palestine'. Arab fears of an eventual Jewish majority were, he said, unfounded:

> The Arabs believe that in the next few years they are going to be swamped by scores of thousands of immigrants from Central Europe, who will push them off the land, eat up the scanty substance of the country and eventually gain absolute control of its institutions and destinies.
>
> As a matter of fact these fears are illusory. The Zionists in order to obtain the enthusiasm and the support which they require are bound to state their case with the fullest ardour, conviction and hope, and it is these declarations which alarm the Arabs, and not the actual dimensions of the immigration which has taken place or can take place in practice. . . .
>
> There really is nothing for the Arabs to be frightened about. All the Jewish immigration is being very carefully watched and controlled both from the point of view of numbers and character. No Jew will be brought in beyond the number who can be provided for by the expanding wealth and development of the resources of the country. There is no doubt whatever that at the present time the country is greatly under-populated.

Churchill then spoke enthusiastically of the results achieved by the Jewish pioneers, of what he had seen at the colony of Rishon le-Zion, and of the benefits to the Arabs of Jewish enterprise:

> I have no doubt that with the proper development of the resources of Palestine, and that if Jewish capital is available, as it may be, for development in Palestine, for the creation of great irrigation works on the Jordan, and for the erection of electrical power stations in the Jordan valley, which can so readily be erected there, there will be year after year, new means of good livelihood for a moderate number of the Jewish community, and the fact that they will be gaining their livelihood by these new means will inure to the general wealth of the whole community, Arabs and Christians as well as of Jews.
>
> I see no reason why with care and progress there, there should not be a

steady flow of Jewish immigrants into the country, and why this flow should not be accompanied at every stage by a general increase in the wealth of the whole of the existing population, and without injury to any of them. That, at any rate, is the task upon which we have embarked, and which I think we are bound to pursue.

We cannot possibly agree to allow the Jewish colonies to be wrecked, or all future immigration to be stopped, without definitely accepting the position that the word of Britain no longer counts throughout the East and the Middle East.

Churchill continued his Middle East survey with a description of British policy towards Transjordan. Abdullah, he said, was 'a very agreeable, intelligent and civilised Arab prince', who, in return for his kingdom and his subsidy, had agreed to maintain order in Transjordan, and to restrain his subjects from both anti-French and anti-British activity.

The whole Middle East settlement, Churchill declared, and all the economies arising from it, depended in the last resort upon 'a peaceful and lasting settlement with Turkey'. A hostile Turkey would be able to disturb Kurdistan and Mesopotamia, and to stir up Arab unrest throughout the Middle East. Peace with Turkey was the 'paramount object' of British policy. Without it, the 'heavy charges' of 1919 would return, and no abatement of them would be possible. Churchill hoped, however, that the decisions of the Cairo Conference, and the territorial agreements arising from it, would be for the best. His speech ended with an appeal to the House of Commons for its support:

I cannot say with certainty that the unknown future which lies before us will enable this policy of reduction and appeasement to be carried out with complete success, but I do believe that the measures which we are taking are well calculated to that end.

I have great confidence in the experts and high authorities who have combined in thinking that they are so calculated, and I advise the Committee to give their assent to them and to give us their support in the difficult and delicate process of reduction and conciliation which lies before us, and on which we are already definitely embarking.

Churchill's speech was a personal triumph. 'It was received,' wrote Colonel Meinertzhagen in his diary, 'with much applause and was an evident success.' 'Winston has had a great success,' Austen Chamberlain wrote to Lloyd George that same day, 'both as to his speech & his policy, & has changed the whole atmosphere of the House on the Middle East question.' On the following day Curzon wrote to congratulate Churchill 'on the brilliancy & success' of his exposition. 'Your Mesopotamian performance,' Lloyd George wrote on June 16, 'was one of your very best. Hearty congratulations on its conspicuous success.' 'I have never known the House more interested in any speech,' Herbert Sidebotham reported to the *Palestine Weekly*, 'or a speaker more easy and confident in his power.'

In the debate that followed Churchill's speech, Lord Winterton spoke enthusiastically of Churchill's achievement. 'The right hon. Gentleman who has just spoken,' he said, 'gives an impression of power and grandeur which is possessed by few persons and institutions with the possible exception of the Pyramids or Lord Northcliffe. Very few Members of this House, or for that matter of the Government either, in these days can hold the attention of a Committee of this House with a closely reasoned and well-knit speech in the manner in which my right hon. Friend has done.'

During his speech, Lord Winterton warned Churchill that once 'you begin to buy land for the purpose of settling Jewish cultivators you will find yourself up against the hereditary antipathy, which exists all over the world to the Jewish race'. But he believed that Churchill had every chance of success 'in eliminating the present really dangerous situation in the Middle East and in casting fresh lustre on the traditions of British Imperial policy'.

34

1921: 'A wonderful and terrible year'

THE possibility of negotiations between Britain and Turkey was much under discussion during the summer of 1921. Churchill's own position was a clear one. 'As you know,' he wrote to Curzon on June 15, 'I am prepared to support hostile measures against Turkey as the sole means of producing a reasonable attitude on their part.' But, he added:

It seems to me vital to use every effort to postpone the Greek offensive and to address Constantine in the sense of our Chequers' conversation. Also to send a really authoritative embassy, armed with the Greek compliance, if possible from France and Britain—at any rate from Britain—to clinch matters with Kemal. If Kemal really agrees to terms like these, we ought not to hesitate to put all forms of pressure upon Greece, including if necessary naval action off Smyrna or the Piraeus, to compel them to close with them.

Lloyd George sought to counter Churchill's arguments, writing to Curzon on June 16 that 'the Turk will not succumb to soft words and that it is only a threat of action that will force him to reason'. It was wrong, Lloyd George added, to underrate the military potential of the Greeks. 'The Turks have done no good fighting for over a generation,' he wrote, 'except when led by British or German officers. Kemal's force is not equipped with either.'

When the Cabinet met in Austen Chamberlain's room at the House of Commons on June 22, Ministers expressed themselves 'very reluctant to miss an opportunity for a conversation with Mustapha Kemal himself', even though they deprecated 'conversations with secondary persons'.

In the last week of June the Greeks refused Britain's advice to open negotiations with Kemal, or at least to await the outcome of any

600

direct British negotiations. They still had confidence in their abilities to defeat the Turks, and to dictate their own terms at Angora. Churchill's anti-Greek sentiments were strengthened when he learned on June 25 that the Greeks, far from agreeing to British mediation, were about to launch a new military offensive. During the day he sent both Lloyd George and Curzon his thoughts on the Greek action:

I am deeply alarmed at the idea of the Greeks starting off in a disheartened manner on this new offensive. It may produce irretrievable disaster if it fails. It simply means that all the policy we agreed upon at Chequers comes to nought. I may add that if the French decline to participate in the naval blockade, either of Greece or Turkey as the case may be, I should still be in favour of our going on alone, as we are fully possessed of the means to do all that is necessary and to do it quite quickly.

'I am sure the path of courage is the path of safety,' Churchill added. 'I think everybody here would approve our stopping the war.'

The Cabinet met on June 25 to discuss the Greek refusal. In his diary Thomas Jones recorded Lloyd George's remark 'that he stood alone as pro-Greek in the Cabinet but that he was willing to treat the Turks and Greeks on an absolute equality'. Churchill expressed his approval of this sentiment, and added 'that he was prepared to blockade whichever of the two proved to be the more provocative'. Three days later, on June 28, news reached London that the Turks had captured Ismid from the Greeks.

On May 29 Churchill's mother had fallen downstairs, while staying with a friend at Mells, in Somerset. As a result of her fall the bones above her left ankle were broken, and gangrene set in. On June 10 her left leg had been amputated above the knee. Within two weeks she seemed to be recovering from the effects of the amputation. 'Danger definitely over,' Churchill telegraphed to Montagu Porch on June 23. 'Temperature going down.' And on June 26 Lady Randolph wrote to Lord Curzon: 'I am getting on famously. My poor departed leg served me well for 67 years & led me into some very pleasant walks. I am not to be pitied—now that my grand pain is over.' But three days later, on the morning of June 29, Churchill was summoned to his mother's bedside. She had suffered a sudden haemorrhage, and was unconscious. That morning, without regaining consciousness, she died.

On learning of Lady Randolph's death, Lord Curzon wrote at once to Churchill:

My dear Winston,

P.M. has just told us here that your dear mother has died of a sudden haemorrhage. I cannot tell you with what deep sorrow & distress I have received this shocking news. Only the day before yesterday I received the wonderful & touching letter from her—to which I referred in conversation with you—probably one of the last which she ever wrote, & therefore greatly to be treasured by me—and I had too rashly anticipated that her amazing courage and spirit would successfully carry her through. This is not to be: and what was an eager hope can now only be a treasured memory.

My memory of your mother goes back to the days when I was an under-graduate at Oxford and she the brilliant wife of a brilliant statesman then rising to fame. During all the years that have passed since then, I have found her—quite apart from the attraction of her radiant personality—to be a true constant and loyal friend, ever warmhearted and generous: and I have no recollection of her that is not instinct with affection & vitality and joy. None who knew her will ever forget her and those who were fond of her living will cherish her memory. The shock will be a very heavy one to you for just as she was a proved & adoring mother, so have you always been a devoted son. But when a woman lives as she told me in her letter she has done—to the age of 67—a life so full of activity and happiness (though she had her sorrows) & triumph death loses something of its tragedy, and the memory of vivid and definite achievement survives.

No one will derive more consolation from this retrospect than yourself: and in a minor degree it will always be a source of joy to her friends.

I am yours ever
Curzon

Churchill replied at once to Lord Curzon's letter:

My dear George,

I found yr letter to her lying on the table downstairs. In a few minutes it wd have been taken up to her. She had had her breakfast, temperature normal—good spirits—suddenly this fatal artery gave. After that one cd not have wished her to survive this day. Another amputation must have ensued at once. Since it had to be, it was better so. The collapse was vy rapid. She was soon beyond the reach of useless pain.

Yr kind and tender letter has just reached me. I do not feel a sense of tragedy, but only of loss. Her life was a full one. The wine of life was in her veins. Sorrows and storms were conquered by her nature & on the whole it was a life of sunshine.

The pangs of these last weeks have been cruel. But they have given her the means of knowing that she was greatly beloved. All her friends of the old brilliant world were around her in spirit. She felt buoyed up in currents of sincere affection. She had nothing to regret. It was a life wh was instinct with joy—wh radiated simple happiness.

I had a vy strong & lasting impression in these last weeks of her supple, vital, gracious personality. It abides with me and my last memories are the most splendid.

I am deeply touched by the kindness of all you write. You have ever been a true friend.

We all keep moving along the road.

Yours ever,
W

Lloyd George wrote at once from 10 Downing Street:

My dear Winston,

I am deeply grieved to hear of your mother's sudden death.

I know how devoted she was to you & you to her & your grief must be profound. I recall now with a saddened pleasure the last occasion upon which I met her. I remember how impressed I was by her vivid personality. She was the life & delight of the party. . . .

On receiving Lloyd George's letter, Churchill replied:

Mr dear P.M.

Thank you so much for yr letter. I know your own warm heart; & that you will understand what the severance of a tie like this means. My mother had the gift of eternal youth of spirit, & never have I felt this more than in these weeks of cruel pain. We hoped that she wd overcome the tides that were setting against her: indeed we were rejoicing that they had been overcome. But since it was to be it was better that the end did come quickly & nearly painlessly. It wd have been a terrible thing to face another amputation after all she had gone through—with practically no hope at the end of it.

I am touched by yr reference to her party wh you came to. She was so delighted to have you there & to give an entertainment in yr honour.

I will come back to my work on Monday, but I hope you will excuse me till then.

Once more thanking you for the kindness of yr letter.

Believe me ever sincerely,

Winston S. Churchill

The news of Lady Randolph's death was announced in the evening papers. Churchill himself telegraphed at once to Montagu Porch:

I deeply grieve to tell you that my mother died this morning from a sudden haemorrage in leg. Her end was quite peaceful and painless. Up till breakfast everything was progressing favourably, temperature normal, good spirits, but loss of blood led to collapse. Everything in human power was done. Accept my most profound sympathy.

On Saturday July 2, Lady Randolph was buried in Bladon Church-yard. Shane Leslie, who was present, described the scene in a letter to Clare Sheridan[1] two days later. 'The feeling shewn was very consider-able,' he wrote, 'and even George West[2] sent a wreath—for auld lang syne. Jack and Winston were like widowers while the poor Porch returns from the end of the world in Nigeria.'

As soon as the service was over, the cortege left the Church, and Lady Randolph was buried next to her first husband. Churchill stood alone for a few moments by his mother's grave, in tears, and threw into the grave a spray of crimson roses.

On the following day Churchill's aunt Cornelia wrote to him:

Dearest Winston,

My heart went out to you as you stood by the little grave & the open one of yr dear Mother, & knew all you must be feeling both in looking back on the scenes of your childhood, & in the thought of your present loss. Solemn thoughts come at such times. Life's work will soon absorb you again, as indeed it is right it should. But don't lose sight of that rift in the heavens which reminds us of the life beyond, & which also can inspire you to right thinking & doing. We need to keep in touch with the unseen. God bless you— Don't think of writing, only every heart was full, & I longed to express it.

In the days following Lady Randolph's death, Churchill's friends hastened to console him. The many sympathetic letters he received were a tribute to the high regard in which his mother was held, and to the wide range of her friends and admirers. Many of the letters evoked an age that was long passed. The former Liberal Prime Minister, Lord Rosebery,[3] wrote:

My dear Winston,

I am beyond measure distressed at the sad news I see in the newspaper this afternoon, which is all the more grievous as she seemed to be going on so well; and I send you my warmest and sincerest sympathy.

I remember her in the full flush of her glorious beauty, when she first

[1] Clare Consuelo Frewen, 1885–1970. Only daughter of Moreton Frewen and Churchill's aunt Clara (Jerome). In 1910 she married Wilfred Sheridan, who was killed in action in France in 1915. Sculptress; among her subjects were the Soviet leaders, Lenin, Trotsky, Kamenev and Dzerzhinsky. In 1947 she became a Roman Catholic.

[2] George Frederick Myddelton Cornwallis-West, 1874–1951. Lieutenant, Scots Guards, 1895–1900. Married Lady Randolph Churchill, 1900; the marriage was dissolved, 1913. Married the actress Mrs Patrick Campbell, April 1914. Lieutenant-Colonel, commanding a battalion of the Royal Naval Division at Antwerp, October 1914. Married Georgette, widow of Adolph Hirsch, 1940.

[3] Archibald Philip Primrose, 1847–1929. Succeeded his grandfather as 5th Earl of Rosebery, 1868. Secretary of State for Foreign Affairs, 1886 and 1892–4. Prime Minister, 1894–5. His younger son, Neil Primrose MP, was killed in action in Palestine in 1917.

married; and from that time to this she has always been the kindest and most friendly of all women.

It must come as a terrible blow in the midst of all your hard work, and she seems to take with her a whole generation of society of which to the end she was so brilliant a member.

I have just come to London, and remember your kind promise to come and see me. But of course nothing would induce me to take advantage of this at such a moment.

Yours always,
A.R.

Churchill's cousin Lord Wimborne wrote:

My dear Winston,

A word of sympathy with you at the present moment.

For her doubtless it was a release from crippled age, but to lose one's mother is to be severed from one's own youth, and begets a new sense of isolation in confronting destiny henceforth.

She too was denied the pleasure of witnessing your prospective success on a greater stage, which I think will not be much longer delayed.

With affectionate sympathy
Ivor

Lord Birkenhead wrote:

My dear Winston,

I cannot tell you how I feel for you. I never like obtruding in the face of such grief as I know you feel but I must write a line of affectionate sympathy.

It is tragic to think of so much brilliancy & joie de vivre extinguished. She gave much to life & her friends even as she asked much. We shall not I think see anyone like her in our day.

Dear Winston it must be a joy to you to reflect upon the constant love and the understanding kindness which she met in such measure at your hands.

It was a wonderful relationship between two wonderful people and its severance will be mourned by others than yourself.

Yours in deep friendship
F.

From Alice Keppel:[1]

My dear Winston—

You will, I know, feel dear Jennie's death most deeply so I want just to tell you of my sympathy, & my own unbounded sorrow. For twenty years, she was a real good friend to me. When things were happy, her gaiety made them more so, & when, sorrow & troubles came, her wonderful sympathy never failed. I shall miss her to my dying day.

---

[1] Alice Frederica Edmonstone, 1869–1947. Daughter of Admiral Sir William Edmonstone. In 1891 she married the Hon. George Keppel. She was a close friend of King Edward VII.

You were such a good son to her & she was justly so proud of you. I saw her in Italy, about two months ago, & she talked about you there, with such pride, & love—I don't think any woman ever lived who had more friends, who really mourn her, & who know, they will never see her like again.

Yr. affectionate old friend
Alice Keppel

Churchill expressed his own feelings in a letter to his close friend Lady Islington,[1] writing to her on July 1:

Dear Anne,

. . . It was a bitter disappointment, just when we had a right to believe she was out of immediate danger. But anyhow she suffers no more pain; nor will she ever know old age, decrepitude, loneliness. Jack & I will miss her vy much: but for herself I do not know whether she has lost much. A long ordeal before her, at the end of wh there cd only be a partial & a limited respite.

Dear Anne—she loved you vy much and always revelled in yr wit & charm.

I wish you cd have seen her as she lay at rest—after all the sunshine & storm of life was over. Very beautiful and splendid she looked. Since the morning with its pangs, thirty years had fallen from her brow.

She recalled to me the countenance I had admired as a child when she was in her heyday and the old brilliant world of the eighties & nineties seemed to come back.

Once more let me thank you *dear*

Yours ever
W

Churchill was momentarily cast down by his mother's death. 'The old brilliant world in which she moved,' he wrote to Lord Crewe[2] on July 4, 'and in wh you met her is a long way off now, & we do not see its like today. I feel a vy great sense of deprivation. Both Jack & I will miss her vy much.'

Following his mother's death, Churchill plunged back quickly into public affairs. He was eager to explain his view of world policy to the Dominion Prime Ministers assembled in London, and during July 4 he circulated a memorandum to the Imperial Conference giving his

[1] Anne Beauclerk Dundas, 1868–1958. A granddaughter of Field-Marshal Lord Napier of Magdala. In 1896 she married Sir John Dickson-Poynder (created Baron Islington, 1910).

[2] Robert Offley Ashburton Crewe-Milnes, 1858–1945. Succeded his father as 2nd Baron Houghton, 1885. Lord-Lieutenant of Ireland, 1892–5. Created Earl of Crewe, 1895. Secretary of State for the Colonies, 1908–10; for India, 1910–15. Created Marquess of Crewe, 1911. Lord President of the Council, 1915–16. President of the Board of Education, 1916. Ambassador to Paris, 1922–8. Secretary of State for War, 1931.

comments on Far Eastern affairs. 'The danger to be guarded against,' he wrote, 'is the danger from Japan.' To forestall such a danger, he proposed an alliance 'between the British Empire and the United States'. Such an alliance, he added, would be 'overwhelmingly effective'.

The Imperial Conference met that day to discuss the renewal of the Anglo-Japanese Alliance of 1902. Churchill spoke strongly against such a step. Japan, he reiterated, was the only real danger to Imperial interests in the Pacific. 'Getting Japan to protect you against Japan,' he had written in his memorandum, 'is like drinking salt water to slake thirst.' Churchill's vigorous argument against renewing the Anglo-Japanese Alliance provoked a lively exchange of notes:

CURZON TO LLOYD GEORGE:

It seems to me entirely wrong that the Colonial Secretary should on an occasion like this air his independent views on a F.O. question.

I would not presume on a Colonial Office question, either to intervene at all or to take a line independent of the C.O.

LLOYD GEORGE TO CURZON:

I quite agree. I have done my best to stopper his fizzing. Montagu, Chamberlain & Balfour would be entitled to join in—so on each item we should have six British speeches. It is intolerable.

AUSTEN CHAMBERLAIN TO CURZON:

I think you are right to show Winston that you profoundly resent his constant & persistent interference. It goes far beyond anything that I at least have ever known in Cabinet even from the most important members of a Govt.

Unless you make him feel that it is a matter which you feel personally I despair of doing anything with him. To a *personal* appeal I think that he is nearly always open (I mean to an appeal on personal grounds).

CURZON TO CHURCHILL:

My dear Winston, I wonder what you would say if on a Colonial Office [question] I felt myself at liberty to make a speech at this Conference—quite independent of the Colonial Office and critical of the attitude adopted by its chief.

CHURCHILL TO CURZON:

You may say anything you like about the *Colonial* Office that is sincerely meant: but there is no comparison between these vital matters wh. affect the whole future of the world and the mere departmental topics with wh. the Colonial Office is concerned.

In these gt matters we must be allowed to have opinions.

When the Imperial Conference met on July 7, the discussion was of European affairs. Churchill was anxious that, in any post-war settlement, France should not find herself isolated and weak. But he prefaced his remarks with caution, and tried not to anger Curzon yet again. 'May I say a word Prime Minister?' he began. 'I only want to say a word from a slightly different angle, but let me say at the beginning . . . that I agree with the Foreign Secretary, it would be most foolish for us to go and thrust an offer of a single-handed guarantee before the French.' But, he went on:

The aim is to get an appeasement of the fearful hatreds and antagonisms which exist in Europe and to enable the world to settle down. I have no other object in view.

I feel that a greater assurance to France would be a foundation for that. First of all, our duty towards France in this matter is rather an obvious one because she gave up her claims—very illegitimate claims as we thought them, but she waived them—to take a strong strategic position along the Rhine which her Marshals advised her to do, and this Anglo-American guarantee was intended to be a substitute to France. We said to her, if you give up the strategical position, England and America will be with you in the hour of need. Well, America did not make good, and one would have thought France all the more would have needed the British Empire, but it is a fact that the Treaty is naturally invalidated by America not having made good and France got neither Britain nor America, nor did she get her strategic frontier on the Rhine. The result of that is undoubtedly to have created a deep fear in the heart of France, and a fear which anyone can understand who looks at the population of the two countries, one declining and already under forty millions—38 millions—and the other bounding up, in spite of all that has happened, with great masses of military youths reaching manhood, and in seven or eight years replacing the losses of the war.

No one can doubt the deep rooted nature of the fear which this poor mutilated, impoverished France has of this mighty Germany which is growing up on the other side of the Rhine. It is this fear, if I may say so with all respect to the Conference which is the explanation and to a certain extent the excuse for the intolerant and violent action which France is taking. If at any time the means arises of reducing that fear, of giving such an assurance, I think we ought to consider it very carefully indeed.

Churchill wanted the Imperial Prime Ministers to look sympathetically at French fears. But he also wanted a positive policy of reconciliation towards Germany, and this too he explained to them:

I am anxious to see friendship grow up and the hatred of the war die between Britain and Germany. I am anxious to see trade relations develop with Germany naturally and harmoniously. I am anxious to see Britain getting all the help and use she can out of Germany in the difficult years that lie before us.

I am very much afraid that any friendly relations which grow up in time between Britain and Germany will be terribly suspect to France. France will say 'You are changing sides; you are going over to the other side. We are to be left to ourselves, and England is more the friend of Germany than of France.'

But I think if a Treaty were in existence which in the ultimate issue, in the extreme issue, bound the British Empire to protect France, against unprovoked aggression, we could always point to that and say, 'No, if you are attacked, there is our scrap of paper; we shall be as good as our word next time as we were last time.' That will give you greater freedom, in my humble opinion, to establish new relations, new co-operation with Germany in the further reconstruction and rebuilding of Europe, and it might well be that being at once the Ally of France and the friend of Germany, we might be in a position to mitigate the frightful rancour and fear and hatred which exist between France and Germany at the present time and which, if left unchecked, will most certainly in a generation or so bring about a renewal of the struggle of which we have just witnessed the conclusion.

A British guarantee to France would not, Churchill insisted, act as a cause of division in Europe. Its aim was to be the reverse. Such a pledge, he said, 'is not connected with the militaristic triumph of one set of nations over another, but aims entirely, in my opinion, at the appeasement and consolidation of the European family'.

Churchill's view of the future of Europe did not prevail. The general mood of the Imperial Conference was one of hostility to France, and reluctance to embark upon any comprehensive scheme of European reconciliation. Yet Churchill's instinct was for appeasement both in Europe and in Asia Minor. During the first weeks of July he continued to hope for a negotiated peace settlement with Turkey. The peace of Iraq, he wrote to General Haldane on July 11, 'depends upon peace along the Northern frontier and the maintenance of friendly relations with the Turkish Empire'. And he added: 'I am doing all I can to promote it from this end.' But on July 11 the Greeks launched a new offensive in Anatolia, and sought once more to advance on Angora, and destroy the Turkish Nationalist Movement. On July 14, during a debate on the Middle East, Churchill told the House of Commons:

This war between the Greeks and the Turks may end this way or it may end that way, but whoever wins, however long it is protracted, it produces continuous, uniform, disadvantage to British interests.

There is no greater interest in the whole of the Middle East than the interest of Britain, and, I believe, of France as well, to secure a cessation of this protracted, vicious, mischievous strife between these two forces, which impoverishes and distracts the whole of the region and leads to every kind of dislocation of our affairs both in Palestine and Mesopotamia.

I could not possibly speak upon this subject of the Middle East without emphasising the need that there is for us to arrive at a satisfactory peace with Turkey and to procure a cessation of the hostilities which, after all these years, are still distracting and ruining the whole of these unfortunate areas of the East.

Lloyd George did not share Churchill's fears of the Graeco-Turkish war harming Britain. He still looked with sympathy on Greek aspirations, and hoped that Turkey would be defeated. On July 20 Frances Stevenson wrote in her diary:

D. very interested in the Greek advance against the Turks. He has had a great fight in the Cabinet to back the Greeks (not in the field but morally) & he & Balfour are the only pro-Greeks there. All the others have done their best to obstruct & the W.O. have behaved abominably. However D. has got his way, but he is much afraid lest the Greek attack should be a failure, & he should be proved to have been wrong. He says his political reputation depends a great deal on what happens in Asia Minor. . . .

In the last week of July there had been fighting in northern Mesopotamia. According to reports reaching Sir Percy Cox in Baghdad, Turkish troops had supported local outlaws in attacks on Arab police posts. On August 2 British aeroplanes bombed rebel forces which had seized the town of Batas; but on August 3 rebel forces, including Turks, occupied Rowanduz. On August 4 Cox telegraphed details of these events to Churchill, adding that they had been accompanied 'by flood of Turkish propaganda violently anti-British'.

On learning of the renewed Turkish activity in northern Mesopotamia, Churchill intensified his efforts to persuade Lloyd George to make peace with Turkey. He was strongly supported by the Middle East Department. A Greek success against the Turks, Major Young minuted on August 9, 'will almost inevitably force the Turkish Nationalists into the arms of the Bolsheviks'. If the Bolsheviks combined with the Turks, he warned, 'there will be a stream of Russian reinforcements pouring down from the Caucasus. Nothing would be easier than for them to make a centre at Diarbekir and from there to encourage the anti-British elements on the Mesopotamian frontier.' A combined 'Turco-Bolshevik movement' against Mesopotamia would, Young added, 'be disastrous'. Churchill approved Young's warnings, initialled them, caused them to be typed out in the form of a letter to Lloyd George which he then signed himself, as if it was his own.

But warnings of the folly of supporting Greece against Turkey did

not impress Lloyd George, whatever their source. On the same day that
Churchill sent his warning, Lord Riddell wrote in his diary:

L.G. is still very pro-Greek and much elated at the Greek military successes.
He said we always regarded the Turk as a first-class fighting man but even
here he has broken down. L.G. told me he believes the Greeks will capture
Constantinople, and he evidently hopes they will. . . .

Early in August Churchill's youngest daughter, Marigold, fell ill.
She was only three and a half years old, and her illness was severe.
'Winston very distressed about his sick child,' H. A. L. Fisher wrote in
his diary on August 19. As their daughter's health worsened, Churchill
and his wife were distraught. 'The child is a little better than she was,'
Churchill wrote to Lord Curzon on August 22, 'but we are still dreadfully anxious about her.' Two days later Marigold died.

On the death of Lady Randolph Churchill in June, Churchill had
received many lengthy condolences and fulsome tributes from her
friends and his own. The death of his daughter was a tragedy for which
words seemed inadequate, and his friends were stunned. 'What torture
for a parent's heart!' Pamela Lytton[1] wrote on hearing the news. 'I can
only pray that as time passes, many precious things will come to you,
to help your wound to heal.'

Churchill received many letters of condolence. His aunt Cornelia
wrote:

My dear Winston,
   What can I say to you in the awful crushing sorrow which has come on you
& dear Clemmie. My heart just aches for you & I can think of nothing but
you two sitting sorrowing in your loss. The only consolation, & it is a great
one, you have each other. I can only pray you may be comforted & enabled
to say 'Thy will be done'.

Yr fond & loving
Aunt C

Sir Archibald Sinclair wrote:

My dear Winston,
   We are so unhappy about poor little Marigold. She was such a lovely,

---

[1] Pamela Frances Audrey Plowden, 1874–1971. Daughter of Sir Trevor Chichele-Plowden.
On 4 November 1896 Churchill wrote to his mother: 'I must say that she is the most beautiful
girl I have ever seen.' In 1902 she married Victor Lytton, later 2nd Earl of Lytton. Their
elder son, Edward, Viscount Knebworth, died in 1933 as a result of an aeroplane accident;
their younger son, Alexander, Viscount Knebworth, was killed in action at El Alamein in
1942.

sparkling, winning little child that we were already completely captivated and we cant bear to think what her loss must mean to you & Clemmie. . . .

Jack writes me that you are going to Loch More this coming week. Do come on to us if you would like a few days quietly painting. The few people we are able to put up in this tiny house will have left by then and we shall be alone for ten days at any rate. We should be so delighted to welcome you & Clemmie here & we could easily motor round to fetch you.

Yrs always
Archie

Lord Beaverbrook wrote:

My dear Winston,

I was so sorry to hear the sad news of Marigold. I hoped so much that she would improve.

It is incomprehensible. She seemed so full of vitality—just a few weeks ago. I thought she could stand any illness & the sudden termination of her life appeared to be impossible.

Please do say to Mrs Churchill that I am sympathising with her in her dreadful grief, although no words of comfort will bring any relief at this time.

Don't answer

Yours ever
Max

Bonar Law wrote:

My dear Winston

I was so distressed to hear your terrible news just as I was leaving last night. I know how you must both be suffering. There is nothing to be said but I am very sorry for you.

Yours sincerely,
A. Bonar Law

Lord Curzon wrote:

My dear Winston,

I see that your very real anxieties were not misplaced and that you have lost your child. This must be a terrible grief to you and your wife. There is something so appealing about the life and so pathetic about the death of the young that the wound of such a bereavement has a very ragged edge.

I hope that you may get clear away and in Nature find some solace.

Sincerely,
Curzon

Lord Grey of Fallodon[1] wrote:

Dear Winston,

You were saying the other day how closely death had pressed home to you this year: and now it has come again in a particularly poignant form. The death of a little child seems to me to be more difficult than any other to reconcile with any scheme we can imagine of the fitness and purpose of things.

But I know you are brave enough to bear suffering & I think you are strong enough to enlarge your outlook & to grow & not to be withered by anything you have to go through. It may be harder still for your wife, who has not your work to pass the time for her. I am very sorry for her & for you.

Yours ever
Edward Grey

Marigold Churchill was buried at the Kensal Green cemetery in London at midday on August 26. Several Press photographers were present at the funeral, but Churchill asked them not to publish the pictures which they had taken, and they respected his request. On September 3 he wrote to Lord Crewe: 'We have suffered a vy heavy & painful loss. It also seems so pitiful that this little life sh'd have been extinguished just when it was so beautiful & so happy—just when it was beginning.'

In mid-September, Churchill went on holiday to Dunrobin, the Duke of Sutherland's castle in Scotland. Churchill had been a life-long friend of 'Geordie' Sutherland, and of his brother Alastair,[2] who had died only four months before. Clementine Churchill stayed in London. 'In the afternoon,' Churchill wrote to her from Dunrobin on September 19, 'I went out and painted a beautiful river in the afternoon light with crimson and golden hills in the background. I hope to make it much better tomorrow. . . .' On September 20 he wrote again:

It is another splendid day: & I am off to the river to catch pictures—much better fun than salmon.

Many tender thoughts my darling one of you & yr sweet kittens. Alas I keep on feeling the hurt of the Duckadilly. I expect you will all have made a pilgrimage yesterday.

[1] Edward Grey, 1862–1933. 3rd Baronet, 1882. Liberal MP, 1885–1916. Foreign Secretary, 1905–16. Created Viscount Grey of Fallodon, 1916. Ambassador on a special Mission to the USA, 1919.

[2] Lord Alastair St Clair Leveson-Gower, 1890–1921. Second son of the 4th Duke of Sutherland. Served in the Royal Horse Guards, and in the Guards Machine Gun Regiment, 1914–18. Awarded the Military Cross; wounded. He died on 28 April 1921, only twenty-nine days after the birth of his only daughter, Elizabeth Millicent Leveson Gower (in 1963 she succeeded her uncle as 24th Countess of Sutherland).

'Tis twenty years since I first used to come here. Geordie & Alastair were little boys. Now Alastair is buried near his father's grave overlooking the bay. Another twenty years will bring me the end of my allotted span even if I have so long. The reflections of middle age are mellow. I will take what comes.

35

Palestine 1921: 'Give the Jews their chance'

CHURCHILL and the officials of his Middle East Department were persistent in their efforts to reconcile the conflicting claims of Arab and Jew in Palestine. But many of the British officials in Palestine, and particularly the senior Army officers, looked with hostility upon Zionist aspirations. On June 16 General Congreve wrote from Cairo to Major Young that the only way to forestall further Arab attacks on Jews was to ensure that 'Arab aspirations are attended to'; and such a policy, Congreve added, 'means Zionist aspirations being greatly curbed'. According to Congreve, Sir Herbert Samuel had been 'warned of the incoming Bolshevists and the growing Arab resentment but would not listen or believe'. Congreve also warned Young, in blunt language, that 'as long as we persist in our Zionist policy we have got to maintain all our present forces in Palestine to enforce a policy hateful to the great majority—a majority which means to fight & to continue to fight and has right on its side'. Congreve's letter ended: 'Don't label us all as anti-Zionists. We only endeavour to see the truth and show it to you. You get the other side very fully I don't doubt.'

The Middle East Department did not encourage overt hostility to the Jewish National Home. 'The real answer,' John Shuckburgh wrote to Churchill on July 1, in a note on Congreve's letter, 'is that we are committed to this policy and have got to make the best of it.'

On June 18 Churchill sent Archibald Sinclair his detailed comments on the continuing Arab demand for representative institutions in Palestine. He believed that it was impossible for Britain to grant any form of representation which would give the Arabs the power to halt Jewish immigration. There was great folly, he warned Sinclair, in 'going out of our way to procure a hungry lion and then walking up to him with a plate of raw beef to see how much he would like to take'.

For more than two weeks Churchill and his advisers had discussed the Arab demand for Representative Government, based on an elected assembly. This was the demand which Churchill had declined to accept at the beginning of the month, but the Arabs were insistent that no other solution would satisfy them. It was essential, Churchill wrote in his letter to Sinclair of June 18, to say to the Arabs: 'We want to give you some elective institutions at once so that you do not feel yourselves left out at the present time. But before we can do this we must have an understanding with your Committee as to what is going to happen about Jewish immigration. We insist upon continuing Jewish immigration within the narrow limits now defined as resources become available. How are you going to safeguard us from not being interfered with by the elective body. . . .'

On June 22 Churchill explained the British position on Zionism to the Dominion Prime Ministers, at a meeting of the Imperial Cabinet. Among those present were the New Zealand Prime Minister, William Massey,[1] and the Canadian Prime Minister, Arthur Meighen.[2] 'The Zionist ideal,' Churchill told them, 'is a very great ideal, and I confess, for myself, it is one that claims my keen personal sympathy.' But the Balfour Declaration, he added, was more than an ideal. It was also an obligation, made in wartime 'to enlist the aid of Jews all over the world', and Britain must be 'very careful and punctilious' he explained, 'to discharge our obligations. . . .' He then outlined his policy as far as Jewish immigration was concerned:

We must insist on the door to immigration being kept open, insist that immigrants are not brought in beyond the numbers which the new wealth of the country, which was created by public works and better agriculture, can sustain.

MR MASSEY: The character of the immigrants?

MR CHURCHILL: Above all, as Mr Massey so justly interjects, by looking strictly to the character of the immigrants, both at the port from which they start for the Holy Land and when they arrive in the country. The stories of Bolshevism have been much exaggerated among them, the numbers

[1] William Ferguson Massey, 1856–1925. Born in Ireland. Went out to New Zealand at the age of 14 to join his parents. Prime Minister of New Zealand from 1912 until his death. New Zealand Representative at the Imperial War Cabinet, 1917–18. New Zealand Representative at the Paris Peace Conference, 1919, and at the Imperial Conference, 1921.

[2] Arthur Meighen, 1874–1960. Canadian Lawyer. Solicitor-General of Canada, 1913; Minister of Mines, 1917; Prime Minister and Secretary for External Affairs, 1920–1; Prime Minister, 1926. Leader of the Conservative Party of Canada, 1941–2.

of those who are infected with this horrible form of mental and moral disease
are not at all great, but I have given to Sir Herbert Samuel, himself a keen
Zionist and a Jew, directions which he is carrying out with vigour, to search
the camps for men of Bolshevik tendencies and to send them out of the
country with the least possible delay, and this is being done. It is not a
question of making war upon opinion, but of not allowing a great experiment
which deserves a fair chance, to be prejudiced by persons who are guilty of a
breach of hospitality.

Arthur Meighen then questioned Churchill about the meaning of a
Jewish 'National Home'. Did it mean, he asked, giving the Jews 'control
of the Government'? To this Churchill replied: 'If, in the course of
many years, they become a majority in the country, they naturally
would take it over.'

On July 5 Dr Weizmann, who had just returned from the United
States, told Colonel Meinertzhagen that he feared for the future of
Zionism. 'He says the British Government is whittling down the Balfour
Declaration,' Meinertzhagen recorded in his diary, 'that immigration
has practically stopped, that the bulk of the British Officers in Palestine
are not in sympathy with the movement and that the Zionists are not
getting those concessions which are necessary for the establishment of
the Home of the Jews in Palestine.' Meinertzhagen shared Weizmann's
worries, writing in his diary on July 5:

Sir Herbert Samuel has been weak. The moment the Jaffa rioting broke
out, he and his staff seem to have been hypnotized by the danger and everything was done to placate the Arab. Immigration was stopped, elective
assemblies were discussed, whereas what the Arab wanted was a good sound
punishment for breaking the peace and killing Jews. The Arab is fast learning
that he can intimidate a British Administration. Samuel has not been able to
stand up to the solid block of anti-Zionist feeling among his military advisers
and civil subordinates. . . .

Meinertzhagen was clear in his own mind about who was responsible
for the failure to give Zionism adequate support, and recorded his
verdict in his diary:

Our main trouble is the apathy of our big men towards Zionism. Winston
Churchill really does not care or know much about it. Balfour knows, and
talks a lot of platitudes but his academic brain is unable to act in any
practical way. Lloyd George has sporadic outbursts of keenness but fails to
appreciate the value to us of Zionism or its moral advantages.

Although Churchill was not prepared to allow an Arab Assembly to
put at risk the Jewish National Home, he did feel that peace could best

be preserved in Palestine by trying to allay Arab fears that the Jewish National Home would eventually lead to a Jewish majority. Yet many Zionists believed that an eventual Jewish majority was essential, if a Jewish National Home was to survive and flourish, and in his article in the *Illustrated Sunday Herald* of 8 February 1920, Churchill himself had looked forward to a Jewish community of three or four million people in Palestine. During the summer of 1921, however, he and his advisers took note of the growing Arab opposition to such a community.

The Arabs believed that Zionism was in retreat. In commenting on Churchill's speech of June 14 to the House of Commons, an article in the Arabic newspaper *El Karmel* noted, on July 6, that Churchill 'wanted to give an interpretation of the Balfour Declaration which would, at least on the surface, have diminished its value; he admitted that the country could not absorb mass immigration, and pointed out that the immigrants had included men who professed Bolshevism'.

A Delegation of Muslim and Christian Arabs was preparing to leave Palestine for London. 'What we can and probably will do,' Young wrote to Congreve on July 6, 'is to put them in touch with the Zionist Organization with a view to arriving at a working arrangement between the two extreme parties.'

On July 14, during the Colonial Office Vote in the House of Commons, there were several references to Palestine. A Conservative MP, Sir John Rees,[1] declared: 'I hope the administration of Palestine, so long as we are connected with it, will not be of an ardently Zionist character, because I think it would be extremely likely to lead to trouble with the Arabs, who, in my view, have far better claims on Palestine than the Jews. . . .' Sir Herbert Samuel, he added, had acted 'very wisely when he put on the screw and prevented further immigration'. These sentiments were echoed by Sir William Joynson-Hicks, who said, in the course of his speech:

I have not been unfriendly to the Zionist movement, but when you are inviting Jews from all over the world to establish a National Home in Palestine, and all that they mean by the term 'National Home', you must be very careful that you do not infringe your obligations of honour to the Arab population. . . .

Of course, if the Jews became the predominant power, it would be open to

---

[1] John David Rees, 1854–1922. Entered the Indian Civil Service, 1875; Additional Member of the Viceroy's Council, 1895–1900. Retired from the ICS, 1901. Chairman of several railway, gold-mining, and tea companies. Liberal MP, 1906–10. Knighted, 1910. Conservative MP for Nottingham East, 1912–22. Created Baronet, 1919. Director, Prisoners of War Information Bureau, 1915–20.

them to pass such laws as they desire, but the Arab has come to feel, rightly or wrongly, that the British Administration of Palestine is becoming to some extent Judean, and that is what is causing the present unrest in that country. I suggest that my right hon. Friend must reconsider some of the terms of the Balfour declaration. If he does not reconsider the terms of that declaration in regard to our obligations of honour to the Arab, it will not be, as he told us last month, 5,000 British troops who will have to be kept in Palestine, but at least another couple of divisions. . . .

Churchill did not reply to these remarks. But he did make a general contrast between Britain's African and Middle Eastern possessions. In the African colonies, he explained, 'you have a docile, tractable population, who only require to be well and wisely treated to develop great economic capacity and utility: whereas the regions of the Middle East are unduly stocked with peppery, pugnacious, proud politicians and theologians. . . .'

Before the Arab Delegation reached London, Dr Weizmann went to see Churchill at the Colonial Office to make his own protest about British policy in Palestine. On July 15 he sent Schmarya Lewin[1] an account of the conversation:

I had a very long argument with Mr Churchill which lasted one hour and a half. As a matter of fact when Mr Churchill first called me, I refused to go, on the ground that I could not discuss with him profitably the situation, because I knew the sort of declarations he would give. Unless Mr Churchill is prepared to grant us definite concessions, it is of no use discussing academic declarations of sympathy. Mr Churchill then called me again, and I went to him and in quite clear terms pointed out to him the vicious circle into which the attitude of the Palestine Administration, and of the Government, is placing us. On the one hand, they complain about Zionism being the burden of the British tax-payer, and when we desire to lighten this burden by developing Palestine and so increasing the wealth and productiveness of the country, they refuse to let us go on with our work because they are fearing an Arab outburst. I think Mr Churchill saw the strength of this argument and after a long discussion he has agreed to my demand that a Conference should be called at which Mr Balfour, Mr Lloyd George, Mr Churchill, General Smuts and Sir Alfred Mond should participate.

[1] Schmarya Lewin (Levin), 1867–1935. Born in Russia. Official Rabbi of Grodno, 1896–97; of Ekaterinoslav, 1898–1904; of Vilna, 1904–6. An ardent Zionist, at the 6th Zionist Congress (1903) he opposed the scheme to settle Jews in Uganda instead of Palestine. Elected to the First Russian Duma as a delegate of the Jewish National List, 1906. A signatory of the Vyborg Declaration, calling for civil disobedience, 1906. Appointed to the Zionist Executive, 1911. One of the initiators of the Haifa Technical School, 1912. Lived in the United States, 1914–23. Settled in Palestine, 1924.

Churchill's apparent hesitations were reflected in the Middle East Department, where doubts were being expressed about the most ambitious of the Zionist proposals, the Rutenberg schemes for electric power in the Jordan and Auja valleys. Gerard Clauson [1] was worried that the concessions to Rutenberg might anger the Arabs, who would ask why Britain was prepared to transfer Government lands to the Jews. Such crown land, he minuted on June 26, 'is *in practice* held on perpetual lease . . . for the Govt to expropriate large chunks of it (as it is bound to do by the terms of the concession) would have a disastrous result politically'. But Hubert Young was insistent that the full concession should be granted. Rutenberg's scheme, he minuted that same day, 'cannot be judged purely on its technical merits. It is the backbone of the Zionist policy of offering employment to Jewish immigrants.' Both Shuckburgh and Churchill supported Young's argument.

Rutenberg himself came to London in July, seeking final approval for his schemes. 'We are all very favourably impressed with Rutenberg here,' Young wrote to Wyndham Deedes on July 18, 'and it certainly seems as if the initiation of his schemes will do more to settle the country than anything else, if we can only get them fairly started.' Young added that Rutenberg himself 'fully realizes the necessity for getting the Arabs to co-operate', and that if Arab landowners who were said to be obstructing the Auja project persisted 'in being unreasonable', the Colonial Office would be prepared to insist on expropriation. Deedes was authorized to warn the Arab landowners to accept the concession. 'We hope that this warning will be enough,' Young added, 'and that once they see that we are determined not to be baulked they will make the best of it and give way.'

In his letter to Wyndham Deedes, Young pointed out that Churchill's Middle Eastern policy still had its critics, and its obstacles. As he explained it:

The 'Times' produced a long leader this morning criticising Winston's policy and suggesting that the sooner we cleared out the better. We must try and bring down the total expenditure to even less than Winston anticipated in his speech, but I do not see how we can make any further reductions in Palestine so long as the political unrest goes on. The whole performance is a desperate gamble and we hop from razor's edge to razor's edge without any

[1] Gerard Leslie Makins Clauson, 1891–1974. Boden Sanskrit Scholar, Oxford, 1911. Entered the Inland Revenue as a 2nd Class Clerk, 1914. 2nd Lieutenant, 1914. Served in Gallipoli, Egypt and Mesopotamia. Captain, 1918. Transferred to the Colonial Office, 1919; Principal, 1920; Assistant Secretary, 1934; Assistant Under-Secretary of State, 1940–51. Knighted, 1945. Chairman of the International Wheat Conference, 1947. Chairman of the International Rubber Conference, 1951. President of the Royal Asiatic Society.

definite prospect of reaching firm ground anywhere. I suppose we shall muddle through somehow, but the Turk is by no means finished with, and, with all respect to our Arab adviser, I have no confidence whatever in the Arabs.

Of the Arab attitude towards the Jewish National Home, Young added: 'they have always misunderstood our policy and it is about time that they should learn what it really means'.

On July 22 Churchill, Lloyd George, A. J. Balfour and Hankey met Weizmann at Balfour's house in London. Weizmann protested that the Balfour Declaration was being whittled away, and that Sir Herbert Samuel in particular was undermining it. On June 3 Samuel had declared, in an official speech, that 'the conditions of Palestine are such as not to permit anything in the nature of mass immigration'. Such a statement, Weizmann pointed out, was 'a negation of the Balfour Declaration'. Churchill asked Weizmann to explain why this was so. Weizmann explained that the Balfour Declaration 'meant an ultimate Jewish majority' whereas Samuel's speech 'would never permit such a majority to eventuate'. According to the Minutes of the meeting, Churchill 'demurred at this interpretation' of Samuel's speech, while Lloyd George and Balfour both agreed 'that by the Declaration they had always meant an eventual Jewish State'.[1]

Weizmann went on to raise the question of two aspects of Jewish activity that had been declared illegal—gun-running in order to protect the Jewish settlements from Arab attack, and the illegal arrival of colonists. At this point Churchill interrupted: 'We won't mind it, but don't speak of it.' Weizmann then asked whether the British intended to grant representative government to Palestine. Such a policy, he stressed, would mean 'giving up Palestine' as far as the Jews were concerned. Before Churchill could answer Lloyd George turned to him and said: 'You mustn't give representative Government to Palestine.' Churchill remarked that he might have to bring the question before the Cabinet, but that any questions effecting the Jewish National Home would, as a matter of course, be 'eliminated from the purview of the representative Government'.

Despite the assurances given by both Churchill and Lloyd George

[1] Earlier, Balfour had taken the opposite view about an eventful Jewish State, having written to Lord Curzon on 21 January 1919: 'As far as I know, Weizmann has never put forward a claim for the Jewish *Government* of Palestine. Such a claim is, in my opinion, certainly inadmissible, and personally I do not think we should go further than the original declaration which I sent to Lord Rothschild.'

during this discussion, Colonel Meinertzhagen still feared that the Zionist ideal was in danger. On July 23 he wrote in his diary:

> Our local administration in Palestine has failed to withstand not only Arab opinion, but local military advice. Both these potent factors are steadily working against Zionism and will, if they can, destroy it. Here in the Colonial Office, Winston is not too sympathetic and I suspect he regards it as a nuisance.

On July 23 Shuckburgh wrote to Churchill, outlining the attitude which he believed should be adopted towards the Arab Delegation. It would be necessary, Shuckburgh wrote, to 'bring to their notice and, if necessary, read over to them word by word, the whole series of public announcements defining British policy in Palestine', starting with the Balfour Declaration, and ending with Churchill's own speech of June 14. It was essential, Shuckburgh wrote, that both Muslims and Christians should accept 'as the basis of all discussion that it is our fixed intention to fulfil our pledges in the matter of the establishment of a National Home for the Jews'. At the same time, Shuckburgh continued:

> . . . we adhere equally firmly to the other part of our pledge, viz: that 'nothing shall be done which may prejudice the civil and religious rights of existing non-Jewish communities in Palestine'. We have given a clear indication of the lines on which we propose to proceed in fulfilment of these pledges. We have made it clear that we have no intention whatever of swamping the non-Jewish elements by the mass immigration of Jews.

Shuckburgh suggested that the Arabs should be advised to start discussions with Dr Weizmann, who had already 'willingly undertaken to discuss matters with them on their arrival', and would be both 'ready and anxious' to come to an understanding with them 'which will afford a firm basis for future co-operation'. But how far the Arabs would be willing to co-operate was a matter for doubt. On July 26 Sir Henry Wilson saw General Evans,[1] a senior Staff Officer in Palestine, and recorded in his diary: 'He is convinced that the Arabs will cut the throats of the Jews & that our force is quite insufficient to prevent this.' Evans added that it was 'preposterous that Sir Herbert Samuel a Jew, should be High Commissioner'.

The Arab Delegation reached London on July 28, but it was nearly three weeks before it began its official discussions. Meanwhile, in the

---

[1] Cuthbert Evans, 1871–1934. 2nd Lieutenant, Royal Artillery, 1891. On active service in South Africa, 1899–1902, and in the Great War, 1914–18 (France, Belgium and Italy). Lieutenant-Colonel, 1915. Staff Officer, Palestine, 1919–23 (with the rank of Brigadier-General).

Middle East Department, the defence of the Balfour Declaration continued. On August 5 Major Young sent Churchill a long and forceful Minute. In it he stressed that both he and Shuckburgh felt that Herbert Samuel had been pressed 'not only by Arabs, but also by British officials who are not in sympathy with Zionist policy', into taking action 'which was not altogether justified' in restricting Jewish immigration. The Cabinet, Young believed, should give Samuel clearer guidelines as to the policy to be pursued. Young himself favoured a policy which, he had written to Churchill on August 1, involved 'the gradual immigration of Jews into Palestine until that country becomes a predominantly Jewish state'.

Young argued that the phrase 'National Home' as used in the Balfour Declaration implied no less than full Statehood for the Jews of Palestine. There could be 'no half-way house', he wrote, between a Jewish State and 'total abandonment of the Zionist programme'. It was, he continued, 'insufficient for us merely to tell the Arab Delegation that we do not intend to waver in our policy—the fact of the matter is that we *have* wavered, and we must be prepared to take a stronger line'.

On August 2 Young discussed the future of Palestine with Dr Weizmann. But his sympathetic attitude did not set Weizmann's mind at rest. On August 10 the Zionist leader wrote to an American friend, Abraham Tulin:[1] 'Whenever you think you have won a real support out of this "other world" it proves at the end to be a mirage and one has to pay bitterly with one's nerves (and) self respect for the few minutes of fictitious joy and satisfaction. And so we stand again before the sphinx.'

Weizmann added: 'At present we have the "Arab Delegation" here, who have come with the avowed purpose of upsetting the Balfour Declaration. Happily they are fifth rate people but they can make a stink and they are supported by an anti-semitic clique and by our Morgenthaus.'[2]

Weizmann's fears that the Arab Delegation would be able to influence British opinion were well founded. On the very day that he was writing his letter, the Delegation was received by the Archbishop of

[1] Abraham Tulin, 1882–1973. Born in Russia. Emigrated to the United States as a child. His interest in Zionism was kindled by the Dreyfus trial in France. Practised law in New York. From 1919 to 1933 he was an American delegate at successive Zionist Congresses. Served as Chief Counsel of the Jewish Agency before the Anglo-American Commission of Enquiry on Palestine, 1947.

[2] A reference to Henry Morgenthau (1856–1946), an American Jewish financier who was strongly opposed to Zionism. From 1913 to 1916 he had been United States Ambassador in Constantinople.

Canterbury, Randall Davidson, who wrote to Churchill later that day, from Lambeth Palace:

> ... I think I ought to tell you that I have received from a good many quarters requests that I should remonstrate against what is thought to be the undue development of a Zionist policy in Palestine, especially with regard to the purchase of land by or on behalf of Jews and their apparent anticipation that in what are called State lands the development will be entrusted to Jews. Even more important is the possible buying out of reluctant sellers if they are non-Jews with a view to giving the lands to Jews.

On August 11 Churchill circulated to the Cabinet a memorandum, written by Major Young, proposing 'the removal of all anti-Zionist civil officials, however highly placed'. Young also advocated the provision of protection for Jewish colonies 'from the wanton attacks of their Arab neighbours'; the punishment of Arab villages who had committed 'violent aggression' on their Jewish neighbours, and gone unpunished; the placing of more reliance on the Zionist Organization 'as a recommending authority' for immigrants; and the early granting of economic concessions to Jewish enterprises 'for works of public utility'. In his covering note Churchill wrote:

> The situation in Palestine causes me perplexity and anxiety. The whole country is in a ferment. The Zionist policy is profoundly unpopular with all except the Zionists. Both Arabs and Jews are armed and arming, ready to spring at each other's throats. . . .
>
> In the interests of the Zionist policy, all elective institutions have so far been refused to the Arabs, and they naturally contrast their treatment with that of their fellows in Mesopotamia.
>
> The present strength of the Imperial garrison is about 8,000 men; and so far from this garrison being reduced, I am more likely to be confronted with demands for increasing it. The War Office estimates for this garrison during the coming financial year 1922–23 are £3,319,000, including expenditure on works and land. It cannot be doubted that this expense is almost wholly due to our Zionist policy.
>
> Meanwhile, Dr Weizmann and the Zionists are extremely discontented at the progress made, at the lukewarm attitude of the British officials, at the chilling disapprobation of the military, and at the alleged weakening of Sir Herbert Samuel.
>
> It seems to me that the whole situation should be reviewed by the Cabinet. I have done and am doing my best to give effect to the pledge given to the Zionists by Mr Balfour on behalf of the War Cabinet and by the Prime Minister at the San Remo Conference. I am prepared to continue in this course, if it is the settled resolve of the Cabinet.

On August 12 the Arab Delegation sent Churchill a memorandum
setting out their demands. Their first was for a National Government,
responsible to a Parliament 'elected by those natives of Palestine who
lived in the country before the war'. Their second was for 'the abolition
of the principle of the creation of a National Home for the Jews in
Palestine'. The Zionist aim, they continued, was the establishment of a
Jewish State in Palestine; such an aim 'threatens our very existence as a
nation'. The third Arab demand was for a total ban on all Jewish
immigration until a National Government had been set up. The fourth
demand was for the cancellation of all laws made since the British
occupation; the fifth demand was for Palestine to be allowed to join 'her
Arab neighbouring sister-states . . . under one confederated government, with one language, one Customs regulations etc. etc.'

On August 15, three days after receiving the Arab memorandum,
Churchill received the members of the Deputation. There were seven
in all, led by Musa Kazim Pasha. At the outset of the discussion
Churchill asked that their talk should be in private 'and that nothing
should appear, except what we agree together should be done'. There
was little use, he went on, 'our making speeches to each other, we have
done that before'. The Secretary to the Delegation, Shibly Jamal,[1] then
read out the Arab memorandum. Churchill insisted that he had no
authority to alter the 'fundamental basis' of British policy, and that the
Balfour Declaration was binding 'on me as well as on you'. He wanted
to discuss with the Arabs 'some satisfactory way of carrying out the
policy, and not merely a way of bringing it to an end'. If they wanted an
elective assembly, he said, they would have to show him in what way it
could be framed and worked 'as not to prevent the execution of the
gradual, but persistent, policy of the British Government in regard to
the Zionists'. This the Arabs refused to contemplate; for they saw it as
undermining their own aspirations to statehood:

SECRETARY:—Just as England is the national home of the Englishmen,
and America is the national home of the Americans, so the Jews want to make
Palestine the national home for Jews. This is what I understand. As they said
they want Palestine to become as Jewish as England is English.
MAJOR YOUNG:—You cannot imagine they want all the Jews in the world
to go and live in Palestine. Nobody could ever imagine that. They cannot

---

[1] Shibly al-Jamal. A Protestant Arab, born in Jerusalem. Taught at the St George's
(Church of England) School in Jerusalem. Before 1914 he moved to Cairo where he made
a fortune as an army contractor. Secretary to the Palestine Arab Delegate to London, 1921–2.
Active in Palestinian Arab politics until the 1940s.

mean that—all the Jews in the world—that Palestine should be to them what England is to us.
SECRETARY:—Then what do they want?

Shibly Jamal then listed the Arab complaints against the Zionists:

It is hard for us to live. A great many of our young men have to leave the country; a great many of the men who are away cannot come back, because the posts and business positions are being gradually taken up by the Jews. It is all right on paper to say the Jews are not going to oust us, it is another thing entirely to put that into practice. We are feeling the pinch of it right away, even at this early time. We really want to ask the Government to explain to us what they mean, because the Jews mean very much more than we think the Government has given them.

Jamal went on to complain of the large number of Jews working for the Government. This, Churchill replied, was because the Arabs 'are not fit to take these posts, they have not sufficient education. . . . There is not enough of modernly trained men.' But Musa Kazim Pasha insisted that the reason so few Arabs were employed was that the British had not 'the inclination' to employ them. The discussion became acrimonious:

SECRETARY:—A great many of the posts to which Jews have been appointed are technical posts, they are just clerical posts. Take the Treasury, there are 89 people in the Treasury and a large number of Jews.
MR CHURCHILL:—How many?
SECRETARY:—The Public Works Department & other Departments. It is everywhere; it is not technical work. It is not that they are more enlightened than we are. We have a great many young people who are waiting to come to the country if the status of the country is defined. A good many of our young men would be quite fit to occupy a great many posts in the Government; it is simply their lack of knowledge of English that keeps them back.
MAJOR YOUNG:—Yesterday you said it was their lack of knowledge of Hebrew.
SECRETARY:—Now they have introduced Hebrew as their language this has become another drawback, not only that they do not know English, but they are required to know Hebrew in some cases. Here we have a few departments. For instance, take in Jerusalem the Legal Department, there are 6 Jews, 3 Christians and 6 Mohammedans.
MR CHURCHILL:—Well, that is not much to complain about is it?
SECRETARY:—Yes it is, because the Moslems form eighty per cent of the people and the Jews six. Take the Public Works, there are 27 Jews, getting £7,312 and 8 Christians getting £1,428, and there is not one Mohammedan in the Public Works. . . .
Then again, what is the idea of making Hebrew the official language when

there is only seven per cent. who know Hebrew. Why should that have been done?

MR CHURCHILL:—All that is implied in the policy of the British Government to support the Zionist movement. You are forgetting all that. You are letting it pass out of your mind. I told you from the beginning that was the declaration that the Jews are to be encouraged to go to Palestine and found there a home for themselves. I told you that.

SECRETARY:—There again we come back to the first point. What is this promise that you made, and what does it mean? Did you promise that you will help them to make Palestine a Jewish State, a Jewish Kingdom.

MR CHURCHILL:—The High Commissioner has expressed very very clearly what is his interpretation of Mr Balfour's pledge. It undoubtedly is intended the Jews shall be allowed to come freely into Palestine in proportion as there is room, and there is a good livelihood, provided of course they develop the resources of the country.

A few moments later, Churchill suggested that while they were in London the Arabs should see Dr Weizmann. But Musa Kazim Pasha replied that 'we do not recognize Dr Weizmann. We recognise the British Government. We like our arguments to be with the Government, because it has the power that can give or take away from us.' But Churchill repeated his advice. 'Have a good talk with Dr Weizmann,' he told them. 'Try to arrange something with him for the next few years.' After seeing Weizmann, he said, they should return to see him. 'After I have seen you again,' he told them, 'if I find you are really making an effort to come to a settlement, and there is some hope of getting a settlement, I will endeavour to persuade the Prime Minister to receive you.' But, Churchill warned, he could do nothing for them if they did not make a serious attempt 'to come to a practical working arrangement' with the Jews.

On August 17, two days after Churchill had received the Arab Delegation, the Cabinet met to discuss the future of the Palestine Mandate. H. A. L. Fisher recorded the discussion in his diary:

Mond is Zionist, Montagu anti-Zionist. Winston anticipates trouble. I propose offering it to America which is welcomed.

The PM indulges in a fancy sketch of the huge population of Palestine in ancient times. The Arabs must not be too much pampered. The Jews are the people for cultivating the soil.

According to the Cabinet Minutes, Ministers were informed 'that recent reports from Palestine were of a disturbing character'. Arabs and Jews were armed, or were arming, and conflict might shortly ensue, 'particularly if the Arab delegation returned to Palestine without having secured a "withdrawal" of the Balfour Declaration'. The Cabinet were then told of two courses open to them; 'they could withdraw from their Declaration, refer the Mandate back to the League of Nations, set up an Arab National Government, and slow down or stop the immigration of Jews: or they could carry out the present policy with greater vigour and encourage the arming of the Jews with a view later on of reducing the numbers of the British garrison and cutting down expenses'.

The Cabinet secretary did not record whether Churchill himself put forward this choice, nor did he record the statements of individual Ministers. But the Minutes did record that in the course of the discussion 'stress was laid' on the fact that the 'honour' of the Government was involved in the Balfour Declaration, and that to go back on this pledge 'would certainly reduce the prestige of this country in the eyes of Jews throughout the world'. It was also argued at one point during the discussion 'that the Arabs had no prescriptive right to a country which they had failed to develop to the best advantage'.

On August 22 the Arab Delegation called on Churchill again at the Colonial Office. He at once rebuked them for refusing to see either Dr Weizmann or Nahum Sokolow, and for being unwilling 'to get to a practical friendly agreement with them'. Churchill then asked if he could speak 'as man to man in a friendly way', and when they agreed he spoke to them without prevarication:

The British Government mean to carry out the Balfour Declaration. I have told you so again and again. I told you so at Jerusalem. I told you so at the House of Commons the other day. I tell you so now. They mean to carry out the Balfour Declaration. They do. What is the use of looking at anything else? The Government is not a thing of straw, to be blown by the wind this way and that way. It is bound to carry out the Declaration. It contains safeguards for the Moslems, just as it contains clauses satisfactory for the Jew. You are not addressing your minds to the real facts of the case. . . .

The Arab Delegation refused to accept the 'facts' of the Balfour Declaration. Churchill asked them to discuss practical steps for 'a friendly arrangement' with the Jews. He could not, he said, discuss principles: 'I am only a servant of higher powers, and I can only act within the limits of my authority.' But Musa Kazim Pasha replied that as the Balfour Declaration was 'the root of the trouble', he still wished to discuss it. 'We are complaining,' he said, 'of our political rights being taken away.'

As the discussion continued, Churchill was drawn into the argument he had sought to avoid, and was irritated by the Arab insistence on discussing the whole principle of Zionism. But Musa Kazim Pasha reiterated that the problems of Palestine arose solely from Britain's promise to the Jews. It was impossible, Churchill replied, for him to discuss past decisions. He had no power, or desire, to repudiate the Balfour Declaration. Nor did he believe that the Jews were in any way a threat to the Arabs:

I have told you again and again that the Jews will not be allowed to come into the country except in so far as they build up the means for their livelihood according to the law. They cannot take any man's lands. They cannot dispossess any man of his rights or his property or interfere with him in any way. If they like to buy people's land, and people like to sell it to them, and if they like to develop and cultivate regions now barren and make them fertile, then they have the right, and we are obliged to secure their right to come into the country and to settle.

Later in the discussion, Churchill stated unequivocably that Britain could not grant representative Government to Palestine, because, as he said, 'we are trustees, not only for the interests of the Arabs but also for the interests of the Jews. We have a double duty to discharge.' The Arabs could not have representative Government, he said, because they could not be given the power to halt Jewish immigration. The British Government, he added, 'wants to see Jews developing and fertilising the country and increasing the population of Palestine'. It was 'a great pity', he continued, that there were so few people in Palestine, which had once been 'three or four times' more populous. He wanted, he said, to see more wealth in Palestine, 'instead of it being occupied by a few people who were not making any great use of it'. It was Britain's intention, Churchill declared, 'to bring more Jews in. We do not intend you to be allowed to stop more from coming in. You must look at the facts.'

The Arab Delegation had been at the Colonial Office for nearly an hour. But before the meeting ended, Churchill spoke to them at length about the need to accept Jewish immigration as a permanent and irrevocable feature of Palestinian life. During his final speech, he declared:

. . . the Jews are a very numerous people, and they are scattered all over the world. This is a country where they have great historic traditions, and you cannot brush that aside as though it were absolutely nothing. They were there many hundreds of years ago. They have always tried to be there. They have done a great deal for the country. They have started many thriving colonies, and many of them wish to go and live there. It is to them a sacred place.

Many of them go there to be buried in the city which they regard as sacred,—
as you regard it as sacred.

Why cannot you live together in amity and develop the country peacefully? There is room for all as long as they are not brought in in great
numbers before there are means of livelihood for them; before the electrical
and other means of power are created which will make waste places fertile;
before the hills have had terraces made upon them; before irrigation and
proper agricultural development. Of course, if they were brought in before
these things were done, you would have reason to complain. . . .

Churchill's speech continued:

Many of the British Officials in Palestine are very, very friendly to the
Arabs, more so than to the Jews. The Jews make continued outcry on that
subject, that the British officials and the British military authorities are unduly
partial towards the Arabs. No one has harmed you, and no one is harming
you. More than one and a half millions of money was invested in Palestine
last year by the Jews, and many years must pass before there can be any
question of Jews having the majority, or having any control or predominant
influence in the Country. . . .

Although it is my duty, as the representative of the Government, to speak to
you in plain and blunt terms so that no one can mistake my language, I can
assure you that I understand your feelings. I do not misunderstand your
feelings; I understand them, and to some extent I sympathise with them. But
I have also to understand the feelings of the other people, and what I am
trying to do is not to shut out the Jew or allow the Arab to shut out the Jew. . . .

Therefore, throw in your lot with us. Work with us hand in hand. Reassure
your people. Bring them along. Take up your share in the government of the
country. Associate yourself with the British Government. Give the Jews their
chance to come and develop the country, and if it does not work and does not
answer, you will have a great chance and plenty of time to show the whole
world that it has not answered and to make your complaint.

The Jews have a far more difficult task than you. You only have to enjoy
your own possession; but they have to try to create out of the wilderness, out
of the barren places, a livelihood for the people they bring in. They have to
bring them in under conditions which make for the general good of the
population, and which supplant no one, and deprive no one of their rights
and liberties. There may be from time to time instances of oppression, but we
will create a machine of government where these matters can be thrashed out
and exposed publicly, where it shall not be a government of autocracy but of
free speech, and of frank and friendly discussion.

But to do that we must be helped.

It would be the height of folly, Churchill warned, for the Arabs to
continue 'to swim round and round the basin in the centre all the time

saying "We want the British Government to enable us to put an end to the Balfour Declaration" '. If that was their only contribution to the debate, he added, the British would be able to say nothing but ' "No, we cannot agree to that" '. Churchill ended his remarks with an appeal to the Arabs which was based, not on political, but on racial grounds:

... it is no good your making out that you are entirely alien to the Jews. The Jews are people whose history from immemorial times has been very closely intermingled with that of the Arabs, and often in the most amicable manner. All history shows the relationship of these two races. It is no good pretending that you are more closely united to the Christians than to the Jews. That is not so. A wider gulf separates us from you than separates you from the Jew. I am talking of the Semitic race.

On August 23 Hubert Young reported on Churchill's discussions with the Arab Delegation to Harry Sacher, who had returned from Jerusalem to London. Young told Sacher 'that Mr Churchill had not received very favourable impression' of the Arab Delegation. During the discussion, Sacher rèiterated the Zionist position that in any future Palestinian constitution, the Zionists 'would desire adequate safeguards for the Jewish National Home'. His fear was that the Arabs might eventually be granted veto powers on Jewish immigration. These worries were shared by Dr Weizmann, who, despite the apparent firmness of Churchill's remarks to the Arab Delegation, doubted that British policy would in the end uphold the promises of the Balfour Declaration.

On August 31, in a long letter to Sir Wyndham Deedes, Weizmann set out his fears in detail. He had not been impressed by Churchill's contribution to the discussion at Balfour's house on July 22. On that occasion, he said, Churchill had tried to defend Herbert Samuel's arguments in favour of restricting Jewish immigration, and had reacted 'sulkily' to Weizmann's questionings. As a result of the meeting of July 22, Weizmann had drawn the conclusion that the British leaders saw no common ground in British and Jewish interests. If this was in fact so, Weizmann told Deedes, 'then this should be told to us honestly and straightforwardly. We are an old people, full of sores. We bleed out of every pore and it is a great sin, which will bitterly revenge itself, if we are simply put off by pious promises.'

Weizmann had been particularly depressed by a remark which Churchill had made to him at the meeting of July 22, when he had stated quite bluntly, as Weizmann told Deedes, that nine-tenths of the British in Palestine were 'opposed to the policy' of a Jewish National Home. In his letter to Deedes, Weizmann commented bitterly that in future the Jews would have to be taught 'to rely only on themselves'. His letter continued:

> Unless there will be a definite change of the course I don't see how we can demand millions from the Jews for an Arab Palestine, how we can continue to pour in about half a million pounds a year into the country. Our lives, our honour are not safe there, our prestige is being ruined, British public opinion which three years ago was distinctly in our favour is being systematically formed against us and I fear chiefly by those '9/10'.
> Of the Balfour Declaration nothing is left but mere lip service. The rock on which the policy has been built up is shattered! I know that all that will have far reaching consequences. But out of this present—terrible crisis, the Zionist idea will emerge triumphantly after much tribulation, because we are indestructible. The God of Israel in His wisdom is trying His people. Ukraine, Poland, Bolshevism—all that is not enough. We must be pogromed in Palestine, submitted there to restrictions and difficulties. Such are the ways of Providence and I believe faithfully that it is all for the good in the end.

Following his meeting with the Arab Delegation, Churchill had called Hubert Young to his room at the Colonial Office, and had outlined to Young his plans for policing Palestine. Writing to R. V. Vernon[1] on August 25, Young described Churchill's plan, and the reasons behind it. 'He said he would decline to employ any British units in Palestine at all,' Young wrote, 'or to have the forces in Palestine connected with Egypt in any way.' Churchill had proposed to use only Indian troops in Palestine; and even then no more than five thousand cavalry and a thousand infantry. Further efforts 'to keep the country quiet', he had decided, must be carried out by a local gendarmerie, for which Sir Herbert Samuel would be asked to spend £200,000 a year. Churchill also wanted the Jews to be given official support in defending their agricultural settlements against Arab marauders. A 'reserve force of Jews', he said, 'must be armed with machine guns and organized for the defence of the Jewish colonies as a recognized Government unit'.

Within the Middle East Department, the refusal of the Arab Delegation either to accept the Balfour Declaration, or to agree to talks with the Zionist leaders, and their demand for immediate self-government,

[1] Roland Venables Vernon, 1877–1942. Entered the Colonial Office, 1900. Private-Secretary to the Governor-General of Australia, 1911–13. Transferred to the Treasury, 1914. Assistant General Secretary, Ministry of Munitions, 1915–18. Deputy Accountant General, Board of Education, 1920–1. Assistant Secretary, Colonial Office, 1921–37. Member of the British delegation at Lausanne for the Turkish Peace Treaty, 1922–3. Financial Adviser to the Government of Iraq, 1925–8. Member of the British Delegation at the International Labour Conference, Geneva, 1929, 1930 and 1935.

was, as John Hathorn Hall[1] minuted on September 3, 'extremely disappointing'. And Gerard Clauson added, two days later: 'Not even the "pro-Arab party" in this country is so foolish as to think that the local popul^n of Palestine is fit to control the Executive.' On September 7 Shuckburgh wrote bluntly to Churchill that the uncompromising attitude of the Arab Delegation 'makes further negotiation with them useless'.

The Zionists continued to press for final British approval of the Rutenberg scheme. But early in September the scheme received a setback. The opponent of haste was Sir Herbert Samuel, who was, Young minuted on September 9, 'reluctant to agree to the signing of the concession until the Arabs agree'. Yet the Arab Delegation in London, Young wrote, 'have put themselves out of court by their attitude on the question of the Balfour Declaration'. Young himself believed 'that we should proceed boldly without obtaining "Arab" consent', and that until the concession was granted, Rutenberg would not be in a position financially 'to secure Arab co-operation'. Young, who was about to go to Palestine himself, wanted to 'press Sir Herbert to concur' in person, and to take Rutenberg with him.

Churchill received Young's proposal while he was in Scotland, where he was staying after the death of his daughter Marigold. Rutenberg wanted to travel to Scotland at once to put his proposals to Churchill personally. He had just received a telegram from Weizmann which, Young informed Shuckburgh on September 10, predicted 'calamity' unless the Zionist Congress at Carlsbad could be informed 'within the next few days' that the concession was to be signed. Rutenberg told Young that he had made plans to go to Scotland on the night Express on September 12. But when Shuckburgh explained to him earlier that day that the Middle East Department were doing everything in their power to conclude the agreement, Rutenberg abandoned his journey. 'I am glad to say,' Shuckburgh wrote to Churchill that day, 'that he does *not* propose to pursue you into Scotland.' Shuckburgh supported the Rutenberg concession as strongly as Young had done, and with the added weight of his senior position, writing to Churchill in his letter of September 12:

[1] John Hathorn Hall, 1894–   . On active service, 1914–18; awarded the Military Cross and the Belgian Croix de Guerre. Entered the Egyptian Civil Service (Ministry of Finance), 1919–20. Assistant Principal, Colonial Office (Middle East Department), 1921; Principal, 1927. Chief Secretary to the Government of Palestine, 1933–7. British Resident, Zanzibar, 1937–40. Governor and Commander-in-Chief, Aden, 1940–4. Knighted, 1944. Governor and Commander-in-Chief, Uganda, 1944–51.

Mr Rutenberg is fully alive to the necessity of treating Arab interests sympathetically, and realises that, without Arab cooperation, his plans cannot succeed. I do not think that any useful purpose wd. be served by asking the Arab Delegation (who have, in effect, broken off negotiations with us) for their formal assent. They would be certain to refuse or waste time in haggling; and even in the unlikely event of their agreeing, their assent wd. bind no one & would in reality carry us no further.

Shuckburgh urged Churchill to give him the authority to 'proceed at once' to try to obtain Herbert Samuel's approval to the concession. This Churchill agreed to do. Shuckburgh thereupon telegraphed to Samuel, in Churchill's name, asking him to accept Rutenberg's assurances that Arabs would be employed as well as Jews in the electrification programme. Samuel was still hesitant, but on September 17 Shuckburgh wrote again to Churchill, asking him to accept Rutenberg's own word as sufficient safeguard, and to authorize the immediate signature of the agreement. Shuckburgh sought an immediate decision. 'If you approve,' he wrote in his letter of September 17, 'I should be vy grateful if you could send me a brief word *by telegram on Monday* authorising me to go ahead. Rutenberg is leaving England almost at once, and it is vy desirable to get the matter settled before he goes. I am sorry to trouble you with all this; but the matter is one in which I could not act without your personal instructions.'

Churchill telegraphed his approval, and on September 22 Shuckburgh wrote to Rutenberg's solicitors: 'I am directed by Mr Churchill to authorize you to sign and deliver to Mr Rutenberg the contract regarding a concession for a hydro-electric scheme in the valley of the River Auja in Palestine and also the contract dealing with a similar concession in connection with the River Jordan.' Shuckburgh's letter set the seal of British approval on a practical scheme, intended by the Zionist leaders to provide the economic basis for the Jewish National Home.

During September, Churchill looked for some means of reducing still further the military cost of the Palestine Mandate. On September 3 he wrote to Lloyd George that 'Palestine simply cannot afford to pay for troops on the War Office scale' and that the need to keep British troops in Palestine was not giving the Colonial Office 'a fair chance to carry out our pledges'. It was, he believed, unnecessary to spend £3,500,000 a year to keep a British force in Palestine, when, for the same amount of money 'we could employ the highest class' of local gendarmerie, such as the Cape Mounted Rifles or the Canadian Police. 'The War Office,' Churchill wrote, 'continue to think in Brigades, Divisions, Columns of Troops, Lines of Communication etc. What is wanted in Palestine is primarily an operation of police.' If the Cabinet would allow him to 'get rid of the British troops altogether', Churchill added, he could not only cut out the cost of troops, but also save 'a full million' in barracks and base facilities. A local police force would have British officers, and the support of aeroplanes and armoured cars controlled by the Royal Air Force; but the bulk of its expenditure would be borne by local funds. An even larger saving could be ensured, Churchill told Lloyd George, if the Cabinet would authorize 'arming the Jewish colonies for their own protection'.

At the end of September Churchill alighted upon a means of creating a Palestine Gendarmerie without delay, thus dispensing altogether with British troops, and possibly obviating the need to arm the Jewish settlers. On September 30 he sent Archibald Sinclair a proposal to transfer the Black and Tans from Ireland to Palestine as soon as they could be spared. The proposal originated from General Tudor, the commander of the Black and Tans, and Churchill accepted it 'subject to such alterations as climatic conditions may require'. In his letter to Sinclair he wrote: 'Colonel Meinertzhagen might get in touch with General Tudor and ascertain from him privately what sort of arrangement would enable us, in the event of an Irish peace, to take over a couple of Black & Tan companies. General Tudor should not, however, broach the matter among his men, as it might raise false hopes.' On October 3 Meinertzhagen informed Churchill that Tudor hoped to raise two thousand troops for Palestine, at a cost 'considerably lower than our estimate of £800,000', thus saving over a million pounds on the original Gendarmerie proposals.

On October 10 Churchill explained his Palestine dilemma in a letter to A. J. Balfour. 'As soon as I am sure,' he wrote, 'that we are not going to have an Arab rebellion this autumn and winter I hope to make a further reduction in the expenses of the garrison.' But, he added, whereas in Mesopotamia it had been possible 'to study the wishes of the people and humour their national sentiment', in Palestine Britain was committed to a policy—'the Zionist policy'—against which 'nine-tenths of the population and an equal proportion of the British officers are marshalled'.

In Palestine itself, General Congreve was openly expressing his dislike for Churchill's Palestine policy. During October 10 he had a long talk with Hubert Young, who had just reached Jerusalem. Young informed the Colonial Office on the following day that Congreve 'told me straight out that he and all his officers were certainly under the impression that His Majesty's Government were in the hands of the Zionist Organization' and that the Middle East Department was 'pursuing an unfair policy in favour of the Jews'.

On October 14 Sir Herbert Samuel sent Churchill a report on the 'uneasy political situation' in Palestine. The failure of the Arab Delegation to have reached a 'detente' while in England would, he wrote, 'almost certainly give rise to a mood of irritation among the Arabs and of alarm among the Jews'. Samuel then put forward a series of proposals which would, he believed, lead to a less dangerous situation. He wanted the Zionists to agree to limit 'immigration of the labouring classes' to those who would have employment waiting for them on 'new enterprises', and he wanted the Zionist Commission to discontinue its political work, and confine itself to cultural and economic questions. Samuel wanted the Zionists to repudiate Dr Weizmann's much-repeated statement that Palestine would in due course become 'as Jewish as England is English'. He also wanted the Zionists to give up their aim of establishing a Jewish State. Hubert Young supported Samuel's proposals. But when they reached the Colonial Office they were at once challenged by Colonel Meinertzhagen, who wrote to Shuckburgh on October 21:

> Weizmann would never agree to Sir Herbert Samuel's declaration and it is unreasonable to ask him to do so. It is demanding certain surrender and suicide on his part. So long as the Balfour Declaration stands we must not ask the Zionists themselves to abandon it.

In the last week of October Churchill, Shuckburgh, Meinertzhagen and Clauson discussed Sir Herbert Samuel's proposals with Dr Weizmann himself, and on November 1 Weizmann reported to the Zionist Executive that he had taken 'an attitude of strong opposition' to all that Samuel had suggested.

The Middle East Department had another cause for dissatisfaction with Sir Herbert Samuel's policies. In an attempt to soothe Arab discontent, Samuel had refrained from enforcing the fine levied from the Arabs of Jaffa for their part in fomenting the Jaffa riots. On October 27 Meinertzhagen wrote angrily to Shuckburgh: 'If we are morally too weak or physically incapable to enforce a just punishment on those guilty of breaches of the peace, we must acknowledge impotence. . . . Apart from our moral obligations to ensure security in Palestine, we

must not submit to injustice on the grounds of weakness or unwillingness to face the Arab threat, which is becoming intolerable.' Shuckburgh joined Meinertzhagen in his protest, minuting on October 28
that Samuel was, quite simply, 'afraid', and he continued: 'The doctrine that offenders may defy us with impunity if only they are strong
enough is clearly an intolerable one.' Shuckburgh proposed that a fine
be levied 'from everybody alike', despite 'the risks involved' of further
disturbances. Churchill noted on November 2: 'As proposed by Mr
Shuckburgh.'

Twice during November Churchill sought to change Samuel's attitude. On November 17 he minuted: 'Sir Herbert Samuel should be held
stiffly up to the enforcement of the fines on Jaffa,' and five days later he
rejected Samuel's representations that the political effects of the imposition of fines should be taken into account. 'It is, in my opinion, essential,' Churchill informed Samuel, 'that Jaffa as well as villages should be
made to realise responsibilities with least possible delay. We cannot
allow expediency to govern the administration of justice.' Were Samuel
to find it difficult to enforce the collection of fines, Churchill added, he
would be willing to arrange for a warship to help uphold the High
Commissioner's authority.

On the fourth anniversary of the Balfour Declaration, violence broke
out again in Palestine. 'A disturbance took place in Jerusalem this
morning,' Samuel telegraphed to Churchill on November 2, 'when a
small crowd of Arab roughs appeared in the Jaffa Road. They were
dispersed by the police but soon after gathered for an attack on the
Jewish quarter. This was averted by the police. Some shots were exchanged between this crowd and the crowd in the Jewish quarter. . . .
Four Jews and one Arab were killed.'

The Middle East Department were angered by the Arab attack, and
by the somewhat feeble action taken to halt it. It was, wrote Gerard
Clauson on November 3, 'a pity that when the first mob gathered the
Police only dispersed it, instead of rounding it up. They knew trouble
was in the wind.' And he added: 'It was quite certain that this demonstration was deliberately organized.' The Arab aim, Meinertzhagen
noted, was to make it impossible for the Government to carry out the
terms of the Balfour Declaration: It was essential, he believed, to 'remove all doubts about our intentions'; otherwise the Arabs would
continue to seek to alter the policy by violence. 'Our attitude towards

the Arab,' Meinertzhagen added, 'has not encouraged his respect for us.'

Not all voices in the Middle East Department felt that the Arabs alone were in the wrong. On November 7 Shuckburgh sent Churchill a long memorandum, pointing out that the Zionist Organization, 'in the person of Doctor Weizmann', enjoyed direct access to 'high political personages outside the Colonial Office'. Shuckburgh had been angered to learn, from Weizmann himself, of the meeting at Balfour's house on July 22, and of Lloyd George's assertion that the 'Jewish National Home' meant a 'Jewish State'. In his memorandum Shuckburgh wrote:

I do not know what may have been the original intention, but it was certainly the object of Sir H. Samuel and the Secretary of State to make it clear that a Jewish State was just what we did not mean. It is clearly useless for us to endeavour to lead Doctor Weizmann in one direction, and to reconcile him to a more limited view of the Balfour pledge, if he is told quite a different story by the head of the Government. Nothing but confusion can result if His Majesty's Government do not speak with a single voice.

Churchill made no comment on Shuckburgh's rebuke. His main concern was expressed on November 12, in a minute to Archibald Sinclair. 'Do please realise,' he wrote, 'that everything else that happens in the Middle East is secondary to the reduction in expense.'

In August the Arab Delegation had rejected Churchill's request that they meet the Zionists for informal talks. But following the Jerusalem riot, Churchill decided to call both sides together for a joint Conference under his own chairmanship. The meeting was fixed for the afternoon of Wednesday November 16, at the Colonial Office. On November 15 Meinertzhagen wrote to Shuckburgh that he hoped that Churchill would impress on the Arab Delegation 'that further violence will not pay'. But at a lunch that same day, given by the Arab Delegation at the Hotel Cecil, Lord Sydenham[1] spoke bitterly against Zionism.

Meinertzhagen doubted whether Churchill would take the initiative in combating the activities of anti-Zionists in England. 'Winston is inclined to pay more attention to reconstituting the Palestine Garrison,' he wrote in his diary, 'than to remedying the political situation'. Meinertzhagen wanted Churchill to make a public declaration of policy

---

[1] George Sydenham Clarke, 1848–1933. Joined Royal Engineers, 1868. On Staff of Royal Indian Engineering College, 1871–80. Secretary to the Colonial Defence Committee, 1885–92; and to the Royal Commission on Navy and Army Administration, 1892–1900. Knighted, 1893. Governor of Victoria, Australia, 1901–4. Secretary to the Committee of Imperial Defence, 1904–7. Governor of Bombay, 1907–13. Created Baron Sydenham of Combe, 1913. Chairman of Central Appeal Tribunal, 1915–16. President, National Council for Combating Venereal Disease, 1915–20. Member of the Air Board, 1916–17.

in favour of the Jewish National Home. But Churchill would not do so, as Meinertzhagen recorded in his diary on November 16. 'Winston,' he wrote, 'has flatly refused to have anything to do with it, referring to it all as a stupid proposition. He suggests no alternative beyond asking the Zionists to come to some amicable arrangement with the Arabs. In other words he is prepared to relegate Zionism to the same policy of drift which has characterized the policy of the Government since the Armistice.'

Churchill asked Sir James Masterton Smith to accompany him to the meeting between the Arab Delegation and the Zionists. On the morning of November 16 Shuckburgh wrote to Masterton Smith that it was 'unfortunate that Lord Sydenham should have made a fiery speech to the Delegation on the very eve of their interview with the Secretary of State'. He also sought to put in a good word for Weizmann:

I hope that the Secretary of State will not make any reference this afternoon to the Zionist tag about making Palestine as Jewish as England is English. This phrase was originally used by Dr Weizmann at the Paris Peace Conference early in 1919. I do not know how it got out, but it has appeared in various newspapers and has excited a certain amount of comment both among Arabs and Zionists. Dr Weizmann has explained to me the circumstances in which it was made and has argued, with some force, that when it was made it was not without justification. He realises that the situation has changed since then. To bring up the expression now would look like a personal reproof to Dr Weizmann. I should be very sorry for this, as I am convinced of the necessity of Dr Weizmann's co-operation in our difficult task. He is much the best and most reliable of the Zionists.

A few hours before the meeting between the Arab Delegation and the Zionists was due to begin, Churchill asked for it to be cancelled, explaining that he was unwell. No new date was set, and on November 22 Shuckburgh wrote to Masterton Smith: 'I understand the Secretary of State's general view to be that the Arabs should be encouraged to come to terms on their own account with the Zionists, and that it is not desirable that any further pronouncement on behalf of His Majesty's Government should be made at present.' The Zionists were depressed by Churchill's apparent neglect. 'Dr W never knows where he has Churchill,' Miriam Sacher[1] wrote to her husband on November 21.

On November 25 Dr Weizmann was again invited to the Colonial

---

[1] Miriam Marks, 1892–   . Born in Wigan, daughter of Michael Marks, founder of Marks and Spencer. She married Harry Sacher in 1916. In 1921 she was a member of the Women's Zionist Delegation to the Carlsbad Zionist Congress. Lived in Palestine, 1921–8; then in England.

Office to discuss Jewish immigration to Palestine. Churchill was not present at the discussion, which was chaired by Shuckburgh. The British officials agreed to re-establish the 'certificate system', which Sir Herbert Samuel had suspended, whereby the Government of Palestine would admit any Jew in possession of a Zionist Organization certificate stating that work was available for him on his arrival. Weizmann was delighted with this decision, writing to his friend David Eder[1] on November 27:

I find the C.O. most friendly and helpful on every concrete matter which is brought up, but the difficulty seems to lie at the other end; then like always in English politics they hate to tackle an angular question and would rather drift than take the bull by the horns and thus they are fiddling and fidgeting about the Arab Delegation without being able to make up their mind. First they wanted me to negotiate with them, then they changed their mind and decided to call us together and make a statement of policy, impose a policy on both parties. At the last moment Churchill changed again and suggested we should negotiate. Now we are invited for Tuesday 29th to the C.O.

At the Colonial Office meeting on November 29, John Shuckburgh took the chair. Churchill had told Weizmann on the previous day that he would make no public announcement, nor was he present at the meeting. The discussion was inconclusive, as Weizmann's account to the Zionist Executive on the following day made clear:

Mr Shuckburgh had opened the proceedings by an appeal to both sides to leave politics aside and co-operate on practical work so necessary in the interests of Palestine. The Arabs declared that the invitation which they had received from Mr Churchill in the first instance had promised a Government pronouncement on policy in Palestine. They asked what had become of this pronouncement. This put the Chairman into an awkward position but he stated that the Colonial Secretary did not consider a statement necessary at the present time. Musa Kazim said he had nothing to add to the demands put forward officially in the Arab Delegation's statement.

On behalf of the Arab Delegation, Musa Kazim Pasha had insisted that he would only negotiate with the Zionists if the Balfour Declaration were not incorporated in the Mandate in its existing form. Shuckburgh told him that 'he could hold out no hope' that the interpretation of the

---

[1] Montagu David Eder, 1865–1936. Born in London, he devoted himself to medical work in London's slums. Member of the Socialist League, 1889. Practised medicine in South America (Doctor of Medicine, Bogota, 1898). Medical Officer, London School Clinic, 1908. Founder, with Ernest Jones, of the Psychoanalytical Association, 1913. In charge of War Shock patients, Malta, 1916. Medical Officer, Neurological Clinic, London, 1917. Member of the Zionist Commission to Palestine, 1918. A relative by marriage of Litvinov, he visited the Soviet Union in 1921 but failed to secure the legalization of Zionist work there. Member of the Executive of the Zionist Organization, London and Jerusalem, 1921–8.

Declaration would be changed. The Arab Delegation were not willing to enter into any further negotiations.

On December 13 Dr Weizmann sent an account of his feelings, and forebodings, to Wyndham Deedes. The Colonial Office's policy, he wrote, seemed designed, not to build a Jewish National Home in Palestine, but rather 'an Arab National Home in which a few Jews will be inserted'.

Churchill knew of Weizmann's discontent. But he took no action to counter the strong anti-Zionist feelings of the British officials in Palestine, nor did he intervene when General Congreve issued an army order which referred at one point to 'the grasping policy of the Zionist extremists', and described the sympathies of the British army as 'rather obviously with the Arabs, who have hitherto appeared to the disinterested observer to have been the victims of an unjust policy, forced upon them by the British Government'. This order had been issued on October 29. Throughout November and December Churchill was urged to denounce it, by Meinertzhagen from within the Colonial Office, and by Sir Alfred Mond. But in a departmental Minute on December 1, Shuckburgh advised him against any action. 'I greatly doubt the advantage of making heavy weather with the War Office over it,' he wrote. And he added: 'It is unfortunately the case that the Army in Palestine is largely anti-Zionist and will probably remain so whatever may be said to it.' Churchill studied the file, and then pronounced, on December 9: 'no action required'. The Zionists were bitterly disappointed, feeling that the enthusiasm generated by Churchill's visit had been whittled away to nothing.

36

Palestine 1922: Defending the Balfour Declaration

A T the beginning of 1922 the Zionists became increasingly alarmed at the growing hostility in England towards the very idea of a Jewish National Home. It seemed to them that the Balfour Declaration itself was at stake. On January 16 the Zionist Executive received a secret note of remarks made by a member of the Arab Delegation to London. These remarks boded ill for the future peace of Palestine. According to the note, a senior British official in Palestine, Ernest Richmond,[1] had told the Arabs that everyone at the Colonial Office hoped that the Rutenberg scheme would fail, so that the concession 'will automatically fall to the ground'.

Richmond's remarks, which so alarmed the Zionists, were based on a misconception. For on January 17 John Shuckburgh wrote to Churchill, setting out the reasons why Rutenberg's electrification scheme was 'to be encouraged'. In his letter he declared:

I admit that the electrification of any portion of the railways in Palestine may at first sight appear quite premature. It may well be asked why the needs of Jaffa and Jerusalem cannot be served by a form of traction which is deemed sufficient for the infinitely heavier traffic between, let us say, London and Liverpool or Paris and Marseilles. The answer is that in this, as in all matters relating to Palestine, we stand under the shadow of the Balfour Declaration. The Rutenberg concession has always been regarded as the most practical example of the policy of setting up a National Home for the Jews. It

[1] Ernest Tatham Richmond, 1874–1954. A member of Lord Cromer's staff in Egypt, 1904. Served in the Public Works Department, Cairo. Served in the Trench Warfare Department of the Ministry of Munitions, 1915–18. Major, Imperial War Commission, Palestine, 1918. Adviser to the Palestine Government on the restoration of the Dome of the Rock, 1919–20. Political Assistant Secretary, Palestine, 1921–2. Arab Adviser to the Palestine Government, 1922–7. Director of Antiquities, Palestine, 1927–8.

is so regarded by the Zionists themselves. We are always trying to divert the attention of the Zionists from political to industrial activities, and preaching to them from the text that their best chance of reconciling the Arabs to the Zionist policy is to show them the practical advantages accruing to the country from Zionist enterprise. For these reasons we have supported and encouraged Mr Rutenberg's projects and I submit that we must continue to support and encourage them so far as circumstances permit.

Churchill agreed with Shuckburgh's submission, and in the continuing negotiations with Rutenberg, it was acted upon as the official view of the Middle East Department.

It was not only towards Zionist industrial enterprise that Churchill's officials acted sympathetically. By the beginning of February they had drafted a Constitution for Palestine which would ensure that no Arab majority could stand in the way of continued Jewish immigration and investment. On February 4 Churchill wrote to his wife:

The Palestine Arabs came to see me this morning and received a draft Constitution which they have taken off to mumble over; we have taken a leaf out of Lenin's book and introduced the principle of 'indirect election', i.e., all the voters in the country elect 400 secondary electors, and these electors again elect 12 members of the Legislative Council.

The Arab Delegation, angered by the rejection of their demand for a majority Government, handed a copy of Churchill's draft to the *Morning Post*. On February 7 Shuckburgh wrote bitterly to Churchill: 'It appears to me that the Arab Delegation has been guilty of an act of treachery such as renders it impossible for us to treat them any longer with the consideration that we have shown them in the past.' Shuckburgh went on to advise Churchill to have 'no further dealings' with them, 'unless they can give us some satisfactory explanation'. No such explanation was forthcoming, only denials.

The campaign against the Balfour Declaration continued. At question time in the House of Commons on February 15 Sir William Joynson-Hicks asked Lloyd George to explain the reason why the Government had promised the Jewish people a national home 'in a country which is already the national home of the Arabs'. Churchill, replying for Lloyd George, declared that such a question was better suited to a full debate 'than by question and answer', and promised to make 'a full statement on policy in Palestine' when he next presented the Middle East estimates.

In the face of mounting criticism of Britain's pledge to the Jews, the Middle East Department decided that Churchill must make a clear public statement of Britain's Palestine policy. On February 21 Dr Weizmann told a meeting of the Zionist Executive that he had just had an interview at the Colonial Office with Sir John Shuckburgh, who had advised him 'not to worry about Arab propaganda'. Shuckburgh added that Churchill would deliver 'a big speech on Palestine' during the Middle East Estimates debate early in March.

The Middle East Department began its defence of the Balfour Declaration on March 1, when Sir John Shuckburgh sent the Arab Delegation a long letter reiterating the Government's determination not to go back on its pledge to the Jews. The letter, which was sent with Churchill's full Ministerial authority, stated emphatically:

Mr Churchill regrets to observe that his personal explanations have apparently failed to convince your Delegation that His Majesty's Government have no intention of repudiating the obligations into which they have entered towards the Jewish people. He has informed you on more than one occasion that he cannot discuss the future of Palestine upon any other basis than that of the letter addressed by the Right Honourable A. J. Balfour to Lord Rothschild[1] on the 2nd November, 1917, commonly known as the 'Balfour Declaration'.

Later in his letter Shuckburgh tried to explain to the Arab Delegation what would be the status of the Jews in Palestine:

When it is asked what is meant by the development of the Jewish National Home in Palestine, it may be answered that it is not the imposition of a Jewish nationality upon the inhabitants of Palestine as a whole, but the further development of the existing Jewish community, with the assistance of Jews in other parts of the world, in order that it may become a centre in which the Jewish people as a whole may take, on grounds of religion and race, an interest and a pride. But in order that this community should have the best prospect of free development and provide a full opportunity for the Jewish people to display its capacities, it is essential that it should know that it is in Palestine as of right and not on sufferance. That is the reason why it is necessary that the existence of a Jewish National Home in Palestine should be internationally guaranteed, and that it should be formally recognised to rest upon ancient historic connection.

For the fulfilment of this policy, Shuckburgh continued, 'it is necessary that the Jewish community in Palestine should be able to increase its numbers by immigration'. But the British Government were willing to insist that this immigration 'cannot be so great in volume as to exceed

[1] Lionel Walter Rothschild, 1868–1937. Zoologist. Trustee of the British Museum, 1899–1937. Conservative MP for Aylesbury, 1899–1910. Major, Royal Bucks Yeomanry. Succeeded his father as 2nd Baron, 1915. A generous benefactor and one of the leaders of world Jewry.

whatever may be the economic capacity of the country at the time to absorb new arrivals'.

The Arab Delegation responded to the Middle East Department's letter on March 3, at a meeting of Arab supporters at the Hyde Park Hotel in London. On March 30 Shuckburgh sent Churchill an account of the meeting. Its object had been to renounce Britain's 'Zionist policy', and the principal Arab speaker, Shibly Jamal, was reported to have used language—as Shuckburgh wrote—'about the necessity of killing Jews if the Arabs did not get their way'.

Churchill's new declaration of policy came, as promised, during the Middle East debate in the House of Commons on March 9. In his speech he stressed that the control of Jewish immigration was an essential feature of his Palestine policy. 'Every effort has been made,' he said, 'to secure only good citizens who will build up the country. We cannot have a country inundated by Bolshevist riffraff, who would seek to subvert institutions in Palestine as they have done with success in the land from which they came.' The immigrants who did arrive, he said, 'bring with them the means of their own livelihood, the Zionist Association expending nearly a million a year in the country'.

Churchill then spoke of the Arab demand for self-determination, and representative government, based on a majority vote. He could, he declared, do nothing which would involve 'falling into a position where I could not fulfil those pledges to which we are committed by the Zionist policy. I am bound to retain in the hands of the Imperial Government the power to carry out those pledges.'

The Zionists were much encouraged by Churchill's declaration. But on that same day, unknown to them, their hopes were being curtailed yet again in Palestine itself. On March 9 Sir Herbert Samuel sent Churchill a draft of his long-term proposals for the administration of Palestine. Samuel declared that he intended to suspend Jewish immigration into Palestine on account of the large number of recent Jewish immigrants, many of whom remained unemployed. 'It is wholly impracticable,' Samuel asserted, 'to make Palestine as Jewish as England is English. . . .'

Samuel's letter described the Arabs of Palestine as 'on the whole a kindly and well disposed people, and by no means turbulent or bloodthirsty'. It went on to warn that the 'economic capacity of the country to absorb labour remains at present small . . .'. As the only labour seeking absorption on a substantial scale was Jewish labour, this concept of an economic absorptive capacity could only act against Jewish immigration. Over a thousand Jewish adult males had entered Palestine between January 1 and February 28, together with over 700 dependants.

The Middle East Department did not feel able to overrule Samuel's decision to suspend Jewish immigration. 'I think we have no alternative,' Shuckburgh wrote to Masterton Smith on March 11, 'but to support the High Commissioner and to do what he asks us. But we must be prepared for a howl from the Zionists. It is a little unfortunate that the Arab Delegation not long ago asked us to suspend immigration until the political question was settled.' Shuckburgh pointed out that the Arabs 'may now boast that they have bullied us into doing what they want. But I am afraid that this cannot be helped.' Masterton Smith passed on Shuckburgh's minute to Churchill, asking whether Churchill wanted to proceed as Samuel proposed. Churchill agreed. In spite of his public declaration supporting the Balfour Declaration, he had accepted Samuel's policy of restricting immigration. This policy seemed to threaten the hopes of an eventual Jewish majority, and looked as if it were in specific answer to the Arab delegation's demands, and threats. Yet despite Samuel's action, there was no falling off in the number of Jewish immigrants, who totalled just over 8,000 a year for each of the years between 1920 and 1923. The Zionists themselves, unable to finance large-scale projects, felt unable to offer work to larger numbers. Even in the two months of so-called suspension of immigration, in May and July of 1921, more than 170 Jewish immigrants arrived in Palestine, and in July 1921, when the ban was lifted, the numbers rose to over 500.[1] Nevertheless, the Zionists were afraid that Samuel's suspension of immigration was a dangerous precedent, which could only encourage the Arabs to resort again to violence in order to restrict Jewish immigration.

In the House of Commons, Churchill continued to defend the Balfour Declaration. During March he found himself having to reply to a series of questions from anti-Zionists, and he was firm in rebutting both their charges and their insinuations. At the same time, he took the opportunity of alerting the Zionists in private, and warning them not to court criticism. In the third week of March he learnt that Rutenberg intended to buy machinery for his scheme from German firms. On March 21 he minuted, to Archibald Sinclair:

[1] Among the immigrants for July 1921 was a Russian-born American Jewess, Goldie Mabowitz (later, as Golda Meir, Prime Minister of the State of Israel, 1969–74).

You had better make it clear to Mr Rutenberg and to the Zionists generally that a policy of placing orders in Germany, while unemployment is so serious in this country, will be used as an additional argument against our providing two millions a year to keep a British garrison to support the Zionist policy.

Churchill was also firmer on the question of Bolshevism in Palestine than his anti-Zionist critics realized. After Sir Herbert Samuel had reported a movement among the extremist immigrants to disrupt the work of the administration, Churchill wrote, in a Colonial Office minute on March 31: 'In my view H.C. shd collect & deport all the leaders of this movement, & he shd be asked to state by telegraph what action he proposes.' The deportation duly took place.

The effect of Churchill's statements of March 9 continued to influence the situation in April. 'I generally think the position here is better,' Sir Alfred Mond wrote to Samuel from London on April 4. 'Churchill's very firm declarations as to the maintenance of the Balfour Declaration have I hope discouraged the Arab Delegation. . . .' But Mond went on to warn Samuel that the Delegation had become, both in the Press, and outside it, 'a focus and a tool of the general Anti-Semitic movement'.

In his speech to the House of Commons on March 9, Churchill had stressed the economies which were being made in Palestine, particularly in defence. During April his plan to replace all British troops in Palestine by a Gendarmerie, paid for principally out of local funds, made good progress. On April 5 he wrote to Archibald Sinclair, urging that as many of the gendarmerie as possible should be mounted, both on horse and on camel. 'The spectacle of these men riding about the country,' he explained, 'is an important element in the whole policy.' On April 11 Colonel Meinertzhagen inspected the men who were already under training at Tregantle, near Devonport. 'All the officers and men,' he wrote in his diary, 'are recruited from the disbanded Black and Tans; they are a magnificent lot of men and should acquit themselves well.'

On May 24 Shuckburgh sent Churchill the final draft of Sir Herbert Samuel's plans for the future of Palestine. In it, Samuel repeated the proposals which he had already sent Churchill on March 9. The proposals were not at all in line with Zionist aspirations. Samuel again reiterated as 'impracticable' the much quoted remark of Dr Weizmann that Palestine would become 'as Jewish as England is English'. The British Government, Samuel insisted, 'have no such aim in view'. Nor did they wish to see 'the disappearance or the subordination of the Arab population, language or culture in Palestine'. Samuel also repeated that the Balfour Declaration did not contemplate 'that Palestine as a whole should be converted into a Jewish National Home, but that such a Home should be founded *in Palestine*'.

Samuel's memorandum went on to state once again that further Jewish immigration could not be permitted to exceed 'whatever may be the economic capacity of the country at any given time to absorb new arrivals'.

Samuel's statement was accepted by Churchill as a guideline for future British policy, and was published as part of the Palestine White Paper of 30 June 1922. The Zionists themselves formally accepted the White Paper. But they were angered by the setting up of so specific an economic condition to future immigration, fearing that unsympathetic, and even anti-Zionist High Commissioners in the future, would abuse the concept of an economic absorptive capacity to halt unfairly some future waves of immigration. Samuel was convinced, however, that his formula was the right one for the peaceful development of Palestine. On June 12 Eric Mills[1] noted, in a departmental minute: 'Sir H. Samuel told me that he thought the country could not support economically more than 6,000 immigrants per annum. If that be so then there is no conceivable chance that the Jews will ever be a majority in Palestine.'

During May the British anti-Zionists began to criticize the Colonial Office for having approved the Rutenberg concession. Lord Northcliffe's *Daily Mail* was particularly vehement against the granting of so important an economic benefit to a Russian Jew. As Northcliffe himself had only recently visited Palestine, these criticisms were thought to have his personal approval. On May 29 Henry Wilson wrote to General Congreve: 'Your Mr Rutenberg & his Palestine monopoly has created quite a stir here.'

In the second week of June Churchill began to prepare his speech for the Colonial Office Vote. This was to be the occasion for the House of Commons to approve the maintenance of the Balfour Declaration as the basis for British policy in Palestine, before the League of Nations finally

---

[1] Eric Mills, 1892–1961. Served with the Government of Palestine, 1919–48. Worked briefly at the Colonial Office, 1921. In 1936 he was Commissioner for Migration and Statistics in Palestine, and also Director of the Department of Immigration. On special duties in Jamaica, 1949; Fiji, 1950; the Anglo-Egyptian Sudan, 1950–1 and British Guiana, 1952–6. In 1931 he wrote the *Report of the Census of Palestine*.

approved the Palestine Constitution. In anticipation of the Vote, strong anti-Zionist forces were mustered to speak in Parliament on behalf of the Arab majority, to demand representative institutions which would enable the Arabs to halt Jewish immigration, and in particular to denounce the Rutenberg concession, which was seen as the beginning of Jewish domination.

On June 21 a Liberal Peer, Lord Islington,[1] introduced a motion in the House of Lords, declaring that the Palestine Mandate was 'inacceptable to this House', because it was 'opposed to the sentiments and wishes of the great majority of the people of Palestine'. The Rutenberg scheme, Islington alleged, would invest the Jewish minority with wide powers over the Arab majority. 'Zionism,' he declared, 'runs counter to the whole human psychology of the age.' It involved bringing into Palestine 'extraneous and alien Jews from other parts of the world', in order to ensure a Jewish predominance. Jewish immigration, he added, would be a burden on the British taxpayer, and a grave threat to Arab rights and development. 'The Zionist Home,' he asserted, 'must, and does mean the predominance of political power on the part of the Jewish community in a country where the population is predominantly non-Jewish.'

Lord Islington's arguments were challenged by Balfour, who, in his maiden speech in the House of Lords, spoke emphatically in favour of Jewish immigration and investment, and denied that the Arabs would suffer in any way as a result. But as the debate continued, it was clear that a majority of the Peers present were bitterly opposed to Zionism and all its works. Lord Sydenham matched Lord Islington in the strength of his anti-Zionism. 'Palestine is not the original home of the Jews,' he said, referring to biblical times. 'It was acquired by them after a ruthless conquest, and they never occupied the whole of it, which they now demand.' The Jews, Lord Sydenham continued, 'have no more valid claim to Palestine than the descendants of the ancient Romans have to this country'. The Romans, he added, had occupied Britain 'nearly as long as the Israelites occupied Palestine, and they left behind them in this country far more valuable and useful work'. The 'only real claim' to Palestine, he believed, 'is that of its present inhabitants'. Sydenham then spoke of the effect of Jewish immigration since 1919:

[1] John Poynder Dickson-Poynder, 1866–1936. Conservative MP for Chippenham, 1892–1905; Liberal MP, 1906–10. In 1896 he married Churchill's friend Anne Dundas. Served in South Africa as a Lieutenant, 3rd Royal Scots, 1900. Created Baron Islington, 1910. Governor of New Zealand, 1910–12. Chairman of the Royal Commission on Indian Public Service, 1912–14. Under-Secretary of State for the Colonies, 1914–15. Parliamentary Under-Secretary for India, 1915–18. Chairman of the National Savings Committee, 1920–6.

Palestinians would never have objected to the establishment of more colonies of well-selected Jews; but, instead of that, we have dumped down 25,000 promiscuous people on the shores of Palestine, many of them quite unsuited for colonising purposes, and some of them Bolsheviks, who have already shown the most sinister activity.

The Arabs would have kept the Holy Land clear from Bolshevism.

A few moments later Lord Sydenham declared:

What we have done is, by concessions, not to the Jewish people but to the Zionist extreme section, to start a running sore in the East, and no one can tell how far that sore will extend.

Zionism will fail . . . but the harm done by dumping down an alien population upon an Arab country—Arab all round in the hinterland—may never be remedied. . . .

The Mandate as it stands will undoubtedly, in time, transfer the control of the Holy Land to New York, Berlin, London, Frankfurt and other places. The strings will not be pulled from Palestine; they will be pulled from foreign capitals; and for everything that happens during this transference of power, we shall be responsible.

Lord Sydenham ended his speech by an appeal to the House of Lords to 'save the Empire from the intolerable situation which the Mandate, as dictated from first to last by the Zionists, will inevitably bring about in Palestine'. Towards the end of the debate, Lord Willoughby de Broke,[1] referring to Balfour's speech, declared: 'I almost wished I was a Jew myself because they came in for some very handsome treatment at his hands.'

The views of the anti-Zionist Lords prevailed. In the division, 60 Peers voted against the Balfour Declaration, and only 29 for it.[2]

On the day after the Lords debate, Hubert Young warned Churchill, in a departmental minute, that the anti-Zionist vote 'will have encouraged the Arab Delegation to persist in their obstinate attitude'. Unless the Lords' vote could be 'signally overruled' by the House of Commons, he wrote, 'we must be prepared for trouble when the Delegation gets back to Palestine'. Young feared an Arab policy of 'non-cooperation' with the British, if the Balfour Declaration were not specifically upheld in the Commons.

[1] Richard Greville Verney, 1869–1923. Conservative MP for Rugby, 1895–1900. Succeeded his father as 19th Baron Willoughby de Broke, 1902. Lieutenant-Colonel, Warwickshire Yeomanry, which he commanded, 1914–18. Author of two books on foxhunting.

[2] Those who voted against the Balfour Declaration included the Duke of Northumberland, Lord Bertie of Thame, Lord Chelmsford, Lord Carson and Lord Raglan. Those who voted in favour of the Declaration included Balfour himself, the Duke of Sutherland, Lord Birkenhead, Lord Lansdowne and Lord Long.

One Arab complaint, which had reached the Middle East Department, was that the Jewish Colonization Association had evicted Arabs from their lands, in order to settle Jewish immigrants in their place. On July 3 Sir John Shuckburgh wrote to Edward Marsh: 'The S of S may like to know, for the purposes of tomorrow's debate, that this lie has been nailed to the counter. So far as we know, none of our critics, in or out of Parliament, have yet fathered this particular story.' The land in question, it appeared, was 'mainly swamps and sand dunes'.

The Colonial Office debate took place on the evening of July 4. Sir William Joynson-Hicks led the attack on Zionist activity in Palestine, and in particular on the Rutenberg concession, by introducing a motion to reduce Churchill's salary by £100. He opened his speech by deploring the fact that the Rutenberg concession contracts had never been submitted to Parliament, and went on to say that it was his wish to set out 'the Arab as against the Zionist intentions'. The Arabs felt, he said, that Palestine was 'within the territories which were to be handed over to the Arab dominions' once Turkey had been defeated. The 'real trouble', Joynson-Hicks went on, was not the Balfour Declaration, but '. . . the way in which the Zionists have been permitted by the Government, practically to control the whole of the Government of Palestine'.

The central point of Joynson-Hicks's attack was that Zionist Jews were being given the senior administrative posts, and that the predominant financial interests and the principal economic concessions throughout Palestine were in their control. 'Palestine,' he declared, 'had been Zionised.' Not only the High Commissioner, but many other leading officials, were Jews. Even Sir Herbert Samuel's son[1] was a junior member of the administration. Arabs who had sought economic concessions had, Joynson-Hicks alleged, been turned away. As for Rutenberg's scheme, it was grandiose but impracticable. Yet the Colonial Office contract 'gives over the development of the whole country to Mr Rutenberg'. Nor was there any provision in the contract 'for any benefit for the manufacturers of Great Britain. There is no clause providing that any orders should be placed in Great Britain at all . . .

---

[1] Edwin Herbert Samuel, 1898–   . 2nd Lieutenant, Royal Field Artillery, 1917. Served on General Allenby's Staff in Palestine, 1918–19. District Officer, Jerusalem, Ramallah and Jaffa, and a member of the Headquarters Staff of the Governor of Jerusalem, 1920–7. Assistant Secretary, Government of Palestine, 1927–30. Assistant District Commissioner, Galilee, 1933–4. Deputy Commissioner for Migration, 1934–9. Postal and Telegraph Censor, Jerusalem, 1939–42. Chief Censor, Palestine, 1942–5; Director of Broadcasting, 1945–8. A director of the *Jewish Chronicle*, London, 1951–70. Senior Lecturer (on British Institutions), Hebrew University of Jerusalem, 1954–69. Succeeded his father as 2nd Viscount, 1963.

We have spent millions of money in Palestine, and sacrificed thousands of lives, and after all this no benefit is to come to England. . . .'

Joynson-Hicks's final attack was upon Rutenberg himself:

I do not wish to make any capital out of the character of Mr Rutenberg, but I think quite seriously I am entitled to say this much, that Great Britain has no right to hand over such vast powers, and such vast possibilities of control over the whole development of Palestine to a man whose character is at least the subject matter of very grave suspicion. Certain statements have been made in the 'Times' newspaper with regard to his actual connection with a very horrible murder, and they have not been contradicted.[1]

Joynson-Hicks ended his speech by asking for a special enquiry into the Rutenberg concession. Another speaker, Sir John Butcher,[2] bitterly attacked Churchill for the powers which the concession gave to Samuel and Rutenberg alike. 'Is that fair,' he asked, 'to the inhabitants of Palestine, or to the interests of the Arabs?'

When Churchill began to reply to these attacks, the House was alert. 'Return to hear Winston on Zionism . . .' H. A. L. Fisher wrote in his diary later that night, 'a brilliant speech. The house rocks with laughter.' Churchill began by pointing out that when one had 'Jews, Russians, Bolshevism, Zionism, electrical monopoly, Government concession, all present at the same moment, it must be admitted that all those ingredients are present out of which our most inexperienced scribe or cartoonist, or our most recently budding statesman, might make a very fine case. . . .' He was therefore surprised, he added, that Joynson-Hicks 'after his long experience of the House of Commons, would rather have given a chance to one of his lieutenants, instead of taking such an easy victim for himself'.

Dealing first with the Balfour Declaration, Churchill pointed out that there had never been 'any serious challenge' in Parliament to that policy, and he continued:

Pledges and promises were made during the War, and they were made, not only on the merits, though I think the merits are considerable. They were made because it was considered they would be of value to us in our struggle to win the War. It was considered that the support which the Jews could give us

---

[1] Rutenberg was said to have been responsible, in 1906, for the murder of Father Gapon, a Russian Orthodox priest who, on 9 January 1905 ('Bloody Sunday'), had led a procession of workers through St Petersburg to present a petition to the Tsar. The procession was fired on, many were killed, and the 1905 revolution began. The revolutionary socialists distrusted Gapon, whom they accused of being a police spy or agent provocateur.

[2] John George Butcher, 1853–1935. Born in Killarney. Barrister, 1878; Queen's Counsel, 1897. Conservative MP for York, 1892–1906 and 1910–23. Created Baronet, 1918. Created Baron Danesfort, 1924.

all over the world, and particularly in the United States, and also in Russia, would be a definite palpable advantage. I was not responsible at that time for the giving of those pledges, nor for the conduct of the War of which they were, when given, an integral part. But like other Members I supported the policy of the War Cabinet. Like other Members, I accepted and was proud to accept a share in those great transactions, which left us with terrible losses, with formidable obligations, but nevertheless with unchallengeable victory.

The Balfour Declaration, Churchill insisted, 'was an integral part of the whole mandatory system, as inaugurated by agreement between the victorious Powers and by the Treaty of Versailles'. These were decisions, he pointed out, 'which the House at every stage approved'. In November 1917, he reminded the House, almost 'every public man in this country' had expressed his opinion on the Balfour Declaration. 'I am going to read now,' he continued, 'not the opinions of ministers of all denominations, not the views of the most gifted writers of every school of thought. I am going to deal only with politicians.' Churchill then quoted twelve statements, all supporting the Balfour Declaration. Some had actually been made by people who now attacked the very policies they had then supported. Lord Sydenham had said:

I earnestly hope that one result of the War will be to free Palestine from the withering blight of Turkish rule, and to render it available as the national home of the Jewish people, who can restore its ancient prosperity.

Sir John Butcher, who, Churchill said, 'has just addressed us in terms of such biting indignation', had earlier been 'almost lyrical on the subject'. Churchill then quoted Butcher's words of 1917:

I trust the day is not far distant when the Jewish people may be free to return to the sacred birthplace of their race, and to establish in the ancient home of their fathers a great, free, industrial community where, safe from all external aggression, they may attain their ideals, and fulfil their destiny.

Churchill's final quotation was from Joynson-Hicks himself, who had written in 1917:

I consider that one of the greatest outcomes of this terrible War will be the rescue of Palestine from Turkish misgovernment, and I will do all in my power to forward the views of the Zionists, in order to enable the Jews once more to take possession of their own land.

Joynson-Hicks's statement of 1917, Churchill commented, 'goes far beyond the Jewish National Home; it is a commonwealth; it is almost a complete expropriation', to which Joynson-Hicks interjected: 'It is not the Rutenberg monopoly.' 'I am coming to that,' Churchill replied. But first, he said, he wanted to draw the House of Commons' attention to the similarity of the comments of Lord Sydenham and Joynson-Hicks; and he continued:

It is very remarkable. Two great minds have moved together. Together they made this immense promise to the Zionists, together they pledged their faith, together they revised their judgement, and together they have made themselves the leaders of the opposition to this Government carrying out their policy.

Churchill offered to 'prolong this list' of those who had supported the Balfour Declaration with such enthusiasm less than five years earlier. But he was content, he said, to 'draw the moral' on the evidence so far:

You have no right to say this kind of thing as individuals; you have no right to support public declarations made in the name of your country in the crisis and heat of War, and then afterwards, when all is cold and prosaic, to turn round and attack the Minister or the Department which is faithfully and laboriously endeavouring to translate these perfervid enthusiasms into the sober, concrete facts of day-to-day administration.

I say, in all consistency and reasonable fair play, that does not justify the House of Commons at this stage in repudiating the general Zionist policy. That would not be in accordance with the way in which affairs of State are conducted by the Imperial Parliament or, at any rate, by the House of Commons.

I appeal to the House of Commons not to alter its opinion on the general question, but to stand faithfully to the undertakings which have been given in the name of Britain, and interpret in an honourable and earnest way the promise that Britain will do her best to fulfil her undertakings to the Zionists.

The House of Commons, Churchill had said earlier in his speech, was 'entirely at liberty' to criticize the administration of the Colonial Office if that administration had been 'wrongly conceived or ill-directed; if it is marked by improper incidents; if it is not, in fact, a reasonable and proper way of carrying out the policy of Great Britain. . . .' The Rutenberg concession, he believed, was not open to any of these criticisms. Indeed, he went on, it was 'the only path open' to him, in pursuing Government policy to secure the establishment of the Jewish National Home. The Rutenberg concession would, he added, safeguard the Arabs against being dispossessed, for it enabled the Jews 'by their industry, by their brains and by their money' to create 'new sources of wealth on which they could live without detriment to or subtraction from the well-being of the Arab population'. Jewish wealth, he believed, would enrich the whole country, all classes and all races:

. . . anyone who has visited Palestine recently must have seen how parts of
the desert have been converted into gardens, and how material improvement
has been effected in every respect by the Arab population dwelling around.
On the sides of the hills there are enormous systems of terraces, and they are
now the abode of an active cultivating population; whereas before, under
centuries of Turkish and Arab rule, they had relapsed into a wilderness.

There is no doubt whatever that in that country there is room for still
further energy and development if capital and other forces be allowed to play
their part.

There is no doubt that there is room for a far larger number of people, and
this far larger number of people will be able to lead far more decent and
prosperous lives.

Apart from this agricultural work—this reclamation work—there are
services which science, assisted by outside capital, can render, and of all the
enterprises of importance which would have the effect of greatly enriching the
land none was greater than the scientific storage and regulation of the waters
of the Jordan for the provision of cheap power and light needed for the industry of Palestine, as well as water for the irrigation of new lands now
desolate.

The granting of the Rutenberg concession did not involve, he said,
'injustice to a single individual'; it did not take away 'one scrap of what
was there before', and it offered to all the inhabitants of Palestine 'the
assurance of a greater prosperity and the means of a higher economic
and social life'. Churchill then asked the House of Commons:

Was not this a good gift which the Zionists could bring with them, the
consequences of which spreading as years went by in general easement and
amelioration—was not this a good gift which would impress more than anything else on the Arab population that the Zionists were their friends and
helpers, not their expellers and expropriators, and that the earth was a
generous mother, that Palestine had before it a bright future, and that there
was enough for all?

Were we wrong in carrying out the policy of the nation and of Parliament
in fixing upon this development of the waterways and the water power of
Palestine as the main and principal means by which we could fulfil our
undertaking?

Critics of the Rutenberg concession had insisted that it was for the
Arab majority to develop the economic wealth of Palestine. Churchill
sought to rebut this argument:

I am told that the Arabs would have done it themselves. Who is going to
believe that? Left to themselves, the Arabs of Palestine would not in a thousand
years have taken effective steps towards the irrigation and electrification of

Palestine. They would have been quite content to dwell—a handful of philo-sophic people—in the wasted sun-scorched plains, letting the waters of the Jordan continue to flow unbridled and unharnessed into the Dead Sea.

There then followed an angry altercation:

Mr MARRIOTT:[1] Is there no Englishman who would have done it for them?

Mr CHURCHILL: I really must remind my hon. Friend that he wrote, in 1917:

'I entirely agree in the declaration of sympathy made by Mr Balfour on behalf of the Government to the Zionist Federation, and trust that the termi-nation of the War may permit the realisation of the hope and intention which he expressed.'

Mr MARRIOTT: I stand by every word of that.

Mr CHURCHILL: It is very easy for my hon. Friend to sit there 'stand-ing by every word,' but he takes every conceivable point that occurs to him against the Government in their endeavour to carry out the Mandate and the imperative commands which he laid upon them. We really must know where we are. Who led us along this path, who impelled us along it? I remained quite silent. I am not in the 'Black Book'. I accepted service on the lines laid down for me. Now, when I am endeavouring to carry it out, it is from this quarter that I am assailed.

Churchill proceeded to explain to the House of Commons that the Government itself did not have the money to develop the irrigation of Palestine. This was true throughout the Colonies. 'The result is,' he added, 'that the development of your possessions is far below what it might be', and that the Government suffered continuously through the fact 'that these great estates are not brought up to a high level of economic development'. For this reason, he had welcomed Rutenberg's application for an electrical concession. The concession itself, he pointed out, 'has been framed in the Colonial Office in exactly the same manner as if it related to East Africa, Nigeria, Ceylon or any other of the Crown Colonies. It has been scrutinized and executed by the agents. Technical matters were submitted to the examination of consulting engineers.' In addition to this, Churchill explained, there would be 'strict Government control' of the prices charged to the consumers for electricity produced under the scheme, and a 'severe limitation on profits', which would, after the company had earned ten per cent of its

[1] John Arthur Ransome Marriott, 1859–1945. Historian and political scientist; author of more than forty books between 1889 and 1946. Secretary to the Oxford University Extension Delegacy, 1895–1920. Conservative MP for Oxford City, 1917–22; for York, 1923–9. Director of the Great Northern Railway, 1919–23. Knighted, 1924.

47. Lloyd George and Churchill, 10 February 1922, leaving 10 Downing Street for the House of Commons

48. Lloyd George, Churchill and Lord Birkenhead, a few moments later, 10 February 1922

50. The Cairo Conference, March 1921. Front row: General Congreve, Sir Herbert Samuel, Churchill, Sir Percy Cox, General Haldane, General Ironside, General Radcliffe. Second row: far left; Gertrude Bell; centre, T. E. Lawrence (above Sir Percy Cox), General Salmond (above Haldane) and Hubert Young (between Ironside and Radcliffe); extreme top, centre, Sir Archibald Sinclair (with bow tie), below him (also with bow tie), Joseph Crosland. Front left; two lion cubs on their way from Somaliland to the London Zoo

49. 'Hats you can't talk through': a cartoon by Strube, 18 January 1921

51. Sir John Shuckburgh

52. At the pyramids, 20 March 1921. Left to right: Clementine Churchill, Churchill, Gertrude Bell, T. E. Lawrence and Churchill's detective, W. H. Thompson

FIDDLING WHILE ROME BURNS.

SPESHUL!!!

NEW LEADER WANTED FOR COMMONS AND GREAT CABINET RESHUFFLE

WINSTON & CHURCHILL PAINTERS AND DECORATERS

IMAGINE BEING CAUGHT LIKE THAT!

53. 'Fiddling While Rome Burns': a cartoon by Poy, *Daily Mail*, March 1921

54. Abdullah, Samuel and Churchill in Jerusalem, March 1921

55. Churchill, Lawrence and Abdullah in Jerusalem, March 1921

56. Churchill at Sir Henry Wilson's funeral, 26 June 1922

57. Churchill at Dundee, after his operation for acute appendicitis, supported by his detective, November 1922

58. Churchill at Dundee, carried by four citizens

59. Churchill at Dundee, waiting to speak

initial investment, be divided equally between it and the Palestine Government. Once fifteen per cent had been received, 'the whole profit' would revert to the Palestine Government, who, after 37 years, would have the 'full right' to buy the whole scheme.

Several MPs had been critical of the concession because it had not been granted to an Arab company. Churchill now answered these criticisms:

It has been stated to-night that 'streams of applications' were coming in from Arabs and British. No stream of applications was coming in. At the time the Rutenberg concession was granted, no other application was before us.

Churchill's assertion was given unexpected confirmation by a Conservative MP, Sir John Norton-Griffiths,[1] who rose from his place to declare that he himself had had the concession offered to him twice, and had refused it. 'It was hawked all over London,' he said, 'and refused by house after house. I have the documents on my file. I would not give a bob for it now.' Churchill then told the House of Commons that before he became Colonial Secretary there had been an application from two inhabitants of Bethlehem, 'one an Arab and one a non-Arab', but they had furnished 'no plans, no estimates, no scheme at all', asking only 'that if there were any concessions going, they would very much like to have them'. For his part, Rutenberg had produced a scheme, in July 1921, 'in the utmost detail, and with considerable backing. . . . No other application was received.' Churchill then told the House of Commons of Rutenberg's own credentials and financial backing:

He is a man of exceptional ability and personal force. He is a Zionist. His application was supported by the influence of Zionist organisations. He presented letters from Mr Edmond Rothschild,[2] the founder of the Zionist colonies, whose whole life has been spent in building up these wonderful colonies in Palestine. These letters offered to place at his disposal from £100,000 to £200,000, on absolutely non-commercial terms, for long periods,

[1] John Norton-Griffiths, 1871–1930. Engineer; Governing Director of Norton Griffiths & Co, public works contractors. Served in the Matabele War, 1896–7, and as Captain Adjutant to Lord Roberts' bodyguard in South Africa, 1899–1900. Conservative MP for Wednesbury, 1909–18; for Wandsworth, 1918–24. Lieutenant-Colonel, 1915; organized the formation of Tunnelling Companies for the Engineer-in-Chief, BEF. Special Mission to Rumania, in connection with oil and corn stores, 1916. Knighted, 1917. Created Baronet, 1922.

[2] Edmond James de Rothschild, 1845–1934. Born in Paris, a member of the banking family. After the Russian pogroms of the 1880s he became a patron of Jewish settlements in Palestine, including Rishon le-Zion. First visited Palestine in 1887. Following Zionist criticism of the patronage system, his settlements were transferred to the Jewish Colonial Association in 1900, but he continued to finance new settlements, and was a pioneer of the wine-industry in Palestine before 1914. Founded the Palestine Jewish Colonization Association, 1923, with the aim of founding further settlements. He died in Paris.

for the development of these irrigation and electrical schemes. He produced plans, diagrams, estimates—all worked out in the utmost detail. He asserted, and his assertion has been justified, that he had behind him all the principal Zionist societies in Europe and America, who would support his plans on a non-commercial basis.

It was the non-commercial aspect of the Rutenberg concession which Churchill wished to stress, for it revealed an aspect of Zionism which had made a profound impression on him. The offer of a major concession in Palestine, he pointed out, had 'fallen extremely flat outside the circles of the Zionist followers'. He continued:

Nearly all the money got up to the present time has come from associations of a Jewish character, which are almost entirely on a non-profit-making basis.

I have no doubt whatever—and, after all, do not let us be too ready to doubt people's ideals—that profit-making, in the ordinary sense, has played no part at all in the driving force on which we must rely to carry through this irrigation scheme in Palestine. I do not believe it has been so with Mr Rutenberg, nor do I believe that this concession would secure the necessary funds were it not supported by sentimental and quasi-religious emotions.

Churchill continued his speech with a defence of Rutenberg himself: 'He is a Jew. I cannot deny that. I do not see why that should be a cause of reproach. . . .' And he then declared:

It is hard enough, in all conscience, to make a New Zion, but if, over the portals of the new Jerusalem, you are going to inscribe the legend, 'No Israelite need apply,' then I hope the House will permit me to confine my attention exclusively to Irish matters.

One argument which had been used against granting the Rutenberg concession was that Rutenberg himself was a Bolshevik. 'Nothing is more untrue,' Churchill declared, and he went on to give the House of Commons an account of Rutenberg's career:[1]

He is a Russian, but he is not a Bolshevist. He was turned out of Russia by the Bolshevists. Had he been a Bolshevist, and had come to ask for a concession from the Colonial Office, I should have told him to go to Genoa.[2]

[1] The Middle East Department had fully prepared this section of Churchill's speech, having learnt beforehand that Rutenberg—as Vernon informed Churchill earlier on July 4— 'feels and resents most bitterly the attacks made upon his personal honour in connection with his political activities in Russia'. Among those who had sent Churchill testimonials praising Rutenberg were Alexander Kerensky (the former head of the Provisional Government) and N. V. Tchaikowsky (the former head of the North Russian Government at Archangel-Murmansk).

[2] Where, in June 1922, Lloyd George had negotiated with the Bolsheviks on the question of the official recognition of the Bolshevik Government.

He was one of those social revolutionaries who combated that tyranny of the then despotic Tsarist Government, and who, after the revolution, did their best to combat the still worse tyranny of the Bolshevist rulers who succeeded to the power of the Tsar. His attitude has been perfectly consistent. . . .

Mr Rutenberg, after being driven out of Northern Russia, went to Odessa. There he was employed by the French during the time of their occupation, and rendered good service in securing the escape of large numbers of persons who were committed to the anti-Bolshevist cause. He was considered a remarkable man, and very good reports about him have been received. At the same time, I have no doubt that his record is one which would not in every respect compare with that of those who have been fortunate enough to live their lives in this settled and ordered country.

Churchill then appealed to the House of Commons not to prevent the Government 'to use Jews, and use Jews freely, within limits that are proper, to develop new sources of wealth in Palestine'. It was also imperative, if the Balfour Declaration's 'pledges to the Zionists' were to be carried out, for the House of Commons to reverse the vote of the House of Lords. 'This vote,' he warned, 'might have a serious result in Palestine. It might lead to violent disturbances . . . to distress and bloodshed.'

Churchill's final appeal was on the grounds of economy. The cost of administering Palestine had fallen, he pointed out, from £8,000,000 in 1920 to £4,000,000 in 1921, and to an estimated £2,000,000 for 1922. Even further reductions would be possible, he declared, if the Colonial Office were allowed to develop the resources of Palestine by means of the Rutenberg scheme. By such a scheme the Government could 'recoup' the money it had spent. He hoped to reduce the annual cost of Palestine to £1,000,000 by 1924. Surely, he asked, such a sum would not be too much to pay 'for the control and guardianship of this great historic land', or for 'keeping the word' Britain had given 'before all the nations of the world'.

The House divided at the end of Churchill's speech. His appeal had been successful. Only 35 votes were cast against the Government's Palestine policy, and 292 in favour.

The success of the Rutenberg Debate effectively freed the Colonial Office from the pressure of anti-Zionists, and left the way clear for presenting the final terms of the Mandate to the League of Nations. On July 5 Churchill telegraphed to Sir Wyndham Deedes—who was administering the Government of Palestine in Samuel's absence—that the House of Commons vote 'has directly reversed House of Lords resolution'. As a result, 'every effort will be made to get terms of mandate approved by Council of League of Nations at forthcoming session and policy will be vigorously pursued'.

On July 22 the League of Nations approved the Palestine Mandate. Henceforth, the anti-Zionists, however strongly they expressed their criticisms, could not uproot the Jewish National Home. 'I am more pleased than I can say at the passing of the Mandate,' Colonel Mein-ertzhagen wrote in his diary on July 22. 'It will once and for all convince the Arabs and their anti-Zionist friends that the Zionist policy has come to stay and that all their obstruction has been of no avail.'

Churchill had taken no part in presenting Britain's case to the League of Nations; that task had been carried out by Balfour himself. But his strong support of Zionist enterprise during the Rutenberg debate had blunted the force of anti-Zionist sentiment. On July 26 Dr Weizmann wrote to Churchill to congratulate him on the approval of the Mandate:

> To you personally, as well as to those who have been associated with you at the Colonial Office, we tender our most grateful thanks. Zionists throughout the world deeply appreciate the unfailing sympathy you have consistently shown towards their legitimate aspirations and the great part you have played in securing for the Jewish people the opportunity of rebuilding its national home in peaceful co-operation with all sections of the inhabitants of Palestine.

The British anti-Zionists were not prepared to accept in silence either the House of Commons vote of July 4 or the League of Nations vote of July 22, making the Balfour Declaration an integral part of the Palestine Mandate. On August 19 Lord Sydenham wrote to *The Times* of how, in Palestine, the Government were pursuing 'a policy of forcing by British bayonets a horde of aliens, some of them eminently un-desirable, upon the original owners of the country'.

Churchill decided to reply to these charges himself. On August 26 he wrote to Lord Sydenham to remind him once more that at the time of the Balfour Declaration, he, Lord Sydenham, had written in support of a 'national home' for the Jews, in Palestine. Churchill's letter continued:

> It seems to me that before you take further part in this particular contro-versy you owe it to the public, and I may add to yourself, to offer some explanation of the apparent discrepancy between these positions. In particu-lar it would be interesting to know what has occurred in the interval to convert 'the Jewish people' for whom you hoped to make Palestine 'the national home' into 'a horde of aliens'. Your opinions as to the expediency of the policy of Zionism may no doubt quite naturally have turned a complete somersault in the last five years, but the relation of the Jewish race to Palestine has not altered in that period. Either, therefore, you were mistaken

then in thinking that the Jews were entitled to regard Palestine as 'the national home' or you are mistaken now in describing them as 'a horde of aliens'.

It is to this point that it would be specially interesting to see you address yourself.

Sydenham sought to defend himself. On August 29 he wrote to Churchill to say that he had been mistaken to support the Balfour Declaration in 1917, and that he now considered that the Jews had 'no more claim to Palestine than the modern Italians to Britain, or the Moors to Southern Spain'. He went on to say, 'I also think that "a horde of aliens" correctly describes the immigrants.' On August 31, Churchill wrote angrily in reply:

I am obliged to you for your letter of the 29th instant, in which you admit that you were grievously mistaken when you promised to support the Zionist policy and have entirely changed your view on the question of establishing a Jewish national home. In the face of so complete an admission, expressed as it is in language of the utmost courtesy, I do not wish to press my point unduly. If, however, the only reasons which have changed you from an ardent advocate into an active opponent are those set out in your letter, I cannot but feel that they are inadequate even where they are not based on misconceptions.

(1) The policy of His Majesty's Government has always been to bring in only 'carefully selected immigrants gradually without grave injury to the inhabitants', or, I may add, any kind of injury to the inhabitants.

(2) Lord Balfour's declaration did not arise from underhand methods of any kind, but from wide and deep arguments which have been clearly explained.

(3) No Jewish Government has been set up in Palestine, but only a British Government in which Jews as well as Arabs participate. A reference to the White Paper recently published should reassure you in this respect.

Churchill ended his letter:

There is, however, one reason for a change of view which I am glad to see you do not give, namely, that it was an easy and popular thing to advocate a Zionist policy in the days of the Balfour declaration, and that it is a laborious and much criticised task to try to give honourable effect at the present time to the pledges which were given then. Still it seems to me that if a public man like yourself has mistakenly supported the giving of the pledge, he should, even if he has changed his mind, show a little forbearance and even consideration to those who are endeavouring to make it good. Might you not well have left to others the task of inflicting censure and creating difficulties and reserved your distinguished controversial gifts for some topic upon which you have an unimpeachable record? To change your mind is one thing; to turn on those who have followed your previous advice another.

Churchill had welcomed the opportunity of making a public rebuttal of the anti-Zionist case. Even so, the Zionist leaders had several reasons for being disappointed in his policies towards them. While publicly he had often emerged as their champion, in the daily administration of his department he had allowed decisions to be reached, often by others, which were to their disadvantage. At the Cairo Conference he had detached Transjordan from the area of the Jewish National Home, despite Weizmann's strong plea that it should be open to Jewish settlement. He had supported Sir Herbert Samuel's decision that Jewish immigration be halted for two months as a result of Arab violence. He had approved Samuel's decision that all future Jewish immigration must be restricted to Palestine's capacity to absorb it. But he had not sought any clear indication of how absorptive capacity would be defined, or to what uses it would be put. He had allowed Dr Weizmann's remark of early 1919, that he hoped to see Palestine as Jewish as England was English, to be given a prominence which no Arab statements had received, and to be specifically contradicted in official Colonial Office correspondence.

But there were other aspects of Churchill's policy which furthered the Zionist cause, and were a bitter disappointment both to the Arabs and to their British supporters. In the face of strong and determined opposition he had reaffirmed the Balfour Declaration as a basic feature of British policy. He had rejected the repeated Arab demands for a total end to Jewish immigration. He had rebutted the Arab Delegation's violent remarks against the Jews. He had brilliantly defended the Rutenberg concession in Parliament and had spoken enthusiastically of Jewish settlement in Palestine. In two major speeches in the House of Commons—the first on 14 June 1921, the second on 4 July 1922—he had spoken with admiration of all that the Jews had achieved in Palestine, of its potential, and of Britain's determination to allow the Jewish National Home to grow and flourish under British protection.

37

'This mysterious power of Ireland'

DURING the first four months of 1921 the Government had pursued, in Ireland, the policy of organized reprisals, which had come into force while Churchill was still Secretary of State for War. But the application of this policy brought no end to the violence, and in April 1921 the process of reconciliation began. The Government had to decide between two policies: the enforcement of martial law to crush Sinn Fein, or a negotiated truce and settlement with the Sinn Fein leaders. On April 22 Lord Derby, using the name of 'Mr Edwards', crossed over to Dublin and had a long, but inconclusive, conversation with De Valera. On April 27 the Cabinet discussed whether or not to proceed with elections in both southern Ireland and Ulster, fully realizing that if they did so, Sinn Fein candidates would be elected throughout the South. Churchill supported the idea of elections, as Thomas Jones' Cabinet notes recorded:

Mr Churchill: How are you worse off if all returned are Sinn Fein than you are now? If Sinn Feins are returned, a wave of feeling will sweep over the nationalist world that the movement is passing from murderous to non-murderous, from non-constitutional to constitutional. The election would be a new situation which might lead to negotiations. I have never been very happy about the Bill, but having got to this point we would stultify ourselves if we shrank back. . . . I would let things take their course.

Lloyd George told the Cabinet that when he had come to the meeting he was 'rather in favour of postponement', but that as a result of the discussion, he now felt that the elections must be held as soon as possible. This was agreed to, and the election date fixed for May 24.

On May 12, less than two weeks before the elections were to be held, the Cabinet met to discuss the possibility of trying to negotiate a truce with the Sinn Fein leaders. 'The present situation,' H. A. L. Fisher told his colleagues, 'is degrading the moral life of the whole country; a truce would mean a clear moral and political gain and you are entitled to take risks to secure that.' Lord French had been succeeded as Viceroy by Lord FitzAlan,[1] an English Catholic, and this, Fisher added, increased the chance of peace; a truce 'would assist his prestige'. Lloyd George feared that the Sinn Fein would take advantage of a truce offer to 'make us ridiculous'. Curzon feared that 'if truce is offered it will break down'. But Churchill again spoke as a conciliator and an optimist:

I am one of the few who holds the same opinion today and yesterday. It is of great public importance to get a respite in Ireland. I don't agree that it would be a sign of weakness. It would be six or eight months ago. Then we were not in a position to make any concessions and we had to stand firm and we did so. Now our forces are stronger and better trained; auxiliaries are stronger; the police are extending their control over the country; our position is vastly better in a material sense; our position is not better from point of view of reaching finality; no great difficulty in going on for a year or two; very unpleasant as regards the interests of this country all over the world; we are getting an odious reputation; poisoning our relations with the United States; it is in our power to go on and enlist constables and Black and Tans; but we should do everything to get a way to a settlement. . . .

If you are strong enough you should make the effort. Where is the disadvantage? There is no military disadvantage. Supposing you appeal to Irish honour. If you do attempt to appease, either the truce will be kept or it will be broken. If kept you'll have tremendous advantage; they'll have great difficulty in getting men to go back; if they break you are in a far stronger position with our public opinion; your troops are all in position; they can begin at any moment and in the interval you'll have got information. It is a matter of psychology when you should time it, but it should be very early and allow a gentler mood to prevail.

The question of a truce was put to the vote. Only five Ministers supported it—Dr Addison, Churchill, H. A. L. Fisher, Robert Munro[2] and

[1] Lord Edmund Bernard Fitzalan Howard, 1855–1947. 3rd son of the 14th Duke of Norfolk. Assumed the name of Talbot, 1876. Adjutant, Middlesex Yeomanry, 1883–8; Lieutenant-Colonel, 11th Hussars, 1900. Conservative MP for Chichester, 1894–1921. A Junior Lord of the Treasury, 1905. Chief Unionist Whip, 1913–21. Parliamentary Under-Secretary, Treasury, 1915–21. Created Viscount FitzAlan of Derwent, 1921. Viceroy of Ireland, 1921–2.

[2] Robert Munro, 1868–1955. Advocate, 1893; King's Counsel, 1910. Liberal MP for Wick Burghs, 1910–16; for Roxburgh and Selkirk, 1916–22. Lord Advocate of Scotland, 1913–16. Secretary for Scotland, 1916–22. Lord Justice-Clerk, 1922–3. Created Baron Alness, 1934. President of the Scottish Savings Committee, 1941–5.

Edwin Montagu. Nine Ministers were opposed—Lloyd George, Balfour, Chamberlain, Curzon, Sir Robert Horne, Edward Shortt, Worthington-Evans, Sir Denis Henry and Lord FitzAlan. Five days later, on Tuesday May 17, Sir Henry Wilson reported 'a bad week end in Ireland, a total of 37 killed including 2 ladies'.

The Irish elections were held on May 24. In Southern Ireland, Sinn Fein candidates were returned unopposed in all but four of the 126 constituencies. Four Unionists were elected for the Trinity College seats in Dublin. They alone met when the Southern Irish Parliament assembled on June 28; they took the oath, and then adjourned, never to meet again.

In northern Ireland the Unionists won 40 seats, the Nationalists and Sinn Feiners 12. Sir James Craig became the first Prime Minister of Northern Ireland, and the political separation of Ulster from the rest of Ireland became a reality.

On the day after the election a company of 120 IRA men seized control of the Customs House in Dublin and set it on fire, destroying most of the records of the Irish Local Government Board. The police moved quickly to dislodge them, and six of the IRA were killed.

When the King opened the Belfast Parliament on June 22 he used the occasion, at General Smuts' suggestion, and with Lloyd George's approval, to appeal to all Irishmen 'to pause, to stretch out the hand of forebearance and conciliation, to forgive and to forget, and to join in making for the land which they love a new era of peace, contentment, and goodwill'. There was no word of reprisals, martial law or the need to crush violence and terror.

On June 23 Churchill wrote to the King:

I cannot resist expressing to Your Majesty the profound thankfulness with wh I welcome Your Majesty's safe return from a duty in Ireland of such great importance to the whole Empire. I am sure that the results of the visit of Your Majesty accompanied by the Queen will help materially to facilitate the reunion of the two islands. Certainly every loyal subject must feel a special debt of gratitude to Your Majesty for the unswerving sense of public devotion wh led to the undertaking of so momentous a journey.

On June 24 the Cabinet met to discuss how to take advantage of the King's speech. 'The appeal had received a favourable reception from the Irish Nationalist Press,' Lloyd George told his colleagues. 'In the course of the last 3 days we have received indications that De Valera is in a frame of mind to discuss a settlement on a basis other than of independence.' Lloyd George suggested sending letters to De Valera and

Craig, inviting them to enter into negotiations. During the discussion Churchill again spoke strongly in favour of trying to reach a settlement. 'I believe in striking while the iron is hot,' he said, 'and I shall be delighted if the P.M. sends this letter.'

The Cabinet decided to send General Smuts to Dublin to see what possibility there might be for opening truce negotiations. Smuts held discussions with four senior Sinn Fein leaders.[1] On July 6 he reported on these discussions to a Conference of Ministers, including Churchill. The Sinn Fein leaders, he said, 'believe they would get a Republic and that the British people would not hold on'. Smuts added that when he had asked if they would accept Dominion status, they had not rejected the idea outright, provided, they said, 'it should not contain limitations which showed distrust of the Irish people'. The settlement, they insisted, 'must be an everlasting peace'.

In his notes on the Conference of Ministers, Thomas Jones observed: 'All through the recent discussions of the Irish problem the most irreconcilable Minister has been Balfour. Churchill had frankly acknowledged the failure of the policy of force.'

Lloyd George decided to call a truce, and was strongly supported in his decision by Churchill. The truce came into operation at noon on July 11. Both sides welcomed an end to the killing, and the Sinn Fein called off all IRA attacks. 'So the murderers have won,' Henry Wilson wrote in his diary on July 9, '& the coward L.G. has gone down on his knees, & all his miserable Cabinet on their hunkers behind him.'

On July 14 Lloyd George met De Valera in the Cabinet room at 10 Downing Street. 'Large Irish crowd waving green flags outside Downing Street,' H. A. L. Fisher wrote in his diary. 'Talk to Hamar in the anti-room. Hamar in great spirits. Bets me a good top hat we shall get a satisfactory settlement.' Six days later, on July 20, Lloyd George presented De Valera with the British Government's proposals. Southern Ireland would be offered Dominion Home Rule, with complete control of finance, taxation, police and army. Britain would retain control of imperial defence, and would prohibit any protective tariffs on trade between the two countries. On August 11 De Valera rejected these proposals, and demanded complete independence.

The Cabinet met that same day to discuss De Valera's reply. As Lloyd George was in France, Austen Chamberlain presided. De Valera's letter, he said, 'had been sent by aeroplane to the Prime Minister and was not available for circulation to Ministers'. But he did give an indication of its contents. 'A.C. described it as a refusal,' Fisher

[1] Eamon de Valera, Arthur Griffith, E. J. Duggan and Robert Barton.

wrote in his diary. 'Very grave.' On August 12 Lloyd George returned to London. That night, at dinner at 10 Downing Street, Lloyd George, discussed the reply to De Valera with Chamberlain, Churchill, Birkenhead, Greenwood and FitzAlan. At the Cabinet on August 13 it was decided that although De Valera's concept of Ireland 'as an independent nation' was 'wholly unacceptable to the Cabinet', negotiations should continue. Lloyd George and De Valera exchanged further letters, and on September 7 the Cabinet met at the Town Hall, Inverness, to discuss the future course of the correspondence. Lloyd George began the meeting by telling his colleagues that the King had 'expressed anxiety' that the Government's reply 'should not be in the nature of an ultimatum or of a character likely to precipitate hostilities'. It was felt, according to the minutes of the meeting, that it would be difficult to advance matters any further 'by correspondence', and that public opinion was 'becoming tired of the prolonged exchange of letters'. The Cabinet then discussed whether or not to impose conditions as a basis for a conference. Thomas Jones recorded Churchill's opinion:

It is too late in the controversy to invite these people to an unconditional conference. In the first instance you saw De Valera without conditions. To allow them to come unconditionally would be to admit tacitly that the British Empire is an open question. We are at the end of our tether but they are not at the end of theirs. They have a great fear in their hearts. I believe you will help them to reason if your reply brings them right up against it. I propose a direct question to them—'If you wish to come to a conference on the basis of the integrity of the Empire, come, if not, not.' The Cabinet should not assume it is going to be a terrible war and I am fortified in my view by the language used by General Macready. It will not be much worse than what has gone on before. We have taken the ground which the world approves. My view was that coercion should be on fundamentals, not on finance. . . .

Lloyd George challenged Churchill's arguments. 'It is a very important decision to make,' he warned, 'and may lead to war in Ireland. I do not agree with the Colonial Secretary that it is a small operation. It is a considerable operation.' Lloyd George added that if there was a break, he hoped it would be 'more thorough than anything we have had yet and a complete smash up of the revolutionaries', to which Churchill replied: 'I do not differ from that.'

It was finally decided to invite De Valera, without prior conditions, to a conference to decide 'how the association of Ireland with the community of Nations known as the British Empire can be best reconciled with Irish National aspirations'. It was also decided to set up a Committee of nine Ministers with 'full powers to deal with the Irish situation which would arise out of the reply which was being sent to Mr de Valera that day'. Churchill was to be a member of the Committee, and as such, one of the negotiators of any Irish settlement.

On September 13 De Valera's answer was brought to Lloyd George at Gairloch, on the west coast of Scotland. In it, De Valera insisted on coming to the conference as the representative of an independent nation. 'The Irish Republic,' he had written, 'would be glad to discuss this question with the Community of Nations known as the British Empire.'

Churchill approved Lloyd George's efforts to bring Sinn Fein back to the conference table. 'If the conference takes place,' he wrote to his wife on September 19, 'and five are chosen by the Sinn Feiners, we shall have an equal number and he will want me. . . . I still believe there will be a peaceful settlement.' On September 21 five Ministers—Churchill, Edwin Montagu, Alfred Mond, Hamar Greenwood and T. J. Macnamara[1]—discussed the state of the negotiations with Lloyd George at Gairloch. As a result of their discussions, it was decided to issue an invitation to De Valera to come to a conference in a month's time, on October 19. Churchill favoured the maximum compromise and concession, provided that the Irish delegates would accept Dominion Status, but he rejected altogether independence and republicanism. On September 24 he set out his views in a speech to his constituents at Dundee. Britain, he declared, could not accept an Irish Republic in any form:

How could they agree to the setting up of a separate foreign Republic in Ireland? How could any one suppose that peace could be found along that road? Not peace, but certain war—real war, not mere bushranging, would follow from such a course. Great Britain would always live in apprehension, which he dared say would be well founded, that Ireland was intriguing against us with other foreign countries, giving submarine bases, or providing facilities for strangling our life and trade. (A Voice—'Bosh!') The only effective check which they could have upon such activities, apart from going to war, would be to erect a tariff wall between Great Britain and Ireland. . . .

If war broke out between the British Empire and the Irish Republic—and in his opinion it certainly would—every Irishman in the British Empire would become an alien enemy, and would be in exactly the same position as the unfortunate Germans who were in this country during the great war.

What a hideous and idiotic prospect unfolded to their eyes! What a crime

---

[1] Thomas James Macnamara, 1861–1931. A school teacher for sixteen years, and subsequently editor of the *Schoolmaster*, 1892–1907. President of the National Union of Teachers, 1896. Liberal MP, 1900–22 (National Liberal, 1922–4). Parliamentary Secretary, Local Government Board, 1907–8 and Admiralty, 1908–20. Minister of Labour, 1920–2.

they would commit if, seeking a brief interval of relief from war, they condemned themselves and their children to such misfortunes. They should be ripping the British Empire and preparing certain war at no distant date— a war in which Britain would be called to the aid of Ulster, and in which the new republic would do their best to embroil their kith and kin in the United States. They could not do this!

The Irish, Churchill went on, must agree to Dominion Home Rule; Britain had nothing more to offer. Loyalty to the Empire was essential. The Irish leaders must ensure that the conference was a success. 'Squander this conference,' he said, 'and peace is bankrupt.'

Under the headline 'An Essay in Statesmanship', *The Times* declared: 'The country will be grateful to MR CHURCHILL for the breadth and lucidity of his speech . . . whether men agree with him or not, MR CHURCHILL's able and calm review of the situation helps to restore confidence.' On October 2 Archibald Sinclair sent his congratulations. 'The chorus of praise in the Press,' he wrote, 'from the loud plaudits of the Times to the grudging & embarrassed comments of the Nation & the Manchester Guardian must have astonished you yourself. It must have been a desperately difficult & delicate task and you achieved a wonderful success.'

The Cabinet met on October 6 to choose the British negotiators. Lloyd George proposed, and the Cabinet accepted, that there should be seven negotiators—Lloyd George himself, Austen Chamberlain, Lord Birkenhead, Worthington-Evans, Churchill, Hamar Greenwood and, whenever constitutional questions were raised, the Attorney-General, Sir Gordon Hewart.[1]

The first session of the conference on Ireland was held at 10 Downing Street on the morning of October 11. In order to spare his Cabinet the embarrassment of having to shake hands with men who were regarded by some of them as murderers, Lloyd George introduced them to the Irish Delegates across the wide table, he alone shaking hands with them. The Delegation was led by Arthur Griffith[2] and Michael Collins.

---

[1] Gordon Hewart, 1870–1943. Called to the Bar, Inner Temple, 1902. Liberal MP, 1913– 22. Solicitor-General, 1916–19. Knighted, 1916. Attorney General, 1919–22. A member of the Cabinet from November 1921 to October 1922. One of the British signatories of the Irish Treaty, December 1921. Created Baron, 1922. President of the War Compensation Court, 1922–9. Created Viscount, 1940.

[2] Arthur Griffith, 1872–1922. Born in Dublin. Worked as a miner on the Rand (South Africa) in the 1890s. Returned to Dublin, where he published a study of the Hungarian national movement. Editor of the *United Irishman*, 1899–1906; of *Sinn Fein*, 1906–14; of *Nationality*, 1915–22. Imprisoned in Wandsworth, 1916. President of the Sinn Fein Party, 1917. Elected to Parliament as a Sinn Fein candidate, 1918. Imprisoned at Gloucester, 1918. Acting President of the Dail, 1919. Imprisoned at Mountjoy, 1920–1. President of the Dail, 1922.

De Valera had refused to come, insisting that, as a 'President', he was senior to Lloyd George.

Lloyd George opened the conference by declaring, in grave tones, that 'the opportunity was a golden one for putting an end to the tragic story of misunderstanding and war between the two countries'. Both parties were eager for peace; a peace, not between oligarchies, as in the past, but 'between the two peoples'. Later in the session, when the Irish objected to Britain's veto on tariff barriers, Churchill commented: 'We are offering you the most terrific guarantee that Ireland can have.' The market would be secure to Ireland, he said, 'quite independently of all the fluctuations of all the political parties'. At the second session that afternoon Churchill was appointed chairman of a joint-committee to discuss naval and air matters.

The British representatives met at noon on October 13, to discuss what position to adopt on defence at the third session. Churchill explained that he had discussed the naval aspects with Lord Beatty, and had discovered what 'little importance' the Admiralty attached to control of the Irish ports. But Lloyd George wanted the Irish to agree to British control of certain ports, which could be handed back 'later'. Thomas Jones' notes recorded Churchill's comment.

Our position is 'We must have free use of the Irish coasts in peace or war for Imperial defence.' Bear Island, Queenstown, Lough Swilly, which is used for manoeuvres and important for guarding the commerce of Liverpool, that we can arrange with the Dominion of Northern Ireland.'

(At the end of the meeting Mr Churchill was told that Lough Swilly was in Donegal and not in Northern Ireland.)

We mean no reference to their internal affairs.

The P.M.: 'It is important to make plain that we do not intend to have political domination.'

The third session of the conference opened shortly after midday on October 13, when the main topic under discussion was tariffs. 'We bind ourselves to receive your stuff without tariffs,' Lloyd George proposed, 'and you bind yourselves to receive our stuff without tariffs.' On the following day the conference met for the fourth time. The principal subject was that of partition and of the future unity of Ireland. Lloyd George told the Sinn Fein delegates that Britain would not 'stand in the way of legitimate persuasion by you' to induce Northern Ireland to join the South. Churchill remarked that South Africa was, at that very moment, 'offering to Rhodesia inducements to come into the Union, customs etc'.

The problem of partition was discussed again at the fifth session of the conference, on October 17, when the Sinn Fein Delegates pressed their case for a united Ireland. According to Thomas Jones' notes, Churchill played no part in the discussion. But on the following day, at the Colonial Office he presided over the joint Sub-Committee on Naval and Air Defence, and rejected a Sinn Fein memorandum insisting that control of naval defence should rest with Dublin. Jones recorded:

Mr Churchill, having glanced at the memorandum, said: 'This able memorandum will shorten the task of this committee, in fact will bring it to an end. It amounts to a reasoned, measured, uncompromising refusal to meet us at any point. It advances the theory to which we could not become a party— that Ireland is a foreign Ireland. . . . The right to build an Irish navy is claimed. I regard this as a mortal blow.

The discussion that followed was at times acrimonious. 'Ireland,' declared Erskine Childers,[1] 'an island with a maritime frontier, is to be denied responsibility for her own naval defence.' Churchill, however, rejected the argument that British control of defence was in any way a denial of Ireland's 'existence as a nation'. The Sinn Fein Delegates were not convinced by Churchill's assurance. On October 19, at a further meeting of the Sub-Committee, Collins and Childers presented Churchill with a memorandum rejecting British control of Irish ports. Two days later, at the Sixth Session of the full conference, Lloyd George insisted that for Britain such control was 'vital to our security against attack'. When Collins denied this, Lloyd George burst out:

We are taking great political risks. The life of the Government is put in issue by our proposals. We were prepared to face that because it is worth while taking risks to get a reconciliation between your great race and ours. To end the feud is worth the risk of our political life, but these incidents will make it impossible. We must know your attitude on certain vital questions. Is allegiance to the King to be finally repudiated? Can you under no conditions accept the sovereignty of the King in the sense that Canada and Australia accept it? Is the communicating link of the Crown to be snapped for ever?

[1] Robert Erskine Childers, 1870–1922. Born in London. A clerk in the House of Commons, 1895–1910. Served with the City Imperial Volunteers in South Africa, 1900. Published *The Riddle of the Sands* (1903), an imaginary account of German preparations for the invasion of England. In July 1914, in his yacht *Asgard*, he landed arms north of Dublin for use by the National Volunteers. Served with the Royal Naval Air Service in the Cuxhaven raid, November 1914, and in intelligence work, 1915–17. Lieutenant-Commander, 1916. Seconded to the Secretariat of the Irish Convention, 1917. Settled in Dublin, 1920. Elected to the Dail, 1921, and appointed Minister of Propaganda. A Chief Secretary to the Irish Delegation to London, 1921. Opposed the Irish Treaty, and served in mobile columns of the Irish Republican Army, 1922. Captured by Free State soldiers, court-martialled in Dublin, and shot, 24 November 1922.

Are you prepared to be associated with the fraternity of Nations known as the British Empire? Do you accept in principle that we must take necessary measures to give us facilities for our security not as a treaty which can be cancelled, but as a fundamental part of an arrangement?

Later in the discussion, Churchill returned to the Collins–Childers memorandum:

Mr Churchill said the ability of the document was marked but it amounted to reasoned rejection of every one of our points, and to a claim of neutrality for Ireland, a neutrality which was to be guaranteed, and which the Irish would take, they said, effective means to protect by building mine craft, etc.—'We cannot be sure that the Irish would have power to keep an effective neutrality. We could not guarantee the confluence of trade in an area where submarines were lurking unless we had Queenstown and other ports . . .'
Mr Collins: 'Mr Churchill, do not you agree that if neutrality were a greater safeguard to you than anything else, it would be a greater value to you than your proposals?
Mr Churchill: 'I do not accept that. A completely honest neutrality by Ireland in the last war would have been worse for us. Ireland's control of her neutrality might be ineffective.' (Compare Norway).

Lloyd George insisted that the Sinn Fein Delegates must accept Britain's claim for the 'necessary facilities to ensure the security of our shores from attack by sea'. The British offer of Dominion Status for Ireland, he concluded, represented 'a greater advance than anything ever made before in the whole history of British statesmanship', and yet he and his fellow negotiators 'have met with no concession from the Irish side'. The session then ended. Two hours before it reconvened on October 24, the Sinn Fein delegates presented a conciliatory document. Lloyd George asked Griffith whether, under his new proposals, the Irish would be 'British subjects or foreigners'. Griffith replied: 'We would be Irish subjects. We would be British subjects. We would assume that Irishmen in England and Englishmen in Ireland would have the same rights.'

The new Irish proposals offered the chance of an agreement. The British delegates thereupon withdrew to Frances Stevenson's room, next to the Cabinet room, for a private consultation. Lord Birkenhead and Austen Chamberlain were both worried that the Sinn Fein delegates would refuse to accept allegiance to the Crown as an essential part of any Treaty. Lloyd George confirmed that this was so. On the afternoon of October 25 Austen Chamberlain negotiated on his own with Griffith and Collins, and during the evening he gave the other British negotiators an account of his discussions. Griffith had insisted that Sinn

Fein would not accept allegiance to the Crown 'unless they got the unity of Ireland'. Churchill's thoughts were divided. He did not want to abandon Ulster, but he did not want Ulster to be a barrier to any Treaty. Thomas Jones recorded his remarks:

Winston: We can't give way on six counties; we are not free agents; we can do our best in include Six in larger Parliament plus autonomy. We could press Ulster to hold autonomy for Six from them instead of from us.

Birkenhead: I rather agree with Winston; our position re Six Counties is an impossible one if these men want to settle, as they do.

Winston: I don't see how Ulster is damnified: she gets her own protection, an effective share in the Southern Parliament and protection for the Southern Unionists.

The Irish conference came to an end, and the formal sessions gave way to a continual round of private meetings. Lloyd George made strenuous efforts to persuade the Conservative leaders to support a Treaty with the Sinn Fein. On Sunday October 30 he dined with Churchill in Sussex Gardens. Lord Birkenhead was also present, and Lloyd George took the opportunity to invite both Griffith and Collins to join them. Thomas Jones recorded in his diary:

As soon as the P.M. reached Churchill's house I got him on the 'phone and told him in Welsh that Griffith and Collins distrusted F.E. and Winston and that it was therefore important that the P.M. should have an interview with Griffith alone before their general conference. This, as I learned afterwards, the P.M. did, he being closeted with Griffith while Collins joined F.E. and Winston. What precisely took place between them all I cannot say but at 11.30 Shakespeare¹ went to fetch the P.M. in his car and the P.M. remarked to him that the interview had been much the most satisfactory. . . .

As the negotiations progressed, Lloyd George had made several personal references to his own resignation. He was not prepared to fight the South, he said, in order to help the North resist a settlement. Churchill deprecated all such talk. 'I urged that Ministers would not escape from their miseries by resignation,' he later recalled in *The World Crisis*. But he also recalled that the 'desire for release' was so general at the beginning of November 'that no one could predict the

¹ Geoffrey Hithersay Shakespeare, 1893–   . Served in the Great War, at Gallipoli and in Egypt. President of the Cambridge Union, 1920. Private Secretary to Lloyd George, 1921–3. Called to the Bar, 1922. National Liberal MP for Wellingborough, 1922–3; Liberal MP for Norwich, 1929–31; Liberal National MP for Norwich, 1931–45. Liberal National Chief Whip, 1931–2. Parliamentary Secretary at the Ministry of Health, 1932–6; and at the Board of Education, 1936–7. Parliamentary and Financial Secretary, Admiralty, 1937–40. Parliamentary Under-Secretary of State, Dominions Office, 1940–2. Created Baronet, 1942.

fortunes of a single day'. On November 9 he wrote direct to Lloyd George, urging him not to contemplate resignation:

The criticism will certainly be made that the Government in resigning have abdicated their responsibility. More especially will this charge be made if the reason given is 'we are debarred by honour from coercing the North, and by conviction from coercing the South'. It will be said, 'here are men united in principle, knowing what they ought to do and what the interests of the country require, who are possessed of an overwhelming Parliamentary majority, including a majority of their own followers, who nevertheless without facing Parliament throw down the commission and declare themselves incapable of action in any direction.'

I greatly fear the consequences of such tactics, no matter how lofty may be the motives which prompt them.

After this has occurred, Mr. Bonar Law will be invited to form a Government. Why should he not do so? Surely he would be bound in honour to do so, if the members of the present Government have declared themselves inhibited from moving in any direction. Why should he not succeed? . . . In the crisis under consideration, the Conservative Party will have to rally to someone. Obviously they will rally to a Conservative leader, forming a Conservative Government, which has come forward to fill the gap created by the suicide of the Coalition; and which will be entitled to carry the standard forward against Labour at an imminent election, and to receive considerate treatment from ex-Ministers who have just thrown up the sponge. The delusion that an alternative Government cannot be formed is perennial. Mr Chamberlain thought Sir Henry Campbell-Bannerman would be 'hissed off the stage'. Mr Asquith was confident that you could not form an administration. But in neither case did the outgoing administration tie its hands in every direction by proclaiming itself honourably bound to do what the situation might require.

Churchill went on to warn Lloyd George that if he resigned 'a very great public disaster might easily ensue, in which a reactionary Conservative Government might go forward to the polls against Labour, with the great central mass of England and Scotland remaining without leadership or decisive influence', and he insisted 'that it is our duty to carry forward the policy about Ireland in which we believe, until we are defeated in the House of Commons, and thus honourably relieved from our duty to the Crown. . . .'

The negotiations continued throughout the second week of November. It was now the turn of Sir James Craig and the Ulster Protestants to raise objections to Lloyd George's proposals for the South. On November 12 Lloyd George summoned the seven original British negotiators—including Churchill—to 10 Downing Street. Thomas

Jones noted in his diary: 'Churchill, ignorant of what the P.M. had been busily doing, urged the importance of bringing Sinn Fein along lest we should lose both Ulster and Sinn Fein, and standing at the fireplace he soliloquised aloud about mediaeval hatreds and barbarous passions which brought men to the stake, still rampant in Ulster.'

Churchill also said, according to Jones, that he was in favour of giving the South 'the status of an Irish State, with an All Ireland Parliament, a position in the Imperial Conference and the League of Nations'. Ulster, he added, 'could have no grievance if she preferred to stay out'.

During the last two weeks of November the negotiations were conducted principally by Lloyd George, Lord Birkenhead and Austen Chamberlain. But Churchill was present when the draft Treaty was handed to the Sinn Fein Delegates on November 29. The Irishmen travelled at once to Dublin with the Draft Treaty. On December 1 they were back in London. That evening Griffith and Collins met Lloyd George, Churchill, Sir Robert Horne and Sir Gordon Hewart to discuss outstanding points. On December 2 they returned again to Dublin. The Dublin Cabinet were divided over whether or not to accept the British terms. De Valera was opposed to acceptance.

On December 3 the Sinn Fein delegates returned yet again to London. Negotiations continued throughout Sunday December 4 and Monday December 5. Churchill followed up every opportunity to find new formulas which could lead to compromise; for the past month he had been discussing the detailed points at issue with several experts. On November 30 he had sent for Harold Laski,[1] who recalled in a letter to a friend a week later:

. . . he told me that things were likely to break down upon the problem of allegiance. So I talked at length upon this as a quantitative problem which need not be met in the formal way of the past. The real thing was to get the safeguards of function which came not from an oath exacted, but a conscience satisfied. He seemed impressed, and when I was going asked me to drop in the next day. When I arrived he had the Attorney-General with him and asked me to repeat my argument. This I did with amplification, and for 1 and $\frac{1}{2}$ hours we argued up and down. Finally the A-G asked if I could put my views (with which he disagreed) into a formula. I suggested an oath 'to the

[1] Harold Joseph Laski, 1893–1950. Political philosopher and historian; the son of Nathan Laski (an influential member of the Jewish community in North-West Manchester, Churchill's former constituency). Lecturer in History, McGill University, Montreal, 1914–16; Harvard University, 1916–20. Vice-Chairman of the British Institute of Adult Education, 1921–30. Member of the Fabian Society Executive, 1922. Lecturer in Political Science, Magdalene College, Cambridge, 1922–5. Professor of Political Science, London, 1926–50. Member of Executive Committee of Labour Party, 1936–49.

Irish State and the King in Parliament as the head of the British Common-wealth'. Churchill was very surprised and said it was a new approach. Then explore it, I said: but the A-G was very hostile and I left with a sense of hopelessness.

On the Saturday I went to town and had a hurried summons from Winston who said that Lloyd George liked my formula and could I develop the point on paper. This I did, and got a note on Sunday saying that L-G would put an almost identical formula before the Cabinet on Monday. The Irish were stiff about it but in the end accepted it in return for a full free trade agreement.

At three in the afternoon of December 5 Lloyd George, Churchill, Austen Chamberlain and Lord Birkenhead met Arthur Griffith, Michael Collins and Robert Barton[1] at 10 Downing Street. In *The World Crisis* Churchill recorded:

The Prime Minister stated bluntly that we could concede no more and debate no further. They must settle now; they must sign the agreement for a Treaty in the form to which after all these weeks it had attained, or else quit; and further, that both sides would be free to resume whatever warfare they could wage against each other. This was an ultimatum delivered, not through diplomatic channels, but face to face, and all present knew and understood that nothing else was possible. Stiff as our personal relations had been, there was by now a mutual respect between the principals and a very deep compre-hension of each other's difficulties.

The Irishmen gulped down the ultimatum phlegmatically. Mr Griffith said, speaking in his soft voice and with his modest manner, 'I will give the answer of the Irish Delegates at nine to-night; but, Mr Prime Minister, I personally will sign this agreement and will recommend it to my country-men.' 'Do I understand, Mr Griffith,' said Mr Lloyd George, 'that though everyone else refuses you will nevertheless agree to sign?' 'Yes, that is so Mr Prime Minister,' replied this quiet little man of great heart and of great purpose. Michael Collins rose looking as if he was going to shoot someone, preferably himself. In all my life I have never seen so much passion and suffering in restraint.

At 6.50 that evening, while awaiting the Irish reply, Lloyd George, Austen Chamberlain, Lord Birkenhead, Churchill and Lord FitzAlan met in Chamberlain's room in the House of Commons. According to Thomas Jones, who was also present, Churchill insisted that if no answer were received by ten o'clock that evening, the Irish should be

---

[1] Robert C. Barton, 1881–   . A cousin of Erskine Childers, and a Protestant from County Wicklow. Served with the British Army, 1914–16. Joined Sinn Fein after the Easter rising, 1916. Director of Agriculture in the Dail Cabinet, 1919. Imprisoned by the British, 1920–1. A Delegate to the Irish Conference, 1921, and a signatory of the Irish Treaty. Secretary for Economic Affairs, 1921–2. He voted in favour of the Treaty, and against De Valera, at the Cabinet of 7 December 1921, but later refused to co-operate with the Provisional Government.

left in no doubt 'as to what we are going to do'. Churchill's own account
of the evening described the sequel:

> The British Representatives were in their places at nine, but it was not until
> long after midnight that the Irish Delegation appeared. As before, they were
> superficially calm and very quiet. There was a long pause, or there seemed to
> be. Then Mr Griffith said, 'Mr Prime Minister, the Delegation is willing to
> sign the agreements, but there are a few points of drafting which perhaps it
> would be convenient if I mentioned at once.' Thus, by the easiest of gestures,
> he carried the whole matter into the region of minor detail, and everyone
> concentrated upon these points with overstrained interest so as to drive the
> main issue into the background for ever.
> Soon we were talking busily about technicalities and verbal corrections,
> and holding firmly to all these lest worse should befall. But underneath this
> protective chatter a profound change had taken place in the spirit and
> atmosphere. We had become allies and associates in a common cause—the
> cause of the Irish Treaty and of peace between two races and two islands. It
> was nearly three o'clock in the morning before we separated. But the agree-
> ment was signed by all. As the Irishmen rose to leave, the British Ministers
> upon a strong impulse walked round and for the first time shook hands.

The Treaty had been signed in the early hours of December 6. On the
following day the Cabinet discussed what to do with Sinn Feiners who
had been convicted of murder. Thomas Jones recorded Churchill's
advice: 'Winston suggested,' he wrote, 'that the Irish should be informed
privately that the extreme sentence will not be carried out.' Churchill's
advice was accepted; the Cabinet conclusions recorded that official
notice would be given privately 'to those prisoners now lying under
sentence of death that the death penalty would not be enforced'.

The Sinn Fein delegates returned to Dublin on December 6. On
December 7 they made out the case for the Treaty before the Sinn Fein
Cabinet ministers. De Valera was bitterly opposed to Dominion Status.
He wanted an Irish Republic, entirely separated from Britain. But four
of the seven Cabinet ministers voted for the Treaty, which was then
debated in the Sinn Fein Parliament, or Dail. On December 15, while
De Valera was still trying to persuade the Dail to reject the Irish Treaty,
Churchill outlined its provisions to the House of Commons, and urged
them to accept it.

Churchill's speech marked a high point of parliamentary exposition,
and was of the utmost importance for the Government. He began with a

description of the 'grim, grave, and, in many cases, shocking realities' of the previous two years. Then he described the slow but increasingly hopeful process of negotiation. During the negotiations, he said, the Sinn Fein delegates had demanded 'an independent sovereign republic for the whole of Ireland, including Ulster'. For their part, the British delegates had insisted 'upon allegiance to the Crown, membership of the Empire, facilities and securities for the Navy, and a complete option for Ulster'. Every one of the British conditions, he went on, 'is embodied in the Treaty'. Of the attitude of Ulster towards the Treaty he declared:

It is no longer open to anyone to say that Ulster is barring the way to the rest of Ireland, that Ulster is forbidding the rest of Ireland to have the kind of government they want. That is all past. These great sacrifices of opinion have been made by that small but resolute community at a time of great, distressing, and protracted anxiety to them, and they have been made for the sake of their common interests in the British Empire. Ulster has boldly said to the rest of Ireland: 'Have the Government you choose; we will do our best to make things go right, and as long as you stay within the British Empire, we close no doors in the future.' That, it seems to me, is what Ulster has said, and I repeat that our debt to her is great.

One day, Churchill said, Ulster would join with Southern Ireland: 'That is our policy.' But such a union would have to be of Ulster's free will, 'and in her own time'. Meanwhile, Britain had accepted 'a complete obligation for the defence of Ulster'.

Churchill then defended the Treaty's acceptance of complete fiscal autonomy for Southern Ireland. This would not harm Britain, he insisted, 'because we are her sole market and her sole source of supply'. As for Southern Ireland's right, under the Treaty, to raise its own army, this, he said, like fiscal autonomy, was a right enjoyed by every Dominion. 'Certain I am,' he added, 'that any force which is raised in Ireland will not be a force beyond the military power of the British Empire.' Churchill spoke next of the naval clauses of the Treaty, whereby Britain was to be 'solely responsible for the security of these islands and the seas around them'. Scarcely any use would be made of these powers, he said, in time of peace. But, he added, 'in time of war or strained relations with a foreign power we have an absolute right to the freest possible use of all harbours and inlets of Ireland, to enable us to undertake the control of coastal waters, the defence of these islands, and the sea routes by which our food is brought to this country'.

Churchill then appealed to those who took 'the extreme view', both at Westminster, and in Dublin, to accept the Treaty as it stood, and not to allow the belief that particular clauses were unsatisfactory to lead to a renewal of fighting:

I cannot believe you will find any body of responsible men here or in Ireland, Liberal or Conservative, North or South, soldier or civilian, who would solemnly declare that on the margin of difference remaining between these extreme views and the Treaty it would be justifiable to lay the land of Ireland waste to the scourge of war, or to drag the name of Great Britain through the dirt in every part of the world. For you cannot embark on such a struggle without being prepared to face conditions of public opinion all over the world which undoubtedly would be profoundly detrimental to your interests. You could not do it without being prepared to inflict the most fearful injury on the land and people of Ireland.

When we have this Treaty, defective, admittedly, from your point of view, but still a great instrument, I ask: Are the differences between the Treaty and the extreme desire worth the re-embarking on war? You cannot do it. If you tried, you would not get the people to support you. On the contrary, you would complain in both countries of their leaders, and they would complain with violence and indignation that they were dragged from their hearths to maltreat each other on pretexts which had been reduced to such manageable dimensions.

It is high time that the main body of Irish and British opinion asserted its determination to put a stop to these fanatical quarrels.

Churchill then pointed to 'a remarkable phenomenon'. On the previous day, in the House of Lords, Lord Carson had denounced Lord Curzon, 'with brilliant and corrosive invective', as a traitor to Britain for having signed the Irish Treaty. And at the same time, in Dublin, De Valera was denouncing Michael Collins 'for a similar offence'. And Churchill went on to ask:

Are we not getting a little tired of all this? These absolutely sincere, consistent, unswerving gentlemen, faithful in all circumstances to their implacable quarrels, seek to mount their respective national war horses, in person or by proxy, and to drive at full tilt at one another, shattering and splintering down the lists, to the indescribable misery of the common people and to the utter confusion of our Imperial affairs.

Earlier in the debate John Gretton[1] had declared that Britain was 'humiliated' by the Irish Treaty, and Rupert Gwynne[2] had described it

---

[1] John Gretton, 1867–1947. Brewer; Chairman of Bass, Ratcliff and Greton Ltd, 1908–45. Conservative MP for South Derbyshire, 1895–1906; for Rutland, 1907–18; for Burton, 1918–43. Privy Councillor, 1926. Created Baron, 1944.

[2] Rupert Sackville Gwynne, 1873–1924. Barrister, 1898. In 1905 he married Churchill's relative, Stella, eldest daughter of 1st Viscount Ridley. Conservative MP for Eastbourne from 1910 until his death. Financial Secretary, War Office, 1923–4.

as 'a surrender'. Churchill denied these charges. It was true, he said, that England was conceding more to Ireland 'than she has as a nation ever been willing to concede before'. But the motive, he insisted, was a noble one—'to end a period of brutal and melancholy violence'. Nor, he added, was Britain's position in the world so poor that she could not afford to take such a conciliatory step:

If we had shown ourselves a feeble nation, fat and supine, sunk in sloth, our mission exhausted, our strength gone, our energies abated, our credentials impaired, if we had shown this lack of quality in the struggle from which we have emerged, then indeed there would be some explanation and justification for such misgivings in the breasts of many gathered here.

But when we have just come out of a world-war with our record such as it is, in which our armies have broken the German line, in which our navies have carried on the whole sea business of the Allies, in which our finances have sustained Europe, when we have come out of all these dangers, and have shown that we are capable of taking a leading part, if not the leading part, in the great struggle which has overthrown the largest and most powerful military Empires of which there is a record—when all these facts are considered, surely we can afford to carry on these Irish negotiations according to a clear, cool judgement of what is best in the country's interest, without being deflected or deterred from any particular course of action by a wholly unjustifiable self-accusation of humiliation.

Churchill went on to describe the concessions given to Southern Ireland as 'a great and peculiar manifestation of British genius'. All Britain's friends, he said, had rejoiced at the settlement; all Britain's enemies 'had been dumbfounded'. Churchill then spoke of the impact of the Irish question in British politics, and of his hopes for a better future:

It is a curious reflection to inquire why Ireland should bulk so largely in our lives. How is it that the great English parties are shaken to their foundations, and even shattered, almost every generation, by contact with Irish affairs? Whence did Ireland derive its power to drive Mr Pitt from office, to drag down Mr Gladstone in the summit of his career, and to draw us who sit here almost to the verge of civil war, from which we were only rescued by the outbreak of the Great War.

Whence does this mysterious power of Ireland come? It is a small, poor, sparsely populated island, lapped about by British sea power, accessible on every side, without iron or coal. How is it that she sways our councils, shakes our parties, and infects us with her bitterness, convulses our passions, and deranges our action? How is it she has forced generation after generation to stop the whole traffic of the British Empire in order to debate her domestic affairs?

Ireland is not a daughter State. She is a parent nation. The Irish are an ancient race. 'We too are,' said their plenipotentiaries, 'a far-flung nation.' They are intermingled with the whole life of the Empire, and have interests in every part of the Empire wherever the English language is spoken, especially in those new countries with whom we have to look forward to the greatest friendship and countenance, and where the Irish canker has been at work. How much have we suffered in all these generations from this continued hostility?

If we can free ourselves from it, if we can to some extent reconcile the spirit of the Irish nation to the British Empire in the same way as Scotland and Wales have been reconciled, then indeed we shall have secured advantages which may well repay the trouble and the uncertainties of the present time.

In the closing moments of his speech, Churchill asked for the 'active and energetic support' of all political parties in carrying out the spirit of the Treaty, and in standing firm 'against all efforts to overthrow it, whether they be in Parliament or out of doors'.

'Winston makes one of his finest speeches in defence of the settlement,' H. A. L. Fisher wrote in his diary that night, and Frederick Guest wrote direct to Churchill: 'Much the best speech I have ever heard you make. Simplicity of style & fervour of advocacy won a genuine reception from all quarters. Splendid, bless you.' Later that day Austen Chamberlain described the impact of Churchill's speech to the King:

He spoke with great force and power and with equal skill and tact. The case of the Agreement could not have been better put. At the same time he paid a tribute to the great services which Ulster had rendered and even to the part which her attitude had had in producing the present Agreement. But it is impossible to summarise the speech. It had a profoud effect upon the House. . . .

In Dublin the arguments for and against the Treaty continued. In the third week of December, before the Dail had reached any decision, Lloyd George asked Churchill to preside over a special Cabinet Committee to arrange the details of the Provisional Government in Dublin which would have to be set up as soon as the Dail ratified the Treaty. On December 21 Churchill circulated a long memorandum setting out the situation which would arise once a Provisional Government were established. This Government, he wrote, would be 'immediately responsible for the whole internal peace and order of Southern Ireland and would take executive control of the country. . . . We do not wish to continue responsibility one day longer than is absolutely necessary.' He added his hope that the Southern Irish would agree to 'the definite assumption of power' on 1 January 1922, following which all British military forces would be withdrawn 'as quickly as convenient'. At the same time both the Royal Ulster Constabulary and the Auxiliaries would be disbanded at Britain's expense, 'advantage being taken', Churchill explained, 'of the decision provisionally arrived at to raise a gendarmerie for Palestine'.

In his memorandum Churchill envisaged a swift transfer of power from Westminster to Dublin; the establishment of Free State Courts 'at the earliest moment', the use of all taxes hitherto raised in Southern Ireland 'for Irish internal administration', and the full responsibility for education and agriculture 'placed on the shoulders of a Free State Minister'. There must, he insisted, be no hanging on to British military or civil control; on the contrary, 'ostentatious preparations to quit should be made everywhere'.

On December 21 Churchill took the chair at a meeting of his Cabinet Committee on the Irish Provisional Government, where his memorandum formed the principal subject of discussion. It was agreed that all the departments of government except the police should be handed over to the Provisional Government 'as soon as possible', and that troops should be withdrawn 'from all outlying places' and concentrated in and around Dublin. According to the minutes of the meeting: 'Emphasis was laid on the desirability of giving some public sign of the withdrawal of troops.'

Churchill's Committee met again on December 22, December 23 and December 24, to work out details of troop withdrawals. 'It is a relief to me to know that Irish affairs are in your hands for the moment,' Wilfrid Scawen Blunt wrote on December 26. But he added: 'I am inclined to think that an immediate peace settlement would have been secured with fewer dissidents if presented with less detail at the start.' Churchill had faith, however, that a detailed, precise settlement would be possible on the basis of the Treaty itself.

When the New Year came, the Dail had still failed to decide whether to ratify the Treaty or not. But Churchill was confident that they would do so. Over the New Year he went for a short holiday, in the South of France, staying with the Countess of Essex.[1] On 2 January 1922, while still on holiday, he wrote to the Prince of Wales:

The Irish event seems to turn well. Arthur Griffith and Michael Collins are men of their word. It was said 'Irishmen have every form of courage except moral courage'. But one cannot say that any more. When the treaty

---

[1] Adele Grant, 1859–1922. Born in New York. In 1893 she married the 7th Earl of Essex (who died in 1916).

was signed after a dramatic struggle, we shook hands on it and pledged ourselves to put it through on both sides without regard to personal or political fortunes. They are certainly doing their part; and we will not fail in ours.

The P.M. has handed the business over to me now: and I am to hurry back from this delightful villa (Lady Essex's) where I have had a few sunny days, to bring the Irish Provisional Government into being at the earliest moment. In spite of all that may be said on the other side—terrible and unanswerable things—I am full of hope and confidence about Ireland. I believe we are going to reap a rich reward all over the world and at home.

38

The Irish Treaty:
'A statue of snow'

═══════

ON 8 January 1922 the Irish Treaty was approved by the Dail by the narrow margin of 64 votes to 57. De Valera, who had argued against the Treaty since the return of his delegates from London a month before, at once resigned as President of the Dail. He then sought re-election, but was defeated on January 9 by the even narrower margin of 60 to 58. 'So Ireland has decided!' General Congreve wrote to Churchill that same day. 'Now I hope we shall not leave a soldier or a penny there & we shall see some pretty doings!'

Churchill had returned to England from the South of France on the evening of January 8. Both Ulster and the Free State were now his personal Ministerial responsibility. On the following morning he called a meeting of his Cabinet Committee on Ireland. The Adjutant-General, Sir George Macdonogh, who was present, told Henry Wilson that Churchill had said to him during the course of the meeting 'that as it now appeared most likely that there would be b—y rows in Ireland, all orders for withdrawing troops must be held up, although it had been previously decided that the moment the Dail ratified the troops were to be instantly withdrawn'. But the Committee had before it evidence of a conciliatory spirit: a message from Alfred Cope[1] that both Collins and Griffith were 'prepared to carry out' the articles of the agreement dealing with amnesty, even though they were not prepared to make any public statement.

Two days later, on January 11, the Prime Minister of Northern

---

[1] Alfred Cope,   –1954. Second Secretary, Ministry of Pensions, 1919–20. Assistant Under-Secretary for Ireland, 1920–2. Knighted, 1922. General Secretary, National Liberal Organisation, 1922–4. Managing Director, Amalgamated Anthracite Collieries Ltd, 1925–35.

Ireland, Sir James Craig, sent Churchill a letter which implied that moderation might still prevail from the Northern side as well. In his letter, Craig wrote: 'I am quite ready to attend a conference between you and the delegates of Southern Ireland . . . so as to ascertain clearly whether the policy of Southern Ireland is to be one of peace or whether the present method of pressure on Northern Ireland is to be continued.' Craig's principal fear was that the constant Sinn Fein denunciation of the Ulster border, as well as repeated raids across the border from the South, might put pressure on Britain to make concessions to the South on where the border was to be drawn. The Ulster leaders were determined not to allow any of the borders of their six counties to be whittled away, and were particularly concerned to keep all of Fermanagh and Tyrone within Ulster, despite the predominantly Catholic population of these two counties.

Churchill took steps to bring Sir James Craig and Michael Collins together, and was hopeful that if Collins could retain power in Dublin, the settlement had a chance of success. On Thursday January 12 Sir Henry Wilson wrote in his diary:

I went over to C.O. before lunch & had a talk with Winston. We have had several assaults on officers & men the last few days & I told him we would not stand it, & we must take over or come out. He agreed & hoped we might begin on Monday. He anticipates peace under Collins but said he would use troops to bolster up Collins.

When Churchill took the Chair at a meeting of his Cabinet Committee on January 12, it was agreed, according to the minutes, that an amnesty was to be issued immediately, and that henceforth the army was 'not to intervene in disturbances without the direct orders of the Viceroy'. This decision was confirmed when the Committee met again on January 13.

On January 15 the Dail met to give its formal approval to the Irish Treaty, and a Provisional Government was appointed with Michael Collins as Prime Minister. The new Government pledged itself to carry out the terms of the Treaty, and to take over all administrative powers previously held by the British Government. On January 16 Lord Fitz Alan handed over Dublin Castle to Michael Collins; whereupon Churchill ordered the evacuation of British troops to begin at once.

Churchill was now determined that Craig and Collins should meet. On January 17 he put this view to his Cabinet Committee. According to the minutes of the meeting 'the Chairman laid great stress on the importance of Mr Collins or Mr Griffith coming to London at the earliest possible moment in order that a meeting might be held between them and Mr Craig'. Churchill did not ignore Conservative hostility to such a meeting, writing to Lord Morley[1] on January 18 that 'the Die-hard Tories are consumed with bitterness against the Irish settlement, and will certainly do their best to wreck it. . . . F.E. helped us tremendously at the critical moment, but at considerable cost to his own position.'

The meeting between Sir James Craig and Michael Collins took place in Churchill's own room at the Colonial Office on January 21. Seven years later he recalled, in *The World Crisis*:

They both glowered magnificently, but after a short, commonplace talk I slipped away upon some excuse and left them together. What these two Irishmen, separated by such gulfs of religion, sentiment, and conduct, said to each other I cannot tell. But it took a long time, and, as I did not wish to disturb them, mutton chops, etc., were tactfully introduced about one o'clock. At four o'clock the Private Secretary reported signs of movement on the All-Ireland front and I ventured to look in. They announced to me complete agreement reduced to writing. They were to help each other in every way; they were to settle outstanding points by personal discussion; they were to stand together within the limits agreed against all disturbers of the peace. We three then joined in the best of all pledges, to wit, 'To try to make things work.'

The immediate outcome of the Craig–Collins discussions was a hopeful one. On January 24 the Provisional Government ordered an end to the economic boycott of Ulster, and free trade began at once between North and South.

On January 30 the Provisional Government made a major gesture of reconciliation, by offering a full amnesty 'to all members of the Naval, Military, Police or civil services of the British Government and all other persons by whom acts of hostility against the Irish people were committed, aided or abetted. . . .' The offer of an amnesty ended with the words: 'We must not suffer ourselves to be outdone by our late enemies in seeking that the wrongs of the past may be buried in oblivion.' This, Churchill wrote to Sir John Anderson[2] on January 31, was a 'bold and

[1] John Morley, 1838–1923. Liberal MP, 1883–95 and 1896–1908. Chief Secretary for Ireland, 1886 and 1892–5. Secretary of State for India, 1905–10. Created Viscount, 1908. Lord President of the Council, 1910–14. One of Churchill's oldest political friends.

[2] John Anderson, 1882–1958. Entered the Colonial Office, 1905; Secretary, Northern Nigeria Lands Committee, 1909. Secretary to the Insurance Commissioners, London, 1913. Secretary, Ministry of Shipping, 1917–19. Knighted, 1919 (at the age of 31). Chairman, Board of Inland Revenue, 1919–22. Joint Under-Secretary of State to the Viceroy of Ireland, 1920. Permanent Under-Secretary of State, Home Office, 1922–32. Governor of Bengal, 1932–7. MP for the Scottish Universities, 1938–50. Lord Privy Seal, 1938–9. Home Secretary

fine declaration', and he asked Anderson to tell Arthur Griffith and Michael Collins: 'The form of the new declaration is very good. We like its tone and style and hope it may be issued as soon as possible. On our side we propose immediately to release the Sinn Fein prisoners now held for pre-truce offences in this country. . . .'

Among the Sinn Feiners for whom the Provisional Government wanted a reciprocal amnesty were several members of the Connaught Rangers who had mutinied in India in 1920. Thirteen of them had been sentenced by court martial to life imprisonment. The War Office were opposed to giving an amnesty to these men, but Churchill pressed Lloyd George to agree. 'The release of the Connaught Rangers is *essential*,' he wrote to him on January 30. 'Unless I get this I cannot settle with the Irish Government.' Churchill's plea was successful. 'LG has now decided to release all the Connaughts. . . .' Henry Wilson wrote in his diary on January 31. 'This is of course on the orders of Collins & is bringing cowardice & politics into the Army with a vengeance.'

The hopeful developments of the last week of January were not followed up in the first few days on February. The Southern Irish were unwilling to accept the borders of Ulster as provisionally defined in the Treaty, and fighting broke out along the border. On February 3 Churchill discussed Ireland with Lord Riddell, who recorded in his diary:

He says the Irish situation is very awkward. He intends to propose arbitration regarding the boundary question, as he thinks this the only way out. He added, 'Everyone in Ireland seems to be unreasonable. The Irish will not recognise that they, like every other civilised people, must adopt reasonable methods for settling differences.'

Churchill was being drawn more and more closely into Irish affairs. In a letter to his wife on February 3 he noted: 'The Irish situation is in the fire again & the reactions of Ulster hostility upon the growing party crisis may be vy serious . . . usually (3 nights out of the last 4) the PM, Max & I dine together. They all think the clouds will break & we shall get through. Anyhow, Courage & Conduct. . . .'

Craig and Collins had met again, in Dublin, on February 2. Craig was determined not to give way on the border issue, and many Conservative MPs supported his stand. 'Yesterday the Irish situation de-

and Minister of Home Security, 1939–40. Lord President of the Council, 1940–3. Chancellor of the Exchequer, 1943–5. Chairman of the Port of London Authority, 1946–58. Created Viscount Waverley, 1952. Order of Merit, 1957.

generated violently,' Churchill wrote to his wife on February 4. Conservative support for Craig's attitude, he added, 'will be formidable. . . . Ireland is sure to bring us every form of difficulty and embarrassment, and I expect I shall have to bear the brunt of it in the House of Commons.' Hopes had faded considerably in the two weeks since Craig and Collins had met in his room at the Colonial Office. And yet, Churchill added, 'I am glad to have this task in my hands, and hope to be able to steer a good course through all the storms and rocks.' 'The new Irish rift is very disappointing,' Clementine Churchill replied on February 7. 'Surely the PM must have misled Collins over the Ulster Boundary? I do hope Craig will not think he has been treated in a slippery way. . . .'

Craig, fearful that Lloyd George would offer Collins a substantial modification of the boundary, saw Lloyd George on February 6 to say that he stood firm on the 1920 borders, and pointed out that Lloyd George himself had said they could not be changed without the sanction of Ulster. Craig also told Lloyd George that he would take no part in the Boundary Commission, set up by the Treaty to decide on any border changes. On February 8 Sinn Fein bands crossed into Fermanagh and Tyrone, and kidnapped several prominent Ulster leaders. The Ulster Government sent armoured cars to the border. That evening Churchill told the House of Commons:

We are going to have a very anxious and difficult time, and no man can say with certainty that a good result will be achieved, but there is a great hope, and it is the only hope, that with patience and with perseverance we may succeed through all the difficulties of this Irish situation in the same way as, 20 years ago, we found our way through the certainly not less baffling and perplexing difficulties of the South African situation.

At any rate, while there is not the slightest ground for optimism or enthusiasm or vain ebullitions of joy and satisfaction, neither is there the slightest ground in anything that presents itself in any portion of this complicated and difficult Irish situation for weakness, disheartenment, or despair.

'The Irish position seems very dark & troubled,' Clementine Churchill wrote to her husband from Cannes on February 10. 'Michael Collins does not appear to be able to control his wild men.' The violence was increasing in intensity. On February 11, at Clones, four police constables were shot dead by the IRA. Between February 11 and 16, thirty people were killed in Belfast. On February 11 Churchill wrote to his wife:

Irish affairs are more & more falling into my hands, & I think I am increasingly gaining control of the event. I am as usual in a gt matter wh I lay my hands on hopeful of the result. We shall see. . . .

I am remaining all alone in London over Sunday to be on the wire to deal with Irish questions. Telegrams arrive continually from both the Northern and Southern Governments. These theatrical Irishmen are enjoying themselves enormously: & apart from a few cruel things vy little blood is shed.

Our position is a vy strong one, *so long as* we adhere to the Treaty. And Ulster's position is a vy strong one *so long as she respects the Law*. I have made it clear I will defend or conceal no illegalities or irregularities of any kind. I will expose them coldly to Parliament whoever is guilty. We must not get back into that hideous bog of reprisals, from which we have saved ourselves.

Elections were to be held in Southern Ireland to obtain a majority vote in favour of the Treaty. By such democratic means did Collins hope to triumph over De Valera, and reassert the rule of law. But whether he would be allowed to do so was not entirely clear. On February 14 General Macready wrote to Churchill from Dublin, where he was supervising the withdrawal of British troops from the South:

It is on the cards, although I personally don't think it likely, that Valera may start a coup d'etat before the elections, or that he may get a majority in favour of a republic at the elections. If British troops are still in the country, should either eventuality take place it would be a help to me to know what may be at the back of the mind of the Government in face of such a contingency. In default of any instructions on the subject, I shall declare Martial Law at once in Dublin, tell the Provisional Government that they will kindly remain quiescent, and I shall take complete charge of the town, railway termini, seaborne traffic, etc.

If either contingency that I have mentioned should occur, it will be no time for hesitation, and for the sake of the lives of those for whom I am responsible, I shall be obliged to act at once.

On the morning of February 14 Churchill's Cabinet Committee met in his room at the Colonial Office to discuss the worsening Irish situation. Henry Wilson told the Committee—as he had told Churchill on the telephone the night before—that it was not enough to send troops to Ulster to protect the border. Nothing could solve the Irish problem, he said, 'except re-conquest which is a formidable thing and can only be done if England is wholeheartedly in favour of it'.

On the morning of February 15 Michael Collins spent several hours at the Colonial Office, where he and Churchill discussed means of reducing tension along the border. The two men agreed to the establishment of two Border Commissions which would operate on each side of the frontier, and regularly exchange information with a view to allaying suspicions and reducing tension. But on the Northern side of the border preparations had already been made to repel any attack from the South; each crossing had been fortified. Such an atmosphere in Ireland did not help the plans for conciliation either on the border, or in London.

On February 16 Churchill introduced the second reading of the Irish Free State Bill to the House of Commons. This Bill, he explained at the start of his speech, 'clothes the Provisional Government with lawful power and enables them to hold an election under favourable conditions at the earliest possible moment'. At present, he pointed out, the Southern Irish Cabinet, established as a result of the Treaty, had 'no legal autonomy'. Every day this situation continued was, he said, 'a reproach to the administration of the Empire'.

There was no question, Churchill told the House of Commons, of Britain recognizing an Irish Republic: 'We have never recognized it, and never will recognize it.' Under the Treaty, Southern Ireland would be a Dominion, owing allegiance to the Crown. He hoped that when elections were held in Southern Ireland 'the Republican idea' would be 'definitely, finally and completely put aside'. If the election were to result in a Republican majority, he went on, Southern Ireland would be 'absolutely isolated from the sympathy of the world, bitterly divided in herself'; but he saw no advantage 'in speculating upon these ugly hypotheses'.

Whatever Southern Ireland were to decide at the elections it was essential, Churchill said, that the law-enforcing efforts of the existing Provisional Government should be given the 'formal sanction' of the House of Commons. Unless this were done, law-breaking, brigandage and even mutiny would undermine the Provisional Government's attempts to win acceptance for the Treaty. Churchill then warned of the dangers if the House of Commons rejected the Free State Bill, and refused to give Michael Collins' Government the seal of constitutional and legal authority:

If you want to see Ireland degenerate into a meaningless welter of lawless chaos and confusion, delay this Bill. If you wish to see increasingly serious bloodshed all along the borders of Ulster, delay this Bill. If you want this House to have on its hands, as it now has, the responsibility for peace and order in Southern Ireland, without the means of enforcing it, if you want to impose those same evil conditions upon the Irish Provisional Government, delay this Bill. If you want to enable dangerous and extreme men, working out schemes of hatred and subterranean secrecy, to undermine and overturn a Government which is faithfully doing its best to keep its word with us and enabling us to keep our word with it, delay this Bill. If you want to proclaim to all the world, week after week, that the British Empire can get on just as well without law as with it, then you will delay this Bill.

But if you wish to give a fair chance to a policy to which Parliament has pledged itself, and to Irish Ministers to whom you are bound in good faith, so long as they act faithfully with you, to give fair play and a fair chance, if you wish to see Ireland brought back from the confusion of tyranny to a reign of law, if you wish to give logical and coherent effect to the policy and experiment to which we are committed, you will not impede, even for a single unnecessary week, the passage of this Bill.

Churchill tried to put at rest the fears of many Conservatives that Ulster had been betrayed, and that the Irish Free State would constitute a terrible danger to the North. Any threat to Ulster, he insisted, would be met 'by the whole force and power, if necessary, of the British Empire'. Ulster could only gain in strength and security by the creation of an autonomous South, for as a result of this, the British Empire, including Ulster, would be 'increasingly detached from the terrible curse of this long internal Irish quarrel'. It was Southern Ireland alone that now suffered from that quarrel. Both Ulster, and Britain, stood aside from the clash between Free Staters and Republicans, between Collins and De Valera, between acceptance of the Treaty, and its rejection. 'All the world is looking at their performance,' Churchill said. 'They are the people at the present time, not Ulster, not Great Britain, whose difficulties and whose task deserve sympathy and support.'

Conservative hostility towards the Treaty centred on the provision for a Boundary Commission. This provision, Churchill insisted, could not be altered. The Treaty itself had been accepted by Parliament on December 16 by an overwhelming majority. The Boundary Commission would therefore come into force as soon as the Treaty came into operation, and the boundaries of Ulster would then be liable to modification and redrawing. The principal dispute, Churchill said, concerned, as it had done before, the boundaries of only two Irish counties, Fermanagh and Tyrone:

I remember on the eve of the Great War we were gathered together at a Cabinet meeting in Downing Street, and for a long time, an hour or an hour and a half, after the failure of the Buckingham Palace Conference, we discussed the boundaries of Fermanagh and Tyrone. Both of the great political parties were at each other's throats. The air was full of talk of civil war. Every effort was made to settle the matter and bring them together. The differences had been narrowed down, not merely to the counties of Fermanagh and Tyrone, but to parishes and groups of parishes inside the areas of Fermanagh and Tyrone, and yet, even when the differences had been so narrowed down, the problem appeared to be as insuperable as ever, and neither side would agree to reach any conclusion. . . .

Then came the great War. Every institution, almost, in the world was strained. Great Empires have been overturned. The whole map of Europe has been changed. The position of countries has been violently altered. The modes of thought of men, the whole outlook on affairs, the grouping of parties, all have encountered violent and tremendous changes in the deluge of the world, but as the deluge subsides and the waters fall short we see the dreary steeples of Fermanagh and Tyrone emerging once again. The integrity of their quarrel is one of the few institutions that has been unaltered in the cataclysm which has swept the world.

That says a lot for the persistency with which Irish men on the one side or the other are able to pursue their controversies. It says a great deal for the power which Ireland has, both Nationalist and Orange, to lay their hands upon the vital strings of British life and politics, and to hold, dominate, and convulse, year after year, generation after generation, the politics of this powerful country.

Churchill accepted the fact, which many Conservatives found un-acceptable, that in certain districts of Fermanagh and Tyrone 'the majority of the inhabitants will prefer to join the Irish Free State'. But he agreed that this fact constituted a 'weak point' in the British Govern-ment's assurances to Ulster. 'I am not concealing it for a moment,' he said. 'I am locating it, defining it and exposing it. This is the weak point. The Boundary Commission . . . affects the existing frontiers of Ulster and may conceivably affect them prejudicially.' Even so, he believed that the Free State Bill offered both North and South a fair solution, and he warned the House of Commons of the dangers of voting against the Bill on account of the boundary issue. Let every member who intended to reject the Bill, he warned, 'ponder carefully and long upon the responsibilities to be assumed and upon the alternatives which were involved, upon the consequences which would surely follow'. It would be better, he believed, to discuss 'passionate questions like the boundary question' after the election in the South, when the Free State had been accepted by a majority vote, and when extremism was on the wane. Southern Ireland, he declared, did not want a Republic—'that is a delusion', he insisted, 'and my hon. Friends are absolutely at sea when they say so. A Republic is an idea most foreign to the Irish mind, associated with the butcheries of Cromwell in their minds, and foreign to the native genius of the Irish race, which is essentially monarchial.'

Churchill's final appeal was to those Conservatives who still believed that the Southern Irish aim was an all-Irish Republic, and who were convinced that the British Government would not, in the last resort, defend Ulster against either border changes or direct attack. Churchill sought to set these fears at rest. 'Not only should we defend every inch of Ulster soil under the Treaty as if it were Kent,' he asserted, 'but we should be bound to take special measures to secure that Ulster was not ruined by her loyalty to us.' And he concluded:

For generations we have been wandering and floundering in the Irish bog; but at last we think that in this Treaty we have set our feet upon a pathway, which has already become a causeway—narrow, but firm and far-reaching. Let us march along this causeway with determination and circumspection, without losing heart and without losing faith. If Britain continues to march forward along that path, the day may come—it may be distant, but it may not be so distant as we expect—when, turning round, Britain will find at her side Ireland united, a nation, and a friend.

Churchill's speech outraged many Conservatives, who refused to put any faith in the alleged moderation of the Free State Government. But many Liberals, and Conservative supporters of the Coalition, found his speech a convincing argument for conciliation. 'Winston speaks with great brilliance,' was H. A. L. Fisher's comment. The House then emptied, Austen Chamberlain informed the King, when Captain Craig[1] rose to move an amendment, refusing to assent to the Boundary Commission, and declaring that any alteration of the boundary would provoke Ulster to resort to force.

The debate continued for two days, and with much recrimination. Captain Foxcroft[2] asserted that Churchill's 'very optimistic speech' was at total variance with the facts: 'We find anarchy in the South and invasion in the North. We find extremists gaining power every day everywhere. We find that the man in power is the man with the gun.' But Austen Chamberlain's half-brother, Neville,[3] urged the House of Commons to reject Captain Craig's amendment, and to accept the Treaty as it stood, declaring that he was 'more convinced than ever' by

[1] Charles Curtis Craig, 1869–1960. Conservative MP for South Antrim, 1903–22; for County Antrim, 1922–9. Captain, 11th battalion, Royal Irish Rifles, 1914–16; wounded and taken prisoner by the Germans, 1916. Parliamentary Secretary, Ministry of Pensions, 1923–4.

[2] Charles Talbot Foxcroft, 1869–1929. Captain 2/4 Battalion Somerset Light Infantry, 1914–16; Assistant Adjutant, 1917–18. Conservative MP for Bath, 1918–23 and 1924–9.

[3] Arthur Neville Chamberlain, 1869–1940. Son of Joseph Chamberlain. Lord Mayor of Birmingham, 1915–16. Director-General of National Service, 1916–17. Conservative MP, 1918–40. Postmaster-General, 1922–3. Paymaster-General, 1923. Minister of Health, 1923, 1924–9 and 1931. Chancellor of the Exchequer, 1923–4 and 1931–7. Prime Minister, 1937–40. Lord President of the Council, May–November 1940.

Churchill's speech that the Boundary Commission would deal fairly and justly with Ulster. When the vote was taken, Captain Craig's amendment received only 60 votes, as against 302 for the Government.

On February 20, the leader of the Liverpool Conservatives, Sir Archibald Salvidge,[1] wrote to Churchill: 'It is not too late, I hope, for me to sincerely congratulate you on your speech in the House last week. I would have written before but have been waiting to weigh up the opinion here, and am pleased to say there is almost unanimous agreement in praise of your very fine achievement.' That same day, Churchill's Cabinet Committee met to discuss a request from Collins for British arms. Collins had asked for 3,500 rifles, and a number of machine guns and armoured cars. Churchill supported his request, but with modifications, and on certain specific conditions. 'The Chairman was disposed,' the Minutes recorded, '. . . to issue immediately to the Provisional Government, 1,000 rifles and 3 or 4 armoured cars, in the clear understanding that these would not be used on the Border, but only for the purpose of maintaining order in the South.' The Committee accepted Churchill's proposal. They also agreed with his suggestion not to give Collins any machine guns 'as yet'.

Churchill spoke every day in the House of Commons during the three days of the Committee Stage of the Irish Free State Bill. 'The Irish Bill, hotly opposed by Die Hards, led by Hugh Cecil. . . .' H. A. L. Fisher noted in his diary on March 1. 'Winston pilots the Bill with great skill and good humour.' Among Churchill's most critical listeners was Henry Wilson, who had ceased to be Chief of the Imperial General Staff on February 19, and had taken his seat in the House of Commons —as Member for North Down—on February 23. Throughout the debate Churchill insisted that 'the character of the Treaty must be upheld'. Of course, he said, Parliament could, if it wished, destroy the Treaty; it could also destroy the Government. But those who had signed the Treaty, as he had, stood by it, and felt 'in honour bound to go through with it'. Every amendment put forward was designed to alter the spirit of the Treaty; all were defeated. During those three days Churchill was continually in the House of Commons, putting the Government's case, and answering its critics.

On March 2, in reply to a major amendment put by Sir Frederick Banbury, aimed at showing that the Irish Delegation had not been

[1] Archibald Tutton James Salvidge, 1863–1928. Chairman, Liverpool Conservative Workingmen's Association, 1892. Alderman, Liverpool City Council, 1898. Chairman of Council, National Union of Conservative and Unionist Associations, 1913–14. Chairman, Liverpool Advisory Committee on Recruiting, 1914–16. Knighted, 1916.

representative of all Irishmen, Churchill declared: 'On behalf of the Government I cannot possibly agree to any amendment which alters, modifies, extends, explains, elucidates, amplifies or otherwise affects the text of the instrument which we call the Treaty.' And he went on: 'if as a result of a Division inspired by his eloquence or the cogency of his arguments, or as the result of his parliamentary resource, experience and knowledge, he were to persuade the House to effect any alteration, modification, amplification etc. of this Treaty instrument, then the Bill would be dead, the Treaty would be dead and the Government would be dead'.

Answering the specific fears of many Conservatives that the Free State might declare its total independence, and set up a Republican Government, Churchill replied:

. . . we are not going to have an Independent Republic in Ireland. I have said so again and again. As far as we are concerned, we should never agree to it in any circumstances whatever. . . . There is absolutely no question of accommodation in that subject, none whatever. None can be suggested, and none whatever would be agreed to. The battle has been joined in Ireland on that issue. There is no weakening on that issue by the men with whom we have signed the Treaty.

On March 3 Churchill continued to insist that the Treaty could not be modified or whittled away. 'We have entered into a bargain,' he said, 'and we are bound to keep our part of the bargain.' On March 6, the third day of the committee stage of the Bill, Churchill urged those who wanted to alter the Treaty not to use their powers to destroy what had been achieved with such difficulty, and with so many hopes. 'The powers of Parliament,' he said, 'are unlimited. Parliament can at any time tear up anything. In its wisdom and in its pleasure it can destroy any arrangement and any constitution, but it is not always wise to exercise to the full the undoubted and the inalienable powers which it possesses.'

Angered by Churchill's defence of the Treaty, and as a final protest, the Conservative 'Die Hards', led by Sir Henry Wilson walked out of the Chamber while Churchill was speaking.

When the Third Reading of the Irish Free State Bill was taken that afternoon, Churchill was insistent that the establishment of the Free State could only be of advantage to Britain. In the course of his speech, which was the concluding one for the Government, he declared to a somewhat uneasy House:

If you strip Ireland of her grievance, if you strip Ireland of the weapon she has hitherto used, if you strip her of the accusation against Great Britain of

being the oppressor, if you strip her of her means of exciting and commanding
the sympathy of almost the whole world, of the support she has received in the
United States, in our own Dominions, indeed, throughout the whole English-
speaking world, if by acting in strict, inflexible, good faith you place Ireland
in the position that if she breaks the Treaty she is in the wrong and you are in
the right, that she is absolutely isolated in the whole world—then, I say, the
strength of your economic position emerges in its integrity.

For many years, Churchill continued, Ireland had played a major
part in British affairs, 'convulsing parties, disturbing Governments,
holding the balance for years. . . . But when Ireland is stripped of her
grievance and stands on her own resources, then, and then alone, will
you know how weak she is, how little power she has to do us harm.'
Churchill ended his speech with an appeal to the House of Commons to
help the Provisional Government to resist the pressure of republicanism
by passing the Free State Bill, and thus recognizing 'that Irishmen are
capable of producing a Government in their own country, and for the
life of their own country, which is not markedly below the standard of
the civilisation of Western Europe'.

On March 9 Austen Chamberlain sent the King an account of the
debate. During the week, he said, the Ulster MPs had 'steadily lost
ground. The more they gave expression to their feelings, the less sympathy the House felt with them.' And he continued:

Mr Churchill wound up for the Government. For some reason he spoke
with less than his usual ease and the House listened rather coldly; but in his
handling of the Irish Questions and his general conduct of this Bill he has
shown parliamentary talent of the highest order and greatly strengthened his
parliamentary position.

During the first two weeks of March the tension, both along the
Ulster border and in Belfast, was at a high pitch. On March 5 a section
of the IRA, rejecting Collins' call for moderation, invaded Limerick.
On March 14, when the Northern Ireland Parliament opened in
Belfast, Sir James Craig announced that Sir Henry Wilson, who had
retired from the Army a month before, was preparing a scheme for the
restoration of order. On March 16 three people were shot dead in
Galway, and fifteen people injured by bomb explosions in Belfast. 'The
state of affairs in Belfast is lamentable,' Churchill had written to Collins
two days earlier. 'There is an underworld there with deadly forces of
its own, and only the sternest and strictest efforts by leading men on
both sides, coupled with ample military and police forces, will produce
that tranquility which is demanded by the interests of Ireland as a
whole.'

On March 17 Churchill's aunt Leonie[1] wrote to him from her home in County Monaghan, on the Free State side of the border with Ulster:

How I've admired yr courage and *patience*—we need to practice both here at present. This transition state is very difficult to cope with. It will be easier after the Elections, when the Govt is properly established. One must be hopeful.

Meantime Jack[2] and all those we can influence try to keep peace—*being the Border*, there is friction. It needs Christian charity, & a sense of humour, to carry one along. The Union Jacks are being silently stored away—the SF flag floats on the orange Hall. The country will vote pro-treaty.

Churchill himself was in optimistic mood. 'There is no doubt Ireland is settling down in many ways,' he wrote to Lloyd George on March 18, 'and the Provisional Government are getting a stronger grip every day. . . . All I can hear points to a heavy defeat of De Valera at the polls. A decisive pronouncement by the Irish people in favour of the Free State and against a Republic will be a dazzling event. . . .'

But the murders continued. During the third week of March IRA raids on Ulster border posts intensified, and a state of continual guerrilla warfare developed throughout the border areas. On March 21 Churchill appealed direct to Michael Collins and Arthur Griffith for them to exert their authority, and reduce the border violence:

An explosion would be disastrous, and even a continuance of the present tension tends to stereotype the border line and make it into a fortified military frontier, which is the last thing in the world you want. I cannot think there is the slightest danger of a raid from the North into the South. If such a raid took place those making it would put themselves in the wrong, and the British Government would take every measure in its power. I am certain that you do not need to be alarmed on this score. Even if it happened it would only do harm to those responsible, just in the same way as the kidnapping raids from Monaghan have done harm to Southern Irish interests.

I am told that I.R.A. (so called) are collecting along the border in increasing numbers. Surely this is not necessary. . . .

You must understand that I am at the same time making the strongest

[1] Leonie Blanche Jerome, 1859–1943. Sister of Lady Randolph Churchill. She married Colonel John Leslie in 1884.

[2] John Leslie, 1857–1944. Lieutenant, Grenadier Guards, 1877. On active service in Egypt, 1882; in South Africa, 1900. Lieutenant-Colonel Commanding the 5th Royal Irish Fusiliers, 1900–8. Retired with the rank of Colonel, 1908. In 1916 he succeeded his father as 2nd Baronet. A Justice of the Peace for County Monaghan.

representations to Sir James Craig to prevent provocative action on the part of his people.

At a meeting of the Cabinet on March 22, Churchill warned that the IRA and Special Constabulary 'had been allowed to come dangerously near each other on the boundary'. He had always believed that the way to avoid a clash was to 'draw a cordon by means of British troops' but this proposal, he said, had been resisted by Sir Henry Wilson. He still thought 'it would be possible to place troops at critical points. . . . He very much dreaded a collision.' It was also essential, he said, 'to press Sir James Craig to meet Mr Collins in conference', and to obtain from Collins 'a repudiation of the revolts on the part of the Irish Republican Army'.

Two days later, on March 24, a particularly repellent murder of a whole Catholic family in Belfast seemed to make some urgent action essential. Late that afternoon Churchill summoned a meeting of his Cabinet Committee. Five Cabinet Ministers were present—Churchill himself, Lord Birkenhead, Austen Chamberlain, Worthington-Evans and Hamar Greenwood. At the start of the meeting, Churchill drew Chamberlain's attention to the Belfast murder. It was essential, he said, to ask Craig and Collins to come to London at once. According to the Minutes of the meeting, Churchill told his colleagues that 'the British Government had a definite responsibility in the matter'. Britain was paying large sums of money for the Protestant B Specials, he explained, 'some of whom had possibly been guilty of these murders'. Churchill suggested drawing a cordon on the border, taking over 'a section of Belfast' under martial Law, and 'bid Collins disband the IRA in the North'.

Churchill's Committee agreed to invite Craig and Collins once more to London as a matter of urgency. 'We cannot believe,' Churchill telegraphed to Craig that evening, 'that if men carrying weight and influence with the opposing factions were to come together, a way could not be found to end these horrors.' Three days later, on March 27, Churchill told the House of Commons that Craig and Collins had agreed to meet in London under his auspices. He also uttered a warning against undue optimism:

I do not pretend to guarantee that there will be good results from this conference. There may be no result at all, except that both sides may go home with more hopeless feelings than before, and the troubles will continue to grow.

We will do our very best, but it rests with Irishmen who care for Ireland to try to bring about a better state of things. They alone can do it.

Great Britain will help, but the initiative, the controlling administration, has passed out of our hands by our own will, deliberately, into the hands of Irishmen. Let them meet together, and endeavour to create in a satisfactory manner a decent future for Ireland.

On the following morning Austen Chamberlain wrote to the King of the 'skill, balance and humour' of Churchill's remarks, 'which have made his handling of this question such a remarkable exhibition of parliamentary talent'. The force of Churchill's argument, Chamberlain added, 'lost nothing by its moderation and good temper. . . .'

On March 28 Craig and Collins reached London. In the House of Commons, Churchill spoke of the continuing murders in Ireland. 'I think one would have to search all over Europe,' he said, 'to find instances of equal atrocity, barbarity, cold blooded, inhuman, cannibal vengeance—cannibal in all except the act of devouring the flesh of the victim. . . .' These horrors, he said, were taking place 'on both sides', and he continued:

We seek only the repression and the termination of these horrors. We have no other object and no other interest. The rest must lie with the representatives of the Irish people across the Channel. Everything we can do to help them to shake themselves free from this convulsion and spasm—due, no doubt, to the tragedies of the past—will be done, and every action which I shall submit from this box must be defended and justified only in reference to that.

Austen Chamberlain was again impressed by Churchill's mastery of the House of Commons. In what was only a short speech, he wrote to the King on the following day, Churchill succeeded 'in maintaining the high reputation he has won as a resolute yet conciliatory debater. The House listened with marked and almost breathless attention to Mr Churchill's comments. . . .'

On the morning of March 29 Churchill prepared the first draft of an agreement between North and South. His draft included the phrase 'Peace to begin from today. . . .' According to his proposals, the two governments would agree to meet at once 'to consider the solution of the boundary question & the furtherance of Irish unity'; the IRA would suspend all activities; and a mixed Catholic–Protestant police force would keep order in Belfast. Later that day four Sinn Fein negotiators,

Collins, Griffith, Duggan[1] and O'Higgins[2] met Craig and Londonderry in Conference in Churchill's room at the Colonial Office. Before proceeding to discuss his draft agreement, Churchill told them that the issues they were to decide involved 'the life and happiness of thousands of poor people'.

Churchill's efforts at reconciliation continued, reaching their climax on March 30. That evening Thomas Jones recorded the day's events in his diary:

From 11.0 onwards there were conferences to-day in Churchill's room at the Colonial Office between him and L. Worthington-Evans, Sir James Craig and Lord Londonderry, Michael Collins and Arthur Griffith. They were engaged in drawing up Heads of Agreement between the North and South. . . .

Considerable progress had been made on the previous day with the draft agreement, Churchill taking great pains to keep its terms secret. He was very anxious that I should not see it, fearing I would tell the P.M. and that in some mysterious way the P.M. would, as he put it, 'pluck all the cherries'. . . .

The conference of the 'Six' continued until five in the afternoon, when the draft agreement was reached. Collins and his fellow Free Staters promised to co-operate 'in every way in their power' to restore peaceful conditions throughout Ireland. For his part, Craig agreed to reorganize the Belfast police so that the special police keeping law and order would consist of equal numbers of Catholics and Protestants. Collins agreed that all border attacks by the IRA would cease. Churchill himself promised a British Government contribution of half a million pounds for relief work in Northern Ireland, one third for the benefit of Roman Catholics and two thirds for Protestants.

The draft agreement was sent to the basement of the Foreign Office, where it was to be printed. Thomas Jones and Lionel Curtis[3] supervised this urgent activity. In his diary Jones recorded:

[1] Edmund John Duggan,   –1936. Solicitor, 1914. Took part in the Easter Rising, 1916. Director of Intelligence, Irish Republican Army. Sinn Fein MP for South Meath, 1918–22. Imprisoned by the British, 1920–1. Member of the Dail, 1921–33. A Delegate to the Irish Conference, 1921, and a signatory of the Irish Treaty, 1922. Secretary for Home Affairs of the Free State Government, 1922–3. Parliamentary Secretary to the President of the Free State, and Junior Minister of Defence, 1927–32. Senator, 1933–6.

[2] Kevin Christopher O'Higgins, 1862–1927. MP (Sinn Fein) for Queen's County, 1918–22. Minister for Home Affairs, Irish Free State, 1922–3; Vice-President and Minister of Justice from 1923 until his death.

[3] Lionel George Curtis, 1872–1955. Served in the South African War as a Private, 1899. Secretary to Sir Alfred Milner in South Africa, 1900. Town Clerk, Johannesburg, 1902–3. Assistant Colonial Secretary, Transvaal, 1903–9. Editor of the *Round Table*, 1909. Professor of Colonial History, Oxford, 1912. Member of the British League of Nations Section at the

It had to be ready by 6.0 but it soon became clear that this was impossible and the full conference was adjourned till 6.30. Churchill himself came to the printing office and finally edited the draft and then he bade me try to keep as close as I could to the Irishmen and do what I could to persuade them to sign. I rang up Jermyn Court Hotel. Collins replied and said he was delayed but that the others had gone to the Colonial Office. For a moment I felt that he was funking but Griffith told me he was detained by his sister and was coming on later. He arrived soon after 6.30 p.m. and was closeted with his colleagues till a few minutes after 7.0 when the full conference started at last, this time being seated round the big round table. Craig, in reply to Churchill, announced that apart from minor verbal alterations he was prepared to sign. O'Higgins, however, raised difficulties at once and continued to do so throughout.

By eight o'clock the final difficulties were overcome, and the agreement was signed. The document, which Churchill read to the House of Commons late that evening, began with a brief but emphatic clause: 'PEACE is today declared'.

The immediate reaction to the Agreement of March 30 was one of wide-spread euphoria. It seemed to advance the Irish Treaty from the stage of hopeful declaration to that of positive action. Joseph Devlin hastened to praise Churchill for his part in it:

May I be permitted to offer my congratulations to the right hon. Gentleman, and to all his colleagues, for the inspired idea which moved him to call this conference together, and I trust, as I pay very free compliments to hon. Members on that bench, that I may also be allowed to congratulate the right hon. Gentleman on the superb tact and ability with which he has conducted all those Irish matters since he has been entrusted with this task.

Defending the agreement in the House of Commons on March 31, Churchill praised Ulster for having 'lent a helping hand to the Irish Free State and to the cause of peace in Ireland'. The Agreement, he said, was intended to bring an end to 'the religious and partisan warfare in Belfast itself and to the acts of repeated injury and counter-injury which have been done by Catholics and Protestants one against the other'. But he also had a warning to make:

. . . there will be forces in Ireland anxious to wreck these arrangements by violent action, by treacherous action, and, if possible, to throw suspicion upon the good faith of those with whom we have entered into a covenant. We must be prepared in our minds for that. We must be prepared for attempts to mar all this fair prospect. We must carefully, even patiently, discriminate in these

Paris Peace Conference, 1919. Secretary to the British Delegation at the Irish Conference, London, 1921. Colonial Office Adviser on Irish Affairs, 1921–4. Companion of Honour, 1949.

matters between the good faith of our friends and the pitiless animosity of our foes.

During the debate that followed Churchill's speech Lord Hugh Cecil spoke to him bitterly about the Treaty and the Agreement: 'Your statue is a statue of snow,' he said, 'which will dissolve under the sunlight of reality.' But one voice of approval and encouragement was that of the industrial arbitrator, Lord Askwith,[1] who wrote to Churchill on March 31:

I cannot refrain from sending a line to congratulate you on your new conciliation success—quickly done, no meteoric splash, *and* achievement. It will not be your fault if there are slips in the future, but it would be trite advice to say 'Keep them together, & keep on keeping them together', if signs of rift loom up.

It may interest you to remark that we were lunching with Ld Knollys[2]—a shrewd observer—today, & he, quite unsolicited, said that it had been a great proof of good *judgement* which might have a remarkable effect on your career, and added 'I think this exercise of judgment brings him nearer to the leadership of the country than any one would have supposed possible. It will modify a great many views.'

The Irish Free State Bill became law on March 31. Churchill had played a major part in introducing it to the House of Commons, in guiding its passage and in beating down the reiterated hostility of an influential group of Conservatives and Unionists. His efforts ensured the Coalition did not break up over Ireland. On April 1 Lord Stamfordham wrote to him from Buckingham Palace: 'Today the King congratulates you upon the successful conclusion of a difficult and responsible task thanks to the skill, patience and tact which you have displayed in handling it and for which you have earned universal gratitude.'

[1] George Ranken Askwith, 1861–1942. Barrister, 1886. Industrial arbitrator. Assistant Secretary, Board of Trade, 1907. Chairman of the Fair Wages Advisory Committee, 1909–19. Knighted, 1911. Chief Industrial Commissioner, Board of Trade, 1911–19. Created Baron, 1919. President of the British Science Guild, 1922–5. Vice-President, Royal Society of Arts, 1927–41. President of the Institute of Arbitrators, 1933–41.

[2] Francis Knollys, 1837–1924. Gentleman Usher to Queen Victoria, 1868–1901. Private Secretary to Edward VII when Prince of Wales and King, 1870–1910. Knighted, 1886. Created Baron, 1902. Private Secretary to George V, 1910–13. Created Viscount, 1911.

39

Ireland 1922: 'Will the lesson be learned in time'

A S soon as the Irish Free State Bill became law on March 31, Republican sentiment was inflamed throughout the areas loyal to De Valera. Throughout Saturday April 1 and Sunday April 2 Belfast was the scene of shootings and burnings. By the end of the weekend one Protestant policeman and four Catholics had been killed, and three Catholic children wounded. On April 2 a rebel section of the IRA paraded through the streets of Dublin. In County Mayo a band of Republicans prevented Michael Collins from addressing a public meeting. At Dundalk De Valera himself denied the legality of both the Provisional and the Northern Governments. 'Valera is daily strengthening,' Henry Wilson wrote in his diary on April 3, '& Collins daily weakening. Collins at Castlebar was ordered to stop speaking and obeyed! We are coming near the Republic.'

Churchill was shaken by the continuation of the violence, and the growing confidence of the Republicans. On April 4 he set out his reflections for his Cabinet colleagues. His memorandum, of thirteen typed pages, was marked 'Secretissime'. The leaders of the Provisional Government, he believed, were men of good faith, who had shown personal courage, who wanted to make the Irish Treaty work, and who were prepared to administer the South as a Dominion. But it had become clear that, despite their good faith, and their personal courage in signing and supporting the Treaty, they were 'obviously afraid of a breach with their extremists and have not shown themselves on any single important occasion capable of standing up to them'. There was no doubt, Churchill added, 'that the Irish have a genius for conspiracy rather than for government. The Government is feeble, apologetic, expostulatory; the conspirators, active, audacious and utterly shameless.'

During the Treaty negotiations, Churchill wrote in his memorandum of April 4, the Sinn Fein delegates had given an assurance that the IRA would obey the Provisional Government. But it had now become clear that 'a very large proportion' of the IRA 'is already openly disloyal to the Provisional Government, and by far the greater part is ardently republican'. This republicanism was spreading unchecked throughout the twenty-six counties of Southern Ireland:

A whole new crop of patriots have now appeared when there is no risk attached to their proceedings. No doubt any desperado feels he has as good a right as Michael Collins to pick up the Government and revenues of Ireland now they are going a-begging. In many cases it is sufficient for the Commandant of an I.R.A. unit to go one way, for his second-in-command to steal a march on him by going the other, or *vice versa*. It is hard to believe that there is any principle which dominates the thoughts of the I.R.A. except the Republican principle.

We have endeavoured to encourage Michael Collins to raise a trustworthy force, and for this purpose I have issued in small instalments up to 3,500 rifles. I am now about to give authority for the issue of another 500. This force, however, is apparently largely unreliable.

Churchill gave several examples of Republican success. In Galway, Free State Troops had been 'treacherously disarmed . . . without making any resistance'. In Cork, the IRA had seized Admiralty munitions of such quantity that they had become 'by far the most heavily armed party in that district'. What he now feared was a Republican revolution in Dublin, in which the Provisional Government 'would no doubt go on parleying until they were bundled into prison or, what is not impossible, make terms with the victorious Republicans'.

If the Republicans seized power outside Dublin, Churchill hoped that Collins and Griffith might agree 'to fight together with the North' to uphold the Treaty. This, he believed, was the direction in which 'we should endeavour to guide events'. But whether the Republicans seized power inside Dublin or outside it, civil war seemed to him almost inevitable. 'I take it for granted, of course,' Churchill continued, 'that we should not recognize or parley with a Republic in any circumstances, and that the mere fact of its being brought into being would constitute an act of war between it and the British Empire.'

Churchill warned his colleagues that once the Republic were declared, Britain would have 'great responsibilities to the refugees who will fly into Dublin or the sea. The aid of the Navy will have to be invoked at many points along the coast.'

The possibility of a war between Britain and an Irish Republic stimulated Churchill's imagination:

In my opinion we should not invade, except where convenient, the territories of this Republic. We should hold Dublin and possibly certain other ports. We should hold the best military line in the North, irrespective of the Ulster Boundary. The most convenient line runs approximately from Dundalk to Ballyshannon. We should proclaim a complete cessation of intercourse with the disaffected Counties, and notify foreign Powers of their effective blockade. This would allow portions of the country, by declaring themselves outside the area of the Republic and taking effective steps to divide themselves from the Republic, to resume their trade with Great Britain.

The effect of a blockade would not starve the Irish people, but it would at a stroke ruin their prosperity. Out of 205 millions exported from Ireland last year, 203 were purchased by Great Britain. This fact is alone decisive.

It is assumed that aerodromes would be established both in the North and in the neighbourhood of Dublin, in order that hostile concentrations may be dealt with from the air, or retaliatory measures taken we if are ourselves aggressively attacked.

In this posture I think we could sit down for a considerable time until Ireland came to her senses, without any great expense or inconvenience.

'I daresay,' Churchill concluded, 'my colleagues will think all these contingencies and the general picture exaggerated, and I still earnestly hope that we shall evade such melancholy events.' But, he added, 'I should not be doing my duty if I did not submit the possibility to the judgment of my colleagues.'

On April 5 the Cabinet discussed Churchill's memorandum. 'LG says we cannot allow a Republican Govt to be set up,' H. A. L. Fisher wrote in his diary. According to the Cabinet Conclusions:

There was general approval of the Prime Minister's proposition that the British Government could not allow the republican flag to fly in Ireland. A point might come when it would be necessary to tell Mr Collins that if he was unable to deal with the situation the British Government would have to do so.

The killings in Ireland continued. On April 6 five demobilized policemen were shot dead in Kerry and Clare. On April 10 the Cabinet decided to send two Companies of troops to protect Lord FitzAlan from being kidnapped 'by enemies of the Free State'. On April 11 Henry Wilson met Churchill in the House of Commons, and talked to him about Ireland:

I asked him what he will do when Valera declared his Republic & the Elections.

He said he would leave troops in Dublin—which I told him was absurd—
& blockade Ireland which I told him would make a war with America,
Germany & Russia. He talked the usual drivel & wound up by saying that
'there was absolutely no thought' of the 'invasion of Ireland'—which I said
simply meant the recognition of the Republic.

On April 12, during the Easter adjournment debate in the House of
Commons, Ireland was again the principal subject of debate. Lord
Robert Cecil criticized the Government for handing over the Government of Southern Ireland 'to men who, whatever their ability, were
absolutely untrained in administration'. He then launched into an
attack on the policy of 'organised arson and organised murder by the
agents of the Crown'; an attack which led to an acrimonious altercation
with Churchill:

Lord R. CECIL: I do not know whether the House remembers what these
reprisals were. . . . Murders were organised in the most brutal way. It is not
disputed, it is admitted, it has been stated by some of the judicial officers of
the Crown. It has never been denied.
Mr CHURCHILL: Those were the statements of the I.R.A.
Lord R. CECIL: What about Balbriggan? It was actually proved——
Mr CHURCHILL: The whole of this matter has been repeatedly made
perfectly clear. When officers of the Crown, military and police, were
ambushed and murdered under circumstances of the grossest treachery, it was
quite impossible to prevent the police and military making reprisals on their
own account. It would exceed the limits of human nature, however lament-
able or however regrettable.
Lord R. CECIL: That is the usual suggestion made by the Government.
Mr CHURCHILL: And you are making the usual suggestion of the
I.R.A.

Later in the debate Sir Henry Wilson—who had emerged as the
leading spokesman of the Conservative MPs from Ulster—urged
Churchill, or one of his colleagues, to go to Ireland and see the conditions there at first hand. 'My country is supposed to be a savage and
barbaric country,' he said, 'but really we have railways and roads and
telegraphs and telephones, and even hotels. It is also true that Belfast is
not so far as Gairloch nor Cork so far as Genoa.'
In replying to the debate, Churchill expressed his surprise at 'the long
stream of vitriolic allegations' with which Lord Robert Cecil had
'affronted the House'. Others, he said, had been consistent in seeking
peace but the 'Noble Lord has only been consistent in finding fault'.
Churchill then defended the actions of the Black and Tans which Cecil
had so severely attacked:

Everyone knows that armed men will not stand by and see one after another of their number shot down by treachery, without to some extent taking the law into their own hands.

Although the Government did their best to restrain them it is perfectly true that we did not punish with full severity persons who had been mixed up in this sort of affair. We have never concealed that.

How could we punish them while there was no other redress open to them, while no court would convict, while no criminals were arrested, while there was no means whatever of affording these men the satisfaction of a sense of self-preservation when they saw comrades weltering in blood from a foul blow?

Churchill then turned to the current situation; the growing strength of Republicanism in the south, and the almost daily killings in Belfast. 'It is, I think, too soon to mock or jeer,' he said. 'Two months ago it was too soon to rejoice. It is still too soon to lament.' He still hoped that the Provisional Government would succeed in persuading a majority of their constituents to vote for the Treaty. It was, he said, only when De Valera felt 'that the majority of the nation' was against him that he began to talk 'of wading through blood and of establishing a Mexican regime'. Churchill still believed that moderation would prevail, and that a majority of Southern Irishmen would accept the Treaty. But as for a Republic, he insisted, that was 'a form of Government in Ireland which the British Empire can in no circumstances whatever tolerate or agree to'.

Ten days later Lord Long wrote enthusiastically to Churchill:

. . . I must send you a line of warm congratulations upon your triumph of last week, & upon the really admirable way in which you have conducted all these difficult Irish affairs.

I accept your wise caution but I am very hopeful & if peace comes it will be mainly due to you.

Churchill was optimistic, but weary, writing to Lloyd George on April 12: 'I am remaining here all through Easter on account of the Irish situation, so I shall demand a holiday on your return. I would give a great deal for ten days painting along the Riviera.' There were, he added, 'all sorts of rumours about a *coup* in Ireland, but my own impression is that nothing serious will occur. On the contrary, I think that public opinion is swinging sourly and sombrely on to the side of the Provisional Government against those who are hampering the prosperity of the whole country.' Churchill told Lloyd George that it seemed to him that Republicanism was becoming 'a *nuisance* instead of a *cause* with the bulk of the people. Things are much quieter in Belfast and on the frontier, and Collins is getting a certain number of trust-worthy riflemen at his disposal.' Churchill concluded: 'I feel better about the whole situation than I did a week ago. But you never know.' That same day Churchill wrote direct to Collins, appealing to him to do everything in his power to halt the spread of Republicanism in the South:

The Cabinet instructed me to send you a formal communication expressing their growing anxiety at the spread of disorder in the 26 Counties. Instead of this, however, I write to you as man to man. Many residents are writing to this country tales of intimidation, disorder, theft and pillage. There is no doubt that capital is taking flight. Credits are shutting up, railways are slowing down, business and enterprise are baffled. The wealth of Ireland is undergoing a woeful shrinkage. Up to a certain point no doubt these facts may have the beneficial effect of rousing all classes to defend their own material interests, and Mr de Valera may gradually come to personify not a cause but a catastrophe.

It is difficult for us over here to measure truly, but it is obvious that in the long run the Government, however patient, must assert itself or perish and be replaced by some other form of control. Surely the moment will come when you can broadly and boldly appeal not to any clique, sect or faction, but to the Irish nation as a whole. They surely have a right to expect you to lead them out of the dark places, and the opportunity is one (the loss of) which history will never forgive. Ought you not to rally round the infant Free State all the elements in Ireland which will wholeheartedly adhere to the Treaty and sign a declaration attaching them to it irrespective of what their former attitudes have been? Would you not find reserves on this basis infinitely more powerful than any you have obtained at the present time? Ought you not to summon your 'far flung people' to your aid? In America, Australia, Canada, New Zealand, there must be hundreds of Irishmen intensely devoted to the welfare and freedom of their native land who would come to see fair play over the Elections and make sure that the people had a free vote.

Churchill told Collins that he felt 'at the tips of my fingers the grow-ing national strength that is behind you, ready for use when the moment comes for no cause but your own'. But he went on to warn Collins that if Southern Ireland moved towards a Republic, the British Government would use 'every scrap of influence' it could command to forestall it. It had been hoped, Churchill added, that the Provisional Government would hold its elections in April. But none had been announced. Any further delay, Churchill declared, would be 'extremely dangerous', and he went on:

Every day that the uncertainty continues must be attended by the pro-gressive impoverishment of Ireland. Nobody can invest or make plans for

production while the threat of civil war, or of a Republic followed by a state
of war with the British Empire, hangs over the country. I trust the end of
May or at the very latest the first week in June will see the issue submitted to
the Irish people. We really have a moral right to ask that the uncertainty as
to whether our offer is accepted or rejected should not be indefinitely prolonged. . . .

Churchill's appeal was in vain; Collins and his Cabinet were quickly
losing control. On April 13 a large force of armed Republicans, led by
Rory O'Connor,[1] seized the Four Courts—the Law Courts of Dublin—
and held them against the Provisional forces. On April 16 armed men
attacked Collins himself in a Dublin Street; he returned the fire, escaped
injury and captured one of the attackers. A week later, on April 22,
Collins was prevented from speaking at Killarney by a posse of armed
men. In Ulster, resistance to Republican attacks had been given a new
incentive by the arrival of Henry Wilson as Sir James Craig's personal
adviser on security. On April 15 Wilson had written in his diary:

. . . the recruitment of 300 more A Specials which I ordered on March 18
has not begun! A man caught 8 days ago with bombs on his person has not
yet been flogged. I am determined to wake up this place, but the real culprit
of course is James Craig away on 'several weeks holidays'. It is disgraceful.

Churchill still put his hopes in the Southern Irish elections. 'There is
no doubt a great deal to be said for the Provisional Government waiting
its moment,' he wrote to Lloyd George on April 17. But he added:
'whether the moment will ever come is another question. . . . A process
of degeneration is going forward, rather than a crisis.' He feared most
of all, he said, that Griffith and Collins would bow to Republican
pressure and postpone the elections indefinitely. 'This wd be disastrous,'
he told Lloyd George, '& may confront us with grave but intangible &
indeterminate issues. I am doing all I can to dissuade Griffith and
Collins from overt weakness.'

On April 19 Churchill sent Lloyd George a more optimistic account
of the Irish situation. 'I think things are worrying along in a favourable
direction . . .' he wrote. And he added: 'There is no doubt that the
personal prestige of Collins, Griffith and McKeown[2] and several other

[1] Rory O'Connor, 1883–1922. Member of the United Irish League, and the Irish Republican Brotherhood. Took part in the Easter rising of 1916. Director of Engineering, Irish
Republican Army. In charge of subversive operations in England. Occupied the Four Courts,
Dublin, 1922; captured by Free State forces, and shot while in prison, 8 December 1922.
[2] Sean McKeown, 1894–1973. A Sinn Fein military leader, known as 'the Blacksmith of
Ballinalee'. Arrested by the British at Mullingar, 1920, and sentenced to death for shooting a
policeman. Released, 1921, as one of the conditions of the Truce. A supporter of the Irish
Treaty. Leader of the National Army of the Irish Free State, with the rank of Lieutenant-

of the Free State leaders has been greatly enhanced by recent events.' There was also no doubt, he wrote, 'that the Free State troops are now standing firm and firing back when attacked. I think the Government is wise to put up with the occupation of the Four Courts until public opinion is exasperated with the raiders. I feel a good deal less anxious than I did a fortnight ago.'

Churchill's optimism derived principally from a letter which General Macready had sent him from Dublin on April 16, a copy of which he had enclosed with his letter to Lloyd George. According to Macready, the time would soon come when Collins and Griffith would be able to 'put their foot down and assert their authority strongly'. If they did this, Macready added, 'I am convinced that they would have the country behind them, except a few hundred, or possibly thousand, extremists like Rory O'Connor & Co., who will resist *any* form of settled Government.' Churchill also sent Lloyd George a letter which Alfred Cope had sent him on April 17, which was likewise hopeful. Cope reported that he had seen both Collins and Griffith on Churchill's behalf, and that both men 'are now alive to the moves of De Valera and I do not think they will consider any agreement for postponing the elections. . . .' As for the continuing siege of the Four Courts, Cope reported that the Provisional Government's policy 'of waiting' was 'understood and generally approved'. Meanwhile, he added, the Provisional Government's forces 'are gathering strength and they hold the ascendancy'.

Throughout April Churchill was providing arms and ammunition for Free State forces in Dublin, Athlone, Sligo and Clare, in the hope that they would be used to combat Republican violence. In mid-April he authorized Alfred Cope to distribute a total of 8,000 rifles and 20 Lewis Guns to the Free State forces. At the same time he rejected a request from Sir James Craig to provide 15,000 rifles for the Northern Irish defence forces. But at the end of the month he decided to help the Northern Government as well as the Free State. As Masterton Smith wrote to Lord Londonderry on April 29:

You will probably be hearing from Sir James Craig the result of the talk that he had with Winston at Sussex Square yesterday morning. Sir James Craig subsequently had a talk with me covering the same ground, and supplementing a long talk that I had with him at Winston's wish a week ago. Sir James Craig was evidently pleased with the talk he had with Winston, and realises that Winston appreciates to the full the difficulties that confront the

General, 1922–4. A member of the Dail from 1925 to 1965; several times Minister of Justice and Minister of Defence. Twice stood unsuccessfully in the Presidential elections.

Northern Government at the present time, and the heavy burden that Sir James Craig and his colleagues are carrying.

Early next week Winston hopes to be able to have a meeting at his house with Lord Cavan[1] and others to explore with care and in detail the requirements for which the Northern Government press. I think you will find that Winston will be able to go a long way towards meeting Sir James Craig's wishes by aiding the equipment for defensive purposes of the Constabulary Forces in Northern Ireland, and by the formation of a depot under the control of the Imperial Military authorities in some convenient place in Northern Ireland (e.g. Carrickfergus) in which could be stored military equipment available for use as and when necessary. I gathered from Sir James Craig that progress on these lines would be helpful to him in enabling him to give assurances to the people of the Six Counties and to allay their fears.

You will, of course, appreciate that Winston's policy must be in accord with the governing principle that the military protection of Ulster is an inalienable right of the Imperial Government.

On April 29 Churchill himself wrote to Michael Collins to congratulate him and Arthur Griffith on 'the spirit and personal courage which you have consistently shown in confronting the enemies of free speech and fair play'. The swing of Irish opinion, he added, seemed increasingly 'towards the Free State and the Treaty and those who stand for them'. Churchill went on to advise Collins to beware of maintaining hostility towards Ulster. It was essential, he said, for Collins and Craig to come together again, to settle the border issue amicably and to act in unison against the extremists of both sides. Collins had complained to Churchill of the killing of Catholics in Belfast. 'Protestants also,' Churchill replied, 'have suffered heavily in the recent disturbances. Belfast goods of very great value, running into millions, have been destroyed. . . .' Churchill appealed to Collins not to turn his back on reconciliation with Ulster, and not to enable the extremists, whether in the South or the North, to take advantage of the prevailing distrust:

Your opponents in the North hope to see a Republic in the South because it will bring about inter alia such a civil war, in which they know they will have the whole force of the British Empire behind them. Your opponents in the South hope to use antagonism against Ulster as a means of enabling them to snatch the power from the hands of the Provisional Government or else

[1] Frederick Rudolph Lambart, 1865–1946. Entered Army, 1885. 10th Earl of Cavan, 1900. Major-General commanding the 4th (Guards) Brigade, September 1914–June 1915. Commanded the Guards Division, August 1915–January 1916. Commanded the XIV Corps in France and Italy, January 1916–18. Commander-in-Chief, Aldershot, 1920–2. Chief of the Imperial General Staff, 1922–6. Field-Marshal, 1932.

involve them in a series of events so tragical that they will break up under the strain. And on both sides the wreckers dread any approach to the idea of a united Ireland as the one fatal, final blow at their destructive schemes.

Churchill tried to assure Collins that Craig 'means to play fair and straight with you'. His letter ended on a stern and warning note:

Although perhaps you get some political advantage for the moment by standing up stiffly against the North, yet every farthing of that advantage is drawn and squandered from the treasure chest of Irish unity. However provoking it may be, I am certain that your interest and that of the cause you serve demands patience and suavity in all that concerns relations with the North. They are your countrymen and require from you at least as careful and diplomatic handling as you bestow on the extremists who defy you in the South. Moreover, they are in a very strong, and in fact inexpugnable, position; and they hold in their hands the key to Irish unity.

When you feel moved to anger by some horrible thing that has happened in Belfast, it may perhaps give you some idea of our feelings in Great Britain when we read of the murder of the helpless, disarmed Royal Irish Constabulary and now, this morning, of what is little less than a massacre of Protestants in and near Cork. Twenty Constabulary men have been shot dead and forty wounded, together with six or seven soldiers, and now these eight Protestant civilians, within the jurisdiction of your Government since the Treaty was signed.

All these men were under the safeguard of the Irish nation and were absolutely protected in honour by the Treaty. Their blood calls aloud for justice and will continue to call as the years pass by until some satisfaction is accorded. As far as I know, not a single person has been apprehended, much less punished, for any of these cruel deeds. Yet we on our side have faithfully proceeded step by step to carry out the Treaty, have loyally done our utmost to help your Government in every way, and have not lost confidence in the good faith and goodwill of those with whom we signed the Treaty.

But do not suppose that deep feelings do not stir on both sides of the Channel. We, too, are a people not altogether to be treated as negligible in the world. No one can read the history of England without perceiving how very serious some of these matters may easily become. It is the business of statesmen not to let themselves be moved unduly by these feelings, however deep and natural, but to try as far as possible to steer away from these dangerous currents and persevere steadily towards the harbour which they have set out to gain.

At any time when you think it useful to have a further meeting with Sir James Craig, I will endeavour to bring it about. I found him reluctant when I addressed him on the subject this last week, but I know that he sincerely desires a peaceful, decent and Christian solution.

During the first week of May Churchill continued to encourage Collins to act in a conciliatory manner towards Ulster, and with firmness towards the Republicans. When, on May 2, he learnt that Collins had ordered a substantial number of rifles from the United States, he telegraphed to Alfred Cope: 'You should do everything in your power to persuade Mr Collins to draw arms from the British Government, which has a large surplus. I am quite ready to continue the steady flow of arms to trustworthy Free State troops.'

On the morning of May 4 Lord Stamfordham saw Churchill and told him that the King was most anxious about 'the very grave condition of things in Ireland'. Later that day Lord Stamfordham sent the King a full account of how Churchill viewed the situation:

Mr Churchill takes a very hopeful view of the situation, though he does not, of course, wish to give assurances for anything that may or may not happen in that extraordinary country and its still more extraordinary people. But he is satisfied that politically speaking things are better and the very fact that the Provisional Government's troops will fight, and have defeated the Irregular troops and turned them out of Kilkenny Castle and captured a large store of whiskey, which had been seized by the latter, is all to the good. In fact he would rather that the fighting continued than that the two sides should be negotiating truces or holding conferences.

He is certain that de Valera is losing ground every day and a large proportion of the population is longing for peace. He also thinks that Michael Collins is right not to take violent and drastic measures in instances such as the seizure of the Law Courts and of the Kildare street Club and that it is better policy to let the public generally realise that they are suffering inconvenience, discomfort, pecuniary loss and general derangement of business, than that they should have a grievance against the Government for the exercise of dragooning and Prussianised methods. For it must be remembered that for the last 700 years the Irish people have been 'agin the Government': and now that they have a Government of their own it would be wise not to encourage that old spirit of opposition.

Though politically Mr Churchill sees improvement, he fully realises that socially and internally the country has degenerated and especially in the matter of robbery and thefts. But, unfortunately, practically speaking the Government have no police and have to depend upon the I.R.A. for keeping the peace.

Mr Churchill, however, stakes everything upon the Elections, which he believes will take place and within the next six weeks and that the result will be an overwhelming majority to the Government. Even if de Valera attempts intimidation, there are 16,000 Polling Booths in the South of Ireland, and they say it would be impossible to exercise any effective control over all of them. If the Government secure this hoped for large majority, they will then be in a position to take a strong line with the people of the country at their back. . . .

On May 9, when Churchill saw Sir James Craig at the Colonial Office, he was able to report to him that Collins had agreed, according to Cope, to accept a single Border Commission, operating on both sides of the border, and presided over by a British officer.

On the morning of May 12 Churchill held a conference at the Colonial Office with General Macready and Alfred Cope, both of whom had come specially from Dublin. Thomas Jones, who was present at the Conference, recorded the pessimistic course of the discussion. Cope told Churchill that in his view the 'rebel' IRA was daily gaining strength, and would soon be able to embroil the British troops in hostilities with all IRA forces. Once this happened, Cope warned, moderation would cease, and Collins would be 'deserted by a large portion of his men'. Jones then recorded Churchill's reaction to this gloomy forecast:

Churchill emphasised very strongly his views as to the undesirability of handing over more arms to Collins until the latter makes it clear that he means really to deal with the rebels, and he expressed the view that Collins's policy of attacking the rebels in their strongholds outside Dublin would lead directly to the repudiation of the treaty since the British Government could not stand by and see their troops murdered. He thought that the Irish signatories to the treaty should be got over at once and a meeting is in fact being arranged for Monday morning. At this meeting he will put to Collins his view; which is that, if Collins will definitely undertake to carry out operations against the rebel strongholds in Dublin itself and clear the capital (which he considers to be an essential step towards the re-establishment in Ireland of the authority of the Provisional Government), the British Government will be prepared to provide him with the necessary equipment such as trench mortars for clearing out these strongholds. Collins's attitude towards these proposals will be regarded by Churchill as a test of his good faith and a proof of his willingness to re-establish order even at the cost of bloodshed. . . .

Later in the conference, Jones recorded, 'Churchill insisted that Collins must demonstrate his power in Dublin itself and became very excited.' On the following day Churchill's excitement turned to anger, when he learnt from Cope that negotiations had begun between Collins and De Valera for 'an agreed election'. Churchill was outraged. 'It seems to me absolutely necessary,' he wrote to Austen Chamberlain on May 13, 'to tell Griffith on Monday that we will have nothing to do with such a farce, nor will we pass any act of Parliament creating the Free State or according a permanent status to the Irish Govt on such a basis.' Unless there were free elections, the Treaty could not be fulfilled. 'The Irish Terrorists,' he added, 'are naturally drawn to imitate Lenin & Trotsky; while we shd take our stand on the will of the people freely expressed. . . .'

Churchill's new-found anger alarmed his subordinates. On May 15 Lionel Curtis told Thomas Jones that both he and Masterton Smith were 'worried' about their Chief. 'So long as matters seemed to be going smoothly in the early days after the Treaty,' Curtis told Jones, 'Churchill was splendid. But now he is so disappointed with the situation that he wants to pull the whole plant out of the ground.'

On May 15 Churchill wrote direct to Collins to protest against any electoral pact between the Provisional Government and the Republicans. His anger was apparent in every sentence:

> I think I had better let you know at once that any such arrangement would be received with world-wide ridicule and reprobation. It would not be an election in any sense of the word, but simply a farce, were a handful of men who possess lethal weapons deliberately to dispose of the political rights of the electors by a deal across the table. Such an arrangement would not strengthen your own position in the slightest degree. It would not invest the Provisional Government with any title to sit in the name of the Irish nation. It would be an outrage upon democratic principles and would be universally so denounced.

> Your Government would soon find itself regarded as a tyrannical junta which having got into office by violence was seeking to maintain itself by a denial of constitutional rights. The enemies of Ireland have been accustomed to say that the Irish people did not care about representative Government, that it was alien to their instincts, and that if they had an opportunity they would return to a despotism or oligarchy in one form or another. If you were to allow yourself to be misled into such an arrangement as is indicated, such action would be immediately proclaimed as justifying to the full this sinister prediction. As far as we are concerned in this country, we should certainly not be able to regard any such arrangement as a basis on which we could build.

The imminent possibility of an electoral Compact between Collins and De Valera shattered Churchill's hopes that Republicanism would be eclipsed. 'The Irish masses,' he reflected bitterly in *The World Crisis*, 'just like the Russians two or three years before, were not to be allowed a voice in their fate. They were to be led by the nose, by a tiny minority making an immoral deal among themselves and parcelling out the nation as if they were cattle. This was more baffling than any of the raids and outrages. It threatened to reduce the whole situation to a meaningless slush.'

The Cabinet met on May 16. Churchill gave his colleagues what Thomas Jones described in his diary as 'a very well balanced appreciation of the situation'. According to Jones's report, Churchill stated his clear belief that if British troops were withdrawn from Dublin, 'a Republic would be declared there'. It might be necessary, Churchill said, to hold Dublin by armed strength as the 'English capital', and to convert it once more into the centre of a small British 'pale' of settlement under permanent military protection. Churchill spoke bitterly to his colleagues about the proposed Collins–De Valera agreement. 'We had a right to be disappointed with the Provisional Government,' he said. 'We thought we were dealing with plenipotentiaries and that we should have an election. But De Valera, recognising that this would have gone against him, had succeeded in delaying it.' The Irish leaders, Churchill explained, 'had been men of violence and conspiracy and had hardly emerged from that atmosphere'.

On May 20 Michael Collins and Eamon De Valera signed their electoral Compact. The Republicans, pledged to destroy the Treaty and renounce the Crown, were to receive 57 seats in the new Parliament; the supporters of the Treaty were to have 64 seats. It was also agreed that as soon as the election had been held, a Coalition was to be formed, consisting of five pro-Treaty Ministers and four anti-Treaty Ministers.

As soon as he learnt of the Collins–De Valera Compact, Churchill invited the Free State leaders to London. Arthur Griffith and Duggan agreed to come; Michael Collins hesitated. 'I feel it my duty,' Churchill wrote to him on May 22, 'most earnestly to urge you not to allow anything to stand in the way of what may easily be a meeting of far-reaching importance.' Collins accepted Churchill's appeal, and the meeting was fixed for May 24. Before it took place, Sir James Craig appealed to Britain for arms to guard the border, and to bring an end to terror in Belfast. The Cabinet approved his request on May 23, and Churchill at once telegraphed the news to Belfast. 'Many thanks for message received,' Craig replied. 'Am greatly relieved.'

Even before the Cabinet decision had been made, Sir James Craig was confident that Britain would now support Ulster in all she did. Elated by this prospect, he announced on May 23 that the Government of Northern Ireland would never accept any change in the border, even if these changes were recommended by the Boundary Commission. This announcement was published in the newspapers on May 23, at the very moment when Collins, Griffith and Duggan were preparing for their meeting with Churchill at the Colonial Office. Churchill wrote at once, in great anger, to Craig:

While I was actually engaged in procuring the assent of my colleagues to your requests, you were making a declaration which was in effect in one passage little short of a defiance of the Imperial Government whose aid you seek. Several of my colleagues have communicated with me this morning in strong protest against a statement of this kind being made by you when you are asking for & receiving our assistance and especially at so critical a moment in Irish affairs. . . .

The effect of such a statement on your part is to make it far more difficult for the Imperial Government to give you the assistance you need, and also it robs the Ministers who will meet the Provisional Government representatives of any effective reproach against Mr Collins for the contemptuous manner in which he has spoken of the Treaty. It has enabled many newspapers in England, on whose support we should have to rely if the worst comes to the worst, to treat the whole Irish situation on the basis of six of one and half a dozen of the other. A very strong effort will undoubtedly be made in favour of a policy of Britain disinteresting herself entirely in Irish affairs, leaving them 'to stew in their own juice and fight it out among themselves'. Such a disastrous conclusion is rendered more difficult to combat by a statement of the kind you have made.

I know you will not mind my speaking quite plainly, because I am doing my best to support you in all that is legitimate and legal. We could not have complained, for instance, if you had said that the Collins–De Valera agreement rendered all co-operation between you and the South impossible. I should have regretted such a statement, but it was entirely one within your rights to make. But it is not within your rights to state that you will not submit to the Treaty which the British Government has signed in any circumstances, and at the same time to ask the British Government to bear the overwhelming burden of the whole of your defensive expenses.

I cannot understand why it was not possible to communicate with me before making a declaration in this sense. I should have thought it would have been quite possible for you to have made a thoroughly satisfactory declaration to your own people in these critical times without taking ground which seems to show you just as ready as Collins or De Valera to defy the Imperial Government if they take a course you do not like. You ought not to send us a telegram begging for help on the largest possible scale and announce an intention to defy the Imperial Parliament on the same day.

Lord Londonderry sought to defend Craig's statement. 'It was you,' he wrote to Churchill on May 25, 'in agreement with the South who introduced the arrangement of a Boundary Commission after *we* had been established by an Act of Parliament. . . . On the spot people concentrate on the points which affect them, and the Boundary is the burning question here.'

On Friday May 26 Churchill spent three hours alone with Arthur

Griffith, discussing the Collins–De Valera Compact. Collins had not yet reached London. Griffith made it clear that he opposed the Compact. On May 27 Collins joined Griffith in the discussions, which continued for three days. Lloyd George and Austen Chamberlain also had a long talk with Collins and Griffith, on the morning of May 30. That same day, after the Free State Ministers had returned to Dublin, Churchill gave the Cabinet an account of his negotiations with them. Both Griffith and Collins had argued that free elections would have been impossible without Republican approval. 'Small bands of armed men,' they said, 'could have seized and destroyed the ballot boxes, and in other ways prevented the free exercise of constitutional rights.'

In his discussions with the British Ministers, Collins had declared his intention to stand by the Treaty, even in conjunction with his Compact with De Valera. He would, after all, still secure a majority of the seats, even if his margin was to be a small one. The elections, he said, would take place in the middle of June, and would uphold the Treaty, and with it the British connection. Churchill, Lloyd George and Austen Chamberlain were impressed by these arguments. Certainly Collins appeared to be seeking a conciliatory solution, within the Treaty, whereas Craig, by his uncompromising statement on the boundary, had issued a direct challenge to the Treaty. Collins pleaded for British support for an Election held under the terms of his compact with De Valera. His plea was successful. Speaking to the Cabinet on May 30 Churchill declared that it 'would not be right' to say that an Election held under the Compact 'would be worthless' and he continued:

. . . some Labour and Independent candidates might be elected, and Mr Collins had received assurances that after the Election some of De Valera's supporters would cross over, because they were convinced that England was loyally carrying out her pledges. The idea was to try and get a non-Party Government, so as to secure tranquillity in Ireland, and at a later stage a proper Election on the main issue.

The Cabinet of May 30 was confronted by two interlocking, and apparently insoluble problems, the ability of the Republicans to sabotage acceptance of the Treaty in the South, and the possibility that the continuing tension on the border would provoke hostilities even between those moderates who accepted the Treaty both in the South and in the North. Churchill told the Cabinet:

The two Governments were further apart from each other than ever, and each blamed the other. Sir James Craig blamed the supporters of De Valera who had succeeded in upsetting the agreement between Craig and Collins on the 31st March, and Collins admitted this. Since the breach and boycott and other measures the I.R.A. had become more effective. Whether it was a case of six of one and half a dozen of the other, he did not know. He would be sorry to try and arrive at any other ratio. The border was in a dangerous situation, and matters were worse in Belfast than they had been. . . .

Churchill defended the Cabinet's earlier decision to send arms to Ulster, and to send them on such a massive scale. Despite what he had just said about 'six of one and half a dozen of the other', he went on to urge his colleagues to appreciate the dangers threatening Ulster, and to realize the imperative need for British support for Craig:

I am bound to say that I think we could do no less, having regard to the gathering of the forces from the South and the ferocious steps used against Ulster. The continuance of disorder of a serious kind in Ulster may be looked for and at any moment patience may be ruptured and we shall find ourselves in an atmosphere where people 'see red'. Ministers should read the Irish papers, such as the 'Freeman'. These papers, published in Dublin—and they are pro-Treaty papers—describe only the murders of Catholics and attribute these horrors to Sir James Craig's Government and the Orangemen. Every outrage on one side is replied to by an outrage on the other in a crescendo of conflict which may bring about an explosion which may put an end to our watching the laboured processes connected with the Constitution.

In reply to questions from the Cabinet, Churchill asserted that had Collins 'taken strong steps' and turned the Republican forces out of the Four Courts, 'the whole situation in Belfast would have improved'. But as Collins had now joined hands 'with avowed Republicanism', Britain could 'hardly wonder that the North had gone back to its extreme and violent position'. And he then stated, as his considered opinion: 'I think we have to give them assurance of help.'

At the end of the Cabinet meeting Lloyd George told Churchill that when he spoke in the House of Commons on the following day, 'every effort should be made not to create the impression that the trouble was in Ulster'.

On May 31 Churchill gave the House of Commons an account of the Irish situation, defending the Collins–De Valera Compact on the grounds that it could lead to 'a cessation of all attacks on Ulster or outrages from the Irish Republican Army within Ulster, to a cessation of the murders of ex-Servants of the Crown, or of Protestants in the South, or of British soldiers'. These, he said, would be 'great advantages'. He still hoped that the elections would give a majority in favour of the Treaty, that Southern Ireland would then proceed to draw up a Constitution, and that the Constitution would link Ireland formally and irrevocably to the British Empire and the British Crown. In this way, the Treaty would survive, and both Republicanism and murder fade away. But Churchill also warned the House of Commons of the grave situation in Southern Ireland, which threatened to make such an outcome illusory:

Banking and business are curtailed; industry and agriculture are languishing; revenue is only coming in with increasingly laggard steps; credit is drying up; railways are slowing down; stagnation and impoverishment are overtaking the productive life of Ireland; the inexorable shadow of famine is already cast on some of its poorer districts.

Will the lesson be learned in time, and will the remedies be applied before it is too late? Or will Ireland, amid the stony indifference of the world—for that is what it would be—have to wander down those chasms which have already engulfed the great Russian people? This is the question which the next few months will answer.

Churchill had spoken in Cabinet in support of Ulster's good faith; in the House of Commons he argued that the leaders of the Provisional Government were likewise not men of guile. 'I do not believe . . .' he said, 'that they are working hand in glove with their Republican opponents with the intent by an act of treachery to betray British confidence and Ireland's good name. I am sure they are not doing that.' Whether Collins and his colleagues would succeed in 'bringing the Treaty into permanent effect' was, he said, 'open to doubt'. But he and the British Cabinet firmly believed 'that they are still trying to do their best'. Churchill ended his speech with an appeal for patience and faith:

We have transferred the powers of government and the whole of the revenues of Ireland to the Irish Ministers responsible to the Irish Parliament. We have done this on the faith of the Treaty solemnly signed by duly accredited plenipotentiaries—for such they were—of the Irish nation, and subsequently endorsed by a majority of the Irish Parliament. This great act of faith on the part of the stronger power will not, I believe, be brought to mockery by the Irish people. If it were, the strength of the Empire will survive the disappointment, but the Irish name will not soon recover from the disgrace. . . .

In his reply, Asquith expressed his 'unqualified admiration' for Churchill's speech. But several Ulster MPs spoke angrily of surrender to the South. John Gretton, Captain Craig, Sir Samuel Hoare and Lord Wolmer[1] all feared that the Collins–De Valera Compact boded ill for the

[1] Roundell Cecil Palmer, Viscount Wolmer, 1887–1971. Eldest son of the 2nd Earl of Selborne and a grandson of the 3rd Marquess of Salisbury. In 1910 he married Churchill's

Treaty and even worse for Ulster. In answer to a question from Henry Wilson, Churchill admitted that British troops were being kept in Dublin partly in case a Republic was declared in the South. A few moments later Churchill reiterated the Government's opposition to any form of Republic in the South:

I have been asked by hon. Members who are in agreement with the hon. and gallant Member for North Down (Sir H. Wilson) whether we will tolerate the setting up of a Republic. I have been asked to give an assurance on that point. I have said, 'No. We will not do so.' In the event of the setting up of a Republic, it would be the intention of the Government to hold Dublin as one of the preliminary and essential steps in military operations.

In his own speech, Sir Henry Wilson took up Churchill's plea for patience:

The Colonial Secretary says we can wait. Can we? All this time murders are going on at the rate of, I should say, about six or seven a day. (HON. MEMBERS: 'Where?') All over Ireland. (HON. MEMBERS: 'Belfast.')

Mr CHURCHILL: I think that there were only three or four murders in Southern Ireland during the last 10 days. The number has been larger in Northern Ireland.

Sir H. WILSON: My point is, can you wait while men are murdered like that?

Churchill made no further reply. The Collins–De Valera Compact had shaken the faith of most supporters of the Treaty. Republicanism seemed almost certain to prevail in the South; and murder to continue in the North. Churchill's appeal for patience, and for faith in the Provisional Government, seemed to some a hopeless one. 'The House was decidedly sceptical,' Henry Wilson wrote in his diary. 'Several spoke against him including myself. . . . Collins and Griffith were in the Distinguished Strangers Gallery & I believe Freddie Guest took them out to lunch. What a scandal.'

Churchill himself lunched after the debate with H. A. L. Fisher, who noted in his diary: 'The Speaker[1] says Winston's speech is the best he has

cousin, Grace Ridley, daughter of the 1st Viscount Ridley. Conservative MP, 1910–40. Assistant-Director, War Trade Department, 1917–18. Parliamentary Secretary, Board of Trade, 1922–4. Assistant Postmaster-General, 1924–9. Succeeded his father as 3rd Earl, 1942. Minister of Economic Warfare, 1942–5. President of the Church Army, 1949–61. His eldest son was killed in action in 1942.

[1] John Henry Whitley, 1866–1935. Liberal MP, 1900–18; Coalition Liberal, 1918–28. A Junior Lord of the Treasury, 1907–10. Deputy Speaker, and Chairman of Ways and Means, House of Commons, 1911–21. Chairman of the Committee on the Relations of Employers and Employed (known as the Whitley Committee), 1917–18. Speaker of the House of Commons, 1921–8. Chairman of the Royal Commission on Labour in India, 1929–31. Chairman of the British Broadcasting Corporation, 1930–5.

ever heard.' This was also Austen Chamberlain's opinion, for on the following day he wrote to the King: 'It was a masterly performance— not merely a great personal and oratorical triumph, though it was both of these, but a great act of statesmanship.'

40

Ireland 1922: 'The unceasing, tormenting struggle'

O N the evening of May 30 Sir James Craig had telegraphed to Churchill from Belfast, to say that forces operating from Southern Ireland were massing on the border, and appeared to be planning concentrated attacks against Londonderry, Strabane and Pettigo. A small body of men, possibly an advance guard, had already crossed the border and occupied the villages of Pettigo and Belleek. Craig asked Churchill for an immediate decision on whether the villages should be recaptured, even if troops had to cross into Free State territory, and maintain themselves there. On the morning of May 31, two hours before his House of Commons statement, Churchill went to 10 Downing Street, where he showed Craig's telegram to Lloyd George, Austen Chamberlain and Worthington-Evans. On Lloyd George's instructions, Collins, Griffith and William Cosgrave[1] were summoned to 10 Downing Street, but as Churchill told the House of Commons later that morning, the Free State leaders had immediately given 'the most unqualified assurance that they were in no way responsible', and had at once 'repudiated the action of these forces in the strongest possible manner'.

At midday, as soon as the debate had ended, Michael Collins went to Churchill's room at the Colonial Office. In *The World Crisis* Churchill recalled how he informed Collins 'that if any part of the Irish Republican Army, either pro-Treaty or anti-Treaty, invaded Northern soil, we would throw them out'. Churchill's account continued:

[1] William Thomas Cosgrave, 1880–1965. Member of the Dublin Corporation, 1909–22; Alderman, 1920–2. Imprisoned after the Easter rising, 1916. Treasurer of Sinn Fein. Sinn Fein MP, 1917–22. Minister of Local Government in the Dail Cabinet, 1919–21. Chairman of the Provisional Government, 1921–2. President of the Irish Free State, 1922–32. Also Minister of Finance, 1922–3, and Minister of Defence, 1934.

He took it quite coolly, and seemed much more interested in the debate. 'I am glad to have seen it,' he said, 'and how it is all done over here. I do not quarrel with your speech; we have got to make good or go under.' We argued a little about Pettigo and Belleek and about Belfast atrocities. Before he left he said, 'I shall not last long; my life is forfeit, but I shall do my best. After I am gone it will be easier for others. You will find they will be able to do more than I can do.' I repeated the phrase of President Brand[1] which I had learned in the days of the Transvaal Constitution Bill, 'Alles zal regt kom' (All will come right).

That afternoon the War Office learnt that both Pettigo and Belleek were definitely in the hands of the Republicans, as was the area between the two villages. Two officers, who had driven from Inniskillen to investigate the situation, had been fired on and had been forced to withdraw.

The Cabinet were perplexed by this new threat. Throughout June 1 they were discussing the draft Free State Constitution which Griffith, Collins and Cosgrave had brought from Dublin, and which was to be the basis of their appeal to the Southern electorate on June 16. The occupation of a small corner of Ulster, however much it was to be deplored, seemed less deplorable than the proposed Constitution for the South, which was, Lloyd George told his colleagues, 'purely republican in character', and as such, unacceptable. The Irish also claimed complete control over their Foreign policy; this too, Lloyd George added, was unacceptable.

For five days the British Cabinet urged the Free State Cabinet to produce an acceptable Constitution. At first it seemed that nothing could be done to move them from their Republican stance, or to reduce their fears of a Republican seizure of power. At the Cabinet of June 1 Churchill told his colleagues that he felt 'very little doubt that the Irish representatives were drifting about in great uncertainty, refusing to face up to either side'. H. A. L. Fisher wrote in his diary: 'Winston thinks Collins really doesn't know what to do. In Ireland he is overwhelmed by the Republican influence. In England he sees reason and avers that he wants the treaty.'

Supported by Churchill and Lord Birkenhead, Lloyd George agreed to see Griffith and Collins once more, to urge them to modify their draft. Meanwhile, at 4.30 that afternoon, Churchill summoned his Cabinet Committee to the Colonial Office. Among those who were asked to

---

[1] Johannes Henricus Brand, 1823–1888. Born in Cape Town. Studied Law in London, 1845–9. President of the Orange Free State, 1864–88. Declined the Presidency of the Transvaal, 1871. A pro-British Boer, he was created GCMG in 1882.

attend were the heads of two of the services, General Lord Cavan and Sir Hugh Trenchard, and the acting head of the Navy, Sir Roger Keyes.[1] At the outset of the meeting Churchill impressed on those present—as the minutes recorded—'the need for the most scrupulous secrecy'. Their object, he explained, was to examine what practical steps Britain could take in the event of southern Ireland 'repudiating the Treaty', and declaring a Republic. The best plan, Churchill believed, would be to cut off the revenue of the new regime. Such a course would not, he said, 'expose this country to any substantial re-entry into Ireland, nor place upon it the responsibility for maintaining all branches of Irish life'. But, he added, if the Republicans were to be deprived of finance, it would 'put a paralyzing pressure on the country . . . and would very likely bring them into line'.

Churchill then outlined how he conceived it possible to cut off any future Republican Government from its revenue. There were four basic 'features' of such a programme. All revenue officers would be withdrawn from Southern Ireland, thus 'paralyzing' the collection of revenue; all 'convenient' customs houses would be occupied by British troops; the Royal Navy would 'divert' all hostile ships away from the occupied customs houses; and some seven or eight 'areas of refuge' would be provided for the 'loyal population'. The Air Force, Churchill added, 'might notify the population of existence of these refuges by the scattering of leaflets'.

During the discussion, Sir Horace Hamilton[2] stated that, if the Admiralty were to help, he saw 'no difficulty' in controlling the customs houses at Dublin, Queenstown and even Limerick. The bulk of the Irish revenue, he pointed out, came from the Guinness Brewery in Dublin. If Dublin alone were controlled by the British, the Republicans would lose £9 million of the annual £18 million revenues drawn from Southern Ireland. Churchill instructed all those present to draw up their plans along the lines suggested.

[1] Roger John Brownlow Keyes, 1872–1945. Entered Navy, 1885. Commodore in charge of submarines, North Sea and adjacent waters, August 1914–February 1915. Chief of Staff, Eastern Mediterranean Squadron, 1915. Director of Plans, Admiralty, 1917. Vice-Admiral in command of the Dover Patrol, 1918. Knighted, 1918. Created Baronet, 1919. Deputy Chief of the Naval Staff, 1921–5. Commander-in-Chief, Mediterranean, 1925–8; Portsmouth, 1929–31. Admiral of the Fleet, 1930. National Conservative MP, 1934–43. Director of Combined Operations, 1940–1. Created Baron, 1943.

[2] Horace Perkins Hamilton, 1880–1971. Entered the Inland Revenue Department, 1904. Transferred to the Treasury, 1912. Private Secretary to Lloyd George, 1912–15. Deputy Chairman, Board of Inland Revenue, 1918–19. Chairman, Board of Customs and Excise, 1919–27. Knighted, 1921. Permanent Secretary, Board of Trade, 1927–37. Permanent Under Secretary of State for Scotland, 1937–46.

During the Cabinet meeting on June 2 there was talk of Churchill's plan to drop leaflets in Republican areas giving the whereabouts of the 'places of refuge'. Thomas Jones recorded how Lloyd George had drawn Churchill out 'into the most vivid details', apparently in complete sympathy with the scheme, asking Sir Robert Horne for his estimate of the cost, 'and then at the end taking care to point out that the discussion was simply aimed at a voyage of exploration. . . .'

At 3.30 that afternoon Churchill met three Belfast Catholics, who had come specially from Ireland to see him. Churchill asked H. A. L. Fisher to help him in the discussion. The meeting took place at the Colonial Office. One of the Catholics said he had been 'brought into the Belfast troubles by the murder of his chauffeur' and that life in Belfast 'was now becoming intolerable'. Churchill urged the Catholics to accept the agreement of March 30, and to work within the Northern Ireland constitution. 'The different parties in Ireland,' he told them, 'were ruining one another, but England would not be involved in their ruin.' The Collins–De Valera Compact, he went on, had made the British Government's position very difficult. According to the minutes, Churchill then declared:

The British Government were playing scrupulously strict with Ireland, and the signature of this pact led them to ask where they stood. Sir James Craig who had been prepared to work with the Provisional Government also demurred to work with the Coalition which included the Republicans. The result was to double the force of evil and to halve the force of good. . . .'

The Collins–De Valera pact, Churchill said, had greatly antagonized Ulster, and had 'doubled' the power of men like Sir Henry Wilson. 'You are being tortured by Wilson and De Valera,' he added.

Republican troops had remained in occupation of Pettigo and Belleek throughout June 1 and June 2. Their presence was a clear flouting of British authority. On June 3, with the approval of the Cabinet, Churchill ordered two companies of British troops to cross from Northern Ireland into the Free State. The attack on Pettigo had begun. By nightfall the village was surrounded, and on June 4 the British troops attacked, and Pettigo was recaptured. During the battle seven Republicans were killed, and fifteen taken prisoner.

Collins, who had returned to Dublin to reconsider the draft constitution, telegraphed to Churchill on June 5 to complain of 'unwarrantable interference' by British troops in Free State territory. Later that same day he informed Alfred Cope that he had heard that the British intended to shell Belleek fort, which was in Free State territory, in order to drive the Republicans from Belleek itself, on the Ulster side of the border. Cope at once telegraphed to Churchill, relaying Collins' urgent appeal that no further British military action should be taken until the Irish Ministers had returned to London.

Churchill summoned his Cabinet Committee on the morning of June 6, and read them Collins' appeal. The Secretary of State for War, Worthington-Evans, pointed out that he had already telegraphed to Dublin that 'the attack on Belleek should be postponed'. Churchill expressed his 'regret' that the military operations had been broken off, telling his colleagues that he had hoped to be able to reply to Collins 'that the operations were now complete'. He also wanted, he said, 'to warn Mr Collins that a continuation of the raiding and firing into Ulster from the Free State could not be tolerated'. Churchill added that in his view the Belleek operation would have 'a salutary effect', showing the Free State leaders 'that His Majesty's Government were ready to act'. Ulster territory, he insisted, 'must be cleared of the raiders from the Free State'.

Before the Cabinet Committee adjourned, Churchill drafted a telegram to Collins, 'which was approved by the Conference', and sent at once to Dublin. In it, Collins was informed 'that Belleek village would be occupied and that if any shots were fired from the fort on Free State territory on British troops in the village the necessary steps would be taken to silence the fire'. The telegram went on to say that 'operations would cease' with the occupation of Belleek, unless there were further provocation from the Free State side.

Churchill's Cabinet Committee reassembled at the Colonial Office at 3 p.m. Churchill proposed setting up internment camps in the Isle of Man, if the camps in Northern Ireland proved too small for the growing number of IRA prisoners. As for the proposed occupation of Belleek, he said, there would be 'no difficulty in justifying the action of the troops. Ulster territory had been invaded, general alarm had been caused in the border districts, shops had been looted and our patrols had been fired upon. . . .'

During the morning Conference, Churchill and his colleagues had discussed an attack by Ulstermen on a British army patrol in Belfast. After the attack, an armoured car patrol of the B Specials had failed to intervene to protect the soldiers. Churchill was as much angered by this example of Protestant violence as he had been by the Catholic activity on the border, telling his colleagues 'that the conduct of the police in the Lancia armoured car was disgraceful and they should be dismissed from the police force'. He went on to say that the incident 'reflected great discredit on Ulster and weakened her position. If there was a repetition of such an incident, His Majesty's Government might be unable to continue to give the Northern Government the assistance they have hitherto been given them.'

On June 7 Lloyd George sent Thomas Jones to see Churchill at the Colonial Office, and to find out what was happening at Belleek. Jones recorded that Churchill was 'most anxious that I should put the Pettigo–Belleek business in as favourable a light as possible'. Jones' record continued:

The conversation became more and more personal. I said now that the Treaty had been put through I felt far less biased in favour of the South. We had put ourselves right and the important thing was to be absolutely fair as between the North and South. Why was not pressure brought on Craig to deal with the murderers in Belfast? (Churchill) said he was doing so and that he had to try to retain the confidence of the Ulster people in him and he had to watch our Parliamentary position: that he could not face Parliament on Monday if he were unable to say what the position in a British village was. I said I recognised fully the great patience he had shewn up to the present in dealing with the Irish situation but that I was very nervous about impulsive action with the troops. He said if the P.M. were going to butt in he could take the business on himself and have his resignation.

Churchill then dictated a letter for Jones to take to Lloyd George at Chequers. In the letter—which reached Lloyd George at six that evening—Churchill gave an account of the further action that was about to be taken against the Catholic forces in Belleek:

The troops, having taken Pettigo, are now preparing to move forward on Belleek village. This is wholly in our territory, and we certainly cannot allow it to remain in the hands of raiders. Before the troops move, however, it is intended that an armoured car or other reconnoitring body under a British officer shall proceed towards the village to ascertain exactly what the situation is and whether the village is held against us or not. If it is not held, it can probably be reoccupied (after giving notice) by a small party without fighting. If, however, our reconnoitring party is driven back, the orders which have been issued to reoccupy the village by force will hold good and will be executed by the troops at their earliest convenience.

Lloyd George considered Churchill's letter overnight. Thomas Jones, who stayed that night at Chequers, recorded in his diary: 'I went to bed but could not sleep for hours as I feared that the troops were moving towards Belleek and that we might have some bloody business on the following day before the PM could intervene.' At breakfast on the following morning, June 8, Lloyd George finally decided to oppose any further military action. Griffith and Collins had returned to London that day with a new draft constitution which no longer embodied the apparent republicanism of the earlier draft.

Lloyd George saw no sense in a show of force, fearing that further action in favour of Ulster might do irreparable harm to the negotiations, and sensing in the whole incident a deliberate exaggeration on the part of Ulster. On June 8 he sent Churchill a strong rebuke. According to Jones, Lloyd George put his views in writing because he 'wanted to have on record his views in case of a breakdown and the publication of documents'. In his letter, a copy of which he sent to the King, Lloyd George declared:

I am profoundly disquieted by the developments on the Ulster border. We are not merely being rushed into a conflict, but we are gradually being manoeuvered into giving battle on the very worst grounds which could possibly be chosen for the struggle. I cannot say whether Henry Wilson and de Valera are behind this but if they are their strategy is very skilful. They both want a break and they both want to fight a battle on this ground. I am not convinced that a break is inevitable. On the contrary, with patience, with the adroitness of which you have such command, I believe we can get through in the end. But even if I am wrong in entertaining these hopes, we should do our best to avoid a conflict except for reasons which would be acknowledged, not merely by our public at home but by the Empire and the whole world as inevitable. Ulster divides British opinion at home and throughout the Empire. It consolidates American opinion against us. The same thing applies to French, Italian and Belgian opinion. But if the Free-Staters insisted on a constitution which repudiated Crown and Empire and practically set up a Republic we could carry the whole world with us in any action we took. That is why the Anti-Treaty-ites are forcing the issue on Ulster.

Moreover, our Ulster case is not a good one;
(1) We have 9,000 troops in Ulster and we are half maintaining and wholly equipping another force of 48,000 Specials. But although the area is not one sixth of that of the Free State and only one third of its population, in two years 400 Catholics have been killed and 1,200 have been wounded without a single person being brought to justice.
(2) It is true that several Protestants have also been murdered, but the murders of Catholics went on at the rate of three or four to one for some time before Catholic reprisals attained their present dimensions: and even now the proportions are two Catholics murdered to one Protestant although the population is two Protestants to one Catholic. It must also be noticed that no Catholic has been arrested. This is a comment on the criticism directed against the Free State because the murderers of thirty seven Protestants have been arrested in that area.
(3) It was reported to us on the authority, I believe, of the Ulster Government

that there were concentrations of Free State troops against Londonderry, Strabane and the Pettigo salient and a serious invasion was predicted. On investigation it was discovered that there were no troops massing against either Londonderry or Strabane and when we got to the Pettigo salient and threatened it by an elaborate maneouvre with two brigades of infantry and one battery of artillery we found twenty-three Free-Staters on Free State territory in Pettigo of whom seven were killed and fifteen captured. If war comes out of this, will it not make us rather ridiculous?

Lloyd George went on to warn Churchill against any further military action against Belleek:

(4) Now I understand we are marching against some rotten barrack at Belleek garrisoned by a friendly blacksmith and a handful of his associates with an equally formidable force. Take this passage out of Colonel Watson's[1] Orders and let it be read in conjunction with the actual facts:—

'*The operation is to be carried out as a military operation by Imperial troops only and in such a manner as to inflict the greatest possible loss on the enemy.*'

Had Belleek been the Hohenzollern redoubt this tone would have been appropriate. McKeown, as you will recollect, is a very strong Treaty man and has publicly denounced de Valera and the Pact. If he should be killed at Belleek it would be a disaster to the cause of reconciliation with the Irish race. Please bear that also in mind.

In his conclusion Lloyd George told Churchill:

Quite frankly, if we force an issue with these facts we shall be hopelessly beaten. There will be a great Die Hard shout which will last for a very short time but we shall have no opinion behind us that will enable us to carry through a costly strangling campaign. Let us keep on the high ground of the Treaty—the Crown, the Empire. There we are unassailable. But if you come down from that height and fight in the swamps of Lough Erne you will be overwhelmed.

You have conducted these negotiations with such skill and patience that I beg you not to be tempted into squandering what you have already gained by a precipitous action however alluring the immediate prospect may be. We have surely done everything that Ulster can possibly expect to ensure its security. Fifty seven thousand armed men ought to be equal to the protection of so small a territory. If they require more they can get them. But if we indulge in provocative action on the frontier, incidents will be inevitable. It is our business as a great Empire to be strictly impartial in our attitude towards all creeds. We have more creeds assembled under our Flag than any Empire in the world and our prestige depends upon maintaining a stern impartiality in our attitude towards them.

[1] Charles Frederick Watson, 1877–1948. Entered the Army, 1898. Major, 1914; Lieutenant-Colonel, 1917; Colonel, 1919. Commanded the Rangoon Brigade, 1927–31.

Early that evening news reached Chequers that Lloyd George's fears had been negated by events. Both the village and the fort of Belleek had been occupied by British troops without loss of life on either side. Some forty Republicans, who had been holding the fort, had escaped without loss. 'As far as we know,' Churchill informed Lloyd George in a letter which was brought to Chequers during the evening, 'the "battle" has been almost bloodless. One soldier has been slightly wounded and no enemy casualties have been found. . . .' On receiving Churchill's letter, Lloyd George 'began to joke', as Jones recorded, 'about the great bloodless Battle of Belleek', and celebrated the victory with champagne.

Belleek and Pettigo were now both under the control of Ulster. 'I am issuing a communiqué explaining that the operations are at an end,' Churchill wrote to Lloyd George, 'that our troops will advance no further, and that no further fighting will take place unless they are attacked. . . .' As soon as 'peaceful conditions' were re-established along the border, he added, the British forces still on Free State territory would be withdrawn 'wholly within the Ulster border-line'.

The negotiations on the draft constitution had continued throughout June 8, during the final stages of the battle of Belleek. Churchill was anxious to defend himself against any charge of recklessness, and on June 8 sent Austen Chamberlain a copy of Lloyd George's rebuke, adding:

My answer to it has been superseded by events but I am sure our case is overwhelming & I shall have no difficulty in justifying everything that has been done to Parliament. The communiqué will have told you the rest. I thought it right to announce our intention to withdraw at the earliest moment to Ulster territory, & Worthy & the soldiers agreed. Progress on the Constitution has been vy satisfactory & Hewart has a good tale to tell tomorrow. The interaction of the local & general situations have been vy worrying but I don't think any harm has been done—rather good indeed—& I am quite sure we cd not have met Parlt on Monday with Belleek in hostile hands.

On June 9 Churchill and Lloyd George discussed the revised draft of the constitution with Arthur Griffith, and the negotiations continued without interruption or setback for the next five days. On June 12 Churchill persuaded Lord Midleton,[1] one of the leading Protestants

---

[1] William St John Brodrick, 1856–1942. Conservative MP, 1880–1906. Secretary of State for War, 1900–3; for India, 1903–5. Succeeded his father as 9th Viscount Midleton, 1907; created Earl, 1920. Two of his three sons were killed in action at Salerno, 1943. In 1901 Churchill had attacked his military policy in a series of speeches published with the title *Mr Brodrick's Army*.

whose home was in the Free State, to meet Griffith, and to discuss the
future position of Protestants in the South. Three days later he was
able to announce in the House of Commons that the British and Free
State negotiators had reached agreement, and that the Southern Irish
Constitution could be submitted to the electorate on the following day.
Several MPs asked for the text of the Constitution to be presented to
Parliament, but Churchill insisted that it was up to 'the Irish Govern-
ment in Ireland' to decide how it was to appear.

The Free State Constitution was published throughout Ireland on the
morning of June 16. Under it, the Irish Free State was to be 'a co-equal
member of the community of nations forming the British Commonwealth of Nations'; all authority was to derive 'from the people'; the
national language was to be Irish, but English would be equally recognized as an official language; the King was to be head of the Legislature,
which would consist of two elected bodies, the Chamber of Deputies
(Dail Eireann) and the Senate; all revenue was to be controlled
by the Dail Eireann, nor could war be declared without the Dail's
consent.

On the same day that the Constitution was published voters went to
the polls to give their verdict on the Treaty. The terms of the Collins–
De Valera Compact were reflected in the results. The pro-Treaty Party,
led by Collins, won 58 seats. The anti-Treaty Party, led by De Valera,
received 35. Labour won 17, Farmers 7, Independents 7 and Dublin
University 4. The result was a victory for Collins, for the Treaty,
and for the new Constitution.

The result of the elections seemed to vindicate Churchill's appeals for
trust in Collins and the Provisional Government. De Valera received no
place in the administration, and the Republicans were disappointed.
On June 17 there was a further setback to the Republican cause, when
Sir James Craig agreed to Churchill's request that there should be a
neutral zone between the Free State and Ulster, in order to prevent any
repetition of the Belleek and Pettigo incident. Craig also agreed that the
zone should be controlled by British troops. Collins had already told
General Macready that he accepted both these decisions.

There now began, throughout Southern Ireland, a struggle between
the Free State and Republican forces. Collins was supported in Dublin;
but even in Dublin, the Four Courts were still held by a band of Republicans. Outside Dublin, the Republicans were in control of wide
areas, including Wexford, Sligo, Waterford, Limerick, Cork and Tipperary. In these areas, the Treaty, the Constitution and the Crown were
openly reviled. The British Government hoped that Collins would be

able to assert his authority throughout the South; but the strength of the Republicans was formidable.

On June 21 Henry Wilson went to the War Office, where Sir Philip Chetwode[1] told him, as he recorded in his diary, 'that at Joe Devlin's instigation Winston had put a proposal to the Cabinet to hand over the South Irish Regts to Collins' Gov\superscript. Imagine anything so mad.' That night Wilson dined at the Trocadero as the guest of the Army Chaplains. At noon on the following day, in his Field Marshal's uniform, he unveiled the War memorial at Liverpool Street Station. From the station he returned, first by underground and then by taxi, to his home in Eaton Place. As he was about to climb the steps to his front door he was shot at by two men. His hand went automatically to his sword hilt, but the shots continued, and Wilson fell. A few moments later he was dead.

The murder of Sir Henry Wilson was thought to be the signal for concerted Republican attacks on all prominent figures connected with the Irish Treaty, or with Ulster. Scotland Yard at once sent two policemen to guard each Cabinet Minister, and the public gallery of the House of Commons was closed. But when Wilson's two murderers were caught they declared that they had acted on their private initiative, and that although they were implacable enemies of the Treaty, and haters of Ulster, their violent action was not part of any wider conspiracy.

A conference of Ministers met later on the afternoon of June 22 to decide what steps to take as a result of Wilson's murder. During the discussion, the revolvers with which Wilson had been shot were brought to 10 Downing Street, and laid on the Cabinet Room table. The four Ministers present, Lloyd George, Austen Chamberlain, Edward Shortt and Churchill were shown a letter found on one of the assassins, which was apparently meant to give, 'to persons planning further outrages, particulars of the lessons to be derived from a previous failure'. There was also, as the Minutes recorded, a 'printed scheme of organization of the Irish Republican Army, in which reference was made to the necessity for an organization in London'.

This evidence convinced the four Ministers that the time had come to force Michael Collins to destroy the power of the Republicans, and of their Army. Specific reference was made to the continuing Republican

---

[1] Philip Walhouse Chetwode, 1869–1950. Entered Army, 1889. Succeeded his father as 7th Baronet, 1905. Brigadier-General, 1914; Major-General, 1916; Commanded the 5th Cavalry Brigade, 1914–15; the 2nd Cavalry Division, 1915–16; the Desert Corps, Egypt, 1916–17; the 20th Army Corps, 1917–18. Took part in the capture of Jerusalem, 1917. Lieutenant-General, 1919. Military Secretary, War Office, 1919–20. Deputy Chief of the Imperial General Staff, 1920–2. Commander-in-Chief, Aldershot, 1923–7. Commander-in-Chief, India, 1930–5. Field Marshal, 1933. Order of Merit, 1936. Created Baron, 1945.

control of the Four Courts in Dublin, 'from which are believed to emanate the principal plots in Southern Ireland, in Northern Ireland and in the United Kingdom, and from where it is reported considerable armaments, including guns are stored'. The Minutes recorded that the four Ministers 'felt it was intolerable that this situation should be allowed to continue, and that the Provisional Government of Ireland ought to be pressed with the matter'.

Lloyd George asked Churchill to draft a letter to Michael Collins, informing him 'that the ambiguous position of the I.R.A. could no longer be ignored' and that it was 'intolerable' that a Republican force 'should be permitted to remain . . . in the heart of Dublin in possession of the Courts of Justice, acting as a centre of murder organization and propaganda'. Lloyd George asked Churchill to include in his letter 'a demand that the Irish Provisional Government, which was now supported by the declared will of the Irish people, should bring this state of affairs to an end'.

Churchill left 10 Downing Street for the Colonial Office, where he drafted the letter. At eight o'clock that evening he returned to 10 Downing Street with the draft, which Lloyd George signed, and which was sent at once to Dublin by special messenger.

That night Churchill decided not to sleep in his bedroom. It would, he told his wife—as she later recalled—be too obvious a place for a would-be assassin to find him. Leaving her in the bedroom, he retired to the attic, where he fixed up a metal shield between himself and the door, and, suitably armed with a service revolver, slept soundly, but determined to do battle should the need arise.

On the morning of June 23, at a further conference of Ministers, it was agreed that there should be an Irish debate in the House of Commons in three days' time, on June 26, and that Churchill 'should be the first speaker for the Government'. It was also agreed:

That he should not confine his statement to this particular outrage, but should review the situation as a whole, accentuating the importance of the recent vote by the Irish people in favour of the Treaty: setting forth how much the British Government had done to enable the Northern Government to protect itself; describing the representations made to the Provisional Government, either by reading the Prime Minister's letter to Mr Collins or otherwise; and generally emphasizing that the root of the trouble was the Irish Republican Army, and that now the Provisional Government has received its vote of confidence from the Irish people the British Government is entitled to insist that the ambiguous position of the I.R.A. must come to an end. . . .

On the morning of June 26 Sir Henry Wilson was given a State funeral at St Paul's Cathedral. That afternoon Churchill told the House of Commons:

We have lost a man who brought to the service of the State two noble gifts, first, a deep love of the British Empire, a passionate desire to see it splendid, powerful, prosperous and safe, which was the animating and dominating passion of his life; and, in addition, he brought to our affairs a luminous and penetrating military vision, which, in its highest manifestations, was not unworthy of the greatest captains and masters of war which this country has ever produced.

As instructed by the conference of Ministers three days earlier, Churchill set out, in his speech of June 26, the reasons why it was now up to Michael Collins to take action against the Republicans, and to assert the authority of the Free State Government throughout southern Ireland. He began by reminding the House of Commons of how, on the night when the Treaty was signed in December 1921, the Government had 'every right to believe, and every reason to believe, that the Irish signatories represented the settled view of the vast majority of the Dail and the united authority of the Sinn Fein Cabinet'. It was only when the delegates had returned to Dublin that De Valera had 'repudiated the action taken by his own plenipotentiaries', but even then that action had been upheld by a majority of the Cabinet. Since then, Churchill declared, De Valera had set to work 'by every means in his power' to prevent the Treaty from being accepted by the Irish people. His principal means, Churchill went on, had been 'the so-called Irish Republican Army', which he then described:

The Irish Republican Army was an association of persons for the purpose of organising attacks upon the Crown forces, ranging from individual murders up to considerable ambuscades. It is not capable, and has not at any time been capable, of fighting any serious action according to the rules of war. Nevertheless, it contains a considerable number of men perfectly ready to suffer imprisonment and execution for what they consider to be their cause.

The influence of De Valera had been such, Churchill continued, as to create 'a series of criminal episodes' throughout the south. Eventually he had been able to force the Provisional Government to guarantee him a minimum number of seats in the Dail. He had exerted his power in every part of southern Ireland, and even in parts of Ulster, using not only 'the mutinous or irregular portion of the Irish Republican Army', but also 'those predatory and criminal elements which exist in every society and come to lead in times of revolution'.

As a result of De Valera's determination to see all Ireland united as a Republic, Churchill went on, the activities of the IRA had been carried on in the North as well as in the South, with terrible results:

Every outrage committed by the Irish Republican Army or by Catholic elements, was repaid with bloody interest. Provocation, reprisals, and counter-reprisals have now built up a ghastly score on both sides, in which, no doubt, the Catholics, being numerically weaker, have got the worst of it, and have suffered about double as many casualties as the Protestants.

No doubt if either side would stop for a month tranquillity would be restored, and justice would overtake the guilty; but we have never been able to obtain sufficient breathing space. There has always been an overlap of atrocity and outrage, the squaring of which has started the hideous process over again.

However, I do not hesitate to say that the prime and continuing cause of all the horrors which have taken place in Belfast is the organisation of these two divisions of the Irish Republican Army in Northern territory, and the continuous effort made by the extreme partisans of the South, to break down the Northern Government and force Ulster against her will to come under the rule of Dublin.

The British Government had taken the view, Churchill said, that the Government of Northern Ireland had to be supported 'at all costs against any attempt to coerce them with submission to the South'. But they had hoped that the Provisional Government in the South would find its own methods of making 'an ordered State'. The Republican occupation of Belleek and Pettigo had shown how difficult such a task would be, but the neutral zone, accepted alike by Collins and Craig, would, Churchill believed, bring a measure of peace to the border at least. He continued:

I hope this experiment will succeed, but, of course, it may fail, as so much else has failed in Ireland. It may fail either locally or because of the pressure of larger external events. If it fails, if the good will that is required for the agreement and the good faith essential for its success are lacking, then it will be necessary for the Imperial Forces to draw a military line between Northern and Southern Ireland.

We shall not be able to draw this line along the existing and tortuous and absurd county boundaries. It will have to follow the best and most convenient chain of military positions, in this case, indicated by long lines of lakes, rivers, and canals. Broadly speaking, the line would run from Dundalk to Ballyshannon, and it will intersect impartially both Free State and Northern territory according to military requirements. Such a line, owing to the configuration of the country, could be held with very much smaller forces, including, of course, the naval forces on the lakes, than are required at the present time to deal with the existing tortuous and sinuous artificial frontiers.

I hope this may be avoided. . . .

Churchill then gave a stern warning to the Republicans, and to those who were reluctant to counter their activities:

The greedy and criminal design of breaking down the Northern Government, either by disorder from within or by incursion from without, has got to die in the hearts of those who nourish it. . . .

The Sinn Fein party has got to realise, once and for all, that they will never win Ulster except by her own free will, and that the more they kick against the pricks the worse it will be for them.

During the past month, Churchill told the House of Commons, there had been 'a rise in temperature and in pressure' throughout Ireland. Those forces, 'not all on one side', who were accustomed 'to use murder as a political weapon', had again become active. Sir James Craig, he said, must do all in his power 'to prevent unlawful reprisals in any form, however great the provocation', in the North. In the South, the time had also come for the Provisional Government to take more determined, and effective action. 'Mere denunciations of murder,' he said, 'however heartfelt, unaccompanied by the apprehension of a single murderer, cannot be accepted.' And he continued:

Hitherto we have been dealing with a Government weak because it has formed no contact with the people. Hitherto we have been anxious to do nothing to compromise the clear expression of Irish opinion. But now this Provisional Government is greatly strengthened. It is armed with the declared will of the Irish electorate. It is supported by an effective Parliamentary majority. It is its duty to give effect to the Treaty in the letter and in the spirit; to give full effect to it, and to give full effect to it without delay.

A much stricter reckoning must rule henceforward. The ambiguous position of the so-called Irish Republican Army, intermingled as it is with the Free State troops, is an affront to the Treaty. The presence in Dublin, in violent occupation of the Four Courts, of a band of men styling themselves the Headquarters of the Republican Executive, is a gross breach and defiance of the Treaty. From this nest of anarchy and treason not only to the British Crown, but to the Irish people, murderous outrages are stimulated and encouraged, not only in the 26 Counties, not only in the territory of the Northern Government, but even, it seems most probable, here across the Channel in Great Britain. From this centre, at any rate, an organisation is kept in being which has branches in Ulster, in Scotland, and in England, with the declared purpose of wrecking the Treaty by the vilest processes of which human degradation can conceive.

The time has come when it is not unfair, not premature, and not impatient for us to make to this strengthened Irish Government and new Irish Parliament a request, in express terms, that this sort of thing must come to an end. If it does not come to an end, if either from weakness, from want of courage, or for some other even less creditable reasons, it is not brought to an end and a very speedy end, then it is my duty to say, on behalf of His Majesty's Government, that we shall regard the Treaty as having been formally violated, that we shall take no steps to carry out or to legalise its further stages, and that we shall resume full liberty of action in any direction that may seem proper and to any extent that may be necessary to safeguard the interests and the rights that are entrusted to our care.

Austen Chamberlain sent an account of Churchill's speech to the King on the following day. 'Mr Churchill,' he wrote, 'opened the debate with a speech of his usual power and effectiveness.' The speech, he added, 'made a great impression on the House'. In the debate that followed Sir Frederick Banbury declared sceptically: 'We have heard before the policy of "No surrender",' and John Gretton asked cynically: 'What is the value of the declaration? We have had before bold declarations made from the Treasury bench.'

That evening Churchill and Lloyd George were together in the Lobby of the House of Commons when they met Bonar Law. 'Although always holding himself in strict restraint,' Churchill recalled in *The World Crisis*, 'he manifested an intense passion. As far as I can remember he said, "You have disarmed us today. If you act up to your words, well and good, but if not——!!" Here by an obvious effort he pulled himself up and walked away from us abruptly.'

As the Irish crisis continued, Churchill spent what spare time he could find searching for a small country property. Messrs Knight, Frank & Rutley, to whom he went for guidance, appointed a special 'negotiator', H. Norman Harding,[1] to help him in his quest, and to accompany him to any potential purchase. Harding later recalled their first drive together:

---

[1] Henry Norman Harding, 1893–   . Began work at Knight, Frank & Rutley as an office boy, 1910. Enlisted as a trooper, 1914; 2nd Lieutenant, Gallipoli, 1915. Served subsequently in Palestine and in France; wounded at Beersheba, 1917, and awarded the Military Cross. Major, 1918. Rejoined Knight, Frank & Rutley, 1920. Senior Partner, Tyser, Greenwood & Co, Chartered Surveyors, 1930–72. Both his brothers were killed in action in 1917, one at Gaza, the other (a chaplain) at Passchendaele. One of his two sons, a pilot, RAF, was killed in a flying accident.

Having sat down, I looked around, and he asked me what I was looking at and I said 'it is the darkest car I had ever been in', and he replied, 'well, you see, it is armoured, and the windows are bullet resisting and I have a loaded revolver' and he produced it, and in front, sitting by the chauffeur, was a gentleman, who, he informed me, was Detective Sergeant Thompson (later, I believe, Chief Inspector), and Mr Churchill said 'he also has a revolver'.

He then turned round, slid back a small shutter, and said 'you see that car behind us' (as far as I remember there were three men in it) 'that car will accompany us 10 miles out of Town, and on our return, will pick us up again and escort us back to the Colonial Office or to my home'.

He then went on to say that 'I have a number of threatening letters each week, some telling me the actual time and method of my death, and I don't like it'.

Churchill did not find it easy to select a property, and Harding's work was strenuous and prolonged. 'He was always asking questions,' Harding later recalled. 'Sometimes he would ask me about Gallipoli.' And he added: 'Mr Churchill was always dressed sombrely with a bow tie, and felt hat; I did not see him in sports clothes. He walked quickly in a purposeful manner and spoke rather slowly and seemed to me to think carefully before doing so.' Harding's recollections continued:

Frequently on these trips, he would doze off, and then wake up and suddenly ask 'what are those two cottages worth'; 'how much would that farm house with 100 acres fetch'; 'what is the value of that residential property'. . . .

One day when we were passing through Guildford a tyre burst with a loud report and he quickly put his hand over his face and said 'drive on, driver, drive on' and we drove down the first side street and pulled up. The weight of the car had cut the tyre to ribbons.

It may be with the threats previously referred to, in his mind, he at first thought that the blowing of the tyre was a shot—I do not know.

The time was about 3 o'clock, and he said 'can we get a drink, Harding' (it was out of hours) but I said I thought it was possible.

About 20 yards along the Road was a small Pub. I knocked on the door and the Publican opened it and said 'We're closed'. I said 'I have Mr Churchill outside and he wants a drink'. He said, 'all right, come in'—so in we went and had a drink while a fresh wheel was being fitted to the car. . . .

On another occasion, Mr Churchill inspected a property in Surrey, giving a rather more thorough examination than usual. When he had finished, he turned to the Owner and said 'you have a lovely property here—I must bring Mrs Churchill to see it'.

When we arrived at the car, he turned to me and said 'that is no good

Harding'. I was very disturbed at this information, and told him so in no unmeasured terms, and that it would have been just as easy for him to have said you have a lovely property but it is not quite what I want. . . .

The next day I telephoned the gentleman in question and tactfully informed him of the position, but it was too late, as I remember the 'Surrey Comet' had a headline saying 'Mr Churchill purchases such and such a property'.

As the summer progressed the problems of Ireland became all-demanding. On June 27 the Republicans themselves took an initiative which forced the Provisional Government to take action. The Assistant Chief of Staff of the Free State Army, General O'Connell,[1] was kidnapped by Republicans in Dublin. Michael Collins at once made plans to attack the Republican enclave at the Four Courts, 'having doubtless learned', Churchill wrote in *The World Crisis*, 'that if he did not march, we would. . . .' During the day, Collins asked General Macready for the loan of two eighteen-pounder guns. Macready at once telegraphed to the War Office, which approved the request, and the two guns were handed over.

The attack on the Four Courts began at four on the morning of June 28. During the afternoon Collins asked Macready for two more guns, which were likewise provided, together with 200 high-explosive shells. But by nightfall the Republicans were still in the Four Courts, while the ammunition for the guns was exhausted. Collins again appealed to Macready, but he declared that he could not provide more ammunition without instructions. Collins, in desperation, telephoned Churchill, who at once contacted the War Office. But General Macready insisted that he could not encroach further on his own supplies which, if Republicanism triumphed, he would need to defend his own garrison.

On June 28, while the battle of the Four Courts continued, Michael Collins wrote bitterly to Churchill about the decision of the Belfast authorities to abolish the system of proportional representation in the local government elections. The existing scheme, Collins wrote, was

[1] J. J. O'Connell, 1887–1944. Born in County Mayo. Graduated from the National University of Ireland. Served in the United States Army, 1912–14. Instructor, Irish Volunteers, 1914. A member of the Volunteer Executive, 1915. Active in the Irish Republican Army, 1916–21. Joined the National Army, with the rank of Lieutenant-General, February 1922. A senior member of the Free State forces, he was subsequently Chief Lecturer, Army School of Instruction, 1924–9; Director of No 2 Bureau (Intelligence Branch), 1929–32; Quartermaster-General, 1932–5; and Officer in Charge of Military Archives, 1935–44.

'enlightened and eminently fair'; yet it had been defeated without opposition in the Northern Ireland Parliament. Collins declared emphatically:

The grave effect of this bill on Nationalist thought in Ulster and in general all over the country, coupled with Sir James Craig's attitude on the Boundary Commission, cannot be exaggerated.

Safeguards for the minority under our jurisdiction have been frequently demanded and readily granted by us. Our people in the North are not slow to notice this, and continually put up to us that their rights under the Craig regime are not protected in the slightest degree.

The introduction of this reactionary bill has greatly strengthened this standpoint, and in consequence, considerably weakened our influence. The effect of this enactment will be to wipe out completely all effective representation of Catholic and Nationalist interests. The Nationalist strongholds of County Fermanagh, County Tyrone, Derry City, as well as several urban and rural districts will go and completely anti-Catholic juntas will reign in their place.

You will agree, I am sure that nothing could be more detrimental to the cause of peace.

The battle continued at the Four Courts throughout June 29, restricted in the main to rifle and machine-gun fire, but uncertain in its outcome. At the British army headquarters, Macready guarded a stock of over 5,000 high-explosive shells, which he refused to hand over to Collins for use in the action. At a Cabinet meeting that morning, Churchill warned his colleagues that Collins himself might be 'entirely defeated'. In that event, Churchill proposed to authorize the immediate recapture of the Four Courts by British troops, who would then be faced 'with the necessity of restoring order in Dublin'. Troops would have to be brought from Ulster, and, to this end, British forces might have to occupy the whole Irish coast from the Ulster border to Dublin itself.

The Cabinet of June 29 also instructed Churchill to telegraph to Collins, urging him to make the fullest possible use of the 300 high-explosive shells that were being sent to him from the British barracks in Dublin. In his telegram Churchill warned Collins that these shells 'will be little use without heavier guns and good gunners', and he added: 'Do not fail to take both. Both are available.' Aeroplanes also, Churchill telegraphed, would be 'available tomorrow'.

The efforts which Collins was making to crush the Republican stronghold were watched with approval in London. The Provisional Government, Churchill told the House of Commons, 'appear to be persisting in their operations with resolution'. When George Lane-Fox[1] asked Churchill what steps he was taking 'to ascertain whether this is really a serious affair or only a sham fight', he replied:

. . . I deprecate very much suggestions which seem to show that the Irish Provisional Government and the troops under their orders are not doing the very best they can loyally and effectively to carry out the Treaty and to maintain order in their country. They are making an effort and they are suffering, and it is quite true of both sides that there is little organisation.

Both sides are weak, but it is certainly not a time to mock at a serious attempt made by men who are striking a blow for freedom, order and ultimate unity of their country.

On June 30 a corner of the Four Courts was captured. The Republicans, despairing of victory, set the building on fire, and then surrendered. During the siege, 30 Free State troops had been killed. Rory O'Connor was captured, imprisoned, and later shot. Elsewhere in Dublin, fighting continued for several days. On July 2 a band of Republicans, led by De Valera himself, barricaded themselves in a square of buildings around Sackville Street. After three days of fierce fighting, the Republicans surrendered. De Valera had managed to escape. On July 6 the Provisional Government issued a proclamation, declaring that it would deal drastically with anarchy, and calling for volunteers for the National Army. The call was widely heeded. The British Government felt that Collins had not failed them. On July 7 Churchill sent Collins a letter marked 'Private and Personal', in which he described the events since the attack on the Four Courts as having in them 'the possibilities of very great hope for the peace and ultimate unity of Ireland, objects both of which are very dear to your British co-signatories'. His letter continued:

I feel this has been a terrible ordeal for you and your colleagues, having regard to all that has happened in the past. But I believe that the action you have taken with so much resolution and coolness was indispensable if Ireland was to be saved from anarchy and the Treaty from destruction. We had reached the end of our tether over here at the same time as you had in Ireland. I could not have sustained another debate in the House of Commons on the old lines without fatal consequences to the existing governing instrument in Britain, and with us the Treaty would have fallen too. Now all is

---

[1] George Richard Lane-Fox, 1870–1940. Barrister, 1896. Conservative MP for Barkston Ash (Yorkshire), 1906–31. Served in the Great War, 1914–17 (wounded). Secretary for Mines, October 1922–January 1924 and November 1924–January 1928. Member, Indian Statutory Commission, 1928–9. Chairman, Pig Products Commission, 1932; Fat Stock Reorganization Commission, 1933. Created Baron Bingley, 1933.

changed. Ireland will be mistress in her own house, and we over here in a position to safeguard your Treaty rights and further your legitimate interests effectually.

Churchill went on to tell Collins that when peace was restored, the ultimate objective of all parties—Britain, the Free State and Ulster—must be the unity of Ireland:

> How and when this can be achieved I cannot tell, but it is surely the goal towards which we must all look steadfastly. There will be tremendous difficulties, vexations and repulses, and no doubt any premature hope will be disappointed. But I have a strong feeling that the top of the hill has been reached, and that we shall find the road easier in the future than in the past. We must endeavour to use the new strength and advantages which are available to secure broad solutions. Minor irritations, however justifiable, must not be allowed to obstruct us or lead us off the track.

As a first step towards unity, Churchill told Collins, he would be seeing Sir James Craig and Lord Londonderry on July 13, and he hoped that Collins would be willing to consider a new 'Collins–Craig pact'. 'You remember,' Churchill wrote, 'how Mr Griffith wrote it all over the blotting pad in my room. There is the key to the new situation.' But, Churchill continued: 'We must wait till the right moment comes and not fritter away growing advantages by premature efforts.'

In his letter to Collins, Churchill described the type of solution which he had in mind:

> . . . from the Imperial point of view there is nothing we should like better than to see North and South join hands in an all-Ireland assembly without prejudice to the existing rights of either. Such ideas would be vehemently denounced in many quarters at the moment, but events in the history of nations, sometimes move very quickly. The Union of South Africa, for instance, was achieved on a wave of impulse. The prize is so great that other things should be subordinated to gaining it. The bulk of people are slow to take in what is happening, and prejudices die hard. Plain folk must have time to take things in and adjust their minds to what has happened. Even a month or two may produce enormous changes in public opinion.

Churchill added a postscript in his letter to Collins. 'I hope you are taking good care of yourself and your colleagues,' he wrote. 'The times are very dangerous.'

Churchill also wrote to Sir James Craig on July 7, asking him if he could turn the 'favourable events' which had taken place in the South 'to the general and lasting profit of Ireland and the Empire'. It might even be possible, Churchill wrote, for Collins to make such a broad offer of co-operation with Ulster as would 'render the intervention of the Boundary Commission unnecessary'. And he continued:

I do not want to hurry you in any way, and I feel that we must see quite clearly what the results of the fighting in the South are going to be. It may carry the Provisional Government very far. Once the position is appreciated and forces are raised with definite aims and principles, people's minds are changed very much: a gulf opens between them and their past. I always live in hopes that we may come back again to your suggestion of the Craig–Collins pact to stand together and settle the outstanding issues in accord. This seems to me to be all the more possible now that you seem to be getting increasing control of the situation in Ulster and now that Collins has definitely drawn the sword.

The events of July seemed to bear out Churchill's hopes for a Free State victory over both republicanism and anarchy. On July 12 Collins set up a War Council, with himself as Commander-in-Chief, to co-ordinate, and accelerate, the establishment of Free State control throughout the South. Already, on July 8, Wexford had been occupied by Free State troops; on July 18 Sligo was captured; on July 21, Waterford; and by the end of the month Limerick and Tipperary.

On August 9 Collins sent Churchill a long protest about Sir James Craig's Local Government Bill for Northern Ireland, the effect of which, he argued, 'is to prejudice the Catholic and Nationalist position in the whole of the North Eastern Counties'. Craig's Bill, he pointed out, fixed the constituency boundaries in such a way as to divide Protestant areas up into several constituencies, but to turn similar Catholic areas into only a single constituency. Collins pleaded with Churchill to prevent this 'gerrymandering':

Do you not see, or have His Majesty's advisers not disclosed, the true meaning of all this? Not merely is it intended to oust the Catholic and Nationalist people of the Six Counties from their rightful share in local administration, but it is, beyond all question, intended to paint the Counties of Tyrone and Fermanagh with a deep Orange tint in anticipation of the operations of the 'Ulster Month' and the Boundary Commission, and so, to try to defraud these people of the benefits of the Treaty.

Collins urged Churchill to intervene against the Northern Ireland Bill, at a time, he wrote, 'when we are seeking any gleam of hope that we can meet the Irishmen of the North East upon some working basis of union'. But the British Cabinet did not feel able to put pressure on Craig to change the Local Government franchise, and Collins' appeal went unheeded.

August opened with further military successes for Collins and his army. On August 2 Churchill told his Cabinet Committee on the Provisional Government of Ireland that 'the establishment of a Republic would not be tolerated'. Eight days later the Republicans were driven from Cork.

On August 12 Arthur Griffith died of a heart attack. 'How sad for Ireland is Arthur Griffith's death,' Clementine Churchill wrote to her husband on August 14. 'I am finding out from Masterton Smith whether you have telegraphed to him to send a wreath; if not I will have it done from us both.' Later in her letter she added:

I have just spoken with Masterton on the telephone & he is going to consult with Mr Cope as to the advisability of sending a wreath & generally speaking as to nature of British Government representation at the Funeral. The fear is if too much is done that the Irish extremists will say Arthur Griffith was too much in with us. It is like the luck of that wretched country to lose the one decent man they had to represent them.

That same day Churchill wrote to his wife. He was still hopeful:

The Irish situation ripens steadily & there shd be a chance of advancing to unity before long. Arthur Griffith's death is a serious blow. But I think we are strong enough now to survive. Poor fellow—he was a man of good faith & good will. I wish he had not died.

On August 14, two days after Griffith's death, the Republicans entered Dundalk, their first successful attack for over a month. But on August 16 they were driven out. Once more the Free State appeared to be in the ascendant. But then, on August 22, Michael Collins himself was killed in an ambush in County Cork. He was only thirty years old, yet for over a year he had been the leading military figure of a nation at war with itself, and one of its principal negotiators with a former foe. Shortly before he was killed, he had sent Churchill a message, through a friend: 'Tell Winston we could never have done anything without him.'

The Provisional Government was afraid that Collins' death would lead the British Government to despair of ever maintaining the Irish Treaty. Churchill was afraid that the Provisional Government would make its peace with De Valera, and drive an iron wedge between the North and South. On August 23 Alfred Cope telegraphed to Lionel Curtis at the Colonial Office that he had assured the Free State leaders that Lloyd George and Churchill would still regard the Treaty as in force, despite the death of two of its four signatories. Cope asked Curtis: 'Please get Mr Churchill to consider sending me a wire, apart from any wire of sympathy, telling me to inform them privately that he has no

anxiety as to their honouring the signatures of A.G. and M.C. to the
Treaty. I am assuming that because A.G. and M.C. are dead we shall
not require the signatures of living men in lieu therefore. Please get Mr
Churchill to confirm this. . . .' On August 24 Churchill telegraphed to
William Cosgrave attempting to calm his fears:

I take the earliest opportunity in this hour of tragedy for Ireland and of.
intense difficulty for the Irish Provisional Government of assuring you of the
confidence which is felt by the British Government that the Treaty position
will be faithfully and resolutely maintained. The death of the two principal
signatories, the retirement of another and the desertion of the fourth, in no
way affect the validity and sanctity of the settlement entered into with the
plenipotentiaries of the Irish nation. On the contrary we are sure that the
Provisional Government and the Irish people will feel it all the more a sacred
duty to carry into full effect the act of reconciliation between the two islands
which was the life-work of the dead Irish leaders, and with which their names
will be imperishably associated.

For our part we hold ourselves bound on the Treaty basis and will meet
good faith with good faith and goodwill with goodwill to the end. You, as acting Chairman of the Provisional Government, and your civil colleagues and
your high military officers, may count on the fullest measure of co-operation
and support from us in any way that is required.

Churchill also telegraphed to Cope, 'for your own guidance,' his
thoughts on the crisis:

The danger to be avoided is a sloppy accommodation with a quasi-
repentant De Valera. It may well be that he will take advantage of the present situation to try to get back from the position of a hunted rebel to that of a
political negotiator. You should do everything in your prower to frustrate
this. . . .

The surrender of the rebels or rebel leaders would of course be all to the
good, but it ought not to be in any circumstances followed by the immediate
reappearance of these men defeated in the field as Members of the Assembly.
Having appealed to the sword and having been defeated, they are out of
politics for the time being and ought to be rigorously shut out. Never fail to
point out in your communications with Cosgrave, Mulcahy[1] and others that
the only hope of a friendly settlement with the North and of ultimate Irish
unity lies in a clear line being drawn between the Treaty party and the
Republicans. Any temporary accommodation which might ease the situation

---

[1] Richard James Mulcahy, 1886–1971. Born in Waterford. A Post Office worker, 1903–16.
Took part in the Easter rising, 1916. Sinn Fein MP for Clontarf, 1918. Chief of Staff, Irish
Volunteers, 1918–21. Assistant Minister of Defence in the Dublin 'Cabinet', 1919–21.
Minister of Defence in the Provisional Government, 1922–4. Commander-in-Chief of the
Provisional Government's forces, 1922–3. Minister for Local Government and Public Health,
Eire, 1927–32; Minister for Education, 1948–51 and 1954–6.

in the South will be obtained only through the raising up of a lasting barrier between the North and the South, whereas firmness may easily make the life-sacrifice of Michael Collins a bond of future Irish unity. Use your utmost endeavours to keep this position constantly before their eyes, making it clear that you have my authority for speaking in this sense.

Churchill instructed Cope to make it clear to the Free State leaders that their fight against the Republicans must go on:

... the authority of the Irish people is still openly challenged; the Commander-in-Chief of the Irish Army and trusted leader has just fallen a victim to the enemy's attack, and it is the duty of those who remain to draw closely together and carry his work to its conclusion. It is also their right. They are the heirs of the authority confided by the people at the polls. Having regard to the continuous assault which is being made upon the Irish Free State, I do not consider that there is the slightest obligation upon the Provisional Government to admit newcomers to their ranks or still less to ask the Dail for further powers at this particular juncture. The election, for instance, of a President to take Mr Griffith's place might well lead to the choice of some extremely doubtful person. . . .

Churchill told Cope that what he feared was 'an absolutely meaningless and incoherent patch up' between the Provisional Government and 'the De Valera fanatics'. But the death of Collins had embittered the situation too much for such an outcome. The Free State had no intention of sharing its authority with those who were its declared enemies. The united South which Collins had hoped to establish was brought no nearer by his death. Churchill was hopeful, however, that some good might come out of the turmoil. On September 12 he wrote to his friend Pamela Lytton:

Ireland about wh you praise me is I think going to save itself. No one else is going to. They are a proud & gifted race & they are up against the grimmest facts. I do not believe they will succumb. But the pangs will be cruel & long. It was interesting to see how when their Parliament met on Saturday there was no oratory or enthusiasm—just awful dead lift effort to save themselves & their country from every ill from ridicule to starvation. And today they are dispersing the pickets of the Post Office servants who are on strike. *Responsibility* is a wonderful agent when thrust upon competent heads.

Throughout the autumn and winter of 1922, the Republicans persevered in their fierce attempts to overthrow the Treaty and to sever all Ireland's links with Britain. Churchill had hoped, with Collins' help, to bring together a secure Free State and a moderate Ulster. This hope did not long survive Collins' death. The Free Staters and the Republicans plunged into a civil war which the people of Britain could only watch, and wonder at. 'Every one assures me that nothing *can* go wrong with the Treaty,' Hazel Lavery[1] wrote to Churchill towards the end of October, 'but one always trembles for the tragic fate that pursues Ireland, there seems no end to it.' And Churchill himself, hearing during October that Cosgrave's uncle had been killed, telegraphed at once to Cosgrave: 'It is indeed a hard service that is now exacted from those who are rebuilding the Irish State and Nation, and defending its authority and freedom.'

Churchill's attitude and actions were appreciated by the Provisional Government. On October 14 Alfred Cope wrote to Edward Marsh: 'You may care to convey the following to Mr Churchill. The leaders here, including the Army leaders, have absolute confidence in Mr Churchill. They have on several occasions expressed to me their appreciation of the manner in which he and the other British signatories are keeping their side of the bargain.' Four days later, on October 19, Lloyd George resigned as Prime Minister, and the responsibility for Irish affairs passed from Churchill's hands. On October 25 he sent Cosgrave a final letter. 'No one knows better than I,' he wrote, 'the unceasing, tormenting struggle which was forced on Mr Arthur Griffith and General Michael Collins from the moment when the treaty between the two nations was signed.' To this Cosgrave replied on October 31:

The valedictory message which you have sent on leaving office touches many chords. Hitherto the exit of a British Cabinet from power has meant for us in Ireland but another milestone on the long dark road of alien government imposed on our nation, shadowed with futility in rule on the one hand and utter bitterness in resistance on the other. But in our day and generation we have found the turn in the road.

On December 6 the Free State came into formal existence. Churchill's part in its emergence had been a leading one. He had worked for nearly a year to reconcile the conflicting passions of North and South. He had believed in, and sought to further, a United Ireland under the British Crown. He had guided complex legislation through a divided Parliament. He had stood firm against the extremists in both South and North. He had refused to be deflected from supporting the Treaty by terror or by the threat of war. At Lloyd George's personal request, he had conducted delicate and prolonged negotiations with the Free State leaders. He had piloted the Treaty through the House of Commons, and had acted in Cabinet as the advocate and spokesman of political compromises, based upon a permanent constitutional link between Britain and Southern Ireland.

41

The War Memoirs: 'A gt chance to put my whole case'

D EEPLY involved though Churchill had been since July 1917 in his work at the Ministry of Munitions, the War Office and the Colonial Office, his mind was often beset by the need to justify his earlier Admiralty administration. Since 27 May 1915—the day on which he had been forced to leave the Admiralty—his work as First Lord had been the subject of constant and often violent criticism. Whenever he was attacked for irresponsibility or recklessness, his determination to write his own account of what he had done was strengthened, and he was confident that once the facts were known they would vindicate his actions. The archive of the Admiralty, he had told his constituents at Dundee on 5 June 1915, 'will show in the utmost detail the part I have played in all the great transactions that have taken place. It is to them that I look for my defence.'

At the end of November 1919 the Dardanelles Commission published its second, and final Report. Churchill was not singled out for blame, and the expedition itself was judged to have been a necessary operation of war. But the mere fact of publication stirred up further controversy, and Churchill decided to publish his own account of his years as First Lord. During the winter of 1919 he sent his drafts to several experts for scrutiny. Each of his chapters was built around the documents which he had acquired while he was First Lord, or had assembled since the end of the war. The linking passages were written out in his own handwriting, largely in red ink, and mostly on the documents themselves. Large sections were dictated to his shorthand writer, Harry Beckenham,[1] and

---

[1] Harry Anstead Beckenham, 1890–1937. Entered Admiralty, 1910. Principal shorthand writer and Assistant Private Secretary to Churchill, 1912–15; to Sir W. Graham Greene, 1916; to Jellicoe when First Sea Lord, 1917; to Wemyss when First Sea Lord, 1918; to Churchill, 1918–22. Secretary to the British Empire Exhibition, Wembley, 1923–5.

then copiously corrected by Churchill himself, mostly in red ink. The typescript was then privately printed, and proofs of particular chapters sent out for expert comment.

Although Churchill had not yet sought a publisher for his history, he had, in March 1920, asked Sir Frederick Macmillan[1] to set up in type his Admiralty minutes and memoranda, so that when he wanted to incorporate them in his narrative, they would be in printed form, and thus easier to use. Macmillan readily agreed to prepare Churchill's material for him. 'I will see that it is printed in a satisfactory form,' he wrote to Churchill on March 24, 'and with all proper regard to secrecy.' While writing, Churchill would often cut out a particular passage from the printed documents, pin the extract in the centre of a blank page of notepaper, add his comments around it, and then draft a linking passage to lead on to the next document. He also scrutinised other people's war memoirs as they were published, and often extracted material from these publications to substantiate his own case.

At the end of October 1920 Churchill decided to make plans for the publication of his memoirs. On November 1 he appointed a firm of literary agents, Curtis Brown Limited, to be his 'exclusive agents' for the negotiation and sale of what he described to them as 'my volume of War Memoirs, which I have in preparation. . . .' His condition was that they guarantee that he receive a gross sum of not less than £20,000 as a result of their efforts. On November 2 Curtis Brown accepted Churchill's condition, and asked for an outline of the book's contents. By the end of November Curtis Brown reported that the publishing house of Thornton Butterworth had offered a cash payment of £9,000 as an advance on any further royalties the book might earn in Britain and the British Empire, and that they had also received an offer of £2,500 for the United States book rights.

Churchill's search for materials continued. There were many gaps in his archive. On November 29 he wrote to Lord Grey of Fallodon:

I wonder if it would be giving you too much trouble to ask you to see whether among your papers you have preserved a letter of mine written to you from Mells in August or September, 1911, about the importance of sending the Fleet to its war stations. If you could let me have a copy of it I should be much obliged.

On December 17 Churchill wrote to the Permanent Secretary to the

---

[1] Frederick Macmillan, 1851–1936. Chairman of Macmillan & Co. Ltd., Publishers. President of the Publishers' Association of Great Britain and Ireland, 1900, 1901, 1911 and 1912. Knighted, 1909. Member of the Royal Commission on Paper, 1916.

Admiralty, Sir Oswyn Murray,[1] asking for copies of his Admiralty minutes and memoranda from October 1911 to February 1912. For the period after that, he added, 'I have a very complete record'. Churchill also asked Murray to send him 'copies of any telegrams drafted and initialled by me from the beginning of the crisis in July, 1914, to the end of the year'. Murray agreed to send Churchill the materials he wanted, and copies of them were made from the archives of the Admiralty.

During December Churchill made good progress with his writing. He also learnt, on December 21, that *The Times* were prepared to pay him £5,000 for the right to serialize his memoirs. This gave him a total of £16,500 in advance cash payments, all non-returnable if the book did badly. For his part, Churchill agreed to deliver the completed manuscript of both volumes not later than 31 December 1922. Churchill had two years to complete his work. On 1 January 1921 he was a guest of Sir Philip Sassoon at Lympne, together with Lloyd George and Lord Riddell. In his diary Riddell recorded:

> I had a long talk with Winston about his book. He says he has written a great part of the first volume. He proposed to dictate 300,000 words, and then cut down the matter and polish it up. He added that it was very exhilarating to feel that one was writing for half a crown a word!
>
> He went upstairs to put in two or three hours' work on the book. When he came down, I said to L.G., with whom I had been talking, 'It is a horrible thought that while we have been frittering away our time, Winston has been piling up words at half a crown each.' This much amused L.G.

In writing his memoirs, Churchill was not only seeking to justify his past actions, but to protect his future reputation. On January 25 he was discussing Britain's Turkish policy in Cabinet when Lloyd George remarked that it was Churchill himself who, at the end of 1914, forced Turkey into war with Britain. Outraged at this accusation in front of his Cabinet colleagues, Churchill wrote to Lloyd George on the following day:

> Some of your statements to me yesterday morning were so staggering that if only to safeguard you from repeating them in the future I must place you in possession of the true facts.
>
> You accuse me of having driven Turkey into the war by seizing the Turkish ships and later by bombarding the Dardanelles forts. It is, of course, true that the Turkish ships were taken over, as our margin of superiority was so small that we could not afford to do without them. Still less could we afford to see

---

[1] Oswyn Alexander Ruthven Murray, 1873–1936. Entered the Admiralty, 1897; Director of Victualling, 1905–11; Assistant Secretary, 1911–17; Permanent Secretary from 1917 until his death. Knighted, 1917.

them transferred to a potentially hostile power. Had these ships gone out to Turkey and been manned by Germans they would have required three or four British Dreadnoughts to cover them and watch them. Thus we should have been 5 or six ships poorer in home waters, and the number of Dreadnoughts in the British and German Fleets would have been within one or two of actual equality. Any other course therefore than that which I took (of course with the assent of the Cabinet) would have jeopardised the very existence of the country. Not less diametrically opposed to the actual facts was your statement that I bombarded the Dardanelles forts in order to force Turkey into actual hostility. The alliance between Turkey and Germany had, as we now know, been signed on the 4th August. The following telegram now in our possession, sent by the German Admiralty to the 'Goeben' at Messina on the 4th August, as follows: 'An alliance has been signed with Turkey: proceed at once to Constantinople.'

On the 27th October the 'Goeben' and 'Breslau', together with several ships of the Turkish Navy, were sent by the Germans with the connivance of Enver Pasha[1] into the Black Sea to bombard various Russian ports (Novorosiisk and Sebastopol) and thus forced Turkey into a state of active hostility. In consequence of this diplomatic relations with Turkey were broken off on Oct 30. It was not until the morning of the 3rd November that the first shots were fired by the British ships in the preliminary bombardment of the Dardanelles forts. It is not possible to over emphasize these simple facts.

However, I fully admit that from the moment when it seemed to me certain that the Turks were playing false about the 'Goeben' and the 'Breslau' and were not carrying out their disarmament and internment as they promised, and that they were clearly in the grip of Germany and of the German ships dominating Constantinople, I strongly urged that we should proceed to make our arrangements with the Christian States of the Balkans without further regard to any consequential action on the part of Turkey. From this point of view I greatly regretted the refusal by Sir Edward Grey of the Greek offer of assistance. I hoped to see Greece, Serbia and Roumania united, first against Austria and if need be against Turkey.

Churchill persevered in his work of explanation and justification. On January 25 Curtis Brown informed him that he was to get even more money from the United States than they had originally supposed. The magazine *Metropolitan* had offered nearly £8,000 to serialize the book,

[1] Enver Pasha, 1881–1922. A member of the Young Turk Triumvirate, 1908. Military Attaché, Berlin, 1909–11. Returned to Turkey and deposed Abdul Hamid, 1909. Served in the Italo-Turkish war at Benghazi, 1912. Lieutenant-Colonel, 1913. Forced the Sultan to transfer power to the Young Turks, June 1913. Appointed himself Major-General and Minister of War, 3 January 1914. Commanded the Turkish Army in the Caucasus, 1915–16. Fled, via Odessa, to Germany, 1918. Helped the Russian General Denikin in the Caucasus against the Bolsheviks, 1919. Supported the Bolsheviks as director of the Asiatic Bureau, Moscow, 1920. Turned against the Bolsheviks, and was killed fighting at the head of an anti-Bolshevik force in Turkestan, as the champion of 'Pan-Turanianism'.

and the publisher Scribner a minimum advance of £5,000 to publish it in the United States. These offers, the letter added, would ensure that Churchill received a total of well over £20,000 for the world rights. They had already secured him £27,000, quite apart from any sales in Europe, or any subsequent royalties the book might earn over and above its advances.

Throughout 1921 Churchill continued his search for documentary materials. Where his own archive was deficient, he sought contemporary evidence from other sources. 'You very kindly said you would let me have copies of some of the letters I wrote to you in the early days of the war,' he wrote to Lord French on May 6. 'I am rather anxious to see what my line was on various episodes.' And on May 30 he wrote to George Lambert:

Very many thanks for sending me the copies of my letters to Fisher. There are four or five letters among them which I had not kept or had mislaid my own copy. It is impossible to re-read them without a heart beat. I am so glad we were friends at the end.

As to the actual publication of Fisher's letters, Churchill wrote:

No doubt they will require a certain amount of editing on account of *obiter dicta* and personal references which would cause pain or do harm. I expect we should easily agree upon this. I would much prefer to publish these letters as letters instead of merely summarising them, as I am entitled to do. . . .
Wasn't it all an awful pity!

Churchill intended to confine his two volumes to his years as First Lord, and to concentrate on the role of sea power in the first nine months of the war. Indeed, the title he had chosen for his book was 'The Great Amphibian', but Scribner, his American publishers, would not accept it, and insisted instead upon another title, 'The World Crisis'.

During June, Churchill received an advance copy of the first official volume on the war at sea, by Julian Corbett.[1] He was relieved to find, at first glance, that it did not seem to criticize his work at the Admiralty in any way. 'I have skimmed up to Chapter 10 with a growing feeling of its awful flatness and sterility,' he wrote to Sir James Masterton

---

[1] Julian Stafford Corbett, 1854–1922. Special Correspondent, *Pall Mall Gazette*, Dongola Expedition, 1896. Lecturer in History, Royal Naval War College, 1903. Admiralty representative, Historical Committee of the Committee of Imperial Defence; in 1915 he agreed to undertake an official naval history, and began work in 1916. Knighted, 1917. Author of the first three volumes of *Naval Operations*, part of the Official History of the Great War, published in 1920, 1922 and 1923 (posthumously).

Smith on June 22. 'So far as I can see it does not seem to affect any interest in which I am concerned, but I should be very much obliged if you would skim through it with your practised eye and let me know.'

Churchill soon began to feel the need for a naval expert to help him. His choice fell upon a former Director of Naval Intelligence, Rear-Admiral Jackson.[1] On July 22 he wrote to Jackson to explain what he wanted of him, and how he himself worked:

I am very glad indeed that you have undertaken to help me in the technical, professional and historical accuracy of my book on the Naval War. Knowing your well-known trustworthiness in all these matters by long experience, I feel there is no one who could do it so well; and it occurred to me that while you were on half pay it might afford an interesting means of filling some of your leisure.

I shall be very glad to see you when you come to London in the first week of August. Meanwhile I send you a draft chapter on the Coronel–Falkland Islands operations. Of course this has been very roughly put together by me. My habit is to dictate in the first instance what I have in my mind on the subject and a body of argument which I believe is substantially true and in correct proportion: and this I hope may be found to be the case as far as possible. But I do not want to make any mistakes, and, on the other hand, the elaborate verifications of dates, places, speeds of ships, numbers, sequence of orders and so forth is a task which I should find it very difficult to undertake with my present occupations.

In addition to checking, correcting and amplifying the account, I should be very glad to have any suggestions or criticisms that may occur to you of the frankest character from the naval point of view. I am most anxious in this work to do justice to the Navy and to the Sea Lords on the Boards of Admiralty with whom I was associated, while at the same time I feel fully justified in showing the part which I played personally and the great responsibilities which from time to time I was forced to assume even in technical matters.

I think this is a very good sample chapter and one in regard to which your assistance will be most valuable. ...

The figures and speeds and times in my account are of course only token figures. In the main I have followed where necessary the account given by Corbett, a copy of whose first volume I am sending you, as you will find it useful.

Looking forward to seeing you soon.

[1] Thomas Jackson, 1868–1945. Entered Navy, 1881. Served with the Naval Brigade during the Burma War, 1885–7. Captain, 1905. Naval Attaché, Tokyo, 1906. Director of Naval Intelligence, January 1912–October 1913 (while Churchill was First Lord). Director of Operations, Admiralty, January 1915–June 1917 (including the planning of the Dardanelles). Commanded the Egypt and Red Sea Division of the Mediterranean Squadron, 1917–19. Vice-Admiral, 1920. Knighted, 1923.

Henceforth, Rear-Admiral Jackson acted as Churchill's principal assistant in assembling and checking his material. In July, while the work continued, the contract was signed with Scribners and, as his first advance payment, Churchill received a cheque for £3,000. A month later, on August 19, he bought a new Rolls-Royce for £2,550.

As Churchill's writing proceeded, he decided to have each draft chapter set up in print, and in the first week of November he sent Thornton Butterworth three chapters from volume one, 'Agadir', 'Antwerp' and 'Coronel and the Falklands', which he wanted them to print at once. At the end of December, Churchill took these proofs with him to the South of France. Lloyd George, who travelled from Paris to Cannes in the same train, was put to work, as Churchill wrote to his wife on December 29:

L.G. read two of my chapters in the train & was well content with the references to himself. He praised the style and made several pregnant suggestions wh I am embodying. I cannot help getting vy interested in the book. It is a gt chance to put my whole case in an agreeable form to an attentive audience. And the pelf will make us feel vy comfortable. Therefore when darkness falls, behold me in my burrow, writing dictating & sifting papers like the Editor of a ha'penny paper.

While he was at Cannes, Churchill worked each day at his book. Both his hostess, Lady Essex, and one of the other guests, Evan Charteris, read the proofs of the early chapters while he continued with the later ones. On 4 January 1922, after six days of writing, he wrote to his wife:

I have been working vy hard morning & evening at the book: & have done more than twenty thousand words. Evan & Adele have both demanded to read the proofs & pronounced it thrilling. Adele gobbled up all the naval part with the greatest avidity. . . .
I expect the first volume will have to divide into two of 80,000 words each. The more I do, the more I feel the need of doing. One thing brings up another. But the first volume (either solitary or twin) is vy nearly done. Only parts of three chapters remain; & then the rest is pure polishing. Considerable sums are payable on handing over the text and much more on publishing.

Churchill added that he hoped the first volume at least would be published in the autumn of 1922. On January 27, when he was once more in England, but his wife in the south of France, he wrote to her again about the financial benefits of the book. 'I am glad the book is so

nearly ready,' he wrote. 'The income will be welcome. I am paying all
sorts of bills. . . .'

In August 1921 Lord Esher had published a short volume entitled
The Tragedy of Lord Kitchener. In it Esher gave an account of the origin
of Churchill's visit to Antwerp which was a complete travesty of the
facts. According to Esher, Kitchener was 'in bed asleep' one night
when:

. . . Mr Churchill, then First Lord of the Admiralty, bursting into the
room, pleaded for the War Minister's permission to leave at once for Antwerp.
In spite of the late hour, Sir Edward Grey arrived in the middle of the discussion, and while he was engaging Lord Kitchener's attention Mr Churchill
slipped away. . . .

Churchill was incensed by the charge that he had acted impetuously,
and without authority. He now had in his possession sufficient contemporary telegrams to disprove Esher's account. He had assumed until
then that such documents would only appear in the official histories,
and that individual writers like himself would be denied the use of
them. Now he felt that he himself must be allowed to publish the secret
documents in full, and on 30 January 1922 he raised the matter in
Cabinet. H. A. L. Fisher, who was present, noted in his diary: 'Is
Winston to be allowed to reply to attacks eg by Esher?' The Cabinet
decided in Churchill's favour, and he at once set about incorporating
the hourly telegrams into his original, less detailed draft. He also quoted
Lord Esher's account, and added, in a footnote:

It is remarkable that Lord Esher should be so much astray; for during the
war I showed him the text of the telegrams printed in this chapter and now
made public for the first time. We must conclude that an uncontrollable
fondness for fiction forbade him to forsake it for fact. Such constancy is a
defect in an historian.

On February 4 Churchill told his wife of the Cabinet's decision to
allow him and others to set out their defence with full documentation:

I held a watching brief during the discussion with some anxiety, but the
Cabinet was very friendly and several of my friends very helpful; and the
general conclusion was strongly in favour of Ministers being allowed to vindicate their actions by publishing the necessary documents, provided this did
not affect current public interests or deal unfairly with the fiduciary relations
of individuals.

Churchill also told his wife: 'That old Admiral Jackson seems to be quite torpid and gives no signs at all.' But the book itself was now near completion, and Churchill wrote a Preface setting out his method, and his intention:

I have made no important statement of fact relating to naval operations or Admiralty business, on which I do not possess unimpeachable documentary proof. I have made or implied no criticism of any decision or action taken or neglected by others, unless I can prove that I had expressed the same opinion in writing *before the event*. . . .

In every case where the interests of the State allow, I have printed the actual memoranda, directions, minutes, telegrams or letters written by me at the time, irrespective of whether these documents have been vindicated or falsified by the march of history and of time.

Churchill went on to explain to his readers that even in his bulky volume the documents published represented 'only a fraction of the whole'. And he added: 'I affirm my willingness to see every document of Admiralty administration for which I am responsible made public provided it is presented in its fair context.' Of his reasons for writing the book, he explained:

It has long been the fashion to disparage the policy and actions of the Ministers who bore the burden of power in the fateful years before the War, and who faced the extraordinary perils of its outbreak and opening phases. Abroad, in Allied, in neutral, and above all, in enemy States, their work is regarded with respect and even admiration. At home, criticism has been its only meed. I hope that this account may be agreeable to those at least who wish to think well of our country, of its naval service, of its governing institutions, of its political life and public men; and that they will feel that perhaps after all Britain and her Empire have not been so ill-guided through the great convulsions as it is customary to declare.

Churchill continued to work on his book whenever he had a spare moment. On August 14 he wrote to his wife from Mimizan: 'I have polished up, polished off & completed the 3 remaining chapters of the book & sent them off to the printer.' On his return to England from France, Churchill asked Edward Marsh to scrutinize the book for grammatical errors and stylistic infelicities. On August 31 they exchanged the following notes:

CHURCHILL TO MARSH: Eddie. You are very free with your commas. I always reduce them to a minimum: and use 'and' or an 'or' as a substitute not as an addition. Let us argue it out. W.
MARSH TO CHURCHILL: I look on myself as a bitter enemy of super-

fluous commas, and I think I could make a good case for any I have put in—
but I won't do it any more! E.
CHURCHILL TO MARSH: No do continue. I am adopting provisionally.
But I want to argue with you. W.

The process of examination and justification had taken up much of
Churchill's spare time for nearly three years. He believed that he had
sufficient materials to tell the story fully, and he had often been engrossed
by the work itself. On 17 July 1915 he had written to his wife: 'Someday
I shd like the truth to be known.' By the end of 1922 he had made
certain that he himself would try to tell it.

42

In Defence of The Coalition

AT the end of December 1921 the Soviet Government approached the
British Government for economic aid. To Churchill, this approach
seemed evidence of grave internal weakness inside Russia, and roused
once more his sense of personal involvement in Russia's fate. On
December 24 he wrote to Lord Curzon to say that in his view Britain
should sponsor a scheme of international activity, by which Britain,
France, Germany and even, if possible, America would undertake 'the
economic reorganization' of Russia. Such a scheme, he wrote, would
involve full recognition of the Bolshevik regime, and a comprehensive
scheme of monetary credits. It would also further his own desire 'to see
France and Germany co-operate in some great work of interest to them
both' and thus prove 'of enormous value to European appeasement'.

In return for receiving the help of so powerful a combination of
states, the Russian Government would have to transform itself internally. For Churchill, this condition was essential. 'I see the gravest
objections,' he wrote, 'to giving all this help and countenance to the
tyrannic Government of these Jew Commissars, at once revolutionary
and opportunist, who are engaged not only in persecuting the bourgeoisie, but are carrying on a perpetual and ubiquitous warfare with the
peasants of Russia.'

Churchill was convinced that the Bolsheviks would agree to alter
their policies in return for foreign aid. They were, he wrote, 'desperately
anxious' to receive money and goods from the west, and in return for
immediate help 'might be prevailed upon to broaden the basis of their
Government and policy. . . .' Churchill believed that the Bolsheviks
would even be willing to bring Savinkov into their Government, and to
moderate their attitude towards both terror, and private property. He
therefore proposed a British initiative, and 'active aid', to bring the
Bolsheviks and their opponents together, and to make it possible for the

hundreds of thousands of Russians who had fled the country since 1917 to return 'and be able to live there again, humble and impoverished but at any rate no longer hunted and tortured to death'. Such British aid, Churchill reiterated, must be conditional upon the Bolsheviks agreeing to 'mollify the tyranny'. And he ended his letter with a phrase which he believed summed up his whole attitude to Bolshevik Russia: 'We want to nourish the dog and not the tapeworm that is killing the dog.'

Curzon sent Churchill's letter to Sir Eyre Crowe,[1] who was not impressed by the scheme, and replied to Curzon on December 28, describing it as totally unrealistic. 'The present Bolshevik regime,' Crowe wrote, 'wants to maintain its power. The idea that they might be willing to relinquish or share their power . . . is one for which I see no evidence. All our information has been to the effect that the sole object in their seeking recognition and obtaining aid is to fortify their own position, and that having once succeeded in doing this they will continue, or reestablish, their absolutist and terrorist regime at all costs.'

At the end of his letter, Crowe wrote scathingly of Churchill's own sources of information on Russia:

Mr Churchill has notoriously always relied on the advice concerning Russia of persons having no standing, no authority, and no direct connection with the centre of Russian affairs. He relied on Koltchak, he relied on Denikin, he was at one time strongly for Wrangel—always men outside Russia, who misled us as to the position *in* Russia. I fear this is happening once again with Savinkoff.

Churchill's scheme got no further. At the end of December he went for a short holiday to the South of France, staying first with Lady Essex and later with Lord Beaverbrook. On 1 January 1922 he sent his wife an account of his activities:

Last night we dined at Monte C. Tomorrow we picnic at Eze. From my room (you know it) I can see the Cap d'Ail Hotel: so linked in my mind with these last few days I saw my poor Mamma. What changes in a year! What gaps! What a sense of fleeting shadows! But your sweet love and comradeship is a light that burns the stronger as our brief years pass.

While in the South of France, Churchill painted, talked politics, worked at his memoirs, gambled a little at the Casino and enjoyed the rarity of complete relaxation from politics. 'I do dumbells every day,' he wrote to the Prince of Wales from Cannes on January 2, 'trying to get

---

[1] Eyre Crowe, 1864–1925. Entered Foreign Office as a Clerk, 1885; Senior Clerk, 1906. Knighted, 1911. Assistant Under-Secretary of State, Foreign Office, 1912–19; Permanent Under-Secretary of State, 1920–5.

my elbow right for next year: not many more polo years at 47!' Two
days later he wrote again to his wife:

Yesterday Monday & today I have painted or am about to paint at
Consuelo's¹ villa. I have done a beautiful picture of Eze which I know you
will want, but wh I cannot give you because Consuelo & Balsan praised it
so much I gave it to them. Now I am doing one of the workmen building their
house—all in shimmering sunshine & violet shades. I have another lovely
theme for today. . . .
A big beastly gt cloud has just come over the mountains & threatens to
spoil my sunshine. Isn't it cruel! And these tiresome stupid inhabitants
actually say: they *want* rain. It is too much.

Churchill also sent his wife news of his companions, and their concerns:

Today I move to the Negresco Nice to stay with Max for a couple of days
& we then return together on Saturday. My dear he was furious with me for
urging him to come out here & then not being at the Montfleury when he
arrived! Such a to do. The P.M. anxiously pacifying him. Bonar stroking
him. Freddie almost in tears (I *did* behave rather badly). So I said I was sorry.
As he continued to sulk I said I had done all I could & said all I cd & that if
that was not enough he cd go to hell. He showed some inclination to take me
at my word: but eventually we were reunited! So much for that.
The P.M. is singularly tame. I have never seen him quite like this. Vy
pleased to have me with him again. He is piling a gt deal on to me now. Next
week will be vy heavy. He seems to me to have much less vitality, than
formerly. But his manner is vy sprightly & his conversation most amusing.
Max is endeavouring to make out that Bonar holds the key of the situation
& says he (B) is vy anti F.E. The election question is quite unsolved. I have
not the remotest idea what they will do. . . .

While he was on holiday, Churchill delighted in keeping his wife informed of what he was doing. Sometimes he sent her long, hand-written
letters, and sometimes dictated typescripts, or 'supplements', as he
called them. For her part, these letters were a necessary comfort during
a difficult time. Since the death of her daughter Marigold the previous
August, she had been overwhelmed by sorrow, and enfeebled by sickness.
During the winter each of her three children—Sarah, Diana and
Randolph—were taken ill. Fears of complications, and of pneumonia,
added to her distress. On December 27—'thirty-two hours since you
quitted this house'—Clementine Churchill sent her husband a long and

¹ Consuelo Vanderbilt, 1877–1964. Born in New York. Married Churchill's cousin, the
ninth Duke of Marlborough, in 1895, at the age of 18. The marriage was dissolved in 1920.
In 1921 she married Colonel Balsan (who died in 1956). She was active in philanthropic
work in England, France and (from 1945) in the United States. She published her autobiography, *The Glitter and the Gold* in 1953.

worried letter describing the events in the house since his departure. Hardly had he left, she wrote, than the household had been stricken with influenza. First the maid, then Randolph, had been taken ill. She had at once ordered a nurse, who proved unsatisfactory, and towards whom she felt 'a distinct sensation of aversion'. During the morning the doctor agreed that the nurse was unsatisfactory, and dismissed her. For the rest of the day, until the new nurse arrived, Clementine Churchill had to look after what she described as her 'miniature hospital' by herself. The strain was too much for her; she felt 'like a squashed fly', and the doctor ordered her to bed, warning that she was suffering from 'nervous exhaustion', and could easily catch influenza herself. On the following day her daughter Diana returned from an aunt's house, having been taken ill during the night. 'In a small way', Clementine Churchill told her husband, the events at their home during the previous twenty-four hours were 'like the beginning of the Great War'.

In her letter of December 27, Clementine Churchill told her husband how glad she was that he was away, and therefore likely to avoid being infected. Three days later she reported that both Randolph and Diana were slowly recovering. But as their health improved, her own weakness increased. At Cannes on January 3, Lady Hozier told Churchill that her daughter was suffering not only from weakness but from breathlessness. 'We must really take the matter in hand,' Churchill wrote to his wife on the following day: 'You want at least two months complete immunity from worries of all kinds. That I am sure wd replenish yr stores of health.' He would soon be home, he added, to look after her. But his absence, although only for ten days, added to her unhappiness. On January 3 she sent him a long letter describing her 'deep misery & depression'; then, a few hours later, she sent him a telegram asking him to burn her letter unopened. On January 4 she wrote to explain that the reason for her depression was that she had received no letter from him until the arrival of a typed letter which, as she wrote, 'was piling Pelium on Ossa coming after one of the most dreary & haunted weeks I have ever lived through'. She was glad, she said, that he was having a few 'sunny carefree days' in France. 'I only wish,' she added, 'I were with you basking in the sun.' There had been many deaths in their neighbourhood from influenza, mostly, as she wrote, 'poor people who did not go to bed in time & were not properly nursed'.[1] Although both she herself and

---

[1] In the forty days between 25 December 1921 and 3 February 1922, over 13,000 people died of influenza in England; in all, 250,000 people died of influenza in England between 1919 and 1922. In the United States, over half a million people died; in India, sixteen million (more than all the battle dead for all countries between 1914 and 1918).

Sarah had escaped influenza altogether, and both Randolph and Diana were recovering, her week in bed had been a terrible experience. 'I wandered in the miserable valley,' she wrote, 'too tired to read much, & all the sad events of last year, culminating in Marigold, passing & re-passing like a stage Army thro my sad heart.'

Churchill had received his wife's telegram, asking him to destroy her letter. But he decided to read it, writing to her on January 4:

My darling,

I cd not bear not opening yr letter in the cream coloured envelope, in spite of yr telegram. In law it was my property once it was delivered to me, & any letter from you is better than none at all. My poor sweet I can see exactly what happened. My 'Supplement' arrived in advance of my own letter. I am so sorry you had such a churlish message. I do so love & value yr being pleased to hear from me, & even the shadow cast by that pleasure when disappointed is dear to me.

I have been thinking so much about you & worrying over yr health. Adele has been charming—praising you so much. I have returned to the Montfleury to the exigent Max. Alas there is no sun today. It actually snowed this morning. So no painting—only book—at wh I have been working hard.

The motor car arrangement was vy satisfactory only 100 frs a day & about 50 extra mileage. I use it a gt deal, skipping to & fro from Cannes to Monte etc.

I must confess to you that I have lost some money here; though nothing like so much as last year. It excites me so much to play—foolish moth. But I have earned many times what I have lost by the work I have done here at my book: and also our shares at home have gone well. I am vexed with myself. Max highly disapproved on every ground. As I was punished by the Cat when I was not at fault, you most now pardon me when I am!

This letter shd reach you Saturday, & I shd reach you myself on Sunday. I am looking forward to coming home. My work will be vy important next week, & then there is the Convention. But how barren these things wd be & how precarious my pleasures & interests if I had not a real issue to come back to & a real sweet to await me there.

Goodnight my darling one
Your ever devoted
W

Churchill returned to England on January 7. The possibility of an early General Election had stimulated him to speak in public on Liberal social policy. Several letters from his constituency had revealed widespread distress in Dundee, accentuated by the rising unemployment. On January 20 he told the National Liberal Council, of which he was a Vice-President, that it was essential for the Government to devise 'better social and industrial conditions for the people', and he declared: 'The workman must know that earnest effort will reap its own reward, that the cost of living will fall. . . .' In his diary, H. A. L. Fisher noted: 'Winston makes an excellent speech . . . beautifully phrased and compacted. The main argument is that Liberalism has finished its destructive work, has secured liberty, and must now conserve its conquests against class aggression on either side.'

In the course of his speech, at which Lloyd George was also present, Churchill also made a strong plea for the maintenance of the Coalition:

He would be a poor patriot who at this juncture sought to divide forces whose continued co-operation is essential to the immediate future of this country. The union and common action of the powerful forces now gathered under the leadership of the Prime Minister will not easily be overthrown. They will endure as long as their endurance is required in the general interests of the nation. As long as we are marching hand in hand with that main interest, intrigue, restlessness, personal vendettas, newspaper agitation, will recoil harmlessly before us.

There was, Churchill argued, one danger above all which the breakup of the Coalition would bring near—a Labour victory. If a 'raw Socialist Government' were to come to power, he warned, it would 'absolutely blast the commercial credit and confidence upon which the economic revival of this country depends'. And he continued:

The Labour, or the Socialist, Party, for that is their true name (hear, hear) have got to learn in the long school of experience, in continuation classes, in night schools in the House of Commons, before they are fitted to carry on the government of the British Empire from an alternative but an equally responsible point of view. We must not be disunited in the face of this danger.

Five days after his speech to the National Liberal Council, Churchill was the main speaker at the 1920 Club. He defended the Coalition's record with tenacity, and spoke bitterly of the Asquithian Liberals:

What do you think of the men who have stood with their hands in their pockets while all this has been going on—jeering, sneering, carping, and cavilling at those who have been doing the work, lolling at ease in comfortable retirement, or trying their best to put a feeble spoke in the wheel of the State? What do you think of the same men who, at the end of a period like this, presume to act themselves up as infallible judges of our efforts and our actions, of our successes or failures, and assume that they will be considered by the nation as persons or as a tribunal entitled to pronounce a final condemnation on all we have done?

They told us how badly we have done, and told us how much better they could have done it themselves. (Cheers.) But they do not stop there. They leave events and address themselves to personalities. They tell us how much better men they are than we are, how much more consistent. All this they repeat with an air of indescribable impudence (Laughter and cheers) to carefully selected audiences, the bulk of whom, like them, in peace or in war, have stood carefully aside from the burden and heat of the day.

In the South of France, where she herself had now gone for a holiday, Clementine Churchill read an account of her husband's speech in *The Times*. She was particularly upset by his remark that for the last two years of the war, after the fall of Asquith's Government in December 1916, the majority of the Liberals had stood aside 'from the burden and heat of the day'. This remark, she wrote on January 28, was 'not quite fair, becos' the Liberals (nearly all) behaved splendidly in the War which is more credit to them than it is to Tories who revel in slaughter & the Army etc. Think of Raymond[1] and Oc Asquith.' Perhaps, she added, 'it was not quite rightly reported?' Churchill replied on February 4: 'You are quite right in fastening on that unfortunately turned sentence. . . . Goonie[2] tells me the old man is very upset and in fact, in accepting her invitation to dinner next week, stipulated that he should not meet me.' But Churchill went on to defend what he had said, and to elaborate on his feelings towards Asquith:

I have always been very courteous and considerate to the old man and looked after Oc for him to the best of my ability in the war. All the same, I cannot forget the way he deserted me over the Dardanelles, calmly leaving me to pay the sole forfeit of the policy which at every stage he had actively approved. Still less can I forget his intervention after I had left the Government to prevent Bonar Law giving me the East African command and to deprive me of the Brigade to which French had already appointed me. Lastly, there was the vacancy in 1916 at the Ministry of Munitions, when he could quite easily have brought me back, as Lloyd George urged him to, but when he preferred to put his money on Montagu. As you know, I am not in the least vindictive; on the contrary, very much the other way. All the same I do not think there can be any doubt on which side the account of injury shows a balance.

Once Asquith was 'removed' from power in December 1916, Churchill continued, 'he stood aside, gave no help, and was ready to profit by any disadvantage that occurred to the Government. . . .' Hence the remarks in his speech of January 25. It was also inevitable, he added, that political controversies would get 'more disagreeable, and not less disagreeable, up to the time the Election takes place'.

[1] Raymond Asquith, 1878–1916. Asquith's eldest son. Called to the Bar, 1904. Lieutenant, Grenadier Guards, 1915–16. Killed in action on the western front, 15 September 1916.
[2] Lady Gwendeline Bertie, 1885–1941. Known as 'Goonie'. Daughter of the 7th Earl of Abingdon. She married Churchill's brother Jack in 1908.

Clementine Churchill was not entirely convinced by her husband's explanations. On February 7 she replied from Cannes:

I am a little sad about the Asquith episode. (I mean that sentence in your speech). All you say about the cold & detached way he treated you on the occasions you mention is more than true. Still it seems to me that as you did *not* mean to reflect upon his war effort & that it *was* merely the way the sentence was turned that gave it that construction it would be handsome and sensible & generous to say so.

Everyone is conscious of his limitations & I daresay that in his dreams & lonely thoughts the old man goes over his war days & tries to prove to himself that he could not have been more energetic. He was as energetic as he could be, but he is not energetic by Nature. He was more energetic then than he is now to get himself back into office.

It is quite a different thing to criticise his unhelpfulness to the Government after the War; but really he would be inhuman if he did not now & then rouse up & try & put a snag in their path. Oh Darling do be a Dove & put it right—to please me & to please yourself. People will only say 'Look how nice Winston is'.

I do not mind hard hitting (at least much) but I do think it is so cruel to say anything about a man's war record. And he has suffered more than we have by the War, by Death.

Churchill had received news of his wife from Archibald Sinclair, who reached London from Cannes on February 7. Later that day Churchill wrote to his wife:

Archie returned this morning and gave vivid & glowing accounts of you. He described yr prowess & agility at tennis . . . in terms wh caused me much pleasure—but also some anxiety (having regard to certain circumstances known only to us both).[1] He described yr accuracy and over hand service etc. I do beg you darling to be careful not only as to general fatigue but also as to particular exertion. But also he cheered me up enormously by the picture wh he painted of yr gt restoration to health & spirits. I am so glad. Do stay until you are really re equipped to fight. I shall need you vy much. The situation is steadily approaching a crisis & you can render me enormous help in the battle.

Clementine Churchill shared her husband's dislike of Lloyd George's Russian policy. 'I don't like this Genoa business,' she had written on February 3. 'Ll G will be rubbing noses with all this Bolshevik riff raff,' she continued, '& playing off the Germans agst the poor French.' The French politicians, she added, were 'a tiresome set of people, but the French people themselves are so brave & hard-working. I don't think we ought to allow them to quarrel with us.' In his letter of February 7 Churchill wrote: 'I am quite in agreement with you about Genoa. I

---

[1] Clementine Churchill was expecting a baby in September.

hate all that orientation. It is not a national British policy but only a purely personal L.G. affair.'

At the beginning of February 1922 Churchill was plunged into a controversy that had been germinating for over six months. Throughout the summer of 1921 the Press had clamoured for greater economy in Government spending, and an 'anti-waste' campaign had been mounted which threatened the stability of the Government. On 2 August 1921 Lloyd George had proposed the appointment of Sir Eric Geddes as head of a special committee charged with proposing major cuts in Government spending. As Geddes was no longer a member of the Government, this proposal provoked strong disagreement. 'I oppose,' H. A. L. Fisher wrote in his diary; 'so does Churchill very vehemently. Baldwin also. However the thing is carried. The PM writes a note to Mond to tell him to support it. The point is the PM is dead tired & wants to throw a sop to the anti-waste before the recess.'

Churchill had resented the idea of someone who was not a Cabinet Minister being entrusted with the task of reducing Government expenditure, especially in the three service Ministries. Such a task, he had told his colleagues, was entirely the responsibility of the Chancellor of the Exchequer, and should not be delegated to someone outside the Cabinet, who had no accountability to Parliament.

By the end of December 1921 the Geddes Committee had recommended drastic reductions in Army, Naval and Air Force expenditure. When Churchill had protested at these conclusions, Lloyd George appointed him Chairman of a Cabinet Committee on Defence Estimates, whose aim was to see how far Defence expenditure could be cut down, without danger to national security. Its other members were Lord Birkenhead, Edwin Montagu and Stanley Baldwin.

Churchill's Committee met for the first time on January 9, and again on January 10 and January 12. At this last meeting, Churchill warned that whatever economies were agreed to, the existing strength of the Navy must be maintained 'to enable us to defend ourselves until we were able to bring the whole fighting resources of the Empire to bear against an enemy'. At a further meeting on January 23 Churchill argued against closing down the Halton Air Training Establishment. These boys, he said, 'were trained in the best possible atmosphere in which the spirit of discipline and loyalty, not only to their service, but also to their country, was instilled in them from the very beginning. . . .'

At his Committee meeting on January 25 Churchill declared that it was 'essential' that Britain maintained a larger naval force than other countries: nevertheless, the naval estimates must still be cut down. Lord Birkenhead supported Churchill in this plea. For a further month Churchill and his Committee examined every aspect of defence expenditure. Lord Beatty agreed to make substantial reductions in naval costs, particularly of oil fuel, coal and ammunition. Trenchard accepted reductions in the area of home defence.

Churchill was pleased with the work of his Committee, believing that its work was both fair and necessary; a constitutional counterweight to Geddes. On January 27 he wrote to his wife:

I have completely succeeded in carrying all my views on the Financial Geddes Report Cte. But the fighting with the Army, Navy & Air on the one hand, & agst L.G. & Geddes & the Stunt Press on the other has been vy stiff.

I don't feel the slightest confidence in L.G.s judgment or care for our national naval position. Anything that serves the mood of the moment & the chatter of the ignorant & pliable newspapers is good enough for him. But I try—however feebly—to think for England. Then on the other hand I have to turn and squeeze Beatty most cruelly to get rid of naval 'fat' as opposed to brain & bone & muscle. It is a vy peculiar ordeal & the vulgar have no idea of it at all.

The Press had campaigned vigorously on Geddes' behalf, portraying Churchill as a man determined to spend Government money on armaments and war. On January 28 Churchill was drawn into an acrimonious dispute with Geddes himself, for that evening, at a dinner in London, Geddes declared that the true aim of the War Office in demanding a large army was 'to enforce their will upon Europe and the world'. Such a statement, Churchill wrote to Geddes on February 15, was a 'monstrous' one, and he added: 'I also resent the bullying campaign directed against the Government with a view to preventing Ministers from discharging their duties calmly.' The innuendoes against Churchill were widespread. 'He is determined,' Frances Stevenson had written in her diary on February 2, 'to oust Horne from the Exchequer, & is trying to defeat the Geddes recommendations & then blame Horne for not economizing.'

On the afternoon of February 16 the Cabinet met to discuss Geddes' proposals for naval economies. H. A. L. Fisher recorded in his diary that Churchill made 'a powerful plea for resisting Geddes' reductions', but that Horne defended them. LG warned his colleagues 'not to attack the Committee, which has done good service and saved us 70 millions'.

Four days later, during another Cabinet meeting on the Geddes report—called at Lloyd George's own request to scrutinize the Geddes recommendations, Churchill, on being criticized, was stung to anger. But he quickly regretted his outburst, writing to Lloyd George that night:

My dear Prime Minister,

I am sorry that a remark escaped me this afternoon wh you may have thought wanting in respect. I feel much the attitude you adopt to the labours of the Committee you entrusted to me; the more so as you have not been able necessarily—to go into the subject as it deserves. But anyhow I hope you will accept my assurance that no one has more regard for you & yr high office among those who serve you than I. The word 'ungrateful' ought not to have been used, & I hope you will efface it from yr memory. I wd have corrected it at once, but thought it wd only mark it the more.

Ever sincerely,
Winston S. Churchill

Lloyd George was not mollified, and on February 22 Churchill learnt that he was not to be summoned to the next Finance Committee of the Cabinet. He wrote at once to protest. 'It is vy difficult,' he declared, 'to form any intelligent opinion on general policy without a knowledge of this central financial position.'

At the Cabinet on February 24 a compromise was reached, worked out by H. A. L. Fisher, who recorded in his diary: 'Winston & the PM cheer up Horne, tell what very remarkable economies he has accomplished etc.' The recommendations of Churchill's Committee had led to a modification of many of the proposed economies, particularly on naval expenditure. Above all, Churchill and his Committee had successfully resisted Geddes' proposal to break up the Air Force into Army and Navy wings, and to rejoin them to their parent services. Yet, at the same time as they had upheld the need for an independent air force, he and his Committee had accepted large-scale cut backs in all the service departments.

On February 21 the Liberal members of Lloyd George's Cabinet met in London to discuss the political future, and the possibility of continuing co-operation between them and the 'Die-Hard' Conservatives, for whom the Government's Irish policy was seen as a betrayal of Ulster and of the Empire. H. A. L. Fisher, who was at the lunch, noted in his diary:

F.E. Guest reports state of feeling of Die-Hards. They hate L.G. and want Derby. Guest and McCurdy[1] both think the election should come soon. Winston & Montagu are strong that we should accomplish our programme & then M thinks L.G. should resign, Winston that he should dissolve & seek another Coalition election.

At the end of February Lloyd George asked Churchill to put his views on the election question in writing. Ideally, Churchill replied on February 27, he preferred the Coalition to continue, and to seek a mandate at the polls. His letter continued:

The objects to be sought are stability at home thus reviving Prosperity, the firm maintenance of the Empire particularly in the East, & the Reconciliation of Ireland through the Treaty.

How can these objects best be attained? Only by maintaining a strong instrument of Government on the centre & the right, & by an early appeal by these united forces to the electorate. In this way the defeat of the Socialist parties will be assured and the country will obtain the period of stability needed for its recovery. Division among these forces on the other hand will result in disaster to all the great & practical causes we have at heart.

How then can division be averted? Can it be best averted by a continuance of the present coalition Government or by the formation of a purely Conservative Government. There is no doubt that a united appeal under your leadership by the forces composing the present coalition if not delayed & made in all good comradeship wd secure a Parliament capable of maintaining the Empire & restoring Prosperity. This wd be the wisest course. . . .

The wisest course might not, however, be open. 'Many Conservatives and Liberals,' Churchill continued, 'are more inclined to look at party interests than to provide against the national danger by wh we are threatened. In these circumstances we are liable to drift, & our forces to degenerate or disperse.' If a break-up of the Coalition were at all likely, Churchill argued, it would be better to bring the Coalition Government to an end without delay:

The Conservatives wd then form a homogeneous administration & wd be at peace among themselves. The Coalition Liberals provided they were not themselves attacked wd give them a general support both in Parliament and at the Election wh cd not be long delayed. Unless a deliberately reactionary policy were initiated, I do not see why this support shd not continue until the period of danger to Society through wh we are passing is over & the results of the British victory in the war have been finally consolidated.

[1] Charles Albert McCurdy, 1870–1941. Barrister, 1896. Liberal MP for Northampton, 1910–3. Food Controller, 1920–1. Coalition Liberal Chief Whip (Joint Parliamentary Secretary to the Treasury), April 1921–October 1922. Chairman, United Newspapers Ltd, 1922–7 (Managing Director, 1925–7). Director, London Express Newspapers Ltd.

Churchill envisaged a new Government in which the Conservatives might have a majority, and therefore choose their own Prime Minister, and to which the former Coalition Liberals would give their support, and be rewarded with office, leaving the Asquithian Liberals, and Labour, in opposition as before. Under such a scheme, Austen Chamberlain might replace Lloyd George as Prime Minister, but Lloyd George receive a high office, as the Leader of a powerful Liberal group. The time had come, Churchill wrote, 'to confront in all friendliness our Conservative colleagues with these two definite alternatives, & that no personal interest or party interest shd intervene'.

On February 28 the Liberal Ministers met again, over dinner at the Savoy, to discuss the future of the Coalition. All of them were concerned by the growing Conservative discontent with a Liberal Prime Minister, and with a shared administration. H. A. L. Fisher recorded the outline of the discussion in his diary:

We have a long talk on what should be done. Winston & Guest for evolution to the right. ESM against. Macnamara (who depends on Tory votes for his seat) all in favour of Coalition. LG thinks continuance of Coalition essential for European peace, and Ireland—but it is necessary there should be discipline. He has offered to resign.

On March 4, speaking at Loughborough in support of General Spears' candidature as a National Liberal, Churchill made a strong plea for a new National Party, made up of both Conservatives and Liberals. 'I am for unity and Coalition. . . .' he declared. 'I look forward also to the day when out of the Coalition there shall arise a strong, united, permanent National Party, liberal, progressive and pacific in its outlook at home and abroad, but resolute also to uphold the traditions of the State and the power and unity of the Empire.' Such a Party, he believed, would be able to win an overwhelming majority at the polls, and form a unified administration, free from the strains and stresses of a two-Party Coalition. Churchill wanted the National Party to adopt a strongly anti-socialist position, and to ensure that the Labour Party remained in isolated opposition. 'A Socialist,' he declared, 'will coax and wheedle you and argue you into ruin, and the Communist will ram ruin down your throat with a bayonet on the Russian plan.'

On March 11 Churchill sent his constituents at Dundee an appeal for continued Liberal and Conservative co-operation. He also took the opportunity to put forward once more his plan for a National Party. His letter was published in *The Times* on March 13. It ended:

Political confusion and violent agitations could only at the present time add to the widespread suffering which has followed in the wake of the war. Britain needs five years of public thrift and trade recovery undisturbed by foreign war or domestic tumult. Only upon this basis and under these conditions shall we be able to help our wage-earning people 'to make a happy fireside clime' and gather resources to succour the weak and poor.

Although Churchill had nowhere attacked the Coalition, rumours began to circulate that his real aim was to oust Lloyd George. 'His tendency is all to the Right,' Lord Beaverbrook wrote to Lloyd George on March 13, 'and his principles becoming more Tory. I am sure he would not fancy being shut up in a coop with you even for a short time because such close collocation within a narrow circle would cloud his own brilliance in the light of your superiority.'

Two days later, on March 15, Beaverbrook again wrote to Lloyd George, attempting to throw doubt on Churchill's intentions. 'He is counting absolutely at the present moment,' Beaverbrook declared, 'on the formation of a new Coalition in which Austen Chamberlain would occupy the position of Lord Salisbury and he would possess the relative influence of Joseph Chamberlain on Conservative Governments. Or, to put it otherwise, he would be to Chamberlain as Premier what Chamberlain has been to you.'

Lloyd George had reason to be concerned about these allegations. On March 17 Charles McCurdy wrote to him that 'Coalition Liberals are commencing to canvass the situation that would arise if the Prime Minister resigned and if Churchill announced his intention of joining forces with the Unionist Government.' But Churchill made no bid to turn either Liberals or Conservatives against Lloyd George.

On March 9 Edwin Montagu had resigned as Secretary of State for India, in protest against Lloyd George's anti-Turk policy, which, he insisted, was alienating the Muslims of India, and undermining the fabric of British rule. The growing Conservative distrust of the Coalition led both Lord Derby and the Duke of Devonshire[1] to refuse Lloyd George's offer of succeeding Montagu at the India Office. These refusals stimulated Conservative unrest, and at a meeting of Conservative MPs at the Constitutional Club on March 17 a majority of those present voted against remaining a part of the Coalition. If the Conservatives withdrew, as a Party, the Coalition could not survive. But

---

[1] Victor Christian William Cavendish, 1868–1938. Liberal Unionist MP, 1891–1908. Financial Secretary to the Treasury, 1903–5. Succeeded his uncle as 9th Duke of Devonshire, 1908. A Civil Lord of the Admiralty, 1915–16. Governor-General of Canada, 1916–21. Secretary of State for the Colonies, October 1922–January 1924.

the vote was not a true indication of Conservative feeling, as Churchill wrote to Lloyd George on March 18:

The Constitutional Club resolution against the Coalition was carried after a great many friendly Conservatives had left the room imagining the proceedings were over. The refusals of Derby and Devonshire to take the India Office are also adverse events, and I wish they could have been avoided. Over all has hung the uncertainty of what you are going to do when you emerge from your mountain retreat.

I do trust that you have benefited by the rest, and that in another week you will be able to come back and survey the position from Headquarters. I think you will find that there is a great consolidation of the Conservative Party and a determination not to be split from the 'Die-hards'. On the other hand, the desire to drive us out is limited to the extreme section. The great bulk would like us to stay. I think the feeling of most of our Liberal colleagues would be in favour of staying. Generally, my feeling is that though the situation has deteriorated, it has become less urgent. These beastly newspapers work everything up in the worst possible way, and I really do not think we ought to let ourselves be hustled by them. Genoa will not be popular with the Conservative Party, but unless the issue of the juridical recognition of the Bolsheviks were raised, I do not see why it should break us up.

'Such are my reflections,' Churchill continued, 'at the end of a week in which I have seen a great many people, and perhaps you will meditate upon this.' On March 20 Churchill told H. A. L. Fisher that the country 'was longing to get back to party conflict, but cannot afford it'. Five days later, on March 25, he publicly supported the Coalition in a speech at Northampton. It would be 'a great disaster', he declared, if the Conservative Party broke up as the Liberals had done, and that the best chance of unity lay in the Coalition. It was essential, he added, that the Coalition Liberals and the Conservatives should combine in order to prevent a Labour Party victory at the Polls. As at Loughborough three weeks earlier, his fiercest remarks were reserved for the Labour movement, 'behind which', he alleged, 'crouched the shadow of Communist folly and Bolshevik crime'.

43

The Genoa Conference

T the beginning of March Lloyd George prepared to go to Genoa for his negotiations with the Russians, with a view to granting British recognition to the Bolshevik regime. On March 5 the Cabinet met to discuss the Russian situation. For almost a year, famine had struck at the provinces along the Volga, and by the end of 1921 as many as ten million people had died of hunger. H. A. L. Fisher recorded in his diary:

> Discussion on aid to Russia. The P.M. and Curzon are favourable. Winston and the rest of the Cabinet against on grounds of (a) Trotsky's expenditure on armaments (b) distress at home. . . .
>
> PM writes from his bed England has always been a leader in humanitarian movements—this is an unexampled catastrophe.

On March 21 Austen Chamberlain wrote to Lloyd George, asking for a Cabinet meeting to discuss the Genoa Conference, and in particular, whether or not Britain was prepared to recognize the Bolsheviks as the legal government of Russia. Chamberlain added that both he and Lord Birkenhead foresaw 'only one difficulty' in regard to Genoa:

> As you know, Winston is the person who has taken the strongest line on this subject. The Lord Chancellor and I have done our best to restrain him; but he has said to both of us that he could not remain a member of the Government if *de jure* recognition were granted by this country to the Soviet Government. Putting aside any feelings of our own, you will readily perceive that our position would be impossible if Winston retired because he was more Tory than the Tory Ministers. It is, therefore, very important that you yourself should see Winston and have a quiet personal talk with him before the Cabinet meeting takes place.

Both Chamberlain and Birkenhead advised Lloyd George against granting *de jure* recognition to the Bolsheviks. The United States,

Chamberlain pointed out, 'has apparently definitely made up its mind not to grant recognition', and France likewise was hesitating. And he continued:

Isolated recognition by us would in any case raise great difficulties among our followers in the House of Commons, and if it led to a breach with Churchill it would be quite fatal to us. I think we are entitled to expect from Russia something more than paper recognition of the ordinary obligations of a civilized State before we grant recognition. Our experience in regard to the assurances given at the time of the trade agreement do not encourage us to place much faith in her word.

Lloyd George was angered by this account of Churchill's attitude, and by Austen Chamberlain's apparent acceptance of Churchill's protest. He was determined, he replied on March 22, to go to Genoa to negotiate recognition. He pointed out that at the Cannes Conference he and Briand had resolved to negotiate with Russia, provided that for their part the Russians would pledge themselves not to make revolutionary propaganda in other countries. These proposed terms, Lloyd George commented, had 'never been challenged by the British Cabinet'. The fact that Briand's successor, Raymond Poincaré,[1] was opposed to recognition, did not alter Lloyd George's determination to go forward with the negotiations on the terms agreed at Cannes. The British delegation to Genoa, he said, would never 'tie themselves to the Chariot Wheels of France'. If the Bolsheviks were prepared to make terms with 'the Western Capitalists', Lloyd George told Chamberlain, 'then it would be folly not to help Russia to return to the community of civilised nations'. As to Churchill, Lloyd George continued:

If Winston, who is obsessed by the defeat inflicted upon his military projects by the Bolshevik Armies, is determined that he will resign rather than assent to any recognition however complete the surrender of the communists and whatever the rest of Europe may decide, the Cabinet must choose between Winston and me.

'I never thought that the restoration of European trade and business was possible,' Lloyd George went on, 'without bringing Russia into the circle.'

During March 22 Lloyd George also wrote to Sir Robert Horne: 'I told you I thought Winston would be a real wrecker. The enclosed

[1] Raymond Poincaré, 1860–1934. Minister of Public Instruction, 1893 and 1895; of Finance, 1894 and 1906. Prime Minister, 1911–13. President of the French Republic, January 1913–February 1920. Prime Minister and Minister of Foreign Affairs, January 1922–June 1924. Minister of Finance, 1926–8. Prime Minister, 1926–9.

correspondence will show you my apprehensions were justified. To go to Genoa under the conditions that would satisfy Winston would be futile and humiliating in the extreme.'

On March 23 Sir Robert Horne wrote to Lloyd George with a full account of the mounting opposition. Churchill, he believed, was the leader of the anti-recognition movement. 'If Winston were appeased,' he wrote, 'I firmly believe that no difficulty would arise with the Unionists other than the Die-hards, provided we got the pledges of the Cannes resolutions publicly & solemnly adopted by Russia.' Horne added that if Churchill took the line that Russia should never be recognized, 'he would get nothing but Die-hard support'; the danger would be if Churchill asked for a period of delay during which the Russians would be asked to 'prove their good faith' by halting all revolutionary propaganda before *de jure* recognition were granted. 'That proposition,' Horne told Lloyd George, 'would, I believe, gain the support of the majority of the Unionists.' Horne continued his letter with a warning that 'if Winston & F.E. were to go out on this matter it would break up the Coalition.' And he added: 'I hope very much that you can persuade Winston. It is no use my trying—nor Austen. . . .'

Austen Chamberlain also wrote to Lloyd George on March 23. He too warned of the danger to the Coalition of Churchill's attitude. 'I beg you to take trouble with Winston,' he wrote, and he continued:

As regards Winston's personal position, you must remember that as a result of the Cabinet discussion before you went to Cannes the Minutes record that the question of according recognition to Russia was reserved, and Winston may well claim, therefore, a free discussion in Cabinet before irrevocable steps are taken . . . he is, as I have said, your follower, and therefore doubly dangerous to me and my colleagues if he parts from us on a question where he would have the sympathy of a large section of Unionist opinion.

Austen Chamberlain added, as a postscript to his letter, that Bonar Law, to whom he had spoken on the previous day, was 'rather anxious about Genoa'. And he warned: 'If we were in real trouble over it, I don't think that I could count on any help from him.'

Lloyd George decided, at Austen Chamberlain's suggestion, to hold a special Cabinet meeting on the evening of Monday March 27, to discuss the recognition of Russia. From the evening of Friday March 24, the weekend was taken up with a spate of Ministerial correspondence and speculation. On March 24 Chamberlain warned Lord Curzon of the 'very difficult situation', and tried to enlist Curzon's support in Cabinet:

You know how violent are Winston's anti-Bolshevik views. He will not oppose the Genoa Conference, but at present he says that he will sooner resign than consent to *de jure* recognition of the Soviet Government. On the other hand the Prime Minister is equally firm that unless he has discretion to give the *de jure* recognition he will not undertake the task, and that if that is the issue the Cabinet must choose between Winston and himself.

Austen Chamberlain went on to explain to Curzon that a concerted effort was being made over the weekend to effect a compromise. Sir Robert Horne was 'doing his best' to persuade Lloyd George to 'modify' his position, while Lord Birkenhead had agreed, in the interests of Coalition unity, to persuade Churchill to accept that recognition of Russia in some form was both necessary and inevitable.

During March 24 Sir Philip Sassoon sought to arouse Lloyd George's suspicions, informing him that, in Lord Beaverbrook's opinion, 'Winston is determined to resign over the Recognition question & join the Die Hards.' Sassoon's letter continued:

Bonar on the other hand thinks that Winston will only go if he can rely on a very serious revolt in the Conservative Party—that this would not arise *unless* you were absolutely 'intransigent' on the question, & that in that case the whole Conservative Party wd go in a body. He had a talk with Austen day before yesterday & he says that Austen is not at all aware of the general disgruntlement that exists. . . .

Horne thinks Winston will burn his boats tomorrow at Northampton. But I shd not imagine he will do more than stage the pyre.

Lloyd George took alarm at this speculation. On the evening of March 24 he telephoned Austen Chamberlain from Wales to ask Chamberlain to persuade Churchill not to say anything in his speech at Northampton that might prejudice the Cabinet's imminent discussion. On the morning of March 25 Chamberlain wrote to Lloyd George:

On receiving your message last night about the speech that Winston is to make to-day, I at once got through to him on the telephone. He assured me that he would say nothing that would prejudice the discussions which we must hold on Monday and Tuesday. I begged him to be very careful, but I admit that I am not wholly at ease as to the line which he will take. I did not use your name in making my appeal to him, for I understood that you would prefer that my intervention should appear as a spontaneous act of my own.

Austen Chamberlain was angry with Lloyd George because, on the previous morning, the *Daily Chronicle* had published a report from Criccieth, clearly inspired by Lloyd George himself, in which it was said that 'Mr Lloyd George will part from his dearest political friend rather than abandon this great fundamental issue of politics.' Was it possible, Chamberlain asked Lloyd George, 'for Winston to regard this as anything but a challenge?'

Chamberlain went on to express his own doubts about the trustworthiness of Russian promises:

> . . . the point to which I would beg you to direct your mind is that of the guarantees which can be offered to, and accepted by us for the fulfilment of the conditions if these are accepted by the Russian Government. Unfortunately we know that they have not kept in good faith the promises made at the time of the signature of the trade agreement. If they had kept their word so far, we could accept their simple word again. But since they have broken that word, something more than their mere word is now required. I believe that this view is almost universal in my party in the House of Commons. . . .

Chamberlain also protested to Lloyd George that he had not brought the Cannes conditions before the Cabinet, although Churchill 'has several times asked for a discussion'.

It was clear from Chamberlain's letter that Churchill's position was not an isolated one. When he spoke that day at Northampton he defended the Coalition, but spoke bitterly about the Bolsheviks. 'We know,' he said, 'how they have destroyed the enormous Russian Empire, and have enthroned themselves among its ruins.'

Lloyd George decided to postpone the Cabinet called for March 27 until the following day. In its place, he summoned a meeting of Ministers at 10 Downing Street on the evening of March 27. Churchill, who opened the discussion, put forward his arguments with tenacity. The question, he said, was 'whether the Soviet representatives would carry out their bargain'; of this he had 'the gravest doubts'. Lloyd George defended his position. He was worried, he said, about 'the frightful prospects of international trade'. These prospects, he warned, 'were hopeless unless peace could be established in Europe'.

Churchill insisted that the Russians must promise, before they were recognized, to desist from revolutionary propaganda. The Cabinet endorsed this condition. They also agreed with his demand that they should be kept fully informed about the course of the discussions at Genoa. As a result of Churchill's insistence, Lloyd George gave an assurance that the Cabinet would be sent an account of the negotiations 'every day', and that both Lord Curzon and Lord Birkenhead would be on the spot for consultations.

Churchill realized that his arguments had been successful. According to the Minutes of the meeting, Lloyd George said 'that in any event' Britain would not grant 'full diplomatic recognition'. In substance, Thomas Jones wrote in his diary on the following day, 'the P.M., as I think, again capitulated to Churchill'.

The Cabinet met again at noon on March 28. Churchill made a strong protest against any dealings at all with Russia, as Thomas Jones recorded:

. . . Churchill in passionate tones full of conviction deplored our dealings with the Bolsheviks. We had concluded a trade agreement on the understanding that if its terms had been broken it could be terminated. Its terms had been flagrantly broken and now we were being asked to go another step to meet the Soviet Government. The account received from our Moscow representative shewed that these leaders had the brains of tortuous conspirators. They were called on to give up the theories to which they had devoted their lives, they would use every effort to make breaches between the Western Powers and would be absolutely cynical in all their dealings with us. They would come to Genoa for the sole purpose of enhancing their prestige at home and would be able to go back and say they had negotiated with the strongest Power of Western Europe. They would sign papers with no intention of honouring them. Meanwhile there were 3,000,000 Russians in exile who would hear of the proposal to grant *de jure* recognition with despair. He was bitterly sorry that at a time of strong Conservative majorities and deep devotion to the monarchy we were to step out to accord this supreme favour and patronage to these people.

Confident of his strength, in view of the previous evening's discussion, Churchill then proposed, as Jones recorded:

. . . that the British Delegates should go to Genoa with a limited discretion, namely that unless the Cannes conditions were accepted in substance there should be no advance in the recognition of the Soviet Government: we were not to act in isolation nor without a general consensus of opinion: in the event of the Russians accepting the conditions and our Delegates being satisfied that they were genuinely seeking to play the game we should give such recognition as was required to make the agreement reach success, but not full ceremonial recognition.

Austen Chamberlain supported Churchill's proposal, which became, Jones noted, 'the operative conclusion of the Cabinet'.

On April 18 Churchill went to Eaton Hall, the Duke of Westminster's house near Chester, in order to play polo for two days. But on the second day he had a serious accident, which he described to Edward Marsh on the following day:

I have had a very disagreeable bump. After we had finished polo I went to give up my pony, not perhaps in the general way, but in the way I always do by throwing my leg over the pony's neck. At this very moment, when my leg was in the air, the pony, who had been very frisky, gave an extraordinary bound, with the result that I was shot down in a somersault with great violence. There was absolutely no means of breaking my fall. I hit on my shoulders and head and my legs curled up under me. Every scrap of wind was knocked out of my body and for some minutes I could not get my breath and rolled about in speechless consternation. However, there is no lasting harm done, but it is very lucky, considering the force with which I hit the ground.

The pressure all concentrated on my breastbone and my ribs and these are all dented in and possibly there may be some minor fractures. I am absolutely powerless to do anything and I cannot even sit up in bed or turn over and lie on my side, but simply lie still on my back, though I have the use of my arms and fingers and am not paralysed in that way. I think I am going to be all right in a few days.

You will naturally understand that I am very shaken and have not been able for the last 36 hours for one moment to find comfort in any position.

To Lord Curzon, who had sent him a letter of good wishes, Churchill wrote on April 24 that he had been 'like a beetle on its back for the last five days, and am only just beginning to be able to turn on one side'. And he added: 'A very little further and you would not have been plagued by me any more.' Churchill's 'only consolation', Sir Philip Sassoon told Lloyd George, was that he was drawing Insurance money for his accident from several different companies, '& is much excited to think that if he had been killed Clemmie wd be wallowing in 1500 pounds!'[1]

On April 16, while the Russians were negotiating at Genoa with the Allies, they announced that they had secretly negotiated a treaty with the Germans at Rapallo. By the terms of the Rapallo Treaty, Russia and

[1] As a result of his accident, Churchill had to give up playing polo for the rest of 1922, despite several efforts to continue. On July 5 he wrote to Lieutenant-Colonel E. D. Miller, CBE, DSO—with whom his polo ponies were stabled: 'The doctors think that it is too much for me to play polo this year in addition to all my work and after my fall. I find myself so exhausted after a match, and it takes me three days to get back to the normal. It is a great disappointment to me, but I must submit.' He sent one of his ponies to Sir Archibald Sinclair, and kept two for himself, for his morning rides in Rotten Row.

Germany declared themselves at peace, renounced all financial liabilities incurred during the revolution, and granted each other most-favoured-nation rights in trade and commerce. On April 24 the hitherto hostile editor of the *Morning Post*, H. A. Gwynne,[1] wrote to Churchill:

It appears to me because of your education and experience you do possess a profound knowledge of foreign politics and you are strong enough to make yourself heard by the Government. Will you not think me impertinent, if I urge you with all the force I can command to set your face against the aggrandisement of Russia & Germany and the weakening of France? Just one strong and reasoned protest would topple over the Genoa house of cards. Will you not, at this most critical moment in our history, take your courage in both hands and give the country a lead in statesmanship and sane and honest politics?

Churchill shared Gwynne's distress at the rapprochment between Britain and Russia. But he had no power to change the policy. He had made his protest before Lloyd George set off to Genoa. Then, he had believed that his protests had been effective. Unable to influence the day-by-day discussions at the Conference, he had hoped that Lord Curzon and Lord Birkenhead would represent his point of view. But Curzon had been too ill to go at all, and Birkenhead was easily swayed by Lloyd George. Thus Lloyd George was as independent at Genoa as he had been at Cannes. On April 24 Churchill wrote angrily to Curzon to point out that Curzon's absence from Genoa had 'sensibly deranged the balance of affairs which the Cabinet counted on and to which I attached so much importance. Austen has repeatedly reassured me by pointing out that you would be present. . . .'

On April 25 the *Morning Post* published the text of a speech delivered by Lord Birkenhead at Genoa on the previous day. Reading it, Churchill felt that even his friend had betrayed him. That morning he drafted a letter of protest:

How can you say 'the right of the Russians to choose their own institutions could not be disputed' when the whole mass of Russia, whether peasants or intellectuals, is absolutely excluded from the slightest means of representation or freedom of expression, when a blasting terror has the whole country in its grip and fixes upon it the rule of a communist sect which does not even estimate itself at more than a few hundred thousand persons? Again, you say 'the Bolsheviks are not fools'. Whoever said they were? These Semitic conspirators are among the highest political intelligence of the world and im-

---

[1] Howell Arthur Gwynne, 1865–1950. Reuter's chief war correspondent in South Africa, 1899–1902. Editor of the *Standard*, 1904–11. Editor of the *Morning Post*, 1911–37. One of Churchill's severest critics at the time of Antwerp and the Dardanelles.

placably devoted to its destruction. What is our country to gain out of this business? The more I ponder and reflect, the more impossible it is to see any advantage to us.

'I had your promise,' Churchill pointed out to Lord Birkenhead 'that you would endeavour to see the views which we have represented together to a very considerable extent given full effect to at the Conference . . . but as far as I can see you have yielded facilely to the influences by which you have been surrounded.'

Churchill decided not to send his letter. On April 26 he drafted—but again did not send—an even longer letter of protest to Lord Curzon.

Although he held back both letters, Churchill did not hesitate to express his anger to those who visited him. On April 28 Sir Philip Sassoon wrote to Lloyd George: 'I went to see Winston yesterday. . . . He is *fulminating* against Genoa & says there is seething public indignation against it—but I fancy that these lava streams are chiefly in the crater of his own breast.' Sassoon added that Churchill was 'terribly annoyed with F.E.'s attitude at Genoa & considers that he has been nobbled by you! In fact he is thoroughly disgruntled. . . .'

On May 4 Churchill learnt that Lord Birkenhead—who was then in Venice—had been summoned back to Genoa by Lloyd George for the final stage of negotiations. On the following day Philip Sassoon wrote to Lloyd George: 'He supposes F.E. could not resist going back there again for "one final hug" with the Bolshies!' For two days Churchill brooded upon his friend's change of attitude. Then, on May 6, he sent him his protest, together with a strong warning. 'My dear Fred,' he wrote:

The absence of Curzon from Genoa altered the balance, & doubled yr responsibility. But from yr telegram sent after you had been but a few days at Genoa & from yr speech I feared that you had ceased to represent in any way the views wh I thought we shared & wh you certainly undertook to safeguard. This caused me great distress: because all my thoughts in future politics turn on working with you, & all that future will be compromised by a fundamental disagreement. It seemed to me disastrous that you shd weaken yr influence with the Conservative party at this juncture by giving a new cause of reproach to yr enemies. The burden wh you partially assumed abt Ireland was surely enough for you to bear at the present moment. Why shd you go out of yr way to add to it by taking up another policy most bitterly & in my judgement most rightly resented by the bulk of those on whom the strength of Britain depends, & with whom we had hoped to act? Moreover if you were a full plenipotentiary attending continually & every day to the work of the Conference, I shd at least feel that you had a real responsibility. But dropping in now & then you become an easy prey to appeals to yr good nature, & thus run a grave risk of being made use of. However I hoped that the harm, such as it was, was done, & that you wd return at any rate not particularly compromised with this unhappy policy——

But now you have been intercepted & summoned to Genoa for the final scene, & of course L.G. wishes to get you in his hand & put the new burden solidly upon you. I know him so well, & my dear friend I know so well what an influence he will have upon you by making appeals to yr chivalry & so persuading you to come into the races with him. Once he has got you well compromised he will feel strong enough to run gt risks agst the House or party, & lines of cleavage may be drawn wh will leave you & me again on different sides.

Churchill believed that there were 'three important safeguards' on which Birkenhead ought to insist:

First—No weakening of the Cannes conditions whether economic or political. This was the pledge given to the Cabinet.

Secondly, the Br Empire surely has a higher claim on Br Credit than the Russian Soviets, & can offer a larger sphere & better security & a more fruitful return.

Thirdly no quarrel with France on account of Russia. Let us try to regain the confidence of France in order to modify her action agst Germany.

By adhering to these three principles you may yet extricate yrself & what is more important this country from the entanglement into wh she has been led by the personal views of one man, & may return home with the credit of having stood firm against temptation. In this way you wd restore & regain yr influence with yr own party & greatly promote those future developments abt wh we have so often talked. Everyone wd rejoice to see that you had played a manly part & had stood by those primary Br national interests to wh you have always been devoted. It is for these reasons as well as on acct of our comradeship that I beg you to reflect on the long consequences that may follow from the steps you take.

This letter is for yr eye alone.

Churchill's protests, although forcefully expressed, did not deflect Birkenhead from his course. But Austen Chamberlain shared Churchill's anxieties. On May 12 he informed Curzon that the majority of Conservative MPs 'do not really like these Russian negotiations or the thought that we may be sacrificing French friendship for the beaux jeux of the Bolsheviks'. The same day Churchill himself went to see Curzon, to discuss Lloyd George's Russian policy. Curzon showed Churchill several Foreign Office telegrams which had come in from Russia. 'Observe. . . .' Churchill wrote to Austen Chamberlain on May 13, 'that the Bolsheviks are going to shoot the seven priests who resisted the pillage of the Churches.'

When Lloyd George returned from Genoa, it was apparent that Churchill's opposition to the immediate recognition of Bolshevik Russia had been successful, at least for the time being. But on May 25 the House of Commons endorsed the policy of negotiation with Russia, and of eventual recognition, by 235 votes to 26. During the debate a Labour MP, Neil Maclean,[1] declared:

No one ever sees the Secretary of State for the Colonies sitting with a smile upon his face when the Prime Minister stands at that box telling of his new ideas with regard to Russia. These ideas are repugnant to the Colonial Secretary and to most members on the other side....

When, towards the end of July, the question of recognizing the Bolsheviks arose once more, Churchill reiterated his total opposition to such a move, writing to Lloyd George on July 26:

My dear PM,
    About the last few words of our talk today—I must make it plain that I feel it quite impossible to recognize the Bolsheviks in view of all that has happened since the Genoa discussions in the Cabinet. The issue does not arise now, & may never arise; but if it does—I do not see the slightest chance of my ever being able to stay. I shd be vy sorry indeed to leave you, but it will be for me a decisive act.
    There has been no improvement of any kind in their character & behaviour, & I do not believe there ever will be.
    This requires no answer & is not written with any other intention than to prevent misunderstanding. You were good enough to say at Fontainebleau that I was a branch that cracked before it broke.

Churchill's warning was not put to the test. Lloyd George had no intention of provoking a political crisis. As for Churchill, he looked forward to an Election, either in late 1922 or early 1923, in which Liberals and Conservatives would fight on a united anti-Socialist platform, and the Coalition be preserved.

Clementine Churchill spent most of July at Barnstaple in Devon. While she was away, Churchill kept her fully informed of his activities

[1] Neil Maclean,   –1953. Organizer of the Scottish Co-operative Wholesale Society. Labour MP for the Govan Division of Glasgow, 1918–50. A Labour Whip, 1919–21 and 1922–3. Chairman of the Parliamentary Labour Party, 1945–6.

in London. 'I have had a vy tiring week,' he wrote on July 15, 'with late sittings in the Commons, & last night a dance at Phillip's at wh I stayed till 2. All my partners were there & I danced 8 times running. Good exercise. . . . Ireland labours in the rough sea & now all the army, navy & air force estimates are coming on top of me, & many other toils as well.' However, he added, 'I have accepted these burdens and must carry them. I can.' Churchill was concerned also with his wife's health. 'I trust you & Goonie will amuse each other,' he wrote, '& be happy together: & that you will collect strength in peace and quietness.'

Churchill himself spent Saturday July 15 as the guest of Mrs Leopold Rothschild,[1] at Gunnersbury Park, just outside London. The weekend conversation was largely about Lord Northcliffe's illness, and the forthcoming Honours debate in the House of Commons. Lloyd George had been accused of abusing the system of political rewards by selling peerages to unknown, and apparently undeserving people. On Sunday July 16 Churchill wrote to his wife:

Darling,

I don't quite know why I came down here. There are several strange people indoors, & outside a total lack of sunshine. So I stayed in bed till lunch. . . .

I meant to tell you yesterday about Northcliffe. He has a strepptococcus infection in his blood & no one has ever got well from this particular disease. His brother is my informant. 'Sic transit gloria mundi'. I cannot help feeling sorry—altho God knows how cruel he was to me in those evil days of 1916.

Our revered leader is no doubt greatly relieved on this score, but on the subject of Honours, or rather Dishonours, he is as timid as a hare. I do not feel in contact with him on this subject that simple conviction of righteousness wh enables a just man to triumph over calumny. He has consented to a Royal Commission to see what steps shd be taken to prevent a Prime Minister from committing abuses of the Prerogative. An awful humiliation out of wh he hopes to slide & slither in a fairly cheap way.

Tender love my dearest one. I do not easily habituate myself to yr absence. Let me know when you will return from yr Devonian excursion. . . .

In a postscript to his letter, Churchill told his wife of Asquith's appearance at the dance given by Philip Sassoon on the previous week. 'The old boy turned up at Philip's party vy heavily loaded,' he wrote. 'The P.M. accompanied him up the stairs & was chivalrous enough to cede him the banister. It was a wounding sight. He kissed a great many people affectionately. I presume they were all relations.' 'Really,'

---

[1] Marie Perugia, 1862–1937. Born in Trieste. She married Leopold de Rothschild in 1881 (he died in 1917). The Churchills were often her guests at Gunnersbury, and at Ascott, near Wing, Buckinghamshire. Her grandson Edmund Leopold de Rothschild was (in 1974) Chairman of N. M. Rothschild & Sons Ltd., merchant bankers.

Churchill added, 'this letter consists in telling "sad stories of the deaths of Kings".'

The Honours debate took place on July 17. Godfrey Locker-Lampson[1] spoke of public suspicions that the honours system had been abused, and called for a public enquiry. Sir Samuel Hoare spoke of how individual peers were constantly advancing from one grade in the peerage to a higher grade, for no apparent reason. Lloyd George denied that financial contributions to Party funds were a decisive consideration in the award of peerages. On July 18 Churchill wrote to his wife:

> The debate on honours was squalid in the extreme & will do nothing but harm to the Govt in the country, & to the country in the Empire. The P.M. was lamentable & is universally pronounced to have made the worst speech of his career. It is indeed a decline. All this year we have suffered from his personal follies—the Election scare—the Resignation scare—the Genoa–Hague fiasco—& now lastly the Honours Gaffe. But for these—things have gone pretty well.

On July 20 Clementine Churchill wrote to her husband: 'The Honours Debate made me blush—our public life is not really squalid but the whole way these last two years have been managed politically makes one doubt.' Churchill shared his wife's unease, writing to her of one of the Peerages that had been attacked: 'The Williamson[2] episode now appears vy murky behind the scenes. I shd have thought his peerage quite justified: but it now appears that the Foreign Office dossier is rather disagreeable. This is a secret.' Churchill also sent his wife some more personal thoughts and news, together with his holiday plans:

> I strongly recommend yr going to the Ritz & pigging it there while passing thro London. . . .
> I hope Parlt will rise on Aug 4. & before that date I shall try to join you at Frinton. If we get reasonable sunshine I shall stay there off and on till you quit; & be with you during Sept till the event is over & you are convalescent.

---

[1] Godfrey Lampson Locker-Lampson, 1875–1946. Served in the Diplomatic Service, 1898–1902. Called to the Bar, 1906. Conservative MP for Salisbury, 1910–18 and for Wood Green, 1918–35. Under-Secretary of State, Home Office, 1923–4 and 1924–5. Under-Secretary of State for Foreign Affairs, 1925–9. Author of several volumes of poetry.

[2] Archibald Williamson, 1860–1931. A Partner in the merchant house of Balfour, Williamson & Co. Director of the Central Argentine Railway; the Lobitos Oilfields and the Anglo-Ecuadorian Oilfields. Liberal MP, 1906–18; Coalition Liberal, 1918–22. Chairman of the Home Office Committee on Taxi-Cabs, 1911; the House of Commons Committee on Short Weight, 1914; the Mesopotamian Commission, 1916 and the Electric Power Supply Committee, 1917. Created Baronet, 1909. Privy Councillor, 1918. Financial and Parliamentary Secretary to the War Office, 1919–21. Created Baron Forres, 1922.

Then I think of going to Benny [the Duke of Westminster] at Mimizan where you can join me as soon as you are fit. Parlt will not meet again till the middle of November. Max is pressing me to go to Deauville for a week early in August. We will talk over all our plans when we meet.

Sarah continues to prosper & Diana is at her examinations. They seem vy difficult & I am glad I do not have to do them!

'Shall we have Autumn meetings in Dundee this year?' Clementine Churchill replied on July 21. 'We might go up there just before Parliament meets in November. How delicious to have a nice long holiday. The Mimizan plan sounds perfect. I will hurry up and recover as quickly as I can so as to be able to join you there.'

On August 2 Churchill wrote to his wife of his dinner the previous night at 10 Downing Street. 'Many speculations on the next Parliament,' he reported. He himself had forecast that the Government would have a majority of between sixty and eighty seats. 'The others,' he wrote, 'were much more pessimistic!' The election need not take place, he added, until the summer of 1923. On receiving her husband's forecast, Clementine Churchill replied perceptively: 'With such an enormous preponderance surely the Tories will want a P.M. of their own?'

On August 4 Churchill sent his wife an account of a small anti-Coalition upset, which did not, however, appear to be a serious danger to the Coalition's survival:

The Tory Under Secretaries[1] visited their Cabinet colleagues again yesterday with further grumbling agst L.G. & the coalition, the purpose of wh was no doubt to indicate how easily England cd be saved by their becoming Secretaries of State instead of being Under Secretary. F.E. scolded them vehemently & they were furious. Increasing political instability will be the feature of the next few months.

On August 4 Churchill left London for Philip Sassoon's house at Lympne, together with Edward Marsh. 'All my work is finished,' he wrote to his wife that afternoon, '& really in the last few days I have accomplished a gt deal (5 millions off the Naval Estimates).'

After a night at Lympne, Churchill and Marsh crossed from Folkestone to Boulogne. Before leaving, Churchill wrote to his wife:

[1] In August 1922 there were four Conservative Under-Secretaries of State: Sir J. Baird (Home Office); Edward Wood (Colonial Office); Lord Winterton (India Office); Sir R. Saunders (War Office). Among the other Conservative Junior Ministers were Sir J. Gilmour (Treasury); Sir P. Lloyd-Graeme (Department of Overseas Trade); Leopold Amery (Admiralty); B. Eyres-Monsell (Admiralty); the Earl of Ancaster (Board of Agriculture and Fisheries); the Earl of Onslow (Local Government Board); Sir A. Montague-Barlow (Ministry of Labour); Sir W. Mitchell-Thomson (Board of Trade) and G. Tryon (Pensions).

Darling,

A Parthian shot of love & kisses. I am just off. I shd have liked to linger here. . . . But I must press on to where the turbulent Max awaits me on the pier at Boulogne. I lie to-night at Deauville! I am arranging to speak in London about October 22nd. Tender love to all of you especially *Diana*, *Randolph*, *Sarah* & above all yourself.

Your loving
W

Lord Beaverbrook and Churchill lunched together at Boulogne and then drove together to Deauville. 'This is just to wish you "Bon Voyage",' Clementine Churchill wrote from Frinton, '& a very happy holiday.'

Churchill sent his wife frequent letters during his holiday. 'The weather is cloudy & today distinctly cold,' he wrote from Deauville on August 7. 'We have vy fine rooms & a splendid lookout.' He was suffering from severe indigestion and was forced, he wrote, 'to consider every mouthful'. He was also very tired: 'So I have gone to bed early each night & have not entered the gambling rooms.' And he added: 'I bathed yesterday. It was freezing. Now I am riding with Jack Wode-house.'[1] On August 8 Clementine Churchill wrote to her husband: 'Lord Northcliffe seems to be dying by inches. What will happen to all his papers? On the other hand Lenin seems to be perking up again.[2] Poor Pig. No luck!' There were also more personal thoughts:

I feel quite excited at the approach of a new kitten. Only 5 weeks now & a new being—perhaps a genius—anyhow very precious to us—will make its appearance & demand our attention. Darling I hope it will be like you.

Three days from now August the 11th our Marigold began to fade. She died on the 23rd.

On August 9 Churchill and Marsh left Deauville by train for Paris. During the journey Churchill wrote to his wife a full account of life at Deauville:

My darling Clemmie,

I am on my road to Paris. The weather at Deauville was vy disappointing—cloudy, cold, floods of rain. I got a little fitful sunshine in the afternoons & painted a small picture & daubed a few canvasses.

Yesterday Max got a temperature from a chill through bathing; & in the

---

[1] John Wodehouse, 1883–1941. Liberal MP for mid-Norfolk, 1906–10. Captain, 16th Lancers; served in France, 1914–17, and in Italy, 1918 (wounded, awarded the Military Cross). Churchill's personal political Secretary, 1922–5. Succeeded his father as 3rd Earl of Kimberley, 1932. Owner of over 11,000 acres in Norfolk. Killed in a German air raid. His brother Edward had been killed in action in 1918.

[2] Lenin, who was suffering from a brain disease, retired from active control of Soviet Russia on 12 December 1922. Thereafter he lived in retirement, dying on 21 January 1924.

night he was pretty rough 102° or more. Today he is better & the doctor
(Frog) declares he will be all right tomorrow. . . .

I rode each day with Jack W: and am really much better so far as indigestion is concerned—& indeed generally. Deauville improved on acquaintance as one got a circle of friends. . . . Fred Cripps[1] is here—gambling and
losing vy heavily. He already owes far more than he can pay, but hopes to
recoup himself by *securing* from the Bolsheviks houses they have *stolen* from
their owners. These he puts in repair & enjoys a leasehold for 20 years. So he
gambles away these ill gotten gains. . . .

The King of Spain arrives this afternoon. His advanced guard in the
shape of a beautiful actress has already installed herself in a sumptuous villa &
many ponies have also arrived.

What a parcel of gossip! But the whole place is full of this sort of thing. I am
not sorry to get away—tho I wd have liked to see Max fully restored before
departing.

Max gave me a most sombre account of Northcliffe's closing scenes. Violent
resistances to treatment, 2 male nurses, gt constitutional strength fighting
with a foul poison, few friends, no children, mania, depression, frenzies.
Lady N[2] receiving the doctor always in the presence of Sir R. Hudson.[3]
Rothermere extremely interested in every turn of the case. Poor wretch—his
worst enemies cd not but grieve for him. Max professed gt sympathy &
sorrow & generally maintained a most correct attitude about the fate of his
formidable rival. It cannot be long now.

My darling sweet I am being frightfully lazy. Literally doing nothing at all.
Bed every night before 12. No gambling—I lost only 300 francs & was frankly
bored by it. I refrained from the sea (after one shivering plunge) & hence
escaped the evil consequences that have befallen Max. I shall look forward to
seeing you all on the 20th.

Tender love
Your ever devoted
W

P.S. Among other notorieties in the rooms I perceived the Shah of Persia[4]

---

[1] Frederick Heyworth Cripps, 1885–   . 2nd son of the 1st Baron Parmoor, and brother
of Stafford Cripps. Director of the Russian and English Bank in Petrograd before 1914.
Captain, Royal Bucks Hussars Yeomanry, 1914. Served at Gallipoli, 1915 (where he was
wounded), in Palestine (where he was awarded the DSO), and in France (Croix de Guerre).
Lieutenant-Colonel, 1917. In 1927 he married Violet, Duchess of Westminster.

[2] Mary Elizabeth Milner, 1867–1963. She married Northcliffe in 1888, a few months
before he launched his first weekly paper, *Answers*. One of the first women to fly as an aircraft
passenger. Active in charitable work, and a Life Governor of the London Hospital. During
the First World War she raised funds for the Red Cross and was appointed GBE for this
work. She and Northcliffe had no children. In 1923, six months after Northcliffe's death she
married Sir Robert Hudson (who died in 1927).

[3] Robert Arundel Hudson, 1864–1927. Joint Treasurer, Westminster Hospitals. Director, Sun
Life Assurance Society. Knighted, 1906. Member, Imperial War Graves Commission, 1919.

[4] The Shah of Persia from 1909–1925 was Ahmed Mirza. His Prime Minister in 1922 was
Qavam-as-Sultaneh (who was replaced in 1923).

also parting with his subjects' cash, handed to him packet by packet by his Prime Minister. Really we are well out of it with our own gracious Monarch!

On the evening of August 9 Churchill dined in Paris with Louis Loucheur. 'He foreshadowed good plans of appeasement for disarmament & for collaboration with Germany,' Churchill wrote to his wife on the following day. But he added: 'The time is not yet ripe.'

After dining with Loucheur in Paris, Churchill took the night sleeper to Bordeaux, from where, still accompanied by Marsh, he went by boat to Mimizan. 'At Bordeaux the skies were brilliant,' Churchill wrote to his wife, 'but by the time our boat had crossed the lake the Almighty had scraped together all the spare clouds he cd find in the Bay of Biscay & now the first rain for six weeks is falling. Quite a fine performance!' Churchill also sent his wife an account of his visit to the Duke of Westminster's stables, and of his holiday plans:

24 magnificent steeds & any number of hounds. I am going to ride every morning early to try to get myself fit. I think the rest is doing me good. I let my mind become almost a blank and simply lollop along without worrying about anything. Even if I am bored I don't mind. I must recharge my batteries.

'I think a gt deal of the "coming kitten",' Churchill added, '& about you my sweet pet. I feel it will enrich yr life and brighten our home to have the nursery started again. I pray to God to watch over us all.'

'I love to think of you resting & painting and riding in that lovely forest,' Clementine Churchill wrote to her husband, and she added:

I am enjoying this garden, but am getting very stationary & crawl even to the beach with difficulty. I long for it all to be over. It has seemed a very long nine months.

My love to Eddie. What does he do all day? You ought to make him try to paint too. I fear there are no ancient Monuments for him to visit quite close. Does he ride with you? I suppose it is the close season for penwipers. Do you fish in the azure lake?

On August 14 Churchill sent his wife an account of his daily life at Mimizan. 'I ride from 7.30 to 9,' he wrote, 'work at my book till lunch, 12.30.' In the afternoons he painted until dinner. 'The days have passed like lightning,' he wrote, and added:

This is really a wonderful part of the world. The people are prosperously poor. Happy, friendly & with lots of vy pretty children. The scenery is not only rich but various. I find it full of beauty & charm. It is quite cool & yet a wonderfully genial climate. The beaches are glorious sand. Today we went to a little place called Conte where a clear river almost entirely tunelled with trees flows over golden strands into the foaming wave. I thought it an ideal spot for a children's holiday. No crowds, no smells, warm bathing, and country, & I suppose cheap as salt water. However do not be alarmed, I am not going to build or buy a house.

Eddie inspired & to some extent aided by me collected shells. We are sending them home so that you can all busy yourselves in matching them. I will give a prize for the nearest approach.

My indigestion lurks around: but I am substantially better & get through each day with only occasional remedies.

I am losing nothing by being away so far as politics are concerned and perhaps for some reasons it is just as well to be cut off them for a bit. . . .

My darling I have thought vy often of you all & most of all of you. Yes I pass through again those sad scenes of last year when we lost our dear Duckadilly. Poor lamb—It is a gaping wound, whenever one touches it & removes the bandages & plasters of daily life. I do hope & pray all is well with you. No letter came by the messenger—but the news is I am sure good news.

Your own adventure is vy near now & I look forward so much to seeing you safe & well with a new darling kitten to cherish. . . .

On August 16, Churchill went to Biarritz. 'Weather cool and brilliant,' he telegraphed to his wife on his arrival, and on the following day he wrote to her: 'I think much of you. I wish you were all out here. It is a sweet land.' On August 18 Churchill returned to Mimizan. Before leaving Biarritz, he sent his wife an account of his activities there:

My darling one,

We have had only about 50% sunlight tho' perhaps today will turn the scale. Montag[1] has arrived, so our conversation proceeds exclusively in French. I have got several nice pictures under way wh only need an afternoon's sunshine to complete them. Montag is vy anxious to teach me & most austere in all his methods. He was positively glad when the sun didn't shine yesterday because I was forced to give attention to the drawing, not having the brilliant light to play with.

Up to last night we successfully resisted the temptation of the Casino, aided by the fact that on our first visit it was closed. Last night however we repaired thither. I had three hands wh got no further than the first coup, & had lost about £40. At the fourth time I passed twice with a 50 Coins bank thus getting back all I had lost. I was so pleased, that I let the bank go—My dear, it passed nine times! So I said goodnight to Mephistopheles & came away, having neither lost nor won.

[1] Charles Montag, 1880–1956. Born in Winterthur, Switzerland. Went to Paris, 1903. Studied painting in Brittany and Provence. Painted mostly landscapes and still life. Exhibited his paintings in Zurich, 1917. He died in Paris.

Tonight we go back to Mimizan, after lunching & painting at St Jean de Luz—taking Montag with us. Being Swiss by extraction, he takes a vy cool view of reparations.

For five more days Churchill stayed at Mimizan, painting, riding and working on his book. On August 22 he left for Paris, and on August 23, having just reached Dover, he telegraphed to his wife: 'Just landed many thoughts darling on this day looking forward much to seeing you all tomorrow.'

September 12 was Churchill's fourteenth wedding anniversary. During the day his wife wrote to him from Sussex Square:

Today we have been married fourteen years quite a long time—full of all sorts of exciting experiences. I am sure that now that the sharp edge of financial anxiety has been removed—if only we could get a little country Home within our means & live there within our means it would add great happiness and peace to our lives.

Churchill had not been idle in his search for a house in the country. On the day after he received his wife's letter, he was offered 'first refusal' on Chartwell Manor, an Elizabethan house near Westerham, in Kent.[1] On September 14 a letter from Knight, Frank & Rutley, Estate Agents, gave him ten days to decide whether to buy the property, at a price of £5,500.

On September 15 Clementine Churchill gave birth to a baby girl, who was christened Mary.[2] That same day Churchill wrote to Knight, Frank & Rutley, offering to buy Chartwell Manor for £4,800. In his letter he explained why his offer was £700 less than the price that had been asked:

The house will have to be very largely rebuilt, and the presence of dry rot in the northern wing is I am advised a very serious adverse factor. Both these considerations tell heavily against the undoubted charm of the situation, and impose financial burdens upon the purchaser of a very heavy character. . . .

If this offer is accepted, I am prepared to complete immediately. On the other hand, I hope an early answer may be given, as I have several other properties under consideration and wish to come to an early decision.

[1] Chartwell belonged to Captain Archibald John Campbell-Colquhoun (died 1945), who had entered Harrow School in 1888, in the same term as Churchill. He had served as a Captain in the Cameron Highlanders, from 1914–18 (wounded). A Justice of the Peace for Dumbarton, where he lived, he inherited Chartwell on the death of his brother William on 15 June 1922, and put it on the market without ever living in it.

[2] Mary Churchill, 1922–   . In 1947 she married Arthur Christopher John Soames (Conservative MP for Bedford, 1950–66, Ambassador to France, 1968–72, Knighted, 1972).

Knight, Frank and Rutley did not accept Churchill's arguments. Later that week he summoned their negotiator, H. Norman Harding, to the Colonial Office. Harding repeated that the price could not be reduced. 'He strode up and down,' Harding later recalled 'using every argument he could think of to lower the price, but I repeated he could have it at the price my Client had named, but if not, he would have to go on searching. Eventually, with a very bad grace, he gave way. This was the only time during my various meetings that he was anything but courteous, kind and considerate. . . .'

Five days later Churchill raised his offer to £5,000, and on September 24 it was accepted. He at once sent a cheque for £500 as an earnest of his intention to buy.

On his return from France at the beginning of September, Churchill had discovered that speculation was once more rife about a possible general election. On September 5 Frederick Guest sent him an estimate of possible voting figures on the assumption 'of a Coalition election'. The Government, he believed, would win 370 seats—including 227 Conservatives and 90 Coalition Liberals—as against a maximum of 250 Opposition seats—of which 200 would be Labour and 50 Asquithian Liberal. On such a basis, if the Coalition were to break up, the Conservatives would be brought to power with 227 seats, with Labour as the main opposition Party, and with the Coalition and Asquithian Liberals in third place, even if their forces were combined. It might also, Guest pointed out, give a majority to a new grouping of Labour and Asquithian Liberals, leaving both Parties of the former Coalition in disarray. Guest's calculations constituted a formidable argument in favour of maintaining the Lloyd George Coalition.

On September 11 Churchill dined with Lloyd George, and found him, as he reported to Lord Balfour on the following day, 'moving rapidly' in favour of an October Election. The main fear, Churchill told Balfour, was that the National Union of Conservative Associations, meeting in November, would 'take disruptive action & pass resolutions wh wd make the P.M.'s position, & perhaps Austen's, impossible, thus entailing a break-up at the very moment when absolute unity in the face of Labour is essential'. Churchill added that Lord Birkenhead was 'greatly exercised about this, & much inclined to an election in October'. Birkenhead's worry was that with every month's delay 'additional Labour candidates wd come into the field, & their general position wd be strengthened'. Churchill himself was not so pessimistic as Birkenhead, but on balance he too favoured an October election, as he explained in his letter to Balfour:

I shd myself have thought that it wd have been possible to get through the National Unions' meeting without a split, the spirit of self-preservation being vy strong among politicians when within a year of an inevitable election. But I must admit that another year or 9 months of continued bickering and nagging by the Die-Hards will add greatly to the opposition we shall have to face in every constituency. It is all grist to the Labour mill. Therefore while I shd have greatly preferred to have waited till next summer in ordinary circumstances, I shall not argue against an October appeal. We have been in for four years out of our five, & our original mandate was somewhat defective on a/c of so many soldier-voters being abroad with the Armies.

On September 12, while Churchill was at Lympne as the guest of Sir Philip Sassoon, he reflected on the political situation in a letter to his friend Pamela Lytton. 'The reign of our revered leader is I apprehend drawing to a close,' he wrote. 'What will happen then? No one can tell. A general election cannot be far off: & with all these millions to vote no one is wise to be to sure.'

44
Iraq 1921–1922:
'An ungrateful Volcano'

IN March 1921 the Cairo Conference had agreed to transform Mesopotamia—or Iraq as it became known—into an Arab kingdom, guarded principally by an Arab army, and linked to Britain by Treaty. Its internal administration would be under Arab control, while the Royal Air Force would safeguard Britain's military interests.

Throughout 1921 and 1922 the principal external threat to a peaceful Iraq was the hostility of the Turks along the remote northern border. In a telegram to Churchill on April 19, Sir Percy Cox pointed out that at the Cairo Conference 'all our deliberations and proposals for prompt reduction of troops' were based on the 'preliminary condition' of a friendly Turkey. Yet no Turkish peace had yet been signed; the Treaty of Sèvres was still unrevised; and anti-British propaganda was being disseminated throughout the Mosul province. Cox told Churchill of the discovery of 'numerous copies of a highly seditious pan-Islamic printed pamphlet in Urdu calling on Indian troops to murder their officers and desert'. At the same time, the Turks were presenting 'gifts of arms' to the leading frontier sheikhs. Churchill and his advisers were not impressed by these alarms. On April 21 Churchill instructed Shuckburgh to tell Cox 'that no alteration in the agreed plan for reducing the garrisons can be allowed. The troops must leave the country at the rate settled.'

At a meeting of the Cabinet on May 31, Churchill explained the progress of his Iraq policy. The British troops were being withdrawn according to plan, he said, and would be replaced by over 8,000 local Arab and Kurdish troops, at an annual cost of only £400,000.

At the beginning of June Churchill learnt from the War Office that aerial action had been taken on the Lower Euphrates, not to suppress a riot, but to put pressure on certain villages to pay their taxes. He

telegraphed at once in protest to Sir Percy Cox. 'Aerial action is a legitimate means of quelling disturbances or enforcing maintenance of
order,' he wrote, 'but it should in no circumstances be employed in
support of purely administrative measures such as collection of revenue.'
In his telegram Churchill went on to warn Cox that, with the 'rapid
diminution' of Britain's military forces in Iraq, 'it must be realized that
aerial action will assume more and more character of bluff and that
there is always risk of our bluff being called. So long as it acts as effective
deterrent well and good, but we must beware of using it on too small
a scale or so frequently that tribes learn to discount it, or in such a
manner as to provoke retaliatory action with which we may not have
adequate means of coping.'

In his reply on June 24, Sir Percy Cox defended the bombing which
had, he said, taken place 'either with my concurrence or at my request'.
Its aim, he said, was to disperse 'a deliberate attempt to defy national
Government' by people who wished to test whether the local authorities
really could call on 'British support'. The results of the bombing, Cox
insisted, had been 'satisfactory' in both cases, resulting in 'a general
improvement in behaviour and a noticeable decrease in highway robbery. . . .' Cox ended his telegram by protesting against 'hyper-critical
strictures upon such action' which were, he said, intended 'to stifle the
growing infant' of air power; and he appealed to Churchill for support,
not censure. Churchill withdrew his rebuke, minuting on Cox's telegram
a short but emphatic reply: 'Certainly I am a great believer in air power
& will help it forward in every way.'

On June 14 Churchill announced his Iraq policy to Parliament.
During the course of his statement he read out a paragraph which had
been suggested by Sir Percy Cox, to the effect that the people of Iraq
could choose their own ruler, and that if they chose the Emir Feisal, he
would have Britain's support. But when Feisal arrived in Basra at the
end of June, it was clear that he expected Britain to be more active on
his behalf. On July 1 Cox telegraphed to Churchill that Feisal 'shows an
inclination to take the line that as he has been sent as British candidate
by His Majesty's Government, it is up to us to do his business for him'.
Cox went on to tell Churchill that he had done his best to combat this
view, and had explained to Feisal 'that while he makes progress it will
daily become more and more easy for us to come into the open and we
will give him all possible help, yet it is most essential that he should
primarily pose as candidate of people with our support and not the
converse, otherwise he will be subject to attack on the score of being a
British puppet'.

Churchill was eager to see Feisal installed in Iraq as soon as possible. On July 5 he sent Cox a 'personal' telegram, asking whether he considered it necessary 'to await results of elections' before proclaiming Feisal as 'Emir of Iraq'. He added: 'I consider there is much to be said in favour of striking while the iron is hot.' Yet although Feisal's candidature suited the British, it was much less ideal for the Arabs of Iraq, for whom he was a foreigner. Several local nationalist candidates were put forward from the three main provinces, Mosul, Baghdad and Basra. But as these candidates were in conflict, Feisal had the double advantage both of being a compromise candidate, and of having the British as his sponsor.

Within the Middle East Department, a series of telegrams were being drafted, and sent to Sir Percy Cox, informing him of Britain's responsibilities to Iraq under the terms of the League of Nations mandate, and seeking to ensure that the coming elections, and Feisal's candidature, came within the proper limits of Britain's authority. Most of these telegrams were drafted by Hubert Young, and amended by John Shuckburgh, Churchill adding his initials only. On the morning of July 9 he was prompted to protest at this procedure, writing to Archibald Sinclair:

All this seems very complicated and I do not think we ought to bombard the High Commissioner with these elaborate instructions. It is quite true that I am responsible for approving all the telegrams you have sent. In the main, however, I think it much better to leave matters to Sir Percy Cox, who alone knows the local situation and who has the greatest possible interest in bringing out a satisfactory result.

There is also too much talk about 'Mandates', 'Mandatories' and things like that. All this obsolescent rigmarole is not worth telegraphing about. It is quite possible that in a year or two there will be no mandates and no League of Nations. Something quite different may have taken their place.

Do let us keep the practical salient points of the policy in our minds and only check Sir Percy Cox when he diverges from them:—

(1) To get another large wave of troops out of the country and so reduce the expenditure to the British taxpayer.

(2) To get Feisal on the throne as soon as possible.

(3) To make whatever arrangements are most likely to conduce to the above objects in regard to Basra (about which the only principle is that we do not put Kurds under Arabs).

I suggest that we repeat these dominant needs to Sir Percy Cox in a telegram and ask him to submit proposals for action.

I am rather worried by all these lengthy detailed telegrams going in my name and at so many being sent. I am sure they must impair the effectiveness of messages which I send myself personally.

Churchill saw Young at noon that same day, and himself drafted a telegram to Cox, which began emphatically: 'Main thing is to secure the early choice of Feisal. . . .' and which ended: 'I am very anxious not to burden you with rigid instructions but to support you in every way in the difficult task you are discharging with increasing measure of success.' Having freed Cox from the problem of how to interpret the conditions of the Mandate, Churchill proceeded to try to relieve him of the problem of military expenditure.

On July 4 Churchill had pressed the Secretary of State for War, Sir Laming Worthington-Evans, to transfer the control of the defence of Iraq from the War Office to the Colonial Office. This transfer had been one of the conditions laid down by Churchill when he agreed to take charge of the Middle East Department. 'I really cannot be expected,' Churchill wrote, 'to take on my Estimates enormous sums for military forces . . . beyond the minimum that is needed,' and he went on to point out that every time he wanted 'a dozen armoured cars' for Iraq 'I have got to fight the W.O. and then the Treasury and then probably the Cabinet before I can get the assistance I require.' Churchill ended his letter: 'We really cannot go on like this.' But the War Office persisted in trying to maintain as large a military force as possible in Iraq, and to find employment there for British troops.

The War Office also put forward proposals for building new military barracks at Baghdad. To this Churchill was utterly opposed, writing to Worthington-Evans on July 16:

. . . I cannot contemplate at the present time the building of permanent barracks. If our policy is successful, we shall in a few years withdraw altogether our troops from the country and there will be nothing there except the Arab forces and possibly our Air establishments. It is intended to run Mesopotamia like an Indian native State and we are certainly not laying out plans for keeping a permanent British garrison there. You have got plenty of good barracks already built for your battalions in Malta and Gibraltar. These are the places where you should surely put those that it is necessary to retain on general grounds . . .

Churchill pointed out to Worthington-Evans that he had embodied all these points in a letter which he had sent to him two months before, and that he had been 'very much surprised not to hear from you in answer to my long and serious letter, and I do beg you to give it your attention. . . .' Worthington-Evans would not accept Churchill's strictures. That same day, General Radcliffe described them as 'preposterous', and he added: 'Even if the system advocated might work more or less happily, thanks to the personal qualifications of the present Secretary of State for the Colonies, it is impossible, as Marshal Foch recently pointed out in discussing the Independent Air Force, to establish a principle on the strength of a personality. . . . Altogether this is a sad case of the ex-gamekeeper turning poacher!'

Churchill continued to assert his authority. That same day, July 16, in a departmental minute, he set out in detail his military proposals. 'The most I can spare,' he wrote, 'is six millions.' All troop allocations must come within that sum. The question of using British or Indian troops must be decided by that yardstick. Any new barracks which were to be built 'must be built out of savings in the present year's expenditure'. The Royal Air Force must take over from the Army during the course of 1922, and 'all the preparations must be begun now'. He himself, he added, was prepared to visit Baghdad before the end of 1921. 'I shall actually be in the neighbourhood of Rome,' he wrote, and from there he thought of going by ship to Alexandria, and thence, by aeroplane across Palestine and Transjordan, to Iraq.

Churchill was eager to take immediate control of the garrisoning of Iraq. During July 17 he and Sir Hugh Trenchard discussed the time-table of the Air Force takeover; but Trenchard warned that it could not be done quickly. Churchill hoped that the transfer could be completed by April 1922. Trenchard felt that October was a more realistic date.

The news from Iraq itself was encouraging. 'Feisal continues to maintain his popularity,' General Haldane wrote to Churchill on July 23, 'and, provided no fanatical pro-Turk assassinates him when he pays his visit to Mosul in the near future, his presence should make for peaceful conditions.' Churchill's relations with Cox were also encouraging, despite earlier disagreements. On July 23 Cox wrote, of Churchill, to Lord Curzon from Baghdad:

I have had rather an unsettled time since I returned to Mesopotamia—as you know I always hoped that the Near East Dept would, and thought it should, be attached to the FO, and I think you will realise, having regard to his attitude in general & toward me personally, in the Cabinet Councils at which I was present, that it was somewhat of a shock to me to find that he of all people was to be my Chief. We did not begin very well, but the Conference at Cairo was useful and we reached a better understanding there; so I hope as far as our personal relations are concerned things will work smoothly. I am afraid though I shall never quite forget, though I have long since forgiven, his remark suggesting that I was in your pocket! You may perhaps remember the occasion. But naturally he had, in changing his post, to change his outlook on things, and I thought he was very good in his running of the Cairo Conference. He was also very friendly to me.

From late July, Churchill embarked upon a long and acrimonious dispute with the War Office, whose estimate of costs he believed to be excessive. On July 26 he sent a minute to R. V. Vernon and Colonel Meinertzhagen, pointing out that the War Office wanted to maintain as many non-combatant as combatant British troops. 'If the War Office insist on establishments like these,' he wrote, 'for the non-combatant services, I will not in any circumstances allow the British infantry or cavalry to remain in the country. We will carry on entirely with Indians and Air Force.' In a 'very secret' note to Archibald Sinclair on July 26, Churchill set 1 October 1922 as the date on which the Royal Air Force would take over control of the defence of Iraq from the Army. Two days later Churchill received a letter from General Haldane, sent from Baghdad on July 12, which gave strong support to the Colonial Office view. Haldane believed that a triple combination of Air Force, Indian troops and Arab levies would be adequate to keep the peace in Iraq. In his letter he praised the work of the Air Force in bombing Arab troublemakers into submission, wrote encouragingly of the development of the Arab levies, and deprecated sending any more British troops to the country at all. 'Aeroplanes are now really feared,' he reported; the Arab levies would be ready by the summer of 1922 'when they might first be wanted'; and the climate was quite unsuitable for British troops. In the past fortnight, he explained, the temperature in Basra had reached 128° Fahrenheit, and he added: 'This is not a white man's country and it is absurd to pretend it is. The British troops hate it, and naturally so. . . .'

Churchill was delighted to receive such confirmation of his three main arguments. 'Please read this letter & enclosures,' he wrote to Lloyd George as soon as he had read Haldane's letter. 'It is *private*, but it will show you the line along wh I want to proceed & am proceeding with success.' Churchill's policy was further advanced when he received, on July 29, Sir Hugh Trenchard's detailed scheme for transfering all responsibility for the defence of Iraq to the Royal Air Force. Two days later Churchill urged his advisers to make plans to 'run a weekly mail for all purposes' from Baghdad to Cairo, and to ensure that when the aeroplanes reached Cairo, there was a ship waiting to carry the mails across the Mediterranean.

Churchill prepared to put his complete proposals to the Cabinet. In a telegram to Sir Percy Cox on August 2, he explained what he wished to do. In October 1921 General Haldane would hand over his command to General Ironside; the new commander would have twelve months to guide the transition from Military to Air Force control; in October 1922 a Royal Air Force officer would take over the command of all British forces in Iraq; from that date 'all financial control or responsibility by the War Office will cease, Colonial Office having plenary powers'. The Air Force would have under its aegis both armoured cars and tanks. 'They also have to learn . . .' Churchill wrote, 'how to feed and supply themselves'; hence the interim year when General Ironside would be in command. During that year, Churchill added, the development of local Arab levies, and of the Arab Army, 'shall be constant'. British troops would be reduced to 2,000 men only. Indian troops would likewise number 2,000. The air force personnel would number about 2,000, all 'high class RAF white personnel'. On the basis of these 6,000 Colonial Office controlled men, and the Arab forces, 'King Feisal's authority' would be maintained. Churchill's letter continued:

> You will readily understand that these proposals will be hotly contested by the War Office. The economy campaign is pressing them very hard now, and they are desperately anxious to quarter at least 7 white battalions in Mesopotamia in order to avoid their possible disbandment. Any such solution will be fatal to Mesopotamian interests. Prime Minister with whom I have conferred, while agreeing generally with the course I have proposed, is pressing me most strongly to go much further, i.e. to pay King Feisal a subsidy and withdraw all troops from the country. This I cannot consent to do. I consider that policy we framed at Cairo and which you have so ably carried thus far must be pursued perseveringly, and that adequate support for the Emir must be forthcoming, and that this must be provided within the limits of the 4 or 5 millions of the Cairo estimate.

> I let you know about these matters, which are very secret, beforehand, in order that you may understand the difficulties I have in resisting excessive demands by the War Office on the one hand and excessive demands for economy and reduction on the other. I shall succeed in doing this if I have your effective support, but if I am unsuccessful I shall not continue responsible in any way for Mesopotamia and I shall if necessary make this clear to the Cabinet in the forthcoming discussion . . .

Churchill also wrote to Worthington-Evans on August 2, pointing out that with Lloyd George wanting no British troops in Iraq, and the War Office wanting a garrison of over 18,000, 'I have the usual difficult middle position to maintain.' For the next three weeks, Churchill worked at the presentation of his case to the Cabinet, and exhorted his officials to provide him with the facts and figures which he needed. On

August 4 he asked Trenchard for a detailed breakdown of the Air Force garrison proposals. That same day, he completed a Cabinet paper entitled 'Policy and Finance in Mesopotamia, 1922–23', in which he declared that he would on no account accept the War Office demand for a garrison of 18,000 men. 'It is of course quite impossible,' he wrote, 'for me to reconcile such a charge with any forecasts or undertakings I have given to Parliament.' It was also impossible, he added, for him to agree with the War Office proposal that over half of those troops should be British, and that they should be as fully supported by clerks, vets, signallers, chaplains, doctors and education officers as they would be in England. 'I cannot in any circumstances face this prospect,' Churchill warned, 'or anything like it. The kind of organisation of the British army which fits it to face a German army under modern conditions is far too costly for a poor, starving, backward, bankrupt country like Mesopotamia.' To throw such a weight of expenditure on so poor a country, he wrote, 'is to crush it, and if no other way can be found than this of holding the country, we had much better give up the Mandate at once'.

Churchill then outlined Trenchard's Air Force scheme, and quoted General Haldane's letters praising the work of the Air Force in maintaining order. Its cost, he pointed out, would be far less than the War Office's scheme, which involved substantial, extraneous Army charges 'not justified by local needs'. Churchill then gave a succinct summary of what he believed Britain's policy should be:

The government of the country will be conducted by an Arab administration under King Feisal, who will act in general accordance with the advice tendered him by the High Commissioner, Sir Percy Cox. All the outlying districts will be garrisoned solely by the local levies and the Arab army, no Imperial troops, British or Indian, being employed. Bagdad itself will be the main air centre, and here will be assembled 1,800 high-class armed white personnel of the Royal Air Force. This force is quite capable of protecting itself in its cantonment against a rising or local disorder in the town or surrounding country. It is capable also of feeding itself indefinitely by air. Radiating from this centre, the aeroplanes will give support to the political officers and the local levies in the various districts, and will act against rebellious movements when necessary. The 3 armoured car companies will be based on the same workshops as those which maintain the aeroplane squadrons. 2 or 3 battalions of infantry will be quartered at Bagdad and 1 or 2 at Basra to maintain local order. These battalions will not be expected to operate as mobile forces at any distance from the towns where they are stationed. . . .

In the event of a general rising necessitating the evacuation of the country, all the Imperial personnel in Bagdad can be brought down the river by the armed vessels, for which special barges carrying high galleries capable of commanding the banks at low water, with machine guns and trench mortar fire, are being prepared by General Haldane. Thus we have every hope of carrying on at a moderate cost, and if the worst comes to the worst we shall retain the means of withdrawing from the country without the need of sending up an expedition. This is the best plan we have been able to make within the financial limits, which are inviolate.

Churchill ended his memorandum with a conciliatory sentence. 'If we desire to part company with the War Office at an early date,' he wrote, 'it is not because we do not value their loyal and skilful aid, but because we simply cannot afford it.' On August 7, before circulating this memorandum to the Cabinet, Churchill sent a copy to Lloyd George. In his covering note he wrote bluntly: 'I must be free from the W.O. & able to peruse my own estimates & prescribe what troops if any we are to take from them. Otherwise I cd not possibly keep my promises to Parliament about reductions, nor cd I present the Estimates.' In his letter, Churchill asked Lloyd George for his support in Cabinet. He also expressed the hope that Lloyd George had followed the details of the Air Force scheme when it had been circulated. Meanwhile, while waiting for the Cabinet to make its decision, he continued to press his advisers to prepare his case. 'My mind is made up upon the policy,' he wrote to Archibald Sinclair on August 11, 'but I wish to be carefully safeguarded in the details.'

During the first two weeks of August a referendum was held throughout Iraq on the question of Feisal's kingship, and on August 15 Sir Percy Cox announced in Baghdad that Feisal had been chosen as King.[1] But in this moment of triumph for British policy, Feisal immediately sought to assert his complete independence. He would not, he said, accept the restrictions on his sovereignty embodied in the terms of the League of Nations Mandate, but wanted a direct Treaty with Britain giving him sovereign powers. He wanted to be King in fact as well as in name, and rejected any position dominated either by Britain or the League.

In an attempt to persuade Feisal to accept British advice, Churchill drafted a personal message to him on August 15. During the day he decided not to send it:

My friend while we have to pay so much for troops & instruments of war to sustain yr Government we must expect that our solemn wishes shall count

---

[1] Although the Hashemites were never universally popular in Iraq, they remained as rulers until 1958.

with you in grave matters. We have no end to seek save the peace & good order of Iraq. We are quite willing without delay to make a treaty with you instead of the present mandatory system. But until there is a regular Government in Iraq there is no one with whom we can make a treaty. You have freely undertaken meanwhile to accept the mandatory system and to that word I hold you. General Gouraud[1] has just written a letter in terms of the utmost bitterness against you & your family in which he predicts that you will repeat in Baghdad the same mistake of falling into the hands of extremists as he charges you with in Damascus. I am confidently expecting you to arm me with the means of answering those who decry the good faith & stability of the Sherifian family by proving over a course of years that the British have been wise to trust them.

Instead of sending this message direct to Feisal, Churchill telegraphed on the evening of August 15 to Sir Percy Cox. His final draft read:

You shd explain to Feisal that while we have to pay the piper we must expect to be consulted about the tune, whether under Mandatory or Treaty arrangements. If he wishes to be a sovereign with plenary powers, he must show that he is capable of maintaining peace & order in Iraq unaided. This will certainly take some years.

We have promised to substitute a Treaty for existing mandatory system. This treaty cannot be made until Feisal's Govt is duly constituted & there is someone to make it with. Draft of Treaty will be telegraphed in a few days & subsequently to be made & ratified in a formal manner. I see no reason why Feisal shd not make a declaration on accepting the Crown, & you & he shd draw this up together. I shd like to see it first. But rather than put off Coronation I am prepared to accept yr decisions. You must keep an eye on the League of Nations etc.

Important thing is Coronation & not upsetting harmonious march of events in Iraq. Feisal has undertaken to accept mandatory system subject to treaty modifications & you shd tell him that I regard this promise as binding on him. However we are actually going further & proposing to make the treaty arrangement with him as soon as possible.

Churchill ended his telegram to Cox on a warning note, intended for Feisal's own ears. 'I am quite sure that if Feisal plays us false,' he wrote, '& policy founded on him breaks down, Br Govt will leave him to his fate & withdraw immediately all aid & military force.'

[1] Henri Gouraud, 1867–1946. Entered the French Army, 1890. Served in the Sudan (twice wounded), 1894–9, and in Morocco, 1911–14. Commanded the 10th Infantry Division, western front, 1914–15 (wounded). Commanded the French Expeditionary Corps at the Dardanelles, May–June 1915 (wounded). Resident General in Morocco, 1916–17. Commanded the 4th Army, 1917–19. Governor of Strasbourg, 1919. French High Commissioner in Syria and Cilicia, and Commander-in-Chief of the French Army of the Levant, 1919–22. Military Governor of Paris, 1923–37.

Sir Percy Cox replied to Churchill's telegram on August 16. Feisal was clearly determined not to give way easily to Britain's demands. He refused absolutely to accept the terms of the Mandate as the justification for Britain's presence in Iraq. Britain's sole status, now that he was King, must be one of 'goodwill and mutual confidence'. A Constitution must be drawn up relating only to the people of Iraq and their government, but making 'no reference' to Iraq's relations with Britain. These relations should be made explicit in a separate Treaty, freely negotiated.

'Generally speaking,' Cox explained, 'he feels his accession must be marked by some definite outward sign of change. If impression is given that he is to be merely a puppet in hands of British his influence will be weak and he will not be able to recover it.'

Amid this storm raised by Feisal, the Cabinet met, on August 18, to discuss the much-postponed question of whether the Colonial Office or the War Office were to garrison Mesopotamia. Churchill put his case for Colonial Office control, based on an Air Force garrison. Worthington-Evans put the case for the War Office. The discussion then turned to whether Britain ought to stay in Iraq at all. Lord Birkenhead and Sir Robert Horne advocated a complete withdrawal. In the event, Churchill's arguments prevailed, and the Cabinet decided that the Air Force scheme should be inaugurated as from 1 October 1922, as Churchill had asked.

At seven on the evening of August 19 Churchill took the chair at a meeting of a special Cabinet Committee set up to work out an Iraq Treaty. Curzon, Montagu and H. A. L. Fisher were the other Members. Churchill told them that he had just received a telegram from Mesopotamia 'that Feisal had been elected by an overwhelming vote'. During the ensuing discussion, it was stressed that Feisal would object 'to ascending the throne with an undefined status'. Following their deliberations, Churchill drafted a telegram to Sir Percy Cox, which was sent from the Colonial Office on the following morning. 'Feisal should be told on my behalf,' Churchill wrote, 'that I have in no way changed to his disadvantage. The only change wh has taken place is that we are now prepared to substitute treaty for existing relations as soon as possible.' But Churchill went on to warn Feisal that even his direct Treaty with Britain must be approved by the League of Nations. 'Under pressure of oil interests,' he told Cox, 'U.S. are making difficulties and we shall have serious difficulties in Council of L of N if they join with the French against Feisal regime. These difficulties might become insurmountable unless we follow absolutely correct procedure.'

Feisal agreed to proceed with the Treaty negotiations. For his part,

Churchill continued to press the Cabinet for 'a good settlement' with Turkey, arguing on September 26, in a memorandum entitled 'Greece and Turkey' that 'a few thousand Turkish troops' sent towards Mosul would force a halt to the withdrawal of British troops from Iraq.

The actual news from Iraq did not bear out Churchill's immediate fears. The border troubles were minor, and the Arab levies beginning to act as an effective police force. 'The tribes are quiet,' General Haldane wrote to Churchill on September 28, 'and have not yet failed wherever they have been employed. . . . The Arab is a born plotter but a coward when Justice comes down upon him swiftly. . . .' Sir Percy Cox reinforced this optimism in a telegram to Churchill on September 29, in which he informed Churchill that although Mustafa Kemal 'will inevitably try to turn Feisal against British', he was 'so satisfied' of Feisal's loyalty to Britain that he was convinced 'it was a risk we can well afford to run'. On October 7 Churchill circulated Cox's telegram to the Cabinet.

On October 5 A. J. Balfour wrote to Churchill from the League of Nations headquarters at Geneva, reminding him that the Iraq Treaty must be agreed upon by the League Council in advance of its final signature. Such agreement, Balfour warned, might prove difficult, particularly as the French would be opposed to 'everything which increases the importance of King Feisal'. The first step, Balfour advised, would be preliminary negotiations with France, Italy, Japan, 'and possibly with America', to explain the Iraq proposals to them.

Churchill rejected Balfour's advice. It was essential to make a Treaty with Feisal as soon as possible, he explained on October 10, in order to strengthen Feisal's position on the throne 'and ensure so far as possible the permanence of his loyalty. If this fails and complete anarchy breaks out we shall have to quit the country with the white people and leave it to complete anarchy'. Churchill had already promised Feisal to negotiate a Treaty at once. The Cabinet had approved the Air Force scheme. The Arab levies were being formed. British troops were withdrawing. These were the facts with which Churchill had to work. 'If the League of Nations cannot arrive at any decision . . .' he warned Balfour, 'we shall have to go on with our administrative work and take the practical steps which the situation requires from time to time; and if the fact that our proceedings are not internationally regularised should cause uncertainty and disturbance in Mesopotamia, the responsibility will rest with the League of Nations.'

On the day that Churchill replied to Balfour, he received encouragement for his belief that peace could be made with Turkey. During

October 10 Colonel Meinertzhagen met General Harington, the commander of the British forces at Constantinople, who was in London on
leave. Harington warned Meinertzhagen that negotiations with Turkey
could not succeed 'so long as Greece has a single soldier in Asia Minor'.
But he added that he himself 'would have no difficulty in negotiating
with Mustapha', although Kemal 'would be averse to dealing with
British politicians whom he considered insincere & pro-Greek'. Meinertzhagen at once reported Harington's remarks to Masterton Smith,
who sent them to Churchill, and Churchill saw Harington before the
General returned to Constantinople.

On October 18 Churchill sent Curzon a personal appeal for a speedy
opening of negotiations with the Turks. 'I really do not think that we
can afford to delay,' he wrote. 'I can't help feeling vy anxious about
Iraq. . . .' Curzon resented Churchill's concern. 'I find it very difficult
to conduct foreign affairs at all,' he wrote to him on November 9,
'under the conditions which are constantly created, not infrequently by
yourself. . . . Negotiations for peace are after all F.O. business not C.O.,
and I wonder what would be your attitude if in the administration of
your department you were subject to the constant interference of a
colleague from which I have to suffer.'

Churchill drafted a reply to this rebuke; then decided not to send it.
'Ever since I entered the Cabinet in 1908,' he wrote, 'it has always been
customary for questions of foreign affairs to be freely discussed by
Ministers at the proper opportunities.' He continued:

There is absolutely no comparison between the issues in foreign affairs and
those which arise in ordinary departments, I have never known foreign
affairs treated as if they were merely a departmental matter. It is a penalty
attached to work of paramount importance, and I never knew Sir Edward
Grey to complain, although his Continental policy was held in the very
tightest grip by the Cabinet . . .

In Iraq itself, Sir Percy Cox had begun to work out the details of the
Iraq Treaty. Hubert Young, who had gone out to Baghdad to help him,
sent the Colonial Office his first full report on October 23. He had seen
Feisal, and impressed upon him the need to incorporate parts of the
Mandate into the Treaty. Young warned Feisal 'that he would
enormously increase our own difficulties if he failed to realize that we
are, at least to a certain extent, responsible to the League for our
treatment of Iraq. . . .'

On November 13 a Conference was held at the Colonial Office to
discuss the defence of Iraq against Turkish attack. On the following

day Churchill telegraphed to Cox that the War Office representatives at the Conference had 'considered it impossible with reduced garrison in Iraq either to repel invasion or to suppress internal disorder', but that the Air Ministry officials had been confident that invasion could be 'if not repelled, delayed', and that all internal disorder could be suppressed. Churchill told Cox that in the Treaty with Feisal, Britain must retain the final control, and liability for both internal disorder and external defence until such time—perhaps fifteen or ten years distant—when 'independent Islamic state of Iraq can stand alone'. But in order to meet Feisal's objections, Churchill advised framing the Treaty in such a way that these defence obligations devolved on Feisal 'in first instance, without prejudice to ultimate responsibility of His Majesty's Government'.

When Cox began to send Churchill a series of telegrams outlining Feisal's point of view, and stressing Feisal's desire for independence in his dealings with foreign powers, Churchill minuted, on November 24:

I am getting tired of all these lengthy telegrams about Feisal and his state of mind. There is too much of it. Six months ago we were paying his hotel bill in London, and now I am forced to read day after day 800-word messages on questions of his status and his relations with foreign Powers. Has he not got some wives to keep him quiet? He seems to be in a state of perpetual ferment, and Cox is much too ready to pass it on here. Whenever Feisal starts talking about Arab aspirations, his sovereign status, and his relations with the French, etc., Cox ought to go into the financial aspect with him and show him that the country on to whose throne he has been hoisted is a monstrous burden to the British Exchequer, and that he himself is heavily subsidised. Let him learn to so develop his country that he can pay his own way, and then will be the time for him to take an interest in all these constitutional and foreign questions.

Churchill had worked out a practical means of avoiding too frequent a clash of opinion with Cox. 'I am very much in favour of abridging this correspondence,' he minuted on December 7, 'and this is best done by allowing considerable intervals to intervene when matters are not urgent before replies are sent.' But this precept did not deter Churchill from taking the initiative when provoked. 'Latest War Office returns give number of Indian followers in Iraq on November 14 as 21,632,' he telegraphed to Cox on December 13. 'This is a shocking figure. Please inform me what is its explanation and what steps you are taking to repatriate and discharge all these people who are living on the British taxpayer. There are 4,000 more Indian followers than there are Indian soldiers.'

While the Treaty discussions continued in Baghdad, Churchill was constantly searching for further means of reducing Britain's defence expenditure in Iraq. On November 10 Colonel Meinertzhagen informed him that over 8,000 Indians were employed as labourers in Iraq, on road-building and barrack maintenance, at a cost in pay of £27 each a year. 'This will never do,' Churchill minuted on the following day. 'Now that the bulk of the Army has gone, these followers must go too.' And he added: 'Propose me a plan for their speedy evacuation.' Four days later, on November 25, he minuted for the whole Middle East Department:

What is all this talk about 9 millions for Mesopotamia next year? There is absolutely no question of anything over 7. Not one farthing more than 7 will be asked for by me, together with 2½ for Palestine. Everything has got to be cut down to this level by any means that you like and at any risk and cost.

In mid-December Churchill found himself in dispute with Colonel Meinertzhagen over the question of using gas bombs in Iraq. Both Sir Percy Cox and Sir Hugh Trenchard wanted a clear indication of Colonial Office policy. On December 14, in a Colonial Office minute, Meinertzhagen argued against gas bombs. 'If the people against whom we use it consider it a barbarous method of warfare,' he wrote, 'doubtless they will retaliate with equally barbarous methods. As I have said before, the Moors of the Riff are killing one Spaniard for every bomb dropped from an aeroplane. Again, say what we may, the gas is lethal. It might permanently damage eyesight, and even kill children and sickly persons, more especially as the people against whom we intend to use it have no medical knowledge with which to supply antidotes.' But Churchill did not accept Meinertzhagen's caution. 'I am ready to authorize the construction of such bombs at once. . . .' he minuted in reply on December 16. 'In my view they are a scientific expedient for sparing life wh shd not be prevented by the prejudices of those who do not think clearly.'

Churchill was content to leave the detailed negotiating of the Iraq Treaty in the hands of Sir Percy Cox, and to rely upon Sir Hugh Trenchard to put into operation the policy of Air Force control of Iraq's defences. In the year since he had taken over responsibility for Mesopotamia, much had changed. 'You can imagine what the state of the country was,' he wrote to his wife on 1 January 1922, 'with all these bitter people, each with his Arab pet, tumbling over each other fighting for power. Now at any rate we have disciplined opinion. I am quite pleased the way things are going.' But Churchill was as alert as before to anything that he considered excessive expenditure. 'There can be no question of building a hospital for £150,000 in Baghdad at the present time,' he minuted on January 9. 'The bulk of the garrison has gone. There can be no new military need.' And he added: 'You really must make these people understand that they are not going to live on our backs for ever. It astonishes me that such ideas should be put forward.'

On February 1 Churchill telegraphed to Sir Percy Cox: 'A fierce economy campaign is on foot here and a very heavy attack is likely to be made upon forthcoming expenditure in Iraq.' Churchill told Cox that Lloyd George still hoped to end Britain's control of Iraq altogether, and, by paying Feisal no more than a million pounds a year, make a Treaty with him 'as a completely independent Sovereign' and withdraw all British troops and officials.

On February 6 Churchill received a memorandum from Lord Trenchard which threatened to set back the timetable of events in Iraq. Trenchard suggested postponing the date for the Royal Air Force takeover from October 1 until the New Year. That same evening Churchill discussed this request for delay with Frederick Guest, who wrote at once to Trenchard, seeking to dissuade him from such a course. Churchill, he wrote, 'was dreadfully upset and says we really must manage October 1st. . . . He pointed out that he quite realized he was sitting on a volcano in the whole matter, and counted upon us, and us alone, to see him through.' Trenchard deferred to Churchill's wishes, and continued with his plans for October 1.

On February 9 Lloyd George took the chair at a Conference of Ministers to discuss Iraq. The question now at issue was whether Britain should not withdraw altogether, as Lloyd George had suggested. Worthington-Evans proposed withdrawing all troops from Mosul and Baghdad, and holding only the port of Basra. There then followed, H. A. L. Fisher noted in his diary, 'a lively contest between W.O. and Winston in support of Air defence. . . . Winston wants to form his own air rifles to protect the aerodromes. . . . W. Evans opposes.' It was finally agreed to uphold the Cabinet decision of the previous August, and allow the Air scheme to go ahead. But Churchill stressed, and his colleagues agreed, that until peace was made with Turkey, the defence needs of Iraq would remain uncertain, and that Britain's ability to protect the country cheaply would remain problematical. Each of the formal conclusions of the Committee was an acceptance of Churchill's arguments of the previous six months.

During the discussion, Churchill had assured the Conference of Ministers that he would keep the cost 'of the whole administration of Iraq' to £7,500,000 for the coming year. He therefore watched carefully for anything that might increase this sum. On February 19 Sir Percy Cox asked for £60,000 to maintain the Iraq railways 'as a going concern' for the remaining short period of British control. Churchill minuted on Cox's telegram: 'No. Not a penny.'

The Cabinet met on February 21 to discuss the draft Iraq Treaty which had been drawn up after three months of negotiations between Sir Percy Cox and Feisal. The only clause in dispute was the one in which Feisal insisted upon 'the right of foreign representation'. The Foreign Office had proposed that 'the British Government should undertake the protection of Iraq nationals' abroad. The Colonial Office favoured general acceptance of Feisal's demand. In the discussion of this conflict, Churchill 'laid stress on the importance of raising an Arab army capable of defending Mesopotamia', and pointed out that Feisal was insistent 'that he should not be a mere puppet monarch'. Curzon challenged Churchill's arguments. The draft Mandate, he pointed out, 'laid down specifically that the British Government would be entrusted with the foreign relations and diplomatic and consular representation of Mesopotamia'. How, he asked, 'was the change now contemplated to be justified to the League of Nations?' Balfour, Britain's representative in the League Council, supported Churchill. The change contemplated, he said, 'was all in the direction of self-determination', of which the League approved. But, he warned, the French Government would 'abominate' the idea of Feisal being allowed to send his own ambassadors abroad, since they had no intention of introducing such a liberal policy for Syria. Lloyd George, while asking the Cabinet 'warmly to congratulate' Churchill on having turned 'a mere collection of tribes' into a nation, proposed sending a telegram to Cox to say that 'the Cabinet felt the greatest reluctance in agreeing to the separate diplomatic and consular representation of Iraq until the State had become an established fact and had made good'. The Cabinet accepted Lloyd George's suggestion.

Feisal had been expected to object strongly to the Cabinet's refusal to allow him any independent representations abroad. But in a letter to Sir Percy Cox written on February 23, he turned his objections to the use of the word 'Mandate' wherever it appeared. 'The people,' he told Cox, 'have acquired a repugnance towards the term "Mandate", its terms and interpretations. . . .' Instead of 'certain ambiguous words', Feisal wanted 'a definite statement providing for a sincere and friendly alliance'. On March 6 John Shuckburgh informed Masterton Smith that Feisal had delivered 'a kind of ultimatum . . . and threatens in effect to drop the treaty negotiations altogether if the point is not conceded to him'. Feisal's objection to the word 'mandate'—which in that context was a new term in every language—was that the actual Arabic word used in the discussions was the same word as that used for 'protectorate', and roused visions of Italian rule in Tunisia and British rule in Egypt; a state of affairs which both he and the Arabs of Iraq very much wished to avoid.

Sir Percy Cox had hoped to see the Iraq Treaty signed at the end of March. But Feisal's desire to exclude all reference to the Mandate made this impossible. 'I do not see any chance of having the treaty through by March 31,' Churchill minuted to Reader Bullard[1] on March 16. The Cabinet, meanwhile, had discussed Feisal's conditions, and rejected them. 'We decide,' H. A. L. Fisher noted in his diary on March 15, 'to press the reluctant Feisal to accept Treaty & Mandate.' Churchill told the Cabinet that, as a special concession, he would be prepared to grant Feisal the foreign representation that he had earlier demanded. But both Curzon and Balfour were strongly opposed to this, and Lloyd George gave them his support. Henceforth, for seven months, the negotiations with Feisal were conducted along lines with which Churchill disagreed.

In the hope of persuading Feisal to change his mind on the question of foreign representation, Churchill wanted T. E. Lawrence to go out to Iraq at once. Lawrence's mission, he wrote in a Cabinet memorandum on March 31, would be 'the best means of clearing up this misunderstanding'. Churchill told his colleagues that he 'set great store' on Lawrence's personal influence with Feisal. But Sir Percy Cox would not agree to Lawrence's visit, telegraphing to Churchill on April 4 that 'in so far as treaty is concerned Lawrence would not cut any ice, while in respect of other matters his presence, granted most loyal intentions on his part—would merely be a source of weakness to me'. Cox feared that Feisal's friendship with Lawrence would stiffen Feisal's resolve.

[1] Reader William Bullard, 1885– . Acting Vice-Consul, Beirut, 1909–10. Vice-Consul, Bitlis, 1910–11. Acting Consul Trebizond, 1912; Erzerum, 1913; Basra, 1914. Civil Adviser to the Military Governor of Basra, 1914–18. Military Governor of Baghdad, 1920. Middle East Department, Colonial Office, 1921. British Agent and Consul, Jedda, 1923–5. Consul, Athens, 1925–8. Consul-General, Moscow, 1930; Leningrad, 1931–4. Knighted, 1936. Minister at Jedda, 1936–9; at Teheran, 1939–46. Director of the Institute of Colonial Studies, Oxford, 1951–6. He published his autobiography, *The Camels Must Go*, in 1961.

Churchill accepted Cox's arguments, and Lawrence remained in London.

The negotiations with Feisal continued throughout the spring and summer. Feisal's continuing insistence upon a specific abrogation of the Mandate was something on which Churchill could not give way. On April 19 he wrote to Sir Percy Cox:

The British Government have no power to abrogate or terminate the Mandate which they hold from the League of Nations, except by resigning once and for all their special position in the country. The other great Powers on the Council of the League of Nations would not agree to Britain having a special position in Iraq unless controlled by the Mandate. America, though not a member of the League, would also refuse consent. There is no possibility, therefore, of Britain freeing herself from the Mandate other than by washing her hands altogether of responsibilities towards Iraq . . .

'There really is no use,' Churchill added, 'searching for vain formulas which disguise the fact that Britain has to obey the League of Nations, and that Iraq must accept our guidance whilst it requires our aid.' There was, he concluded, a single alternative to futile negotiations, and that was total British withdrawal. 'We could begin the evacuation immediately after the hot weather,' he pointed out, 'and all British troops and civilians could be out of the country before the end of the Christian year. If this is the King's wish he should say so. . . . The British nation would rejoice to be relieved from a burdensome charge devoid of the slightest advantage to them. . . .'

Feisal persisted in his course, demanding the Treaty, but rejecting the Mandate. 'Feisal is most unreasonable. . . .' Churchill wrote to Curzon on April 24. 'He asked for the Treaty. It has been so shaped as to give him the fullest measure of satisfaction. If he now declines to sign, I propose to leave matters in an undefined and indeterminate condition and see which happens next.' Churchill was in no hurry, he added, to present to Feisal 'what I expect will be the inevitable ultimatum'.

At the beginning of July T. E. Lawrence decided to resign. On July 4 he sent John Shuckburgh a formal letter of resignation:

It seems to me that the time has come when I can fairly offer my resignation from the Middle East Department. You will remember that I was an emergency appointment, made because Mr Churchill meant to introduce changes in our policy, and because he thought my help would be useful during the expected stormy period.

Well, that was eighteen months ago; but since we 'changed direction', we have not, I think, a British casualty in Palestine or Arabia or the Arab provinces of Irak. Political questions there are still, of course, and wide open, there always will be, but their expression and conduct has been growing steadily more constitutional. For long there has not been an outbreak of any kind. . . .

While things run along the present settled and routine lines I can see no justification for the Department's continuing my employment—and little for me to do if it is continued. So if Mr Churchill permits, I shall be very glad to leave so prosperous a ship. I needly hardly say that I'm always at his disposal if ever there is a crisis, or any job, small or big, for which he can convince me that I am necessary.

Shuckburgh took Lawrence's request to Churchill, with the recommendation that it be accepted. That same day Churchill wrote to Lawrence:

I very much regret your decision to quit our small group at the Middle East Department of the Colonial Office. Your help in all matters and guidance in many has been invaluable to me and to your colleagues. I should have been glad if you would have stayed with us longer. I hope you are not unduly sanguine in your belief that our difficulties are largely surmounted. Still, I know I can count upon you at any time that a need arises, and in the meanwhile I am glad to know that you will accept at least the honorary position of Adviser on Arabian Affairs.

Four months after his resignation, Lawrence set down, in a letter to R. D. Blumenfeld,[1] his thoughts on Churchill's achievements as Colonial Secretary. 'If we get out of the Middle East Mandates with credit,' he wrote on November 11, 'it will be by Winston's bridge.'

At the end of July, the Middle East Department began to press Feisal to sign the draft Treaty. But Feisal was insistent that the Mandate should be specifically revoked. On July 31 Reader Bullard minuted that 'it wd not be worth while trying to maintain a special position in Iraq without the authority of the Mandate behind us'. Bullard went on to point out 'the serious defects in Faisal's character which the last year has revealed'; he was, in Sir Percy Cox's opinion, 'crooked and

[1] Ralph D. Blumenfeld, 1864–1948. Born in the United States. Entered journalism as a reporter on the *Chicago Herald*, 1884. London Correspondent of the *New York Herald*, 1887–93. News Editor of the *Daily Mail*, 1900–2. Editor of the *Daily Express*, 1902–32. Founder of the Anti-Socialist Union. Chairman of the *Daily Express* from 1933 until his death.

insincere'. Bullard was pessimistic about the future of the Iraq Treaty. 'When it was decided to send Faisal to Iraq,' he recalled, 'the decision was taken on the assumption that he would play straight with us. It was always a forlorn hope. . . .'

On August 3 Churchill tried to break the deadlock by inviting Feisal to London. The suggestion had originated with Sir Percy Cox. But Feisal refused to come unless he were given an assurance of a successful solution of the Mandate problem, and—as Young noted on August 15— 'with permission to announce, before leaving Iraq, that we have conceded the principle of emancipation from the Mandate'.

Feisal's refusal to come to London provoked much hostile comment in the Middle East Department. T. E. Lawrence was asked for his advice, and suggested—as Masterton Smith reported to Churchill on August 16 —that unless Feisal signed the Treaty 'within a specified time (say a week or so) we will drop the Treaty and carry on without it'. But Churchill did not favour such a drastic course. The Treaty, he pointed out in a departmental minute on August 17, 'was Feisal's plan, not ours. We consented in order to meet his views. If he obstructs the Treaty & will not sign it, it is for him to suggest a method of avoiding the deadlock.' And Churchill added: 'I see not the slightest reason for hurry on our part.'

In the third week of August a series of telegrams from Sir Percy Cox made it clear that Feisal was encouraging anti-British feeling throughout Iraq, and that he clearly felt able to ignore the lack of any formal Treaty. 'Feisal is playing a very low & treacherous game with us,' Churchill wrote to Lloyd George on August 23. During August 25 Churchill drafted a telegram to Feisal warning him that the British would act 'in whatever way may seem best suited to secure the peace and order of Iraq, for which they hold the Mandate under the League of Nations'. But for the Mandate, Churchill pointed out, 'the immediate status of Iraq would be no more than that of a Turkish province in British military occupation'. On August 26 Sir Percy Cox telegraphed that Feisal had been taken ill. Churchill held back his telegram.

Britain's future position in Iraq was endangered on August 26, when the Turks, fearing yet another Greek offensive, launched their own attack on the Greek forces in Asia Minor. The French and Italians, who had been anxious to make peace with Turkey for more than a year, provided the Turks with arms and equipment. The Greeks believed that

Britain would support them; three weeks earlier, on August 4, Lloyd George had told the House of Commons that the Turks were untrustworthy barbarians, and had praised Greek military prowess. He had also stated that Britain would no longer refuse Greece the right to blockade the Turkish coast.

The Turkish attack was immediately successful, and by August 31 the Greek troops were in flight, retreating precipitately towards the coast. This sudden Turkish success threatened to disrupt the whole Iraq settlement. On September 1 Churchill wrote to Lloyd George:

I am deeply concerned about Iraq. The task you have given me is becoming really impossible. Our forces are reduced now to very slender proportions. The Turkish menace has got worse; Feisal is playing the fool, if not the knave; his incompetent Arab officials are disturbing some of the provinces and failing to collect the revenue; we overpaid £200,000 on last year's account which it is almost certain Iraq will not be able to pay this year, thus entailing a Supplementary Estimate in regard to a matter never sanctioned by Parliament; a further deficit, in spite of large economies, is nearly certain this year on the civil expenses owing to the drop in the revenue.

I have had to maintain British troops at Mosul all through the year in consequence of the Angora quarrel; this has upset the programme of reliefs and will certainly lead to further expenditure beyond the provision. I cannot at this moment withdraw these troops without practically inviting the Turks to come in. . . .

Churchill pointed out that there was 'scarcely a single newspaper— Tory, Liberal or Labour', which was not 'consistently hostile' to Britain's remaining in Iraq, and that the 'enormous reductions' in expenditure for which he had been responsible had 'brought no goodwill'. If an alternative Government were formed in Britain, Churchill warned, whether it were Labour, Conservative, or Asquithian Liberal, it could gain great popularity by ordering the 'instant evacuation' of Iraq. 'Moreover,' Churchill added 'in my own heart I do not see what we are getting out of it.'

Churchill told Lloyd George that he would like to send an ultimatum to Feisal, stating that unless Feisal were to 'beg us to stay and to stay on our own terms in regard to efficient control, we shall actually evacuate before the close of the financial year'. He wanted, he said, to put this ultimatum 'in the most brutal way'; if Feisal were not prepared to accept it, 'I would actually clear out.' At present, Churchill wrote, 'we are paying eight millions a year for the privilege of living on an ungrateful volcano out of which we are in no circumstances to get anything worth having.'

Lloyd George was opposed to withdrawal from Iraq. He rejected Churchill's proposed ultimatum threatening total evacuation. In his reply on September 5 he criticized the decision of the Asquith Cabinet—eight years before—to attack the Turks in Mesopotamia. His criticism was a strong one, but he also defended the Arab policy, for which he himself had been responsible:

The whole problem has arisen out of the decision to attack the Turks in Mesopotamia. Strategically, I think that decision was faulty. To be effective we had to leave our base on the sea for hundreds of miles in a torrid country utterly unfit for white fighting. We ought to have concentrated on Gallipoli and Palestine or Alexandretta. The Taurus was then unpierced. The decision was taken when I was hardly on the fringe of the War Cabinet. You were in it. Having provoked war with the Turk we had to fight him somewhere, but the swamps of the Tigris were a badly chosen battleground.

Whatever, however, the merits or demerits of the original decision to fight in Mesopotamia, it certainly is responsible for our difficulties now; and tracing the story back to that decision, I do not see how any of our subsequent troubles could have been avoided.

It was quite clear to me when I became Prime Minister that we could not afford to relax our campaign against the Turks in that region. Such a decision, after the withdrawal from Gallipoli, and the surrender of a British army at Kut, would have weakened our position throughout the Mahomedan world.

Having beaten the Turk both in Iraq and in Palestine, we could not at the Armistice have repudiated all our undertakings towards the Arabs. We were responsible for liberating them from Turkish sovereignty, and we were absolutely bound to assist them in setting up Arab governments, if we were not prepared to govern them ourselves . . .

Lloyd George went on to criticize both Churchill and his predecessors for failing 'during our years of occupation' to prospect for oil in Iraq. It was the possible existence of oil, he believed, which made it impossible to leave Iraq out of pique. 'If we leave,' he wrote, 'we may find a year or two after we have departed that we have handed over to the French and Americans some of the richest oilfields in the world—just to purchase one derisive shout from our enemies.' And Lloyd George ended: 'On general principles, I am against a policy of scuttle, in Iraq as elsewhere. . . .'

In his reply on September 6, Churchill hastened to dissociate himself from Lloyd George's rebuke about the origins of the Mesopotamia campaign pointing out that:

The Government of India and Crewe were the prime movers in the original expedition to Basra and though of course both you and I were members of the

War Committee of the Cabinet at that time and are therefore responsible, the matter did not seem at that time to be one of very great importance, and amid the press of much greater events I do not think we took any part in the discussion. On the question of advancing to Baghdad itself, which arose in June or July 1915, a much more serious decision was taken and here again we were both members of the War Committee, though I was a very waning influence at that time. Still, here again we are clearly both responsible. After that I agree that there was no way out during the war except by fighting and winning . . .

Churchill went on to challenge Lloyd George's assertion that Britain's victory over Turkey made it obligatory for her to take Iraq under her protection. In his view, Churchill wrote, 'we were undoubtedly free to decline the Mandate for Iraq and quit the country as rapidly as our troops could be withdrawn'. Nevertheless, he added: 'Like you, I am very much against a policy of scuttle and after your clear expression of opinion you may be sure I shall do all in my power to avoid it.'

In his letter to Lloyd George on September 6, Churchill pointed out that Sir Percy Cox had spoken firmly to Feisal, and that the King's obduracy had begun to wane. 'For the moment,' he wrote, 'the position is very much easier.' And he went on to point out that if peace could be made with Turkey, 'a very great easement would result'. Everything now depended upon the outcome of the Graeco-Turkish war, which had reached a new intensity. 'It may well be,' Churchill wrote to Lloyd George, 'that out of the lamentable events now taking place in Anatolia may come a decision upon which a stable peace with Turkey may be made'. If so, Iraq would no longer be open to Turkish intrigue, with the resulting fears of high military expenditure, and Feisal would soon accept the much delayed and much disputed Treaty. Churchill had been prepared to abandon Iraq to its fate. Lloyd George was determined to remain. Both of them had now to await the result of events in Turkey itself.

45

The Chanak Crisis

THROUGHOUT the first week of September, the Greeks retreated in chaos towards Smyrna, with the Turks in constant
pursuit. On September 5 a force of Royal Marines landed at Smyrna
to supervise the evacuation of all British subjects. During the day the
French Government urged the Greeks to sue for an armistice, and the
British High Commissioner at Constantinople, Sir Horace Rumbold,
telegraphed to Lord Curzon that any such armistice must involve 'the
immediate and orderly evacuation of Asia Minor by Greeks'. Lloyd
George's hopes of a powerful Greek State in Anatolia were at an end.

When the Cabinet met at 10 Downing Street at noon on September 7,
Curzon advised the Cabinet to follow Sir Horace Rumbold's advice, to
encourage the Greeks to seek an armistice, and to agree to the evacuation of all Greek forces from Asia Minor. But as far as European Turkey
was concerned, Curzon told the Cabinet that he 'earnestly hoped that
we should not abandon the Gallipoli Peninsula or at present abandon
Constantinople to the Turks'.

Churchill supported Curzon's view. The Turks must be allowed to
control Asia Minor; that had always been his view. But European
Turkey must remain under Allied control; on this he was insistent. The
Cabinet minutes recorded Churchill's remarks:

> The line of deep water separating Asia from Europe was a line of great
> significance, and we must make that line secure by every means within our
> power. If the Turks take the Gallipoli Peninsula and Constantinople, we
> shall have lost the whole fruits of our victory, and another Balkan war would
> be inevitable.

Lloyd George expressed his doubts that the Greek army had suffered
'a complete *débâcle*', and made no comment about the future of
Anatolia. But he agreed with both Curzon and Churchill that the

Turks must not be allowed to occupy the Gallipoli peninsula, telling the Cabinet:

> In no circumstances could we allow the Gallipoli Peninsula to be held by the Turks. It was the most important strategic position in the world and the closing of the Straits had prolonged the war by two years. It was inconceivable that we should allow the Turks to gain possession of the Gallipoli Peninsula and we should fight to prevent their doing so. The Peninsula was easily defended against a great Sea Power like ourselves and if it were in the occupation of a great Sea Power it would be impregnable. . . .

Lord Lee of Fareham, who had recently returned from a visit to Constantinople, pointed out that the Peninsula itself 'was occupied by French and Italian troops'. There were no British troops there, he said, although there was a small British detachment at Chanak, on the Asiatic shore of the Dardanelles. Lord Lee was afraid, as he told his colleagues, 'that the French might surrender the Peninsula to the Turks'. Lloyd George replied that this danger should be met 'by strengthening our naval forces' at the Dardanelles, and that, in order to guard Constantinople against attack, the Turks should be told that 'the British Fleet should certainly fire on them' if they tried to cross the Bosphorus.

On September 9 the first Turkish troops entered Smyrna, followed on September 10 by Mustafa Kemal himself. Mustafa Kemal's future intentions were unclear. On September 10 Sir Horace Rumbold telegraphed to Curzon from Constantinople that the Commander-in-Chief of the British Forces in Turkey, General Harington, possessed secret information 'to show that Nationalist forces are considering the question of occupation of the Asiatic shore of the Bosphorus and also Chanak'. Harington had no information about any threat either to the Gallipoli Peninsula or to Constantinople. Nevertheless, although both the Asiatic shore of the Bosphorus, and the town of Chanak, were in Asia Minor, Harington felt the Allies should not allow the Turks to encroach upon them. Both lay in the 'neutral zone' set up by the Allies in the Treaty of Sèvres as an area into which none but Allied troops could go. Rumbold reported Harington's proposal:

> He considered that measures should be taken immediately to guard against this action and asked for a demonstration of allied unity by despatch of small French and Italian contingents to show the flag in neutral zones now only held by British troops as well as for general assurances of allied solidarity in this matter. He also asked that allied governments should immediately intimate to Angora government that they would not tolerate any violation of neutral zone.

© Martin Gilbert

CONSTANTINOPLE AND THE

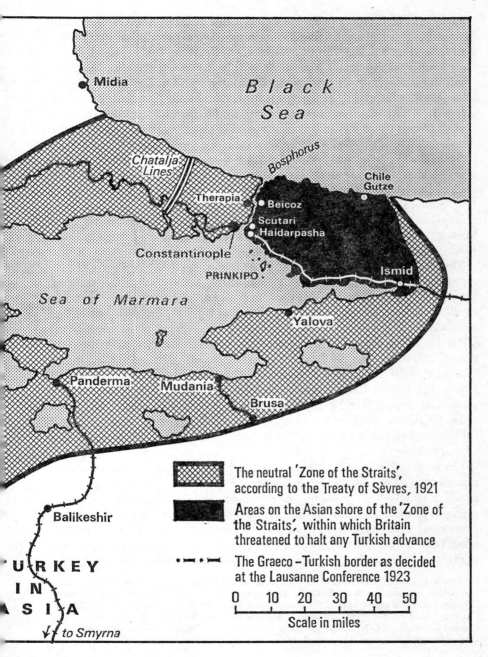

The neutral 'Zone of the Straits', according to the Treaty of Sèvres, 1921

Areas on the Asian shore of the 'Zone of the Straits', within which Britain threatened to halt any Turkish advance

The Graeco–Turkish border as decided at the Lausanne Conference 1923

Scale in miles

STRAITS, 1921–1922

General Harington's proposal was not discussed by the Cabinet until September 15. But in the five intervening days his advice gained in importance. The Turkish forces, victorious at Smyrna, turned towards the Greek units on the Sea of Marmora, within the 'neutral zone'. Even the small British force at Chanak seemed endangered. On September 11 the War Office informed Harington that he should evacuate Chanak altogether. The Cabinet of September 7 had expressed the hope that the British troops there would be transported to the European shore, for the direct defence of the Gallipoli Peninsula. Harington, however, preferred to keep them at Chanak, on the Asiatic shore, as a rear-guard, and to this the War Office agreed. That same day, Harington sent the British Officer in charge of the Ottoman War Office, Colonel Shuttleworth,[1] to take command of the Chanak force of a thousand men, and on September 12 the battleship *Ajax*, which had been ordered north from Smyrna, anchored in the Narrows between Chanak and the Gallipoli Peninsula.

Despite the uncertain situation in Anatolia, the Middle East Department continued to press Feisal to sign the Iraq Treaty. On September 11 Hubert Young informed Churchill that Feisal was now ready to agree to allow Britain to 'support an application by Iraq for membership of the League of Nations', once the Treaty was signed. This constituted effective, if retrospective, acceptance of the Mandate, and Young reported that Sir Percy Cox 'expresses himself satisfied'. But many observers feared that the victories of the Turkish Nationalists might revive Feisal's obstinacy, and stimulate nationalist favour throughout Iraq. On September 13 Archibald Sinclair wrote to Churchill: 'You must be full of anxiety for your tender Arab plant in Iraq with this furious storm raging on—and threatening to spread from—the Asia Minor horizon'.

On September 14 Churchill wrote to Lord Curzon that it would be another ten days or so before the renewed negotiations with Feisal could reach a conclusion. 'I should like also to know which way the cat is going to jump in the Dardanelles,' he wrote; and he went on: 'You must remember that my task has been to build bricks without straw and to blow bubbles without soap; and that at any rate our commitments are enormously reduced and that we are only riding at single anchor.' 'This

---

[1] Digby Inglis Shuttleworth, 1876–1948. Entered Army, 1896; Major, 1914. Lieutenant-Colonel, Mesopotamian Expeditionary Force, 1917–19. Commanded the 39th Infantry Brigade in the Caucasus, 1919–20. Colonel, 1920. President, Allied Commission of Control, Ottoman War Office, 1920–2. Commanded the 83rd Infantry Brigade, Chanak, 1922–3. Colonel Commandant, Jullundur Brigade, India, 1924–8. Major-General, 1929. Quartermaster General, Northern Command, India, 1930–2. Knighted, 1937.

wealth of metaphor,' Churchill added, 'may be reconciled if goodwill is used at each stage.'

Throughout September 13 and September 14 the Turkish Nationalist forces advanced towards the neutral zone, driving the Greeks before them in disorder. A few hours before the Cabinet met on September 15, Lloyd George wrote to Lord Curzon: 'I feel that we might do more to organize Balkan support,' both against Turkey, and to neutralize 'French & Italian intrigue'. 'The country,' he added, 'would be behind us in any steps we took to keep the Turk out of Europe. The Slavs & Roumanians would gladly supply troops.'

At the Cabinet on September 15, Worthington-Evans, with the help of a map, showed how 7,600 Allied troops in the neutral zone, including Constantinople, confronted 6,000 Turks near Ismid, 5,000 near Chanak and a further 40,000 moving northwards from Smyrna. Curzon spoke against any military attempt to halt the Turkish advance; Sir Horace Rumbold, he said, had warned in a telegram of September 13, that it would not be safe 'to try to bluff' Mustafa Kemal. But Lloyd George maintained his determination to keep the Turks out of Europe, if necessary by force, and Churchill expressed his entire agreement with Lloyd George. Like Lloyd George, he had been shocked by the Turkish slaughter of Armenians throughout 1921, and by the destruction of so much Greek life and property at Smyrna itself. During the discussion, Churchill told the Cabinet:

He thought the Government were justified in insisting that the Straits should be kept open and in refusing to be thrown out of Constantinople, even up to the point of having to maintain the position by force. This was not an impossible position to sustain. Liberal opinion would be a good deal influenced by the recent atrocities and conservative opinion would not be willing to see the British flag fired on.

Churchill hoped that if the British were to reinforce their troops at Constantinople with an extra Division, the French would do likewise. He also thought 'that Greece, Serbia and Roumania should all contribute forces for holding vital points'. This, he said, in addition to the Italian troops already there, 'would be to confront the Turkish forces with six flags instead of three flags, which was in itself something of a League of Nations'.

Lloyd George supported Churchill's argument. 'No country had an interest in the freedom of the Dardanelles,' he interrupted, 'comparable with that of Roumania.' Churchill then continued with an appeal for Australian, New Zealand and other imperial troops:

However fatigued it might be, he thought that the Empire would put up some force to preserve Gallipoli, with the graves of so many of its soldiers, and they might even be willing to do this without the co-operation of France. As regards Thrace, however, there would be a grave danger if the British Government were isolated and depicted as the sole enemy of Islam. Our safety in this matter was to keep as close as possible with France. He thought we ought to obtain as much as we could for Greece, but we ought not to be placed in the position of being the sole and isolated champion of Greek claims.

Austen Chamberlain agreed that 'diplomacy ought to have force behind it', and argued in favour both of British reinforcements, and of the bringing in of other Powers 'which were vitally concerned'. But he added a warning:

Previously the argument had been that if we held Gallipoli we could send forces into the Marmora, that these forces could dominate Constantinople and so dominate Turkey. Was this true? We were now at Constantinople and we did not appear to be able to dominate Turkey. The British Government could go to Brusa or Angora. Before embarking on this plan he would like to know whether we were to hold the position in the Straits permanently. . . .

Churchill replied that what he envisaged was 'some international force' which would remain in permanent occupation of the neutral zone, not only of the Gallipoli Peninsula on the European shore, but also Chanak and Ismid, which were both in Asiatic Turkey.

Lloyd George supported Churchill. He was 'convinced', he said, 'that the Allied forces must not be driven out of their position nor run away before Mustapha Kemal'. Britain, he insisted, had 'a supreme interest in the freedom of the Straits', and at once should ask the Serbs, the Rumanians and the Greeks what they 'were prepared to do' to help Britain. What he had in mind, he explained, was that by combining British, Greek, Rumanian and Serb forces 'a considerable Army would be available.' And he added: 'Mustapha Kemal ought to know that if he crossed the Straits with 60,000 rifles he would be met by 60,000—to say nothing of the British Fleet. The time had come to do something concrete.'

Lloyd George's determination was decisive. Only Curzon uttered a warning 'against building too enthusiastically on these proposals'. Hamar Greenwood suggested that Australia and New Zealand 'ought to be asked to co-operate', and Worthington-Evans agreed that any reinforcements that were sent 'should be Imperial in character'. Two battalions of British troops, he added, would be sent at once from Malta and Gibraltar, and to this the Cabinet agreed. In answer to a question from Lloyd George, as to 'what transport was available to the Turks for crossing the Straits and the Sea of Marmora', Lord Lee of Fareham pointed out that he had given orders to the Naval Commander-in-Chief, Vice-Admiral Brock,[1] to prevent the Turks from crossing'.

The Cabinet of September 15 were unanimous that the Neutral Zone must be defended by force, and instructed Churchill to draft a telegram which Lloyd George could then send to the Dominions informing them of this decision, and seeking their support 'in the despatch of military reinforcement'. In his draft Churchill described the advance of the Turkish forces, and he continued:

These armies, which have so far not had any serious resistance to encounter from disheartened Greeks, are estimated at between sixty and seventy thousand men, but timely precautions are imperative. Grave consequences in India and among other Mohammedan populations for which we are responsible might result from a defeat or from a humiliating exodus of the Allies from Constantinople. . . .

The announcement of an offer from all or any of the Dominions to send a contingent even of moderate size would undoubtedly exercise in itself a most favourable influence on the situation.

Churchill took his draft telegram to Lloyd George shortly before seven o'clock in the evening, and Lloyd George approved it without alteration. The telegram was then ciphered, and shortly before midnight copies were sent to each of the Dominion Prime Ministers.

The Cabinet of September 15 had also decided that the public should be told of the nature, and gravity, of the Turkish situation. That evening Churchill discussed the crisis with Lloyd George at 10 Downing Street, and after lunch on September 16 the two men agreed upon a communiqué to the Press, which was issued in time for the evening papers. The British Government, they declared, 'regard the effective and permanent freedom of the Straits as a vital necessity for the sake of which they are prepared to make exertions'. The British aim, the communiqué continued, was a Conference at which efforts would be made 'to secure a stable peace with Turkey', but, the communiqué added:

---

[1] Osmond de Beauvoir Brock, 1869–1947. Entered the Navy, as a cadet, in 1874. Assistant Director of Naval Mobilization, 1910. Rear-Admiral, 1915. Served at the battle of Jutland, 1916. Chief of Staff to the Commander-in-Chief, Grand Fleet, 1916–18. Knighted, 1917. Deputy Chief of the Naval Staff, 1919–21. Succeeded Sir John de Robeck as Commander-in-Chief Mediterranean, May 1922. Admiral, 1924. Commander-in-Chief, Portsmouth, 1926–9. Admiral of the Fleet, 1929.

. . . such a Conference cannot embark upon its labours, still less carry them through with the slightest prospect of success, while there is any question of the Kemalist forces attacking the neutral zones by which Constantinople, the Bosphorus, and the Dardanelles are now protected.

The British and French Governments have instructed their High Commissioners at Constantinople to notify Mustapha Kemal and the Angora Government that these neutral zones established under the flags of the three Great Powers must be respected.

The Press communiqué went on to warn that 'it would be futile and dangerous, in view of the excited mood and extravagant claims of the Kemalists, to trust simply to diplomatic action'. And it continued:

Adequate force must be available to guard the freedom of the Straits and defend the deep-water line between Europe and Asia against a violent and hostile Turkish aggression. That the Allies should be driven out of Constantinople by the forces of Mustapha Kemal would be an event of the most disastrous character, producing, no doubt, far-reaching reactions throughout all Moslem countries, and not only through all Moslem countries but through all the States defeated in the late war, who would be profoundly encouraged by the spectacle of the undreamed-of-successes that have attended the efforts of the comparatively weak Turkish forces.

Moreover, the reappearance of the victorious Turk on the European shore would provoke a situation of the gravest character throughout the Balkans, and very likely lead to bloodshed on a large scale in regions already cruelly devastated. It is the duty of the Allies of the late war to prevent this great danger, and to secure the orderly and peaceful conditions in and around the Straits which will allow a conference to conduct its deliberations with dignity and efficiency and so alone reach a permanent settlement.

The communiqué then explained that Britain had appealed to Rumania, Serbia, Yugoslavia and Greece to prevent the 'deadly consequences' of Turkish control of the Straits, and of a possible 'union' of Turkey and Bulgaria. 'The whole trade of the Danube flowing into the Black Sea is likewise subject to strangulation,' it warned, 'if the Straits are closed.' The Government, it added, had also invited the Dominions to send contingents of troops 'in the defence of interests for which they have already made enormous sacrifices and of soil which is hallowed by immortal memories of the Anzacs'. Orders had already been given, the communiqué concluded, to Sir Charles Harington and to the British fleet, 'to oppose by every means any infraction of the neutral zones by the Turks or any attempt by them to cross to the European shore'.

This Press communiqué, issued on September 16, was published in the Canadian, Australian and New Zealand Press before Lloyd George's secret telegram to the Dominion Prime Ministers had been decoded by them. The result was a feeling in the Dominions, and particularly in Australia and Canada, that they were being hustled unfairly into a commitment. The Australian Prime Minister, William Hughes,[1] replied: 'In a good cause, we are prepared to venture our all; in a bad one, not a single man.' The Canadian Prime Minister, Mackenzie King,[2] refused to send any Canadian troops. The South African Prime Minister, General Smuts, was silent. Only New Zealand and Newfoundland responded favourably to Lloyd George's appeal. In Britain the tone of the Press communiqué was widely thought to be too bellicose, and provoked, particularly among the Conservatives, the fear that Lloyd George was leading the country precipitately into war. On September 18 the *Daily Mail* demanded in its main headline: 'STOP THIS NEW WAR!' and added that the Press communiqué was 'deliberately designed to promote a most disastrous and costly war'. On September 19 the paper told its readers that not a single Dominion soldier should be allowed to lose his life 'in order that Mr Winston Churchill may make a new Gallipoli'.

At Chanak itself, British military forces accumulated. On September 15 Admiral Brock had reached the Dardanelles on board his flagship, *Iron Duke*, and two days later the battleship *Marlborough* arrived. The five seaplanes of the carrier *Pegasus* carried out daily air reconnaissances over the neutral zone, and Colonel Shuttleworth was superseded by a more senior officer, Major-General Marden.[3]

When the Cabinet met at noon on September 18, Worthington-Evans told his colleagues that in General Harington's opinion 'prompt action by us might have a deterrent effect' upon Kemal. Harington had added that if the French 'were sincere in their promises', of support at Constantinople itself, he was hopeful of holding out in the City 'for three or four weeks'. Only the Chief of the Imperial General Staff, Lord Cavan, was pessimistic. At Chanak, he said, only a thousand British

[1] William Morris Hughes, 1864–1952. Educated in Wales and London. Emigrated to Australia, 1884. A Labour MP in the 1st Federal Australian Parliament. Prime Minister of Australia, 1915–23. Australian Delegate to the Paris Peace Conference, 1919. Minister for External Affairs, 1921–3; for Health and Repatriation, 1934–7; for External Affairs, 1937–9; for Industry, 1939–40. Attorney-General, 1939–40. Minister for the Navy, 1940–1.
[2] William Lyon Mackenzie King, 1874–1950. Born in Ontario, Canada. Fellow in Political Science, Harvard University, 1897–1900. Editor of the *Labour Gazette*, Canada, 1900–8. Liberal MP in the Canadian Parliament, 1908–49. Leader of the Liberal Party of Canada, 1919. Leader of the Opposition, 1919–21. Prime Minister of Canada, 1921–6, 1926–30 and 1935–48. Secretary of State for External Affairs, 1935–46. Order of Merit, 1947.
[3] Thomas Owen Marden, 1866–1951. Entered Army, 1886. Commanded the 114th Infantry Brigade, 1915–17; the 6th Division, 1917–19. Major-General Commanding the British Troops in Constantinople, 1920–3. Commanded the Welsh Division, 1923–7.

troops aced as many as 52,000 Turks. 'The Kemalists,' he warned, 'could push that small force into the sea within a fortnight. If we lost Chanak the troops in Constantinople would be cut off.' To attempt to reconquer Chanak would then mean 'a big war', and the use of at least 300,000 troops. But Lloyd George replied that Cavan's estimate of the Turkish strength was 'far in excess' of what Harington had reported, and that he shared Harington's view 'that if it was seen that we were taking immediate action to reinforce our troops . . . Kemal would probably be deterred from attacking us'.

The discussion turned to the means of finding extra troops to send to Chanak. Churchill informed his colleagues that if the situation demanded it, the British troops in Iraq could be 'withdrawn altogether' and sent to the Dardanelles. He considered it 'essential', he added, 'that our forces should be increased at the earliest possible moment so as to prevent their being rushed by the Kemalists'. He also urged that heavy howitzers should be mounted on the Gallipoli Peninsula 'at once'. Lloyd George supported him. Such action, he said, 'would be very important from a diplomatic point of view' and would impress on the French Britain's determination not to retreat.

The Cabinet met again five hours later. The First Lord of the Admiralty, Lord Lee of Fareham, stated his belief 'that the Navy would be able to keep open the Dardanelles even if the Turks were at Chanak'. A further thousand British troops, he said, 'fully equipped with ammunition and supplies', would reach Chanak in eleven days' time, on September 29. Sir Robert Horne was insistent that if the Kemalists advanced into the neutral zone 'it was an act of war', and Lloyd George declared that 'it was desirable that it should be made clear that we were serious, and it would be a good thing if it became generally known in Constantinople, of the action we were taking to send troops, aeroplanes and ships. . . .' Later in the discussion Lloyd George expressed his belief that 'by a show of force and firmness it was possible that fighting might be prevented'. At his suggestion, the Cabinet agreed to send three more battleships to the eastern Mediterranean.

Churchill made only one intervention at the evening Cabinet of September 18, pointing out that there would be no collision between Turkish and British troops when the Kemalists crossed into the neutral zone, but only when they reached the outskirts of Chanak itself. And he added: 'It was important that Kemal should be informed that the advance of his troops into the neutral zone would be regarded as a hostile act, so that our aerial forces could act against the Kemalist troops the moment they infringed the zone.'

During October 18 the French Government announced that its own contingent of troops, both at Chanak and Ismid, would be withdrawn. The Italians immediately followed the French example. The French High Commissioner, General Pellé,[1] had left Constantinople on the previous day for Smyrna, without informing the other Allies, and with the intention of entering into separate negotiations with Kemal. But General Harington was determined not to allow the French defection to affect Britain's position at Chanak. On September 19, as soon as the French and Italian troops had withdrawn, he telegraphed to General Marden:

> You should hold Chanak as long as possible with the forces I have available. I am communicating the decision to the Government. In my opinion in view of the French withdrawing from Chanak, Kemal will challenge British policy there. In all probability he will stop to reflect, if you stop him there with naval support. Your stand there may avert further trouble.

The Cabinet met again on the morning of September 19. Churchill reported that the Government of Newfoundland 'had indicated their support of the attitude taken up by the British Government'. Lord Birkenhead persuaded his colleagues to agree to make the news public. Lord Curzon, who had just returned from Paris, reported the gloomy news that French opinion was 'hardening' against any conflict with the Turks. And he added a note of warning. 'The Turks,' he said, 'once back in Constantinople, would obey no law or regulations as to the size of their Armies, and Eastern Thrace would become to all intents and purposes a Turkish possession.'

Most Cabinet Ministers were in an inflexible mood. Austen Chamberlain said that if the withdrawal of French support meant the loss of Constantinople, Britain was still determined 'to hold Gallipoli if necessary alone'. Lord Lee of Fareham remarked that he hoped Britain would not evacuate Constantinople 'unless absolutely necessary', and added that France 'had long been striving for the dominant position at Constantinople'. Churchill struck a note of warning and of caution, telling his colleagues:

> . . . all our misfortunes had arisen in the past from trying to do that for which we had not got the strength. By trying to hold both places with insufficient troops it might lead to a military disaster which would be still

---

[1] Maurice Cesar Joseph Pellé, 1863–1924. Served before 1914 in the French Artillery, and as Military Attaché in Berlin. On the Staff of General Joffre, 1914–16. Commanded the 15th Corps on the western front, 1917–18. Head of the French Military Mission to Czechoslovakia, 1919–20. High Commissioner in Constantinople, 1921–2, and in Syria, 1923–4.

more disastrous for our prestige. The Turks would always hate whatever European power was dominant at Constantinople.

Later in the discussion, Churchill was able to report more news from the Dominions. New Zealand had joined Newfoundland in offering to send forces to Gallipoli. But, he added, the Canadian Government had sent a cautious message, stating that because of 'public opinion' in Canada, parliamentary approval would be needed 'before definite assistance could be sent'. Churchill's colleagues agreed with his suggestion that the Canadian Government should be told at once 'that it had not been considered necessary in London to summon Parliament, and it was hoped the necessity for this would be averted'.

Towards the end of the meeting, Austen Chamberlain suggested that it was in Britain's 'vital interest' to retain command 'of the Straits of Gallipoli'. In answer to a question from Lloyd George, Lord Cavan said that 20,000 troops would be sufficient to defend the Gallipoli Peninsula from any Turkish land attack across the Bulair lines, assuming the Turks had already entered Constantinople and were in control of Eastern Thrace.

General Harington had complete confidence in the Cabinet's policy. Nor did he feel the need for Dominion troops. On September 20 he telegraphed to the War Office:

If we continue to show our determination, I am of opinion that the British will be able to carry through the task without them so that I do not consider you need feel concern for their action. According to my information his (Kemal's) ministers are being summoned to Smyrna to-morrow for a conference. Evidently this is to decide whether he will take England on with her Dominions. My own opinion is they will not dare to do so.

The Australian refusal to send troops to Chanak was a serious public setback for the policy decided upon by the Cabinet on September 15. During September 20 Lloyd George asked Churchill to send a second appeal, this time in his own name. That afternoon Churchill sent Hughes a long telegram, apologizing for the appearance of the public communiqué before the arrival of the secret telegram, explaining that the mistake had only happened because of the suddenness of the crisis, and appealing to Hughes to change his mind. Australian troops, Churchill explained, were needed as part of an imperial force. And he concluded:

You will remember how often it is said that the Great War itself might have been averted if Great Britain had taken up a plain and clear position at the beginning of the fateful week. The Prime Minister therefore, as result of Cabinet decision, sent you the telegram you have received. . . .

Hughes was still not convinced that Australian interests were at stake, and refused to send any troops to Turkey. A second appeal to Mackenzie King was likewise unsuccessful. But the Cabinet persevered in its policy, and on September 20 Harington was instructed that the defence of Chanak was his first duty.

Lord Curzon was in Paris on September 20. In a stormy interview, Poincaré informed him that 'French public opinion would not admit of a shot being fired against a Turk,' and that as far as France was concerned, the Turks 'could cross to Europe when they pleased'.

A Conference of seven Ministers, together with their senior advisers, met at 10 Downing Street on the evening of September 20.[1] A telegram was read out from Lord Curzon, to the effect that the French Government were not prepared to give any military assistance against the Kemalists. Churchill spoke strongly against any weakening of the British position. There could be 'no greater blow to British prestige', he declared, 'than the hurried evacuation of Chanak in face of Turkish threats'. It was, he said, 'most desirable that Chanak should be held, even at the expense of British evacuation of Ismid and Constantinople'. Lloyd George agreed that 'the threat to Chanak was a blow to Great Britain alone', and that it should be held 'even if we had to re-inforce from Ismid'. Churchill then told his colleagues that he had received a telegram from New Zealand, to the effect that 5,000 New Zealanders had already volunteered for service. Both Austen Chamberlain and Churchill spoke of the need to warn the Kemalists not to march on Chanak. The meeting then adjourned.

Three hours later, at nine-thirty, the seven Ministers met again, to hear a further telegram from Curzon, in which the Foreign Secretary not only reported on the continuing French refusal to make a stand against the Kemalists, but added his own advice, that Britain should herself 'resist from any action likely to provoke immediate hostilities'. But Lloyd George insisted that all steps should be taken 'to expedite as much as possible the arrival in Gallipoli' of reinforcements from Egypt.

During the meeting, at Lloyd George's request, Churchill drafted a telegram to General Harington, which he read out to the Conference.

[1] The seven Ministers were Lloyd George, Austen Chamberlain, Worthington-Evans, Sir Robert Horne, Lord Peel, Lord Lee of Fareham and Churchill. The advisers present were Lord Cavan (Chief of the Imperial General Staff), Sir Hugh Trenchard (Chief of the Air Staff), Sir Ernle Chatfield (Assistant Chief of the Naval Staff), Sir William Tyrrell (Assistan Under-Secretary of State, Foreign Office) and Sir Edward Grigg.

The telegram was approved by all present. In it, Harington, was informed that Chanak was 'of more importance than Constantinople or Ismid'; that he should move his troops and guns accordingly; and that he should warn Mustafa Kemal 'against any violation of the neutral zones'. If a serious collision were to occur at Chanak, the telegram continued, 'we shall take that as a definite challenge to the power of the British Empire, mobilise our two divisions and call for volunteers to reinforce and supplement them'; Australia, New Zealand and even Greece would be asked to give military support; and although Greek help could not entirely be relied upon, 'if we are forced to fight we will take all help we can get from any quarter'.

On the morning of September 21 the *Daily Mail* demanded: 'GET OUT OF CHANAK', and reported that 'Stop the War' meetings had been held in London and the provinces on the previous evening. During the morning a deputation of thirty members of the T.U.C. General Council went to 10 Downing Street to protest to Lloyd George against any possible war with Turkey.[1] The Cabinet met as soon as the deputation had gone. Churchill reported that a thousand men of the Royal Air Force—'for the most part highly skilled mechanics and unarmed'—were on their way back to England from Mesopotamia, and could, if necessary 'be sent in as reinforcements'. Austen Chamberlain pointed out that even the Trade Union deputation had agreed that the Straits must be defended, in order to keep the war out of Europe, although they had made it clear 'that the country would not be willing to make any military exertions in respect of Thrace'.

Lloyd George, however, was determined both to keep the Turkish forces out of Europe, and to defend the neutral zone. On September 22 he appointed Churchill chairman of a Cabinet Committee to exercise day-to-day control over the military, naval and air force movements. The two other members of the Committee were the First Lord of the Admiralty, Lord Lee of Fareham, and the Secretary of State for War, Sir Laming Worthington-Evans. They held their first meeting on the evening of September 22. The First Sea Lord, Lord Beatty, who was present, had circulated copies of a letter he had received that afternoon from Sir Maurice Hankey. The letter read:

. . . the Prime Minister's view is that no Kemalist forces must be allowed to cross the salt water. The moment a Kemalist gets afloat he must be dealt

[1] The TUC deputation chose as its three spokesmen J. H. Thomas (General Secretary of the National Union of Railwaymen and later Secretary of State for the Colonies), Ben Tillett (the dockers' leader) and Margaret Bondfield (National Union of General and Municipal Workers, and in 1929 the first woman Cabinet Minister).

with. If he believes that there is danger of Kemalist forces crossing the Straits, the Admiral must use his discretion to take any action which he deems essential to prevent this.

The Chief of the Imperial General Staff, Lord Cavan, told Churchill's Committee that the Turks had lost their main advantages 'by delay', and that Harington should be able 'to hold his own' for four or five weeks. 'Ultimately however,' Lord Cavan concluded, 'it was difficult to see how Mustapha Kemal's pretensions could be disposed of if our troops remained on the defensive . . . it would be necessary sooner or later to defeat his army, and perhaps even to advance and to occupy his capital, for which very large forces would be required.'

On September 22 Churchill wrote to Lloyd George to inform him that the War Office had agreed to send General Harington substantial reinforcements of heavy artillery, which would reach the town in fourteen or fifteen days. The heaviest weapons were sixteen 8-inch howitzers, which, Churchill wrote, 'will be very formidable indeed'. Churchill added that one thousand airmen, at that moment on their way to Iraq on board the *Braemar Castle*, could be diverted to Constantinople 'in two or three days', and could keep order in the city, thus releasing the Irish Guards for service in the war zone. But, he warned, the airmen were 'badly wanted in Mesopotamia and should be allowed to resume their journey at the very earliest moment'.

On September 23, a detachment of some 200 Turkish troops had crossed into the neutral zone south of Chanak, and moved to the village of Eren Keui, less than ten miles from Chanak. Advancing closer to Chanak, they soon came within sight of the British troops, but did not open fire. When asked to withdraw, they refused. A further 800 Turks rode up to the British position. The British, without firing, then withdrew, behind their fortified positions. The Turks did not follow them. 'The situation was quite unanticipated,' Colonel Shuttleworth telegraphed to General Harington later that day. 'Peaceful penetration by armed men who did not wish to fight, and yet refused either to withdraw or to halt, had not been foreseen.' On September 24 Harington replied that the British forces must avoid any 'unnecessary' engagements with Turkish troops.

Churchill's Cabinet Committee met again on September 23. During the discussion Lord Lee raised the question of public opinion:

LORD LEE stated that it had been suggested at the Cabinet that it was necessary to instruct the public as to the significance of the Chanak position to secure the freedom of the Straits. Several newspapers which had not been unfriendly to the policy of the Government were now urging the abandonment of the Chanak position. It was clear that they did not understand the need for the military occupation of Chanak to ensure the freedom of navigation of the Straits. They seemed to think that naval action would be sufficient to keep the Straits open.

MR CHURCHILL remarked that there was now general agreement that although the loss of Chanak would not close the Straits to ships of war, it would fatally compromise the use of the Straits by merchant shipping. The freedom of navigation of the Straits cannot exist with the Turks in military possession of the Asiatic shore of the Dardanelles. He requested that the Naval and Military authorities should confer and draw up a brief communiqué, 400 to 500 words, explaining the military need for holding Chanak.

On September 23 Curzon, Poincaré and the Italian Ambassador to France, Count Sforza,[1] announced, in a joint Note issued from Paris, that they 'viewed with favour' the Turkish claim to European Turkey, including Adrianople, and that as soon as a peace treaty had been signed, all Allied troops and administrators would leave Constantinople, In the interim, they promised, if the Turks respected the neutral zone, no Greek troopships would be allowed in the Sea of Marmora.

This 'Paris Note' of September 23 was at once telegraphed to the Turks. But it was some days before there was any reply.

The Turks continued to confront the British troops at Chanak without violence. Meanwhile, the British force there was being strengthened daily. On September 25 a thousand British troops arrived at Chanak from Egypt, thus doubling the size of the garrison. In London, the *Daily Mail* kept up its barrage of dissent. The people of Britain, it declared on September 25, 'will not stand another avoidable war of any sort, and still less a wanton war'.[2]

During the day the Turkish forces returned to Eren Keui. 'Here they remained,' Churchill later recalled in *The World Crisis*, 'contumaciously

---

[1] Count Carlo Sforza, 1873–1952. Entered the Italian Diplomatic Service, 1896. Minister to China, 1911–15; to the Serbian Government in Exile, 1915–18. Italian Representative in Albania and Corfu, 1915–18. Italian High Commissioner, Constantinople, October 1918–June 1919. Minister for Foreign Affairs, June 1920–July 1921. Ambassador to France, February–October 1922. In October 1922 he refused an offer to join Mussolini's Government. Leader of the Democratic Opposition in the Italian Parliament, 1922–6. Minister without Portfolio in Marshal Badoglio's Government, 1944. President of the Consultative Assembly, 1945–6. Minister for Foreign Affairs, 1947–51.

[2] The *Daily Mail* criticisms were discussed at a Conference of Ministers on September 27. Sir Laming Worthington-Evans was instructed to send a personal letter to the Editor 'informing him that he had been apprised by General Harington that the morale of the troops in the Near East was being affected by the tenor of these articles'. The Editor was to be warned 'that the Government would have to take steps to secure that the military position was not prejudiced'. He was also to be reminded 'that the Turkish agents were making use of these articles for the purpose of Nationalist propaganda'.

and encroachingly, but with much politeness and parleying; and in undoubted violation of the neutral zone.' That same day, in a personal
letter to Archibald Sinclair, Churchill reflected on the crisis, and
explained his own position:

Thank God that awful pro-Greek policy against which we have so long
inveighed has come to an end. We have paid an enormously heavy price for
nothing. However, at the very end I have had to throw in my lot with L.G. in
order to try to make some sort of front against what would otherwise have
been a complete Turkish walk-over and the total loss of all the fruits of the
Great War in this quarter. They make a great deal of fuss about the com-
munique which I drafted for the P.M. at his request and which he issued. All
the same, I am convinced, that if we had not got a move on there would be no
question of the Turks accepting the terms we have now offered, and even
now it is possible that they will prove uncontrollable.

General Harington was anxious to negotiate a settlement direct with
Mustafa Kemal. Both he and Sir Horace Rumbold believed that the
Paris Note of September 23 would be acceptable to the Turks, and make
a military confrontation unnecessary. On September 26 Harington telegraphed to Lord Cavan: 'Losing a lot of lives hanging on is what I want
to guard against. . . . Why not start at once and give Turkey Constantinople and Maritza . . . and so end it all.' Harington urged Cavan
to remember that 'Turks are within sight of their goal and are naturally
elated.' That same day, Sir Horace Rumbold wrote to Lancelot Oliphant[1] at the Foreign Office:

Brock, Harington and I have throughout had in mind the absolute necessity of avoiding any action which might lead to war. We feel the last thing our
country wants is to have another war and that the average man does not care
a straw whether Eastern Thrace and Adrianople belong to the Greeks or
Turks. In my view both are absolute barbarians and have recently proved it.
We imagine our country *would* fight for the freedom of the Straits, but for
nothing else.

When Churchill's Committee met on the evening of September 26,
Churchill himself spoke of the possible meeting between Harington and
Mustafa Kemal, and of the effect such a meeting would have on the
continuing flow of British reinforcements to the East. Churchill told his
Committee:

[1] Lancelot Oliphant, 1881–1965. Entered Foreign Office, 1903. 3rd Secretary, Constantinople, 1905–6; at Teheran, 1909–11. Returned to the Foreign Office, 1912; Assistant
Secretary, 1920; Counsellor, 1923; Assistant Under-Secretary of State, 1927–36; Deputy
Under-Secretary of State, 1936–9. Knighted, 1931. Ambassador to Belgium, 1939; captured
by the Germans and interned, June 1940–September 1941. Resumed his duties as Ambassador
to Belgium (to the Government in Exile, in London), 1941–5.

It appeared that the meeting between General Harington and Kemal could not commence for another 48 hours; at this meeting no offer to suspend despatch of reinforcements should be made but Kemal was likely to demand that no further British reinforcements should be despatched to the Near East as a condition of his attending the projected Peace Conference. His demand could hardly arrive before 29th or 30th September and by this latter date practically all our available combatant reinforcements would be on the sea. We could accordingly offer that no further fighting units would be forwarded from British ports except those already at sea, and the names of the ships conveying these reinforcements could be specified if desired.

Churchill went on to say that he approved of the idea of the despatch of reinforcements becoming an object for negotiation, but that the demand 'must come from Kemal'. In the meantime, he added, 'H.M. ships conveying reinforcements should proceed with all possible despatch.'

General Harington approved of these efforts. 'It was awfully good of you and Winston to switch off the "Braemar Castle",' he wrote to Trenchard on September 27. And he continued: 'My trouble is that Mustafa has got 3 parties inside my neutral zone at Chanak, and I want to get them out! I am using every form of persuasion for the moment, but if that fails, a combined force—Navy, Army and Air Force—will be compelled to descend upon them. However, I think we shall do it by threat of force in the end.'

On September 27 the seaplane carrier *Pegasus* was joined by the *Argus*, with six seaplanes and four fighters. That day a Committee of Ministers met in Churchill's room at the Colonial Office. The five Ministers present were Austen Chamberlain, who took the Chair, Curzon, Churchill, Worthington-Evans and Lord Lee of Fareham. Worthington-Evans read out a telegram from General Harington 'in which it is reported that he is now in touch with Kemal Pasha', with a view to arranging a meeting. In answer to a question by Churchill, the Chief of the Imperial General Staff, Lord Cavan, spoke pessimistically of Britain's ability to hold Chanak if it were actually attacked.

Lord Cavan's advice was to withdraw all but one battalion from Chanak to the Gallipoli Peninsula, and, if politically possible, to withdraw from Chanak altogether. 'If it were decided to evacuate Chanak now,' he said, 'we might claim that our action was a "beau geste", and explain that our object was to avoid the risk of a collision. . . .'

Austen Chamberlain was opposed to Lord Cavan's suggestions, which were, he said, 'based on purely military considerations'. He was of the opinion 'that we could not now withdraw from Chanak with credit to ourselves. . . . He would regard such a withdrawal as an humiliation to the British Empire.' Churchill remarked that he 'concurred in Mr Chamberlain's views', but he went on to suggest a possible point of compromise and negotiation. If it were possible, he said, 'to ensure the immunity of the neutral zone by withdrawing from Chanak, we should accept such an arrangement at once. . . .' He doubted, however, that Kemal himself would agree so easily to leave the shores of the Dardanelles, seeing that his troops had arrived there 'without firing a shot'.

The discussion then turned to the military situation at Chanak itself. In reply to a question from Churchill, Lord Cavan said that the Turks had a force of 23,000, the British a force of 3,500. A further 5,000 British troops were due to arrive by October 9.

Lord Lee of Fareham felt that these figures gave too pessimistic a picture, and urged his colleagues not to talk of abandoning Chanak. Encouraged by Lord Lee's statement, Churchill remarked 'that it clearly emerged that the forces at Chanak could hold out until reinforcements arrived'. It was desirable also, he said, 'not to exaggerate the power of Kemal's artillery'. Although Kemal undoubtedly had some 8 in. and 6 in. field guns, 'his supply of ammunition was probably limited and the difficulty of transporting ammunition across broken country to the shores of the Dardanelles must be very great'.

The 'inner' Cabinet met that evening at 10 Downing Street. Churchill told his colleagues that he was 'very uncomfortable' at the weakness of the Chanak garrison. He wanted to establish a clear sequence of military priorities. If both Chanak and Constantinople had to be evacuated, he pointed out, 'the whole of the British forces' in Turkey could then concentrate at Gallipoli. This plan, he said, 'involved no serious risk, and had the very great merit that it would mystify, confuse and hold up the enemy'.

Lloyd George rejected Churchill's argument. He wanted Chanak to be defended. He would not accept the theory 'that a 4 mile perimeter was indefensible'; the Navy, he said, could make the coast roads leading to the perimeter 'unusable'.

Churchill still feared that the Chanak position was a dangerous one to maintain. But Lloyd George was insistent that it should be held, telling his colleagues 'that the evacuation of Chanak, having regard to all that had happened, would be the greatest loss of prestige which could possibly be inflicted on the British Empire'. If Britain had to 'scuttle' from Chanak, he declared, 'our credit would entirely disappear'. But Churchill added quickly that there was certainly one more disastrous event than evacuation, and that was 'a British defeat at Chanak involving compulsory abandonment of that position'.

The discussion turned almost entirely upon whether or not Chanak could be held. Lord Beatty spoke of the 'very effective help' which the Navy would be able to give. There was some discussion about calling in Greek help to reinforce the Chanak garrison, and it was agreed that Worthington-Evans should telegraph to the British Military Attaché in Athens, General Hoare-Nairne,[1] 'asking him to report with the least possible delay as to the number and character of the Greek troops available in Athens, Thrace and elsewhere, and to give the appreciation of their probable fighting qualities.' As soon as the Cabinet was over, Curzon returned to the Foreign Office and wrote to Austen Chamberlain:

I was very much alarmed at the idea put forward by Winston & the P.M. that we should once again seek the precarious and as I think worthless alliance of the Greeks, and very likely find ourselves once more at war with Turkey—with Greece alone on our side.

Nothing in my opinion would reconcile the country to such a development, and it would I think bring about the fall of the Govt.

It would also destroy at one blow the allied unity which I was sent to Paris to endeavour to rebuild.

During the evening of September 27, news reached London that Kemal had rejected the British demand to withdraw his troops from the neutral zone. At ten that evening Churchill telegraphed to the Dominion Prime Ministers: 'The reply is most unsatisfactory. Mustafa Kemal ignores the neutral zone and he affirms that Turkish troops are following up the defeated Greek army.' In rejecting the British demand, Kemal had accused the British of dropping bombs near his troops. 'So far as we know,' Churchill told the Dominion Prime Ministers, 'this is untrue.' Kemal also declared that Greek warships were anchored off Constantinople; but this too, Churchill telegraphed, was false, as all Greek warships had, according to Harington, left the Bosphorus. A further complication, Churchill added, was that a revolution had broken out in Greece, and that Venizelos, Kemal's determined adversary, was once again striving to return to power.

That night Churchill dined with Lloyd George at Sir Philip Sassoon's house in Park Lane. He was angry at Kemal's rejection of the British terms. Sir Maurice Hankey, who was present at the dinner, recorded

---

[1] Edward Spencer Nairne, 1869–1958. 2nd Lieutenant, Royal Artillery, 1888. Assumed the surname Hoare-Nairne, 1910. Lieutenant-Colonel, 1914. Brigadier-General, 1915. Mentioned in despatches six times, 1914–18. Military Attaché, Athens and Belgrade, 1920–3.

the conversation in his diary: 'We talked late into the night. Winston, hitherto a strong Turko-phile had swung round at the threat to his beloved Dardanelles and become violently Turko-phobe and even Phil-Hellene.' Lloyd George was also stimulated by the news of Kemal's refusal, and Venizelos' apparent success. As Hankey went on to record:

All the talk was of war. By violating the neutral zone the Turks had released us of the already hated condition re Eastern Thrace in the Paris invitation to a conference. We were not strong enough to keep them from crossing the Bosphorus into Europe. So let them into Europe, we holding meanwhile to Chanak to enable us to keep open the Dardanelles. In Thrace the Turks would come up, not against Constantine's tired, ill-commanded and dispirited army, but against a national resistance, inspired by Venizelos and the revolution, invigorated by having the British Empire at its back, and with its old Generals restored. By the time Mustapha Kemal is beaten and held we shall be strong enough to move up from Chanak to Ismid, where, with a relatively small force we shall cut his communications and compel a humiliating surrender. Such was the burden of the talk.

Three times on September 28, Conferences of Ministers met to discuss the crisis. That morning they had received confirmation of the military and naval revolution in Greece, the purpose of which, it now emerged, was to ensure that Eastern Thrace did not fall into Turkish hands without a fierce fight. Lloyd George took the leading part in all three discussions. 'If necessary,' he declared at the morning meeting, 'we should defend the Dardanelles alone. We had made a public announcement to that effect, and if we receded from that position we should humiliate ourselves before the whole world, Eastern and Western.' Lord Birkenhead then spoke forcefully in support of Lloyd George's attitude, and Sir Laming Worthington-Evans asked that mobilization 'should not be unduly delayed'. Churchill said little. When, at the second meeting, the discussion turned upon what part Britain should play in keeping the Greek and Turkish forces apart in Eastern Thrace, he was prompted to make a formal statement of protest 'pointing out that his desire was to bring this war to a close and to avoid the state of equipoise and the policy of "keeping the ring" '.

As a result of these three Ministerial Conferences, General Harington was informed that he was free to 'withdraw the British forces from Constantinople' if, by so doing, it would assist in the defence of 'Chanak or Gallipoli'. It was also agreed to telegraph to Harington 'promising full support if he is compelled to fight'. During the day a series of decisions had been reached, each of which was intended to persuade Kemal to respect the neutral zone. If he did not 'retire' from the zone at once, Sir

Horace Rumbold was told, then the British would cancel a promise of the Paris Note of September 23, forbidding Greek warships to enter the Sea of Marmora.

Late on the evening of September 28, Churchill telegraphed an account of the day's discussions to the Dominion Prime Ministers. His telegram was in three parts. Part one read:

Situation at Chanak continues extremely critical and unsatisfactory. Yesterday at 3.15 p.m. a Turkish column was moving out of Erenkeui apparently to seize the heights above Chanak and the officer in command of Chanak was authorised by General Harington to fire upon it if it would not turn back. We do not know yet what has happened. Apparently Kemal himself has gone to Angora and he is not expected to give an answer to the allied note for a week. His forces meanwhile are concentrating steadily towards both the Ismid and Chanak neutral zones, and at any moment fresh violations may take place.

Part two of Churchill's telegram referred to the events in Greece, and their implications:

The Greek revolution is a new and formidable complication. The main object of the Army and Navy revolutionaries appears to be to make a strenuous fight for Thrace, and Greece will be a very different proposition from what she was under Constantine if they recall Venizelos and put him at the helm. Kemal on the other hand will be more anxious than ever to break through into Europe in order to smash the Greeks before they can reorganise. Events, therefore, seem to me to cause increasing anxiety.

Part three of the telegram set out the British Government's decision, confirmed at the three Ministerial Conferences that day, not to abandon the Asiatic shore of the Dardanelles:

We are still absolutely determined to defend ourselves at Chanak where we are growing stronger each day. General Harington is being told that if he is seriously attacked we shall mobilize and despatch 2 divisions and will call for volunteers to supplement these forces. It is worth noting that the forces will not be so unequal as they appear from a mere enumeration of divisions since a Turkish division is rather less strong than one British Brigade.

In Constantinople itself, both Harington and Rumbold saw the possibility of a peace settlement, provided it were based on the Paris Note of September 23, granting the Turks ultimate sovereignty over Constantinople and Eastern Thrace. But in London, where the mood of the

Turks was more difficult to gauge, Lloyd George, Churchill and Austen Chamberlain saw the Turkish entry into the neutral zone as a permanent threat to British interests.

At a Conference of Ministers, meeting at 10 Downing Street on the morning of Friday September 29, the mood was a stern one. Churchill was confident that the troops at Chanak could hold their positions. Lloyd George was determined not to accept any compromise based upon threats. The Ministers had before them a telegram from Rumbold, sent from Constantinople on September 28, in which he put forward a compromise which, he believed, would be acceptable to Kemal and induce him to act with moderation. The Greeks he suggested, should at once be instructed to withdraw all their forces in Thrace to the western bank of the Maritza River. Curzon joined Lloyd George and Churchill in rejecting Rumbold's suggestion. 'The High Commissioner's proposals,' the Ministerial minutes recorded, 'would be tantamount to a new concession to Mustapha Kemal at a time when he was flagrantly contravening the condition in the Paris Note that he should observe the neutral line. . . .' The Ministers also rejected a proposal from the French High Commissioner, General Pellé, that British troops should withdraw from Chanak as soon as Harington's proposed meeting with Kemal had begun. On this point the Ministers accepted Rumbold's warning 'namely', as the Minutes recorded, 'that we could not withdraw as the Kemalists could then mount guns and be in a position to render the passage of the Straits difficult if they are dissatisfied with the progress of the Conference'.

Having rejected the compromises put forward by Rumbold and Pellé from Constantinople, the Ministers proceeded to seek a solution of their own. Worthington-Evans reported the view of the War Office General Staff that Kemal's reason for delaying his attack at Chanak was to build up a large enough force to overwhelm the British garrison. Intelligence sources believed that Kemal planned to attack the Chanak garrison on the following day, and that the Russian Government were pressing him to take action against Britain. The Ministers adjourned while the three Service Chiefs, Cavan, Beatty and Trenchard, met to 'formulate their views' of what should be done. The Service Chiefs decided that in order to protect the British forces at Chanak, it was necessary to send an ultimatum to Kemal. The Ministers reassembled, and the idea of an ultimatum was approved. They then approved a telegram to Harington, warning him that if the Kemalists continued to build up their strength around Chanak 'the defensive position will be imperilled', and that, in the view of the Service Chiefs 'the moment to avert the disaster has

arrived'. Harington was therefore instructed to tell the Turks that unless
their forces were withdrawn by an hour to be settled by Harington
himself 'all the forces at our disposal—naval, military and aerial—will
open fire'.

The War Office sent Harington the terms of the ultimatum at two on
the afternoon of September 29. He was also instructed, according to the
Ministerial Conference, that the time limit which he eventually decided
upon 'should be short and it should not be overlooked that we have
received warning regarding the date—September 30th, from our intelligence'. At half past five on the afternoon of September 29, Churchill
sent the Dominion Prime Ministers an account of the morning's
decisions, and of the ultimatum. He added that the situation at Chanak
itself was, according to General Harington, 'becoming impossible', and
that the number of Turks in the neutral zone around the city had more
than doubled, from 2,000 to 4,500, since the previous day. Churchill also
informed the Dominion Prime Ministers that 'from secret information'
the Cabinet had learnt that 'the Bolsheviks are strongly pressing the
Turks into aggressive courses'.

A further Conference of Ministers met at ten o'clock on the evening
of September 29 at Curzon's house in Carlton House Terrace. Austen
Chamberlain took the Chair. Curzon opened the meeting by urging his
colleagues, in the strongest terms, to cancel the ultimatum and to telegraph this decision to Harington that night. Lord Birkenhead spoke in
favour of maintaining the ultimatum. There was the 'gravest risk', he
said, in deferring action. Lord Lee, Austen Chamberlain and Churchill
likewise supported the ultimatum. According to the minutes of the
Conference:

THE SECRETARY OF STATE FOR THE COLONIES said he sympa-
thized most deeply with the Foreign Secretary, who was bound to assure
himself, like Sir Edward Grey in 1914, that no stone had been left unturned
to preserve peace, and he felt he had the full right to clear his conscience in
the matter. After all, it was his duty more than anyone else's. He agreed,
however, in the opinions expressed that it was not physically possible to defer
action without the gravest risk. It might upset the whole situation. It would
almost certainly make General Harington feel that he did not know where he
was. He would probably say to himself that the Government had 'cold feet'.
Moreover, a counter order issued at the last moment might prove only
partially effective. Consequently the Cabinet could not undo what had been
done after very careful consideration.

He himself, however, did not take a tragic view of the situation, and had by
no means lost hope that there might still be a peaceful settlement. He did not

think the action to be taken on the morrow would exclude conversations being reopened in a few days' time. The Turks might scurry off with some loss. He thought it quite possible, however, that this might not result in war. It must be borne in mind that Mustapha Kemal was at war with the Greeks, and his aim was to pursue them into Thrace. So far as he was concerned, the British force at Chanak was an irrelevance. He could hardly believe that Mustapha Kemal wished to embroil himself with us. What Mustapha Kemal thought and what had been dinned into him was that the British could be trampled on and ignored. He might get over that idea if a lesson were given him locally at Chanak.

Churchill believed that the ultimatum would result in negotiation, not war. His argument was well-received, and the conference decided that the ultimatum should stand. Austen Chamberlain then told the Conference 'that the Prime Minister's view accorded with the conclusion that had been reached'.

The Cabinet met on the morning of Saturday September 30. Lloyd George expressed his concern that General Harington had not yet acknowledged receipt of the ultimatum, which had been sent to him over twenty hours before. The Cabinet also discussed five telegrams which had been received during the night from Sir Horace Rumbold. It was clear from these telegrams that both Rumbold and Harington felt that the wisest course would be for Harington to begin negotiations with Kemal without any prior conditions, and that even the conciliatory terms of the Paris Note should no longer be insisted upon.

Lord Curzon commented 'that General Harington was paying rather too much attention to the political situation, which should be left to Sir Horace Rumbold, and not paying sufficient attention to the military situation'. But a few months later it became clear that Harington's judgement had been sound, for Worthington-Evans reported that a telegram from Kemal to Harington had 'just been received by the Navy', in which Kemal assured Harington that he had given orders to the Turkish troops at Chanak not to 'provoke any incident' within the neutral zone. Kemal had also offered, if British troops withdrew from the Asiatic shore of the Dardanelles, that Turkish forces on the Dardanelles 'would retire slightly'. This was the first intimation that Kemal was willing to avoid a clash with Britain, and to negotiate a truce.

At the end of the Cabinet meeting, Curzon told his colleagues that he hoped 'that firing had not yet taken place' at Chanak, as he felt that the telegrams from Constantinople indicated that Kemal 'was more reasonable' and that he would be willing to open negotiations with Harington quite soon. It must never be forgotten, Curzon added, 'that although Kemal "put forward extravagant demands", this was always the custom of the Oriental'. The Cabinet then adjourned, to await Harington's reply about the delivery of the ultimatum.

At Constantinople General Harington received the news of Kemal's willingness to negotiate simultaneously with the Cabinet's ultimatum. He at once consulted Sir Horace Rumbold, who agreed that if the ultimatum were delivered, the chances of opening negotiations with Kemal might be jeopardized. Harington thereupon telegraphed his reply to London. But at five o'clock that afternoon, before it had arrived, the Cabinet met again at 10 Downing Street. Their anxiety was intense. Had Harington already acted on the ultimatum? What time limit had he given it? Was the time limit about to expire? Were hostilities about to begin? In a statement to his colleagues, Lloyd George set out his feelings, and justified the ultimatum:

Mustapha Kemal had paid no heed to the Paris Note or to the warnings of General Harington, and continued to pour cavalry and perhaps artillery into the neutral zone. These troops were very insolent in their demeanour. They walked up to the wire entanglements of the British forces and made grimaces through them. The General Staff had advised that our troops were being netted in and that in a short time this process would render them ineffective because the positions that were being taken up by the Turks would make their situation impossible. The three Staffs had examined the question and had considered it essential that something should be done to clear up this situation. The Conference of Ministers had therefore decided on the previous afternoon that General Harington should arrange for notice to be given to the local Commander of the Turkish forces outside Chanak, that if his troops were not withdrawn by a fixed time, all the forces at our disposal—naval, military and air—would be used to reject them. Nothing had been heard in reply to this telegram, which had been despatched on the previous afternoon and this was rather perplexing.

The Cabinet hoped that General Harington's reply would reach them while they were in session. But it did not do so, and after Lloyd George had pointed out that the French 'had offered us no support whatsoever', but that the Australians were now willing to send a force, the meeting was adjourned. As the meeting ended, Lloyd George asked his colleagues to 'remain within easy reach' in case Harington's reply should arrive during the evening. On returning to the Colonial Office Churchill telegraphed to the Dominion Prime Ministers: 'Cabinet assembled at

4 o'clock and waited till 6 without receiving any information of importance from Constantinople. Ministers are now waiting to reassemble at half an hour's notice.'

During the early evening, while he was at the Colonial Office, Churchill set out for his Cabinet Committee a Note on the Turkish situation. In it he wrote:

The more the situation is surveyed, the more the strategic advantages of the British position at Chanak and Gallipoli will become patent. The dilemma which faces Kemal will be painful in the extreme. He has either to break his teeth against the British at Chanak while the Greek armies grow stronger every day, or else to hurry into what is virtually a death-trap in Thrace. . . .

It was for these reasons, Churchill concluded, that he believed Kemal would recognize 'the futility . . . of a serious and prolonged effort against the British at Chanak'. Kemal was more likely, Churchill believed, to agree to negotiations. 'In this case,' he pointed out, 'we shall have attained our present objects without serious hostilities.'

During the afternoon of September 30, a message had reached the Foreign Office in London from the British Ambassador in Paris, Lord Hardinge, to the effect that Poincaré had dissociated himself from any possible ultimatum to the Turks. At a quarter to ten that night Churchill telegraphed to the Dominion Prime Ministers that the French Government 'would not consider themselves bound by any responsibility for any development that might result from the action which General Harington had been authorised to take.'

At the end of his telegram, Churchill added a 'Private and Personal' comment:

Considering M. Poincaré has left our men alone on the Asiatic shore and has said that in no circumstances could he kill a single Turk it would appear that measures taken for the safety of our troops are our own business principally.

The Cabinet met again at half past ten that night, with Lloyd George in the chair. General Harington's reply had not yet arrived. But two telegrams had just reached the Foreign Office from Sir Horace Rumbold, which made it clear, as the Cabinet were told, that the ultimatum 'had not been acted on by General Harington'. Sir Maurice Hankey, who was present at the Cabinet, later informed Balfour—who was at Geneva—of the Cabinet's response:

There was, to put it mildly, a considerable reaction on this news. There was some annoyance in certain quarters (Churchill & Co.) with Harington for not

having answered before, and I think everyone felt a little that after his telegrams about the seriousness of the situation (which had of course led to the
'ultimatum') we had been 'spoofed'.

According to the Cabinet Minutes, 'extreme concern was expressed'
about the safety of the British forces at Chanak, which the Chief of
Staff had, on the previous day, said were in imminent danger. Misgivings were again expressed as to whether Harington 'was giving
sufficient attention to the military situation'. He was not, after all, at
Chanak itself, but in Constantinople, and appeared to be 'intensely
preoccupied with the political situation'. There was also anger at his
failure to reply to what were described as the 'peremptory orders' sent
to him on the previous afternoon.

The Cabinet waited until after midnight for Harington's reply, but
it still had not come. The Cabinet minutes recorded the 'concern' of
Ministers:

That Sir Horace Rumbold and General Harington should apparently
contemplate a meeting between the General and Mustapha Kemal at
Mudania while the Turkish Nationalists, in defiance of several remonstrances
and warnings, were still actively violating the essential condition laid down in
the Paris Note of September 23rd, that the Government of Angora should
undertake not to send troops, either before or during the Conference, into the
neutral zones.

The Cabinet continued to sit after midnight. According to the
Minutes, there was much anger at the 'apparent progressive deteriora-
tion' of Britain's political position and prestige, as a result of Kemal's
refusal to respect the neutral zone. One Minister pointed out that
Kemal's attitude was particularly galling when it was remembered that
Turkey was 'an enemy whom we had defeated decisively in the Great
War and who possessed only a remnant of his former strength'.

Shortly before one o'clock in the morning, General Harington's long-
awaited telegram reached the War Office. The Cabinet were at once
informed that it had arrived, and demanded to see it. But they were
told that the telegram was in cipher, in six separate parts, and would
take several hours to decode. The Cabinet thereupon broke up, and
arranged to meet nine hours later, at ten in the morning.

The Cabinet met at 10 Downing Street at ten on the morning of
Sunday October 1, as planned. General Harington's telegram had been

decoded during the night, and each Minister was given a copy. Sir Horace Rumbold's advance report of it had been correct; Harington was unambiguous in his decision to delay the Cabinet's ultimatum. In Part one of his telegram, not all of which had been completely deciphered, he declared:

I share Cabinet's desire to end procrastinations of Kemal and I note decision of Cabinet but I would earnestly beg that matter be left to my judgment for moment. There is no question (3 groups omitted) British forces until Kemalists bring up serious force of guns and infantry. To have some 4000 so called cavalry at close quarters is only a minor affair and General Marden has said that his position is strong enough to hold out against anything except a very serious attack. He has 6 fine British Battalions supported by most tremendous gunfire both military and naval—and by air. We must be guided by facts and (?) that is (?) how far distant Kemalist infantry and guns are.

Part two of Harington's telegram read:

To me it seems very inadvisable just at moment when within reach of distance of meeting between Allied Generals and Kemal which Hamid[1] says will be in two or three days and Angora Government are penning their reply to allied note that I should launch Avalanche of fire which will put a match to mine here and everywhere else and from which there will be no drawing back. I have incessantly been working for peace which I thought was the wish of His Majesty's Government. To suppose my not having fired so far at Chanak has been interpreted as sign of weakness is quite wrong because I have been very careful to warn Hamid that I have (2 groups undecipherable) powers of England behind me and that I shall not hesitate to use it if time comes. General Marden has full powers from me to strike when he thinks fit.

In Part three of his telegram, Harington wrote:

I had very carefully considered whether, as we are so far not at war with Kemal, the Turkish cavalry could be best dealt with by using the minimum force to effect my object or whether I should at once employ full force. In order to avoid England being interpreted as aggressor I decided on the former. You must remember the repercussions on Christian population here of any actions at Chanak. If we plunged this city into a panic it would be deplorable and they are very frightened after Smyrna. The action I am now to take means in my opinion the beginning of very serious hostilities and I realize I cannot get further reserves.

[1] Hamid Hasancan Bey. Administrator of the Ottoman Bank, 1912–25. Joined the Board of Directors of the Turkish Red Crescent Society as an expert in financial matters, 1913. Constantinople representative of the International Organization for the Protection of Children, 1920. Constantinople Agent of the Angora Government, 1921–2.

My only reserve of troops is in Constantinople. I may have to withdraw from there and it means the desertion of Christian (?Women) and (?Children).

Part four of the telegram continued:

If British forces left here suddenly I am, as I said yesterday horrified to think what would happen. Confidence has re-appeared in last few days since reinforcements marched in and I was every day feeling more hopeful that I might see the end with principle of the neutral zones preserved without firing a shot and with British flag flying high here. It all hangs in my opinion, on what can be effected in Thrace. . . .

Such were Harington's reasons for not immediately carrying out the Cabinet's instructions. In the fifth section of his telegram he described how, at Chanak itself, the situation was 'improving daily', and gave details of General Marden's activities in building up a defensive line of outposts ringing Chanak from Nagara point to Kephez. 'He has now got elbow room he requires,' Harington pointed out, 'and in a few days will be nearing maximum strength. . . .' It was also evident, he added, that 'Kemalists have had orders not to attack'.

In part six of his telegram, Harington declared that the situation at Chanak 'was never dangerous', and he continued:

Will you at once confirm or otherwise whether my judgment is overruled. I am meanwhile working out how long it would take for Turks to get behind neutral line and preparing ultimatum. If Kemal's reply to my last request is unsatisfactory I am all in favour of issuing. He does not intend to attack Chanak seriously in my opinion. It looks as if he is working up for Ismid. In 9 days he might produce as much as 18 Divisions (Rifle strength 45–50,000) on Yarimje frontier though he would presumably keep a central reserve between the Sea of Marmora and Balikesri. This is his reason for procrastination. Have shown this to Brock and Rumbold who agree.

General Harington's telegram was discussed that morning by the Cabinet, but no decision was reached on whether or not to insist that he deliver the ultimatum. At midday a telegram reached the Foreign Office from Sir Horace Rumbold, announcing that Mustafa Kemal had agreed to meet General Harington at Mudania, in order to discuss the future of the neutral zone, Thrace and the Straits. The British Cabinet met again at 3 o'clock that afternoon. It was agreed that Harington 'need not send the ultimatum . . . unless he considered the situation demanded it'. But he was to be reminded that however the Mudania negotiations developed, his was 'the primary responsibility for the security of our position at Chanak', and that 'the safety of our troops rested with him'. Churchill himself drafted the Cabinet's telegram to Harington. 'If you are no longer in immediate danger of being netted in,' he wrote, there was 'no need' to deliver the ultimatum. He went on:

You are indeed right in supposing that H.M.G. earnestly desire peace. We do not however desire to purchase a few days peace at the price of actively assisting a successful Turkish invasion of Europe. Such a course wd deprive us of every vestige of sympathy & respect & particularly in the United States. Nor do we believe that repeated concessions & submissions to victorious orientals is the best way to avert war.

The crisis at Chanak itself was over; henceforth the future of the neutral zone, and of Thrace, depended upon the negotiations at Mudania. The afternoon Cabinet of October 1 instructed Harington that his 'sole function' at Mudania was to fix 'the line to which the Greeks were to be asked to withdraw in Eastern Thrace'. But they knew that Harington's own opinion was that the Greeks should withdraw behind the Maritza, as the Turks demanded.

The Cabinet accepted the new situation. But they were still not certain whether the Turks intended to keep the peace. During the afternoon of October 1 Lord Curzon telegraphed to Sir Horace Rumbold, on the Cabinet's instructions: 'We cannot contemplate Mudania meeting being spun out from day to day, in order to enable Mustapha Kemal to strengthen his position at Ismid with a view to invading Europe.' And at seven o'clock that evening Churchill telegraphed to the Dominion Prime Ministers:

In my personal opinion it is very doubtful whether any solid result will follow from this conference. Mustapha Kemal has been marching and moving the main body of his troops northwards towards the Ismid Peninsula without intermission since the fall of Smyrna. General Harington now reports that Kemal will be able in nine days' time to bring 18 divisions, comprising between forty and fifty thousand fighting men, up to the edge of the neutral zone across the Ismid Peninsula, that is to say, that on about the fourth or fifth day of the conference he will be ready to advance in strength towards Constantinople. General Harington and the High Commissioner both consider that Kemal's procrastination has been due to his wish to have his concentration completed in good time and so be in a position to carry matters with a high hand at the conference. . . .

Churchill went on to forecast, as 'the most reasonable probability', an invasion of the Ismid neutral zone by Mustafa Kemal 'on or immediately after the 10th October'. He added that if the Turks invaded Thrace across the Bosphorus, the British forces at Chanak would not have to bear 'any heavy attack'. And he went on to defend the Cabinet's decision to keep control of Chanak and the Straits, even at the risk of war:

It would seem that up to the present the British decision to hold Chanak at all costs has been vindicated, and that although we were assured by Marshal Foch that 100,000 men would be needed, in fact we shall not be shaken from it in spite of our small numbers. The position of the British forces at Chanak and on Gallipoli, coupled with our naval power, is one of enormous strategic advantage, and should enable us to safeguard British vital interests in the Straits whatever may happen until larger Imperial forces can be brought there should need arise.

To the Australian Prime Minister, William Hughes, Churchill added a personal paragraph, informing him that the despatch of Australian troops would have 'a very steadying effect upon opinion in this country, which while thoroughly sound is naturally puzzled by the complexity of this tangled problem'.

At half past ten on the evening of October 1, Churchill sent the Dominion Prime Ministers details of what Britain's terms would be at the Mudania Conference. In return for Allied help in securing a Greek withdrawal in Thrace, the Turks would have to agree 'not to send troops either before or during final peace conference into neutral zones and not to cross Marmora or Straits'. The Cabinet were also worried about Turkish activity in the Mosul area, and, as Churchill explained to the Dominion Prime Ministers, Harington had been instructed to tell Kemal that no agreement would be reached over Thrace 'while Kemalist forces are taking hostile action against Iraq and Kurdistan'. All such action must be suspended. 'While we are endeavouring to make peace in Europe,' Churchill explained, 'Kemal cannot go on making war in Asia.'

On Monday October 2 General Harington went on board the battle-ship *Iron Duke*, and sailed from Constantinople to Mudania. To the annoyance of the Cabinet, Mustafa Kemal announced that he himself would not go to the conference, but would be represented by the Commander of his Western Army, General Ismet.[1] 'This is a pity,' Churchill

[1] Ismet, 1884–1974. Born in Smyrna. Captain, General Staff of the 2nd Army (Edirne), 1906. Major, Army of the Yemen, 1912. Colonel, 1915. Commanded the 4th Corps, 1916; the 20th Army Corps, 1917. Under-Secretary for War, 1918. Chief of the General Staff of the

telegraphed to the Dominion Prime Ministers on October 2. But the Conference, he added, would continue. Churchill also reported that the French politician, Franklin-Bouillon,[1] who had just returned from seeing Kemal at Angora, had stated 'that he has persuaded Kemal and Kemal has persuaded the Angora Assembly to be reasonable'. According to Franklin-Bouillon, Churchill added, 'Kemal has ordered an *arrêt absolu* of all his troops and expects us to discontinue all our disembarkations'. But Churchill continued: 'We shall certainly not do this so far as troops already on the seas are concerned.'

In his telegram to the Dominion Prime Ministers on October 2, Churchill set out his personal fears of what he believed would happen if General Harington's negotiations were unsuccessful. His views, he said, were 'particularly secret and for the exclusive information of your Cabinet'. He did not say whether any of his own Cabinet colleagues shared them. His tone was alarmist:

If Mudania breaks down and Kemal advances upon Constantinople, a very terrible situation will arise. We are not strong enough to defend the tip of the Ismid Peninsula and prevent the Turks from reaching the Bosphorus. It is doubtful whether the Navy will be able to collect all the means of transportation across the Bosphorus, as the daily life of Constantinople is to a very great extent dependent upon water transport. A rising in Constantinople is almost certain when the Kemalists arrive at the water's edge.

Unless the French at the eleventh hour make a loyal effort in the interests of humanity, we shall have to evacuate the British colony and make ourselves secure at Gallipoli. The peril of the Christian population of Constantinople numbering hundreds of thousands will be great. It is melancholy that Europe cannot find thirty or forty thousand men to ward off such a calamity. . . .

The British Consul-General in Smyrna, Sir Harry Lamb,[2] had sent Lord Curzon a full account of the destruction of Smyrna in the second week of September. On reading Lamb's account Churchill was horrified by all that had happened. In his telegram to the Dominion Prime Ministers on October 2, he described the event in detail:

Nationalist Forces, 1920. Commanded the Turkish troops in Western Anatolia at the 1st and 2nd battles of Inönü, 1921. Lieutenant-General, 1922. Foreign Minister, 1922–23. Prime Minister, 1923–4 and 1925–37. Given the name of Inönü. President of Turkey, 1938–50. Leader of the Opposition in the Turkish Parliament, 1950–60. Prime Minister, 1961–5. Leader of the Opposition, 1965–72.

[1] Henri Franklin-Bouillon, 1870–1939. Entered the Chamber of Deputies, 1910. Minister of State in Charge of Propaganda, 1917. In charge of negotiations with Mustafa Kemal, 1921–2. Known to the British in Constantinople as 'boiling Frankie'.

[2] Harry Harling Lamb, 1857–1948. Entered Consular Service, 1885. Chief Dragoman, British Embassy, Constantinople, 1903–7. Consul-General, Salonica, 1907–13. Employed in the Foreign Office, London, 1914–18. Knighted, 1919. Consul-General, Smyrna, 1921–3.

The Greek rearguard burnt every village they could reach in their retreat and killed many Turkish inhabitants. The Turkish troops entered Smyrna under perfect restraint. Even when a Turkish officer was wounded by a bomb thrown by an Armenian no reprisals were allowed. Three days afterwards, however, when superior Turkish authorities had arrived and the matter had been maturely considered, the whole Armenian quarter was methodically delivered to pillage, rape and massacre. Sir Harry Lamb counted 20 corpses in 50 yards during the infernal orgy. Out of 900 females rescued by a British destroyer, only 20 were between the ages of 15 and 35.

To obliterate the horror, fires were started on the windward side of the Armenian quarter and restarted to windward as particular areas burned themselves out. These fires were also carried to the European quarter equally on the windward side, and even the bundles of the refugees on the quay, according to the Consul General, were besprinkled with petrol by the Turks and lighted up. The Turkish quarter was undamaged.

180,000 refugees have been taken off and dumped down in Greece mainly by British agency. For a deliberately planned and methodically executed atrocity Smyrna must, according to the facts reported by the Consul General, find few parallels in the history of human crime.

'Our fear,' Churchill added at the end of his telegram, 'is that Constantinople may soon afford the same spectacle on a much larger scale.'

The Mudania Conference opened on Tuesday October 3. Harington was confident that he would reach agreement with Ismet, and for three days the negotiations proceeded smoothly. Ismet agreed to accept the Paris Note of September 23, and at Chanak the Turkish forces withdrew a thousand yards from the British lines. On October 4 Churchill telegraphed to the Dominion Prime Ministers: 'The British War Office appreciation confirms the continuance of the Turkish concentration towards the Ismid Peninsula.' But the general feeling was that the crisis had ended, and that Harington, who had prudently decided to hold back the Cabinet's ultimatum five days earlier, was likely to secure a satisfactory agreement. Such was the feeling of calm that on October 3 Frederick Guest had asked Churchill to allow the thousand RAF personnel, who had been diverted to the Dardanelles 'at the time of the panic', to continue on their journey to Iraq. Guest added that Lord Cavan had agreed that the men were no longer needed at the Dardanelles. 'The longer they are kept,' he wrote, 'the greater is the danger that they will get involved in administrative inter-Allied duties in Thrace, from which it would be very difficult to extricate them.' Churchill noted in the margin: 'Yes, I agree.' The Chanak crisis seemed to be coming rapidly to an end.

On the morning of October 4, H. A. L. Fisher went to see Lloyd George at 10 Downing Street. The Prime Minister was more concerned with the political situation at home than with Chanak. 'His mind is clearly set upon a General Election at once,' Fisher recorded in his diary, 'and on retirement *either* before the election or after it.' Lloyd George told Fisher that he did not envisage that the Coalition could survive. The Coalition Liberals, he feared, would win only 50 seats, the Conservatives 200. The result, he told Fisher, would be that:

The diehards & Labour & Liberal wll overturn the Govt. An alternative coalition will be formed. Edward Grey, Salisbury,[1] Bob Cecil. Asquith will probably not join. In any case he (LG) thinks a Liberal Party will not be dominant. Liberalism done for. All the Liberal side will be represented by Labour.

Almost unnoticed during the Chanak crisis, Churchill's Iraq policy had reached its apogee. On October 1, as planned, the Royal Air Force assumed full responsibility for the defence of Iraq. Ministerial control of all military affairs was transferred to the Secretary of State for Air, Churchill's cousin Frederick Guest, and Sir John Salmond became the first Air Force officer to be appointed commander-in-chief of a complete defence force both on land and in the air. On October 5, the Iraq Treaty itself was finally accepted by King Feisal, and was ready for signature in both Britain and Iraq. That afternoon Churchill informed the Cabinet that the final Treaty draft 'conformed in all respects to the requirements of the League of Nations', while at the same time fulfilling the Cabinet's own aim of seeing Iraq transformed into 'an independent Arab State bound to Great Britain during the mandatory period by Treaty relations'. Churchill told the Cabinet that Feisal had undoubtedly become more conciliatory in the final months of negotiation as a result both of his own illness, and of Sir Percy Cox's 'energetic action' in suppressing all extremism and revolt. Churchill then told his colleagues:

Trouble with the Turk was the time for friendship with the Arab, and inasmuch as the Treaty was extremely favourable to Arab aspirations the publication of its terms would undoubtedly have an excellent effect and would enable Feisal to unite the Arabs against any Turkish attack. The Treaty did not commit Great Britain to giving any definite military or

---

[1] John Edward Hubert Gascoyne-Cecil, Viscount Cranborne, 1861–1947. Conservative MP, 1885–92 and 1893–1903. Succeeded his father (then Prime Minister) as 4th Marquess of Salisbury, 1903. President of the Board of Trade, 1905. Lord President of the Council, October 1922–January 1924. Lord Privy Seal, 1924–9. Leader of the House of Lords, 1925–9.

financial assistance; it merely provided for the making of supplementary agreements dealing with military and financial arrangements. If warlike operations could be avoided it seemed probable that next year the cost to the British Exchequer of Mesopotamia would be reduced to £4,000,000 as compared with £8,000,000 in the present year and £32,000,000 two years ago.

The Cabinet accepted the Iraq Treaty with little enthusiasm. An unnamed Minister remarked that 'there might be some doubt as to the possibility of King Feisal being able to maintain a civilised and stable Government in Iraq', and he added: 'The genius which the Arabs had displayed in the Middle Ages for administration had apparently disappeared.' It was then formally agreed to approve 'the proposals for the Treaty'. Not Iraq, but Turkey, was the Cabinet's principal concern on October 5. During the day the Mudania negotiations ran into unexpected difficulties. The French politician, Franklin-Bouillon, who had been acting as a mediator behind the scenes since the negotiations had begun, persuaded the Turks not to accept all the British conditions. 'Kemalists have been most unreasonable,' Churchill telegraphed to the Dominion Prime Ministers at eight that evening, 'repeatedly threatening force and declining to make any concession. Franklin-Bouillon has been an unmitigated nuisance. . . .' The Frenchman, he added, had 'no doubt made many promises at the expense of British interests'. During the day, Harington returned from Mudania to Constantinople for consultations with the Allied High Commissioners. In London, the Cabinet met at half past eleven that night. A telegram from Sir Horace Rumbold made it clear that the Turks were insisting upon the right to occupy Eastern Thrace at once. They were also refusing to evacuate the neutral zone. The French and Italian High Commissioners, General Pellé and Marquis Garroni,[1] wanted to give way to the Turkish demands. Rumbold opposed any further concessions. But, as H. A. L. Fisher recorded in his diary:

The Cabinet quite clear that without French cooperation it will not fight & prevent Turk getting to Constantinople & Thrace. It appears that Curzon, Mond, Boscawen[2] were all for moderation. . . .

[1] Marquis Eugenio Camillo Garroni, 1852–1935. Prefect of Genoa, 1896–1912. Senator, 1905. Italian Ambassador in Constantinople, 1912–15 and High Commissioner, 1920–2. Head of the Italian Delegation at the Lausanne Conference, 1922–3.

[2] Arthur Sackville Trevor Griffith-Boscawen, 1865–1946. Conservative MP for Tonbridge, 1892–1906; for Dudley, 1910–21; for Taunton, 1921–2. Knighted, 1911. Commanded a battalion in France, 1915. Parliamentary Secretary, Ministry of Pensions, 1916–19; Board of Agriculture and Fisheries, 1919–21. Minister of Agriculture and Fisheries, 1921–2. Minister of Health, 1922–3. Chairman, Royal Commission on Transport, 1928–31; Transport Advisory Council, 1936–45; Inland Transport War Council, 1939–45.

There was little enthusiasm in Britain for making the Mudania negotiations an issue of peace or war, and it was widely believed that the Cabinet were being pushed forward by a small group of irresponsible Ministers. 'I am told,' Colonel Meinertzhagen wrote in his diary on October 5, 'that Winston is at the back of this crazy policy and really wished to fight the Turk.'

Throughout October 5 Rumbold and his fellow High Commissioners in Constantinople discussed the Turkish demands with Harington. In the early hours of October 6 Rumbold telegraphed to Curzon that both Pellé and Garroni had 'argued strongly in favour of yielding to Turks', and that both of them had also favoured the restoration of Eastern Thrace to Turkey before any peace treaty, and without guarantees for the minorities. Garroni had insisted that 'if war resulted', the world 'would attribute it to unwillingness of Allied High Commissioners and generals to take responsibility for concessions which were of small account'. Rumbold had disagreed. 'I replied,' he told Curzon, 'that world would attribute it to intractability of Turks, that the more we yielded to Turks the more demands they would make and that the next might well be evacuation of Constantinople, that General Harington, Admiral Brock and I had done our utmost to avoid war, that there were limits to forbearance of His Majesty's Government and that I must now report facts to my Government and leave it to them to appreciate whether in refusing these demands they were prepared to contemplate war.'

During October 6 Churchill sent a full account of the discussions to the Dominion Prime Ministers. Basing his narrative on Sir Horace Rumbold's telegrams, received that morning, Churchill set out some of the details of the breakdown of the Mudania conference:

Protocol had been drafted as result of three days' discussion with Ismet Pasha giving great and important concessions to Turks ... but Ismet demanded at the last moment that Eastern Thrace should be given to the Turks before the Peace Treaty and that the Allies should withdraw their missions and any military contingents sent to support missions in maintaining order. This demand runs counter to Allies' joint note of September 23rd. Karagatch, a suburb of Adrianople on the western bank of the Maritza was also demanded by the Turks. This demand also ignores allied proposal of September 23rd. Ismet intimated that if the allied generals did not agree to his proposals he would set his troops in motion. After some discussion, Ismet agreed to do nothing until 2.30 this afternoon which is 11.30 Greenwich time. . . .

The Cabinet met on the morning of October 6 to consider Sir Horace

Rumbold's telegrams, and approved his decision not to moderate the British proposals. At midday Lord Curzon crossed over to Paris to try to persuade the French Government to support the British in this firm approach. At midnight, Curzon and Poincaré began their discussion. On October 7 Churchill informed the Dominion Prime Ministers of the result of their meeting, and of the situation at Chanak and Mudania:

There is no doubt the French are alarmed by the growing demands of the Kemalists. A further effort will now probably be made in concert to procure a temporary settlement on the basis of allied troops of the three nations taking over Eastern Thrace for one month pending the assembly of the Peace Conference. M. Venizelos would press the Greeks to agree to this and to the withdrawal of their troops.

General Harington has returned to Mudania with the other Generals. He has not disembarked from the 'Iron Duke' pending further instructions. He reports a better atmosphere prevails.

There is a great deal of bluff in the Turkish proceedings. . . .

The most satisfactory news is that the Turks have not begun their advance, in spite of the fact that they are being kept waiting and will still be kept waiting at Mudania.

We are of course making it perfectly clear that we are going to stay at Chanak and that they have got to evacuate the Chanak neutral zone. All our troops should be in to-day, a very formidable artillery is now in position at Chanak, and aviation is developing every hour.

Political criticism of the Government's handling of the Chanak crisis was growing. On October 6, in a speech at Dumfries, Asquith had criticized the conduct of diplomacy 'by amateurs in Downing Street'. Asquith's criticisms were published in all the newspapers on the morning of October 7. But they were overshadowed by a letter published that same morning in *The Times*, from Bonar Law. The former Leader of the Conservative Party, who since March 1921 had taken no part in politics, declared that Britain could only keep the Turks out of Constantinople or Eastern Thrace if the Allied powers, including the United States, agreed to join in such action. It would be wrong, Bonar Law warned, for Britain, as the leading Mohammedan power, 'to show any hostility or unfairness to the Turk'. Without at least French support, all military action should be avoided. 'We cannot act alone,' Bonar Law declared, 'as the policeman of the world.'

Bonar Law's letter reflected the public distress at the possibility of a war with Turkey, in which Britain would have no allies. In fact, that very morning, Curzon had secured Poincaré's support in the event of a final breakdown of the Mudania Conference, while, at Constantinople,

Sir Horace Rumbold was putting Turkish fears at rest by assuring the Kemalists that Britain had no intention of embroiling the Turks in a conflict with Greece over Eastern Thrace. These developments were still secret when Bonar Law's letter was published on October 7. Nevertheless, his appeal for peace caught the public imagination. Churchill himself telegraphed to the Dominion Prime Ministers: 'Bonar Law in a timely letter today expresses a very general view.'

During October 7 it became clear that Bonar Law's letter was being widely interpreted as a direct challenge to the Coalition. Many Conservatives welcomed it as a sign that at last, albeit belatedly, the former Conservative leader was prepared to challenge Lloyd George, and, if necessary, force the Conservative Party out of the Coalition altogether. Churchill saw the danger at once. Later that day he wrote to his Constituency Chairman, James Robertson:[1]

Broadly speaking, I agree with Mr Bonar Law, in his letter published today, that the British Empire cannot become the policeman of the world. Our burdens are too heavy, our losses have been too great, and our responsibilities too numerous and too complex for us to undertake single-handed the task of maintaining the Treaties by which the Great War was closed. It would be our duty to take our stand by the side of other Great Powers in endeavouring to prevent the war between Turkey and Greece spreading again to Europe. If, however, no common action can be arranged, events will have to take their course. The responsibility will not surely be ours. We had adhered faithfully to the engagements we made with our allies and in particular to the agreement reached in Paris only a fortnight ago. It is not fair to Britain to put all the burdens on her.

Up to this point, Churchill's letter accurately reflected Bonar Law's cautionary sentiments. But Churchill then continued:

Do not, however underrate how serious the consequences of a violent Turkish inroad into Europe may be. It will certainly mean war and massacre in Thrace, and no one call tell how far the conflagration may spread. Even after this conflict is finished the evil consequences will endure and Europe in another generation will reap a harvest of blood and tears which might all have been prevented without great expense or effort by common action and loyalty between the signatories of the Treaty of Sèvres.

The freedom of the Straits stands on a different footing. Here we have a vital British and Imperial interest to guard. It is also one which we are quite

[1] James Constable Robertson, 1849–1932. Chartered accountant. Senior Partner in the firm of Moody Stuart and Robertson, Dundee, 1875. An early and active promoter of Investment Trust Companies, for which he travelled regularly to the United States and Canada. For several years he was City Treasurer, Dundee, and President of the Dundee Liberal Association. He was a generous contributor to Liberal Party funds.

capable of guarding if necessary by ourselves. I do not think we ought to retire from Chanak or surrender the Gallipoli Peninsula until conditions are established at a formal peace conference which secures the great waterway of the Straits for the enjoyment of the whole world under the effective custody of the League of Nations. Such is the policy we have consistently pursued and to which we adhere, and I am convinced that it offers the best chance of that peaceful settlement which is the supreme object of our desires.

When the Cabinet met on the morning of October 7, Ministers learned that Poincaré would probably agree to support Britain's contention that a month must elapse between the signature of any agreement with the Turks, and the occupation of Eastern Thrace by Turkish troops. By this formula, Britain would be able to maintain its insistence upon an unhurried settlement, but on terms that the Turks would accept. When the Cabinet was over, H. A. L. Fisher noted in his diary: 'Walk away with Peel,[1] who states his anxiety last week at Winston & FE's warlike policy. . . .'

The Cabinet met again that evening. Poincaré had finally accepted Britain's formula, and General Harington was instructed to reopen the Mudania negotiations. General Ismet, who had no desire for a direct military confrontation with the Greeks in Thrace, then accepted a compromise which had originated from Sir Horace Rumbold, for an inter-allied Commission to replace the Greeks in Eastern Thrace during the month before the Turks were allowed to return. The negotiations continued during October 9 and throughout the following day. Agreement was finally reached, after an all-night session, at 7.15 on the morning of October 11. A Convention was signed to come into force at midnight on October 14. Under the terms of the Convention, Allied troops were to occupy eastern Thrace for thirty days. Three military Commissions, headed by a French, a British and an Italian officer, were to take over from October 16 the civil administration of eastern Thrace and the Greek authorities would return to Greece. At Chanak, the Turks were to withdraw 15 kilometres from the coast, and not increase the number of their troops. On the Ismid peninsula the Turks were likewise to withdraw behind the neutral zone. The Allies were to remain in occupation of Constantinople, Ismid, Chanak and the Gallipoli Penin-

[1] William Robert Wellesley Peel, 1867–1937. Conservative MP, 1900–6 and 1909–12. Succeeded his father as Viscount Peel, 1912. Chairman of the London County Council, 1914. Chairman of the Committee on the Detention of Neutral Vessels, 1916. Under-Secretary of State for War, 1919–21. Chancellor of the Duchy of Lancaster and Minister of Transport, 1921–2. Secretary of State for India, 1922–4 and 1928–9. Created Earl, 1929. Lord Privy Seal, 1931. Member of the Indian Round Table Conference, 1930–1. Chairman, Burma Round Table Conference, 1931–2; the Palestine Royal Commission, 1936–7.

sula until a formal peace treaty had been negotiated between them and Turkey. Until a peace treaty was signed, the Turks would neither transport troops into Eastern Thrace, nor raise an army from the Turkish population there.

News of the signature of the Mudania Convention reached London during the afternoon of October 11, and brought much relief. At a quarter to ten that night Churchill telegraphed news of the Convention to the Dominion Prime Ministers:

After much obstinacy the Turks have signed a good agreement of which the text has been published The neutral zones are to be respected and all Turkish troops are to retire at once behind lines drawn in Ismid zone just east of Chile Gutze and in Chanak zone 16 kilometres from coast between Kara Bigha and Besika Bay. Greeks are allowed 45 days to evacuate Eastern Thrace and Allied troops are meanwhile going to prevent panic and massacre there and to arrange for peaceful transference. . . .

Churchill's telegram continued:

Situation is now greatly relieved and we may hope for a peaceful outcome. We have been greatly hampered by the repeated failures of support from our Allies and also by factious and vicious Party and Press campaign in this country. We have for the time being however preserved in spite of this all the essential interests. . . .

At eleven o'clock that evening Churchill telegraphed again. It was his final message to the Dominion Prime Ministers. In it he revealed once more his bitterness against France and Italy. His message read:

If as may be hoped we are approaching the end of this crisis I trust I may venture once more to ask you to make every allowance, in case of any defect in procedure, for the sudden emergency which arose and the need of firm and instant action at a time when we were confronted single handed with the headlong advance of the Turks and when our Allies were prepared to take everything lying down.

Sir Horace Rumbold, who had helped to carry out the Cabinet's policy, believed that it had been a wise one. 'Factors which probably determined the Turks to sign,' he telegraphed to Lord Curzon that same day, 'were our display of force and their knowledge that we would use it in the last resort.'

The Chanak crisis was over. British policy had succeeded in averting war. But in the public mind it was widely believed, not only that both Churchill and Lloyd George had hoped for war with Turkey, but also that they had been disappointed when it was averted. On October 12

Alice Keppel wrote to Sir Horace Rumbold: 'the fighting "bloods" at home have been straining at the leash. Winston is longing to drop the paint brush for his sword and L.G. murmuring at every meal, "*We will fight to the end*". . . .' On October 17 Sir Maurice Hankey recorded in his diary: 'I walked across the Park with Churchill one evening towards the end of the crisis and he quite frankly regretted that the Turks had not attacked us at Chanak, as he felt that the surrender to them of Eastern Thrace was humiliating, and that the return of the Turks to Europe meant an infinity of troubles. I don't think the Prime Minister felt very differently.'

46

The Fall of the Coalition

DESPITE the peaceful outcome of events in Turkey, the political crisis in England continued. Even before Bonar Law's letter to *The Times* on October 7, an independent Conservative, Reginald Clarry,[1] had announced his intention of challenging the Coalition at the forthcoming Newport by-election, due to be held on October 18. Clarry's decision provoked much speculation. On October 8, H. A. L. Fisher dined at 10 Downing Street, recording in his diary that night:

After the ladies leave the P.M. talks of electoral chances. If the Conservative wins at Newport the Coalition is dead. If Labour wins, the Coalition may go on. L.G. principally concerned to carry Austen, Birkenhead and Balfour with him.

As a result of the evening's discussions, Fisher was convinced that Lloyd George favoured 'a prompt dissolution with a view to the Govt being overthrown by the Diehards & Liberals & Labour. . . .' Two days later, on October 10, the Conservative members of Lloyd George's Cabinet discussed the wisdom of an election in the near future, on a Coalition basis. The Chief Whip, Sir Leslie Wilson,[2] who was asked to attend, objected strongly to such a plan, preferring to see the Conservatives go to the polls as an independent Party, with their own

---

[1] Reginald Clarry, 1882–1945. Engineer. Secretary to the Swansea Gas Company; Managing Director of the Duffryn Steel and Tin Plate Works, Glamorgan. Adviser to the Ministry of Munitions, 1915–18. Conservative MP for Newport, 1922–9 and 1931–45. Knighted, 1936.

[2] Leslie Orme Wilson, 1876–1955. 2nd Lieutenant, Royal Marine Light Infantry, 1895; Captain, 1901. Severely wounded during the war in South Africa, 1899–1901. Conservative MP for Reading, 1913–22; for South Portsmouth, 1922–3. Lieutenant-Colonel Commanding the Hawke Battalion, Royal Naval Division, at Gallipoli, 1915; in France, 1916. Severely wounded in France, 1916. Parliamentary Assistant Secretary to the War Cabinet, 1918. Chairman of the National Maritime Board, 1919. Parliamentary Secretary, Ministry of Shipping, 1919. Chief Unionist Whip (Parliamentary Secretary to the Treasury), 1921–3. Knighted, 1923. Governor of Bombay, 1923–8; of Queensland, 1932–46.

leader. Only one Conservative Minister supported him, the President of the Board of Trade, Stanley Baldwin. Both Wilson and Baldwin were overruled. When news of the meeting reached 10 Downing Street Lloyd George is said to have remarked to Churchill: 'Does little Baldwin think he can turn us out?'

Later that day Churchill called to see Baldwin at the Board of Trade. According to Lucy Baldwin's[1] subsequent account of the meeting, Churchill 'proceeded to harangue' her husband 'upon the disloyalty of anyone daring to leave the PM'. Baldwin listened in silence until Churchill warned him that in any open split 'there'll be some pretty mud-slinging', to which Baldwin retorted: 'That would be a pity because some pretty big chunks could come from the other side.'

At the Conservative Ministers meeting of October 10, Austen Chamberlain had argued strongly in favour of maintaining the Coalition because he thought it could win the election if it held together. Two days later he wrote to Lord Birkenhead that he proposed to take the initiative by calling a meeting of all Conservative MPs: 'to tell them bluntly that they must either follow our advice or do without us, in which case they must find their own Chief and form a Government *at once*. They would be in a d—d fix!'

On October 13 Austen Chamberlain defended the Coalition in a speech at Birmingham, and appealed to the Conservatives to continue to work with the Lloyd George Liberals. If the Coalition broke up, he warned, the Labour Party might obtain a majority. Such an event, he declared, would endanger national safety.

The Mudania Convention came into force on October 14, ensuring the possibility of a peaceful outcome to the Turkish crisis. That same day Lloyd George himself spoke in defence of his policy at the Manchester Reform Club. He denied that the Chanak crisis had brought Britain to the brink of war. 'We have not been warmongers; we have been peacemakers,' he declared. It had been essential, he said, not to surrender British control at the Dardanelles. 'Vital for us,' he explained, 'vital to humanity, we could not have those Straits barred without giving away the biggest and the most important prize which we won by our victory over Turkey in the Great War. . . .' To Asquith, and to all other Liberal critics, Lloyd George declared:

---

[1] Lucy Ridsdale, –1945. Daughter of Edward Ridsdale, a former Master of the Mint, she married Baldwin in 1892. She was awarded the OBE for her work during the Great War, and in 1937, after her husband's third premiership, she received the DBE. According to two of Baldwin's biographers (Middlemas and Barnes): 'Without Lucy Baldwin, he would probably never have had a political career. . . . With her own breezy and unquestioning faith, she gave him above all confidence in himself.'

Mr Asquith has asked why we did not emulate the patient, forbearing policy which Lord Grey displayed in 1914 towards the Germans, instead of indulging in the amateur tactics of Downing Street today? Well, the old patient and forbearing policy of 1914 ended in the most disastrous war which this world has ever seen. The amateur diplomacy of 1922, has at any rate, brought peace.

On October 16 Lord Londonderry wrote to Churchill from County Down, comparing Chamberlain's speech at Birmingham and Lloyd George's at Manchester: 'I think,' he wrote, 'Austen made a poor effort virtually saying that he was quite satisfied because the Conservatives got enough posts in the Government. L.G. made a good one and glossed over his rotten Greek policy which nearly landed us into war.' Londonderry ended his letter: 'I wish you would somehow become P.M.'

Churchill had invited both Liberal and Conservative Ministers to dine with him on Sunday, October 15, at Sussex Square, in order to discuss the future of the Coalition. Lloyd George and Lord Birkenhead were to be the chief advocates of the Coalition. On the day of the dinner Lord Curzon wrote from Carlton House Terrace:

My dear Winston,
   I regret that I am unable to come to your dinner tonight. I have told Austen the reasons which he will explain.

Yours sincerely,
Curzon

Churchill's dinner of October 15 was a testing point for the Conservative Ministers, each of whose loyalty to Lloyd George's leadership was essential if the Coalition were to survive. The forthcoming meeting of all Conservative MPs at the Carlton Club seemed an opportunity to put the case for a Coalition election, and to win majority support. Austen Chamberlain agreed to put to the Carlton Club meeting the arguments in favour of fighting the forthcoming election as a Coalition, under Lloyd George's continuing leadership.

Churchill planned to speak at Bristol on October 17, to put the case for a Coalition election, and to defend its policies. But on the morning of Monday October 16 he felt unwell, and during the day he complained to Edward Marsh of pains in his side. That evening it was announced from the Colonial Office that he was suffering 'from acute gastro-enteritis and was strictly confined to bed'. On October 17 his doctors decided that it would be necessary to operate for appendicitis, and during the day he was moved to a nursing home in Dorset Square.[1]

[1] Churchill had three medical advisers during his illness: Lord Dawson, Sir Crisp English and Dr Hartigan. Appendicitis was, in the 1920s, a far more serious illness than it later

From his sick bed Churchill could take no part in the political crisis. At five o'clock that Tuesday afternoon Lloyd George called a meeting of all the Liberal Ministers in his Government. H. A. L. Fisher, who was present, recorded in his diary:

The P.M. says either the Tories will reject Austen next Thursday or they will accept him. If (a) the Coalition is broken; if (b) then we go on as a Coalition. In either event he contemplates the future with confidence. . . .

Churchill could only follow these events from the nursing home. 'I am sorry to see from the newspapers,' James Allison[1] wrote from Dundee on October 17, 'that you were indisposed. I trust that your illness will quickly pass away.' On October 18—the day of the Newport by-election —Churchill dictated a letter to Allison, setting out his plans in the event of an early General Election:

I cannot tell whether I shall have to be operated on or not. If I am I shall be out of the fight altogether, but will send an Election address as soon as I have sufficiently recovered. The Lord Chancellor will come up in any case, and will make exertions. I am trying to get Mr Pratt,[2] the late Scottish Whip, who is well-known in Dundee, to represent me. Also Captain Guest will put in some time if he is not too heavily attacked in Dorsetshire.

'I will send you a fuller message,' Churchill added, 'when I know what the verdict of the doctors is.' That night he was operated on for appendicitis.

The result of the Newport by-election was announced on the morning of Thursday October 19. The independent Conservative was elected, with a majority of 2,090. In 1918 the seat had been won by a Coalition-Liberal. The victory of a non-Coalition candidate strengthened the determination of the Conservative MPs to assert their independence. On hearing the Newport result H. A. L. Fisher wrote in his diary: 'This I feel at once means the end of Coalition.'

---

became. Thus, in 1925 over 1,600 males died of acute appendicitis, while in 1971 there were only 185 such deaths.

[1] James Allison, 1866–1951. Practised as a solicitor for more than sixty years; Borough Prosecutor, Newport, Fife, 1895–1949. Lecturer in Scottish Law at Dundee University College, 1899–1945. Chairman of the Court of Referees, Dundee (under the Unemployment Insurance Act). Chairman of the Dundee Munitions Tribunal, 1915–19; CBE, 1920. Acting Chairman of the Dundee Liberal Association, 1922.

[2] John William Pratt, 1873–1952. Warden of Glasgow University Settlement, 1902–12. Member of the Glasgow Town Council, 1906. Coalition Liberal MP for Linlithgow, 1913–18; for Cathcart, 1918–22. A Lord Commissioner of the Treasury, 1916–19. Parliamentary Under-Secretary for Scotland, 1919–22. Knighted, 1922.

That morning the Conservative MPs met at the Carlton Club, to discuss the future of the Coalition with the Conservative Ministers, both MPs and Peers. Austen Chamberlain opened the meeting with a plea for the maintenance and indispensability of the Coalition. Using the arguments he had used at Birmingham six days earlier, he reiterated that there was no divergence of policy between the Conservative and Liberal wings of the Government. At once there was a barrage of dissent, in which cries of 'Ireland', 'Egypt', 'India' and 'Newport' were heard. The next speaker was Stanley Baldwin, President of the Board of Trade. Speaking as a member of Lloyd George's Cabinet, he warned that Lloyd George had already destroyed the Liberal Party, and was in the course of destroying the Conservatives also, by depriving them of their power of independent action.

Bonar Law spoke in support of Baldwin. It was more important, he said, to keep the Conservative Party united than to win the next election. Despite an appeal from Balfour, who argued forcefully in favour of maintaining the Coalition, a substantial majority of those present voted to withdraw their support from Lloyd George.

Deprived of the support of a majority of the Coalition's MPs, Lloyd George had no alternative but to resign. That afternoon he went to Buckingham Palace and advised the King to send for Bonar Law. Bonar Law agreed to become Prime Minister, provided he were elected leader of the Conservative Party. On returning to 10 Downing Street, Lloyd George sent a formal letter to all his Cabinet. The one to Churchill read:

My dear Secretary of State for the Colonies,

I write to inform you that I have tendered my resignation and that of the Government to the King this afternoon. I understand that His Majesty will be graciously pleased to accept these resignations as soon as he is assured that an alternative Government can be formed.

I should like to take this opportunity of thanking you for your valuable services during your tenure of office under my premiership.

Ever sincerely,
D. Lloyd George

This letter was delivered to Churchill at the nursing home. During the afternoon Thomas Jones discussed the crisis with Sir James Masterton Smith and Lionel Curtis, noting in his diary: 'We all deplored the unkind fate that had kept Churchill out of all this.'

On October 20 Hankey, Sir John Anderson and Sir James Masterton Smith were driving together to the Guildhall. On the following day Hankey recorded in his diary:

Masterton Smith told us a characteristic story of Winston Churchill. . . .
On coming to from his anaesthetic he immediately cried 'Who has got in for
Newport? Give me a newspaper'. The doctor told him he could not have it
and must keep quiet. Shortly after, the doctor returned and found Winston
unconscious again with four or five newspapers lying on the bed.

Churchill remained in the nursing home, recuperating slowly from
his operation, and too ill to work or write. On October 23 Lloyd George
went to see him 'on his bed of sickness', as Hankey recorded in his diary.
'Apparently Winston's pet aversion is Curzon,' Lloyd George told
Hankey, for Churchill had told Lloyd George: 'I am going to write
some letters next week and one of them will let Curzon have it.'
Churchill's bitterness arose because, as he later recorded in *Great Contemporaries*, Curzon had definitely assured the Coalition Ministers that
he would stand with them when the crisis came, but at the last moment,
he 'threw his weight against us'.

The news of Churchill's illness brought him many letters. On October
22 General Tudor wrote from his Gendarmerie headquarters in Palestine:

My dear Winston,
    I am so sorry to see that you have had to be operated on for appendicitis. I
hope you will soon be fit again. It is a great blow that with the change of
Govt you may not remain at the Colonial Office. Everybody knew whilst you
were there they would be properly backed up if things got difficult. I am
personally extremely sorry I shall no longer be under you. You have been a
real good friend to me. My present post is most interesting & I am more than
satisfied to be here. Your idea of using the 'Black & Tans'—& the British
Gendarmerie have inherited the name here!—has been a great success. They
have had a great influence already in keeping things quiet.
    I think the press attacks on Lloyd George for standing up to the Turks are
abominable. The Muslims are uppish enough at the Turkish victories as it is.
If we had not faced them as we did, our prestige in the Mohammedan world
would, in my opinion, have suffered very much more.

Yrs ever
H. H. Tudor

    General Harington also wrote to Churchill on October 22, from Con-
stantinople:

My dear S of S,
    I am sorry to see you are laid up with appendicitis. I do hope you will soon
be fit and about again as I realize how hard it must be for you to be laid up at
this moment. I have been trying to get a moment to write and thank you for
all your help over sending me the 1000 R.A.F. on the 'Braemar Castle' and I

appreciated it so much. They were a very fine body of men and did every-thing possible to help. I released them as soon as I could as I knew how much they were required elsewhere. Everyone has been so kind and I am quite overwhelmed with all the support sent to me. I only hope we are now on the road to peace. I am much impressed by General Raffet Pasha[1] who has arrived here to take over Eastern Thrace. The evacuation is very difficult and heart rending but I hope we shall get through without massacre and burning.

Again thanking you and hoping you will soon be fit again.

Yrs very sincerely,
Tim Harington

Churchill's constituency Party were anxious to know his view of the political crisis, and of the immediate future. On October 22 he sent a telegram to the President of the Dundee Liberal Association, James Robertson, in which he declared:

I am the vice-chairman of the National Liberal Council. I propose to stand as a Liberal and a Free-trader, but I shall ask the electors to authorize me to cooperate freely with sober-minded and progressive Conservatives in defend-ing the lasting and central interests of this realm and its wide Empire against the very dangerous attacks now about to be levelled upon them by the Socialist and Communist forces, as well as against the almost equally serious menace of downright reaction from the opposite quarter.

I shall appeal to the Liberals and Conservatives of Dundee to stand shoul-der to shoulder against the Labour and Communist candidates and to give their support to Mr MacDonald[2] and to me. If they should once again honour me with the right to speak in their name in the new Parliament 'Country before Party' shall be my guiding rule.

The Dundee Conservatives were puzzled by Churchill's telegram. He had declared himself a Liberal as before, but in appealing for a united front against Socialists and Communists, he was asking for the main-tenance of a Coalition that no longer existed. The Conservatives resolved to ask Churchill where he stood on the issues which troubled them,

---

[1] Raffet Pasha, 1881–1963. Born in Constantinople. A graduate of the Ottoman War Academy, he served in Palestine, 1915–17, rendering outstanding services on the Gaza front. Joined Mustafa Kemal, 1919. Commanded the 3rd sub-Army at Sivas, 1919–20. Member of the First National Grand Assembly, 1920. Minister of the Interior, 1921–1 ; of Defence, 1921–2. Member of Parliament, 1922–6 and 1939–50. He changed his name to Refet Bele.

[2] David Johnstone Macdonald, 1857–1940. A Dundee Engineer, and one of the best-known engineers in Scotland. Director of the Dundee branch of Lord Roberts' Memorial Workshop. Assessor of the General Tribunal, Dundee. A leading member of the Dundee Veterans' Garden City Association. Chairman of the Dundee Juvenile Advisory Committee. Chairman of the Scottish Committee for the training of discharged and disabled officers and men, 1915–21. Adopted as a National Liberal Candidate for Dundee on 13 June 1921; defeated at the General Election on 15 November 1922. Member of the Departmental Enquiry into Education and Industry in Scotland, 1927.

before deciding whether or not to put forward a candidate of their own.

On October 23, on a resolution proposed by Lord Curzon and Stanley Baldwin, at a meeting of Conservatives at the Hotel Cecil, Bonar Law was elected leader of the Conservative Party. He went at once to Buckingham Palace, and was appointed Prime Minister. The new Ministerial appointments were announced on October 24, and on the morning of October 25 Lloyd George's Ministers went to Buckingham Palace to hand over their Seals of Office. H. A. L. Fisher recorded in his diary that the King congratulated him on the Government's firm policy towards Turkey. Later that day Lord Stamfordham wrote to Churchill, who was still in bed:

The King desires me to say, firstly that he trusts you are making steady progress and that you must not impede it by your natural eagerness to join the Political Fray!—and further to express his great regret that you were unable to be present here this morning to hand over your Seal of Office and take leave of His Majesty. The King will, however, look forward to seeing you when you are convalescent—he will be back in London on the 2nd November.

May I add my own earnest hope that you will soon be well again.

Each of the Conservative members of the Coalition Government who had spoken against Lloyd George at the Carlton Club, or otherwise opposed the Coalition, received Cabinet Office in the new administration. Lord Curzon retained his position as Foreign Secretary and Stanley Baldwin was appointed Chancellor of the Exchequer. The four leading Conservative members of Lloyd George's Government who had wanted the Coalition preserved received no office under Bonar Law: these were Lord Birkenhead, Lord Balfour, Austen Chamberlain and Sir Robert Horne.

In the last week of October, Colonel Meinertzhagen was travelling by armoured car in the Syrian desert. During the journey he contacted Royal Air Force headquarters in Amman by wireless, and asked who had been appointed Colonial Secretary in Churchill's place. The reply came back: 'The Duke of Devonshire, thank God a gentleman.' On October 29 Meinertzhagen recorded in his diary:

So Winston is gone. For many reasons I am sorry. He has a brilliant brain and is as quick as lightning. He acts almost entirely by instinct and is usually right though easily led astray by some enthusiast. He was a hard master to serve, working like a Trojan himself and expecting equally hard work from his staff.

47

'I thought his career was over'

PARLIAMENT was dissolved by Royal Proclamation on
October 26, and elections were fixed to take place on November
15. Because of his operation for appendicitis, Churchill had to conduct
his election campaign, as he had watched the political crisis, from his
sick bed. He could no longer call upon the services of Edward Marsh
who, as a civil servant, remained at the Colonial Office as the Duke of
Devonshire's Private Secretary. But his Assistant Private Secretary and
shorthand writer, Harry Beckenham, remained with him, and it was to
Beckenham that Churchill dictated an election message on October 27.
The message, which was published in *The Times* on October 28, opened
with an attack on the new Government. 'It is absurd to suppose,' he
wrote, 'that Mr Bonar Law has a vital resourcefulness or constructive
capacity superior to that with which Mr Lloyd George was endowed;
and he continued:

How far the new Administration is equipped with Parliamentary and
popular figures well-known in the homes of the people and long established in
the public life of the nation you will be able to judge for yourselves. But when
I think of the gravity of the hour, of its formidable problems, of its measureless
uncertainties, I marvel at the temerity and presumption which have squandered so many friendly forces and stripped the State of much serviceable
experience and power.

The new Government, Churchill continued, had 'slighted' the position and authority of the House of Commons. 'Four out of five Secretaries of State,' he pointed out, 'are in the House of Lords. Most of the
principal personages of the Administration are Peers.'

Churchill went on to say that although he was standing as 'a Liberal
and a Free Trader', he hoped that the Conservatives of Dundee, who
had supported him 'with so much public spirit and disinterestedness'

since the formation of Asquith's Coalition in 1915, would continue to give him their support. There was one danger, he asserted, which made it essential for Liberals and Conservatives to continue to work together:

... when we turn our eyes from this newly-fledged Administration to the formidable Socialist attack which is gathering in the opposite quarter, we must see how great is the need for patriotic men and men of sincere goodwill to stand together. We cannot afford to be divided on minor issues when the whole accumulated greatness of Britain is under challenge. A predatory and confiscatory programme fatal to the reviving prosperity of the country, inspired by class jealousy and the doctrines of envy, hatred and malice, is appropriately championed in Dundee by two candidates[1] both of whom had to be shut up during the late war in order to prevent them further hampering the national defence. . . .

The Labour vote, Churchill warned, 'will be a very heavy one'. Only a united opposition could defeat it.

It was to Ireland to which Churchill then turned. 'I rejoice,' he wrote, 'to have been associated with the Irish Treaty and to have been in charge of Irish affairs during the whole of the present year.' And he continued:

Much of the bitterness which suddenly exploded at the Carlton Club was due to the fury of the Die-Hards at the Irish Treaty. This was the deed they could not forgive and for which they were determined to exact vengeance. But in spite of many disappointments and difficulties and heart-breaking delays the Treaty settlement is going to live and prosper.

Of the Chanak crisis, Churchill wrote with satisfaction and confidence, informing his constituents: 'I am very proud indeed to have taken part in the decisions and energetic action of the British Cabinet which prevented the Turks from carrying a new war into Europe. . . . So far from excusing the course we adopted I regard my association with it as one of the greatest honours in my long official life.' Speaking

---

[1] Georges Edmond Morel-de-Ville, 1873–1924. Born in France, the son of a French Ministry of Finance Official and an English Quaker lady. Educated in England. Naturalized (as E. D. Morel), 1896. Founded the Congo Reform Society, 1904. A Vice-President of the Anti-Slavery Society. Author of many books and pamphlets critical of British foreign and colonial policy. Editor of *Foreign Affairs*. Adopted as Liberal candidate for Birkenhead, 1914, but resigned on the outbreak of war, declaring that Grey's foreign policy was a main cause of war. Imprisoned for six months, 1917. Joined the Independent Labour Party, 1918. Labour MP for Dundee from November 1922 until his death two years later.

William Gallacher, 1881–1965. Chairman of the Clyde Workers Committee, 1914–18. Imprisoned for 3 months in 1921. Vice-Chairman of the British Communist Party, 1922. Member of the Executive Committee of the Communist International, 1924 (and again in 1935). Imprisoned for 12 months in 1925. Communist MP for West Fife, 1935–50. Chairman of the Communist Party of Great Britain, 1943–56; President from 1956 until his death.

of Lloyd George himself, Churchill declared his full support, and added: 'I am sure that among the broad masses of faithful, valiant, toiling, Britain-loving men and women whom he led to victory, there will still be found a few to wish him well.'

'And now,' Churchill continued, 'I have to make a most melancholy confession. For the time being I am helpless. I cannot stir a yard to defend myself or the causes about which I care. I must entrust my fortunes to the Liberal Association of Dundee.' And he ended his message: 'I leave myself in your hands.'

On October 29 Alfred Mond wrote to Churchill to urge an immediate reconciliation of the two Liberal factions. Churchill's illness, he said, 'has really been a disaster', both for 'your personal suffering and for your absence from the Councils in these critical days'. Mond wanted Lloyd George and Churchill to work together for a united Liberal platform. After all, he wrote, Churchill had declared that he was standing as a Liberal. But the Coalition Liberals, under Lloyd George's guidance, were at that very moment trying to negotiate an agreement with the Conservatives, whereby each would agree not to oppose the other in certain constituencies. Mond ended his letter with a strong personal appeal for 'Liberal Reunion', telling Churchill: 'Where ever I go all the Liberals I meet are simply dying for it. You and I are young men and can afford to wait for a great Liberal Revival.[1] It may keep us out of office a year or two, but it ought eventually to land you in the Premiership.'

In his reply, Churchill defended Lloyd George's decision to seek electoral bargains with the Conservatives, writing on October 31:

In the prevailing confusion everyone must fight his corner as best he can, and I do not at all blame you for the line you have taken. In Dundee, however, I am supported not only by an intact Liberal Association represented by far the predominant party in the city, but also by the Unionist Association, with whom I have made no bargain of any kind. . . . On the other hand, I am preserving the good and friendly relations which exist with the Unionists in my constituency who are sincerely united with me in resisting the two Socialist candidates. . . .

You must remember that we are under great obligations to the Unionists who have taken their lives in their hands and sacrificed so much to be loyal to Lloyd George. I am certainly not going to lose contact with them. You will find my criticisms of this Government of duds and pipsqueaks will not diminish as the combat deepens.

[1] In October 1922 Churchill was forty-seven years old and Sir Alfred Mond fifty-four. Churchill joined the Conservative Party in 1925, Mond in 1926.

As the election campaign progressed, Lord Beaverbrook offered to pay the election expenses of any Conservatives who were willing to stand against otherwise unopposed Lloyd George candidates. Churchill, however, had finally secured the support of the Dundee Conservatives, and no Conservative candidate was put up against him.

While he was still in the nursing home, Churchill drafted a fierce denunciation of Lord Beaverbrook's activities:

The Electors all over the country wd do well also to pay attention to the following facts. Behind Mr Bonar Law stands Lord Beaverbrook the gt Canadian financier. This vy gifted man with his millions & with his newspaper the 'Daily Express' is to a large extent the driving force animating the new Prime Minister. Lord Beaverbrook has a Transatlantic view of politics & with his influence over the Prime Minister he is at this moment probably the nearest approach to a Tammany Boss this country has ever witnessed. Do the Conservative party realise how much their fate & fortunes are in the hands of this strange wayward genius? Do they realise how much they will be in his hands if the schemes he is now carrying forward shd succeed? Do they realise the risks to the general political structure of this country of the cold blooded & unscrupulous policy wh he is pursuing. . . .

Churchill went on to condemn Beaverbrook's attempt to finance Conservative candidates in constituencies where Lloyd George's candidates were as yet unopposed. This, he warned, would split the anti-Socialist vote, and give the Labour Party a chance of victory.

Churchill also drafted a statement attacking two of the candidates who were to oppose him, E. D. Morel and William Gallacher. Morel's efforts, Churchill declared, had always been directed against Britain. He belonged 'to that band of degenerate international intellectuals who regard the greatness of Britain and the stability and prosperity of the British Empire as a fatal obstacle to their subversive sickness'. Churchill then turned his invective upon William Gallacher, citing Gallacher's wartime strike activities and post-war anti-capitalist speeches as proof that he was not a patriot. For such speeches and incitement, Churchill pointed out, Gallacher had already been imprisoned; and he went on to declare:

These crazy and ferocious outpourings and this long record of malignant if ineffectual blows struck at the prosperity and even at the existence of this country give a sufficient idea of the character and conduct of the new aspirant to the honour of representing Dundee in Parliament. From some points of view, however, their crudity renders them less pernicious and certainly less harmful than the more slimy and insidious propaganda of his companion and comrade Mr Morel.

The campaign in Dundee had begun in Churchill's absence. On October 30 the *Dundee Courier* published a reply by E. D. Morel, answering Churchill's accusation that he was not fit to be elected because he had been imprisoned during the war, and because he had been a leading advocate of a negotiated peace. 'As between Churchill and myself,' Morel told the *Courier*, 'it simply comes to this. I was working for peace before the war. He was working for war before the war. I tried to shorten its duration, not by peace at any price but by conference. He was for prosecuting it at any price.' Since November 1918, Morel added, he had worked for 'reconstruction and reconciliation', whereas Churchill 'has promoted fresh wars'.

On November 1 Churchill was well enough to leave the nursing home in Dorset Square. But he was still not well enough to leave his bed. Meanwhile, the Asquith Liberals had decided not to let him be the sole representative of Liberalism in Dundee, and had supported the candidature of R. R. Pilkington[1] on behalf of the Independent Liberal Party. When, on November 3, the *Manchester Guardian* supported this action, Churchill wrote angrily to C. P. Scott that he had previously understood the newspaper's policy to be opposed to 'purely wrecking and splitting candidatures between Liberals', as well as to 'the pursuance of personal vendettas'. Churchill's letter continued:

I expect you are pretty well ashamed in your heart of hearts at the line your caucus is taking in its bitter malevolence. If I had the health and strength to come to the Free Trade Hall I would concentrate the reprehension of the Liberals of the city upon the untimely pettiness of the action which is taken in their name.

Since October 30 Churchill had been represented in Dundee by one of his personal private secretaries, Lord Wodehouse. On November 4 Wodehouse was joined by General Spears, who had just been nominated unopposed, as a Coalition-Liberal for Loughborough. Wodehouse and Spears helped organize Churchill's committee rooms, made plans for the distribution of his election manifesto—which was expected within a few days—and organized the visits of those who were coming to Dundee to speak on his behalf. Fifty years later Spears recalled: 'I knew nothing about politics. Jack Wodehouse knew nothing about politics. There we both were—rivals only in ignorance.'

Churchill was keen that his wife should represent him during the

[1] Robert Rivington Pilkington,   –1942. Born in Australia. Called to the English Bar, 1893. Practised in Australia, 1894–1921. King's Counsel, 1906. Independent Liberal Candidate, Dundee, 1922. Liberal MP for Keighley, 1923–4.

final ten days of the campaign, and she agreed to go, although her daughter Mary was only seven weeks old. While his wife was on her way to Scotland, Churchill took steps to complete the purchase of Chartwell, and to arrange for its conversion. He had already asked a leading architect, Philip Tilden,[1] to design several extensions to the house, and Tilden had spent most of the afternoon with him. 'He wants very much,' Churchill wrote to his wife from London on November 6, 'to get decisions about the children's wing, in order that that can be ready by Christmas. . . .' Churchill added a more personal note:

I do hope you were not too tired by your long journey. I felt it was a great effort for you to cart yourself and your kitten all that way last night. Jack W. telephoned this morning that you were all right and were addressing a meeting this evening. Do take it easy. The mere fact of your presence will I am sure be highly beneficial.

Clementine Churchill made her first speech of the campaign on the evening of November 6, at Larch Street Hall. At the outset of the meeting, before she had arrived in the hall, the audience began to cough and sneeze; for sneezing powder had been released into the hall. 'The meeting was in a state of uproar,' the *Courier* reported, 'almost from beginning to end.' The first speaker was the former Parliamentary Under-Secretary of State for Scotland, J. W. Pratt, who was continually interrupted, and unable to finish his speech. Many of the hecklers were supporters of the Communist Candidate, William Gallacher. Clementine Churchill reached the hall while the shouting was at its height, and Pratt still trying to speak. In answer to a question as to whether Churchill worked for his money, Pratt replied 'that he had been one of the hardest workers the country had ever known'. This prompted sceptical cheers, and cries of 'Good old Gallacher'. Clementine Churchill then rose to speak. The *Courier* reported the ensuing scene:

Mrs Churchill was well received. Her opening sentence was, 'I am pleased to see you are all alive and kicking in Dundee——
A Voice—It's a good job we're living.
Mrs Churchill said she only wished her husband had not been prevented through his illness from coming to that meeting. He had been very ill. . . .
Although he had been prevented coming to Dundee, she felt confident that

[1] Philip Armstrong Tilden, 1887–1956. Architect, and decorator in murals. Among the houses on which he worked were Sir Philip Sassoon's houses, Port Lympne, and 25 Park Lane; and Lloyd George's house, Bron-y-de, at Churt in Surrey. He also exhibited black-and-white drawings at the Royal Academy, and designed bookplates. A Governor of the Old Vic Theatre, and of Sadlers Wells. President of the Devon and Cornwall Architectural Society. Author of a novel, *Noah* (1932) and a volume of memoirs, *True Remembrances*.

the great majority of the men and women of Dundee would not take advantage of that, and she would not be a bit surprised if he got a much bigger majority at this election. (Uproar) She would not like to feel that after all these years when he had been able to come to Dundee and fight they should take advantage because he was not able to come to Dundee.

A Woman—Play the game, Mrs Churchill, play the game. Don't use that sentimental argument about your man being ill. (Loud laughter.)

Mrs Churchill—Whatever you may think you know jolly well that he is an energetic, strong man, and I am quite certain that the great majority of the electors of Dundee will vote for him.

On the morning of November 7 Churchill's election address was published in *The Times*. He stood, he said, as a Liberal, but wished to make it 'quite clear' that he would not desert either Lloyd George, or 'the high-minded Conservatives who have stood by him and who are now exposed to the malicious intrigues alike of the "Die-hard" and "Wee Free" factions.' The Conservative Government, he added, was based 'on far too narrow a basis', to offer Britain political security. He continued:

But if the character and composition of the Government remind us of the days of King George III rather than of his present Majesty King George V, the policy which has been announced by the new Prime Minister carries us back almost into the Middle Ages. On every occasion when he has spoken, Mr Bonar Law has described his policy as one of negation, that is to say, 'Do nothing.' I cannot conceive that such a policy is possible in the modern world. I am sure it will not bring tranquillity.

Anyone who is acquainted with the grim social and economic conditions affecting the people, who knows the problems of our great cities, the clamant demands of public health, of housing, of education; everyone who understands the helplessness of large masses of people at the present time under the hard conditions of their environment, be he Liberal or be he Conservative, must know that no policy of negation will suffice. . . .

Such a message of negation will strike a knell of despair in the heart of every earnest social worker and of every striver after social justice. It cannot be accepted by any generous-hearted man or woman. Every broad-minded Unionist, every ardent Liberal, every Tory Democrat with a spark of the spirit of Disraeli or Lord Randolph Churchill in his breast must repudiate it.

Churchill then surveyed his opponents:

Apart from our old friend Mr Scrymgeour and our new friend Mr Pilkington, who may be safely left to expound their doctrines to their particular sectaries, we are confronted with a very serious and formidable attack of the two Socialist and Communist candidates. . . . Britain's difficulty has been their opportunity; Britain's triumph has been their mortification; Britain's downfall is their supreme objective. Mr Gallacher is only Mr Morel with the courage of his convictions, and Trotsky is only Mr Gallacher with the power to murder those whom he cannot convince.

Churchill urged the 'patriotic trade unionists' among his constituents not to support 'this pair of dangerous and dismal revolutionaries'. He himself, he said, would, if elected, 'carry forward the cause of social reform', on Liberal, and on Radical lines.

After Churchill's election address was issued from London, he began to deal with his constituents' questions. Those about Education he sent to H. A. L. Fisher for an answer, those about Health to Sir Alfred Mond. On November 7, Mond, in sending Churchill some information about health, wrote, of Churchill's election address: 'I do envy you your gift of coining phrases which will live.'

On the evening of November 7 Clementine Churchill again addressed the voters of Dundee. She was one of the speakers at the Caird Hall. But the uproar was even more intense than it had been on the previous night, and the audience, of over 3,000 people, would allow none of the speakers to complete their remarks. Clementine Churchill later recalled: 'The women of Dundee didn't like a woman getting involved in politics.' And General Spears commented: 'Clemmie appeared with a string of pearls. The women spat on her.'

Despite continual interruptions, which forced her on several occasions to sit down, Clementine Churchill managed to put forward several arguments on her husband's behalf. The *Courier* reported:

A barrage of cries and interruptions ensued, but Mrs Churchill carried on smilingly.

In the course of further efforts to destroy her speech Mrs Churchill appealed, 'Do be kind and let me get on'. She then treated the whole affair laughingly, and her smiles won the interrupters to comparative silence once again.

Clementine Churchill continued her campaign on November 8, speaking at one meeting in the afternoon, and three in the evening. General Spears later recalled: 'Clemmie's bearing was magnificent— like an aristocrat going to the guillotine in a tumbril.' At St Salvador's Hall, the *Courier* reported, 'she encountered a "Red Flag" element which persistently attempted to destroy order. . . .' On entering the Hall she had been received 'with applause and hisses'; an hour and a half later she left, as the meeting 'broke up in disorder'. At the Down-field Public Hall she referred to her husband's part in the Irish Treaty:

There were some things a Coalition Government could do that a purely party Government could not do, and one was the Irish settlement. (Applause.) She did not want to blow her husband's trumpet, but he did have a very great share in the Irish settlement. (Applause.) She remembered meeting in the street a little time ago a rather strong political opponent of her husband, who said. 'Well, I always knew Winston was a great fighter, but I did not know he was a great peacemaker.' (Applause.)

Clementine Churchill worked indefatigably. On November 7 Lord Wodehouse was also taken ill, adding to the problems of the Churchill organization. Churchill himself had now decided to go to Dundee, although he still had his stitches in from the operation. Meanwhile the attacks upon him by his opponents mounted in intensity. On November 8 Edwin Scrymgeour, who combined a radical socialist political philosophy with his prohibitionist ethic, declared that he was 'against any thought of civil war, but it would not surprise him, if there were one, if Mr Churchill were at the head of the Fascisti party'.[1]

On the night of November 8 Clementine Churchill sent her husband an account of the campaign so far:

The situation here is an anxious one but I comfort myself by remembering how in past election times when we got pessimistic Sir George Ritchie used to say with confidence that you would be returned. Mr Pratt is absolutely *invaluable*. He is such a good speaker & very conciliatory & tactful. He is delighted with his prospective Knighthood. Jack Wodehouse is recovered & is working again tooth & nail. . . .

If we win (which I pray & believe we will) we really must put in some time & work here & *re-organise* the whole organisation which was in chaos. Of course I feel the minute you arrive the atmosphere will change & the people will be roused. If you bring Sergeant Thompson etc tell him to conceal himself tactfully as it would not do if the populace thought you were afraid of them. The papers are so *vile*, they would misrepresent it & say you have bought detectives because you were afraid of the rowdy element. They are capable of anything.

If you feel strong enough I think besides the Drill Hall Meeting which is pretty sure to be broken up you should address one or two small open meetings. Every rowdy meeting rouses sympathy & brings votes & will especially as you have been so ill. Even in the rowdiest foulest place of all the people tho' abusive were really good-natured. To shew you the sort of place it was there were placards all round the walls with not as you might guess 'no spitting' or 'no smoking' or 'no swearing' allowed but 'Obscene Language not allowed'! . . .

[1] Mussolini had come to power in Italy on 30 October 1922, not only as Prime Minister, but also as President of the Fascist Council, Minister of the Interior and Minister of Foreign Affairs. He was only thirty-nine years old.

I am longing to see you & so is Dundee—I shall be heartbroken if you don't get in. I find what the people like best is the settlement of the Irish Question. So I trot that out & also your share in giving the Boers self government. The idea against you seems to be that you are a 'War Monger', but I am exhibiting you as a Cherub Peace Maker with little fluffy wings round your chubby face. I think the line is not so much 'Smash the Socialists' as to try with your great abilities to help in finding a solution of the Capital & Labour problem & I tell them that now you are free from the cares & labours of office you will have time to think that out & work for it in the next Parliament.

My darling, the misery here is appalling. Some of the people look absolutely starving. Morel's Election address just out *very moderate* & in favour of only constitutional methods. So one cannot compare him with Gallacher.

Your loving
Clemmie

That evening Lord Birkenhead spoke on Churchill's behalf at the Caird Hall. Clementine Churchill was among those on the platform. Birkenhead devoted most of his speech to a vicious attack on E. D. Morel, whose French origins he derided. 'France was a very great country,' he said, 'and, on the whole, he liked a man to stick to the country, particularly if it was a great one, in which he was born.' To the accompaniment of increasing applause and delight, Birkenhead repeated Morel's original French name again and again, in sarcastic tone. Were there to be a grave international crisis, he went on, there would be no point in the electors having chosen either Morel or Gallacher: 'Both would be in gaol. That was not much good to Dundee.'

Clementine Churchill was disappointed, and angered by Birkenhead's speech. 'He was no use at all,' she later recalled, 'he was drunk.'

On the evening of November 10, Churchill left London by train for Dundee, reaching his constituency on the morning of November 11, and going straight to his campaign headquarters at the Royal Hotel. That evening he spoke at the Caird Hall, at a meeting of his supporters. He was too ill to stand, but spoke, sitting, from a special platform; and spoke for over an hour and a half. His first remarks were in praise of the late Coalition, which had, he said, 'laboured—and laboured successfully—to improve and rebuild the credit of the country, to pay our debts, and to pay our way'. Britain was the only nation in Europe, he declared, which had re-established its financial position 'unshaken and unshakable'.

Churchill then defended the Coalition's policy during the Chanak crisis, telling his constituents, as the *Courier* reported:

It was a new war that had to be stopped. It was a new war which they endeavoured to stop. It was a new war which at the time when Mr Lloyd George left office was definitely stopped. (Cheers.) That was an achievement which to his dying day he would be proud to have participated in. . . . Someone would say to him 'Ah! but a risk was run.' Quite true, a risk was run. Risks were run every time the lifeboat went out into the storm, but such risks had never deterred men, aye, and women, too, of British blood from doing their duty. (Cheers.)

The Coalition, Churchill said, had been overthrown because the Tory Die-hards hated the men who had made the Irish Treaty. And yet, he pointed out, Bonar Law's Government had promised to carry out the Treaty, and he rejoiced that this was so. It was now up to Irishmen, he said, to work towards peace and unity: 'The Irishman has got to con-quer himself or perish. Nobody can do it for him.' When Churchill described Arthur Griffith and Michael Collins as 'those Irish patriots', a heckler cried out: 'How many did they murder,' to which Churchill replied: 'Ah, this is no time to add up the catalogue of injuries. This is the time to pass the sponge of oblivion, merciful oblivion, across the horrid past.'

Churchill then spoke of his rival candidates. E. D. Morel, he said, was certainly 'a man of intellectual eminence and distinction', nor did he deny that he had wanted to make peace in 1917 from 'the most high-minded motives'. If a man faced hardship and imprisonment for his opinion, Churchill continued, 'you do not deny him at all the reputa-tion of being conscientious, but if a man is conscientiously bent on my destruction, although I may admire his methods, I resist his action'. Churchill then spoke of the Temperance candidate:

As for Scrymgeour, he was always with them. (Laughter.) They admired his persistency and his fidelity to the principles which he advocated; still, a vote given to him, apart from being a testimony to the views which he held and the opinion which he had championed for so many years, was a vote which he did not think would have any direct bearing upon the great issues being fought out in Dundee.

At this point, Clementine Churchill gestured to her husband that Scrymgeour himself was in the audience. Churchill, according to the *Courier*, 'smiled broadly'.

Churchill appealed for an end to 'party turmoil', and the inaugura-tion of a period 'of stability and recuperation from which a victorious nation might regain its strength'. And he ended his speech with a brave, but painful gesture, which the *Courier* recorded:

Ah! ladies and gentlemen, said Mr Churchill, rising to his feet, let us stand together—(cheers)—let us be united, let us tread the sober middle way amid the confusion and perplexity of the present time. Let us send forth from Dundee to the whole of Great Britain a message. Let us send forth from Scotland and from Britain to the whole world a message of strength and of conviction, of encouragement and valour, a message which will resound far beyond the limits of this small island and carry its good cheer to the suffering, struggling, baffled, tortured humanity the wide world o'er. (Loud cheers.)

Churchill then sat down, exhausted by his speech, and in pain at having stood up for his peroration. But at least the audience had been made up mostly of his supporters. Two days later, on the evening of November 13, he had a quite different, and frightening experience. That night he was due to speak at the Drill Hall. A vast crowd had come to hear him, but hundreds were turned away for lack of space, and the gates to the Hall were padlocked. So great was the crush, however, that one of the gates burst open, and the crowd surged forward towards the Hall. The police guarding the hall at once advanced, driving the crowd back with their batons. 'Several who were in the front of the rush,' the *Courier* reported, 'are suffering from the effects of the successful efforts of the police to keep the crowd under control.'

Inside the Hall the waiting audience seemed, according to the *Courier*, 'electrified' by the possibility of a meeting which promised to be 'of an unusual character'. Churchill himself arrived at half-past seven, and was received 'with rounds of cheers intermixed with howling and booing'. A special raised seat had been prepared for Churchill, as at the Caird Hall, so that he could speak while sitting down. But he decided not to use it at the start. General Spears, who had accompanied Churchill to the hall, later recalled:

Everyone was standing. As Winston forced himself up on his feet, the enormous packed meeting surged back as if they had been hit in the face. But they quickly found their voice again, and yelled and yelled. They would not let him speak. As fatigue overtook him he fell back. The crowd at once surged forward. They had planted posts to protect the platform, but the upsurge was so great that the posts bent, and it looked for a moment as if the mob were going to overwhelm the platform.

After several minutes of booing and hissing, Churchill managed to speak. The *Courier* recorded the course of his remarks:

I have not had much opportunity, he began, to prosecute—(A Voice—'Why don't you go to Manchester this time?')—(laughter)—my campaign in Dundee. A lot of people have been criticising me—(A Voice—'You deserve it')—but whether I deserve it or not I have a right to make my answer. (Cheers.)

Continued interruptions were accompanied by cries of 'Shut up' from the other section of the audience.

Mr Churchill said no man was condemned unheard in Britain. The election campaign had been in progress for nearly three weeks, and he was only able to come here last Saturday, and this was the second great meeting he had had the chance of addressing, and as the poll was on Wednesday—(A Voice—'You will be at the bottom of the poll.') 'If I am going to be at the bottom of the poll,' interjected Mr Churchill, 'why don't you allow me my last dying kick.' (Cheers.) He had only got three days in which to state his case to the electors of Dundee. It was perfectly clear when they were very crowded, when many of them, he feared—(A Voice—'You are a political failure.' laughter)—were very uncomfortable and crowded together, it was perfectly clear they could not conduct a public meeting—(interruptions)—unless everyone looked after one. (A Voice—'Do be serious.' laughter.) 'If they do,' continued Mr Churchill, 'we can have an important political discussion; and if they don't we can have a bear garden.' (Uproar.)

Churchill tried to persuade the audience to give him a hearing. If the disturbances were to continue, he said, he would 'go home to bed without having to argue a lot of difficult questions'; but in a democracy, the right to speak must be upheld 'in a peaceful and in an orderly manner'. And he continued:

This I do say to you. As a matter of fair bargain, if you are going to let me speak at all, you must let me say whatever I choose. I am not going to be muzzled and to be told that I am going to attack this man or that; that I must not say anything against this candidate and that candidate. Not at all. If anybody has got a shrewd rejoinder to make let them make it, but let us at any rate survey broadly the situation.

Churchill could go no further. From the audience came the cry: 'What about the Dardanelles?' When Churchill replied that he was not going to try to put any arguments forward unless he was listened to 'in silence', there was another howl from the audience, and then Churchill spoke again:

'If about a hundred young men and women in the audience choose to spoil the whole meeting, and if about a hundred of these young reptiles—(cheers and uproar)—choose to deny to democracy, the masses of the people, the power to conduct great assemblies, the fault is with them, the blame is with them, and the punishment will be administered to them by the electors. (cheers and booing.) Now you see what the Gallacher crowd are worth. (Cheers and uproar.) Now you see the liberty you have if the country were run by them—(cheers and interruptions.)—no sense, no brains, just breaking up a meeting that they would not have the wit to address. (Cheers.) The electors will know how to deal with a party whose only weapon is idiotic clamour.' (Cheers.)

According to the *Courier*'s account of the meeting:

At this stage pandemonium broke out anew, and when comparative quietness again prevailed Mr Churchill said he had addressed public meetings for the last five and twenty years, and he never remembered having addressed one which was not willing to listen to a political argument. 'Perhaps you would like to hear some other speaker for the time being, in which case I will be glad to give way. I am quite willing to listen to some other speaker.'

Subsequent interruptions lasted for nearly five minutes. Mr Churchill waited patiently, remarking—'They will soon get tired.' ('Send him home,' cried a voice.)

Churchill could say no more. He abandoned his speech, and suggested that he answer questions instead. There was at once 'a fusillade of questions', and it was some minutes before speakers could be persuaded to ask their questions one at a time. Five questioners managed to make themselves heard above the catcalls and uproar. Then the spate of questions increased. No single one could be heard among the others. 'The howling mob intensified their efforts in producing a perfect rabble of vocal discord,' the *Courier* reported. Churchill remained seated during the outcry. Finally, while the noise continued unabated, he rose, in the hope of saying a few concluding words. According to the *Courier*'s account:

His opening sentence was marked by an effort to sing the 'Red Flag', but it soon died away.

He said—Ladies and gentlemen, I thank you most sincerely for the attentive hearing—(applause)—you have given me, and I think you have vindicated in a most effective manner the devotion of the Socialist party to free speech. You have shown, it has been shown, clearly that a handful of rowdies can break up a great meeting, and can prevent ten times their number from transacting their public business. (Applause.) We may be interrupted here tonight, but we will carry out our purpose at the poll. (Applause). We will stand up for the rights of British citizens, the rights and liberties of British citizens against the supporters of the Socialist candidates who, if they have their way, would reduce—(uproar)—this great country to the same bear garden to which they have reduced this great meeting. (Applause, and booing.)

Churchill sat down amid what the *Courier* described as 'the disturbance of the meeting-wreckers', and in reply to several of the platform party he declared—'No, I am finished.'

That night Churchill's detective slept across the door of his room in the hotel. Every time a cork popped, General Spears later recalled, 'we thought it was Winston being shot'.

Throughout the campaign, Churchill had been criticized relentlessly by the two Dundee newspapers, the *Courier* and the *Advertiser*, both of whom were owned by the same man, D. C. Thomson.[1] On November 14, the day before polling was to take place, Churchill revealed the strength of his anger to a small and sympathetic audience at Broughty Ferry. It was, he said, 'not only the communist and socialist tag, rag and bobtail', which indulged in undemocratic practices. The press was equally to blame. D. C. Thomson 'has equally set his face against the free expression of opinion'. During the course of his speech Churchill declared:

You have the Liberal and the Conservative newspaper owned by the same man and produced from the same office on the same day. Here is one man, Mr Thomson, selling Liberal opinions with his left hand and Conservative opinions with his right hand at the same moment. That is an extraordinary spectacle. I say that if such conduct were developed in private life or by politicians in public life every man and woman in the country would say, 'That is very double-faced. You cannot believe the two.' What would be said, I would like to know, of a preacher who preached Roman Catholicism in the morning, Presbyterianism in the afternoon, and then took a turn at Mohammedanism in the evening? He would be regarded as coming perilously near a rogue. It would be said of a politician who made Socialist speeches in Scotland, Conservative speeches in England, and Radical speeches in Wales—you would say he was downright dishonest. . . .

Here we get in the morning the Liberal Mr Thomson through the columns of the Liberal 'Dundee Advertiser' advising the Liberals of Dundee to be very careful not to give a vote to Mr Churchill because his Liberalism is not quite orthodox. This is the Mr Thomson, the same Mr Thomson, who failed to get elected as chairman of the Conservative Party, telling the Liberals to be very

[1] David Couper Thomson, 1861–1954. Born in Dundee, son of William Thomson, Shipowner. Founder of the publishing company of D. C. Thomson & Co, 1905. Managing Director of more than twelve Scottish newspapers, including the *Dundee Courier*, the *Dundee Argus*, the *Dundee Advertiser*, the *Evening Telegraph*, the *Weekly Post*, the *Weekly Welcome*, *Red Letter* and the *Sunday Post*. In 1922 he started his first comic paper, the *Rover*. In the late 1930s he launched *Dandy* and *Beano*.

careful of the company they keep, warning the Liberal Association that they have strayed from the true fold, and that by any attempt to stretch a friendly hand to progressive Conservatives they are running perilously in danger of jeopardising their political soul.

At the same time, the same moment, you have the Conservative, the 'Die-Hard' Mr Thomson, through the columns of the Conservative 'Dundee Courier', advising the Conservative electors of Dundee to be very careful lest in giving a vote to Mr Churchill they should run the risk of building up opposition to the new Conservative Government; and you get the same man behind these two absolutely differently served up dishes, hot or cold, roast or boiled, seasoned or unseasoned, according to taste, and both brought out by the same cook from the same kitchen. Behind those two, I say, you get the one single individual, a narrow, bitter, unreasonable being eaten up with his own conceit, consumed with his own petty arrogance, and pursued from day to day and from year to year by an unrelenting bee in his bonnet.

Churchill was convinced that it was Thomson's attitude towards him which had created the gulf between himself and the majority of his constituents, telling his audience: 'I have had a couple of years of ceaseless detraction, spiteful, malicious detraction. Anything that I have done which has been of advantage to this city . . . anything which has been in accordance with the wishes of my constituents has been whittled away or crabbed or put in some obscure position.' And he warned:

. . . it comes to the day—it is reaching the point—when public men will have to stand up against it. I do not speak against the papers. They are ably and well conducted, but against the man behind the papers, and he is the man I hold up here in the district where he lives to the reprobation of his fellow-citizens.

Churchill's outburst did him no good. On November 15, the morning of the election, the *Courier*'s editorial remarked: 'Whatever may be his chances at the poll today, there can be no doubt that Mr. Winston Churchill is in a vile temper. He takes no pains to conceal the fact. Like the disappointed man on the station platform he kicks out any anybody who happens to be near him.' The editorial continued: 'He has sprayed Labour with invective, has sprinkled many doses of it upon his rival candidates—Mr Pilkington, Mr Morel, Mr Scrymgeour, and Mr Gallacher—and now he has turned the full blast of his vituperation upon the Dundee newspapers. Whose turn it will be tomorrow God only knows.'

The *Courier* advised the people of Dundee to vote for Pilkington and Macdonald. Throughout November 15 the electors went to the polls. But they elected neither Churchill, nor Pilkington nor Macdonald, but the Prohibitionist and the Socialist. The result of the Election was declared on November 16:

E. Scrymgeour (Independent)	32,578	elected
E. D. Morel (Labour)	30,292	
D. J. Macdonald (National Liberal)	22,244	
W. Churchill (National Liberal)	20,466	
R. R. Pilkington (Independent Liberal)	6,681	
W. Gallacher (Communist)	5,906	

Churchill was without a seat in Parliament for the first time in twenty-two years. Fourteen years earlier, when he had first been elected for Dundee, Scrymgeour had received only 655 votes.[1] On November 16, in his speech of farewell at the Liberal Club Rooms, Churchill declared: 'My heart is devoid of the slightest sense of regret, resentment or bitterness; on the contrary I look back over those eventful years in which we have lived and fought through together, and I feel I can have done nothing in these stormy times without your loyal and sustained support.' Churchill also spoke to his supporters about the principal victor:

In Mr Scrymgeour's victory they saw the victory of a man who stood for endurance, and also for moral orderly conceptions of democratic reform and action. They would find he (Mr Scrymgeour) would have a useful part to play in representing Dundee, where there was such fearful misery and distress and such awful contrast between one class and another. He did not in the least grudge Mr Scrymgeour his victory.

Churchill added that he hoped his supporters would forgive him, if he said no more, for he was 'far from well'. That night he left Dundee for London. As he left his hotel, a crowd of students followed him to the station, where, according to the *Courier*, 'they bore down on him and quickly surrounded him'. But their purpose was a friendly one, as the *Courier* reported:

With his roystering retinue behind, Mr Churchill walked up to the far end of the platform to the waiting train smoking a cigar and smiling broadly. Before entering the carriage he shook hands cordially with the students, who were singing with great gusto the Varsity song, 'Ygorra,' altering the last line to finish 'Churchill Ygorra.' One or two Irish students in the party were specially demonstrative, and one waxed so enthusiastic that he lost his eye glasses, which were trampled and broken under the feet of the crowd swaying round the carriage door. Heedless of his loss, this enthusiastic Irishman again and again called for 'Cheers for Churchill,' his slogan being 'Up Churchill,

[1] In 1908, after he had first accepted the invitation to stand for Dundee, Churchill wrote to his mother: 'It is a life seat and cheap & easy beyond all experience.'

up Collins. Collins believed in you, we believe in you.' Mrs Churchill who was smiling cheerily, then shook hands all round, and there were further cries of 'Cheers for Mrs Churchill.'

'Say a few words, Mr Churchill,' was an appeal which after a few moments' hesitation he did not let pass unheeded. Leaning out of the compartment window, Mr Churchill said he expressed from the very bottom of his heart his appreciation of those boys coming down. They were very kind. He referred to the happy associations which he had had with Dundee during all those fifteen years he had represented the city. He had always been a democrat, and had always believed in the right of the people to make their own institutions. He bowed to that now, even though he thought that it was misguided. 'Accept my heartfelt gratitude, you boys,' went on Mr Churchill, 'for the kindly thoughts which have caused you to come down here when others are away celebrating other things. (Loud cheers and laughter.) Nothing has given me greater pleasure,' he added, 'than the fact that during the last year that I have represented Dundee I have been able to do something for old Ireland.'

This reference to Ireland sent the Irish students of the party into further ecstacies, and renewed cries of 'Good old Churchill' resounded up and down the station.

The engine whistle shrieking its warning of departure, Mr Churchill made his final adieus, and as the train moved off he said 'Goodbye, boys,' and, leaning out of the window, waved his hat to his loudly-cheering followers until the lights of the train were swallowed up in the darkness of the night.

'His is perhaps, the most sensational defeat of the whole election,' the *Daily Telegraph* declared on November 17. 'Politically,' wrote the *Daily Mail*, 'Mr Churchill has had as many lives as the proverbial cat, but the indictment against him is a long one.'

The result of the election was an overwhelming victory for Bonar Law and the Conservatives, who won 345 seats, as against 142 for the Labour Party. Lloyd George's National Liberals won only 62 seats, the Asquithian Liberals 54, pushing them into third and fourth place, and giving them, even if combined, a smaller representation than that of the Labour Party.

Churchill's defeat at Dundee provoked great sympathy among his friends and former colleagues. On November 17 Lord Londonderry wrote:

My dear Winston,

I am more distressed over the result of your election than I am capable of expressing in words. It seems quite incomprehensible to me. I know how much you will feel it from so many different points of view. I feel however that a good rest now, and especially after your serious operation, will not be at all a bad thing, and I have no doubt that a seat can and will be found for you as soon as you want one. . . .

Let me beg of you to have a good rest. These operations take more out of you, than one with your fiery spirit and boundless energy ever can realize. I know all about it because I have gone through a lesser operation than yours and it took me more than 6 months to feel completely recovered.

Love to you all my dear Winston,

Yours affectionately,
Charley

Humbert Wolfe,[1] who had worked under Churchill at the Ministry of Munitions throughout 1918, wrote on November 17:

Will you acquit me of impertinence if I write to say how profoundly I resent the Dundee result? You won't want to hear from an individual I guess at the verdict on your public record, which you may safely trust to history. But perhaps you will let me remind you how deep & how permanent is the affection, which you inspire in all who have the honour to serve you. We all (I know!) felt what happened as a blow personal to ourselves. It is of course the most transitory of reverses, but as it may cast a momentary shadow you may care to be assured that when you & Mrs Churchill waited for the result & still more when you heard it you were not alone.

On November 18, T. E. Lawrence wrote to his former chief, whose employ he had left in order to join the Royal Air Force:

Dear Mr Churchill

This is a difficult letter to write—because it follows on many unwritten ones. First I wanted to say how sorry I was when you fell ill, and again when you had to have an operation. Then I should have written to say I was sorry when the Government resigned. I meant to write & congratulate you on getting better: but before I could do that you were in Dundee and making speeches. Lastly I should write to say that I'm sorry the poll went against you—but I want to wash out all these lost opportunities, & to give you instead my hope that you will rest a little: six months perhaps. There is that book of memoirs to be made not merely worth £30,000, but of permanent

---

[1] Humbert Wolfe, 1886–1940. Born in Milan, of German-Italian Jewish parentage. Educated at Bradford Grammar School and Wadham College, Oxford. Entered the civil service, 1908. At the Board of Trade he played a leading part in the organization of Labour Exchanges and Unemployment Insurance. Controller, Labour Regulation Department, Ministry of Munitions, 1915–18. Director of Services and Establishments, Ministry of Labour, 1919–21; Head of the Department of Employment and Training, 1934–7; Deputy Secretary, 1938. A poet and literary critic, his first volume of poetry was published in 1920. He wrote or edited over 40 books, and translated Greek, German and French poems and plays.

value. Your life of Lord Randolph shows what you could do with memoirs. Then there is the painting to work at, but I feel you are sure to do that anyhow: but the first essential seems to me a holiday for you. It sounds like preaching from a younger to an elder (and is worse still when the younger is an airman-recruit!) but you have the advantage of twenty years over nearly all your political rivals: and physically you are as strong as any three of them (do you remember your camel-trotting at Giza, when you wore out your escort, except myself, & I'm not a fair competitor at that!) and in guts and power and speech you can roll over anyone bar Lloyd George: so that you can (or should) really not be in any hurry.

Of course I know that your fighting sense is urging you to get back into the scrimmage at the first moment: but it would be better for your forces to rest & rearrange them: & no bad tactics to disengage a little. The public won't forget you soon, & you will be in a position to choose your new position and line of action more freely, for an interval. I needn't say that I'm at your disposal when you need me—or rather if ever you do. I've had lots of chiefs in my time, but never one before who really was my chief. The others have needed help at all times: you only when you want it. . . .

'I'm more sorry about Winston than I can say,' Lawrence wrote to Edward Marsh on November 18. 'I hope the Press comment is not too malevolent. It's sure to hurt him though. What bloody shits the Dundeans must be.' This was not Churchill's own verdict. That same day he wrote to H. A. L. Fisher: 'If you saw the kind of lives the Dundee folk have to live, you would admit they have many excuses.'

Churchill's defeat caused widespread comment. 'Winston too, is out,' Sir Ian Hamilton's wife[1] wrote in her diary on November 17, 'and wept bitterly at Dundee the papers say; Winston denies this and told Ian he did not care: he is off to *Rome* for four months as he hears there are such good tennis courts at the Embassy. . . .' and on November 19 Lord Esher wrote to Sir Philip Sassoon: 'The women put Winston out. When he loses his temper, he looks so damned ugly. Otherwise it was ten to one, in Dundee, on a Whiskey bottle versus a Pussyfoot.'

On November 19 J. L. Garvin[2] commented on Churchill's defeat in his 'Political Notes' in *The Observer*. 'Personally he is a brilliant and lovable human being,' Garvin wrote, 'Before the Chanak scare his Parliamentary gifts had come to the pitch in his handling of the Irish

---

[1] Jean Muir, 1863–1941. Daughter of the ship-owner Sir John Muir, 1st Baronet. She married Ian Hamilton in 1887 (when he was a Major, Gordon Highlanders, and ADC to the Commander-in-Chief, East Indies). She and her husband bought Lullenden from Churchill in 1921.

[2] James Louis Garvin, 1868–1947. Editor, *The Observer*, 1908–42. Editor, *Pall Mall Gazette*, 1912–15. Editor-in-Chief, *Encyclopaedia Brittanica*, 1926–9. His only son was killed in action in 1916 on the western front.

Treaty. In the variety and force of his powers, he was shown to be not inferior to any other personality whatever.' But then, Garvin added, 'he spoilt it all by the Chanak manifesto'. In his article, Garvin summed up the feelings of those who, although sympathetic towards Churchill, feared that there was some flaw in his character which might mar his rise to the premiership. As Garvin wrote:

> Mr Churchill is not yet fifty. Behind him there lies an immense length and range of administrative experience and political performance. In vivid, yet deliberate exposition, in massive yet glowing appeal, he has no equal. Yet whether he ever comes to the very top or not, will depend upon the answer to one old question. The tendency to rush into warlike enterprises—and general-ly to build on first impressions—has been the very bane of his life, and unless he corrects that bias all else will be in vain.
>
> If Mr Churchill takes a little time for reflection on all this, Dundee may be the best thing that ever happened to him. . . .

Churchill reflected continuously on his defeat. On November 21 he wrote to Lord Stamfordham, setting out his thoughts on the election campaign, and describing his plans for the immediate future. 'It was very trying,' he wrote, 'having to do three days of electioneering with a serious wound so newly healed. It was quite impossible for me to defend myself in so short a time. I have always held Dundee by speeches and argument and at least three weeks is required to deal with such a large number of electors.'

'His Majesty is very sorry about the Dundee Election,' Lord Stam-fordham replied on November 22, from Buckingham Palace, 'but of course realises how heavily handicapped you were after your severe operation. But the Scotch Electorate is rather an incomprehensible body!' On November 24 Churchill's former headmaster, Bishop Welldon,[1] wrote from the Deanery, Durham: 'My dear Churchill. You will, I think, allow me as an old friend to express my regret, I could almost say my indignation, at your loss of your seat in the House of Commons. Ingratitude, I am afraid, is apt to be one of the vices of democracy. But it is sometimes an advantage to a statesman that he should be temporarily excluded from the House of Commons. . . .'

---

[1] James Edward Cowell Welldon, 1854–1937. Headmaster of Harrow School, 1885–98. Bishop of Calcutta, 1898–1902. Canon of Westminster, 1902–6. Dean of Manchester, 1906–18. Dean of Durham, 1918–33. On 28 September 1896, while Churchill was on his way to India, Welldon wrote to him: 'I implore you not to let your wild spirits carry you away to any action that may bring dishonour on your school or your name. It is impossible that I should not hear of your follies and impertinences if you are guilty of them, and you will recognise that you put a severe strain upon my friendship if you ask me to treat you as a friend when other people speak of you with indignation or contempt.'

Welldon added: 'I do not doubt that your star will rise again and will shine even more brightly than before.'

The new Parliament was opened on November 27. Without either a place in the Cabinet or a seat in Parliament, Churchill had no reason to delay any further the publication of his memoirs. On November 23 he informed his literary agent, Curtis Brown, that he hoped to be able to send *The Times* sufficient text for serialization 'in about a month'.

Churchill planned to leave England on November 30—his forty-eighth birthday—for a four-month holiday in the Mediterranean. Before leaving he dined with Sir Alfred Mond, who, having dis-associated himself from Lloyd George during the election and having stood as an independent Liberal, had held his seat. Among those present was Lloyd George's former private secretary, Geoffrey Shakespeare, who, at his first attempt, had just been elected to Parliament as a Lloyd George Liberal. 'Winston was so down in the dumps,' Shakespeare later recalled, 'he could scarcely speak the whole evening. He thought his world had come to an end—at least his political world. I thought his career was over.'

48
Retrospect: 'Ponder, & then *act*'

D URING the six years of Lloyd George's premiership, Church-ill's enthusiasm for public life was intense and productive. Be-tween 1917 and 1922 he accepted responsibility not only for the work of his own Departments, but for many other tasks which he was asked to carry out in the spheres of economy, defence and foreign affairs. These tasks were heavy ones. 'After nearly 14 years of experience of administrative departments,' he wrote to Lloyd George at the beginning of September 1919, 'I have never seen anything to compare with the difficulties of the questions now pressing for decision, while the daily routine business in volume exceeds several times the greatest pressure known before the war.'

Churchill welcomed the responsibility which Lloyd George gave him. He worked long hours, demanded a great deal from his subordinates, spoke often both in Parliament and in public, continued to write for the Press, and was active not only in Cabinet, but also in a series of im-portant and time-consuming Cabinet Committees. 'This has been a really hard-worked week for me,' he wrote to his wife from the Colonial Office on 27 January 1922: 'Continual speeches & discussions on one grave subject after another. A foretaste perhaps of what is to come.'

As an administrator, Churchill was a careful and considerate chief; in setting out the guidelines by which his subordinates were to work, he showed himself appreciative of their problems. 'The men at the top should not be overworked,' he wrote to General Macdonogh on 20 January 1919, a week after reaching the War Office. 'There should be plenty of them, each should have his sphere, and they should have leisure and a good deal in hand.' It was impossible, Churchill added, to carry out any major administrative task 'without delegation of powers and a really big machine at the top'. At the Ministry of Munitions in 1917, and as head of the Middle East Department in 1921, Churchill set up entirely new administrative machinery to deal with previously uncoordinated problems. To each Department of which he was head, he brought in officials with a wide range of expertise, encouraged them to use their initiative, scrutinized what they did, stirred them to action by constant questioning and supported their policies when they went forward to the Cabinet for decision.

One of the main administrative problems throughout Lloyd George's peacetime premiership was the reduction of Government spending. To this task Churchill and his officials devoted a large portion of their time. Churchill's Estimates speeches, both as Secretary of State for War, and as Colonial Secretary, were intricate, comprehensive, and often inspiring, explanations of why economies were needed, and how they could be made. His work at the Middle East Department centred on the need to save Britain from unnecessary expense abroad. For over a month Churchill guided his Departmental officials in working out the basis of a comprehensive scheme for reducing expenditure in Mesopotamia and Palestine; then, at the Cairo Conference in March 1921, he prevailed upon his Colonial officials to accept his plans for economy. Throughout his two years as Colonial Secretary he was vigilant in restricting extravagance, and finding cheaper methods of keeping order. By September 1922 he had reduced Britain's annual expenditure in the Middle East from £45,000,000 to £11,000,000.

Churchill's colleagues and subordinates were much impressed by his administrative skills. On 17 July 1917 Christopher Addison noted in his diary: 'There is no more capable chief of a department than he is.' On 22 October 1922 General Tudor wrote to Sir Hugh Trenchard, of Churchill's two years at the Colonial Office: 'Everyone felt, while he was there, that if things did get bad they would be thoroughly backed up.'

The work for which Churchill was most praised during Lloyd George's premiership was his handling of the Irish negotiations in 1922. 'Firmness,' he told the House of Commons on 31 May 1922, 'is needed in the interest of peace as much as patience.' During the negotiations he showed both qualities to a high degree. At daily meetings, often conducted under conditions of great strain, he had soothed the suspicions and allayed the fears of both South and North. The Free State leaders were particularly appreciative of his understanding. Shortly before his death in August, Michael Collins sent a message to London: 'Tell Winston we could never have done anything without him,' and on 23 September 1922, after the negotiations were concluded, William Cosgrave sent Churchill a private letter, thanking him for his 'sympathetic insight, tact and breadth of view.'

Churchill's closest friends had always recognized his political courage. On 13 October 1915 Edward Marsh had written to Archibald Sinclair: 'the worse things go, the braver and serener he gets—it was the feeling of being condemned to inactivity that was so terribly *depressing* to him'. Seven years later, on 11 November 1922, T. E. Lawrence wrote to R. D. Blumenfeld: 'The man's as brave as six, as good-humoured, shrewd, self-confident & considerate as a statesman can be: & several times I've seen him chuck the statesmanlike course & do the honest thing instead.'

In times of crisis, Churchill's courage enabled him to give a firm lead and good guidance. Recognizing this quality, Lloyd George often sought his advice during the six years of his premiership. When danger threatened, as it did during the German breakthrough of March 1918, he turned to Churchill for moral support. Three years later, at a time when Britain was supporting the Greek offensive against Turkey, he wrote to Lloyd George, on 25 June 1921: 'I am sure the path of courage is the path of safety. . . . I think everybody here would approve our stopping the war.' On 27 February 1922, when the Coalition was in difficulties, he again sent Lloyd George advice—at Lloyd George's request: 'What is best for the nation & Empire. . . .' Churchill wrote, 'must alone decide. Decisions must be taken, & those who take them must not shirk from facing the consequences. We must not squander the gt forces wh are still in our hands by vacillation, ambiguity, or fear of not pleasing everybody.'

Churchill constantly demanded clear policies and definite decisions. Many of his most forceful letters, memoranda and speeches were those in which he urged decisive policies in place of drift and delay. On 19 January 1918, after outlining to Lloyd George the policies he believed essential if defeat were to be avoided, he wrote: 'Ponder & then *act*.'

At the time of the Paris Peace Conference, Churchill urged a generous, speedy and humane peace with Germany, and opposed any threat to renew war if the Germans refused to sign the Treaty. On 28 February 1919 he told the War Cabinet that he wished to see Germany 'treated humanely and adequately fed, and her industries restarted. He had little patience with the cranks of various kinds who denied that Germany suffered any privations at all.' On 20 May 1919, in a long and forceful letter to Lloyd George, he set out his hopes and fears. 'In my opinion,' he wrote, 'it is of profound importance to reach a settlement with the present German Government, and to reach it as speedily as possible.' He continued:

The newspapers and public opinion at home, so far as it is vocal, claims the enforcement of the most extreme terms upon the vanquished enemy. . . .

The same crowd that is now so vociferous for ruthless terms of peace will spin round to-morrow against the Government if a military breakdown occurs through the dwindling forces which are at our disposal. It is one thing to keep a compact force for a long time in comfortable billets around Cologne in a well administered and adequately rationed district. It is quite another to spread these young troops we have over large areas of Germany holding down starving populations, living in houses with famished women and children, and firing on miners and working people maddened by despair.

Disaster of the most terrible kind lies on that road, and I solemnly warn the Government of the peril of proceeding along it. A situation might soon be reached from which the British moral sentiment would recoil. I consider that we shall commit a political error of the first order if we are drawn into the heart of Germany in these conditions. We may easily be caught, as Napoleon was in Spain, and gripped in a position from which there is no retreat and where our strength will steadily be consumed. . . .

In his letter Churchill went on to warn Lloyd George of the practical difficulties of trying 'to carve up and distribute at pleasure the populations of three or four enormous Empires with a few hundred thousand war-weary conscripts', and he declared:

Now is the time, and it may be the only time, to reap the fruits of victory. 'Agree with thine adversary whilst thou art in the way with him'. Everything shows that the present German Government is sincerely desirous of making a beaten peace and preserving an orderly community which will carry out its agreement. It seems to me quite natural that they should put forward a series of counter propositions, and we ought to take these up seriatim with patience and goodwill and endeavour to split the outstanding differences. In this way we shall get a genuine German acceptance of a defeated peace and not be drawn into new dangers measureless in their character.

The British Empire is in a very fine position at the present moment, and we now require a peace which will fix and recognise that position. Let us beware lest in following too far Latin ambitions and hatreds we do not create a new situation in which our advantages will largely have disappeared. Settle now while we have the power, or lose perhaps for ever the power of settlement on the basis of a military victory.

Churchill was always critical of unclear policies or undue delay. On 4 August 1919, in a letter to Lloyd George about the need for a new and clear defence policy, he wrote: 'I am full of sympathy for you in the immense burden wh you bear. . . . But if you are to have the rest wh is needed to recover yr buoyancy and creative power, it is essential that you shd beforehand give the decisions wh will allow yr lieutenants to act effectively.' Two months later, on 10 October 1919, during the Cabinet's hesitations about helping the anti-Bolsheviks in Russia, Churchill wrote to Lord Curzon: 'Forgive this fury. We are so near immense events. And yet there is time to baulk them.' Two years later he was again vexed when, having asked the Cabinet repeatedly for a decision on the question of a final British military withdrawal from the Caucasus, Lord Curzon counselled delay. On 19 October 1921 Churchill sent him a personal appeal:

All right. I agree to wait till next week. But I am very anxious. We are dawdling to disaster. . . . Egypt, India, Mesopotamia, Palestine and Turkey all flatter and cheat by turn the partisans of every view. Every cock can find some morning on which to crow. We are simply flopping about without a resolute, consistent policy: or rather with the interplay of several resolute consistent policies.

Throughout 1920 and 1921 a policy for which Churchill pressed most persistently was a settlement between France and Germany, aimed at avoiding a second European war. He argued that Britain should take the lead in offering secure guarantees both to France and to Germany, in order to enable them to live together without fear of attack. On 7 July 1921 he told the Imperial Conference in London that if Britain could become 'the Ally of France and the friend of Germany', she should then be in a position 'to mitigate the frightful rancour and fear and hatred which exist between France and Germany at the present time and which, if left unchecked, will most certainly in a generation or so bring about a renewal of the struggle of which we have just witnessed the conclusion'. His aim, he declared, was 'to get an appeasement of the fearful hatreds and antagonisms which exist in Europe and to enable the world to settle down'. And he added: 'I have no other object in view.'

Churchill saw appeasement as a positive and firm policy. 'We must base ourselves,' he had told the House of Commons on 22 March 1920, 'not upon force, though a certain amount of force is needed, but upon a sagacious, shrewd, prudent and conciliatory policy in many directions.' Such a policy, Churchill believed, must be based upon strength, not turned to through weakness. Britain must be strong, he argued; her strength must be always based upon a name for 'fair dealing'; and she must be seen to be the advocate of 'an earnest desire to promote the general peace and well-being of mankind'. During the Chanak crisis in the autumn of 1922 he advocated a strong policy, supported by the threat of military action, believing this to be the only way to avert war with Turkey. But he also warned his colleagues not to rely on bluff in any such confrontation. In Cabinet on 19 September 1922 he declared 'that all our misfortunes had arisen in the past from trying to do that for which we had not got the strength'.

Churchill's breadth of vision, and his concern, was not restricted to foreign affairs. Throughout the post-war period he consistently pressed for a constructive and humanitarian social policy, and wanted it to be given priority. As soon as the war ended he advocated the nationalization of the railways, an end to private monopolies and a punitive tax on war profits. 'Why *should* anybody make a great fortune out of the war,' he wrote to Lloyd George on 21 November 1918. 'While everybody has been serving the Country, profiteers & contractors & shipping speculators have gained fortunes of a gigantic character.' Churchill wanted a punitive tax on all profits over £10,000. During 1920 he took a lead in pressing upon Lloyd George the need to devise a comprehensive scheme to combat unemployment in Britain, and to provide adequate housing. He understood the distress of the working class, and was sympathetic towards it. Speaking at Dundee on 10 December 1918 he argued that there should be 'just laws to regulate the acquisition of wealth', 'discrimination between earned and unearned income' and 'most important of all . . . decent minimum standards of life and labour'. Monopolies, he argued, should be controlled 'in the general interest', and taxation should be levied only in proportion 'to ability to pay'. Churchill clung tenaciously to these beliefs. On 4 August 1919 he wrote to Lloyd George:

I don't wonder there is an ugly spirit abroad when everyone can see a whole new class of millionaires who made their fortunes while 5/6ths of the industries of the country were in suspension or abeyance & every little shopkeeper who cd march was serving in the trenches. This sense of injustice rankles in every heart and is in my opinion at the root of our troubles & governmental weakness.

Churchill had already taken a lead in the Cabinet in pressing for a positive and imaginative policy towards the unemployed. On 28 September 1921 he had circulated a memorandum entitled 'The Unemployment Situation', in which he had written:

The problem of unemployment now before us deserves to be treated on some basis of general principle which for good or ill we can expound and defend when we meet our constituents. It is not possible for a civilised State with a large portion of its members living in luxury and the great bulk of its members living in comfort to leave a proportion of its citizens with neither work nor maintenance. No doubt the standard of maintenance must vary with the resources of the State, and in hard times it must be reduced to the absolute minimum so as to encourage and, indeed, compel the most earnest efforts to seek economic employment. But we must have some answer to give in regard to every class of workpeople who are affected by the present trade depression. In answer to the question, which can be posed by hundreds of thousands of men to-day: 'What am I to do?' we must have an absolutely clear-cut reply. It may not be popular, but it must be comprehensive, and it must be complete. We cannot say, for instance: 'You had better starve.' We cannot say: 'You had better go to the work-house': the workhouses could not hold a tenth part of the numbers affected.

Churchill urged 'prompt and searching examination', by committees of experts, of every scheme of unemployment relief. He wanted the State to take a direct part in stimulating industrial growth, possibly by export credit schemes 'which would stimulate foreign countries to place work with British factories'. He opposed any short-term solution, such as cash subsidies to private firms, which would, he warned, be 'fatal to the economic future of our industry'. Above all, he wanted the Government to seek 'clear guidance upon this great subject' from economic experts, after which the Cabinet should 'formulate definite opinions'. But these pleas were in vain, for foreign affairs and Ireland had come to dominate, and almost to overwhelm, the Government's daily work.

On 8 October 1921 Churchill sent Lloyd George a long personal letter, reiterating earlier demands for a clear policy in the field of fiscal policy:

. . . I remember two long discussions wh we had together—the first nearly a year ago in the Hyde Park Hotel after a dinner at wh Max & Rothermere were present, & the second in Lympne at the beginning of this year. In each case I had the feeling that we made great progress in cutting our way into the heart of the post-war monetary & financial mystery, & the contributions of yr own thoughts, so far as they went, seemed to me of incomparable value & far more searching than I have heard on this subject from anyone else.

But it seemed to me that all this process stopped short of reaching any conclusion of a definite character on which a policy or even a provisional policy cd be based; & the fact is undoubtedly as I have stated in my memorandum, that we have not at the present time got a clear view on the fundamental questions to wh I have drawn attention. *I* certainly do not pretend to have a clear view upon them, tho' I have a feeling that if we went on hammering away for say a week or two we shd get to the bottom of it & frame a definite policy wh cd be announced, explained, & defended, & wh wd carry us through the temporary & baffling fluctuations wh are affecting us so violently at the present time.

It is quite true that owing to yr vy great skill in navigation we have avoided many dangerous rocks & shoals, & in the Coal strike have come through one of the greatest industrial hurricanes that have ever blown. But for all that we are drifting about in a fog without a compass.

Churchill was emphatic in his pleas for a more egalitarian social policy. But as a Liberal Minister in an overwhelmingly Conservative Coalition, he could never persuade his colleagues to accept them. He was not surprised, in the light of his own repeated demands for radical social legislation, when the electorate rejected the Coalition in 1922, and he lost his seat in Parliament, after having been an MP for twenty-two years.

Although Churchill was upset by his defeat in 1922, he saw it as the legitimate expression of popular discontent. His belief in Parliamentary democracy was deeply held; he was convinced that all policy decisions, however controversial, could be explained fully to Parliament, fought for in Parliament, and carried out with Parliamentary approval. During the military crisis of April 1917 he urged Lloyd George to take Parliament into his confidence in a secret session, so that it could form an instructed view of war policy. On 27 January 1919, at the height of the demobilization controversy, he wrote privately to Lloyd George: 'the manly course—and the honest course—is to take Parliament fully into our confidence and rely on the good sense of the nation'.

Churchill's belief in the importance of Parliament was firmly rooted in the House of Commons and he opposed all plans to increase the power of the House of Lords. Serious consequences might ensue, he told the House of Lords Reform Committee on 26 October 1921, 'from any attempt to revive those powers which had been taken away' ten years before. 'Parliament,' he declared in a memorandum on 7 December 1921, 'exists as a vehicle for giving effect to the public will', and in a long memorandum printed for the Cabinet on 21 June 1922, he argued against any increase in the power of the House of Lords because of the danger of any whittling away of 'free elections and fair Parliamentary debate'. All forms of 'Sovietism', he insisted, must be confronted by the 'supreme and dominating' argument: 'Convince the people, get a majority, and then you will be able to carry out your schemes. But till you get a majority which changes the law by lawful means, you will have to obey the law.'

Churchill was prepared to act on his own precept, and to try to explain his actions in detail in order to win acceptance for them in Parliament. Indeed, it was as a parliamentary orator that he made his greatest impact during Lloyd George's premiership. Throughout the four years of war Churchill's speeches had inspired great audiences.

After the war his powers of speech seemed to increase still further. Lloyd George often called on Churchill to present the Government's case, particularly when it was a weak or much criticized one. In the Amritsar debate of 1920 he soothed a hostile Parliament, and insisted that Liberal concepts alone could govern the Indian empire. During the debates on the Irish crisis in 1921 he was able to inspire a sceptical House of Commons, and bring some hope to a desperate situation. In the Rutenberg debate of 1922 he not only mollified the numerous critics of Britain's Palestine policy, but also upheld the Balfour Declaration against the hostile verdict of the House of Lords. Both as Secretary of State for War, and as Colonial Secretary, his Estimates speeches frequently calmed the strong clamour for economy, by detailed, careful and masterly accounts of the precise financial position. His humour was another feature of his Parliamentary speaking, and on several occasions he was able to reduce a tense or hostile House of Commons to laughter.

Sometimes Churchill himself was surprised by his oratorical powers. For over twenty years he had never spoken in a parliamentary debate without first writing out in full what he wanted to say. But on 8 February 1922, after he had gone to the House of Commons less than an hour before he was due to speak about Iraq, he decided to speak without notes, writing to his wife two days later:

It was really a great success: no worry, nor work, but quite an agreeable experience. With the first two or three sentences I got the House laughing, and thereafter they simply would not leave off. Although when it was written down and read it looked fairly simple, yet almost every phrase produced a laugh of its own. I think I have really got my full freedom now in debate, and I propose to make far less use of notes than ever before.

Churchill's mastery of debate impressed all who heard him. After the Irish debate of 31 May 1922, Austen Chamberlain wrote to the King:

Mr Chamberlain does not wish to bore Your Majesty by frequent repetition of his admiration for Mr Churchill's great and growing parliamentary qualities, but he humbly commends to Your Majesty's particular attention a speech faultless in manner and wording, profoundly impressive in its delivery and of the first consequence as a statement of policy. It gripped the attention of the House from the opening sentences and held it, breathlessly intent, to the end.

On 17 November 1922, after Churchill had lost his Parliamentary seat, the *Daily Telegraph*, long one of his sternest critics wrote: 'The House of Commons loses for a time its most brilliant and dazzling speaker.'

Much of Churchill's hatred of Bolshevism, and of the Labour Party, sprang from his belief that the ultimate aim of both was the destruction of Parliamentary democracy and free speech. In a speech at Sunderland on 2 January 1920 he had denounced those in Britain who were attracted by Bolshevik theories, telling his audience:

We believe in Parliamentary Government exercised in accordance with the will of the majority of the electors constitutionally and freely ascertained. They seek to overthrow Parliament by direct action or other violent means . . . and then to rule the mass of the nation in accordance with their theories, which have never yet been applied successfully, and through the agency of self-elected or sham-elected caucuses of their own.

They seek to destroy capital. We seek to control monopolies. They seek to eradicate the idea of individual possession. We seek to use the great main-spring of human endeavour as a means of increasing the volume of produc-tion on every side and of sharing the fruits far more broadly and evenly among millions of individual homes. We defend freedom of conscience and religious equality. They seek to exterminate every form of religious belief that has given comfort and inspiration to the soul of man. . . .

Churchill's fears of the collapse of democratic values led him to attack the Labour Party, with increasing frequency and venom, as unfit to govern. These attacks roused the fierce hostility of all Labour sup-porters. Yet Churchill was convinced that socialism was a divisive and anti-patriotic force, telling a Cabinet Committee on Defence Estimates on 23 January 1922 that he wanted to reduce the amount spent on naval recruits, as most of them were trade unionists 'and could not be entirely relied upon to give loyal and devoted service'. He believed that loyalty to the State and parliamentary democracy were the twin pillars of an ideal polity, and he saw the Labour Party as the enemy of both.

During 1919 Churchill's most intense thoughts were devoted to organizing and encouraging anti-Bolshevik activity in Russia. For more than a year he submitted his colleagues to a barrage of anti-Bolshevik memoranda, appeals and letters. He also made his feelings public in a series of passionate and uncompromising speeches. The story of his part in the Intervention reveals how, once he believed in a particular course of action, he would cling to it, regardless of public opinion, Press hostility, or the growing indifference of his colleagues. It was his un-compromising anti-Bolshevik attitude that convinced many observers that his convictions always led to obsessions, and confirmed many

people in the view expressed by the Conservative *Morning Post* on
11 January 1919: 'There is some tragic flaw in Mr Churchill which
determines him on every occasion in the wrong course.'

By January 1919 Churchill was convinced that unless Bolshevism
were overthrown, western democracy and civilization would be
destroyed. A typical outburst appeared in an article he published in the
Weekly Dispatch on 22 June 1919, when he wrote of Lenin, Trotsky and
the other Bolshevik leaders:

Theirs is a war against civilised society which can never end. They seek as the
first condition of their being the overthrow and destruction of all existing
institutions and of every State and Government now standing in the world.
They too aim at a worldwide and international league, but a league of the
failures, the criminals, the unfit, the mutinous, the morbid, the deranged, and
the distraught in every land; and between them and such order of civilisation
as we have been able to build up since the dawn of history there can, as
Lenin rightly proclaims, be neither truce nor pact.

As soon as he became Secretary of State for War in January 1919,
Churchill demanded a clear policy, and the despatch of military re-
inforcements to help protect the British troops who had been sent to
Russia long before he had gone to the War Office. Lloyd George had
agreed to send reinforcements. At the same time, Churchill urged collective Allied action to restore democratic institutions in Russia. The Allies
were mainly concerned, however, with the future of Germany, not of
Russia, and no clear policy was forthcoming. On 14 February 1919 the
Cabinet sent Churchill to the Paris Peace Conference in order to get an
Allied decision on whether to continue to intervene with military forces,
or to continue the policy of negotiations which had been set in train by
the Allied invitations to the Bolsheviks and anti-Bolsheviks to a Conference at Prinkipo. Although Churchill was in favour of the Prinkipo
negotiations, he suggested while in Paris that the Allied military Staffs
should work out a comprehensive plan for full-scale war in the event of
the Prinkipo plan breaking down. It was this suggestion which first
alienated him from many of his colleagues. The Allies failed to reach any
decision. Henceforth, Churchill's pleas for a decision became more
intense; this too isolated him from the Cabinet.

On 4 March 1919 the Cabinet finally decided to evacuate Archangel.
Churchill accepted this decision with reluctance, and continued to
make strong anti-Bolshevik speeches. When his senior War Office
advisers pressed him to send more men to North Russia to make at
least one more forward movement, towards Kotlas, he accepted their

advice, and actually obtained Cabinet sanction for it. At the same time, he argued fiercely with Lloyd George and Curzon for the recognition of Admiral Kolchak as ruler of all Russia. Later, when the anti-Bolshevik forces were beaten back in Siberia—and the Kotlas plan abandoned—Churchill turned his energies towards supporting General Denikin in South Russia. But his appeals on Denikin's behalf met with growing indifference from his colleagues, and growing hostility from the Press.

Churchill continued to make his anxieties known, both in the Cabinet and in public. On 29 July 1919, during the Cabinet's discussion on the possibility of an armistice with Soviet Russia, and total evacuation of all British troops, he expressed his deep dislike of any such reconciliation, telling his colleagues that he 'could not conceive that we could sink so low'. Later that day, when he informed the House of Commons that all British troops were to be evacuated from Archangel, he declared: 'I can never clear my mind from a sense of anxiety.'

Throughout July, August and September Churchill repeatedly appealed for both British and Allied help for all the anti-Bolshevik leaders, including General Yudenitch, who planned to capture Petrograd. But the Cabinet rejected his appeals. 'To see gt matters go so ill,' he wrote to Lloyd George on 6 September 1919, '& to be powerless to avert the disasters, is always painful.'

Churchill's appeals reached a pitch in September, when British support for the anti-Bolshevik forces was waning, and yet, as he saw it, those very forces were on the verge of victory. Lloyd George became angered by Churchill's singlemindedness, and on 22 September 1919 he accused Churchill of having 'strained policy' over the Kotlas expedition. 'I am frankly in despair,' he wrote, going on to ask: '. . . why waste your energy and usefulness in this vain fretting which completely paralyses you for other work?' And he added: 'I wonder whether it is any use making one last effort to induce you to throw off this obsession which, if you will forgive me for saying so, is upsetting your balance.'

Lloyd George wanted Churchill to concentrate on other urgent problems, such as the need for strict economies in War Office expenditure, but Churchill replied by defending his position in detail. The Kotlas plan, he argued, had been suggested by three senior military advisers whom Lloyd George himself had chosen. Britain's Russian policy, he pointed out, was not his policy, but the Cabinet's. As for the Russians, he wrote, 'I cannot feel a sense of detachment from their tragical scene.'

As the anti-Bolshevik campaign reached its climax early in October 1919, Churchill's demands became even more intense. In frequent letters to his colleagues he urged support for Denikin. But in the second half of October, Denikin's army began to be driven towards the south, and Churchill's loneliness and isolation became complete. 'LG is getting very sick about Denikin,' H. A. L. Fisher noted in his diary on 3 November 1919, and five days later, to Churchill's consternation, Lloyd George announced a new policy, that of reconciliation with the Bolsheviks.

Churchill's anguish grew because of his fears of what Bolshevism could do to Europe and western civilization. He feared above all a hostile and militaristic Russia which, in alliance with Germany, would create the conditions for future war, and undermine all the achievements of victory and peacemaking. On 21 November 1919 he tried to explain his position to the French Minister of Munitions, Louis Loucheur:

Understand, my friend, that I am not thinking of any immediate danger, but only of the dangers of five or ten years hence. I fear more than I can express the re-union of Russia and Germany, both determined to get back what they have lost in the war, the one through being our ally, the other through being our foe, and both convinced that acting together they will be irresistible. . . .

I am young enough to have to look ahead so far as the future of my own country is concerned, and I am bound to say, speaking of the years which lie before us, that I should deeply regret to see England involved in such a hopeless situation.

For more than a month, Churchill continued to fight for Denikin. He was alone; on 19 December 1919 he learned that he was not even being consulted on some major problems relating to Russia. By the end of the year he realized that the anti-Bolshevik cause was lost. 'Was there ever a more awful spectacle in the whole long history of the world,' Churchill asked his audience at Sunderland on 2 January 1920, 'than is unfolded by the agony of Russia?' On 16 January 1920, when the Allies announced that they intended to begin trading with the Bolsheviks, Churchill was incensed. To his closest friends he spoke seriously of resignation. After talking to Lloyd George that evening, Sir Henry Wilson noted in his diary: 'He thinks Winston has gone mad.'

Churchill did not resign. Instead, he continued to express his hatred of Bolshevism in articles, speeches and memoranda, and to warn of the dangers of Bolshevism spreading either into Europe or towards India. It was the tyrannical aspect of Lenin's regime that most roused his fury. Writing in the *Illustrated Sunday Herald* on 25 January 1920 he declared:

A Tyrant is one who allows the fancies of his mind to count for more in deciding action than the needs, feeling, hopes, lives and physical well-being of the people over whom he has obtained control. A tyrant is one who wrecks the lives of millions for the satisfaction of his own conceptions. So far as possible in this world no man should have such power, whether under an imperialist, republican, militarist, socialist or soviet form of Government. . . .

On 1 May 1920 Churchill set out his view of Bolshevik tyranny in a Cabinet memorandum. The Bolsheviks, he wrote, have 'committed, and are committing unspeakable atrocities, and are maintaining themselves in power by a terrorism on an unprecedented scale, and by the denial of the most elementary rights of citizenship and freedom'.

Churchill was never reconciled to the idea of negotiating with the Bolsheviks. Six months later, on 18 November 1920, the Cabinet decided that the Bolsheviks could pay for British exports with the gold which they had acquired after the revolution. Churchill was totally disturbed by this decision, which he opposed passionately. 'He was quite pale,' Sir Maurice Hankey wrote in his diary, 'and did not speak again during the meeting.' That evening, Churchill left London for Oxford, where he made a vitriolic speech against the Bolsheviks. When, in April 1922, Lloyd George decided to recognize the Bolsheviks, the intensity of Churchill's feelings had not diminished. He was only prevented from resigning by a personal appeal from Lord Birkenhead.

Churchill's hostility towards Bolshevism dominated nearly two years of his work for Lloyd George, and plunged him into fierce and frequent disagreements with all his colleagues. His commitment to the causes he believed in was total; when opposed, he fought back with increasing passion. He seemed at times insensitive to the feelings of his colleagues and unable to see where to stop his barrage of demands. It was this persistence which wearied, irritated and at times angered those with whom he worked, and whom he sought, often in vain, to convince.

When the policies which Churchill advocated were taken seriously, he was confident and composed. But when his policies were rejected, or belittled he became morose, angry and inflexible. The quality of his judgement seemed to vary with these contrasting moods. When thwarted, his judgement could go awry, and he often allowed himself to be cast down by an overwhelming sense of responsibility and foreboding. By repeatedly expressing his anxieties in public, he was blamed for a policy which was not his own.

Churchill's friends and colleagues were frequently puzzled by the intensity of his feelings, and found him at such times difficult to work with, irritating and uncompromising. On 20 January 1921 Sir Henry Wilson wrote to General Congreve: 'He has many good qualities, some of which lie hidden, and he has many bad ones, all of which are in the shop window.' Whenever he was criticized, Churchill made enormous efforts to defend himself. His war memoirs were part of this process of self-defence, and many passages in them were provoked by criticism of his past actions voiced both in the Press and also in private conversation. In a letter to Lord Curzon on 15 November 1921 Austen Chamberlain commented: 'Winston is a very able and a very interesting colleague, but he is often very difficult in council.' After H. A. L. Fisher and Lloyd George had discussed the premiership together, on 18 February 1922, Fisher recorded in his diary: 'The PM says the two great qualities for a Prime Minister are patience and courage. Winston will be defective in patience.' On 2 March 1922 Edwin Montagu said of Churchill, to H. A. L. Fisher: 'Nobody learns more readily from experience or yields with more difficulty to argument.' Three weeks later, Austen Chamberlain wrote to Lloyd George: 'He is, of course, at times very much a man of one idea, and his vehemence sometimes makes him a difficult partner in Cabinet.' But, Chamberlain added, 'he is not unreasonable at bottom; he is not impervious to a personal appeal. . . .'

Churchill was always quick to respond to the call of friendship. 'I do not harbour malice,' he wrote to his wife on 15 February 1921. 'Perhaps I wd be a stronger character if I did.' And he added: 'Personally I always forgive political attacks or ill-treatment not directed at private life.'

Churchill's friendship with Lloyd George was a complex one. Between 1917 and 1922 the two men worked closely together, often in daily conclave. But in 1916 that friendship—already more than ten years old—had almost been destroyed, for Churchill had blamed Lloyd George for his political isolation after he had been forced to leave the Admiralty. On 9 June 1915 he had written to Sinclair that between himself and Lloyd George 'tout est fini'. In December 1916 he had again written with bitterness of Lloyd George's refusal to find him a place in the new Coalition, and on 17 April 1917 he had publicly criticized Lloyd George's Government in the House of Commons for its 'undue love of the assertion of arbitrary power'. Yet the two men came together again during the early summer of 1917, and soon re-established their pre-war intimacy.

As the war progressed, Churchill's admiration for Lloyd George's achievements grew; there was no other politician whom he so respected. When the war was over, on 16 October 1919, he asked the King to grant Lloyd George the Distinguished Service Order. In his letter he wrote:

As the Prime Minister must have made 30 or 40 journeys to France and was on several occasions in zones where shells were falling, and as all these journeys were made in strict performance of necessary duty of the highest possible consequence, Mr Churchill considers that the grant of the War Medals in these circumstances will be in every respect appropriate.

The King expressed reluctance to grant such an honour to Lloyd George alone, feeling that all Cabinet Ministers might have a claim. But Churchill wrote again, on November 17: 'There is no doubt that the purely military work done by Mr Lloyd George stands on an entirely different plane to that done by other Cabinet Ministers. . . .'[1]

Throughout the six years of Lloyd George's premiership Churchill constantly sent him long and personal letters with frank advice, warnings and encouragement. The two men exchanged harsh words when they disagreed. On 6 November 1918 Edwin Montagu noted that Churchill was speaking 'if not open treason, open disgruntlement'. But despite the efforts of outsiders to magnify these disagreements, reconciliation was never far away. 'I breakfasted and lunched with the PM,' Churchill wrote to his wife on 24 January 1919. 'It is a good thing to get in touch again. We were diverging a good deal.' And he added: 'I think I influence him to a considerable degree, & there is no one with whom he talks so easily.' Even during their worst disagreements—over Russia —Churchill still sought to win Lloyd George's approval, and to preserve their friendship. 'I do hope,' he wrote to Lloyd George on 20 September 1919, 'that you will not brush away lightly the convictions of one who wishes to remain your faithful lieutenant and looks forward to a fruitful and active cooperation.' And on 24 March 1920, at a moment of intense disagreement, Churchill wrote to Lloyd George: 'My interests as well as inclinations march with yours, & in addition there is our long friendship wh I so greatly value. . . .' In a good cause, he added, 'I wd gladly at yr side face political misfortune.'

In the spring of 1921 the intimacy between Churchill and Lloyd George seemed once more to wane. Churchill had been embittered by his failure to become Chancellor of the Exchequer, and mooted the idea of a 'national' or an 'anti-socialist' party, with himself at its head. This was the only time in six years when they stopped seeing each other, except for formal meetings in Cabinet. At times of deepest disagreement,

---

[1] Speaking to the House of Commons on 28 March 1945, after Lloyd George's death, Churchill recalled the wartime years 'when I watched him so closely and enjoyed his confidence and admired him so much'. He went on to describe 'two characteristics of his which seemed to me invaluable in those days: first, his power to live in the present yet without taking short views; and secondly, his power of drawing from misfortune itself the means of future success'.

both Lloyd George and Churchill could be particularly harsh about each other, especially to third parties. On 27 January 1922, when Lloyd George was pressing his colleagues to accept severe cuts in naval expenditure, Churchill wrote to his wife: 'I don't feel the slightest confidence in LG's judgment or care for our national naval position. Anything that serves the mood of the moment & the chatter of the ignorant and pliable newspapers is good enough for him. But I try—however feebly—to think for England.' Four months later, on 8 June 1922, when Lloyd George was vexed with Churchill's handling of the crisis at Belleek, on the Ulster border, Thomas Jones noted in his diary: 'the PM compared Winston to a chauffeur who apparently is perfectly sane and drives with great skill for months, then suddenly he takes you over the precipice'. Lloyd George added that he thought 'there was a strain of lunacy' in Churchill.

The friction between Churchill and Lloyd George was usually short-lived. The two men worked closely together for long periods. On 31 January 1922 Churchill wrote to his wife: 'The PM piles business on me, & I really am deciding large matters over the whole field of Government in a way I never have done before.' Later in the year Lloyd George entrusted Churchill with the final and most intricate of the Irish negotiations, and during the Chanak crisis, despite their previous disagreements on Turkish policy, they worked together in the closest co-operation. Churchill responded to Lloyd George's trust in him, and during the General Election of 1922 he denounced—from his sickbed—all those who sought to end Lloyd George's authority. In his message to the electors on 27 October 1922 he declared:

In the political confusion that reigns, and with causes so precious to defend, I take my stand by Mr Lloyd George. I was his friend before he was famous. I was with him when all were at his feet. And now to-day when men who fawned upon him, who praised even his errors, who climbed into place and Parliament upon his shoulders, have cast him aside, when Wee Free fanatics think the time has come to pay off old scores, when Mr McKenna, the political banker, emerges from his opulent seclusion to administer what he no doubt calculates is a finishing kick, I am still his friend and lieutenant.

Throughout Lloyd George's premiership, Clementine Churchill had continued to give her husband outspoken advice. She wrote frankly about such matters as Ireland, rejecting her husband's view that reprisals were necessary against Sinn Fein; and she constantly urged him to adopt a less hostile and negative attitude towards the Labour Party. In January 1919 she believed that it was wrong of him to take on the combined duties of Secretary of State for War and Air. Her instinct was always for moderation and caution. During their search for a country property she was worried that he was becoming too much involved in something he did not fully know about, and wrote, on 11 July 1921: 'Let us beware of risking our newly come fortune in operations which we do not understand & have not the time to learn & to practice when learned. Politics are absolutely engrossing to you really, or *should* be & now you have Painting for your leisure & Polo for excitement and danger.' She also warned him against quarrelling openly with Lloyd George. 'I do feel,' she wrote in the same letter, 'that as long as he is P.M. it would be better to hunt with him than to lie in the bushes & watch him careering along with a jaundiced eye.'

Clementine Churchill also spoke strongly to her husband about his character. On 29 October 1918, while he was in France, she wrote:

. . . Do come home and look after what is to be done with the Munition Workers when the fighting really does stop. Even if the fighting is not over yet, your share of it must be & I would like you to be praised as a reconstructive genius, as well as for a Mustard Gas fiend, a Tank juggernaut & a flying Terror. Besides the credit for all these Bogey parts will be given to subordinates . . .

Can't the men Munition Workers build lovely garden cities & pull down slums in places like Bethnal Green, Newcastle, Glasgow, Leeds, etc. & can't the women Munition Workers make all the lovely furniture for them, babies' cradles, cupboards etc. . . . .

Do come home & arrange all this.

In this same letter Clementine Churchill reminded her husband of how long he had been in France, away from her. This was true of much of his time as Minister of Munitions, when his official duties took him out of England almost every month, and later when he lived in the Ministry building. Whenever he was away, his wife felt his absence strongly. Sometimes he would go on holiday without her. After the failure of his Russian plans early in 1920 he had gone boar hunting with General Rawlinson near Bordeaux. Throughout 1921, a year of great personal loss for both of them, he was often away from her both on official business and on holiday. In the year following the death of their daughter Marigold in the autumn of 1921, she frequently referred in her letters to her terrible sadness and loneliness. This was particularly acute in December 1921 and January 1922, when, after her husband's departure to France on holiday, her children were taken gravely ill with influenza, and she had collapsed from exhaustion.

Churchill understood his wife's feelings, and his letters to her were sympathetic. 'I reproach myself vy much,' he wrote on 12 September 1918, 'for not having been more to you.' But the demands of his public work in each of his Ministries, the often relentless pressure of his Cabinet Committees, and his need sometimes to find solace in painting, hunting and the conversation of friends, meant that he could not always be with her to comfort her.

Churchill was deeply affected by the recurring tragedies of the war. Since August 1914 the death of friends in action had been a source of much personal sorrow and sombre reflection. On 22 March 1917 he wrote to Archibald Sinclair: 'The war weighs heavy on us all & amid such universal misfortune & with death so ubiquitous and life so harsh, I find a difficulty in setting pen to paper,' and on 10 May 1917 he begged the House of Commons, then in secret session, not to tolerate 'fresh, bloody and disastrous adventures' on the western front. Ten days later his friend Valentine Fleming[1] was killed in action; Churchill wrote his obituary in *The Times* on May 25. Four days later he wrote to his wife, from France: 'Never for a moment does the thought of this carnage & ruin escape my mind. . . .'

In his parliamentary speeches Churchill reiterated the need for mechanical support on a large scale, for protective devices in attack, and for the use of tanks on a large enough scale to accelerate victory and save lives. Mechanical devices of all kinds, he wrote in the *Sunday Pictorial* on 8 April 1917, 'augment the power of the human hand and shield the sacred chalice of human life'. He strongly opposed the Passchendaele offensive of 1917, and was relieved when it had ended. On 23 February 1918, after a visit to the Ypres salient, he wrote to his wife: 'Nearly 800,000 of our British race have shed their blood or lost their lives here during $3\frac{1}{2}$ years of unceasing conflict. Many of our friends & my contemporaries all perished here. Death seems as commonplace & as little alarming as the undertaker. Quite a natural ordinary event, wh may

[1] Valentine Fleming, 1882–1917. Educated at Eton and Magdalen College, Oxford. Called to the Bar, 1907. Captain, Queen's Own Oxfordshire Hussars, 1909; Major, 1914. Conservative MP for South Oxfordshire from 1910 until his death. Served on the western front from October 1914. In November 1914 he had written to Churchill: 'Its going to be a *long long* war in spite of the fact that every single man in it wants it stopped *at once*.' Killed in action 20 May 1917. Father of Peter Fleming the explorer and Ian Fleming the novelist.

happen to anyone at any moment, as it happened to all these scores of thousands who lie together in this vast cemetery, ennobled & rendered forever glorious by their brave memory.'

Churchill was depressed during 1919 by the inability of the victor states to halt the slaughter in Russia, and feared to forecast when or how that conflict would end. 'I have had so many bitter experiences in the last five years,' he wrote to J. A. Spender on 10 October 1919, 'and have seen so many fine chances thrown away or hopelessly delayed, that I refrain from making predictions about the future. . . .'

Churchill understood the public desire for peace, and on 28 July 1920, at the time of the Russo-Polish war, he wrote in the *Evening News* of the British people: 'They are thoroughly tired of war. They have learnt during five bitter years too much of its iron slavery, its squalor, its mocking disappointments, its ever dwelling sense of loss.'

During 1921 the death of his mother, his daughter, and several close personal friends had intensified Churchill's unhappiness, and made him deeply aware of the passing of time. On hearing of the death of Lord Ranksborough[1] he wrote to Lord French, on 6 May 1921: 'Alas, our poor Ranksborough is no more. The world thins very quickly in these days.'

Churchill's sadness at the death of friends and his sense of the advancing years was a marked feature of his private correspondence. On 20 September 1921 he wrote to his wife: 'Another twenty years will bring me to the end of my allotted span even if I have so long. The reflections of middle age are mellow. I will take what comes.'

Churchill's melancholy reflections were not confined to personal matters. Since the end of the war he had grown increasingly despondent about world affairs, and often spoke of his belief that sinister forces were at work throughout the world, seeking to undermine the unity of the British Empire. On 4 November 1920, during a speech in the City of London, he spoke of 'a world wide conspiracy against our country, designed to deprive us of our place in the world and rob us of victory'. Britain, he said, would be on its guard. Conspiracy would fail. And he went on:

Having beaten the most powerful military empire in the world, having emerged triumphantly from the fearful struggle of armageddon, we should

---

[1] John Fielden Brocklehurst, 1852–1921. Entered the army, 1874. On active service in Egypt, 1882 and 1884–5; in South Africa, 1899–1901. Major-General commanding the 3rd Cavalry Brigade, Natal, 1899; present at the defence of Ladysmith. Equerry to Queen Victoria, 1899–1901. Retired from the army with rank of Major-General, 1908. Created Baron Ranksborough, 1914.

not allow ourselves to be pulled down and have our Empire disrupted by a malevolent and subversive force, the rascals and rapscallions of mankind who were now on the move against us. Whether it be the Irish murder gang, the Egyptian Vengeance Society, the seditious extremism in India, or the arch-traitors we had at home, they should feel the weight of the British arm. It was strong enough to break the Hindenburg line; it would be strong enough to defend the main interests of the British people. . . .

It was not only in public that Churchill denounced any surrender to anti-imperial forces. When the Government accepted Lord Milner's report on Egyptian self-government, he was outraged. When Lord Curzon—a former Viceroy of India—supported the policy in Cabinet, Churchill passed him a note, on 26 January 1922: 'It leaves me absolutely baffled why you shd be on this side, or why you shd have insisted on keeping Egyptian affairs in yr hands only to lead to this melancholy conclusion. It grieves me profoundly to see what is unfolding.'

Churchill's sense of a world whose values were in turmoil was heightened by the work he did—first at the War Office and then at the Colonial Office—in writing his war memoirs. On War Office notepaper he set out his reflections on the nature of the events of 1914 to 1918:

The Great War through which we have passed differed from all ancient wars in the immense power of the combatants and their fearful agencies of destruction, and from all modern wars in the utter ruthlessness with which it was fought. All the horrors of all the ages were brought together, and not only armies but whole populations were thrust into the midst of them. The mighty educated States involved conceived—not without reason—that their very existence was at stake. Neither peoples nor rules drew the line at any deed which they thought could help them to win. Germany having let Hell loose kept well in the van of terror; but she was followed step by step by the desperate and ultimately avenging nations she had assailed. Every outrage against humanity or international law was repaid by reprisals—often of a greater scale and of longer duration. No truce or parley mitigated the strife of the armies. The wounded died between the lines: the dead mouldered into the soil. Merchant ships and neutral ships and hospital ships were sunk on the seas and all on board left to their fate, or killed as they swam. Every effort was made to starve whole nations into submission without regard to age or sex. Cities and monuments were smashed by artillery. Bombs from the air were cast down indiscriminately. Poison gas in many forms stifled or seared the soldiers. Liquid fire was projected upon their bodies. Men fell from the air in flames, or were smothered often slowly in the dark recesses of the sea. The fighting strength of armies was limited only by the manhood of their countries. Europe and large parts of Asia and Africa became one vast battlefield on which after years of struggle not armies but nations broke and ran. When all was over, Torture and Cannibalism were the only two expedients that the civilised scientific Christian States had been able to deny themselves: and these were of doubtful utility.

Churchill brooded on the fact that the war had not really ended in November 1918, and that its evil effects would not soon wear off. On 9 April 1919 he wrote to Lloyd George of the 'gravity and tragedy' of events in Europe since the armistice. A year later, on 24 March 1920, he wrote again to Lloyd George: 'We may well be within measurable distance of universal collapse and anarchy throughout Europe & Asia.' Three days later he wrote to his wife:

I have been reading Philip Gibbs'[1] book about the war—very impressive and terrible, also extremely well written. If it is monotonous in its tale of horror, it is because war is full of inexhaustible horrors. We shall certainly never see the like again. The wars of the future will be civil and social wars, with a complete outfit of terrors of their own. . . .

While writing his own book about the war, Churchill often reflected on the pre-1914 world, and on its relative calm. In an early draft of his war memoirs he wrote:

Children were taught of the Great War against Napoleon, as the culminating effort in the history of the British peoples, and they looked on Waterloo & Trafalgar as the supreme achievements of British arms by land & sea. These prodigious victories, eclipsing all that had gone before, seemed the fit & predestined ending to the long drama of our island race, which had advanced over a thousand years from small & weak beginnings to the first position in the world.

Such, Churchill went on, was the self-confidence of 'the palmy days of Queen Victoria'; and he often reflected on those days in conversation with his friends. On 17 January 1920 Frances Stevenson noted in her diary: 'Winston waxed very eloquent on the subject of the old world & the new, taking up arms in defence of the former. . . .'
Churchill was deeply disturbed by the collapse of settled values and ancient institutions. In his election speech on 11 November 1922 he

---

[1] Philip Gibbs, 1877–1962. An editor at Cassell and Company, publishers, 1898. Entered journalism, 1902; Literary editor, the *Daily Mail*. War correspondent, for the *Daily Chronicle*, in the Balkans, 1912, and on the western front, 1914–18. Author of over fifty novels and a further twenty-five historical works, including *Realities of War* (1920). Knighted, 1920.

gave public vent to the feelings which he had so often expressed in private. In the notes for his speech he set out his thoughts as follows:

> What a disappointment the Twentieth Century has been
> How terrible & how melancholy
>   is long series of disastrous events
>   wh have darkened its first 20 years.
> We have seen in ev country a dissolution,
>   a weakening of those bonds,
>   a challenge to those principles
>   a decay of faith
>   an abridgement of hope
>   on wh structure & ultimate existence
>   of civilized society depends.
> We have seen in ev part of globe
>   one gt country after another
>   wh had erected an orderly, a peaceful
>   a prosperous structure of civilised society,
>   relapsing in hideous succession
>   into bankruptcy, barbarism or anarchy.

Churchill then spoke of each of the areas which were in turmoil: China and Mexico 'sunk into confusion'; Russia, where 'that little set of Communist criminals . . . have exhausted millions of the Russian people'; Ireland, scene of an 'enormous retrogression of civilisation & Christianity'; Egypt and India, where 'we see among millions of people hitherto shielded by superior science & superior law a desire to shatter the structure by which they live & to return blindly & heedlessly to primordial chaos'. He then went on to warn of the future:

> Can you doubt, my faithful friends
>   as you survey this sombre panorama,
>   that mankind is passing through a period marked
>   not only by an enormous destruction
>   & abridgement of human species,
>   not only by a vast impoverishment
>   & reduction in means of existence
>   but also that destructive tendencies
>   have not yet run their course?
> And only intense, concerted & prolonged efforts
>   among all nations
>   can avert further & perhaps even greater calamities.

List of Sources

I have divided this list of sources into three parts: a page by page list of original documents; a person by person list of previously unpublished individual recollections; and an alphabetical list of printed sources. I have used printed sources almost entirely for the contemporary material which they contain, principally the texts of speeches and extracts from diaries.

PART ONE
ORIGINAL DOCUMENTS

CHAPTER 1. 'THE SHADOW OF THE DARDANELLES', 1915–1917: **p. 1**, Churchill to Sinclair, 5 July 1915 (Sinclair papers); **p. 2**, Churchill to John Churchill, 15 July 1916 (John Churchill papers); Churchill to Sinclair, 29 Nov. 1916 (Sinclair papers); Churchill to Sinclair, 10 Dec. 1916 (Sinclair papers); **p. 4**, Carson to Bonar Law, 20 Dec. 1916 (Bonar Law papers); Churchill to Sinclair, 20 Dec. 1916 (Sinclair papers); **p. 5**, Marsh to Sinclair, 21 Dec. 1916 (Sinclair papers); Churchill to Fisher, 25 Jan. 1917 (Fisher papers); **p. 6**, Hankey diary, 16 Feb. 1917 (Hankey papers); Churchill's two memoranda of mid-Feb., 1917 (Churchill papers); **p. 9**, Churchill to Lloyd George, 10 March 1917 (Lloyd George papers); Churchill notes to the Dardanelles Commission, mid-March 1917 (Churchill papers); **p. 11**, Scott diary, 16 March 1917 (Scott papers); **p. 13**, Churchill to Sinclair, 22 March 1917 (Sinclair papers); **p. 14**, Churchill to Sinclair, 11 April 1917 (Sinclair papers); **p. 16**, Addison to Lloyd George, 27 April 1917 (Lloyd George papers); **p. 17**, Lloyd George to Painlevé, 19 May 1917 (Lloyd George papers); **p. 19**, Churchill to his wife, 29 May 1917 (Spencer-Churchill papers); **p. 20**, Henry Wilson diary, 29 May 1917 (Wilson papers); **p. 21**, Sir H. Norman to Lloyd George, 31 May 1917 (Lloyd George papers); Esher to Haig, 30 May 1917 (Philip Sassoon papers).

CHAPTER 2. 'A DANGEROUSLY AMBITIOUS MAN', 1917: **p. 23**, Curzon to Bonar Law, 4 June (Bonar Law papers); Derby to Lloyd George, 8 June (Lloyd George papers); **p. 24**, Wilson diary, 30 June (Wilson papers); Addison to Lloyd George, 4 June (Lloyd George papers); Rothermere to Lloyd George, mid-June (Lloyd George papers); **p. 25**, Curzon to Lloyd George, 8 June (Lloyd George papers); Younger to Lloyd George, 8 June (Lloyd George papers); **p. 26**, Cowdray to Lloyd George, 9 June (Lloyd George papers); Northcliffe to Churchill, 13 June (Churchill papers); Guest to Lloyd George, 18 June (Lloyd George papers); **p. 28**, Creedy note, 18 July (Derby papers); **p. 29**, Long to Lloyd George, 18 July (Lloyd George papers); **p. 30**, Amery diary, 18 July (Amery papers); Seely to Churchill, 20 July (Churchill papers); Esher to Churchill, 24 July (Churchill papers); Lady Wimborne to Churchill, 18 July (Churchill papers); Lloyd George to Bonar Law, undated (Bonar Law papers); **p. 42**, Derby to Sassoon, 22 July (Sassoon papers).

CHAPTER 3. MINISTER OF MUNITIONS, 1917: **p. 33**, Hankey diary, 22 July (Hankey papers); Churchill to Lloyd George, 22 July (Lloyd George papers); Black to Churchill, 25 July (Churchill papers); **p. 35**, Smuts to Churchill, 31 July (Churchill papers); Munro to Churchill, 1 Aug. (Churchill papers); **p. 37**, Churchill to Balfour, 2 Aug. (Churchill papers); **p. 38**, Churchill to Layton, 3 Aug. (Churchill papers); Churchill to Newman,

5 Aug. (Churchill papers); **p. 39,** Churchill to Kent, 6 Aug. (Churchill papers); Churchill to Worthington-Evans, 12 Aug. (Churchill papers); **p. 40,** Robertson to Derby, 15 Aug. (Derby papers); Derby to Lloyd George, 16 Aug. (Lloyd George papers); **p. 41,** E. Geddes to Lloyd George, 16 Aug. (Lloyd George papers); Churchill to Lloyd George, 19 Aug. (Churchill papers); **p. 42,** Long to Bonar Law, 23 Aug. (Bonar Law papers); Churchill memorandum, 18 Aug. (Churchill papers); **p. 44,** Churchill to Lloyd George, 9 Sept. (Churchill papers).

CHAPTER 4. 'GIVE ME THE POWER', 1917–1918: **p. 45,** Churchill circular letter, 10 Sept. 1917 (Churchill papers); **p. 48,** Churchill to Loucheur, 17 Sept. (Churchill papers); **p. 49,** War Cabinet, 2 Oct. (Cabinet papers 23/4); Haig to Derby, 3 Oct. (Churchill papers); Churchill to Northcliffe, 5 Oct. (Churchill papers); Brand to Churchill, 5 Oct. (Churchill papers); **p. 50,** War Cabinet, 9 Oct. (Cabinet papers 23/4); **p. 51,** Amery diary, 10 Oct. (Amery papers); **p. 52,** Churchill to Ellis, 6 Sept. (Churchill papers); **p. 54,** Churchill notes of 2, 5 and 7 Nov. (Churchill papers); Churchill to General Barnes, 15 Nov. (Churchill papers); Churchill to Maclay, 15 Nov. (Churchill papers); **p. 55,** Churchill to Lloyd George, 19 Nov. (Churchill papers); Derby to Churchill, 19 Nov. (Churchill papers); **p. 57,** Churchill to Lloyd George and Derby, 21 Nov. (Cabinet papers 23/4); Churchill to Milner, 10 Nov. (Churchill papers); **p. 59,** Churchill to Maclay, 21 Nov. (Churchill papers); **p. 60,** Churchill Minute, end Nov. (Churchill papers); Wilson diary, 3 Dec. (Wilson papers); **p. 61,** Wilson diary, 30 Oct. (Wilson papers); Churchill War Cabinet paper, 8 Dec. (Churchill papers); **p. 62,** Churchill to Sinclair, 29 Dec. (Sinclair papers); **p. 63,** War Cabinet, 24 Dec. (Cabinet papers 23/4); Churchill memorandum, 31 Dec. (Churchill papers); **p. 64,** War Cabinet, 4 Jan. (Cabinet papers 23/5); Churchill to Lloyd George, 7 Jan. (Lloyd George papers); **p. 65,** Churchill note, 21 Jan. (Churchill papers); Churchill to Lloyd George, 22 Jan. (Lloyd George papers); **p. 66,** Churchill to Lloyd George, 19 Jan. (Churchill papers); **p. 67,** Churchill to Rothermere, 26 Jan. (Churchill papers); Churchill to his wife, 17 Feb. (Spencer-Churchill papers); **p. 68,** Churchill to his wife, 21 Feb. (Spencer-Churchill papers); Churchill to his wife, 25 Feb. (Spencer-Churchill papers); **p. 72,** Churchill memorandum, 5 March (Churchill papers); **p. 73,** Hankey diary, 8 March (Hankey papers); Geddes to Churchill, 8 March (Churchill papers); Churchill to Geddes, 10 March (Churchill papers); Wilson diary, 8 March (Wilson papers); **p. 74,** War Cabinet, 11 March (Cabinet papers 23/5); Churchill memorandum, 16 March (Churchill papers); **p. 75,** Lord Wimborne to Churchill, 16 March (Churchill papers); Churchill to Wimborne, 18 March (Churchill papers).

CHAPTER 5. 'WITHIN AN ACE OF DESTRUCTION', 1918: **p. 80,** Spiers diary, 23 March (Spears papers); **p. 80,** Sassoon to Esher, 23 March (Esher papers); Maurice diary, 23 March (Maurice papers); **p. 81,** Wilson diary, 23 March (Wilson papers); Hankey diary, 23 March (Hankey papers); Churchill to Lloyd George, 24 March (Churchill papers); **p. 82,** Wilson diary, 24 March (Wilson papers); Maurice diary, 25 March (Maurice papers); **p. 83,** Hankey diary, 25 March (Hankey papers); Churchill telegram to munition works, 26 March (Churchill papers); Hankey diary, 26 March (Hankey papers); **p. 84,** Wilson diary, 26 March (Wilson papers); Wilson diary, 27 March (Wilson papers); Munition workers telegrams, 27 March (Churchill papers); **p. 85,** Lloyd George to Clemenceau, 28 March (Lloyd George papers); **p. 86,** Wilson diary, 28 March (Wilson papers); Lloyd George to Davies, 28 March (Lloyd George papers); **p. 88,** Amery diary, 28 March (Amery papers); **p. 89,** Churchill to Lloyd George, two telegrams of 29 March (Lloyd George papers); **p. 90,** Maurice diary, 28 March (Maurice papers); Lloyd George to President Wilson, 29 March (Lloyd George papers); **p. 91,** Churchill to Clemenceau, 29 March (Churchill papers); Spiers to Henry Wilson, 29 March (Spears papers); Clementine Churchill to her husband, 29 and 30 March (Spencer-Churchill papers); Wilson diary, 30 March (Wilson papers); **p. 98,** Churchill to his wife, 31 March (Spencer-Churchill papers); **p. 99,** Churchill to Lloyd George, 31 March (Lloyd George papers); **p. 100,**

Churchill to Clemenceau, 31 March (Churchill papers); Clemenceau to Jusserand, 31 March (Churchill papers); **p. 101**, Amery diary, 31 March (Amery papers); Churchill to Lloyd George, 31 March (Lloyd George papers); **p. 102**, Churchill to Lloyd George, two telegrams of 1 April (Lloyd George papers); **p. 103**, Wilson diary, 3 April (Wilson papers); Churchill to Asquith, 6 April (Churchill papers).

CHAPTER 6. 'NO PEACE TILL VICTORY', 1918: **p. 105**, Churchill to Loucheur, 6 April (Churchill papers); **p. 106**, Spiers diary, 10 April (Spears papers); Churchill to Docker, 17 April (Churchill papers); **p. 107**, Churchill to Lloyd George, 18 April (Churchill papers); **p. 108**, Churchill to Duke of Westminster, 22 April (Churchill papers); **p. 110**, Churchill to Loucheur, early May (Churchill papers); **p. 111**, Churchill to Lloyd George, 15 April (Churchill papers); Churchill to Lloyd George, 4 May (Churchill papers); **p. 112**, Churchill to Lloyd George, 15 May (Churchill papers); **p. 113**, Churchill to Haig, 10 May (Churchill papers); **p. 115**, Porch to Churchill, 1 June (Churchill papers); **p. 116**, Churchill to his wife, 4 and 6 June (Spencer-Churchill papers); Hankey diary, 4 June (Hankey papers); **p. 117**, Churchill to his wife, 10 June (Spencer-Churchill papers); **p. 118**, Churchill to Sinclair, 7 July (Sinclair papers); Haig to Churchill, 20 June (Churchill papers); Churchill to Lloyd George, 15 June (Lloyd George papers); **p. 119**, Churchill to Lloyd George, 17 June (Lloyd George papers); Churchill memorandum, 6 July (Churchill papers); **p. 120**, Churchill to Lloyd George, 9 July (Churchill papers); **p. 121**, Churchill to Harington, 17 July (Churchill papers); War Cabinet, 19 July (Cabinet papers 23/7); Churchill to Lloyd George, 22 July (Lloyd George papers); War Cabinet, 4 Jan. (Cabinet papers 23/5); **p. 122**, Churchill letter, 18 June (Churchill papers); Churchill memorandum, late June (Churchill papers); Churchill speech, 4 July (Churchill papers); **p. 123** Beaverbrook to Churchill, 4 July (Churchill papers); Sinclair to Churchill, early July (Churchill papers); **p. 124**, Churchill to Sinclair, 11 July (Sinclair papers); **p. 125**, Churchill statement, 9 July (Churchill papers); **p. 126**, War Cabinet, 16 July (Cabinet papers 23/7); War Cabinet, 22 July (Cabinet papers 23/7); **p. 127**, War Cabinet, 24 July (Cabinet papers 23/7); Wilson diary, 27 July (Wilson papers); **p. 128**, Lloyd George statement, 26 July (Churchill papers); Wilson diary, 30 July (Wilson papers); Churchill message, 3 Aug. (Churchill papers).

CHAPTER 7. 'THE SORT OF LIFE I LIKE', 1918: **pp. 131–3**, Churchill to his wife, 10 Aug. (Spencer-Churchill papers); **p. 131**, Churchill to Haig, 8 Aug. (Churchill papers); Haig to Churchill, 9 Aug. (Spencer-Churchill papers); **p. 133**, Churchill to Seely, 10 Aug. (Churchill papers); Churchill to Lloyd George, 10 Aug. (Churchill papers); **p. 134**, Churchill to his wife, 14 Aug. (Spencer-Churchill papers); Clementine Churchill to her husband, 13 Aug. (Spencer-Churchill papers); **p. 135**, Churchill to his wife, 17 Aug. (Spencer-Churchill papers); Clementine Churchill to her husband, 15 Aug. (Spencer-Churchill papers); Churchill to his wife, 15 Aug. (Spencer-Churchill papers); **p. 136**, Churchill to Haig, 16 Aug. (Churchill papers); Rawlinson to Wilson, 29 Aug. (Wilson papers); Churchill to Lloyd George, 17 Aug. (Lloyd George papers); Sutherland to Churchill, 17 Aug. (Lloyd George papers); **p. 137**, Churchill to Loucheur, 18 Aug. (Churchill papers); **p. 138**, Clementine Churchill to her husband, 18 Aug. (Spencer-Churchill papers); **p. 140**, Esher to Sassoon, 10 Aug. (Sassoon papers); **p. 141**, Churchill to his wife, 23 Aug. (Spencer-Churchill papers); **p. 142**, Churchill to Baruch, 7 Sept. (Churchill papers); **pp. 141–3**, Churchill to his wife, 8 and 9 Sept. (Spencer-Churchill papers); **p. 144**, Churchill to Lloyd George, 10 Sept. (Churchill papers); **pp. 147–9**, Churchill to his wife, 10, 12 and 15 Sept. (Spencer-Churchill papers).

CHAPTER 8. 'THE COMING OF VICTORY', 1918: **p. 152**, Haig to Churchill, 3 Oct. (Churchill papers); **pp. 152–4**, Churchill speeches, 7, 8, 11 and 15 Oct. (Churchill Press Cutting albums); **p. 156**, Churchill to Tudor, 4 Nov. (Churchill papers); **p. 160**, Churchill to Lloyd George, 7 Nov. (Churchill papers); **p. 161**, Lloyd George to Churchill, 8 Nov.

(Churchill papers); **p. 163**, Churchill to Lloyd George, 9 Nov. (Churchill papers); **p. 166**, Wilson diary, 11 Nov. (Wilson papers).

CHAPTER 9. 'ELECTIONEERING AND CABINET MAKING', 1918: **p. 167**, Churchill speech, 18 Nov . (Churchill papers); **p. 168**, Foggie to Churchill, 21 Nov. (Churchill papers); Churchill to Foggie, 22 Nov. (Churchill papers); **p. 169**, Beaverbrook to Churchill, 26 Nov. (Churchill papers); Churchill to Lloyd George, 21 Nov. (Lloyd George papers); **p. 170**, Churchill speech, 26 Nov. (Churchill papers); **p. 172**, Churchill to his wife, 27 Nov. (Spencer-Churchill papers); **p. 173**, Churchill to Perks, 4 Dec. (Perks papers); **p. 174**, Churchill to his wife, 13 Dec. (Spencer-Churchill papers); **p. 175**, Amery to Lloyd George, 27 Dec. (Lloyd George papers); **p. 176**, Churchill to Lloyd George, 26 Dec. (Lloyd George papers); **p. 179**, Churchill to Lloyd George, 29 Dec. (Churchill papers); Marsh to Esher, 1 Jan. 1919 (Esher papers); Bonar Law to Lloyd George, 3 Jan. 1919 (Lloyd George papers); Wilson diary, 9 Jan. 1919 (Wilson papers).

CHAPTER 10. DEMOBILIZATION, 1919: **p. 181**, Wilson diary, 10 Jan. (Wilson papers); Churchill to Haig, 11 Jan. (Churchill papers); **p. 182**, Wilson diary, 12 Jan. (Wilson papers); **p. 183**, ditto, 15 Jan.; **p. 183**, Churchill to Austen Chamberlain, 16 Jan. (Churchill papers); Chamberlain to Churchill, 16 Jan. (Churchill papers); **p. 184**, Bonar Law to Lloyd George, 17 Jan. (Lloyd George papers); Wilson diary, 17 Jan. (Wilson papers); Marsh to Esher, 17 Jan. (Esher papers); Churchill to Lloyd George, 18 Jan. (Churchill papers); **p. 185**, Churchill memorandum, 18 Jan. (Lloyd George papers); **p. 186**, Churchill to Lloyd George, 19 Jan. (Lloyd George papers); Hankey to Jones, 18 Jan. (Hankey papers); Lloyd George to Churchill, 18 Jan. (Churchill papers); Churchill to Lloyd George, 20 Jan. (Lloyd George papers); **p. 187**, Wilson diary, 21 Jan. (Wilson papers); J. T. Davies to Churchill, 21 Jan. (Churchill papers); **p. 188**, Wilson diary, 22 Jan. (Wilson papers); Churchill to Bonar Law, 22 Jan. (Churchill papers); **p. 189**, Wilson diary, 23 Jan. (Wilson papers); ditto 24 Jan.; Churchill to his wife, 24 Jan. (Spencer-Churchill papers); **p. 190**, Bonar Law to Lloyd George, 25 Jan. (Lloyd George papers); Lloyd George to Churchill, 27 Jan. (Churchill papers); Churchill to Lloyd George, 27 Jan. (Churchill papers); **p. 191**, Churchill to Northcliffe, 27 Jan. (Churchill papers); Northcliffe to Churchill, 31 Jan. (Churchill papers); Wilson diary, 28 Jan. (Wilson papers); Churchill to Lloyd George, 29 Jan. (Churchill papers); **p. 192**, Guest to Lloyd George, 30 Jan. (Lloyd George papers); Wilson diary, 31 Jan. (Wilson papers); Chamberlain to Churchill, 30 Jan. (Churchill papers); Haig to Churchill, 31 Jan. (Churchill papers); **p. 193**, Churchill to Haig, 31 Jan. (Churchill papers); **p. 195**, Churchill to Lloyd George, early Sept. (Churchill papers); **p. 196**, Finance Committee of the Cabinet, 17 Oct. (Cabinet papers 27/71).

CHAPTER 11. SECRETARY OF STATE FOR AIR, 1919: **p. 197**, Churchill note, 12 Jan. (Churchill papers); **p. 198**, Churchill to Long, 18 Jan. (Churchill papers); Long to Lloyd George, 1 Feb. (Lloyd George papers); **p. 199**, Trenchard recollections (Trenchard papers); Trenchard memorandum, 4 Feb. (Trenchard papers); **p. 200**, Churchill to Long (Churchill papers); **p. 201**, Sykes to Churchill, 10 Feb. (Churchill papers); **p. 202**, Churchill to Seely, 15 Feb. (Churchill papers); **p. 203**, Churchill to Birkenhead, end Feb. (Churchill papers); Trenchard to Churchill, 3 March (Churchill papers); **p. 204**, Churchill to Trenchard, 3 March (Churchill papers); Churchill to Seely, 5 March (Churchill papers); **p. 205**, Clementine Churchill to her husband, 9 March (Spencer-Churchill papers); Trenchard to Churchill, 19 March (Churchill papers); Churchill to Trenchard, 18 March (Churchill papers); **p. 206**, Trenchard to Salmond, June (Trenchard papers); Churchill notes, 10 June (Churchill papers); **p. 207**, Churchill to Seely, 20 June (Churchill papers); **p. 208**, Trenchard to Churchill, 2 July (Churchill papers); **p. 210**, Haldane to Churchill, 19 July (Churchill papers); **p. 211**, Lady Londonderry to Churchill, mid-July (Churchill papers); **p. 212**, Churchill to Birkenhead, 1 March (Churchill papers); Wilson diary, 11, 12 and 31 July (Wilson papers); **p. 213**, Churchill to Lloyd George, 4 Aug. (Churchill papers); Seely to Churchill, 10 Nov. (Churchill papers); **p. 214**, Churchill to Seely, 11 Nov. (Churchill papers); Sykes to Churchill, 4 March (Sykes papers); **p. 215**, Sykes to Churchill, July (Sykes papers); **p. 216**, Salmond to Trenchard, 10 April (Trenchard papers); Trenchard to Salmond, 5 Sept. (Trenchard papers); **p. 217**, Churchill to Trenchard, 20 Feb. 1920 (Churchill papers); Trenchard to Churchill, 12 March 1920 (Churchill papers); **p. 218**, Trenchard memorandum, March 1921 (Trenchard papers); Churchill Cabinet note, March 1921 (Trenchard papers).

CHAPTER 12. RUSSIA IN TURMOIL, 1917–19: **p. 219**, War Cabinet, 26 Dec. 1917 (Cabinet papers 23/4); **p. 220**, War Cabinet, 14 Dec. 1917 (Cabinet papers 23/4) and 26 Dec. 1917 (Cabinet papers 23/4); Churchill to Beaverbrook, 23 Feb. 1918 (Beaverbrook papers); **p. 221**, Churchill to Lloyd George, 17 June 1918 (Lloyd George papers); Churchill memorandum, 22 June 1918 (Churchill papers); War Cabinet, 16 July 1918 (Cabinet papers 23/7); **p. 217**, War Cabinet, 22 July 1918 (Cabinet papers 23/7); **p. 225**, Scavenius to Copenhagen, 2 Sept. 1918 (Churchill papers); Churchill War Cabinet paper, 3 Sept. 1918 (Churchill papers); War Cabinet, 4 Sept. 1918 (Cabinet papers 23/7); **p. 226**, War Cabinet, 6 Sept. 1918 (Cabinet papers 23/7) and 18 Oct. 1918 (Cabinet papers 23/8) and 10 Nov. (Cabinet papers 23/8) and 14 Nov. 1918 (Cabinet papers 23/8); **p. 228**, Churchill memorandum, end 1918 (Churchill papers); **p. 229**, Imperial War Cabinet, 31 Dec. 1918 (Churchill papers); **p. 230**, Henry Wilson memorandum, 21 Jan. 1919 (Churchill papers); **p. 233**, War Cabinet, 10 Jan. 1919 (Cabinet papers 23/9); Wilson diary, 10 Jan. 1919 (Wilson papers); **p. 234**, Wilson diary, 12 and 13 Jan. 1919 (Wilson papers); Churchill to Maynard and Ironside, 14 Jan. 1919 (Churchill papers); **p. 235**, Wilson diary, 20 Jan. 1919 (Wilson papers); Mary Borden diary, 24 Jan. 1919 (Spears papers); Churchill to Lloyd George, 27 Jan. 1919 (Churchill papers); **p. 236**, Wilson to Churchill, 27 Jan. 1919 (Lloyd George papers); **p. 237**, Churchill Minute, 29 Jan. 1919 (War Office papers 32/5676); Wilson diary, 30 Jan. 1919 (Wilson papers); Wilson to Churchill, 31 Jan. 1919 (Churchill papers); Churchill to Lloyd George, 3 Feb. 1919 (Churchill papers); **p. 238**, General Staff memorandum, 31 Jan. 1919 (Lloyd George papers); Lloyd George to Churchill, 5 Feb. 1919 (Churchill papers); Churchill to Lloyd George, 5 Feb. 1919 (Churchill papers); **p. 239**, Churchill to Harington and Thwaites, 6 Feb. 1919 (War Office papers 32/5684); War Cabinet, 12 Feb. 1919 (Cabinet papers 23/9); **p. 241**, Wilson diary, 13 Feb. 1919 (Wilson papers); War Cabinet, 13 Feb. 1919 (Cabinet papers 23/9); Wilson Minute, 12 Feb. 1919 (War Office papers 32/5677); **p. 242**, Churchill Minute, 14 Feb. 1919 (War Office papers 32/5677).

CHAPTER 13. MISSION TO PARIS, 1919: **p. 244**, Council of Ten, 14 Feb. (Lloyd George papers); **p. 246**, Kerr to Lloyd George, 15 Feb. (Lloyd George papers); **p. 247**, Wilson diary, 15 Feb. (Wilson papers); Churchill to Lloyd George, 15 Feb. (Churchill papers); **p. 248**, Harington to Ironside, 15 Feb. (War Office papers 106/1153); Radcliffe memorandum, 16 Feb. (War Office papers 106/1169); **p. 249**, Lloyd George to Kerr, 16 Feb. (Lloyd George papers); Churchill to Balfour, 16 Feb. (Churchill papers); **p. 250**, Balfour to Churchill, 16 Feb. (Churchill papers); Churchill to Lloyd George, 16 Feb. (Churchill papers); **pp. 251 and 255**, Wilson diary, 17 Feb. (Wilson papers); **p. 251**, Lloyd George to Churchill, 16 Feb. (Churchill papers); **p. 252**, Kerr to Lloyd George, 17 Feb. (Lloyd George papers); Wilson diary, 16 Feb. (Wilson papers); Lloyd George to Churchill, 17 Feb. (Churchill papers); Churchill to Lloyd George, 17 Feb. (Churchill papers); **p. 253**, Churchill draft, 17 Feb. (Churchill papers); **p. 256**, Colonel House diary, 17 Feb. (House papers); **p. 256**, Churchill to Lloyd George, 17 Feb. (Churchill papers).

CHAPTER 14. 'I KNOW OF NO RUSSIAN POLICY', 1919: **p. 257**, Churchill to Wilson, 19 Feb. (Churchill papers); **p. 258**, Montagu to Churchill, 20 Feb. (Churchill papers); Lloyd George to Churchill, 20 Feb. (Churchill papers); **p. 259**, Churchill draft, 21 Feb. (Churchill papers); **p. 260**, Wilson diary, 21 Feb. (Wilson papers); Churchill to Harington,

22 Feb. (War Office papers 32/5679); War Cabinet, 24 Feb. (Cabinet papers 23/9); **p. 261**, Ironside to War Office, 23 Feb. (War Office papers 106/1153); Ironside to Churchill, 27 Feb. (Churchill papers); Churchill to Lloyd George, 27 Feb. (Churchill papers); **p. 262**, Churchill to Lloyd George, 2 March (Churchill papers); H. A. L. Fisher diary, 4 March (Fisher papers); Wilson diary, 4 March (Wilson papers); Churchill to Wilson, 4 March (War Office papers 32/5682); Churchill to Harington and Radcliffe, 5 March (War Office papers 32/6582); **p. 263**, Interdepartmental Conference, 6 March (Foreign Office papers 371/3661); **p. 265**, War Cabinet, 6 March (Cabinet papers 23/9); Churchill to Lloyd George, 8 March (Churchill papers).

CHAPTER 15. 'THE BOLSHEVIK TRYANNY IS THE WORST', 1919: **p. 268**, Churchill to Lloyd George, 14 March (Churchill papers); **p. 269**, War Cabinet, 17 March (Curzon papers); **p. 270**, Wilson diary, 26 March (Wilson papers); Radcliffe memorandum, 27 March (Churchill papers); **p. 271**, Churchill to Curzon, 28 March (Curzon papers); Curzon to Churchill, 29 March (Churchill papers); Churchill to Foch, 28 March (Churchill papers); War Cabinet, 31 March (Cabinet papers 23/9); **p. 272**, Churchill to Clemenceau, 1 April (Churchill papers); **p. 273**, Churchill to Lloyd George, 2 April (Churchill papers); Lloyd George to Churchill, 3 April (Churchill papers); Wilson to Churchill, 3 April (Churchill papers); Clemenceau to Churchill, footnote **p. 273**, 9 April (Churchill papers); **p. 274**, Churchill to Lloyd George, 4 April (Churchill papers); Churchill to Harington, 4 April (Churchill papers); Churchill to Harington, second letter of 4 April, Harington to Churchill, 4 April; Churchill to Harington, 9 April and War Office minute, 24 April (all from War Office papers 32/5749); 3 April, Churchill appeal to soldiers in North Russia (Churchill papers); **p. 275**, Churchill to Lloyd George, 6 April (Churchill papers); Fisher diary, 8 April (Fisher papers); **p. 276**, Churchill to Lloyd George, 10 April (Churchill papers); **p. 278**, Churchill speech, 11 April (Churchill Press Cutting Albums); Churchill to Harington, Thwaites and Macdonogh, 16 April (Churchill papers). Also, **p. 271**, War Cabinet, 14 Nov. 1918 (Cabinet papers 23/8).

CHAPTER 16. 'NOW IS THE TIME TO HELP', 1919: **p. 280**, General Staff memorandum, 15 April (Churchill papers); **p. 282**, Maynard to War Office, 17 April (Churchill papers); Wilson to Briggs, 19 April (Churchill papers); Churchill to Wilson, 22 April (Churchill papers); **p. 283**, Churchill to Chamberlain, 22 April (Churchill papers); Wilson diary, 23 April (Wilson papers); Knox to War Office, arrived 25 April (Churchill papers); Maynard to War Office, 25 April (Churchill papers); **p. 284**, Churchill to Lloyd George, 26 April (Churchill papers); **p. 285**, Wilson to Churchill, 28 April (Churchill papers); Churchill to Lloyd George, 28 April (Churchill papers); **p. 286**, Savory to his mother, 26 April (Savory papers); War Cabinet, 29 April (Cabinet papers 23/10); Wilson to Churchill, 30 April (Churchill papers); Churchill to Curzon, 1 May (Curzon papers); Curzon to Churchill, 2 May (Churchill papers); **p. 287**, Churchill to Wilson, 3 May (Churchill papers); Wilson diary, 1 May (Wilson papers); Wilson to Churchill, 1 May (Churchill papers); War Office to Ironside, 4 May (Churchill papers); Churchill to Wilson, 5 May (Churchill papers); **p. 288**, Churchill to Lloyd George, 5 May (Churchill papers); Churchill to Wilson, 5 May (Churchill papers); Lloyd George to Churchill, 6 May (Churchill papers); Churchill to Lloyd George, 7 May (Churchill papers); **p. 289**, Curzon Minute, 9 May (Foreign Office papers 371/4095); Churchill to Harington, 12 May (War Office papers 32/5687); **p. 290**, Churchill speech, 14 May (Churchill Press Cutting Albums); Ironside to Churchill, 18 May (War Office papers 106/1153); **p. 291**, Knox to War Office (Churchill papers); Churchill to Lloyd George, 21 May (Lloyd George papers); **p. 292**, Gough to War Office, 25 May (War Office papers 32/5692); **p. 293**, Clive to Foreign Office, 30 May (War Office papers 32/5692); Churchill to Harington, 2 June (War Office papers 32/5692); Churchill to Gough, 6 June (War Office papers 32/5692); **p. 295**, Hoare to Churchill, 31 May (Churchill papers); **p. 296**, Hodgson to Foreign Office, 3 June (Foreign Office papers 371/4095); **p. 297**, Wedgwood to Churchill, 7 June, and Churchill's reply,

13 June (Churchill papers); Knox to War Office, 8 June (Churchill papers); Ironside to War Office, 6 June (Churchill papers); **p. 298**, Wilson diary, 10 June (Wilson papers); Wilson to Churchill, 10 June (Churchill papers); War Office to Knox, 10 June (Churchill papers); Wilson diary, 11 June (Wilson papers); War Cabinet, 11 June (Curzon papers); **p. 299**, Wilson diary, 16 June (Wilson papers); War Cabinet, 18 June (Curzon papers); Radcliffe to Churchill, 18 June (War Office papers 32/5693); **p. 300**, Churchill to Bonar Law, Curzon and Chamberlain, 20 June (War Office papers 32/5693); Curzon to Churchill, 20 June (War Office papers 32/5693); Ironside to War Office, 19 June (War Office papers 32/5693); Chamberlain to Churchill, 20 June (War Office papers 32/5693); Churchill to Harington, 21 June (War Office papers 32/5693); War Cabinet, 27 June (Curzon papers); **p. 301**, Hankey diary, 7 July (Hankey papers); Wilson diary, 7 July (Wilson papers); War Cabinet, July 9 (Curzon papers).

CHAPTER 17. 'THE WHOLE FATE OF RUSSIA', 1919: **p. 303**, War Cabinet, 29 May (Cabinet papers 23/10); **p. 304**, Curzon to Churchill, 10 June (Churchill papers); Churchill to Curzon, 11 June (Churchill papers); **p. 305**, Curzon draft, early June (Foreign Office papers 371/3667); War Cabinet, 27 June (Curzon papers); **p. 306**, Wilson diary, 30 June (Wilson papers); Churchill to Wilson, 1 July (War Office papers 32/5697); **p. 307**, War Office conference, 2 July (War Office papers 32/5697); War Cabinet, 4 July (Curzon papers); **p. 308**, Briggs memorandum, received 9 July (War Office papers 32/5697); Wilson diary, 25 July (Wilson papers); **p. 309**, War Cabinet, 25 July (Cabinet papers 23/11); **p. 310**, Wilson to Churchill, 26 July (Churchill papers); **p. 311**, Fisher diary, 27 July (Fisher papers); Wilson diary, 28 July (Wilson papers); War Cabinet, 29 July (Cabinet papers 23/11); **p. 314**, War Cabinet, 1 Aug. (Cabinet 23/11); **p. 315**, Rawlinson diary, 31 July (Rawlinson papers); **p. 316**, Rawlinson diary, 9 and 12 Aug. (Rawlinson papers); War Cabinet, 12 Aug. (Cabinet papers 23/11); **p. 318**, Churchill to Curzon, 14 Aug. (Churchill papers).

CHAPTER 18. 'MR CHURCHILL'S PRIVATE WAR', 1919: **p. 320**, Hankey diary, 17 Aug. (Hankey papers); Churchill to Clemenceau, 19 Aug. (Churchill papers); **p. 321**, Churchill to Lloyd George, 23 Aug. (Churchill papers); Churchill to Balfour, 23 Aug. (Churchill papers); Churchill to Lloyd George, Balfour and Curzon, 24 Aug. (Churchill papers); **p. 322**, Churchill to Wilson, two letters of 24 Aug. (Churchill papers); Wilson to Churchill, 28 Aug. (War Office papers 32/5246); **p. 323**, Churchill to Wilson, 31 Aug. (Churchill papers); Wilson to Churchill, 5 Sept. (War Office papers 32/5750); Churchill to Wilson, 6 Sept. (War Office papers 32/5751); Lloyd George to Balfour, Churchill and Curzon, 30 Aug. (Lloyd George papers); **p. 325**, Churchill speech to deputation, end Aug. (Churchill papers); **p. 326**, Churchill to Lloyd George, 6 Sept. (Churchill papers); **p. 327**, Churchill to Curzon, 10 Sept. (Curzon papers); Churchill to Wilson, 9 Sept. (Churchill papers); Churchill to his mother, 16 Sept. (Shane Leslie papers); **p. 328**, Wilson to Churchill, 11 Sept. (Churchill papers); Churchill to Wilson, 13 Sept. (Churchill papers); Clementine Churchill to her husband, 14 Sept. (Spencer-Churchill papers); Wilson to Churchill, 16 Sept. (Churchill papers); Churchill to Curzon, 17 Sept. (Churchill papers); **p. 329**, Wilson to Churchill, 18 Sept. (Churchill papers); Fisher diary, 18 Sept. (Fisher papers); **p. 330**, War Cabinet, 18 Sept. (Cabinet papers 32/12); Churchill to Holman, 18 Sept. (Churchill papers); Churchill to Holman, 20 Sept. (Churchill papers); Churchill to Lloyd George, 20 Sept. (Churchill papers); Churchill to Lloyd George, letter of 22 Sept. (Churchill papers); Churchill to Lloyd George, memorandum of 22 Sept. (Churchill papers); Churchill Cabinet memorandum of 16 Sept., circulated 22 Sept. (Cabinet papers 24/89); **p. 331**, Lloyd George to Churchill, 22 Sept. (Churchill papers); **p. 333**, Churchill to Lloyd George, 22 Sept. (Churchill papers); **p. 335**, Fisher diary, 23 Sept. (Fisher papers); War Cabinet, 24 Sept. (Cabinet papers 23/12); **p. 336**, Yudenitch to Churchill, 24 Sept. (Churchill papers); Churchill memorandum, 25 Sept. (Cabinet papers 23/12); **p. 337**, Churchill to Kolchak, 5 Oct. (Churchill papers); Churchill to Curzon, 5 Oct. (Churchill papers);

p. 339, Churchill to Lloyd George, 6 Oct. (Lloyd George papers); War Cabinet, 7 Oct. (Cabinet papers 23/12); **p. 340,** Churchill to Lloyd George, 9 Oct. (Churchill papers); **p. 341,** Churchill to Denikin, 9 Oct. (Churchill papers); **p. 342,** Lloyd George to Churchill, 7 Oct. (Churchill papers); Churchill to Lloyd George, 10 Oct. (Lloyd George papers); Churchill to Denikin, 10 Oct. (Churchill papers); Churchill press statement, 13 Oct. (Churchill papers); **p. 343,** Churchill to Curzon, 9 Oct. (Churchill papers); Curzon minute, 10 Oct. (Foreign Office papers 371/3663); Churchill to Curzon, 10 Oct. (Churchill papers); **p. 344,** Churchill to Lloyd George, 10 Oct. (Lloyd George papers); **p. 345,** Churchill to Spender, 10 Oct. (Churchill papers); **p. 346,** General Staff memorandum, 10 Oct. (War Office papers 32/5700); Churchill memorandum, 14 Oct. (Churchill papers); **p. 348,** Wilson diary, 16 Oct. (Wilson papers); Churchill to Yudenitch, 17 Oct. (Churchill papers).

CHAPTER 19. 'GENERAL DENIKIN'S RETREAT', 1919: **p. 350,** Churchill to Ritchie, 18 Oct. (Churchill papers); Wilson diary, 20 Oct. (Wilson papers); **p. 351,** Churchill to Curzon, 21 Oct. (Churchill papers); Churchill instructions to Haking, 21 Oct. (Churchill papers); Churchill to Curzon, covering note, 21 Oct. (Curzon papers); **p. 352,** Cabinet Finance Committee, 22 Oct. (Cabinet papers 27/71), ditto, 24 Oct. (Cabinet papers 27/71); **p. 354,** Fisher diary, 31 Oct. (Fisher papers); Fisher diary, 3 Nov. (Fisher papers); **p. 355,** Fisher diary, 4 Nov. (Fisher papers); **p. 356,** Fisher diary, 6 Nov. (Fisher papers); Wilson diary, 7 Nov. (Wilson papers); Churchill to Lloyd George, 7 Nov. (Lloyd George papers); **p. 357,** Cabinet, 9 Nov. (Cabinet papers 23/18); Churchill memorandum, 12 Nov. (Churchill papers); Fisher diary, 12 Nov. (Fisher papers); **p. 358,** Churchill to Holman, 19 Nov. (Churchill papers); **p. 359,** Churchill to Wilson, 20 Nov. (Churchill papers); Churchill to Loucheur, 21 Nov. (Loucheur papers); **p. 360,** Churchill to Reading, 29 Nov. (Churchill papers); Wilson diary, 2 Dec. (Wilson papers); **p. 361,** Churchill to Holman, 11 Dec. (Churchill papers); Churchill to Denikin, 11 Dec. (Churchill papers); **p. 362,** Clemenceau–Lloyd George meeting, 12 Dec. (Cabinet papers 23/18); Cabinet, 12 Dec. (Cabinet papers 23/18); **p. 363,** Wilson diary, 15 Dec. (Wilson papers); Churchill memorandum, 15 Dec. (Churchill papers); Wilson diary, 20 Dec. (Wilson papers); Wilson diary, 28 Dec. (Wilson papers); Churchill to Wilson, 31 Dec. (Churchill papers).

CHAPTER 20. THE TRIUMPH OF THE BOLSHEVIKS, 1920: **p. 365,** Churchill speech, 2 Jan. (Churchill Press Cutting Albums); **p. 366,** Churchill to Wilson, 5 Jan. (Churchill papers); Churchill to Curzon, 5 Jan. (Curzon papers); Holman to Churchill, 8 Jan. (Churchill papers); **p. 367,** Holman to Churchill, 9 Jan. (Churchill papers); Yudenitch to Churchill, 10 Jan. (Churchill papers); **p. 368,** Churchill to Holman, 11 Jan. (Churchill papers); **p. 369,** Churchill to Wilson, 11 Jan. (Churchill papers); Wilson diary, 14 Jan. (Wilson papers); Fisher diary, 14 Jan. (Fisher papers); Cabinet, 14 Jan. (Cabinet papers 23/20); Churchill to Lloyd George, 14 Jan. (Churchill papers); **p. 370,** Wilson diary, 15 Jan. (Wilson papers); Wilson diary, 16 Jan. (Wilson papers); **p. 371,** Wilson diary, 17 Jan. (Wilson papers); **p. 372,** Wilson diary, 18 Jan. (Wilson papers); **p. 373,** Wilson diary, 19 Jan. (Wilson papers); Cabinet, 19 Jan. (Churchill papers); **p. 374,** Churchill to his wife, 20 Jan. (Spencer-Churchill papers); Churchill to Lloyd George, 28 Jan. (Lloyd George papers); **p. 376,** Cabinet, 29 Jan. (Cabinet papers 23/20); Churchill to Holman, 3 Feb. (Churchill papers); **p. 378,** Fisher diary, 9 Feb. (Fisher papers).

CHAPTER 21. 'EVERYBODY WISHING TO MAKE THEIR PEACE', 1920; **p. 380,** Holman to Denikin, 16 Feb. (Churchill papers); Churchill to Wilson, 21 Feb. (War Office papers 32/5711); Supreme Allied Council, 25 Feb. (Lloyd George papers); **p. 381,** Churchill to Holman, 25 Feb. (Churchill papers); Radcliffe to Wilson, 1 March (War Office papers 32/5712); Wilson to Churchill, 1 March (War Office papers 32/5712); Churchill to Holman, 5 March (Churchill papers); **p. 382,** Fisher to Lloyd George, 13 March (Lloyd George papers); Churchill to Harington, 18 March (War Office papers 32/5713); Churchill to

Harington, 15 March (War Office papers 32/5713); Churchill to Lloyd George, 18 March (Lloyd George papers); **p. 383**, Churchill to Holman, 22 March (Churchill papers); Churchill minute, 23 March (War Office papers 32/5714); Wilson diary, 29 March (Wilson papers).

CHAPTER 22. 'THE HAIRY PAW OF THE BABOON', 1920: **p. 384**, Churchill to Lloyd George, 24 March (Churchill papers); **p. 385**, Churchill to his wife, 26 March (Spencer-Churchill papers); **pp. 385–7**, Churchill to his wife, 26, 27, 29, 30 and 31 March (Spencer-Churchill papers); **p. 387**, Clementine Churchill to her husband, 31 March (Spencer-Churchill papers); **p. 388**, Fisher diary, 31 March (Fisher papers); Cabinet, 31 March (Cabinet papers 23/20); Thwaites to Wilson, 1 April (War Office papers 32/5708); Churchill to Lloyd George, 31 March (Lloyd George papers); Churchill to Wilson, 9 April (War Office papers 32/5716); **p. 389**, Churchill to Lloyd George (Churchill papers); **p. 391**, Churchill to Hankey, 13 May (Churchill papers); Hankey to Churchill, 13 May (Churchill papers); Churchill to Wilson, 1 May (Churchill papers); **p. 392**, Churchill memorandum, 1 May (Marsh papers); **p. 393**, Wilson diary, 5 May (Wilson papers); **p. 395**, Churchill memorandum, 11 May (Cabinet papers 24/106); Churchill to Lloyd George, 14 May (Churchill papers); **p. 396**, Churchill to Radcliffe and Thwaites, 19 May (Churchill papers); **p. 397**, Wilson diary, 19 May (Wilson papers); Churchill to Curzon, 20 May (Churchill papers); **p. 398**, Cabinet, 21 May (Cabinet papers 23/21); Fisher diary, 21 May (Fisher papers); Churchill to Curzon, 22 May (Curzon papers); **p. 399**, Conference of Ministers, 28 May (Cabinet papers, 23/21); **p. 400**, Hankey diary, 31 May (Hankey papers).

CHAPTER 23. THE AMRITSAR DEBATE, 1920: **p. 401**, Bonar Law to Churchill, 7 July (Churchill papers); **pp. 402, 410** and **411**, Fisher diary, 8 July (Fisher papers); **pp. 402, 403** and **410**, Sunderland to Lloyd George, 9 July (Lloyd George papers); **p. 411**, Davidson to Curzon, 17 July (Curzon papers).

CHAPTER 24. 'THE POISON PERIL FROM THE EAST', 1920: **p. 412**, British Government to Wrangel, 3 June (Churchill papers); Cabinet, 3 June (Cabinet papers 23/21); Cabinet, 11 June (Cabinet papers 23/22); Churchill to Milne, 11 June (Churchill papers); **p. 413**, Churchill memorandum, 21 June (Churchill papers); Fisher diary, 1 July (Fisher papers); Churchill to Lloyd George, Bonar Law and Balfour, 1 July (Churchill papers); **p. 414**, Churchill to Bonar Law, 16 July (Churchill papers); Wilson diary, 19 July (Wilson papers); Fisher diary, 20 July (Fisher papers); Cabinet, 20 July (Cabinet papers 23/22); Churchill to Wilson, Harington and Macdonogh, 20 July (Churchill papers); **p. 418**, Derby to Lloyd George, 6 Aug. (Lloyd George papers); **p. 419**, Lloyd George to Churchill, 4 Aug. (Churchill papers); Cabinet Finance Committee, 6 Aug. (War Office papers 32/5745); **p. 420**, Churchill to Milne, 6 Aug. (Churchill papers); D'Abernon to Curzon, 6 Aug. (Curzon papers); Fisher diary, 7 Aug. (Fisher papers); Anglo-French Conference, 8 Aug. (Cabinet papers 23/22); **p. 421**, Fisher diary, 10 and 11 Aug. (Fisher papers); Sapieha to Curzon, 13 Aug. (Rumbold papers); **p. 422**, Marsh to Churchill, 19 Aug. (Churchill papers); Churchill to Marsh, 20 Aug. (Churchill papers); Cabinet, 17 Aug. (Cabinet papers 23/22); **p. 423**, Wilson diary, 18 Aug. (Wilson papers); Churchill to Lloyd George, Bonar Law and Balfour, 18 Aug. (Lloyd George papers); Kamenev to Chicherin, 12 and 13 Aug. (Cabinet papers 24/111); Litvinov to Chicherin, 13 Aug. (Cabinet papers 24/111); Kamenev to Litvinov and Lenin, 14 Aug. (Cabinet papers 24/111); Churchill to Thwaites, 23 Aug. (Churchill papers); Kamenev to Lenin, 20 Aug. (Cabinet papers 24/111); **p. 424**, Churchill covering note, 24 Aug. (Lloyd George papers); **p. 425**, Wilson diary, 23 and 24 Aug. (Wilson papers); Churchill to Lloyd George, 26 Aug. (Churchill papers); **p. 426**, Churchill memorandum, 29 Aug. (Churchill papers); **p. 428**, Wilson diary, 2 Sept. (Wilson papers); Conference of Ministers, 2 Sept. (Cabinet papers 23/22); **p. 429**, Fisher diary, 9 Sept. (Fisher papers); Cabinet, 10 Sept. (Cabinet papers 23/22); Churchill to Thwaites,

17 Sept. (Churchill papers); **p. 430**, Churchill memorandum, 21 Sept. (Cabinet papers 24/111); Cabinet, 21 Sept. (Cabinet papers 23/22); Fisher diary, 24 Sept. (Fisher papers); Sunderland to Lloyd George, 6 July (Lloyd George papers).

CHAPTER 25. RUSSIA'S 'BLOODSTAINED GOLD', 1920: **p. 431**, General Staff report, 13 Oct. (Churchill papers); Churchill to Lloyd George, 17 Oct. (Churchill papers); **p. 432**, Churchill to Lloyd George, 26 Oct. (Lloyd George papers); Churchill memorandum, 27 Oct. (Churchill papers); **p. 433**, Churchill to Curzon, 29 Oct. (Churchill papers); **p. 434**, Cabinet, 11 Nov. (Cabinet papers 23/23); de Robeck to London, received 11 Nov. (Lloyd George papers); Churchill to Lloyd George, 11 Nov. (Lloyd George papers); **p. 435**, Churchill memorandum, 16 Nov. (Churchill papers); **p. 436**, Cabinet, 17 Nov. (Cabinet papers 23/23); **p. 438**, Birkenhead to Churchill, 17 Nov. (Churchill papers); **p. 439** and **440**, Hankey diary, 18 Nov. (Hankey papers); Cabinet, 18 Nov. (Cabinet papers 23/23); **p. 441**, Hankey diary, 19 Nov. (Hankey papers).

CHAPTER 26. IRELAND, 1919–1920: 'LET MURDER STOP': **p. 445**, Wilson diary, 18 Jan. (Wilson papers); Brade to Churchill, 2 Feb. (War Office papers 32/9300); **p. 446**, Churchill to French, 10 April (Churchill papers); **p. 447**, Wilson diary, 22 Dec. (Wilson papers); **p. 449**, Clementine Churchill to her husband, 27 March (Spencer-Churchill papers); Churchill to his wife, 31 March (Spencer-Churchill papers); **p. 450**, Wilson diary, 14 April (Wilson papers); Churchill to Lloyd George, 10 May (Churchill papers); Wilson diary, 11 May (Wilson papers); **p. 451**, Wilson diary, 13 and 21 May (Wilson papers); **p. 453**, Wilson diary, 2 June (Wilson papers); Hankey diary, 28 May (Hankey papers); Fisher diary, 2 June (Fisher papers); **p. 454**, Long to Churchill, 14 June (Churchill papers); Wilson diary, 25 June (Wilson papers); Churchill to Wilson, 25 June (Churchill papers); **p. 455**, Churchill to Harington and Trenchard, 1 July (Churchill papers); **p. 456**, Wilson diary, 12 July (Wilson papers); **p. 457**, Conference of Ministers, 25 Aug (Cabinet papers 23/22); **p. 458**, Wilson diary, 30 Aug. (Wilson papers); Macready to Churchill, 1 Sept. (War Office papers 32/9537); **p. 459**, Churchill to Charteris, 13 Sept. (Churchill papers); Wilson diary, 13 Sept. (Wilson papers); Churchill to Wilson and Macdonogh, 18 Sept. (War Office papers 32/9537); **p. 460**, Wilson diary, 21 and 22 Sept. (Wilson papers); **p. 461**, Radcliffe to Wilson, 23 Sept. (War Office papers 32/9537); Wilson diary, 23 Sept. (Wilson papers); Fisher diary, 24 Sept. (Fisher papers); Churchill to Leslie, 2 Oct. (Leslie papers); **pp. 462–3**, Wilson diary, 12 Oct., 2 and 3 Nov. (Wilson papers); **p. 463**, Churchill to Lloyd George, 3 Nov. (Churchill papers); **p. 464**, Thomson to Churchill, 9 Nov. (Churchill papers); **p. 465**, Wilson diary, 16 and 22 Nov. (Wilson papers); **p. 466**, Wilson diary, 26 Nov. (Wilson papers); **p. 467**, Churchill to Gilmartin, 14 Dec. (Churchill papers); **p. 469**, Gilmartin to Churchill, 17 Dec. (Churchill papers); **p. 470**, Churchill to Gilmartin, 27 Dec. (Churchill papers); Wilson diary, 29 Dec. (Wilson papers); **p. 471**, Clementine Churchill to her husband, 18 Feb. 1921 (Spencer-Churchill papers).

CHAPTER 27. TURKEY IN DEFEAT, 1919–1920: **p. 472**, Churchill to Lloyd George, 1 May 1919 (Churchill papers); **p. 473**, Churchill to Balfour, 12 and 23 Aug. (Churchill papers); Churchill to MacMunn, 30 Aug. (Churchill papers); **p. 476**, Churchill to Lloyd George, 1 Sept. (Lloyd George papers); Churchill to Lloyd George, 22 Sept. (Churchill papers); Milne to Churchill, 20 Oct. (War Office papers 32/5733); **p. 477**, Wilson diary, 7 Nov. (Wilson papers); Radcliffe Minute, 12 Nov. (War Office papers 32/5733); Wilson to Churchill, 13 Nov. (War Office papers 32/5733); Churchill Note, 6 Jan. (Churchill papers); **p. 478**, Churchill memorandum, 7 Feb. (Churchill papers); Montagu to Churchill, 10 Feb. (War Office papers 32/5620); Churchill to Lloyd George and Bonar Law, 12 Feb. (War Office papers 32/5620); **p. 479**, Churchill to Milne, 17 March (Churchill papers); Wilson diary, 19 March (Wilson papers); War Office notes, 19 March (Churchill papers); **p. 480**, Curzon to Lloyd George, 9 April (Lloyd George papers); Churchill to Lloyd George, 24 March (Churchill papers); Churchill to General Haldane, 1 April

(Aylmer Haldane papers); **p. 481**, Churchill memorandum, 1 May (Cabinet papers 24/106); **p. 483**, Wilson diary, 1 May (Wilson papers); Churchill to Austen Chamberlain, 10 May (Churchill papers); Meeting of Ministers, 18 June (Cabinet papers 23/21); **p. 484**, Churchill to Lloyd George, 13 June (Churchill papers); **p. 485**, Wilson diary, 16 June (Wilson papers); Churchill memorandum, 7 June (Cabinet papers 24/107); **p. 486**, Churchill to Lloyd George, 13 June (Churchill papers); Wilson diary, 15, 16 and 17 June (Wilson papers); **p. 487**, Cabinet, 17 June (Cabinet papers 23/22); Wilson diary, 19 June (Wilson papers). Also **p. 484**, Churchill to Moser, 30 Jan. 1908 (Churchill papers) and Churchill memorandum, 25 Oct. 1919 (Churchill papers).

CHAPTER 28. 'THESE THANKLESS DESERTS', 1920: **p. 490**, Cabinet, 7 July (Cabinet papers 23/22); Wilson diary, 15 July (Wilson papers); **p. 491**, Wilson diary, 16, 20 and 30 July (Wilson papers); Thomas Jones to Lloyd George, 30 July (Lloyd George papers); **p. 492**, Cabinet Finance Committee, 3 Aug. (Cabinet papers 27/71); Churchill to Lloyd George, 5 Aug. (Lloyd George papers); **p. 493**, Wilson diary, 6 Aug. (Wilson papers); Cabinet, 12 Aug. (Cabinet papers 23/22); Churchill to Lloyd George, 26 Aug. (Lloyd George papers); **p. 494**, Churchill to Haldane, 26 Aug. (Churchill papers); Churchill to Trenchard, 29 Aug. (Churchill papers); Wilson diary, 30 Aug. (Wilson papers); Churchill to Haldane, 30 Aug. (Churchill papers); **p. 495**, Churchill to Venizelos, 31 Aug. (Churchill papers); Churchill to Curzon, 31 Aug. (Curzon papers); Churchill to Lloyd George, 31 Aug. (Churchill papers); **p. 496**, Churchill to Ritchie, 7 Sept. (Churchill papers); Wilson diary, 20 Sept. (Wilson papers); **p. 497**, Fisher diary, 12 Oct. (Fisher papers); Churchill memorandum, 23 Nov. (Churchill papers); **p. 498**, Thwaites to Churchill, 30 Nov. (War Office papers 32/5773); Aga Khan to Montagu, 2 Dec. (Churchill papers); **p. 499**, Churchill to Lloyd George, 4 Dec. (Churchill papers); **p. 501**, Churchill memorandum, 16 Dec. (Churchill papers); Curzon to Derby, 22 Nov. (Derby papers); Churchill to Derby, 21 Dec. (Churchill papers); Derby to Churchill, 23 Dec. (Churchill papers); **p. 502**, Congreve to Churchill, 15 Nov. (War Office papers 32/5770); **p. 503**, Conference of Ministers, 1 and 2 Dec. (Cabinet papers 23/23); Churchill to Hankey, 10 Dec. (Cabinet papers 23/23); **p. 504**, Cabinet, 13 Dec. (Cabinet papers 23/23); Wilson diary, 13 Dec. (Wilson papers); **p. 506**, Wilson diary, 23 Jan. 1921 (Wilson papers).

CHAPTER 29. CREATING THE MIDDLE EAST DEPARTMENT, 1921: **p. 507**, Cabinet Finance Committee, 7 Dec. 1920 (Cabinet papers 27/71); Cabinet, 31 Dec. (Cabinet papers 23/23); **p. 509**, Churchill to Lloyd George, 4 Jan. 1921 (Lloyd George papers); Churchill notes, 4 Jan. (Lloyd George papers); Hankey diary, 7 Jan. (Hankey papers); **p. 510**, Churchill to Curzon, 8 Jan. (Curzon papers); Churchill to Lloyd George, 8 Jan. (Lloyd George papers); Churchill to Cox and Haldane, 8 Jan. (Churchill papers); **p. 511**, Churchill to Curzon, 9 Jan. (Churchill papers); Churchill to Cox, 10 Jan. (Churchill papers); **p. 512**, Shuckburgh notes, 12 Jan. (Churchill papers); Churchill to Cox, 10 Jan. (Churchill papers); **p. 513**, Churchill to Lloyd George and Curzon, 12 Jan. (Churchill papers); **p. 514**, Churchill to Lloyd George, 12 Jan. (Churchill papers); Haldane to Churchill, 13 Jan. (Churchill papers); **p. 515**, Cox to Churchill, 13 Jan. (Churchill papers); Cox to Churchill, 15 Jan. (Churchill papers); Geiger to Sinclair, 13 Jan. (Churchill papers); Hirtzel to Churchill, 14 Jan. (Churchill papers); Lawrence to Marsh, 17 Jan. (Churchill papers); **p. 516**, Churchill to Cox, 16 Jan. (Churchill papers); **p. 517**, Curzon to Churchill, 17 Jan. (Churchill papers); Churchill to Haldane, 19 Jan. (Churchill papers); Haldane to Churchill, two telegrams of 19 Jan. (Churchill papers); Hirtzel Minute, 21 Jan. (Churchill papers); **p. 518**, Masterton Smith to Churchill, 22 Jan. (Churchill papers); Churchill to Hirtzel, 23 Jan. (Churchill papers); **p. 519**, Churchill to Lloyd George, 24 Jan. (Churchill papers); Churchill to Haldane, 27 Jan. (Churchill papers); Hirtzel to Churchill, 25 Jan. (Churchill papers); Churchill to Worthington-Evans, 27 Jan. (Churchill papers); **p. 520**, Churchill to his wife (Spencer-Churchill papers); Milner to Samuel, 5 Feb. (Samuel papers); Churchill to his wife, 6 Feb. (Spencer-Churchill papers); **p. 522**, Churchill to his advisers, 7 Feb. (Churchill papers); Churchill to Cox, 7 Feb. (Churchill papers); Churchill to Haldane, 7 Feb. (Churchill papers); Churchill to Hirtzel, 7 Feb. (Churchill papers); **p. 523,** Cabinet notes, probably 7 Feb. (Churchill papers); **p. 524,** Hirtzel to Churchill, 9 Feb. (Churchill papers); Clementine Churchill to her husband, 7 Feb. (Spencer-Churchill papers); **p. 525,** Churchill to his wife, 9 Feb. (Spencer-Churchill papers); Churchill to Long and Curzon, 8 Feb. (Churchill papers); Rawlinson to Churchill, 10 Feb. (Churchill papers); **p. 526,** Churchill to Curzon, 10 Feb. (Churchill papers); Curzon to Churchill, 15 Feb. (Churchill papers); **p. 527,** Churchill to Lloyd George, 12 Feb. (Churchill papers); Masterton Smith to Churchill, 13 Feb. (Churchill papers); **p. 528,** Cabinet, 14 Feb. (Cabinet papers 23/23); **p. 528,** Curzon to his wife, 14 Feb. (Curzon papers); Churchill to his wife, 14 Feb. (Spencer-Churchill papers); **p. 530,** Churchill to his wife, 15 Feb. (Spencer-Churchill papers); Also, **p. 523,**[Creedy to Worthington-Evans, 16 March 1921 (Churchill papers) and Churchill to Curzon, 1 Jan. 1917 (Curzon papers).

CHAPTER 30. 'I AM DETERMINED TO SAVE YOU MILLIONS', 1921: **p. 531,** Churchill to his wife, 16 Feb. (Spencer-Churchill papers); Churchill to Austen Chamberlain, 16 Feb. (Churchill papers); **p. 532,** Churchill to Curzon, 16 Feb. (Churchill papers); Arnold Wilson memorandum, 16 Feb. (Colonial Office papers 730/13); Churchill memorandum, 18 Feb. (Churchill papers); **p. 533,** Clementine Churchill to her husband, 18 and 20 Feb. (Spencer-Churchill papers); Churchill to his wife, 19 and 21 Feb. (Spencer-Churchill papers); **p. 535,** Venizelos report, 16 Feb. (Churchill papers); Churchill to Lloyd George, 22 Feb. (Churchill papers); **p. 536,** Shuckburgh to Churchill, 23 Feb. (Colonial Office papers 733/1); Churchill to Shuckburgh, 24 Feb. (Colonial Office papers 733/1); **p. 537,** Curzon to Churchill, 24 Feb. (Churchill papers); Churchill to Curzon, 25 Feb. (Churchill papers); Churchill to his wife, 24 Feb. (Spencer-Churchill papers); Middle-East Department memorandum, end Feb. (Churchill papers); **p. 539,** Churchill to his wife, 26 Feb. (Spencer-Churchill papers); **p. 540,** Churchill to Lloyd George, 28 Feb. (Lloyd George papers); Zionist Organization Minutes, 1 March (Central Zionist Archive); Weizmann to Churchill, 1 March (Weizmann papers); **p. 543,** Weizmann to Samuel, 10 March (Weizmann papers).

CHAPTER 31. THE CAIRO CONFERENCE, MARCH 1921: **p. 544,** Trenchard to Churchill, 11 March (Churchill papers); Trenchard to Churchill, 11 March (Churchill papers); **p.545,** Trenchard to Salmond, 12 March (Trenchard papers); **pp.545–56,** Cairo Conference Minutes, 12–22 March (Churchill papers); **p. 555,** Churchill to Bonar Law, 18 March (Churchill papers); Churchill to Marsh, 18 March (Churchill papers); Marsh to Churchill, 18 March (Churchill papers); Wilson diary, 19 and 21 March (Wilson papers); **p. 556,** Wilson diary, 29 March (Wilson papers); T. E. Lawrence to Robert Lawrence, 20 March (Lawrence papers); **p. 557,** Fisher diary, 22 March (Fisher papers).

CHAPTER 32. VISIT TO JERUSALEM, 1921: **pp. 560–2, 569–70** and **572,** Churchill conversations with Abdullah (Churchill papers); **pp. 562–4,** Palestinian Arab memorandum, 28 March (Churchill papers); **pp.564–6,** Churchill reply to the Palestinian Arabs, 28 March (Churchill papers); **pp. 567–8,** Jewish National Council memorandum (Churchill papers); **pp. 568–9,** Churchill reply to Jewish National Council, 28 March (Churchill papers); **p. 569,** Ruppin diary, 28 March (Ruppin papers); **p. 570,** Sokolow speech, 29 March (Central Zionist Archive); Churchill speech, 29 March (Central Zionist Archive); **p. 571,** Sacher to Simon, 30 March (Sacher papers); **p. 573,** Dizengoff to Churchill, 30 March (Churchill papers); Churchill speech in Tel-Aviv, 30 March (Central Zionist Archive); Meerovitch to Churchill, 30 March (Churchill papers).

CHAPTER 33. THE MIDDLE EAST SETTLEMENT, 1921: **p. 576,** Churchill memorandum on future of Transjordan, 2 April (Churchill papers); Churchill to Curzon, 5 April (Curzon papers); Conference of Ministers, 11 April (Cabinet papers 23/25); **p. 577,** Wilson diary,

12 April (Wilson papers); **p. 578**, Churchill to Hankey, 13 April (War Office papers 32/5237); Hankey to Churchill, 13 April (War Office papers 32/5237); Churchill to Chamberlain, 14 April (Chamberlain papers); **p. 579**, Chamberlain to Churchill, 16 April (Churchill papers); Stamfordham to Churchill, 18 April (Churchill papers); Blanche Hozier to Churchill, 17 April (Churchill papers); **p. 580**, Conference of Ministers, 19 April (Cabinet papers 23/25); **p. 581**, Chamberlain to his sister, 8 May (Chamberlain papers); Beaverbrook to Borden, 12 May (Beaverbrook papers); notes passed between Churchill and Chamberlain, early May (Churchill papers); **p. 584**, Sidebotham note, 28 April (Central Zionist Archive); Samuel to Churchill, 2 May (Colonial Office papers 733/3); Churchill to Samuel, 3 May (Colonial Office papers 733/3); Samuel to Churchill, 3 May (Colonial Office papers 733/3); Churchill to Sinclair, 4 May (Colonial Office papers 733/3); Young Minute, 18 May (Colonial Office papers 733/16); Churchill Minute, 18 May (Colonial Office papers 733/16); Samuel to Churchill, 8 May (Churchill papers); **p. 586**, Churchill to Samuel, 12 May (Colonial Office papers 733/3); Young Minute, 13 May (Colonial Office papers 733/3); Churchill to Samuel, 14 May (Colonial Office papers 733/3); **p. 587**, Moslem resolution, 12 May (Colonial Office papers 733/16); Young Minute, 17 May (Colonial Office papers 733/16); Deedes to Young, 18 May (Colonial Office papers 733/17); Lawrence to Churchill, 19 May (Churchill papers); **p. 588**, Marlowe to Northcliffe, 30 May (Northcliffe papers); Cabinet, 31 May (Cabinet papers 23/25); Fisher diary, 31 May (Fisher papers); **p. 589**, Churchill to Samuel, 2 June (Colonial Office papers 733/3); Jewish National Council telegram, 3 June (Central Zionist Archive); Samuel to Churchill, 5 June (Churchill papers); Sokolow–Churchill interview, 5 June (Central Zionist Archive); **p. 590**, Wilson diary, 31 May and 1 June (Wilson papers); Fisher diary, 1 and 2 June (Fisher papers); Churchill to Lloyd George, 2 June (Churchill papers); **p. 591**, Cabinet Committee, 2 June (Cabinet papers 27/133); **p. 592**, Wilson diary, 9 June (Wilson papers); Churchill to Lloyd George, 9 June (Churchill papers); Lloyd George to Churchill, 10 June (Churchill papers); Curzon to Lloyd George, 10 June (Lloyd George papers); Churchill to Curzon, 11 June (Curzon papers); **p. 593**, Curzon to Churchill, 13 June (Churchill papers); Churchill to Curzon, 13 June (Churchill papers); Lloyd George to Chamberlain, 14 June (Lloyd George papers); Lloyd George to Curzon, 14 June (Churchill papers); **pp. 594** and **598**, Curzon to Churchill, 15 June (Churchill papers); **p. 598**, Chamberlain to Lloyd George, 14 June (Lloyd George papers); Lloyd George to Churchill, 16 June (Churchill papers).

CHAPTER 34. 1921: 'A WONDERFUL AND TERRIBLE YEAR': **p. 600**, Churchill to Curzon, 15 June (Churchill papers); Lloyd George to Curzon, 16 June (Lloyd George papers); Cabinet, 22 June (Cabinet papers 23/26); **p. 601**, Churchill to Lloyd George and Curzon, 25 June (Lloyd George papers); Churchill to Porch, 23 June (Churchill papers); Lady Randolph to Curzon, 26 June (Curzon papers); **pp. 601-6**, letters to Churchill on his mother's death, June–July (Churchill papers); **p. 602**, Churchill to Curzon, 29 June (Curzon papers); **p. 603**, Churchill to Lloyd George, 29 June (Lloyd George papers); Churchill to Porch, 29 June (Churchill papers); **p. 604**, Leslie to Clare Sheridan, 4 July (Leslie papers); **p. 606**, Churchill to Lady Islington (Islington papers); Churchill to Crewe, 4 July (Crewe papers); **p. 607**, Churchill memorandum, 4 July (Churchill papers); Ministerial exchange of notes, 4 July (Curzon papers); **p. 608**, Imperial Conference, 7 July (Churchill papers); **p. 609**, Churchill to Haldane, 11 July (Churchill papers); **p. 610**, Cox to Churchill, 4 Aug. (Churchill papers); Young Minute, 9 Aug. (Colonial Office papers 730/4); **p. 611**, Fisher diary, 19 Aug. (Fisher papers); Churchill to Curzon, 22 Aug. (Curzon papers); **pp. 611-13**, letters to Churchill on his daughter's death, Aug. (Churchill papers); **p. 613**, Churchill to Crewe, 3 Sept. (Crewe papers); Churchill to his wife, 19 and 20 Sept. (Spencer-Churchill papers).

CHAPTER 35. PALESTINE 1921: 'GIVE THE JEWS THEIR CHANCE': **p. 615**, Congreve to Young, 16 June (Colonial Office papers 733/17A); Shuckburgh to Churchill, 1 July

(Colonial Office papers 733/17A); Churchill to Sinclair, 18 June (Churchill papers); **p. 616**, Imperial Cabinet, 22 June (Lloyd George papers); **p. 618**, Young to Congreve, 6 July (Colonial Office papers 733/17A); **p. 619**, Weizmann to Lewin, 15 July (Weizmann papers); **p. 620**, Clausen Minute, 26 June (Colonial Office papers 733/3); Young Minute, 26 June (Colonial Office papers 733/3); Young to Deedes, 18 July (Colonial Office papers 733/17A); **p. 621**, Samuel speech, 3 June (Central Zionist Archives); Meeting at Balfour's house, 22 July (Weizmann papers); **p. 622**, Shuckburgh to Churchill, 23 July (Colonial Office papers 733/13); Wilson diary, 26 July (Wilson papers); **p. 623**, Young to Churchill, 5 Aug. (Colonial Office papers 733/10); Weizmann to Tulin, 10 Aug. (Weizmann papers); **p. 624**, Randall Davidson to Churchill, 10 Aug. (Colonial Office papers 733/14); Young memorandum, 11 Aug. (Churchill papers); Churchill memorandum, 11 Aug. (Churchill papers); **p. 625**, Arab memorandum, 12 Aug. (Central Zionist Archives); **pp. 625–7**, Churchill discussion with Arab Deputation, 15 Aug. (Central Zionist Archives); **p. 627**, Fisher diary, 17 Aug. (Fisher papers); Cabinet, 17 Aug. (Cabinet papers 23/26); **pp. 628–31**, Churchill discussion with Arab Deputation, 22 Aug. (Central Zionist Archives); **p. 631**, Young–Sacher discussion, 23 Aug. (Weizmann papers); Weizmann to Deedes, 31 Aug. (Weizmann papers); **p. 632**, Young to Vernon, 25 Aug. (Colonial Office papers 733/13); **p. 633**, Hall Minute, 2 Sept. (Colonial Office papers 733/16); Shuckburgh to Churchill, 7 Sept. (Colonial Office papers 733/16); Young Minute, 9 Sept. (Colonial Office papers 733/6); Young to Shuckburgh, 10 Sept. (Colonial Office papers 733/6); Shuckburgh to Churchill, 12 Sept. (Colonial Office papers 733/6); **p. 634**, Shuckburgh to Churchill, 17 Sept. (Colonial Office papers 733/15); Shuckburgh to Rutenberg's solicitors, 22 Sept. (Colonial Office papers 733/6); Churchill to Lloyd George, 3 Sept. (Churchill papers); **p. 635**, Churchill to Sinclair, 30 Sept. (Churchill papers); Meinertzhagen to Churchill, 3 Oct. (Colonial Office papers 733/15); Churchill to Balfour, 10 Oct. (Churchill papers); **p. 636**, Young to Colonial Office, 12 Oct. (Colonial Office papers 733/10); Churchill to Samuel, 14 Oct. (Churchill papers); Meinertzhagen to Shuckburgh, 21 Oct. (Colonial Office papers 733/10); Weizmann to Zionist Executive, 1 Nov. (Central Zionist Archives); Meinertzhagen to Shuckburgh, 27 Oct. (Colonial Office papers 733/10); **p. 637**, Shuckburgh Minute, 28 Oct. (Colonial Office papers 733/10); Churchill note, 2 Nov. (Colonial Office papers 733/10); Churchill Minute, 17 Nov. (Colonial Office papers 733/7); Churchill Minute, 22 Nov. (Colonial Office papers 733/7); Samuel to Churchill, 2 Nov. (Colonial Office papers 733/7); Clauson Minute, 3 Nov. (Colonial Office papers 733/7); Meinertzhagen note, 3 Nov. (Colonial Office papers 733/7); **p. 638**, Shuckburgh to Churchill, 7 Nov. (Colonial Office papers 733/15); Churchill to Sinclair, 12 Nov. (Churchill papers); Meinertzhagen to Shuckburgh, 15 Nov. (Colonial Office papers 733/7); **p. 639**, Shuckburgh to Masterton Smith, 16 Nov. (Colonial Office papers 733/7); Shuckburgh to Masterton Smith, 22 Nov. (Colonial Office papers 733/7); Miriam Sacher to her husband, 21 Nov. (Sacher papers); **p. 640**, Weizmann to Eder, 27 Nov. (Weizmann papers); Weizmann to Zionist Executive, 30 Nov. (Weizmann papers); **p. 641**, Weizmann to Deedes, 13 Dec. (Weizmann papers); Congreve order, 29 Oct. (Churchill papers); Shuckburgh Minute, 1 Dec. (Colonial Office papers 733/7); Churchill note, 9 Dec. (Colonial Office papers 733/7). Also, **p. 621** n. 2, Balfour to Curzon, 21 Jan. 1919 (Curzon papers).

CHAPTER 36. PALESTINE 1922: DEFENDING THE BALFOUR DECLARATION: **p. 642**, Zionist Executive note, 16 Jan. (Central Zionist Archives); Shuckburgh to Churchill, 17 Jan. (Colonial Office papers 733/29); **p. 643**, Churchill to his wife, 4 Feb. (Spencer-Churchill papers); Shuckburgh to Churchill, 7 Feb. (Colonial Office papers 733/33); Zionist Executive discussion, 21 Feb. (Weizmann archives); **p. 644**, Shuckburgh to Arab Delegation, 1 March (Central Zionist Archives); **p. 645**, Shuckburgh to Churchill, 30 March (Colonial Office papers 733/37); Samuel to Churchill, 9 March (Churchill papers); **p. 646**, Shuckburgh to Masterton Smith, March 11 (Colonial Office papers 733/37); **p. 647**, Churchill to Sinclair, 21 March (Colonial Office papers 733/33); Churchill Minute, 31 March (Colonial Office papers 733/19); Mond to Samuel, 4 April (Samuel papers);

Churchill to Sinclair, 5 April (Colonial Office papers 733/18); Samuel draft, 24 May (Colonial Office papers 733/34); **p. 648**, Mills Minute, 12 June (Colonial Office papers 733/22); Wilson diary, 29 May (Wilson papers); **p. 650**, Young Minute, 22 June (Colonial Office papers 733/22); **p. 651**, Shuckburgh to Marsh, 3 July (Colonial Office papers 733/22); **p. 659**, Churchill to Deedes, 5 July (Colonial Office papers 733/35); **p. 660**, Weizmann to Churchill, 26 July (Weizmann papers); Churchill to Sydenham, 26 Aug. (Churchill papers); **p. 661**, Sydenham to Churchill, 29 Aug. (Churchill papers); Churchill to Sydenham, 31 Aug. (Churchill papers).

CHAPTER 37. 'THIS MYSTERIOUS POWER OF IRELAND', 1921: **p. 665**, Churchill to the King, 23 June (Royal Archives); **p. 666**, Wilson diary, 19 July (Wilson papers); Fisher diary, 14 June (Fisher papers); Cabinet, 11 Aug. (Cabinet papers 23/26); Fisher diary, 11 Aug. (Fisher papers); **p. 667**, Cabinet, 13 Aug. (Cabinet papers 23/26); Cabinet, 7 Sept. (Cabinet papers 23/27); **p. 669**, Sinclair to Churchill, 2 Oct. (Churchill papers); **p. 674**, Churchill to Lloyd George, 9 Nov. (Lloyd George papers); **p. 681**, Fisher diary, 15 Dec. (Fisher papers); Guest to Churchill, 15 Dec. (Churchill papers); Chamberlain to the King, 15 Dec. (Royal Archives); Churchill memorandum, 21 Dec. (Cabinet papers 27/153); **p. 682**, Cabinet Committee, 21 Dec. (Cabinet papers 27/153); Blunt to Churchill, 26 Dec. (Churchill papers); Churchill to the Prince of Wales, 2 Jan. 1922 (Churchill papers).

CHAPTER 38. THE IRISH TREATY: 'A STATUE OF SNOW', 1922: **p. 684**, Congreve to Churchill, 9 Jan. (Churchill papers); Wilson diary, 9 Jan. (Wilson papers); **p. 685**, Craig to Churchill, 11 Jan. (Churchill papers); Wilson diary, 12 Jan. (Wilson papers); Cabinet Committee, 12 and 17 Jan. (Cabinet papers 27/153); Churchill to Morley, 18 Jan. (Churchill papers); **p. 686**, Churchill to Anderson, 31 Jan. (Churchill papers); **p. 687**, Churchill to Lloyd George, 30 Jan. (Lloyd George papers); Wilson diary, 31 Jan. (Wilson papers); Churchill to his wife, 3 and 4 Feb. (Spencer-Churchill papers); **p. 688**, Clementine Churchill to her husband, 7 and 10 Feb. (Spencer-Churchill papers); **p. 689**, Churchill to his wife, 11 Feb. (Spencer-Churchill papers); Macready to Churchill, 14 Feb. (Churchill papers); Cabinet Committee, 14 Feb. (Cabinet papers 27/153); **p. 693**, Fisher diary, 16 Feb. (Fisher papers); **p. 694**, Salvidge to Churchill, 20 Feb. (Churchill papers); Cabinet Committee, 20 Feb. (Cabinet papers 27/153); Fisher diary, 1 March (Fisher papers); **p. 696**, Chamberlain to the King, 9 March (Royal Archives); Churchill to Collins, 14 March (Churchill papers); **p. 697**, Leonie Leslie to Churchill, 17 March (Churchill papers); Churchill to Lloyd George, 18 March (Churchill papers); Churchill to Collins and Griffith, 21 March (Churchill papers); **p. 698**, Cabinet, 22 March (Cabinet papers 23/29); Cabinet Committee, 24 March (Cabinet papers 27/153); Churchill to Craig, 24 March (Austen Chamberlain papers); **p. 699**, Chamberlain to the King, 28 and 29 March (Royal Archives); Churchill draft agreement, 29 March (Colonial Office papers 739/5); **p. 700**, Colonial Office conference, 29 March (Colonial Office papers 739/5); **p. 702**, Lord Askwith to Churchill, 31 March (Churchill papers); Stamfordham to Churchill, 1 April (Churchill papers).

CHAPTER 39. IRELAND 1922: 'WILL THE LESSON BE LEARNED IN TIME': **p. 703**, Wilson diary, 3 April (Wilson papers); Churchill memorandum, 4 April (Churchill papers); **p. 705**, Fisher diary, 5 April (Fisher papers); Cabinet, 5 April (Cabinet papers 23/30); Wilson diary, 11 April (Wilson papers); **p. 707**, Long to Churchill, 22 April (Churchill papers); Churchill to Lloyd George, 12 April (Lloyd George papers); **p. 708**, Churchill to Collins, 12 April (Churchill papers); **p. 709**, Wilson diary, 15 April (Wilson papers); Churchill to Lloyd George, 17 April (Lloyd George papers); Churchill to Lloyd George, 19 April (Lloyd George papers); **p. 710**, Macready to Churchill, 16 April (Lloyd George papers); Cope to Churchill, 17 April (Lloyd George papers); Masterton Smith to Londonderry, 29 April (Churchill papers); **p. 711**, Churchill to Collins, 29 April (Churchill papers); **p. 713**, Churchill to Cope, 2 May (Churchill papers); Stamfordham to the King, 4 May (Royal Archives); **p. 714**, Churchill to Chamberlain, 13 May (Chamberlain papers); **p. 715**, Churchill to Collins, 15 May (Churchill papers); **p. 716**, Churchill to Collins, 22 May (Churchill papers); Churchill to Craig and Craig's reply, 23 May (Churchill papers); **p. 717**, Churchill to Craig, 24 May (Chamberlain papers); Londonderry to Churchill, 25 May (Churchill papers); **p. 718**, Cabinet, 30 May (Cabinet papers 23/30); **p. 721**, Wilson diary, 31 May (Wilson papers); Fisher diary, 31 May (Fisher papers); **p. 722**, Chamberlain to the King (Royal Archives).

CHAPTER 40. IRELAND 1922: 'THE UNCEASING, TORMENTING STRUGGLE': **p. 724**, Cabinet, 1 June (Cabinet papers 23/30); Fisher diary, 1 June (Fisher papers); **p. 725**, Cabinet Committee, 1 June (Cabinet papers 27/153); **p. 726**, Cabinet, 2 June (Cabinet papers 23/30); Colonial Office discussion, 2 June (Colonial Office papers 906/25); Collins to Churchill, 5 June (Cabinet papers 27/153); **p. 727**, Cabinet Committee, 6 June (Cabinet papers 27/153); **p. 728**, Churchill to Lloyd George, 7 June (Churchill papers); **p. 729**, Lloyd George to Churchill, 8 June (Churchill papers and Royal Archives); **p. 731**, Churchill to Lloyd George, 8 June (Lloyd George papers); Churchill to Chamberlain, 8 June (Chamberlain papers); **p. 733**, Wilson diary, 21 June (Wilson papers); Cabinet, 22 June (Cabinet papers 23/30); **p. 734**, Conference of Ministers, 23 June (Cabinet papers 23/30); **p. 738**, Chamberlain to the King, 27 June (Royal Archives); **p. 740**, Collins to Churchill ,28 June (Chamberlain papers); **p. 741**, Cabinet, 29 June (Cabinet papers 23/30); **p. 742**, Churchill to Collins, 7 July (Churchill papers); **p. 743**, Churchill to Craig, 7 July (Churchill papers); **p. 744**, Collins to Churchill, 9 Aug. (Chamberlain papers); **p. 745**, Cabinet Committee, 2 Aug. (Cabinet papers 27/153); Clementine Churchill to her husband, 14 Aug. (Spencer-Churchill papers); Cope to Curtis, 23 Aug. (Lloyd George papers); **p. 746**, Churchill to Cosgrave, 24 Aug. (Lloyd George papers); Churchill to Cope, 24 Aug. (Lloyd George papers); **p. 747**, Churchill to Pamela Lytton, 12 Sept. (Lytton papers); **p. 748**, Hazel Lavery to Churchill, end October (Churchill papers); Cope to Marsh, 14 Oct. (Colonial Office papers 739/2); Churchill to Cosgrave, 25 Oct. (Colonial Office papers 739/2); Cosgrave to Churchill, 31 Oct. (Colonial Office papers 739/2).

CHAPTER 41. THE WAR MEMOIRS: 'A GT CHANCE TO PUT MY WHOLE CASE', 1919–1922: **p. 751**, Macmillan to Churchill, 24 March 1919 (Churchill papers); Churchill to Curtis Brown, 1 Nov. 1920 (Churchill papers); Churchill to Grey, 29 Nov. 1920 (Churchill papers); **p. 752**, Churchill to Murray (Churchill papers); Churchill to Lloyd George, 26 Jan. 1921 (Churchill papers); **p. 754**, Churchill to French, 6 May 1921 (Churchill papers); Churchill to Lambert, 30 May 1921 (Churchill papers); Churchill to Masterton Smith, 22 June 1921 (Churchill papers); **p. 755**, Churchill to Jackson, 22 July 1921 (Churchill papers); **p. 756**, Churchill to his wife, 29 Dec. 1921 and 4 Jan. and 27 Jan. 1922 (Spencer-Churchill papers); **p. 757**, Fisher diary, 30 Jan. 1922 (Fisher papers); Churchill to his wife, 4 Feb. 1922 (Spencer-Churchill papers); **p. 758**, Churchill to his wife, 14 Aug. 1922 (Spencer-Churchill papers); Churchill–Marsh notes, 31 Aug. 1922 (Marsh papers). Also, **p. 759**, Churchill to his wife, 17 July 1915 (Spencer-Churchill papers).

CHAPTER 42. IN DEFENCE OF THE COALITION, 1922: **p. 760**, Churchill to Curzon, 24 Dec. 1921 (Churchill papers); **p. 761**, Crowe to Curzon, 28 Dec. 1921 (Curzon papers); Churchill to his wife, 1 Jan 1922 (Spencer-Churchill papers); Churchill to the Prince of Wales, 2 Jan. (Churchill papers); **p. 762**, Churchill to his wife, 4 Jan. (Spencer-Churchill papers); **p. 763**, Churchill to his wife, 4 Jan. (Spencer-Churchill papers); Clementine Churchill to her husband, 4 Jan. (Spencer-Churchill papers); **p. 764**, Churchill to his wife, 4 Jan. (Spencer-Churchill papers); Fisher diary, 20 Jan. (Fisher papers); **pp. 766–7**, Clementine Churchill to her husband, 28 Jan., 3 and 28 Feb. (Spencer-Churchill papers); Churchill to his wife, 4 Feb. (Spencer-Churchill papers); **pp. 767–8**, Churchill to his wife, 7 Feb. (Spencer-Churchill papers); Cabinet Committee, 12 and 23 Jan. (Cabinet papers 27/164);

p. 769, Cabinet Committee, 25 Jan. (Cabinet papers 27/164); Churchill to his wife, 27 Jan. (Spencer-Churchill papers); Churchill to Geddes, 15 Feb. (Churchill papers); Fisher diary, 16 Feb. (Fisher papers); **p. 770**, Churchill to Lloyd George, 20 and 22 Feb. (Lloyd George papers); Fisher diary, 24 Feb. (Fisher papers); **p. 771**, Fisher diary, 21 Feb. (Fisher papers); Churchill to Lloyd George, 27 Feb. (Churchill papers); **p. 722**, Fisher diary, 28 Feb. (Fisher papers); **p. 773**, Beaverbrook to Lloyd George, 13 and 15 March (Lloyd George papers); McCurdy to Lloyd George, 17 March (Lloyd George papers); **p. 774**, Churchill to Lloyd George, 18 March (Churchill papers); Fisher diary, 20 March (Fisher papers). Also, **p. 768**, Fisher diary, 2 Aug. (Fisher papers).

CHAPTER 43. THE GENOA CONFERENCE, 1922: **p. 775**, Fisher diary, 5 March (Fisher papers); Chamberlain to Lloyd George, 21 March (Chamberlain papers); **p. 776**, Lloyd George to Chamberlain, 22 March (Lloyd George papers); Lloyd George to Horne, 22 March (Lloyd George papers); **p. 777**, Horne to Lloyd George, 23 March (Lloyd George papers); Chamberlain to Lloyd George, 23 March (Lloyd George papers); **p. 778**, Chamberlain to Curzon, 24 March (Chamberlain papers); Sassoon to Lloyd George, 24 March (Lloyd George papers); Chamberlain to Lloyd George, 25 March (Lloyd George papers); **p. 779**, Meeting of Ministers, 27 March (Cabinet papers 23/29); **p. 781**, Churchill to Marsh, 20 April (Marsh papers); **pp. 781** and **782**, Churchill to Curzon, 24 April (Churchill papers); **pp. 781** and **783**, Sassoon to Lloyd George, 28 April (Lloyd George papers); **p. 781**, n. 1, Churchill to E. D. Miller, 5 July (Churchill papers); **p. 782**, Gwynne to Churchill, 24 April (Churchill papers); Churchill to Curzon, 24 April (Churchill papers); Churchill to Birkenhead, 25 April (Churchill papers); **p. 783**, Sassoon to Lloyd George, 5 May (Lloyd George papers); Churchill to Birkenhead, 6 May (Churchill papers); **p. 784**, Chamberlain to Curzon, 12 May (Curzon papers); Churchill to Chamberlain, 13 May (Chamberlain papers); **p. 785**, Churchill to Lloyd George, 26 July (Lloyd George papers); **pp. 786-93**, Churchill to his wife, 15, 16, 17 and 20 July, and 2, 4, 7, 9, 10, 14, 18 and 23 Aug., and 12 Sept. (Spencer-Churchill papers); **pp. 788-9** and **p. 791**, Clementine Churchill to her husband, 4, 8 and 10 Aug. (Spencer-Churchill papers); **p. 793**, Churchill to Knight, Frank & Rutley, 15 Sept. (Churchill papers); **p. 794**, Guest to Churchill, 5 Sept. (Churchill papers); Churchill to Balfour, 12 Sept. (Churchill papers); **p. 795**, Churchill to Pamela Lytton, 12 Sept. (Lytton papers).

CHAPTER 44. IRAQ 1921–1922: 'AN UNGRATEFUL VOLCANO': **p. 796**, Cox to Churchill, 19 April 1921 (Churchill papers); Churchill to Shuckburgh, 21 April (Churchill papers); **p. 797**, Churchill to Cox, early June (Colonial Office papers 730/2); Cox to Churchill, 24 June (Colonial Office papers 730/2); Churchill Minute, end June (Colonial Office papers 730/2); Cox to Churchill, 1 July (Colonial Office papers 730/3); **p. 798**, Churchill to Cox, 5 July (Colonial Office papers 730/3); Churchill to Sinclair, 9 July (Colonial Office papers 730/3); **p. 799**, Churchill to Cox, 9 July (Churchill papers); Churchill to Worthington-Evans, 4 and 16 July (Churchill papers); **p. 800**, Radcliffe Minute, 16 July (War Office papers 32/5898); Churchill Minute, 16 July (Colonial Office papers 730/17); Haldane to Churchill, 23 July (Colonial Office papers 730/17); Cox to Curzon, 23 July (Curzon papers); **p. 801**, Churchill to Vernon and Meinertzhagen, 26 July (Colonial Office papers 730/15); Churchill to Sinclair, 26 July (Colonial Office papers 730/15); Haldane to Churchill, 12 July (Lloyd George papers); Churchill to Lloyd George, 28 July (Lloyd George papers); Churchill Minute, 31 July (Colonial Office papers 730/15); **pp. 801-2**, Churchill to Cox, 2 Aug. (Churchill papers 17/6); **p. 802**, Churchill to Worthington-Evans, 2 Aug. (Churchill papers); **p. 803**, Churchill Cabinet paper, 4 Aug. (Churchill papers); **p. 804**, Churchill to Lloyd George, 7 Aug. (Lloyd George papers); Churchill to Sinclair, 11 Aug. (Churchill papers); Churchill draft to Feisal, 15 Aug. (Churchill papers); Churchill to Cox, 15 Aug. (Lloyd George papers); **p. 806**, Cox to Churchill, 16 Aug. (Colonial Office papers 730/4); Cabinet Committee, 19 Aug. (Cabinet papers 23/27); **p. 807**, Churchill memorandum (Churchill papers); Haldane to Churchill,

28 Sept. (Churchill papers); Cox to Churchill, 29 Sept. (Churchill papers); Balfour to Churchill, 5 Oct. (Colonial Office papers 730/16); Churchill to Balfour, 10 Oct. (Colonial Office papers 730/16); **p. 808**, Meinertzhagen note (Colonial Office papers 733/5); Churchill to Curzon, 18 Oct. (Churchill papers); Curzon to Churchill, 9 Nov. (Churchill papers); Churchill draft reply, mid-Nov. (Churchill papers); Young to the Colonial Office, 23 Oct. (Colonial Office papers 730/18); **p. 809**, Churchill to Cox, 14 Nov. (Colonial Office papers 730/7); Churchill Minute, 24 Nov. (Colonial Office papers 730/16); Churchill Minute, 7 Dec. (Colonial Office papers 730/7); Churchill to Cox, 13 Dec. (Churchill papers); Churchill to his wife, 1 Jan. 1922 (Spencer-Churchill papers); **p. 811**, Churchill Minute, 9 Jan. (Churchill papers); Churchill to Cox, 2 Feb. (Churchill papers); Guest to Trenchard, 6 Feb. (Trenchard papers); Fisher diary, 9 Feb. (Fisher papers); **p. 812**, Conference of Ministers, 9 Feb. (Cabinet papers 23/29); Cox to Churchill, and Churchill Minute, 19 Feb. (Colonial Office papers 730/30); Cabinet, 21 Feb. (Cabinet papers 23/29); Feisal to Cox, 23 Feb. (Colonial Office papers 730/20); **p. 813**, Shuckburgh to Masterton Smith, 6 March (Colonial Office papers 730/20); Churchill Minute, 16 March (Colonial Office papers 730/20); Fisher diary, 15 March (Fisher papers); Churchill memorandum, 31 March (Churchill papers); Cox to Churchill, 4 April (Churchill papers); **p. 814**, Churchill to Cox, 19 April (Churchill papers); Churchill to Curzon, 24 April (Churchill papers); Lawrence to Shuckburgh, 4 July (Lawrence papers); Churchill to Lawrence, 4 July (Churchill papers); Lawrence to Blumenfeld, 11 Nov. (Lawrence papers); Bullard Minute, 31 July (Colonial Office papers 730/23); **p. 816**, Young note, 15 Aug. (Colonial Office papers 730/23); Masterton Smith to Churchill, 16 Aug. (Colonial Office papers 730/23); Churchill Minute, 17 Aug. (Colonial Office papers 730/23); Churchill to Lloyd George, 23 Aug. (Lloyd George papers); Churchill draft to Feisal, 25 Aug. (Colonial Office papers 730/23); **p. 817**, Churchill to Lloyd George, 1 Sept. (Lloyd George papers); **p. 818**, Lloyd George to Churchill, 5 Sept. (Churchill papers); Churchill to Lloyd George, 6 Sept. (Lloyd George papers).

CHAPTER 45. THE CHANAK CRISIS, 1922: **p. 820**, Rumbold to Curzon, 5 Sept. (Rumbold papers); Cabinet, 7 Sept. (Cabinet papers 23/31); **p. 821**, Rumbold to Curzon, 10 Sept. (Rumbold papers); **p. 824**, Young to Churchill, 11 Sept. (Colonial Office papers 730/24); Sinclair to Churchill, 13 Sept. (Churchill papers); Churchill to Curzon, 14 Sept. (Churchill papers); **p. 825**, Lloyd George to Curzon, 15 Sept. (Lloyd George papers); Cabinet, 15 Sept. (Cabinet papers 23/31); **p. 827**, Churchill draft telegram, 15 Sept. (Churchill papers); Press communiqué, 16 Sept. (Churchill papers); **p. 829**, Hughes to Churchill, 17 Sept. (Churchill papers); Cabinet, 18 Sept. (Cabinet papers 23/31); **p. 831**, Harington to Marden, 19 Sept. (Rumbold papers); Cabinet, 19 Sept. (Cabinet papers 23/31); **p. 832**, Harington to War Office, 20 Sept. (Rumbold papers); Churchill to Hughes, 20 Sept. (Churchill papers); **p. 833**, Conference of Ministers, 20 Sept. (Cabinet papers 23/39); Churchill to Harington, 20 Sept. (Cabinet papers 23/39); **p. 834**, Cabinet, 21 Sept. (Cabinet papers 23/39); Hankey to Beatty, 22 Sept. (Cabinet papers 23/31); **p. 835**, Churchill to Lloyd George, 22 Sept. (Lloyd George papers); Shuttleworth to Harington and reply, 23, 24 Sept. (Rumbold papers); Cabinet Committee, 23 Sept. (Cabinet papers 23/31); **p. 837**, Churchill to Sinclair, 25 Sept. (Churchill papers); Harington to Cavan, 26 Sept. (Rumbold papers); Rumbold to Oliphant, 26 Sept. (Rumbold papers); Cabinet Committee, 26 Sept. (Cabinet papers 23/31); **p. 838**, Harington to Trenchard, 27 Sept. (Trenchard papers); Cabinet Committee, 27 Sept. (Cabinet papers 23/21); **p. 839**, Inner Cabinet, 27 Sept. (Cabinet papers 23/21); **p. 840**, Curzon to Chamberlain, 27 Sept. (Chamberlain papers); Churchill to Dominion Prime Ministers, 27 Sept. (Churchill papers); **p. 841**, Hankey diary, 27 Sept. (Hankey papers); Conferences of Ministers, 28 Sept. (Cabinet papers 23/31); **p. 842**, Churchill to Dominion Prime Ministers, 28 Sept. (Churchill papers); **p. 843**, Conferences of Ministers, 29 Sept. (Cabinet papers 23/31); **p. 844**, Churchill to Dominion Prime Ministers, 29 Sept. (Churchill papers); **p. 845**, morning Cabinet, 30 Sept. (Cabinet papers 23/31); **p. 846**, afternoon Cabinet, 30 Sept. (Cabinet papers 23/31); **p. 847**, Churchill note,

30 Sept. (Churchill papers); Churchill to Dominion Prime Ministers, 30 Sept. (Churchill papers); evening Cabinet, 30 Sept. (Cabinet papers 23/31); Hankey to Balfour, 1 Oct. (Hankey papers); **pp. 849–50,** Harington telegram, 30 Sept. (Churchill papers); **pp. 850–1,** afternoon Cabinet, 1 Oct. (Cabinet papers 23/31); **p. 851,** Churchill to Harington, 1 Oct. (Cabinet papers 23/31); **pp. 851** and **852,** Churchill telegrams to Dominion Prime Ministers, 1 Oct. (Churchill papers); **p. 852,** Churchill to Hughes, 1 Oct. (Churchill papers); Churchill to Dominion Prime Ministers, 2 Oct. (Churchill papers); **p. 854,** Churchill to Dominion Prime Ministers, 4 Oct. (Churchill papers); Guest to Churchill, 3 Oct. (Air Ministry papers, 8/55); **p. 855,** Fisher diary, 4 Oct. (Fisher papers); Cabinet, 5 Oct. (Cabinet papers 23/31); **p. 856,** Churchill to Dominion Prime Ministers, 5 Oct. (Churchill papers); Fisher diary, 5 Oct. (Fisher papers); **p. 857,** Rumbold to Curzon, 6 Oct. (Foreign Office papers 371/7899); **pp. 857** and **858,** Churchill to Dominion Prime Ministers, 6 and 7 Oct. (Churchill papers); **p. 859,** Churchill to Robertson, 7 Oct. (Churchill papers); **p. 860,** Fisher diary, 7 Oct. (Fisher papers); **p. 861,** Churchill's two telegrams to Dominion Prime Ministers, 11 Oct. (Churchill papers); Rumbold to Curzon, 11 Oct. (Foreign Office papers 371/7902); **p. 862,** Alice Keppel to Rumbold, 12 Oct. (Rumbold papers); Hankey diary, 17 Oct. (Hankey papers).

CHAPTER 46. THE FALL OF THE COALITION, 1922: **p. 863,** Fisher diary, 8 Oct. (Fisher papers); **p. 864,** Lucy Baldwin memorandum (Baldwin papers); Chamberlain to Birkenhead, 10 Oct. (Chamberlain papers); **p. 865,** Londonderry to Churchill, 16 Oct. (Churchill papers); Curzon to Churchill, 15 Oct. (Churchill papers); **p. 866,** Fisher diary, 17 Oct. (Fisher papers); Allison to Churchill, 17 Oct. (Churchill papers); Churchill to Allison, 18 Oct. (Churchill papers); Fisher diary, 19 Oct. (Fisher papers); **p. 867,** Lloyd George to Churchill, 19 Oct. (Churchill papers); **p. 868,** Hankey diary, 20 and 23 Oct. (Hankey papers); Tudor to Churchill, 22 Oct. (Churchill papers); Harington to Churchill, 22 Oct. (Churchill papers); **p. 869,** Churchill to James Robertson, 22 Oct. (Churchill papers); **p. 870,** Stamfordham to Churchill, 25 Oct. (Churchill papers).

CHAPTER 47. 'I THOUGHT HIS CAREER WAS OVER', 1922: **p. 873,** Mond to Churchill, 29 Oct. (Churchill papers); Churchill to Mond, 31 Oct. (Churchill papers); **p. 874,** Churchill notes about Beaverbrook, end Oct. (Churchill papers); Churchill notes about his election opponents, end Oct. (Churchill papers); **p. 875,** Churchill to C. P. Scott, 3 Nov. (Churchill papers); **p. 876,** Churchill to his wife, 6 Nov. (Spencer-Churchill papers); **p. 878,** Mond to Churchill, 7 Nov. (Churchill papers); **p. 879,** Clementine Churchill to her husband, 8 Nov. (Spencer-Churchill papers); **pp. 885–6,** Churchill speech, 14 Nov. (Churchill papers); **p. 888,** Londonderry to Churchill, 17 Nov. (Churchill papers); **p. 889,** Wolfe to Churchill, 17 Nov. (Churchill papers); **pp. 889–90,** Lawrence to Churchill, 18 Nov. (Churchill papers); **p. 890,** Lawrence to Marsh, 18 Nov. (Marsh papers); Churchill to Fisher, 18 Nov. (Fisher papers); Lady Hamilton's diary, 17 Nov. (Lady Ian Hamilton papers); Esher to Sassoon, 19 Nov. (Sassoon papers); **p. 891,** Churchill to Stamfordham, 21 Nov. (Churchill papers); Stamfordham to Churchill, 22 Nov. (Churchill papers); Bishop Welldon to Churchill, 24 Nov. (Churchill papers); **p. 892,** Churchill to Curtis Brown, 23 Nov. (Churchill papers). Also, **p. 891** n. 1, Welldon to Churchill, 28 Sept. 1896 (Churchill papers).

CHAPTER 48. RETROSPECT: 'PONDER & THEN *ACT*', 1917–1922: **p. 893,** Churchill to Lloyd George, early Sept. 1919 (Churchill papers); Churchill to his wife, 27 Jan. 1922 (Spencer-Churchill papers); Churchill to Macdonogh, 20 Jan. 1919 (War Office 32/9300); **p. 894,** Tudor to Trenchard, 22 Oct. 1922 (Trenchard papers); **p. 895,** Marsh to Sinclair, 13 Oct. 1915 (Sinclair papers); Lawrence to Blumenfeld, 11 Nov. 1922 (Lawrence papers); Churchill to Lloyd George, 25 June 1921 (Lloyd George papers); Churchill to Lloyd George, 27 Feb. 1922 (Churchill papers); Churchill to Lloyd George, 19 Jan. 1918 (Churchill papers); War Cabinet, 28 Feb. 1919 (Cabinet papers 23/9); Churchill to Lloyd George, 20

May 1919 (Lloyd George papers); **p. 896**, Churchill to Lloyd George, 4 Aug. 1919 (Churchill papers); **p. 897**, Churchill to Curzon, 10 Oct. 1919 (Churchill papers); Churchill to Curzon, 19 Oct. 1921 (Churchill papers); Imperial Conference, 7 July 1921 (Churchill papers); **p. 898**, Cabinet, 19 Sept. 1922 (Cabinet papers 23/29); Churchill to Lloyd George, 21 Nov. 1918 (Lloyd George papers); Churchill to Lloyd George, 4 Aug. 1919 (Churchill papers); Churchill memorandum, 23 Sept. 1921 (Cabinet papers 24/128); **p. 899**, Churchill to Lloyd George, 8 Oct. 1921 (Lloyd George papers); **p. 900**, Churchill to Lloyd George, 27 Jan. 1919 (Lloyd George papers); House of Lords Reform Committee, 26 Oct. 1921 (Cabinet papers 27/113); Churchill memorandum, 21 June 1922 (Cabinet papers 27/113); **p. 901**, Churchill to his wife, 8 Feb. 1922 (Spencer-Churchill papers); Chamberlain to the King, 31 May 1922 (Royal Archives); **p. 904**, Cabinet, 29 July 1919 (Cabinet papers 23/11); Churchill to Lloyd George, 6 Sept. 1919 (Churchill papers); Lloyd George to Churchill, 22 Sept. 1919 (Churchill papers); Churchill to Lloyd George, 22 Sept. 1919 (Churchill papers); **p. 905**, Fisher diary, 3 Nov. 1919 (Fisher papers); Churchill to Loucheur, 21 Nov. 1919 (Loucheur papers); Wilson diary, 16 Jan. 1920 (Wilson papers); **p. 906**, Churchill memorandum, 1 May 1920 (Marsh papers); Hankey diary, 18 Nov. 1920 (Hankey papers); Wilson to Congreve, 20 Jan. 1921 (Wilson papers); **p. 907**, Chamberlain to Curzon, 15 Nov. 1921 (Curzon papers); Fisher diary, 18 Feb. 1922 (Fisher papers); Fisher diary, 2 March 1922 (Fisher papers); Austen Chamberlain to Lloyd George, 23 March 1922 (Lloyd George papers); Churchill to his wife, 15 Feb. 1921 (Spencer-Churchill papers); Churchill to Sinclair, 9 June 1915 (Sinclair papers); **p. 908**, Churchill to the King, 16 and 17 Nov. 1919 (Royal Archives); Churchill to his wife, 24 Jan. 1919 (Spencer-Churchill papers); Churchill to Lloyd George, 20 Sept. 1919 (Lloyd George papers); Churchill to Lloyd George, 24 March 1920 (Lloyd George papers); **p. 909**, Churchill to his wife, 27 and 31 Jan. 1922 (Spencer-Churchill papers); **p. 910**, Clementine Churchill to her husband, 11 July 1921 and 29 Oct. 1918 (Spencer-Churchill papers); **p. 911**, Churchill to his wife, 12 Sept. 1918 (Spencer-Churchill papers); Churchill to Sinclair, 22 March 1917 (Sinclair papers); Churchill to his wife, 29 May 1917 and 23 Feb. 1918 (Spencer-Churchill papers); Fleming to Churchill, Nov. 1914 (Churchill papers); **p. 912**, Churchill to Spender, 10 Oct. 1919 (Churchill papers); Churchill to French, 6 May 1921 (Churchill papers); Churchill to his wife, 20 Sept. 1921 (Spencer-Churchill papers); **p. 913**, Churchill to Curzon, 26 Jan. 1922 (Curzon papers); World Crisis drafts (Churchill papers); **p. 914**, Churchill to Lloyd George, 9 April 1919 (Churchill papers); Churchill to Lloyd George, 24 March 1920 (Lloyd George papers); Churchill to his wife, 27 March 1920 (Spencer-Churchill papers); **p. 915**, Churchill notes, 11 Nov. 1922 (Churchill papers).

PART TWO
AUTHOR'S RECORDS OF INDIVIDUAL RECOLLECTIONS

Recollections of Peregrine S. Churchill, quoted on **p. 18**; of the Hon. Randolph S. Churchill, **p. 19**; of Captain Gilbert Hall, RAF, **pp. 114, 138–9, 140, 141**; of Baroness Asquith of Yarnbury, **pp. 277–8**; of Brigadier Douglas Roberts, **pp. 306, 346**; of Major-General George Wood, **pp. 358, 367**; of Mrs Jessie Crosland, **p. 557**; of Baroness Spencer-Churchill, **pp. 734, 880**; of H. Norman Harding, **pp. 738–40, 794**; and of General Sir Edward Louis Spears, **pp. 875, 885**.

PART THREE
PRINTED SOURCES

The Memoirs of King Abdullah: quoted on **p. 560**.

Christopher Addison, *Four and a Half Years*: Addison's diary, quoted on **pp. 25, 26, 32, 127–8, 894**.

Harold Bellman, *Cornish Cockney*: quoted on **p. 32**.

The Diary of Lord Bertie 1914–1918: quoted on **p. 71.**

Robert Blake (ed.), *The Private Diaries of Douglas Haig:* quoted on **pp. 21, 46, 47, 76, 110, 141, 147, 182, 183, 139, 193, 256.**

British Weekly: quoted on **p. 374.**

Winston S. Churchill, articles by, in the *Strand* magazine: quoted on **p. 56**; in *Cosmopolitan:* quoted on **pp. 86–8, 92–8**; in *Nash's Pall Mall:* quoted on **pp. 209–10**; in the *Weekly Dispatch:* quoted on **pp. 305, 903**; in the *Illustrated Sunday Herald:* quoted on **pp. 375, 453–4, 484, 905**; in the *Evening News:* quoted on **pp. 417–18, 912**; in the *Sunday Express:* quoted on **p. 441**; in the *Sunday Pictorial:* quoted on **p. 911.**

Winston S. Churchill, *Great Contemporaries:* quoted on **pp. 56** (footnote) and **868.**

Winston S. Churchill, *The World Crisis:* quoted for the Secret Session of 1917, **p. 17**; the choice of Ministry of Munitions, **p. 28**; the Italian defeat at Caporetto, **p. 53**; the battle of Cambrai, **p. 62**; conversations with General Tudor, **pp. 77** and **79**; the crisis of March 1918, **pp. 80, 82** and **85**; the battle of June 1918, **p. 117**; Chilean nitrates and Bernard Baruch, **p. 142**; the coming of the armistice, **pp. 164–6**; the Russo-Polish war, **p. 419**; Ireland, **pp. 673–4, 676, 677, 686, 715, 723–4, 738** and **745**; the Antwerp expedition of October 1914, **p. 757**; the aim of his war memoirs, **p. 758**; and the Chanak crisis, **pp. 836–7.**

Daily Express: quoted on **pp. 231, 311, 315.**

Daily Herald: quoted on **pp. 295, 297, 321, 419.**

Daily Mail: quoted on **pp. 179, 197, 829, 834, 836, 888.**

Daily Telegraph: quoted on **pp. 464, 888, 901.**

Mark de Wolfe-Howe (ed.), *Holmes–Laski Letters:* a Laski letter quoted on **pp. 675–6.**

Dundee Advertiser: quoted on **pp. 173, 178.**

Dundee Courier: leading article quoted on **p. 169**; Churchill's Labour opponent quoted on **p. 875**; Mrs Churchill's speeches quoted on **pp. 876–7, 878–9**; Churchill's speeches quoted on **pp. 880–5, 886–8.**

El Karmel: quoted on **p. 618.**

Egyptian Gazette: quoted on **pp. 557, 559.**

Lord Esher, *The Tragedy of Lord Kitchener:* quoted on **p. 757.**

Freeman's Journal: quoted on **p. 448.**

Sir Aylmer L. Haldane, *The Insurrection in Mesopotamia 1920:* quoted on **p. 490.**

Lord Hankey, *The Supreme Control:* quoted on **p. 244.**

Hansard: quoted on **pp. 7–8, 11–12, 13–15, 27–8, 39–40, 57, 59, 67–8, 109–10, 193–4, 201–2, 211–12, 214, 270, 276, 293, 295, 296–7, 302, 314, 355–6, 379–80, 395, 397, 402–10** (the Amritsar debate), **415–16, 421, 447–8, 449, 468–9, 479, 488, 504–5, 512, 540, 574, 594–8, 599, 609–10, 618–19, 643, 645, 649–50, 651–9** (the Rutenberg debate), **677–81, 688, 690–3, 694–6, 698–9, 701–2, 706–7, 719–21, 723, 732, 735–8, 741–2, 785, 894, 897, 904, 907, 908** n. 1, **911.**

Christopher Hassall, *Edward Marsh:* Marsh's letters quoted on **pp. 46, 47, 48, 149–50, 154, 155–6, 158.**

David Kirkwood, *My Life of Revolt:* quoted on **pp. 36–7.**

A. W. Lawrence (ed.), *T. E. Lawrence by His Friends:* recollections of Captain Maxwell Coote quoted on **p. 558.**

Major-General Sir Frederick Maurice, *The Life of General Lord Rawlinson of Trent:* Rawlinson diary quoted on **pp. 315, 316.**

Jan M. Meijer (ed.), *The Trotsky Papers 1917–1922*: Trotsky's and other Bolshevik telegrams quoted on **pp. 296, 325, 346–7, 352, 358.**

Meinertzhagen, Colonel Richard, *Middle East Diary*: quoted on **pp. 582–3, 598, 617, 622, 638, 639, 647, 660, 857, 870.**

Keith Middlemas (ed.), *Whitehall Diary*, volume one: Thomas Jones diary quoted on **pp. 270, 370, 378, 780, 867**; volume three (Ireland), quoted on **pp. 452–3, 456–7, 466–7, 663–4, 666, 667–8, 668, 670–2, 673, 675, 677, 700, 701, 714, 715, 716, 728–9, 731, 909.**

Morning Post: quoted on **pp. 26, 29, 30, 37, 179–80, 903.**

Observer: quoted on **pp. 890–1.**

Official History of the Ministry of Munitions: Churchill speech quoted on **p. 43.**

Palestine: quoted on **p. 575.**

Palestine Weekly: quoted on **pp. 544, 552, 556, 557, 599.**

Pall Mall Magazine: quoted on **p. 20.**

W. J. Reader, *Architect of Air Power* (the Life of Lord Weir): Churchill's questionings quoted on **pp. 43–4.**

Charles à Court Repington, *Diary*: quoted on **p. 115.**

Lord Riddell, *War Diary*: quoted on **pp. 3, 8, 34.**

Lord Riddell, *Intimate Diary of the Peace Conference and After*: quoted on **pp. 210, 213, 251, 371, 391** (footnote), **395, 413, 416, 487–8, 508, 611, 687, 752.**

Siegfried Sassoon, *Siegfried's Journey*: quoted on **pp. 150–1.**

Sunday Pictorial: quoted on **pp. 14, 27.**

Sunday Times: quoted on **p. 23.**

Sir Frederick Sykes, *From Many Angles*: quoted on **pp. 201, 215–16.**

A. J. P. Taylor (ed.), *Lloyd George – A Diary*: Frances Stevenson's diary quoted on **pp. 16, 18, 371, 372, 374, 581, 582, 610, 769, 914.**

The Times: quoted on **pp. 35** (leading article); **50** (Churchill speech); **50–1** (German comment); **64** (munitions agreement); **83** (Churchill speech); **126** (Churchill statement); **197–8, 206, 321** (leading articles); **404, 410** (the Amritsar debate); **418, 419** (Russian policy; **660** (Lord Sydenham letter); **668–9** (Churchill speech on Ireland); **764–5** (Churchill speech on Liberalism); **765** (Churchill attack on Asquithian Liberals); **772–3** (Churchill letter to his constituents); **858** (Bonar Law's Chanak letter); **871, 909** (Churchill's election message of 27 Oct. 1922); **877–8** (Churchill's election address of 7 Nov. 1922).

Major-General Sir Hugh Tudor, *The Fog of War*: Tudor's diary quoted on **pp. 79, 156.**

S. D. Waley, *Edwin Montagu*: Montagu's diary quoted on **pp. 159–60, 908.**

West Africa: quoted on **p. 115.**

Zionist Review: quoted on **p. 575.**

Index

Compiled by the Author

Churchill, Winston Leonard Spencer
1919—*continued*

executions by the anti-Bolsheviks, 293; criticized, 295; warns against undue optimism, 296–7; his hopes for General Ironside's Kotlas operation, 298–302; defends his Russian policy, 302; puts his faith in General Denikin, 303–19; appeals to Clemenceau about South Russia, 320–1; criticizes British policy, 322; rebuked by Lloyd George, 323–5; defends himself against Lloyd George, 326–7; hopes to see the Bolsheviks 'definitely beaten', 328–30; again rebuked by Lloyd George, 331–3; again defends himself against Lloyd George, 333–5; bitter about British policy towards the Baltic States, 336–7; believes the Bolshevik regime is 'doomed', 337; urges help for Denikin, 338–9, 341–2; warns Denikin against anti-semitism, 342–3; wants to arm Poland, 344; writes of the 'wonderful progress' of the anti-Bolsheviks, 345; 'Victory is in sight', 346–8, 350–1; in dispute with Lloyd George, 354–5; defends his policy, 345–6; urges 'more vigorous' action against the Bolsheviks, 357–8; seeks to avert Denikin's defeat, 358–64; warns of 'the very great evils that will come upon the world' as a result of British policy towards Russia, 364; his policy towards Ireland during 1919, 443–7; his policy towards Turkey during 1919, 472–7

1920: describes 'the agony of Russia', 365; defends General Yudenitch, 366; advises General Denikin to seek an armistice, 368–9; in Paris, 370–4; his Russian policy criticized, 374, and defended, 375; and Denikin's defeat, 376–7, 379–83; his 'evil policy' rebuked, 378; his advice to Lloyd George on European affairs, 384–5; in Paris, 385; on holiday near Bordeaux, 386–8; in Paris, 389–90; opposes British negotiations with the Bol-

Churchill, Winston Leonard Spencer
1920—*continued*

sheviks, 391; hopes for a Polish victory over the Bolsheviks, 395–7; bitter about 'the uninstructed state of public opinion', 398; favours 'a comprehensive agreement' with the Bolsheviks, 399–400; orders the withdrawal of British troops from South Russia, 412–13; warns that Britain will soon be left 'quite alone', 414; discusses the possibility of aid to Poland, 415; supported by Lloyd George, 415–16; defends Polish policy, 417–18; fears 'a measureless array of toils and perils', 419; and the climax of the Russo-Polish war, 420–2, 427; urges the immediate expulsion of the Bolshevik negotiators then in England, 422–5, 428–30; his forecast for Europe, 426–7; seen as 'a bold, bad man', 430; continues to resist Lloyd George's plans for trade and negotiations with Soviet Russia, 431–41; decides to resign, 438, but dissuaded, 438–9; argues against the policy of 'frightfulness' in India, 401–11; defends military reprisals in Ireland, 447–8; writes of a 'diabolical streak' in the Irish character, 449; Lloyd George enlists the help of, 450; and the search for more troops to send to Ireland, 451; wants special tribunals to try murderers in Ireland, 452; advocates a firm policy against Sinn Fein, 452–6; and the actions of the 'Black and Tans', 456, 458–69; urges 'official' reprisals, 463–4; given a personal detective, 465; his advice on Ireland, to Shane Leslie, 461, and to the Archbishop of Tuam, 467–8, 470; supports a truce in Ireland, 470; urged by his wife to adopt a moderate policy towards Ireland, 471; urges the need to retain Constantinople, 477–8; urges peace with Turkey, 479, 480; advocates replacing troops by aircraft in Mesopotamia, 481–2, 483; his early interest in Zionism, 484;